D1288855

A
MARK TWAIN
LEXICON

A
MARK TWAIN
LEXICON

BY

ROBERT L. RAMSAY, Ph. D.

AND

FRANCES G. EMBERSON, Ph. D.

NEW YORK
RUSSELL & RUSSELL · INC
1963

FIRST PUBLISHED IN 1938
REISSUED, 1963, BY RUSSELL & RUSSELL, INC.
L. C. CATALOG CARD NO: 63—9325

PRINTED IN THE UNITED STATES OF AMERICA

CONTENTS

TO

Alma B. Martin

Emma O. Woods

Avera Leolin Taylor

Florence Potter Stedman

Georgia House Watson

Ernestine Ernst

Amelia Madera

Everette M. Webber

Donald C. Thompson

True Gaines

Margaret Sellars Edwards

whose Master's Theses on the vocabulary of single volumes of Mark Twain's work helped to lay the foundation for the present study of his entire vocabulary.

PREFACE

This LEXICON had its beginning in a dozen Master's Theses upon as many separate works by Mark Twain. These studies of his vocabulary were written from 1929 to 1935 in the Graduate School of the University of Missouri, under the direction of Professor R. L. Ramsay, by Frances G. Emberson and the other students whose names appear on the opposite page. In 1932 Dr. Emberson produced her dissertation for the Ph.D. degree on *The Vocabulary of Samuel L. Clemens from 1852 to 1884,* and in 1935 her study entitled *Mark Twain's Vocabulary: a General Survey,* published in The University of Missouri Studies (X. 3). To this work reference should be made for a general discussion of the formation and growth of Mark Twain's vocabulary and its special aspects, and for a complete bibliography of his work and the critical and lexicographical sources.

Grateful acknowledgment for aid received at many points must be made to colleagues at the University of Missouri in the Departments of Agriculture, Botany, German, History, Journalism, Mathematics, Romance Languages, and English, who have willingly responded to what Mark Twain would have called "pestering" inquiries on numerous problems of vocabulary that led into their special fields; to obliging local printers, photographers, poker and billiard players, and cooks and housewives; and especially to Captain Edward Heckmann of Columbia, Missouri, captain and pilot on the "Sergeant Prior," a Government inspection steamer in the Omaha division of the U. S. Engineering Office, who has held for over thirty years a pilot's license on the Mississippi, the Missouri, and the Yukon Rivers and their tributaries. Captain Heckmann is a Mark Twain enthusiast, and he has taken a personal and very kindly interest in helping to elucidate many knotty points of nautical and steamboat terminology. We are also deeply indebted to the University of Missouri, its presiding authorities, and its Committee on Publication, for their liberal support and encouragement which has made this publication possible, and their forbearing patience in awaiting its protracted completion. Our greatest obligation is to Professor H. M. Belden of the University of Missouri for his devoted and indispensable assistance, advice, and criticism at all stages of the work from its preparation to its final proofreading. Without his constant collaboration and wise counsel this LEXICON would never have been accomplished.

The LEXICON makes no attempt to include the whole of Mark Twain's extraordinarily large vocabulary. Merely those elements of it have here been brought together that seemed best to illustrate the man and his many-sided genius, the America all of whose ways and works he loved, or at least knew, and the English language to whose development in America he significantly contributed. Still less, of course, is it in any sense a concordance to his works, for the quotations that have been chosen, after discarding more than have been retained, have been selected for the single purpose of throwing light upon the meaning and history of the words under which they are placed. We hope, however, that merely as a collection of extracts from his wit and wisdom this dictionary may not be without interest to readers and lovers of Mark Twain, as well as to specialists in his literary production and his language, and that to some extent it may even serve as a finding list for his good things.

From *AN AMERICAN PRIMER*, by Walt Whitman

"It is a truth that the words continually used among the people are, in numberless cases, not the words used in writing, or recorded in the dictionaries by authority."

"The Real Dictionary will give all words that exist in use, the bad words as well as any."

"It is the glory and superb rose-hue of the English language, anywhere, that it favors growth as the skin does."

"Do you suppose the liberties and the brawn of These States have to do only with delicate lady-words? with gloved gentleman words?"

"American writers are to show far more freedom in the use of words. Ten thousand native idiomatic words are growing or are today already grown, out of which vast numbers could be used by American writers, with meaning and effect—words that would be welcomed by the nation, being of the national blood."

A CLASSIFICATION OF MARK TWAIN'S VOCABULARY

"He could curl his tongue around the bulliest words in the language
when he was a mind to"

A total of nearly eight thousand words, combinations, and meanings[1] have been selected from the vocabulary of Mark Twain's published writings for inclusion in this LEXICON. They have been chosen with four aims in mind. We have tried, so far as possible, to collect all of his Americanisms, both those already recognized as such and those considered doubtful or merely possible or hitherto unrecognized. We have tried to collect all of his new words, formations, and usages, especially those for which he supplies the only recorded example or an example earlier than any hitherto recorded; these include both those which he deliberately coined and those which he merely discovered in the vernacular or elsewhere and was the first to use in writing. We have tried to collect all of his archaisms, both those he used consciously because of their archaic flavor and those he employed merely because they were survivals in the speech around him. Finally, we have included, without aiming at completeness, certain miscellaneous groups of words which seemed to be significant or interesting for various reasons.

These very diverse classes have been discriminated in the LEXICON by letters (A and ?A, B¹, B², and B³, C and ?C, D, and E) placed in brackets just after the headword in each entry. They are by no means mutually exclusive; the same entry is often marked by two or more letters because it seems to belong at the same time to two or more classes. These symbols of classification are carefully defined below, in our "Explanatory Note" on pp. cxvf. Here it seems desirable to explain and illustrate them further by assembling significant groups and lists under each of our four main classes.

---

1 The exact total of entries in the LEXICON is 7802. An original total of over ten thousand was reduced by extensive eliminations, largely from among the B³ and D words.

I. MARK TWAIN'S AMERICANISMS

*"Some of these old American words do have a kind of bully swing
to them; a man can express himself with 'em."*

Of the 7802 entries in the LEXICON, 2329 have been marked A as Americanisms, and 2743 ?A as Unrecorded or Doubtful Americanisms, making a total of
5072 possibly American words.

A Words. As is explained below (p. cxv), we have chosen to use the term
"Americanism" in its broadest possible sense, and we have accepted the judgment
of the OXFORD ENGLISH DICTIONARY in this matter whenever it was available,
marking all words as A which are so classed in it, whether as American words or
things, as American by origin or survival, as American exclusively or inclusively,
as American by explicit statement or implicit inference.

The omission or denial of such classification by other dictionaries has not
been considered a sufficient reason for questioning the Americanism of an entry,
although such conflicts of judgment have always been recorded. The judgments
of our three great American dictionaries in this matter are amazingly conflicting
and arbitrary; and to have attempted to weigh them in the balance against the
OXFORD would have led us to inextricable confusion. No criticism, of course, would
lie against them for choosing to adopt a narrower definition of Americanism than
the very broad one adopted in this LEXICON, if only that definition had been
clearly stated and consistently followed. Unfortunately no precise statement of
policy with regard to Americanisms has been made by any of them, nor, so far
as we have been able to discover, has any uniform policy been followed.

Whatever conception of an Americanism may have been in the minds of
the distinguished editors of WEBSTER'S, the STANDARD, and the CENTURY dictionaries, it was obviously not the same conception. Each of them, and the UNIVERSAL
as well, has chosen in many cases to stand in a minority of one, by omitting the
American label for words or uses which are so called by all the others. In the
case of the UNIVERSAL, Professor Wyld's intention would seem to have been to
report only upon present British usage, and hence not to describe as American
any words that have gained full adoption in Great Britain. This consideration
may explain his omission of the label from many entries which are called American
in all other dictionaries, and which are certainly American at least in origin.
The following instances are noted in the LEXICON[2]: *armory, baggage, boom,* v.,
cavort, cinch, v., *combine,* sb., *to strike oil, plunder* (baggage), *porter-house
steak, preempt, rope in* (ensnare), *run,* v. (conduct a business), *rye* (whiskey),
sidewalk, stump, sb. and v. (political sense), *ticket* (political sense), and *white*
(honorable).

No similar general principle is discernible in the practice of WEBSTER'S, the
STANDARD, or the CENTURY. Among their inconsistencies may be mentioned the

2   Reference should be made, for all words cited in this and the following lists, to the
LEXICON. Their right to rank as real Americanisms is claimed, of course, only for the
particular sense in which each is employed by Mark Twain, as illustrated in the entries
given.

curious circumstance that WEBSTER'S considers the attributive use of the word *boss* as American, but not its substantive use, except in the sense of a political boss, nor its use as a verb; whereas the STANDARD labels both substantive and verbal use as American, but not the attributive use; and the CENTURY calls all three uses *U.S.!* The following are among the very numerous entries for which WEBSTER'S omits the American classification for no apparent reason, since the other American dictionaries are united against it: *aboard, avenue, bargain-counter, boodle, boom,* sb., *break-down, bucket-shop, bunco, bushwhacking, by and large, to pass in one's checks, chewing-gum, chirk,* v., *cocktail, corral,* v., *to eat crow, cutter, Dutchman* (for German), *to fill the bill, flyer, gallinipper, gobble, graft,* sb., *hard-boiled, hellion, holt, hoodlum, honest Injun, lasso,* sb. and v., *machine* (political sense), *mileage, nation* (for damnation), *navy yard, to keep one's eyes peeled, planked* (fish), *raft* (a lot), *rank,* v. (take precedence), *right off, rugged* (robust), *sand* (pluck), *shackly, show,* sb. (opportunity), *silverite, smouch, sophomore, sun-up, taffy* (flattery), *tanglefoot* (whiskey), *vamose the ranch,* and *vestibuled* (train).

The following are among similar examples in which the STANDARD stands alone in omitting the American classification: *backwoods, branch, candy-pull, dominie, to get the drop on, to fly around, frontier, gouge,* v., *grade,* sb., *grist, groggery, half-breed, hunky, jibe, parlor-car, plant* (bury), *plumb,* adv., *to pull up stakes, stove-pipe* (hat), *tough* (vicious), *transom,* and *way-station.*

The following are Americanisms in all but the CENTURY: *adobe, chin,* v., *China-tree, from the word go, hurricane-deck, mail,* v., *to feel mean, nifty, nub* (of a story), *penitentiary, piazza, raise* (rear), *spread-eagle,* and *ten-pins.*

The following are unrecognized as Americanisms by either WEBSTER'S or the STANDARD: *back-country, back number, to ball up, to belittle, booming, brash, buckwheat cake, close call, cold deck, divide,* sb., *down cellar, down-town, express,* sb., *fixings, to fix up, to have the floor, fresh* (impudent), *hackman, hefty, easy mark, nonpareil* (type), *pap, railroading, rig* (vehicle), *spat,* sb. (dispute), *squatter, swale, to take and, to talk back, town-site,* and *yellow journalism.*

The following Americanisms are unlabelled by either WEBSTER'S, the STANDARD, or the CENTURY: *air-line, alleyway, axman, barker, billy, bindery, block, blooded, brakeman, bulletin-board, buzz-saw, catch-all, coal-oil, confidence-game, cuspidor, derby, driveway, elevated road, exclamation point, to play hookey, Irish potato, layout, low-down, mosquito-bar, mull over, nary, off-color* (this was called American in the 1911 ed. of WEBSTER'S, but not in the 1935 ed.), *old-timer, pitch in, pretzel, profanity, real estate, road* (railroad), *roundabout* (jacket), *seven-up, singed cat* (fig. use), *skyscraper, stateroom, tenderloin, thoroughbrace, thunder-gust, tide-water, use around* (to frequent), *out of whole cloth, wire-worker,* and *witness-stand.*

Finally, the following examples may be given of words or meanings which seem to be indubitably American, upon the evidence presented by the OXFORD

DICTIONARY and confirmed by Mark Twain, although they are not so recognized by either WEBSTER's, the STANDARD, the CENTURY, or the UNIVERSAL: *to back down, bed-rock, bluff, burglarize, cache, celluloid, chute, claim,* sb., *clearing, crowbar, crowd* (company), *cuteness, daily,* sb., *daisy* (slang use), *dander, deck of cards, disgruntled, doughnut, dumb-waiter, euchre, in a fix, to fizzle out, flapjack, foothill, to gas, go-ahead,* a., *to gravel, immigrant, iron-clad,* sb., *land-slide, lengthy, to let on, lot* (plot of land), *mammoth,* a., *mass-meeting, measurably, morgue, morning-glory, mucilage, one-horse,* a., *outfit, overalls, overland, pantalettes, pantaloons, pants, peddle, pry* (prize), *rapids, rattle* (confuse), *rowdy, self-made man, shanty, tenement-house, thug* (ruffian), *trolley, underbrush, up-country, vacation, waffle-iron, wash-basin,* and *waste-basket.*

The multitudinous "blind spots" with which our American lexicographers are afflicted in the matter of recognizing Americanisms are perhaps merely manifestations of the universal human blindness to one's own peculiarities and idiosyncracies. At times, however, their reluctance to use the American label seems to amount almost to an inferiority complex,—as if it were a reproach instead of a distinction to acknowledge the national stamp upon so large a part of the English vocabulary!

?A Words. When it comes to the doubtful and unrecorded Americanisms, that is, words, combinations, and meanings which are not called American by the OXFORD, the case is somewhat different. There are of course degrees of doubt. A few of the entries so marked in our LEXICON, which are labeled as Americanisms only by one or two minor authorities, must be considered extremely doubtful; e.g. the following are called American only in Bartlett: *alley* (marble), *brummagem, make-up, muddle,* sb., *potter,* v. (denied by Farmer and Clapin); only in Farmer: *authoress, mansard roof, nous* (intelligence); only in Mencken: *second-hand, life-preserver, sugar-bowl;* only in Thornton, and doubted by him: *bread-and-butter* (livelihood), *let alone,* v. phr., *shady* (disreputable); only in Horwill: *a half, semi-civilization;* only in DIALECT NOTES: *numskull, phiz, ramshackle, rattletrap, seedy;* only in AMERICAN SPEECH: *neck-and-neck* (denied by Horwill), and the ironical use of *nice.* In none of these cases does the nature of Mark Twain's usage appear to bring any convincing support to the lone advocate of an American classification, opposed as his judgment is to the evidence presented in the OXFORD of earlier and continuous British usage.

In some cases the OXFORD is apparently itself in doubt, inasmuch as, although it has refrained from making any definite pronouncement, it has found earlier American examples for the word or meaning than any in British writers; e.g., *ahold of, alive* (swarming with), *to back water, to bark, battery (Mining* sense), *billiardist, billionaire, the blues, cabinet minister, casting, copyrighted, cry-baby, insurance-policy, interview, jollification, labor-union, to make one's mark, to meet (Naut.* sense), *monthly,* sb., *muggins, object* (no object), *pork-packer, royalty* (payment to an author), *to run the blockade, Sabbath-school, sick,* v., *slack* (of the trousers), *slack water, smoke-house, soothing-syrup, tow-path, transcontinental, twilight,* v., *up-stream, utilize, to make it warm for,* and *weekly,* sb.; or, in the case of words now gone out of use in Great Britain, later American examples, e.g. *cooper-shop, lady-finger, lanky, onto, paling-fence, stretch* (to exaggerate), and *weave* (to sway the body); or even when its only examples are American, e.g. *Athenaeum, berrying, carding-machine, ice-storm, lamp-lighting, mind-cure, mule-race, newspaper-office, newspaper-reporter, to take one's number, Old School Baptist, Old World, prohibition* (of intoxicating drinks), *on tap, tar-baby, tax-return,* and *washpan.* In most of these cases, the nature of the term and the nature and authority of Mark Twain's usage are sufficient, it seems to us, to swing the balance in favor of a definite acknowledgment of the Americanism of the word or usage.

There are stronger grounds for such acknowledgment when the Americanism of a word or meaning is supported both by the nature of Mark Twain's usage and the judgment of at least one American authority. Hence there is little doubt of the genuine Americanism of the following, although they are called American only by Thornton: *bank-robbery, booky, hair-trigger, hard cash, heaves, high-grade, ice-cream, low-grade, outstart, point* (river sense), *slang* (abuse), and *wood,* v.; also in his third volume now appearing in DIALECT NOTES: *multi-millionaire, overflow-meeting, poster, soulful, spot cash,* and *tramp* (vessel). These are called American only in Mencken: *ach, aggravate, ass, to ballast, bank-account, bath-tub, to canvass, chromo, clothes-pin, copper-bellied, fad, funny, ground-wire, healthy* (healthful), *hello, ice-water, machine-shop, oyster-supper, to do one proud, specialty, standpoint, switchback, ticket-office, toggery,* and *underhanded.* These are Americanisms only in Horwill: *acclimated, acclimation, all of, all over, to beat the band, business-suit, contact* (association), *hand-spring, initiation fee, jarred, jolt, latch-string, raise,* sb. (increase in price), *to train with, wheelman, whoop,* and *write up.* The Americanism of the following is supported only by the contributors to DIALECT NOTES: *acrost, to back up, to bang, to let be, bitters, body* (a person), *one's born days, case-knife, to catch up, cattle* (of men and women), *cedar pencil, chaffy, chatterbox, cheeky, chicken-hearted, clothes-horse, coal-scuttle, cobble-stone, cobbling, comforter* (scarf), *kinfolks, king-bee, measly, mightily, mighty* (very great), *palings, patent-medicine, quality* (upper classes), *simon-pure, tow-headed,* and *unbeknownst.* These are so called only by contributors to AMERICAN SPEECH: *admire* (wonder), *air-shaft, bloke, carpet-bag, cold shoulder, to sleep in one's cravat, deck passage, desperadoism, to doctor, to fuzzle, hunterman, landing* (river sense), *nugget, putrefied* (for petrified), *rig* (costume), *sandbar, scatteration, spunk-water, stage* (landing-stage), *steamship, swag, turn out* (get out of bed), *turn to* (set to work), *tush* (tusk), *whack* (bargain), and *independent as a wood-sawyer's clerk.* A few words have actually been called Americanisms only by WEBSTER'S, the STANDARD, or the CENTURY: *air-tight stove* (W), *assay-office* (S), *coal-barge* (C), *free silver* (S), *hair-ball* (W), *hog-chain* (C), *to stand the racket* (S), *tintype* (S), and *torch-light procession* (S).

The most interesting cases, so far as the present study is concerned, are those for whose Americanism Mark Twain is himself the sole but, in our opinion, a sufficing authority. His usage is not, of course, a compelling reason unless he has employed the word in a definitely American connection, or has applied it specifically to American things, or has used it in passages of consciously vernacular flavor, in such a way as to indicate unmistakably that he felt it as an Americanism. It is always upon the implications of the context, taken as a whole, that the value and weight of Mark Twain's authority for the Americanism of a word depends. Most convincing are, naturally, occurrences in the dialog of books like TOM SAWYER or ROUGHING IT or THE AMERICAN CLAIMANT, or anywhere in HUCKLEBERRY FINN or CAPTAIN STORMFIELD or THE CONNECTICUT YANKEE, which are composed in the vernacular throughout. But wherever he speaks consciously, or makes his characters speak, as Americans, his usage is good evidence for the Americanism of his language.

It is least compelling, perhaps, in cases (marked ?AB³ in the LEXICON) where the OXFORD supplies earlier British examples; e.g., *to average, bell-punch, to book, common* (low-class), *to lead up to, negro minstrel, nigger minstrel, nigger-trader, paddle-box, stylographic,* and *syndicate.*

It is stronger, at least for the American origin of the word or usage, in cases (marked ?AB²) where Mark Twain has supplied an earlier example than the earliest given in the OXFORD; e.g., *absent-minded, accident insurance, for all of, all through, as* (as may be), *barbed wire, bar-soap, Bible-class, blasting-powder, boshy, cement, to slip a cog, colossal, combination* (of a safe), *to call it a day, endowment* (insurance), *handle-bar, foreign missions, mud-valve, mule-headed, nail-keg* (hat), *to come natural to, object-lesson, osteopathy, quartz-mill, on the quiet, reading-matter, to read up, respectworthy, to rule out, to run across, sloppy* (sentimental), *slush* (rubbishy literature), *stack* (a quantity), *war-correspondent,* and *war-footing.*

It is strongest in cases (marked ?AB¹) where Mark Twain is the sole authority for a word or meaning that is not found in the OXFORD at all, although given in one or more of the American dictionaries; e.g., *to ache* (long for), *airing, alongside of, to set amidships, article* (an immaterial thing), *to bank, on one's back, back-breaking, balmy, to ride bareback, battle-flag, battle-lantern, billet, bill of particulars, blind lead, buyer thirty, cabbage* and *cabbage-leaf* (of tobacco), *the "code," header, to jockey, night-owl, potato-gun, red-hot* (fresh), *river-front, like sin, slim Jim, statistic* (sing. form), *to string out, to be talked out,* and *tribute* (encomium); or in cases where Mark Twain's word or meaning is not found in any dictionary; e.g., *absolutely, alum-basket, arm-loop, around* (reported), *ashcat, to travel on asphalt, auction-block, baby-wagon, to know one by the back, backing-bell, just out of the band-box, to bang away, to give one down the banks, barb lace, blind reef, blip, to brace back, to breast, breast to breast with, breastboard, to brick up, high-light, ice-breaker, to meeky, mock trial, nail-grab, no name for it, need,* v. (deserve), *nigger-corner, notice,* sb., *off-watch, paper-collar, paust, pilot* (river sense), *privilege of the floor, quick-motioned, railbed, ready-bell, remainders* (corpse), *river-pilot, on the good side of, Simplified Speller, singing-geography, sny, sounding-boat, spinning-stick, spring-line, to step over* (cross the ocean), *strong suit* (fig.), *td* and *tf*, *third clerk*, *twain* (*Naut.* sense), *whistle-lever, wind-reef, witch-pie,* and *World's Fair.*

Of special interest in this connection are words or meanings used by Mark Twain that have been hitherto recorded only in Wright's ENGLISH DIALECT DICTIONARY. Mark Twain's use of these British dialect words argues that they must somehow have traveled to America, for otherwise it is hard to see how he could have known them. Examples are: *bulrusher, draw* (a puff at a pipe), *duffy, flummery* (in dress), *the Good Place, greasy* (water), *haddock, hanging-bout, night-times,* adv., *soothering, whack,* v., and *working-folks.* Among them are a few whose Americanism is recognized by Wright: *nonesuch,* sb., *regular* (thorough), *slab* (of cake), *sprint,* v., *stead of, that's the ticket, trembly, unregular, without* (unless), and *worsen.*

Allied to these are cases (marked ?AC) of words or meanings labeled by the OXFORD as obsolete or archaic. Their appearance in Mark Twain's vernacular at a later date than the latest British example in the OXFORD indicates that they should also be classed as American survivals. Examples are: *afront of, artist* (a proficient), *ballocks, to belch, betwixt, to blood, carcass, cleanliness* (moral sense), *comfortable* (reassuring), *dent* (indentation in a river-bank), *fulsome* morally foul), *larboard, lay to, in the nick of time, noble* (notable), *outlander, oversize,* v., *printing-house, put to* (hitch), *of record, shad* (as term of abuse), *strap* (for strop), *superscription, table-room, warming-pan, washer,* and *wicket.*

*   *   *

Mark Twain's Americanisms may next be considered and grouped from the point of view of their signification and content. They fall naturally into three main divisions, each of which may be further sub-divided. The first of these larger sections comprises those terms that reflect his own life and his special fields of interest. The second division brings together words that depict his America in its more general aspects, physical and geographical, environmental and social, political and historical. The third includes expressions and usages that particularly illustrate the spirit and tendencies of what has been called the "American language."[3]

A.   MARK TWAIN's SPECIAL FIELDS OF INTEREST

*"I have been everything, from a newspaper editor down to a
cowcatcher on a locomotive."*

Ten groups have been selected. Five of them reflect his principal professions and occupations, as riverman, traveler, miner, printer, and writer; and five his particular preoccupations and hobbies: machinery and invention, business and speculation, games and sports, food and drink, medicine and religion.

3   In the lists that follow no distinction has been made between certain and doubtful Americanisms; a few non-Americanisms have also been included for illustrative purposes. See the LEXICON for the exact status of each item.

1. *River and Nautical Terms*

This field made by far the largest contribution to Mark Twain's vocabulary.

a. The River and Its Aspects

ballast	head (of an island)	sawyer
bank-caving	head-mark	seepage
bar	high-river	shoal-mark
Big Water	high water	shoal up
blind reef	high-water-stained	shoal-water
bluff	horse-shoe	side-mark
boil, sb.	landing	slack water
break, sb.	landing-cabin	slick (water)
cave, v.	levee	snag
cave in	levee-rim	snagging
cave off	lower river	sny, sb.
chute	low-water	square crossing
clear-water, a.	make down	stage (level of water)
Coast	mark	stage (landing stage)
crevasse	Muddy, sb.	stern-mark
crossing	muddy-water, a.	tide-water
crossing-mark	on the river	timber-front
cut bank	pass, sb.	tourbillon
cut-off	point, sb.	towhead
dent	quarter, v.	tow-path
down the river	rapids	upper river
down-stream	reach, sb.	upper-river, a.
drift	reef-bench	up-river, a. and adv.
drift-canoe	rise, sb.	up-stream
drift-log	river-edge	up-streaming
drift-wood	river-front	water-glimpse
easy water	river-glimpse	water-lot
ferry-landing	river-inspector	water-supply
gorge	river-road	wind-reef
greasy water	sandbar	wing-dam
Great Waters	sand-reef	work down

b. River-Boats and Their Operation

ahead, to come	backing-bell	broad-horn
ark	back water	by and large
after-cabin	barge	boat-hand
after-davit	berth-saloon	cabin
after-deck	boiler-deck	cabin-guard
amidships	breast, v.	cabin-mate
back and fill	breast-board	cable-chain

cable-locker

canal-boat

canoe, sb. and v.

canoe-bottom

cathead

cattle-scow

chimney-guy

clerk

clew-iron

close (pilot)

coal-barge

coal-flat

coal-passer

coop

cramp, v.

cub

cub-engineer

cub-pilot

cylinder-head

deck-awning

deck-hand

deck-load

deck-passage

deck-passenger

deck-sweep

deck-washer

deep, sb.

doctor

dug-out

ease all

engine-bell

fetch

fiddle

fife-rail

flat, sb.

flat-boat

flat-boatman

fog-horn

fore-and-aft

foretopmaststuddingsail

gang-plank

garboard-strake

get in

gingerbread

guard

guard-deep

hail

half

head-line

head-on

helm-a-lee

hog-chain

hold on

hurricane deck

inside, prep. and sb.

jockey, v.

keelboat

keelboating

keelboatman

larboard

large

lay to

leads, to lay in the

leadsman

leeward

line

liner

locker-bunk

locker-sofa

log raft

longshoreman

lumber-raft

marks, in or into her

mark twain

meet, v.

mizen-yard

mud-clerk

mud-valve

night-hawk

oar-handle

off-watch

old man

outside, adv. and sb.

paddle-box

partner

passenger-list

passenger-packet

pilot

pilot-apprentice

pilot-house

piloting

pirogue

pole, v.

quarter, sb.

rack-heap

raft

rafting

raftsman

raft-voyage

ready-bell

relief-steamer

river-pilot

round to

round trip

roustabout

safe

safeness

sail-boat

saloon

scant

scoop, v.

scoopful

scow

scrape

scratch

second clerk

set back

shake up

ship, v.

ship up

shore up

shove up

show a pair of heels

side-wheel

signal-lantern

skid, sb.

smell, v.

smoke-stack

snag-boat

snatch

snub

sounding

sounding-barge

sounding-boat

sounding-pole

sounding-yawl
spar, v.
speaking-tube
spread open
spring-line
stage-plank
starboard
state-room
steamboat
steamboat-boiler
steamboatful
steamboating
steamboat-landing
steamboatman
steamboat-owner
steamer
steam-ferry
steam-ferryboat
stern-line
stern-wheel
stern-wheeler
storm-quarters
straighten down
straighten up

striker
texas
texas-deck
texas-hall
texas-tender
third clerk
tie up
timber-raft
torch-basket
tow-boat
trading-scow
transient, sb.
transom
tug-load
turn over
twain
two-taps-and-one
under-clerk
unloaden, v.
up-anchor, v.
up-bound
up-steam, v.
'vast
verge-staff

voyageur
walk, v.
watch, go off
watch below
water-reading
way-freight
way-passenger
way-port
way-traffic
weather-gasket
whale, v.
wharf-boat
wharf-rat
wheel
wheel-house
whistle-lever
white-ash
wood, v.
wood-boat
wood-flat
wood-sawyer's clerk,
   independent as a
yawl, a. and v.

c. Other Nautical Expressions

battle-lantern
clipper
clipper-ship
cobbling
combing
crowd, v.
Cunarder
hard tack
haul down one's colors
ironclad
land-dinner
life-preserver
man-of-war-like
ply, v.

run the blockade
sailor-knot
sailor-people
sailor-talk
sailor-way
sea-wonder
ship-going
ship-house
ship of war
shipping, to take
ship-talk
ship-time
sky-scraper
soup-and-bouille

steamship
steamshipping
steel ship
storm-rack
thwartships
tonnage
tramp
twin-screw
water-spout
wicked (sea)
yacht, v.
yachting-contest

d. Metaphorical and Transferred Uses

aboard
aft
aground

anchor out
after
back water

board, to stay by the
boom
break, sb.

breakers ahead   *foul,* v.   *reef*
bring up standing   *hail from*   *reel off*
by and large   *hard up*   *riffle, try* or *make the*
brace back   *head, full*   *sail,* v.
calk, v.   *head, half*   *sail in*
cave, v.   *head off*   *set back*
cave in   *heave*   *shoal water*
center, to catch on the *high water*   *slew,* v.
channel-finder   *holystone,* v.   *slush*
close-reef, v.   *inboard*   *snag*
cork, v.   *ironclad*   *square away*
crowd, v.   *keel over*   *steer clear of*
dead-center   *lay by*   *tidal wave*
dead-lights   *lay on the oars*   *turn in*
deck, on   *load up*   *turn out*
drift, v.   *mainbrace, to splice the* *turn to*
ease up   *manifest,* sb.   *unfurl*
fetch   *mark twain*   *wake,* sb.
fly light   *navigate*   *wash,* sb. and v.
fore-hatch   *pile-driving*   *watch-and-watch*
fore-top   *raise*   *yare*
forward   *rake,* sb.   *yarning*

2. Travel and Means of Transportation

His other occupations monopolized sections of his life; this one was lifelong and almost continuous. The terms listed under (d), which he doubtless picked up on his journeys, might of course have been multiplied indefinitely.

a. Horses and Stagecoaching

armloop   *horse-car*   *riata*
beat, sb.   *lariat*   *rig*
buggy   *lasso*   *rope in*
bus   *lope*   *saddle-bag*
chock up   *mud-wagon*   *saddle-blanket*
cinch   *mule-path*   *saddle-horn*
corduroy   *mule-power*   *shell-road*
cross-lots   *mule-rush*   *sleigh-runner*
cutter   *mule-race*   *stage*
dray-horse   *mustang*   *stage-coaching*
dray-pin   *pack-mule*   *stage-office*
hack   *pack-train*   *station-boss*
hack-driver   *passenger-coach*   *station-man*
hackful   *plug*   *sulky*
hackman   *quarter-horse*   *sumpter*
horseback-riding   *ranger-saddle*   *tapadero*

thoroughbrace   top-buggy   watering-depot

toll-road   wagon   way-station

b. Railroading

air-line	gravel-train	railway official
baggage	hand-car	recheck
baggage-check	hot-box	road
baggage-coupon	hotel-car	rock-cutting
baggage-master	invalid-car	schedule
baggage-smasher	iron horse	schedule-time
baggage-van	ladder-railroad	seat-back
baggage-wagon	ladder-railway	section
billet	lay over	sleeper
book, v.	lightning express	sleeping-car
brakeman	line	sleeping-section
branch-road	mail, v.	small baggage
car	mail-matter	smoker
cattle-car	mail-train	smoking-car
check, v.	mountain-railway	smoking-compartment
coach-candle	palace-car	spur
coal-train	palatial car	state-room
conductor	parlor-car	stop over
connect, v.	passenger-car	switchback
couple-up	paster	switchman
cow-catcher	peanut-boy	switch off
depot	plunder	through-freight
detained-baggage, a.	Pullman	through-line
division	Pullman car	ticket-money
double-gauge	rail, by	ticket-office
express	rail it	tie, sb.
expressman	railbed	track, off the
express-train	railroad	train-boy
fare-ticket	railroad-building	train-time
fly the track (fig.)	railroading	trunk-line
freight	railroad man	vestibuled
freightage	railroad president	way-train
freight-car	railroad-train	whistle, v.
freighting	rails	wood-and-water-station
grade	railway-center	

c. Other Conveyances

bicycle	header	street car
cable-car	machine	surface-line
elevated road	motor-car	velocipede
handle-bar	racing-mobile	wheelman

d. Traveler's Terms

Alp-climber	*memento-factory*	*relic-peddler*
Alp-climbing	*memento-seeker*	*step over*
chaleteer	*Morgue*	*summer-resort*
crevasse	*noon*, v.	*summer-resorter*
Cunarder	*nooning*	*tear-jug*
hula-hula	*Old Master*	*tourist-book*
lanai	*Old World*	*tourist-resort*
make good time	*palace-hotel*	*traveling-bag*
memento	*poi*	*yodel*

3. *Western and Mining Terms*

Next to the river, his Western experience colored Mark Twain's vocabulary more than any other chapter of his life.

a. Frontier Language (including ranching, lumbering, oil-drilling, and land speculation)

axman	*frontier*	*lumberman*
bag, v.	*gouge*	*meat, to be one's*
barbed wire	*guide-board*	*notice*, sb.
bareback, to ride	*hive*, v.	*outfit*, sb. and v.
bark on, with the	*hog-wallow*	*overland*
beat, sb.	*homestead*	*oil, to strike*
bead, to draw a	*horn-blow*	*oil-derrick*
bee-line	*hunterman*	*oil-region*
bee-tree	*husky*, sb.	*pard*
bull-driver	*jerked* (beef)	*petroleum-city*
cache	*John*	*point*, v.
cattle-pen	*jump*	*prairie-fire*
cattle-raiser	*jumper*	*preempt*
center, to drive	*land-boom*	*prove title*
center-driving	*land-dealer*	*ranch*, sb. and v.
chock up	*land-office business*	*ranch-life*
cord	*land-speculator*	*ranchman*
cord wood	*latch-string*	*range*, sb.
corral	*lay* (a claim)	*rawhide*, v.
cow-boy	*layout*	*relocatable*
cowhide	*line-shot*	*round-up*
cowhiding	*locate*	*round up*, v.
desperadoism	*location*	*sand-mound*
emigrant	*locator*	*sand-wave*
emigrant-train	*log cabin*	*saw-buck*
Far West	*lots, across*	*saw-log*
finger-board	*lumber-camp*	*scout*

settlement
shanty
shebang
sheep-drover
sheep-run
sight, v.
sighting-iron
squatter
stakes, to pull up
stale (track)
stampede

tenderfoot
tenderfooted
torpedo
tracks, in one's
trading-post
trail
transcontinental
tree, v.
vamose
vigilance committee
West

Western
Westerner
Wild West
wood-rank
woods, in the
woods, out of the
woods, to take to the
wood-sawing
wood-sawyer
woodsy

b. Mining (see especially the passage quoted under *arrastre*)

air-shaft
angle
arrastre (arastra)
assay-office
battery
bed-rock
blasting-powder
blind lead
blind vein
bonanza
casing
cement
cement-mine
chimney
chunk
claim
clean up
concentrator
dip
dirt
discovery
drift
find
fire-assay
flat, sb.
flume
foot
foot-casing
foot-wall
Forty-Niner
free gold
Golconda
gold-miner

gold-pan
gold-strike
hanging wall
hardpan
hoisting works
horn
horse
hydraulic
incline
indication
ingot
lead, sb.
ledge
lode
mining-broker
mining-camp
mining-tax
mud, to sell for the
nugget
outcropping
pan, sb. and v.
panful
pan out
paust
pay-rock
pick and shovel, v.
pig
placer
placer-diggings
pocket
pocket-miner
pocket-mining
powder-can

powder-keg
prospect, sb. and v.
prospecting
prospector
quartz-mill
quartz-milling
quartz-miner
riffle
saleratus
salt, v.
salting
sawdust mine
side drift
silver-claim
Silverland
silver-miner
silver-mining
slug
sluice, sb. and v.
sluice-box
spur
strike, sb. and v.
strike it lucky
strike it rich
surface-miner
tailings
tailing-pile
tamp
trash-dust
wash-up
wild cat (mine)
worked-out (mine)

4. *Printing and Journalistic Terms*

Printing was the first trade whose technicalities he mastered; journalism and publishing always remained the second strings to his bow.

a. Printing and Binding

agate	frisket	plant out
assemble	hand-tooled	poster
bindery	hell-box	poster-fence
bogus	hell-matter	printing-house
break, sb.	jeff	proof-reading
break line	job-printing	roll, v.
case-man	job-office	sit, sb.
coarse print	job-work	slap
comp	jour	solid matter
composing-gait	jour printer	standing-galley
compositor	justifier	steel plate
d box	k box	sub, sb. and v.
display-head	nonpareil	subbing
display-heading	occasional, sb.	take, sb.
display sheet	one-liner	thin-spaced
divinity circuit	out, sb.	turn over
double-starred	perfecting press	two-liner
even, to make	pie (pi)	
fence, v.	pied	

b. Newspapers and Magazines

ad	item	personal, sb.
Adam-newsboy	leader	personal-gossip, a.
beat, v.	leader-writer	pictorial paper
chock up	letter-correspondence	press-notice
city-editor	local editor	reading-matter
daily, sb.	local item	regular, sb.
continued story	magazine-agent	reporter-material
double-columned	magazining	reportorial
dramatic editor	monthly, sb.	salutatory, sb.
editor-critic	mustard-plaster	scare-head
editorial	newspaper-bag	scoop
evening paper	newspaper-clipping	society item
exchange, sb.	newspaper-hawking	special, sb.
fat, sb.	newpaperless	td and tf
floating (item)	newspaper-office	war-correspondence
funny paragraph	newspaper-picture	war-correspondent
health-journal	newspaper-reporter	weekly, sb.
interview, v. and sb.	news-scrap	writing-parlor
interviewer	notice	yellow journalism

c. Publishing

canvass, v.	*royalty*	*syndicating*
copyrighted	*subscription*	
copyright-preserving	*syndicate*	

5. *Writing and Speaking Terms*

Naturally there are only a few distinctive Americanisms in this group. A high proportion of them are obviously deliberate coinages or metaphorical adaptations of Mark Twain's own.

a. Literary

Arabian-Nighty	*poet-orator*	*Shakesperiod*
authoress	*robber-book*	*storiette*
authoring	*romance-literature*	*Stratfordian*, sb. and a.
literary (littery)	*romance-reading*	*Stratfordolater*
Picciola	*romaunt*	*Swinburnian*
Pickwickian	*sensation-story*	*tourist-book*
pirate-book	*Shakespeare*	*Twainiana*
poet-lariat	*Shakespeare-adoring*	
poet-laureatic	*Shakespearite*	

b. Technical and Critical

adjective-piling	*humorism*	*phrase-juggler*
adjective-stump	*humor-lover*	*picturesquenesses*
appendix-basket	*involuted*	*pile it on*
book, like a	*jack-leg* (novelist)	*poetastical*
book-material	*jamble*	*repetitious*
booky	*journeyman*	*repetitiousness*
boshy	*jumbulacious*	*revamp* (revise)
complacency-signal	*labored-out*	*rot*
drool, v.	*lightning*, a.	*sappy*
flapdoodle	*literature-preserver*	*slush*
flat out	*localized*	*snapper* (of a story)
flatting	*magnanimous-*	*snappy*
go, sb.	*incident*, a.	*stage-direction*
gruel	*motif*	*starchy*
gush, v.	*mush-and-milk*	*Sweet Singer*
gushy	*nickel-plated*	*synopsize*
hack-grinding	*noble-episode*, a.	*thunder-and-lightning*, **a.**
half-sole (revise)	*nub* (of a story)	*under-description*
hand-painted	*over-description*	*write up*
hifalutin	*over-fondle*	*yare*, v.
hog-wash	*over-terseness*	*yellow-covered*
holystone, v. (revise)	*panegyrics*	
humor	*pemmican* (style)	

c. Language and Grammar (see especially the passage quoted under *kahkah-poneeka*)

addition (name)	*governess-German*	*Simplified Speller*
American language	*guide-English*	*Simplified Spelling*
argot	*had,* sb. and v.	*slang* (3 senses)
Carnegian (spelling)	*hard-boiled* (grammar)	*slangy*
Carnegieize	*human* (see M.T.'s	*spell down*
Choctaw (language)	comment)	*spelling-fight*
choice (English)	*hyphenated name*	*thesaurus*
compounding-disease	*Injun-English*	*trade-form*
debauch (one's	*king-parenthesis*	*trade-phrasing*
grammar)	*language, strong*	*transcontinental*
English-murdering	*leaky* (grammar)	(sentence)
fine language	*letter-perfect*	*Unabridged*
fourth dimension	*middle name*	*undictionarial*
(grammar)	*palaver*	*Verbarium*
freemasonry	*phrase-family*	*Webster-Unabridged*
Germanic	*raven* (language)	*word-sense*
given name	*reparenthesis*	*Yankee* (language)

d. Speech and Pronunciation

book-talk	*phonetics (fonetics)*	*speech-vehicle*
costermonger	*pull one's words*	*swing* (of a word)
dialect-speaking	*rattler* (long word)	*talk-machinery*
horse-talk	*sailor-talk*	*turn,* v. (of the voice)
lawyer-talk	*ship-talk*	*utterance-point*
lightning-heeled (word)	*slobber*	*word-musician*
long talk	*snip out*	*yap*
miscall	*soldier-talk*	*yawp*

e. Oratory and Lecturing

Chautauqua	*lecture-raid*	*orator of the day*
highway	*lecture-season*	*platform*
house-emptier	*lecture-tour*	*platform-business*
house-filler	*lecturing-trip*	*reader*
lecture-agent	*lyceum*	*reading,* vbl. sb.
lecture-hall	*lyceum-system*	

6. *Mechanical Inventions and Scientific Terms*

An inventor himself, Mark Twain was always keenly interested in every sort of mechanical device and discovery, and an assiduous reader in many fields of science.

a. Machines and Inventions (see especially the passages quoted under *bicycle* and *cotton-gin*)

air-blast	*ice-machine*	*radiator*
annunciator	*king-bolt*	*safety-box*
bell-punch	*ladder railroad*	*scrap-book*
bicycle	*lift*, sb.	*self-binder*
bone-filter	*lightning-rod*	*self-pasting* (scrap-book)
cable	*long-distance*	*sewing-machine*
cablegram	*loom-work*	*shaft*
cable telegraph	*loop-engineering*	*sleeping-car*
cable telephone	*lucifer* (match)	*steam-sawmill*
carbon film	*machine*	*steamship*
carding machine	*machine-shop*	*steel ship*
celluloid	*mill-saw*	*stylographic*
centrifugal	*motor-car*	*telegraph*
chromo	*miller-gun*	*telelectrophonoscope*
corn-sheller	*palace-car*	*telelectroscope*
cotton-gin	*palace hotel*	*telephone*
dry battery	*pantograph*	*tintype*
electric call	*paper-collar*	*trolley*
electric car	*phonograph*	*type-channel*
elevator	*photo*	*type-machine*
flouring-mill	*phrenophone*	*vacuum-pan*
flutter-mill	*porcelaintype*	*weet-weeter*
grain-elevator	*raceway*	*wood-sawing* (machine)
hair-trigger	*railroad*	
ice-factory	*racing-mobile*	

b. Finger-Printing

finger-mark	*loop*	*record*
finger-print	*pattern*	*takings*
grease-print	*plate*	*throw up*
identifier	*paw-mark*	

c. Miscellaneous Scientific and Mechanical Expressions

asteroid	*Edisonian*	*mounting-peg*
casting	*engineer*, v.	*Oolitic*
Central	*focus*	*phonographer*
clear-burning	*ground-circuit*	*point* (of lightning rod)
daguerreotype-case	*ground-connection*	*post-Pleosaurian*
dead-center	*ground-wire*	*pre-geologic*
derrick	*machinist*	*science*
Edisonially	*Mesozoic*	*scientifics*

scrap-book, v.	telescoper	typewriter-copyist
scrap-booking	telescopulariat	type-writer, v.
Silurian	telescopulist	typewriter-table
tap, on	type-copy	zinc-plated
telegram	type-girl	
telegraph-pole	type-setter	

7. Business and Speculative Terms

His dearest dream was to become a big business man and a financial magnate; his keenest disappointment that he always failed to do so.

a. Investment and Speculation

at (Comm. sense)	flyer	seller ten
bank, v.	four prices	short, sb.
bank account	freeze out	short, to sell
bargain-counter	futures	short on, to go
bear, v.	gilt-edged	six figures
Board	go security	squeeze
boom, sb. and v.	gobble	stake, v.
bucket-shop	good thing	Standard Oil Trust
bull, v.	ground floor	stock, v.
bunco	horse	stock in, to take
buyer thirty	horse-trade	stock-board
buy into	incorporatorship	stockholder
call, upon	indorse	sure thing
cash in	inflated	taker
checks, to pass in one's	long on, to be	trade, sb. and v.
clean out	margin, sb. and v.	trade off
combine, sb.	margin-business	Trust
copper, v.	market-report	unload
corner, v.	negotiate	unwatered
declare	operation	Wall Street
defaulter	operator	war-price
deficit	plant, v.	water, v.
dicker	pool, sb. and v.	watered
dividend-cooking	racket	whirl, sb.
feeler	raise, sb.	wild cat (bank)
fence, sb.	rose-tinted	world-trade

b. Monetary and Financial Expressions

bank-bill	boodle	copper, sb.
bill	broke	continental
billion	bust, v.	dead broke
billionaire	busted	dollar
bit	cent	eagle

fip
five, sb.
five-center
flat broke
flush
greenback
half-dime
half-dollar
hard cash
mill
millionaire
million-pounder
milray
money in it
multi-billionaire

multi-millionaire
nickel
one-hundred-millionaire
one-pounder
postal currency
rag dollar
receipt, v.
red, sb.
rock
safe, sb.
safe-deposit
safe-door
safe-key
seller ten
shekel

shin-plaster
sixpence
slug
spondulicks
stake, v.
tael
three-dollar
twenty, sb.
twenty-dollar
two-millionaire
V
wherewithal
wild cat (money)
yellow-boy
yellow-jacket

c. Insurance Terminology

accidental insurance
accident insurance
endowment

insurance-agency
insurance-policy
life-policy

paid-up (insurance)
policy business

d. Business Occupations and Miscellaneous Commercial Expressions

article
barber-shop
barker
bindery
boss
boycott
clothing-store
concern
cooper-shop
corner-grocery
distributing-house
drugstore
drummer
dry goods
establishment
fire-auction
hang up
hardware

hardware store
ice-man
instalment plan
junk-shop
lagniappe
line
milk-route
order-book
output
parlor
peddle
plank, v.
plant, sb.
pork-house
pork-millionaire
pork-packer
pork-packing
pungle

real estate
saloon
salt-warehouse
shop, a.
shop-right
square, v.
square up
stand, sb.
stonemason
store, sb. and a.
store, to keep
thread-spinner
tin-monger
trade-form
trade-mark
variety store
washer
washerman

8. *Amusements and Sporting Terms*

If there was a single game, sport, or social diversion of his time in which Mark Twain did not at one time or another take an absorbing interest, we have failed to discover it.

a. Cards and Gambling

age, to hold the	*gift*	*Quaker*
and (deuces-and)	*high*	*raffle off*
and (kings-and)	*high-low-jack*	*raise*
ante	*hold over*	*raise out*
bet	*Jack*	*risk*, v.
blind, sb.	*jack-pair*	*see*
bower, right	*jack-pot*	*seven-up*
buck, pass the	*kings-and*	*stand pat*
chip in	*layout*	*straddle*
corner, sb.	*lone hand*	*straight flush*
deck of cards	*low*, sb.	*strong suit*
draw, sb. and v.	*old sledge*	*sure thing*
dummy-whist	*pass*, v.	*threes*
euchre	*pile, to go one's*	*throw a card*
fill	*play*, v.	*throw up*
flush, sb.	*poker*	*tiger*
full, sb.	*poker-clergy*	*trump*
gambling-den	*pool*, sb.	*Trumps*
game, the	*pot*	
game of chance	*put up*	

b. Billiards

bank, v.	*English*	*scratch*
billiardist	*fifteen-ball pool*	*set up*
billiard-parlor	*fluke*	*string*
billiard-room	*freeze*	*tally-keeper*
carom, v.	*leather*	*three-ball game*
cocked hat	*outlay*	
crotch, v.	*punch*, v.	

c. Baseball

balk, to make a	*catcher*	*nine*, sb.
ball-proof	*daisy-cutter*	*right fielder*
base	*drive*, sb.	*short-stop*
baseball	*earned run*	*slide*, v.
bat, at	*fielding*	*steal a base*
bat, hot from the	*goose-egg*	*team*
bat, step to the	*home-plate*	*whitewash*, v.
call game	*inning*	
call the game	*keep game*	

d. Theatrical Terms

circus	*charading*	*mock trial*
circusing	*minstrel*	*make-up*

negro-minstrel
nigger-minstrel
nigger-show
opera house
panoramist

play-acting
show-people
sideshow
stage-carpentering
stage-courtier

stage-direction
stage-fright
stage-whispering
stand, sb.
supe

e. Other Sports and Social Amusements

band-wagon
berryings
break-down
break-down-dancing
blow-out
candy-pull
candy-pulling
clog-dancing
cocking main
corn-shucking
dough-face
Fair
fair-grounds
fandango
fantastic, sb.
grand-stand
gully-keeper

hay-ride
home-stretch
horse-billiards
hula hula
jollification
junketing
keeps
knucks
larks, to play
marvel (marble)
Midway
muggins
mule-race
mumble-the-peg
neck (a neck ahead)
neck-and-neck
nutting-expedition

philippina
Pigs in Clover
pillow-fight
pleasure-resort
pleasuring
pumpkin-show
quarter-horse
schottische, sb. and v.
shivaree
skylarking
ten-pins
ten-strike
toboggan-slide
Verbarium
Virginia reel
World's Fair

9. *Eating, Drinking, and Smoking Terms*

He loved to talk about eating and drinking more than to practise them; but in the matter of smoking he probably practised even more than he preached.

a. Eating and Culinary Expressions (see especially the passages quoted under *batter-cake* and *biscuit*)

ash-cake
Baltimore perch
barbecue
batter-cake
bear-meat
biscuit
biscuit-punch
black bass
blue-point
buckwheat cakes
butter-bean
candy
cantelope

canvas-back duck
cherry-stone clam
chestnut cake
chewing-gum
chickory
chitlings
chuck
clabber
cobbler
cook-book
corn-beef
corn-bread
corn-crust

corn-dodger
corn-meal
corn-pone
cracker
cranberry
croaker
dog-in-a-blanket
doughnut
drawn butter
drench, sb.
dried-apple-pie
duffy
ear, on the

eating-room
eating-station
egg-bread
emptings
European plan
feeding-house
feeding-place
flap-jack
fruit-cake
granite
gravy
grease-biscuit
greens
grub
gum-drop
half-shell, on the
hard-boil, v.
hard-boiled
hash
hoe-cake
hog and hominy
hominy
ice-cream
Indian meal
Irish potato
lady-finger
left-over
light-bread
Limburger
liquorice
liver-sausage
maple sugar

maple syrup
Milam (apple)
molasses
molasses candy
moon
mush-and-milk
muskmelon
oleomargarine
oyster-supper
partridge
pemmican
pie, apple
pie, mince
pie, peach
planked (fish)
poi
pone
pop-corn
porter-house steak
possum
prairie-hen
pretzel
pumpkin
pumpkin-pie
rare (meat)
restaurant
Saratoga potatoes
sausage-stuffing
shad, Conneticut
slapjack
slum
slumgullion

soft-shell crab
soup-and-bouille
sour-crout
spoon-vittles
spread, sb.
square meal
squash
stand-up, sb.
string-bean
succotash
sweet-potato
table, to set a good
table-fare
table-room
tenderloin
terrapin
tomato
trout, brook
trout, lake
truck
turkey, roast
turkey, wild
victual (vittles)
waffle-iron
waffle-mould
wheat, good as
wheat-bread
whitebait
woodcock
yam

b. Drinking and Terms for Intoxication (see especially the passage quoted under cocktail)

aguardiente
bar-keep
bar-keeper
bar-room
beer-mill
beer-saloon
bitters
Bourbon
brandy-smash
bust, on a

bung-starter
chain-lightning
cobbler, sherry
cocktail
corn-whisky
delirium tremens
doggery
drunk, sb.
dry
dryness

earthquake
eggnog
exhilaration
eye-opener
fire-water
forty-rod whisky
fuzzle, v.
gin-mill
gin-sling
groggery

half-seas-over	rum-hole	teetotalism
hic!	rum-mill	temperance
ice-water	rummy	tight
illuminate	rum-shop	tipple, sb.
influence, under the	rye	town drunkard
lager	saloon	valley tan
liquor-drinking	saloon-keeper	vodka jug
liquor saloon	sample-room	wet down
loon, drunk as a	scorpion-bile	whisky
make it	Scotch	whisky-drinking
mellow	set up	whisky-habit
moonshiner	snuggery	whisky-jug
persuader	sour-mash	whisky-mill
piper, drunk as a	spree, sb. and v.	whisky-shelf
poison-swilling	spreeing	whisky-soaked
prohibition	stone-fence	whisky-sodden
prohibitionist	straight (whisky)	whisky-straight
punch, Santa Cruz	sudden death	wine-bag
Red Ribbon	tanglefoot	wine-sipper
rum	teetotaler	

c. **Smoking**

cabbage	nigger-head	tobacco
cabbage-leaf	old soldier	tobacco-chewing
cigar (seegar)	plug	tobacco-commerce
corn-cob pipe	seed-leaf	tobacco-curing
dog-hair	smokable, sb.	tobacco-field
dog-leg	smoking party	tobacco-juice
double-butt-ender	snifter	tobacco-lover
draw, sb.	special-brand	tobacco-smoke
Havana	stogy	tobacco-stemmer
leaf tobacco	stub	toby
long-nine	stub-hunter	wrapper

10. *Medical and Religious Terms*

Medicine and religion interested Mark Twain more deeply and absorbed more of his attention than any other subjects that ever entered his mind. It is impossible to draw the border-line between them in his thinking; he knew all the sects and debated most of the problems of them both, although he never committed his final allegiance to any one of them. The one he should have joined is the American denomination known as the River Brethren.

a. **Health and Disease**

blind staggers	chills and fever	dry gripes
chills, cold	chills-racked	dyspeptic

heaves   *rugged*   *squalmish*
janders   *run down*, v.   *up and around* (conval-
lay up   *sick*   escent)
madhouse   *sick-list*   *wabbles*
rheums   *small-poxed*
Riggs's disease   *smallpox-pitted*

b. Death and Burial

bone-yard   *death-room*   *post-mortuary*
burial-case   *death-stroke*   *remainders*
casket   *diseased* (deceased) *reward, go to one's*
city of the dead   *graveyard*   *send-off*, sb.
death-agony   *immortelle*   *sepulture*
death-damp   *jewel-box*   *tower of silence*
death-grip   *obituarial*   *tribute*
death-light   *plant*, v.   *undertaker-outfit*

c. Remedies and Healing Methods (see especially the passage quoted under
    afarabocca)

afarabocca   *doctor-book*   *paregoric*, v.
alipta   *elecampane*   *patent-medicine*
allopath   *Electropath*   *regular*, sb.
anacardium   *farmacopia*   *rheum ponticum*
attractive, sb.   *farmeopath*   *saw-bones*
bathcure   *galingale*   *soothing-syrup*
bay-berry   *grape-doctor*   *sozodont*
bay rum   *grape-system*   *spider's web*
blatta byzantina   *herb-doctor*   *spignel*
blue mass   *Indian doctor*   *styrax calamita*
calamus odoratus   *macedonian*   *surgery-practice*
camphene   *moschata*   *water-cure*
carnabodium   *mud-cure*   *xylaloes*
celtic   *osteopath*   *xylobalsamum*
coftus   *osteopathic*   *zedoary*
corpobalsamum   *osteopathy*
doctor, v.   *pain-killer*

d. Christian Science and the "Mind-Sects"

absent treatment   *capitation-tax*   *claim*, sb.
annex   *Christian Science*   *demonstrate*
annex polisher   *Christian Scientifically* *demonstration*
Association   *Christian-Scientism* *Divine Science*
Bible-Annex   *Christian Scientist* *Eddyty*

Eddy-worship	*Mental Scientist*	*pastor emeritus*
faith-curist	*mental telegraphy*	*prayer-cure*
faith-doctor	*Metaphysical*	*Reader*
First Member	*mind-cure*	*Science*
harmonious	*mind-curist*	*Science Pope*
healer	*mind-sect*	*Scientist*
matteration	*mortal mind*	*Scientist-Church*
Mental Science	*Mother Church*	*self-deification*

e. Spiritualists

materialization	*materializer*	*Spiritualism*
materialize	*materializing*	*Spiritualist*
materializee	*medium*	*Spiritualistic*

f. Mormons

Destroying Angel	*Latter-Day Saint*	*Mormon, sb.* **and** *a.*
Gentile	*Morisite*	*Mormondom*

g. Other Denominations and Religious Bodies (see passages quoted under *Adventist, Allopath,* and *Congregationalist*)

Adventist	*Disciples*	*Millerite*
ascensionist	*dissentering*	*Nationalist*
Blavatsky-Buddhist	*Dowie*	*Old School Baptist*
Campbellite	*Dunkards*	*Peculiar People*
Catholic	*Dunker-Baptist*	*Plymouth Brethren*
Christadelphian	*Episcopal*	*Reformed*
Christian Catholic	*Episcopalian*	*River Brethren*
Christian Connection	*Evangelical*	*Salvation Warriors*
Christian Missionary	*Free Will Baptist*	*Shaker*
Association	*Harrisite, Laurence*	*Universalist*
Church of God	*Oliphant*	*Waldenstromian*
Congregationalist	*Methodist*	*Winebrennarian*

h. Miscellaneous Religious Expressions

amen-corner	*dominie*	*Kingdom*
ascension-robe	*doxology-works*	*Kingdom-Come*
Bad Place	*exhorter*	*lay preacher*
Bible-class	*experience* (religion)	*line out*
camp-meeting	*get* (religion)	*meeting-house*
Christian	*glorify*	*miracle-factory*
Christian-missionary, v.	*Good Book*	*missions, foreign*
contribution-box	*Good Place*	*missionary,* v.
contribution-plate	*gospel-mill*	*missionarying*
contribution-purse	*gospel-sharp*	*mourner*

mourners' bench	religiouswise	Sunday-school
nigger-corner	Reverend, sb.	Sunday-school book
nigger-gallery	rice Christian	thee (Quaker use)
notice, sb.	Sabbath-school	this-worldly
Other Place	Santa Claus	upper bench (Quaker
Other Side	sensation-preacher	use)
pastorate	sewing-society	world's people (Quaker
preforeordestination	sociable, sb.	use)
professor	society (Quaker use)	yonder (other world)

i. Folklore and Superstition

hair-ball	whip-poor-will	witch-dread
haunt	witch, v.	witch-hazel professor
spunk-water	witch-business	witch-pie
tar-baby	witch-cat	witch-terror
weaken down	witch-commissioner	

B. MARK TWAIN'S AMERICA

The ten groups included in this division were not so immediately close to Mark Twain's heart as those given above; but every aspect of America interested him, and his vocabulary demonstrates his intimate acquaintance with American geography and nature, and with all the races and classes that make up the American people, as well as with their life, their habitations, their possessions, their dress, their manners, their politics, and their history.

1. The Land and the Landscape

a. Toponymic Terms

American, sb. and a.	Coast	Kanaka
Americanism	Congress water	Klondike
Americanized	Cotton States	Mexicanized
American language	District of Columbia	mid-Atlantic
Arkansaw	East, sb. and adv.	Middle States
Aztec	Eastern	Missouri
Bad Lands	Far West	Missourian, sb. and a.
Banner State	Far-Western	Mound City
Bermuda	Great Plains	Muddy
Big Water	Great Republic	Nevadian
Blue Grass	Great Waters	New Englander
Blue Hen's Chickens	Gulf Stream	New Yorker
Bourbon	Halifax	Niagara
Californiaward	Hannibal	North
Chautauqua	Havana	Northern
Cherokee Strip	jimpson-weed	Northerner

Oklahoma	*Southerner*	*Virginia reel*
Old Dominion	*Southern-looking*	*Wallachian*
Old Virginia	*Southern-style*	*Wall Street*
Pacific-coaster	*Southron*	*Washoe*
Panama hat	*State*	*Washoe zephyr*
Plains	*States, the*	*Waterbury*
plainsman	*Sucker*	*West,* sb. and adv.
Potomac	*Susquehannian*	*West, out*
Quaker City	*Tahoe*	*Western*
Rocky Mountains	*Tennessean*	*Westerner*
St. Louis (St. Looey)	*Territorial*	*West-Pointer*
Saratoga potatoes	*Territory*	*Wild West*
Saratoga trunk	*texas*	*Yank*
Silverland	*un-American*	*Yankee*
South, sb. and adv.	*Union*	*Yankee-land*
South, down	*Valley*	*Young America*
South Carolinian	*Virginia (Virginny)*	
Southern	*Virginian*	

b. Topographic Terms

alkali	*continental*	*layout*
back-country	*creek*	*outdoors,* sb.
back-lot	*divide*	*prairie*
back-settlement	*dornick*	*rolling* (land)
backwoods	*foot-hill*	*scar*
bayou	*Forks*	*section*
belt of timber	*gap*	*sink,* sb.
bench	*gore*	*slough*
bottom	*gulch*	*slue*
branch	*hollow*	*swale*
bluff	*ice-barren*	*swamp*
canebrake	*knob*	*timber-land*
cañon	*lake-front*	*up-country,* sb., a.,
cañon-bed	*land-slide*	adv.
cañon-side	*lay* (of the land)	

2. *Nature*

a. Fauna

alligator	*black bass*	*bullfrog*
anaconda	*blackbird*	*buzzard*
angle-worm	*black fish*	*canvass-back duck*
antelope	*bronco*	*cat-bird*
Baltimore perch	*buffalo*	*cat-fish*
beaver	*bug*	*chicken*

chicken-cock	locust	rooster
chipmunk	martin-box	sea-otter
coon	mocker	sheep-head
coyote	mosquito	silver-gray fox
crawfish	mud-cat	skip-jack
crayfish	mud-dobber	skipper
daddy	mud-turkle	skunk
daddy-longlegs	mud-turtle	snapping-turtle
doodle-bug	night-hawk	sun-perch
fiddler	opossum	tarantula
fire-bug	panther	terrapin
fishing-worm	partridge	tree-toad
fox-squirrel	pheasant	trout
gallinipper	pigeon	tumble-bug
garter	pinch-bug	turkey
garter-snake	pocket-pup	turkey, wild
gopher	polecat	turkey-call
grand-daddy-longlegs	pompano	turkeylet
hoop-snake	possum	turtle
house-snake	prairie-chicken	varmint
jackass	prairie-dog	water-moccasin
jackass rabbit	prairie-hen	water-turkey
jay	prairie-rattlesnake	whip-poor-will
June-bug	puff-adder	whitebait
katydid	quail	wild cat
king-bee	rabbit	wild goose
king-fisher	racer (snake)	woodcock
lady-bug	rat terrier	wood-pheasant
lightning-bug	rattlesnake	yellow-jacket

b. Flora

American creeper	corn	magnolia
autumn-butter	cottonwood	manzanita
bagasse	cypress	morning-glory
bay-berry	dog-fennel	mountain-cabbage
Big Tree	garden-truck	mullen-stalk
bulrusher	grease-wood	palmetto
butternut	gum	pawpaw
bunchgrass	hickory	peanut
cane	horse-chestnut	persimmon
cantelope	huckleberry	phlox
cat-tail	Indian corn	pie-plant
chapparal	jimpson-weed	pine, white
cherimoya	live-oak	pine, yellow
chili-bean	locust-tree	pine-knot

pinery
pitch-pine
plantain
potato
prairie-pink
pulu
pumpkin
raspberry
redwood
sage-brush
sage-bush
sarsaparilla

sequoia gigantea
simlin
Spanish moss
squash
sugar-bush
sumac-berry
summer-grape
sunflower
sycamore
timber
tobacco
tomato

tomato-vine
torch-plant
truck
tule
underbrush
walnut, black
walnut, English
walnut-hull
white-oak
witch-hazel
yam

c. Weather

burster
cyclone
hurricane
ice-storm
norther
Old Probabilities
rain-dog

snow-drive
snow in
snow-storm
snow under
squally
storm-buffeted
storm-wash

thunder-burst
thunder-gust
tornado
Washoe zephyr
weather
weather-clerk

3. Race, Class, and Occupation

a. Indians and Indian Terms

Aztec
audience-room
Blackfoot
brave, sb.
buck
campoodie
cayuse
Cheyenne
Choctaw
council-fire
Digger
half-breed
half-white
hatchet, to bury the
heap much
hostile, sb.
hunting-ground
Indian
Indian doctor

Indian file
Indian mound
Indian sign
Injun
Injun-English
lodge, sb.
manito
medicine-man
medicine-sack
mishemokwa
moccasin
moccasined
pale-face
pappoose
Pawnee
pipe of peace
Piute
powwow, sb. and v.
Red Man

Reds
Redskin
sachem
sagamore
saw-saw-quan
scalp, sb. and v.
scalp-dance
scalp-lock
Shoshone
Sioux
Son of the Forest
squaw
squaw-man
Tammany
Thunder-Bird
tomahawk, sb. and v.
totem-post
wampum
war-paint

war-party	war-whoop	wigwam
war-path	war-whooping	Young-Man-Afraid-of-
war-plume	wickyup	his-Shadow

b. Negroes and Negro Terms

abolition	Mars, Marse	Old Mistress (Ole
abolitionist	moke	Missus)
auction-block	mulatto	pickaninny, a.
Aunt	negro-minstrel	plantation hymn
auntie	negro-stealer	quarters
banjo	negro-trader	runaway-nigger
Brer	nigger	slave auction
buck	nigger-bill	slave-lord
cake-walk	nigger-corner	slave state
contraband, sb.	nigger-gallery	slave-wench
darky	niggerkin	slave-worked
free papers	nigger-minstrel	Uncle
free soil	nigger-show	wench
Free State	nigger-stealer	white-wooled
juba	nigger-trader	
kinky	Old Master (Ole Marse)	

c. Other Americans

alkali-spider	Greaser	outlander
American	hand	Patrick
backwoodsman	help	white, low
Dutch	hired girl	white, poor
Dutchman	immigrant	working-folks
F. F. V.	John	working-people
First Family	Mick	

4. Country and City Life

a. Rural Terms

ashhopper	fence-post	round-log, a.
bake-oven	fence-rail	smoke-house
back-log	garden-acre	smoke-house raising
chicken-farm	out back	sugar-camp
country-place	out-cabin	sugar-hogshead
country-woven	plantain-patch	sugar-plantation
dornick	plantation	sugar-trough
farm, for a	planter	work-animal
farmer-class	potato-patch	work-mule
farmer-preacher	prairie-farm	work-stock
farm-help	prairie-land	
farm-land	rail-fence	

b. Urban and Village Terms

alley
alleyway
almshouse
asphalt, to travel on
asphaltum-paved
Athenaeum
avenue
back-alley
banquette
block
burnt district
board-fence
calaboose
citified
cobble-stone

down-town
driveway
fire-boy
fire-department
hook-and-ladder
independent (fireman)
lamp-lighting
lot, sb.
morgue
palings
paling-fence
plank fencing
plank sidewalk
plaza
pocket (blind alley)

poorhouse
shade-tree
side-walk
sky-scraper
square
street-crossing
street-lamp
tavern
tenement-house
town-site
up-town
water-lot
workhouse

5. *Houses and Furniture*

a. Dwellings and Building Terms

adobe
back hall
back-room
back yard
broom closet
bush house
Big House
cabin
card-room
clapboard
crib
doby
dressed-stone, a.
ell
frame, sb.
frame house
frame shop
front yard
guest-room

home-place
house-porch
keybox
L
lanai
living-room
manor-house
mansard roof
mud-stripe
music-room
ombra
piazza
porch
porch-roof
puncheon floor
scantling
scuttle
second floor
second-story

setting-room
shed-roof
shanty
shebang
shingle, sb. and v.
shingle-bundle
shingle-nail
stair-step
sitting-room
stoop
transom
two-story
waiting-parlor
wall-paper
water-paint
window-hole
window-slit
wooden-shuttered
work-parlor

b. Furniture and Furnishings

baby-wagon
bar (mosquito)
baseburner

bath-tub
bureau
carpeting

carpet-stuff
clothes-horse
cot-bed

cot-bedstead
cuspidor
dog-iron
double-bed
dumb-waiter
ingrain
kindlings
kindling-wood
lambrequin
mosquito-bar
night-key
rag carpet
rag carpeting
rocker

rocking-chair
Saratoga trunk
shake-down
shuck-mattress
shuck tick
sofa-back
spittoon
splint-bottom
splint-bottomed
split-bottom
split-bottomed
spring mattress
stove-lid
stove-pipe

stove-polish
stove-wood
tick
tidy
wash-basin
washboard
wash-bowl
washpan
wash-sink
washstand
waste-basket
whatnot
window-box
window-shade

6. Dress

arctics
band-box, out of the
bang, sb.
bangless
barb lace
belt
blinder
boiled shirt
brogan
buckskin-seated
calico
claw-hammer coat
cloud
comforter
crush hat
derby
dress-pattern
dress-reform
duds
duster
ear-drop
eighteens
fixings
flummery
frills
full-dress suit
galluses
gallus-buckle

handkerchief-turban
harness
high-collared
high-quarter (shoes)
high-water (coat)
hoop-skirt
imperial
jeans
jeans-clad
kid-glove
lap-robe
leggins
linsey-woolsey
low-necked
low-quarter (shoes)
morning-suit
nail-kag
nail-keg
night-garment
overalls
overcoat
overskirt
Panama hat
pantalettes
pantaloons
pants
paper-collar
part (of the hair)

patent-leathers
peek-a-boo waist
peeled (bald)
plug hat
plug tile
puff-sleeved
pyjamas (pajamas)
rag
rig
roundabout
ruffle-cuffed
sack
scoop-shovel (bonnet)
second-hander
serape
shirt-bosom
slack (of trousers)
slop-shop
spike-tailed coat
stiff-brim
stogy (boots)
stove-pipe
stove-pipe hat
sun-bonnet
Sunday best
Sunday-dressed
suspenders
swallow-tail

tile
toggery
toilet
tow-linen
trimmings
trunks
truss

truss point
turban
upholster, v.
vest-pocket
walking-costume
walking-suit
waterfall

white-aproned
white-kid-gloved
wideawake, sb.
work-clothes
work-gown
working-gown
yarn socks

7. Implements and Instruments

banjo
bucket
buzz-saw
cag
carpet-bag
carpet-sack
catch-all
clothes-pin
coarse-comb
crowbar
grip
gripsack
globe-lamp
hand-bag
ice-pitcher
invalid-chair
jack-knife

jack-plane, v.
jew's-harp
jug
kerosene lamp
kit
kite-line
kodak
lattice-box
leather (pocket-book)
melodeon
mucilage
orchestrelle
pitcher
porte-monnaie
skillet
spinning-stick
stem-winder

sugar-bowl
sugar-shovel
sun-umbrella
tack-hammer
tallow-dip
tallow-drip
tin-can
tin cup
tin-ware
toilet-article
traps
turkey-wing
turnip
valise
wallet
warming-pan
Waterbury

8. Weapons and Military Terms (including pugilistic terms)

Barlow knife
billy
bowie
bowie-knife
butcher-knife
case-knife
cross-counter
derringer
drive the center
flank, v.
flint-lock
Gatling
Gatling gun
heeled
home-guard
left-hander
lifter

love-box
love-tap
long spoon
machete
monitor
navy
navy revolver
orderly sergeant
pepper away
pepper-box
picket-watch
pull (a gun)
repeater
retire upon
revolver
rifle-pistol
seven-shooter

shooter
shot-gun
six-shooter
slung-shot
smooth-bore
sock, v.
sockdologer
split, v.
square off
square oneself
swab
swivel
taps
vivandiere
war-canoe
war-fleet
war-footing

9. *American History*

abolition
blockade, to run the
Blue Laws
border-ruffian
bounty-jumping
buccaneer
bushwhacker
carpet-bagger
Civil War
Confederate
Continental
Copperhead
Father of His Country
Federal
filibuster
Fourth of July
Hail Columbia

Halifax, go to
home of the brave
Independence Day
institution
Jackson, by
Jacksonian
jayhawker
kitchen cabinet
land of the free
liberty-pole
Lost Cause
Pilgrim
Potomac, all quiet on
  the
pro-slavery
Rebel
reconcentrado

repudiation
Rough Rider
secession
secessionist
sedition
Stars and Stripes
star-spangled banner
tory
Union (3 senses)
Unionism
Unionist
War, befo' the
Washingtonian
white-sleeve badge
Yankee

10. *American Politics, Government, and Law*

Attorney-General
anti-
baby-act
back-pay
Bland dollar
buncombe
buzz, v.
cabinet minister
cabinet secretary
Cadet of Temperance
campaign
campaigner
candidacy
canvass, v.
Capitol
caucusing
Congress
congressional
congressman
convention
convention-packer
county
county-hospital
county-seat

courthouse
Delegate
Democrat
Department
district attorney
docket, on the
dodge, sb.
eagle, to fly the
executive family
executive session
exequatur
floor, get the
free silver
free trade
gavel
get through
go over
government-bond
government-office
Governor
graft
Grand Old Party
Great Republic
gubernatorial

heeler
high-tariff
Honorable
House
insanity plea
Interior Department
Justice, Chief
justice of the peace
large, at
law-dog
lawing
Legislature
libel suit
lobby
lobbyist
log-rolling
long term
lynch
lynching
lynch-law
machine politics
marshall
mass-meeting
mileage

mud-sill
mugwump
Nationalism
Nationalist
navy yard
office-seeker
Organic Act
outlaw, v.
overflow-meeting
party-collar
penitentiary
personal-assault
plank, sb.
platform
police
police-parade
polls
polling-day
postal service
Postmaster General
President
presidential
primary, sb.
privilege of the floor

prosecuting attorney
pull (arrest)
red-tape
Representative
Republican, sb. and a.
roster
roundsman
run, v.
Secretary of State
Senate
Senator
see, v.
sergeant-at-arms
sheriff
sheriff's sale
silverite
sovereign
Sovereign State
Speaker
state-prison
station-house
stealing-raid
steal, sb.
straight ticket

straw bail
stump, sb. and v.
suffrage
Tammany
tar and feather
tax-collar
tax-gatherer
tax-payer
tax-return
Third House
ticket
torch-light procession
township
War Department
Whig
White Cap
White House
wire-worker
witness-stand
Woman's Rights
worker
Yellow Terror

C. MARK TWAIN AND THE AMERICAN LANGUAGE

Many aspects of the development of the English language in America may be illustrated and studied better from Mark Twain's vocabulary than from that of any other American writer. Six of them have been chosen here because they are especially revealing both for the spirit of the American vernacular and for Mark Twain's own genius: his form-words, his adverbs, his idioms, and certain special classes of his verbs, his epithets, and his exclamations.

1. *Mark Twain's Uses of the Form-Words*

Mark Twain's "empty" or symbolic words, among which are included articles, pronouns, prepositions, conjunctions, auxiliary and "faded" verbs, show many uses that are distinctive and characteristically American.

a (six uses)
acrost
afront of
after
agin (two uses)
ahold of

all of
all of, for
all over (two uses)
all through
all-to
all-around (two uses)

along (three uses)
along about
alongside
alongside of
an
and (two uses)

anti-
any
anyways
anywheres
around (two uses)
around about
ary
as (two uses)
at (four uses)
away
back, at one's
back, by the
back, on one's
back of (three uses)
back of, in
backways
betwixt
by-and-by
by and large
can
do (four uses)
doff
don
down (six uses)
-er, -est, suffixes
every last
every which way
everything, like
everywheres
forasmuch
for that
for to
forward of
forwards
forwhy
get (25 uses)
go (20 uses)
have (6 uses)
hern
his'n
how
in
in it
inside

it
least
leastways
lieves
like
like to
like as if
longside
may
nary
nigh
no
nohow
nor (two uses)
nothing
nothing, like
nowheres
nuther
of (four uses)
off
offen (off'n)
off of
on (four uses)
once (wunst)
onto
or
ourn
out (four uses)
out-and-out
out back
outen
outside
overthwart
owing to
-s, suffix
she
same
sith
so
so as, so's
so as that, so'st
some
somewheres
somers

soon as
stead of
subscriber (=I, me)
that, adv. use
that-air
that-away
the (three uses)
thee
theirn
there (two uses)
they (=there)
this-away
this-here
to (five uses)
t'other
toward
twice (twiste)
un (on, of)
until, prep.
up (three uses)
we-all
what
whenas
whereat
wherefore
whereunto
which (two uses)
whilst
whit
whither
whoso
withal
without, conj.
ye, art.
ye, pron. (two uses)
yes
yez
yon
yonder
yonder-way
you-all
yourn
yours truly (=I, me)

2. *Mark Twain's Adverbs*

Mark Twain shows a marked fondness for the old native suffixless or "flat" adverbs, which are sometimes unjustly stigmatized as ungrammatical uses of the adjective. At the same time he coins a number of new adverbs with the standard *-ly* suffix.

absolutely	maybe	short
almighty	measurably	shoutingly
awful	mightily	sight
bad	mighty	sinfully
bald-headed	Mondays	slick
blame	monstrous	slightually
beautiful	mornings	smart
cantankerously	mortal	sort of
clear	most	square
consarned	mushily	squarely
considerable	nation	straight
cruel	nattily	straight along
curious	near	straight-off
dead	nights	summers
dead-head	night-times	supposably
dearly	nobbily	sure
directly	noble	swearing
distressed	plenty	thundering
drawly	plumb	thwart-ships
dreadful	point-blank (pine-	tight
everlasting	blank)	tolerable
fair	poison (pison)	toothsomely
first-off	powerful	three-leggedly
first-rate	precious	unbrahminically
forevermore	private	uncommon
good	processionally	uncomplimentarily
heap	real	up-country
heap much	rearwards	up-river
illy	right (three senses)	up-town
indeedy	right along	urgingly
languishy	right and left	valleywards
large	right away	vinegarishly
limber	right-down	way
literally	right off	winters
lively	right so	world
longly	rip	worm-fashion
loud	Saturdays	
loudly	sharp	

3. *Mark Twain's Idioms*

John Millington Synge declared that in a good play "every speech should be as fully flavored as an apple or a nut." The flavor of Mark Twain's style is always racy of the American soil; and it owes this quality largely to the prodigious store of native phrases and idioms which he employs. Many of them are unrecorded in the dictionaries; a few of them have been deliberately manufactured by Mark Twain, or twisted into novel shapes. In the list that follows idioms not found in the OXFORD have been starred; those not found in any dictionary have been double-starred.

to be after doing something
to hold the age
*to come ahead
*to set amidships
**and (kings-and)
**and (deuces-and)
around about
**to travel on asphalt
*to be at oneself
*at that
*to read the baby-act
at one's back
*on one's back
**to know one by the back
*in back of
to give one a back-cap
to take a back seat
the Bad Place
to make a balk
to beat the band
**just out of the band-box
**to give one down the banks
**to bank the fires
*to ride bareback
with the bark on
hot from the bat
**step to the bat
to draw a bead on
to see or *hear the beat of*
*to hold the belt
you bet
name your bet
to bite the dust
to run the blockade
the blues

the Blue Hen's Chickens
**to stay by the board
the whole bilin'
like a book
one's born days
one's bottom dollar
**at the bottom of the ladder
the grand bounce
*breakers ahead
**breast to breast with
to take one's breath
**children by brevet
to bring up standing
to pass the buck
to have the bulge on
**the grand bulge
to have to burn
*to burn one's bridges
*buyer thirty
to take by and large
to raise Cain
*to call game
**to call the game
**to take into camp
*to set one's cap for
**blame my cats
to let the cat out of the bag
**that cat wouldn't fight
**to bark one's shins on the cathead
**to catch on the center
**to walk chalk
a right smart chance
**to keep the change
to pass in one's checks
**to sell a clam

a close call
**a close fit
**cold chills
a cold deck
the cold shoulder
to come it over
*to come a game on
come Christmas
**come out of that
to sleep in one's cravat
to shake the cross
to eat crow
to cut one's stick
to take a dare
**dark as the inside of a cow
in the dark of the moon
dark and bloody
to call it a day
for dear life
*dear-me-suz
to be on deck
**in the last degree
*to go on the dipe
the Big Dipper
on the docket
dog in a blanket
**to have in the door
***to sell down the river
***to drive the center
to get the drop on
**like a duck
***to fly the eagle
**fliers of the eagle
**on the ear
on earth
to take it easy
to have all one's eggs in one basket
**to suck eggs
**elbow to elbow
to run emptyings
*to get even
*to make even
**every last
every which way

**like everything
**to get one's eye on
***to keep an eye out for
to say or ask fair
**for a farm
*in full feather
**a fighting liar
to come out flat-footed
*to make one's flesh crawl
to go up the flume
*to fly light
to fly the track
**to get a focus on
*to set one's foot down
**to go up to four prices
free to say
to put on frills
to make the fur fly
like fury
to knock galley-west
**to fall over the garboard-strake
to get religion
**no getting around
like all get out
*Gilderoy's kite, higher than
to be blue about the gills
to give good day, night
one's given name
from the word go
to go security
to go better
to feel good
to make good
the Good Book
*the Good Place
a good thing
*to go to do (something)
to go to grass
to hunt grass
**old Grayback from Wayback
*to hold one's grip
to be grit
great guns!
half-seas-over
*on the half shell

**half-wheel-deep
go to Halifax
*to have one where the hair is short
**to be in one's hair
hand over fist
*to have one's hand in
*to take a hand
**with one hand tied behind
to fly off the handle
to get the hang of
to hang fire
**to work in harness with
**at the dropping of a hat
to bury the hatchet
*to haul down one's colors
out of one's head
**to shut one's head
**heart-and-heart
*so help me
how is that for high?
*to hitch teams together
to go the whole hog
hog and hominy
**on the ice
on thin ice
*to be in it with
honest Injun
*by jabers
**by Jackson
the jig is up
**at one jump
on the jump
the jumping-off place
**to keep door
**to keep game
for keeps
**kiss-the-Bible, sb.
the whole kit and biling
know-it-all, a.
*land-office business
**land of the free
*strong language
at large
**to play larks

to see the last of
to lay low
to lay on the oars
*to lay open
to lay tongue to
**to lay in the leads
to get left
not a leg to stand on
let or hindrance
to let down softly
one's level best
**to lift the roof
out of one's line
where one lives
*to make one's liver curl
lo and behold you
easy as rolling off a log
to be long on
*look-a-here (looky here)
as drunk as a loon
across lots
to splice the main-brace
**to make it
to make good time
to make one's mark
easy mark
*in or into her marks
**mark twain
*what is the matter of
**mercy sakes
to give one the mitten
there is money in—
**my sainted mother!
to fling mud
**to sell for the mud
**no name for it
to come natural to
to say one nay
**to need killing
in the neighborhood of
the Never-Never Country
**to live in the Never-Never Country
new chum
*a new deal

*next-to-impossible
in the nick of time
nip and tuck
**No Man's Land
**like nothing
**nuck and tip
to take one's number (2 senses)
nuts to or for
no object
what's the odds?
to strike oil
**on the river
to be on it
one while
**the orator of the day
to do the other thing
from this out
overthwart and endlong
to hold one's peace
to keep one's eyes peeled
**to pick a fuss
**to pick and shovel
in a Pickwickian sense
*to go all to pieces
**to go one's pile
on pins and needles
drunk as a piper
the pipe of peace
more's the pity
to poke fun at
*to put up a poor mouth
like all possessed
*All quiet on the Potomac
**the privilege of the floor
to do one proud
**to prove title
**to pull one's words
to put in the time
on the quiet
to stand the racket
**to drop the rag
**to knock all to rags
*the ragged edge
rag-tag and bob-tail
by rail

**to know enough to come in out
of the rain
to know enough to come in when
it rains
**to rain brickbats
to raise the mischief
*to rake and scrape
**to ride a rampage
with great random
to give one rats
**rat's nest in one's hair
a good ready
of record
a red rag to a bull
**to go to one's reward
to ride on a rail
**to try a riffle
to make the riffle
to read the riot act
*to rip and tear
to keep the run of
to run the blockade
**in a rush
**run to cover
**on salary
**like scat
a screw loose
*to keep shady
to be no great shakes
*to give one the cold shake
*a shake (three shakes) of a
sheep's tail
**to shut up one's shell
to give up the ship
to take shipping
**to drop into the shoes of
**until someone's shoes are vacant
*to go short on
Now you're shouting
**to put in one's shovel
to show a pair of heels
to get shut of
**to be on the good side of
not by a long (considerable) sight
*like sin

a singed cat—better than one
  looks
that's the size of it
to skin the cat
*slim Jim
**to be soft on
**Son of the Forest
**son of toil
**my souls!
  down South
the spit and image of
to be spoiling for
**to throw up the sponge
to knock the spots out of
to put up the spout
**to spread open
a square deal
a square meal
**to square oneself
to pull up stakes
to stand from under
to stand pat
*to stand a show
to stay one's hand
**staying capacity
to steal a base
to steer clear of
**to be stuck after
to take stock in
to keep store
to vote the straight ticket
straw bail
**a stray cat
a street Arab
**to strike one's average
**to strike bottom
**to strike it lucky
to strike it rich
on a string
at one's string's end
one's strong suit
**to be strong with
to knock the stuffing out of
to be up a stump
**to suck one's fingers

*a suit of hair
**sure as guns
**to swap knives
  in a sweat
*the Sweet Singer of
*to set a good table
to take and
to take hold
to take hold of
**to take in one's sign
to talk back
**to talk off
to be talked out
on tap
to tar and feather
thank goodness
at that
to be all there
there you are
**to throw a card
in a tight place
**to keep a tight tongue
to have a good time
*to have a time
**to beat one's time
**time being, adv.
**to a fraction
**to not to
by the same token
to tell t'other from which
**a tough nut
off the track
in one's tracks
**a trick worth six of that
**to get a trip
in troth
to take the tuck out of
the tune the old cow died on
**not to turn a feather
**at the turn of noon
**two-taps-and-one
**up and around
up and doing
*used to was
to vamose the ranch

*to take a walk
to walk on air
*befo' the War
to make it warm for
**warm shoulder
to be on the war-path
**to take in washing
to go off watch
to be on the watch-out
down——way
from way-back
*out West
*good as wheat

*a low white
a poor white
out of whole cloth
**a witch-hazel professor
**in the woods
out of the woods
**to take to the woods
*as independent as a wood-saw-
yer's clerk
the world's people
to think the world of
yellow journalism

4. Mark Twain's Verbs of Motion

Mark Twain loved the native American verbs of motion, mostly rapid, and of departure, mostly abrupt. His amazing stock of these verbs, and his invention of others, do much to account for the dynamic quality of his style.

avalanche
bang away
bat, step to the
beat around
boom
break for
bulge in
bull
bum around
cavort
chalk, to walk
circulate
clear
clear out
clip along
close in on
close up on
cut
cut one's stick
cut out
dig out
drift
drop over
fetch
fetch up
fire out

flip out
fly around
fly light
fly the track
fool along
fool around
foot it
fur fly, make the
get
git
get after
get along
get at
get down to
get in
get-out, like all
get up and
give way
go
go it
go for
haul off and
head-on, go
head, go full
heel it
hog, to go the whole

hoist
hoof it
hop
hum
hump oneself
hump it
hump-up
jerk
jigger
jockey
jolt
jump
knock around
lam
lay for
lay into
lay on the oars
lay out
let into
let out and
lick, to keep up one's
lift the roof
light into
light on
light out
loaf

lope
make good time
make at
meander
meeky
meet her
mosey
on it, to be
out with
pile down
pile in
pile it on
pitch in
plunk through
polish off
pull out
push along
put
raid
reel off
rip
rip and tear
rip out
run
rush through
rustle
sail
sail in
sasshay
scatter
scoot
scrabble
scrape
scratch
scurry
set at, take a
shake up
shin
shove
skaddle
skeet

skin
skip
skip out
slam
slash
slash out
slat
slew around
slide
slope
slosh around
snake
snap
snatch
snatch on
snip out
snoop
snort, get up and
sock it to
sockdologer
spin
split
spook around
spread
spread open
sprint
square away
square off
squirm
stampede
stand from under
start in
start out
step out
step over
straddle
strike
stroll
stump it
swap about
swing round

swush
take and
take on
take out
tear around
thrash around
trapse (traipse)
trot out
turn to and
unfurl one's heels
up and
up-anchor
up-steam
vamose the ranch
waddle
walk
walk, take a
walk on air
wallow
waltz
warm up
wash
watch-out, be on the
weaken down
weave
wend
whack
whale
whip
whirlwind
whistle
whoop
whoopee, raise
whoopjamboree
whoopjamborehoo
whoop up
woods, take to the
worry along
yank
yare

5. *Mark Twain's Terms of Praise and Abuse*

Mrs. Elizabeth Mary Wright in her *Rustic Speech and Folklore* says that the speakers of English dialects have over 1,300 ways of telling a person he is a fool;

but even an English peasant might learn new ways of performing this useful function with neatness and dispatch, and also of expressing his admiration, from a study of Mark Twain's stock of epithets.

a. Commendatory Epithets (often used in a "sarcastified" sense)

In the matter of commendation he runs the gamut from the tepid *fair-to-middling*, through his favorite adjectives-of-all-work *nobby*, *gaudy*, and *gay*, to the heights of eulogy with *chain-lightning*, *white*, and *made of angel-clay*. The highest summits of eminence are reserved for Mrs. Eddy, when he characterizes her as both an *"Is"* and a *"The."*

angel-clay, made of	*grit, to be*	*peach-bloomy*
bird	*high-grade*	*pleasant-spoken*
brick	*high-light*	*quality*
bully	*high-mightiness*	*rattler*
Captain	*high muck-a-muck*	*respectworthy*
card	*high-toned*	*ripper*
chain-lightning	*high up*	*rustler*
chipper	*homely*	*safe*
chirk	*honey*	*sharp*, sb.
clean-cut	*hunky*	*sightly*
clever	*husky*	*simon-pure*
Colonel	*influential*, sb.	*smart*
cute	*Is*, sb.	*smasher*
daisy	*Judge*	*snappy*
diamond-breastpin	*kid-glove*	*star*
dusty	*lady*	*starchy*
fair-and-square	*level head*	*staving*
fair-to-middling	*likely*	*stunner*
fat	*live-looking*	*stunning*
fill the bill	*Major*	*swell*
first-class	*mogul, great*	*Squire*
gamy	*mogul, grand*	*tony*
gaudy	*much*	*taffy*
gay	*natty*	*The*, sb.
General	*nice*	*there, to be all*
gent	*nifty*	*trig*
go-ahead	*nobby*	*trim-built*
gold-leaf	*noble*	*up and doing*
gorgeous	*nonesuch*	*white*
Old Grayback from	*nuts*	*whole-hearted*
Wayback	*onion*	*wide-awake*
great	*peach*	

b. Depreciatory Epithets

Characteristically enough, his terms of abuse are over three times as numerous as those of commendation. It is noteworthy also that he has about twice as many epithets implying inferiority of intelligence in various members of the "damned human race" as he does for reflecting upon their moral standards.

abortionist	*clam*	*girly-girly*
ash-cat	*common*, a.	*goody-goody*
back number	*copper-bellied*	*gorilla*
bandoleer	*corpse-maker*	*gouger*
beat, sb.	*crank*	*grafter*
big-bug	*crook*	*granny*
biggity	*crouter*	*grouty*
big-head	*crybaby*	*gutter-scum*
bilk	*dead-beat*	*gutter-snipe*
blame-fool	*dude*	*haddock*
blatherskite	*dudess*	*hard-boiled*
blister	*duffer*	*hard-looking*
bloat, sb.	*dumb*	*hard lot*
bloke	*easy game*	*has-been*
body-snatcher	*egg-sucking*	*heeler*
bogus	*fake*	*heifer*
boshy	*famine-breeder*	*herumfrodite*
brash	*fighting liar*	*hifalutin*
brummagem	*file*, sb.	*hog-wash*
buccaneer	*fire-bug*	*homely*
budge, sb.	*flapdoodle*	*hoodlum*
bug	*flashy*	*horse-thief*
bull-headed	*flat*, sb.	*howler*
bummer	*flathead*	*huckleberry*
buncombe	*folderol*	*hunks*
buzzard	*foo-foo*	*infant-schooly*
cabbage	*fool*, a.	*iron-clad*
carrot	*foxy*	*iron-jawed*
cattle	*fraud*	*irreverencer*
chatterbox	*freak*	*jackass*
cheap-john	*fresh*	*jack-at-all-science*
cheeky	*fulsome*	*jack-leg*
chicken	*fussy*	*jack-legged*
chicken-hearted	*gallus*	*jack-pair*
chicken-livered	*galoot*	*jake*
chowder-headed	*gangly*	*jambled*
chuckle-head	*gashly*	*jumbulacious*
chuckle-headed	*gawk*	*kennel-rat*
chump	*gawky-looking*	*know-it-all*

labrick
languishy
lanky
larrikin
leather-head
leather-headed
left-handed
lewd
light-weight
loafer
loud
louse-brat
low-down
low-grade
low-rate
lubber
lummox
lunkhead
mark, easy
mean
measly
Methusalem-numskull
moonshiny
moss-backed
mud-cat
mud-dobber
mud-sill
mud-turtle
muff
muggins
mule-headed
mullet-headed
mustang
nickeled
nickel-plate
nickel-plated
night-hawk
night-owl
numskull
no-account
offal
off-color
oil-derrick
one-horse
ornery

outrage
pall-bearer
pesky
pestiferous
petrifaction
phantom
pie-plant
policy-Christian
poor-quality
puddinghead
pumpkin-head
putrid
putty-hearted
rag-tag and bob-tail
ramshackle
ramshackly
rancid
rapscallion
rat
rattletrap
rat-trap
ratty
ratty-looking
riffraff
rip
rocky
rot
rotten
rough, sb.
rough, a.
rough-scruff
rowdy, sb.
rowdy, a.
rubbish
ruck
saphead
sapheaded
sappy
scab
scalliwag
scrawny
screaky
scrimp-nosed
scruffy
seedy

shad
shady
Shakesperiod
sheep-witted
shenanigan
shyster
sinful
singed cat
slab
sloppy
slouch
slouchy
small-fry
smarty, sb.
smarty, a.
smirky
snail-belly
soft-soaper
softy
sophomoric
sorry
sorry-looking
specter
sprite
spoony
squaw-man
Stratfordolater
stump-tail
super-high-moral
superstition-monger
swindle
tough-headed
tedious
third-quality
third-rate
thin
thug
tin, a.
tough
tough nut
trap-robber
ugly customer
un-American
wharf-rat
white, low

white, poor	wild cat	yellow
wild-brained		

6. Mark Twain's Profanity and Indelicacy

"He wove a glittering streak of profanity through his garrulous fabric that was refreshing to a spirit weary of the dull neutralities of undecorated speech."

Undoubtedly Mark Twain knew even more "cusswords" and vulgarisms than are here listed; but if Mrs. Clemens and Mr. Howells managed to suppress a good many at their birth, and Mr. Paine polished others away (cf. our note in the Lexicon under *guts*), at least a good many more managed to escape into his published works than the dictionaries have had the courage to include.

a. Profanity and Substitutes therefor

all-fired	devil-fire	jabers! be
Bad Place	deviltry	Jackson! by
bad words	ding-busted	jings! by
blame-fool	dod-dern!	ker-
blasphemous	dog, v.	la!
blast	dog my cats!	lackaday!
bloody	dog-goned	land!
blooming	drat	land! good
body o' me!	drot	land! my
Caesar's ghost!	durn, v. and sb.	land's sake!
Cain, to raise	egod!	laws!
cats! blame my	geewhillikins!	laws-a-me!
Charlie!	Gemini (by Jiminy,	laws-goodness!
chebang!	etc.)	lawsy!
consound	good day!	lo and behold you!
crash-word	goodness!	lordy!
cuss	goody!	magnify (one's English)
cussed	gracious!	marry!
cussedness	grandmother! your	mercy sakes!
cussing	granny! your	Moses! suffering
cussword	Great Scott!	mother! my sainted
d———	guns! great	mph!
dadblame	Hail Columbia!	my!
dadfetch	hell	nation (for damnation)
damfool	hell-bent	never-never, v.
damnation	hellfired	'Od's bodikins!
dang	hellion	'Od's body!
dashed	hell's-mint	'Od's my life!
dear-me-suz!	help (so help me)	ouch!
dern, a., v., sb.	her-blam!	Other Place
derned	irruption	pfew!

pfit!
plagued
profanity
profanity-mill
sacre bleu!
sakes alive!
Sam Hill
Sanhedrin! by the great
scat!
Sheol!
Scott!

sho!
shucks!
Sirree-bob!
so boy!
soul (my souls!)
swan, v.
thunderation!
thundering
tush!
tropics (Hell)
ugh!

umf!
waly!
well-a-well!
whoopee
whoop-jamboree
whoop-jamborehoo
whoosh!
would God!
zip!

b. Indelicate Terms and Euphemisms (see the discussion in the LEXICON under *rear*)

ass
assification
assified
bollock
barrel
breed, v.
brevet, children by
brothel-daddy
brothel-knight
carcass

cravat, to sleep in one's
fig-leaf, v.
fly-blister
guts
innards
herumfrodite
jackass
jackassful
leg-shop
leman

quiffsplitter
rear
rear-skirts
roger, v.
shag, v.
south end
thunder-gust
top, v.
warm-blooded

II. MARK TWAIN'S NEW WORDS

*"He exploited three hundred and sixty-five red-hot
new eagernesses every year of his life"*

Of the 7802 entries given in the Lexicon, 3384 have been marked B¹, signifying that the word, the combination or idiom, or the meaning is not given in the Oxford English Dictionary or its Supplement. Many of these, of course, have been included in other lexicographical authorities, particularly in Webster's, the Standard, or the Century; but a still larger number that are found in the Oxford have been omitted by these so-called unabridged dictionaries. The exact total of words, combinations, and meanings here listed and illustrated from Mark Twain's vocabulary which are missing in Webster's is 3584; in the Standard, 4025; in the Century, 4240. Hence the supplementing of existing authorities, so far as Mark Twain's vocabulary is concerned, has been one of the principal tasks of the present work.

In addition, 958 entries have been marked B², signifying that while found in the Oxford, the word, combination, or meaning was used by Mark Twain at an earlier date than, or one as early as, the earliest quotation there given. By adding our B¹ and B² entries together, we obtain a total of 4342, for which our quotations from Mark Twain supply what is so far the earliest recorded literary evidence.

Obviously no claim can be made that the whole of these 4342 new words or usages were first coined by Mark Twain, or even that they were first written down by him. In many cases there was doubtless earlier use as yet unnoted; of these a few have been discovered and mentioned by us. In a far larger number of cases, Mark Twain was in all probability merely the first to observe the word, combination, or meaning in the vernacular usage around him and to employ it in his writings. No exact estimate of the number of his actual coinages has been attempted, and none could well be made; but it seems evident that they were astoundingly numerous. We trust that we have been able to include most of them in our Lexicon.

A. Entries Not in the Oxford but Given in Other Authorities

B¹ Words. Of the 3384 entries which we have labeled as B¹, that is, as not to be found in the Oxford, 668 are found in other authorities. Of these, 317 occur only in a single authority. The largest contribution here is made by Webster's, which includes just 150 words, combinations, or meanings not found in any other dictionary.

1. Entries Explained Only in a Single Authority

a. In Webster's alone:

Words: *foresightedness, recheck, retying, scoopful, sentimenter, smirchless, uncledom, unrisky,* and *warbly.*

Combinations (including idioms and special constructions): *absent treatment, after-deck, alongside of, ash-pile, awe-compelling, axle-grease, on one's back, in back of, barrel-hoop, beflagged, belief-compelling, bell-button, benevolent-looking, blind lead, boat-hand, breast-board, bright-colored, carriage-body, chair-arm, continued story, cream-yellow, death-grip, divinity-circuit, fellow-conspirator, fellow-villager, fire-assay, flood-time, free gold, furnace-stoker, golden buck, Great Plains, half-intoxicated, half-minded, hard-driven, hard-looking, heart-line, high-ceiled, ice-bridge, lake-front, large-mouthed, low-hung, marble-topped, mid-Atlantic, non-cultivation, non-participant, over-gently, over-plump, over-sentimental, passenger-list, pest-ridden, rake and scrape, ranch-life, right-fielder, river-front, river road, safe-door, sand-reef, school-slate, shop-right, silver-miner, silver-tipped, Simplified Spelling, six-fingered, skip out, slaughter-pen, slim Jim, slim-shanked, smooth-surfaced, steamboatman, steel pen, stiff-jointed, stove-wood, tea-planting, teething-ring, telephone-wire, Friends of the Temple, thick-fingered, thread-spinner, ticket-taker, to have a time, tin cup, toilet article, torch-lighted, twenty-dollar, typewriter-table, ultra-pious, up-bound, water-paint, well-sustained, well-tanned, world-celebrated,* and *yellow-splotched.*

Meanings: *after, agin, airing, billet, blow up, bogus, bouquet, bum, Catholic, cough, crotch, duffer, effect, five, fix up, Germanic, gift, godspeed, head-line, hopping, horse-chestnut, hydraulic, identifier, importance, jolt, Judge, judge-advocate, justice of the peace, keeps, strong language, modify, orgy, paid-up, pepper-box, pocket, red-hot, scatteration, scrunch, shaft, shooting, shut off, slash out, smarty, stale, swear off, Sweet Singer, the, tourbillon,* and *tribute.*

b. In the STANDARD alone (27):

Words: none

Combinations: *air-blast, Christian Missionary Association, engineer-in-chief, faith-doctor, fifteen-ball pool, ground-connection, great* or *grand mogul, mortal mind, plunkety-plunk, sheriff's sale, sour-mash, stick down,* and *swap around.*

Meanings: *allow, battery, beat, cabbage* (two senses), *cabbage-leaf, continental, foot, heap, puff-adder, scout, slide, snuffle,* and *water-lot.*

c. In the CENTURY alone (18):

Word: *labrick.*

Combinations: *beer-saloon, so help me, job-work, long-descended, in her marks, potato-gun, to go short on, standing-galley,* and *working-plans.*

Meanings: *article, compositor, gain, harness, pass, product, tavern-keeper,* and *terror.*

d. In the UNIVERSAL alone (11):

Word: *unwatered.*

Combinations: *breakers ahead, to haul down one's colors.*

Meanings: *breed, ignorant, languors, load up, organize, rear, shed,* and *talons.*

e. In Wright's DIALECT DICTIONARY alone (23):

Words: *bulrusher, duffy, night-times,* and *soothering.*

Combinations: *around about, Good Place, greasy water, hanging-bout, hide up, know on,* and *working-folks.*

Meanings: *comb, draw, flummery, fuss up, going on, haddock, happen, learn, least, limber, ranting,* and *whack,* v.

f. In DIALECT NOTES alone (34):

Word: *dingnation.*

Combinations: *Bad Place, Big House, Caesar's ghost, chicken-cock, come a game on, dad-blame, dear-me-suz, ding-busted, dod-dern, dog-pelter, easy game, goods-box, hi-yi, knock around, look-a-here (looky-here), low-quarter, what is the matter of, mud-turkle, to put up a poor mouth, cold shake, so boy,* and *yarn socks.*

Meanings: *blubber, chap, cheap-john, cork, gabble, granny, give up, infest, let on, navigate,* and *throw off on.*

g. In AMERICAN SPEECH alone (15):

Word: *hunterman.*

Combinations: *carpet-sack, Great Waters, spunk water,* and *independent as a wood-sawyer's clerk.*

Meanings: *illuminate, jamble, lay by, manor-house, meander, no, shag, sightly, slug,* and *whack,* sb.

h. In other authorities (39):

Six entries are explained only in Bartlett: *sozodont, pocket-miner, good as wheat,* and special meanings of *annexation, use,* and *wet down.* Nine are found only in Farmer: *burnt district, to go on the dipe, to make one's liver curl, palatial car, Santa Cruz punch, turned around, befo' the War, low white,* and Mark Twain's meaning for *body-snatcher.* Two are given only in Clapin: *berth-saloon* and *plantain-patch.* Four are found only in Thornton: *to hitch teams together, to be in it,* and special senses of *circumstance* and *shut down.* Three are supplied by Mencken: *government-bond* and Mark Twain's meanings for *corpse-maker* and *Forks.* Three are given only in Horwill: *limit-rope, out West,* and one meaning of *junior.* Tucker is the only authority to explain the combination *ragged edge* as used by Mark Twain. Finally, eleven terms not included in any of the lexical authorities used in this study have been explained from other sources: *to give one down the banks, Comanche, herumfrodite, Milam, Morisite, to roger, sny, td, tf, Waldenstromian,* and *Waterbury.*

2. Entries Explained in More than One Authority

Of the entries not included in the OXFORD, 351 are found in more than one other authority. For exact details see the LEXICON.

Words:

adios	*indeedy*	*skyugle*
ary	*lanai*	*soary*
biggity	*materializee*	*somers*
blubbery	*missionarying*	*squalmish*
campoodie	*Missourian*, a.	*unconcreted*
Cap	*Pawnee*	*undiscredited*
Cheyenne	*pestiferous*	*unsagacious*
Choctaw	*Piute*	*Verbarium*
disenjoy	*pungle*	*Virginny*
Dowie	*rawhide*	*Washingtonian*
druther	*reconcentrado*	*Washoe*
electropath	*reflush*	*Winebrennarian*
elocute	*skaddle*	*wisht*
gangly	*skeet*	*worlded*

Combinations and Idioms:

to come ahead	*buyer thirty*	*drawn butter*
air-tight stove	*buy into*	*dry battery*
all over	*canned goods*	*earned run*
all right	*to set one's cap for*	*to get even*
almond-eyed	*drawing-room car*	*to make even*
American language	*car-load*	*extra-hazardous*
to set amidships	*cattle-car*	*fair-to-middling*
assay office	*cherry-stone clam*	*Father of His Country*
to be at oneself	*chicken-livered*	*in full feather*
at that	*chills and fever*	*F. F. V.*
to read the baby-act	*Christian Catholic*	*fig-paste*
bank-account	*Christian Connection*	*fishing-worm*
to ride bareback	*Church of God*	*flat-broke*
battle-flag	*city of the dead*	*to make one's flesh crawl*
battle-lantern	*clew-iron*	*fly light*
bill of particulars	*cocking-main*	*foo-foo*
Bland dollar	*common-run*	*to set one's foot down*
blind vein	*cylinder-head*	*foretopmaststuddingsail*
blue-mass	*dead-bell*	*free silver*
breach of trust	*death-damp*	*game of chance*
breast-deep	*dig in*	*Gilderoy's kite*
buckle in	*dime-museum*	*gold-miner*
to burn one's bridges	*Divine Science*	*to go to do something*

grand-daddy-longlegs
guest-room
to have where the hair is
   short
on the half shell
to have one's hand in
hand-tooled
hard lot
to heel it
hello-girl
hell's mint
herb-doctor
hickory-bark
high-collared
high muck-a-muck
home-plate
horse-post
hot and heavy
iron-jawed
iron-rust
by jabers
kinfolks
land-office business
lap-robe
laws-a-me
lay open
leg-shop
light-bread
Lost Cause
Mental Science
mind-transference

new deal
next-to-impossible
nowheres
old-gold
old master
peek-a-boo waist
to go all to pieces
plague-sore
all quiet on the Potomac
to raffle off
Riggs' disease
to rip and tear
River Brethren
Rough Rider
rum-mill
rum-shop
salt-horse
Sam Hill
say (s'I, s'e, sh-she)
seat-back
self-communion
self-upbraiding
semi-civilization
sequoia gigantea
setting-room
to keep shady
a shake of a sheep's tail
sick-list
signal-lantern
silver-gray fox
like sin

Sirree-bob
skip-jack
slave-lord
slobber over
snake-charming
soft-footed
South Carolinian
spike-tailed coat
spool of thread
to stand a show
straight-up-and-down
suit of hair
to set a good table
to tear around
this-away
thrash around
thunder-burst
toe-hold
train with
used to was
to take a walk
Washoe zephyr
water-turkey
way-traffic
we-all
whisky-mill
Wild West
wine-bag
to work down
Young America

Meanings:

ache
ambuscade
annunciator
antelope
Attorney-General
Auntie
back-up
back water
bank
bar
batch

belt
bitters
blister
break
break down
break up
breed
build
bullyrag
bust
call game

central
ceramics
chunk
cobbling
cobweb
code
cold
Colonel
cord
corded
counter-mine

crack
cut out
dead-lights
directly
diseased
distressed
dose
draw out
East (two uses)
Evangelical
Fair
fantastic
fat
fetch around
fill up
fix
folderol
freeze (two senses)
gait
gingerbread
go through
greens
grip (two senses)
grit
hang up
haul off
haunt
header
healer
heifer
hello
high water
hoist
horseshoe
horsy
hot
House

howling
involuted
jam
jockey
lay over
leather (two senses)
life-line
light into
liquid
march-past
meet
memento
night-hawk
night-owl
nip
non-conforming
opera house
plug
point
poison
pot
primary
rabbit
radiator
rag
rattler
reader
Rebel
roll
Scientist
scoop
scratch (two senses)
second floor
second-story
set
shake-up
she

show up
slab
slather
slick
sluice
snap
softly
sovereign
Sovereign State
special
spring chicken
squeeze
star
statistic
string
string out
sublimity
suggester
swab
sweat
take in
take out
talk out
tavern
threes
trap
turn in
turtle
Uncle
water-cure
whoop
whooping
work
work off
yap
yellow-boy
yellow-covered

B. ENTRIES HITHERTO UNRECORDED IN ANY AUTHORITY

After deducting the entries listed in the previous section, there remain 2716 for which we have been able to discover no dictionary authority whatever. Here, if anywhere, we may feel confident that Mark Twain's own invention was at work, although, as we shall see, not in every case. These terms may most conveniently be grouped as New Words, including both those formed from old words by the aid of familiar prefixes and suffixes and those made "out of whole cloth"; New Combinations, including new phrases, constructions, and idioms; and New Meanings, including unrecorded metaphorical and transferred senses, humorous twists of meaning, and words used in novel grammatical functions.

1. New Words

Mark Twain's new words fall naturally into three divisions, which may be discriminated as formations, distortions, and inventions.

a. Formations from Familiar Elements

Mark Twain exercised the greatest freedom in extending the domain of the familiar suffixes and prefixes. His favorite suffixes, for nouns, are *-er*, *-ing*, *-ness*, and *-ship*; for adjectives, *-y*, *-able*, *-less*, *-ing*, *-like*, and *-looking*; for adverbs, *-ly* and *-s*.

He uses the noun-suffix *-er* freely both for agents or persons, as in *Alp-climber, Black-Forester, boomeranger, bulletin-boarder, coat-turner, house-emptier, house-filler, Nineteener, Pacific-coaster, Perhapser, psychologizer, crouter, diaperer, grouper, irreverencer, summer-resorter, surface-miner, telescoper, three-year-older, thumb-sucker, weet-weeter*, and for things, as in *five-center, ice-breaker, million-pounder, one-liner, one-pounder, price-raiser, second-hander, stencher*, and *two-liner*. He was also fond of forming new verbal substantives in *-ing*, as in *Alp-climbing, call-boying, chambermaiding, charading, chopping-up, circusing, cussing, dusting, empering, encrusting, excursioning, fortuning, Great-Scotting, keelboating, note-booking, originating, panning-out, scrap-booking, smouching, steamshipping, straightening out, that-is-ing, upstreaming, war-whooping*, and *washing-around*. For the suffix *-ness* he has coined the words *bulliness, chipperness, frivolishness, sickheartedness*, and *unendurableness*; for the suffix *-ship, brigadier-generalship, bullyship, chameleonship, claimantship*, and *old-comradeship*. Other noun-suffixes employed are *-ian* in his *Brontosaurian, Carnegian, Edisonian*, and *Nevadian; -ist* in *ascensionist* and *telescopulist; -ite* in *Harrisite* and *Shakespearite;* the feminine *-ess* in *braggartess* and *dudess;* the diminutive *-let* in *doglet* and *turkey-let;* for abstract nouns *-ty* in *awarity, conjecturability, Eddity, -tude* in *balditude*, and *-ation* in *assification* and *matteration;* and for collectives *-dom* in *Arthurdom, lyncherdom*, and *-ry* in *subjectry*. Others used but once may be seen in the words *catology, manologist, Christian-Scientism, panegyrics, chaleteer, presentee, orchestrelle, pattie, poppy*, and *Twainiana*.

For forming new adjectives he uses the suffix *-y* in *Arabian-Nighty, brick-yardy, bridgy, chuckly, comrady, graveyardy, infant-schooly, night-breezy, peach-bloomy, rose-leafy, spider-webby*, and *splattery; -able* in *begettable, bettable, chewable, forecastable, functionable, matable, relocatable, uncashable, unget-aroundable, unreinstatable*, and *unseatable; -less* in *bangless, Bibleless, dog-fightless, exitless, gossipless, historyless*, and *newspaperless;* the participial adjective suffix *-ing* in *arriving, expediting, dissentering, millinerizing, swearing-off*, and *war-whooping;* and the elements *-like* in *candelabrum-like, cell-like, man-*

of-war-like, terrace-like, worklike, and, chief favorite of all, *-looking* in *animal-looking, aristocratic-looking, cat-tail-looking, comical-looking, dusty-looking, fair-looking, fancy-looking, gawky-looking, happy-looking, horrible-looking, live-looking, mixed-up-looking, ragged-looking, ratty-looking, Roman-looking, rural-looking, Southern-looking, undertaker-looking, unprepossessing-looking,* and *villain-looking.* Other adjective suffixes used are the participial *-ed* in *cool-brained, double-starred, mile-posted, mortar-boarded, puff-sleeved; -fied* or *-ified* in *assified, chimneyfied, sarcastified; -ful* in *homeful, jackassful, steamboatful; -ish* in *Mayoritish* and *roosterish; -ic* in *Japanesic* and *poet-laureatic;* and *-al, -ial,* or *-ical* in *obituarial, unanecdotical,* and *undictionarial.* Others used but once may be seen in *Susquehannian, jumbulacious, puzzlesome,* and *ship-going.*

The chief adverb suffix is of course *-ly,* sometimes extended to *-ably, -ially, -ually, -ically,* or *-edly,* as in *advertisedly, Christian-Scientifically, Edisonially, elephantinely, gallusly, hearably, killingly, slightually, three-leggedly, unbrahminically, uncomplimentarily, vinegarishly.* Mark Twain has also extended the use of the old adverb suffix *-s,* (q. v. in the LEXICON), to the unrecorded *Mondays, night-times, Saturdays, summers,* and *winters.* Others employed are *-wise* in his *businesswise, familywise, religiouswise,* and *-ward* in *Californiaward, tavernward.* For verbs he occasionally uses the suffix *-ize: Carnegieize, millinerize.*

Mark Twain is equally fond of extending the use of certain prefixes in the formation of new words. The list is as follows: *acrack; after-davit, after-development; all-sorrowfully; back hall, back lot, back-room; between-days; disapplaud, disinvite, disorbit; engame; ever-augmenting, ever-glorious, ever-progressing, ever-vigilant; ex-Congressman, ex-convict, ex-desperado, ex-Governor, ex-keelboatman, ex-Member, ex-official, ex-slave; far-receding, far-sounding; fellow-barber, fellow-pilot, fellow-savant, fellow-second, fellow-trader, fellow-unfortunate; half-apologetic, half-bank, half-confession, half-confidence, half-doubt, half-generation, half-massacred, half-petticoat, half-stretch, half-uttered, half-wheel-deep, half-white; long-agone, long-coveted, long-departed, long-discarded, long-liver, long-oval, long-pent, long-pent-up, long-speech, long-talked-of, long-vanished; mid-movement, mid-nothingness; much-nicked; multi-billionaire; never-diminishing; non-progressionist, non-association, non-associationist; off-watch; out-cabin, out-engineer, out-superintend; over-conspicuous, over-described, over-description, over-flatter, over-terseness; post-college; self-acquittal, self-conferred, self-deification, self-pasting; super-high-moral, superhonorable; under-description, underwaiter.*

It is of course not always easy to draw the line between words formed with prefixes or suffixes, as in the above lists, and the compound words listed in the next section, made by joining two or more words of approximately equal importance.

b. Humorous Distortions

Mark Twain's liberties with the language took on a more daring range when he passed from the manufacture of new formations, more or less regular, to deliberate distortions. One of his favorite humorous devices was the "blend," i. e., the telescoping together of two different words, as when he called himself a "procrastinaturalist," a mixture of procrastinator and naturalist, or a natural procrastinator. Some of the "blends" listed below may have been the products of the humorous genius of the American vernacular rather than that of Mark Twain himself, as was probably the case with the familiar "consound" (a union of "confound" and "consarned"?). The component parts of the others are either obvious or have been discussed in the LEXICON.

consound	*procrastinaturalist*
chicken-livered	*psychosuperintangibly*
electroincandescently	*refresh up*
endiometrical	*sanchrosynchrostereoptically*
oligarcheologically	*Shakesperiod*
perscontation	*she-brew*
phrenophone	*Stratfordolator*
poet lariat	*telelectrophonoscope*
polytechnique	*telescopulariat*
poundiferous	*vermifuginous*
preforeordestination	*Wallachian*

Another group of humorous coinages may be better described as deformations or whimsical alterations:

alipta	*coftus*	*rheum ponticum*
bandoleer	*dissenwhich*	*ring-streaked-and-*
bangalore	*farmacopia*	*striped*
bathostic	*farmeopath*	*rough-scruff*
blatta byzantina	*foreslander*	*simultane*, v. (a "back-*
brontosaur	*hybernian*	*formation")*
calamus odoratus	*Macedonian*	
celtic	*moral* (as sing. sb.)	

Still a different group is made up of Mark Twain's alienisms, nonce borrowings from the foreign languages which always fascinated him so much, or humorous adaptations in English springing from too literal translation. German was by all odds his favorite foreign speech, and from it he took or adapted *cattie, ceramiker, Geschirr, Meisterschaft, niggerkin, paust (?), Schlag, Zug,* and the four fearsome German compounds listed under *effect*. A somewhat larger number are borrowed from French: *allons, apprehend, arrest, batter, by-blue, empocket, equilibree, gage, gros de laine, longly, misery, mount, palmiste,* and *ventre saint gris.* From Italian come *colazione, facchino, ombra, Picciola,* and *revolveration.* From Portuguese probably sprang the inspiration for his new coin the *milray.* From Latin, of a sort, came his use of *exequatur, extraordinariensis, maxillaris superioris, os frontis,* and *populo.* From the American Indian tongues he took *checaudum, mishemokwa,* and *saw-saw-quan.* On his visit to far-off India he helped himself to *bheel, Chaur, choke-cloth,* and *Kaet.* Finally he found amusement in some specimens of foreigner's English, which yielded him the words *perfuse* and *signation,* as well as several examples of the twisting of grammatical function which will be listed below.

Last of all may be listed a group of "pseudo-words," all of which are either errors on Mark Twain's part, or misprints of the proof-readers with whom he fought a life-long battle, or else "polishings" perpetrated upon him after his death by his devoted editor (see comment in the LEXICON under *guts:*

banderillo (for *banderillero*)   *outlay* (for *layout*)
beaten out (for *beat out*)   *pulu* (for *tule*)
begattings (for *begats*)   *post-Pleosaurian* (for *post-*
east-by-east (for *nor'-east-by-east*)   *Plesiosaurian*)
daintly (for *daintily*)   *white-sleeve badge* (for *white-slave*
chirinoya (for *chirimoya* or   *badge?*)
   cherimoya)   *wise-drawn* (for *wire-drawn?*)

c. Pure Inventions

These include onomatopoetic and nonsense coinages. In the former subdivision may be listed:

blimblammin'   *ker-blim*   *umf*
blip   *ker-chunk*   *whoopee*
chebang   *mph*   *whoop-jamborehoo*
chow-wow   *pfew-few*   *who-whoo,* v.
her-blam   *phit*
ker-blam   *swush*

Last of all come the pure nonsense inventions. In this group the sheer joy which Mark Twain felt in playing with words, a joy which he shared with Jonathan Swift and Lewis Carroll and James Joyce, is at its height. He let himself go most recklessly in the passages quoted under *afarabocca* and *kahkahponeeka,* but frequently elsewhere shows his ability to create words out of nothing. Especially interesting from a psychological point of view are the "dream-words" vouched for in "My Platonic Sweetheart." The complete list is as follows:

afarabocca   *corpobalsamum*   *hopow*
atreous   *dingblatter*   *kahkahponeeka*
balragoomah   *diramic*   *kazark*
Bgwjjilligkkk   *flirk*   *mmbglx*
bolwoggoly   *gmwkwllolp*   *nappersocket*
bong-a-bong   *gnillic*   *owdawakk*
bopple   *gowkarak*   *poopoo*
bzzzzzzzeeeee   *haboolong*   *puckittypukk*
carnabadium   *hogglebumgullop*   *schnawp*

sinon	*swosh-swosh*	*xhvloj*
slowwk	*wawhawp*	*yokky*
sufa	*wlgw*	

2. New Combinations

When Mark Twain wrote in the Appendix to his A Tramp Abroad: "In our newspapers the compounding-disease lingers a little to the present day," he was perhaps unconsciously satirizing himself; for if ever there was a writer who had the "compounding-disease" it was Mark Twain. The prodigious number of compounds and combinations used by him and not recorded in any dictionary, of which the total number included in the Lexicon is 1414, may perhaps best be grouped, following the lead set by the Oxford, into Special and Obvious Combinations. Special Combinations are defined by the Oxford in its "Preface" to Vol. I (p. xiii) as combinations, whether formally connected by the hyphen or virtually by the unity of their signification, in which that signification is more or less specialized, such as *air-line* or *eyewash*. Obvious Combinations, on the other hand, are those in which each word retains its full meaning, the relation betwen them falling under one or other of the ordinary grammatical categories; e.g., *camp-fire, eye-syringe*. The distinction is not always an easy one to make; and some combinations which we have, with a certain amount of hesitation, assigned to the one class would perhaps have been assigned to the other by the editors of the Oxford, had they discovered their existence. A third group has also been required by the nature of Mark Twain's vocabulary, made up of what we have called Nonce Combinations, because they seem, like the new words in the preceding section, to have been deliberately manufactured for the occasion or for humorous effect. Two special subdivisions of this third group have been listed separately: the Multiple Compounds or Phrase-Words, and the Compounds Made on German Models.

a. Special Combinations

In the comprehensive table of statistics furnished in its "Preface" to Vol. X, the Oxford enumerates 47,800 Special Combinations out of its grand total of 414,825 words, not including the Supplement. The additional Special Combinations here included do not seem to have been coined by Mark Twain, but rather taken by him from current use. Because of their specific application, their exact meaning cannot be gathered merely from their component parts, and hence they are in need of definition or brief explanation. There seems to be no legitimate reason why all of these should not be included in a real unabridged dictionary, especially since they are found in the works of an author of the standing of Mark Twain.

The term Special Combination, as here employed, includes special phrases, constructions, and idioms; but it has not seemed necessary to list again Mark Twain's unrecorded idioms, which are double-starred in the list given on pp. xlv-l.

accidental insurance
alkali-spider
along about
alum-basket
anchor out
and (deuces-and)
apple-paring
arm-loop
auction-block
baby-wagon
back-alley, a.
backing-bell
Ballarat fly
Baltimore perch
barb lace
bath-cure
beat around
beer-mill
Big Water
billiard-parlor
billiard-saloon
biscuit-punch
blame-fool, a.
blind reef
blood-kin, a.
blue-clay, a.
boiler-factory
bone-filter
book-talk
boxing-mill
boy-life
branch-road
breakdown-dancing
breakfast-horn
bridal tour
broom-closet
bust out
cabinet secretary
cactus tree
Cadet of Temperance
candy-striped
cannon-swab
capitation tax
carrying capacity
cave off

center-driving
chattel slavery
cold chills
change off
chills-racked
chimney-guy
chip into
clarifying-tank
clock-hand
close down
close fit
close up on
coach candle
coarse hand
coarse print
coarse whisper
comb up
common charge
contribution-plate
contribution-purse
conversation-voice
cotton-domestic
country place
county-hospital
couple-up
court-clerk
creation-dawn
crossing-mark
crossing-stone
cross off
curtain-calico
darken up
d box
deaf-and-dummy
devil-fire
display-head
display-heading
display-sheet
distributing-house
doctor-book
double-columned
double-gauge
double-starred
dragoon-revolver
dramatic editor

draw off
dray-pin
dressing-bureau
dress-pattern
drop over
dry-goods box
dry gripes
Dunker-Baptist
duty-visit
ear-socket
eased-up
effect-collecting
elbow-mate
elbow-neighbor
electric call
electric car
emigrant-train
expert accountant
famine-breeder
fifteen-puzzle
fine language
finger-ball
fire-auction
fire-boy
fire-faced
first-best
First Family
First Member
fool along
foot-casing
free papers
fringe off
funny-paragraph
gamble-money
gambling-palace
garden-acre
glory-fire
go-ahead bell
good licks
goo-goo, v.
goose-milk
gospel-mill
grape-doctor
grape-system
grease-biscuit

grease-jet
grease-print
Great Republic
gully-keeper
hack-grinding
hair-lifting
hair-spine
ham-rag
hand-print
hanging-eve
hay-ride
heart-and-heart
heat-shimmer
high-mightiness
high-quarter
high-tariff
home-shot
home-trail
horn-blow
horse-bill
horse-talk
hyphenated name
Indian doctor
Injun-English
insanity plea
insurance-agency
invalid-car
ivy-mailed
k box
kennel-rat
killing-grudge
kings-and
kiss-the-Bible
labored-out
ladder railroad
ladder railway
ladle in
land-dinner
lap-bred
law-dog
laws goodness
lay preacher
leather-face
letter-correspondence
letter-crossing

lie in with
life-policy
life-stream
lightning-heeled
lightning-shod
light-throwing
lime-town
line shot
local editor
local item
lock-pick
long spoon
long talk
long term
loop-engineering
love-box
love-duel
lower river
low-rate
marble-time
marble-yard
march-out
market-report
medicine-sack
memorial-spoon
Mental Scientist
Methusalem-numskull
middle name
Mother-Church
mounting-peg
mud-cure
mud-stripe
mud-wagon
mule-rush
mush up
nail-grab
nickel-clad
nigger-bill
nigger-corner
nigger-gallery
nigger-show
occasion of state
Old Master
Old Mistress
Old Virginia

Other Place
Other Side
out back
pain-proof
palace-shop
paper-collar
parenthesis-mark
passenger-packet
patch-eyed
patent-leathers
peanut-boy
peanut-commerce
peel off
personal-assault, a.
personal-gossip, a.
picket-watch
pictorial paper
pine-grown
plantation-hymn
plug-tile
pocket-mining
poison-swilling
porcelaintype
postal service
prairie-pink
press-notice
privileged sex
pumpkin show
push along
quarter-hour
quick-motioned
racing-mobile
racing-pressure
rack-heap
rag dollar
rag-lamp
rag-store
railbed
rain-dog
rat's nest
rat-trap
ready-bell
rear-skirts
Red Ribbon
reef-bench

retire upon
rifle-match
rifle-pistol
ring in with
rock-cutting
round-log, a.
rummage around
runaway-nigger
rush through
safety-box
Saratoga potatoes
Scientist-Church
scoop-shovel, a.
scorpion-bile
scrimp-nosed
second clerk
sensation-preacher
sensation-story
Shark God
sheet-bath
shoal up
show-people
shrimp-colored
side drift
side-mark
signal-lantern
silver-gray fox
singing-geography
slave-auction
slave-wench
slave-worked
sleeping-section
slow-motioned
small-baggage
smoking-compartment
snatch on
snip out
society item
sounding-barge
sounding-boat
sounding-pole
sounding-yawl
spinning-stick
spiral twist
spring-line

spring step
square crossing
stage-carpentering
stage-courtier
stage-office
stage-plank
stage-whispering
station-man
staying capacity
steel plate
steel ship
stern-mark
stick through
stiff-brim
stock-board
storm-quarters
storm-rack
stove-lid
straight along
straighten down
straighten up
strangling cloth
string along
sugar-plantation
sugar-shovel
sugar-trough
sumach-tobacco
Sunday-school-book
sworn-off
tailing-pile
tallow-drip
tear-jug
telephone-station
texas-hall
thin-spaced
third clerk
three-ball game
through-freight
through-line
thug-book
thug-chief
timber-front
tin-monger
tobacco-curing
tobacco-stemmer

tomb-lantern
torch-basket
town-dog
town-drunkard
trading-scow
trap-robber
trim-built
trim-chiselled
trowel in
tuck down
tumbling-bug
type-channel
type-girl
type-machine
typewriter copyist
Tyrolese warbling
upper bench
upper river
upper-river, a.
verge-staff
war-correspondence
war-ethics
war-plume
war-price
watch below
watch-room
watering-depot
water-reading
weaken down
weather-gasket
wheat-bread
whisky-shelf
whisky-soaked
whistle-lever
white-wooled
wind-reef
witch-pie
wood-rank
World's Fair
writing-parlor
Yellow Terror

b. Obvious Combinations

In the nature of things, the free or obvious combinations in the language are capable of almost infinite multiplication, and no dictionary is to be blamed for not including all of them. The OXFORD does, however, include 59,755 of them, and many that have escaped its notice have been given in other dictionaries, as has been noted above. The omission of those listed below from all the dictionaries is not seldom made more surprising in view of their inclusion of closely parallel combinations, many of which have been cited for comparison under the respective entries in the LEXICON.

alligator-hide	bone-racking	castle-graced
angular-limbed	bone-wrenching	cat-fight
ant-deposit	book-material	cattle-scow
art-architecture	boot-polishing	cement-mine
ascension-robe	boot-toe	century-long
asphaltum-paved	bow-end	channel-finder
audience-room	bramble-infested	channel-interruption
awning-post	brass-buttoned	character-reader
badge-holder	breakfast-station	character-reading
baggage-coupon	breeches-button	charity-founder
baggage-van	bridge-pier	cheerful-tinted
bank-caving	buckle-hole	cheer-killing
bank-robbery	buckskin-seated	chestnut-cake
baseball match	bug-eaten	chestnut-woman
battle-chant	bull-driver	chicken-fight
battle-gallery	buzzard-roost	chromo-portrait
battle-stretch	cabin-guard	cigar-peddler
battle-tragedy	cable-locker	circus-bill
bead-basket	cable-telegraph	circus-poster
bead-reticule	calf-butchering	claim-owner
bed-leg	campaign-directing	class-teacher
bell-tap	camrod	clean-scraped
bench-manager	candle-factory	clear-water, a.
bench-shaped	cane-head	clock-strike
Bible-text	cannon-thunder	close-cowled
bier-bearer	cañon-bed	close-ranked
bit-champing	canvas-box	cloud-breeder
blood-smeared	canvas-canopied	cloud-effect
bloody-jawed	canvas-covered	cloud-height
blubber-grease	cargo-room	cloud-shoal
blue-uniformed	car-hook	cluster-diamond
blunt-toed	carpet-stuff	coal-flat
bone-bruising	caste-brother	coaling center
bone-mashing	caste-custom	coal-smoke

coal-train
coarse comb
coffee-stain
coffin-box
comfit-box
compass-shelf
conscience-soothing
copper-tinged
corner-grocery
cranberry-farm
crater-summit
crooked-handled
curiosity-breeding
cypress-top
daguerreotype-case
day-gear
death-picture
death-room
death-sentinel
death-stroke
death-warning
deck-awning
deck-sweep
deck-washer
deep-thinker
deer-horn
desert-frequenting
desert-making
dew-fashioned
dialect-speaking
diamond-boom
diamond-breastpin
diamond-crater
diligence-time
dim-hearkening
dim-hoping
dining-house
dirt-caked
dirt-preferring
disaster-breeding
disease-breeder
dog-hair
doll-clothes
donkey-voiced
dream-failure

dream-haze
dream-people
dream-picture
dream-stuff
dream-thought
dream-yacht
dress-change
dressed-stone
dried-apple-pie
drift-canoe
dust-rag
dynamite-can
easy-working
eating-station
editor-critic
elephant-driver
elephant-fight
elephant-legged
elephant-waisted
elevator-load
end-feather
engine-bell
English-murdering
entrance-door
erect-haired
euchre-party
evening-paper
examination-day
exhibition-ground
eye-contenting
fact-life
faith-straining
fancy-topped
fare-ticket
farmer-class
farm-help
fear-bound
ferry-landing
fickle-tempered
figure-artist
figure-drawing
fire-building
fire-hued
fire-spouting
firmament-clogging

firmament-obliterating
first-uttered
fish-bladder
fishing-things
flame-front
flame-jet
flint-arm
flint-picker
flood-wasted
flower-harvest
foot-casing
footing-up
forest-bordered
fortune-making
foul-witted
fountain-jet
four-hour
fox-hearted
fragment-strewn
freight-car
freight-pile
fresh-crowned
frog-shaped
fruit-peddler
fruit-wagon
funnel-topped
furniture-mender
gallows-buckle
gallows-builder
game-shop
gas-illuminated
gas-office
gate-guard
gentle-flowing
gentle-humored
gentleman-servant
gentle-spirited
girl-soldier
glacier-paved
glade-furrowed
glass-inclosed
glass-smooth
globe-shadowing
gold-sack
gold-strike

gout-smitten
granite-bound
granite-hearted
granulating-pipe
green-spectacled
grizzly-headed
grove-plumed
guard-deep
guide-in-chief
gutter-scum
habit-sodden
hackful
ham-bone
hand-free
handkerchief-turban
hand-painted
hate-inspiring
hay-cutting
health-journal
hearse-horse
heart-lift
heart-secret
heart-torturing
heel-blistered
hemp-colored
hero-heart
hiding-quarters
high-laced
high-river
high-water-stained
hill-city
history-building
history-creating
history-sodden
hoisting-works
homage-payer
home-knit
home-mate
honor-reward
horizon-rim
horse-bite
horse-holding
house-corner
house-minion
house-porch

house-thief
howdah-house
humor-lover
hundred-faceted
ice-arch
ice barren
ice-bead
ice-cavern
ice-coated
ice-crest
ice-factory
ice-wave
idiot-asylum
imagination-stunning
inch-mark
iron-armed
ivy-grown
jackass-voiced
joy-flame
joy-song
kangaroo-chasing
kite-line
knife-sheath
labor-dirt
lake-reservoir
landlord-apprentice
late-night, a.
law-equipment
lawyer-farmer
league-striding
league-wide
lease-roll
lecture-season
letter-sack
levee-rim
libel suit
liberation-party
liquor-drinking
listening-distance
livery-flunkey
locker-bunk
locker-sofa
log raft
love-quarreling
love-sign

luxury-loving
magazine-agent
manhood-testing
manure-pile
maple-sugar camp
marble-topped
marble-visaged
measure-defying
meat-feast
meditation-breeder
melon-rind
memento-seeker
memory-exhibition
memory-expert
messenger-splendor
meteor-flight
mile-wide
million-voiced
mining-broker
mining-tax
miracle-performance
mist-dimmed
modern-born
modern-style
modest-salaried
money-loss
money-necessity
morocco-covered
moss-bearded
moss-hung
mother-instinct
mountain-climber
muddy-water, a.
mule-hoof
mule-mounted
mule-path
mule-road
muscle-training
musketry-clatter
mystery-dispelling
nerve-web
new-gold, a.
new-time, a.
newspaper-bag
newspaper-hawking

newspaper-picture
news-scrap
night-garment
night-marching
nine-log, a.
nougat-peddler
oar-handle
oil-stench
one-limbed
order-restoring
Oxford-trained
pain-giving
palace-bordered
paper-overlaid
parent-honoring
peanut-peddler
pebble-splash
petroleum-city
pistol-case
pitcher-bearer
plank fencing
plank sidewalk
plant-root
platform-business
plotting-place
poet-orator
police-parade
policy business
polite-letter, a.
poor-quality, a.
porch-roof
poster-fence
powder-can
powder-keg
prentice-fashion
previous-engagement, a.
prism-fringed
pure-white
purple-plumed
quarantine-blockade
quarantine-term
quartz-milling
quartz-miner
race-aversion
race-prejudice

raft-voyage
ragged-filagree
ragged-topped
railroad-building
railroad president
railway-center
railway official
ranger-saddle
recreation-time
reform-compelling
refreshment-peddler
relic-peddler
relief-steamer
resin-colored
river-edge
river-glimpse
river-inspector
river-pilot
romance-literature
romance-reading
romance-tinge
roof-clustered
rubbish-pile
sack-pile
sad-visaged
safe-key
salt-warehouse
sample-grain
sand-mound
sand-wave
satin-clad
sausage-stuffing
scepter-wielding
school-bully
school-knapsack
screw-shape
searching-expedition
sea-wonder
servant-tipping
seventh-rate
shark-fisher
sheep-drover
shingle-bundle
side-gaze
side-glimpse

side remark
silk-and-velvet, a.
silken-clad
silver-bowed
silver-claim
simple-natured
sky-piercing
sky-towering
sleeping-bench
sleeping-mixture
slim-legged
slop-tub
slow-dragging
slow-drifting
smoke-charged
smoke-house raising
snake-charming
snow-block
snow-hooded
snow-summit
snow-wreathed
sober-colored
sofa-back
soldier-camp
soldier-cap
soldier-plume
soldier-shoe
soot-blackened
sore-faced
Southern-style
space-annihilating
spiral-shaped
spirit-contenting
spume-spray
steamboat-boiler
steamboat-landing
steamboatman
steamboat-owner
steam-ferry
steam-ferryboat
steam-sawmill
step-papa
stern-countenanced
stiff-jointed
stiff-standing

stone-benched
storm-buffeted
storm-scarred
strange-shaped
street-crossing
stump-toed
sugar-hogshead
Sunday-service
surf-beat
surf-wave
surgery-practice
table-fare
tea-grounds
tea-planting
ten-ounce
text-meaning
theater-actor
theft-raid
third-quality
thirteen-jointed
thirty-cord
three-carat
three-dollar
three-log
three-word
tiger-fight
tight-buttoned
tight-legged
tin-patched
tobacco-commerce
tobacco-field
tobacco-juice

tobacco-lover
tomato-vine
tomb-desecrator
torch-lighted
tourist-book
tourist-resort
trial-time
trouble-weighted
tug-load
turning-room
turnip-barrel
turnip-shaving
two-acre
umbrella-drippings
valor-breeding
vanity-snubbing
van-leader
vengeance-hungry
vengeance-prompted
vermin-tortured
victory-flush
vine-embowered
vision-seer
vodka-jug
waiting-parlor
walking-costume
walking-suit
walnut-hull
war-fleet
war-telegram
war-tribe
water-canteen

way-place
way-port
weather-defying
well-gnawed
whip-stroke
whisky-habit
whisky-jug
white-aproned
white-kid-gloved
white-shuttered
window-slit
wine-bag
wine-sipper
witch-business
witch-cat
witch-commissioner
wooden-shuttered
wood-sawing
work-animal
work-clothes
work-gown
working-gown
working-moment
work-mule
work-stock
work-parlor
worm-fashion
yachting-contest
Zeus-worshipping
zinc-plated

c. Nonce Combinations

These collocations differ from those listed above in that they all sound like deliberate coinages. Most of them were made with humorous intent; some, such as *peach-vine* and *watermelon-tree*, may be described as pure nonsense combinations. As a rule their meaning is sufficiently obvious from the context. Whether or not they should all be included in the dictionary is a debatable question. A nonce-word might be defined as one that has been nominated for membership in the language; and certainly many of those nominated by Mark Twain, such as his *angel-clay*, *mind-sect*, *poker-clergy*, *soul-butter*, *speech-vehicle*, *word-musician*, and *word-sense*, deserve to be seconded and elected!

accident-ticket
accident-title
acquaintanceship-
   breeder
Adam-clam
Adam-newsboy
Adam-nugget
adjective-piling
adjective-stump
advance-advertisement
adventure-bristling
air-torpedo
alligator-bed
alligator-boat
alligator-pilot
alligator-reef
alligator-water
all-the-time, a.
angel-clay
Annex-polisher
appendix-basket
appetite-cure
artificial-flower, a.
autumn-butter
bald-summited
beaver-trowel
birth-commission
bladder-balloon
Blavatsky-Buddhist
bliss-business
board-clatter
boiled-cauliflower, a.
bone-spray
boss-pilotical
boy-admiration
boy-Paradise
brain-machine
brain-plow
brain-territory
brimstone-shovel
brook-connection
buck-angel
burglar-time
business-brain
business-eye

business-head
business-idea
business-talent
butter-timber
cat-assizes
catch-sentence
cat-knowledge
cattle-friend
century-wave
character-fabric
church-machinery
city-capture
civilization-tool
claw back
clay-plugged
climate-proof
clock-caked
coal-venture
coffin-clad
compassion-inspiring
complacency-signal
complaint-system
composing-gait
compounding-disease
conspirator-in-chief
convention-packer
conversation-mill
copying-gait
copyright-preserving
corn-crust
corpse-face
corpse-room
corpsy-white
counter-yell
courteously-discourteous
craft-equipment
crash-word
culture-wagon
darkish-paly
day-thought
death-disk
death-toilet
debt-factory
deportment-tournament
discovery-fever

discussion-mortar
dividend-cooking
Double-Man
Double-Man-Bird
doxology-works
engineer-in-general
everything-in-which
exaggeration-mill
fan-distributor
farmer-preacher
fisher-loafer
fish-interior
flea-pasture
flesh-bulk
frog-span
fry, minor
furniture-scout
garlic-exterminator
general-talk
general-ways
ghost-bag
ghost-stuff
gnat-and-bull
governess-German
grace-of-God, a.
grasshopper-soup
Grindstone, Old Red
guide-English
hackman-general
hackman-gondolier
hail-barge
hailstorm-discourager
happiness-machine
hearing-orifice
heifer-paddock
highwayman-term
history-mill
history-tank
hospital-bird
hotel-devil
hotelward-bound
idiot-factory
imagination-
   manufactured
imagination-mill

induction-talent
inspiration-works
insurance-chromo
inventor-tribe
jack-at-all-science
jack-pair
king-feature
king-parenthesis
landing-cabin
laughter-and-chatter
lawyer-talk
lawyer-way
lecture-double
lecture-raid
lecture-shirmish
leg-power
lightning-vivid
literature-preserver
loot-basket
machine-expense
magnanimous-
    incident, a.
mamma-partridge
mamma-turkey
man-bird
man-factory
man-mystery
mansion-and-brewery
margin-business
marriage-week
memento-factory
memento-magazine
mental telegraphic
mental telegraphist
mental telegraphy
miller-gun
millionaire, hundred-
million-pound, a.
mind-extinguished
mind-sect
mind-telegraphing
miracle-factory
mob-tide
mote-magnifying
mother-title

mud-turtle-shaped
mule-power
myriad-accomplished
never-never, v.
noble-episode, a.
oldest-alumnus, a.
one-hundred-millionaire
outer-border
parenthesis-disease
parlor-desperado
party-collar
passenger-bear
passenger-dog
passenger-kennel
patriot-maker
paupershod
paw-mark
peach-vine
phrase-family
phrase-juggler
picture-proclamation
pilot-apprentice
pilot-farmer
pirate-book
pocket-pup
poker-clergy
policy Christian
pork-millionaire
presumption-tadpole
profanity-mill
prophecy-enthusiast
prophecy-gun
prophecy-savan
purse-reach
puzzled-up
quarter-civilization
quarter-god
quiffsplitter
rascal-nest
reporter-material
return-entertaining
revolution-breeder
rhyme-jingle
roached-backed
road-pegging

road-straggler
robber-book
ruffle-cuffed
sailor-people
sailor-talk
sailor-way
salvation-notion
Salvation-Warrior
sand-quarry
sausage-wreath
sawdust-mine
scalp-plant
Science-Pope
scrape-up
seven-stepped
seventeen-jointed
several-barreled
Shakespeare-adoring
Shakespeare-law
she-college
sheep-signal
shell-shower
ship-house
ship-talk
sighting-iron
sign-name
silent-assertion, a.
silk-spinner
Silverland
Simplified Speller
siphon-squirting
six figures
sky-blues
slander-mill
slave-lethargy
slave-tyrant
slush-boy
slush-plastered
smoke-mark
smoking-party
snow-drive
soap-and-candle
socialist-hated
soda-squirt
soda-squirter

sofa-shifter

sofa-skirmisher

soldier-people

soldier-talk

soldier-way

soldier-wile

sore-back, a.

sorrow-sowing

soul-blistering

soul-butter

soul-capture

soul-scorching

soul-staining

speaker-list

special-brand, a.

specter-earl

specter-knight

speech-vehicle

spelling-fight

spider-strand

spring-book

statue-rigid

stealing-raid

steel-pen-coated

storm-gloom

storm-wash

stub-hunter

suffering-machine

suicide-average

Sunday-dressed

superstition-monger

supplication-mill

supremacy-bell

suspicion-point

sweeper-out

swill-room

talking-walk

talk-machinery

tax-collar

teacher-factory

tea-group

test-remark

think-works

thought-machine

thought-machinery

thunder-tramp

tick-running

tiger-average

tiger-persuader

time-passer

torch-plant

trade-form

trade-phrasing

trade-taffy

trash-dust

trunk-lie

truss point

truth-monger

twin-monster

undertaker-eye

undertaker-furniture

undertaker-outfit

utterance-point

vague-murmuring

war-colossus

war-firmament

war-tempest

war-tiger

waste-paper-littered

watch-tinker

water-career

water-glimpse

watermelon-tree

weather-failure

Webster-Unabridged

white-sleeve

who-whoo, v.

witch-dread

witch-terror

wit-mechanism

woman-assemblage

wonder-dream

wood-and-water-station

word-musician

word-sense

writing-gait

year-worn

zenith-scouring

d. Multiple Compounds or Phrase-Words

Among the nonce combinations a special place must be reserved for what may be called Mark Twain's multiple compounds. Such grotesque collocations as those in the following list, which must have been in his mind when he spoke of words like "a seventeen-jointed vestibuled railroad-train," or of "a clatter of syllables as long as a string of sluice-boxes," made an irresistible appeal to his sense of the ridiculous:

American-Colonial-Dutch peddler-and-Salt Cod-McAllister, a.

Annual-Veteran-who-has-Voted-for-Every - President-from -Washington - down - and -Walked - to-the-Polls -Yesterday - with-as-Bright-

an-Eye-and-as-Firm-a - Step - as-Ever, sb.

beer-and-anecdote, a.

blessings-of-civilization, a.

blubber-and-slush, sb.

brother-on-the-half-shell, sb.

Could-Have-Beener, sb.
devotion-to-passengers'-safety, a.
double-butt-ender, sb.
God-Bless-Our-Home, sb.
Happy-Land-of-Canaan, sb.
Hail-Columbia, sb.
Hark-from-the-Tomb, sb.
Home-of-the-Brave, sb.
ich-habe-gehabt-haben, sb.
jabber-jabber-jabber, v.
Land-of-the-Free, sb.
Might-Have-Beener, sb.
must-have-been, sb.
Must-Have-Beener, sb.
Now-I-lay-me-down-to-sleep, a.

Noyoudont, sb.
That-settles-it, a.
Thou-hast-wounded-the-spirit-that loved-thee, a.
thousand-times-offered, a.
three-children-born-at-a-birth, a.
'tisn't-anything-I-can-do-it-any-time-I-want-to, sb.
We-Are-Warranted-in-Believinger, sb.
what-have-I-done, a.
wish-you-didn't-have-to-try, a.
Without-a-Shadow-of-Doubter, sb.
Young-Man-Afraid-of-his-Shadow, sb.

e. Compounds Made on German Models

Perhaps the clue to Mark Twain's fondness for compound words is to be found in the following list. At least it may be said that with his particular predilection for them, he was predestined to fall in love with the German language, as he did, just as soon as he made its acquaintance. Doubtless his interest in German reinforced his native linguistic tendencies in this and other respects. When his Connecticut Yankee wished to reach the acme of impressiveness (see under *effect*), he turned instinctively to German compounds, and apparently manufactured more terrific ones for the occasion than were even to be found in the German phrasebooks. The following English compounds are evidently modeled directly upon German originals (see note in each case); and doubtless there were many others whose immediate source of inspiration is not so apparent.

barrel-round
beer-hall
beer-jolly
brothel-daddy
brothel-knight
coal-pitch-raven-black
collar-sewer
duelling-day
duelling-house
duelling-place
duelling-room
ear-boxing

hare-foot
hunterman
kernel-sound
knight-stroke
light-ray
liver-sausage
locked-hair
louse-brat
life-day
life-day (another sense)
mask-law
order-maker

pleasure-walk
sham-duel
sham-supplication
student-corps
thumbkin
thumb-sucker
word-of-honor-breaker
world-celebrated
world-girdling
world-trade
world-wonder

3. New Meanings

Mark Twain's linguistic inventiveness is manifested quite as much in discovering new uses for old words as it is in creating new words or in manufacturing new combinations. His new meanings fall naturally into much the same sub-divisions. First have been listed those cases where the meanings he employs do not seem to be really new or original with him, but merely taken from current use, though hitherto overlooked by all the dictionaries; these have been called Un-recorded Transfers. Next come the cases whre he has used old words in new gram-matical functions; and next those where he has turned old abstract words into con-cretes. Last are given his Nonce Uses and humorous twists of meaning, with a separate subdivision for his pure nonsense uses, including his puns and malapro-pisms.

a. Unrecorded Transfers

absolutely
around, adv.
ash-cat
assemble
Association
and (two new senses)
at
back of (one sense)
bad words
bar, v.
barren
beat, sb. (one sense)
Bermuda
boxing (two senses)
bracketed
breakdown, sb.
breakown, sb.
break down, v. trans. (two senses)
break up, v.intr.
breast, v.
brick
brick up
brisken
bugle
bull, v.
bundle
calk, sb.
call, v.
call the game
campaigner
canvass, v.
carbon film
card

catch, sb.
circus, v.
classic, sb.
clean, v.
clerk
clerkly
clog, sb.
close, a.
clouds, in the
cold, a.
come in
coop
crazy
crossing
crowd, v.
cry, sb.
cub
cylinder
darling, a.
death-light
demonstrate
demonstration
down on
draw, v. (one sense)
drench, sb.
earth, on
earthquake
ecstasy
eggs, to suck
egg-sucking
eloquence
eloquent
emigrant
emit

feeding-house
feeding-place
fence, v.
fetch (one sense)
fetch around (two senses)
fetch away
fiddle, sb.
fighting
finisher
fish-belly
fixed (one sense)
floating
fore-and-aft
freemasonry
friend
gage, v.
gaudy
get after
get along
get at
get in
get into
get up and
give
glass-eyed
glorify
good day, int.
hail, sb.
harmonious
harness, v.
harvest, v.
have
have it

head
head-mark
hive, v.
hold, sb.
hold on (one sense)
holt, sb.
horn
horse (one sense)
howler
huckleberry
immortelle
independent
Indian sign
inside
Jack
jerk, v.
joker
jolt, sb.
journeyman
kid
Kingdom
knock out
large, adv.
letter-perfect
let out (one sense)
level (one sense)
life-history
light on
line (one sense)
lodging-money
look around
lose
machinist
Metaphysical
Missourian, sb.
moonshiny
Nationalist
neck
need
No Man's Land
notice (three senses)
Old-English
on (one sense)
out, adv. (one sense)
outside, adv. (one sense)

outside, sb.
panoramist
pantograph
partner
pastorate
pastor emeritus
Patrick
pattern
persuader
pilot
plant, v. (one sense)
plant out
plate
platform (one sense)
play, v. (two senses)
played
point, sb. (one sense)
point, v.
poison, v.
police
powwow, sb. (one sense)
pull, sb.
pull, v. (one sense)
pull down
pull off
pull on
pulpit
punch, v.
putty-hearted
put up, v. (one sense)
Quaker
Quaker City
raging
rap
Reader
record
recruit, v.
recruiting
relieve
risk
round to
run, v. (one sense)
run to
rusty

safe, a.
safeness
Sanhedrim
scant, adv.
scar
see through
serfdom
set back (two senses)
shake up (one sense)
she (Am. use)
ship up
shove up
show-up, sb.
slop-shop (one sense)
snatch
snuffy
sour up
spider's web
split, v.
split, sb.
spread open
start
step over
stick, v. (one sense)
stock, v.
Stratfordian, sb. and a.
strong suit
subscriber
sudden death
suffer
swing round
take down
taker
take up (one sense)
taking, ppl. a.
takings (two senses)
Tammany
tending, vbl. sb.
thesaurus
they (for *there*)
throw off
throw up (three senses)
transient, sb.
Trumps
turn, v. (one sense)

turn over (two senses)	*Union* (one sense)	*water-drip*
twain	*Valley*	*water-spout*
twenty	*volcanic*	*wood-pheasant*
uncover	*volcano*	
under-clerk	*wabbles*	

b. New Functions

Mark Twain is constantly taking liberties with the traditional parts of speech. He delights in turning nouns, adjectives, or interjections into verbs, verbs, adjectives, or adverbs into nouns, adjectives into adverbs or adverbs into adjectives, transitive verbs into intransitive or *vice versa*, or in making almost anything into an interjection by dint of an exclamation point. In so doing he is of course merely pushing further than most writers do an ancient tendency of the English language; but none of the particular changes here listed is sanctioned by any dictionary.

a for *an* before vowel-sounds	*dray-horse*, v.	*paregoric*, v.
ah, v.	*dreamy*, v.	*pick and shovel*, v.
alas, v.	*excursion*, v. trans.	*polish off*, v.intr.
angrily, a.	*foreground*, v.	*post up*, v.intr.
argument, v.	*funnel*, v.	*put-in*, sb.
atomy, a.	*grail*, v.	*quintessential*, sb.
authentic, sb.	*grandmother*, int.	*rip*, adv.
baking, adv.	*ground-circuit*, v.	*Ross*, v.
baldheaded, adv.	*had*, sb.	*rotten*, adv.
beautiful, adv.	*handspring*, v.	*run-to-cover*, sb.
begat, sb.	*happen*, sb.	*sarcasm*, v.
bombshell, v.	*hard-boil*, v.	*seventy-four-gun*, a.
chain-mail, v.	*holy grail*, v.	*shed*, v. intr.
Charlie, int.	*hosanna*, v. intr.	*shut down*, v. intr.
Christian-missionary, v.	*hump up*, v. trans.	*shut off*, v. intr.
Christian-Scientist, a.	*Imperishable*, sb.	*sire*, v.
claw, v. trans.	*indoors*, sb.	*smokable*, sb. sing.
clear-water, a.	*Is*, sb.	*squirm*, v. trans.
corruptible, sb.	*jaw*, v. trans.	*sqush*, v. intr.
cotton-seed, v.	*jew's-harp*, v.	*stove-polish*, v.
cracked-pot, a.	*jigger*, v. trans.	*suck back*, v. intr.
crooked-skeleton, a.	*jigger*, sb.	*swearing*, adv.
cross-counter, v.	*languishy*, adv.	*tadpole*, v.
deficit, v.	*loud*, adv.	*The*, sb.
detained-baggage, a.	*majesty*, v.	*third-rate*, sb.
discretion, v.	*new-paint*, v.	*triple-lock*, v.
doubtless, sb.	*noble*, adv.	*type-copy*, v.
drawly, adv.	*outdoors*, sb.	*type-writer*, v.
	pale, sb.	*unswell*, v. trans.

up-stream, v.	*what,* v.	*yare,* v.
waddle, v. trans.	*whet up,* v. intr.	*yez,* pron. sing.
warm-up, sb.	*yacht,* v. trans.	

c. Abstracts as Concretes

Closely allied to the group of changes just listed, but constituting so marked a feature of his style that it deserves a separate place, is Mark Twain's treatment of abstract nouns. The vigor and vitality of his style owes not a little to his fondness for making concretes out of abstracts. The process is of course an old one in the development of the English vocabulary; cf. Poutsma's GRAMMAR OF LATE MODERN ENGLISH, II (1914) xxv 241: "In English many abstract nouns admit of being used in an individualized meaning, with an ordinary plural . . . But there is a considerable number of abstract nouns which hardly admit of being used in the plural. Such among many others are *bravery, compassion, courage, freedom, happiness, haste, honesty, hunger, hurry, integrity, luck, might, moderation, obedience, patience, pity, quiet, sadness, temperance, willingness, wisdom.* When necessity arises to express plural instances of the notions for which these nouns stand, certain individualizers, such as *piece, bit,* etc., are often put into requisition." Cf. also the discussion of this phenomenon by Jespersen, MODERN ENGLISH GRAMMAR, II (1914) 125-131, in the section entitled "Individualization and Concretion," especially p. 129. Jespersen gives examples of concrete plurals of abstract nouns, chiefly in *-ness,* from Sterne, Jane Austen, Wordsworth, Kipling, etc.: *flatteries, benevolences, bitternesses, childishnesses, civilities, consciousnesses, egoisms, happinesses, meannesses, perfectnesses, uglinesses, uneasinesses, waywardnesses, weaknesses, nothingnesses, thicknesses, likenesses* (= portraits), most of which are given in the dictionaries. Mark Twain, however, uses the process more freely than any of the authors mentioned.

The following cases, among many others not retained in the present LEXICON, are mentioned in one or more of the dictionaries:

brilliancies (W)	*Importances* (W)	*neglects* (OED *rare;* so
emptinesses (OED)	*inconsequentialities*	W; not *rare* in S C)
fames (C)	(C *rare*)	*nobilities* (OED)
furtivenesses (OED)	*intellects* (Now *arch* or	*privacy* (OED *rare;* so
generosities (OED *rare;*	*vulgar* in OED W S C	W; not *rare* in S C)
not *rare* in W S C U)	Wr)	*sobrieties* (OED)

The following concretes used by Mark Twain are not given in any dictionary:

blacknesses	*despairs*	*gentlenesses*
bullinesses	*despondencies*	*gorgeousnesses*
bushwhackings	*drearinesses*	*heredities*
collaborations	*dulnesses*	*hospitalities*
conjecturabilities	*eagernesses*	*immortalities*
conspicuousnesses	*forlornities*	*inharmoniousnesses*
demurenesses	*gaudinesses*	*irreconcilabilities*

irreverencies	picturesquenesses	servilities
languors	poverties	shabbinesses
monotonies	reassurings	sobrieties
neutralities	remotenesses	sweetnesses
pettings	repulsivenesses	unconsciousnesses

In the following cases abstract nouns are used in a new concrete sense in the singular: *comradeship, humorism, relevancy, non-necessity.* Cf. also Mark Twain's use of adjectives as concrete nouns: *corruptibles, imperishables, influentials, quintessentials, sentimentals.* Cf. also the phrase *to play larks.* Once, however, Mark Twain has turned a concrete word into an abstract, when he uses *powwow* in the sense of noisiness, confusion, instead of its usual sense of a noisy meeting.

d. Nonce Uses

Like the Nonce Combinations listed above, these variations seem to be deliberate, that is, metaphorical transfers invented for the occasion or for humorous effect. A large share of Mark Twain's characteristic humor lies in these whimsical twists of meaning.

aberration	boiler-iron	cobwebby
able	bony	colicky
abortionist	boost, sb.	conflagration
after, a.	bore, v.	costermonger
agony	bother, v.	crime
aground	bounce, v. (one sense)	crimson
air	brace back	cyclone (one sense)
alongside	break, sb. (one sense)	daddy
alongside of	breeze	dark and bloody
annex	breeziness	dead-center
assertive	brickbat	deliriously
bacillus	bring up standing	deploy
ball-proof	browse	drink up
balmy	buccaneer	drippings
bank the fires	bulky	drive, sb.
bannered	cannibal	drugged
barrel	capable	Egyptian
bat, step to the	carrot	eighteens
belt, to hold the	cave-dweller	elect
bet, name your	chance	electing
blandly	Choctaw (one sense)	emeute
blasphemous	chortle	establishment
blast	clan	exalted
Blue Hen's Chickens	close-reef, v.	executive family
(error)	clothes-horse	exhilaration

extract, v.
fat, sb.
fat up, v.
fight along
firm, sb.
flange
flush, v.
forehatch
forty-rod
four-ace, a.
freckle, v.
freight up
frog
game-bag
geologic
glorifier
gold-leaf, a.
gourd
gruel
Hadji
Hail Columbia, sb.
half-breed (one sense)
half-sole, v.
Hannibal
hare-lip
hash
high-light
high water
highway
hindquarters
hock-joint
holystone, v.
hop, v.
inflamed
influence
inhabit
invoice
ironclad, sb. (two senses)
ironclad, a.
jewel-box
kid-glove, a.
kitchen cabinet
lay by
lay on the oars

land, v. (one sense)
leak, v. (two senses)
leaky
load up (three senses)
love, v.
magnify
manifest
mark twain
martyr-maker
mash, v.
Memnon
mesozoic
mill, sb.
mizen-yard
morganatic
moribund
mosque
moss, v.
mud-dobber
mud-turtle
mush-and-milk, a.
mustang (one sense)
mustard-plaster
navigate
nickeled
nickel-plate
nickel-plated
Oklahoma
onion
output
outrage
outvote
over-fondle
owing
palaver
pall-bearer
pauperize
paw, v.
perturbate
petrifaction
petrified
phantom
phillippina
picturesque
pie (one sense)

piety-hive
pile-driving
pit, v.
planked
pray
pregeologic
prehistoric
prism
proceed
processionally
raid, sb.
raid, v. (two senses)
raider
railroad (one sense)
raise, sb. (one sense)
raise, v. (one sense)
rake, sb. (two senses)
rancid
raven
reel off
relic
remainders
reorganize
richen
right, sb.
roast, v.
rose-tinted
sarcasm, sb.
scatter
science
scollop
scorch
sedition
service
shadbelly
shade, v.
Shakespeare, sb.
shoal water
shop, a.
short
shouting
shoutingly
shuck, v.
sick, a. (one sense)
silvery

single-barreled	starchy	thunder-and-lightning, a.
sizable	Star-Spangled Banner	trade, a.
slogan	step out	tropical
small-poxed	stone-breaker	tropics
smallpox-pitted	strawberry, v.	twin-screw
snail-belly	stray cat	unfurl
snuggle, sb.	stump-tail, a.	unirrigated
sour on	sugar-coated	unlimber
south, a. (one sense)	Sundays	velvet-head
south end	suppress	waltzing
specter	swallow off	warble
spectral	swell, v.	warm-blooded
sponge, to throw up the	Swinburnian	war-party
spread, v.	swing, sb.	watch, to go off
sprite	swoon, sb.	whimper
square away	the (one sense)	whirl, sb.
stage-direction	third degree	whoop, sb.
Standard Oil Trust	throttle down	yonder

e. Quips and Quibbles

Here, as with the nonsense words listed above (p. lxvi), Mark Twain follows farthest the promptings of the comic spirit in the direction of finding sheer amusement for himself and his readers in the manipulation of the language. His sallies range from deliberate puns, his King Charles's head in this respect being *canon* and its family:

battery	howitzer	shifty
caliber	levee, v.	smooth-bore
canon	lick, v.	swivel
forty-niner	pain-giving	tael
full	phonographer	

through a liberal sprinkling of malapropisms:

accessionary	derange	putrified
amorphous	dogmatic	rabbit
anonymous	extradition	ransom
ayah	frisket	redoubt
basso-relievo	gules	solar sister
bituminous	howdah	strangulated sorosis
chamois	hypothenuse	technical
chamois-hunter	king-bolt	ultimate
chamois-pasture	meretricious	vivandiere
culverin	oesophagus	
depredation	organic	

to sheer nonsense uses:

anisodactylous	*holophotal*	*pachydermata*
anthropomorphous	*hydrocephalous*	*plesiosaurian*
antiphonal	*hypodermic*	*rampant*
apocryphal	*idyllic*	*refragability*
apodictical	*lamellibranchiate*	*refrangibility*
bend	*lymphatic*	*Silurian*
cathead	*maxillary*	*sirocco*
coleoptera	*nombril*	*superimbrication*
conchyliaceous	*oblique*	*ultramarine*
dephlogistic	*odic*	*wombat*
discrepantly	*Oolitic*	*xylobalsamum*
garboard-strake	*ornithorhyncus*	*yare*

———————————•———————————

It is something of a revelation to find that more than twenty-seven hundred words, combinations, and meanings employed by so important a writer as Mark Twain have been omitted from all of our dictionaries. A plausible defence might be made for not including all his nonsense inventions and uses, his humorous distortions of form or sense, his nonce compounds, or even all of his obvious combinations. The fact that one will look in vain in any dictionary for over one third of the entries in the present Lexicon, in the Oxford for over 40%, in Webster's[4] for over 45%, in the Standard for over 50%, and in the Century for nearly 55% of them, is not so disturbing as the further fact that the readers of one of our American classics will fail to find, even in our American dictionaries, any definition of such authentic and familiar words as *advertisedly, consound, functionable, keelboating,* or *puzzlesome,* or of such combinations as *apple-paring, baby-wagon, back-room, boy-life, contribution-plate, display-head, dress-pattern, fine language, middle name, parenthesis-mark, pocket-mining, Saratoga potatoes, Sunday-School-book, war-correspondence,* or *World's Fair,* or of such idioms as *just out of the band-box, at the bottom of the ladder, to sell down the river, to keep an eye out for, to make a hooraw over, with one hand tied behind one, the privilege of the floor,* or *to go to one's reward,* or such meanings and uses as Mark Twain's for the words *and, at, classic, crossing, emigrant, thesaurus,* or even *pilot!*

4 No doubt it is due to modesty that Webster's has omitted from its pages the term *Unabridged,* sb., defined in the Oxford as "A copy of the 'unabridged edition' of Webster's Dictionary," and also the not unfamiliar combination *Webster-Unabridged!*

C. ENTRIES FOR WHICH MARK TWAIN PROVIDES THE EARLIEST EVIDENCE

B² Words. The LEXICON includes 958 entries for which Mark Twain provides an earlier quotation than (or one as early as) the earliest quotation given in the OXFORD DICTIONARY.

At the risk of repetition, it should be remarked once more that the evidence presented for Mark Twain's priority should of course be taken for what it is worth. The fact that he furnishes the earliest examples so far recorded affords no proof that he invented *accident-insurance* or the *instalment plan, newspaper reporters* or *war-correspondents, syndicating* or *royalty* for authors, *whisky-drinking* or *whoopee, foreign missions* or the *fourth dimension;* but it does indicate that he took an early and a lively interest in all of these things, and it suggests a search for still further evidence in the editions of future dictionaries[5].

The B² entries are here listed under four sub-divisions. The first of these includes words, combinations, and meanings for which the first OXFORD quotation is taken from Mark Twain; the second those for which we have found a Mark Twain quotation of the same date as the first quotation given in the OXFORD; the third those for which Mark Twain provides an earlier quotation or quotations; and the fourth those which are given by the OXFORD without any dated examples, but which are illustrated in Mark Twain's work.

1. *Earliest OED Evidence Taken from Mark Twain*

In some of these cases the Mark Twain quotation has been wrongly dated in the OXFORD. The correct date in each case is supplied in the LEXICON.

aboard	*buck, to pass the*	*close down on*
back-cap, to give one a	*bunch,* v.trans.	*cluster-pin*
back-pay	*business*	*cocoon,* v. (fig.)
bake-shop	*casing (Mining)*	*cold deck*
barbed wire	*cavalieress*	*continental, give a*
blacksnake, v.	*chin,* v.	*copper,* v.
blind, sb. *(Poker)*	*Chinadom*	*cramp,* v.
bolting	*Chinawoman*	*cross-lot,* a.
bric-a-bracker	*clack-clack*	*cub*
bric-a-brackery	*clack-clacking*	*cub-engineer*
bridge, v.	*clattery*	*cub-pilot*
bridge-building	*clean up (Mining)*	*daisy-cutter*

5 Several instructive cases of what may be called "linguistic rivalry," in which we may see Mark Twain hesitating between rival candidates for the naming of a new invention, device, or institution, may be studied in the LEXICON under the entries for *accidental insurance* vs. *accident insurance, editorial* vs. *leader, finger-mark* vs. *finger-print, grease-print,* or *paw-mark, palatial car* vs. *palace-car, parlor-car, Pullman car,* or *Pullman,* the verb *typewriter* vs. *typewrite,* and the substantive *typewriter* vs. *typewriter copyist, typist,* or *machinist.*

dare, take a
dead-certain
dead-earnest
dead-head
deadwood, a.
defectless
dern, a.
dig out
discriminate
doodle-bug
double-team, v.
easy water
ell
exhumer
fig-leaf, v.
freeze out
freight up
fringe out
fumigator
get-out, like all
get through
going-over
gospel-sharp
grain elevator
grass, to hunt
guy, v.
hat-rack
hell-matter
hold over
honest, adv.
hoo-hooing
horse-billiards
husky
incorporatorship
indictive
Injun, honest
jack-plane, v.
jake
jokist
jour printer
jump, on the
lamp-lighting
land-dealer

lattice-box
law-office
leather-headedness
lecture-agent
lecture-tour
lecturing-trip
lifter
love-tap
lunkhead
Mick
milk-route
moon (biscuit)
Muddy, sb. (for the
    Mississippi)
muck (fig.)
mud-puddle
mule-headed
mullet-headed
nail-kag
nail-keg (hat)
navy (revolver)
newspaper-office
newspaper reporter
nigger-head (tobacco)
nutting-expedition
old lady (wife)
Old School Baptist
on it, to be
one while
outlaw, v.intr.
outside (in the open sea)
pard
pile down
quail-shot
rain (to come in when
    it rains)
raise the mischief
rattler
sail in
Saratoga trunk
schottische, v.
scratch, v.
send-off, sb.

shebang
sheep-witted
shoal-mark
shower (bath)
shuck tick
skeleton, v.
slat, v.
slathers
slurring, ppl.a.
snagging, vbl.sb.
soft-soaper
softy, a.
soothing-syrup
splint-bottom, a.
square off
start in
station-boss
sway-backed
swing, v. (control)
switchback, sb.
tapadero
Tennessean
texas-deck
this-worldly
tree-box
unfloatable
up-ended
waffle-mould
waltz, v.trans.
washpan
watch-and-watch
watch-out, sb.
way-back, from
way-freight
way-train
weaken (give way)
whale-backed
whang, sb.
white (honorable)
whiz (bargain)
wood-boat
yawl, v.
young-girl, a.

2. Earliest OED Evidence of Even Date with Mark Twain

anyways	go-as-you-please, a.	side, a.
blockade	jackass, a.	slump, v.
boom, v.intr.	justifier	smarty, sb.
bounty-jumping	know-it-all, a.	smell (Naut. sense)
canoe, v.	lambrequin	solid (of color)
cave-in	left, to get	stretchy
checks, to pass in one's	mugwump	swindle, sb.
clam (fig.)	osteopathy	syndicating
cog, to slip a	plant (bury)	take up (begin)
contraband, sb.	pleasuring	telelectroscope
cuss-word	puttering	Tube
cut through	rearwards	two-story, a.
day-before-yesterday	run the blockade	whistle, v. (fig.)
figure-head	rustler	white, poor
geewhillikins	sharp, sb.	whitebait

3. Earlier Evidence from Mark Twain than the Earliest in OED

Before each item in the following list has been placed the number of years by which Mark Twain's use has priority over the earliest quotation in the OXFORD. For items starred, the earliest OXFORD quotation is from Mark Twain, but a still earlier Mark Twain quotation is noted in the LEXICON.

a. Mark Twain Priority of One to Five Years

5 accident-insurance	4 butter-bean	2 emery-bag
5 arctic	1 call off	1 fair-minded
4 away, adv.	4 can, v. (=may)	1 fidgety
2 backdown, sb.	1 card-room	1 fixed
4 backless	2 cash in	4 flat, sb.
2 ball up	4*chuckleheadedness	5 flathead
5 bank, v.	1 close-fitting	1 Forty-Niner
2 bath-house	5 cold-storage, a.	2 forty-rod whisky
5 beatenest	5 colossal	5 four-story
4 berrying	1 crow, to eat	5 frills
4 Big Tree	2 curl up	1 frozen
1 bite the dust	2 cut-up, sb.	1 full-fledged
5 boss-ship	4*dead-loads	1 furtivenesses
3 bow-and-arrow, a.	2 desperadoism	4 get (git)
5 brain-racking	1*dish-rag	1 get at (=assail)
4 brass-mounted	4 doll-face	5 gin-mill
2 brontosaurus	5*down to date	4 Golconda
1 bulk, v.	4 down grade	3 hair-oil
4 bulletin-board	2 drainage-basin	3 handspring
4 bum, v.intr.	2 effusion	3 hanging wall

1 *headline*
3 *heart-sinking*
2 *hefty*
4 *helm-a-lee*
1 *hifalutin*, a.
5 *Himalayan* (fig.)
3 *hog*, v.
2 *hog-chain*
3 *hum*, v. (fig.)
5 *incline*, sb.
1 *inning*, sing form
5 *instalment plan*
1 *jeans*, a.
3 *John* (=Chinaman)
1 *junk-shop*
2 *kindlings*
4 *lay over* (excel)
2*lazy, v.
3 *league-long*
5 *left-over*
1 *level* (head)
3 *liberty-loving*
1*lightning, a.
5 *Limburger*
1 *line out*
4 *lint* (raw cotton)
1 *liquor saloon*
5 *locate* (a claim)
1 *long-distance* (telephone)
1 *machine politics*
2 *maple syrup*
4 *massed*, ppl.a.
3 *morning-suit*
3 *motif*
4 *mud, to fling*
2 *mud-valve*
1 *muggins* (game)
5 *mule-race*

3 *mushy*
2 *newspaper-clipping*
3 *nobbily*
5 *nutritiousness*
3 *overskirt*
3 *own up*
3 *pan*, sb.
2 *panful*
2 *paper-stock*
1 *passenger-car*
5 *pickaninny*, a.
3 *picknicking*
1*pile it on
1 *played out*
1 *poetastical*
4 *pull out* (leave)
3 *raggedy*
3 *rail, by*
4 *rails*
4 *reading-matter*
2 *retire*, v.trans.
2 *ride on a rail*
3 *rough* (hard on)
5 *ruck*
2 *scour*
2*scrap-book, v.
2 *see* (Poker)
1 *shake* (cast off)
4 *shaving cup*
1 *sheet-music*
2 *shifty*
2 *show* (opportunity)
5 *silver-mining*
1 *sitting-room*
5 *skin* (make off)
1 *sleeper* (R.R.)
2 *slumgullion*
4 *smarty*, sb.
2 *smile, I should*

1 *snappy*
1 *spot cash*
5 *spreeing*
2 *stage-fright*
2 *stand-off*, sb.
5 *start out*
3 *steal a base*
4 *steel* (engraving)
4 *stock in, take*
1 *street-lamp*
3 *sure thing*
5 *tackle* (drink)
3 *take in* (in a journey)
5*talk back
3 *tally-keeper*
5 *telegraph-pole*
3 *tick* (bed)
5 *tidal wave* (fig.)
4 *tongue-lashing*
4 *tow-headed*
3 *trade-mark*
4**tuck out of, take the*
5 *tunnel-like*
1 *type-setter*
4*upholster (fig.)
2 *vacation*
4 *vaporously*
1 *walk* (Naut. sense)
1 *walking-delegate*
2 *war-correspondent*
1 *whirlwind*, v.
3 *whisky-straight*
4 *window-box*
2 *witness-stand*
4 *womenfolks*
2 *world of, think the*
2 *worry along*

b. Mark Twain Priority of Six to Ten Years

9 *absent-minded*
10 *absent-mindedness*
10 *along*, adv.

7 *bat* (Baseball)
8 *bloodthirstily*
10 *blooming*

10 *boil down*
7*bug out
6 *cable-chain*

7 cañon-side
7 cement (Mining)
6 chitling
7 claim, v.
10 clankety-clank
10 claw-hammer coat
9 cluster-ring
10 cobble-stone, attrib.
8 collapse, v.trans.
9 collection-plate
7 condemn
10 corner, sb. (Poker)
8 cotton-seed meal
8 cotton-seed oil
8 dashed
7 dear life, for
7 dern, v.
6 dress-reform
9 drop on to
8 durn, sb.
8 ear-splitting
7 endowment insurance
8 executive session
10 fair field
7 fip
7 first-class
7 fix up
10*flume, up the
8 flutter-mill
6 foremanship
6 fourth dimension
9 freshness (imperti-
nence)
10 full-dress suit
8 galley-west, to knock
7 get out (leak out)
8 girly-girly
6 giveaway, sb.
9 gouge, v.
10 go up
9 grab for
9 gracious, int.
9 grass-carpeted
9 gushy
7 hand-bag
6 heat-lightning

10 high-grade
6 hot (fig. use)
7 housetop, on the
8 ice, on thin
6 invalid-chair
10 iron-railed
9 jarred
6 jeans, sb.
10 jeans-clad
8 jimjams
8 kerosene-lamp
6 knock out (fig.)
7 lack for
9 lay tongue to
10 lay up (take to one's
bed)
8 leg to stand on, not
a
8 loop (in finger-print-
ing)
8 mailing
10 meat, to be one's
10 mind-curist
7 mosey, v.
8 mucilage
7 mucilage-bottle
9 nutshell, v.
10 order-book
7 organ-tone
6 pepper away
10 pet aversion
8 Pigs in Clover
8 pins and needles, on
6*pipe up
8 pleasure-resort
6*plug (horse)
7 plug hat
6 pool, sb. (Betting)
10 pump-house
7 quartz-mill
8 ragged-looking
10 red rag to a bull
10 rough (ill)
6 royalty (to an au-
thor)
7 run across

10 sailor-knot
6 saloon-keeper
8 scoop, v. (dredge)
9 scoop, v. (appropri-
ate)
8 screaky
9 shenanigan
8 short, to sell
6 shrinkage (fig.)
6 silver-miner
6 size of it, that is the
7 size, v.
9 sluice-box
10 snowstorm (fig.)
7 sounding, vbl.sb.
6 spell, for a
8 spring, v. (fig.)
6 spring-mattress
8 stack up
7 stand, sb. (Theatr.)
8 star-stuff
9 stick it out
10 straddle (Poker)
9 stuck, ppl.a.
7 swab, sb.
8 switch off
9 sword-play
6 tan (thrash)
7 tattoo-mark
8 toe-ring
9 toothsomely
7 torch-light procession
8 up-anchor, v.
10 Wall Street (fig.)
6 walnut, English
8 war-path, to be on
the (fig.)
8 watered (fig.)
10 water-supply
7 wax-white
7 whisky (a drink of)
7 whisky-drinking
8 whisky-sodden
7 whitewash, v.
8 work (cheat)

c. Mark Twain Priority of Ten to Twenty Years

15 *agin*, prep.
14 *air-ship*
20 *all over*
14 *bath-tub*
20* *begin with*
11 *blood-kinship*
12 *board* (Stock Exchange)
18 *boshy*
19 *brashly*
17 *breath-taking*
17 *brogan*
12 *broke*
14 *building-material*
18 *bull-pup*
13 *burglar*, v.
16 *busted*
11 *call*, v. *(Poker)*
17 *candy-shop*
14 *car-wheel*
18 *center* (target)
16 *chain-lightning* (fig.)
16 *circus* (fig.)
15 *coal-passer*
20 *collect*, v. absol.
19 *combination* (of safe)
12 *congratulatory*
17 *conscience, in all*
19 *coroneting*
16 *count*, v. absol.
12 *counting-house,* attrib.
14 *criminal lawyer*
13 *crook*
16 *culvert*, v.
11 *Daughter*
16 *death-agony*
13 *dinner-pail*
17 *draw*, sb. *(Poker)*
11 *drift*, v. (fig.)
19 *drinking-water*
12 *drowsing*, a.

15 *dryness (Politics)*
17 *duck* (fig.)
14 *electric storm*
15 *emptyings, to run*
11 *eyes, up to the*
15* *fantods*
15 *fife-rail*
15 *fill*, v. *(Poker)*
11 *first-off*
11 *fly-specked*
19 *fly the track*
15 *fool around*
14 *freightage*
15 *front*
12 *fumigating*
15 *get* (catch)
11 *get* (worry)
14 *get* (have got to)
13 *get around (no getting around)*
11 *get down to*
15 *get out of*
16 *giant swing*
20 *Good Book*
17 *go over*
17 *gorgeous*
15 *gorilla* (fig.)
11 *government office*
18 *granite (granita)*
12 *granny* (stupid)
12 *gravel-train*
11 *guns, great*
18 *hair-trigger* (fig.)
14 *handle-bar*
12 *hoist*, v.
11 *ice-storm*
11 *indication (Mining)*
12 *inflated*
15 *initiation fee*
20 *Interior Department*
15 *Jacksonian*
18 *jammed*
13 *judge, county*

15 *ker-slam*
13 *ker-whop*
15 *layout* (of land)
12 *layout* (of cards)
11 *littered-up*
17 *make good time*
17 *Mars, Marse*
15 *Mexicanized*
17 *milestone*, v. (fig.)
15 *missions, foreign*
14 *money in, there is*
11 *moss-backed*
18 *mountain-railway*
14 *mushily*
20 *nail-file*
20 *number, take one's* (one sense)
15 *object-lesson*
13 *odds? what's the*
15 *old man* (in address)
17 *old-time*, a.
18 *over-kind*
19 *part* (of hair)
15 *pass*, v. *(Euchre)*
20 *pie* (treat)
12 *pillow-fight*
15 *pity, more's the*
13 *pot-shaped*
19 *profile paper*
15 *protoplasm* (fig.)
19 *putrid* (beastly)
19 *put up* (stake)
18 *put up* (interpret)
11 *quarter*, v.
11 *ranch*, sb.
18 *ranch*, v.
18 *ratty*
20 *read up*
16* *ready, a good*
16 *rest up*
16 *riddle*, v. (fig.)
13 *rig* (vehicle)
20 *right and left*, adv.

15 *right-hearted*
13 *roundsman*
16 *saddle-blanket*
11 *sage-brush*
18 *salting,* vbl.sb.
11 *salutatory,* sb.
13 *Science* (Christian Science)
19 *scorcher*
15 *scrooch*
12 *send up* (prices)
18 *seven-shooter*
13 *shake up* (upset)
18 *shove* (put out)
12 *show a pair of heels*
11 *shut down,* v.intr.
15 *side-show* (fig.)
12 *side-table*
12 *sight, not by a con-siderable*
20 *simon-pure*
19 *sinfully* (fig.)
15 *slam,* v. (fig.)

13 *sloppy*
19 *slug,* sb.
12**South,* adv.
20 *spiritualize*
13 *spread* (show off)
12 *square deal*
20 *square up*
14 *stagger,* sb.
11 *steal,* sb.
18 *stern-line*
18 *straighten out*
16 *striker* (green hand)
14 *string, on a*
18 *stuff* (fighting mater-ial)
19 *sultry* (fig.)
20 *tack-hammer*
18 *tailor-man*
11 *take,* sb. (*Printing*)
12*take up (a collec-tion)
18 *talky-talk*
14 *talon-like*

18 *tax-return*
18 *tend* (take care of)
15 *ten-day,* a.
14 *texas-tender*
11 *to* (involved in)
11 *tough* (vicious)
13 *tower of silence*
12 *train-time*
20 *two-hour,* a.
11 *urgingly*
14 *valleywards*
19 *vest-pocket,* a.
14 *walk on air*
11 *wallow* (*Hum.* sense)
11 *waste-basket,* v.
14 *winded*
13 *window-hole*
18 *worked-out*
15 *worker* (Politics)
18 *workhouse*
20 *worrisome*
18 *yawl,* a.

d.   Mark Twain Priority of More than Twenty Years

32 *agate* (*Typog.*)
22 *all of, for*
25 *avalanche,* v.
35 *barkeep*
21 *bar-soap*
22 *bat, hot from the*
23 *breezy*
24 *business-suit*
21 *centrifugal,* sb.
26 *chattily*
27 *close out*
44 *cold, to knock*
21 *cow-shed*
37 *day, call it a*
33 *dog-fight* (fig.)
45 *ease off*
42 *fash*
28 *globe-lamp*
26 *gorge*

24 *go under*
21 *ground wire*
33 *hard-boiled* (fig.)
44 *head-on*
23 *hic,* int.
23 *high-keyed*
24 *high-toned*
44 *horn, to blow one's*
26 *hot air* (fig.)
26 *hula hula*
21 *hump it*
21 *jolt,* sb. (fig.)
32 *keybox*
44 *kneip*
39 *knock out of* (fig.)
22 *My land!*
21 *last of, to see the*
34 *lawsy,* int.
25 *line* (stock of goods)

25 *linsey-woolsey*
43 *locust* (17-year)
24 *log, easy as rolling off a*
28 *low-necked*
24 *mean,* v. (emphatic use)
41 *mill-saw*
21 *natural to, come*
23 *no-account,* sb.
23 *number, take one's* (one sense)
25 *occasional,* sb.
39 *old-maidy*
39 *other thing, to do the*
21 *out, from this*
26 *overtasked*
22 *panoply,* v.
33 *patent-medicine*

21 *peek-hole*
23 *phit*, int.
33 *pleasant-spoken*
36 *pop*, sb. (turn)
23 *post-mortuary*
30 *quiet, on the*
22 *raise out*
21 *rats* (sarcasm)
26 *regular*, sb.
23 *reminiscing*
26 *respectworthy*
43 *riot act, to read the* (fig.)
21 *rule out*
21 *saddle-bag*, v.
28 *saddle-colored*
30 *sail* (move smoothly)
54 *scruffy*
22 *ship-time*
21 *shredding*, ppl.a.
29 *shucks*, int.

35 *sit* (situation)
28 *skim*, sb.
25 *skirmish*, v. (search)
47 *sleep up*
39 *slum* (hash)
27 *slush* (rubbishy literature)
22 *small-fry*
31 *sorry-looking*
24 *spar*, v.
31 *spree*, v.trans.
22 *square*, adv.
24 *stack*, sb. (a lot)
23 *stand-up*, sb.
25 *stay* (the stomach)
34 *streaky*
23 *strike it rich*
26 *sub* (*Printer's* use)
24 *sun-umbrella*
24 *tangle-headed*
24 *there you are*

25 *Third House*
46 *thinkful*
24 *tooth-wash*
21 *t'other from which, to tell*
23 *touch off*
26 *turn on* (fig.)
28 *up and doing*
22 *war-footing*
24 *wash*, v. (fig.)
25 *way* (*down——way*)
22 *weather-clerk*
48 *whoopee*
26 *whoosh*
22 *wild cat* (bills)
28 *work-stock*
21 *yarning*
30 *yodeler*
31 *you-all*

4. *Given in OED without Any Dated Evidence*

abolition speech
aggravation
all through
as (as possible)
atrocious
barge
Bible-class
bicentennial, a.
biscuit-toss
blasting-powder
blind-drunk
book-cased
boot-heel
breach-of-promise
breech-clout
broken-legged
bucket
bullet-hole
bung-starter
cabin-mate
call-boy

cannon-smoke
car, coal
car-seat
case-knife
case-man
cedar-pencil
charged (fig.)
circus-ring
Civil War
close-shaven
cobbler (pie)
cocked hat (game)
composite, sb. (Photog.)
consolation-race
copper-bellied
corn-beef
crayfish
cross, shake the
crushed-strawberry, a.
crystal (of watch)
daddy-longlegs

deck, on (fig.)
declare (dividend)
Delegate
dim-lighted
doctor, v.intr.
dream-life
dreamy-eyed
durn, v.
dust-storm
duty-call
eagle (coin)
ear-drop
eggs in one basket
engineer, mining-
English (Billiards)
false start
fashion-plate
flooding
fly-blister
freight
gambling-den

gas-bill
gills, blue about the
goodness, so help me
grain-sack
hard-worked
heavy-weight
hell-box
high-low-jack
history-making
Honorable
house-snake
ice-machine
ice-pitcher
insurance policy
iron-moulder
jings, by
job-office
ker-chunk
killing (fig.)
line, out of one's
location (mining claim)
machine (bicycle)
magazining, vbl.sb.
materializer
mining-camp

mother-heart
music-room
nonpareil (Am. sense)
oil-derrick
over-express
overland, a.
over-patient
paladin (fig.)
parlor-magic
pay-rock
petting, ppl.a.
phonographer
photograph-album
play, v. (two senses)
polling-day
poultry-raising
prayer-cure
provision-basket
puddinghead
pumpkin-head
Reformed
right along
right-feeling
same, adv.
Secretary of State (Am.

sense)
seller ten
sergeant-at-arms (Am.
    sense)
shad, Connecticut
Sheol
shove (set out)
slab (of cake)
stage (omnibus)
study up
subbing
surface-line
ten-pound, a.
theirn
thick-legged
thousand-mile, a.
three-month, a.
ticket-money
ticket-office
tow-head
whisky-drinking, ppl.a.
wild-brained
works (Hum. sense)

D. NINETEENTH CENTURY COINAGES ADOPTED BY MARK TWAIN

B³ Words. In the preparation of this study, a large number of comparatively recent words and usages were collected for which Mark Twain does not provide earlier evidence than the OXFORD. These adoptions by Mark Twain of earlier nineteenth century coinages, which have been marked B³, might serve to throw light on the development of the English language in America and the spread of new words and new ideas to the American continent and the Mississippi Valley. Considerations of space, however, have compelled the omission of most of them in the present LEXICON. With a few exceptions, B³ words have been retained only when they fall also under the classification of Americanisms (AB³) or of archaisms (B³C). The exceptions, 104 in all, consist of B³ words retained either to throw light on related words or other senses of the same word:

acclimatized
after-cabin
all right
back, at one's
bathotic

concrete, v.
conductor
crevasse
duffer
emptinesses

finger-print
lady
lark
nigger
nobilities

old man   *slangy*   *squatter*
owing to   *slap*, v.   *statistics*
saloon (two senses) *slobber*, v.   *straight-off*, adv.
shady   *slop-shop*, sb.   *Stratfordian*
sick, a.   *slow*   *swindle*, v.
skeletonize   *slush-bucket*   *tin*, a.
slang (two senses) *sobrieties*

or because they belong to one or another of Mark Twain's fields of special interest (see above, pp. xiiif.):

allopath   *half*   *scrap-book*
argot   *leader*   *snuggery*
asteroid   *leader-writer*   *solid matter*
bicycle   *lift*   *speaking-tube*
break, sb.   *motor-car*   *spur*
break-line   *outcropping*   *stage-coaching*
comp   *Peculiar People*   *steamer*
dancette   *Plymouth Brethren* *Sunday-school*
delirium tremens   *rise*, sb.   *tonnage*
fluke   *Scotch*, sb.

or because they seemed characteristic, even though not original; that is, British or Australian expressions which attracted him by their crispness or picturesqueness, or whimsical twists of meaning such as he would infallibly have invented if they had not already been invented before him—"Mark Twainisms before Mark Twain" (cf. note under *plant*, sb.):

bail up (Austr.)   *engineer*   *school board*
bar sinister   *gone*, ppl.a.   *settle*
bloody   *good thing*   *sheep-run* (Austr.)
brick   *larrikin* (Austr.)   *ship*, v.
burster (Austr.)   *mainbrace, splice the* *shudder*, v.trans.
cast-iron   *Never-Never Country*   *sinful*
catch it   (Austr.)   *snaffle*
catch out   *new chum* (Austr.)   *spout, up the*
comrade, v.   *particular*, a.   *squatter* (Austr.)
concert, European   *Pickwickian sense, in a* *stick up* (Austr.)
cook, v.   *plant*, sb.   *stopper*
cut, v.   *rabid*   *stump*, v.
dog in a blanket   *rice Christian*   *sundowner* (Austr.)
economize   *sawbones*

III. MARK TWAIN'S ARCHAISMS

*"From time to time I dipped into old Sir Thomas Malory's enchanting
book, and fed at its rich feast of prodigies and adventures, breathed in the fragrance of its
obsolete names, and dreamed"*

The LEXICON includes 601 entries which have been marked C as Archaisms, and 142 which have been marked ?C as Doubtful Archaisms, making a total of 743.

C Words. The Archaisms, comprising those recognized as such by the OXFORD DICTIONARY, fall into two clearly distinct divisions according as they are or are not so used by Mark Twain. The first group have here been called Conscious Archaisms, i.e., words, combinations, or meanings which were deliberately employed by him to give an archaic coloring to his style. The second have been listed as American Survivals, because they were obviously not felt as archaisms by Mark Twain, and because there is evidence that they persisted in American usage, at least in the vernacular, after they had become archaic in Great Britain. A third group is formed by words or usages labeled *Rare* or *Nonce Words* in the OXFORD, since these are clearly archaic in a different sense. The Doubtful Archaisms form a fourth division, which will be explained more fully below. Finally come a short list of words marked D, i.e., words filling gaps in the OXFORD evidence.

A. CONSCIOUS ARCHAISMS

Mark Twain's intense and lifelong interest in the past both of civilization and language bears witness to the latent strain of romanticism which formed an integral ingredient in his many-sided genius. His archaisms, although of course they are most in evidence in his PRINCE AND PAUPER, CONNECTICUT YANKEE, and JOAN OF ARC, are by no means confined to these reconstructions of past history, but pervade, as our quotations show, his entire work. His keen sensitiveness to the archaic flavor of a word or meaning makes him an almost infallible judge of the fact of obsolescence in any case of doubt or conflict.

Hence the frequent failure of other dictionaries to class as obsolete or archaic words so classed by the OXFORD DICTIONARY and clearly so recognized by Mark Twain has not been regarded as sufficient reason for labeling them as doubtful archaisms, although such divergence is always noted in the LEXICON. As in the case of the doubtful Americanisms (see above, pp. viiif.), the pronouncements of WEBSTER's, the STANDARD, the CENTURY, and the UNIVERSAL are too conflicting and too erratic in this matter to afford a firm basis for the recognition of archaisms. Thus it seems quite impossible to discover any consistent principle or reason why a word or sense that is recognized as archaic or obsolete by all other authorities should have been denied that classification in WEBSTER's alone, as has been the case with *fare* (go), *favor* (appearance), *overthwart*, prep.; or in the STANDARD alone, e.g., *assoil, parlous, to make reverence;* or in the CENTURY alone, e.g., *certes, go* (walk), *meseems, of a surety;* or only in WEBSTER'S and the CENTURY, e.g., *circumforaneous, to cry mercy, malison, passing,* adv., *stead,* v.; or only in the STANDARD and the CENTURY, e.g., *bereave* (rob), *beshrew, goodwife, grievous* (oppressive), *marry,* int., *mayhap, peradventure, prithee, serving-man, servitor, straight* (immediately). For this reason also the judgment of the OXFORD, supported by that of Mark Twain, has been regarded as decisive against the combined absence of such judgment on the part of WEBSTER'S, the STANDARD, and the CENTURY, as in the cases of *fountain, halt* (lame), *hap,* sb., *hie, hold* (stop), *mart, pilgrim, pluck,* v., *prove* (test), *purfle, scourge;* or even against WEBSTER'S, the STANDARD, the CENTURY, and the UNIVERSAL, as with *abide, apparel, doff, don, entrails, forsooth, full* (full of food), *grandam, grisly, head-piece, heavy* (grave), *lightly* (quickly, nimbly), *lubber, mislike* (dislike), *sepulture,* and *Sire* (used in address to a monarch).

The complete list of his Conscious Archaisms is as follows:

abide	*carve*	*dure*
agone	*certes*	*eftsoons*
alack	*chance* (impersonal use)	*emergence*
all-to	*chieftain*	*emprise*
an, conj.	*circumforaneous*	*enow*
ancient	*circumstance*	*entrails*
apparel, v.	*clapperdudgeon*	*entreat*
asbestos	*clerkly*	*errand* (message)
assoil	*closet* (private apartment)	*erst*
attire		*esquire*
attractive, sb.	*clyme*	*fair,* a.
aventre	*cofferer*	*fantasy*
bawdkin	*commandment* (order)	*fare,* v. (go)
bereave (rob)	*consider of*	*fault,* v.
beseen	*craft*	*favor* (appearance)
beshrew	*cry mercy*	*fear,* v.refl.
bethink	*dame*	*feeble,* v.
bewray	*damosel*	*fell,* sb.
bide	*dell*	*female,* sb.
bitter	*despatch*	*finger-mark*
body o' me	*dight*	*foin*
boon	*disapparel*	*forasmuch*
boulevard	*doff*	*force, no*
brast	*dole*	*forfend*
broidery	*dolphin*	*forsooth*
bulk	*don*	*for that*
cabinet (room)	*donjon-keep*	*fountain*
cannel-bone	*doublet*	*fret*
cantle	*doubt,* v. (fear)	*full* (full of food)
carle	*doxy*	*ghost, deliver up the*

go (=walk)
good (one use)
good lack, int.
goodman
Goodman
goodwife
goodwilly
gramercy
grandam
grievous
grisly
halidome
halt
hand (a man of his hands)
hap, sb.
harbour, v.
he (any he)
head-piece
heavy (grave)
helm
hie
hight
hold (stop)
idlesse
i'fegs
Jewry
lackaday
lap (hem in)
largess
leal
leech
leman
let (hinder)
lewd
Lieutenant of the Tower
lightly (easily)
lightly (quickly)
like to
like, v. (please)
list, v.
long-agone
lubber
make at
malison

mar (hinder)
marry, int.
mart
maunder, sb.
mayhap
meet, a.
meseems
mislike
morrow
mort
moschata
murrey
mystery (trade)
na
natheless
naught
nay, to say one
nigh
nor (neither)
nothing, adv.
observance (respect)
'Od's bodikins
'Od's body
'Od's my life
of (=on)
or, conj. (=ere)
overthwart
overthwart and endlong
pardy
parlous
passing, adv.
paynim
peace, v.
pensioner
peradventure
perchance
pike
pilgrim
please-it-you
pluck, v.
pounce
pourpoint
poursuivant
prentice
prentice-fashion

prentice-hand
prentice-work
prithee
prove (test)
purfle
quaint
quality (high birth)
quoth
raiment
random, with great
random, v.
rayed
redoubtable
religiouswise
remember, v.refl.
repent, v.refl.
reverence, to make
rheums
riband, sb. and v.
right, adv. (very)
right so
romaunt
ruffler
samite
scoffing, vbl.sb.
scorch
scourge, sb. and v.
scrip
seed (offspring)
sepulture
serving-man
servitor
shipping, to take
Sir (Fair Sir)
Sire
Sirrah
Sirrah, attrib.
sith
skill (to matter)
skill (to help)
smoke (to suspect)
sooth, sb., a., adv.
sore, adv.
sorry (dismal)
spignel

staff	*trow*	*whereunto*
stay (sustain)	*truss*	*whilst*
stay (hinder)	*tush*, int.	*whipping-boy*
stay one's hand	*unhand*	*whit*
stead, v.	*unholpen*	*whither*
steed	*unnethes*	*whoso*
straight (immediately)	*until*, prep.	*wit*, sb. and v.
stripe (lash)	*vanity*	*withal*
surety, of a	*varlet*	*woe is me*
sweet (in address)	*voided*	*wonderly*
tabard	*waiting-woman*	*wont*, sb.
tarry	*ware*, a. and v.	*world*, adv.
tide, v.	*warrant*, v.refl.	*wot*
timbrel	*wax*, v.	*would God*
tinct	*ween*	*woundily*
tissue	*well*, a.	*xylaloes*
Tom o' Bedlam	*wend*	*ye*, art.
toward, a.	*whenas*	*yesternight*
trencher	*whereat*	*yield*
troth, in	*wherefore*	*yon*
troublous	*whereso*	

To these should be added the following archaic spellings and inflectional forms: *a* (*an* before sounded *h* in accented syllables), *accompt* (for *account*) *alway* (for *always*), *baronette* (for *baronet*), *becomen, damosel, even* (*e'en*), *get* (past tense *gat*), *good even* (*good den*), *heave* (past tense *hove*, for *hoved?*), *help* (past tense *holp*, pa.pple. *holpen*), *hold* (pa.pple. *holden*), *mummery* (*mommarye*), *murther* (for *murder*), *'Od's my life* (*Odds*), *salvage* (for *savage*), *unholpen* (for *unhelped*), *unnethes* (for *uneaths*), *ween* (past tense *wend*), *work* (pa.pple. *wrought*).

B. AMERICAN SURVIVALS

(See also the archaic spellings and inflections which survive in American usage, in the lists given on pp. cvii and cix.)

a (for *an* before vowel sounds)	*artist*	*carcass*
	ballock	*cattle* (of persons)
a, prep.	*bank-bill*	*certain-sure*
addition	*be, let*	*China*, a.
admire	*belch*	*chop off*
afeared	*betwixt*	*cleanliness* (moral sense)
afront of	*body*	*collide* (fig.)
airy	*budge*	*come Christmas*
ambition, v.	*buzz*, v.	*comfortable* (encouraging)
as (for *that*)	*cabin*	

considerable, adv.
corded
cruel, adv.
curious, adv.
dam, v.
dangersome
dark of the moon
declination
dent
discover
dominie
dull, v.
dust, v.
Dutch
Dutchman
eating-room
egod
evidence
exceptions to, take
fair, to say or ask
fair daylight
faix
fall
fandango
feel of
festoon, v.
fetch (six obs senses)
file, sb.
fire-red
fitten
flapjack
fool, a.
for to
forwards
forwhy
fox-fire
frame, sb.
free to say
fulsome
furbish up
fuzzle
gag, v.
gang
gashly
gay

give good day, night
glad, v.
go security
God-a-mercy
guess out
halver
hanker
have (redundant)
homely
howdy
howsoever
human, sb.
in, adv. (involved)
intellects
irruption
jings, by
king-bee
la, int.
lanky (of hair)
larboard
lawing
lay (for lie)
lay in (scheme)
lay off (take off)
learn (teach)
lights (lungs)
like (was likely)
like, conj. (as)
like, conj. (as if)
like as if
likely (suitable)
limber (limp)
lively, adv.
loaden, v.
low-water, a.
madhouse
maybe
mean, a.
meeting-house
Methusalem-numskull
mightily
mile (pl. form)
mind (remind)
miscarry (misbehave)
molasses

monstrous, adv.
mornings, adv.
mortal, adv.
most, adv. (almost)
much, a. (important)
mum, a.
mutual (common)
nail, v. (prove)
near, adv.
negotiate (traffic)
nick of time, in the
nip, v. (steal)
noble (notable)
nonesuch, sb.
nuther
of (after vbl.sb.)
of (for with)
off (distant)
off of
orderly sergeant
outen
outlander
overdo
oversize
party (person)
pig (of silver)
piper, drunk as a
pitcher
poison, a.
pretty (agreeable)
printing-house
private, adv.
professor (professing
    Christian)
put (make off)
put to (attach to ve-
    hicle)
quality (people of good
    birth)
raise, v. (for rise)
rare (underdone)
ratsbane
reciprocate
record, of
regular, sb.

relict
riffraff
right, adv. (altogether)
rip, sb.
sadful
same, adv.
say-so
scaffolding
scant, adv.
scare at
scatteration
scoff, v.trans.
scrabble (scramble)
scrape, v.
screak, v.
screaky
scuttle
seldom, a.
shad (term of abuse)
sixpence
slap, v.
so as (so's)
so as that (so'st)
solid (substantial)
soon as

stall, v.
stead of
stick, v.
stout (strong)
strap (strop)
stroll, v.trans.
study, v.
superscription
sweat, v. (fume)
sweeten (cajole)
table-room
tangle (confuse)
tax-gatherer
td
tedious
telegraph (telegram)
tf
that, adv.
to (for at)
tolerable, adv.
transom
tush (tusk)
twain
un (on, of)
undigestible

unloaden, v.
unregular
unreverent
uppish
vanish, sb.
warming-pan
warm up
washer
way (a ways)
way, adv.
weave (sway the body)
well-a-well
which (of persons)
wicket
wireworker
without, conj.
woman (wife)
wonted, pa.pple.
wonted, ppl.a.
word (speech)
ye (sing.)
ye (for you)
yonder-way

C.   RARE WORDS AND NONCE WORDS

alight
barber, v.
changement
concreted
crackless
despairs
differ, v.trans.
easement
Englishry
fidgety (one sense)
generosities
gurgly
gymnastic, sb.
indictive
influential, sb.

inventionless
laugh, sb.
neglects, sb.pl.
numberable
pappy
particle
procrastinated
product (offspring)
quivery
ribby
rigidify
screech, v.trans.
scuffle, sb. (controversy)
sex, the
shifty (shifting)

shining (eminent)
shore up (fig.)
shrunk-up
strip, v.
think, sb.
thinker (mind)
thinkful
top, v.
velocipede
wake, sb.
whirlwind, v.
worlded
yawl, v.

D. DOUBTFUL ARCHAISMS

?C Words. About the obsolescence of these words there is genuine doubt, either because the OXFORD is itself doubtful or in conflict with other authorities, or because its judgment is apparently in conflict with that of Mark Twain. The reasons for considering the case a doubtful one are explained for each of them in the LEXICON. They fall naturally into two divisions, according as they are or are not felt as archaisms by Mark Twain.

1. Felt as Archaic by Mark Twain

A few of these terms were evidently felt as obsolete or archaic by Mark Twain, and used by him for their antiquated flavor, in spite of the doubt or conflicting judgment of one or more dictionaries.

betide	hassock	vagabond
blithe	keep	warder
comely	let or hindrance	Southron
depute	megalophonous	waly, int.
gear	spin (to run)	worsen
haberdashery	stead (in his stead)	

2. Not Felt as Archaic by Mark Twain

A much larger proportion of the doubtful archaisms are apparently not felt or used as obsolete or archaic by Mark Twain. Among these a number might have been included with the list given above of American Survivals; for although possibly archaic in Great Britain they have certainly continued in use in America.

accommodations	hustings	play-acting
ass	jamble	sail-boat
bad, adv.	lady-finger	scantling
balk, make a	laws, int.	scrabble (scrawl)
clear, adv.	lay on (impute to)	shed, v.intr.
cooper-shop	lay out (expound)	sky-scraper (sky-sail)
dauber	lay to (Naut. sense)	soary
declination	left-handed (sinister)	spell, v. (take turns)
Gemini (Jimminy)	liver	trim-built
get (gotten)	maybe	undisposed
hoist (remove)	peeled (bald)	
housekeeper	pied	

In a few cases, either the terms or the things they denote were in living use when Mark Twain employed them but have in the opinion of some authorities since become obsolete or obsolescent.

beaver (hat)	*lucifer* (match)	*tavernward*
Chinaman	*palace-car*	*whatnot*
East, sb. and adv.	*parlor-car*	*wheat-bread*
(M. T.'s sense)	*tavern*	*West, Western*
hansom	*tavern-keeper*	(M.T.'s sense)

In other cases, there is no reason to consider the word as particularly American, but it is apparently by no means obsolete for Mark Twain, in spite of the opinion of some dictionaries.

ally (connection by marriage)	*flat*, v.	*obscene*
belief (faith)	*flatting*	*peace, hold one's*
bone (bone of contention)	*foreignize*	*post*, v.
canvass (examine physically)	*general* (common to several persons)	*ration*, v.
chance, v. (with personal subject)	*guts*	*saint*, v.
	half-god	*sharp*, v.
coat, to turn one's	*horse-laughter*	*ship of war*
coil (ado)	*idiotcy*	*softly*, int.
day-dawn	*interject*	*toilet* (costume)
dead-wall	*interlard*	*token, by the same*
dearly (keenly)	*it* (for *he*)	*tourbillon* (whirlpool)
distraught	*lack for*	*trick*, sb. (knack)
drift (of time)	*like* (likely to)	*trunks* (trunk-hose)
drift (intention)	*line* (lineage)	*ungenuine*
fast (grip)	*loom-work*	*vacate* (render inoperative)
filch, sb.	*manhood* (manliness)	*waste*, v. and a.
fire-new	*marvel*, v.	*wicked* (of the sea)
	massy	
	money-sack	

Finally, there is an interesting group of words and uses that may be called "Mark Twain's Reinventions." They undoubtedly once existed in the language and then became obsolete, but Mark Twain was apparently unaware of their former existence and coined them over again!

aft (fig. use)	*inconsequentiality* (concrete use)
apodictical	*inroader*
arrest (stop)	*life-day* (day in one's life)
caliber (social standing)	*life-day* (life-time)
debauch (spoil)	*longly*
disinvite	*moral*, sb. sing.
empocket	*ornithologer*
gage (wager)	*poverties* (concrete use)
hand (of an insect)	*traditioner*

E. WORDS FILLING GAPS

D Words. In the preparation of the LEXICON a considerable number of words, combinations, and meanings filling gaps of forty years or more in the evidence of the OXFORD DICTIONARY were collected and marked as D Words. Most of these were discarded, however, for lack of space. A few, only 33 in all, have been retained because they belong to Mark Twain's special fields of interest, or because they serve to throw light on other words. Among them his 22 heraldic terms, all of which occur in a single passage cited under the word *coat-of-arms*, might well have been included above among his archaisms; although they are not technically obsolete, they are certainly so in effect to the average American reader.

Heraldic Terms:

azure	*embattled*	*or*, sb.
base	*engrailed*	*sable*
chevron	*fesse*	*saltire*
chief	*field*	*scutcheon*
coat-of-arms	*gules*	*supporter*
couchant	*indented*	*vert*
crest	*invected*	
dexter	*nombril*	

Other D Words:

admit	*deep four*	*styrax calamita*
allow	*humor*	*weather*
calk, v.	*mark*	*zedoary*
Christian (human being)	*quarter*	

IV. MISCELLANEOUS GROUPS

E Words. The LEXICON contains 247 entries marked E, denoting miscellaneous peculiarities of Mark Twain's orthography or of his inflections. There have also been added at the end lists of his favorite words, of words or uses that seem to have been wrongly interpreted or described by previous authorities, and of problem words or usages on which an attempt has been made to throw new light, or on which still further light is needed.

A. PECULIARITIES OF SPELLING

Most, though not all, of these indicate peculiarities of pronunciation. Of them the following are American.

accounts of, on
acrost
agin, adv.
agin, prep.
allow ('low)
along ('long)
Arkansaw
arrastre (arastra)
ax (for ask)
ballock (bollock)
beatenest (for beatemest)
boiled (biled) shirt
brakeman (for brakesman)
Brer (for Brother)
by-and-by (bimeby)
cag (for keg)
chaw
chaw up
checkered
chimney (chimbley)
chimney-guy (chimbly-guy)
conflagrate (conflaggerate)
concerned (consarned)
coyote (ki-yo-tie, ky-o-te)
creature (cretur, cratur)
cracky (for crikey)
creek (crick)
deaf (deef)
depot (depo, deepo)
emptings (for emptyings)
faix
faze (phase)

fellow (feller)
gaily (for gala)
gallows (galluses)
gallows, a. (gallus)
gallows-buckle (gallus-buckle)
gallowsly (gallusly)
gape, sb. (gap)
gape, v. (gap)
Gemini (Jimminy, geeminy)
get (git)
gimcrack (jimcrack)
go (gwine to)
haunt (ha'nt)
hinder (hender)
hoist (hyste)
indorse (for endorse)
Injun (for Indian)
jail (for gaol)
janders (for jaundice)
jew's-harp (juice-harp)
joint (jint)
Jubiter (for Jupiter)
leggings (leggins)
let (lemme, less)
liquorice (licorice, lickerish)
machete (for matchet)
mamma (momma)
marvel (for marble)
Methusalem-numskull (for
   Methusaleh-)
Miss (for Mrs.)
moldy (for mouldy)

moustached (mustached)   scalliwag (for scalawag)
mud-turkle (for -turtle)   share (sheer)
mullen-stalk (for mullein-)   shut (shet)
mumble-the-peg (mumble-peg,   simlin (simblin)
    mumbletypeg)   slazy (for sleazy)
muskmelon (mushmelon)   smouch (smooch)
mud-dobber (for -dauber)   so as (so's)
nap of the neck (for nape)   so as that (so'st)
nuther (for nother)   somers (for somewheres)
Old Master (Ole Marster, Marse)   sour-crout (for sauerkraut)
Old Mistress (Ole Missus, Missis)   spoil (spile)
once (wunst)   squalmish (for squeamish?)
parcel (passel)   stomp (for stamp)
pie (pi)   that-air (for that there)
plow, v. (for plough)   they (for there)
point (pint)   this-here (thish-yer, this h-yere)
point-blank (pine-blank)   tramp (tromp)
poison, a., adv., v. (pison, pizen)   trample (tromple)
porte-monnaie (port-money)   trapse (traipse)
pumpkin (punkin)   twice (twiste)
pyjamas (pajamas)   un (for on)
raspberry (razberry)   unbeknownst (unbeknowens)
rather (ruther, druther)   uncommon (oncommon)
reputation (ruputation)   verdigris (verdigrease)
rubbish (rubbage)   victual (vittles)
saddle-bag, v. (saddle-baggs)   Virginia (Virginny)
St. Louis (St. Looey)   well-a-well (for wellaway)
sarsaparilla (sassaparilla)   whip-poor-will (whippowill)
sauce, sb. and v. (sass)   wickyup (wickiup, wickieup)
saucer (sasser)   yellow (yaller)
saucy (sassy)   yes (yas)
say (s'I, s'e, sh-she)

The following orthographical variants seem to be due to Mark Twain himself, either by error or by deliberate phonetic intention:

cadess (for caddess)   genre (johnry)
ceramic (keramic)—German?   google (for gurgle?)
ceramiker (keramiker)—German?   herumfrodite
ceramics (keramics)—German?   larboard (labboard)
cherimoya (for chirinoya)   leeward (looard)
daintly (for daintily)   literary (littery)
elecampane (allycum pain)   medieval (meedyevil)
elocute (yellocute)   miaow (meow, maow, me-yow,
fash (for fach)   me-yo)
forward (for'rard)   Paris (Pairree, Parry)

paust (for German *posten?*)
perhaps (*praps*)
phew (*pfew-few*)
phonetics (*fonetics*)
Picciola (*pitchiola*)
puddinghead (*pudd'nhead*)
pyrotechnique
scare (*skyer*)
screaky (*skreeky*)
starboard (*stabboard*)

suggest (*sejest*)
tapadero (*tapidaro*)
thwartships (*thortships*)
tule (*tuler*)
umf (*mph*)
wallop (*whollop*)
yodel, sb. and v. (*jodel*)—German?
yodeler (*jodeler*)—German?
yodeling (*jodeling*)—German?

Other variants:

cañon (*canyon*)
chirk (*cherk*)
cigar (*seegar*)
clew-iron (*clue-iron*)
dorian (*durian*)
eight (for *eighth*)
fess (*fesse*)
filigree (*filagree*)
Gaekwar (*Gaikowar*)
galingale (*galangals*)
grizzly (*grisly*)

naivety (for *naïveté*)
ne'er-do-well (*ne'er-do-weel*)
philippina (*philopena, phillipene*)
prophecy-savan (for *-savant*)
sheep-head (for *sheepshead*)
soup-and-bouille (for *soup-and-bully*)
sumpter (*sumter*)
what (*phwat*)
windrow (*winrow*)
xylobalsamum (*zylo-*)

B. PECULIARITIES OF INFLECTION

The following are American in provenance:

be (*warn't* for *wasn't*)
bring (*brung*)
catch (*catched*)
climb (*clumb*)
creep (*crope*)
dare (*dasn't, didn't dast*)
dive (*dove*)
do (*don't* for *doesn't*)
do (past tense *done*)
drownded
eat (*et*)
-*er*, -*est* (with polysyllables)
get (*gotten*)
give (past tense *give*)
go (pa.pple. *went*)
have (*hain't*)
hear (*hearn*)

heave (*hove*)
heave (*hove* for *hoved?*)
help (*holp, holpen*)
hern (for *hers*)
his'n
look (*look-a-here, looky-here*)
may (*mought*)
mile (pl. form)
of (for *have*)
ourn (for *ours*)
ought (*hadn't ought*)
Portygee (sing. form)
set, sot (for *sit, sat*)
skin (past tense *skun*)
speak (past tense *spake*)
theirn (for *theirs*)
wisht (for *wish*)

wore-out (for *worn-out*)
ye (sing. use)

ye (for *you*)
yourn (for *yours*)

Other peculiarities:

arcana (as sing.)
beaten out (for *beat out*—pseudo-refinement)
kneip, kneips (for *Kneipe, Kneipen*)
smile (past tense *smole*—humorous form)

thee (for you—Quaker use)
think (past tense *thunk*—humorous form)

For archaic forms and inflections see above, p. ci.

C. MARK TWAIN'S FAVORITE WORDS

The fifty words here listed seem to have given Mark Twain especial pleasure, judging by the frequency with which he used them. Perhaps they are characteristic of his personality and bent of mind. Only a selection of quotations using them has been given in the LEXICON from a much larger number that might have been cited.

anti-	*high-toned*	*shin*, v.
article	*layout*	*shove*, v.
ass	*lazy*, v.	*shucks*
blatherskite	*light-throwing*	*Silurian*
body (person)	*load up*	*slosh*, v.
book, v.	*low-down*	*slouch, no*
brick (fig. use)	*mark twain*	*smouch*, v.
bully, a.	*nobby*	*starchy*
crowd, v.	*orgy*	*statistic* (sing form)
drift, v.	*oversize*, v.	*swindle*, sb.
faze, phase	*particular*, a.	*tackle*, v.
fetch	*petrified*	*the* (emphatic use)
fix	*pie*	*tote*
gaudy	*pilot*	*waltz*
gay	*play*, v.	*whoop*
get	*profanity*	*work* (special sense)
harvest, v.	*raft* (a lot)	*work off*

D. Errors in Previous Dictionaries

A few errors in detail, or what seem to us to be such, have been noted in previous dictionaries and other authorities on Mark Twain. They are here brought together for convenient reference.

All the dictionaries disagree hopelessly over the distinction in usage between *forward* and *forwards;* they all give definitions that are inadequate for Mark Twain's usage of the words *picturesque, pilot, tender-footed,* and *Third House;* and they are mistakenly agreed in affirming that the substantive *wherewithal* always requires the article.

The OXFORD seems mistaken or inadequate, although followed by one or more of the other dictionaries, in its definitions for *boiler-deck, get to, hard-boiled, life-history, lightning,* a., *mugwump, to go one's pile, sail,* v., *shebang, shove,* v., *Sweet Singer, towhead, turtle, from wayback,* and *wheel-house;* in the restriction of usage which it ascribes to *poor white* and *yam;* and in saying that *you-all* may be either singular or plural. It is strangely inconsistent in its capitalization of such words as *State, South, Southern,* and the like. It appears to be wrong in claiming a British origin for the phrase *to go the whole hog,* and in its derivation for the phrase *to make* or *try the riffle;* in calling the verb *marvel* archaic, and in denying the existence of a singular form of the substantive *statistics;* and in finding no example for *Pigs in Clover* or for the *fourth dimension* until the twentieth century.

WEBSTER'S makes unfounded statements about the origin of the American sense of the verb *boom;* calls Mark Twain's pronunciation of the words *literary* and *perhaps* "especially British"; provides a doubtful derivation for the word *skaddle;* and gives an inadequate definition for the word *skyugle,* in which it is followed by the STANDARD. Farmer gives a surprising meaning for the word *stogy.* Mr. Mencken, it seems to us, has written too hastily about American ignorance of the meaning of the term "dissenters" (see under *dissentering*), and about the earliest uses of *nuts* and *yawp;* he also makes an odd mistake about the adjective *gaily.* Mr. Horwill is wrong, in our opinion, in declaring the use of *a half* instead of *half a,* and of the prefix *semi-,* to be American, and also in his late date for the American use of the phrase *in the neighborhood of.* Contributors to AMERICAN SPEECH have made rash statements about the origin of *hellion* and *whoopee;* Mr. Paine about the invention by Mark Twain of the bicycling expression *to take a header;* and Mr. Leacock about Mark Twain's "typical" twist of meaning for the substantive *plant.*

But the most remarkable statement of all is to be found in the UNIVERSAL, under the word *North* (q.v.). Perhaps it is no part of the essential equipment of a British lexicographer to be familiar with the difference between the North and North America, or to know the exact location of Mason's and Dixon's line!

E. PROBLEM WORDS

For the following entries previous dictionaries and other authorities have failed either to supply any explanation or at least to give as much information as seemed desirable. A special effort has been made in each case to solve the very various problems presented, and all available sources have been consulted. Criticisms of our solutions will be appreciated. In several cases no sufficient or satisfactory solution has been found, and any further light upon them will be sincerely welcomed.

alum-basket
and (deuces-and)
anti-, prefix
autumn-butter
bheel
biggity
boom, v.
buckwheat cake
d box and *k box*
dusty
-er, -est, suffixes
fifteen-puzzle
gully-keeper
guts
Hannibal
harness, v.
Harrisite
herumfrodite
jayhawker
Kaet
kings-and
like, a.
line-shot
mark twain

meeky, v.
Meisterschaft
Milam
miller-gun
milray
mishemokwa
Miss (for *Mrs.*)
Morisite
Muddy, sb.
Nationalist
nickeled (new use)
night-hawk
no (new use)
object, no (Am. origin?)
ombra (origin?)
osteopathy (Am. origin?)
paust
paper-collar
porcelaintype
Picciola
pictorial paper
rear
reading-matter

sawdust-mine
scar (*spec.* sense)
she (Am. use)
sny
spinning-stick
spring-line
string (Billiards)
tar-baby
tax-collar
td and *tf*
the (Am. use)
three-ball game
verge-staff
Waldenstromian
war-correspondent (Am. origin?)
weather
wheat-bread
whisky-shelf
white-sleeve badge
wood-sawyer (independent as a wood-sawyer's clerk)
yellow journalism

LEXICON

EXPLANATORY NOTE

The entries in the LEXICON are arranged in the following order: first the *word or combination,* followed by the *symbols of classification,* in brackets; second, the *quotation or quotations;* third the *lexicographical information,* in parentheses.

Word or Combination. A separate entry is made for each word, combination, or meaning. On the first line of each entry has been placed the headword or combination, in the form used by the OED; or, if not found in the OED, as nearly as possible on the same principles. With it is given an abbreviation denoting its part of speech. This is followed by any variant form actually used by Mark Twain, or if used as part of a phrase or idiom, by the exact usage exemplified.

Quotations. Illustrative quotations, arranged in chronological order, are given in the following form: first, the quotation, exactly as found in the source referred to, but freely condensed, omissions being indicated by suspension points; second, the year of its earliest publication, or that of its original composition or delivery if that is known to have been earlier than its publication; third, the title in abbreviated form, as given in the *Finding List* (pp. 267-278), of the work or volume from which the quotation has been taken, with its date if different from the original date, and its volume, chapter, and page number.

A selection has been made from the quotations available, with preference given to the earliest and those which best illustrate the meaning. In order to avoid, so far as possible, the repetition of quotations, free use has been made of cross-references from word to word. This practice has permitted the use, in a number of cases, of longer quotations, transcribed but once, exemplifying related groups of words, as for instance under *Adventist, afarabocca, allopath, arrastre, batter-cake, bicycle, biscuit, budge, cent, coat-of-arms, cocktail, Congregationalist, cotton-gin, effect, kahkahponeeka,* and others.

Lexicographical Information. This is given after the quotations and is placed in parentheses. First is given the treatment of the word in the OED or its Supplement (OEDS). This comprises the OED number or letter for the particular meaning illustrated, any terms of description or classification used by the OED, the OED dates for its earliest or latest examples, or both, and the OED definition; but the definition is often abbreviated or omitted when, as is so often the case in Mark Twain's writing, his quotations seem to have full and adequate "defining value." Then follow the treatment and classification of the word or usage in other lexicographical authorities, given in summary form, except when they disagree with the OED or supplement it. For words, combinations, or meanings not found in the OED, the best available authority is cited. Those not found in any previous dictionary are defined or discussed so far as seems needful. For the lexicographical abbreviations used, see below (p. cxviii).

Symbols of Classification. The letters placed in brackets after the headword or combination in each entry are intended to bear the following significations.

A=Americanism. The term "Americanism" is used in this LEXICON in its widest sense, both of words and things; but no entry has been classed as A without authority.

Words and meanings found in the OED are classed as A (1) if definitely so called by the OED, whether without qualification ("*U.S.*"), or as of American origin ("*Orig.*

U.S."), or as of American survival ("*Now U.S.*"), and also whether described as exclusively American or as also used in other parts of the English-speaking world; or (2) if described by the OED as American by reference, i. e., as denoting an object or an idea which is American by origin, habitat, or custom, such as American plants and animals, groups and movements, institutions and inventions. (Included here are all terms characterized as "*Baseball*" or "*Poker*" or the like; also the technical vocabulary of Christian Science, Mormonism, Simplified Spelling, etc.) The authority of the OED is regarded as decisive, even though the distinctive Americanism of the term is ignored or denied by other dictionaries, as it so often is by American lexicographers; but all conflicting judgments are cited in every case.

Words and meanings not found in the OED (B¹ entries) are classed also as A (1) if so called in any of the other general dictionaries (W, S, C, or U), or in Wr; or (2) if included in any of the special dictionaries of Americanisms (B, F, Cl, Th, T, M, or H) or in lists of American terms supplied in DN or AS; or (3) if American by necessary inference from related words or from Mark Twain's own description or usage.

?A=Unrecorded or Doubtful Americanism. Used for cases where authority is conflicting or nonexistent.

Words and meanings found in the OED, but not called by it "*U.S.*", are classed as ?A (1) if so called by any other authority (but note that, as stated above, conflicts of the opposite sort, where the OED does call the word "*U.S.*" and other dictionaries do not, are not regarded by us as a rule as doubtful cases); or (2) if the OED, although not definitely calling the word or meaning American, gives for it earlier American examples, or in the case of obsolete words, later American examples, as happens with especial frequency in the Supplement (OEDS) where attention is expressly directed to the discovery of "Earlier U.S. exs.", thus indicating that the editors of the OED were themselves in doubt about the Americanism of the word; or (3) if Mark Twain himself uses it with distinctive American implications, or himself supplies an "Earlier U.S. ex." that has not been discovered by the OED (B² words).

Words and meanings not found in the OED at all (B¹ words) are classed also as ?A (1) if the other authorities are wrong in our judgment in ignoring or denying its Americanism; or (2) if not found in any dictionary, but in our judgment clearly deserving to be added to the list of genuine Americanisms.

Our reasons for differing with authority, or venturing to supplement it, are always indicated. We have done so chiefly on the ground of Mark Twain's own usage, believing as we do that his judgment about the American provenance or flavor of a word or phrase is almost infallible. We do not, of course, maintain that the mere fact that Mark Twain has used a word, even if (as with our B¹ and B² entries) he supplies the earliest recorded example of its use, is sufficient reason for calling it an Americanism. Many such words are obviously personal coinages; that is, they are "Mark Twainisms" rather than Americanisms. The test is always whether Mark Twain's usage, in its context and with its implications, indicates that he felt it as a part of the American vernacular. The decision, naturally, is not always an easy one. For numerous examples of the various sorts of conflict and doubt that have presented themselves, see our discussion above (pp. x-xiii). It is for this reason that we have preferred to class all such words and meanings as ?A rather than as A.

For both A and ?A entries, the date of the earliest OED quotation is always given, followed by dots when there are later quotations in the OED; e.g., OED 1780..Still earlier examples, if supplied by Thornton or other authorities, are also noted.

B=New words. (For these also the earliest OED date is always given.)

B¹=Words or meanings not found in the OED at all.

B²=Words or meanings for which Mark Twain supplies an earlier example than (or one as early as) the earliest given in OED or OEDS. Also used for cases where the earliest OED quotation is taken from Mark Twain.

B³=Words or meanings for which the OED furnishes earlier evidence than is found in Mark Twain, but not earlier than 1800. No complete list of B³ words has been attempted. Such words have been retained only when they fall also under other classifications, when they help to explain other words, or when they serve to illustrate one of Mark Twain's special fields of interest.

C=Archaisms. Used for words or meanings called by the OED *obsolete, obsolescent, archaic, rare, literary, poetic, nonce-words,* or the like, or marked with a †.

?C=Unrecorded or Doubtful Archaisms. Used (like ?A) for cases of conflict between authorities or absence of authority; where the OED is itself doubtful; or where Mark Twain's own authority is in conflict with it. His extensive use of archaisms, and his keen sense for the archaic flavor of a word, make his judgment on this point, where it can be determined, almost as decisive as for Americanisms. (As with A words, we have not regarded the frequent failure of W, S, C, and U to class as archaic a word or meaning which is so classed by the OED as constituting a real conflict of authorities, although we have always recorded their omissions or denials.)

For C and ?C entries, the date of the latest OED quotation is supplied, preceded by dots; e.g., OED..1820. Usually the earliest date is given as well; e.g., OED 1610.. 1820.

D=Words filling Gaps. Used for words or meanings for which our quotations from Mark Twain fill gaps of forty years or more in the OED evidence. The label D has been used only with entries not labelled A, B, or C. No complete list of D words has been attempted. As with the B³ words, the D words have been retained only when they seemed of special interest for other reasons.

The gap which our quotations help to fill is indicated by a dash; e.g., a quotation dated 1869 IA (from *Innocents Abroad*) may be followed by the notation OED 1840— 1890; or one dated 1909 ISD (from *Is Shakespeare Dead?*) by the notation OED 1840.. 1890—.

E=Miscellaneous Peculiarities, mainly of form, spelling, or pronunciation. No complete list of E words has been attempted; our study is primarily of Mark Twain's vocabulary, not of his grammar or his orthography. But interesting peculiarities have been noted.

Dictionary references and dates for E words have been given only so far as they are pertinent to the peculiarities involved.

LEXICAL REFERENCES AND ABBREVIATIONS

AS—*American Speech*, vols. I-XII, 1926-1938

B—John R. Bartlett's *Dictionary of Americanisms*, 4th ed., 1877

C—*The Century Dictionary and Encyclopedia*, Rev. ed., 1911

Cl—Sylva Clapin's *New Dictionary of Americanisms*, 1902

DN—*Dialect Notes*, vols. I-VI, 1890-1938

F—John S. Farmer's *Americanisms Old and New*, 1889

H—H. W. Horwill's *Dictionary of Modern English Usage*, 1935

K—A. G. Kennedy's *Bibliography of Writings on the English Language from the Beginning of Printing to the End of 1922*, 1927

M—H. L. Mencken's *The American Language*, 4th ed., 1936

Mait—James Maitland's *American Slang Dictionary*, 1891

OED—*A New English Dictionary on Historical Principles*, ed. James A. H. Murray, Henry Bradley, W. A. Craigie, and C. T. Onions, 10 vols., 1888-1928

(Curiously bitter feelings, on both sides, seem to have been aroused over the question of whether to use the abbreviation OED or NED in referring to the great dictionary produced at Oxford. Considerations of convenience of reference and growing custom have led us to persist in using OED, in spite of critical rebukes. We should even like to be permitted to refer to it summarily as the "OXFORD" on occasion, without intending to be unduly deferential to the University of Oxford in doing so. The dictionary is hardly "New" any longer, nor is it yet old enough to justify its name by an association with New College, Oxford!)

OEDS—*Supplement* to the OED, issued 1933

S—*The New Standard Dictionary of the English Language*, 1930

T—Gilbert M. Tucker's *American English*, 1921

Th—Richard H. Thornton's *American Glossary*, 2 vols., 1912

Th. III—Thornton's third or supplementary volume, now being published in *Dialect Notes*, vol. VI, Part III, 1931, and subsequent issues.

(When Thornton gives a quotation dated earlier than the earliest given in OED or OEDS, his date is added just after the abbreviation: thus Th,1801, or Th.III,1790)

U—H. C. Wyld's *Universal Dictionary of the English Language*, 1932

W—Webster's *New International Dictionary of the English Language*

(References are to the Second Edition of 1935, unless otherwise stated)

Wr—Joseph Wright's *English Dialect Dictionary*, 6 vols., 1898-1905

(The sections of Great Britain and the United States from which dialect terms are reported in Wright's *English Dialect Dictionary*, in *Dialect Notes*, and in *American Speech* are occasionally added, after the abreviations Wr, DN, or AS, when they throw light on Mark Twain's usage.)

The lexical authorities listed above have been referred to, in most cases, in the following order: OED OEDS W S C U Wr B F Cl Th T M H DN AS; but OED is usually left unmentioned when OEDS gives earlier examples or fuller information. The absence of a word or meaning has been noted only in OED W S C, since only these four dictionaries have aimed at completeness. Page references for the lexical authorities are added only for AS, which lacks an alphabetical index.

OTHER ABBREVIATIONS

(For the abbreviations used after the quotations for the titles of Mark Twain's works, see the *Finding List* in the *Appendix,* pp. 267-278)

a., adj............adjective	*Lit.*............Literary
a (as *a*1300)............*ante,* before	M.T.............Mark Twain
absol.............absolutely	*Naut.*............Nautical
adv.............adverb	*obs.*............obsolete
Am.............American	orig.............original, -ly
app.............apparently	pa.pple.............past participle
arch.............archaic	pa.t.............past tense
art.............article	phr.............phrase
Astron.............Astronomy	pl.............plural
attrib.............attributive, -ly	*poet.*............poetic
c.............century	ppl.............participle
c (as *c*1300)............*circa,* about	ppl.a.............participial adjective
colloq.............colloquial, -ly	prep.............preposition
comb.............combination	prob.............probably
Comm.............Commercial use	pron.............pronoun, or
concr.............concrete, -ly	pronounced
conj.............conjunction	refl.............reflexive
const.............construction	*rhet.*............rhetorical
dial.............dialect, -al	sb.............substantive
dict.............dictionary	*Sc.*............Scotch
ellipt.............elliptical, -ly	sing.............singular
Eng.............England, English	sp.............spelled, or spelling
esp.............especially	*spec.*............specifically
exc.............except	*Theol.*............Theology
fig.............figurative, -ly	trans.............transitive
freq.............frequently	*transf.*............transferred sense
gen.............general, -ly	*Typog.*............Typography
Geol.............Geology	U.S.............United States or
Her.............Heraldry	Americanism
Hist.............History	v.............verb
hum.............humorous, -ly	vbl.sb.............verbal substantive
int.............interjection	*Zool.*............Zoology
intr.............intransitive	†.............obsolete or obsolescent
lit.............literal, -ly	

a, art. *a* for **an** before sounded *h* in unaccented syllables. [?A] *"If the signs are to be trusted, even your educated classes* [speaking to an Englishman] *used to drop the 'h.' They say 'humble' now, with the clear 'h,' and 'heroic,' and 'historic,' etc., but I judge that they used to drop those 'h's because your writers still keep up the fashion of putting an 'an' before those words instead of an 'a.' This is what Mr. Darwin might call a 'rudimentary' sign that an 'an' was justifiable once, and useful—when your educated classes used to say 'umble, and 'eroic, and 'istorical. Correct writers of the American language do not put 'an' before those words."* 1882 "Concerning the American Language" 267. *It has a historical side. I do not say 'an' historical side, because I am speaking the American language. I do not see why our cousins should continue to say 'an' hospital, 'an' historical fact, 'an' horse* 1899 *Speeches* (1910) 403. (M.T.'s unjust accusation that British writers continue to say 'an' hospital and 'an' horse shows that he never got the difference between British and American usage entirely clear in his mind. For a correct statement, cf. OED Headnote: "Bef. sounded *h, an* was retained after 1600, and sometimes after 1700, as *an house, an heifer, an hermitage*...In *unaccented* syllables, many, perhaps most, writers still retain *an* bef. sounded *h*...as *an historian*..though this is all but obsolete in speech, and in writing *a* becomes increasingly common in this position." The last OED ex. of *an* bef. sounded *h* in acc. syls. is dated 1732: *an hermitage.* For American non-use of *an* bef. sounded *h* even in unacc. syls., as *a historical*, cf. Cl and M, esp. the discussion in M p. 351. Cf. also AS.IV.442f.; V.82. Not A in W S C)

a, art. **an** for **a** before sounded *h* in accented syllables. [C] *The king and Merlin went until an hermit* 1889 CY iii 47 (A conscious archaism; cf. above. For M.T.'s usual usage cf. *"A pirate don't have to do anything when he's ashore, but a hermit he has to be praying considerable"* 1876 TS xiii 118)

a, art. **a** for **an** before vowel-sounds. [AB¹] *That sand-bar was a aggravating thing* 1856 *Adv. of T. J. Snodgrass* (1928) 22. *She'd been gone a hour and a half* do. 44 (Called A in DN.II,III, from s.e.Mo., n.w.Ark., s.Ill., s.Ind., e.Ala. This usage not in OED W S C. A feature of M.T.'s native dialect which he entirely discarded after his earliest production; it is never found in TS, HF, etc.)

a, prep. [?AC] *"You can work when you're a mind to, Tom"* 1876 TS iii 34. *"Hellum-a-lee—hard a port! Stand by to meet her!"* do. xiii 116. *"If he done it a-purpose"* 1880 TA xxiii 226. *If he had got into such an amazing condition as that a-purpose* 1892 AmCl xxiv 253 (OED A worn-down proclitic form of OE prep. *an, on.* 9. Manner. *Obs.* 1230..1695. So W S C Wr. A in Cl DN.III,IV)

a, prep. [AC] *Bimeby the second clerk came a staggerin' in* 1856 *Adventures of T.J. Snodgrass* (1928) 26. *"I was a-askin' Tom whah you was a-sett'n' at"* 1883 LM xliv 449. *"What is this country a-coming to?"* 1884 HF vi 43 (OED 13. *arch* or *dial*...Most of the southern dialects, and the vulgar speech both in England and America, retain the earlier usage. 1523..1845. So W S C Wr. A in Cl M)

a, v. for **have.** [?AC] See *have.*

aberration, sb. [B¹] *The pictures were fearful as to color..."Explain—explain these aberrations,"* said *Tracy* 1892 AmCl xvi 163 (Hum. nonce use)

abide, v. [C] *"They would not abide your coming"* 1889 CY xiv 169 (OED 12, *arch*..1859. Not *arch* in W S C U Wr)

able, a. [B¹] *And it ought to be the ablest weather that can be had* 1892 AmCl Pref. (Hum. nonce use)

aboard, prep. [AB²] *We stepped aboard the train* 1869 IA xii 79. *They stepped aboard a crowded car* 1892 AmCl xii 124 (OEDS 1c. In, or into, a train. *U.S.* 1869, this quot..So S C F CL T H. Not A in W)

abolition, sb. **abolition speech.** [AB²] *He made abolition speeches in the open air* 1894 "Scrap of Curious History" (1917) 184 (OED 1b. The abolition of the slave trade, which...in the U.S. became a great political question, so as to be spoken of familiarly as 'abolition.' Hence *attrib.* as an 'Abolition speech.' No ex. Comb. not in W S C U)

abolitionist, sb. [A] *It* [the jail] *was surrounded with chains and companies of soldiers to prevent the rescue of McReynold's nigger by the infernal Abolitionists* 1853 *Hannibal Journal* Sept. 6. *All of a sudden he proclaimed himself an abolitionist—straight out and publicly! He said that negro slavery was a crime, an infamy* 1894 "Scrap of Curious Hist." (1917) 184 (Cf. above. OED b. 1790..So W S C U F Cl Th T M)

abortionist, sb. [B¹] *The pictures were fearful... "People actually pay money for these calumnies?" "They actually do...And these abortionists could double their trade"* 1892 AmCl xvi 163 (Hum. nonce use)

absent-minded, a. [?AB²] *He would immediately look wise...and walk off with his nose in the air and his cap turned wrong side before, trying to appear absent-minded and eccentric* 1870 SNO (1875) 217. *He is absent-minded or unapprehensive of danger* 1872 RI iii 32. *"Bless my soul, I'm so absent-minded when I get to thinking"* 1873 GA xlv 412. *He grew weary at last, and then indifferent and absent-minded* 1876 TS v 58. *He is drowsy and absent-minded; there is no tenacity to his mind* 1880 TA xliii 509 (OED 1879, only ex. Not A in W S C U)

absent-mindedness, sb. [?AB²] *"In my absent-mindedness I forgot it"* 1869 IA xiii 122 (OED 1879, only ex. Not A in W S C U)

absent treatment, sb. [AB¹] *She was a Christian Science doctor and could cure anything...She would give me "absent treatment" now, and come in the morning* 1899 "Chr. Sc. and the Book" 585 (W: Mental treatment of disease in the patient's absence. This *spec* Christian Science term is not in OED S C)

absolutely, adv. [?AB¹] *"Do you mean to say that if he was all right and proper otherwise, you'd be indifferent about the early part of the business?" "Absolutely."* 1892 AmCl xxiv 255 (An emphatic affirmative=Yes. This common use is not noted in OED W S C)

accessory, a. [B¹] *"Arrest these two witnesses on suspicions of being accessionary after the fact to the murder* 1896 TSD xi 529 (Hum. malapropism for *accessory*)

accidental-insurance, sb. [?AB¹] *He had what the accidental insurance people might call an extra-hazardous polish* 1869 IA xxxvii 401 (Comb. not in OED W S C. Perhaps an earlier form for *accident-insurance*; cf. below)

accident-insurance, sb. [?AB²] *Ever since I have been a director in an accident-insurance company I have felt that I am a better man* c.1875 "Accident Insurance" *Speeches* (1910) 250 (OEDS 1880..Comb. not in W S C)

accident-ticket, sb. [B¹] *You couldn't clean up a tournament and pile the result without finding one of my accident-tickets in every helmet* 1889 CY xxx 382 (Nonce comb.)

accident-title, sb. [B¹] *Orion...got that accident-title through Governor Nye's absences* 1906 *Autob* (1924) II 350 (Nonce comb. for *accidental title*)

acclimated, ppl.a. [?AB³] *The fever at length got tired of tormenting the stout young engineer...and left him very thin, a little sallow, but an "acclimated" man* 1873 GA xvi 153 (OED 1856..So W S C. A in H)

acclimation, sb. [?AB³] *The acquisition of a habit of taking every morning before breakfast a dose of bitters, composed of whiskey and asafoetida, out of the acclimation jug* 1873 GA xvi 154 (OEDS 1832..So W S C. A in H)

acclimatized, ppl.a. [B³] "*Bring it out—I am prepared—acclimatized, if I may use the word*" 1897 FE xiii 146 (OED 1855..So W S C U)

accommodations, sb.pl. [?A?C] *Some of those other people will have to drift around to two or three hotels in the rain, before they find accommodations* 1880 TA xxxii 353. *Lakeside was a pleasant little town of five or six thousand inhabitants...It had church accommodations for 35,000* 1904 "Bequest" (1906) i 1 (OED 7. Room and suitable provision for the reception of people. Formerly mostly in *plural.* 1722.. OEDS Later *U.S.* exs. of *pl.* use. 1804..1879. The *pl.* use is A in H; not A or *obs* in W S C)

accompt, sb. [CE] "*An Sir Kay had had time to get another skin of sour wine into him, ye had seen the accompt doubled*" 1889 CY iii 44 (OED *arch* form of Account..1741. So W S C)

account, sb. **on accounts of.** [?AB¹E] "*I forgot all about driving slow on accounts of being glad and full of thinking*" 1884 HF xxxiii 339 (*Pl.* form not in OED W S C)

ach, int. [?AB³] *The poor devil...so laughed at... ach, the vulgar, crawling, insufferable tramp* 1892 AmCl i 22 (OED Not Eng. unless meant for an emphatic and strongly aspirated form of *ah!* Used in German and Celtic. 1865.. So W S. A in M: another example of debased German. Not in C)

ache, v. [?AB¹] *I saw she had been aching to have me ask it* 1893 "Esquimau Maiden's Romance" (1900) 144 (W: To wish ardently, to long. *colloq.* So U. Cf. Suffer, below, used in same sense. This use not in OED S C)

acquaintanceship-breeder, sb. [B¹] *The inundation ...used, evidently, as a mere ice-breaker and acquaintanceship-breeder* 1883 LM xxxix 412 (Nonce comb.)

a-crack, a. [B¹] *I drew near the door...it was a-crack and I glanced in* 1883 LM xxxvi 392 (Not in OED W S C. Cf. ajar, OED 1786..)

acrost, prep. [AE] "*One day a feller...come acrost with his box*" 1865 "Jumping Frog" (1875) 34. "*I didn't want to run acrost them devils, even if they was dead*" 1876 TS xxx 227 (A in DN.I,III. This form not in OED W S C)

ad, sb. [?AB³] See *fence,* v. 1886. "*For just a modest little one-line ad, it's a corker*" 1889 CY xvi 192. See also *plant out* 1906 (OEDS 1868..So W S C. A in F Cl M)

Adam-clam, sb. [B¹] *A procession of ancestors that stretches back a billion years to the Adam-clam or grasshopper...from whom our race has developed* 1889 CY xviii 216 (Nonce comb.)

Adam-newsboy, sb. [B¹] *One greater than kings had arrived—the newsboy...The Adam-newsboy of the world went round the corner* 1889 CY xxvi 338 (Nonce comb.)

Adam-nugget, sb. [B¹] *It is the Adam-nugget of this mine, and its children run up into the millions* 1897 FE xxv 242 (Nonce comb.)

adding on, vbl.sb. [?AB¹] *Like the dropping off and adding on of logs in a raft* 1898 "Stirring Times in Austria" (1900) 286 (Neither *adding on* nor *to add on* is given in OED W S C)

addition, sb. (?AC) *I write my family name without additions* 1892 AmCl vii 72 (OED 4. Something annexed to a man's name to show his rank, occupation, place of residence, etc.; 'style' of address. *Obs.* W: *obs.* exc. *Low.* S C: *Low.* Apparently a survival in vulgar Am. use)

adios, int. [AB¹] "*You are the loser by this rupture, not me. Adios.*" *I then left* 1871 *Screamers* x 58 (A in DN.I. Not A in W S C. Not in OED)

adjective-piling, vbl.sb. [B¹] *We listened to an old-fashioned speech, full of that adjective-piling, mixed metaphor, and windy declamation which was regarded as eloquence in that ancient time* 1885 "Private History of Campaign" 195 (Nonce comb.)

adjective-stump, sb. (B¹) *He plowed through these papers, removing unnecessary flowers and digging up some acres of adjective-stumps* 1878 "About Magnanimous-Incident Literature" 617 (Nonce comb.)

admiration-compelling, ppl.a. [B¹] *He was going to make brilliant and easy and admiration-compelling use of these treasures* 1909 ISD iv 43 (Nonce comb.)

admire, v. [?AC] *Many will admire to see what a good memory you are furnished with* 1899 "Historical Dates" (1917) 143. *They would "admire" to see a "Gentile" force a Mormon to fulfil a losing contract in Utah* 1872 RI xiv 114 (OED 1. To wonder, marvel. d. with inf. *obs* or *dial.* So W S C U Wr. A in AS.IV.474)

admire, v. (A) *My companion said he did not admire to smell a whale; and I adopt his sentiments while I scorn his language* 1864 SS (1926) ii 128. *I always admired to study Raphael's art* 1889 CY vii 84 (OEDS 1d. *U.S.* To like, be desirous *to do* something. 1770..So W B F Cl Th M H DN.II. Not A in S C Wr T)

admit, v. [D] *I am not here to testify against myself— I can't be expected to do so, a prisoner in your own country is not admitted to do so* 1899 *Speeches* (1910) 130 (OED 1c. To allow *to do* anything. 1413..1747—. This use not in W S C U)

adobe, sb. [AB³] *The station buildings were made of sundried, mud-colored bricks, laid up without mortar— adobes, the Spaniards call these bricks, and Americans shorten it to 'dobies* 1872 RI iv 40 (OED Adopted in U.S. from Mexico, 1834.. So W S B F Cl Th M DN.I AS.VII.432. Not A in C)

advance-advertisement, sb. [B¹] *There were other advance-advertisements. One of them appeared just before Caesar Augustus was born* 1917 "Interpreting the Deity" 268 (Nonce comb.)

Adventist, sb. [?AB³] *It is hair-splitting differences of opinion over disputed text-meanings that have divided into many sects a once united Church...The list...compiled by Rev. Dr. H. K. Carroll, was published, January 8, 1903, in the New York Christian Advocate: Adventists (6 bodies). Baptists (13 bodies). Brethren (Plymouth) (4 bodies). Brethren (River) (3 bodies). Catholics (8 bodies). Catholic Apostolic. Christadelphians. Christian Connection. Christian Catholics (Dowie). Christian Missionary Association. Christian Scientists. Church of God (Winebrennarians). Church of the New Jerusalem. Congregationalists. Disciples of Christ. Dunkards (4 bodies). Evangelical (2 bodies). Friends (4 bodies). Friends of the Temple. German Evangelical Protestant. German Evangelical Synod. Independent congregations. Jews (2 bodies). Latter-day Saints (2 bodies). Lutherans (22 bodies). Mennonites (12 bodies). Methodists (17 bodies). Moravians. Presbyterians (12 bodies). Protestant Episcopal (2 bodies). Reformed (3 bodies). Schwenkfeldians. Social Brethren. Spiritualists. Swedish Evangelical Miss. Covenant (Waldenstromians). Unitarians. United Brethren (2 bodies). Universalists. Total of sects and splits— 139.* 1907 CS II vii 193-4 (OEDS A member of any of the various religious sects holding millenarian views.. Second Adventist, orig. the fuller designation of the followers of William Miller (died 1849)..a Millerite. 1876.. So W S C . A in B F Cl T)

adventure-bristling, ppl.a. [B¹] *The Bering Strait whale-fishery...that adventure-bristling trade* 1909 ISD iv 44 (Nonce comb.)

advertisedly, adv. [B¹] *When an alien observer turns his telescope upon us—advertisedly in our own special interest—a natural apprehension moves us to ask, What is the diameter of his reflector?* 1895 "What Bourget Thinks" 49 (Not in OED W S C)

afarabocca, sb. [B¹] *The doctor...said he would write a prescription; which he did. It was one of Galen's; in fact, it was Galen's favorite, and had been slaying people for sixteen thousand years...Galen was still the only medical authority recognized in Missouri..."Take of* *afarabocca, henbane, corpobalsamum, each two drams and a half: of cloves, opium, myrrh, cyperus, each two drams; of opobalsamum, Indian leaf, cinnamon, zedoary, ginger, costus, coral, cassia, euphorbium, gum tragacanth, frankincense, styrax calamita, celtic, nard, spignel, hartwort, mustard, saxifrage, dill, anise, each one dram; of xylaloes, rheum ponticum, alipta, moschata, castor, spikenard, galangal, opoponax, anacardium, mastich, brimstone, peony, eringo, pulp of dates, red and white hermodactyls, roses, thyme, acorns, pennyroyal, gentian, the bark of the root of mandrake, germander, valerian, bishop's weed, bayberries, long and white pepper, xylobalsamum, carnabadium, macedonian, parsley seeds, lovage, the seeds of rue, and sinon, of each a dram and a half; of pure gold, pure silver, pearls not perforated, the blatta byzantina, the bone of the stag's heart, of each the quantity of fourteen grains of wheat; of sapphire, emerald and jasper stones, each one dram; of hazel nuts, two drams; of pellitory of Spain, shavings of ivory, calamus odoratus, each the quantity of twenty-nine grains of wheat; of honey or sugar a sufficient quantity. Boil down and skim off.*" 1894 TET vii 412 (Hum. invention)

afeard, ppl.a. [?AC] See *corner,* v. 1884; *hail,* sb.1884. *We told him we would help him and he needn't be so afeard* 1896 TSD iv 354 (OED *Rare* in lit. after 1700.. it survives everywhere in the popular speech. *c*1000.. 1868. OEDS 1807..1911. So W C Wr. A in S F Cl DN.I,II,III,V AS.II.486; V.202,265, Ozarks; VI.97)

a–front of, prep. [?AC] "*When he got a-front of us he lifts his hat*" 1884 HF xxxiii 340 (OED *obs.* 1557..1622. So W. S. Not *obs* in C Wr)

aft, adv. [?B¹?C] *Her hair was frizzled into a tangled chaparral, forward of her ears; aft it was drawn together* 1870 SNO (1875) 153 (OED 1. *gen.* Behind, in the rear. *Obs.* 937. *Naut.* in W S C U. Here more likely a hum. twist of the *naut.* sense than a survival)

after, prep. **to be after doing something.** [?AB¹] "*If yez want to see Mr. Daly, yez'll have to be after going to the front door and buy a ticket*" *c*1890 *Speeches* (1910) 81 (W: In the act of; at the point of, given to; as, to be after putting curses on people. *An Irishism.* Both M.T. and W seem to have misunderstood the use of the phrase in the Anglo-Irish dialect; cf. P. W. Joyce, *English as We Speak It in Ireland,* where it is explained (pp.84f.) as merely a substitute for the perfect tense: thus "I am after finishing my work" = I have finished. Not an *Irishism* in Wr: *After* used with a progressive tense to denote that an action is about to take place. The phrase is not mentioned in OED S C U)

after, a. [B¹] *Negroes and ruffians with heads clean shaven, except a kinky scalplock back of the ear, or rather upon the after corner of the skull* 1869 IA viii 78. *The depression forward of their after shoulders* [of cattle] 1869 IA lix 636 (Hum. extension of the *naut.* sense, OED 4 Nearer the rear, hinder, posterior. 1200..So W S C U)

after–cabin, sb. [B³] *They spoke glibly of the "after-cabin"* 1869 IA iv 38 (OED *naut.* 1833, only ex. Not in W S C)

after–davit, sb. [B¹] *The captain stood on the stern, by the after-davits* 1907 "Capt. Stormfield" 42 (Comb. not in OED W S C)

after–deck, sb. [B¹] *Fifteen or twenty Africanders sat up singing on the afterdeck in the moonlight* 1897 FE lxiv 632. *They were reclining in lazy luxury under the awning of the after-deck* 1904 "*Bequest*" (1906) vii 38 (W: The part of a deck abaft midships. Comb. not in OED S C)

after–development, sb. [B¹] *Now that the after-developments of the Clayton case have run their course.* .1898 "From the London Times of 1904" (1900) 143 (Comb. not in OED W S C)

agate, sb. [AB²] *The type is mostly agate and minion* 1853 *Letters* (1917) I 26 (OED 4.*Typog.* The American name of the type called in England *ruby.* 1891, only ex. So W S C H)

age, sb. **to hold the age.**]AB³] *This government "holds the age" on him* 1898 "Austrian Edison" (1900) 266. *How could I talk when he was talking? He "held the age," as the poker-clergy say* 1907 "Chaps. from Autob." 569 (OEDS 6b. The 'eldest hand' in a game of poker. 1882.. So W S C U Cl T)

aggravate, v. [?A] *He'd git the blues and feel kird o' scrubby, aggravated, and disgusted* 1871 *Screamers* ii 16. See *mad* 1872. "*I've seen cats aggravated in more ways than one*" 1894 TET ii 334 (OED 7. To exasperate, provoke. 1611.. *Dial* and *colloq* in W S C U. A in M)

aggravating, ppl.a. [?A] *No sound is quite so inane, and silly, and aggravating as the "hoo hoo" of a cuckoo clock* 1880 TA xxvi 263. See also *dead-earnest* 1883 (OED 3. *fam.* 1775.. *Dial* and *colloq* in W S C U)

aggravation, sb. [?AB²] *I heard lately of a worn and sorely tried American student who used to fly to a certain German word* [*damit*] *for relief when he could bear up under his aggravations no longer* 1880 TA App.D 614 (OED 6. *fam.* No ex. *Colloq* in W S C U)

agin, adv. [?AB¹E] See *allow* 1873. "*Blame my skin if I ain't gone en forgit dat name agin!*" 1892 AmCl viii 81 (W: *dial* var. of Again. This form not in OED S C)

agin, prep. [?AB²E] *There was a flush out agin him* 1867 SNO (1875) 74. *To lean his back agin the chimbly* 1880 TA iii 40. "*We can't buck agin him*" 1882 SWE 102 (OED *dial var.* of Again, prep.=Against; often used jocularly. 1878..So W. A in Cl M DN.I. Not in S C)

agone, ppl.a. [C] "*Some two and forty years agone the good count rode hence*" 1869 IA xxi 212. "*Thou wilt not miscall thyself, as they say thou didst a little while agone?*" 1881 PP v 63. See also *bonanza* 1881 (OED *arch* and *poet.* 1601..1846. So W S C Wr)

agony, sb. [AB¹] *The first draft or original agony of the wail "In the Sweet Bye and Bye"* 1889 CY xvii 202 (An extension of the sense in S: *Slang, U.S.* Trivial custom, fashion, or fad. So F. This sense not in OED W C)

aground, a. [B¹] *And so 'twill be when I'm aground— These yearly duns will still go round* 1875 SNO 62 (Buried: hum. nonce meaning)

aguardiente, sb. [AB³] *Oranges, bananas, aguardiente* [in Nicaragua] 1866 *Notebook* (1935) v 38 (OEDS In southwestern U.S., native whisky. 1826..So S C B F Cl. This sense not in W)

ah, v. [B¹] *We went oh-ing and ah-ing in admiration* 1897 FE ix 111 (Nonce use)

ahead, adv. **to come ahead.** [AB¹] *Ealer rang to "come ahead," full steam* 1883 LM xx 238 (Naut. phrase, A in B Cl. Not in OED W S C)

ahold of, prep. [?AB³] "*Got to set stock-still for six whole months before it can take a-hold of a prowling, thieving, infernal, white-shirted free nigger!*" 1884 HF vi 43 (OEDS 1879..Earliest exs. U.S. W: *dial.* Not in S C)

ain't, v. [?AB³] "*I ain't got no frog*" 1865 "Jumping Frog" (1875) 34. "*Ain't he played me tricks enough like that?...I ain't got the heart to lash him*" 1876 TS i 19 (OEDS *dial* variant of *hain't,* have not. All exs. U.S. 1845..A in M DN.I,II,III,V. Not A in W S C Wr T)

air, sb. [?AB¹] "*He's all air, you know—breeze, you may say—and he freshens them up*" 1892 AmCl iii 42 (Giving oneself airs; buoyance, optimism. This sense not in OED W S C; but cf. airy and breezy, below)

air–blast, sb. [B¹] *At the last moment Paige concluded to add an air-blast...I went on footing the bills and got the machine really perfected at last* 1890 *Autob* (1924) I 77 (Cf. S: An air-current directed on a dynamo-commutator to prevent sparking. Not in OED W C)

airing, vbl.sb. [?AB¹] *All the papers in America would have found out that I was a wife beater, and they would have given it a pretty general airing, too* 1873 *Speeches* (1923) 52 (W: An exposure to public notice. This sense not in OED S C)

air-line, sb. [AB³] *I bought tickets for each railroad in the United States...but the Alexandria and Boston air-line* 1856 *Adv. of T. J. Snodgrass* (1928) 21 (OEDS A direct or "bee" line. Chiefly *U.S.* 1813..So F Cl Th T M H. Not A in W S C)

air-shaft, sb. [?A] See *arrastre* 1909 (OED Passage for the admission of air into a mine or tunnel. 1692.. So S C U. A in AS.IV.368. Not in W)

air-ship, sb. [B²] *My air-ship was delayed by a collision with a fellow from China* 1874 *Letters* (1917) I xiv 232 (OEDS 1888..So W S C U)

air-tight stove, sb. [AB¹] *Airtight stove (new and deadly invention)* 1883 LM xxxviii 400 (W: A sheet-iron stove the draft of which can be almost entirely shut off. *U.S.* Not A in S C. Comb. not in OED)

air-torpedo, sb. [B¹] *Colonel Sellers was the inventor of the famous air-torpedo, which came very near destroying the Union armies in Missouri and the city of St. Louis itself* 1873 GA xviii 171 (A prophetic coinage, even yet not quite realized)

airy, a. [?AC] *If we chance to discover that from Dan to Beersheba seemed a mighty stretch of country to the Israelites, let us not be airy with them, but reflect that it was and is a mighty stretch when one cannot traverse it by rail* 1869 IA xlvi 479. See also *hay-scales* 1872; *hot air* 1873; *biggety* 1883 (OED 8a. Assuming airs, making lofty pretensions. *obs.* 1606. Not *obs* in W S C Wr. A in B Cl T)

alack, int. [C] *"Alack, I had believed the rumor disproportioned to the truth"* 1881 PP v 63 (OED Now *arch, poet,* or *dial.* 1480..1842. So W S Wr. Not *arch* in C U)

alarmist, sb. [?AB³] *The alarmist was a horseman* 1885 "Priv. Hist. of Camp." 200 (OED 1802..So W S C U. A in Th,1800 T M)

alas, v. [B¹] *"Alas!" "What're you alassin' about?"* says the baldhead 1884 HF xix 183 (Hum. nonce use)

alight, v. [B³C] *At eleven o'clock we alighted upon a sign which manifestly referred to billiards* 1869 IA xii 116 (OED 8. To come upon anything without design; to light upon. *Rare.* 1858, only ex. So W S C)

alipta, sb. [B¹] See *afarabocca* 1894 (Hum. coinage, perhaps suggested by *aliptic,* a. W: *Old Med.,* Pertaining to inunction; or by *alipata,* sb. W: Blind-your-eyes, an Australian tree (*Excoecaria agallocha*), called also *milky mangrove, poison tree*)

alive, a. [?A] *I could not remember that there was much furniture in the room when I went to bed, but the place was alive with it now* 1880 TA xiii 118. See also *fiddler* 1883 (OED 6. In a state of commotion; swarming with things in motion. 1808...OEDS Earlier U.S. ex. 1789. Not A in W C U. Not in S)

alkali, sb. [AB³] *That awful five days journey, through alkali sagebrush, peril of body, and imminent starvation* 1870 SNO (1875) 240. *One of that species of desert whose concentrated hideousness shames the diffused and diluted horrors of Sahara—an "alkali" desert* 1872 RI xviii 142. *A slick alkali flat which was surfaced like steel* 1902 "DBDS" (1928) 320 (OEDS 3b. *U.S. attrib.* 1869.. So W S B F Cl T. Not A in C U)

alkali-spider, sb. [AB¹] *"My mother was all American—no alkali-spider about her, I can tell you"* 1906 "Horse's Tale" 328 (Comb. not in OED W S C; but cf. OEDS Alkali, sb. 3c. One who lives in or frequents an alkali region. *U.S.* 1907)

all, a. **all of**. [?AB³] *It must have been all of fifteen minutes—fifteen minutes of dull, homesick silence—before that long horse-face swung round upon me again* 1883 LM xviii 220. *It was all of twenty years since any one of them had known what it was to be equipped with any remaining snag or remnant of a tooth* 1889 CY xx 240 (OEDS A.6. As much as, altogether, quite. 1856. So S. A in H. This construction not in W C U)

all, a. **for all of**. [?AB²] *Most knights would have thought of nothing but getting his armor; but so I got his bandana, he could keep his hardware for all of me* 1889 CY xxii 143 (OEDS A.6. As far as concerned. 1911, only ex. Phrase not in W S C U)

all, adv. **all over**. [AB²] *If you are anywhere where it won't do for you to scratch, why you will itch all over in upward of a thousand places* 1884 HF ii 6. See also *soldier-plume* 1884. (OEDS All over. 1b Everywhere. *U.S.* 1904..So H. Not A in W S Wr. This sense not in C U)

all, adv. **all over**. [?AB¹] *"That is European management, all over! An inch a day—think of that!"* 1880 TA xxxix 456 (S: Exactly, completely, thoroughly. *colloq.* So C U Wr. A in H. This sense not in OED W)

all, adv. **all through**. [?AB²] *"She's a Sellers all through!"* 1892 AmCl v 57 (OED C.11. No ex. Phrase not in W S C U)

all, adv. **all-to**. [C] *He dislodged me with a stone... which "all-to brast" the most of my bones* 1889 CY iv 54 (OED C.14. The fact that the *to* belonged to the verb was lost sight of. *obs.* c1000..1637. So W Wr. Not in S C U)

all-around, a. [AB³] *I might have tried as much as a year to think of such a strange thing as an all-around left-handed man and I could not have done it* 1899 "Hist. Dates" (1917) 159 (OEDS *U.S.* = All-round. 1883..Comb. not in W S C)

all around, adv. [AB³] See *hand-shake* 1880. *They agreed that I filled the bill all around* 1893 "Banknote" (1928) 108. *It was awkward all around, but more particularly in the case of Rowena* 1894 TET, intro. 312 (OEDS *U.S.* = All-round, adv. 1878..Comb. not in W S C)

alley, sb. [A] *To reproduce a Jerusalem street, it would be necessary to up-end a chicken coop and hang it before each window in an alley of American houses* 1869 IA liii 558. See *tenement-house* 1880. *That alley is a lonesome little pocket that runs along one side of the New Gadsby* 1892 AmCl vi 68 (OEDS 3b. A back-lane running parallel with a main street. *U.S.* 1729..So H. Not A in W S C)

alley, sb. [?A] *"Jim, I'll give you a marvel. I'll give you a white alley...And it's a bully taw"* 1876 TS ii 27 (OED var. Ally. Supposed to be a diminutive abbreviation of *alabaster.* A choice marble or taw. 1720..So W S C. A in B T.)

alleyway, sb. [AB³] *He looked into the detective's room across a little alleyway ten or twelve feet wide* 1902 "DBDS" (1928) 325 (OEDS orig. *U.S.* 1869..So H DN.IV,V. Not A in W S C)

all-fired, a. [AB³] *"With the all-firedest pleasure in the world, madam"* 1857 *Adv. of T. J. Snodgrass* (1928) 42 (OED *slang.* Chiefly *U.S.* 1837..So S Wr B F Cl Th,1835 T M DN.IV. Not A in W. Not in C)

alligator, sb. [A] *"I take nineteen alligators and a bar'l of whiskey for breakfast when I'm in robust health, and a bushel of rattlesnakes and a dead body when I'm ailing"* 1883 LM iii 45 (OED 1. A genus of saurian reptiles...of which the various species are found in America. 1568..So W S C U B F Cl T M)

alligator-bed, sb. [AB¹] *"Where the river is wide and shoal [there are] places they call alligator-beds"* 1883 LM xxiv 204 (Hum. nonce comb.)

alligator-boat, sb. [AB¹] *"An alligator-boat? What's it for?" "To dredge out alligators with"* 1883 LM xxiv 203 (Hum. nonce comb.)

alligator-hide, sb. [AB¹] *"All the government shoes are made of alligator-hide"* 1883 LM xxiv 206. (Comb. not in OED W S C; but cf. C: Leather made from alligator skin is widely used)

alligator-pilot, sb. [AB¹] *"All A1 alligator-pilots ...could tell alligator-water as far as another Christian could tell whiskey"* 1883 LM xxiv 205 (Hum. nonce comb.)

alligator-reef, sb. [AB¹] *"You can tell a sand-reef... but an alligator-reef doesn't show up"* 1883 LM xxiv 205 (Hum. nonce comb.)

alligator-water, sb.[AB¹]See *alligator-pilot* 1883(Hum. nonce comb.)

allons [B¹] [From a letter] *"You hear me. Allons. Blucher."* 1869 IA xix 189 (Nonce borrowing. Cf. Whitman's use, as mentioned by Miss Louise Pound, *American Mercury*, Feb. 1925. So M)

allopath, sb. [B³] *When I look around me, I am often troubled to see how many people are mad. To mention only a few: the Atheist, the Infidel, the Agnostic, the Baptist, the Methodist, the Christian Scientist, the Catholic, and the 115 Christian sects, the Presbyterian excepted, the 72 Mohammedan sects, the Buddhist, the Blavatsky-Buddhist, the Nationalist, the Confucian, the Spiritualist, the 2,000 East Indian sects, the Peculiar People, the Theosophists, the Swedenborgians, the Shakers, the Millerites, the Laurence Oliphant Harrisites, the Grand Lama's people, the Monarchists, the Imperialists, the Democrats, the Republicans (but not the Mugwumps), the Mind-Curists, the Faith-Curists, the Mental Scientists, the Allopaths, the Homoeopaths, the Electropaths, the—but there's no end to the list!* 1902 "Chr. Sc." 757 (OED 1830..So W S C U)

allow, v. [D] *"Why, Biljy, it beats the Nonesuch, don't it?"* The duke allowed it did 1884 HF xxv 249 (OED 5. To admit something claimed; to acknowledge, grant, concede; to accede to an opinion. 1643.. 1858—. So W S C U. It is doubtful whether M.T. meant the word in this, its "correct" sense, for it is his only ex.; it is perhaps better taken in the sense below)

allow, v. [AB³] *People allowed there'd be another trial to get me away from him* 1884 HF vi 40. *He allowed that I was his property, the captive of his spear* 1889 CY, foreword 21. *A lot of other animals...that Tom allowed was Jackals* 1894 TSA ix 355 (OED 7. To come to the conclusion, to form the opinion, or state as an opinion formed. In Eng. and Amer. dialects. 1580..1872, first Amer. ex.. OEDS Earlier U.S. exs. 1843.. A in S Wr B F Cl Th,1801 M H DN.II As.V.388, VII.90, IX.320. *Dial* in W C T)

allow, v. also '**low**. [AB¹E] *"Tuck his crap down... hit warn't no time for to sell, he say, so he fotch it back ag'in 'lowin' to wait tell fall"* 1873 GA i 21. *So he went away, but he said he 'lowed to "lay" for that boy* 1876 TS i 24. *The first fellow said he 'lowed to tell it to his old woman—she would think it was pretty good* 1884 HF vii 55. *"Pa, he 'lowed he'd break up and go down and live with Uncle Ben"* 1884 HF xx 190. *"So I 'lowed to drown myself en git out o' my troubles"* 1894 PW xviii 18. *"He allowed we would steal the bogus swag"* 1896 TDS iii 352. *"I've tucked mine [halo and wings] away in the cupboard, and I allow to let them lay there"* 1908 "Capt. Stormfield" 268 (S: To have in mind as an intention; propose, intend; used esp. in the southern U.S. So T DN.II. This sense not clearly distinguished from the one above in W, and not given at all in OED C U. Cf. OEDS: Also used in the aphetic form '*low*; so W S C)

all right, a. [B¹] *"I reckon it's all right—chance it, anyway"* 1880 TA iii 39 (Satisfactory, correct. This extremely common adj. phrase is not given in OED, although its adv. use is mentioned under Right, adv.; cf. below. Given in W S C)

all right, adv.phr. [B³] *"If you call this camping-out, all right—but it isn't the style I am accustomed to"* 1869 IA xli 436. *"Well, all right, have it your own way"* 1892 AmCl iv 53 (OED Right, adv. 15c. Used to express acquiescence or assent. 1837.. So W S C)

all-sorrowfully, adv. [B¹] *Then all-sorrowfully he made his last dispositions* 1902 "Belated Russian Passport" (1928) 187 (Comb. not in OED W S C; but cf. OED all-sufficiently, 1649)

all-the-time, a. [B¹] *He made preparations for that first and last and all-the-time duty* 1892 AmCl vii 71 (Comb. not in OED W S C; but cf. OED All-ages, All-or-nothing, a., 1843)

ally, sb. [?C] *Finally there was a quiet wedding at the Towers... The Sellerses were to go to England with their new allies for a brief visit* 1892 AmCl xxv 269 (OED 1. Connexion by marriage. *Obs. c*1400..1592. So W. Not *obs* in S C, and app. not so felt by M.T.)

almighty, adv. [?AB³] *You never saw a narrow-minded, self-conceited, almighty mean man in your life but he had stuck in one place ever since he was born* 1867 Speeches (1923) 30. *He talked freely with Philip about Ruth, an almighty fine girl, he said* 1873 GA xxxi 284 (OED 2. *slang.* Mighty, great, exceedingly. 1824..So W S. A in F Cl Th. Not in C)

almond-eyed, a. [B¹] *An unsuspecting, almond-eyed son of Confucius* 1870 SNO (1875) 118 (W: Having the somewhat almond-shaped eye characteristic of the Mongolian race. So S C U. Not in OED)

almshouse, sb. [?A] *Drag him to the rumshop...thence to the almshouse* 1883 LM xxxii 360 (OED 1440..1858. So W C U. A in S Cl T H)

along, adv. [AB²] *Along in the fall the invitation came* 1873 GA xxx 275. *Far along in the day, we saw one steamboat* 1883 LM xxviii 204. *My father was a blacksmith, my uncle was a horse-doctor, and I was both, along at first* 1889 CY, foreword 19. *He was along toward fifty* 1897 FE xxi 290. *I am well along, and my memory is not as good as it was* 1899 "My First Lie" (1900) 159 (OEDS 1b. Some way on in the progress of time. *U.S.* 1883.. All exs. from M.T. So C. Not in W S)

along, adv. also '**long**. [?AE] *"Come ahead on the starboard, straighten up and go 'long, never tremble"* 1909 ISD i 6 (OED 2. With vbs. of motion. 1300..So Wr U. A in B Cl. This use not in W S C. Cf. OED Headnote: Aphetic '*long*, 14th-17th c.)

along, adv. to be along. [?AB³] *"They're finishing one up, but they'll be along as soon as it's done"* 1892 AmCl xvi 162 (OEDS 2b. To come to a place, to call. Only ex. *U.S.* 1831. Phrase not in W S C)

along about, adv.phr. [?AB¹] *You start out with a friend along about eleven o'clock* 1870 SNO (1875) 82 (Phrase not in OED W S C)

alongside, adv. [B¹] *"I started for town in the wagon, and when I was halfway I saw a wagon coming...I says 'Hold on!' and it stopped alongside"* 1884 HF xxxiii 337 (Close by the side of. The gen. sense not in OED. Probably a hum. transf. from the *naut.* sense, OED a. Close to the side of the ship. 1707.. Given in W S C)

alongside of, prep. [?AB¹] *"Dat jist ain't nothin' at all, 'longside o' what I knows"* 1894 PW ix 549 (W: As compared with. *colloq.* This fig. sense not in OED S C)

alongside of, prep. [?AB¹] *He laid me out with a crusher alongside of the head* 1889 CY, foreword 20 (At or upon the side of. This sense not in OED W S C. An extension from OED b. Parallel to or close by the side of; side by side with. 1781..)

Alp-climber, sb. [B¹] *This was not a make-believe home of the Alp-climber* 1880 TA xxxvi 411 (Comb. not in OED W S C)

Alp-climbing, vbl.sb. [B¹] *Alp-climbing was a different thing from what I had supposed* 1880 TA xxxiv 379 (Comb. not in OED W S C)

alum-basket, sb. [?AB¹] *Pyramidal what-not in the corner, the shelves occupied chiefly with bric-a-brac of the period...three "alum" baskets of various colors—being skeleton-frame of wire, clothed on with cubes of crystallized alum in the rock-candy style—works of art which were achieved by the young ladies* 1883 LM xxxviii 404 (Comb. not in OED W S C)

alway, adv. [C] *'Twas his way, alway, to say one thing and mean another* 1881 PP xii 143. *We tarry not here alway, but must answer at the last day* 1889 CY xxxii 410

(OED. Surviving only in poetry or as an archaism. 885..1868. So W S C U)

ambition, v.trans. [?AC] *These have exalted him, enthused him, ambitioned him to higher and higher flights* 1906 "WIM" (1917) v 105 (OED 1. To move to ambition. *obs.* 1628, only ex. So W. The *trans.* sense not in S C. Cf. Ambition, v.intr., A in Cl Th,1688; not A in OED W S C)

ambuscade, v.trans. [B¹] *The band of toughs that ambuscade them* [policemen] *on lonely beats* 1892 AmCl iii 45 (W: To waylay. So S C U. The *trans.* sense not in OED; cf. OED *intr.* To lie in ambuscade. 1592..)

amen–corner, sb. [AB³] *Her old place in the amen-corner* 1894 PW viii 337 (OEDS That part of a meeting house occupied by persons who assist the preacher with occasional and irregular responses. *U.S.* 1868..So W S C Th.III T M DN.II,V)

American, a. [AB³] *Intensely and practically American by inhaled nationalism* 1892 AmCl vi 67. *There isn't a single human characteristic that can be safely labelled "American"...There is only one thing that can be called by the wide name "American". That is the national devotion to ice-water* 1895 "What Bourget Thinks" 52 (OEDS 2c. *U.S.* spec.1846..So W S C U Th)

American, sb. [AB³] *"Digger, Chinaman, Greaser, and American"* 1865 SS (1926) 161. *"I am a free-born sovereign, sir, an American"* 1869 IA xi 100. *"If I ain't an American there ain't any Americans, that's all!"* 1880 TA xx 192. *Whenever we meet as Northerners and Southerners, we part as Americans* c.1880 *M.T. the Letter-Writer* (1932) iii 43. *Dead Americans of distinction* 1892 AmCl ii 27 (OED 2. A native of America of European descent; *esp.* a citizen of the U.S. 1809, first ex. for "citizen of the U.S."..So W S C U Th)

American, sb. [AB³] *None of them ever thought of translating Obadiah's curse into classic American* 1883 LM App.C 610. See also *Blackfoot* 1906 (OEDS 5. American English. 1837.. So W S AS.IV.474. This sense not in CU)

American–Colonial–Dutch peddler – and – Salt Cod–McAllister, a. [B¹] *Four generations of American-Colonial-Dutch peddler-and-Salt Cod-McAllister nobility* 1892 AmCl v 58 (Hum. nonce comb.)

American creeper, sb. [AB³] *On the peak of the hill is an old arbor roofed with bark and covered with the vine you call the "American creeper"—its green is almost bloodied with red* (letter from Quarry Farm, near Elmira, N. Y., to Dr. John Brown of Edinburgh, Scotland) Sept. 4, 1874 *Letters* (1917) I xiii 226 (OEDS American 3. American ivy, the Virginia creeper. 1859. So B. Cf. OED Virginia creeper 1870 Dickens *E. Drood* ii, "The Virginia creeper on the cathedral wall has showered half its deep-red leaves down on the pavement." *American creeper* is identified in Wr as Canary Creeper, *Tropaeolum Canariense,* in Devonshire; this with its orange-colored flowers would be impossible here. Comb. not given in W S C U)

Americanism, sb. [A] *I have met many Americans there, and it has been very gratifying to me to find that nearly all preserved their Americanism. I have found they all like to see the Flag fly* 1893 *Speeches* (1910) 313 (OED 1. Attachment to, or political sympathy with, the U.S. OEDS Earlier U.S. ex. 1797..So W S C)

Americanism, sb. [AB³] *One very peculiar feature of Mr. Stanley's character is his indestructible Americanism ...He is a product of institutions which exist in no other country on earth* 1886 *Speeches* (1910) 158 (OED 2. Anything peculiar to, or characteristic of, the U.S. 1833..So W S C U T M)

Americanized, ppl.a. [A] *His audiences will be composed of foreigners who...have not yet had time to become Americanized* 1906 *Autob* (1924) II 292 (OEDS 2. 1797 ..So W S C U B F Th T M DN.VI)

American language, sb. [AB¹] *"I heard you fellows gassing away in the good old American language"* 1880 TA xx 192. *"Concerning the American Language"* (title) 1882. *I am speaking the American language* 1899 *Speeches* (1910) 403 (Comb. not in OED W C. Given in S M)

amidships, adv. to set amidships. [?AB¹] *The "Cyclone" was the sweetest thing to steer that ever walked the waters. Set her amidships, in a big river, and just let her go* 1883 LM xxiv 271 (S: On the fore-and-aft line; as, to put the helm amidships. So C. Phrase not in OED W. Cf. Lead, sb., To lay in the leads, below)

amorphous, a. [B¹] *He said that the emu had an amorphous appetite and would eat bricks* 1897 FE viii 101 (Hum. malapropism, for enormous?)

an, art. for a. [C] See *a,* art., above.

an, conj. [C] *"Marry", quoth the peasant, "an it please your worships"* 1869 IA xxi 212. *"Tom Canty, an it please thee, sir"* 1881 PP iii 40 (OED 2.=if. *arch* and *dial.* 1542..1859. So W S C Wr)

anacardium, sb. [A] See *afarabocca* 1894 (OED Anacard. 1. The Cashew-nut; the fruit of *Anacardium occidentale,* a West Indian tree. 1541..1847. So W S C)

anaconda, sb. [AB³] *These Britons were used to long fasts, and knew how to bear them; and also how to freight up...after the style of the Indian and the anaconda* 1889 CY xiii 153 (OED Specific name of a large S.Am. boa. 1836..So W S C U Th)

anchor out, v. [?AB¹] *He was planted solid as a church, and he couldn't no more stir than if he was anchored out* 1865 "Jumping Frog" (1875) 34. *There was a pig and a small donkey and a hen anchored out, close at hand, by cords to their legs* 1877 "Some Rambling Notes" iii 722 (Comb. with *out* not in OED W S C)

ancient, a. [C] *Some bundles of ancient and dirty straw* 1881 PP i27 (OED 1. Of or belonging to time past. *arch.* 1490..1793. Not *arch* in W S C U)

ancient, a. [C] *I touched an ancient common-looking man on the shoulder* 1889 CY ii 32 (OED 6. Of living beings: aged, old. *arch.* c1340..1849. So S C U. Not *arch* in W Wr)

and, conj. [AB¹] *"All of us so put to it for to get along and families so large"* 1873 GA ii 33. *"To think I went and whipped him for taking that cream, and I never to see him again in this world, poor abused boy!"* 1876 TS xv 131. *"How did you get hold of the raft again, Jim—did you catch her?" "How I gwyne to ketch her en I out in de woods?"* 1884 HF xviii 170. *"It ain't right for you to talk so to him, and him a stranger and so far from his people"* 1884 HF xxvi 263 (Wr 2: To introduce a nominative absolute, with ellipsis of the verb. *Scotch.* Cf. Poutsma, *Grammar of Late Modern English,* I.2.729. Noted as a feature of Kentucky folk-speech, AS.VI.272. This usage is not mentioned in OED W S C. It is explained in P.W. Joyce's *English as We Speak It in Ireland,* pp.33,34, as a literal translation in Irish English of a Gaelic idiom. A similar explanation is given in M p. 451n. of the Am. use of "the familiar Irish 'John is dead and him always so hearty'." But M.T.'s use of it affords no support to the theory of Irish origin)

and, conj. kings-and, deuces-and. [AB¹] *His last acts was to go his pile on "Kings-and"* (calculatin' to fill, but which he didn't fill), *when there was a "flush" out agin' him, and naterally, you see, he went under. And so he was cleaned out, as you may say, and he struck the home trail, cheerful but flat broke* 1867 "Answers to Correspondents" SNO (1875) 74. *"This poor old Richards has brought my judgment to shame. He is an honest man: I don't understand it but I acknowledge it. Yes, he saw my deuces-and with a straight flush, and by rights the pot is his. And it shall be a jack-pot, too, if I can manage it."* 1899 "MCH" (1900) 56 (Neither 'kings-*and*' nor 'deuces-*and*' is explained in any dictionary, and neither combination seems to be any longer in use. Present-day poker experts —those whom M.T. called the "poker-clergy"—so far as it has been possible to consult them, are far from agreed in their interpretations. 'Kings-*and*', in the passage cited, would clearly seem to mean two pair, one pair being kings, and the fifth card being discarded in the fallacious hope of improving the hand to a full house. By analogy, 'deuces-*and*' should be two pair also, one of the pairs being deuces. But it seems unlikely that a two-pair hand should ever have been named from the lower pair. Other interpretations are that 'deuces-*and*' means either a full house with three deuces in it, or else merely a pair of deuces with the other three cards valueless. If the last interpretation is the correct one, M.T. would seem to have intended a contrast, metaphorically, between the lowest possible combination in poker, a deuce pair, and the highest, a straight flush. The man who corrupted Hadleyburg really had nothing at all in his hand; he was "bluffing," as the devil usually is, and the stranger acknowledges that against the wiles of the devil honesty, the highest hand of all, will win every time if it is only played. With this emphatic use of *and* compare the common American tennis expressions "game-*and*" and "thirty-*and*" for what the British call "game-all" and "thirty-all"; also the still more familiar Americanism "ham-*and*" for a restaurant order of ham and eggs. It is surprising that no dictionary has as yet condescended to notice any of these expressions, or to comment upon this peculiar and growing American use of an emphasized *and*.)

angel-clay, sb. [B¹] *She seemed to me to be made out of angel-clay* 1897-8 *Autob* (1924) I 129 (Comb. not in OED W S C. This is perhaps M.T.'s happiest coinage)

angle, sb. [?AB¹] See *arrastre* 1909 (The *spec* mining sense seems not to be in OED W S C; but cf. OED Angle-meter: an instrument for measuring angles, esp. for ascertaining the dip of geological strata; a clinometer. No ex. So W S C)

angle-worm, sb. [?AB³] *They didn't do as horses or cats or angle-worms would have done* 1889 CY xxiii 268 (OED 1875, only ex. So W S C. A in Cl T DN.I)

angrily, a. [B¹] *The infliction on us of a placard fairly reeking with wretched English...e.g. Peter is described as "Argumenting in a threatening and angrily condition at Judas Iscariot"* 1889 IA xix 190 (Hum. alienism)

angular-limbed, ppl.a. [B¹] See *cypress-top* 1883 (Comb. not in OED W S C)

animal-looking, ppl.a. [B¹] *A party of black-robed, animal-looking Italian monks* 1869 IA liii 401 (Comb. not in OED W S C)

anisodactylous, a. [B¹] *I spoke right out and called him an anisodactylous plesiosaurian conchyliaceous ornithorhyncus. He lived only two hours* 1906 "Simplified Spelling" 220 (Nonsense use)

annex, sb. [B¹] *He often went out with me to the small lecture towns in the neighborhood of Boston...It took about a month to do these Boston annexes* 1898 *Autob* (1934) I 156 (Suburb; perhaps by extension from the sense in OED 4. A supplementary building; a wing. 1861..This sense not in OED W S C)

Annex, sb. [AB¹] *Mrs. Eddy's apocalyptic Annex* 1902 "Chr. Sc." 760 ("Key to the Scriptures," a sort of appendix to *Science and Health*. This sense not in OED W S C. The Christian Science use may have been borrowed from the Episcopalian. Cf. C: The Book Annexed: a book containing the alterations in the American Book of Common Prayer of the Protestant Episcopal Church, proposed in 1880)

Annex-polisher, sb. [AB¹] *She reserves the authority to make a Reader fill any office connected with a Science Church—advertising agent, Annex-polisher, leader of the choir* 1907 CS II vii 187 (Hum. nonce comb., from above)

annexation, sb. [?AB¹] *Forcible annexation would be "criminal aggression"* 1901 "To the Person Sitting in Darkness" 169 (A in B: In the restricted sense of the addition of new territory to that of the U.S., and often with the accessory idea of unlawful acquisition. The *spec* Am. use of the word is not mentioned in OED W S C)

Annual-Veteran-who-has-Voted-for-Every-President-from-Washington-down-and-Walked-to-the-Polls-Yesterday-with-as-Bright-an-Eye-and-as-firm-a-Step-as-Ever, sb. [B¹] 1883 LM lx 584 (Hum. nonce comb.)

annunciator, sb. [AB¹] *The burglar-alarm let fly about two o'clock. I turned up the gas, looked at the annunciator, and turned off the alarm* 1906 *Autob* (1934) II 78 (A in F: A word used in connection with electrical apparatus; a warning-bell. Not A in C. This *spec* sense not in OED W S)

A No.1, a. [AB³] *Tons of A No.1, fourth-proof, hard-boiled, hide-bound grammar* 1886 *Speeches* (1923) 137 (OED A IV 2. *fig.*, familiar and savoring of commercial phraseology: *A1*, or in the U.S. *A No.1*, used adjectively for 'prime, first-class.' 1851..So W S C U B F Cl M H. M.T. also uses the less distinctively Am. form *A1*; cf. *He ranked A1* 1875 OTM 571. *The A1 Barber Shop* 1875 SNO 139)

anonymous, a. [B¹] *So Tom said, " Now for the non-namous letters." "What's them?" I says. "Warnings to the people that something is up"* 1884 HF xxxix 399 (Hum. malapropism)

ant-deposit, sb. [B¹] *The exactest simile I can devise is to compare these villages to ant-deposits of granulated dirt* 1880 TA xxviii 288 (Comb. not in OED W S C)

ante, v. [AB³] *Smiley would ante up money on him as long as he had a red* 1865 "Jumping Frog" (1875) 30. *"I'd bet a hundred dollars he will ante his way right into the United States Senate when his territory comes in. He's got the cheek for it."* 1873 GA xiii 124. See also *buck, pass the* 1872, 1902 (OEDS *U.S.* To bet, to stake; to pay. 1845.. So W S C B F Cl Th T M DN.III)

antelope, sb. [AB¹] See *buffalo* 1869. *We had breakfast—fresh antelope steaks* 1872 RI xii 105 (The American antelope or *Antilocapra*, otherwise known as the cabrit or pronghorn. So W S C. This sense not in OED)

anthropomorphous, a. [B¹] *" You can see how searchingly and co-ordinately interdependent and anthropomorphous it [Christian Science] all is"* 1899 "Chr. Sc. and the Book" 588 (Nonsense use?)

anti-, prefix. [?AB³] *Edward, as a boy, had interested himself in penny missionary affairs, anti-tobacco organizations, anti-profanity associations* 1880 "Edward Mills" 227. *The anti-temperance mass-meeting* 1882 SWE 123. *There was a strong rum party and a strong anti-rum party... Half of the company was composed of rummies and the other half of anti-rummies* 1894 PW xi 556. *The teetotalers and the anti-teetotalers* 1894 TET iv 335. *The price per vote was paid in doughnuts. Some of us organized a third party. Those who didn't like us called us the Anti-Doughnut party...I was an Anti-Doughnut in my boyhood, and I'm an Anti-Doughnut still. The modern designation is Mugwump* 1901 *Speeches* (1910) 120. *Prohibition and anti-prohibition* 1909 ISD xi 128 (OED 4. Attrib. phrases, consisting of *anti-* governing a sb.. Their widely extended modern use seems partly the result of an independent analysis of the phrase...*anti-* may here be considered as a naturalized preposition, equivalent to *against*. 1837..Cf. also OED 8. Abstract substantives, formed on...the phrases in 4. 1846.. Of the *spec* combs. used by M.T., OED has only *anti-temperance* 1842 and *anti-tobacco* 1864. So W, which gives also *anti-prohibition*. C gives only *anti-prohibition*. Cf. also OED *anti-teetotalism* 1856. None of them are given in S U. Cf. M: "Words in *anti-* are numerous in English, but they seem to be even more numerous in American, esp. in the field of politics. For a full discussion of the notable Am. expansion of this prefix, see A.W.Read in AS.VII.3.14f.)

antiphonal, a. [B¹] *He said those skeletons were two million years old, which astonished her and made her Kentucky pretensions look small and pretty antiphonal, not to say oblique* 1906 "Horse's Tale" 328 (Nonsense use)

any, adv. [AB³] *Palestine has not changed any since those days* 1869 IA xlviii 504. See also *richen* 1883 (OEDS At all. *dial* and *U.S.* 1817..So F Cl Th T M H. Not A in W S C Wr)

anyways, adv. [?AB²] *"Anyways, I've got my opinion"* 1865 "Jumping Frog" (1875) 33 (OED 2. *dial* or *illiterate.* 1865, only ex. So W S C Wr. A in Th,1848 M DN. III AS.V.207, Ozarks; XI.352, e.Texas)

anywheres, adv. [AB¹] *If he even saw a straddle-bug start to go anywheres..."* 1865 "Jumping Frog" (1875) 31. See also *quality* 1884 (A in Th,1856 Th.III,1815 M DN.III AS.XI.352. Not A in W S. Not in OED C)

apart, adv. [C] *"But that is apart; lead on!"* 1881 PP xvii 204 (OED 5. Aside, away from consideration. *arch.* 1477..1827. Not *arch* in W S C U)

apocryphal, a. [B¹] *He said he could furnish spiral-twist* [lightning-rods] *that would stop a streak of lightning at any time and "render its further progress apocryphal"* 1870 SNO (1875) 21 (Nonsense use)

apodictical, a. [?C] *"This Apodictical Principle is the absolute Principle of Scientific Mind-Healing"* 1899 "Chr. Sc. and the Book" 589 (OED *arch.* Of apodictic nature; absolutely demonstrable. *a*1638..1860. Or intended as a hum. malapropism? Not *arch* in W S C U)

apparel, v. [C] *"Now I will apparel him, feed him"* 1881 PP xiii 154 (OED *arch.* 5. 1362..1832. Not *arch* in W S C U)

appendix–basket, sb.]B¹]*Some of his best stock is hid in an appendix-basket behind the door* 1894 "Defence of Harriet Shelley" 111 (Hum. nonce comb.)

appetite–cure, sb. [B¹] *"At the Appetite-Cure"* (title) 1898 (1900) 151. *I was on my way back to Vienna from the Appetite-Cure in the mountains* 1899 "Chr. Sc." 585 (Hum. nonce comb.)

apple–paring, sb. [?AB¹] *If you will throw a long, pliant apple-paring over your shoulder, it will pretty fairly shape itself into an average section of the Mississippi* 1875 OTM 192 (A paring or peeling from an apple. Comb. not in OED W S C; but cf. OED Apple-paring 1879, in different sense, and Paring 3. A shaving 1382..)

apprehend, v. [B¹] *During three months he not has nothing done but to him apprehend to jump* ['Retranslated' from the French *apprendre;* the original version of the "Jumping Frog" has *"He never done nothing for three months but learn that frog to jump"*] 1875 SNO 41 (Hum. alienism)

Arabian–Nighty, a. [B¹] *How strange and remote and Arabian-Nighty it all seems!* 1901 "To My Missionary Critics" 530 (Hum. nonce comb.)

arcana, sb.sing. [E] *"There it is—the whole sublime Arcana of Christian Science in a nutshell"* 1899 "Chr. Sc. and the Book" 587 (Apparently intended as a sing. form here. Cf. OED: In 17th-18th c. the pl. form *arcana* was occas. treated as sing., with pl. *arcanas.* This usage not in W S C)

archipelagoed, ppl.a. [B²] *A mighty porterhouse steak ...archipelagoed with mushrooms* 1880 TA xlix 572 (OEDS 1880, this quot. Not in W S C)

arctic, sb. [AB²] *He shook the snow of his native city from his arctics* 1878 "Loves of Alonzo and Rosannah" 327. *I found I had left my arctics in the* [theater] *box... He was back with the shoes in three minutes...he accomplished that miracle by saying, "Way, gentlemen, please—coming to fetch Mr. Corbett's overshoes"* 1894 *Letters* (1917) II xxxiv 604. *"Don't wear your arctics in the White House"* 1906 Autob (1924) II 154 (OEDS 2. *U.S.* 1883.. So SF Cl T H DN.I. Not in W C)

argot, sb. [B³] *A man can't handle glibly and easily and comfortably and successfully the argot of a trade at which he has not served* 1909 ISD i 15 (OED 1860..So W S C U)

argument, v. [B¹] See *angrily,* a. 1869 (Hum. alienism)

aristocratic, a. [?AB³] *Rowena-Ivanhoe College is the selectest and most aristocratic seat of learning for young ladies in our country* 1892 AmCl iv 53 (OED 2. Grand, stylish. 1845..So W S C U. A in B F DN.III)

aristocratic-looking, a. [?AB¹] *Most aristocratic-looking white man that ever lived* 1883 LM xlvii 474 (Comb. not in OED W S C. Cf. above)

ark, sb. [AB³] *A settler's scow or ark which is coming up the stream* 1895 "Cooper's Literary Offences" 6. *Drifting arks and stone-boats* 1898 MS (1916) i 1 (OED 4. *spec* in U S., a large flat-bottomed boat formerly used on rivers. 1882, only Am. ex. Cf. B: These boats first mentioned in 1799. So W S C F Cl Th,1802)

Arkansaw, sb. [AE] *Arkansaw would certainly have hanged Baker* 1880 TA xlvii 545. See *corpse-maker* 1883. *"He's the best-naturedest old fool in Arkansaw"* 1884 HF xxi 213 (This sp. not in OED W S C. For the pron., see M)

arm–loop, sb. [?AB¹] *We got down our coats from the armloops where they had been swinging all day* 1872 RI iv 37. *He jumped into the hack...passed his arms through the loops and hung on...he hung tight to the arm-loops* 1893 TSA i 22 (Comb. not in OED W S C)

armory, sb. [AB³] *The Rock Island establishment is a national armory and arsenal* 1883 LM lviii 567 (OED 5. *U.S.* 1841..So W S C. Not A in U)

around, adv. [AB³] *The owner was around—and not only around, but with his friends around also* 1869 IA xxxii 350. *She artlessly said that she would be "around" when school let out* 1876 TS xviii 156. See *artificial-flower* 1883. *Howells, Lowell, Holmes, Harte...all common everyday names in those people's habitat, names commonly borne by everybody around* 1902 M.T. the Letter Writer (1932) ii 25 (OED 5b. *U.S.* Somewhere near. OEDS 1828..So W S C U B F Cl T DN.III)

around, adv. [?AB¹] *It was around, this long time, that the concern was tottering* 1894 *Letters* (1917) II xxxiv 614 (Reported, generally said. This sense not in OED W S C; but cf. OEDS quot.1873: "It is told around for a fact that I could tell great confessions," *U.S.*)

around about, adv.phr. [?AB¹] *Hadleyburg was the most honest and upright town in all the region around about* 1899 "MCH" (1900) 1 (Comb. not in OED W S C. Given in Wr)

arrastre, sb. Spelled **arastra.** [?AB³E] *I have been a quartz miner in the silver regions... I know all the palaver of that business; I know all about discovery claims and the subordinate claims; I know all about lodes, ledges, outcroppings, dips, spurs, angles, shafts, drifts, inclines, levels, tunnels, air-shafts, "horses," clay casings, granite casings; quartz mills and their batteries; arrastras, and how to charge them with quicksilver and sulphate of copper; and how to clean them up, and how to reduce the resulting amalgam in the retorts, and how to cast the bullion into pigs; and finally I know how to screen tailings...I know the argot of the quartz-mining and milling industry familiarly* 1909 ISD vii 74 (OED An apparatus for grinding and mixing ores. 1881..So W. A in S C B F Cl AS.V.145. The sp. *arastra* not in OED, but given in all Am. dicts.)

arrest, v. [B¹?C] *A stranger at the camp him arrested with his box* ["Retranslated" from the French *arrêter;* the original version of the "Jumping Frog" has *"A stranger in the camp come acrost him with his box"*] 1875 SNO 41 (Hum. alienism. M.T. was hardly aware that the Eng. word once had the same meaning: OED 5a. To cause a person to stop. *Obs* in literal sense since 1600. So W. This sense not in S C)

arriving, ppl.a. [B¹] *No answer to that telegram; no arriving daughter* 1892 AmCl v 57 (This use not in OED W S C. Cf. OED vbl.sb. 1375..)

art–architecture, sb. [B¹] *I am speaking of art-architecture...there is no more architecture of that breed discoverable in this long stretch of ugly and ornamentless three-storied house front than there is about a rope walk or a bowling alley* 1904 *Autob* (1924) I 197 (Comb. not in OED W S C. Cf. OED Art-furniture, 1870)

art–critic, sb. [B²] *The government appointed a commission of art-critics* 1869 SNO (1875) 226 (OED 1879. Comb. not in W S C)

Arthurdom, sb. [B¹] *A dollar and a half apiece...was the price of a blooded race-horse in Arthurdom* 1889 CY xxii 280 (Not in OED W S C. Coined on the model of Christendom, heathendom, etc.)

article, sb. [?AB¹] *Weather is a literary specialty, and no untrained hand can turn out a good article of it* 1892 AmCl,pref. *Till these practically dead people are replaced with the genuine article...do.* xxv 272. *Supply a good business article of climate* do. xxv 272 (C: A particular immaterial thing; a matter. This sense not in OED W S. Cf. OED 14. A commodity; a piece of goods or property; a thing material. 1804.. Cf. also Wr: A term of contempt for an inferior or worthless person or thing. A characteristically Am. twist of meaning)

artificial–flower, a. [B¹] *The trouble with the Southern reporter is—Women...His mind totters, he becomes flowery and idiotic...He knows well enough how to handle a pen when the women are not around to give him the artificial-flower complaint* 1883 LM xlv 461 (Hum. nonce comb.)

artist, sb. [?AC] *"Merlin don't amount to shucks, as a magician... He oughtn't to set up for an expert—anyway not where there's a real artist"* 1889 CY v 64 (OED 4a. A skilled performer, a proficient. *Obs.* 1594..1793. So W C U. Not *obs* in S)

ary, a. [AB¹] *That feller 'd offer to bet on it, and take ary side you please* 1865 "Jumping Frog" (1875) 31 (C: Any; a modification of *e'er a* or *ever a. Prov. Eng.* and *U.S.* So Wr Th,1852 T M DN.I,II,IV,V AS.III.8, Ozarks; V.268; VI.230; VII.90. Not A in W S. This form not in OED; but cf. OED Ever, adv. 8a. Ever a, e'er a, now vulgar. Cf. also OED Arrow: vulgar corruption of e'er a, ever a. 1749..)

as, conj. [?AC] *"Did you ever see us before?" "No sah; not as I knows on"* 1884 HF xxxiv 353 (OED 28. Introducing a noun sentence, after *say,know,think,etc. Obs* and replaced by *that,* but still common in *dial.* 1483..1856. So W Wr. A in C: *colloq* New England. A in B DN.III. This use not in S)

as, adv. [?AB²] *"Shucks, I'll be just as careful. Now lemme try"* 1876 TS ii 30. *He would sit up that night till the town was as still and dark, and then he would sneak there* 1893 TSA i 20 (OED 5c. As can be imagined, as may be, as possible; cf. Latin *quam* in *quam maximum.* No exs. This use not in W S C. It may be noted that when TSA was reprinted in book form in 1894, the *as* here was omitted)

asbestos, sb. [C] *What I cannot help wishing is, that Adam and Eve had been postponed, and Martin Luther and Joan of Arc put in their place—that splendid pair equipped with temperaments not made of butter, but of asbestos* 1910 "Turning Point of My Life" (1917) 139 (OED 1. A fabulous stone, the heat of which, when once kindled, was alleged to be unquenchable. *Obs.* 1387.. 1750. So S C. This sense not in W. It is evident from the context that what M.T. here has in mind is not the familiar incombustible mineral, OED 3, but the little known unquenchable stone—however he had heard of it!)

ascensionist, sb. [AB¹] *Twenty-five years ago, a multitude of people in America put on their ascension robes... and made ready to fly up into heaven at the first blast of the trumpet. But the angel did not blow it. Miller's resurrection day was a failure. The Millerites were disgusted... The ascensionists came down from the mountain* 1869 IA xxxix 416 (A Millerite; a believer in the doctrines of William Miller (died 1849), an American preacher who interpreted the Scriptures as foretelling the early coming of Christ and the end of the world. This *spec* sense not in OED W S C)

ascension robe, sb. [AB¹] See *ascensionist* 1869. (Cf. above. Comb. not in OED W S C)

ash–cake, sb. [AB³] *Recipe for an Ash-Cake...Rake away a place among the embers, lay it there, and cover it an inch deep with hot ashes. When it is done, remove it; blow off all the ashes but one layer; butter that one and eat...It has been noticed that tramps never return for another ash-cake* 1880 TA xlix 575 (OED *U.S.* A cake baked in or under the ashes of a fire. 1824.. So B F Cl Th T DN.II,III. Not A in W S C Wr)

ash–cat, sb. [?AB¹] *They* [Italian women] *sit in the alleys and nurse their cubs. They nurse one ash-cat at a time, and the others scratch their backs against the doorpost and are happy* 1869 IA xxv 262. *The poor little ash-cat was already more wonted to his strange garret than a mature person could have become in a full month* 1881 PP xvi 195 (A ragamuffin; a child of the slums. This sense not in OED W S C. Cf. S: Prov. Eng., One who sits habitually by the fire; a lazy person; dreamer. So Wr)

ash–hopper, sb. [AB³] *There was an ash-hopper by the fence, and an iron pot, for soap-boiling* 1873 GA i 18. *"I went around and clumb over the back stile by the ash-hopper"* 1884 HF xxxii 329 (OEDS 8b. *U.S.* A lye cask, resembling a hopper in a mill. 1843.. So W S B F Cl. Not in C)

ash–pile, sb. [B¹] *The houses had little gardens around them, but they didn't seem to raise hardly anything in them but jimpson-weeds, and sun-flowers, and ash-piles* 1884 HF xxi 209. *A pile of ashes is all that's left...Round that ash-pile glowing, In brooks their tears keep flowing* [German, ein Häuflein Asche] 1891 *Slovenly Peter* (1935) 7 (Comb. not in OED S C. Given in W)

asphalt, sb. to travel on asphalt. [?AB¹] *"Mary was herself not unlearned in the lore of pain"—meaning by that that she had not always travelled on asphalt* 1894 "Defence of Harriet Shelley" 109 (Apparently, to be in comfortable circumstance; to live amid prosperous surroundings, where the streets are paved with asphalt. Cf. below. Phrase not in OED W S C)

asphaltum–paved, ppl.a. [B¹] *A long walk through smooth, asphaltum-paved streets...brought us at last to the principal thoroughfare* 1869 IA x 96 (Comb. not in OED W S C)

ass, sb. [?A ?C] *"Taking you by and large, you do seem to be more different kinds of an ass than any creature I ever saw"* 1875 OTM 285. *Everybody went on making a wonderful to-do over that ass, as if he had done something great* 1875 OTM 570. See *chucklehead* 1883. *This armor-plated ass* 1889 CY ix 111. *"Have you been training with that ass again—that radical, if you prefer the term, though the words are synonymous?"* 1892 AmCl i 21. *The average man is what his environment and his superstitions have made him; and their function is to make him an ass* 1898 "At the Appetite Cure" (1900) 160 (OED 2. An ignorant fellow, a perverse fool, a conceited dolt. Now disused in polite literature and speech. A in M. Not *obs* nor A in W S C U. In view of M.T.'s predilection for the word, the OED dictum about its disuse in "polite" literature seems exaggerated. But perhaps his writing is not to be called "polite" in the OED sense! Cf. also *assification* and *assified,* below)

assay–office, sb. [AB¹] *The assay-offices of Nevada* 1869 IA xviii 179 (S: *U.S.* A laboratory for examining ores. Not A in W C. Not in OED)

assemble, v. [B¹] See *comp*, sb. 1909 (Not in OED W S C in this *spec* printers' sense)

assertive, a. [B¹] *He examined his clothes. They were rather assertive, it seemed to him* 1892 AmCl vii 75 (Obtrusive, 'loud'. This sense not in OED W S C)

assification, sb. [?AB¹] *He can properly display the assification of the whole system* 1897 FE lxi 607 (Asininity, stupidity. Not in OED W S C)

assified, ppl.a. [?AB¹] *Often a quite assified remark becomes sanctified by use and petrified by custom* 1902 "Does the Race of Man Love a Lord?" 433 (Asinine, senseless. Not in OED W S C. Cf. OED Assify, v. To make an ass of. 1804, only ex.; so W S)

Association, sb. [AB¹] *She organized her first Christian Science "Association"... The first of these* [subsequent] *moves was to aggrandize the "Association" to a "Church"* ... *The former name suggested nothing, invited no remark, no criticism, no hostility; the new usage invited them all* 1907 CS II vi 153 (This *spec* use for the early Christian Science organization is not given in OED W S C. Cf. W S C for its use among Congregationalists, Baptists, and Evangelicals. In view of this widespread American ecclesiastical significance of the word, with which M.T. may have been unfamiliar, his assertion that it "suggested nothing" is too strongly put)

assoil, v. [C] *"By the slaughtered body of St. Parley, whom God assoil!"* 1872 RI xv 123 (OED 1. *arch.* 1297.. 1840. So W C U. Not *arch* in S)

asteroid, sb. [B³] *Often a hen who has merely laid an egg cackles as if she had laid an asteroid* 1897 FE v 97 (OED 1. 1802..So W S C U)

at, prep. [A] *Laura liked to hear about life at the East* 1873 GA xix 183 (OEDS Used with the cardinal points of the compass, to indicate parts of the country. *U.S.* 1646..So B Cl AS.VII.154. This use not in W S C)

at, prep. **where...at**. [AB³] *A Southerner talks music...But there are some infelicities, such as...the addition of an "at" where it isn't needed... You hear gentlemen say, "Where have you been at?" And here is the aggravated form—heard a ragged street Arab say it to a comrade: "I was a-askin' Tom whah you was a-sett'n' at"* 1883 LM xliv 449. *It is time to foot up again and "see where we are at"* 1907 CS II vii 175 (OEDS 1d. Used superfluously after *where*. *U.S.* 1859..So Wr B Cl T M H DN.II AS.III.11, Ozarks; VII.19,387. S: *colloq*, Southern U.S. W: *colloq*. Not in C)

at, prep. **to be at oneself**. [AB¹] *Joan was always at herself* 1895 JA II iv 93. *Tom Sawyer was the levelest head I ever see, and always at himself and ready for anything you might spring on him* 1896 TSD i 345. *He was not entirely at himself when he told that one* 1899 "My First Lie" (1900) 167 (A in DN.I: To be in a condition equal to the performance of a task; s.Ill., s.e.Mo., e.Ala. Cf. Wr: Sound, healthy in mind and body. This phrase not in OED W S C)

at, prep. **at that**. [AB¹] *It was all downhill, too, and very muddy at that* 1880 TA xlii 489 (Into the bargain; in addition, as well. A in B F Cl Th,1830 T. Not A in W S. Phrase not in OED C)

at, prep. [?AB¹] *"Do you know what the margins would foot up, to buy it at sixty days?"* 1897 FE xiii 145 (With an agreement or contract to complete the transaction in the specified time. This frequent commercial use not in OED W S C)

Athenaeum, sb. [?AB³] *A great mass-meeting was to be held on a certain day in the new Athenaeum* [at Keokuk, Iowa, in 1861] 1883 LM lvii 557 (OED 2b. A building or large room in which books, magazines, and newspapers are kept for the use of members or of the public; a library; a reading-room. 1822, only ex. U.S. Not A in W C. This sense not in S)

atomy, a. [B¹] *Alps which...had little atomy Swiss homes perched upon grassy benches along their mist-dimmed heights* 1880 TA xxxv 398 (Not in OED W S C as adj. Cf. OED Atomy, sb. 1. An atom, mote. 1595..)

atreous, a. [B¹] *At the time it* [the solution] *seemed luminous with intelligence. She added that it was "quite atreous"... The words seemed to mean something, I do not know why* 1912 "My Platonic Sweetheart" (1922) 20 (A "dream-word", not in any dictionary)

atrocious, a. [B²] *The atrocious name grated harshly on my ear* 1869 IA xiii 130. *A peculiarly atrocious chromo* 1892 AmCl iii 47 (OED 3. *colloq*. Very bad, execrable. *Modern*. No ex. So W S C U)

atrocity, sb. [B²] *He tendered me a toothwash atrocity of his own invention* 1871 SNO (1875) 261 (OED 4. *colloq*. A very bad blunder, violation of taste, etc. 1878, only ex. So W S C)

attire, v. [C] *"Who helpeth them undress at night? who attireth them when they rise?"* 1881 PP iii 42 (OED 3b. Now only *literary*. *c*1350..1859. So W S C U)

attitudinizing, ppl.a. [?AB³] *The concert was one of those fragmentary drearinesses that people endure because they are fashionable...the attitudinizing tenor, with his languishing "Oh, Summer Night"* 1873 GA xxxi 285 (OED 1853..So W S C. A in B F T)

Attorney-General, sb. [AB¹] See *claim-owner* 1861 (A legal official of a State, who is empowered to act in all cases in which the State is a party. So W C H. The only Am. sense given in OED S is the national one, used as a name of a member of the President's cabinet)

attractive, sb. [C] *Under the head of "Attractives" he introduces Paracelsus, who tells of a nameless "Specific"* 1890 "Majestic Literary Fossil" 441 (OED 1. *Med*. A 'drawing' medicament. *Obs*. 1607..1786. So W. Not in S C)

auction-block, sb. [?AB¹] *The Hawkins hearts had been torn to see Uncle Dan'l and his wife pass from the auction-block into the hands of a negro-trader* 1873 GA vii 78. *The auction-block came into my personal experience* 1889 CY xxxiv 448 (The block from which slaves were auctioned. Comb. not in OED W S C. Cf. OED Auction-pulpit)

audience-room, sb. [?AB¹] *The* [Indian] *chief's house contained an audience-room forty feet square* 1883 LM ii 39 (Comb. not in OED W S C. Cf. OED Audience-chamber, Audience-hall)

Aunt, sb. [AB³] *'Aunt Rachel' was sitting respectfully below our level, on the steps—for she was our servant, and colored* 1874 SNO (1875) 202. *In the little log cabin lived a bedridden white-headed slave woman...We called her "Aunt" Hannah, Southern fashion* 1897-8 *Autob* (1924) I 99 (OEDS 1c. *U.S.* 1835..So W S F Cl DN.II. This sense not in C)

auntie, sb. [AB¹] *At the door stood a negress with a bright turban on her head, to whom Philip called: "Can you tell me, auntie, how far it is to the town of Magnolia?"* 1873 GA xvi 156 (W: Often used in the southern U.S. of an aged negro woman. So S Cl Th,1852 DN.III. This *spec* sense not in OED C)

authentic, sb. [AB¹] *Now we'll soon see who's the Claimant and who's the Authentic* 1892 AmCl xxiv 254 (The rightful or genuine owner. Not in OED W S C with ref. to a person. Cf. S: A genuine or authoritative book, as distinguished from a counterfeit or apocryphal one)

authoress, sb. [?A] *The authoress quite innocently and unconsciously gives the whole business away* 1906 "WIM" (1917) 33 (OED Now used only when sex is purposely emphasized. 1478..1865. So W S C U. A in F T)

authoring, vbl.sb. [?A] *Their authorship was claimed by most of the grown-up people who were alive at the time, and every claimant had one plausible argument in his favor, at least—to wit, he could have done the authoring* 1909 ISD ix 104 (OED 1742, only ex. Not in W S C. Cf. author, v., A in M)

autumn-butter, sb. [B¹] *Whenever we come upon one of these intensely right words in a book or a newspaper, the resulting effect is physical as well as spiritual...it tingles exquisitely around through the walls of the mouth, and tastes as tart and crisp and good as the autumn-butter that* *creams the sumac-berry* 1906 "Howells" (1917) 229 (Comb. not in OED W S C. Doubtless a reminiscence of M.T.'s boyhood days in Missouri. Some of the botanists consulted think he was referring to the Smooth Sumach (*Rhus glabra*) found everywhere in the state, which bears berry-like drupes in panicles that in autumn are clothed with crimson hair yielding a slight waxy exudate. Three of the highest botanical authorities, however, Professors Aven Nelson of the University of Wyoming, Fred A. Barkley of Montana State University, and William J. Robbins of the University of Missouri, think the species of sumach that M.T. had in mind was *Rhus trilobata*, also known as squawbush or skunkbush, which is equally common in the Mississippi Valley states. The berries of this variety are coated with a much denser pubescence or pulp, which is tan in color. Boys eat the fruit of both for their pleasantly acid taste, and they are even said sometimes to have been made into jelly. In any event, M.T.'s name is probably of his own coinage in later life, for 'autumn' is altogether a book-word in Missouri)

avalanche, v. [B²] *Every time we avalanched from one end of the stage to the other, the Unabridged Dictionary would come too* 1872 RI iv 38 (OEDS 1897..So W. Not in S C)

aventre, v. [C] *He dressed his shield, and they aventred their spears* 1889 CY xv 80 (OED *Obs.* 1557..1596. So W S C)

avenue, sb. [A] *That superb avenue bordered with patrician mansions* 1869 IA xi 100. *By and by the procession went filling down the steep descent of the main avenue* 1876 TS xxix 219 (OED 4. A fine wide street; used esp. in the U.S. OEDS 1780..Cf. S: Used often in the U.S. without reference to the character of the street. So C H. Not A in W)

average, v.trans. [?AB³] *They measure a stranger by the eye, and begin to average him as soon as he gets into their camp* 1866 *Speeches* (1923) 8. *I remonstrated against sending this note, because it was so mixed up that the landlord would never be able to make head or tail of it; but Blucher said he guessed the old man could read the French of it and average the rest* 1869 IA xix 189. *The blacksmith averaged the stalwart soldier at a glance* 1881 PP xxii 276 (OED 1. To estimate, form an opinion as to. 1831..This sense not in W S C)

average, v.intr. [?AB³] *I like my relative Jim very much, and as a Clemens he averages away up* 1899 *M.T. the Letter Writer* (1932) vi 90 (OED 2. To average oneself at, to amount to. 1821..This sense not in W S C)

awarity, sb. [B¹] *His brush pawed away at the canvas, almost without his awarity—awarity, in this sense, being the sense of being aware, though disputed by some authorities* 1892 AmCl xx 206 (Nonce word)

away, adv. [AB²] *Away in the middle of the day* 1869 IA lii 556. *Within another month I was away down, down, down, supplicating with tears and anguish* 1892 AmCl ii 31. *Away late that night we were coming up town* 1893 "Traveling with a Reformer" (1900) 352. *Then No. 4 jumped for the boat, and fell into the water away astern* 1895 "Cooper's Literary Offences" 7. *He must rise away above that* 1899 "My Debut" (1900) 70. See also *average,* v. 1899; *cañon* 1902; *chimney* 1906 (OEDS 11b. Used with intensive force, chiefly with advs. as *away back, down, up,* etc.=far. *U.S.* 1873..So Wr M H. Not A in W S C)

awe-compelling, ppl.a. [B¹] *This awe-compelling miracle* 1880 TA xliii 503. *My awe-compelling fireworks* 1889 CY xiv 166. *The old man's awe-compelling words and manner* 1892 AmCl xix 193 (Comb. not in OED S C. Given in W)

awful, a. [?AB³] See *slush* 1869. *"It's an awful distance—ten or twelve hundred mile"* 1873 GA xxxiii 307. *His father would curse him and thrash him first, and... the awful grandmother would do it all over again and improve on it* 1881 PP ii 29. *It was awful—awfuler than you can ever imagine* 1889 CY xliv 574 (OED 4. Frightful, monstrous, and hence as a mere intensive deriving its sense from the context. 1834..So W S C. A in B F Cl DN.III)

awful, adv. [?AB³] *"She talks awful, but talk don't hurt"* 1876 TS ii 13. *"Aunt Polly is awful particular about this fence"* do. ii 30. *"It's awful undermining to the intellect, German is"* 1880 TA xxvii 281. *"He's English—they're awful particular"* 1892 AmCl xi 107 (OEDS 4b. Awfully. *slang.* 1846.. So W S C. A in B F Cl DN.II)

awning-post, sb. [B¹] *There was as many as one loafer leaning up against every awning-post* 1884 HF xxi 209 (Comb. not in OED W S C)

ax, v. for **ask** [?AE] *"Mars Tom gwine to ax me to whitewash"* 1876 TS ii 27 (OED Down to nearly 1600 the regular lit. form, and still used everywhere in *dial.* So W S C Wr. A in B F Cl M DN.V AS.IV.474, V.206, Ozarks)

axle-grease, sb. [B¹] *"The idea!...This illiterate hostler, with his skull full of axle-grease.."* 1900 *Autob* (1924) I 179 (Comb. not in OED S C. Given in W)

axman, sb. [A] *The gay fellow...was the admiration of the camp servants, axmen, teamsters, and cooks* 1873 GA xvii 159 (OEDS 1. *U.S.* 1671..So Th. Not A in W S C)

ayah, sb. [B¹] *I shall come riding my ayah with his tusks adorned with silver bells and ribbons* 1895 *Letters* (1917) II xxxv 629 (Hum. malapropism)

Aztec, sb. [A] *"America was occupied a billion years and more, by the Injuns and Aztecs"* 1908 "Capt. Stormfield" 273 (OEDS 1787..So W S C)

azure, a. [D] See *coat-of-arms* 1883 (OED 3. *Heraldry.* The blue color in coats of arms. a1330..1838—. So W S C U)

baby-act, sb. **to read the baby-act.** [AB¹] *He said the Jew was pushing the Christian to the wall all along the line...In fierce language he demanded the expulsion of the Jews. When politicians come out without a blush and read the baby-act in this frank way, unrebuked, it is a very good indication that they have a market back of them* 1899 "Concerning the Jews" (1900) 268 (To use cowardly or unworthy tactics, behave childishly; in recent phraseology, to show the "inferiority complex." Cf. C: A colloquial name for the legal defence of infancy; hence *to plead the baby-act*; to attempt to excuse excessive or feigned ignorance or stupidity on the ground of inexperience. So W S: *colloq.* A in Th.III, 1873. This *fig* extension of meaning not in OED; but cf. OEDS Baby act. *U.S.* An act or statute for the protection of minors. 1873..)

baby-wagon, sb. [?AB¹] *In front of Wilson's porch stood Roxy, with a...baby-wagon* 1894 PW ii 31 (Not in OED W S C; but cf. OEDS Baby-carriage, Baby-coach. *U.S.* 1903..)

bacillus, sb. [B¹] *Twenty million priests, fakeers, holy mendicants, and other sacred bacilli* 1897 FE li 494 (Hum. nonce use)

back, sb. **at one's back.** [B³] See *close-fit* 1884; *pull through* 1892. *He could not carry on his government without a majority vote in the House at his back* 1898 "Stirring Times in Austria" (1900) 292 (OED 23. Supporting. 1879, only ex. this sense. So W. Not in S C)

back, sb. **on one's back.** [?AB¹] *I would have had ...the Church on my back in a minute* 1889 CY x 119 (W: Assailing. The opposite of *at one's back*. Cf. C: To be severe on one for any fault or foolish act. Phrase not in OED S)

back, sb. **to know one by the back.** [?AB¹] *"I don't want no better friend than Buck Fanshaw. I knowed him by the back."* 1872 RI xlvii 333. *"De man dat think he kin settle a 'spute 'bout a whole chile wid a half a chile doan' know enough to come in out'n de rain. Doan' talk to me 'bout Sollermun, Huck; I knows him by de back"* 1884 HF xiv 122. *"I know you—I know you 'by the back,' as the gamblers say* 1897 FE xxviii 276 (To know thoroughly. Phr. not in OED W S C; but cf. OED To the back: to the backbone, all through, 1588.. Perhaps an allusion to marked cards, as suggested by the quot. from FE)

back, adv. **back of.** [A] *He had a little one-horse log church down back of his plantation* 1884 HF xxxiii 339. *Back of it a graceful fringe of leaning palms* 1897 FE vii 91. *Some of us lived in the new part, the rest in the old part back of it* 1898 *Autob* (1924) I 125 (OED 14. Behind. *U.S.* OEDS 1694.. So W Cl Th H DN.VI. Not A in C U Wr. Not in S)

back, adv. **back of.** [AB³] *"Have you got some secret project in your head which requires a Bank of England back of it to make it succeed?"* 1892 AmCl xviii 182 (This *fig* sense not distinguished from the above in OED, but cf. quots. 1875. Given in W C as *colloq U.S.* Not in S)

back, adv. **back of.** [AB¹] *To be vested with enormous authority is a fine thing...There was nothing back of me that could approach it, unless it might be Joseph's case...I stood here, at the very spring and source of the second great period of the world's history* 1889 CY viii 95 (Before; backward of in time. This further extension in meaning not in OED W S C; but cf. OED Back, adv. 4. In time past, backward in time. 1711.. So W; *colloq* in S C)

back, adv. **in back of.** [AB¹] *The picture represents a burning martyr. He is in back of the smoke* 1899 "How to Make History Dates Stick" (1917) 165 (W: Behind. Phr. not in OED S C. An obvious variation of the above)

back, v. **to back and fill.** [AB³] *Amid the frenzy of the bells the engines began to back and fill in a furious way* 1875 OTM 287 (OEDS 16b. To recede and advance. *U.S.* 1848.. So F Cl Th M H DN.VI. Not A in W. Phr. not in S C)

back-alley, a. [AB¹] *He said they were back-alley barbers disguised as nobilities* 1894 PW xvii 223 (Not in OED W S C; but cf. OEDS Alley, sb. *U.S.* 1729..)

back-breaking, ppl.a. [?AB¹] *Did you ever notice how back-breaking and tiresome it was?* 1870 *Bequest* (1906) 214. See also *bone-bruising* 1894 (W: Greatly taxing one's strength or endurance. Comb. not in OED S C)

back-cap, sb. **to give one a back-cap.** [AB²] *"Now I didn't fear no one giving me a back-cap (exposing his past life) and running me off the job"* [given as thieves' argot] 1883 LM lii 514 (OEDS *U.S.slang.* 1883, this quot...Not in W S C; but cf. W S C: Backcap, v. To disparage, speak ill of. *U.S.* A in F Cl)

back-country, sb. [A] *He was talking to some of the back-country members about the approaching fall elections* 1864 SNO (1875) 164. See also *dodge* 1869; *receipt* 1897 (OEDS Chiefly *U.S.* b. attrib. 1787.. So B F Cl Th,1755 TM AS.II.347, VIII.2.77. Not A in W S. Not in C)

back down, v. [AB³] *As I had committed myself I would not back down* 1880 TA xliv 515. *"He'd wobble." "And back down?" "Every time"* 1892 AmCl xxi 214 (OEDS 19. orig.*U.S.* 1849.. So B F Cl T DN.III. Not A in W S C U)

back-down, sb. [?AB²] *"She had the grit to pray for Judas if she took a notion—there warn't no back-down to her"* 1884 HF xxviii 289. *"It's a clean back-down! He gives up without hitting a lick!"* 1894 PW xxi 236 (OEDS *colloq.* 1886.. So W C U. A in S Cl DN.III)

back hall, sb. [B¹] *Tom...passed through the other door into the back hall* 1894 PW xix 22 (Comb. not in OED W S C; but cf. OED Back chamber 1653, Back kitchen 1784, Back parlour 1759)

backing bell, sb. [?AB¹] *The pilot...putting his hand on the backing-bell rope...*1883 LM xxiv 264 (Comb. not in OED W S C. Cf. go-ahead bell, below)

backless, a. [B²] *A coffin stood upon two backless chairs* 1873 GA ii 31 (OED 1877.. So W C. Not in S)

back-log, sb. [A] *I've got a noble wood fire going— that is, part of it is wood. The back-log is a plumber. He came up here and interrupted me...Whenever you catch a plumber, you just make a back-log of him. I always do* 1881 *M.T. the Letter Writer* (1932) iii 36 (OED Chiefly in U.S. 1684.. So W B F Cl Th T M H DN.III AS.II.347, VII.92. Not A in S C)

back lot, sb. [?AB¹] *Our King is shut up in a narrow little patch of the kingdom—a sort of back lot, as one may say* 1895 JA I vii 850 (Comb. not in OED W S C; but cf. OED Back court, etc., and W Backlotter. See also lot, sb., below)

back number, sb. [AB³] *Postal service? France is a back number there* 1895 "What Bourget Thinks" 49 (OEDS *colloq.* orig. *U.S.* 1866.. So C Th M H DN.IV, VI. Not A in W S)

back pay, sb. [?AB²] *Nearly all the back pay members contemplate making the round trip with us, in case their constituents will allow them a holiday* 1875 SNO 310 (OEDS Payment to cover a past period of time. Earlier U.S.exs. 1874, this quot.. Cf.F: Back Salary Grab. During the 42nd Congress, 1871-73, a bill was passed to increase salaries...The popularly obnoxious feature of the Act was that it gave *back-pay* for the entire Session to the very men who had the measure under consideration. A in H. Not A in W. Comb. not in S C)

back-room, sb. [B¹] *The preacher stepped softly to a back-room door* 1880 TA xlii 488 (Comb. not in OED W S C; but cf. OED Back chamber, etc.)

back-seat, sb. **to take a back seat.** [AB³] *I had carefully prepared myself to take rather a back-seat in that ship, because of the uncommonly select material* 1869 IA ii 26. *Whenever one was talking and letting on to know all about such things, Jim would say: "What do you know 'bout witches?" and that nigger was corked up and had to take a back seat* 1884 HF ii 10 (OED Seat, sb. 27c. orig. *U.S. fig.* 1868.. A in B F Cl Th,1863 M AS.II.348. Not A in W. Phr. not in S C)

back-settlement, sb. [?A] *That was only a mud-turtle of a back-settlement lawyer* 1896 TSD xi 527 (OED 1759 .. So W C Wr. A in Cl Th.III. Comb. not in S)

back up, v.trans. [?AB³] *Backed up the petition with many depositions and affidavits* 1871 SNO (1875) 110. *"A body's got his hands full without going around making up other people's say-so's"* 1883 LM xxiv 268. *I beseech you, swear one more oath, and back it up with cash* 1884 *Speeches* (1923) 2 (OED 8. To support materially or morally. 1865.. So W S C U Wr. A in DN.III)

back up, v.intr. [AB¹] *He then backed up against Pompey's statue, and squared himself to receive his assailants* 1864 SNO (1875) 165 (The intr. sense not in OED S C. A in DN.III. Not A in W)

backward, a. [?A] *"There's plenty that ain't backward about doing it"* 1883 LM xxiv 268 (OED 6. Reluctant. 1599.. So W S C U Wr. A in B F Cl T DN.III)

back water, v. [?AB³] *"Set her back, John"...They backed water* 1884 HF xvi 139 (OEDS 15b. Earlier U.S. ex. 1806.. Not A in W S C)

back water, v. [?AB¹] *I have taken the largest house in New York, and cannot back water* 1867 *Letters* 1917 I vi 124 (B: To retreat; a Western metaphor derived from steamboat language. So W F Cl T M DN.III. This *fig* sense not in OED S C)

backways, adv. [?AB¹] *A crab...couldn't travel any way but sideways or backways* 1889 CY ix 106 (Not in OED W S C. Cf. Wr: Backways on: backwards, hind before. Cf. anyways, above)

backwoods, sb. [AB³] *He was a grazier or farmer from the back woods of some western state* 1883 LM xxxvi 387 (OED Wild uncleared forest-land; e.g., that of N. Am. 1834.. So W C U B F Cl Th M DN.III AS.IV.5. Not A in S)

backwoods, sb. [AB³] *His backwoods costume would not be needed in St. Louis* 1873 GA xiii 126. *An agonized voice, with the backwoods "whang" to it* 1875 OTM 448 (Cf. above. OED b. attrib. 1822.. So W. Not A in S. Not attrib. in C)

backwoodsman, sb. [?A] *No one can care less for a lord than the backwoodsman* 1902 "Does the Race Love a Lord?" 434 (OEDS 1793.. So S. A in W C B Cl Th DN.VI AS.IV.5,17)

back yard, sb. [?AB³] See *handspring*, v. 1877; *front yard* 1897 (OEDS Earlier U.S. exs. 1837.. A in M. Not A in W S H. Comb. not in C)

bad, adv. [?A?C] *He didn't try no more to win the fight, and so he got shucked out bad* 1865 "Jumping Frog" (1875) 32 (OED. Badly. *obs.* OEDS Delete *obs* and add U.S.exs. 1816.. A in B F Cl T M DN.III. Not A in W Wr. This use not in S C)

Bad Lands, sb. [AB³] *"I was with...the expedition in the Bad Lands"* 1906 "Horse's Tale" 342 (OEDS *U.S.*1868.. So W B F Cl M H. Not in S C)

bad off, a. [?AB³] *"Where a man hasn't a regular trade he's pretty bad off in this world"* 1892 AmCl xi 117 (OEDS U.S. exs. 1817.. A in Wr. Not in W S C)

Bad Place, sb. [AB¹] *"O Lord, we's ben mighty wicked, an' we knows dat we 'zerve to go to de bad place"* 1873 GA iii 37. *Then she told me all about the bad place ...She said she was going to live so as to go to the good place* 1884 HF i 4 (A in DN.IV: used for Hell in Va. Not A in Wr. Phr. not in OED W S C)

bad words, sb. [?AB¹] *Tom Holmes says more bad words than any other boy in the village* 1883 LM liv 532 (Profanity. This sense not in OED W S C)

badge-holder, sb. [B¹] *The badge-holders stood upon their privilege* 1880 TA vii 66 (Comb. not in OED W S C)

bag, v. [?AB³] *In Germany, when you load your conversational gun, it is always best to throw in a Schlag or two and a Zug or two, because...you are bound to bag something with them* 1880 TA App.D 611. (OED 6. *colloq.* 1818.. So W S C U Wr. A in Cl DN.I)

bagasse, sb. [?AB³] *The refuse of the [sugar-cane] stalks, which they [in New Orleans] call bagasse* 1875 OTM 450 (OED 1854.. So W S U. A in C B F Cl Th,1835 DN.VI)

baggage, sb. [A] *When we see a monk sitting on a rock, looking tranquilly up to heaven, with a human skull beside him, and without other baggage, we know that it is St. Jerome...He always went flying light in the matter of baggage* 1869 IA xxiii 238. See also *express* 1872; *check*, v. 1875; *wharf-boat* 1884; *peanut-commerce* 1897; *paster* 1902 (OEDS *U.S.* 1748.. So W S C B F Cl Th T M H AS.IV.5. Not A in U)

baggage-check, sb. [AB³] *A battered old New York Central baggage-check* 1893 "Esquimau Maiden's Romance" (1900) 147 (OEDS 1888.. So W C F Cl Th, 1847 T M H. Not in S)

baggage-coupon, sb. [AB¹] *"I couldn't get these tickets and baggage-coupons changed for St. Petersburg"* 1902 "Belated Russian Passport" (1928) 175 (Cf. above. Comb. not in OED W S C)

baggage-master, sb. [AB³] *An Erie baggage-master* 1880 TA xlviii 566 (Cf. above. OEDS 1849.. So W S C H)

baggage-smasher, sb. [AB³] *Their English would discredit the baggage-smasher* 1907 CS II xv 289 (Cf. above. OEDS 1859.. So W S B F Cl Th M H AS. XII.114, quot.1856. Comb. not in C)

baggage-van, sb. [AB¹] *Drays and baggage-vans were clattering hither and thither in a wild hurry* 1875 OTM 190 (Cf. above. Comb. not in OED S C. Given in W)

baggage-wagon, sb. [AB¹] *Take him the baggage-wagon* 1869 IA lvii 616 (Cf. above. Comb. not in OED S C in this sense. Given in W)

bail up, v. [B³] See *hold up* 1897 (OED 2. To 'stick up' and disarm travelers. *Australian.* 1880. So S C Wr. Not in W)

bake-oven, sb. [?AB³] *The Devil's Bake-Oven [at Grand Tower, Missouri]—so-called, perhaps, because it does not powerfully resemble anybody else's bake-oven* 1883 LM xxv 274 (OEDS Earlier U.S.exs. 1812.. A in S B F Cl Th AS.VIII.2.77. Not A in W Wr. Not in C)

bake-shop, sb. [?AB²] *There are the bake-shops... all clean-scraped and neat* 1869 IA xxxi 327 (OED 1872, this quot., wrongly dated. So W. A in F Cl T. Comb. not in S C)

baking, adv. [B¹] *And baking hot, of course!* 1899 "My Debut" (1900) 81 (Bakingly. The adv. use not in OED W S C. Given in U)

balance, sb. [AB³] *The balance of your letter pleases me exceedingly* 1862 *Letters* (1917) I iii 80. *I then paid the balance of my passage money* 1869 IA i 24 (OEDS 21. Remainder. orig. *U.S.* 1805.. So W S B F Cl Th T M H DN.III. *Colloq* in C U)

bald-headed, a. [AB¹] *I prophesied myself bald-headed trying to supply the demand* 1889 CY xxvii 352. *"Can't you keep away from that greasy water? pull her down! snatch her! snatch her baldheaded!"* 1909 ISD i 6 (To the limit; used as a mere intensive. This use not in OED W S C; but cf. OEDS To go bald-headed for, *colloq. phr.* orig. *U.S.*: to dash or charge forward without heeding danger or obstacles. 1846.. So U B F. Not A in Wr. Cf. also F: Snatched bald-headed, used of a person defeated in a fight)

balditude, sb. [B¹] *"Trouble has brung these gray hairs and this premature balditude"* 1884 HF xix 187 (Not in OED W S C. Hum. coinage?)

bald-summited, ppl.a. [?AB¹] *A bald-summited superintendent who had been a towheaded Sunday-School mate of mine* 1883 LM liv 538 (Comb. not in OED W S C. Hum. coinage, with allusion to the sense in OEDS Bald, sb. A mountain summit naturally bare of forest, esp. in the southern Appalachians. *U.S.* 1849..)

balk, sb. **to make a balk**. [AB³?C] *She kept a corner of her eye on the servants to see that they made no balks in handling the body and getting it out* 1889 CY xvi 195 (OED 5. *fig.* To blunder, go wrong. *obs.* 1430..1661. So Wr. Not *obs* in W S C U. OEDS 5b. *U.S.* Used of an illegal motion by the pitcher in *Baseball,* 1867..)

Ballarat fly, sb. [B¹] *We had one of those whizzing green Ballarat flies in the room, with his stunning buzzsaw noise* [at Gisborne, New Zealand] 1897 FE xxxiv 315 (Comb. not in OED W S C)

ballast, v. [?AB³] *Shaving the bank down...and ballasting it with stones* 1883 LM xxviii 302 (OED 6. 1864. So W S C U W. A in M: orig. *U.S.*)

ballock, sb. [?ACE] *He did tell of a man his father knew that had a double pair of bollocks* 1880 *Fireside Conversation, 1601* (OED *obs* in polite use. c1000..1800. So W C. Not in S. This sp. nowhere recorded; its use by M.T. indicates that he took the word from oral rather than written tradition, for it undoubtedly represents current Am. *colloq* pronunciation)

ball-proof, sb. [?AB¹] *Being ball-proof, they* [Arthurian knights at baseball] *never skipped out of the way* 1889 CY xl 518 (Hum. *Baseball* application of the sense in W: Incapable of being penetrated by small-arm projectiles. So C. Comb. not in OED S)

ball up, v. [AB²] *It will "ball up" the binderies again* 1885 *Letters* (1917) II xxv 465 (OEDS 8b. *U.S.* To bring into a state of entanglement or difficulty. 1887.. So Cl T. Not A in W S. Not in C)

balmy, a. [?AB¹] *Here was another balmy place to be in: I had forgotten the child's name!* 1880 TA xxv 252 (Such as to drive one insane. An extension of the sense applied to persons, OEDS 7. 'Soft,' weak-minded, idiotic. *slang.* 1851.. So W Wr. This sense not in S C)

balragoomah, sb. [B¹] See *kahkahponeeka* 1880 (Hum. invention)

Baltimore perch, sb. [AB¹] See *biscuit* 1880 (Comb. not in OED W S C)

band, sb. **to beat the band**. [?AB³] *"It certainly beats the band!* 1905 "Helpless Situation" (1906) 121 (OEDS 4b. To surpass everything. 1900.. So U. *Slang* in W. A in H. Phr. not in S C)

band-box, sb. **just out of the band-box** [?AB¹] *They are all...exceedingly neat and cleanly; they look as if they were just out of a band-box* 1869 IA xxxviii 408. *The streetcar conductors and drivers wore pretty uniforms which seemed to be just out of the bandbox* 1880 TA i 19 (This very familiar phrase not in OED W S C)

banderillo, sb. [B¹] *"Scattering the nimble banderillos in every direction"* 1906 "Horse's Tale" 545 (Not in OED W S C. A doubtless unintentional mistake for Banderillero, OED The bull-fighter who uses banderillas. 1864..)

bandoleer, sb. [B¹] *One of the most trying defects which I find...in these bangalores, these buccaneers, these bandoleers, is their spirit of irreverence* 1909 ISD xii 134 (Hum. nonce modification of Bandolero, OEDS A highwayman or robber. 1832..)

band-wagon, sb. [AB³] *The band-wagon of a circus* 1869 IA xvii 167 (OEDS 7. *U.S.* 1855.. So M H Th. III DN.VI. Not A in W C. Not in S)

bang, v. [?AB³] *"Don't just bang anything you ever heard of?* 1883 LM liii 527. *"I tell you, it just bangs anything I ever heard of"* 1884 HF xli 419 (OED 6 *colloq.* To beat, surpass. 1808.. So W S C Wr. A in DN.V)

bang, v. [?AB³] *The high classes wore their hair banged across the forehead* 1889 CY xxvii 344 (OED Bang, v.² To cut the front hair square across. 1882.. Cf. OED Bang, sb. orig. *U.S.* 1880.. A in F Cl T. Not A in W S C U)

bangalore, sb. [B¹] See *bandoleer* 1909 (Robber, rascal; hum. nonce coinage)

bang away, v. [?AB¹] *Clarence was still alive and banging away* 1889 CY xxxvi 467 (To work as usual, keep occupied. This sense not in OED W S C; but cf. Wr Bang along: to work with rapidity)

bangless, a. [?AB¹] *The slaves were bangless* 1889 CY xxvii 344 (Coined from Bang; see above. Not in OED W S C)

banjo, sb. [A] See *break down*, v. 1873 (OED A corruption of *Bandore*, through Negro slave pronunciation. OEDS 1774.. So W S C U B F Th,1764 T M)

bank, sb. **down the banks**. [?AB¹] *"He give me down the banks for not coming and telling him"* 1884 HF xxvii 280 (A scolding, a reprimand. Phr. not in OED W S C. Given as an Irish idiom in P.W.Joyce, *English as We Speak It in Ireland,* p.250. Cf. the similar phr. *to give anyone down the country* = to call to account, A in DN.III)

bank, v. **to bank the fires**. [?AB¹] *In plain terms, do they shut up shop, draw the game, bank the fires?* 1889 CY xxii 276 (To stop, discontinue operations. This *fig* sense not in OED W S C. Cf. *lit.* sense in OED 10. 1860..)

bank, v. [?AB¹] See *string* 1872 (W: Billiards. To drive a ball to the bank or cushion. So S. The *billiards* sense of neither sb. nor verb is given in OED C)

bank, v. [?AB²] *I can "bank" in the neighborhood of $100 a month* 1859 *Letters* (1917) I ii 43. *He made money then, and sent it always to his wife to bank it for him* 1870 SNO (1875) 166. *She banked two hundred a year from the salary* 1904 "Bequest" (1906) i 2 (OED 3. 1864.. So W S C U. A in Cl)

bank-account, sb. [?AB¹] *She began to get miserly as her bank-account grew* 1870 SNO (1875) 166. *He started a bank-account, in a small way—and mentioned the deposit casually to friends* 1873 GA xxv 231 (A in M. Not A in W S C. Not in OED)

bank-bill, sb. [AC] See *State* 1853 (OED Formerly, and still sometimes in the provinces, and in the U.S., synonymous with Bank-note. 1709..1863. A in W S C U Cl M H)

bank-caving, ppl.a. [?AB¹] *The turbulent, bank-caving Missouri* 1883 LM xxii 252 (Cf. cave, v., below. Comb. not in OED W S C)

banking, ppl.a. [B²] *A weird picture, that small company of frantic men fighting the banking snows* 1867 SNO (1875) 372 (OED Forming into banks. 1867, this quot. This use not in W S C)

bank-robbery, sb. [?AB¹] *"Confess? Merely that bank-robbery?"* 1892 AmCl xix 195 (Comb. not in OED W S C; but cf. OEDS Bank-robber 1799, U.S. quot., and A in Th)

bannered, ppl.a. [B¹] *He was out at the door and flying through the palace grounds in his bannered rags* 1881 PP iii 137 (Banner-like, flapping. This sense not in OED W S C)

Banner State, sb. [AB³] *I was born in the "Banner State," and by "Banner State" I mean Missouri* 1901 *Speeches* (1910) 255 (OEDS 6b. *U.S.* 1840.. So Th M H. Term not in W S C)

banquette, sb. [?AB³] *The young colored population of New Orleans were much given to flirting, at twilight, on the banquettes of the back streets* 1875 OTM 722 (A in T: Sidewalk, in some Southern cities. So S C B F Cl. Not A in W or OED 1842..)

bar, sb. [AB¹] See *boil*, sb., *cramp*, v., *work down*, all 1875 OTM. *Three miles below St. Petersburg, at a point where the Mississippi River was a trifle over a mile wide, there was a long, narrow, wooded island, with a shallow bar at the head of it* 1876 TS xiii 114.

No bars, snags, sawyers, or wrecks in his road 1883 LM
xl 416. *His straw hat blew off and fell in the creek, and
floated down and lodged against a bar* 1897 FE ii 43 (A
in DN.VI: A well known word...common on the sea-
coast, but in the West almost always used in connection with rivers; it became current in 1849. The distinctive river use of the word is best defined in S: An
alluvial deposit forming a shallow place or an island
in a river or at its mouth. So C: A bank of sand,
gravel, or earth forming a shoal in any body of water.
Inadequate to the Am. use of the word is the definition
in OED 15. A bank of sand, silt, etc., across the mouth
or a river or harbor, which obstructs navigation. 1586
.. So W)

bar, sb. [AB³] *"Get their bed ready...and see that you
drive all the mosquitoes out of their bar"* 1894 TET vii
415 (OEDS *U.S.* A mosquito net. 1835.. So Th,1797,
under *Bear.* Not in W S C. Cf. mosquito-bar, below.
For the origin and early history of the word, see E.H.
Cris well, *Lewis and Clark: Linguistic Pioneers* (Uni-
versi ty of Missouri Ph.D. dissertation, in manuscript,
1936) vol. II, pp. 351, 374. Dr. Criswell explains it as
an Americanized pronunciation of the old word *bere*
or *bier*, covering. Cf.also A.W.Read, AS.X.196)

bar, v. [?AB¹] *The others bar medicines, and claim
ability to cure...through the application of their mental
forces alone* 1899 "Chr. Sc. and the Book" 594 (Forbid,
exclude from use. This sense not in OED W S C. An
extension of the use in OED 8. To exclude from consideration, set aside. 1481..1809)

barbecue, sb. [AB³] *They ran up the Cannibal flag
and had a grand human barbecue* 1871 SNO (1875) 156.
*Whenever there was a barbecue, or a circus, or a baptizing,
we knocked off for half a day* 1886 *Speeches* (1910) 184
(OED 4. *U.S.* 1809.. So W S C U B F Cl Th T M
DN.VI AS.II.348,VII.432)

barbed wire, sb. [?AB²] *If they couldn't persuade a
person to try...a barbed wire fence...they removed him
and passed on* 1889 CY xl 512 (OED Wire. 1e. Earlier
barb wire. 1889, first quot. for *barbed wire*.. So W S
C U)

barber, v. [?AC] *We were dressed and barbered alike*
1889 CY xxvii 346 (OED *Rare.* 1606, 1816. So S C.
Not *rare* in W Wr. A in Cl)

barber-shop, sb. [?AB³] *We hunted for a barber-shop*
1869 IA xii 113. See also *candy-striped* 1893 (OEDS
Earlier U.S.ex. 1829.. A in Th M=Eng. Barber's
shop. Not in W. Comb. not in S C)

barb lace, sb. [?AB¹] *The Grand Duchess had on a
white Alpaca robe, with the seams and gores trimmed
with black barb lace* 1869 IA xxxvii 397 (Comb. not in
OED W S C; but cf. C: Barb 6. A band or small scarf
of lace, or other fine material, worn by women at the
neck or as a head-dress)

bareback, adv. **to ride bareback.** [?AB¹] *He could ride
bareback and know and feel that he was safe* 1880 TA
xxvi 269 (W: To ride without using a saddle. So U
Wr. Not in OED S C as adv., but cf. OED Bare-
backed, a. 2. 1628..)

bargain-counter, sb. [AB³] *The Christian-Science
Mother-Church and Bargain-Counter in Boston peddles
all kinds of spiritual wares to the faithful* 1903 "Chr.
Sc." 2 (OEDS *U.S.* Also *fig.* 1888.. So S C Th.III M
H. Not A in W)

barge, sb. [AB²] See *broadhorn* 1875 (OED 6. *U.S.*
No ex. So S C. The Mississippi River vessel so named
is described in B F Cl. This sense not in W)

bark, sb. **with the bark on.** [AB²] *"That is the word,
with the bark on it!"* 1872 RI xv 124; also 1902 "DBDS"
(1928) 342 (OEDS *U.S.* A rough or unpolished
form. 1872, this quot. So F Cl H DN.I. Not in W S C)

bark, v. [?AB³] *The Dictionary "barked" the Secretary's elbow* 1872 RI iv 29. *He went head over heels over
the tub of salt pork and barked both shins* 1884 HF vi

44 (OED 3c. To scrape or rub off the skin. Earliest
ex. U.S. 1850.. Not A in W S C U Wr)

bar-keep, sb. [?AB²] *In my time they used to call the
"barkeep" Bill, or Joe, or Tom, and slap him on the
shoulder* 1883 LM xxii 251 (OEDS 1918.. A in M H
DN.IV. Not in W S C)

bar-keeper, sb. [?A] See *baggage-wagon* 1869; *corn-
whiskey, exhilaration, hang it up,* and *upholster*—all
1873 GA. *The wholesale liquor dealer's son became the
bar-keeper on a boat* 1875 OTM 71. See also *salary* 1883
(OED 1712.. So W S C. A in F (under Bartender)
Th T M H)

barker, sb. [A] *Her barkers (what a curious name! I
wonder if it is copyrighted)...persistently advertise to
the public her generosity* 1907 CS II vii 200 (OEDS 2.
One who calls out or 'spiels' at the entrance of a cheap
shop or show to attract customers. Chiefly *U.S.* 1700..
So H. Not A in W S C)

Barlow knife, sb. [A] *A brand new "Barlow" knife
worth twelve and a half cents* 1876 TS iv 43. *"A bran-
new Barlow knife worth two bits in any store"* 1884 HF
ix 78 (OEDS *U.S.* From the name of the maker.
1779.. So W S Th DN.II,III,IV. Not in C)

baronet, sb. [C] *"My father is a baronet—one of the
smaller lords, by knight service."* (Footnote) *He refers to
the order of baronets, or baronettes—the barones minores,
as distinct from the parliamentary barons; not, it need
hardly be said, the baronets of later creation* 1880 PP xii
142 (OED 1. orig. A word meaning young, little, or
lesser baron, found as a title from the 14th c. *obs.*
1400..1662. So W S C)

baronette, sb. [CE] See *baronet* 1880 (OED This sp.
16th c. Not in W S C)

barrel, sb. [B¹] *"He will tell it...every time he hath
gotten his barrel full"* 1889 CY iii 45 (Not in OED W
S C of a human being. Cf. OED 8. The belly and loins
of a horse, ox, etc. 1703. So W U Wr)

barrel-hoop, sb. [B¹] *"An old iron barrel-hoop"* 1884
HF xxxv 360 (Comb. not in OED S C. Given in W)

barrel-round, a. [B¹] *A fleshy cub and barrel-round*
[German, kugelrund] 1891 *Slovenly Peter* (1935) 17
(Comb. not in OED W S C; but cf. OED Barrel-shaped,
1869)

barren, a. [B¹] *She is nearly barren of troublesome
conventions and artificialities* 1892 AmCl xx 204 (Free,
devoid of something objectionable. This sense not in
OED W S C. Given with opposite sense in OED 6:
Bare of intellectual wealth, destitute of attraction or
interest, poor. 1387..1846)

bar-room, sb. [?AB³] *I found Simon Wheeler dozing
comfortably by the bar-room stove* 1865 "Jumping Frog"
(1875) 30. *Philip was shown into the dirty barroom. It
was a small room, with a stove in the middle, set in a long
shallow box of sand, for the benefit of the "spitters," a
bar across one end* 1873 GA xxix 270 (OED 1809.. So
W S C. A in Th DN.VI)

bar sinister, sb. [B³] See *coat-of-arms* 1883. *Our tribe
had always been short of the bar sinister* 1889 CY viii
101 (OED 8. In popular but erroneous phrase, the
heraldic sign of illegitimacy. 1823, only ex. So W S
C U)

bar-soap, sb. [?AB²] *Near it was a pail of water, and
a piece of yellow bar-soap* 1872 RI iv 41 (OEDS Soap
made up into bars, as distinguished from soap in cakes
or tablets. 1893.. Comb. not in W S C)

base, sb. [D] See *coat-of-arms* 1883 (OED 8. *Heraldry.* The lower part of a shield. 1611..1706—. So W
S C U)

base, sb. [AB³] *It's about the gaudiest thing in the
book, if you boom it right along and don't get left on a
base* 1888 "Meisterschaft" 463. See also *slide,* v. 1889
(OEDS 15c. *Baseball.* 1869.. So W S C U)

baseball, sb. [AB³] *Baseball is the very symbol, the
outward and visible expression of the drive and push and*

*rush and struggle of the raging, tearing, booming nine-
teenth century* 1889 *Speeches* (1923) 145 (OED The
national field-game of the U.S. 1815.. So S U B F Cl T
M. Not A in W C)

baseball match, sb. [AB[1]] *Rogers bent himself...in
the modern attitude of the catcher at a baseball match*
1894 TET v 377 (Cf. above. Comb. not in OED W S C)

base-burner, sb. [AB[3]] *We should have seen the plebeian fireplace vanish away and a recherché, big base-
burner wiith isinglass windows take position and spread
awe around* 1904 "Bequest" (1906) iv 23 (OEDS *U.S.*
1874.. So B F Cl Th. Not A in W S C)

basso-relievo, a. [B[1]] *I was charmed by the manner
in which the basso-relievo sofa shifter performed his part*
1864 SS (1926) iii 132 (Hum. nonce use: basso-relievo
=bas-relief, work carved in low relief, here used in the
sense of the musical terms basso-continuo, basso-
ripieno, etc.)

basting, vbl.sb. [?A] See *bone-racking* 1881. *I got a
merciless basting, but I did not mind it* 1898 *Autob*
(1924) I 139 (OED 1590..1833. So W C U Wr. A in Cl.
Not in S)

bat, sb. [AB[2]] *He put his hoop away, and his bat;
there was no joy in them any more* 1876 TS xii 107. *The
umpire's decision was usually his last; they broke him
in two with a bat* 1889 CY xl 519 (OEDS 3c. In baseball.
U.S. 1883.. So W S C T)

bat, sb. **at bat.** [AB[3]] *When a Bessemer was at the
bat and a ball hit him, it would bound a hundred and
fifty yards sometimes* 1889 CY xi 518 (OEDS *U.S.*
1883.. So S C. Phr. not in W)

bat, sb. **hot from the bat.** [AB[2]] *"Whoever may ask
us a Meisterschaft question shall get a Meisterschaft
answer—and hot from the bat!"* 1888 "Meisterschaft"
459. *The stories had to come hot from the bat, always.
They had to be absolutely original and fresh* 1906
"Chaps. from Autob." 710 (OEDS Hot off the bat.
U.S. 1910, only ex. Not in W S C)

bat, sb. **step to the bat.** [AB[1]] *"Step to the bat, it's
your innings"* 1889 CY vii 88 (Here *fig*=Proceed, go
ahead, take your turn. Phr. not in OED W S C)

bat, v. **to bat an eye.** [AB[3]] *Unhandkerchiefs one eye,
bats it around tearfully* 1883 LM xliii 438 (OED 2. dial
and *U.S.* To move the eyelids quickly. 1847.. So W
S C Wr B F Cl Th DN.II)

batch, sb. [AB[1]] *I don't want any more of your statistics; I took your whole batch and lit my pipe with it*
1867 SNO (1875) 72. *Yet it* [the Mississippi Valley] *is
much the youthfullest batch of country that lies around
there anywheres* 1883 LM i 23. See *slap,* v. 1886; *flush,*
v. 1888. *They asked him to lend them a batch of the
work to read at home* 1894 PW xi 553. (A in AS.II.348:
A large quantity of any material. So U Wr. This vague
sense not in OED W S C. An Am. extension of the
sense in OED 5: A quantity produced at one operation; a brewing. *arch.* 1713..1878)

bath-cure, sb. [B[1]] *"Grape-cure, bath-cure, mud-cure
—it is all the same"* 1898 "At the Appetite-Cure"
(1900) 162 (Comb. not in OED W S C]

bath-house, sb. [B[2]] *This water is conducted in pipes
to the numerous bath-houses* 1880 TA xxi 200 (OED
1882, only ex. So W S C)

bathing-house, sb. [?AB[3]] *There are several of these
big bathing-houses* 1880 TA xxxv 394 (OEDS 1816..
Earliest ex. *U.S.* A in C. Not A in S. Not in W)

bath-tub, sb. [?AB[2]] *He had carried off my red
blanket and my bath-tub* 1870 SNO (1875) 221. *"We
got mixed in the bath-tub when we were only two weeks
old, and one of us was drowned"* 1875 "Encounter with
an Interviewer" 31 (OED 1884.. So W S C. Not in U.
A in M: Am. *bath-tub* =Eng. *bath*)

bathostic, a. [B[1]] *Been reading Daniel Webster's
Private Correspondence. Have read a hundred of his
diffuse, conceited, "eloquent," bathotic (or bathostic)*

letters written in that dim Past 1880 *Letters* (1917) I xx
384 (Nonce word)

bathotic, a. [B[3]] See *bathostic* 1880 (OED Nonce-
wd. = Bathetic, on superficial analogy of *chaotic.* 1863
only ex. So S. Not in W C)

batter, v. [B[1]] *"She can batter in jumping—elle peut
batter en sautant—all frogs of the county of Calaveras"*
["Retranslated" from the French; the original version
of the "Jumping Frog" has *"He can outjump ary frog
in Calaveras· county"*] 1875 SNO 42 (Hum. nonce-
borrowing)

batter-cake, sb. [?AB[3]] *It was a heavenly place for a
boy, that farm of my uncle John's... The sumptuous
meals—well, it makes me cry to think of them. Fried
chicken, roast pig; wild and tame turkeys, ducks, and
geese; venison just killed; squirrels, rabbits, pheasants,
partridges, prairie-chickens; biscuits, hot batter-cakes, hot
buckwheat cakes, hot "wheat bread," hot rolls, hot corn
pone; fresh corn boiled on the ear, succotash, butter-beans,
string-beans, tomatoes, peas, Irish potatoes, sweet potatoes; buttermilk, sweet milk, "clabber;" watermelons,
muskmelons, cantaloupes—all fresh from ·the garden;
apple pie, peach pie, pumpkin pie, apple dumplings,
peach cobbler—I can't remember the rest. The way that
these things were cooked was perhaps the main splendor
...The North thinks it knows how to make corn bread,
but this is mere superstition. Perhaps no bread in the
world is quite so good as Southern corn bread, and perhaps no bread in the world is quite so bad as the Northern
imitation of it* 1897-8 *Autob* (1924) I 97 (OED Batter
1c. 1853, only ex. So W S. A in F: An inseparable
adjunct to the early morning meal in the South. It is
made of Indian meal. So Cl DN.VI. Not in C)

battery, sb. [?AB[3]] *This mill was a six-stamp affair.
Six tall, upright rods of iron rose and fell in an iron box
called a battery* 1872 RI xxxvi 252. See also *arrastre*
1909 (OEDS 7. *Mining.* Earlier U.S. exs. 1861.. Not
A in W S C)

battery, sb. [AB[1]] *"There's no telling how much he
does weigh when he is out on the war-path and has his
batteries belted on"* 1906 "Horse's Tale" 327 (S: A revolver. *Slang, western U.S.* This sense not in OED
W C)

battery, sb. [B[1]] *I dare say he is Archdeacon now—
he was a canon then—and he was serving in the Westminster battery, if that is the proper term—I do not
know, as you mix military and ecclesiastical things
together so much* 1907 *Speeches* (1910) 37 (Hum. nonce
use; pun on the artillery sense of Battery, OED 5.
1590.. Cf. canon, howitzer, swivel, etc., below)

battle-chant, sb. [B[1]] *The impressive strains of a
battle-chant* 1880 TA xxxvii 432 (Comb. not in OED
W S C)

battle-flag, sb. [?AB[1]] *Now, old fellow, take in your
battle-flag out of the wet* 1892 AmCl xv 161 (Comb. not
in OED. Given in W S C)

battle-gallery, sb. [B[1]] *They picture no French defeats in the battle-galleries of Versailles* 1869 IA xvii 159
(Comb. not in OED W S C; but cf. OED Battle-piece,
1711)

battle-lantern, sb. [?AB[1]] *When Farragut advanced
upon Port Hudson on a dark night—and did not wish
to assist the aim of the Confederate gunners—he carried
no battle-lanterns, but painted the decks of his ships
white* 1883 LM xlv 456 (C: A lantern placed at each
gun on the gun-deck of a ship of war. So W. Comb. not
in OED S)

battle-stretch, sb. [B[1]] *We were getting down into the
upper edge of the former battle-stretch by this time* 1883
LM xxvi 281 (Comb. not in OED W S C; but cf. OED
Battlefield, 1812)

battle-tragedy, sb. [B[1]] *Davoust and Massena, who
wrought in many a battle-tragedy* 1869 IA xv 140 (Comb.
not in OED W S C)

bawdkin, sb. [C] *Long robes of bawdkin powdered with gold* 1881 PP xi 125 (OED *obs exc. Hist.* A rich embroidered stuff. *c*1300..1861. So W S C)

bay-berry, sb. [A] See *afarabocca* 1894 (OED 2. In U.S., the fruit of the wax-myrtle. OEDS 1687..So W S C B F Cl Th M H. Not A in U)

bayou, sb. [AB³] See *relief-steamer* 1883. *"Bound for one of them bayous or one-horse rivers away down Louisiana way"* 1896 TSD ii 346 (OED Used chiefly in the southern states of N.Am. OEDS 1806.. So W S C U B F Cl Th T M DN.I,II,IV,VI. See also *Nation* LIX.361,381; *Mod. Lang. Notes* VII.395)

bay-rum, sb. [?AB³] *Next he [the barber] poked bay rum into the cut place with his towel* 1871 SNO (1875) 258 (OEDS Earlier U.S. exs. 1846.. A in B. Not A in W S C U)

be, v. **warn't.** [?AE] *"Tom, it was middling warm in school, warn't it?"* 1876 TS i 20. *"There warn't anything really the matter"* 1884 HF i 2. So *passim* in M.T. (OED This form *dial* and in 18th c. dramatists. So Wr. A in B AS.V.205, Ozarks. Not in W S C)

be, v. **to let be.** [?AC] *Pray let the little stranger be!* 1891 *Slovenly Peter* (1935) 9 (OED 4. *arch.* 1297..1869. Not *arch* in W S C. *Dial* in Wr. A in DN.III)

bead, sb. **to draw a bead on.** [AB³] *By the time you have "drawn a bead" on him you see that nothing could reach him where he is now* 1873 RI v 50. *There was the old man...just drawing a bead on a bird with a gun* 1884 HF vii 48 (OED 5d. Phr. of U.S. origin. 1841.. So W S B F Cl Th T M. Not A in C U)

bead-basket, sb. [B¹] *A sudden flash in the air of... bead-baskets and moccasins* 1869 SNO (1875) 70 (Comb. not in OED W S C)

bead-reticule, sb. [B¹] *I came upon a noble Son of the Forest sitting under a tree, diligently at work on a bead-reticule* 1869 SNO (1875) 67 (Comb. not in OED W S C)

bear, v. [?AB³] *Buyers are too weak to bear the market, while sellers are amply prepared to bull it* 1869 IA xxxiv 368 (OEDS trans., of the market. 1861.. So W C. A in S B T AS.X.196)

bear-meat, sb. [AB³] *His meals were restricted to bear-meat* 1898 "At the Appetite-Cure" (1900) 161 (OEDS *U.S.* 1816.. So F. Not in W S C)

beat, sb. [?AB¹] *The stage company had everything under strict discipline and good system. Over each two hundred and fifty miles of road they placed an agent or superintendent, and invested him with great authority. His beat or jurisdiction...was called a "division"* 1872 RI vi 54 (This sense not in OED W S C; but cf. OEDS 10d: In Alabama and Mississippi, the principal subdivision of a county; a voting-precinct. 1893..)

beat, sb. **to see** or **hear the beat of.** [AB³] *"I never did see the beat of that boy!"* 1876 TS i 18. *"I never heard the beat of it"* 1884 HF xxxiii 342. *"His beat don't exist, I reckon"* 1892 AmCl iv 56 (OEDS 15. *U.S.*, chiefly *dial.* Only in phr. To see, or hear, the beat of. 1834.. So S B F Th T DN.IV. Not A in W. Not in C. The OED restriction to the phr. quoted is disproved by the quot. from AmCl)

beat, sb. [AB³] *"I could swear they was beats and bummers"* 1884 HF xxviii 285. *"Do you know, that beat wouldn't believe him!"* 1894 TSA x 393 (OEDS 16. *U.S.* An idle, worthless, or shiftless fellow. 1877.. So F Th T H DN.IV. Not A in W S C)

beat, v. [?AB³] *"Well, this beats anything!"* 1875 OTM 219. *"It beats anything that was ever heard of!"* 1894 PW xi 555 (OED 10. To overcome or conquer in battle; in mod. use in any other contest; to surpass, excel. 1802, first ex. mod. use. So W S C U. A in B Cl Th DN.II)

beat, v. [?AB¹] *There was no time to spare if I would beat the other correspondents* 1899 "My Debut" (1900) 72 (S: In newspaper slang, to "make a scoop." The verb not in this sense in OED W C; but cf. Beat, sb.

OEDS 15c. *U.S.* A success scored against rivals by a reporter or newspaper. 1875.. The sb. is listed as A in F Cl H; not A in W S C U)

beat around, v. [?AB¹] *Last week I was beating around the Lake of Four Cantons* 1892 "Switzerland" (1917) 195 (Comb. not in OED S C; but cf. OED 26b. to beat about 1713.. 26c. to beat about the bush 1572.. Cf. also W: to beat around the bush)

beatenest, a. [AB²E] *"It's the beatenest thing I ever struck"* 1884 HF xiii 114. See also *break down* 1894 (OEDS *U.S. dial.* 1833.. Earliest forms beatemest, beatomest, beatinest. App. from *beat 'em* with superl. suffix *-est*, later apprehended as from *beating* ppl.a. 1889, first quot.for beatenest. A in F Th M DN.I,II, III,IV AS.II.348. Not in W S C)

beat one's time. See *time*, sb.

beat out, v. Pa.pple. **beat out, beaten out.** [AB¹E] *I was all beat out and blistered* 1869 IA xlvii 491. *Livy is too much beaten out with the baby, nights, to write* 1880 *Letters* (1917) I xx 390. *"The horses is about beat out"* 1884 HF viii 63 (OED 39g. *U.S.* To exhaust. 1780, only ex. So W S C Wr B T DN.III,IV. Cf. OED W S C Beat, ppl.a. Overcome by hard work or difficulty. 1832.. No dict. gives beaten out in this sense, which was probably an effort at refinement on M.T.'s part—or his editor's)

beautiful, adv. [?AB¹] *"Oh, it was done beautiful—beautiful!"* 1875 OTM 223 (The adv. use not in OED W S)

beaver, sb. [?C] *"He'd take off his new white beaver"* 1884 HF xxiv 237 (OED 3. A hat made of beaver's fur ...formerly worn. 1528..1885. *Obs* in Wr. Not *obs* in W S C U)

beaver-trowel, sb. [B¹] *"And fishy fin where should be paw, And beaver-trowel tail"* 1897 FE viii 107 (Nonce comb.)

become, v. [C] *"Where are all my noble knights becomen?"* 1889 CY xlii 535 (OED 1. To arrive, betake oneself, go. *obs.* 885..1727. So W S C)

bed-leg, sb. [B¹] *"Saw the bed-leg in two"* 1884 HF xxxv 357 (Comb. not in OED W S C)

bed-rock, sb. [AB³] *This stuff had run under him and cemented him fast to the "bed-rock"* 1870 SNO (1875) 241. See *pot-shaped* 1880. *When you come right down to the bed-rock, knight-errantry is worse than pork* 1889 CY xix 233. *We are down to the bed-rock, financially speaking* 1892 AmCl v 63 (OEDS *Geol.*,also *fig.* orig. *U.S.* 1850.. So F Cl Th.III T M H. Not A in W S C U)

bee-line, sb. [?AB³] *Precisely straight west of the city in a bee-line* 1866 *Letters* (1917) I v 115 (OEDS Earlier U.S.exs. 1830.. A in B F Cl Th M DN.III,VI. Not A in W S C U)

beer-and-anecdote, a. [B¹] *The Emperor's dinner, and its beer-and-anecdote appendix, covered six hours of diligent industry* 1907 "Chaps. from Autob" 568 (Nonce comb.)

beer-hall, sb. [B¹] *Some of them go, with wife and children, to a beer-hall, and sit quietly and genteelly drinking a mug or two of ale and listening to music* 1869 IA xix 187. See also *bilked* 1902 (Comb. not in OED W S C. After German Bierhaus, Bierschenke?)

beer-jolly, a. [B¹] *A...jam of howling and hurrahing people, whose beer-jolly faces stood out strongly in the glare from the manifold torches* 1881 PP xxix 344 (Comb. not in OED W S C. After German bierfrölich, bierlustig?]

beer-mill, sb. [?AB¹] *We went to a beer mill to meet some twenty Chicago journalists* 1879 *Letters* (1917) I xix 367. *Vienna beer...particularly the Pilsener which one gets in a small cellar up an obscure back lane, at that little beer-mill* 1898 "At the Appetite-Cure" (1900) 147 (Comb. not in OED W S C. Formed on the model of the Americanism *gin-mill*, q.v.)

beer-saloon, sb. [?AB¹] *A great beer-saloon in the Friedrichstrasse, Berlin* 1902 "Belated Russian Passport" (1928) 171 (Comb. not in OED W S. Given in C. Cf. saloon, below)

bee-tree, sb. [?AB³] *One can imagine a family of bears taking pride in the historic fact that an ancestor of theirs took violent possession of a bee-tree some centuries ago* 1888 *Notebook* (1935) xx 197 (OEDS Earlier U.S. exs. 1817.. A in B Th. Not A in W S C)

beflagged, ppl.a. [B¹] *The huge camp of beflagged and gay-colored tents* 1889 CY xxxix 497 (Comb. not in OED S C. Given in W)

begat, sb. [B¹] *He was now reading what to them seemed a quite unemotional chapter—that one about how Moses begat Aaron, and Aaron begat Deuteronomy, and Deuteronomy begat St. Peter...That a man should break all down over the Begats, they couldn't understand* 1907 "Chaps. from Autob" 570 (Hum. nonce use)

begatting, vbl.sb. [B¹] *That a man should break all down over the begattings* [the same passage as above, as edited by Mr.Paine] *Autob* (1924) I 342 (Nonce word. Obviously one of Mr.Paine's "improvements")

begettable, a. [B¹] *He has not yet been begotten, and in fact he is not begettable* 1902 "Does the Race Love a Lord?" 441 (Not in OED W S C)

begin with, v. [AB²] *"There ain't a book that begins with it. It lays over 'em all"* 1877 "Some Rambling Notes" ii 590. See *raft-voyage* 1891. *For illuminating purposes and economy combined, there's nothing in the world that begins with sewer-gas* 1892 AmCl xvii 180. *She steps with such style...indeed, our workingwomen cannot begin with her as a road decoration* 1897 FE xxxviii 347. *"We haven't any such comets—ours don't begin"* 1907 "Capt. Stormfield" 41 (OEDS 1f. *U.S.* To compare in any degree with. 1897, only ex., above quot. from FE. So Wr Cl. Not in W S C)

behave, v. [?A] *"Why don't you try to behave?"* 1884 HF i 4 (OED 1b. To conduct oneself well. 1691.. So W S C U. A in Wr DN.IV)

belch, v. [?AC] *He belched out a double handful of shot* 1865 "Jumping Frog" (1875) 34 (OED 4a. To vomit. *obs.* 1558..1768. Not *obs* in W S C U)

belief, sb. [?C] *By the mental and spiritual clock it was still the Age of Belief in Austria* 1898 MS (1916) i 1 (OED Belief was the earlier word for what is now commonly called *faith*...the word *faith* in course of time almost superseded *belief*, esp. in theological language, leaving *belief* in great measure to the merely intellectual process or state...Thus 'belief in God' no longer means as much as 'faith in God'...1b. Trust in God; the Christian virtue of faith. *arch* or *obs.* 1375.. 1840. So W S. Not *arch* or *obs* in C. Although the distinction drawn between *belief* and *faith* in OED W S undoubtedly holds good as a rule, the older meaning of *belief*, in the light of such passages as the above, is surely not so obsolescent as they affirm)

belief-compelling, sb. [B¹] *Such belief-compelling sincerity of tone and manner!* 1896 JA II xvi 439 (Comb. not in OED S C. Given in W)

belittle, v. [A] *The drifting years belittle certain gods of his admiration* 1873 GA x 104. *Earthly empire overshadows and belittles the pomps and shows of a village* 1896 JA III xiv 404 (OED Appears to have originated in U.S. 2. To cause to appear small; to dwarf. OEDS 1782.. So C B F Cl Th DN.VI AS.IV.473, VII.318. Not A in W S)

belittle, v. [?AB³] *"Archy is all right, and it don't become anybody to belittle him, I can tell you"* 1902 "DBDS" (1928) 327 (OED 3. To depreciate, decry the importance of. OEDS Earlier U.S.exs. 1836.. A in C B Th T M. Not A in W S U)

bell-button, sb. [B¹] *Sellers reached out and touched a bell-button in the wall* 1892 AmCl viii 79 (W: A push-button to ring a bell. This sense not in OED S C)

bell-punch, sb. [?AB³] *The clergyman did not include me among the leading citizens who took the plates around for collection. I complained...and he replied, "I would trust you—if you had a bell-punch"* 1900 *Speeches* (1910) 190 (OEDS 1883.. S: A ticket-punch having a signal-bell, used to record fares collected, and serving as a check on the conductor. So W C. Cf. B 1877 Gong-punch: an instrument used by conductors; a bell-punch)

bell-tap, sb. [B¹] *Some started to get out, but loitered; no bell-tap to land* 1875 OTM 223 (Comb. not in OED W S C; but cf. OED Bell-chime, 1819; Bell-toll, 1861)

belongings, sb. [?AB³] *A sale of all his belongings at something approaching their value* 1902 "DBDS" (1928) 294 (OED 2. 1817.. So W S C U. A in B F Cl)

belt, sb. [?A] *He snatched a navy revolver from his belt and fired* 1869 SNO (1875) 47 (Cf. OED 1. A strip of leather...used to encircle the person...and to support various articles of use. a1000.. So W S C U. Here *spec.* of the pistol-belt worn in the West)

belt, sb. **belt of timber**. [?AB¹] *The belt of timber that fringes the North Platte* 1872 RI iv 46 (Phr. not in OED W S C. Cf. OED 2b. Used of the physical features of the landscape. 1810..)

belt, sb. **to hold the belt**. [?AB¹] *He easily held the belt for honesty in that country* 1906 *Autob* (1924) II 307 (Here *fig.* Cf. C: to hold the championship in pugilism. Phr. not in OED W S)

belt, v. [?AB¹] *"They* ['genies'] *don't think nothing of pulling a shot-tower up by the roots, and belting a Sunday-School superintendent over the head with it"* 1884 HF ii 21 (W: *slang*, to inflict a blow upon, as with the fist; to strike. So S C U Wr. A in Cl DN.I,III. This sense not in OED; but cf. OEDS Belt, sb. A heavy blow or stroke. 1899, only ex.)

bench, sb. [AB³] *They were camped on the second bench of the narrow bottom of a crooked, sluggish stream* 1873 GA xvii 161. See also *atomy* 1880, for a similar but not identical use (OED 7. In U.S. a level tract between a river and neighboring hills. OEDS 1811.. So W Th H DN.VI. Not A in S C)

bench-manager, sb. [?AB¹] *She would govern the whole combination as easily as a bench-manager governs a dog-show* 1907 CS II x 264 (Comb. not in OED W S C. Cf. bench-show, below)

bench-shaped, ppl.a. [?AB¹] *Right under us a narrow ledge rose up out of the valley, with a green, slanting, bench-shaped top* 1880 TA xxxv 385 (Comb. not in OED W S C. Cf. bench, above)

bench-show, sb. [?AB³] *I had often heard of bench-shows...I had supposed they were lectures that were not well attended. It turned out now, that it was not that, but a dog-show* 1897 FE xlv 415 (OEDS U.S. quot. 1887, only ex. A in H. Not A in W S C)

bend, sb. [B¹] See *coat-of-arms* 1883 (Cf. OED 3. Heraldry. An ordinary formed by two parallel lines drawn from the dexter chief to the sinister base of the shield...Bend sinister: a similar ordinary drawn in the opposite direction: one of the marks of bastardy. c1430 ..1872—. So W S C U. Tom Sawyer's "bend or in the dexter base" is nonsense, with perhaps a suggestion of the "sinister" implication)

bend, sb. [AB¹] See *cottonwood* 1875. *The stream has bends in it, a sure indication that it has alluvial banks, and cuts them; yet these bends are only thirty and fifty feet long...This leviathan had been prowling down bends which were but a third as long as itself* 1895 "Cooper's Literary Offences" 5 (A in DN.VI: Used of a river... in the Southwest, and in most of the Far Western states. This *spec* river sense not in OED W S C)

benevolent-looking, ppl.a. [B¹] *A mild, benevolent-looking gentleman* 1872 SNO (1875) 237 (Comb. not in OED S C. Given in W)

bereave, v. [C] *"It was not I who bereaved thee of thy paltry goods"* 1881 PP xxii 275 (OED 3. To snatch away, take away by violence. *obs.* c1320..1718. So W. Not *obs* in S C)

Bermuda, sb. [?AB[1]] *Irish potatoes (choice Bermudas) five dollars* 1877 *Autob* (1924) I 9 (This meaning not in OED W S C)

berrying, vbl.sb. [?AB[2]] *Berrying, circusing, and all sorts of things which boys delight in* 1880 "Edward Mills" 326 (OED U.S. quot. 1884, only ex. Not A in S. Not in W C)

berth–saloon, sb. [AB[1]] *He entered the berth-saloon of the boat* 1897 FE iii 57 (A in Cl. Comb. not in OED W S C)

beseen, ppl.a. [C] *As fair a place as any on earth and richly beseen* 1889 CY iii 47 (OED 7. *obs* or *arch.* 1450..1629. So W S. Not *obs* in C)

beshrew, v. [C] "*Beshrew me, but I marvel that they do not require to breathe for me also!*" 1881 PP vi 81 (OED 3b. *arch.* 1566..1856. So W U. Not *arch* in S C)

bet, v. **you bet.** [AB[3]] "*The mosquitoes are pretty bad about here, madam.*" "*You bet!*" "*What did I understand you to say, madam?*" "*You Bet!*" 1872 RI ii 27. "*I'll get you there on time,*" *and you bet he did, too* 1872 RI xx 152. "*You bet I took that chance at once*" 1883 LM lii 514 (OED b. *slang,* chiefly in *U.S.* Be assured. OEDS Has long ceased to be peculiarly *U.S.* 1868.. A in S C F Cl AS.I.153. Phr. not in W)

bet, sb. **name your bet.** [?AB[1]] "*If you do not like the terms, name your bet. I scorn to stand on expenses now*" 1869 IA lviii 625 (State your terms. Phr. not in OED W S C)

bethink, v. [C] "*Collect thy scattered wits—bethink thee—take time, man*" 1881 PP xiii 156 (OED 7. *obs.* c1000..1649. So W S Wr. Not *obs* in C)

betide, v. [?C] *Tide me death, betide me life, saith the king* 1889 CY xlii 536 (OED 1. To befall. c1250..1870. So S C U. *Obs* in W)

bettable, a. [B[1]] *It is bettable that that harmless cataclysm...excited not a person in Europe but me* 1904 "Italian without a Master" (1906) 182 (Not in OED W S C)

between–days, sb. [B[1]] *She always collected her half of his pension punctually...Every now and then she paid him a visit there on between-days, also* 1894 PW x 552 (Comb. not in OED W S C; but cf. OED Between-whiles, adv. 1678.. OEDS Between-time, sb. 1909)

betwixt, prep. [?AC] *The two or three days betwixt this and the plenty that awaits us* 1881 PP xiii 153. "*He set down on the ground betwixt me and Tom*" 1884 HF ii 9 (OED 1. Now somewhat *arch* in lit.Eng. Still in *colloq* use in some dialects. 931..1865. So W Wr. Not *arch* in S C)

bewray, v. [C] "*My mind miscarrieth, bewraying simple language in such sort that the words do seem to come endlong*" 1889 CY xix 232 (OED Erroneous form of Beray. Generally mis-spelt by modern writers. *obs* or *arch.* 1. To disfigure, dirty, befoul. 1701, first ex.of the erroneous form..1863. The confusion is not mentioned in W S C, but they agree that both words are *obs.* M.T. seems to have mistaken the sense as well as the spelling of the word; he was evidently under the impression that it meant to disarrange, distort)

Bgwjjilligkkk, sb. [B[1]] "*By his own dread name I command it—BGWJJILLIGKKK!*"...*Merlin admitted, afterward, that that spirit's own mother could not have pronounced that name better than I did* 1889 CY xxiii 292 (Hum. invention)

bheel, sb. [B[1]] *They* [the Thugs] *preferred to get to one of their regular burying-places (bheels) if they could* 1897 FE xlvii 444 (Not in OED W S C. Probably not the same word as Bheel=Jheel, a pool, marsh, given in W. See under Kaet, below)

Bible–annex, sb. [AB[1]] *We know that the Bible-annex was not written by Mrs. Eddy* 1899 "Chr. Sc. and the Book" 572. *We have Mrs.Eddy's and the Angel's little Bible-annex in eight styles of binding* 1903 "Chr. Sc." 2 (M.T.'s satirical name for "Science and Health, with a Key to the Scriptures." Not in OED W S C)

Bible–class, sb. [?AB[2]] *The local minister had read sixteen 'notices' of Sunday-school and Bible-class and church and sewing-society and other meetings* a1870 Letter in Clara Clemens, *My Father* (1931) 11. *The Senator wrought in Bible classes, and nothing could keep him away from the Sunday-Schools* 1873 GA liii 478. "*She got me put in the bible-class in Sunday School*" 1883 LM lii 515 (OED A class for the study of the Bible. No ex. Not in W S C)

Bibleless, a. [B[1]] *Some poor Bibleless pagan of the South Seas* 1875 GA liii 478 (Not in OED W S C)

Bible–text, sb. [B[1]] *This poor boy baits his hook with a macerated Bible-text* 1897 FE lxi 600. See also *billy* 1906 (Comb. not in OED C. This sense not in W S)

bicentennial, a. [B[2]] *The bicentennial anniversary of this illustrious event* 1883 LM xxvii 297 (OED Occurring every two hundred years. No ex. Given in W S C U)

bicycle [B[3]] *Here they came—five hundred mailed and belted knights on bicycles* 1889 CY xxxviii 488. *A Republican simplicity...has invented and exported to the Old World the palace-car, the sleeping-car, the tram-car, the electric trolley, the best bicycles, the best motor-cars, the steam-heater, the best and smartest systems of electric calls and telephonic aids to laziness and comfort, the elevator, the private bath-room (hot and cold water on tap), the palace hotel, with its multifarious conveniences, comforts, shows, and luxuries, the—oh, the list is interminable!* 1899 "Diplomatic Pay" (1928) 239 (OED 1868.. So W S C U. In spite of M.T.'s claim, there are no convincing grounds for Am. priority with either the word *bicycle* or the thing)

biddable, a. [?AB[3]] *She was a quite biddable creature and goodhearted* 1889 CY xii 145 (OED Of Scotch origin. Obedient, docile. 1826.. So W S C U Wr. A in B F)

bide, v. [C] "*Canst not bide still an instant?*" 1881 PP xiii 157 (OED 2. To remain or continue. *arch.* 893..1871. Not *arch* in W S C Wr)

bide, v. [C] "*There bides not the man in this kingdom that would be desperate enough*" 1889 CY v 62 (OED 5. To sojourn, dwell. *arch.* c1280..1821. So U. Not *arch* in W S C)

bier–bearer, sb. [B[1]] *The bier-bearers deliver the body to some low-caste natives* 1897 FE lii 500 (Comb. not in OED W S C)

big–bug, sb. [AB[3]] "*You think you're a good deal of a big-bug, don't you?*" 1884 HF v 31 (OEDS orig. *U.S.* 1830.. So S B F Cl Th DN.III AS.II.55,348. Not A in W C U Wr. See also George T. Flom, "The Etymology of *Big-Bug*", *Mod.Lang. Notes* XVII.60)

biggity, a. [AB[1]] *The captains were very independent and airy—pretty 'biggity,' as Uncle Remus would say* 1883 LM lviii 570 (W: var. of bigotty, from bigot. Conceited or conceitedly self-important; saucily independent. *Chiefly Dial.* S: var.of bigoty. *Colloq., So. U.S.* Full of conceit, obstinate, stubborn. A in F Cl T DN.I,II,III,IV,V. Neither biggity, bigotty, nor bigoty is given in OED C. The derivation in W S from an unrecorded bigotty or bigoty, which may be a "ghost-word," seems doubtful. The negroism biggity may perhaps more plausibly be explained as a *colloq.* var. of big-head-y, from big-head; see below. For the phonetic change involved, cf. the development of beatenest, above)

big–head, sb. [AB[3]] *I got the big-head early in the game* 1901 *Speeches* (1910) 341 (OEDS *U.S.* 2.*fig.* Arrogance, conceit, 'swelled head.' 1853.. So S B F Cl Th,1805 T DN.VI. This sense not in W C)

Big House, sb. [AB[1]] "*I had a pow'ful good start, 'case de big house 'uz three mile back f'om de river*" 1894 PW xviii 18 (A in DN.II,IV,V: s.e.Mo., Va., Ky.: The large, or living house, as opposed to the summer kitchen, slave quarters, etc. This sense not in OED W S C)

20 THE UNIVERSITY OF MISSOURI STUDIES

Big Tree, sb. [AB²] *Calaveras possesses some of the grandest natural features...such as the Big Trees* 1865 SS (1926) 163. *The person who imagines that a Big Tree sprout is bigger than other kinds of sprouts is quite mistaken* 1907 CS II i 103 (OED The Sequoias or Wellingtonias of the Sierra Nevada. OEDS 1869.. So W S C B F Cl)

Big Water, sb. [AB¹] *The boat was slipping along, swift and steady, through the big water in the smoky moonlight* 1896 TSD iii 351 (The Mississippi River, from the supposed Indian etymology of its name. Not in OED W S C)

bilk, sb. [?A] *"This duffer, this scrub, this bilk!"* 1892 AmCl xv 156. *"This bilk here—this loud-mouthed sneak"* 1902 "DBDS" (1928) 356 (OED 4. A cheat. 1790..1836. OEDS Later U.S.exs. 1869..1873. A in B: used in the Far West. A in F Cl T. Not A in W S C U Wr)

bilked, ppl.a. [?A] *The cab flew farther and farther from the bilked beer-hall* 1902 "Belated Russian Passport" (1928) 178 (OED Cheated, 'done' out of one's due. 1682, only ex. So W S C Wr. Bilk, v., is A in Cl)

bill, sb. [AB³] *"Gave me a $50 green back...I asked him to take the bill back and give me a job"* 1883 LM lii 514. See *cent* 1889. *He held out the wild-cat bill* 1894 PW viii 336 (OEDS 9c. A bank-note. *U.S.* 1817.. So W S C Wr Cl M H)

bill, v. [?A] *He [the king] was billed for the king's evil—to touch for it* 1889 CY xxvi 330 (OED 4. To announce or advertise by bill. 1694..1884. So W S C U. A in Th H)

billet, sb. [?A] *The king was in a rage in a moment; he seized a billet of wood* 1881 PP xvii 205 (OED 1. A thick piece of wood. 1361..1846. So W S C U Wr. A in Cl DN.I,II)

billet, sb. [?AB¹] *They get their baggage billets, at last, and then...the disheartening business of trying to get them recorded and paid for* 1880 TA xxxii 352 (W: A written order or ticket. This R.R. sense not in OED S C)

billiardist, sb. [?AB³] *I have a billiardist on the premises* 1906 Letters (1917) II xlv 799 (OEDS A billiard player. Earliest exs. U.S. 1879.. Not A in W S C)

billiard-parlor, sb. [?AB¹] *One day a stranger came to town and opened a billiard-parlor* 1906 Speeches (1910) 269 (Comb. not in OED W S C; but cf. parlor, below, A in this sense)

billiard-room, sb. [?AB³] *The thronged billiard-rooms of St. Louis* 1875 OTM 250. See *card-room* 1875. *The tavern billiard-room* 1902 "DBDS" (1928) 315 (OEDS Earlier U.S. exs. 1816.. Not A in W U. Comb. not in S C)

billiard-saloon, sb. [B¹] *Bogart's billiard-saloon was a great resort for pilots* 1875 OTM 196 (Comb. not in OED W S C. Cf. saloon, below, not A in this sense)

billion, sb. [AB³] *I sat under the telling of it hundreds and thousands and millions and billions of times* 1889 CY ix 111. *"Billions in it—billions!"* 1892 AmCl iii 46. See also *star-stuff* 1894 (OED 2. In U.S., as in France: A thousand millions. So H: Am.billion=Eng. milliard. So W S C U Th T M)

billionaire, sb. [?AB³] See *breech-clout* 1899 (OED The possessor of property worth a billion or more of the recognized standard coin of the realm. Earliest ex. from O.W.Holmes, *Elsie Venner*. 1861.. Not A in W. Rare in S C!)

bill of particulars, sb. [?AB¹] *The party whose outside tallied with this bill of particulars* 1883 LM xlvii 471 (W: A written exhibit of the items constituting the demand for which a suit is brought. So S C. This legal phr. not in OED)

billy, sb. [AB³] *Beating his handful of humane defenders with Bible texts and billies* 1906 Autob (1924) II 11 (OEDS 1b. A policeman's baton. *U.S.* 1859.. So B F Cl T H. Not A in W S C)

bindery, sb. [AB³] *I got nervous and came down to help hump-up the binderies* 1885 Letters (1917) II xxv 465 (OED First in U.S. 1828.. So F Cl T M. Not A in W S C)

bird, sb. [?AB³] *These independent birds knew no law. They seldom obeyed the king* 1895 JA II xiii 547 (OEDS 1e. jocularly: A man, a 'cove'. 1853.. So U. Colloq or slang in W. A in Th,1842 M. This sense not in S C)

bird, sb. [AB³] *"My, what a fine bird we are! We must have orders!"* 1883 LM xviii 221. *Those nightmares they call his "celebrated Hampton Court cartoons!" Raphael was a bird* 1889 CY vii 84. *The widow...promised herself high satisfaction in showing off her fine foreign birds* 1884 PW vi 333 (OEDS 4b. *U.S.slang.* An exceptionally smart or accomplished person (freq. ironical). 1842.. So Th M. Not A in W S U. This sense not in C)

bird, sb. [AB³] *The machine does at last seem perfect; and just a bird to go!* 1890 Letters (1917) II xxx 531 (OEDS 4b. *U.S.slang.* A first-rate animal or thing. 1856.. So Th. This sense not in W S C)

birth-commission, sb. [B¹] *No exterior contributor, no birth-commission, conferred these possessions upon him* 1902 "Defence of Gen. Funston" 614 (Comb. not in OED W S C)

biscuit, sb. [AB³] *I have selected a few dishes, and made out a little bill of fare, which will go home in the steamer that precedes me, and be hot when I arrive—as follows: Radishes. Baked apples, with cream. Fried oysters; stewed oysters. Frogs. American coffee, with real cream. American butter. Fried chicken, Southern style. Porterhouse steak. Saratoga potatoes. Broiled chicken, American style. Hot biscuits, Southern style. Hot wheat-bread, Southern style. Hot buckwheat cakes. American toast. Clear maple syrup. Virginia bacon, broiled. Blue points, on the half shell. Cherrystone clams. San Francisco mussels, steamed. Oyster soup. Clam soup. Philadelphia terrapin soup. Oysters roasted in shell, Northern style. Soft-shell crabs. Connecticut shad. Baltimore perch. Brook-trout, from Sierra Nevadas. Lake-trout, from Tahoe. Sheepshead and croakers from New Orleans. Black-bass from the Mississippi. American roast beef. Roast turkey, Thanksgiving style. Cranberry sauce. Celery. Roast wild turkey. Woodcock. Canvasback duck, from Baltimore. Prairie-hens, from Illinois. Missouri partridges, broiled. Possum. Coon. Boston bacon and beans. Bacon and greens, Southern style. Hominy. Boiled onions. Turnips. Pumpkin. Squash. Asparagus. Butter-beans. Sweet-potatoes. Lettuce. Succotash. String-beans. Mashed potatoes. Catsup. Boiled potatoes, in their skins. New potatoes, minus the skins. Early Rose potatoes, roasted in the ashes, Southern style, served hot. Sliced tomatoes, with sugar or vinegar. Stewed tomatoes. Green corn, cut from the ear and served with butter and pepper. Green corn, on the ear. Hot corn-pone, with chitlings, Southern style. Hot hoe-cake, Southern style. Hot egg-bread, Southern style. Hot light-bread, Southern style. Buttermilk. Iced sweet milk. Apple dumplings, with real cream. Apple pie. Apple fritters. Apple puffs, Southern style. Peach cobbler, Southern style. Peach pie. American mince pie. Pumpkin pie. Squash pie...Ice-water* 1880 TA xlix 574-5. See *mean*, a. 1884; *wheat-bread* 1885. *The hand that picked up a biscuit carried it to the wrong head* 1894 TET ii 337. See *batter-cake* 1897. *You can stand in Vienna and toss a biscuit into Kaltenleutgeben* 1898 "At the Appetite-Cure" (1900) 148 (OED 1. A kind of crisp dry bread more or less hard..but even the characteristic of hardness implied in the name is lost in the sense 'A kind of small, baked cake, usually fermented, made of flour, milk, etc., used, according to Webster, in U.S. No exs. OEDS exs. of U.S. sense 1828..So W S C Wr F Cl M H)

biscuit-punch, sb. [AB¹] *Scale armor whose scales are represented by round holes—so that a man's coat looks as if it had been done with a biscuit-punch* 1889 CY ii 37

(Biscuit-cutter; the implement used to 'cut out' American biscuits. Comb. not in OED W S C)

biscuit-toss, sb. [B²] *A sheer summitless and bottomless wall of rock...across a gorge or crack a biscuit's toss in width* 1880 TA xxxv 386 (OED Biscuit-throw. No ex. Not in W S C)

bit, sb. [A] *A very small establishment, with a few rolls of "bit" calicoes on half a dozen shelves* 1877 *Autob* (1924) I 8. See also *Barlow knife* 1884 (OED 8b. Applied in the southern States of N.Am. to fractions of the Spanish dollar, or to their value in current money: usually one-eighth of a dollar. 1683.. So W S C Wr B F Cl Th T H DN.I,II,III,V)

bit-champing, vbl.sb. [B¹] *Then a rest followed, with the usual sneezing and bit-champing* 1872 RI xviii 144 (Comb.not in OED W S C)

bite, v. **to bite the dust.** [?AB²] *One more pilgrim had bitten the dust* 1869 IA xl 419 (OED 16. To fall in death. 1870, only ex. U.S.)

bitter, a. [C] *"The laws be so bitter and so diligently enforced"* 1881 PP xvii 211 (OED 5. Causing pain or suffering, cruel, severe. *obs. a*1000..1635. Not *obs* in W S C U)

bitters, sb. [?AB¹] See *acclimation,* sb. 1873; *Sir* 1884 (C: Spirituous liquor in which bitter herbs or roots are steeped. So W S. A in DN.III. This sense not in OED; but cf. OEDS 3. *colloq=*bitter beer. 1856..)

bituminous, a. [B¹] See *technical* 1872 (Hum. malapropism)

black bass, sb. [AB³] *Black bass from the Mississippi:* see *biscuit* 1880 (W: Any one of three widely distributed and highly prized fresh-water game fishes of eastern N.Am. So S C B F Cl DN.,III. OED lb 1840...mentions only: A fish of the Perch family found in Lake Huron)

blackbird, sb. [A] *He* [the Indian crow] *reminds one of the American blackbird* 1897 FE xxxviii 354 (OEDS U.S. exs. 1643.. So W S C H)

black fish, sb. [?A] *We had a pleasant ten days' run from New York to the Azores islands...We saw the usual sharks, black fish, porpoises, etc.* 1869 IA v 48 (OED 2. A small species of whale. Earliest ex. U.S. 1796.. A in B F Cl. Not A in W S C)

Blackfoot, sb. [AB³] *Lay a row of moccasins before me—Pawnee, Sioux, Shoshone, Cheyenne, Blackfoot, and as many other tribes as you please,—and I can name the tribe every moccasin belongs to by the make of it. Name it in horse-talk, and could do it in American if I had speech* 1906 "Horse's Tale" 327 (OED 1. The name of a tribe of N.Am. Indians. 1842.. So W S C)

Black Forester, sb. [B¹] *Manure is evidently the Black Forester's main treasure* 1880 TA xxii 210 (Inhabitant of the Black Forest, Germany. Not in OED W S C)

blacknesses, sb.pl. [B¹] *The other animals...are free from the blacknesses and rottennesses of his* [man's] *character* 1906 *Autob* (1924) II 8 (Concrete use not in OED W S C)

black-snake, sb. [A] *When they were black-snakes, we fled, without shame* 1897-8 *Autob* (1924) I 103 (OED 1. A name given to several dark-colored snakes...in U.S. 1688.. So W S C)

blacksnake, v. [AB²] *"I lay I'll blacksnake you within an inch of your life!"* 1870 SNO (1875) 271 (OEDS U.S. 1875, this quot... So F Cl. Not in W S C as verb)

bladder-balloon, sb. [B¹] *He had the aspect of a bladder-balloon that's been stepped on by a cow* 1889 CY xxxii 415 (Comb. not in OED W S C)

blame, v. [AB³] *"Why, blame my cats if he don't weigh five pound!"* 1865 "Jumping Frog" (1875) 35. *"Why, blame it all, we've got to do it"* 1884 HF ii 14. *"Blame my skin if I hain't gone en forgit dat name agin!"* 1892 AmCl viii 81 (OEDS 7a. *dial* and *U.S.* Used as an imprecation, in the imperative mood. 1835.. So Wr B T DN.II,III,V. Not A in W. This use not in S C)

blame, v. **blamed if.** [AB³] See *horrible-looking* 1884. *"Blamed if I haven't seen him keep it up a level two hours and a half"* 1892 AmCl xvi 169. *"I'm blamed if I can see my way through it"* 1894 PW xiii 777 (OEDS 7b. *dial* and *U.S.* In passive, in phr. (I'm) blamed if (etc.) 1867.. So S Wr B F Cl T DN.III. Not A in W. This use not in C)

blame, adv. [AB³] *"He's my tick and I'll do what I blame please with him, or die!"* 1876 TS vii 74 (OEDS 7c. *dial* and *U.S.* 1843.. So S. Not A in W. This use not in C)

blamed, ppl.a. [AB³] *"Blamed old rip!"* 1876 TS ix 89. *"I'd a blamed sight ruther carry the claim myself"* 1880 TA xxvi 270. *The blamedest, jambledest, idiotic sermons you ever struck* 1896 TSD xi 537 (OEDS *dial* and *U.S.* 1. 1840.. So S Wr B F Cl T DN.III,V. Not A in W. Not in C)

blamed, adv. [AB³] *"Well, it's blamed mean, that's all"* 1876 TS viii 84 (OEDS *dial* and *U.S.* 2. 1845.. So S B F T. Not A in W Wr. Not in C)

blame-fool, a. [AB¹] *"Talk about trying to cure warts with spunk-water, such a blame-fool way as that!"* 1876 TS vi 65 (Comb. not in OED W S C. Cf. above)

Bland dollar, sb. [AB¹] *"Being a Bland dollar don't make it a dollar just the same"* 1892 AmCl v 59 (W: *U.S.* The silver dollar coined under the Bland-Allison Act of 1878. So Th.III: Named after Mr. Richard P. Bland of Missouri. Term not in OED S C; but cf. OED Dollar 5. Buzzard dollar, a name applied in derision to the U.S. silver dollar of 412½ grains, coined in accordance with the Bland bill of 1878)

blandly, adv. [B¹] *He peered blandly out into the blackness* 1875 OTM 451. *The howler would...swim blandly away* 1894 PW iv 330. *Then the paper in which it was suppressed blandly copies the forbidden matter into its evening edition* 1898 "Stirring Times" (1900) 289 (Smoothly, imperturbably, with irritating superiority. This ironical sense not in OED W S C. Cf. OED: Mildly, gently, pleasingly. 1827..)

blanket-bag, sb. [?AB³] *Porters to carry provisions ...and also blanket bags for the party to sleep in* 1880 TA xxxvi 413 (OED 1856, only ex. U.S. Comb. not in W S C)

blasphemous, a [B¹] *If educated people can hear such blasphemous grammar...and be unconscious of the deed* 1883 LM xxvi 288 (Atrocious, execrable; deserving blasphemy. This hum. transf. sense not in OED W S C)

blast, sb. [B¹] *I gave the P.O.Department a blast in the papers about sending misdirected letters of mine back to the writers* 1874 *Letters* (1917) I xiii 226 (Severe criticism; scathing condemnation. This *fig* sense not in OED W S C; but cf. OED 8. A 'blowing up' by gunpowder, an explosion. 1635..)

blast, v. [B¹] *Sally...resolved to blast him out of his serenity* 1892 AmCl xxv 264 (This *fig* sense not in OED W S C. Cf. OED 5. To blow up by explosion. 1758..)

blast, v. [?A] *"Blast it, boy!"* 1883 LM iii 61 (OEDS 10. Freq. in imprecations. 1634.. So C U. A in M DN.V. This expletive use not in W S)

blasting-powder, sb. [?AB²] *We bought a two-horse wagon and put eighteen hundred pounds of bacon, flour, beans, blasting-powder, picks, and shovels in it* 1869 IA xxvii 285. *No hint milder than blasting-powder or nitroglycerin would be likely to move the bores out of listening distance* 1870 SNO (1875) 99. *A tin can of blasting-powder, which they placed upon the candle-box* 1902 "DBDS" (1928) 311 (OED 6. No ex. So W. Not in S C)

blatherskite, sb. [AB³] *She was a perfect blatherskite; I mean for jaw, jaw, jaw* 1889 CY xii 145. See *larrikin* 1897. *"You cowardly blatherskite, say that again!"* 1898 "Stirring Times" (1900) 317. See *sultry* 1899. *He will not hesitate to vote for the blatherskites if his "party* *honor" shall exact it* 1907 CS II 359. See *herumfrodite* 1909 (One of M.T.'s favorite words. OED *U.S. colloq.* 1848.. So F T DN.I,IV AS.V.219. Not A in W S C Wr)

blatta byzantina, sb. [B¹] See *afarabocca* 1894 (Not in OED W S C; but cf. C: Blatta..the cockroach or common black beetle, introduced from the East into Europe and America, is *Blatta (Periplaneta) orientalis*)

blatter, v. [?A] *So the king he blattered along, and managed to inquire about pretty much everybody* 1884 HF xxv 248 (OED 1. To prate or speak volubly. 1555..1865. So S C. *Dial* in W Wr)

Blavatsky-Buddhist, sb. [B¹] See *Allopath* 1902 (Nonce comb. Madame Elena Petrovsky Blavatsky (1831-1891) was a Russian theosophist and traveler in India)

blessings-of-civilization, a. [B¹] *The Blessings-of-Civilization Trust, wisely and cautiously administered, is a Daisy* 1901 "To the Person Sitting in Darkness" 165 (Hum. nonce comb.)

blimblammin', vbl.sb. [B¹] *"Dey say Sollermun de wises' man dat ever live...Would a wise man want to live in de mids' er sich a blimblammin' all de time?...A wise man 'ud take en buil' a biler-factry; en den he could shet down de biler-factry when he want to res'"* 1884 HF xiv 120 (Hum. coinage)

blind, sb. [AB²] *"Now you talk! You see my blind—straddle it like a man!"* 1872 RI xlvii 333 (OEDS 9. In poker, a stake put up by a player before seeing his cards. 1872, this quot...So W S C F Cl Th.III T DN.VI)

blind, a. [C] *"How is a body ever going to get through this blind place at night?"* 1875 OTM 446 (OED 6. Enveloped in darkness; dark, obscure. *arch.* 1000..1809. So W S C)

blind-drunk, a. [B²] *"Poor blind-drunk Uncle Lige"* 1865 SS (1926) 192. *I judged he would be blind drunk in about an hour* 1884 HF vi 45 (OED 15. So intoxicated as to see no better than a blind man. No ex. So W Wr. Not in S C)

blinder, sb. [AB³] *I took off the sun-bonnet, for I didn't want no blinders on then* 1884 HF xi 96 (OED 2. A blinker for a horse. Chiefly *U.S.* 1809.. So Th T H. Not A in W S C Wr)

blind lead, sb. [?AB¹] *A "blind lead" is a lead or ledge that does not "crop out" above the surface* 1872 RI xl 280 (Comb. not in OED S C. Given as mining term in W)

blind reef, sb. [?AB¹] *She must pick her intricate way through snags and blind reefs* 1875 OTM 224 (A *spec* river term. Comb. not in OED W S C; but cf. OED Blind, a. 9. Covered or concealed from sight. 1513..)

blind staggers, sb. [?AB³] *The horse-doctor...would give me something to turn the cold in the head into the blind staggers* 1899 "Chr. Sc. and the Book" 590 (OEDS 16. All exs. U.S. 1838.. Not A in W. Comb. not in S C)

blind vein, sb. [?AB¹] *Mr. Fair...no doubt looking for cross lodes and blind veins—came across a body of rich ore* 1906 *Autob* (1924) I 272 (W: Not appearing in an outcrop at the surface. So S. Comb. not in OED C)

blip, sb. [?AB¹] *We took him a blip in the back and knocked him off* 1894 TSA xii 540 (A sudden blow. Not in OED W S C)

bliss-business, sb. [B¹] *Mrs. Driscoll enjoyed two years of bliss...then she died, and her husband and... Mrs. Pratt continued the bliss-business at the old stand* 1894 PW v 332 (Nonce comb.)

blister, sb. [?AB¹] *"I never seen anything like that old blister for clean out-and-out cheek"* 1884 HF xxix 303. *The princess and two of her ladies-in-waiting...a couple of the tryingest blisters I ever saw* 1889 CY xx 246 (S: A troublesome or annoying person; a nuisance. So Wr. This sense not in OED W C. Given as A in the sense of "extortioner" in Th,1854 DN.IV)

blithe, a. [?C] *"Come—ye shall see a blithe sight"* 1889 CY xvii 206 (OED 2. Merry, gay, mirthful. *Rare* in mod.Eng.prose or speech. 1000..1807. 2b. transf. of

things. More common. 1300..1857. Not *rare* in W S C U Wr)

bloat, sb. [AB³] *The sun looked through the tall cocoa-nut trees like a blooming whiskey bloat through the bars of a city prison* 1872 RI lxxi 513 (OEDS 2. One soaked in liquor; a drunkard. *U.S.* 1861.. So F Cl Th.III. Not A in W S. This sense not in C)

block, sb. [A] *"Take a walk around the block!"* 1869 IA xxvi 283. See *graveyard* 1870. *They moved up the river street three blocks, then turned to the left up a cross street* 1876 TS xxix 222. *Blocks of tall new buildings of the most sumptuous sort* 1880 TA xlviii 555. See also *frame shop* 1893 (OED 14. Used esp. in U.S. and Canada. OEDS 1796.. So B F Cl Th T M H DN.I,III,V AS.I.491. Not A in W S C)

blockade, sb. *to run a blockade.* [?AB²] *Inquired about chances to run the blockade and visit the Alhambra at Granada* 1869 IA lix 636 (OED 1b. 1869, only ex. U.S. Not A in W S C U. The phr. may have originated in the U.S. during the Civil War)

bloke, sb. [?AB³] *"I made up my mind to be a square bloke"* [given as thieves' argot] 1883 LM lii 511 (OED *slang*. Man, fellow. 1851.. So W S C U. A in AS.IV.338)

blood, v. [?AC] *"I blooded the ax good"* 1884 HF vii 52 (OED 2. To wet or smear with blood. *?Obs* or *dial.* 1593..1862. So S. *Arch* in W C)

blooded, ppl.a. [A] *He put his blooded steed to his utmost speed to show him off* 1866 *Speeches* (1923) 13 (OEDS 3. Chiefly *U.S.* 1778.. So B F Cl Th M. H. Not A in W S C)

blood-kin, a. [B¹] *The seven hundred inhabitants are all blood-kin to each other* 1880 TA xix 173 (Comb. not in OED W S C)

blood-kinship, sb. [B²] *They testify their blood-kinship with each other* 1872 RI App. 583 (OED 1883, only ex. Not in W S C)

blood-smeared, ppl.a. [B¹] *She took up the young child of the murdered woman in her blood-smeared hands* 1870 SNO (1875) 190 (Comb. not in OED W S C)

blood-thirstily, adv. [B²] *A bloodthirstily interesting little Montana book* 1872 RI x 84 (OED 1880.. So W S. Not in C)

bloody, a. [B³] *The bloody machine offered but a doubtful outlook* 1893 *Letters* (1917) II xxxiii 593 (OED 10. In foul language, a vague epithet expressing anger, resentment, detestation. 1840.. So Wr. *Low slang* in W S C)

bloody-jawed, ppl.a. [B¹] *This granite-hearted, bloody-jawed maniac of Russia* 1890 *Letters* (1917) II xxx 536 (Comb. not in OED W S C)

blooming, ppl.a. [B²] See *bloat* 1872 (OED 4. Often euphemistic, for bloody or the like. 1882.. *Slang* in W S C U)

blow, v. [?AB³] *"Pap got drunk, and went a-blowing around and cussing"* 1884 HF v 35. See also *meat-feast* 1889 (OED 6b. To fume, storm. *colloq.* 1863..So W S C Wr. A in B F Cl Th,1840 Th.III,1789 T M)

blow-out, sb. [?AB³] *We had a blow-out at Dan's house and a lively talk over old times* 1868 *Letters* (1917) I viii 142. *"What's all this blow-out about anyway?" "It's one of the widow's parties"* 1876 TS xxxiv 264. *Here comes along a man who slashes out nearly four dollars on a single blow-out* 1889 CY xxxii 415. See also *starchy* 1894 (OEDS 2. A 'feast' or 'feed'. *colloq.* 1824.. So W S C Wr. A in B F Th T M DN.II)

blow up, v. intr. [?AB¹] *Redpath tells me to blow up. Here goes!* 1871 *Letters* (1917) I x 189 (W: To become explosively angry or abusive. This sense not in OED S C; but cf. the trans. use in OED 25b. To scold, rail at. *colloq.* 1827..; which sense is called A in B)

blubber, sb.[AB¹] *That may be good Dutch Flat poetry, but...it is too smooth and blubbery; it reads like buttermilk gurgling from a jug...There is genius in you, but too much blubber* 1867 SNO (1875) 75 (A in DN.IV: Empty talk, chatter. This sense not in OED W S C)

blubber–and–slush, sb. [?AB¹] *"What we take for thinking is just blubber-and-slush"* 1902 "DBDS" (1928) 326 (Hum. nonce comb. Cf. above)

blubber–grease, sb. [B¹] *She had been absently scraping blubber-grease from her cheeks* 1893 "Esquimau Maiden's Romance" (1900) 136 (Comb. not in OED W S C)

blubbery, a. [?AB¹] See *blubber* 1867 (W: Like blubber; gelatinous and quivering. So S. Not in OED C. Cf. b ubber, above)

blue, sb. **the blues.** [?AB³] See *sky-blue,* sb. 1872. *Polly's heart was nearly broken; the "blues" returned in fearful force* 1873 GA xxviii 261. *Her blues were gone; she was in high feather* 1894 PW viii 337 (OED 12. For 'blue devils'. *colloq.* 1807. . Earliest quot. from W. Irving. A in AS.XI.293. Not A in W S U. Not in C)

blue–clay, sb. [B¹] *Any person who is familiar with me knows how to get at the jewel of any fact of mine and dig it out of its blue-clay matrix* 1906 *Autob* (1924) I 293 (Comb. not in OED W S C; but cf. OEDS Blue earth, Blue ground: the dark soil, normally greyish-blue, in which diamonds are found; so W)

Blue Grass, a. [AB³] *She was of the best blood of Kentucky, the bluest Blue Grass aristocracy* 1906 "Horse's Tale" 328 (OEDS *U.S.* 3b. ellipt. as adj. 1889. So W S C B F Cl Th,1784 T M DN.VI)

Blue Hen's Chickens, sb. [AB¹] *"I's one o' de ole Blue Hen's Chickens, I is! 'Ca'se, you see, dat's what folks dat's bawn in Maryland calls deyselves, an' dey's proud of it"* 1874 SNO (1875) 203 (Clearly a mistake for Delaware. Cf. OEDS Blue Hen *U.S.* The State of Delaware. 1830. . So W S C B F Cl Th M DN.VI)

bluejay, sb. [A] *"There's more to a bluejay than any other creature"* 1880 TA ii 36 (OEDS *U.S.* A N.American jay. 1709. . So W S C Th)

Blue Laws, sb. [A] *One hears much about the "hideous Blue Laws of Connecticut"* 1881 PP Gen.Note 410 (OEDS *U.S.* 1781. . So W S C B F Cl Th,1775 M)

blue–mass, sb. [?AB¹] *Commenced by eating one dozen large blue-mass pills, box and all* 1867 SNO (1875) 78 (W: *Pharm.* A preparation of finely divided mercury; called also blue pill. So S C. A in H. Comb. not in OED U; but cf. OED Blue pill, 1794. .)

blue point, sb. [AB³] See *biscuit* 1880 (OEDS *U.S.* Used ellipt. to designate a small well-flavoured oyster from the south shore of Long Island. 1832. . So W S C)

blue–uniformed, ppl.a. [B¹] *A blue-uniformed brass-buttoned little page* 1873 GA xlv 405 (Comb. not in OED W S C)

bluff, sb. [A] See *wood,* v. 1859. *They landed near the Third Chickasaw Bluffs* 1883 LM ii 36. *From the tall bluffs above the bridge Rouen was become again a delight to the eyes* 1896 JA III xv 405 (OED. First used in N. America, and still mostly of American landscapes. 1737. . B: In America applied to a high bank presenting a steep front along a river. So Cl Th T M DN.II,III,V, VI, in s.w.Mo., n.w.Ark., s.Ill. AS.II.32, IV.6. Not A in W S C U)

bluff, sb. [AB³] *A high "bluff" sandbar in the middle of a stream* 1873 GA iv 42. *"It wasn't a bluff reef...It wasn't anything but a wind reef"* 1875 OTM 288. See also *scoot,* v. 1884; *sqush,* v. 1884 (OEDS *attrib.* 1861. . Cf. above)

bluff, sb. [AB³] *It was a "bluff", you know. At such a time it is sound judgment to put on a bold face and play your hand for a hundred times what it is worth* 1889 CY xxxix 505 (OED.2. First used in U.S. 1848. . So C F Cl Th T M DN.II. Not A in W S U)

bluff, v. [AB³] *I was not bluffing this time. I meant what I said; I could do what I promised* 1889 CY xl 510. *In preparing for armed revolution and in talking revolution, were the Reformers "bluffing", or were they in earnest?* 1897 FE lxvii 668 (OED.3. Of U.S. origin. 1882. . OEDS 1854. . So C B F Cl Th,1850 T M. Not A in W S U)

blunt-toed, a. [B¹] *His clumsy, blunt-toed shoes with thick cork soles* 1870 SNO (1875) 232 (Comb. not in OED W S C)

board, sb. [AB²] *I was an expert in all details of stock traffic...My time was my own after the afternoon board, Saturdays* 1893 "Banknote" (1928) 116 (OEDS 8b The Stock Exchange. *U.S.* 1905. . So defined in W, but called *Colloq.Brit.* This sense not in S C)

board, sb. **to stay by the board.** [B¹] *We stayed by the board and put it through on that line* 1889 CY xxii 271 (To stick to it, persist, remain steadfast; opposite of 'to go by the board.' Phr. not in OED S W C. Cf. OED 12b. To go by the board: to go for good and all, be 'carried away'. 1856. .)

board–clatter, sb. [B¹] *Wolf accompanied him with his board-clatter* 1898 "Stirring Times" (1900) 307 (Nonce comb.)

board–fence, sb. [A] *The lad...scrambled up the high board fence, and disappeared over it* 1876 TS i 18 (OEDS *U.S.* A close fence made with boards. 1725. . So B. Comb. not in W S C)

boat–hand, sb. [B¹] *The passengers had an hour's recreation while the boat-hands chopped the bridge away* 1875 OTM 450 (Comb. not in OED S C. Given in W)

body, sb. **body of me.** [C] *"Body o' me! I have driven the needle under my nail!"* 1881 PP xiii 153 (OED 4. Used as an oath. *obs.* 1530. .1828. Not *obs* in Wr. Phr. not in W S C)

body, sb. [?AC] See *natty* 1871. *He will put himself to any amount of trouble to oblige a body* 1871 SNO (1875) 157. See *eagle* 1872. *"Does a body's whole soul good to look at you!"* 1873 GA v 57. See *muck* 1876; *line, out of one's* 1881; *back up* 1883; *land's sake* 1884. *I could make anything a body wanted* 1889 CY pref. 12. See also *mullet-headed* 1893 (OED 13. Formerly, as still *dial,* exactly equivalent to the current 'person'; but now only as a term of familiarity, with a tinge of compassion. 1297. .1833. So W S C U Wr. A in DN.I,II,III. A favorite usage with M.T.)

body–snatcher, sb. [AB¹] *They say that the long-nosed, lanky, dyspeptic-looking body-snatchers, with the indescribable hats on...are the old, familiar, self-righteous Pharisees we read of in the Scriptures* 1869 IA xlviii 505. *The journal always referred to me afterwards as "Twain, the Body-Snatcher"* 1870 SNO (1875) 313 (A in F: A western term of revilement. This use not in OED W S C)

bogus, a. [AB³] *I despise bogus brick columns, plastered over with mortar* 1853 Letter in *Iowa Journal of Hist.* (1929) 411. *The merchant bit the coins, and then he said, These be bogus* 1869 IA xl 427. *The small bogus king has a...cussed time of it on the throne* 1880 *Letters* (1917) I xx 377. *The home of the bogus miracle become the home of the real one* 1889 CY xxiv 302. See also *allow* 1896; *chromo-portrait* 1903 (OED A cant word of U.S. OEDS 2. adj. 1839. . So W S C U B F Cl Th,1827 T M DN.VI)

bogus, sb. [AB¹] *We couldn't afford "bogus" in that office...Well, we did have one or two kinds of "bogus"... To make up for short matter we would "turn over ads"— turn over whole pages and duplicate it. The other "bogus" was deep philosophical stuff, which we judged nobody ever read; so we kept a galley of it standing, and kept on slapping the same old batches of it in every now and then* 1886 *Speeches* (1910) 184 (W: Miscellaneous matter, not news, printed in an early edition and to be replaced by news. *Slang, U.S.* This sense not in OED S C)

boil, sb. [AB³] *These tumbling "boils" show a dissolving bar and a changing channel* 1875 OTM 289 (OEDS 4. *U.S.* 1826. . So W: A swirling upheaveal of water at the surface of a river or the sea. This sense not in S C)

boil down, v. [B²] *This one had loved her husband with all her might, and now she boiled it all down into hate* 1870 SNO (1875) 121 (OED 8.*fig.* 1880, only ex. So W S C)

boiled–cauliflower, a. [B¹] *Elderly man—a drinker. Boiled-cauliflower nose in a flabby face* 1897 FE xli 382 (Nonce comb.)

boiled shirt, sb. sp. **biled shirt.** [AB³E] *A nigger on the box in a biled shirt and a plug hat* 1872 RI xlviii 334. *If a man wanted a fight...all he had to do was to appear in public in a white shirt or a stove-pipe hat... They had a particular and malignant animosity toward what they called a "biled shirt"* do. lvii 416 (OEDS Boiled, ppl.a. 2. *U.S.* A white or dress shirt. 1869.. So W B F M H DN.III,IV, e.Ala., w. Ind., Minn. AS.V.59, Neb. Comb. not in S C. Cf. W: *illit.* and hence often humorously *biled shirt*)

boiler–deck, sb. [AB³] *The boiler-deck, the hurricane-deck, and the texas-deck are fenced and ornamented with clean white railings* 1875 OTM 70. *The boiler-deck—i.e., the second story of the boat, so to speak—was as spacious as a church* 1875 OTM 220. *Ealer sank through the ragged cavern where the hurricane-deck and the boiler-deck had been, and landed in a nest of ruins on the main deck* 1909 ISD i 18 (OEDS *U.S.* The lower deck of a steamer, lying immediately above the boilers. 1830.. So W Th. Not in S C. The OED definition is wrong, as is shown both by the quots. above from M.T. and by the OED quot. for 1830: the boiler-deck was not the lower, but part of the upper deck, and *above* the main deck)

boiler–factory, sb. [B¹] See *blimblammin'* 1884. *It's like a boiler-factory for racket* 1888 *Letters* (1917) II xxviii 500 (Comb. not in OED W S C. Used by M.T. as a synonym for noise or pandemonium)

boiler–iron, sb. [B¹] See *triple-lock,* v. 1876. *She was a W.C.T.U., with all that that implies of boiler-iron virtue and unendurable holiness* 1904 "Bequest" (1906) v 28 (Used by M.T. as a symbol of moral rigidity. This *fig* sense not in OED W S C)

boiling, sb. **the whole bilin'.** [?AB³] *"I thought maybe you'd fetch the whole bilin' along with you"* 1873 GA xvii 164. *"The whole bilin' of 'm's frauds!"* 1884 HF xxix 304 (OED 4. The 'whole lot'. slang. 1837.. So W U Wr T. A in B Th.III,1786 DN.I,II,III,IV. Phr. not in S C)

bolting, vbl.sb. [B²] *No five minute boltings of flabby rolls, muddy coffee* 1869 IA xii 109 (OED 4. Hasty swallowing. 1872, this quot., wrongly dated. This sense not in W S C. Given in Wr.)

bolwoggoly, sb. [B¹] See *kahkahponeeka* 1880 (Hum. invention)

bombshell, v. [B¹] *They got used to being bombshelled out of home* 1883 LM xxxv 379 (Not as verb in OED W S C)

bonanza, sb. [AB³] *"Three days agone, I struck a manure mine!—a Golconda, a limitless Bonanza, of solid manure"* 1880 TA xxii 212. *Glance over the headings in the telegraphic page—a perfect bonanza of texts, you see!* 1906 *Autob* (1924) I 282 (OEDS *U.S.colloq.*1847.. So W S C U B F Cl Th T M)

bone, sb. [?C] *Pride of profession is one of the boniest bones in existence—if not the boniest* 1902 "The Bee" (1917) 284 (OED 7. Bone of contention: formerly simply *bone*...in allusion to the strife which a bone causes between dogs. 1562...1692. This use not in W S C. App. not felt as *arch* by M.T.)

bone–bruising, ppl.a. [B¹] *His native cheerfulness unannihilated by his back-breaking and bone-bruising passage* 1894 TET v 369 (Comb. not in OED W S C; but cf. OED Bone-crushing 1676, Bone-breaking 1808, etc.)

bone–filter, sb. [B¹] *The great sugar-house was a wilderness of tubs and tanks and vats and filters...the bone-filter to remove the alcohol* 1883 LM xlviii 479 (Comb. not in OED W S C)

bone–mashing, ppl.a. [B¹] *The bone-mashing good-fellowship handshake of the mines* 1902 "DBDS" (1928) 354 (Comb. not in OED W S C)

bone–racking, vbl.sb. [B¹] *"Bone-rackings and bastings be plenty enow in this life"* 1881 PP xviii 226 (Comb. not in OED W S C)

bone-spray, sb. [B¹] *Look at the wax-work head... then the feet, all beads and joints and bone-sprays, an imitation X-ray photograph!* 1905 "Czar's Soliloquy" 321 (Nonce comb.)

bone-wrenching, ppl.a. [B¹] *A lively, muscle-straining, bone-wrenching...pastime, climbing the Pyramids* 1869 IA lviii 622 (Comb. not in OED W S C)

bone-yard, sb. [AB²] *"Some roughs jumped the Catholic bone-yard, and started in to stake out town-lots in it"* 1872 RI xlvii 334 (OEDS *U.S.* 1872, this quot. So W F Cl T AS.XI.201. Not A in S C)

bong-a-bong, sb. [B¹] See *kahkahponeeka* 1880 (Hum. invention)

bony, a. [B¹] See *bone* 1902 (Nonce use. Cf. note under *bone,* above)

boodle, sb. [AB³] *The stately nation called Christendom, returning from pirate raids...with her pocket full of boodle* 1900 E&E, intro. p. xxxiv (OEDS 2b. *U.S.* 1884.. So S C B F Cl Th,1858 T M DN.VI. Not A in W)

book, sb. **like a book.** [AB³] *"Prince Bossloffsky knows me, knows me like a book"* 1902 "Belated Russian Passport" (1928) 184 (OEDS 1c. *U.S.colloq.* 1829.. So B F Th. Not A in W S C)

book, v. [?AB³] *Booked for the excursion* 1869 IA ii 27. *In the college prison—booked for three months* 1880 TA App. C 599. *Booked for the penitentiary* 1883 LM xix 228. *Angelo books himself for one table, I book myself for the other* 1894 TET ii 339. *The eclipse had been booked for only a month away* 1889 CY vii 86. *I thank the society cordially for these invitations, although I am booked elsewhere and cannot come* 1901 *Speeches* (1910) 343. *"I am booked through to Paris"* 1902 "Belated Russian Passport" (1928) 175 (OED 4. To engage, enter for a seat or place. 1826.. So W S C U. F says this sense was originally an Americanism, but is now one of the most common British colloquialisms. The claim to Am. priority is not borne out by the OED quots. M considers it distinctively British. Whether Am. or not, it was a favorite word with M.T.)

bookcased, ppl.a. [B²] *The room beyond, where the precious library is bookcased* 1904 *Autob* (1924) I 212 (Given in OED, no ex. Not in W S C)

book–material, sb. [B¹] *I shan't be able to pick up the kind of book-material I want* 1882 *Letters* (1917) I xxii 418 (Comb. not in OED W S C; but cf. OED Book-matter 1548)

book-talk, sb. [B¹] *"No more commonplace language, either, but rattling, out-and-out book-talk!"* 1880 TA ii 36 (Comb. not in OED W S C; but cf. OED Book-language, 1645; Book-word, 1851; Book-speech, 1871)

booky, a. [?AB³] *The most permanent lessons in morals are those which come, not of booky teaching, but of experience* 1880 TA xlvii 554. See also *clerkly* 1897 (OED colloq. 1880,this quot...OEDS Earlier U.S.ex. 1832.. A in Th. Not A in W S C)

boom, sb. [AB³] *The "boom" was something wonderful. Everybody bought, everybody sold* 1883 LM lvii 556. *The boom collapsed and left his hitherto envied young devil of an heir a pauper* 1894 PW iv 331. See also *Christian Science* 1902 (OEDS *U.S.* 1875.. So S C F Cl Th.III T M H. Not A in W!)

boom, v.intr. [AB²] *Mr. Jeff Thompson was the most popular engineer who could be found for his work...In his own language, he "just went booming"* 1873 GA xvii 160. *"There's two hundred thousand dollars coming, and that will set things booming again"* 1873 GA xxvii 245. *I'm booming these days—got health and spirits to waste* 1883 *Letters* (1917) I xxiii 434. See *cut bank* 1884. *Sellers arrived sodden with grief and booming with glad excitement* 1892 AmCl iv 52. See also *Hail Columbia* 1902; *corner,* sb. 1904 (OED *U.S.* 1. 1879.. OEDS For *U.S.*, read *'orig.U.S.',* and add earlier exs. 1873 1875. So W S C F Cl Th,1850 Th.III,1715 T M H. In view of the quots. cited in Th and OEDS, it is hard to understand how W came to make the statement:

"The first use of *boom* in this sense was probably in the St. Louis *Globe-Democrat*, July 18, 1878: 'The Grant movement is *booming*'. The author of the phrase, J. B. McCullagh, derived it from sense 2: To move with a booming noise, as a ship under full sail." F says the term originated in California. Mark Twain was probably not its inventor, but he has a clear priority of five years over McCullagh.)

boom, v.trans. [AB³] See *base,* sb. 1888 (OED *U.S.* 2. To give a 'boom' to; to push, puff, force upon public attention. 1879.. So W S C B Cl Th M H. Not A in U)

boomeranger, sb. [B¹] *There must have been a large distribution of acuteness among those naked, skinny aboriginals* [Australian Bushmen], *or they couldn't have been such unapproachable trackers and boomerangers* 1897 FE xxi 207 (Not in OED W S C; but it seems hardly possible that M.T. should have coined it)

booming, ppl.a. [AB³] *I haven't had such booming working days for many years* 1883 *Letters* (1917) I xxiii 434. *"We can just have booming times—they don't have no school now"* 1884 HF xvii 151. See also *baseball* 1889; *push,* sb. 1889 (OED 2. Flourishing, advancing on a tide of prosperity. *U.S.* 1879.. So C F Cl Th,1850 M H. Not A in W S!)

booming, ppl.a.[?AB¹] *"I was jist a-bilin'! Mad? I was jist a-boomin'!"* 1874 SNO (1875) 244. *"They was booming mad, and gave us a cussing"* 1884 HF xxiv 242 (Furious; in a high state of excitement. This further extension of the sense above is unnoted in OED W S C)

boon, sb. [C] *"I and my old wife have prayed fervently or the good boon of a son"* 1871 SNO (1875) 172. *He cannot have the boon of death* 1898 *"About Play-Acting"* (1900) 218 (OED 3. The matter prayed for or asked. *obs or arch. c1175..1823.* So W S C U)

boost, v. [AB³] *"You ought to have seen the bull boosting up the sand like a whirlwind"* 1872 RI vii 63. *"All you want is somebody to steady you and boost you along on the right road"* 1892 *"Switzerland"* (1917) 207 (OED *U.S.colloq.* To lift or push from behind. Also *fig.* OEDS 1826.. So W S C U B F Cl Th.III,1815 T M AS.I.661f.)

boost, sb. [?AB¹] *"They grind out a couple* [of pictures] *a day when they strike what they call a boost—that is, an inspiration"* 1892 AmCl xvi 163 (This sense not in OED W S C; but cf. OED sb. 2: A lift; a shove up. *U.S. colloq.* OEDS 1825..; so W S C U Cl Th T M AS.I.661)

boot-heel, sb. [B²] *He stretches his legs till the rims of his boot-heels rest upon the floor* 1870 SNO (1875) 99 (Given in OED, no ex. Not in W S C)

boot-polishing, vbl.sb. [?AB¹] *He found himself, when a boy, a sort of street Arab... He speedily took to boot-polishing* 1873 GA liv 487 (Comb. not in OED W S C; but cf. OED Boot-black. Chiefly *U.S.* 1864.. So H: Am. boot-black=Eng. shoe-black. Cf.also W: boot-polisher)

boot-toe, sb. [B¹] See *sleigh-runner* 1876 (Comb. not in OED W S C)

bopple, sb. [B¹] See *kahkahponeeka* 1880 (Hum. invention)

border-ruffian, sb. [AB³] *I am a border-ruffian from the State of Missouri* 1881 *Speeches* (1910) 19 (OEDS *U.S.* 1856.. So W: One of those pro-slavery men of Missouri who, during the Border War, used to cross the border into Kansas and Nebraska to vote illegally or to intimidate the anti-slavery settlers. So S F Cl Th. Not in C)

bore, v. [B¹] *I bored through Middlemarch during the past week* 1885 *Letters* (1917) II xxv 454 (To suffer boredom while reading. This intr. use not in OED W S C)

born days, sb. [?A] *"Well, I never seen the beat of it in my born days"* 1884 HF xxxiii 343 (OED *colloq.* 1742.. So W S C Wr. A in DN.II,III)

boshy, a. [?AB²] *I read your boshy criticisms on the opera with the most exquisite anguish* 1864 SS (1926) 132 (OEDS 1882, only ex. Not in W S C)

boss, sb. [AB³] *"That's Captain L—, the owner of the ship—he's one of the main bosses"* 1869 IA iii 35. *He said he would show who was Huck Finn's boss* 1884 HF vi 38. *My title would be The Boss* 1889 CY viii 102. See also *cent* 1889. *He was a born boss, and loved to command, and to jaw and dispute with inferiors and harry them and bullyrag them* 1897 FE lx 588 (OED An American equivalent of 'master'. OEDS 1806.. So S C U B F Cl Th T M H DN.II. Not A in W!)

boss, sb.attrib. [AB³] *Pictures by old Swiss masters— old boss sign-painters, who flourished before the decadence of art* 1880 TA xxvi 263. *"This is the boss dodge, there ain't no mistake 'bout it"* 1884 HF xxv 251. *"I'm an American in principle and a German at heart, and it's the boss combination"* 1892 *"Switzerland"* (1917) 205. (Cf. above. OEDS c1840.. A in W C B F Th. *Slang* in S. Curiously, W considers the attrib. use as *U.S.* but not its sb. use, except in the meaning of a political boss, whereas S pronounces exactly the opposite)

boss, v. [AB³] *They regulated and bossed all such matters* 1866 *Speeches* (1923)16. *Fetter and handcuff that river, and boss him* 1883 LM xxviii 302. *I would boss the whole country inside of three months* 1889 CY ii 35 (OED *U.S.* So S C U B F Cl Th M. *Colloq* in W)

boss-pilotical, a. [B¹] *The distance that lay between the lofty boss-pilotical attitude and my lowly one* 1909 ISD i 9 (Hum. nonce word)

boss-ship, sb. [AB²] *The thing that would have best suited my nature would have been to resign the Boss-ship and get up an insurrection* 1889 CY xiii 159 (OEDS *U.S.* 1894.. So W H. Not in S C)

bother, v. [B¹] *"Now, doctor, don't you come bothering around me with that dictionary bosh"* 1869 IA x 90. *You consider it best to go to your hotel and sleep an hour or two while the sun bothers along over the Atlantic* 1873 GA xxiv 217 (To blunder along, make an aimless fuss or ado; used vaguely without implying positive vexation or trouble-making. This sense not in OED W S C. Cf. OED 3. intr. To give trouble to others or to oneself; to make a fuss, be troublesome. 1774..)

botheration, sb. [?AB³] *A cozy and delightful human nest, shut away from the world and its botherations* 1880 TA xxii 214 (OED *colloq.* Petty vexation. 1801.. So W S C U. A in Th DN.V AS.II)

bothersome, a. [?AB³] *No bothersome peddlers* 1869 IA xii 107. *"A bothersome lot they'll be, too"* 1884 HF ii 15 (OED Troublesome. 1834.. So W S C Wr. A in B F T)

bottom, sb. [A] See *bench* 1873. *Hogs soon went wild in them bottoms after they had got away from the prairie-farms* 1884 HF vii 51 (OED 4b. An alluvial hollow. c1325..1803. OEDS Now esp.*U.S.* 1817.. A in F Cl T M H DN.III,VI AS.II.30. Not A in W S C Wr)

bottom, sb. [A] *Gould and Carry soared to six thousand three hundred dollars a foot! And then—all of a sudden out went the bottom, and everything...went to ruin and destruction* 1872 RI xiii 341 (OEDS 11c. In *fig* phrases such as 'The bottom falls out,' etc. 1637.. Phr. not in W S C. A in F)

bottom dollar, sb. [AB³] *"You bet your bottom dollar, Johnny, it ain't easy"* 1880 TA xx 194 (OEDS *U.S.* One's last dollar, usually in allit. phrase with *bet.* 1866.. So B Cl Th M. *Colloq* in W U. Not in S C)

bottom facts, sb. [AB³] *"There ain't only one or two ways when you come down to the bottom facts of it"* 1883 LM xliii 440 (OEDS *U.S.* The fundamental facts. 1877.. So B F Cl Th. Not A in W S C U)

bottom of the ladder, sb. [B¹] *Pudd'nhead was still toiling in obscurity at the bottom of the ladder* 1894 PW v 332 (Phr. not in OED W S C)

boulevard, sb. [C] *The end of this bridge was defended ...by one of those fortresses called a boulevard* 1899

JA II xvii 444 (OED The French word originally meant the horizontal portion of a rampart. No ex. So W S C)

bounce, sb. **the grand bounce**. [AB³] *There was no possible way of crowding her in...I saw I must simply give her the grand bounce* 1894 TET intro. 313 (OEDS 3b. *U.S.* An act of bouncing or ejecting. 1877.. So W S C B F Cl)

bounce, v. [AB³] *"They'll bounce you the minute you get a little old and worked out"* 1892 "Switzerland" (1917) 207 (OEDS 8b. To eject summarily. *U.S.* 1882.. So W S C B F Cl Th.III,1876 T H)

bounce, v. [?AB¹] *"If you give me much more of your sass I'll take and bounce a rock off'n your head"* 1876 TS i 23 (To make rebound; to toss or throw at. This sense not in OED W S C)

bound, ppl.a. [AB³] *The queen was bound to hang him for killing her kinsman* 1889 CY xviii 221 (OED 7e. In U.S., determined, resolved. 1844, only ex. U.S. sense. This sense A in W S C Wr B Cl H. Not A in T)

bounty-jumping, vbl.sb. [AB²] *Bounty-jumping excitements and irritations* 1881 "Curious Experience" 38 (OEDS 1881, only ex.U.S. A in W F. Not in S C. Cf. Bounty-jumper, A in OED W S C B Cl Th.III T)

bouquet, sb. [B¹] *The butter was perhaps good enough ...but it had more bouquet than was necessary* 1892 AmCl xii 119 (W: The distinctive aroma of a wine; hence, any aroma. Only of wine in OED S C)

Bourbon, sb. [AB³] *A long row of bottles, with Old Bourbon, and Old Rye, and Old Tom in them* 1864 SS (1926) 126 (OEDS 4. Whiskey of a kind originally made in Bourbon County, Kentucky. *U.S.* 1857.. So W S C B F Cl Th T)

bow-and-arrow, a. [B²] *A kind of bow-and-arrow arrangement, you see: the causeway the arrow* 1896 JA II xvii 444 (OEDS attrib. 1899.. Comb. not in W S C)

bow-end, sb. [B¹] *They gradually tapered from a nine-log breadth at their sterns, to a three-log breadth at their bow-ends* 1880 TA xiv 123 (Comb. not in OED W S C)

bower, sb. [?AB³] *"Down he fetched a right bower"* 1877 Speeches (1910) 5. *There was simply nothing to be done but play their right bower* 1889 CY xxxix 502 (OED In the game of Euchre the name of the two highest cards, exc. the 'joker', called right and left bower respectively. OEDS 1858.. So W S C U. A in B F Cl Th T M)

Bowery, sb. [AB³] *Whenever he expressed a feeling he did it in Bowery slang* 1905 Speeches (1910) 244 (OEDS *U.S.* b. attrib. 1862.. So W S C F Th M)

bowie, sb. [AB³] *"Bob's been carved up some with a bowie"* 1884 HF xviii 166. *"Set down!" says the judge, pulling his bowie and laying it on his pulpit* 1896 TSD x 529 (OEDS *U.S.* 1846.. So W B F Th. Not in S C)

bowie-knife, sb. [AB³] *Our dandy drew from his bosom a formidable looking bowie-knife* 1852 "The Dandy Frightening the Squatter" (1930) 448. *Injun Joe's bowie-knife lay close by, its blade broken in two* 1876 TS xxxiii 253. *He had always done his murders with a bowie-knife* 1883 LM lv 542. See also *machete* 1885 (OEDS *U.S.* 1836.. So W S C U B F Cl Th AS.VI.249, VII.432, XII.77)

boxing, vbl.sb. [B¹] *Lambrequins dependent from gaudy boxings of beaten tin gilded* 1883 LM xxxviii 405 (A metal fixture or bracket used to support window-hangings. Cf. S: The casing or niche into which window-shutters fold back. Neither sense given in OED W C)

boxing, vbl.sb. [B¹] *Locust trees with trunks protected by wooden boxing* 1893 PW i 234 (A tree-box; a wooden casing used to protect a tree-trunk. This *spec* sense not in OED W S C)

boxing-mill, sb. [B¹] *Me and Tom had a foot-race and a boxing-mill* 1894 TSA viii 353 (Comb. not in OED W S C; but cf. OED Mill, sb. 6. A pugilistic encounter 1825..)

boy, sb. [A] *"It's the same old boy, Nancy, just the same old boy—ain't he?"* 1873 GA i 30 (OED 2b. Used

instead of 'man' in certain localities, e.g., Cornwall, Ireland, the far West of the U.S. 1730.. Not A in S C U Wr. This use not in W)

boy-admiration, sb. [B¹] *He will become an example and a boy-admiration* 1902 "Defence of Gen. Funston" 623 (Nonce comb.)

boycott, sb. [AB³] *A trade-union boycott in a religious disguise* 1899 "Concerning the Jews" (1900) 266 (OED *U.S.* An application of Boycotting. Now often written without capitals. 1880.. Not A in W S C U)

boy-life, sb. [B¹] *I confined myself to the boy-life out on the Mississippi* 1891 Letters (1917) II xxxi 541 (Comb. not in OED W S C)

boy-Paradise, sb. [B¹] *That distant boy-Paradise, Cardiff Hill (Holliday's Hill)* 1906 Autob (1924) II 179 (Nonce comb.)

brace back, v. [?AB¹] *The mule would sit down and brace back, and no one could budge it* 1885 "Private Hist. of Campaign" 196 (Phr. not in OED W S C. Probably a var. and fig use of the *Naut.* brace aback, OED: To draw (the yards) in, so as to lay the sails aback. 1762. So W C)

brace up, v. [AB³] *"Now you're doing well—good again— don't hurry—there, now you're all right—brace up—go ahead"* c1880 "Taming the Bicycle" (1917) 292. *He gripped my hand hard, and braced up, and was all right* 1893 "Banknote" (1928) 123. *All that was needed...was that Wilhelm should brace up and do something that should cause favorable talk* 1898 MS (1916) x 130. (OEDS 5c. *U.S.*1809.. So S C F Cl T. Colloq in W)

bracketed, ppl.a. [B¹] *Bracketed over what-not...an outrage in watercolor* 1883 LM xxxviii 504 (Supported by a small shelf or bracket. This sense not in OED W S C)

braggartess, sb. [B¹] *If I had called her a braggart, I suppose you would have polished her into a braggartess, with your curious and random notions about the English tongue* 1900 Autob (1924) I 184 (Hum. nonce formation)

brain-machine, sb. [B¹] *Men perceive, and their brain-machines automatically combine the things perceived* 1906 "WIM" (1917) v 72 (Comb. not in OED W S C)

brain-plow, sb. [B¹] *To discover a great thought—an intellectual nugget—right under the dust of a field that many a brain-plow had gone over before* 1869 IA xxvi 266 (Comb. not in OED W S C)

brain-racking, ppl.a. [B²] *"My very footfalls time themselves to the brain-racking rhythm"* 1892 AmCl i 20 (OED 1897.. So C. Not in W S)

brain-territory, sb. [B¹] *The periodical unconsciousnesses began to extend their spell gradually over more of my brain-territory, and at last I sank into a drowse* 1880 TA xiii 115 (Comb. not in OED W S C)

brakeman, sb. [AB³E] *Every third man wears a uniform...whether he be marshall of the empire or a brakeman* 1869 IA xii 108. *The legation furniture consists of a minister or ambassador with a brakeman's salary* 1902 "Belated Russian Passport" (1928) 190 (OED Brakesman, sb. 2. In U.S. Brakeman. The guard. OEDS 1843.. So B F Cl Th.III M H. Not A in W S C)

bramble-infested, ppl.a. [B¹] *We came to a bramble-infested inclosure* 1869 IA xlviii 505 (Comb. not in OED W S C)

branch, sb. [A] See *slue* 1873. *He crossed a small "branch" two or three times, because of a prevailing juvenile superstition that to cross water baffled pursuit* 1876 TS viii 79 (OED 2b. *U.S.spec.* A small stream or brook. OEDS 1674.. So W C B F Cl Th T M H DN.VI. Not A in S)

branch-road, sb. [AB¹] *By contrast, these pleasant cars call to mind the branch-road cars at Maryborough* 1897 FE xxxi 290 (Cf. road, below, A in the sense of railroad. Comb. not in OED W S C; but cf. OED Branch-line, 1846..)

brandy-smash, sb. [AB³] See *cocktail* 1869 (OEDS *U.S.* 1855.. So S F Cl Th. Not A in W C)

brash, sb. [AB³] "*I warn't feeling very brash, there warn't much sand in my craw*" 1884 HF viii 62. *Maybe he had been a trifle too "brash"* 1892 AmCl xv 158 (OEDS *U.S.* Rash, impetuous. 1837.. So C Cl Th,1824 M DN.I,II AS.IX.320. Not A in W S Wr)

brashly, adv. [AB²] *I mixed into this business a little too brashly, so to speak, and without due reflection* 1865 SS (1926) 179 (OED *U.S.* 1884.. Not in W S C)

brass–buttoned, ppl.a. [B¹] *A glittering array of helmeted and brass-buttoned police* 1898 "Stirring Times" (1900) 336 (Comb. not in OED W S C)

brass–mounted, ppl.a. [B²] *A blue-uniformed, brass-mounted little page put a note into his hand* 1873 GA xlv 405. See also *corpse-maker* 1883 (OED 1877, only ex. So W. Comb. not in S C)

brast, v. [C] See *all-to* 1889 (OED Northern form of *burst. dial* and *arch.* 1300..1865. So W S C)

brave, a. [C] "*A brave lodging for such as we, is it not so?*" 1881 PP xxv 298 (OED 3b. Worthy, excellent. *arch.* 1577..1850. So S C. Not *arch* in W U Wr)

brave, sb. [AB³] See *paleface* 1869 (OED 1. Since 1800 applied chiefly to warriors among the N.Am.Indians. 1837, first ex. this sense.. So W S C B F Cl Th.III T M)

breach–of–promise, a. [B²] *Sometimes there is a breach-of-promise case* 1906-10 *Autob* (1924) I 15 (OED *spec* for breach of promise to marry. *Mod.*, no ex. So W S C U)

breach of trust, sb. [B¹] *When...they sold the negro, it only became a breach of trust, not stealing* 1883 LM xxix 315 (W: Violation of one's duty in a matter entrusted to one. So S C. Phr. not in OED)

bread–and–butter, sb. [?A] *What you needed...was more bread-and-butter learning* 1892 AmCl xi 117. "*Don't report him at all, for then you risk his bread and butter*" 1893 "Travelling with a Reformer" (1928) 349 (OED 2. Means of living. 1836.. So W S C. A in Th: Is this a Jeffersonian coinage? 1820, letter of Jefferson. But cf. OEDS 1732..)

break, sb. [AB³] *They was all about to make a break for him* 1883 LM iii 44 (OEDS 4b. A rush. *U.S.* 1834.. So W F Cl DN.I. Not A in S C)

break, sb. [B³] See *set up*, v. 1902 (OED 6a. Billiards. A consecutive series of successful strokes. 1865.. So W S C U)

break, sb. [B¹] *Singers...would some day get tired of doing her hymns...A seven-stanza break might well be a calamitous strain upon a soloist* 1907 CS II vii 217 (A continuous or unbroken run. Perhaps an extension of the *billiards* sense above. This musical sense not in OED W S C; but cf. OEDS 6c, where it is used of an unbroken railway journey. *colloq.* 1898.)

break, sb. [AB¹] *He never would have made a break like that if he hadn't been a little off his balance* 1892 AmCl xvi 170. *I did suffer during a year or two from the deep humiliation of the episode* [i.e.,M.T.'s disastrous Boston speech]. *One day that lamented break of mine was mentioned* 1906 Speeches (1910) 8 (W: *U.S.* An awkward social blunder or embarrassing remark. So S Cl Th.III,1890 T H. Not in OED C U; but cf. OEDS 8e. A bad break: a serious mistake. *U.S.*1883..)

break, sb. [AB³] *That silver streak in the shadow of the forest is the "break" from a new snag* 1875 OTM 289. *Beaver Dam Rock was out in the middle of the river now, and throwing a prodigious "break"* 1883 LM xxv 278. *She passed many a snag whose "break" could have told her a thing to break her heart* 1894 PW xvi 821. *You would see a blinding splash or explosion of light on the water; then that blotch of light would take the corkscrew shape and imposing length of the fabled sea-serpent, with ...every curve of its body and the "break" spreading away from its head* 1897 FE ix 109 (OEDS 10. A broken or disturbed portion on the surface of water. *U.S.* 1852.. So S. This sense not in W C)

break, v. intr. **to break for.** [AB³] See *traps* 1857. *I didn't wait to kiss good-by, but went overboard and broke for shore* 1883 LM iii 60. *If your boat got away from you,*

on a black night, and broke for the woods, it was an anxious time with you 1883 LM xxviii 300. "*He will join his Meung garrison to his army and break for Paris*" 1895 JA II vi 149. *I asked Mr. Barclay if he had ever heard of another woman* [than Eve] *who, being approached by a serpent, would not excuse herself and break for the nearest timber* 1909 ISD ii 21 (OEDS 38b. To make a dash. *U.S.* 1834.. So Th.III DN.II,VI. This sense not in W S C)

break down, v.intr. [?AB¹] "*Ef dat ain't de beatenes' tale ever I struck. Fist gits to de place whah de intrust is gittin' red-hot, en down she breaks*" 1894 TSA vii 258 (To break off, stop, desist. This sense not in OED W S C)

break–down, sb. [?AB¹] *General break-down—long pause* 1888 "Meisterschaft" 462 (A breaking-off, cessation. Transferred from the preceding verb-sense. This sense not in OED W S C; but cf. OED 1. A collapse, *lit.* and *fig.* 1832.. The OED sense is called A in B T)

break down, v.intr. [?AB¹] "*A remarkable letter here, which I want to read to you, if I can do it without breaking down*" 1883 LM lii 509. See also *begat* 1907 (U: To burst into tears. W: To give way, as to grief or despair. So S C. A in B. This sense not in OED)

break down, v.trans. [?AB¹] *This thought broke her down, and she wandered away, with tears rolling down her cheeks* 1876 TS xvii 145 (To reduce to tears. An extension of the intr. sense above. Not in OED W S C)

break–down, sb. [AB³] *Turned themselves loose on a regular old-fashioned keel-boat breakdown* 1883 LM iii 49. *The boys and girls would soon be arriving now, and hungry for a good, old-fashioned break-down* 1893 "Californian's Tale" (1906) 112 (OED 2. A riotous dance. *U.S.* 1864.. So S C U B Cl T M DN.III. Not A in W)

break down, v.trans. [?AB¹] *The twang of a banjo became audible as they drew nearer, and they saw a couple of negroes, from some neighboring plantation, "breaking down" a juba in approved style* 1873 GA xvi 157 (A transf. verb usage from the preceding sb. This sense of the verb not in OED W S C)

breakdown–dancing, ppl.a. [?AB¹] *Whiskey-drinking, breakdown-dancing rapscallions* 1883 LM xviii 571 (Cf. above. Comb. not in OED W S C)

breaker, sb. **breakers ahead.** [B¹] *As soon as I'd got through the breakers that was laying just ahead of me—explanations, I mean* 1884 HF xlii 427 (U: Future difficulties. Phr. not in OED W S C)

breakfast–horn, sb. [?AB¹] *He broke off there, because we heard the breakfast-horn blowing* 1884 HF xxxv 361 (Comb. not in OED W S C. Cf. OED Breakfast-bell, 1842)

breakfast–station, sb. [B¹] *Just beyond the breakfast station we overtook a Mormon emigrant-train* 1872 RI xii 97 (A stage-coach station where passengers ate breakfast. Comb. not in OED W S C)

break–line, sb. [B³] See *solid matter* 1906 (OEDS Typogr. The last line of a paragraph. 1808.. So W. Comb. not in S C)

break up, v. trans. [?AB¹] *He went on, pouring out a most pathetic stream of arguments and blasphemy, which broke Joan all up, and made her laugh* 1895 JA II xii 545. *He said he was all broken up to think I'd gotten a green watermelon* 1906 Speeches (1910) 230 (W: *Colloq.* To unsettle or disconcert completely; to upset, confuse—often with *all*; as, he was all broken up by the news. A in F. This sense not in OED S C. Cf. break down, above)

breakup, v.intr. [?AB¹] See *countermine* 1895 (To be completely disconcerted or nonplussed; cf. above. This sense not in OED W S C)

breast, sb. **breast to breast with.** [?AB¹] *Always keeping breast to breast with the drum-major in the great work of material civilization* 1892 AmCl viii 80 (Abreast of. Phr. not in OED W S C. Cf. breast, v., below)

breast, v. [?AB¹] *The Amaranth drew steadily up till her jack-staff breasted the Boreas's wheelhouse* 1873 GA

[i]v 49 (To come or draw abreast of. This sense not in OED W S C. Cf. breast, v., A in Th.III,1850: To oppose manfully. In its *fig* uses, the word seems originally American)

breast–board, sb. [?AB[1]] *Every detail of the pilot-house was familiar to me, with one exception—a large-mouthed tube under the breast-board* 1883 LM xxiv 264. *In the pilot-house...on the compass-shelf under the breast-board* 1909 ISD i 17 (W: A board placed at the breast-beam—the beam where the quarter-deck or forecastle breaks. Curiously, this definition is omitted in the Second Edition of W. Not in OED S C)

breast–deep, a. [B[1]] *Water that is breast-deep* 1880 TA xxxv 394 (Comb. not in OED S. Given in W C)

breath, sb. **to take one's breath.** [?AB[2]] *He said it placidly, but it took our breath for a moment, and made our hearts beat* 1898 MS (1916) 14 (OEDS 5c. 1898, this quot...A in H: The common Eng. expression *take one's breath away* seems to have lost *away* in crossing the Atlantic. Phr. not in W S C)

breath–taking, ppl.a. [?AB[2]] *A sort of breath-taking surprise* 1880 TA xxxiii 359 (OEDS 1897.. So W. Not in S C. Cf. above)

breech–clout, sb. [B[2]] *A billionaire in a paper-collar, a king in a breech-clout, an archangel in a tin halo* 1899 "Diplomatic Pay and Clothes" (1928) 239 (Comb. given in OED W S C. No ex.)

breeches–button, sb. [B[1]] *An Englishman offered a pound sterling for a single breeches-button* 1880 TA xl 472 (Comb. not in OED W S C)

breed, sb. [?AB[1]] *All the different breeds of rockets* 1889 CY xxiii 288. *Can you get the name of the breed for me?...I've got to have the cigars* 1900 *M.T. the Letter Writer* (1932) vi 84 (W: In loose popular language, a species or variety. So U. This sense not in OED S C)

breed, v. [?AB[1]] *The rightful heir did go to America... got married, and began to breed savages* 1892 AmCl i 19 (U: Sometimes used forcibly, but coarsely, of human beings. This usage not in OED W S C)

breeze, sb. [?AB[1]] See *air* 1892 (Assurance, impudence, liveliness. This sense not in OED W S C; but cf. breezy, below)

breeziness, sb. [?AB[1]] *A freshness and a breeziness and an exhilarating sense of emancipation* 1872 RI ii 25 (Assurance, self-confidence. This sense not in OED W S C; but cf. breezy, below)

breezy, a. [?AB[2]] *Said in almost his breezy old-time way* 1873 GA li 470. *"His breezy impudence is... colossal"* 1892 AmCl i 24. *In his breezy and exhilarating fashion* 1902 "Belated Russian Passport" (1928) 178 (OEDS esp. Characterized by brisk vigour or activity. 1896.. W: Pertly smart; sprightly in a cheeky way. *colloq.* So S C U. A in B F Cl)

Brer, sb. [AB[3]E] *It turned Brer Merlin green with envy* 1889 CY vii 85. *You read between the lines what this author says about Brer Albucasis* 1890 "Majestic Literary Fossil" 440 (OEDS *U.S.* Negro pron. of Brother. 1880.. So W S C)

brevet, sb. **children by brevet.** [AB[1]] *Lax court morals and the absurd chivalry business were in full feather...religion was the passion of the ladies, and the classifying their offspring into children of full rank and children by brevet their pastime* 1883 LM i 27 (Supposititious or illegitimate children. A popular jest during and after the Civil War; cf. Brevet-wife and Brevet-hell in F. This improper sense not in OED W S C; but cf. OED Brevet, sb. 2. *spec.* in the Army, a document conferring nominal rank on an officer but giving no right to extra pay. 1689..)

bric–a–bracker, sb. [B[2]] *I am content to be a bric-a-bracker* 1880 TA xx 169 (OED *colloq* or *humorous.* 1880, this quot. Not in W S C)

bric–a–brackery, sb. [B[2]] *The true devotee in any department of bric-a-brackery* 1880 TA xx 187 (OED 1880, this quot. So W. Not in S C)

brick, sb. [B[3]] *He is a Christian in the truest sense of the term, and unquestionably a brick* 1866 *Letters* (1917) I vi 122. *It is but a just and graceful tribute to woman to say of her that she is a brick* c1870 *Speeches* (1910) 105. *"Now that corpse was a brick...everyway you took him he was a brick"* 1871 SNO (1875) 247 (OED 6. *slang* or *colloq.* 1840.. So W S C U. A piece of distinctively British slang, which M.T. took to his heart)

brick, sb. [?AB[1]] *When I read that they let a bed-ridden man down through the roof of a house in Capernaum to get him into the presence of the Savior, I generally had a three-story brick in mind* 1869 IA xlviii 504. *If we could have looked out through the eyes of these dreamers, we should have seen their tidy little wooden house disappear, and a two-story brick take its place* 1904 "Bequest" (1906) iv 23 (A brick house. This sense not in OED W S C)

brick, v. **to brick up.** [?AB[1]] *"I only used it as a metaphor". That word kinder bricked us up for a minute. Then Jim says: "Mars Tom, what is a metaphor?"* 1893 TSA iv 124 (To stop, give pause to, reduce to silence. This *fig* sense not in OED W S C; but cf. OED 1. To build or close up with brick-work. 1648..)

brickbat, sb. [B[1]] *A large part of the pupil's "instruction" consists in cramming him with obscure and wordy "rules"...It would be as useful to cram him with brickbats...Their memories had been stocked, but not their understandings. It was a case of brickbat culture, pure and simple* 1887 "English as She is Taught" (1917) 254 (Hum. nonce meaning)

brickyardy, a. [B[1]] *A plain, perfectly flat, dust-colored, and brickyardy, stretching limitlessly away in the dim gray light* 1897 FE xlix 460 (Not in OED W S C)

bridal tour, sb. [B[1]] *She was newly married, and was on her bridal tour* 1880 TA xxxv 388 (Comb. not in OED W S C; but cf. OED Wedding-journey, 1881)

bridge, v. [B[2]] *A speculator bridged a couple of barrels with a board* 1869 IA xiii 125 (OED 1c. To span or cross as with a bridge. 1872, this quot., wrongly dated.. So S C. This sense not in W)

bridge–building, vbl.sb. [B[2]] *He wrote some papers... especially upon bridge-building* 1873 GA xxiii 216 (OEDS 1873, this quot. So W. Not in S C)

bridge–pier, sb. [B[1]] *Hoping to see one of them* [rafts] *hit the bridge-pier and wreck itself* 1880 TA xiv 124 (Comb. not in OED W S C)

bridgy, a. [B[1]] *The Bridge* [London Bridge] *had its aristocracy who always talked bridgy talk and thought bridgy thoughts, and lived in a long, level, direct, substantial bridgy way* 1881 PP xii 135 (Hum. nonce use)

brigadier–generalship, sb. [B[1]] *"You had been rewarded with a brigadier-generalship in the regular army"* 1907 "Chaps. from Autob." 490 (Comb. not in OED W S C)

bright–colored, ppl.a. [B[1]] *Putting a bright-colored flower in his button-hole* 1892 AmCl xx 208 (Comb. not in OED S C. Given in W)

brilliancies, sb.pl. [B[1]] *Every remark he made delighted his hearers. Presently he had saved up quite a repertoire of brilliancies* 1873 GA xxxiv 317. *I was working off these humorous brilliancies on him and getting no return* 1906 *Speeches* (1910) 400 (W: An instance of the quality. This *concrete* sense not in OED S C)

brimstone–shovel, sb. [B[1]] *"He's probably out of his troubles before this; it's a hundred to nothing he's selecting his brimstone-shovel this very minute"* 1904 "Bequest" (1906) ii 8 (Hum. nonce comb.)

bring, v. Pa.pple. **brung.** [?AE] *"Trouble has brung these gray hairs"* 1884 HF xix 187 (OED This form 19th c. *dial.* So W Wr. A in B F Th,1833 T M DN.II,III,V. Not given in S C)

bring up standing, v. [?AB[1]] *When our brigade first went into camp on the Potomac, we used to be brought up standing, occasionally, by an ear-splitting howl of anguish*

1880 TA xxiii 222 (Phr. not in OED W S C. Probably a *var.* and *fig* use of the *Naut. bring up all standing;* cf. S: To come to anchor before the sails are taken in, stop abruptly)

brisken, v. [?AB¹] *All sorts of little knickknacks and gimcracks around, like girls brisken up a room with* 1884 HF xxvi 258 (To smarten up; to trim. This sense not in OED W S C. Cf. OEDS 1. To make brisk or lively. 1799.. ; so W S C Wr. Exactly this sense, however, is given for Brisk, v. OED 3a. To smarten up; to dress finely; to trim. *obs.* 1592..1861. Probably an Am. var. and survival)

broad-horn, sb. [AB³] *On the great rise, down came a swarm of broad-horns from "Posey County," Indiana* 1875 OTM 448. *The river's earliest commerce was in great barges—keelboats, broadhorns* 1883 LM iii 41 (OEDS 1. A large flat-bottomed boat formerly used on the Mississippi and Ohio rivers. 1819.. So W S C B F Cl Th T DN.VI)

brogan, sb. [AB²] *He wore a slouch hat and brogans* 1869 SNO (1875) 67. *A countrified cub lounged in, crossed his mighty brogans* 1880 TA xxiii 224 (OEDS *U.S.* 1886.. So DN.II,III. Not A in W S C Wr)

broidery, sb. [C] *It is pretty to see her* [Mrs.Eddy] *keep putting forward ...Boards of This and That, and other broideries and ruffles of her raiment* 1907 CS II vii 207 (OED Now *poetic.* 2. *fig.* 1782..1844. *Arch* in W S C)

broke, ppl.a. [?AB²] *"Bymeby my ole mistis say she's broke, an' she got to sell all de niggers on de place"* 1874 SNO (1875) 204 (OEDS 3. Ruined financially. 1886.. So W. A in C Cl M DN.II,III. Not in S)

broken-legged, ppl.a. [B²] *The broken-hearted artist and the broken-legged statue* 1869 SNO (1875) 225 (Comb. given in OED W, no ex. Not in S C)

bronco, sb. [AB³] *My father was a bronco* 1906 "Horse's Tale" 328 (OED A native horse of California or New Mexico. OEDS 1869.. So W S C U B F Cl Th T M)

brontosaur, sb. [B¹] *Professor Osborn and I built the colossal skeleton brontosaur that stands fifty-seven feet long and sixteen feet high in the Natural History Museum* 1909 ISD iv 41 (This form not in OED W S C)

Brontosaurian, sb. [B¹] *Two of these cults are known as the Shakespearites and the Baconians, and I am the other one—the Brontosaurian* 1909 ISD v 51 (Hum. coinage)

brontosaurus, sb. [B²] *The mighty brontosaurus came striding into camp* 1905 "Eve's Diary" 73 (OEDS 1907.. So W S C U)

brook-connection, sb. [B¹] *I placed the brook-connection under the guard of three boys* 1889 CY xliii 557 (Nonce comb.)

broom-closet, sb. [?AB¹] *If you hurry...a house, you are nearly sure to find out by and by that you have left out... a broom-closet, or some other little convenience* 1883 LM li 503 (Comb. not in OED W S C. Cf. Broom, sb. A in H: What Americans call a broom does not exist in England, while Eng. *brooms* are more like Am. *long-handled brushes.* So S C B; not A in OED W)

brothel-daddy, sb. [B¹] *Many happy phrases were distributed through the proceedings. Among them were... "Brothel-daddy!"... "Brothel-knight!"* 1898 "Stirring Times in Austria" (1900) 328 (Comb. not in OED W S C. A literal rendering of German *Bordellvater,* or *Hurenvater,* keeper of a house of ill fame)

brothel-knight, sb. [B¹] See *brothel-daddy* 1898 (Comb. not in OED W S C. Formed after German *Hurenjäger, Hurenknecht, Bordellgänger,* whoremonger)

brother-on-the-half-shell sb. [B¹] *An adoptive brother of mine...my brother-on-the-half-shell* 1901 "To My Missionary Critics" 531 (Hum. nonce comb.)

browse, v. [B¹] *"They'll drag the river for me...and go browsing down the creek that leads out of it to find the robbers that killed me"* 1884 HF vii 53. *"She browse around the hills and scour the woods with me—alone?"*

1889 CY x 132 (To move here and there over the ground, scout, wander about; a hum. transfer from animals to human beings. This sense not in OED W S C)

brummagem, a. [?A] *She was merely prejudiced against the brummagem article* 1892 AmCl xxii 234 (OED 1b. Counterfeit, sham. 1637.. So W S C U. A in B T)

brush house, sb. [AB³] *We concluded to build a "brush" house* 1872 RI xxii 172 (OEDS *U.S.* Dwelling made of cut brushwood. 1853. Comb. not in W S C. Brush in this sense is A in OED C B Cl Th,1774 DN.VI; not A in W S U)

bub, sb. [AB³] *"Well, I shall have to tear myself away from you, bub"* 1872 RI v 51. *"Don't cry, bub"* 1873 GA xiii 112 (OEDS *U.S.colloq.* A form of familiar address to boys or men. 1845.. So W S C B F Th T M DN. I,III)

buccaneer, sb. [AB¹] See *bandoleer* 1909 (U: An unscrupulous adventurer. This extension of the orig. sense not in OED W S C. Cf. OED 2. A name given to piratical rovers who formerly infested the Spanish coasts in America.1690..; so W S C U)

buck, sb. [AB³] *There was nigger boys in every tree, and bucks and wenches looking over every fence* 1884 HF xxii 218 (OEDS 2d(b). A negro man. Chiefly *U.S.* 1842.. So W S C Wr B F Cl Th T H DN.II,III. Not A in U)

buck, sb. [AB³] See *hat* 1889. *A great shut-in meadow, full of Indian lodges...the squaws busy at work, and the bucks busy resting* 1906 "Horse's Tale" 332 (OEDS 2d (c). A male Indian. Chiefly *U.S.* 1860.. So W S C B F Cl Th T H)

buck, sb. **buck angel.** [AB¹] *"By gracious! I feel as cocky as a buck angel"* 1902 "Belated Russian Passport" (1928) 190 (A male angel. An irreverent extension of M.T.'s)

buck, sb. **buck Indian.** [AB³] *The camp has...a dozen vagrant buck Indians in rabbit-skin robes* 1902 "DBDS" (1928) 307 (OEDS 3. 1840.. Comb. not in W S C. Cf. above)

buck, sb. **to pass the buck.** [AB²] *"You ruther hold over me, pard. I reckon I can't call that hand. Ante and pass the buck"* 1872 RI xlvii 332. *His method was to keep saying: "I am well!...I have no disease; there's no such thing as disease! All is Mind, All-Good, Good-Good, Life, Soul, Liver, Bones, one of a series, ante and pass the buck!"* *I do not mean that that was exactly the formula used, but that it doubtless contains the spirit of it* 1902 "Chr. Sc." 764 (OEDS 12. *U.S.* To shift responsibility. 1872, above quot.. So W. Phr. not in S C)

buck, v. **to buck against,** [AB³] *"It ain't no use. We can't buck agin him"* 1882 SWE 102. *That bullet-wound in Tom's leg was a tough thing for Nat Parsons to buck against, but he bucked the best he could* 1893 TSA i 21 (OEDS *U.S.* 2. Chiefly *fig.* 1859.. So W S C B F Cl Th T H)

bucket, sb. [AB²] *Tom appeared on the sidewalk with a bucket of whitewash* 1876 TS ii 26. *I took the bucket and gourd* 1884 HF vii 50 (OED In U.S...a round wooden pail with arched handle. No ex. Am. sense. So S C Wr B Cl T DN.II,III,IV,VI AS.IX.320. Not A in W)

bucketshop, sb. [AB³] *Somebody corners the market and down goes your bucketshop* 1889 CY xix 232 (OED *U.S.* 1882.. So S C U F Cl Th,1881 T M H. Not A in W)

buckle in, v. [?AB¹] *I buckled in and read all of those books* 1880 TA xx 194 (Wr: To set to work. A in Cl. Comb. not in OED W S C in this sense; but cf. OED Buckle to: To set to work, apply oneself vigorously. 1712..)

buckle-hole, sb. [B¹] *On this day the starvation regimen drew its belt a couple of buckle-holes tighter* 1899 "My Debut" (1900) 91 (Comb. not in OED W S C)

buckskin–seated, ppl.a. [?AB¹] *Our buckskin-seated pantaloons* 1869 IA lvi 440 (Comb. not in OED W S C; but cf. OEDS Buckskin, sb. Later U.S.ex.1878. A in C F Cl Th T. Not A in W S)

buckwheat cake, sb. [A] *Everything she looked at reminded her of that poor old negro woman, and so the buckwheat cakes made her sob* 1871 SNO (1875) 157. *The angel suddenly sweeping down out of a better land and setting before him...a plate of hot buckwheat cakes, with transparent syrup,—could words describe the gratitude of this exile?* 1880 TA xlix 572. See also *batter-cake* 1897 (OEDS *U.S.*1774.. So C F Th M DN.I,II. Not A in W S. Cf. also the remark in OED Buckwheat, sb. "The seed is in Europe used as food for horses, cattle, and poultry; in N.America its meal is made into 'buckwheat cakes,' regarded as a dainty for the breakfast-table." This rare intrusion of humor into the OED is traced back in an entertaining article by Mr. Allen Walker Read, "The History of Dr. Johnson's Definition of 'Oats'," *Agricultural History* VIII (July, 1934) 81-94, to the famous jest in Johnson's Dictionary: "Oats: A grain which in England is generally given to horses, but in Scotland supports the people". Mr. Read writes: "Is it possible that an 'oats-consciousness' can be found in the great *Oxford English Dictionary*? The first editor, James A. H. Murray, was a pure Scotchman out of Roxburghshire, and as a student of words from his early youth he must have conned Johnson's definition of oats time and again... Here is the same antithesis: 'food for horses, cattle, and poultry' on the one hand, and 'a dainty for the breakfast, table' on the other—perhaps a more subtly stinging contrast even than Johnson's. Is it possible that Sir James Murray could write this without a twinkle in his eye?")

budge, sb. [?AC] *He inquired how many persons the gang numbered now. The "Ruffler," or chief, answered: "Five and twenty sturdy budges, bulks, files, clapperdogeons, and maunders, counting the dells and doxies and other morts"* 1881 PP xvii 211 (OED *obs. slang.* 1706.. 1751. So W S C. A in F Cl: An accomplice who gains access to a building during the day, for the purpose of being locked in, so as to admit his fellow-thieves that night. Since M.T. borrowed all the "canting terms" in this passage direct from *The English Rogue*, London, 1665, chap. V, pp. 38f., as he acknowledges in a footnote, it is doubtful whether he was familiar with this word as an Am. survival)

buffalo, sb. [A] *Scurrying through the Great South Pass and the Wind River Mountains, among antelope and buffaloes, and painted Indians on the war path* 1869 IA xii 107. *He would see buffaloes and Indians* 1872 RI i 19 (OED 1c. Applied in popular unscientific use to the American Bison. OEDS 1635.. So W S C B F Cl T AS.II.31, IV.4,6,VII.4)

buffalo–hide, sb. [A] *The monoply of buffalo-hides* 1883 LM ii 31 (OED 1703, only ex. Comb. not in W S C)

buffalo–hunt, sb. [AB³] *We joined a party who were just starting on a buffalo-hunt* 1872 RI vii 161. *They took him out on a buffalo-hunt when he visited our country* 1873 GA xvii 164 (OED 1856.. Comb. not in W S C)

buffalo–range, sb. [AB³] *There's not a buffalo-range in the whole sweep of the Rocky Mountains and the Great Plains that we don't know* 1906 "Horse's Tale" 327 (OEDS 1837.. Comb. not in W S C)

buffalo–robe, sb. [AB³] *Doormats and buffalo-robes* 1872 RI xxi 160 (OEDS 1806.. A in S C B F T. Comb. not in W)

bug, sb. [A] See *chaw up* 1856. *They will counterfeit a fly, or a high-toned bug, or a ruined coliseum, within the cramped circle of a breastpin* 1869 IA xxiv 246. *Men without title...were creatures of no more consideration than so many animals, bugs, insects* 1889 CY viii 97 (OED 1. A name given vaguely to various insects, esp. of the beetle kind. Now chiefly *dial* and in U.S. OEDS Earlier U.S. ex. 1785.. So W U Wr B F Cl Th M H DN.VI. Not A in S C T)

bug, sb. [? A] *Look at Henry the Eight... He used to marry a new wife every day, and chop off her head next morning...That's the kind of a bug Henry was* 1884 HF xxiii 232 (OED 1b. A person of assumed importance. 1771.. *Obs* in W. A in F M DN.II,IV,V. Not in S C)

bug–eaten, ppl.a. [AB¹] *A slouch hat whose broken rim hung limp and ragged about his eyes and ears like a bug-eaten cabbage leaf* 1880 TA xxiii 224 (Comb. not in OED W S C. Cf. bug, above)

buggy, sb. [A] *We enjoy ourselves much more than we could in a buggy jolting over our cobblestone pavement at home* 1869 IA xxiii 229. See also *second-hand* 1880; *woods, take to the* 1894; *cutter* 1904 (OED Those in use in America have four wheels; those in England and India, two. 1773.. So W S C F Cl Th DN.I,III)

bugle, sb. [AB¹] *Tore his coat, clutched his throat, And split him in the bugle* 1865, from a "poem" quoted in Paine's *Biography* I 275 (A in DN.V, California: Head. Here: nose or mouth. This sense not in OED W S C)

bug out, v. [AB²] *"His dead-lights were bugged out like tompions"* 1877 "Some Rambling Notes" i 446. *"Wouldn't their eyes bug out to see'em handled like that?"* 1883 LM xxxvi 391. *Jim's eyes bugged out when he heard that; and I reckon mine did too* 1884 HF xix 185. *I hain't ever seen eyes bug out and gaze without a blink the way theirn did* 1896 TSD xi 531 (OEDS *U.S.* To bulge out. 1884, quot.from HF.. So W S F Cl DN.I,III. This sense not in C)

build, v. [AB¹] *The old lady pulled her spectacles down; they were her state pair, the pride of her heart, and were built for "style"* 1876 TS i 17 (A in Th: To construct anything, e.g., "These cravats are built on the same principle". 1852.. So B F Cl. Not A in W C U. This extended sense not in OED S)

building–material, sb. [B²] *All the streets were obstructed with building-material* 1883 LM lx 586 (OEDS 1897. Comb. not in W S C)

bulge, sb. **to have the bulge on.** [AB³] *"Well, you've ruther got the bulge on me. Or maybe we've both got the bulge somehow"* 1872 RI xlvii 332. *"Now I guess I've got the bulge on you by this time!"* 1880 TA iii 40. *The boys had too good a start...they had the bulge on the men again* 1884 HF viii 174 (OEDS 3c. Usually with *the*: the advantage or upper hand. *slang, orig. U.S.* 1860.. So S C F Th T DN.II,III. Not A in W)

bulge, sb. **the grand bulge.** [AB¹] *The thing was working very well, Tom said...So he said, now for the grand bulge* 1884 HF xxxix 402 (The great design, the grand scheme. Phr. not in OED W S C. Cf. with dif. sense OEDS 3d. The big bulge: a rise in shares. *U.S.*1908)

bulge, v. [AB³] *Here comes a couple of the hounds bulging in from under Jim's bed* 1884 HF xxxvi 372 (OEDS 5. To rush in. *U.S.* 1834.. So W. This sense not in S C)

bulk, sb. [C] See *budge* 1881 (OED An assistant to a file or pickpocket. *obs.slang.* 1673..1725. Not in W S C)

bulk, v. [B²] *This idea is many times larger than all her borrowings bulked together* 1907 CS II vii 171 (OEDS 6. To put together for transport. 1908.. Here *fig.* So W: To assemble in large aggregates. This sense not in S C)

bulky, a. [B¹] *The sage takes that in without a strain, but the following case was a trifle too bulky for him*, as his comment reveals 1890 "Majestic Literary Fossil" 442 (Difficult of belief, 'steep', 'staggering', a 'tall' story. This hum. twist of meaning not in OED W S C)

bull, v. [?AB³] See *bear*, v. 1869. *At the instigation of Rhodes, to bull the stock market* 1897 FE lxv 653 (OED 2. Stock Exchange. 1842.. So W S C U. A in B AS.II.46)

bull, v. [?AB¹] *Up-stream boats...bull right up the channel against the whole river* 1884 HF xvi 144. *The old fool he bulled right along* 1884 HF xxvii 276 (To push ahead, persist stubbornly, like a bull. This sense not in OED W S C. Cf. bull-headed, below)

bull-driver, sb. [B¹] *Mr. John Backus..a cattle raiser from interior Ohio...Backus went twenty better... "Five hundred better", said the foolish bull-driver* 1883 LM xxxvi 394 (Cattleman, drover. Not in OED W S C)

bullet-hole, sb. [B²] *A friend drops in to swap compliments with you, and freckles me with bullet-holes.* 1869 SNO (1875) 49. *They kept him so leaky with bullet-holes that "he couldn't hold his vittles"* 1872 RI ix 76 (Given in OED, no ex. Not in W S C)

bulletin-board, sb. [AB²] *They had a great public bulletin-board in Pompeii—a place where announcements for gladiatorial combats, elections, and such things, were posted* 1869 IA xxxi 333. *A great display sheet on the bulletin-board of a newspaper-office* 1873 GA lvii 518. See *notice* 1876. *I had started a number of these people out...sandwiched between bulletin-boards bearing one device or another* 1889 CY xvi 189 (OEDS 2b. *U.S.* 1873.. Not A in W S C)

bulletin-boarder, sb. [AB¹] *The bulletin-boarder referred to was...a brave knight* 1889 CY xx 239 (Nonce word)

bull-frog, sb. [A] *The collecting of seeds and peculiar bull-frogs for the Smithsonian Institute* 1869 IA ii 27 (OED Name given to certain large American frogs. OEDS 1704.. So W S C F Cl Th M)

bull-headed, ppl.a. [?AB³] *"Let it go, if you're so bull-headed about it"* 1884 HF xxxviii 391 (OED *fig.* Blindly impetuous, blockheaded. 1818.. So W S C. A in F Cl)

bulliness, sb. [AB¹] *"Kind of swell medieval bulliness and tinsel about it"* 1883 LM xlv 459. *I knowed he would be changing it around every which way as we went along, and heaving in new bullinesses wherever he got a chance* 1884 HF xxxiv 349 (Not in OED W S C. Coined from bully, a., below. Note the *concrete* use in the second quot.)

bull-pup, sb. [B²] *"And he had a little small bull-pup"* 1865 "Jumping Frog" (1875) 32. *"I am going to buy a new drum, and a sure 'nough sword, and a red necktie, and a bull-pup, and get married"* 1876 TS xxv 194 (OED A young bull-dog. 1883, only ex. Not in W S C)

bully, a. [AB³] *He at that jam, and said it was bully* 1867 SNO (1875) 52. *"I'm coming along bully"* 1869 IA iv 40. *Some of these old American words do have a kind of bully swing to them; a man can express himself with 'em* 1880 TA xx 194. *He could curl his tongue around the bulliest words in the language when he was a mind to* 1883 LM iii 55. *A real bully circus* 1884 HF xxii 221. See *soul-butter* 1884. *The interviewer said that I characterized Mr. Birrell's speech the other day at the Pilgrim's Club as "bully." Now, if you will excuse me, I never use slang to an interviewer* 1907 Speeches (1910) 388 (OED *U.S* and *Colonies.* 1855.. So S C U B F Cl Th T M H DN.III,IV,V. Not A in W)

bullyrag, v. [?AB¹] *A dog might tackle him and bullyrag him and bite him, and Andrew Jackson would never let on but what he was satisfied* 1865 "Jumping Frog" (1875) 32. *He found him in the back room of a little low doggery, very tight, and a lot of loafers bullyragging him for sport* 1884 HF xxxi 316. See also *pungle* 1884; *boss,* sb. 1897 (W: To abuse or vex by scolding, teasing, etc.; to badger. So S C. A in B Cl Th M DN.IV. This sense not in OED)

bullyship, sb. [B¹] *Brooks apologized and retired from his bullyship* 1908 Autob (1924) II 124 (Nonce word: the profession or status of bully)

bulrusher, sb. [?AB¹] *After supper she got out her book and learned me about Moses and the Bulrushers* 1884 HF i 2 (Wr: used in Northumberland for *bulrush.*

Not in OED W S C. Perhaps this *dial* form found its way to America)

bum, v.intr. [AB²] *I bummed around that banquet hall from 6 in the evening until 2 in the morning* 1879 Letters (1917) I xix 373 (OEDS *U.S.colloq.* 1a. To knock about; to wander around, loaf. 1883.. So W. This sense not in S C)

bum, v.trans. [AB¹] *He can't bum a living at home* 1892 AmCl xv 156 (W: To get by sponging. *slang, U.S.*This sense not in OED S C)

bummer, sb. [AB³] *An awkward express employee let it fall on the bummer's foot* 1872 RI lv 402. *I wound up with something about such-and-such a devastating agent being "as terrible as an army with bummers"* 1881 Speeches (1923) 103. See also *beat,* sb. 1884; *larrikin* 1897 (OEDS *U.S.* slang. An idler, lounger, loafer. 1856.. So W S C Wr B F Cl Th M T DN.IV)

bunch, v.trans. [AB²] *The speaker bunched his thick lips together like the stem end of a tomato* 1873 GA i 21. See *layout,* sb. 1877. *The cavern was as big as two or three rooms bunched together* 1884 HF iv 74 (OEDS *U.S.* 1873, quot from GA.. So B F Cl Th.III T H. Not A in W S C)

bunch-grass, sb. [AB³] *"Bunch-grass" grows on the bleak mountainsides of Nevada* 1872 RI iii 34 (OED 7. N.America. OEDS 1837.. So W S C B F Cl Th DN. VI)

bunco, v. [AB³] *I certainly did bunco a Yankee—as these people phrase it* 1905 King Leopold's Soliloquy 7 (OED *U.S. slang.* 1883.. So S C U F Cl Th T M. Not A in W)

buncombe, sb. [AB³] *He said that the reward offered for the lost knife was humbug and buncombe* 1894 PW xvii 822 (OED *U.S.* in origin. 2. 1862.. So W S C U B F Cl Th,1827 T M)

bunco-steerer, sb. [AB³] *I will make short work of these bunco-steerers* 1889 CY xx 344 (OEDS *U.S.* slang. A swindler. 1876.. So W S C U F Cl Th.III M)

bundle, sb. [B¹] *It appears that his "bundle" (his book of humorous matter) fails of a market in Holland* 1909 "Capable Humorist" 13 (Here *spec* of a peddler's pack. This sense not in OED W S C)

bung-starter, sb. [?AB²] *The coppersmith bird's note at a certain distance away has the ring of a sledge on granite...at another distance it has a more woodeny thump, and sounds just like starting a bung. So he is a hard bird to name with a single name; he is a stonebreaker, coppermith, and bung-starter* 1897 FE lvi 540 (Cf. OED Coppersmith, sb. 2. The popular name in India of the Crimson-breasted Barbet.1862.. M.T.'s other two names for the Indian bird seem to be his own invention, the latter, bung-starter, being taken from the civilization of his native land. Cf. M: Am. bung-starter = Eng. beer-mallet. So Cl. Not A in OED W S C; given in OED without ex.)

bunk, sb. [?A] *When she went to her foul steerage bunk at last, it was not to sleep* 1894 PW xvi 821. *I am living at a miner's boarding-house, and it is an awful place: the bunks, the food, the dirt—everything* 1902 "DBDS" (1928) iii 299 (OEDS 1780.. So W S C U. A in B Cl T DN.III AS.VII.166)

bunk, v. [?AB³] *We voted that the old man should bunk with us* 1902 "DBDS" (1928) ix 354 (OEDS Earlier exs. U.S. 1840.. A in W B F Cl DN.III AS.VII.11. Not A in S C U)

bureau, sb. [AB³] *Tom contrived to scarify the cupboard...and was arranging to begin on the bureau* 1876 TS iv 43. *She put...a pair of nail-scissors under the bureau* 1902 "DBDS" (1928) ii 290 (OEDS 1b. A chest of drawers. *U.S.* 1819.. So W B Cl Th,1742 T M H. Not A in S C U)

burglar, v. [B²] *"They used to hear about him robbing and burglaring now and then"* 1896 TSD i 345 (OEDS b. 1909.. *Colloq.* in W. The use as verb not in S C)

burglar-time, sb. [B¹] *"The money is still here, and it is fast getting along toward burglar-time"* 1899 "MCH" (1900) 6 (Nonce comb.)

burglarize, v. [AB³] *Those people who burglarized our house in September—we got back the plated ware they took off* 1909 Speeches (1910) 333 (OED *U.S.* To rob burglariously. OEDS 1871.. So F T M. Not A in W S C U)

burial-case, sb. [AB³] *Your high-toned, silver-mounted burial-case, your monumental sort, that travel under black plumes at the head of a procession and have a choice of cemetery lots* 1870 SNO(1875) 198. *He lay in a metallic burial-case* 1906 Autob (1924) I 308 (OEDS *U.S.* 1851.. Not A in W S C)

burn, v. **to have to burn.** [AB³] *I had lots of them—yes, uncles to burn, uncles to spare* 1907 Speeches (1910) 409 (OEDS 8d. To have in abundance. orig. *U.S.* 1897 .. So Th.III H. Phr. not in W S C)

burn, v. **to burn one's bridges.** [B¹] *It might be pardonable to burn his bridges behind him* 1892 AmCl x 94 (W: To burn one's boats or bridges: to cut off all means of retreat. So S C. OED 9c.*fig.* only To burn one's boats, 1886, only ex.)

burnt district, sb. [AB¹] *The broken pillars, the doorless doorways...were wonderfully suggestive of the "burnt district" in one of our cities* 1869 IA xxxi 328. *One would be able to tell the "Burnt District" by the radical improvement in its architecture...One can do this in Boston and Chicago. The "burnt district" of Boston was commonplace before the fire* 1883 LM xli 424. *Some of these scars...form a city map on a man's face; they suggest the "burned district"* 1880 TA vii 65 (A in F: So frequent and devastating have been large fires in many of the cities of the Union that the term 'burnt district' to signify the part destroyed by fire has become quite familiar. Comb. not in OED W S C)

burster, sb. [B³] *Then came a "burster"—kind of hurricane—out of the south—the twin of the Texas "norther"—and knocked the mercury down 36 degrees in four hours* 1895 Notebook (1935) xxiii 262 (OED 2. In Australia. 1879. So W S C)

bus, sb. [?AB³] *I sat in the front end of the 'bus, directly under the driver's box* 1853 Letters (1917) I i 27. *We were coming down-town on top of the bus* 1899 "My First Lie" (1900) 164 (OED A familiar shortening of Omnibus. 1832.. So U. Colloq in W S C. A in B F Cl Th M DN.IV AS.V.275)

bushwhacker, sb. [AB³] *A minister of the Gospel living out West is sometimes chased around considerable by the bushwhackers* 1864 SS (1926) 129 (OED *U.S.* 2. Applied in the Am. Civil War to irregular combatants who took to the woods. 1862.. So W S C B Cl Th T M)

bushwhacking, sb. [AB³] *Those were troublous days in Hawkeye...between Unionists and Confederate occupations, sudden maraudings and bushwhackings and raids* 1873 GA xviii 169. *He knew something about... bushwhacking around for ogres* 1889 CY xxv 323 (OED *U.S.* 1864.. So S C B F Cl Th,1813. Not A in W)

business, sb. [?A] *Some of the effects of this ditching business* 1875 OTM 192. *The absurd chivalry business* 1883 LM i 27. *Ragsdale's leper business* 1884 Letters (1917) II xxiv 440 (OED 18. Vaguely. An affair, concern, matter. Now usually indicating some degree of contempt or impatience. 1605.. So W C U. A in AS.VI. 257. This sense not in S)

business, sb. [B²] *When he destroyed the Church and burned the idols, he did a mighty thing for civilization and his people's weal—but it was not "business"* 1897 FE iii 53 (OEDS 21c. Action having a commercial basis or value. 1897, this quot. This sense not in W S C)

business-brain, sb. [B¹] *One must respect the business-brain that produced it* 1907 CS II vii 171 (Comb. not in OED W S C)

business-eye, sb. [B¹] *Mrs.Eddy was born with a far-seeing business-eye* 1907 CS II x 263 (Comb. not in OED W S C)

business-head, sb. [B¹] *This idea came out of no ordinary business-head* 1907 CS II vii 171 (Comb. not in OED W S C)

business-idea, sb. [B¹] *It outclasses the best business-idea yet invented* 1907 CS II vii 170 (Comb. not in OED W S C)

business-suit, sb. [?AB²] *We saw eight or ten wooden dummies grouped together, clothed in woolen business suits* 1880 TA xlviii 556 (OEDS 1904, only ex. So W. A in H: Am. business-suit = Eng. lounge-suit. Comb. not in S C)

business-talent, sb. [B¹] *This is another exhibition of her business-talent* 1907 CS II vii 176 (Comb. not in OED W S C)

businesswise, adv. [B¹] *A man who was very wealthy, whom no one would venture to call a fool, either business-wise or otherwise* 1885 Autob (1924) I 47 (Comb. not in OED W S C)

bust, sb. [AB³] *"Santa Maria!—zis ze bust!—zis ze pedestal!" "Ah, I see...Is this the first time the gentleman was ever on a bust?" That joke was lost on the foreigner—guides cannot master the subtleties of the American joke* 1869 IA xxvii 293 (OED *U.S.* spec. A frolic; a spree. 1860.. OEDS 1856.. So S B F Cl Th,1850 M. Not A in W C U)

bust, v. [AB³] *"Here I've sot a-bustin' muskeeters"* 1872 RI ii 27. *"If she'll let up on some of the roughest things, I'll smoke private and cuss private, and crowd through or bust"* 1876 TS xxxv 272. *"The truth's a-busting on him now!"* 1896 TSD iv 353 (OED *Dial* or *vulgar* pron. of Burst, esp. in U.S. OEDS 1839.. So B F M AS.IV.292; V.201,Ozarks. Not A in W S C U)

bust, v. [AB¹] *"Take in a poor man, and...he'll bust himself on a single lay-out"* 1883 LM xliii 438 (W: *slang, U.S.*: To make bankrupt. So S C B F Cl. This sense not in OED, exc. as implied in Busted, below)

busted, ppl.a. [AB²] *"If there was a horse-race, you'd find him flush or you'd find him busted at the end of it"* 1865 "Jumping Frog" (1875) 31. See *cuss,* sb. 1867; *dornick* 1869; *chance,* sb. 1870. *Just a rubbish-pile of battered corpses and...busted hardware* 1889 CY xix 234 (OEDS *U.S. colloq.* Broken, bankrupt, ruined. 1881.. So W S B F Cl T M DN.I. Not A in C U)

buster, sb. [AB³] *"He tackled some of them regular busters"* 1865 SS (1926) 159 (OED 2a. *slang,* chiefly *U.S.* Something that 'takes one's breath away.' OEDS 1845.. So S Wr B F Cl. Not A in W C)

bust out, v. [?AB¹] *I had the misfortune to "bust out" one author of standing. They had his manuscript, with the understanding that they would publish his book if they could not get a book from me...So that manuscript was sent back to its author today* 1868 Letters (1917) I viii 146. *"Wunst I had foteen dollars, but I took to specalatin', en got busted out"* 1884 HF viii 70 (To cause the failure of; to ruin, bankrupt. Comb. not in OED W S C)

butcher-knife, sb. [AB³] *A rusty old butcher-knife and a whet-stone* 1881 PP xx 254. *Extracted a butcher-knife from his boot* 1883 LM lvii 562. *A butcher-knife without any handle* 1884 HF ix 78 (OEDS *U.S.* A large knife used by butchers. 1822.. So Th. Not in W S C)

butter-bean, sb. [?AB²] See *biscuit* 1880; *batter-cake* 1897 (OEDS 1884.. So W. A in S: A variety of Lima bean cultivated in the U.S. So C DN.VI)

butternut, sb. [A] *Against the wall stands a tall glass-fronted bookcase—the material, American butternut* 1904 Autob (1924) I 205 (OED 1. The White Walnut tree of N.Am. 1783.. So W S C U Cl Th,1781 M)

butternut, a. [AB³] *The tall Missouri youth...the butternut lad* 1873 GA xvii 159 (OED 3. The color of the Southern uniform in the American War of Secession..hence *absol.*, a Confederate, a Southerner. 1861.. So W S C B F Cl Th T)

butter–timber, sb. [B¹] *Men who had freighted their stomachs with strips of leather from old boots and with chips from the butter-cask...all full of leather...and butter-timber* 1899 "My Debut" (1900) 103 (Nonce comb.)

buyer, sb. **buyer thirty.** [?AB¹] See *seller* 1869. (W: The option is called *buyer four, ten, thirty,* etc. according as it is good for four, ten, thirty, etc. days. So S C. Not in OED; but cf. OEDS Seller, cited below)

buy into, v. [?AB¹] *Three years ago if a man...went over to Washoe and bought into a good silver mine...* 1867 "Inquiry About Insurances" 79 (W: To obtain a place, footing, or interest by purchase in. So C. A in F. Comb. not in OED S; but cf. OED Buy in. 6c. To purchase stock or shares. 1826..)

buzz, v. [?AC] *He diligently "buzzed" and "button-holed" Congressmen in the interest of the Columbia River scheme* 1873 GA xxiv 226 (OED 7. To whisper to, tell privately; to incite by suggestions. *obs.* 1637.. 1692. Not *obs* in W Wr. A in F Cl T. Not in S C)

buzzard, sb. [AB³] *"The idea of coaxing a sick man's appetite back with this buzzard fare is clear insanity"* 1898 "At the Appetite Cure" (1900) 153 (OEDS 1c. The species of vulture more fully called turkey-buzzard. *U.S.* 1851.. So W S C F Cl H)

buzzard–roost, sb. [AB¹] *After suffocating body and mind...in that intolerable old buzzard-roost* 1889 CY iv 53 (Comb. not in OED W S C)

buzz–saw, sb. [AB³] See *Ballarat fly* 1897 (OEDS *U.S.* A circular saw. 1860.. So Cl Th.III T M H. Not A in W S C)

by–and–by, adv.phr. **bymeby.** [AE] *"But bymeby she roused up like, and looked around wild"* 1873 GA ii 32. See *broke* 1874. *"Her chile was de king bimeby"* 1893 PW iii 239 (OED 4. Before long. In U.S., vulgarly *by'mby.* OEDS 1825, first ex.this pron. So W S C B F Cl Th,1786)

by and large, adv.phr. **to take by and large.** [AB³] *Taking it "by and large," as the sailors say, we had a pleasant ten days run from New York to the Azores Islands* 1869 IA v 47. *"Taking you by and large, you do seem to be more different kinds of an ass than any creature I ever saw"* 1875 OTM 285 (OEDS orig. *U.S.* To regard in a general aspect. 1833.. So S C B F Cl Th T H DN.II,VI. Not A in W)

by–blue, adv.phr. [B¹] *"By-blue! if you have see two birds upon a fence, he you should have offered to bet which of those birds shall fly the first"* ["Retranslated" from the French *parbleu*; the original version of the "Jumping Frog" had: *"Why, if there was two birds setting on a fence, he would have bet you which one would fly first"*] 1875 SNO 39 (Hum.nonce borrowing)

bzzzzzzzeeeee, sb. [B¹] See *kahkahponeeka* 1880 (Hum. invention)

C

cabbage, sb. [?AB¹] *Smoking one of those cabbage cigars the San Francisco people used to think were good enough for us in those times* 1870 SNO (1875) 272 (Inferior tobacco, as if made out of cabbage-leaves. So S. This sense not in OED W C)

cabbage, sb. [?AB¹] *This whole swindle is a creation of one of those cabbages that used to be the head of one of those Departments* 1887 *Letters* (1917) II xxvi 482 (Blockhead, idiot. So S. This sense not in OED W C)

cabbage, v. [?AB³] *That one lay in the plate of the man from whom I had cabbaged the lot* 1893 "Concerning Tobacco" (1917) 276. *No matter which member of her clerical staff shall furnish the explanations, not a line of them will she [Mrs. Eddy] ever allow to be printed until she shall have approved it, accepted it, copyrighted it, cabbaged it* 1907 CS II vii 195 (OED To pilfer. b. transf. 1862.. So W S C Wr. A in F Cl DN.III)

cabbage-leaf, sb. [?AB¹] *"No Connecticut cabbage-leaf product, but Havana, $25 the box!"* 1907 "Chaps. from Autob" 681 (Cf. above. This sense not in OED W C. Given in S)

cabin, sb. [?AC] *Unionville consisted of eleven cabins and a liberty-pole* 1872 RI xxviii 203. *Old Jim's cabin that he was captivated in, the time we set him free* 1896 TSD vi 356 (OED 1. A temporary shelter of slight materials, *Obs.* a1400..1869. H: the Am. use of the word, to denote a small and roughly built cottage, is now *obs* in Eng. A in AS.VII.166. Not *obs* or A in W S C U Wr)

cabin, v. [?A] *Dan Twing and I and Dan's dog "cabin" together* 1862 *Letters* (1917) I iii 85 (OED.1.intr. 1586.. Used by Parkman 1865 of Am. Indians. Not A in W S C. Cf. above)

cabin, sb. [?A] See *carriage-body* 1869; *state-room* 1883. *Inside, a far-receding snow-white "cabin;" porcelain knob and oil-picture on every stateroom door* 1883 LM xxxix 406. (OED.5. A room or compartment in a vessel for sleeping or eating in. An apartment or small room in a ship for officers or passengers. 1382.. The first clear ex. of the latter use is dated 1835. So W S C U. The *spec* steamboat usage is not mentioned by any dict.)

cabinet, sb. [C] *Edward took Tom to a rich apartment in the palace which he called his cabinet* 1881 PP iii 40 (OED 3. A small chamber or room, *arch* or *obs.* 1565..1822. So W S C. Not *arch* in U)

cabinet minister, sb. [?AB³] *The first reception took place at a Cabinet Minister's—or rather, a Cabinet Secretary's—mansion* 1873 GA xxxii 290 (OED Cabinet, sb.13. No ex. OEDS Earlier U.S.ex. 1806. Not A in U. Cf. H: The term cabinet minister is unknown in America, where cabinet secretary takes its place. So M. The OEDS quot. shows that this distinction did not always hold good. Comb. not in W S C)

cabinet secretary, sb. [AB¹] See above (Comb.not in OED W S C U; but they all recognize that the U.S. "Cabinet" is composed of Secretaries rather than Ministers)

cabin-guard, sb. [?AB¹] *"It has been up on the ladies' cabin-guard two days"* 1875 OTM 569 (The 'guard,' or lateral extension of the deck, outside the ladies' cabin. Cf. cabin, sb., above, and guard, sb., below. Comb. not in OED W S C)

cabin-mate, sb. [?AB²] *Will the new candidate explain...the little circumstance of his cabin-mates... losing small valuables from time to time?* 1870 SNO (1875) 312 (OED no ex. Not A in C; but cf. Cabin, sb., above. Comb. not in W S)

cable, v. [?AB³] *Harris wanted to cable his mother* 1880 TA xiv 124. See also *poppy* 1892 (OED 3. 1871.. So W S C U. A in F Cl; but not A in T AS.IX.70)

cable-car, sb. [?AB³] *Melbourne has an elaborate system of cable-car service* 1897 FE xvi 161 (OEDS 1887.. So W S C. A in T AS.IX.70: used in California in 1873)

cable-chain, sb. [B²] *His cultivation reconciles him to see the floating of iron cable-chains and other unfloatable things* 1880 TA xxiv 237 (OED 1886. So W. Comb. not in S C)

cablegram, sb. [?AB³] *He sent his cablegram* 1891 "Mental Telegraphy" 100 (OED 1868.. So W S C U. A in B F Cl Th.III T M DN.VI AS.IX.70)

cable-locker, sb. [B¹] See *reader* 1869 (Comb. not in OED W S C)

cable telegraph, sb. [?AB¹] *If we had had the cable telegraph in those days, this blood would not have been spilt* 1883 LM xlviii 476 (Comb. not in OED W S C. Cf. cable, above)

cable-telephone, sb. [?AB¹] *I resume by cable-telephone where I left off yesterday* 1898 "From the London Times of 1904" (1900) 128 (Cf. cable, above. Comb. not in OED W S C)

cache, sb. [AB³] *In a "cache" among the rocks we found the provisions* 1872 RI xxii 169 (OEDS *U.S.* 1b. A hole or mound made by American pioneers to hide stores. 1817.. So B F Cl Th M DN.V AS.VII.3,169. Not A in W S C U T)

cactus tree, sb. [B¹] *The cactus tree—candelabrum-like* [at Durban, South Africa] 1897 FE lxv 646 (Comb. not in OED W S C)

cadess, sb. [B³E] *Has he heroes and heroines who are not cads and cadesses?* 1903 *Letters* (1917) II xlii 737 (OED Caddess, nonce-wd. 1870. So S. Not in W C)

Cadet of Temperance, sb. [AB¹] *In Hannibal, when I was about fifteen, I was for a short time a Cadet of Temperance, an organization which probably covered the whole United States during as much as a year. It consisted in a pledge to refrain, during membership, from the use of tobacco* 1906 *Autob* (1924) II 99 (Comb. not in OED W S C. Cf. Mencken on the use of *cadet* in the Salvation Army)

Caesar, int. [AB¹] *Refused three times—warned to quit once—accepted at last!—and beloved!—Great Caesar's ghost, if there were a church in town with a steeple high enough to make it an object, I would go out and jump over it* 1868 Letter in Clara Clemens, *My Father* (1931) 15. *"Caesar's ghost!" commented Tom, with astonishment* 1894 PW xi 555. *"My word!" In cold print it is the* [British] *equivalent of our "Ger-reat Caesar!"* 1897 FE xxii 221 (This use not in OED W S C. A in DN.V. Cf. Great Caesar's ghost! A in DN.III.IV,V)

cag, sb. spelled kag. [?ACE] *"Collar that kag of nails!"* 1883 LM xxviii 303. *Like setting down on a kag of powder* 1884 HF xxviii 282. See also *eat,* v.1884. (OED The forms cag and kag 17th c. Now corrupted to *keg.* 1. A small cask. *obs.* 1452..1797. So C. *Dial* in W S. A in Wr DN.I,Missouri; III,IV AS.VI.57. Cf.M: The sp. *cag* for *keg* was preferred by Webster in his Dict. of 1806)

Cain, sb. to raise Cain. [AB³] *"Every time he got money he got drunk; and every time he got drunk he raised Cain around town; and every time he raised Cain he got jailed"* 1884 HF vi 37 (OEDS 1b. Orig. *U.S.* 1840.. So B F Cl Th M DN.II. Not A in W S C U)

cake-walk, sb. [AB³] *The negroes have a name for this grave deportment-tournament: a name taken from the prize contended for. They call it a Cake-Walk* 1894 "Defence of Harriet Shelley" 109 (OEDS 1a. A walking-competition among negroes of the southern U.S. 1889.. So W S C U Cl Th M)

calaboose, sb. [A] *The small jail (or "calaboose")* 1883 LM lvi 548. *Once in the calaboose they would be disgraced* 1894 PW xiii 775. *Hardy was surrounded by a strong guard and safely conveyed to the village calaboose* [in Hannibal, Missouri] 1894 "Scrap of Curious Hist." (1917) 185 (OEDS *U.S.* Negro French of Louisiana. The name in New Orleans and adjacent parts of the U.S. for a common prison. 1797.. So W S C U B F Cl Th T M DN.I,III,e.Ala.)

calamus odoratus, sb. [B¹] See *afarabocca* 1894 (Hum. variation of *Calamus aromaticus*, given in OED 1741. Not in W S C)

calculate, v. [AB³] *An old fellow with a carpet bag calculated it was good exercise to walk to Quincey* 1856 *Adv.of T.J.Snodgrass* (1928) 22. *He ketched a frog one day and said he cal'lated to educate him* 1865 "Jumping Frog" (1875) 33. See *and* 1867; *stub-hunter* 1869; *head off* 1870; *night-owl* 1880; *spree* 1883. *I calculated to educate the commonwealth up to it if I pulled through* 1889 CY iv 53. *I judged I had some reputation..and I calculated to keep it* 1907 "Capt.Stormfield" 42 (OEDS 7. U.S. colloq. To think, 'reckon;' to intend, purpose. 1805.. So W S C U B F Cl Th T M DN.II,III,IV,V)

calculated, ppl.a. [?A] *Attractions calculated to draw—and they did* 1892 AmCl iv 55 (OED 2. Apt, likely. 1722.. So W S C U. A in B F Cl)

calf–butchering, vbl.sb. [B¹] *Rightly viewed, calf-butchering accounts for "Titus Andronicus"* 1909 ISD iv 39. Comb. not in OED W S C)

caliber, sb. [B¹?C] *Then there was Colonel Cecil Burleigh Essex, another F.F.V. of formidable caliber* 1893 PW i 234 (OED 2. *fig.* a. Degree of social standing or importance, quality, rank, *obs*.1567..1870. So W. Not *obs* in S U. This sense not in C. Probably not a survival in M.T.'s vocabulary, but a new creation: a hum. twist of meaning along the lines of his favorite pun; cf. his jokes on *canon, howitzer, swivel,* etc.)

calico, sb. [AB³] *They were made of tolerably fanciful patterns of calico* 1873 GA i 19. *Two dirty old calico dresses* 1884 HF ix 78 (OED 2c. Applied in U.S. to printed cotton cloth, coarser than muslin. 1841.. So W S C B F Cl M H DN.II AS.IV.6,15, from Freneau, 1809; VII.170. Not A in U)

Californiaward, adv. [AB¹] *The spume-flakes were beginning to blow thinly Californiaward* 1877 *Speeches* (1910) 1 (Comb. not in OED W S C)

calk, sb. [?AB¹] *There is every bit as much reasonable material in it for a big calk like either of us to cry over* 1865 SS (1926) 193 (A derogatory epithet or term of abuse; cf. 'swab.' Not in OED W S C)

calk, v. [D] *The more I calk up the sources the more I leak wisdom* 1872 RI pref. *We calked the windows with clothing* 1872 RI xii 104 (OED 2. orig. *Naut.* To stop up the crevices of. 1609..1796—1884. So W S C U. This verb may help to explain the obscure sb. above; the waste material used in calking up crevices might well supply an invidious epithet)

call, sb. [?AB³] *He bought about twice as much more, deliverable upon call* 1889 CY xlii 532. See also *put up* 1904 (OED 11b. *Commercial.* A demand for the payment of money on the Stock Exchange. 1860. So W C U. A in S B T H)

call, v. [AB²] See *buck, pass the* 1872; *hold over* 1872. *Forty-nine times out of fifty no one dares to "call," and you rake in the chips* 1889 CY xlix 506 (OED 1e. In *Poker,* to call upon one's opponents to show their hands. 1883. So W S C Th.III M)

call, v. [B¹] *Business wasn't very brisk in the telegraphic line...I said..."Lively, now, call Camelot"* 1889 CY xxxvii 477 (To make a telegraphic call. This sense not in OED W S C; but cf. OEDS 1f. To make a telephone call. 1882..)

call, v. to call game. [AB¹] *Neither of us had had any rest...both of us waiting for the other to call game... When she got tired of the game at last, she rose from almost under my hand and flew aloft* 1906 "Hunting the Deceitful Turkey" 58 (A in W S: *Baseball.* To stop or suspend a game. Here *fig.* This sense not in OED C)

call, v. to call the game. [?AB¹] *Figuratively speaking, game's called...Go to the bat. I mean, get to work* 1889 CY xv 175. *By virtue of the authority in me vested, I declare the fair open. I call the ball game* 1907 *Speeches* (1910) 285 (*Baseball.* To start, open, give the signal

for the game to begin. This sense, curiously just the opposite of the one above, not in OED W S C)

call–boy, sb. [B²] *The landlord-apprentice serves as call-boy, then as under-waiter* 1880 TA App.A 586 (OED 15c. A youth employed in a hotel to answer the bells. No ex. So W S C)

call–boying, vbl.sb. [B¹] *I would like to know who did the call-boying and the play-acting...for he* [Shakespeare] *became a call-boy* 1909 ISD iv 47 (Not in OED W S C; but cf. OED Call, sb. 15a. A youth employed in the theatre. 1794.. So W S C U)

call off, v. [?AB²] *He drew on me for $56,000. Then I asked him to take the book and call it off* 1901 *Speeches* (1910) 344 (OEDS 30c. To rescind, draw back from 1902.. So W U. Not in S C)

camp, sb. to take into camp. [?AB¹] *He had six sons left for Sir Marhaus and me to take into camp* 1889 CY xix 234. See *unload* 1889. *The pawnbroker could get both rewards by taking him into camp with the swag* 1894 PW xv 818 (To capture, defeat, take prisoner. Phrase not in OED W S C)

campaign, sb. [?AB³] *They call my tribe customary hard names in their campaign speeches* 1884 *Speeches* (1923) 115. See also *Republican* 1906 (OEDS 5. Earlier U.S. exs. 1871.. A in C B F Cl Th.III T M H. Cf. B: The English use "canvass" with this meaning. Not A in W S U)

campaign–directing, ppl.a. [B¹] *The war-making, campaign-directing wanton of France* 1889 CY viii 95 (Comb. not in OED W S C)

campaigner, sb. [?AB¹] *Two of the best known of the Hartford campaigners for Blaine* 1884 *Speeches* (1923) 115 (A political supporter or advocate. Cf. campaign, sb., above. This sense not in OED W S C)

Campbellite, sb. [AB³] *The celebrated founder of the new and widespread sect called Campbellites arrived in our village from Kentucky* 1906 *Autob* (1924) II 279 (OED A follower of Alexander Campbell, a religious teacher of Virginia. 1881.. OEDS Earlier U.S.exs. In def. for 'of Virginia' read 'in Pennsylvania.' 1830.. So W S C B F Th AS.II.30. The nervousness shown by the OED about the great American reformer's state is rather amusing; he lived and worked, of course, during his long life (1788—1866) in both Virginia and Pennsylvania, as well as Kentucky, Missouri, and other states, but he was born in Ireland, and came to America only in 1809)

camphene, sb. [?AB³] *"He drinks everything that is fluid: milk, water, castor oil, camphene"* 1882 SWE 14 (OED A terpene contained in camphor oil. 1839.. So W S C. A in B F Cl T)

camp–meeting, sb. [AB³] See *skirmisher* 1864. *If there was a camp-meeting he would be there reg'lar to bet on Parson Walker* 1865 "Jumping Frog" (1875) 31. *A piece of music that would warm them up like a camp-meeting revival* 1875 SNO 360. See also *missionarying* 1884 (OEDS A religious meeting held in the open air or in a tent, chiefly among Methodists in America, and usually lasting for some days. 1803.. So W S C B F Cl Th,1801 M AS.II.30)

campoodie, sb. [AB¹] *Endor heads the list. It is worse than an Indian campoodie. The hill is barren, rocky and forbidding* 1869 IA li 541 (W: An Indian village, southwestern U.S. Cf. AS.VII.426: California "gold-rush" English. Not in OED S C)

camp out, v. [?AB³] *"If you call this camping out, all right—but it isn't the style I am used to"* 1869 IA xli 436 (OED 1837.. So W S C U. A in Cl)

camrod, sb. [B¹] *"When you run out of lightning-rods, put up ramrods, camrods, stair-rods, piston-rods—anything"* 1870 SNO (1875) 24 (Comb. not in OED W S C; but cf. OED Cam-shaft, Cam-wheel, etc.)

can, v. [?AB²] *"Can I have a big coach-candle fixed up just at the head of my bed?* 1890 *Speeches* (1910) 260 (OEDS B. 6b. To be allowed, to be given permission.

1894.. So W U. S: a misuse. C: Chiefly *colloq.* A in Cl M DN.III)

candelabrum–like, a. [B¹] See *cactus-tree* 1897 (Comb. not in OED W S C)

candidacy, sb. [?AB³] *It took weeks to decide a candidacy, because many pilots were so long absent on voyages* 1875 OTM 728 (OED 1852.. So W S C. A in B F Th T M H)

candle–factory, sb. [B¹] *"It's one of the oldest and noblest of the three hundred and sixty-four ancient German principalities...It's got a rope-walk and a candle-factory and an army* 1904 "Bequest" (1906) vii 43 (Comb. not in OED W S C)

candy–pull, sb. [AB³] *My sister gave a "candy-pull" on a winter's night* 1898 *Autob* (1924) I 135 (OEDS *U.S.* A party of young people at which toffy is made. 1873.. So W C. Not A in S)

candy–pulling, sb. [AB³] See *West,* sb. 1874 (OEDS *U.S.* 1854. So W DN.III,V. Not A in S. Not in C)

candy–shop, sb. [?AB²] *I have felt all the time like a boy in a candy-shop* 1869 IA xxviii 307 (OEDS 1886. Cf. M: A half-Briticism for Am. candy-store = Brit. sweetshop. Cf. OED Candy, *U.S.*; So F Cl H AS.I.492. Comb. not in W S C)

candy–striped, ppl.a. [AB¹] *The candy-striped pole... indicated merely the humble barber shop* 1893 PW i 234 (Cf. above. Comb. not in OED W S C)

cane, sb. [AB³] *A scheme to plant a swamp with cane to grow paper-stock* 1873 GA xv 40. See also *vacuum-pan* 1883 (OEDS 1c. Canes collectively. *U.S.* 1836.. So C. This use not in W S)

cane–brake, sb. [A] *They passed the mouth of the Ohio; they passed the cane-brakes* 1883 LM ii 35 (OEDS *U.S.* 1784.. So W S C B F Cl Th T M)

cane–head, sb. [B¹] *All the young clerks stood in the vestibule sucking their cane-heads* 1876 TS v 54 (Comb. not in OED W S C)

canned–goods, sb. [?AB¹] *Sally got to taking apples; then soap; then maple-sugar; then canned-goods* 1904 "Bequest" (1906) vi 33 (A in Cl, for British "tinned goods." Not A in S C. Comb. not in OED W; but cf. OEDS Canned, ppl.a. Earlier U.S.ex. 1859; A in B F M H)

cannel–bone, sb. [C] *"Doublets of crimson velvet, voyded low on the back and before to the cannel-bone"* 1881 PP xi 125 (OED *obs.* 2. The collar-bone. c1420.. 1656. So W. Comb. not in S C)

cannibal, sb. [B¹] *None of your flabby, tough meat that's laid in a cupboard in a damp cellar all night and tastes like a hunk of old cold cannibal in the morning* 1884 HF xxxiii 344 (Hum. nonce meaning)

cannon–smoke, sb. [B²] *So I set there and watched the cannon-smoke and listened to the boom* 1884 HF viii 58 (OED Cannon, sb. 9. No ex. Comb. not in W S C)

cannon–swab, sb. [B¹] *The head a cannon-swab of solid hair combed straight out from the skull* 1897 FE vii 94 (Comb. not in OED W S C)

cannon–thunder, sb. [B¹] *The cannon-thunder rages* 1883 LM xxxv 377 (Comb. not in OED W S C)

canoe, sb. [A] See *voyageur* 1883. *I dropped the canoe down the river under some willows* 1884 HF vii 53. See also *dent* 1884; *traps* 1884 (OED From Haytian, the native name found in use by Columbus. 2. In civilized use: A small light sort of boat or skiff propelled by paddling. 1799.. So W S C U. A in B F Cl M DN.IV, VI AS.IV.6,15)

canoe, v. **to canoe it.** [AB²] *The old man said, come along, let Sid foot it home, or canoe it* 1884 HF xli 416 (OED *colloq.* To do the journey in a canoe. 1884. So W. Phr. not in S C. Cf. above)

canoe–bottom, sb. [AB¹] *He came down on his head in the canoe-bottom* 1894 PW iv 330 (Cf. canoe, above. Comb. not in OED W S C)

canon, sb. [B¹] *She lived with her uncle Fulbert, a canon of the cathedral of Paris...She then returned to*

her uncle, the old gun, or son of a gun, as the case may be 1869 IA xv 142 (Hum. twist: the one pun that M.T. could never resist. Cf. howitzer, battery, swivel, smoothbore, etc.)

cañon, sb. Also **canyon.** [AB³E] *It was ribbed with sharp deep ridges and cloven with narrow cañons* 1869 IA v 50. *Echo Canyon is twenty miles long. It was like a long, smooth, narrow street, with a gradually descending grade, and shut in by enormous perpendicular walls of coarse conglomerate, four hundred feet high in many places, and turreted like mediaeval castles* 1872 RI xii 106. *"It's away down the gorge"...The crowd poured down the canyon* 1902 "DBDS" (1928) vii 333 (OEDS A physical feature characteristic of the Rocky Mountains and the western plateaus of N.Am. 1834.. So W S C B F Cl Th T M DN.I,IV,VI AS.VIII.3. 8. Cf. OED Canyon: a phonetic spelling. 1870. So U)

cañon–bed, sb. [AB¹] *Plodding its patient way down the mountain-sides and canyon-beds* 1872 RI xii 101 (Comb. not in OED W S C. Cf. above)

cañon–side, sb. [AB²] *He could watch the sleeted rain drive along the canyon-sides* 1872 RI xii 101 (OED 1879. Comb. not in W S C)

cantankerously, a. [?AB³] *"You are most cantankerously particular about a little thing"* 1894 TET v 389 (OED 1868.. So W S C. A in Th DN.III,IV)

cantelope, sb. [?A] See *batter-cake* 1897. *Trying to make up our minds whether to drop the watermelons, or the cantelopes, or the mushmelons* 1884 HF xii 102 (OED Cantaloup. Chiefly *U.S.* 1839.. OEDS Delete 'Chiefly U.S.' 1739.. Not A in W S C U T. A in F DN.III)

cantle, sb. [C] *Sir Gawaine and Sir Marhaus smote together with their swords, that their shields flew in cantles* 1889 CY xv 181 (OED 2. A sliver, a slice. *Obs.*.1627. Not *obs* in W S C Wr)

canvas–back duck, sb. [AB³] See *biscuit* 1880 (OEDS 2. A North American duck. 1809.. So W S C U B F Cl Th T M H DN.IV)

canvas–box, sb. [B¹] *This was a cluster of little canvas-boxes—palanquins* 1897 FE l 476 (Comb. not in OED W S C)

canvas–canopied, a. [B¹] See *hand-car* 1897 (Comb. not in OED W S C)

canvas–covered, a. [B¹] *A canvas-covered ham* 1869 IA xxxvii 394. *A canvas-covered modern trunk* 1873 GA lxi 553 (Comb. not in OED W S C)

canvass, v. [?C] *He canvassed his system. No ailment was found* 1876 TS vi 60 (OED 4b. To investigate or examine physically. *obs.* 1622. W: *rare.* Not *obs* nor *rare* in S C)

canvass, v. [?A] *He had seen them around the polls "canvassing"* 1883 LM xxxiv 373 (OED 6. To solicit votes previously to an election. 1681..1831. So W S C U. A in M: a term for American campaigning. Its Americanism is denied for this sense by B F Cl T H. Cf. campaign, v., above)

canvass, v. [?AB¹] See *subscription* 1907 (To promote or push the sale of a book. This sense not in OED W S C)

cap, to set one's cap for. [?AB¹] *"I'm going to set my cap for you, you dear old thing!"* 1892 AmCl xv 160 (Phr. not in OED, which has only: 9. To set one's cap at. *colloq.* 1822.. Given as *colloq* with either *at* or *for* in W S C)

Cap, sb. [AB¹] *"Well, Cap, what you done with your wings?"* 1908 "Capt.Stormfield" 266 (S: abbrev. of Captain. A in M DN.IV. Not in OED W C)

capable, a. [B¹] *Designing a particularly rare and capable gown for herself* 1892 AmCl xx 207 (Here, by a hum. twist of meaning: Showing capability in the maker. This sense not in OED W S C)

capitation tax, sb. [?AB¹] *No member, young or old, of a Christian-Scientist church can retain that membership unless he pay "capitation tax" to the Boston Trust* *every year* 1903 "Chr.Sc." 3 (This *spec* Chr.Sc. sense not in OED W S C. For gen. sense cf. OED 1776. .)

Capitol, sb. [A] *The President was up to the Capitol* 1893 TSA i 22. *A policeman at the Capitol building* 1892 AmCl xii 128 (OEDS 2. *U.S.* The edifice occupied by the congress of the U.S. 1795 . .So W S C U M. Cf. *Nation* XLVII.457, LX.361, with quot. dated 1699)

Captain, sb. [?A] *"When we first came here, I was Mr. Sellers, and Major Sellers, and Captain Sellers, but nobody could ever get it right, somehow; but the minute our bill went through the House, I was Colonel Sellers every time"* 1873 GA lvii 515 (OED 12. As a term of address, without implying any office or rank. *familiar* or *slang.* 1607. .1862. So S. A in M H AS.IX.205. This use not in W C)

car, sb. [AB³] *I took my seat in the car* 1856 *Adv. of T.J.Snodgrass* (1928) 24. *Changing cars at Terre Haute, Indiana* 1872 SNO (1875) 287. See *peanut-boy* 1873; *sleeper* 1881. *"That swindle has gone through without change of cars"* 1894 TET v 363. See also *branch-road* 1897 (OEDS 2. In the U.S. the term has become restricted almost entirely to vehicles designed for travelling on railways, or on tramways. 1831. . So W S C U B F Cl T M H)

car, sb. **coal-car.** [AB²] *Long trains of coal-cars, laden and unladen, stood upon sidings* 1873 GA lxiii 569 (OED 2. *U.S.* No ex. So W S C)

car, sb. **drawing-room car.** [AB¹] *A lady timidly entered the drawing-room car* 1873 GA xxix 264 (Comb. not in OED. Given in W S C B Cl)

carbon film, sb. [B¹] *These carbon films that got burnt out long ago and cannot now carry any faintest thread of light* 1906 "Howells" (1917) 237 (Here = filament. This sense not in OED W S C)

carcass, sb. [?AC] See *chunk* 1852; *shy,* v. 1880. *They won't ever hunt the river for anything but my dead carcass* 1884 HF vii 53 (OED 1. No longer used, in ordinary language, of the human corpse. 1340. .1750. So W S C)

card, sb. [?AB¹] *It occurred to Mr. Barnum that he needed a "card." He suggested Jumbo* 1897 FE lxiv 639 (A leading attraction. *Card,* without adj., in this sense not in OED W S C; but cf. OED *Sure card:* A person whose agency, or the use of whose name, will ensure success. 1579. .1826)

carding-machine, sb. [?A] *He got the other* [arm] *pulled out by a carding-machine* 1867 SNO (1875) 255 (OEDS 1789, only ex.U.S. Not A in W S C)

card-room, sb. [B²] *We shall have billard-rooms, card-rooms, music-rooms* 1875 SNO 307 (OED 1876. So W S C)

cargo-room, sb. [B¹] *I was carrying about as many short answers as my cargo-room would admit of* 1875 OTM 219 (Comb. not in OED W S C)

car-hook, sb. [AB¹] *Killing him with a car-hook* 1873 GA liv 489 (Cf. car, above. Comb. not in OED W S C)

carle, sb. [C] *"I would take the shabby carle"* 1881 PP xxvii 319 (OED 2. A churl. *Scotch* or *arch.* a1300. .1882. So W S Wr. Not *arch* in C)

car-load, sb. [AB¹] *That whole car-load of people* 1872 SNO (1875) 295 (Cf. car, above. Comb. not in OED. Given in W S C. Cf. OED *Carful, U.S.*)

carnabodium, sb. [B¹] See *afarabocca* 1894 (Nonsense coinage?)

Carnegian, a. [AB¹] *Suppose all the newspapers and periodicals should suddenly adopt a Carnegian system of phonetic spelling* 1906 "Carnegie Spelling Reform" 488 (Nonce word)

Carnegieize, v. [AB¹] *We would not disturb the Bible's spelling, but leave it as it is—no one would ever think of Carnegieizing it* 1906 "Carnegie Spelling Reform" 488 (Nonce word)

carom, v. [?AB³] *The sidewalks are not often wide enough to pass a man on without caroming on him* 1869 IA xxx 316. *Croquet, a game where you don't carom on*

anything of consequence 1869 IA App. 645 (OED Applied to the stroke so called in Billiards. 1860. . So W S C. A in B F T M H)

carpet-bag, sb. [?AB³] See *calculate* 1856. *The man thrust him from the car, and then flung his carpet-bag, overcoat, and umbrella after him* 1873 GA xxix 266. *A sharp-looking gentleman, with a carpet-bag of the old-fashioned kind* 1884 HF xxix 296 (OEDS Earlier U.S. exs. 1830. . A in AS.VII.12. Not A in W S C U)

carpet-bagger, sb. [AB³] *"Poor old carpet-bagger!"* 1869 CRG (1919) 129 (OED *U.S.* Political *slang.* Immigrant from the Northern into the Southern states. 1868. . So W S C U B F Cl Th T M H AS.V.220)

carpeting, sb. [?A] *A dim hall that was clad in ancient carpeting, faded, worn-out* 1869 IA lviii 615 (OEDS Earlier U.S.exs.1758. . Not A in W S C U)

carpet-sack, sb. [AB¹] *Women with reticules and bandboxes were trying to keep up with husbands freighted with carpet-sacks* 1875 OTM 190. *"They found where the thief had got his disguise out of his carpet-sack to put on"* 1896 TSD xi 533 (A in AS.VII.12, Nebraska, 1861. Comb. not in OED W S C)

carpet-stuff, sb. [?AB¹] *A carpet-bag of the old-fashioned kind, made out of carpet-stuff* 1884 HF xxix 296 (Comb. not in OED W S C)

carriage-body, sb. [B¹] *We sit in the cushioned carriage-body of a cabin* [in a Venetian gondola] 1869 IA xxiii 229 (Comb. not in OED S C. Given in W)

carrot, sb. [B¹] *It was I that got that grovelling and awe-smitten worship! I. . .this carrot!* 1905 "Czar's Soliloquy" 326 (This sense not in OED W S C. Cf. Shakespeare's "He was, for all the world, like a forked radish" 2 *Hen.IV* III. ii.334)

carrying capacity, sb. [B¹] *The boats were not able to keep up with the demands made upon their carrying capacity* 1883 LM lviii 570 (Comb. not in OED W S C; but cf. OED Carrying-power, 1878)

carry on, v. [?AB³] *"We do have such carrying-on"* 1869 IA xxiii 231. *"Don't it s'prize you de way dem kings carries on, Huck?"* 1884 HF xxiii 230. *"They carry on a good deal, but that's their fun"* 1892 AmCl xi 106 (OEDS 52e. *colloq.* To behave or 'go on' in some conspicuous way. 1828. . So W S C U Wr. A in B T M DN.III,IV,V, Ozarks)

car-seat, sb. [AB²] *We improvised tables by propping up the backs of car-seats* 1872 SNO (1875) 294 (OED Car, sb. 6. esp. in U.S. No ex. So S. Comb. not in W C)

carve, v. [C] *"Sir Miles, carve me this rabble to rags!"* 1881 PP xxii 277 (OED 1. *obs.* To cut: formerly the ordinary word for that action in all its varieties c1000 . .1560. So W C. This gen. sense not in S)

car-wheel, sb. [AB²] *A patent car-wheel he had bought an interest in* 1873 GA lxiii 572. *An improved railway car-wheel* 1883 LM xlviii 485 (OEDS Car, sb. 6. esp. in U.S. 1887. So W S C)

case-knife, sb. [?AB²] *"If we don't want the shovels, what do we want?" "A couple of case-knives"* 1884 HF xxxv 364 (OED b. A large kitchen or table knife. No ex. So W S C U. A in DN.II,III)

case-man, sb. [B²] *I saw the operator set at the rate of 3000 ems an hour, which, counting distribution, was but little short of four case-men's work* 1890 Autob (1924) I 71 (OED *Printing:* a compositor. No ex. C: *rare.* Not in W S)

cash in, v. [AB²] *"I'm going to cash-in a whole three hundred on the missionaries"* 1904 "Bequest" (1906) ii 10 (OEDS *U.S.* 2d.trans. To pay in to a bank. a1906. . So M. Not A in W S. Not in C)

casing, vbl.sb. [AB²] *"It's a blind lead—hanging wall—foot wall—clay casings—everything complete!"* 1872 RI xl 218. *The vein which contains the silver is sandwiched in between casings of granite* 1872 SNO (1875) 284. See also *arrastre* 1909 (OEDS 2c. *U.S. Mining.* 1872, this quot. So S C AS.II.87. Not in W in this sense)

casket sb. [AB³] *"There's one thing in this world which a person won't take in pine if he can go walnut; and won't take in walnut if he can go mahogany; and won't take in mahogany if he can go an iron casket with silver door-plate and bronze handles. That's a coffin"* 1883 LM xliii 438 (OED 3. A coffin. *U.S.* 1870.. OEDS *spec* one of a rectangular form. 1863.. So W S C Cl Th T M H AS.V.214,XI.201. Cf. jewel-box, below)

caste–brother, sb. [B¹] *All night long eighteen principal citizens did what their caste-brother Richards was doing at the same time* 1899 "MCH" (1900) 28 (Comb. not in OED W S C)

caste–custom, sb. [B¹] *There were other resemblances between Maori tabu and Hindoo caste-custom* 1897 FE xxxv 320 (Comb. not in OED W S C; but cf. OED Caste-feeling, 1875)

casting, vbl.sb. [?AB³] *He went rattling and clanking out like a crate of loose castings* 1889 CY ix 111 (OEDS 3. *concr.* Earlier U.S. exs. 1817.. Not A in W S C)

cast iron, a. [B³] *I opened up in cast iron German* 1883 LM xxxi 339. *My cast iron duty is to my audience —it leaves me no liberty and no option* 1885 *Letters* (1917) II xxv 450 (OED 2b.*fig.* Rigid, stern, unbending. 1830.. So W S C U)

castle–graced, ppl.a. [B¹] *Castle-graced crags and ridges* 1880 TA xix 175 (Comb. not in OED W S C)

cat, sb. **blame my cats.** [?AB¹] *"Why, blame my cats if he don't weigh five pound!"* 1865 "Jumping Frog" (1875) 35 (Doubtless a variation of *dog my cats*, q.v. Phr.not in OED W S C. Cf. Mencken's comment on Galsworthy's use of *cats* as an exclamation, under the impression that it is American)

cat, sb. **to let the cat out of the bag.** [?A] *"What are we going to do—lay around there till he lets the cat out of the bag?"* 1884 HF xli 414 (OED 13. To disclose a guarded secret. 1760.. So W S C U. A in Mait. AS. II.47, W.Va.)

cat, sb. **that cat wouldn't fight.** [?AB¹] *"First I thought I would leave France out and start fresh. But that wouldn't do, would it?...That cat wouldn't fight, you know"* 1869 IA iv 41 (That plan is not satisfactory. Phr.not in OED W S C)

cat-assizes, sb. [B¹] See *lawyer-talk* 1909 (Nonce comb.)

cat–bird, sb. [A] *A cat-bird, the Northern mocker, lit in a tree* 1876 TS xiv 122 (OED An American thrush. 1731.. So W S C U Cl Th M)

catch, sb. [B¹] *There was a sudden catch of her voice* 1892 AmCl ii 29 (This sense not in OED; but cf. OED 1. quot. for 1884, 'catch in the breath'. Given in W S C U)

catch, v. past tense **catched.** [?AE] *He ketched a frog one day* 1865 "Jumping Frog" (1875) 33. *I catched a catfish and haggled him open with my saw* 1884 HF viii 61; so *passim* in HF (OED This form 14th-18th c. C: rare. Dial in W Wr. A in M DN.I,II,IV AS.I.232. Not in S)

catch, v. **to catch it.** [B³] *I "caught it" for letting Mrs. Howells bother and bother about her coffee* 1875 *Letters* (1917) I xv 265. *There would be nothing so good in this world as to see that pet model "catch it"* 1876 TS iii 37 (OED 41. To get a threshing or a scolding. *colloq.* 1835.. So W S C U)

catch-all, sb. [AB³] *The white man's complexion... seems to have been designed as a catch-all for everything that can damage it* 1897 FE xli 383 (OEDS *U.S.* A general receptacle. 1838.. So Th T. Not A in W S C)

catcher, sb. [AB³] See *baseball match* 1894 (*Baseball.* OED 1886. So W S C)

catch out, v. [B³] See *snow under* 1889. *I am caught out worse than ever before, in the matter of letters* 1894 *Letters* (1917) II xxxiv 602. *As the judge was caught out himself, his reprimand was not very vigorous* 1894 TET

v 374 (OEDS 51c. *fig.* To catch in a mistake, catch napping in the act. 1815.. So W S. Comb. not in C)

catch–sentence, sb. [B¹] *I made six pictures with a pen, and they did the work of the eleven catch-sentences* 1899 "How to Make Hist. Dates Stick" (1917) 142 (Comb. not in OED W S C; but cf. OED Catch-phrase, 1850; OEDS Catch-question, 1860..)

catch up, v. [?AB³] *Let the introduction work along and catch up at its leisure* 1892 AmCl v 61 (OEDS 53e. To overtake. 1886.. So W S C U. A in DN.V)

catdom, sb. [?AB³] *She was not an ordinary cat, but moving upon a plane far above the prejudices and superstitions which are law to common catdom* 1907 "Chaps. from Autob" 2 (OEDS The world of cats. 1888.. Not in W S C. A in DN.V)

cat–fight, sb. [B¹] *Momentary outburst of a terrific cat-fight* 1892 AmCl xvii 179 (Comb. not in OED W S C)

catfish, sb. [AB³] See *sun-perch* 1876. *I have seen a Mississippi catfish that was more than six feet long* 1883 LM ii 32. *Not a solitary word of it all could those catfish make head or tail of* 1889 CY xxv 321. See also *lifter* 1894; *trot-line* 1909 (OED 1b. A N.Am. freshwater fish. Also *fig.* 1817.. So W S C U B F Cl T M DN.VI AS.IV.6, Freneau, 1809)

Catholic, sb. [?AB¹] *Catholics (8 bodies).* See *Adventist* 1907 (W: Any of various churches which claim apostolic succession. Not given for minor religious bodies in OED S C)

cathead, sb. **to bark one's shins on the cathead.** [B¹] See *garboard-strake* 1904 (Nonsense use: to do what is impossible or absurd. Cf. OED *Naut.* A beam projecting almost horizontally at each side of the bows of a ship. 1626.. This phr. not in OED W S C)

cat-knowledge, sb. [B¹] *One may say of him "all cat-knowledge is his province"* 1909 ISD v 52 (Comb. not in OED W S C)

cat-nap, sb. [?AB³] *I thought I would take jest one little cat-nap* 1884 HF xv 129 (OED Cat, sb. 18. 1856. So W S C. A in F AS.II.47)

catology, sb. [B¹] *The kitten...could have studied catology in a garret* 1909 ISD v 53 (Nonce word)

cat-tail-looking, a. [AB¹] *"One er dem big cat-tail-lookin' mullen-stalks"* 1884 HF xxxviii 373 (Comb. not in OED W S C. Cf. W: Cat-tail, sb. In England called the Reed-Mace. A in B AS.II.27)

cattie, sb. [B¹] See *pattie* 1891 (After German *Kätzchen* or *Katzlein.* Not in OED W S C)

cattle, sb. [?AC] *"If any of these cattle had known enough to get it out of her"* 1865 SS (1926) 159. *A despotism has no use for anything but human cattle* 1892 AmCl xviii 185 (OED 7b. of men and women. *arch..* 1823. Not *arch* in W S C U. A in DN.IV,V)

cattle-car, sb. [AB¹] *He had travelled two-thirds of a night and a whole day in a cattle-car* 1898 *Autob* (1924) I 150 (Comb. not in OED C. Given in W S. Cf. car, above)

cattle-friend, sb. [B¹] *I had given my attention to saving my poor cattle-friend* 1883 LM xxxvi 392 (Here: cattle-man friend. Nonce comb.)

cattle-pen, sb. [?AB³] *They are like the cattle-pen of a ranch* 1899 "How to Make Hist. Dates Stick" (1917) 141 (OED Cattle, sb. 8b. 1837. So W S C U. A in F: Land used for grazing purposes.)

cattle-raiser, sb. [?AB³] *He was a cattle-raiser from interior Ohio* 1883 LM xxxvi 388 (OEDS Cattle, sb. 8a. 1870.. Comb. not in W.S.C. A in F Cl)

cattle-scow, sb. [B¹] See *change, keep the* 1897. (Comb. not in OED W S C; but cf. OEDS Cattle-boat, 1860..)

caucusing, vbl.sb. [A] *A recess of half an hour was then taken and some little caucusing followed* 1872 SNO (1875) 291 (OED. In *U.S.* 1788.. So W S C B Cl Th T M H DN.V)

cavalieress, sb. [B²] *Every street was packed with charging cavaliers and cavalieresses* 1872 RI lxvi 476 (OED Nonce-wd. 1872, this quot. F: One of Mark Twain's individualisms. So T M. Not in W S C)

cave, v. [?AB³] *An hour in the caved mines...it still has a propensity to cave in places...the caving and settling of the tremendous mass was still going on* 1872 RI lii 381. *The muffled crash of a caving bank in the distance* 1873 GA iii 35 (OEDS 1b. Earlier U.S.exs. 1848.. Not A in W S C U)

cave, v. [?AB³] *"Well, I jist march on dem niggers...an' dey jist cave away befo' me an' out at de do'"* 1874 SNO (1875) 207. *All the ladies are seasick...The Scotchman's wife has "caved"* 1877 *Notebook* (1935) 127 (OEDS 2b. *slang.* Earlier U.S. exs. 1858.. A in B. Not A in W S C U)

caved–in, ppl.a. [?AB³] *People shut up in caved-in mines* 1898 "At the Appetite-Cure" (1900) 155 (OEDS Cave, v. 3c. 1865.. So W S C. Cf. Cave in, below)

cave–dweller, sb. [B¹] *There being but three thousand of these cave-dwellers...in Vicksburg* 1883 LM xxxv 378 (Here *spec* of refugees from bombardment at the siege of Vicksburg. Cf. in gen. sense OED 5. Troglodyte. 1865.. So W S C U)

cave in, v.intr. [?A] *Of course these mines cave in, in places, occasionally* 1872 RI lii 381. *The whole face of the stream was black with...great trees that had caved in and been washed away* 1875 OTM 448 (OED All the earliest instances in print are from America. OEDS 1707.. A in B F Cl Th M DN.III AS.II.86. Not A in W S C U)

cave in, v.trans. [?AB³] *The tropical sun was beating down and threatening to cave the top of my head in* 1872 RI lxiv 460 (OEDS 3. Earlier U.S.exs. 1857.. A in F Th. Not A in W S C U)

cave–in, sb. [?AB²] *Looked like there had been a cave-in in the bank there* 1884 HF xii 99 (Cf. above. OED 1884. So W S C)

cave off, v. [?AB¹] *Spots where the masonry had caved off and left dangerous gaps* 1880 TA xlii 486 (A variation upon *cave in.* Comb. not in OED W S C)

cavort, v. [AB³] See *straddle,* v. 1865. *It was the unholiest gang that ever cavorted through Palestine* 1868 *Letters* (1917) I vii 143. See *rasp,* v. 1874. *Galloping and cavorting and yelling and banging* 1883 LM xxvi 287. *There was four or five men cavorting around on their horses* 1884 HF xviii 172 (OEDS *U.S. vulgar* 1830.. So W S C B F Cl Th T M DN.I,II,III,V,VI. Not A in U)

cayuse, sb. [AB³] *The island shrunk into a fish, and the mastodon dwindled down to a Cayuse pony* 1864 SS (1926) 127 (OEDS *U.S.* A common Indian pony. 1857.. So W S C F Cl Th M DN.II AS.IV.129, VI.230)

cedar–pencil, sb. [?AB²] *It seems to come as natural as it is to put your friend's cedar-pencil in your pocket* 1869 IA xxxvii 398 (OED Cedar, sb. 4. No ex. A in DN.III: Alabama term for lead-pencil. Comb. not in W S C)

cell–like, a. [B¹] *We took candles and descended into the dismal cell-like chambers* 1869 IA lv 589 (Comb. not in OED W S C)

celluloid, sb. [AB³] *Celluloid teeth, nine dollars a set* 1889 CY xv 183 (OED Invented in America...as a material for dental plates. 1871.. Not A in W S C U)

celtic, sb. [B¹] *Se afarabocca* 1894 (Cf.W: Celtic nard or spikenard. Not in OED S C)

cement, sb. [?AB²] *Every pound of the wonderful cement was worth well-nigh two hundred dollars* 1872 RI xxxvii 259 (OED 5. *Mining.* Gravel firmly held in a silicious matrix. 1881.. So S C. *Colloq* in W)

cement–mine, sb. [?AB¹] *The whole region was a cement-mine—and they make the finest kind of Portland cement there now* 1906 *Autob* (1924) II 215 (Cf. above. Comb. not in OED W S C)

cent, sb. [A] *A penny in Arthur's land and a couple of dollars in Connecticut were about one and the same thing: just twins, as you might say, in purchasing-power...I could have paid these people in beautiful new coins from our own mint...I had adopted the American values exclusively. In a week or two now, cents, nickels, dimes, quarters, and half-dollars, and also a trifle of gold, would be trickling in thin but steady streams all through the commercial veins of the kingdom* 1889 CY xiv 165. *A thing that gratified me a good deal was to find our new coins in circulation—lots of milrays, lots of mills, lots of cents, a good many nickels, and some silver...yes, and even some gold...I asked for change for a twenty-dollar gold piece...They changed my twenty, but I judged it strained the bank a little, which was a thing to be expected, for it was the same as walking into a paltry village store in the nineteenth century and requiring the boss of it to change a two-thousand-dollar bill for you all of a sudden ...People had dropped the names of the former moneys, and spoke of things as being worth so many dollars or cents or mills or milrays now* 1889 CY xxxi 396 (OED 4. In the U.S., the hundredth part of a dollar. 1782.. So W S C U B F Cl T M DN.V)

center, sb. to catch on the center. [AB¹] *His voice caught on the center occasionally* 1869 IA iv 45 (To change pitch, as when a boy's voice 'breaks.' A steamboat-engine metaphor; cf. Herbert Quick's *Mississippi Steamboatin'*, 1926, p. 196: "Many a cub went to the throttle, trembling in fear that he would center his engine and so make a lot of work for men who would have to turn the wheel past this center point with levers." This sense not in OED W S; but cf. OED 5. A form of bearing in a lathe, 1680.. Cf. also dead-center, below)

center, sb. [?AB²] *They kept them dodging bullets for half an hour before they managed to drive the center* 1869 IA ix 84. *" You've hit it; you've driven the center, you've plugged the bull's eye of my dream"* 1892 AmCl xviii 183 (OED 9. The part of a target between the bull's eye and the "outer." 1887. So W S C)

center–driving, ppl.a. [?AB¹] *Is there a long-range, center-driving, up-to-date Mauser-magazine for elephant?* 1907 CS II ii 117 (Cf. above. Comb. not in OED W S C)

central, sb. [AB¹] *I used to wake...and say "Hello, Central!" just to hear her dear voice* 1889 CY xv 183 (S: An operator of a telephone exchange. So W. A in H: takes the place of the Eng. *exchange.* This sense not in OED C)

centrifugal, sb. [?AB²] See *vacuum-pan* 1883 (OEDS 6. As sb., a centrifugal machine. 1904. So W S C. A in AS.VI.14)

century–long, a. [B¹] *A dead saint enters upon a century-long career* 1883 LM xlii 432 (Comb. not in OED W S C; but cf. OEDS Centuries-long, a. 1908..)

century–wave, sb. [B¹] *Gazing out over the ocean of Time—over lines of century waves* 1869 IA lviii 629 (Comb. not in OED W S C)

ceramic, a. Spelled **keramic.** [B³E] *The whole keramic world would be informed* 1880 TA xx 185 (OED. Also keramic. 1. Of or pertaining to pottery. 1850.. So W S C U)

ceramiker, sb. Spelled **keramiker.** [B¹E] *The true keramiker, or the true devotee in any department of brick-a-brackery* 1880 TA xx 187 (Not in OED W S C. A nonce borrowing from German Keramiker? Cf. OEDS Ceramicist, 1930)

ceramics, sb. Spelled **keramics.** [B¹E] *My chief solicitude was about my collection of Keramics* 1880 TA xx 184 (Specimens of pottery. This sense not in OED. Given in W S C, with both spellings)

certain–sure, a. [?AB³C] *"All the cranks in the kingdom load up the mails with certain-sure quack cures for him"* 1901 "Two Little Tales" (1928) 205 (OED Certain, adv. 3. Emphasizing *sure. obs* or *dial.* 1804.. 1875. *Dial* in Wr. A in B Cl Th. Comb. not in W S C)

certes, adv. [C] *"Certes, this hour's experience has taught me..."* 1881 PP xii 146 (OED *arch.* Of a truth, certainly. a1250..1870. So W S U Wr. Not *arch* in C)

chaffy, a. [?AB³] *He was as chaffy as he was sixty years ago, too, and swore the Archbishop and I never walked to Boston* 1874 *Letters* (1917) I xiv 233 (OEDS Given to chaff or chaffing. 1855.. So W S C. A in DN.IV)

chain-gang, sb. [?AB³] *"The Austro-Hungarian Monarchy is the patch-work quilt, the Midway Plaisance, the national chain-gang of Europe"* 1898 "Stirring Times" (1900) 285 (OED Chain, sb. 19. A gang or number of convicts chained together while at work, etc. Here *fig.* 1858.. So W S C U. OEDS Earlier U.S. ex. 1841. A in M H)

chain-lightning, sb. [AB²] *"By jiminy, but he's chain-lightning!"* 1902 "DBDS" (1928) 338 (OEDS *U.S.* 1. Lightning in the form of a continuous flash; forked lightning. *fig* 1918.. So U B F Cl T DN.III. Not A in W S C)

chain-lightning, sb. [AB³] *Our reserve, whom we had kept out of sight and full of chain-lightning, sudden death, and scorpion-bile all day, came filing down the street as drunk as loons* 1865 SS (1926) 163 (OEDS *U.S.* 2. A raw brand of whisky. 1843.. So F Cl. Not A in W. Not in S C)

chain-mail, v. [B¹] *A chromo of some Ohio politician which had been retouched and chain-mailed for a crusading Rossmore* 1892 AmCl xxi 223 (To provide with chain-mail armor. Not in OED W S C as verb)

chair-arm, sb. [B¹] *They drop limp and pensive over the chair-arms* 1870 SNO (1875) 99 (Comb. not in OED S C. Given in W)

chaleteer, sb. [B¹] *I explained to the head chaleteer just how the thing happened* 1880 TA xxxviii 438 (Proprietor of a chalet. Not in OED W S C)

chalk, sb. **to walk chalk.** [?AB¹] *"If anybody come meddlin' wid you, you jist make 'em walk chalk"* 1874 SNO (1875) 204 (To behave oneself, mind one's own business. Phr. not in OED W S C. A blend of two idioms, but with not quite the same significance as either: (1) OEDS *Walk one's chalks:* To go away, be off. Earlier U.S.exs. *slang* 1836.. So W S C; and (2) W S C: *Walk the chalk, walk the chalk mark* or *line:* To act always with strict propriety, to keep "straight;" from the testing of a man's sobriety by making him try to walk on a straight line chalked to the floor. *colloq.* Not in OED)

chambermaiding, vbl.sb. [B¹] *She would go chambermaiding on a steamboat* 1894 PW iv 332 (Not in OED W S C)

chameleonship, sb. [B¹] *No help for this chameleon? ...It is in his chameleonship that his greatest good fortune lies* 1906 "WIM" (1917) 46 (Not in OED W S C)

chamois, sb. [B¹] *In Lucerne...I made another discovery...The chamois is a black or brown creature no bigger than a mustard seed...it arrives in vast herds and skips and scampers all over your body, inside your clothes* 1880 TA xxv 240 (Hum. nonce use, for flea. Ct. rabbit, below)

chamois-hunter, sb. [B¹] *The romancers always dress up the chamois-hunter in a fanciful and picturesque costume, whereas the best way to hunt this game is without any costume at all* 1880 TA xxv 241 (Hum. nonce use; cf. above)

chamois-pasture, sb. [B¹] *Harris's body was simply a chamois-pasture; his body was populous with the little hungry pests* 1880 TA xxxv 391 (Hum. nonce use; cf. above)

chance, sb. **a right smart chance.** [AB³] *"I'm acquainted with a right smart chance of gals in Keokuk"* 1856 *Adv. of T.J. Snodgrass* (1928) 13. *"There's a right smart chance of people here that'd like to know who killed him"* 1884 HF xi 88 (OEDS 4b. *U.S.dial.* 1819.. So

W Wr B F Cl Th T DN.II,III,IV,V,VI AS.II.350. Not in S C)

chance, sb. [B¹] *The 'chance' men are all busted and the 'science' men have got the money* 1870 SNO (1875) 161 (Nonce use for those who believe 'old sledge' to be a game of chance, not of science)

chance, v.intr. [C] *"If it so chance that we be separated, let each make for London Bridge"* 1881 PP x 118 (OED 1a. With impersonal *it* as subject. *arch.* 1393.. 1863. Not *arch* in W S C)

chance, v.intr. [?C] *He might possibly chance to need a sermon* 1883 LM lii 517 (OED 1c. With personal subject and inf. c1400..1867. Somewhat *arch.* Not *arch* in W S C)

chance, v.trans. [?AB³] See *salt-horse* 1887. *"I reckon it's all right—chance it, anyway"* 1880 TA iii 39. *Sufficient justification for chancing any dangerous thing* 1893 "Extracts from Adam's Diary" (1901) 765 (OED 4. To risk, venture. *colloq.* 1859.. So W S C U. A in B F T)

chancy, a. [?AB³] *The struggle for life was difficult and chancy in the islands in those days* 1897 FE iii 53 (OED 3. *colloq* or *dial.* 1860.. So W S C U. Cf. the expression *chancy if*=doubtful if, A in DN.II,1V)

change, sb. **to keep the change.** [?AB¹] *The Flora is about the equivalent of a cattle-scow...They smuggle her into passenger service, and "keep the change"* 1897 FE xxxii 301 (To pocket the profit; to appropriate an illegitimate increment or differential. Phr. not in OED W S C. But cf. OED Change, sb. 7c. *To take one's change out of:* to take one's revenge. 1830.. Also OEDS *Not to get any change out of:* to get no return or result from)

changement, sb. [C] *That song worked an instant and thorough "changement" in her* 1880 TA xvi 142 (OED *rare.* 1584..1801. So W S C. Used by M.T. as an alienism)

change off, v. [?AB¹] See *run to* 1873. *I experimented with the stogy. Then, once more, I changed off, so that I might acquire the subtler flavor of the Wheeling toby* 1910 *Speeches* 267 (Comb. not in OED W S C)

channel-finder, sb. [?AB¹] *I also had the highest opinion of his acquired qualifications as a channel-finder* 1906 "Carl Schurz, Pilot" 727 (Comb. not in OED W S C. A part of M.T.'s river vocabulary?)

channel-interruption, sb. [B¹] *Saharas of sand... (barring the channel-interruptions)* 1897 FE xlix 465 (Comb. not in OED W S C)

chap, sb. [AB¹] *There's a new baby down stairs* [Jean, born 1880]...*Little chaps like that can't be comfortable on a long journey, you know* 1881 *M.T. the Letter Writer* (1932) iii 37 (A babe or child, whether male or female. A in DN.II,III,V, So.Ill., Ala., Ozarks. This use not in OED W S C. Cf. OED 2b. *humorously* applied to a female. 1768.. So Wr)

chaparral, sb. [AB³] *Her hair was frizzled into a tangled chaparral* 1870 SNO (1875) 153. See *manzanita* 1872. *A thick growth of chaparral extended down the mountain-side* 1902 "DBDS" (1928) 314 (OEDS *U.S.* Dense tangled brushwood, composed of low thorny shrubs, brambles, briars, etc., such as abounds on poor soil in Mexico and Texas. 1845.. So W S C U B F Cl Th T M DN.I AS.VII.434)

character-fabric, sb. [B¹] *The unprincipled newspaper adds a baseness to a million decaying character-fabrics every day* 1903 "Defence of Gen. Funston" 615 (Comb. not in OED W S C)

character-reader, sb. [B¹] *A man just made out of the condensed milk of human kindness, yet with the ability to totally hide the fact from any but the most practiced character-reader* 1892 AmCl xxv 269 (Comb. not in OED W S C)

character-reading, vbl.sb. [B¹] *Master the difficult science of character-reading* 1892 AmCl xxi 217 (Comb. not in OED W S C)

charading, vbl.sb. [B¹] *Their stage facility was a result of their charading practice* 1907 "Chaps. from Autob." 242 (Not in OED W S C)

charged, ppl.a. [B²] *The talk and the beer flow for an hour or two, and by and by the professor, properly charged, gives a cordial good night* 1880 TA iv 48 (OED 4. To fill with liquor. No ex. Not in W S C)

charity-founder, sb. [B¹] *This madness for being noticed and talked about...has raised up...little and big politicians, and big and little charity-founders* 1898 "Memorable Assassination" (1917) 172 (Comb. not in OED W S C)

Charlie, int. [?AB¹] *Oh, Charlie!* (comment on one of Stella's bons mots: "The Doctor's nails grew dirty by scratching himself") 1868-1910 *Margins on "Swift"* (1935) 49. (An exclamation denoting fastidious disgust. Cf. *Charley boy, Cholly,* slang terms for an effeminate man or dandy. Not in OED W S C as int.)

chattel slavery, sb. [?AB¹] *Despotisms and aristocracies and chattel slaveries* 1899 "My First Lie" (1900) 162 (Comb. not in OED W S C; but cf. OED Chattel, sb. 4e. Used, chiefly rhetorically, by emancipation writers and others, of slaves or bondsmen. 1649..1865. Cf.also Chattelhood, sb., A in Th.III, 1870)

chatterbox, sb. [?AB³] *He and the innocent chatterbox whom I met on the Swiss lake are the most unique and interesting specimens of Young America I came across* 1880 TA xxxviii 444 (OED 1814.. So W S C U. A in DN.IV)

chattily, adv. [B²] *Talk began. It flowed along chattily and sociably* 1894 PW xi 552 (OEDS 1920. So W S. Not in C)

Chaur, sb. [B¹] See *Kaet* 1897 (Not in OED W S C)

Chautauqua, sb. [AB³] *Save it for processions, and Chautauquas, and World's Fairs* 1905 *Speeches* (1910) 432 (OEDS 2. *U.S.* 1903. So W S M DN.III AS.VII. 406, IX.232. Not in C)

chaw, v. [?ACE] *I got to set down and chaw over a lot of gold-leaf distinctions* 1884 HF xxxv 363 (OED A byform of Chew...very common in 16th-17th c...now esteemed vulgar. 2c. To ruminate upon, brood over. *a*1558..1845. So W S C. A in Wr M DN.I,II,III,IV AS.V.203, Ozarks; XI.30, e.Texas, but now disused)

chaw up, v. [AB³E] *"I stood at the little press until nearly 2 o'clock, and the flaring gas-light over my head attracted all the varieties of bugs which are to be found in natural history...The little press "chawed up" half a bushel of the devotees, and I combed 976 beetles out of my hair the next morning* 1857 Letter in the *Iowa Journal of Hist.* (1929) 424. *"Set whar you are, gentlemen. Leave him to me; he's my meat... You lay there tell the chawin'-up's done"* 1883 LM iii 44. See also *reputation* 1884 (OED 3. *slang,* chiefly *U.S.* To demolish, 'do for.' 'smash.' 1844.. So C B F Cl M. Not A in U. Not in W S)

cheap-john, a. [AB¹] *The "Vicar of Wakefield," that strange menagerie of thratrical cheap-john heroes and heroines who are always showing off* 1897 FE lxii 612 (In poor taste, low-bred, vulgar. A in DN.III,IV, Arkansas. This sense not in OED W S C; but cf.OED Cheap-john,sb. A travelling hawker. 1826..)

chebang, int. [AB¹] *There rang O'er all the place the loud "cheBang!"* 1891 *Slovenly Peter* (1935) 14 (This form not in OED W S C; but cf. OEDS Ker-, prefix. *U.S.vulgar:* also co-, che-. See also Mencken on the prefix che- in America, p.146)

checaudum, sb. [?AB¹] *Giving the peculiar yell, and a howl as if the sounds came from the depths of his stomach, and what is called checaudum* 1883 LM App.D 616 (Presumably an Indian word. Not in OED W S C)

check, sb. to pass in one's checks. [AB²] *"He'll pass in his checks before sun-up"* 1870 CRG (1919) 97. *"One of the boys has passed in his checks, and we want you to give him a good send-off"* 1872 RI xlvii 332. *"When the market breaks and every knight in the pool*

passes in his checks, what have you got for assets? Just a rubbish-pile of battered corpses" 1889 CY xix 235 (OED 15. *U.S.* 1870. Cf. also OED Pass, v. 63. To die. *slang.* 1872.. A in S C B F Cl Th DN.IV AS.XI. 200. Not A in W)

check, v. [AB³] *Baggage checked through to any point on the route* 1875 SNO 308. See also *baggage-master* 1880 (OEDS 16c. *U.S.* 1860.. F: Equivalent to the English "to book." So Cl Th T. Cf. H: No longer peculiar to America. Not A in W S C)

checkered, ppl.a. [AE] *He wore a checkered neckerchief with the ends hanging down* 1869 SNO (1875) 45 (OED A variant spelling of Chequered, esp. in U.S. So M H. This sp. not A in W S C)

cheek, sb. [?AB³] *I declined that honor—not because I hadn't cheek enough* 1867 *Letters* (1917) I vii 133. See also *ante,* v.1873; *blister* 1884; *sublimity* 1892 (OED 4b. *colloq.* Effrontery. 1852.. So W S C U. A in B)

cheeky, a. [?AB³] *"Coming out so cool and cheeky with that imaginary blue-arrow mark"* 1884 HF xxx 310 (OED *colloq.* 1857.. So W S C U. A in DN.IV)

cheerful-tinted, a. [B¹] *Floors clothed with soft, cheerful-tinted carpets* 1869 IA xliv 459 (Comb. not in OED W S C)

cheer-killing, a. [B¹] *Shouldering the whole show is such a cheer-killing responsibility* 1877 *Letters* (1917) I xvii 311 (Comb. not in OED W S C)

cheese, v. cheese it. [?AB³] *"Cheese it, pard"* 1872 RI xlvii 336 (OED Thieves' slang: Run away, have done. 1812.. So W S C Wr. A in B F M DN.II,III AS.XI.294)

cherimoya, sb. Spelled **chirinoya.** [AE] *The cocoa palm grows [in the Sandwich Islands] and the coffee tree, the mango, orange, banana, and the delicious chirinoya* 1866 *Speeches* (1923) 18 (OED 1. A small tree, a native of Peru. 1736.. B: Of West Indies and South America. So W S C F. OED gives var. sp. chirimoya; M.T.'s sp. -noya is probably a misprint)

Cherokee Strip, sb. [AB³] *"Where are you from?" ..."Cherokee Strip"* 1892 AmCl ii 30 (OEDS A part of the State of Oklahoma inhabited by Cherokees. 1889. So W Th.III,1869. Name not in S C)

cherry-stone clam, sb. [AB¹] See *biscuit* 1880 (W: a small quahog, or round clam. *U.S.* So H. Comb. not in OED S C)

chestnut, sb. [AB³] *The serpent informed her [Eve] that "chestnut" was a figurative term meaning an aged and mouldy joke* 1893 "Extracts from Adam's Diary" 764 (OED 7. *slang.* Said to have arisen in U.S. 1886.. So S C F Cl Th T. *Colloq* in W U)

chestnut-cake, sb. [B¹] *A chunk of chestnut cake* 1893 PW intro. 233 (Comb. not in OED W S C; but cf. OED Chestnut-bread, 1846)

chestnut-woman, sb. [B¹] *"Tell the chestnut-woman about your watermelon cure"* 1901 "Two Little Tales" (1928) 208 (Comb. not in OED W S C; but cf. OED Chestnut-seller, 1883)

chevron, sb. [D] See *coat-of-arms* 1883 (OED 2. *Heraldry.* A charge or device on the escutcheon, consisting of a bar bent like two meeting rafters. *Chevron in chief:* one which rises to the top of the field. 1395.. 1872—. So W S C U)

chewable, a. [B¹] *What nourishment we can get from boot-legs and such chewable matter* 1866 "Forty-Three Days" 111 (Not in OED W S C)

chewing-gum, sb. [AB³] *"What I like is chewing-gum"* 1876 TS vii 75. *"If he tells them [genies] to build a palace forty miles long out of di'monds and fill it full of chewing-gum...they've got to do it"* 1884 HF iii 21 (OEDS *U.S.* 1864.. So S C U F Th,1836 M. Not A in W)

Cheyenne, sb. [AB¹] See *Blackfoot* 1906 (Not in OED C. Given in W S)

chicken, sb. [AB³] *The chickens go to roost an hour before schedule-time* 1896 JA II xvi 439 (OEDS 1d.

dial or *colloq* as coll. sing. for fowls of any age. *U.S.* 1829.. Cf.H: In Am. sometimes loosely used in the sense of *fowl*...Hence Am. *chicken-yard*=Eng. *fowl-run*. So DN.II,III. Not A in W S C. Mencken, p.233, oddly cites this use of *chicken* as a Briticism)

chicken, sb. [?A] *"Don't you try to come that game, my chicken"* 1872 RI xxxi 224 (Cf. OED 3b. Applied to one who is timorous. 1611.. So W S. In *colloq* Am. use the word does not necessarily imply the suggestion of timidity. This sense not in C)

chicken-cock, sb. [AB¹] *"Well, thish-yer Smiley had rat-terriers and chicken-cocks"* 1865 "Jumping Frog" (1875) 33 (Game-cock. A in DN.II,VI: A rooster, s.e.Mo. Not in OED W S C)

chicken-coop, sb. [?A] See *alley* 1869. *The sort of door which in the South the negro attaches to his chicken-coop* 1904 *Autob* (1924) I 211 (Cf. chicken, above. OED 1789.. So W S. Not in C)

chicken-farm, sb. [?AB³] *His idea was to buy that place and start a chicken-farm* 1906 *Autob* (1924) II 324 (Cf. chicken, above. OEDS 1895. So W. Comb. not in S C)

chicken-fight, sb. [?AB¹] *If there was a chicken-fight, he'd bet on it* 1865 "Jumping Frog" (1875) 31 (Cf. chicken, above. Comb. not in OED W S C)

chicken-hearted, a. [?A] *They call him "hare-foot," which is the German equivalent for chicken-hearted* 1880 TA vi 62 (OED 1681.. So W S C U. A in DN.III, IV,V)

chicken-livered, a. [AB¹] *Of all the childish, idiotic, chuckle-headed, chicken-livered superstitions* 1889 CY v 62. *A chicken-livered slave, with no more pride than a tramp* 1890 *Autob* (1924) I 75 (A blend of *chicken-hearted* and *white-livered*. A in AS.V.129: Maine dialect. Comb. not in OED W S C. Given in U)

chicory, sb. [?AB³] *Continue the boiling and evaporation until the flavor and aroma of the coffee and chicory has been diminished to a proper degree* 1880 TA xlix 376 (OED 2. Ground and roasted as an addition to, or substitute for, coffee. 1853.. So W S C U. A in H: Am. *chicory*=Eng. *endive*. So M, adding that Am. *endive*=Eng. *chicory*)

chief, sb. [D] See *coat-of-arms* 1883 (OED 3. Heraldry. The head or principal part of the escutcheon, occupying the upper third of the shield, and divided from the rest by a line which may be straight, indented, embattled, wavy, etc. *a*1440..1864—. So W S C U)

chieftain, sb. [C] *Several military chieftains with sounding titles* 1869 IA ii 26 (OED 2. A military leader. *arch* or *poet*. *c*1330..1847. So W. Not *arch* in S C U)

chili-bean, sb. [AB¹] See *slum* 1865 (A in DN.III. Comb. not in OED W S C; but cf. OED Chilli, tropical Am. plant)

chills, sb. **cold chills.** [?AB¹] See *streak*, v. 1884. *It made the cold chills creep over me* 1889 CY ii 33. *The cold chills trickled down my back* 1896 TSD vii 361 (The shivers, 'gooseflesh.' Not in OED W S C)

chills and fever, sb. [AB¹] *It was a famous breeder of chills and fever* 1883 LM lv 546 (Fever and ague. A in S B F Cl DN.III. Comb. not in OED W S C)

chills-racked, ppl.a. [AB¹] *Crazy rail fences...with one or two jeans-clad, chills-racked, yellow-faced male miserables roosting on the top rail* 1875 OTM 449 (Chills, pl.=fever and ague is A in DN.II,III, s.Ill. and s.e.Mo. Neither the pl. form nor the comb. is in OED W S C)

chimney, sb. Spelled **chimbley.** [?AE] *I couldn't get up the chimbley; it was too narrow* 1884 HF vi 39. *He had just strength enough to crawl up on the comb and lean his back agin the chimbley* 1880 TA iii 40 (OED This form *dial* and *vulgar*, 18th and 19th c. So W S C Wr. A in Cl M DN.I,III,IV,V AS.V.206, Ozarks; XI. 237, e.Texas)

chimney, sb. [?AB³] *They examined this body of rich ore and found that there was a very great deposit of it. They thought it was a "chimney", belonging probably to the California, away up on the mountain-side, which had an abandoned shaft* 1906 *Autob* (1924) I 272 (OEDS 9. Mining. An ore-shoot. 1873.. So W S C. A in AS.V. 145: Colorado mining term, a richer spot in a lode as distinguished from a poorer one)

chimneyfied, ppl.a. [B¹] *Our skyscrapers...in the daylight are—well, too chimneyfied and too snaggy* 1900 *Speeches* (1910) 124 (Not in OED W S C. A hum. coinage?)

chimney-guy, sb. Spelled **chimbly-guy.** [?AB¹E] *It was a steamboat that had killed herself on a rock. The lightning showed her very distinct. She was leaning over, with part of her upper deck above water, and you could see every little chimbly-guy clean and clear* 1884 HF xii 102 (A steel cable used to fix and hold the smoke-stack in place. Comb. not in OED W S C; but cf. OED chimney, sb. 5a. The tunnel which carries off smoke from a steam-boat. 1825, only ex. So S C. W rashly calls this use *Brit.* For sp., cf. above)

chin, v. [AB²] *When I stood before the "Republican" office and looked up at its tall unsympathetic front, it seemed hardly me that could have "chinned" its tower ten minutes before* 1870 *Screamers* (1871) 77 (OEDS 3b. To talk to, to address, esp. boldly and impudently. *U.S.* 1871, this quot.. So W S B F Cl DN.II. Not A in C)

China, sb. [C] *An old Chinaman named Quong, non-progressionist, was the chief China minister at Washington* 1885 *Autob* (1924) I 22 (OED 2a. Used as simple attrib. Now generally superseded by *Chinese*. 1589..1868. Not in W S C as attrib.)

Chinadom, sb. [?AB³] *The combined stenches of Chinadom and Brannan Street slaughter houses* 1872 RI lxiii 456 (OEDS Earlier U.S. ex. 1872, this quot.. Not A in S. Not in W C)

Chinaman, sb. [AB³?C] *"Digger, Chinaman, Greaser, and American"* 1865 SS (1926) 161. See *China*, sb. 1885 (OED 2. A native of China. Earliest ex. U.S. 1854.. Not A in W: Now being superseded by *Chinese*, which is preferred exc. in derogatory uses. Not A or *arch* in S C U)

China-tree, sb. [AB³] *"The slack water ends here, abreast this bunch of China-trees"* 1875 OTM 218 (OEDS 2b. *U.S.* The Azedarac. 1819.. So W S Th. Not A in C)

Chinawoman, sb. [?AB²] *There are few white servants and no Chinawomen so employed* 1872 RI liv 392 (OEDS 1872, this quot.. So W. Not in S C)

chin-music, sb. [AB³] *"The thing I'm on now is to roust out somebody to jerk a little chin-music for us"* [i.e., to preach a funeral sermon] 1872 RI xlvii 332. *"A young sprig from the East blustered up...and began to sass the conductor with his chin-music"* 1873 GA xxix 267 (OEDS *U.S.* Talk, chatter. 1844.. So W S B F Th DN.IV,V AS.II.350, W.Va.; V.121, Maine. In AS.IV.430, this is mistakenly listed among phrases invented by Tad Dorgan, cartoonist, who died in 1929. Not in C)

chip, sb. [?AB³] See *call*, v. 1889. *He was gambling —with his family for "chips"* 1906 "WIM" (1917) iii 33 (OEDS 2d. A counter used in games of chance. 1851.. So W S C. A in Cl T)

chip in, v. [?AB³] *"Pard, he was a great loss to the town. It would please the boys if you could chip in something like that and do him justice...Put that in, pard"* 1872 RI xlvii 336. *The Child of Calamity chipped in again* 1883 LM iii 47. *The old man he was on hand...chipping in a little Scripture now and then* 1884 HF xxviii 294 (OED 8. *colloq*. To interpose smartly. 1870.. So W S C U Wr. A in B F Cl Th T M DN.I)

chip into, v. [?AB¹] *They chip into a conversation whenever they want to* 1892 AmCl viii 81 (Cf. above. Comb. not in OED W S C)

chipmunk, sb. [AB³] *A vague file of chipmunk tracks stringing through the dust* 1909 ISD xi 131 (OED A ground-squirrel of N.Am. 1842.. So W S C U B F Cl Th T DN.I,III)

chipper, a. [AB³] *One neat and chipper suit of spotless muslin* 1880 TA xlii 489. *A gay and chipper essay* 1880 TA App.F 627. *We wished we hadn't been quite so chipper* 1893 TSA i 24 (OED *U.S.* Lively, brisk, cheerful. 1837.. So W S C B F Cl T DN.I)

chipper, v. [AB³] *After they'd jumped overboard and took a swim it chippered them up a good deal* 1884 HF xxi 204 (OED *dial* and *U.S.* 2. 1873. So W S C)

chipperness, sb. [AB¹] *Then he worked up a hollow chipperness of manner* 1894 PW viii 339(Cf. above. Not in OED W S C)

chirk, v. [AB³] *I see Jim chirk up to listen* 1894 TSA xii 544. *Tom chirked and joined in the fun himself* 1894 PW xxi 237 (OEDS 3. To cheer up. *U.S.colloq.* 1844.. So S C Wr B F Cl Th T DN.I,III. Not A in W)

chirk, a. Spelled **cherk**. [AE] *There's a cherk and natty something about N. Y. dress* 1877 Notebook (1935) xiii 132 (OEDS *U.S.colloq.* Lively, cheerful. 1789.. So W S C B F Cl Th T DN.V. Under Chirk, v., OED gives the form *cherk* as 15th-17th c. So C. This form not in W S)

chirpy, a. [?AB³] *Straightway his horror softens down to a sort of chirpy contentment* 1906 "Entertaining Article" 221 (OED *colloq.* Cheerful. 1837.. So W S C U. A in F Cl Th)

chitling, sb. [AB²] See *biscuit* 1880 (OED Another form of 'chitterling.' 1. Widely used in Eng.dials. and in U.S. 1886.. So DN.III AS.V.17, Ozarks. Not A in W S C)

chock, v. [AB³] *Where do they* [the newspapers] *get matter to fill up a page in this little island* [Mauritius]? *... They discuss Madagascar and France... They chock up the rest with advice to the government* 1897 FE lxiii 621 (OEDS 1b. To fill in as packing. *U.S.* 1868. So F Cl. Not A in Wr. This sense not in W S C)

chock, v. [?AB³] *A Boer teamster chocking his wagon-wheel on a steep grade with a diamond as large as a football* 1897 FE lxix 701 (OED 2. To make fast, wedge. 1854. So W S C U Wr. A in Th DN.III)

chocolate-colored, ppl.a. [?AB³] *A single block of chocolate-colored wood* 1880 TA xxxii 346 (OEDS Earlier U.S.ex. 1819.. Not A in W. Not in S C)

Choctaw, sb. [AB¹] *A Chinese captain and a Choctaw crew* 1859 Letter in New Orleans Daily Crescent (W: An Indian of a tribe of Muskhogean stock, formerly of Alabama. So S U. Not in OED C)

Choctaw, sb. [AB¹] *I spoke in the purest German, but I might as well have spoken in the purest Choctaw for all the good it did* 1880 TA xviii 163. See also *kahkahpo-neeka* 1880; *sailor-talk* 1909 (The Choctaw language, taken as a type of unintelligible gibberish. This sense not in OED W S C)

choice, a. [?A] *They were choice in their English* 1875 OTM 221 (OEDS 3b. Discriminative. Earlier U.S. ex. 1775.. Not A in W S C U)

choke-cloth, sb. [B¹] *They were taught how to strangle a person with the sacred choke-cloth* 1897 FE xlvi 428 Comb. not in OED W S C)

chomp, v. [A] *"The Frenchman had his bottle of wine and plate of food...and was 'chomping' like a horse"* 1897 FE lv 528 (OED var.of Champ. *U.S.and dial.* 3. 1558.. So S B Cl M DN.I,II,III. Not A in W C Wr)

chop off, v. [?AC] See *flat out* 1894 (OED 8b. To break off abruptly. *obs.* 1620, only ex. Not in W S C)

chopping-up, vbl.sb. [B¹] *The interior of this barrack is so chopped up that one cannot deal in exact numbers when trying to put its choppings-up into statistics* 1904 Autob (1924) I 198 (Nonce formation)

chore, sb. [A] *"Do you have to do all the 'chores'?"* 1878 "Some Rambling Notes" iv 15 (OEDS 1. *dial* and *U.S.* A small piece of domestic work. 1758.. So W S C U Wr B F Cl Th T M DN.III,V,VI)

chortle, v. [B¹] *Whenever Mrs. Eddy notices that she is chortling along without saying anything, she pulls up with a sudden irrelevancy* 1907 CS II ii 122 (OED A factitious word invented by Lewis Carroll, app. as a blend of *chuckle* and *snort*. 1872.. As M.T. uses it, the word carries no suggestion of *chuckle*, but means rather to gabble, run on unintelligibly)

chouse, v. [?A] *Some villains were trying to chouse some negro orphans out of $700* 1897 "Pen-Picture" (1917) 352 (OED *colloq.* To dupe, cheat. 1659.. So W S C U. A in F Cl)

chowder-headed, ppl.a. [?AB³] See *let out*, v. 1871 (OED *dial.* Thick-headed. 1819.. So W S. C: A dial. form of Cholter-headed. A in B F Cl DN.II,IV,V)

chow-wow, int. [B¹] *"Set her back on the stabboard! Ting-a-ling! Chow! chow-wow!"* 1876 TS ii 29 (Nonce formation)

Christadelphian, sb. [AB³] See *Adventist* 1907 (OED A religious sect founded in the U.S. by Dr.Thomas in 1833. 1873.. So W S C)

Christian, sb. [D] *"All AI alligator-pilots...could tell alligator-water as far as another Christian could tell whiskey"* 1883 LM xxiv 205 (OED.3a. *colloq* and *dial*. A human being, as distinguished from a brute. A common sense in the Romanic langs. 1591..1818—. So W S C U Wr. This sense is oddly called *Eng.* in S C)

Christian Catholic, sb. [AB¹] See *Adventist* 1907 (W: In full, Christian Catholic Apostolic Church in Zion. A religious organization chiefly centered at Zion City, near Chicago, Illinois, formed in 1896 by John Alexander Dowie (d.1907). So S C. Not in OED)

Christian Connection, sb. [AB¹] See *Adventist* 1907 (W: An Am. sect formerly called by some Christian Connection, and later, Christian Church (General Convention of the Christian Church). They were united with the Congregational Church (U.S.) in 1931, under the new name Congregational and Christian Church. So S C. Not in OED)

Christian–missionary, v. [B¹] *To go Christian-missionarying with infidel tracts in your hands* 1886 "What Amer. Authors Think" 634 (Nonce comb. Cf. missionary, v., below)

Christian Missionary Association, sb. [AB¹] See *Adventist* 1907 (S: A loosely federated group of independent unsectarian churches, for the most part in Kentucky. Not in OED W C)

Christian Science, sb. [AB³] See *absent treatment* 1899. *The Christian-Science "boom" is not yet five years old* 1902 "Chr.Sc." 761. See also *church-machinery* 1907. (OEDS. Founded on principles formulated by Mrs. Mary Baker Glover Eddy of Concord, New Hampshire, U.S.A. 1863.. So W S C U F)

Christian–Scientifically, adv. [AB¹] See *harmonious* 1903 (Nonce formation)

Christian Scientism, sb. [AB¹] *The coming great march of Christian Scientism through the Protestant dominions of the planet* 1902 "Chr.Sc." 757 (Nonce formation. Cf.OED Scientism: The habit and mode of expression of a man of science, 1897)

Christian Scientist, sb. [AB³] *"All Christian Scientists know the book by heart"* 1899 "Chr.Sc.and the Book" 589. See also *Allopath* 1902; *Congregationalist* 1906; *Adventist* 1907 (OEDS 1881.. So W S C U F Cl AS. II.68)

Christian–Scientist, a. [AB¹] *A Christian-Scientist church* 1903 "Chr.Sc." 3 (The attrib. use not in OED W S C)

chromo, sb. [?AB³] *We finally decided to send him a chromo* 1883 LM xxxii 360. *Whenever I enjoy anything in art it means that it is mighty poor. The private knowledge of this fact has saved me from going to pieces with enthusiasm in front of many and many a chromo* 1891 "At the Shrine of St.Wagner" 227. See also *chain-mail*, v. 1892 (OED 1868.. So W S C U. A in M)

chromo–portrait, sb. [?AB[1]] *Aureoled chromo-por-traits and bogus autographs of Mrs. Eddy* 1903 "Chr. Sc." 4 (Cf. above. Comb. not in OED W S C)

chuck, sb. [AB[3]] *I wish I was near you so I could send you chuck (refreshments)* [given as thieves' argot] 1883 LM lii 515 (OEDS Now chiefly *U.S.* 1. Food, grub. 1850.. So S Wr F Cl M DN.III,IV,V AS.II.399, IV.339. Cf. Chuck-box, Chuck-wagon, A in H. Not A in W. Not in C)

chuckle–head, sb. [?A] *There wasn't a human being in this town but knew that boy was a perfect chucklehead; perfect dummy; just a stupid ass, as you may say* 1883 LM liii 526 (OED 1731.. So W S C U Wr. A in F Cl T DN.II)

chuckle-headed, a. [?A] See *chicken-livered* 1889. *"If there's anybody that's fool enough to go on such a chuckle-headed errand"* 1892 AmCl xv 157 (OED Block-headed. 1764.. So W S C U Wr. A in F Cl T)

chuckleheadedness, sb. [?AB[2]] *Opaque perception, dense and pitiful chuckleheadedness* 1876 *Letters* (1917) I xvi 289. *With the native chuckleheadedness of the heroine of romance* 1880 TA xv 133 (OED 1880, this quot. So W S. A in F. Not in C)

chuckly, a. [B[1]] *Stevenson, smiling a chuckly smile, said...*1904 *Autob* (1924) I 248 (Not in OED W S C)

chug–chug, v. [AB[3]] *There warn't no sound but the screaking of the woodwork and the chug-chugging of the machinery down below* 1896 TSD ii 347 (OEDS Chug, sb. orig. *U.S.* 1894.. So DN.V. Not A in W S C)

chump, sb. [?AB[3]] *A two-dollar-and-a-half chump with a thirty-dollar style* 1889 CY xxxv 455. (OED 3 *fig.* 1883.. So W S C U. A in Wr Cl M T DN.II,IV)

chunk, sb. [A] See *dornick* 1869; *fox-fire* 1884. *The old bower leaped into the air in chunks* 1889 CY vii 89. *A chunk of chestnut-cake* 1893 PW intro. 233. *An erudition he [Shakespeare] was acquiring hunk by hunk and chunk by chunk* 1909 ISD iv 46 (OED *colloq* and *dial,* esp. common in U.S. 1. 1691.. So S B F Cl Th DN. III,V,VI. This sense not A in W C U Wr)

chunk, sb. [AB[1]] *"Local" contemplates suicide. He resolves to "extinguish his chunk" by feeding his carcass to the fishes of Bear Creek* 1852 *Hannibal Journal,* Sept. 16. *"Mary, get me a silk thread, and a chunk of fire out of the kitchen"...The old lady made one end of the silk thread fast to Tom's tooth with a loop and tied the other to the bedpost. Then she seized the chunk of fire and suddenly thrust it almost into the boy's face* 1876 TS vi 63. *Matches were hardly known there in that day. They saw a fire smoldering upon a great raft a hundred yards above, and they went stealthily thither and helped themselves to a chunk* 1876 TS xiii 115.*"Fetch me a lantern or a chunk of fire here, boys"* 1883 LM iii 58 (A in DN. III: A partly consumed piece of firewood, e.Ala. Cf. Th,1821: "In the room of andirons, many families make use of what are here [Ohio] called *chunks,* which are the two brands of a large forestick, or billets of wood cut on purpose for this use." This sense not in OED W S C)

church–machinery, sb. [B[1]] See *Reader* 1907 [Comb. not in OED W S C)

Church of God (Winebrennarians). [AB[1]] See *Adventist* 1907 (W: Church of God in North America. A denomination of Christians in the U.S., founded by John Winebrenner in Pennsylvania in 1830. So S C. Not in OED)

chute, sb. [A] *He actually ran the chute of Glasscock's Island, downstream, in the night* 1859 Letter in *New Orleans Daily Crescent. Sometimes she* [the steamboat] *approached a solid wall of tall trees as if she meant to break through it, but all of a sudden a little crack would open just enough to admit her, and away she would go plowing through the "chute" with just barely room enough between the island on the one side and the mainland on the other* 1873 GA iv 42. *" You don't run close chutes on a falling river, upstream"* 1875 OTM 447 (OED A French word adopted in N.America: a rapid descent in

a river. 1725.. So B F Cl Th T M DN.VI. Not A in W S C U)

cigar, sb. Spelled **seegar.** [E] See *solid* 1884 (OED This sp. 18th c. 1735. So W S. A in DN.II. Not in C)

cigar-peddler, sb. [B[1]] *In Italy, as in France, the Government is the only cigar-peddler* 1893 "Concerning Tobacco" (1917) 278 (Comb. not in OED W S C)

cinch, v. [AB[2]] *They never cinch a Californian's horse tight enough to suit him* 1866 *Speeches* (1923) 13 (OED *U.S.* To girth tightly. 1875.. So W S C F Cl Th T M DN.I. Not A in U)

cipher, v. [?AB[3]] *It was impossible to comprehend that it was a very large building. I had to cipher a comprehension of it* 1869 IA xxvi 271. *The Shakespearite conduc's his assuming upon a definite principle...which is: 2 and 8 and 7 and 14, added together, make 165... You cannot get a habit-sodden Shakespearite to cipher up his materials upon any other basis* 1909 ISD v 51 (OEDS lb. To work out mathematically. Earlier U.S. exs. 1825.. Not A in W S C U)

cipher, v. [AB[3]] See *mumble-the-peg* 1870. *She puzzles her brain to cipher out some scheme for getting it into my hands* 1872 RI xv 124. See *Unabridged* 1875. *"Leave me alone to cipher out a way so we can run in the daytime"* 1884 HF xx 191 (OED lc. To cast in the mind, think out. *U.S.colloq.* 1837.. So W F Th DN.V. Not A in S C)

cipherable, a. [?AB[3]] *The proper measure...is cipherable merely upon the littleness or the vastness of the disappointment* 1900 "My Boyhood Dreams" 255 (OED 1888. So W S. Not in C. Cf. above)

circulate, v. [?AB[3]] *We shan't circulate in Florence until Livy shall be well enough to take a share in it* 1892 *Letters* (1917) II xxxii 571 (OED 5b. intr. Of persons: To go about in a social circle, 'go the round'. 1863.. So W S. A in Cl H DN.V. This sense not in C)

circumforaneous, a. [C] *"Summon hither the per-functory and circumforaneous Tumble-Bug"* 1875 SNO 145 (OED Now *rare* or *obs.* Wandering, vagrant. 1650..1827. So S. Not *rare* or *obs* in W C)

circumstance, sb. [C] *"In all the wide circumstance of this planet"* 1894 TET v 393 (OED lb. Circumference. *obs.* 1509, only ex. Not in W S C)

circumstance, sb. [AB[1]] *Next comes King John, and he was a poor circumstance* 1899 "How to Make Hist. Dates Stick" (1917) 155 (A in Th: Anything to speak of, 1836; used positively, 1838. Only with negatives in OEDS 7c. A fact or thing of importance. *U.S.* 1836.. So W S B F Cl H DN.III. This sense not in C)

circus, sb. [?A] *A circus came* 1876 TS xxii 178. See also *barbecue* 1886 (Cf. OED 2. A circular arena surrounded by tiers of seats, for the exhibition of equestrian, acrobatic, and other performances. 1791.. So W S C U. The Am. circus is a distinctive institution, with three or more arenas or rings, and other special features.)

circus, sb. [AB[2]] *Constantinople was—well, it was an eternal circus* 1869 IA xxxiii 358. *"Mulberry Sellers with an office! Why, they'd come from the ends of the earth to see a circus like that"* 1892 AmCl iii 41 (OEDS 2c. A disturbance or uproar; also an 'exhibition', a 'show'. orig. *U.S.colloq.* 1885.. So S. This sense not in W C)

circus, v. [?AB[1]] *"Boys, these are our own tracks, and we've actually been circussing round and round in a circle for more than two hours"* 1872 RI xxxi 228 (This sense not in OED W S C)

circus-bill, sb. [?AB[1]] *A monstrous inscription in Turkish characters wrought in gold mosaic that looks as glaring as a circus-bill* 1869 IA xxxiii 363 (Cf. above. Comb. not in OED W S C)

circusing, vbl.sb. [?AB[1]] *The boys played circus for three days...and then circusing was abandoned* 1876 TS xxii 178. See also *berrying* 1880 (Playing circus. Cf. above. Not in OED W S C)

circus-poster, sb. [?AB[1]] *Barnum wants to paste*

circus-posters on him [the elephant] 1882 SWE 25 (Cf. above. Comb. not in OED W S C)

circus-ring, sb. [?AB²] *What we saw was simply a circular crater...In the center of the great circus-ring thus formed was a ragged upheaval* 1869 IA xxix 324 (OED Circus, sb. 8. No ex. Comb. not in W S C)

citified, ppl.a. [?AB³] *He had a citified air about him that ate into Tom's vitals* 1876 TS i 22 (OEDS 1855.. So W C. A in S B F T M AS.XII.115, with Am. quot. 1855)

city-capture, sb. [B¹] *This stately old-time criminal, with his meditated insurrections and city-captures* 1883 LM xxix 312 (Nonce comb.)

city-editor, sb. [AB³] *I had been serving as city editor on Mr. Goodman's Virginia City "Enterprise"* 1906 *Autob* (1924) I 350 (OEDS The editor who superintends local news. *U.S.* 1889.. So W S C. Cf. M: In England = financial editor)

city of the dead, sb. [B¹] *The phrase "city of the dead" has all at once a new meaning...Many of the cemeteries are beautiful* (A cemetery. Phr. not in OED C. Given in W S)

civilization-tool, sb. [B¹] *Would it not be prudent to get our civilization-tools together?* 1901 "To the Person Sitting in Darkness" 165 (Nonce comb.)

Civil War, sb. [AB²] *In the Civil War he* [the Jew] *was represented in the armies and navies of both the North and the South* 1899 "Concerning the Jews" (1900) 282 (OED 3b. *U.S.* No ex. So W S C)

clabber, sb. [?A] See *batter-cake* 1897 (OED 2. Bonny-clabber: milk naturally curdled. 1634.. So W S C Wr. A in F Cl Th DN.II,III,VI)

clack, sb. [?A] See *spot*, v. 1880. *"If you didn't want to hear my clack, what did you keep intruding your conversation on me for?"* 1895 JA II i 136 (OED 6. Loquacious talk. 1440.. So W S C U. A in DN.II,IV)

clack-clack, sb. [B²] *I heard another one coming—for I recognized his clack-clack* 1870 SNO (1875) 193 (OEDS A repeated clacking noise. 1870, this quot. Not in W S C)

clack-clacking, vbl.sb. [B²] *Presently up the street I heard a bony clack-clacking* 1870 SNO (1875) 192 (OEDS 1870, this quot. Not in W S C)

claim, sb. [AB³] *I have already laid a timber claim on the borders of a lake* 1861 *Letters* (1917) I iii 59. *We the undersigned claim five claims of two hundred feet each (and one for discovery) on this ledge or lode of oyster shells* 1869 IA xxix 414. See also *taker* 1897; *arrastre* 1909 (OEDS 3. *spec* in U.S. and Australia. A piece of land allotted and taken. 1817.. So B F Cl T DN.II,III AS.VII.9, 427. Not A in W S C U)

claim, sb. [AB³] *He calls it his "claim"...which is Christian Science slang for "ailment". The Christian Scientist has no ailment... Upon his attention an imaginary disturbance sometimes obtrudes itself which claims to be an ailment, but isn't* 1902 "Chr.Sc." 764. *In Christian Science terminology, "claims" are errors of mortal mind, fictions of the imagination* 1903 "Mrs. Eddy in Error" 508 (OEDS 5. 1898.. Not in W S C)

claim, v. [AB²] *It is claimed that they were accepted gospel twelve or fifteen centuries ago* 1869 IA lxi 539. *I do not claim that I can tell a story as it ought to be told* 1895 "How to Tell a Story" (1900) 225. See also *tracker* 1897 (OEDS 2c. Often loosely used, esp, in U.S., for contend, maintain, assert. 1876.. So B F Cl T M H DN.III. Not A in W S C U)

claim agent, sb. [AB³] *Colonel Mulberry Sellers, Claim Agent* 1892 AmCl ii 28 (OEDS 1888.. A in F Cl M H. Not A in W. Not in S C. Cf. above)

claimantship, sb. [B¹] See *lewd* 1892 (Formed from Claimant in the sense of pretender to a title. Not in OED W S C)

claim-owner, sb. [AB¹] *I went out with the Attorney-General and the claim-owner* 1861 *Letters* (1917) I iii 61 (Cf. claim, above. Comb. not in OED W S C)

Claims Department, sb. [AB¹] *I got through the Claims Department* 1870 SNO (1875) 105 (Cf. claim, above. Comb. not in OED W S C)

clam, sb. [AB²] See *let out*, v. 1871. *These innumerable clams had permitted it so long that they had come...to accept it as a truth* 1889 CY xii 154 (OED 2. *U.S.* A term of contempt. 1871.. So DN.IV. This sense not in W S C)

clam, sb. **to sell a clam**. [?AB¹] *"Just go in and toot your horn, if you don't sell a clam"* 1872 RI xlvii 334 (To do business of any kind. Phrase not in OED W S C)

clan, sb. [B¹] *We are plodding along about as usual... Mrs.Clemens takes care of the clan* 1899 *M.T. the Letter Writer* (1932) vi 86 (Here: the family. A transf. use from the one in OED 1. A number of persons claiming descent from a common ancestor; a tribe. c1425.. This sense not in OED W S C)

clankety-clank, sb. [B²] *I heard the clankety-clank that plate-armor makes* 1895 JA II xv 565 (OEDS 1905.. Comb. not in W S C)

clapboard, sb. [A] *It was laid in between a rafter and the clapboards of the roof* 1884 HF vi 39 (OED 1b. In U.S. A board, thinner at one edge, used to cover the sides or roofs of houses, each board being made to overlap that below it. 1641.. So W U B F Cl Th,1632 M DN.II,III,VI. Not A in S C)

clarifying-tank, sb. [?AB¹] *Through the clarifying-tanks to discharge the molasses* 1883 LM xlviii 479 (Used in the sugar-houses in La. Comb. not in OED W S C)

clapperdudgeon, sb. [C] See *budge* 1881 (OED *arch* A cant name for a beggar born. 1567..1863. So W S M. Not *arch* in C)

classic, a. [B¹] *It was the twins knocking out a classic four-handed piece on the piano* 1894 PW vi 335 (Of acknowledged excellence as a musical work. This sense not in OED W S C, which have only the use of the word with ref. to literature and art!)

class-teacher, sb. [B¹] *When I was a Sunday-school scholar..I began to ask questions, but my class-teacher was reluctant about answering them* 1909 ISD ii 20 (Comb. not in OED W S C; but cf. OEDS Class-teaching, 1892)

clattery, a. [B²] *A small piano in the room, a clattery, wheezy, asthmatic thing* 1880 TA xxxii 341 (OED *colloq* 1880, this quot. So W S. Not in C)

claw, v. [B¹] *I held my breath and began to claw the boat away from danger* 1875 OTM 217 (This trans. use not in OED W S C. Cf. OED 7. *Naut.* Claw off, intr. 1696..)

claw back, v. [B¹] *The "Jumping Frog": in English, Then in French, Then Clawed Back into a Civilized Language once more by Patient, Unremunerated Toil* (title) 1875 SNO 28 (Hum. nonce use, with a suggestion of the naut. meaning)

claw-hammer coat, sb. [?AB²] *What a furbishing up of claw-hammer coats and white silk neckties!* 1869 IA xxxvi 389 (OED *colloq.* A tail-coat for evening dress. 1879.. So W C U. A in S F Cl Th,1869 T M)

clay-plugged, ppl.a. [B¹] *Our ivory Teeth...now own disgust Of clay-plug'd cavities* 1900 "My Boyhood Dreams" (1928) 260 (Nonce comb.)

clean, v. [?AB¹] *"He went for 'em. And he cleaned 'em, too!"* 1872 RI xlvii 334 (To dispose of. This sense not in OED W S C; but cf. OEDS Clean out. 4c. To deal effectively with; to eject. *U.S.* 1866..)

clean-cut, a. [?AB³] *The Pyramids, rising above the palms, looked very clean-cut, very grand and imposing* 1869 IA lviii 620 (OED 1843.. So W S C U. A in F Cl Th)

cleanliness, sb. [?AC] *He was our joint lawyer, and I had every confidence in his wisdom and cleanliness* 1890 *Autob* (1924) I 75 (OED In the earliest quots., it is used, like the adj., of moral purity. 1430..1786, last ex. moral sense. Not *obs* in W S. This sense not in C)

clean out, v. [?AB³] See *and* 1865. "*I'm cleaned out, done for, except my plantation and private mansion*" 1873 GA xl 357 (OED 4b. *slang*. To deprive of cash. 1812.. OEDS Later U.S. exs. A in W S C Th)

clean-scraped, ppl.a. [B¹] See *bake-shop* 1869 (Comb. not in OED W S C)

clean up, v. [AB²] *The machinery was stopped, and we "cleaned up". That is to say we...washed the mud patiently away till nothing was left but the long-accumulating mass of quick-silver* 1872 RI xxxvi 255. See also *arrastre* 1909 (A in Cl: In gold-mining, the operation of separating the gold after the auriferous gravel has been for a certain length of time through the sluices. Cf. OED Clean, v. 3. To clean by taking up dust or dirt. 1872, this quot. Here a technical mining term, not recognized as *spec* in OED W S C)

clear, a. [AB³] *A clear waste of raw material* 1869 IA xix 184 (OED 25. *U.S.slang*. Pure, 'real'. 1837.. So C. Not A in W S)

clear, adv. [?A?C] *He brought us clear down to the ground* 1873 GA i 27. *It has clear out-grown the town I used to know* 1883 LM lvii 562. *Ladies and gentlemen in England had remained no cleaner in their talk...clear up to a hundred years ago; in fact clear into our own nineteenth century* 1889 CY iv 55 (OED 5. Completely, quite, entirely. *obs.* 1513.. 1690. OEDS Later U.S.exs. 1835, 1845. A in H DN.II,III. Not A or *obs* in W S C U Wr)

clear, v. [?AB³] *I cleared for that country in the overland stage-coach* 1906 *Autob* (1924) II 291 (OEDS 13. *intr.* To depart. Early U.S. ex. 1839.. A in C U. W S have only 'clear out' in this sense. A *Naut.* metaphor?)

clear-burning, ppl.a. [B¹] *The government has set up a clear-burning lamp* 1883 LM xxviii 299 (Comb. not in OED W S C)

clear-cut, a. [?AB³] *Cypress-top standing out, clear-cut against the sky* 1883 LM xliii 445 (OED 1855.. So W S C. A in F Cl Th)

clearing, vbl.sb. [AB³] *Dense forests which extended for miles without farm, wood-yard, clearing, or break of any kind* 1883 LM xxx 325 (OEDS 4. *U.S.* A piece of land cleared for cultivation. 1817.. So B F Cl Th T M. Not A in W S C U)

clear out, v. [?AB³] *George and I cleared out again* 1858 *Letters* (1917) I ii 37. "*Clear out, and settle it in the kitchen*" 1892 AmCl viii 81. *She resolved to clear out and see the world* 1894 PW iv 332. *They would burn her if she did not clear out now while she had a chance* 1895 JA II xiv 551 (OEDS 26d. *colloq.* To be off. Earlier U.S.ex. 1816.. A in F Cl Th T. Not A in W S C U)

clear-water, a. [?AB¹] *They talked about differences between clear-water rivers and muddy-water rivers... Clear-water rivers with gravel bottoms change their channels very gradually* 1875 OTM 446 (Comb. not in OED W S C; but cf. OED Clear, a.3b. Free from sediment. 1483.. This sense of Clear is A in Cl T)

clerk, sb. [?AB¹] *I sent him to our clerk to work his way for a trip, by measuring wood piles, counting coal boxes, and other clerkly duties* 1858 *Letters* (1917) I ii 37 (An official on a steamboat. This *spec* sense not in OED W S C. Cf. *underclerk*, below)

clerk, v. [?A] See *establishment* 1869 (OED *colloq.* To act as clerk. 1551.. A in W S C B F Cl M H DN.III. Cf. OEDS Clerk, sb. 6d. A shop-assistant. *U.S.* 1840..)

clerkly, a. [C] *Clerkly English, booky English, acquired in the schools* 1897 FE lxi 599 (OED 2. Scholarly, booklearned. *arch.* 1523..1835. So W S C U)

clerkly, a. [?AB¹] See *clerk*, sb. 1858 (Cf. OED 4. Of or belonging to an office clerk. 1845.. So W S C. Here, transf., of the duties of a clerk on a steamboat)

clever, a. [A] "*When you* [i.e., the English] *say 'clever', you mean 'capable'; with us the word used to mean 'accommodating'*" 1882 "Concerning the Ameri-

can Language" 268 (OEDS 8c. Of persons: Good-natured, amiable. *U.S.colloq.* 1758.. So W S C B F Cl Th M DN.II,III,IV,V AS.X.234)

clew-iron, sb. Spelled **clue-iron**. [B¹E] *The clew-iron which we are trying to make serve for the broken block works very indifferently* 1866 "Forty-Three Days" 111. *The clue-iron will, I am afraid, soon cut the rope* 1899 "My Debut" (1900) 97 (C: A shackle-shaped iron at the clues of large sails. So S. Not in OED W. Cf. OED Clue: a later sp. of Clew in all surviving senses)

climate-proof, a. [B¹] *A kind of patent climate-proof compensation-balance* 1888 "Meisterschaft" 461 (Comb. not in OED W S C)

climb, v. pa. t. **clumb.** [?AE] *I clumb up the shed and crept into my window* 1884 HF ii 16. So *passim* in HF (OED This form 14th-15th c. *Dial* in Wr. A in M DN.I,II,IV,V AS.I.232,V.264. Not in W S C)

clinch, v. [A] *Both clinched and began to gouge and beat each other* 1869 SNO (1875) 210 (OED 2d. To close and struggle at close grips. Now *U.S.* 1652..1860. Not A in W S C)

clincher, sb. [?A] *As an affectionate clincher of the reconciliation, Sally declared she had now banished Lord Berkeley from her mind* 1892 AmCl xxii 233. *Mrs.Eddy adds this clincher: "The candidates shall be elected by a majority of the First Members present"* 1907 CS II vii 180 (OED 4. A conclusive statement; a 'settler'. *colloq.* OEDS Earlier U.S.exs. 1784.. A in DN.III. Not A in W S C U)

clip, sb. [?AB³] *She fetched first one and then another of them a clip* 1884 HF xxxii 330 (OED 4. A smart blow. 1830..1860. OEDS Later U.S. exs. 1869..1913. A in Wr B F Cl DN.III. Not A in W S C)

clip, v. [AB³] *A slower boat clipping along in the easy water* 1875 OTM 724 (OEDS *U.S.* 7. To move quickly 1833.. So Wr DN.III. Not A in W S C)

clipper, sb. [AB³] *The Hornet was a clipper of the first class and a fast sailer* 1899 "My Debut" (1900) 74 (OEDS Formerly chiefly applied to the sharp-built raking schooners of America. 1824.. So C DN.III. Not A in W S U)

clipper-ship, sb. [AB³] *The superb clipper-ship sailed out of New York harbor* 1866 "Forty-Three Days" 104 (OED = Clipper. 1853.. So W C B Cl. Comb.not in S)

clock-caked, a. [B¹] See *bell-ringing* 1880 (Nonce comb.)

clock-hand, sb. [B¹] *The clock-hand pointed to seven* 1880 TA x 93 (Comb. not in OED W S C; but cf. OED Clock-finger, the hand of a clock. No ex.)

clock-strike, sb. [B¹] *Waiting through the still eternities for the clock-strikes* 1885 "Priv. Hist. of Campaign" 201 (Comb. not in OED W S C)

clog, sb. [?AB¹] *Great Spanish spurs whose little iron clogs and chains jingled with every step* 1872 RI iv 42. (Not in OED W S C; but cf. OED 2c. A block or lump tied to anything for use or ornament, e.g. to a key. 1325..1562)

clog-dancing, vbl. sb. [B¹] *Among his various industries was clog-dancing in a "nigger" show* 1898 *Autob* (1924) I 155 (Comb. not in OED. Given in W S C U. Cf. OED Clog-dance, 1881)

close, a. [?AB¹] See *safe*, a. 1859; *chute* 1875 (Of a river pilot: Skilful in coming near, but not too near, to the shore or other obstructions. This *spec* sense, evidently felt as a localism by M.T., is prob. a transf. from the sense in OED 15c. *Naut.* 1627.., cf.quot.1871, "A close sailer to the wind." Neither sense is given in W S C)

close call, sb. [AB³] "*Now we are safe*", I said, "*but it was a close call*" 1889 CY xxx 378. *I brushed her tail-feathers as I landed on my stomach—a very close call, but still not quite close enough* 1906 "Hunting the Deceitful Turkey" 57 (OEDS orig. *U.S. colloq.* A near thing. 1887.. So Th.III M H. Not A in W S. Phr. not in C)

close–cowled, ppl.a. [B¹] *The robed and close-cowled harlequins* 1869 IA xxi 213 (Comb. not in OED W S C)

close down, v.intr. [?AB¹] *The night presently closed down* 1883 LM liv 536 (This sense not in OED W S C)

close down on, v.trans. [?AB²] *They have set a gunboat to watch the vessel night and day, with orders to close down on any revolutionary movement in a twinkling* 1869 IA xxiv 254 (OEDS 16. Also *fig,* to exercise repression. 1869, this quot. A in H. Not in W S C)

close fit, sb. [?AB¹] *This was the most awful trouble and the most dangersome I ever was in. Stead of being fixed so I could take my own time and have Mary Jane at my back when the close-fit come, here was nothing in the world betwixt me and sudden death* 1884 HF xxix 305. *I'm straining to reach St.Pierre de Boeuf, but it's going to be a close fit, I reckon* 1891 *Letters* (1917) II xxxi 552 (Cf.close call, above. Phr. not in OED W S C)

close–fitting, ppl.a. [B²] *Close-fitting wings like the tails of a dress-coat* 1869 IA xi 101 (OED 1870. So W. Not in S C)

close in on, v.trans. [?AB³] See *freeze out* 1867. *They closed in on him and chased him into the river* 1883 LM xxvi 288. *Closing in on the equator this noon* 1897 FE iv 65 (OEDS 17e. To draw in upon. Earlier U.S. ex. 1829.. Not A in W C. Not in S)

close out, v.trans. [AB²] *The fall would have been only one hundred feet, but it would have closed me out as effectually as one thousand* 1880 TA xlvi 538 (OEDS 19b. To finish off. U.S. *fig.* 1907. An extension of the *comm.* sense, to close out a stock of goods. A in H. Not A in W S C)

close–ranked, ppl.a. [B¹] *His close-ranked merchandise stretched from one city to the other* 1883 LM xxii 257 (Comb. not in OED W S C)

close–reef, v.trans. [?AB¹] *I close-reefed my ears, that is to say, I bent the flaps of them down* 1880 TA xiii 116 (Hum. extension of the *naut.* sense in OED: To take in all the reefs of a sail. 1738.. *Naut.* sense in W S C)

close–shaven, ppl.a. [B²] *Some were close-shaven, all over* 1869 IA lviii 618 (OED Close, adv. 2. No ex. So W. Not in S C)

closet, sb. [C] *Her Majestie...had to her closet certain that doe write plays, bokes, and such like* 1880 *Fireside Conversation, 1601. He would give order to admit Humphrey to the royal closet whenever he might come* 1881 PP xiv 174 (OED 2. The private apartment of a monarch. obs exc. Hist. c1340..1868. Not obs in W S C U)

close up on, v.trans. [?AB¹] *By and by I closed up abreast of his tail. Do you know what it was like? It was like a gnat closing up on the Continent of America* 1907 "Capt.Stormfield" 41 (To draw near to, close in on. An extension of the *mil.* sense in OED 21e. To come together so as to leave no gaps, esp. of ranks of soldiers. 1835.. Not in W S C)

clothes–horse, sb. [?AB¹] *I could see her [England] erect statues and monuments to her unspeakable Georges and other royal and noble clothes-horses, and leave unhonored the creators of this world—after God—Gutenberg, Watt, Arkwright, Whitney, Morse, Stephenson, Bell* 1889 CY xxxiii 419 (One whose principal function is to wear and show off clothes; a mannequin. Not in OED W S C; but for lit. sense cf. OED:An upright wooden frame on which clothes are hung out to dry or air. 1806..So W S C U. A in DN.V)

clothes–pin, sb. [?AB³] *She had just carved out a wooden chief that had a strong family resemblance to a clothespin* 1869 SNO (1875) 68 (OED 1866. So W S C. A in M: Am. clothespin = Eng. clothespeg)

clothing–store, sb. [AB³] *The clothing-store merchant wished to consume the corner-grocery man with envy* 1869 IA xxvi 278 (OEDS U.S. A draper's shop. 1837.. So M. Comb. not in W S C)

cloud, sb. [?AB³] *She threw over her shoulders a fluffy thing called a "cloud" in that day* 1893 PW iii 238 (OED 8. A light, loose-knitted woolen scarf worn by ladies. a1877. So W S C U. A in B F Cl)

cloud, sb. in the clouds. [B¹] *Rowena was in the clouds; she walked on air* 1894 PW vi 333 (Uplifted, in high spirits. Strangely, this sense not in OED W S C U. Cf. OED In the clouds: obscure, fanciful, unreal; generally combining the notions of obscurity and elevation. 1649.. So W S C. U: preoccupied with one's thoughts)

cloud–breeder, sb. [B¹] *The cloud-breeder was revealed at last...it was manifest that all the sour weather had come from this girl's dread that Tracy was lured by her rank* 1892 AmCl xxiii 242 (Comb. not in OED W S C)

cloud–effect, sb. [B¹] *Frequently, in Australia, one has cloud-effects of an unfamiliar sort* 1897 FE xxiv 230 (Comb. not in OED W S C)

cloud–height, sb. [B¹] *The friends would have a tedious long journey down out of those cloud-heights* 1880 TA xxvii 274 (Comb. not in OED W S C)

cloud–shoal, sb. [B¹] *Swimming through the cloud-shoals* 1880 TA xlviii 562 (Comb. not in OED W S C)

cloud up, v. [?AB³] *No matter how much it might cloud up later, it always began with a clear sky* 1892 AmCl xxiii 239 (OEDS 7. Earlier U.S. ex. 1834.. A in B F Cl DN.III. Not A in S C. Not in W)

cluster–diamond, sb. [B¹] *Stand behind a bar, wear a cluster-diamond pin, and sell whisky* 1872 RI xlviii 339 (Comb. not in W S C; but cf. below)

cluster–pin, sb. [B²] *The gold in his finger ring was worth forty-five dollars; he wore a diamond cluster-pin* 1873 GA xxxiii 301 (OEDS Cluster, sb. 4. 1873, this quot. Comb. not in W S C)

cluster–ring, sb. [B²] *She has jewelry bunched on the side of her nose also, and showy cluster rings on her toes* 1897 FE xxxviii 347 (OEDS Cluster, sb. 4. 1906. Comb. not in W S C)

clutter, v. [?A] *"We'll have the cave so cluttered up... that there won't be no place for the robbers"* 1884 HF ii 15 (OED 6. Now chiefly *dial* and U.S. 1674.. OEDS Delete U.S. A in Wr DN. II,III,IV. Not A in W S C U)

clyme, sb. [C] *"Clime" was the cant term for a sore, artificially created* 1881 PP xxii 272 (OED Cant. obs.. 1725. Not in W S C)

coach candle, sb. [AB¹] *I observed that the colored porter of the sleeping-car had his eye on me... "Can I have a big coach candle fixed up just at the head of my bed?"* 1890 *Speeches* (1910) 260 (Cf. OED Coach, sb. 1d.. in U.S. esp. a sleeping-car. 1866.. Comb. not in OED W S C)

coal–barge, sb. [?AB³] *Acres of lumber-rafts and dozens of big coal-barges* 1883 LM xxviii 298 (OED Coal, sb. 15a. 1827. So W. A in C. Not in S)

coal–flat, sb. [?AB¹] *He took a berth on a Pittsburgh coal-flat, or on a pine raft* 1883 LM iii 41 (Comb. not in OED W S C. Cf. flat, below)

coaling center, sb. [B¹] *Grand Tower was a great coaling center and a prosperous place* 1883 LM xxv 275 (Comb. not in OED W S C; but cf. OED Coaling-station, 1870)

coal–oil, sb. [AB³] *"Out with that coal-oil, now, lively, lively!"* 1883 LM xxviii 304 (OEDS U.S. 1858.. So B M DN.I,II,IV. Not A in W S C)

coal–passer, sb. [?AB²] *The coal-passers moved to their duties in the profound depths of the ship* 1869 IA xxxviii 405 (OED Coal, sb. 16. One who passes coal on to the furnace of a steam boiler. 1884. So W S C)

coal–pitch–raven–black, a. [B¹] *There came a-walking past the door A coal-pitch-raven-black young Moor* [German, ein kohlpechrabenschwarzer Mohr] 1891 *Slovenly Peter* (1935) 8 (Hum. nonce comb.)

coal–scuttle, sb. [?AB³] *An odd-looking craft, with a vast coal-scuttle slanting aloft on the end of a beam* 1883 LM xxiv 266 (OED 1. Coal-box, coal-scoop. a1825.. So W S C U Wr. A in DN.I,III)

coal–smoke, sb. [B¹] *The coal-smoke turns it into an antiquity* 1883 LM xxii 252 (Comb. not in OED W S C)

coal–train, sb. [B¹] *"The coal-train is coming"* 1873 GA xlix 443 (Comb. not in OED W S C)

coal–venture, sb. [B¹] *Aleck had given the coal speculation a twelvemonth in which to materialize... The coal-venture had returned with its rich freight* 1904 "Bequest" (1906) iv 22 (Nonce comb.)

coarse comb, sb. [?AB¹] *"I've got an old coarse comb in my pocket."...I'd jest give 'em a tech of "Auld Lang Syne" on it...Out come the old comb and a piece of paper to put on it* 1856 *Adv. of T. J. Snodgrass* (1928) 6. See also *jew's harp,* sb. 1884 (A comb with large or widely separated teeth; opposite of a *fine comb*. This *spec* sense not in OED W S C; but cf. OED Coarse, a. 2. Opposed to *fine.* 1582..)

coarse–hand, sb. [?AB¹] *She asked me if I could read writing, and I told her "no, only coarse-hand"* 1884 HF xviii 169 (Comb. not in OED W S C)

coarse print, sb. [?AB¹] *"I don't want no better book than what your face is. A body can set down and read it off like coarse print"* 1884 HF xxviii 287 (Comb. not in OED W S C)

coarse whisper, sb. [?AB¹] *I said, in a kind of a coarse whisper, "Jim!" and he answered up, right at my elbow* 1884 HF xii 108. *The undertaker slid around...making no more sound than a cat...he shaded his mouth with his hands, and says, in a kind of a coarse whisper...* 1884 HF xxvii 272 (Here used for "stage whisper", or what is technically known in phonetics as "whispering voice"; cf. J. S. Kenyon, *Am. Pronunciation,* sect. 36, 51. This sense not in OED W S C. Cf. OED Coarse, a. 3d. Of sound: Rough and harsh; *spec* in *Pathol.* of certain sounds heard on auscultation in diseased conditions of the chest. 1879..)

Coast, sb. [AB³] *The great sugar-plantations border both sides of the river. Everything was trim and trig and bright along the "coast"* 1883 LM xl 421 (OEDS *spec.* One or other bank of the Mississippi near its mouth. 1812.. So Th DN.IV. This sense not in W S C)

coat, sb. **to turn one's coat.** [?C] *To turn one's coat once makes one...a Mugwump* 1884 *Speeches* (1923) 114 (OED 13. †To turn one's coat: To change or abandon one's principles. 1576. Not *obs* in W S C U)

coat–of–arms, sb. [D] *"Jim's got to do his inscription and coat of arms. They all do." Jim says: "Why, Mars Tom, I haint got no coat o' arm."...Tom set to work to think out the coat of arms... He says: "On the scutcheon we'll have a bend or in the dexter base, a saltire murrey in the fess, with a dog, couchant, for common charge, and under his foot a chain embattled, for slavery, with a chevron vert in a chief engrailed, and three invected lines on a field azure, with the nombril points rampant on a dancette indented; crest, a runaway nigger, sable, with his bundle over his shoulder on a bar sinister; and a couple of gules for supporters, which is you and me; motto, Maggiore fretta, minore atto. Got it out of a book—means the more haste the less speed."..."What's a fess?" "A fess—a fess is—you don't need to know what a fess is. I'll show him how to make it when he gets to it." "Shucks, Tom," I says, "I think you might tell a person. What's a bar sinister?" "Oh, I don't know. But he's got to have it. All the nobility does."* 1883 HF xxxviii 386 (OED Heraldry. 2. 1562..1833—. So W S C U)

coat–turner, sb. [B¹] *What sort of spectacle is it when such a coat-turner turns his coat again...after a nomination?* 1884 *Speeches* (1923) 114 (Comb. not in OED W S C; but cf. OED Coat-turning, 1888)

cobbler, sb. [AB³] See *cocktail* 1869. *I witnessed the spectacle of an Englishman ordering an American sherry cobbler of his own free will and accord* 1875 SNO 180 (OED 3. *colloq.* A drink made of wine, sugar, lemon, and pounded ice; so Bartlett *Dict.Amer.*1809.. A in W S C B F Th M)

cobbler, sb. [AB²] See *biscuit* 1880; *batter-cake* 1897 (OED 4. A sort of pie. *U.S.Western.* No ex. So W S C B F Cl T DN.II,III)

cobblestone, sb. [?AB²] *Jolting over our cobblestone pavements at home* 1869 IA xxiii 230 (OED attrib. 1879. So W S C. A in DN.III)

cobbling, ppl.a. [?AB¹] *The sea was very wicked—the waves broken and dangerous—what sailors call a "cobbling" sea* 1866 "Forty-Three Days" 105 (W: Becoming choppy. So S. A in DN.V. This sense not in OED C)

cob–house, sb. [A] *We have just that as "evidence", and out of its meagre materials the biographer builds a cobhouse of conjectures* 1894 "Defence of Harriet Shelley" iii 363 (OEDS *U.S.* A house built by children out of corn-cobs, hence applied *fig* to any insecure or unsubstantial scheme, etc. 1774.. So Th. Not A in S C. Not in W)

cob–pipe, sb. [AB³] *Buck and his ma and all of them smoked cob pipes* 1884 HF xvii 151. *We lazied the rest of the pleasant afternoon away, some smoking cob pipes* 1885 "Priv.Hist.of Campaign" 197 (OEDS *U.S.* A tobacco pipe made from a corn-cob. 1847.. So S F Th. Not in W C)

cobweb, sb. [B¹] *These four held the graceful cobweb [bicycle] upright while I climbed into the saddle* c1880 "Taming the Bicycle" (1917) 287. *Wilson began to study Luigi's palm, noting carefully... the cobweb of finer and more delicate marks and lines* 1894 PW xi 554 (W: A slight or flimsy network or texture. So C. This *fig* sense not in OED; but cf. OED 3.*fig.* Fanciful fine-spun reasoning. So S)

cobwebby, a. [B¹] *My head is pretty cobwebby yet* 1894 *Letters* (1917) II xxxiv 616. *The brooding depression, the cobwebby mouth...that come of dissipation* 1894 TET iii 352. *They were clothed invisibly in the damp and cobwebby mould of antiquity* 1906 *Autob* (1924) II 218 (No *fig* use given in OED W S C)

cocked hat, sb. [AB²] *Next we started cocked hat—that is to say, a triangle of three pins* 1907 "Chaps. from Autob" 335 (OED 3. A game similar to nine-pins. *U.S.* No ex. Not A in W S C)

cocking–main, sb. [?AB¹] *The "cocking-main" is an inhuman sort of entertainment* 1883 LM xlv 458 (W: A series of cockfights. So S C. Comb. not in OED; but cf. OED Main of cocks, 1760..; also Cock-main, 1890)

cocktail, sb. [AB³] *We ferreted out another French imposition—a frequent sign to this effect; "All Manner of American Drinks Artistically Prepared Here." We procured the services of a gentleman experienced in the nomenclature of the American bar...Our General said, "We will take a whiskey-straight."..."Well, if you don't know what that is, give us a champagne cocktail." "...Well, then, give us a sherry cobbler."..."Give us a brandy smash!"...The uneducated foreigner could not even furnish a Santa Cruz Punch, an Eye-Opener, a Stone-Fence, or an Earthquake* 1869 IA xv 148. *It was almost religion, there in the silver mines, to precede such a meal with whiskey cocktails* 1872 SNO (1875) 283 (OEDS 3. Chiefly *U.S.* 1806.. So S C U B F Cl Th T M AS.I.159. Not A in W)

cocoon, v. [B²] *We cocooned ourselves in the proper red blankets* 1880 TA xxviii 296 (OED 2.To swathe. 1881, this quot. So W S C)

code, sb. [?AB¹] *He was an authority on the "code"* 1893 PW i 234 (C "The code": Code of honor, the social customs and rules of procedure which support and regulate the practice of dueling. So S. This sense not in OED W)

coffee–stain, sb. [B¹] *A tablecloth mottled with grease-spots and coffee-stains* 1869 IA xxxviii 404 (Comb. not in OED W S C)

cofferer, sb. [C] *"My cofferer shall look to it"* 1881 PP iii 42 (OED *obs* exc. *Hist.* 1b. An officer of the royal household. 1538..1860. So W S C)

coffin-box, sb. [B¹] *There was my coffin-box back again* 1882 "Invalid's Story" 95 (Comb. not in OED W S C)

coffin-clad, a. [B¹] *In the seat thus pirated, sat two Americans, greatly incommoded by that woman's majestic coffin-clad feet* 1880 TA xlvii 547 (Nonce comb., with ref. to the size of her shoes)

coftus, sb. [B¹] See *afarabocca* 1894 (Not in OED W S C. Perhaps an error for Costus; cf. OED:The herb also called Alecost or Costuary. 1712. M.T. may have been misled by the similarity between f and s in the old medical book he was using)

cog, sb. **to slip a cog**. [?AB²] *I got in a word now and then when he slipped a cog and there was a vacancy* 1909 ISD i 8 (OEDS 1c. To make a single unexpected mistake. 1909. So W C. *Slang* in S)

coil, sb. [?C] *Well, here was a coil to be in!* 1893 "Banknote" (1928) 112 (OED *arch* and *dial*. 3. Ado, 'business'. 1593..1877. So W. Not *arch* in S C U Wr, and app. not so felt by M.T.)

colazione, sb. [B¹] *By labor-union law the colazione must stop* 1904 "Italian with Grammar" (1906) 196 (Nonce borrowing from Italian: Conference, collation)

cold, a. **to knock cold**. [AB²] *It was the sudden surprise of it that knocked us so kind of cold* 1884 HF xxxvii 376 (OEDS 1c. Used to denote the effect on a person of a severe blow or shock. *U.S.* 1928. So W. Phr. not in S C)

cold, a. [AB¹] *"The suspense is over, Sally—and we are worth a cold million!"* 1904 "Bequest" (1906) v 29˙ (Absolute, indubitable. This sense of the adj. not in OED W S C; but cf. OEDS 10b. In adverbial use: Absolutely, without any mitigation. *U.S.slang*. 1889.. So W C DN.II,IV; not in S C)

cold, a. [AB¹] *"Now they're stuck. Can't find it. Here they come again. Now they're hot. Cold again. Hot again. Red hot! They're p'inted right, this time"* 1876 TS ix 89 (W: Distant from anything concealed.So S C. A in B Cl. This sense not in OED; doubtless it is an extension of OED 12.*Hunting*. Said of scent in opposition to 'hot' or 'warm'. 1592.. OEDS Later U.S. exs.)

cold deck, sb. [AB²] *I never have gambled without a "cold deck" in my pocket* 1868 Screamers (1871) 97. See also *ring in* 1888 (OEDS *U.S. Poker*: A pack of cards which have been arranged beforehand. 1868, this quot. So F Cl M DN.IV AS.IV.339. Not A in W S. Not in C)

cold shoulder, sb. [?AB³] *Senator Dilworthy had been a Unionist...but was that any reason why Colonel Sellers, who had been a Confederate...should give him the cold shoulder?* 1873 GA xx 186. *If one would have friends and be popular, instead of having the cold shoulder turned upon him, he must be prosperous* 1892 AMCl xii 127. Cf. also *warm shoulder* 1916 (OED Used *fig*. 1816.. So W S C U. A in AS.XI.294)

cold-storage, a. [?AB²] *"Saintly and unsmirched Truth-Seekers, in whose cold-storage souls a lie would freeze to death if it got there!"* 1902 "Was It Heaven?" (1906) 82 (OED Storage. sb. 2b.*fig*. 1907. Not *fig* in W S C)

coleoptera, sb. [B¹] *A bat is beautifully soft and silky. I know all about these coleoptera* 1897 Autob (1924) I 104. See also *pachydermata* 1897 (Nonsense use)

colicky, a. [B¹] See *melodeon* 1884 (Sounding like a sufferer from colic. This sense not in OED W S C)

collaborations, sb. [B¹] *They are collaborations; the one artist does the figure, the other the accessories* 1892 AmCl xvi 163 (*Concrete* sense not in OED W S C; but cf. OED: United labor, esp. in literary, artistic, or scientific work. 1860..)

collapse, v.trans. [?AB²] *We burst a boiler; broke a shaft; collapsed a flue* 1883 LM xxv 277. See also *wilt*, v. 1889 (OEDS 3. 1891.. So W S. Not in C)

collar-sewer, sb. [B¹] *Gregory deals in shirts, cravats, etc. One of the cards bore these words: "Much-respected Deputy and collar-sewer"* 1898 "Stirring Times" (1900) 319 (Comb. not in OED W S C; but cf. OED Collar-dresser, 1890. A rendering of German Halsbandnähende?)

collect, v. [?AB²] *Smyrna has been utterly destroyed six times. If her "crown of life" had been an insurance policy, she would have had an opportunity to collect on it* 1869 IA xxxviii 409 (OEDS 1b. absol. A contraction for 'to collect payments'. 1889.. So W. A in F Cl T H. This use not in S C)

collection-plate, sb. [B²] *The collection-plate began its rounds* 1880 TA xxiv 234 (OEDS 1889. Comb. not in W S C)

collide, v. [?AB³C] *Telephone me when you are coming; otherwise we shall fail to collide* 1907 *M.T. the Letter Writer* (1932) ix 131 (OED 3b. To come together without conflict. *rare*. 1877, only ex. Not in W S C. Cf. for the ordinary sense of the word OED 2.To come into collision, come forcibly into conflict. When first used of railway trains or ships in collision, c1860-70, it was much objected to as an Americanism. [Perhaps for this reason it was avoided by M.T.] This sense is called A in B F Cl Th M; not A in W S C)

Colonel, sb. [AB¹] See *Captain* 1873. *"My wife says, 'Colonel'—she will call me Colonel spite of everything I can do"* 1873 GA v 57. *What's a Colonel in our South? ...They're all colonels down there* 1892 AmCl xi 115. *I have been personally acquainted with over eighty-four thousand persons who have served for a year or two on the staffs of our multitudinous governors, and through that fatality have been generals temporarily, and colonels temporarily* 1902 "Does the Race of Man Love a Lord?" 442 (A in B: A title of courtesy. So W F Cl M H DN. II,III,V AS.IX.204. This use not in OED S C)

colored, ppl.a. [?AB³] See *Aunt* 1874. *Jim, the small colored boy* 1876 TS i 19. *An occasional picturesque colored person on the bank* 1883 LM xliv 445. See also *farm-help* 1884; *coach-candle* 1890; *get religion* 1893 (OED 2c. Of the negro race. 1866.. So W U. A in S C B F Cl Th,1760 T M)

colossal, a. [?AB²] See *breezy* 1892. *A colossal sense of humor* 1892 AmCl xxi 218. *The 19th century made colossal progress* 1905 Letters (1917) II xliv 769. *Colossal graft* 1906 "Unpublished Chapters" (1922) 456 (OEDS c. Stupendous, 'immense'. *colloq*. 1897. So W S C U)

Colt, sb. [AB³] *I found a revolving pistol which looked strangely like a modern Colt* 1869 IA xiii 125 (OEDS Named for Samuel Colt, Am. inventor. 1852.. So W U. Not in S C)

Columbiad, sb. [AB³] *A sheet was wound around me until I resembled a swab for a Columbiad* 1867 SNO (1875) 303 (OED 2. A kind of heavy howitzer formerly used in the U.S. army. 1861.. So W S C Th.III. Cf. OED quot. 1861: "a piece of ordnance very thick in the breech, and lightened off gradually from the trunnions to the muzzle")

Comanche, sb. [AB¹] *Ordered me out of the pilot-house with more than Comanche bluster* 1883 LM xix 231. *They had the hardihood to offer General Grant the very same royalty which they would have offered to any unknown Comanche Indian* 1885 Autob (1924) I 35. *Many of the terms...would have made a Comanche blush* 1889 CY iv 55 (Not in OED W S C)

comb, sb. [?AB³] *From the eaves to the comb of the roof* 1869 IA xviii 174. See *chimney* 1880. (OEDS 6e. The crest or ridge of a roof. *dial*. Earlier U.S.ex. 1845.. Not A in W S Wr. This sense not in C)

comb, sb. [?AB¹] *The moon come a-swelling up out of the ground, now, powerful big and round and bright, behind a comb of trees, like a face looking through prison bars* 1896 TSD v 355 (Wr: A clump of trees, *Lancashire*. This sense not in OED W S C)

combination, sb. [?AB²] *They commanded him to reveal the "combination", so that they could get into the safe* 1880 "Edward Mills" 228 (OEDS 9. Combination lock. 1909.. So W S. This sense not in C. Cf. *safe*, below)

combine, sb. [AB³] *They're a "combine"...who band themselves together to force their lowly brother to take what they choose to give* 1889 CY xxxiii 427. *They were in every board of directors of every prodigious combine in the country* 1904 "Bequest" (1906) vi 30 (OED b. *U.S. colloq.* 1887.. So W S C F Cl Th M. Not A in U)

combing, ppl.a. [AB³] *Far-reaching ranks of combing whitecaps* 1883 LM li 502 (OED 1857.. Cf. OED Comb, v. 5.To roll over, break with a white foam. App. of U.S.origin. 1808.. Not A in W S C)

comb up, v. [?AB¹] *You had to wash, and eat on a plate, and comb up, and go to bed and get up regular* 1884 HF vi 38 (This intr. use not in OED W S C)

come, v. **to come it over.** [?A] *"Give the rest of 'em the slip...I'll come it over 'em the same way"* 1876 TS vii 74 (OED 28b. To play or practise (a dodge or trick), esp. *over* any one. *slang* and *colloq.* 1785.. So W Wr. A in B F Cl DN.II,III. Phr. not in S C)

come, v. **to come a game on.** [?AB¹] *" You are coming some fresh game or other on me"* 1869 IA xix 189. *If they tried to come any such game on him* 1884 HF vi 40 (Cf. above. This phr., with *on*, not in OED W S C. A in DN. II,III)

come, v. **come Christmas.** [?AC] *A servant in that selfsame family for twenty-seven years come Christmas* 1871 SNO (1875) 137. *"How long you been in heaven?" "Twenty-seven years, come Christmas"* 1907 "Capt. Stormfield" 48 (OED 35. The present conj. used with a future date following as subject. *arch* and *dial.* 1420.. 1888. Not *arch* in W S Wr. A in DN.III,IV,V, s.e.Mo. Phr. not in C)

come in, v. [AB¹] *" He will ante his way right into the United States Senate when his territory comes in"* 1873 GA xiii 124 (To enter the Union as a State, acquire statehood. This sense not in OED W S C; but cf. W: To assume official station or duties; as, when Lincoln came in)

comely, a. [?C] *" He hath a comely face"* 1881 PP xix 237. *A comely young girl* 1883 LM xlix 492. *"Your comely little English lass"* 1892 AmCl xi 116 (OED 1b. Fair, pretty; in modern use implying a lower and homelier style of personal beauty, which pleases but does not excite admiration. *c*1340..1888. Not *arch* in W S C)

come off, v. [?AB³] *A grand affair of a ball...came off at the Occidental some time ago* 1867 SNO (1875) 256. *"The weddings will never come off; all that is past"* 1904 "Bequest" (1906) viii 45 (OED 61j. To take place. 1825.. So W S C. A in Cl DN.III)

come on, v. [?A] *He cast his eye aloft...and said it was coming on to blow* 1880 TA xvii 156. *About ten o'clock it come on to rain and blow and thunder and lighten like everything* 1884 HF xx 193 (OED 62c. To come so as to prevail disagreeably; said of night, winter, bad weather. 1400..1886. So W Wr. A in DN.II. This sense not in S C)

come out, v. [?AB³] *The Baconian assumers have come out ahead of the Shakespearites* 1909 ISD v 50 (OED 63d. To emerge from a contest. 1848.. So W. A in B: *Come off* would be more agreeable to English usage. So F Cl H. This use not in S C)

come out, v. [?A] *She ought to realize, now that she has "come out", that this is a right and proper time to change a part of her style* 1899 "Diplomatic Pay" 31 (OED 63o. To make formal entry into 'society'. 1782..1850. So W S C. A in B Cl)

come out, v. **come out of that.** [?AB¹] *I saw a long spyglass on a desk...and reached after it..."Hands off! Come out of that!"* 1869 IA iii 35 (Drop it, let it alone. Phr. not in OED W S C)

comfit-box, sb. [B¹] *They passed their jeweled comfit-boxes one to another* 1895 JA II xxiii 891 (Comb. not in OED W S C)

comfortable, a. [?AC] *Pap he hadn't been seen for more than a year, and that was comfortable to me; I didn't want to see him no more* 1884 HF iii 18 (OED 1. Encour-

aging, reassuring. *Obs* or *arch*...1869. So S C. Not *obs* or *arch* in W)

comforter, sb. [?AB³] *Two boys with caps down over their ears and their red comforters streaming out behind* 1881 M.T. the Letter Writer (1932) iii 36 (OED 6. A long woollen scarf. 1833.. So W S C U. A in DN.III)

comical-looking, ppl.a. [B¹] *He was the most comical-looking creature that can be imagined* 1869 IA xi 101 (Comb. not in OED W S C)

commander-in-chief, sb. [A] *The future illustrious commander-in-chief of the American armies* 1879 Speeches (1910) 68 (OED 10b. In U.S., vested in the President, but the title is often unofficially applied to the acting general officer of highest rank. 1778.. So W S C)

commandment, sb. [C] *"Give commandment that I be hanged"* 1881 PP xv 184 (OED 1. Command, order. *arch.* 1250..1868. Not *arch* in W S C)

common, a. [?AB³] *"White folks done it...en not on'y jis' common white folks nuther"* 1893 PW iii 239 (OED 14b. Low class. 1866.. So W S C. A characteristic usage in the Southern States)

common charge, sb. [B¹] See *coat-of-arms* 1883 (Probably an error for *ordinary*, sb.: OED 15. Her. A charge of the earliest, simplest, and commonest kind.. The principal charges so classed are the Chief, Pale, Bend, Bend-sinister, Fess, Bar, Chevron, Cross, and Saltire. 1610.. So W S C. Tom has contrived to work in no fewer than five of the nine "ordinaries" in his coat-of-arms.)

common-run, a. [B¹] *He has done more than enough to pull sixteen common-run great men down* 1897 FE lxix 710 (Comb. not in OED C. Given as sb. in W S)

comp, sb. [B³] *If a man should write a book and in it make one of his characters say, "Here, devil, empty the quoins into the standing galley and the imposing stone into the hell-box; assemble the comps around the frisket and let them jeff for takes and be quick about it," I should... know that the writer was only a printer theoretically, not practically* 1909 ISD vii 73 (OED An abbrev. 6. in Printer's phrase, of Compositor. Said to be originally for companion, i.e. member of a companionship of compositors. 1870.. Not in W S C)

compassion-inspiring, ppl.a. [B¹] *The little shame-faced girl...performed a compassion-inspiring curtsy* 1876 TS xxi 169 (Nonce comb.)

compass-shelf, sb. [B¹] See *breast-board* 1909 (Comb. not in OED W S C)

complacency-signal, sb. [B¹] [His style] *how compact, without a complacency-signal hung out anywhere to call attention to it* 1906 "Howells" (1917) 231 (Nonce comb.)

complaint-system, sb. [B¹] *"A crying defect in the complaint-system"* 1893 "Travelling with a Reformer" (1900) 357 (Comb. not in OED W S C)

complected, ppl.a. **dark-complected, light-complected.** [AB³] *Monstrous bluffs on both sides of the river—ragged, rugged, dark-complected* 1883 LM lix 574. *"Here is the dark-complected hand with a potato on its fork...there, the light-complected head's got it"* 1894 TET ii 337. *Red angels, with now and then a curiously complected diseased one* 1908 "Capt.Stoddard" 273 (OEDS *U.S. dial* or *colloq.* 1822.. So W S C B F Cl Th T M H DN.I,II,III, IV,V AS.II.351)

composing-gait, sb. [B¹] *My writing-gait is... twenty-four words per minute...There isn't any definite composing-gait* 1899 "Simplified Alphabet" (1917) 260 (Nonce comb.)

composite, sb. [B²] *She took nine pictures on top of each other—composites* 1892 Letters (1917) II xxxii 564 (OED 6d. No ex. So W C U. Not in S C)

compositor, sb. [B¹] *The Paige Compositor marches alone and far in the lead of human inventions* 1889 Letters (1917) II xxix 508 (A type-setting machine. So C. Only of persons in OED W S)

compounding–disease, sb. [B¹] *We used to speak of a thing as a "never-to-be-forgotten" circumstance, instead of cramping it into the simple and sufficient word "memorable"...In our newspapers the compounding-disease lingers a little to the present day* 1880 TA App. D 613 (Nonce comb.)

comrade, v. [B³] *Comrading with the poor and humble on equal terms* 1892 AmCl xxiii 245. *I say he* [General Grant] *comraded with them, and that is the proper term, though he would not have given the relationship so familiar a name himself* 1898 *Autob* (1924) I 154 (OED b. intr. 1865.. So W S. Not in C)

comradeship, sb. [B¹] *When my comradeship moved hence upon their labors,...I got me to needed rest* 1889 CY xxiv 301. *Beloved members of the old comradeship whose names have long ago been carved upon their gravestones* 1906 *Autob* (1924) II 204 (A band or group of comrades. This *concrete* sense not in OED W S C)

comrady, a. [B¹] *She laughed her affectionate comrady laugh* 1895 JA II vi 148 (Not in OED W S C)

concentrator, sb. [?AB³] *I watched the "concentrators" at work—big tanks containing mud and water and invisible diamonds* 1897 FE lxix 702 (Cf. OED 3. An apparatus by which mechanical concentration of ores is performed. 1873. So W S. A in C: esp. in the U.S. Here, similar apparatus for separating diamonds, used in South Africa)

concern, sb. [?AB³] See *fix*, v. 1869. *The stores and houses was most all old, shackly, dried-up frame concerns* 1884 HF xxi 209 (OED 11. Any material contrivance or object, usually with some amount of depreciation. 1834..1856. OEDS Later U S. exs. 1873..1888. Not A in W S C)

concerned, ppl.a. Spelled **consarned**. [AB³E] "*Them other fellers is a consarned sight meaner'n him*" 1856 *Adv. of T. J. Snodgrass* (1928) 11 (OEDS 3. *U.S. slang.* Confounded, deuced. 1834.. So S C B F T DN.III,V AS.IV.475, quot.1803. Not in W)

concert, sb. **the European Concert**. [B³] *I would rather see him* [the Devil] *and shake him by the tail than any other member of the European Concert* 1899 "Concerning the Jews" (1900) 255 (OEDS ld. 1879.. So S C U. Phr. not in W)

conchyliaceous, a. [B¹] See *anisodactylous* 1906 (Nonsense use)

concrete, v. [B³] *This exercise soon concreted itself into habit* 1894 PW iv 329 (OEDS 3. 1864.. So W S C U)

concreted, ppl.a. [B³C] *This time the threat was in a concreted condition* 1906 *Autob* (1924) II 228 (OED 2. = Concrete. *rare*. 1875, only ex. Not *rare* in W S C)

condemn, v. [AB²] *He condemns a whole street at a time, assesses the damages, pays them, and rebuilds superbly* 1869 IA xiii 128 (OEDS 7b. *U.S.* To pronounce judicially as converted to public use. 1876. So Th.III. Not A in W S C)

condition, sb. [AB³] *He was sent to Yale. He went handsomely equipped with "conditions"* 1894 PW v 332 (OEDS 8. In U.S. colleges: studies or subjects in arrears. 1832.. So W S C Th H DN.II)

conductor, sb. [B³] *By the side of the driver* [of the stagecoach] *sat the "conductor"* 1873 RI ii 25. *The streetcar conductors and drivers wore pretty uniforms* 1880 TA i 19. *My daughters are frequently robbed by conductors on the surface lines* 1906 *M.T. the Letter Writer* (1932) xii 156 (OED 7. The official who has charge of the passengers and collects fares on an omnibus or tram car. 1837.. So W S U M. This sense not in S C)

conductor, sb. [AB³] *The conductor of the 4:33 express was a duke* 1889 CY xl 512. *They sent for the parlor-car conductor* 1893 "Travelling with a Reformer" (1900) 361. See also *shut down* 1893 (OED 7. The official who has charge of the passengers and collects fares..in the U.S., on a railroad train. The *guard* on an English railway has similar but less com-

prehensive functions. 1856.. OEDS 1839.. So W S C U B F Cl Th T M H)

Confederate, sb. [AB³] See *cold shoulder* 1873. "*Confederates are just as eager to get at the treasury as Unionists*" 1873 GA xxxviii 347 (OED 3. *U.S. Hist.* 1861.. So W S C U B F Cl T)

Confederate, a. [AB³] See *secessionist* 1872; *bushwhacking* 1873. *I was in the Confederate army* 1885 "Priv.Hist of Campaign" 193. See also *shinplaster* 1889 (OED 3b. 1861.. So W S C U B F Cl H)

confidence–game, sb. [AB³] "*It was a confidence-game. We played it on a julery-shop in St.Louis*" 1896 TSD iii 349 (OEDS 10. orig. *U.S.* 1867.. So B F Th. III H DN.IV. Not A in W S C)

conflagrate, v. Spelled **conflaggerate**. [E] *The use of the steam fire injuns when a house would conflaggerate* 1857 *Adv. of T.J.Snodgrass* (1928) 39 (This form not in OED W S C)

conflagration, sb. [B¹] *A cheap curtain calico thing, a conflagration of gaudy colors and fantastic figures* 1893 PW iii 238 (This sense not in OED W S C)

congratulatory, a. [B²] *Friends flocked after them, jubilant and congratulatory* 1873 GA xlv 414 (OED 2. 1885, only ex. So W S C U)

Congregationalist, sb. [A] *Why were the Congregationalists not Baptists...and the Episcopalians Millerites, and the Millerites Hindoos, and the Hindoos Atheists, and the Atheists Spiritualists, and the Spiritualists Agnostics...and the Mohammedans Salvation Warriors, and the Salvation Warriors Zoroastrians, and the Zoroastrians Christian Scientists, and the Christian Scientists Mormons—and so on?* 1906 "WIM" (1917) iii 44. See also *Adventist* 1907 (OED A member of a Congregational church. 1692.. So W S C. Cf. OED Congregational, a. 3. After the 17th c., *Independent* was chiefly used in England, while *Congregational* was decidedly preferred in New England..in the 19th c. the latter name has also prevailed in Great Britain. So S C DN.V. Not A in W)

Congress, sb. [A] *Furnish this country with a Congress that knows enough to come in out of the rain* 1892 AmCl iii 46. *There is no distinctively native American criminal class except Congress* 1897 FE viii 99 (OED 7. The national legislative body of the U.S. 1765.. So W S C U B F Cl M DN.V,VI AS.IV.6)

Congressional, a. [A] *The Senator beamed with his own Congressional wit* 1873 GA xxxv 320. *A most Congressional expression—one eye on the constituency and one on the swag* 1897 FE lxv 645 (OED 2. Pertaining to the Congress of the U.S. 1796.. So W S C U B F Cl T M DN.V AS.IV.6)

Congressman, sb. [A] See *dodge*, sb. 1869; *steal*, sb. 1873. "*A jay hasn't got any more principle than a Congressman*" 1880 TA ii 37. See *slobber over* 1892. *Fleas can be taught nearly anything that a Congressman can* 1906 "WIM" (1917) vi 82 (OEDS. A member of Congress in U.S. 1780.. So W S C U B Cl Th T)

Congress water, sb. [AB³] "*Looky here*", I says, "*did you ever see any Congress water?*" "*Yes.*" "*Well, did you have to go to Congress to get it?*" 1884 HF xxvi 260 (OED A mineral water from Congress Springs, Saratoga, N.Y. 1865.. So S C. Not in W)

conjecturability, sb. [B¹] *The two Great Unknowns, the two Illustrious Conjecturabilities!* 1909 ISD iii 27 (Not in OED W S C; but cf. OED Conjecturable, 1656.. Note the *concrete* use)

connect, v. [AB³] *The stage still remained vacant—the distinguished stranger had failed to connect* 1883 LM lvii 558. *The ten-year rearrangement was due a year ago, but failed to connect* 1897 "Stirring Times in Austria" (1928) 294 (OED 5b. Of a railway train, etc. *U.S.* 1856. So W Th.III. Not A in S C U)

conniption, sb. [AB³] *The bare sight of it give him a conniption* 1893 TSA i 20 (OED *U.S.vulgar.* Hysterical excitement. 1860.. So W S C U B F Th,1859 T M DN.I,III)

conscience, sb. **in all conscience.** [B²] *Last year their taxes were heavy enough, in all conscience* 1869 IA xliii 443 (OED 10. By all that is right or reasonable. *colloq.* 1886, only ex. So W S C U)

conscience–soothing, ppl.a. [B¹] *"Every man will be glad of these conscience-soothing falsities"* 1898 MS (1916) ix 129 (Comb. not in OED W S C; but cf. OED Conscience-pacifying, 1671)

consider, v. **to consider of.** [C] *"I will consider of her punishment"* 1881 PP iii 41 (OED 11. Now somewhat *arch.* 1568..1891. Not *arch* in C. This usage not in W S)

considerable, a. [AB³] *The privilege costs considerable money* 1876 TS ii 32. *I know considerable French* 1880 TA xxvii 276. *"I've done considerable in the doctoring way"* 1884 HF xix 183. *A noble brass warming-pan which he thought considerable of* 1884 HF xxxvii 384. See also *stand a show* 1884 (OED 6. *U.S.colloq.* A large quantity of.. also *absol.* much, a good deal 1816.. So W F Cl Th.III DN.III AS.II.31. Not A in S C)

considerable, sb. [A] *A brick gave me a considerable of a jolt in the back* 1869 SNO (1875) 47 (OEDS 2. A fair amount, quantity, etc. of something. *U.S.* 1745.. So W B F Cl Th T H. Not A in S C)

considerable, adv. [?AC] *Sometimes he was chased around considerable by the bushwhackers* 1864 SS (1926) 129. *"De Hebrew Chil'en dat went frough de fiah...was burnt considerable"* 1873 GA iii 39. *By and by she let it out that Moses had been dead a considerable long time* 1884 HF i 2. See also *frill, nigger-trader, cussword, set back, shake up,* all 1884 HF; also *leeward* 1908 (OED 7. *Obs* or *dial.* ..1843. So W. OEDS Later U.S.exs...1884. A in B F Cl Th.III T M DN.III. Not in S C)

consolation–race, sb. [B²] *The consolation race for beaten mules* 1883 LM xlv 464 (OED 3b. One open only to those competitors who have been unsuccessful in the preceding events. No ex. So W C U. Not in S)

consound, v. [?AB¹] *"Mr. Longfellow, Mr. Emerson, and Mr. Oliver Wendell Holmes—consound the lot!"* 1877 *Speeches* (1910) 2 (Not in OED W S C. A blend of *confound* and *consarned?*)

conspicuousnesses, sb. [B¹] *In both of these conspicuousnesses I was gratified to recognize a resemblance to myself* 1907 *"Ch. from Autob."* 563 (An instance of the quality. This *concrete* sense not in OED W S C)

conspirator–in–chief, sb. [B¹] *"All but the dead know how to name the two conspirators-in-chief"* 1896 JA II xv 436 (Comb. not in OED W S C)

Constantinopolitanischerdudelsackspfeifenmachers– gesellschafft, sb. [B¹] See *effect* 1889 (Hum. coinage)

contact, sb. [?AB³] *The most momentary contact with such a spirit would have ennobled her whole character* 1892 AmCl viii 83 (OED 2. *fig.* 1818.. So W U. A in H: Am. contact=Eng. association or acquaintanceship. The *fig* sense not in S C)

continental, sb. [AB²] *"He didn't give a continental for anybody"* 1872 RI xlvii 334 (OED 2. *Amer. Hist.* A currency note issued by the Continental Congress during the war. 1872, this quot. So W S C F Th,1841 T M DN.III AS.IV.4, from Freneau, 1809. Cf.also OEDS 2b. Not to care a continental. *U.S.* 1897)

Continental, a. [A] *The ghost of Washington in warning attitude, and in the background a troop of shadowy soldiers in Continental uniform* 1869 IA xix 195 (OED 3.*Amer. Hist.* 1775.. So W S C B F Cl Th)

continental, a. [B¹] *That continental stretch of dry prairie which stood for his imagination was afire* 1892 AmCl iii 41. *A continental spread of white shirt front* 1898 *"Stirring Times"* (1900) 327 (S: Of continental bread thor proportions; huge. This sense not in OED WC)

continued story, sb. [B¹] *Some of the less important dailies give one a tablespoonful of a continued story every day* 1880 TA App. F 627 (Comb. not in OED S C. Given in W)

contraband, sb. [AB²] *The whole to be kept in parlor order by two likely contrabands at big wages* 1862 *Letters* (1917) I iii 75 (OED 4. *U.S.* Used during the American Civil War for: A negro slave, *esp* a fugitive or captured slave. 1862.. So W S C B F Cl Th T H)

contribution–box, sb. [?AB³] *"In church you are always down on your knees, with your eyes buried in the cushion, when the contribution-box comes around"* 1865 SNO (1875) 78 (OEDS Contribution, sb. 5. Earlier U.S. ex. 1845.. Not A in S. Comb. not in W C)

contribution–plate, sb. [?AB¹] *It is strictly religious furniture, like...a contribution-plate* 1899 *"Concerning the Jews"* (1900) 280 (Comb. not in OED W S C. Cf. above)

contribution–purse, sb. [?AB¹] *There were the stiff pews; the black velvet contribution purses attached to long poles, flanking the pulpit a*1870 Letter in Clara Clemens, *My Father* (1931) 10 (Comb. not in OED W S C. Cf. above)

convention, sb. [AB³] *The Republican party was to make its nominations in the Convention* 1906 *Autob* (1924) II 318 (OED 5c. *U.S.* In party politics. 1817.. So C B F Cl H. Not A in W S U)

convention–packer, sb. [AB¹] *The convention packers know they are not obliged to put up the fittest man for the office* 1884 *Speeches* (1923) 126 (Comb. not in OED W S C. Cf. above)

conversation–mill, sb. [B¹] *It plugged up her conversation-mill, too...and that was a gain* 1889 CY xiv 166 (Nonce comb.)

conversation–voice, sb. [B¹] *Talk into a phonograph in an ordinary conversation-voice* 1891 *Letters* (1917) II xxxi 543 (Comb. not in OED W S C)

cook, v. [B³] *Yesterday a lunatic burst into my quarters and warned me that the Jesuits were going to "cook" (poison) me in my food* 1897 FE xxxv 320 (OED 4. To ruin, spoil, 'do for'. *slang* 1851.. So W. Not in S C)

cooked, ppl.a. [?AB³] *The company whose director had declared a "cooked" or false dividend* 1870 SNO (1875) 244 (OED 2. *fig.* 'doctored'. 1861.. So W S C. A in B T)

cook–book, sb. [AB³] *I have often furnished recipes for cook-books* 1880 TA xlix 575 (OEDS *U.S.* 1865.. So W S C Th.III M H. Cf. H: Am. cook-book=Eng. cookery-book)

cool–brained, ppl.a. [B¹] *Stupid preachers and teachers work more damage to religion than cool-brained clergymen can fight away again* 1869 IA xxxviii 409 (Comb. not in OED W S C; but cf. OED Cool-headed, 1777)

coon, sb. [AB³] See *biscuit* 1880. *I remember the 'coon and possum hunts* 1898 *Autob* (1924) I 114 (OED *U.S.* 1839.. So W S C U B F Cl Th T M DN.III,IV)

coonskin, sb. [AB³] *He traded a quart of thick molasses for a coonskin and a cake of beeswax* 1873 GA i 22 (OEDS *U.S.* 1818.. So W S C. Cf. above)

coop, sb. [B¹] *He staggered away and fell over the coop of the skylight* 1869 IA iii 33 (A protecting grating or cover? No *naut* sense in OED W S C; but cf. OED 4. A protecting grating about a tree, etc. 1750, only ex.)

cooper–shop, sb. [?A:C] *"I hid in de ole tumbledown cooper-shop"* 1884 HF viii 67. *He was a journeyman cooper and worked in the big cooper-shop* 1894 *"Scrap of Curious Hist."* 184 (OED Cooper, sb. 5. †cooper-shop =cooper's shop. 1632, only ex. OEDS Delete † and add later U.S. exs. 1801..1894. This form not given in W S C)

cop, sb. [?AB³] *I never write "policeman", because I can get the same price for "cop"* 1906 *"Simplified Spelling"* 220 (OED *slang* 1859.. So W S C U. A in Th.III M AS.IV.339)

copper, sb. [A] *The new boy took two broad coppers out of his pocket* 1876 TS i 24 (OED 2. A cent of the U.S. 1788.. So W S C DN.I,III,V. Not A in U) copper, v. [AB²] *"The safe way is to copper the operation"* 1883 LM xxviii 304 (OEDS 2.. To bet against. *U.S. fig.* 1883, this quot... So W. Not A in S C)

copper-bellied, a. [?AB²] See *corpse-maker* 1883 (OED Copper, a. 10e. No ex. Comb. not in W S C. A in M)

Copperhead, sb. [AB³] *He gave the Copperheads and the Democratic party a most admirable hammering every week* 1898 *Autob* (1924) I 147 (OED 2. *U.S.* A nickname given, during the Civil War, to a northern sympathizer with the Secessionists of the south. 1863.. So W S C B F Cl Th T M DN.III,V AS.VIII.4.50)

copper-tinged, ppl.a. [B¹] *A slender little maid, with plaited tails of copper-tinged brown hair down her back* 1906 *Autob* (1924) II 64 (Comb. not in OED W S C; but cf. OED Copper-coloured, 1697)

copying-gait, sb. [B¹] *My copying-gait is 1,440 words per hour* 1899 "Simplified Alphabet" (1917) 260 (Nonce comb.)

copyrighted, ppl.a. [?AB³] *Unabridged dictionaries are revised and newly copyrighted every ten or twelve years* 1905 "Concerning Coypright" 6. See also *barker* 1907 (OEDS Earlier U.S.ex. 1806.. Not A in W S C U)

copyright-preserving, ppl.a. [B¹] *The requirements of the copyright-preserving law* 1905 "Concerning Copyright" 7 (Nonce comb.)

cord, sb. [AB¹] *Tom got cords of glory* 1896 TSD xi 537 (A in B: A large quantity, *Western.* So F Cl Th, 1616. This sense not in OED W S C)

corded, ppl.a. [?AB¹C] *Bedsteads of th. "corded" sort, with a sag in the middle* 1883 LM xxxviii 405 (S: Made of cord or rope; as, a corded ladder. *Obs.* Not *obs* in C U. Not in OED W)

corduroy, a. [AB³] *A word as stirring as a ride over a corduroy road* 1871 *Screamers* 11. *The merry electric car replaced the melancholy bus, the macadamized road the primitive corduroy* 1899 "Chr.Sc.and the Book" 592 (OEDS *U.S.* Applied to a road constructed of trunks of trees laid together transversely. 1822.. So U B F Cl T H DN.V AS.II.351, VI.97. Not in W S C)

cord wood, sb. [A] *I had cordwood enough to run the family for two years* 1871 SNO (1875) 31. See also *rise*, sb.1884 (OED Wood for fuel. Now chiefly in America. 1638.. So B Cl Th M. Not A in W S C)

cork, v. [?AB¹] See *back-seat* 1884. *It was an emergency that had never happened in his experience before, and it corked him... He looked stunned, confused; he couldn't say a word* 1889 CY xxiv 306 (To shut up, reduce to speechlessness. Cf. OED 2b. transf. To stop up as with a cork. 1650.. So W S C. The OED gives no ex. of the word as applied to a person. Probably M.T. had in mind the Am. dial. use mentioned in DN.III, from n.w.Ark.: To get the better of; to make ridiculous,—in which sense the word is probably another form of *calk*, to stop up)

corker, sb.]?AB³[See *ad* 1889. *"As a mental tour de force it is without a mate."* *"It seems to be a corker."* *I blushed for the word, but it was out before I could stop it* 1899 "Chr.Sc.and the Book" 587 (OEDS 2b. A 'stunner'. *slang* and *dial.* 1877.. So W C U Wr. A in DN. II,V. This sense not in S)

corn, sb. [A] See *biscuit* 1880; *magnify* 1885; *batter-cake* 1897 (OEDS 5. *U.S.* Maize or Indian corn. 1608.. So W S C U B F Cl Th T M H DN.V,VI)

corn-beef, sb. [?AB²] *The First Comptroller of the Corn-Beef Division* 1870 SNO (1875) 105 (OED Corn, sb. 11. No ex. A in M: Am.pron. of *corned-beef*; also DN.III. Comb. not in W S C)

corn-bread, sb. [AB³] *His small sister was sopping corn-bread in some gravy* 1873 GA i 22. See also *hunk* 1884; *batter-cake* 1897 (OEDS *U.S.* 1823.. So W S C B F Cl Th.III H)

corn-cob, sb. [A] *Huck Finn had also brought a few corn-cobs to make pipes with* 1876 TS xiii 115. See also

shuck mattress 1907 (OEDS *U.S.* 1797.. So W S C U B F Cl Th M H)

corn-cob pipe, sb. [AB³] See *leaf tobacco* 1873. *Jim had plenty corn-cob pipes and tobacco; so we had a right down good sociable time* 1884 HF xxxvi 372. *My uncle... smoking his corn-cob pipe* 1897 *Autob* (1924) I 103 (OEDS *U.S.* 1829.. So W F Cl Th. Not in W C)

corn-crib, sb. [A] *A long corn-crib served as sleeping quarters for the battalion* 1885 "Priv. Hist. of Campaign" 195. See also *tobacco-curing* 1897 (OEDS *U.S.* 1716.. So W S C B F Cl Th M DN.III AS.II.30)

corn-crust, sb. [AB¹] *A hard piece of corn-crust started down my throat* 1884 HF xxxvii 376 (Corn-bread crust. This comb. not in OED W S C)

corn-dodger, sb. [AB³] *Jim he got out some corn-dodgers and buttermilk* 1884 HF xviii 176. *Corn-dodgers, buttermilk, and other good things* 1897-8 *Autob* (1924) I 109 (OEDS *U.S.* Made of the meal of Indian corn, baked very hard. 1834.. So W S C B F Cl Th M H DN.I,II,III AS.VII.168. With the OED def. cf. Th, quot.1834: A soft cake of wheat or maize; and DN.III: A corn-cake of any kind)

corned, ppl.a. [?A] *We found him...in a saloon, haranguing a gang of "corned" miners* 1872 *Speeches* (1910) 272 (OED 5. *slang.* Intoxicated. 1785.. So W S C. A in Th DN.III)

corner, sb. [AB²] *"They went to playing euchre at ten cents a corner"* 1866 *Speeches* (1910) 5 (OEDS 13. Poker term. 1876. So W. Not in S C)

corner, sb. [AB³] *A corner so stupendous that, by comparison with it, the most gigantic corners in subsequent history are but baby things* 1899 "Concerning the Jews" (1900) 261. *For forty-eight hours Aleck's imaginary corner had been booming* 1904 "Bequest" (1906) 44 (OED 14. *Comm.* A speculative operation.. of *U.S.* origin. 1857.. So C B F Cl Th,1853 T. Not A in W S U)

corner, v. [AB³] *Worried him, as dogs do with a cornered cat* 1892 AmCl xv 160 (OED 3. To drive into a corner. App. of *U.S.* origin. 1841.. So Th,1824. Not A in W S C U)

corner, v. [AB³] *I felt sort of cornered, and was afeard I was looking it, too* 1884 HF xi 91. *Wilson...cornered him up so close that he had to confess* 1894 PW xv 819 (OEDS 3b.*fig.* To put into a position of difficulty or embarrassment. Chiefly *U.S.*. 1824.. So B F Cl Th DN.III. Not A in W S C U)

corner, v. [AB³] See *bucketshop* 1889 (OEDS 4. *Comm.* orig. *U.S.* 1821.. So S C B F Cl Th T M. Not A in W U)

corner-grocery, sb. [AB¹] See *clothing-store* 1869 (A in Th,1862 DN.III. Comb. not in OED W S C; but cf. OED Grocery, sb. 4a. *U.S.*)

corn-field, sb. [A] *Get the Indians to burn a corn-field for him* 1871 SNO (1875) 111. See also *mushmelon* 1884; *rail-fence* 1897 (OEDS b. *U.S.* 1634.. So W C U H AS.II.28. Not in S)

corn-meal, sb. [AB³] *A fifty-pound sack of corn-meal* 1884 HF vi 41 (OED In U.S., meal of maize or Indian corn. OEDS 1831.. So W S C F Cl M AS.II.30)

corn-pone, sb. [AB³] See *biscuit* 1880. *It was "baker's bread"—what the quality eat; none of your low-down corn-pone* 1884 HF viii 58. See also *batter-cake* 1897 (OED Southern *U.S.* A kind of Indian corn bread made with milk and eggs. 1860.. Cf.W: corn bread, esp. when made without milk or eggs. A in S C B F Cl M H)

corn-sheller, sb. [AB³] *You can make a corn-sheller appear well that won't shell any corn* 1867 *M.T. the Letter Writer* (1932) i 17 (OEDS *U.S.* 1825.. So W S C)

corn shuck, sb. [AB³] *My bed was a straw tick—better than Jim's, which was a corn shuck tick* 1884 HF xx 191 (OEDS *U.S.* Corn husk. 1845.. So W S B F Th,1811 M DN.III. Not in C)

corn-shucking, vbl.sb. [AB³] *He would not have sent his daughter to a state ball in a corn-shucking costume, nor to a corn-shucking in a state ball costume* 1899 "Diplomatic Pay" (1928) 232 (OEDS *U.S.* 1819.. So W S C B F H DN.I,III,IV)

corn–stalk, sb. [A] *It will be well for the farmer to begin setting out his corn-stalks* 1870 SNO (1875) 235 (OEDS 1. *U.S.* 1697.. So W S C B F Cl M DN.III)

corn whisky, sb. [AB³] *The bar keeper shoved along the counter a bottle of apparently corn whiskey* 1873 GA xiii 130 (OEDS *U.S.* 1843.. So S. Comb. not in W C)

coroneting, vbl.sb. [B²] *The time for the simultaneous coroneting of the nobles shall arrive* 1881 PP xxxii 366 (OEDS Coronet, v. 1900.. Not in W S C)

corpobalsamum, sb. [B¹] See *afarabocca* 1894 (Not in OED W S C)

corpse–face, sb. [B¹] *Into it drifted that black figure with the corpse-face* 1898 "About Play Acting" (1900) 216 (Comb. not in OED W S C)

corpse–faced, a. [B¹] See *black-robed* 1898 (Comb. not in OED W S C)

corpse–maker, sb. [AB¹] *"I'm the old original iron-jawed, brass-mounted, copper-bellied corpse-maker from the wilds of Arkansaw!"* 1883 LM iii 45 (A in M, as part of the River "tall-talk." Comb. not in OED W S C)

corpse–room, sb. [B¹] *I gathered myself together and flew to the corpse-room* 1883 LM xxxi 351 (Comb. not in OED W S C)

corpsy–white, a. [B¹] *Large bouquet of stiff flowers in corpsy-white wax* 1883 LM xxxviii 404 (Comb. not in OED W S C)

corral, sb. [AB³] *He puts them in the corral, or the mourner's bench* 1864 SS (1926) 129 (OED An enclosure for horses, cattle, etc., chiefly in Spanish America and U.S. Also transf. 1849.. So Th.III M. Not in W S C U in transf. sense)

corral, v. [AB³] *A half-dozen tents were pitched under the trees; horses and oxen were corralled at a little distance* 1873 GA xvi 157 (OEDS U.S. 1. 1846.. So S C B F Cl Th T M DN.I AS.VI.250,VII.432,VIII.1.28. Not A in W)

corral, v. [AB³] *The flattest old sermon a man can grind out is bound to corral half a dozen* 1865 SS (1926) 167. *That sort of thing would corral their sympathies* 1871 SNO (1875) 297. *"He had already corralled two tricks"* 1877 *Speeches* (1910) 5. *Money enough to corral the shop-keeper's respect* 1889 CY xxxi 401 (OEDS 3. *U.S. colloq* or *slang*. To secure, capture. 1860.. So W C B F Cl Th T M DN.I AS.VIII.1.28. This sense not in S)

corruptible, sb. [B¹] *One convention offering a Democratic and another a Republican list of—corruptibles!* 1873 GA xxxiii 302 (Not as sb. in OED W S C; but cf. W: The Incorruptible. Robespierre, so called by his admirers)

costermonger, sb. [B¹] *One hears such words as 'piper' for paper... This pronunciation is "costermonger."* *All over Australasia this pronunciation is nearly as common among servants as it is in London among the uneducated* 1897 FE xi 129 (Low English, esp. vulgar London speech. This sense not in OED W S C; but cf. OED Costermonger. c. As a term of contempt or abuse. 1597..1809)

cot–bed, sb. [?AB³] *The beautiful queen of Washington drawing-rooms...sat shivering on her cot-bed in the darkness of a damp cell in the Tombs* 1873 GA xlvi 425 (OEDS U.S. exs. 1838.. Not A in S C. Comb. not in W)

cot–bedstead, sb. [?AB³] *White-pine cot-bedsteads* 1872 RI xxi 162 (OEDS U.S. ex. 1849. Comb. not in W S C)

cotton–bale, sb. [?AB³] *He clung to a cotton-bale* 1883 LM xlix 491 (OEDS Earlier U.S.ex. 1840.. Not A in W C. Comb. not in S)

cotton–domestic, sb. [AB¹] *You stretch a great sheet of "cotton-domestic"* 1869 IA xxvii 286 (Comb. not in OED W S C; but cf. OED Domestic, sb. 4. *U.S.*)

cotton–gin, sb. [?A] *What great births you have witnessed! The steam press, the steamship, the steelship, the railroad, the perfect cotton gin, the telegraph, the phonograph, photogravure, the electrotype, the gaslight, the electric light, the sewing machine, and the amazing, infinitely varied and innumerable products of coal tar, those latest and strangest marvels of a marvellous age* 1889 "Letter to Walt Whitman" (1926) 174 (OED Cotton, sb. 10. 1796.. So U. A in W S C B as an American invention)

cotton–planter, sb. [?AB³] *A cotton-planter's estimate of the average margin of profit on planting* 1883 LM xxxiii 366 (OEDS Cotton, sb. 9a. 1808.. So W S C. Cf. planter, below)

cotton plantation, sb. [?AB³] *They came wandering back, worn out and used up on the cotton plantations* 1892 AmCl iii 38 (OEDS. Cotton, sb. 9a. 1819.. Comb. not in W S C. Cf. plantation, below)

cotton–seed, v. [B¹] *"Maybe you'll butter everybody's bread...but we'll cotton-seed his salad for him"* 1883 LM xxix 414 (Not in OED W S C)

cotton–seed meal, sb. [B²] *Ground and mixed with ensilage of cotton-seed meal* 1883 LM xxxiii 367 (OED 1891. So W S C)

cotton–seed oil, sb. [?AB²] *Manufactories of wagons, carriages, and cotton-seed oil* 1883 LM xxix 323 (OED 1891. So W S C. A in F Cl)

Cotton State, sb. [AB³] *In the cotton States, after the war, the simple and ignorant negroes made the crops for the white planter on shares* 1899 "Concerning the Jews" (1900) 263 (OEDS Any one of the cotton-growing States. 1845.. So C Th.III DN.VI. This sense is not in W S, which restrict the term to Alabama)

cottonwood, sb. [A] *The old one-limbed cottonwood in the bend* 1875 OTM 221. *I clumb up into the forks of a cottonwood that was out of reach* 1884 HF xviii 172 (OEDS The name of several species of poplar in U.S. 1787.. So W S C U B F Cl Th M AS.II.30)

couchant, a. [D] See *coat-of-arms* 1883 (OED 2. *Heraldry*. Of an animal: Represented as lying with the body resting on the legs and the head lifted up. c1500.. 1864—. So W S C U)

cough, v. [B¹] *A steamboat coughing along up-stream* 1884 HF xix 178 (W: To make a noise like that of coughing. This transf. sense not in OED S C)

Could–Have–Beener, sb. [B¹] See *Perhapser* 1909 (Nonce comb.)

council–fire, sb. [A] *"Does she mourn over the extinguished council-fires of her race?"* 1869 SNO (1875) 69 (OEDS A fire kindled by the N. Am. Indians when in council. 1753.. So W S C B F Cl)

count, v. [?AB²] *Chang consented to be baptized at the same time that Eng was, on condition that it should not 'count'* 1869 "Siamese Twins," in SNO (1875) 209. *I had already published one little thing...but I did not consider that that counted* 1899 "My Debut" (1900) 70 (OED 14b. To enter into the account. absol. 1885.. So W S C U Wr. A in DN.III)

counter–mine, sb. [B¹] *When he said that bright thing, I broke all up. I remember exploding its American counter-mine once, under that grand hero, Napoleon* 1895 "What Bourget Thinks" 61 (Here, *fig*: counterpart, corresponding stroke. This sense not in OED. Given in W S C)

counter–yell, sb. [B¹] *Yells from the Left, counter-yells from the Right* 1898 "Stirring Times" (1900) 299 (Comb. not in OED W S C)

counting–house, sb. [B²] *I can perch on this counting-house stool* 1870 SNO (1875) 219 (OED *attrib* 1882. So W S C U)

count out, v. [AB³] *I can make the money without lecturing. Therefore, old man, count me out* 1870 *Letters* (1917) I x 172 (OEDS Count, v. 15. Orig. *U.S.* 1854.. So Th. Not A in W S U. Not in C)

country place, sb. [B¹] *It had once been somebody's country place* 1892 AmCl ii 28 (Comb. not in OED W S C)

country-woven, a. [B¹] *The station-men wore panta-loons of coarse, country-woven stuff* 1872 RI iv 24 (Comb. not in OED W S C)

county, sb. [A] *The county and township elections were carried on these issues alone* 1865 SS (1926) 160 (OED 3. In the U.S., the political and administrative division next below the State. 1683.. So W S C B H)

county-hospital, sb. [?AB¹] *A stuffy sort of pallet [in the Turkish bath in Constantinople] which was not made of cloth of gold, or Persian shawls, but was merely the unpretending sort of thing I have seen in the negro quarters of Arkansas...It was more suggestive of the county hospital than anything else* 1869 IA xxxiv 380 (Poorhouse? Comb. not in OED W S C; but cf. County-house = poorhouse, A in F Th.III T)

county-seat, sb. [AB³] *A town that was county-seat of a great important county* 1883 LM xxxii 363. *A slave came flying from Palmyra, the county-seat* 1894 "Scrap of Curious Hist." (1917) 185 (OEDS *U.S.* 1815.. So W S C. Cf. H: Am. county-seat = Eng.county town)

couple-up, v. [?AB¹] *Whenever she [Mrs.Eddy] dis-covers that she is getting pretty disconnected, she couples-up with an ostentatious "But"* 1907 CS II ii 122 (Comb. not in OED W S C. A *fig* use of the sense in OED Couple, v. 2d. *Mech.* To connect railway carriages by a coupling. 1841..)

court-clerk, sb. [B¹] *Training in a court-clerk's office* 1909 ISD v 52 (Comb. not in OED W S C; but cf. Clerk of Court, W S C)

courteously-discourteous, a. [B¹] *It embarrassed me a little to confess this fact, right on the heels of that cour-teously-discourteous letter* 1906 "Unpublished Chaps." (1922) 315 (Nonce comb.)

courthouse, sb. [?A] *These very eyes had looked upon the county courthouse—which was said to have a tin roof* 1876 TS iv 49 (OEDS 1b. Common in U.S. 1667.. Not A in W S C)

cow-boy, sb. [AB³] *"Thinks he can play himself on folks for a cowboy!"* 1892 AmCl xii 107. *Brander Mat-thews wanted to be a cowboy* 1900 "My Boyhood Dreams" 258 (OEDS 3. In the western U.S...a man employed to take care of grazing cattle on a ranch. 1877.. So W S C U B F Cl Th,1725 M H DN.II,VI AS.V.53,57)

cow-catcher, sb. [AB³] *I have been everything, from a newspaper editor down to a cow-catcher on a locomotive* 1869 *Letters* (1917) I ix 165. *It carries the usual "cow-catcher" in front of the locomotive* 1873 GA xliii 391. (OED *U.S.* An apparatus fixed in front of a locomotive engine 1838.. So W U B F Cl Th T M H. Not A in S C)

cowhide, sb. [AB³] *He struck her across the face with his cowhide* 1902 "DBDS" (1928) 187 (OEDS 3. *U.S.* A strong whip made of the raw or dressed hide of the cow. 1818.. So C B F Cl Th T DN.III. Not A in W S U)

cowhide, v. [?AB³] *He said he'd cowhide me till I was black and blue if I didn't raise some money for him* 1884 HF v 34 (OEDS *trans.* Earlier U.S.ex. 1820. A in B F Cl Th M DN.III. Not A in W S C T)

cowhiding, vbl.sb. [?AB³] *Every now and then I'd borrow two or three dollars off of the judge for him, to keep from getting a cowhiding* 1884 HF vi 37 (OED 1832.. So W. A in B Th M DN.III. Not in S C)

cow-shed, sb. [B²] *"Be it in the home of luxury or in the humble cow-shed"* 1865 SNO (1875) 78 (OED 1886. So U. Comb.not in W S C)

coyote, sb. [AB³E] *The country is fabulously rich in gamblers, sharpers, coyotes (pronounced ki-yo-ties), poets, preachers, and jackass rabbits* 1861 *Letters* (1917) I iii 54. *The regular coyote—pronounced ky-o-te—of the farther deserts* 1872 RI v 48. See also *mad*, a. 1872 (OEDS The prairie-wolf of the Pacific slope of N.America. 1834.. So W S C U B F Cl Th.III M DN.I AS.I.152. The trisyllabic pron. on which M.T. insists is given the preference in OED S, and is the only pron. indicated in C; but W lists the dissyllabic pron. first)

crack, v. [?AB¹] *"Jump up and crack yo' heels!"* 1884 HF xvi 137 (W: To cause to make a sharp noise; as, to crack a whip. So S C. This sense not in OED)

cracked-pot, a. [B¹] *The cracked-pot clangor of the church-bells* 1880 TA xxxvi 401 (Comb. not in OED W S C)

cracker, sb. [A] *"Toast part of a cracker until it begins to brown"* 1894 TET vii 413. See also *soggy* 1898 (OEDS 9. A thin hard biscuit. Now chiefly *U.S.* 1739.. So S C U B F Cl Th M H DN.III,VI AS.V.21. Not A in W T)

crackless, a. [C] *Solid blackness—a crackless bank of it* 1883 LM lviii 571. See also *exitless* 1909 (OED *rare.* 1616, only ex. Not *rare* in C. Not in W S)

crack on, v. [?AB³] *When the shoalest water was struck, he cracked on the steam* 1875 OTM 451. *France and Italy...cracked on such a rattling impost that cotton-seed olive oil couldn't stand the raise* 1883 LM xxxix 413 (OED 21.trans. To clap on. *colloq.* 1850, only ex. OEDS Later U.S.exs. 1883, these quots. A in B F Cl T. Not A in W S. This sense not in C)

crack up, v. [?AB³] *"Looky here, Tom, being rich ain't what it's cracked up to be"* 1876 TS xxxv 271 (OEDS 8. To praise, eulogize. Earlier U.S.exs. 1829.. A in Th M. Not A in W S. This sense not in C)

cracky, int. [?AB³E] *"Cracky! What did they give you?"* 1870 SNO (1875) 100. *"Cracky, I wisht I was"* 1876 TS xxvi 200 (OED var. of Crikey. OEDS Crackey or Crackee. U.S. exs. 1854.. A in DN.II,III. Not A in W S C)

craft, sb. [C] *Merlin had done such a craft that Pelli-nore saw not Arthur* 1889 CY iii 48 (OED 3b. A spell or enchantment. *obs.* c1205..1533. So W. This sense not in S C)

craft-equipment, sb. [B¹] *Shakespeare's multifarious craft-equipments* 1909 ISD vii 67 (Nonce comb.)

cramp, v. [AB²] *"A boat hates shoal water. Stand by—wait—wait—keep her well in hand. Now cramp her down! Snatch her! snatch her!"* 1875 OTM 286. *Twenty times a day we would be cramping up around a bar* do. 446. *"Cramp her up to the bar! What are you standing up through the middle of the river for?"* do. 447. *"I told you not to cramp that reef! G'way from the wheel!"* 1883 LM xviii 223 (Cf. OEDS 4c. trans. and intr. To deflect or turn to one side. *U.S.* 1883, quot from OTM. A in DN.III,IV,V, as applied to a carriage or wagon. But M.T.'s meaning seems rather: To come close to, graze. Not in W S C)

cranberry-farm, sb. [AB¹] *The marshy slush of his cranberry-farm* 1907 "Capt. Stormfield" 48 (Comb. not in OED W S C; but cf. OED Cranberry: the name seems to have been adopted by the N. Am. colonists. 1672..)

cranberry sauce, sb. [A] See *biscuit* 1880 (OEDS 1767.. A in H. Not A in S. Comb. not in W C. Cf. above)

crank, sb. [AB³] *The foreign crank who carried million-pound bills in his vest pocket* 1893 "Banknote" (1928) 117. *The man with a new idea is a crank until the idea succeeds* 1897 FE xxxii 297. See also *certain-sure* 1901 (OED 5. *U.S. colloq.* 1881.. So C F Cl Th T M DN.IV. Not A in W S U)

crash-word, sb. [B¹] *The profanity was not good... with the crash-word in the middle instead of at the end* 1889 CY xxxv 457 (Nonce coinage)

crater-summit, sb. [B¹] *The grassy crater-summit of Mount Eden* 1897 FE xxxiii 308 (Comb. not in OED W S C)

cravat, sb. **to sleep in one's cravat**. [?A] *"If the ex-cited fools hadn't made that rush, we'd 'a' slept in our cravats tonight—cravats warranted to wear, too—longer than we'd need 'em"* 1884 HF xxx 310 (OED 1b. *fig.* in ref. to hanging. 1678.. A in AS.XI.200. Phr. not in W S C)

crawfish, v. [AB³] *I crawfished as good as I could about ten yards* 1884 HF xii 105 (OEDS *U.S.colloq.* To retreat. 1848.. So W S C B F Cl Th M DN.I,II,III, IV,V)

crayfish, sb. [AB²] *A tall pyramid of scarlet crayfish* 1883 LM xliv 446 (OED 3. Applied to the American genus *Cambarus.* No Am. quot. A in B F Th,1805. Not A in W S C U)

crazy, a. [?AB¹] *Crazy rail-fences* 1875 OTM 449 (Crooked, irregular, uncertain in direction. This sense not in OED W S C; but cf. OED Crazy quilt, *U.S.* 1886..)

cream-yellow, a. [B¹] *Hill-tops with ribbony roads and paths squirming and snaking cream-yellow all over them* 1897 FE lv 530 (Comb. not in OED S C. Given in W)

creation-dawn, sb. [B¹] *The old, old creation-dawn scheme of ultimately launching me into the literary guild* 1910 "Turning-Point of My Life" (1917) 140 (Comb. not in OED W S C; but cf. OED Creation-day, 1667)

creature, sb. Spelled **cretur, cratur.** [?AE] *"All of us was saved but Bill Whipple—and oh, he was the best cretur!"* 1884 HF xiii 114. *See this frowsy "cratur"— Pah! it's Struwwelpeter!* 1891 *Slovenly Peter* (1935) 2 (OED 3b. A human being. *c*1290.. A in F Cl Th DN. I,II,III. Not A in W S C. OED gives the sp. *cretur* as 18th c., *crater* as 19th c. Cf. OEDS Critter: freq.U.S. dial.var. So M. Cf.DN.II: Creature in the Cape Cod dial. was *creeter* when referring to a person, *critter* of a bull)

creek, sb. Spelled **crick.** [AE] *Paddling up some obscure creek* 1869 IA i 19. *A picture of Higgins wading out into the creek* 1871 SNO (1875) 93. *"Dey hid her in a crick 'mongst de willows"* 1884 HF xviii 171 (OED In many parts of U.S. *crick* is the common pron. 2b.In U.S. and British Colonies: brook, small stream, or run. 1674.. So W S C B F Cl Th T M H DN.III,V,VI AS.V.158, X.256)

creep, v. Past tense **crope.** [AE] *"So he crope in—and the next minute out he crope again"* 1896 TSD vii 361 (OED This form 1420..1883. Common in U.S. among the negroes and poorer whites. So M DN.III AS.V.264, Ozarks. Not A in W S C Wr)

crest, sb. [D] See *coat-of-arms* 1883 (OED 3. *Heraldry.* A figure or device borne above the shield and helmet in a coat of arms. *a*1400..1837—. So W S C U)

crevasse, sb. [B³] See *ice-bridge* 1880 (OED 1. A fissure in the ice of a glacier. 1823.. So W S C)

crevasse, sb. [AB³] *The negroes had given up all thoughts of a crevasse there, as the upper levee had stood so long* 1883 LM App. A 596 (OEDS 2. *U.S.* A breach in a levee. 1812.. So W S C B F Cl Th T M)

crib, sb. [?AB³] *The pompous name of this ramshackle old crib—Rossmore Towers* 1892 AmCl xx 201 (OED 3b. *Thieves' slang:* A dwelling-house. 1812.. So W S C U Wr. A in Th.III)

crime, sb. [B¹] *Some of these terrors [pictures] were landscapes, and some libelled the sea...all were crimes* 1892 AmCl ii 27 (This sense not in OED W S C. Cf. atrocity, terror, etc.)

criminal lawyer, sb. [B²] *Everybody in the courtroom knew Mr.Braham, the great criminal lawyer* 1873 GA liv 486 (OED 1887, only ex. Comb. not in W S C)

crimson, a. [B¹] *You can't talk pale inconsequentialities when you've got a crimson fact* 1883 LM xlv 455 (Actual, concrete, real; used as a graphic intensive. This sense not in OED W S C; but cf. OED *bloody* and the other intensives there mentioned)

croaker, sb. [A] See *biscuit* 1880 (OED Applied to several N. Am. fishes. 1676. So W S C B F Cl)

crook, sb. [AB²] *Our newspapers glorify the "Black Crook"* 1873 *Speeches* (1923) 48 (OEDS 13. One whose conduct is crooked. orig. *U.S.* 1886.. So F Cl Th T M

H. Not A in W S C. Mencken mistakenly assigns 1878 as the date when the word was first used in this sense)

crooked-handled, ppl.a. [B¹] *A crooked-handled cane* 1884 HF xxi 217 (Comb. not in OED W S C; but cf. OED Crooked-backed, 1865; OEDS Crooked-necked, 1796..)

crooked-skeleton, a. [B¹] *Given a crooked-skeleton disposition, no power nor influence in the earth can mould a permanently shapely form around it* 1902 "Defence of General Funston" 613 (Comb. not in OED W S C)

cross, sb. **to shake the cross.** [?AB²] *"If I would shake the cross (quit stealing)...it would be the best job I ever done"* [given as thieves' argot] 1883 LM lii 511 (OED 29.*slang.* No ex. So C. A in F. Phr. not in W S)

cross-counter, v. [B¹] *The skirmishers counter and cross-counter* 1864 SS (1926) 149 (Not in OED W S C as verb, but cf. OEDS Cross-counter, sb. A blow at the head delivered across an opponent's lead-off with the other hand. 1889, only ex. So W)

cross-cut, a. [?A] *They ruined an old cross-cut saw* 1889 CY ix 108 (OEDS 1. 1645.. So W S C U Wr. A in Th DN.III)

crossing, vbl.sb. [?AB¹] *It was about the plainest and simplest crossing in the whole river* 1875 OTM 573. *I made out to see that the drift of the current was towards the left-hand shore, which meant that I was in a crossing* 1884 HF xvi 145. *See sounding-barge* 1906. *We had sounded a tangled patch of crossings known as Hell's Half Acre* 1909 ISD i 13 (The crossing over of the current from one side of a river to the other. This *spec* sense not in OED W S C; but cf. OEDS Cross-over, sb. 4, in same sense. 1902)

crossing-mark, sb. [?AB¹] *By and by even the shoal water and the countless crossing-marks began to stay with me* 1875 OTM 286 (Cf. above. Comb. not in OED W S C)

crossing-stone, sb. [?AB¹] *Go on until you know every street-crossing, the character, size and position of the crossing-stones* 1875 OTM 571 (Comb. not in OED W S C. A distinctively Am. device for getting across a muddy street?)

cross-lot, a. [AB²] *The dwelling where Ruth lived, the cross-lot path she traversed to the Seminary* 1873 GA xxi 199. *Three hours of awful cross-lot riding* 1889 CY xx 240 (OEDS *U.S.* attrib. 1873, this quot. So W S B F Cl Th T DN.III. Not in C. Cf. lot (across lots), below)

cross off, v. [?AB¹] *Miss Watson was in ahead of me and crossed me off* 1884 HF iv 25 (To thwart, head off. The comb. with *off* not in OED W S C; but cf. OED Cross, v. 14b. To thwart, oppose, go counter to. *c*1555..)

crotch, v. [?AB¹] *He sent his ball flying around the table at random, and it crotched a ball that was packed against the cushion* 1907 "Chaps. from Autob" 682 (W: *Billiards.* To play into a crotch. Not given as verb in OED S C)

crouter, sb. [?AB¹] *I was a settin in the parlor of my Dutch boardin house,—I board among the crouters so as to observe human natur in a forren aspeck* 1856 *Adv.of T.J.Snodgrass* (1928) 3 (A German, eater of sourcrout or sauerkraut. Not in OED W S C; but cf. OEDS Crout-eating. 1886: "A crout-eating Dutchman")

crow, sb. **to eat crow.** [AB²] *Hawley is howling for Blaine, Warner and Clark are eating their daily crow in the paper for him, and all three will vote for him* 1884 *Letters* (1917) II xxiv 443 (OEDS 3. *U.S. colloq.* To be forced to do something extremely disagreeable and humiliating. 1885.. So S C F Cl Th H. Not A in W)

crow-bar, sb. [A] *"It doesn't need a crow-bar to break your way into society there as it does in Philadelphia"* 1873 GA xix 183 (OEDS orig. *U.S.* 1797.. So DN.III. Not A in W S C U)

crowd, sb. [AB³] *"It almost blew the heads off the whole crowd"* 1873 GA i 29 (OEDS 2c, *U.S.* A company. 1840.. So B F Cl Th T M H. Not A in W S C U)

crowd, v.intr. [?A] *"If she'll let up on some of the roughest things, I'll crowd through or bust"* 1876 TS xxxv 272 (OED 2. To press, drive; said orig. of a ship. 937.. So W S C U. A in H)

crowd, v.trans. [?AB¹] *"Meet her, meet her! didn't you know she'd smell the reef if you crowded it like that?"* 1909 ISD i 6 (To press close to, approach too near. This sense not in OED W S C)

crowd, v.trans. [AB³] *" You ought to respect their little prejudices...and put up with their little foibles, until they get to crowding you too much"* 1872 SNO (1875) 322. *He was too crowded for time* 1876 TS iii 34. *"We obey orders and leave the consequences where they belong. But I am willing to admit this much: we do crowd the orders a trifle when we get a chance"* 1876 "Facts concerning the Recent Carnival of Crime" 646. *We can't get crowded for money for eight months yet* 1894 *Letters* (1917) II xxxiv 615. *They crowded him so that he had to give himself up* 1897 FE xlvii 441. *I'm a crowded and busy poor devil* 1901 *M.T. the Letter Writer* (1932) xiii 167 (OED 7c. To press upon or beset. *U.S. colloq* 1851. So Th H. This sense not in W S C. One of M.T.'s favorite words, perhaps because of its nautical origin)

cruel, adv. [?AC] *All the people there were cruel anxious to see her* 1896 JA II xiv 435 (OED 5. Exceedingly, very. *obs* exc. *dial.* 1573..1860. So W Wr. *Colloq* in S C U. A in B F Cl)

crushed-strawberry, a. [B²] *Figured silk of a fiendish crushed-strawberry tint* 1904 *Autob* (1924) I 205 (OED Crushed, ppl.a. 3. No ex. Given in W. Comb. not in S C)

crusher, sb. [?AB³] *He laid me out with a crusher alongside the head* 1889 CY pref. 20 (OEDS 2. A crushing blow. 1888. So S C. This sense not in W)

crusher, sb. [?AB³] *"What if he commands you to stay?" That was a crusher—and sudden* 1896 JA II xiii 304 (OED 2. *colloq.* Something which overwhelms or overpowers. 1840.. So W S C)

crush hat, sb. [?AB³] *His fiddle under one arm and his crush-hat under the other* 1894 "Defence of Harriet Shelley" 109 (OED 1838.. So W S C U. A in B F Cl)

cry, v. to cry mercy. [C] *"Good your majesty, I cry you mercy!"* 1881 PP viii 99 (OED 1b. c1225..1672 *obs.* So U. Not *obs* in W C. Not in S)

cry, sb. [B¹] *I know that it must be low-grade music, because it so moved me...that I was full of cry* 1880 TA xxiv 236 (Silent tears, desire to weep. This sense not in OED W S C; but cf. OED Cry, v. 10. To weep..even where no sound is uttered. 1532..)

cry-baby, sb. [?AB³] *"We'll let the cry-baby go home to his mother, won't we, Huck?"* 1876 TS xvi 137 (OEDS Earlier U.S.exs. 1851.. Not A in W S C U)

crystal, sb. [?AB²] *Said the crystal [of my watch] had got bent!* 1870 SNO (1875) 20 (OED 6. The glass of a watch-case. No ex. So W S C. A in M H)

crystal-clear, a. [B²] *These big blocks were hard, solid, and crystal-clear* 1883 LM xxxix 410 (OED Crystal, a. 2a. No ex. Given in W. Not in S C)

cub, sb. [?AB¹] *"Mary, that cub has got the whooping-cough"* 1869 SNO (1875) 228. See *ash-cat* 1869; *pluck*, v. 1881; *'vast*, int. 1883. *Young Kaspar was...a fleshy cub* 1891 *Slovenly Peter* (1935) 17. *She put her cub in Tommy's elegant cradle* 1893 PW iii 239 (A brat; contemptuous name for an infant in arms, baby. This sense not in OED W S C. Used of an older child in OED 3. An uncouth, unpolished youth. 1601.. So W.)

cub, sb. [AB²] *The pilot not on watch takes his "cub" or steersman* 1875 OTM 567. *I was a cub on a country weekly* 1886 *Speeches* (1910) 182. See also *non-pareil* 1889. *Four years later I became a "cub" on a Mississippi steamboat* 1909 ISD vi 61 (OED 3b. An apprentice or beginner. *U.S.* 1883, quot.from OTM, wrongly dated. So S M H. This sense not in W C)

cubby, sb. [?AB³] *Up garret was a little cubby with a pallet in it* 1884 HF xxvi 257 (OEDS 1. Cubby hole. Earlier U.S. ex. 1868.. A in Wr Th.III. Not A in W C. Not in S)

cub-engineer, sb. [AB²] *They learned to disappear when the ruthless "cub" engineer approached* 1875 OTM 71 (OEDS 5. 1883, this quot. Not in W S C)

cub-pilot, sb. [AB²] *Our friend Sergeant Fathom, one of the oldest cub pilots on the river* 1859 Letter in *New Orleans Daily Crescent*. *I want to be a cub-pilot* 1875 OTM 75. *I was a cub pilot on the Mississippi in the late '50s* 1906 *Autob* (1924) I 296. *A compliment...not likely to set anything afire, not even a cub-pilot's self-conceit* 1909 ISD i 9 (OEDS 5. 1883, quot. from OTM. A in H. Comb. not in W S C)

culture-wagon, sb. [B¹] *To leave that powerful agency [the theater] out is to have the culture-wagon with a crippled team* 1898 "About Play Acting" (1900) 224 (Nonce comb.)

culverin, sb. [B¹] *Von Berlichingen shut his daughter up in his donjon-keep, or his oubliette, or his culverin, or some such place* 1880 TA xv 133 (Hum. malapropism)

culvert, v. [B²] *"Culverts enough to culvert creation itself!"* 1873 GA xxvii 248 (OED To provide with culverts. 1889. So W S U. Not in C)

Cunarder, sb. [?AB³] *He pointed out where the Cunarders lay when in port* 1873 GA lv 494 (OEDS One of a line of steamships between Liverpool and New York. Earlier U.S.exs. 1869.. Not A in W. Not in S C)

cunning, a. [AB³] See *too-too*, a. 1893. *One of those large farm-houses, with a cunning little porch under the deep gable* 1899 "Chr.Sc.and the Book" 585 (OED 6. *U.S.colloq.* Quaintly interesting or pretty. 1854.. So W S C U B F Cl Th T M H AS.V.214)

curiosity-breeding, ppl.a. [B¹] See *joker* 1905 (Comb. not in OED W S C)

curious, a. [?A] See *eggnog* 1869. *A curious commingling of earnest and persiflage* 1873 GA xxxv 325. See *puzzled-up* 1884. *It was a curious kind of spectacle, and interesting* 1889 CY ii 36. *Curious rivers they are; low shores a dizzy distance apart, with nothing between but an enormous acreage of sand-flats* 1897 FE xlix 465. See also *dried-apple-pie* 1906 (OED 16. Deserving or exciting attention on account of its novelty or peculiarity; somewhat surprising; strange, singular, odd. (The ordinary current objective sense. 1715.. So W S C U. A in B F Cl DN.V)

curious, adv. [?AC] *She was looking at me pretty curious, and smiling a little* 1884 HF xi 90 (OED 18. quasi-adv. *Obs.* 1593..1834. This use not in W S C)

curl up, v. [?AB²] *Women curled up and quit in every direction* 1889 CY xxiii 290 (OED 5d. *Sporting.* To give up, to collapse. 1891.. So W U. This sense not in S C)

curtain-calico, a. [AB¹] *" Here are the costumes for the parts". He got out two or three curtain-calico suits* 1884 HF xx 194. *She had caught sight of her new Sunday gown—a cheap curtain-calico thing* 1893 PW iii 238 (Cf. calico, above. Comb. not in OED W S C)

cuspidor, sb. [A] *Bright, fanciful cuspidores* 1875 OTM 220. *A cuspidor with the motto, "In God We Trust"* 1902 "Belated Russian Passport" (1928) 190 (OED *U.S.* 1779.. So U B F Th T M. Not A in W S C)

cuss, sb. [AB³] *He polished off with a kind of general cuss all around* 1884 HF vi 40 (OED *U.S. colloq* or *slang*. 1. An execration.1848.. So W S C B T M DN.III)

cuss, sb. [A] *The poor cuss is busted and gone home* 1867 SNO (1875) 74. See also *potter*, v. 1896; *fifteen-puzzle* 1902 (OEDS *U.S. colloq* or *slang*. 2. Applied to persons. 1775.. So W S C B F Cl Th M DN.II,IV)

cuss, v. [AB³] See *bust*, v.1876. *He broke loose and cussed himself black in the face* 1880 TA iii 39. *He... cussed me for putting on frills and trying to be better than him* 1884 HF v 33 (OEDS Vulgar *U.S.* 1835.. So W S C B F Cl M DN.III,IV,V)

cussed, ppl.a. [AB³] *" Nothing'll soothe him down but them cussed books"* 1869 IA lvii 445. See *bogus*, a. 1880. *A cussed thief!* 1883 LM iii 58. *This cussed nonsense!* 1884 HF xxx 311 (OEDS Vulgar *U.S.* pron. of Cursed. 1840.. So W S C F Cl Th M DN.V)

cussedness, sb. [AB³] *They just do them out of pure cussedness* 1867 SNO (1875) 252. *None of us can have as many virtues as the fountain-pen, or half its cussedness* 1897 FE lxviii 687 (OED *U.S.colloq* or *slang*. 1866.. So W S C B F Cl Th T M DN.III)

cussing, vbl.sb. [AB¹] See *booming* 1884; *good-by* 1884 (Not in OED W S C)

cuss-word, sb. [AB²] *He didn't give a continental for anybody. Beg your pardon, friend, for coming so near saying a cuss-word* 1872 RI xlvii 334. *They...used considerable many cuss-words* 1884 HF xxi 229 (OED *U.S. colloq* or *slang*. 1872.. So W S C B F Cl Th T M DN. II,III)

cut, v. [B³] *"This chap had a falling out with his father...and just cut for this country"* 1892 AmCl xi 107 (OED 19. *slang* or *colloq*. To run away, make off. 1844.. So S C U Wr. This sense not in W. A distinctively British piece of slang)

cut, v. **to cut one's stick.** [?AB³] See *vamose*, v. 1866 (OED 43. *slang*. To take one's departure. 1825.. So W S C. A in B F Cl DN.III AS.XII.115)

cut bank, sb. [AB³] *In about a minute I come a-booming down on a cut bank with smoky ghosts of big trees on it. That cut bank was an island* 1884 HF xv 127 (OEDS A bank formed by a river cutting into it. *U.S.* 1836.. So DN.VI. Comb. not in W S C)

cute, a. [AB³] *The judge thought that these quips and fancies of Wilson's were neatly turned and cute* 1894 PW v 332 (OEDS 2. *U.S.* Attractive, taking, 'cunning.' 1834.. So S U Wr B F Cl Th M H DN.III,V. Not A in W C)

cuteness, sb. [?A] *I was obliged to admire my cuteness in foreseeing this very thing* 1889 CY xxxiv 442 (OED Acuteness. 1768..1807. *colloq*. OEDS Later U.S.exs. 1845..1903. A in Wr B F Cl Th DN.III. Not A in W S C U)

cut-off, sb. [A] *Below Red River Landing, Raccourci cut-off was made* 1875 OTM 193. *These cut-offs have curious effects: they have thrown several rivertowns out into the rural districts* 1883 LM i 23 (OEDS 2. A new and shorter passage cut by a river through a bend. *Western U.S.* 1773.. So W S C B F Cl Th T M H)

cut out, v. [?A] *No girl could withstand his charms. He "cut out" every boy in the village* 1875 OTM 71 (OED 56f. To get in front of a rival. 1738.. So W S C U Wr. A in DN.I,III AS.II)

cut out, v. [AB¹] *You ought to have seen the bull cut out after him* 1872 RI vi 63 (A in DN.III. S: *colloq*. This sense not in OED W C)

cutter, sb. [AB³] *"We'll have a horse and buggy for summer, and a cutter and a skin lap-robe for winter"* 1904 "Bequest" (1906) ii 6 (OEDS 3. A small light sledge or sleigh. *Canada* and *U.S.* 1804.. So S C B F Cl Th T H DN.III. Not A in W)

cut through, v. [?AB²] *The river will cut through and move the mouth down five miles more* 1883 LM liii 523 (OED 9c. 1883. So W. Comb. not in S C. Cf. *cut-off*, above)

cut under, v. [?AB³] *I am not going to cut under on the trade* 1870 CRG (1919) 62. *The other magician had been cutting under me* 1889 CY xxiv 309 (OEDS 58. To cut out by underselling. Earlier U.S. ex. 1859.. A in B F T DN.III. Not A in W S. Not in C)

cut-up, sb. [AB²] *The ground floor...is cut up into twenty-three rooms. With eighty cut-ups in this house...* 1904 *Autob* (1924) I 200 (A pun on the sense in OEDS 1b. A person who 'cuts up' or capers. *U.S.slang.* a1906.. Not A in w. This sense not in S C)

cut up, v. [?AB³] *Tom was so cut up he couldn't take any intrust in him* 1896 TSD ix 524 (OED 59h. To distress greatly. 1844.. So W S C U. A in B Cl DN.III)

cut up, v. [AB³] *As for Queen Victoria and Lord Derby, they may cut up as much as they like* 1852 *Hannibal Journal*, Sept, 16 (OEDS 59o. To 'kick' up a disturbance. *U.S.* a1848.. So B Cl Th DN.I,II,III. Not A in W S C)

cyclone, sb. [?AB³] *A cyclone blew him some three miles and knocked down a tree with him* 1883 LM xlviii 482. *The evoking of cyclones and other kinds of electric storms* 1892 AmCl xxv 272 (OED 1b. A hurricane or tornado. 1856.. So W U. A in S C M)

cyclone, sb. [AB¹] *Cyclones of frantic joy* 1889 CY xviii 223. *A perfect cyclone of satisfaction from the Left* 1898 "Stirring Times in Austria" (1898) 302. *"The telegram, it was just a cyclone!"* 1892 AmCl v 58. *The cyclone of laughter* 1902 "DBDS" (1928) 350 (A *fig* extension of the above. This use not in OED W S C)

cylinder, sb. [B¹] *Ask them on what terms they will rent me a phonograph for three months and furnish me cylinders enough to carry 75,000 words* 1891 *Letters* (1917) II xxxi 543 (Here *spec* of a phonograph cylinder. This sense not in OED W S C)

cylinder-head, sb. [?AB¹] *"What kep' you?—boat get aground?" "It warn't the grounding...We blowed out a cylinder-head"* 1884 HF xxxii 332 (S: The metal plate or cover closing the end of a cylinder in an engine. So W. Comb. not in OED C)

cypress, sb. [A] *I paddled about a mile up a crick amongst the cypress woods* 1884 HF xix 180 (OED 2a. Bald, Black, or Deciduous Cypress, a native of America. 1794. So W S C F Cl AS.II.30

cypress-top, sb. [AB¹] *A ragged and angular-limbed and moss-bearded cypress-top, standing out, clear-cut against the sky* 1883 LM xliv 445 (Comb. not in OED W S C. Cf. above)

D

d—, int. [?AB³] "*D— the old woman!*" 1894 PW xv 817 (OED 3. Used euphemistically for damn. 1861.. So C. A in DN.V. Not in W S)

dad, sb. dad blame, dad fetch. [AB³] "*He had some er de dad-fetchedes' ways I ever see*" 1884 HF xiv 121. "*Dad fetch the whole business!*" do. xxvii 275. "*Why, Mars Tom, I doan' want no rats. Dey's the dadblamedest creturs to 'sturb a body*" do. xxxviii 391. "*Dad blame dat revival*" 1893 PW ii 237 (OEDS A deformation of God. *U.S.*, esp. with verbs and pa.ppls. 1834.. So W Wr F Th DN.III,IV,V, in s.e.Mo., n.w.Ark., e.Ala. Not in S C)

dad-blame, a. [AB¹] "*It's de dad-blame witches*" 1884 HF xxxiv 354 (A in DN.III,IV,V. Not given as adj. in OED W S C)

daddy, sb. [B¹] *The patriotic "daddies" who beat time hadn't a stump of a leg left* 1856 Letter in *Iowa Journal of Hist.* (1929) 424 (Nonce use: short for daddy-long-legs. See below)

daddy-long-legs, sb. [?AB²] *Three dignified daddy longlegs, perched near the gas burner* 1856 Letter in *Iowa Journal of Hist.* (1929) 423 (OED b. An arachnid of the genus *Phalangium.* No. ex. So W S. A in C B T DN.I. Cf. grand-daddy-long-legs, below)

daguerrotype-case, sb. [B¹] *A daguerrotype case... containing the sweetest girlish face...that I had ever seen* 1893 "Californian's Tale" (1906) 107 (Comb. not in OED W S C)

daily, sb. [AB³] *The average German daily is made up solely of correspondence* 1880 TA App.F 627. *Here* [Minneapolis] *there are three great dailies, ten weeklies, and three monthlies* 1883 LM lx 589 (OEDS orig. *U.S.* 1833.. So B Th. Not A in W S C U)

daintly, adv. [B¹C] *His boots were daintly polished* 1873 GA xxxiii 301 (*Obs* in W S C. This form not in OED. Possibly a misprint here)

daisy, sb. [A] *She was a daisy* 1889 CY xiv 170. See also *blessings-of-civilization* 1901 (OED 5. *slang*, chiefly *U.S.* A first-rate thing or person. 1757.. So Wr F Cl Th T DN.IV. Not A in W S C U)

daisy-cutter, sb. [AB²] *I've seen him catch a daisy-cutter in his teeth* 1889 CY xli 533 (OED 2. *Baseball.* A ball so batted as to skim along the ground. 1889, this quot.. So W S C U)

dam, v. [C] "*Sired by a hurricane, dam'd by an earthquake*" 1883 LM iii 45 (OED *obs. rare.* 1577, only ex. Not in W S C)

dame, sb. [C] *He was not to lose this thrifty dame's society so easily* 1881 PP xix 243 (OED 2. A housewife. Now *arch* or *dial.* 1330..1855. So W Wr. Not *arch* in S C U)

damfool, sb. [?AB³] "*Yes sir, he's a dam fool, that's the way I put him up*" 1893 PW i 235 (OEDS *colloq.* 1886.. A in M DN.IV. Comb. not in W S C)

damnation, int. [?A] "*Damnation, I'm going to be roasted alive*" 1894 TET vii 416. (OED 3a. 1604..1836. So W S C U. A in DN.V)

damosel, sb. [CE] "*Look upon this damosel! note her wasted form*" 1869 IA xxi 214 (OED Damsel. 1. Modern poets and romantic writers, led by Sir W. Scott, have recalled the 16-17c. *damosel* to express a more stately notion than is now conveyed by *damsel.* 1300..1615, 1813..1884. So W S. Not *arch* in C U)

dancette, sb. [B³] See *coat-of-arms* 1883 (OED A modern formation from *Dancetté.* 1. Heraldry. A fesse with three indentations. 1864. So W S C)

dander, sb. [AB³] *There is only one thing that gets my "dander" up* 1853 Letters (1917) I i 27. "*He 'pears to know just how long he can torment me before I get my dander up*" 1876 TS i 19 (OEDS *U.S. colloq* and *dial.* 1834.. So Wr B F Cl Th,1801 DN.III,IV. Not A in W S C U)

dang, v. [?A] "*Oh, dang it now, don't take on so*" 1884 HF xiii 113 (OED A euphemistic substitute for Damn. 1793.. So S C Wr. A in F DN.III,V. Not in W)

danger-line. sb. [?AB³] *The lawmakers have no limit, no danger-line* 1898 "Stirring Times in Austria" (1900) 330 (OEDS 1890. So W S C. A in Th.III DN.VI)

dangersome, a. [?AC] *He had ciphered out his idea about how to run in daylight without it being dangersome for Jim* 1884 HF xx 195. See also *close-fit* 1884 (OED *obs exc. dial.* 1567..1885. OEDS Earlier U.S. exs. 1850.. A in Th. Not A in W S C Wr)

dare, v. Negative forms: **dasn't, didn't dast** [AB¹E] See *fighting* 1876. *She was afraid to go to bed, but she dasn't set up* 1884 HF xxxix 401. *Old pigeon-holed things, of the years gone by, which I or editors didn't dast to print* 1906 Letters (1917) II xlv 796. *The same old argument—the one I couldn't answer, because I dasn't* 1909 ISD i 16 (S: These forms *dial.U.S.* So M DN.I,III,IV,V AS.IX.319, XI.348: Ill., Ohio, Neb., e.Texas, N.Y., N.E. These forms not given in OED W C)

dare, sb. to take a dare. [?AB²] "*I dare you to knock it off, and anybody that'll take a dare will suck eggs*" 1876 TS i 8 (OEDS Earlier U.S. exs. 1876, this quot.. A in DN.I AS.IX.319. Not A in W S C Wr)

dark, a. dark as the inside of a cow. [?AB¹] *Once, at night, in one of those forest-bordered crevices behind an island which steam-boatmen intensely describe with the phrase "as dark as the inside of a cow"* 1875 OTM 448 (Phr. not in OED W S C)

dark, sb. the dark of the moon. [?AC] *I remember how very dark that room was, in the dark of the moon* 1897 Autob (1924) I 113 (OED † 1651..1801. OEDS Later U.S. exs. 1872..1889. A in F Cl. Not A in W S C)

dark and bloody, a. [AB¹] *Pies whose conception and execution are a dark and bloody mystery to all save the cook who created them* 1869 IA xii 109. "*Here I register a dark and bloody oath that you shan't sing*" do. xxii 218 (Hum. variation on the supposed meaning of the name Kentucky. Cf. OEDS Dark and bloody ground. *U.S.* the state of Kentucky. 1832.. So W S B F Cl Th AS.V.260. Phr. not in C)

darken up, v. [?AB¹] *Pretty soon it darkened up and begun to thunder and lighten* 1884 HF ix 74 (Comb. not in OED W S C; but cf. Wr Darken in: to grow dark or dusk in the evening)

darkish-paly, a. [B¹] *Col. Grangerford...had a darkish-paly complexion, not a sign of red in it anywhere* 1884 HF xviii 160 (Nonce comb.)

darky, sb. [?AB³] See *spittoon* 1873; white-wooled 1873. *A stalwart darky once gave offence at a negro ball in New Orleans by putting on a good many airs* 1875 OTM 722 (OED 3. *colloq.* 1840.. So W S C U. A in B F Cl Th,1775 T M)

darling, a. [B¹] *I have just now fallen upon a darling literary curiosity* 1887 "English as She Is Taught" (1917) 241. *He thought it would be darling fun To see that hunter skip and run* 1891 Slovenly Peter (1935) 13. *These were the darlingest words the poor vacillating young apostate had ever heard* 1892 AmCl xiv 147 (Delightful, dear, 'precious.' This sense not in OED W S C. Cf. the different meaning given in OEDS: Sweetly pretty or charming, 'sweet.' Affected. 1854..)

dashed, ppl.a. [?AB²] "*Well, I'll be dashed*" 1873 GA xvii 161. "*You dash-dash-dash-dashed split between a tired mud-turtle and a crippled hearse-horse*" 1875 OTM 73. See also *egg-sucking* 1875. "*Stop that dashed bailing, or we shall be aground*" 1880 TA xvii 158 (OED 3. *slang* or *colloq.* A euphemism for 'damned.' 1881.. So W S C U. A in DN.V)

dauber, sb. [?A?C] "*And what may a mechanic get—carpenter, dauber...and the like?*" 1889 CY xxxiii 420 (OED 1. A plasterer. *obs.* 1300..1825. So W. Not *obs* in C Wr. Not in S)

Daughter, sb. [AB²] *The institution called the Daughters of the Royal Crown has established itself. Nobody eligible but American descendants of Charles II* 1900

Speeches (1910) 357 (OEDS 1c. Used in pl. in the names of various women's societies. *U.S.* 1911. Cf. D.A.R. in W. This use not in S C)

day, sb. **to call it a day.** [?AB²] *It would have been best for Merlin...to quit and call it half a day* 1889 CY xxii 271 (OEDS 20b. To consider that one has done a day's work. 1926, only ex. Phr. not in W S C)

day–before–yesterday, sb. [AB²] *If there was a day-before-yesterday I was not there when it happened* 1905 "Eve's Diary" 25 (OEDS *U.S.* 1905, only ex. Not in W S C)

day–dawn, sb. [B³?C] *Before day-dawn Judge Thatcher and the handful of searchers with him were tracked out, in the cave* 1876 TS xxxii 250 (OED Chiefly poetic. 1813.. So W S C)

day–gear, sb. [B¹] *There was no sufficient change from day-gear to night-gear* 1897 FE xlix 459 (Comb. not in OED W S C. Cf. OED Day-clothes, 1856)

day–thought, sb. [B¹] *We have wild and fantastic day-thoughts* 1906 "WIM" (1917) 67 (Nonce comb.)

d box, sb. [?AB¹] *I can see that printing office of prehistoric times yet...its "d" boxes clogged with tallow, because we always stood the candle in the "k" box nights* 1886 *Speeches* (1910) 185 (Not in OED W S C. In this passage M.T. has in mind the printer's case in use in the U.S. In the American printer's case, the small partition for the "k" type has always been located in the top row of the "lower case," near the center line and just to the left of the big "e" box. It thus affords a very convenient place for a candle, and the "d" box, which is directly under it, would naturally receive the candle-drippings. The "lay of the case" in England is different, and would not suit the passage at all. In the diagram of it given in R. B. McKerrow's *Introduction to Bibliography for Literary Students,* 1927, p. 9, said to have remained much the same since the seventeenth century until quite recent times, the k's are put in the upper case, and the partition they occupy in America is filled by the digraph "œ")

dead, adv. [?AB³] *The king stopped dead in his tracks* 1889 CY xxvii 350 (OED 1b. With absolute or abrupt cessation of motion. 1856.. So W S C U Wr. A in T DN.III)

dead–beat, sb. [AB³] *Rapscallions and dead-beats is the kind the widow and good people takes the most interest in* 1884 HF xiii 116 (OEDS *slang U.S.* A sponger, loafer. 1875.. So W B F Cl Th T M DN.IV,V. Not A in S C)

dead–bell, sb. [?AB¹] *That dead-bell rang out a blood-curdling alarum* 1883 LM xxxi 350 (C: same as death bell. So Wr. Comb. not in OED W S)

dead broke, a. [?AB³] *They couldn't seem to have no luck, so at last they got just about dead broke* 1884 HF xxxi 315 (OEDS Broke, ppl.a. 3. dead broke. Earliest exs. U.S. 1851.. A in B F Cl Th T M DN.III,IV. Comb. not in W S C)

dead–center, sb. [B¹] *Where the dead-center of that town used to be* 1883 LM xxxii 362 (A *fig* use, doubtless transf. from M.T.'s steamboat experience. Only literal use in OED W S C U; cf. OED *Mech.* 1. Dead-point: that position of a crank at which it is in a direct line with the connecting rod, and at which therefore the force exerted tends to thrust or pull instead of turning the crank. 1874.. So W S C U. On steamboat usage cf. center, to. To catch on the center, above)

dead–certain, a.[?AB²] *"We'll cottonseed his salad for him...that's a dead-certain thing"* 1883 LM xxxix 414 (OEDS 1883, this quot.. Comb. not in W S C)

dead–earnest, a. [?AB²] *The grimmest and most dead-earnest of reading-matter* 1875 OTM 288. *Ritchie's good-natured badgering was pretty nearly as aggravating as Brown's dead-earnest nagging* 1883 LM xviii 223 (OEDS 1883, this quot. Comb. not in W S C. A in F Cl)

dead–head, sb. [AB³] *"Tell this lad that I'm a friend of yours and a dead-head"* 1889 CY xxxvii 479 (OEDS 3. *U.S.* A person admitted without payment. 1848.. So S C B F Cl Th T M DN.III,1V. Not A in W U)

dead–head, adv. [AB²] *Senators and Representatives ...always traveled "dead-head" both ways* 1873 GA xxx 275 (OEDS *U.S.* 3b. Used predicatively without article. 1873, this quot... This use not in W S C)

dead–lights, sb. [?AB¹] See **bug out** 1877 (W S: eyes. *Sailors' slang.* This sense not in OED C; but cf. OED 1. *Naut.* A shutter fixed outside a porthole. 1726)

dead loads, sb. [AB²] *"The old man's got dead loads of books"* 1869 IA lvii 616. *"There's dead loads of peat down there"* 1873 GA xxvii 247. *"There's a lot of dead-limb trees—dead loads of 'em"* 1876 TS xxv 192 (OEDS *U.S.* 1873, this quot. So B,1859 Cl DN.II,III, s.e.Mo., n.w.Ark., e.Ala., N.Y. Not in W S C)

dead set, sb. [?AB³] *I made a dead set at him* 1889 CY xxxiii 418 (OED Set, sb. 10c. A pointed attack. 1835.. So W S C U. A in B F)

dead–sure, a. [?A] See **night-hawk** 1873. *"Undertaking is...the dead-surest business in Christendom"* 1883 LM xliii 438 (OEDS 1589..1906. So S C. A in T. Comb. not in W)

dead–wall, sb. [?C] *The afflicted lover will read "Go to Love's Bakery" on the dead-walls and telegraph poles, and be saved* 1864 SS (1926) 138 (OED 1670..1868. So S C U. *Arch* in W: a blank wall)

deadwood, a. [?AB²] *"Are you in real deadwood earnest, Tom?"* 1876 TS xxxv 289 (OEDS 4. Used *attrib* as an intensive. 1876, this quot. Not in W S C)

deaf, a. Spelled **deef.** [AE] *It made me deef with the noise* 1884 HF viii 60 (OED This pron. is still widely diffused dialectally and in the U.S. So Cl Th,1824 M DN.I,II,III AS.V.203, XI.15, Ozarks, e.Texas. *Arch* and *dial* in W Wr. This sp. not in S C)

deaf–and–dummy, sb. [?AB¹] *Tom said it would take him days to get so he wouldn't forget he was a deef and dummy sometimes, and speak out before he thought* 1896 TSD viii 521 (Comb. not in OED W S C; but cf. AS.VI.97: Deaf-and-dummer: A deaf and dumb person, Erie Canal. Cf. also OED Dummy, sb. A dumb person, *colloq.* 1598..1849. So W Wr)

dear, a. **for dear life.** [B²] *The fiddlers sawed away for dear life* 1880 TA x 98 (OED 5c. As though one's life were at stake. 1887.. So W S U. Phr. not in C)

dearly, adv. [?C] *I dearly wanted to see the islands* 1899 "My Debut" (1900) 71 (OED 3c. Deeply, keenly. *obs.* 1590..1602, all exs. from Shakespeare. So W S C. Not *obs* in Wr. This sense is certainly familiar in current use)

dear–me–suz, int. [AB¹] *"Dear-me-suz...it's more than I believe they could"* 1904 "Bequest" (1906) iv 25 (A in DN.IV. Not in OED W S C; but cf. OED Dear, a. Used interjectionally. *Dear save us,* 1719)

death–agony, sb. [B²] *Gasp for breath just as men do in the death-agony* 1867 SNO (1875) 304. *Seeing one of their number in his death-agony* 1883 LM xx 243 (OED 1883, only ex. So W S C U)

death–damp, sb. [B¹] *And then he would die—out in the cold world, with no friendly hand to wipe the death-damps from his brow* 1876 TS iii 40 (S: The cold sweat sometimes preceding death. So W C. Comb. not in OED)

death–disk, sb. [B¹] *The Death Disk* [title] 1901 (1928) 268 (Nonce comb.)

death–grip, sb. [B¹] *The man's death-grip still held fast to the bars* 1883 LM lvi 549 (Given in W. Comb. not in OED S C; but cf. OED Death-grapple, 1834)

death–light, sb. [B¹] *The queen rose up majestic, with the death-light in her eyes* 1889 CY xvii 204 (Determination to the death. This sense not in OED W S C; cf. OED 1. Death-fire, a luminous appearance supposed to be seen over a dead body. 1823; also 2. A light burning in a death-chamber. 1871)

death–picture, sb. [B¹] *With trembling lips and with tears in his voice, he gave them that heroic death-picture* 1892 AmCl viii 82 (Comb. not in OED W S C)

death–room, sb. [B¹] *I saw many poor fellows removed to the "death-room"* 1883 LM xx 243 (Comb. not in OED W S C; but cf. OED Death-chamber)

death–sentinel, sb. [B¹] *I imagined myself a death-sentinel drowsing there alone* 1883 LM xxxi 339 (Comb. not in OED W S C)

death–stroke, sb. [B¹] *The old man shrank suddenly together like one who had received a death-stroke* 1894 PW xii 773 (Comb. not in OED; but cf. OED Death-struck, 1622. Given in W S C)

death–toilet, sb. [B¹] *She resolved to make her death-toilet perfect* 1893 PW iii 238 (Nonce comb.)

death–warning, sb. [B¹] *The death-warning had nothing dismal about it for her* 1895 JA II vi 147 (Comb. not in OED W S C; cf. OED Death-sentence, 1811)

debauch, v. [?C] *No one in the world speaks blemishless grammar...therefore it would not be fair to exact grammatical perfection from the peoples of the Valley; but they and other peoples may justly be required to refrain from knowingly and purposely debauching their grammar* 1883 LM xxvi 289 (Cf. OED 4b. To damage or spoil in quality. *obs.* 1633, only ex. So W S C. M.T.'s use here may be a survival of this *obs* use applied to things; but it is more likely to be merely a bold *fig* application of the usual sense applied to persons; cf. OED 2. To seduce from virtue or morality. 1603..1879)

debt–factory, sb. [B¹] *Godwin's little debt-factory of a bookshop* 1894 "Defence of Harriet Shelley" 359 (Nonce comb.)

debut, v. [?AB³] *If she fails to d²but this time, I will never bet on her again* 1876 *Letters* (1917) I xvi 280 (OED To make one's début. 1830.. So W. A in M. Use as a verb not in S C)

deck, sb. deck of cards. [A] See *euchre* 1866. *"Give them candles and a couple of decks of cards"* 1870 SNO (1875) 160 (OED 5. A pack. Since 17th c. *dial* and *U.S.* 1593... So Wr B F Cl Th M H DN.III. Not A in W S C U)

deck, sb. on deck. [AB²] *"Tilbury set that trap for you...and fully expects you to blunder into it. Well, he is going to be disappointed—at least while I'm on deck"* 1904 "Bequest" (1906) iv 18. *Angels are always on deck when there is a miracle to the fore* 1889 CY xxii 273 (OED *Naut. fig U.S.* At hand; ready for action. No ex. Not A in W S C)

deck–awning, sb. [B¹] *One lolls in a long chair all day under deck-awnings* 1897 FE xxxvi 324 (Comb. not in OED W S C)

deck–hand, sb. [?AB³] *Wonder if she wouldn't like to cut wood, be a deck-hand, or something of that sort?* 1853 *Hannibal Journal*, May 25. See *sounding-boat* 1858. *A deck-hand stood on the bow and hove the lead* 1873 GA iv 42. See also *stage-plank* 1875; *roustabout* 1875; *mark twain* 1909 (OEDS Earlier U.S. exs. 1844.. Not A in W S C U)

deck–load, sb. [?A] *A solid deck-load of immigrants and harvesters* 1883 LM lviii 571 (OEDS Earlier U.S. exs. 1757.. A in DN.II. Not A in W C. Comb. not in S)

deck passage, sb. [?AB³] *He said his parents were wealthy, and he only traveled deck passage because it was cooler!* [Footnote] *Steerage passage* 1875 OTM 217. *"That warn't enough to take us fourteen hundred mile, deck passage nor no other way"* 1884 HF xx 191 (OEDS U.S. exs. 1837.. A in AS.II.27. Not A in W C. Comb. not in S)

deck–passenger, sb. [?AB³] *Four hundred deck passengers—and not very many of them were astir* 1883 LM xx 238 (OEDS U.S. exs. 1835.. Not A in W C. Comb. not in S)

deck–sweep, sb. [B¹] *A slush-plastered deck-sweep* 1869 IA xxxviii 404 (Comb. not in OED W S C; but cf. OED Deck-swabber, 1883)

deck–washer sb. [B¹] *The deck-washers...send a bucket of water sloshing along the side of the ship* 1897 FE iv 73 (Comb. not in OED W S C)

declare, v. [B²] *"The first semi-annual dividend... might even be declared within three months"* 1904 "Bequest" (1906) ii 9 (OED 5d. To announce officially a specified dividend as payable. No ex. So S C. This sense not in W)

declare, v. [?AB³] *"You's a-jokin, ain't you?" "Clah to goodness I ain't"* 1894 PW viii 337 (OED 6b. Used as a mere asseveration. 1811.. So W S C U. A in DN.III,V)

declination, sb. [?A?C] *Tracy had been expecting this invitation, and had his declination all ready* 1892 AmCl xiv 147 (OED 6. Refusal, declinature. *?Obs.* 1612.. 1884. Not *obs* in W S C Wr. A in S C B F T H)

deducer, sb. [B¹] *The Observer of Peoples has to be a Classifier, a Grouper, a Deducer, a Generalizer* 1895 "What Bourget Thinks" 49 (Not in OED W S C)

deep four, sb. [D] *Two leadsmen sprang to their posts, and in a moment their weird cries rose on the night air... "Deep four!"* 1873 GA iv 46. See also *leadsman* 1875 (OED Deep, sb. 8. *Naut.* A term used in estimating the fathoms intermediate to those indicated by marks on the 20-fathom sounding-line. The marks are at 2, 3, 5, 7, 10, 13, 15, 17, 20 fathoms; the 'deeps' or 'dips' are therefore 1, 4, 6, 8, 9, 11, 12, 14, 16, 18, 19. 1769..1867—. So W S C)

deep–thinker, sb. [B¹] *The deep-thinkers didn't merely laugh* 1901 *Speeches* (1910) 153 (Comb. not in OED W S C; but cf. OED Deep-thinking, 1768)

deer–horn, sb. [B¹] *Gilt deer-horns over the big bell* 1883 LM xxxviii 406 (Comb. not in OED S C. Given in W)

defaulter, sb. [?AB³] *"I gave you three weeks...to prove that you are not a defaulter"* 1880 TA xxii 212 (OEDS c. One who fails properly to account for money entrusted to his care. Earlier U.S. ex. 1806.. Not A in W S C U)

defectless, a. [B²] *An absolutely defectless memory* 1883 LM xlviii 485 (OED 1883, this quot.. So W S C)

deficit, v. [B¹] *"Don't you deffersit me no more deffersits"* 1884 HF xxx 313 (Nonce use)

degree, sb. in the last degree. [B¹] *The airs these little insect governments put on are in the last degree ridiculous* 1869 IA xxx 320 (This phr. not in OED W S C. Cf. OED 6b. To a degree, 1737; to the last degree: to the utmost measure. 1639..)

Delegate, sb. [AB²] See *West,* out 1873. *"I am a Congressional Delegate from Cherokee Strip"* 1892 AmCl ii 34 (OED 3. *U.S.* a. The representative of a Territory in Congress. No ex. So W S C)

deliriously, adv. [B¹] *They are not as deliriously beautiful as the books paint them* 1869 IA xlvii 502 (Here hum.: causing delirium. OED W S C define delirious, deliriously: Affected with delirium; madly, frantically)

delirium tremens, sb. [B³] *He died a natural death— of delirium tremens* 1883 LM lvi 548. See *drunk,* sb. 1884. *It seems to me that "Deerslayer" is just simply a literary delirium tremens* 1895 "Cooper's Literary Offences" 12 (OED 1813.. So W S C U)

dell, sb. [C] See *budge* 1881 (OED *Rogues' Cant. arch.* A young girl. 1567..1834. So W S C)

Democrat, sb. [A] See *Whig* 1896; *Allopath* 1902; *mugwump* 1902. *The transparencies which the Democrats would carry in their torch-light procession* 1906 *Autob* (1924) II 330 (OED 2. *U.S. politics.* 1798.. So W S C U F Cl H AS.IV.17)

Democratic, a. [AB³] *He voted the Democratic ticket* 1873 GA xxxiii 302. See also *Copperhead* 1898 (OED 2. *U.S. politics.* 1800.. So W S C U F H AS.IV.7)

democrat wagon, sb. [AB³] *A democrat wagon stood outside the main gate with my trunk in it* 1906 *Autob* (1924) II 106 (OED 3. *U.S.* A light four-wheeled cart with several seats one behind the other, and usually drawn by two horses. 1890.. So W S C Th H DN.III AS.XI.303)

demonstrate, v. [AB¹] *There is an account of the restoration to perfect health of a fatally injured horse, by the application of Christian Science. That horse had as many as fifty "claims." How could he demonstrate over them?* 1902 "Chr.Sc." 768 (Cf. below. This *spec* Christian Science sense not in OED W S C)

demonstration, sb. [AB¹] *Now and then an interesting new addition to the Science slang appears on the page. We have "demonstrations" over chilblains and such things. It seems to be a curtailed way of saying "demonstrations of the power of Christian-Science Truth over the fiction which masquerades under the name of Chilblains"* 1902 "Chr.Sc." 765. (This *spec* Chr.Sc. sense not in OED W S C)

demoralized, ppl.a. [?AB³] *The enemy were totally demoralized* 1873 GA xlv 413. *It flooded Tracy's demoralized soul with waters of refreshment* 1892 AmCl xiv 147 (OED 1817.. So W S C U. A in B M. Noah Webster's claim to have invented the word is mentioned by OED S C B M DN.VI)

demurenesses, sb.pl. [B¹] *Ruth...fascinated him with her little demurenesses and half-confidences* 1873 GA xxii 212 (This *concrete* use not in OED W S C)

dent, sb. [?AC] *I run the canoe into a deep dent in the bank* 1884 HF vii 55 (OED 1. An indentation in the edge of anything. *obs.* 1552..1700. This *gen.* sense not in W S C. M.T.'s use may show that it is an Am. survival)

Department, sb. [A] See *spittoon* 1873; *cabbage,* sb. 1887. *"I was not able to get the man's message to the Director-General of the Shoe-Leather Department"* 1901 "Two Little Tales" (1928) 197 (OED 3b. *spec.* In the U.S. the word is used in the titles of the great branches of administration. 1791.. So W S C B F Cl H)

dephlogistic, a. [B¹] *"If the recalcitrant and dephlogistic messenger of heaven strikes you"* 1870 SNO (1875) 23 (Nonsense use. Cf. OED † Relieved of inflammation. 1787, only ex. Word not in W S C)

deploy, v. [B¹] *If she hadn't deployed suddenly to the right, it would have driven her into the floor* 1867 SNO (1875) 78 (Hum. nonce usage. Cf. OED *Mil.* To spread out troops. 1768.. So W S C U)

deportment-tournament, sb. [B¹] See *cake-walk* 1894. (Nonce comb.)

depot, sb. Also sp. **depo, deepo.** [AB³E] *When we got to the depo, I went around to get a look at the iron horse* 1856 *Adv. of T. J. Snodgrass* (1928) 23. *You cannot pass into the waiting-room of the depot until you have secured your ticket* 1869 IA xii 108. *"That's the place for...the deepo"* 1873 GA xvii 165 (OED 5. *U.S.* A railway station. 1842.. So W S C U B F Cl Th,1836 T M. Cf. H: Now largely *obs.* See also OEDS Depo. U.S. var. of Depot. 1819.. This sp. not in W S C)

depredation, sb. [B¹] *Shekels, the Seventh Cavalry's dog...is out on depredation, and I can't get hold of him* 1906 "Horse's Tale" i 329 (Hum. malapropism; for expedition?)

depute, v. [?C] *The King deputed five great nobles to ride in solemn state* 1896 JA II xii 299 (OED 1. To appoint, assign, ordain. *obs.* 1425..1683. Not *obs* in W S C U)

derange, v. [?AB¹] *The hotel-devils lazily deranged a breakfast for us* 1878 *Letters* (1917) I xviii 340 (Hum. malapropism. A reminiscence of Mrs. Malaprop's "nice derangement of epitaphs?" On the word in its ordinary sense, cf. M: Seems to have been given currency by George Washington. Not A in OED 1776.. W S C)

derby, sb. [AB³] *I would wear a derby or nothing* 1900 *Speeches* (1910) 87 (OED 2. *U.S.* A stiff felt hat with rounded crown and narrow brim. 1888. So M H. Not A in W S C)

derelict, a. [AB³] *The committee has been derelict in its duty* 1872 SNO (1875) 292 (OED 2. Delinquent. *U.S.* 1864.. So W S C H)

dern, sb. [AB³] *"I wouldn't give a dern for spunkwater"* 1876 TS vi 65. *"I wouldn't give a dern for a millioun n um"* 1884 HF xiv 122. See also *matter* 1896 (OEDS var. of Darn, vulgar pron. of Damn. *U.S.* 1874.. So B F. This sb. use not in W S C)

dern, a. [AB²] *"I'd druther they was devils a dern sight"* 1876 TS ix 84. *"Where was you born?" "In Florida, Missouri." "Dern sight better stayed there!"* 1883 LM xviii 219 (OEDS *U.S.* var. of Darn a. 1876, this quot... The adj. use not in W S C)

dern, v. [AB²] *Old Hays...says, "Dern that cat"* 1876 TS vi 67. *"Dern the dern fog"* 1884 HF xix 179 (OEDS *U.S.* var. of Darn v. 1883.. So C Wr M DN.V. Not A in W S)

derned, ppl.a. [AB³] *"Derndest mudcat I ever saw!"* 1883 LM xviii 223. See *spondulicks* 1884. *"He wanted me to challenge that derned Italian savage"* 1894 PW xiii 775 (OEDS *U.S.* var. of Darned. 1873.. So C M. Not A in S. Not in W)

derrick, sb. [?AB³] *I couldn't have got up again... without a derrick* 1889 CY xi 136. *When it [Adam] stands, it spreads itself apart like a derrick* 1905 "Eve's Diary" 26 (OED 2c. 1856.. So W S C U. A in Cl T DN.II)

derringer, sb. [AB³] *The pawnbroker gave us an old derringer with a bullet as big as a hickory nut* 1901 *Speeches* (1910) 142 (OEDS *U.S.* A small pistol with large bore 1854.. So W S C)

desert-frequenting, a. [B¹] *The desert-frequenting tribes of Indians will eat anything they can bite* 1872 RI v 52 (Comb. not in OED W S C)

desert-making, vbl.sb. [B¹] *"These harryings and burnings and desert-makings in the Transvaal"* 1901 "To the Person Sitting in Darkness" 167 (Comb. not in OED W S C)

despairs, sb. [C] *His deep glooms, his despondencies, his despairs* 1906 *Autob* (1924) II 269 (OED 1b. *Rarely* in plural. 1560..1655. *Concrete* sense not in W S C)

despatch, v. [C] *"Despatch, in the name of all the devils!"* 1881 PP xxi 261 (OED 9. To make haste. *obs* or *arch.* 1581..1833. So W S C)

desperadoism, sb. [?AB²] *Desperadoism in the "flush times"* of Nevada 1872 RI xlviii 343 (OED Nonce-wd. 1874, only ex. A in AS.VIII.4.50: Nebraska pioneer English. Not in W S C)

despondencies, sb. [B¹] See *despairs* 1906 (Concrete sense not in OED W S C)

Destroying Angel, sb. [AB³] *We took supper with a Mormon "Destroying Angel." "Destroying Angels," as I understand it, are Latter-Day Saints who are set apart by the Church to conduct permanent disappearances of obnoxious citizens* 1872 RI xii 106 (OEDS =Danite: A member of an alleged secret order of Mormons. 1857.. So W S C F)

detained-baggage, a. [B¹] *These enthusiastic admirers ...hired the tavern's detained-baggage lockup* 1902 "DBDS" (1928) 325 (Comb. not in OED W S C)

deuce, sb. **deuces-and.** [AB¹] See *and* 1899 (A poker hand, for the exact nature of which see the discussion under *and.* Comb. not in OED W S C)

devil-fire, sb. [?AB¹] *"Look! See there!" whispered Tom. "What is it?" "It's devil-fire. Oh, Tom, this is awful"* 1876 TS ix 88 (Will-'o-the-wisp, St. Elmo's fire. Comb. not in OED W S C)

deviltry, sb. [A] *They think it is hatching deviltry* 1869 IA xxxiv 374. *We judged they were studying up some kind of worse deviltry than ever* 1884 HF xxxi 315. See also *witch-business* 1894 (OEDS Corruption of Devilry. *Dial Eng.* and *U.S.* 1788.. So Th H DN.II. Not A in W S C Wr)

devotion-to-passengers'-safety, a. [B¹] *The company owning the vessel would discharge him and make a devotion-*

to-passengers'-safety advertisement out of it. 1897 FE
xxxiii 311 (Nonce comb.)

dew–fashioned, ppl.a. [B¹] *It was good to take in
God's untainted, dew-fashioned air once more* 1889 CY
xix 230 (Comb. not in OED W S C)

dexter, a. [D] See *coat-of-arms* 1883 (OED 1. *Heraldry*. The opposite of *sinister*. The dexter side of... a
shield is to the *left* of the spectator facing it. 1562..
1882—. So W S C U)

dialect–speaking, ppl.a. [B¹] *He would make those
dialect-speaking raftsmen understand him* 1880 TA xviii
164 (Comb. not in OED W S C; but cf. OED Dialect-
speaker, no ex.)

diamond–boom, sb. [AB¹] *The South African diamond-
boom began* 1897 FE lxix 700 (Comb. not in OED
W S C; but cf. OEDS Boom, sb., orig. *U.S.* 1875..)

diamond–breastpin, sb. [?AB¹] See *kid-glove*, a. 1873,
1875 (Comb. not in OED W S C; but cf. Breast-pin,
A in H: Am. breast-pin=Eng. brooch; not A in OED
W S C)

diamond–crater, sb. [B¹] *The most interesting con-
vulsion of nature in South Africa was the diamond-crater*
1897 FE lxix 699 (Comb. not in OED W S C)

diaperer, sb. [B¹] *The Earl of Berkeley...fastened a
napkin about his neck; for the great post of Diaperers to
the Princes of Wales was hereditary in this nobleman's
family* 1881 PP vii 89 (Not in OED W S C. Here
M.T. seems to have invented a mythical office, but he
does not explain its duties in full detail)

dicker, v. [AB³] *Punch pictured me all a-flutter with
rags, dickering with a beef-eater for the Tower of London*
1893 "Banknote" (1928) 119 [OEDS *U.S.* To bargain
in a petty way, to haggle. 1802.. So W S C B F Cl Th
T M DN.III,V)

differ, v.trans. [C] *There was a subtle something about
her beauty that differed it from the human types
of your experience* 1895 JA II xvi 743 (OED 2. To distinguish, differentiate. Now *unusual.* a1400..1867.
Rare in W S C. Dial in Wr)

dig, sb. [?AB³] *"I guess you were about to give me
another dig, anyway"* 1894 PW xi 553 (OED 4b. *fig.*
1840.. So W S C U. A in B Cl Th T DN.II,V.)

Digger, sb. [AB³] *"Digger, Chinaman, Greaser, and
American"* 1865 SS (1926) 161. *The Diggers—those degraded savages who roast their dead relatives, then mix
the human grease and ashes of bones with tar, and "gaum"
it thick all over their heads* 1869 IA xx 205 (OED 2c.
N. Am. Indians. 1837.. So W S C U B F Cl Th)

dight, v. [C] *"It is enchanted and dight in a base
aspect"* 1889 CY xx 243 (OED 10. To clothe, dress,
array. The pa.pple. *dight* is used by Scott, and in later
poetic and romantic language; it appears to be often
taken as an *arch* form of *decked.* c1200.. 1887. So W
S C U)

dig in, v. [AB¹] *"We ain't got no time to bother over
that,"* he says; *"we got to dig in like all git-out"* 1884 HF
xxxviii 386 (A in DN.III: To begin operations vigorously. Not A in W S. This sense not in OED C; but
cf. OEDS 1c. *fig.* To study hard. *U.S.* 1789..)

dig out, v. [AB²] *I was about to dig out from there in a
hurry* 1884 HF xix 180 (OED 13c. To depart, elope.
U.S. colloq. 1884, this quot... So W C F Cl DN.III,
IV,V. Not A in S)

diligence–time, sb. [B¹] *It was diligence-time—the
half-dozen big diligences would soon be arriving from
Geneva* 1880 TA xliii 499 (Comb. not in OED W S C)

dilly–dallying, vbl.sb. [?AB³] See *fool around* 1895
(OED 1879. So W S C U Wr. A in DN.V)

dime, sb. [A] See *cent* 1889; *Jubiter* 1896; *non-
necessity* 1904 (OED 2. A silver coin of the U.S.A.
1786.. So W S C U B F Cl Th T M DN.III,V)

dime–museum, sb. [AB¹] *He scoffed at them as...
dime-museum freaks* 1894 PW xvii 822 (W: An exhibition of curiosities, monstrosities, etc. So C U T. Comb.
not in OED S. Cf. above)

dime–novel, sb. [AB³] *He was a ravenous devourer of
dime novels and sensation-story papers.* 1881 "Curious
Experience" 46 (OEDS 1865.. So W S C U B F Cl
Th. Cf. above)

dim–hearkening, a. [B¹] *"There's something divine
about his art—soulful...dim-hearkening on the void horizon"* 1892 AmCl xvi 169 (Comb. not in OED W S C;
but cf. OED Dim-brooding, 1837)

dim–hoping, a. [B¹] *"If the remains should actually
come, and be put before that poor old dim-hoping soul"*
1892 AmCl ix 93 (Comb. not in OED W S C)

dim–lighted, a. [B²] *Through it a dim-lighted path led
a quarter of a mile* 1897 Autob (1924) I 106 (OED Dim,
a. No ex. So W. Not in S C)

dingblatter, sb. [B¹] See *kahkahponeeka* 1880 (Hum.
invention)

ding–busted, a. [AB¹] *"Well, now, I be ding-busted!"*
1884 HF xiv 123 (A in DN.V. Not in OED W S C; but
cf. Ding, used imprecatively, A in W B F)

dingnation, sb. [AB¹] *"Who in the dingnation's a-
going to pay for it?"* 1884 HF xiii 114 (A in DN.III:
Damnation. Not in OED W S C)

dining–house, sb. [B¹] *All his course is lined with the
prettiest of shops and the most inviting dining-houses*
1880 TA xlvii 549 (Comb. not in OED W S C)

dinner–pail, sb. [AB²] *Bring your dinner-pail with
you* 1891 "At the Shrine of St. Wagner" (1917) 222
(OEDS *U.S.* 1904. So C. Not A in W. Comb. not in S)

dipe, sb. **to go on the dipe.** [AB¹] *"Was thinking i
would have to go on the dipe (picking pockets) again"*
[given as thieves' argot] 1883 LM lii 513 (A in F, this
quot. Not in OED W S C; but cf. OED Dip, sb. 10.
Thieves' slang. A pickpocket; also pocket-picking.
1859..)

dipper, sb. **the Big Dipper.** [AB³] *Constellations that
never associated with the "Big Dipper"* [i.e., Ameri-
cans] *were so tired of* 1869 IA i 19. *The Great Bear remained the Great Bear for thousands of years...But as
soon as it became the property of the United States, Congress changed it to the Big Dipper* 1897 FE v 80 (OEDS
5b. The popular name in the U.S. 1842.. So S C B F
Cl Th T H DN.IV. Not A in W U)

diramic, a. [B¹] *"Them effects is on account of the
superior refragility, as you may say, of the sun's diramic combination"* 1869 IA x 90 (Nonsense coinage)

directly, adv. [?AB¹] *This was a very pretty compliment, and it put us on the pleasantest terms directly—I
use the word in its English sense..."Directly," in the
American language, signifies "after a little while"* 1882
"Concerning the American Language" 268. *Pretty soon
it darkened up, and...directly it begun to rain* 1884 HF
ix 74 (W: Soon, before long. So S C U Wr. A in M.
This sense not in OED)

dirt, sb. [?AB³] *A "prospect" is what one finds in the
first panful of dirt* 1872 RI lxi 443. See also *panning out*
1872; *placer-diggings* 1872; *horn* 1893 (OED 3c. The
alluvial deposit from which gold is separated by washing; =Washdirt. Earliest ex. U.S. 1857.. A in B F
AS.VII.429. Not A in W S C)

dirt–caked, ppl.a. [B¹] *She sat bowed, with her dirt-
caked fingers idly interlocked in her lap* 1889 CY xviii
219 (Comb. not in OED W S C; but cf. OED Dirt-
incrusted, no ex.)

dirt–cheap, a. [?AB³] *Has this government ever heard
of a publisher who would get out a dirt-cheap edition
without being compelled to do it?* 1905 "Concerning
Copyright" 8 (OED 1821.. So W S C U. A in DN.III)

dirt–preferring, a. [B¹] *He was a...dirt-eating and
dirt-preferring slave* 1884 Speeches (1923) 118 (Comb.
not in OED W S C; but cf. OED Dirt-loving, no ex.)

disapparel, v. [C] *Hendon disappareled the boy* 1881
PP xiii 151 (OED *obs.* To undress. 1580..1652. Not
obs in W C. Not in S)

disapplaud, v. [B¹] *The several clauses of his motion
were loudly applauded by these allies, and as loudly dis-*

applauded—if I may invent a word—by such of the Opposition as could hear his voice 1898 "Stirring Times" (1900) 334 (Nonce word)

disaster–breeding, ppl.a. [B¹] *That lying and disaster-breeding verdict* 1869 IA xii 110 (Comb. not in OED W S C)

Disciple, sb. [AB³] See *Adventist* 1907 (OED 3. pl. The name of a denomination of Christians, a branch of the Baptists, which originated in the early part of the 19th c. and is chiefly found in the U.S.; called also Campbellites. OEDS The name Disciples was suggested by Alex. Campbell in 1832. 1835.. So W S C B F)

discover, v. [C] *Becky moved on, without discovering herself* 1876 TS xviii 157 (OED 6. To reveal the identity of. *arch*. 1320..1865. So W U. Not *arch* in S C)

discovery, sb. [AB³] See *claim,* sb. 1869; *arrastre* 1909 (OED 3d. *U.S. Mining.* The first finding of the mineral deposit in place upon a mining claim. 1812.. Not A in W S. This sense not in C)

discovery–fever, sb. [B¹] *Columbus's great achievement gave him the discovery-fever* 1899 "How to Make Hist. Dates Stick" (1917) 164 (Nonce comb.)

discrepantly, adv. [B¹] *"There's such a discrepancy between your age and your looks," he said. "Oh, that's nothing," I said; "I was born discrepantly"* 1906 *Speeches* (1910) 300 (Nonsense use. Cf. OED With discrepancy; in contrary ways. 1603, only ex. So W S U)

discretion, v. [B¹] *If your Majesty should equip young Bright with discretion, it is an even guess that he would discretion you out of house and home in two or three years* 1893 "Petition to the Queen" (1928) 363 (Nonce use)

discriminate, v. [B²] *I did not propose to be discriminated against on account of my nationality* 1880 TA ii 153. *"Is he gwine to 'scriminate 'twixt 'em?"* 1893 TSA iii 118 (OED 3b. To make an adverse distinction with regard to. 1880, this quot... So W S U. This sense not in C)

discussion–mortar, sb. [B¹] *He slipped from the presence, to keep from getting brayed in his wife's discussion-mortar* 1904 "Bequest" (1906) 17 (Nonce comb.)

disease–breeder, sb. [B¹] *The water in the gutters used to be stagnant and slimy, and a potent disease-breeder* 1883 LM xli 427 (Comb. not in OED W S C)

diseased, ppl.a. [AB¹] *Pretty soon all hands got to talking about the diseased, and how good he was, and what a loss he was* 1884 HF xxv 254. *They told how they had heard Uncle Silas threaten the diseased, at one time and another* 1896 TSD x 528 (AS.VI.272: used for *deceased* in Ky. Dial. in Wr. This use not in OED W S C)

disenjoy, v. [B¹] *It was a poor and mean distinction, and I early learned to disenjoy it* 1906 *Autob* (1924) II 257 (Not in OED. Given in W S C)

disgruntled, ppl.a. [AB³] *The tanner was a disgruntled man* 1899 "MCH" (1900) 37 (OED Now chiefly *U.S.* 1847.. So Wr B F Cl Th,1682 T. Not A in W S C U)

dished, ppl.a. [?A] *Look at the waxwork head—the projecting ears—the knotted elbows—the dished breast—the knife-edged shins* 1905 "Czar's Soliloquy" 321 (OED b. Shaped like a dish. 1737..1816. So W S C Wr. Cf. Dished face, A in Th.III 1901: One that is concave in profile; Dish-faced, A in DN.III AS.V.129)

dish–rag, sb. [AB²] *It really pretended to be tea, but there was too much dish-rag and sand in it* 1872 RI iv 44. *"We used to have a calf that et apples and just chawed up dishrags like nothing"* 1873 GA vii 81 (OEDS *U.S.* a. A dish-cloth. 1873, this quot. Not A in W S C)

disinvite, v. [?C] See *punch,* v. 1889 (OED To retract an invitation. *obs.* 1580..1665. So C. Not *obs* in W S. More likely, as M.T. uses it, to be a fresh coinage than a survival)

disorbit, v. [B¹] *We should have struck them as world strikes world when disorbited constellations crash into the Milky Way* 1896 JA II xvi 438 (Not in OED W S C)

display–head, sb. [B¹] *The biggest line in the display-head announces his own death!* 1892 AmCl vii 76 (Comb. not in OED W S C; but cf. OED Display-letter, -type, work, all 1888)

display–heading, sb. [B¹] *According to the display heading—"Rich Woman Fell Down Cellar"* 1907 "Chaps. from Autob" 4 (Comb. not in OED W S C. Cf. above)

display–sheet, sb. [B¹] See *bulletin–board* 1873 (Comb. not in OED W S C. Cf. above.

disremember, v. [?AB³] *"I disremember her name"* 1884 HF xiii 114 (OEDS Earlier U.S. exs. 1815.. A in Wr B F Cl Th DN.I,II,III,IV,V AS.II.486, V.425, Ozarks. Not A in W S C T)

dissentering, ppl.a. [?AB¹] *Blamed if he didn't inquire...about Peter's business, and about Harvey's, which was a dissentering minister* 1884 HF xxiv 241 (Not in OED W S C; but cf. OED Dissenterish, 1841. Mencken says rashly (p. 249): "The American language, of course, knows nothing of *nonconformists* or *dissenters.*")

dissenwhich, v. [B¹] *"He tuck 'n' dissenhurrit him"* ..."*Dissenwhiched him?*" 1894 PW viii 338 (Hum. nonce coinage)

distraught, ppl.a. [?C] *She was so distraught and silent* 1892 AmCl xx 205 (OED *arch* 1. Mentally distracted. 1393..1877. Not *arch* in W S C U Wr)

distressed, adv. [AB¹] *Making them pens was a distressed tough job* 1884 HF xxxviii 385 (Extremely, plaguedly. A in B F. This use not in OED W S C)

distributing–house, sb. [B¹] *Venice was...the distributing-house from whence the enormous trade of the Orient was spread* 1869 IA xxii 217 (Comb. not in OED W S C)

district attorney, sb. [AB³] *The district attorney opened the case for the state* 1873 GA liv 493 (OEDS District, sb. 6. *U.S.* 1856.. So W. Not A in S C. Cf. H: Am. district attorney = Eng. public prosecutor)

District of Columbia, sb. [A] *Head of the order in the District of Columbia* 1892 AmCl xx 206 (OEDS *U.S.* 1792.. So W S C)

dive, v. Past tense **dove.** [AE] *"We all went overboard and dove under the wheel"* 1884 HF xx 191 (OED This form 19th c. *U.S.* and Eng. *dial.* So W Wr B F Cl Th,1806 M H DN.II,III AS.III.3, Ozarks. Not A in S C T)

divide, sb. [AB³] *We were to meet at dawn on the "divide" overlooking Mono Lake* 1872 RI xxxvii 261. See also *town-site* 1873; *gulch* 1905 (OED 2. *U.S.* and *Colonies.* A watershed. 1807.. So C U B F Cl Th T M H DN.VI. Not A in W S)

dividend–cooking, ppl.a. [?AB¹] *My scathing satire upon the dividend-cooking system* 1879 SNO (1875) 244 (Comb. not in OED W S C. Cf. cooked, above)

Divine Science, sb. [B¹] *By command left in her Will, the term "Christian Science" was changed to "Divine Science" as soon as her Church's universal dominion in the earth was secure* 1903 "Chr.Sc." 180 (S: In Christian Science, the spiritual faith of those who acknowledge God's supreme power on earth as in heaven. W: A branch of the New Thought movement. Term not in OED C)

divinity–circuit, a. [B¹] *We have Mrs. Eddy's "Miscellaneous Writings," at noble big prices, the divinity-circuit style heading the extortions* 1903 "Chr.Sc."2 (W: Style of binding used esp. on Bibles, in which the flexible leather cover bends over so as to protect the edges of the leaves. Comb. not in OED S C; but cf. OED Divinity-calf, 1895)

division, sb. [AB³] *A certain division superintendent of the Consolidated road* 1893 "Travelling with a Reformer" (1900) 361 (OEDS 10g. A section of a railway line. *U.S.* 1887.. So W H. This sense not in S C)

divvy, v. [?AB³] *"That's it! Divvy! divvy! Be kind to the poor"* 1899 "MCH" (1900) 51 (OEDS *colloq.* To go shares. Earlier U.S. exs. 1881.. A in Wr Th M DN.IV AS.IV.339. Not A in W S C)

do, v. [?AB³] *Nothing would do Tom but he must crawl to where Jim was, on his hands and knees, and play something on him* 1884 HF ii 10 (OEDS 20b. To do for, suffice, satisfy. *trans. colloq.* 1846.. So W S C U Wr. A in B F Th T)

do, v. don't=does not. [?AE] *Sometimes the patient gets well, but as a general thing he don't* 1869 IA ix 84. *"She talks awful, but talk don't hurt, anyways it don't if she don't cry"* 1876 TS ii 27 *His loose grammar was the fruit of careless habit, not ignorance...I heard a Westerner, who would be accounted a highly educated man in any country, say, "Never mind, it don't make no difference, anyway." A life-long resident who was present heard it, but it made no impression upon her* 1883 LM xxvi 289. *They* [Southerners] *haven't any "doesn't" in their language; they say "don't" instead* 1883 LM xxvi 449 (OED A. 2c. 1741, 1831. OEDS Am. exs. 1670.. 1862. A in M. Not A in W S C)

do, v. pa.t. done. [AB³E] *"I think it done him good"* 1873 GA xxxiii 307 (OEDS A. 3d. *dial* and *U.S.* 1847.. So B F M DN.I,II,III. Wr: *dial.* This form not in W S C)

do, v. to be done with. [A] *I am done with official life for the present* 1872 SNO (1875) 269. *We are done with poverty* 1873 GA xlv 415 (OED 8b. Chiefly *Irish, Scotch, U.S., dial.* 1766.. A in Th. The idiom is not given in W S C)

do, v. that will do. [?A] *"That will do, sir—that will do"* 1870 SNO (1875) 104 (OED 20. That is sufficient. 1596.. So W S C U. A in F Th,1846)

dob, v. [AB¹] *"Dob his address and general destination onto it with a blacking brush"* 1871 SNO (1875) 247. *"He jes' shuck his head, dat painter did, en went on a-dobbin'"* 1893 TSA iii 118 (Variant of Daub, v., A in F DN.III. Not in OED W S C. A dif. word from OED Dob, v., var. of Dab, v. To set or put down with a sharp, abrupt motion. 1821.. So W Wr)

doby, sb. [AB³] *Old romantic doby castle of a fort on top of steep grass dome* 1866 *Notebook* (1935) 39. See also *adobe* 1872 (OEDS *U.S. colloq* shortening of Adobe. 1857.. So W S C DN.V)

docket, sb. on the docket. [A] *"What's the next thing on the docket?"* 1892 AmCl xix 197 (OED 5. *Law. U.S.* 1790.. So W Th T M H DN.VI. Not A in S C)

doctor, sb. [AB¹] *The engineer drowsed around and allowed chips to get into the "doctor" and shut off the water supply from the boilers* 1875 OTM 191 (W: An independent steam pump with a working beam, used on Western river steamers. *U.S.* Not A in S C. This sense not in OED)

doctor, v.intr. [?AB²] *We lay idle in Frankfort 4 days, doctoring* 1892 *Letters* (1917) II xxxii 568 (OED 4b. No ex. So S. *Colloq* in W C. A in AS.II.352, V.17, 122, W.Va., Ozarks, Me.)

doctor-book, sb. [B¹] *"There'll be a new disease in the doctor-books"* 1902 "DBDS" (1928) 356 (Comb. not in OED W S C)

dod-dern, v. [AB¹] *He ejaculated: "Well, I'll be dod-derned!"..."Dod dern" was the nearest he ventured to the luxury of swearing* 1883 LM xviii 220 (A in DN.II, III. Comb. not in OED W S C; but cf. OEDS Dod-, used as intensive with verbs and pa.pples. *U.S. vulgar.* 1859.. So Wr F)

dodge, sb. [?AB³] *The removal of the capital is one of those old, regular, reliable dodges that are the bread and meat of back country congressmen* 1869 *Letters* (1917) I ix 161. *"How you did fool 'em, Huck! Dat wuz de smartes' dodge!"* 1884 HF xvi 142. See also *boss* 1884 (OED 3. *colloq.* and *slang.* A clever or adroit expedient. 1842.. So W S C U)

doff, v. [C] *"Doff thy rags, and don these splendors, lad!"* 1881 PP iii 44 (In ordinary *colloq* use in north of England; elsewhere, since 16th c., a lit. word with an arch flavor. 1350..1859. So Wr. Not *arch* in W S C U)

dog, v. [AB³] *"Tain't a dream! Somehow I most wish it was. Dog'd if I don't, Huck!"* 1876 TS xxvii 209. *He said...dog'd if he wanted to risk his neck* 1880 TA xxvi 268. *"Say, who is you? Whar is you? Dog my cats if I didn' hear sumf'n"* 1884 HF ii 12. *"Dog my cats if it ain't all I kin do to tell t'other fum which"* 1893 PW iii 239 (OED 8. *U.S. slang.* Used in imprecations. 1860.. So B F DN.III,IV,V AS.VII.28. Not in W S C)

dog-fennel, sb. [?A] *Your dog-fennel is such a tasteful ornament to any yard* 1856 Letter in *Iowa Journal of Hist.* (1929) 424 (OED A name for Stinking Camomile, *Anthemis cotula:* so called from its bad smell. 1523.. So W S C Wr. OEDS U.S. exs. 1873)

dog-fight, sb. [B²] *They* [German newspapers] *contain...no information about prize-fights or other dog-fights* 1880 TA App. F 626. *She's got a perfectly immense reputation—draws like a dog-fight* 1892 AmCl ix 84 (OEDS 2. transf. A general shindy or mêlée. 1913.. So W. This sense not in S C)

dog-fightless, a. [B¹] *They were good listeners...in a dog-fightless interval* 1889 CY ii 38 (Nonce comb.)

doggery, sb. [AB³] See *bullyrag* 1884 (OEDS *U.S. vulgar.* A low drinking saloon. 1835.. So W S C B F Cl Th T M DN.II.30)

doggoned, a. [AB³] *"He'd be doggoned if he ever expected to see that railroad any mo'"* 1873 GA xvii 167 (OED c. *U.S. slang* 'Confounded.' 1860. So W S C B F Cl Th M DN.I,II,III,IV,V *Nation* LIV.303. Cf. Wr Dog on it: a mild oath)

dog-hair, sb. [B¹] *I have never seen any cigars that I really could not smoke, except those that cost a dollar apiece. I have examined those and know that they are made of dog-hair* 1893 "Concerning Tobacco" (1917) 278 (Comb. not in OED W S C)

dog in a blanket, sb. [B³] *Stewed prunes for dessert—on Sundays "dog in a blanket"* 1893 "About All Kinds of Ships" 156 (OED 18. A rolled currant dumpling or jam-pudding. *colloq.* 1867. So Wr. Not in W S C)

dog-iron, sb. [AB³] *They had big brass dog-irons that could hold up a saw-log* 1884 HF xvii 153 (OED Andiron. 1883. So W S Wr. A in F DN.IV,V, in s.w.Mo., Va., Newfoundland. Not in C)

dog-leg, sb. [AB³] *"I had my pipe en a plug er dog-leg en some matches"* 1884 HF viii 69 (OEDS 2. Applied to an inferior quality of tobacco. *U.S.* 1863.. So Th.III. This sense not in W S C)

doglet, sb. [B¹] *A dog stood drinking at a pump—The way he made that doglet jump!* 1891 *Slovenly Peter* (1935) 4 (Not in OED W S C; but cf. OED Dogling, 1830)

dogmatic, a. [B¹] *She was able to keep it until there was a dogmatic gathering in the neighborhood, then she would ...surprise them all, from pocket-pup to mastiff* 1903 "Dog's Tale" 11 (Hum. nonce use)

dog-pelter, sb. [AB¹] *We have never been able to choose a dog-pelter without celebrating the event with a dozen knock-downs* 1864 SNO (1875) 163 (DN.II: An imaginary official; used as a term of contempt in s.e.Mo., s.Ill. Comb. not in OED W S C)

dole, sb. [C] *"Maledictions light upon him, misfortune be his dole!"* 1889 CY iii 46 (OED 4. Portion or lot in life. *arch.*1500..1838. So S C U Wr. Not *arch* in W)

dollar, sb. [A] *"A hundred dollars an acre!"* 1873 GA i 24. See *cent* 1889. *A piece of biscuit the size of a silver dollar* 1899 "My Debut" (1900) 89 (OED 3. The standard unit of the gold and silver coinage of the United States. 1782.. So W S C U B F Cl M DN.II)

doll-clothes, sb. [B¹] See *bric-a-brac* 1880 (Comb. not in OED W S C)

doll-face, sb. [B²] *The doll-faces of other painted babes* 1880 TA l 579 (OED 1884, only ex. So W. Comb. not in S C)

dolphin, sb. [C] *I told him about Louis sixteenth... and about his little boy the dolphin* 1884 HF xiv 122 (OED 8. Dauphin. This form *rare* after 1670. 1494..

1708. So C. Not in W S. M.T. 's acquaintance with this old form perhaps came from Shakespeare's use of it in 1 Hen.VI, I.i.92)

domestic, sb. [AB³] *The mansion is* 10 x 12, *with a "domestic" roof...*"*Domestic*" *is not water-proof* 1862 *Letters* (1917) I iii 85. *They had white domestic awnings in front* 1884 HF xxi 209 (OED 4. esp. in U. S. Home-made cotton cloths, bleached or unbleached, for common use. 1846..So W S C B F Cl Th,1840 H DN.II,III)

dominie, sb. [?AC] *The master always prepared himself for great occasions by getting pretty well fuddled...The dominie had reached the proper condition on Examination Evening* 1876 TS xxi 168 (OED 1. A schoolmaster, a pedagogue. Now chiefly *Sc.* 1612...1870. So W S C Wr)

dominie, sb. [AB³] *Judge and counsel* [in a trial in Kentucky] *called Deacons Burke and Johnson, and Dominies Wirt and Miggles, to testify* 1870 SNO (1875) 160 (OED 2. In U.S., the title of a pastor of the Dutch Reformed Church...whence in New York, New Jersey, etc., extended colloquially to ministers or parsons of other churches. Commonly pronounced, after the Dutch, with a long o. 1824.. So W C F Th M DN.IV: in general use in the Catskills. Not A in S)

don, v. [C] See *doff*, v. 1881 (OED *arch.* 1. 1567.. 1879. Not *arch* in W S C U Wr)

donjon-keep, sb. [B³CE] See *culverin* 1880. "*Prisoners don't have geese running around the donjon-keep*" 1884 HF xxxv 360 (OED Donjon, *arch* sp. of Dungeon. This comb. under Dungeon, sb. 1b. 1808.. Not *arch* in W S. Not in C)

donkey-voiced, ppl. a. [B¹] *When you wish to raise a fine donkey--voiced Shanghai rooster, you do it with a lasso* 1870 SNO (1875) 83 (Comb. not in OED W S C)

doodle-bug, sb. [AB²] "*Doodle-bug, doodle-bug, tell me what I want to know*" 1876 TS vii 82 (OEDS *U.S.* A tiger-beetle. 1876, this quot..So W S C B F Cl Th.III T DN.I,III,IV AS.II.352)

door, sb. **to have in the door.** [?AB¹] *He'd see in a minute how he'd been imposed on, and how the other dog had him in the door, so to speak* 1865 "*Jumping Frog*" (1875) 52 (To have at a disadvantage, in a tight place. Phr. not in OED W S C)

dorian, sb. [E] See *durian*.

dornick, sb. [AB³] *I have found him breaking a stone in two, and labelling half of it "Chunk busted from the pulpit of Demosthenes", and the other half "Dornick from the Tomb of Abelard and Heloise"* 1869 IA xxxv 385 (OEDS *U.S.* A pebble, stone, or small boulder, 1840.. So W S C B F Cl Th T DN.II,III,V AS.II.353)

dose, sb. [?AB¹] *I met my match and I got my dose* 1889 CY Intro. 19 (S: Anything disagreeable given as a prescription or an infliction. So C U. This sense not in OED W)

dot, sb. **to a dot.** [AB³] *His epithet described that boy to a dot* 1880 TA xxviii 287."*That's Lord Berkeley to a dot*" 1892 AmCl xxi 213 (OEDS 4b. Exactly, precisely. *U.S.* 1854.. Th.III DN.VI. Not A in W S Wr. Phr. not in C)

double-barreled; ppl.a. [?A] *He possessed a single-barreled fame before; he will possess a double-barreled fame now* 1880 *Speeches* (1923) 83. *A Double-Barreled Detective Story* (title) 1902 "DBDS" (1928) 285. See also *flint-lock* 1904 (OEDS 2. *fig.* Having a double reference. Earlier U.S. ex 1777.. A in Th. Not A in W S C U)

double bed, sb. [?AB²] "*We got a room upstairs with a cot and a double bed in it*" 1896 TSD iv 352 (OEDS 1925.. So W U. Comb. not in S C)

double-butt-ender, sb. [B¹] *Give me the name of the cigars you brought here with you the other day...The box that came are the old-fashioned double-butt-enders* 1900 *M.T. the Letter Writer* (1932) vi 84 (Nonce comb.)

double-columned, ppl.a. [B¹] *His past utterances will be double-columned with his present ones* 1884

Speeches (1923) 120. *Here are samples from recent articles from her unappeasable pen; double-columned with them are a couple of passages from the Annex* 1899 "Chr.Sc. and the Book" 592 (Placed in parallel columns for purposes of comparison. Comb. not in OED W S C)

double-gauge, sb. [B¹] *It is a narrow-gauge road to the frontier and a broader gauge thence to Melbourne... All passengers fret at the double-gauge* 1897 FE xiv 153 (Comb. not in OED W S C)

Double-Man, sb. [B¹] *The Double-Man.....was paired together to the end that while one part slept the other might watch* 1875 SNO 174 (Nonce comb. for Siamese twins. Cf. OED Double- 2. 1691)

Double-Man-bird, sb. [B¹] *Near the Double Man-bird was found an ancient record* 1875 SNO 174 (Nonce comb. Cf. above)

double-starred, ppl.a. [B¹] *It is double-starred in Baedeker* 1880 TA xxii 211 (Comb. not in OED W S C)

doublet, sb. [C] "*They were dressed in...doublets of murrey and blue cloth*" 1881 PP ix 105 (OED 1. A close-fitting body-garment worn by men from the 14th to the 18th c. *Obs* exc. *Hist.* 1326..1835. So W U Wr. Not *obs* in S C)

double-team, v. [AB²] "*Old man*," *said the young one*, "*I reckon we might double-team it together; what do you think?*" "*I ain't undisposed.*" 1884 HF xix 183 (OEDS *U.S.* b. With *it:* To act in combination. 1884, this quot. So Th.III,1865 M. Comb. not in W S C)

doubt, v. [C] "*Knowst' thou the Latin?*" "*But scantily, sir, I doubt*" 1881 PP iii 42 (OED 5b. To fear. *arch* and *dial.* 1300..1820. *Obs* in W. Not *arch* or *obs* in S C)

doubtless, sb. [B¹] *We set down the five known facts* [about Shakespeare] *by themselves; then we set down the "conjectures" and "suppositions" and "maybes" and "perhapses" and "doubtlesses"* 1909 ISD ii 23 (Nonce use)

doughface, sb. [AB³] *Those giddy young ladies came tiptoeing into the room where she sat reading at midnight by a lamp. The girl at the head of the file wore a shroud and a doughface; she crept behind the victim, touched her on the shoulder, and she looked up and screamed, and then fell into convulsions* 1883 LM liii 528 (OEDS 1. *U.S.* A mask made of dough. 1809.. So M DN.III. Not in W S C)

doughnut, sb. [AB³] "*Next minute you'd see that frog whirling in the air like a doughnut*" [In the French translation "doughnut" is "un beignet;" in the retranslation it becomes "grease-biscuit"] 1865 "*Jumping Frog*" (1875) 33. *And while she closed with a happy Scriptural flourish, he "hooked" a doughnut* 1876 TS iii 34. See also *gum-drop* 1889; *anti* 1901 (OED Local Eng. and U.S. 1809.. So B F Cl Th H DN.I,III AS.I.150,II.109,XII.102. Not A in W S C U Wr T)

Dowie, sb. [AB¹] See *Adventist* 1907 (W: Name applied to the Christian Catholic Church, q.v. So S C. Not in OED)

down, a. [?A] "*Things have been getting worse and worse...I don't go out of the house, I feel so down*" 1873 GA vi 65. See also *away* 1892 (OED 18. Downcast or depressed. *colloq.* 1610..1865. So W S C. A in DN.III)

down, a. **to be down on.** [?AB¹] "*I was down on sich doin's*" 1874 SNO (1875) 205. "*If there's one thing an alligator is more down on than another, it's being dredged*" 1883 LM xxiv 268 (To be opposed or averse to; to dislike. Cf. W: To dislike and treat harshly. *colloq.* So C. Not *colloq* in S. A in B F Cl. This sense not in OED; cf. OED 27a. To be aware of, to be 'up to.' *slang.* 1793.. Also OED 27b. To fall upon, attack. 1815..)

down, adv. **down to date.** [?AB²] "*I've got part of him down to date, anyway*" 1892 AmCl xxi 211. *He was down to date with them, too* 1897 FE xxv 244 (OEDS 15. Formed after *up to date.* 1897, this quot... So W S C)

down, prep. **down cellar**. [AB³] *I know how a frozen apple looks, in a barrel down cellar in the winter-time* 1897 *Autob* (1924) I 112 (OEDS 1c. In the cellar or basement. *U.S.* 1855.. So B F Cl. Not A in W S. Phr. not in C)

down, prep. **down the river**. [AB¹] *Percy Driscoll slept well the night he saved his house-minions from going down the river* 1893 PW iii 238. *If the threat to sell an incorrigible slave "down the river" would not reform him, nothing would—his case was past cure* 1898 *Autob* (1924) I 124 (Into slavery on the Lower Mississippi, considered harsher and more dreaded. Phr. not in OED W S C)

down, v. **to down with**. [?A] *"Blamed if he didn't down with another right bower!"* 1877 *Speeches* (1910) 5 (OED 4. To put or throw down. 1599.. So W Wr. A in DN.IV. This use not in S C)

down grade, sb. [?AB²] *A "down grade," a flying coach* 1872 RI xvii 141 (OEDS Earlier U.S. exs. 1876.. Not A in W S C U)

down-stream, adv. [?AB³] See *upstreaming* 1875. *You can't back a raft up-stream, you can't hurry it down-stream* 1880 TA xvii 152. *There was Jackson's island about two mile and a half down-stream* 1884 HF vii 55 (OED 1864. So W S C. Here *spec* of the Mississippi)

down-town, sb. [AB³] *The coachman arrived from down-town* 1875 SNO 88. *He said he was going down-town* 1884 HF vi 40. See also *bus* 1899 (OEDS The lower or business part of town. *U.S.* 1851.. So F Cl Th M AS.I.491. Not A in W S. Not in C)

doxology-works, sb. [?AB¹] *"You are the head clerk of the doxology-works next door?"* 1872 RI xlvii 332 (Church. Comb. not in OED W S C)

doxy, sb. [C] See *budge* 1881 (OED *Vagabond's Cant*. Orig. the term for the unmarried mistress of a beggar or rogue. 1530..1857. So W S C U Wr)

dragoon–revolver, sb. [B¹] *The colonel appeared... with a dragoon-revolver in his hand* 1869 SNO (1875) 46 (Comb. not in OED W S C)

drainage–basin, sb. [B²] *No other river has so vast a drainage-basin* 1883 LM i 22 (OEDS 1885, only ex. So W S C U)

dramatic editor, sb. [B¹] *Willie Winter...dramatic editor of the "New York Tribune"* 1907 "Chaps from Autob" 486 (Comb. not in OED W S C)

drat, int. [?AB³] *Drat my buttons if I wasn't astonished* 1856 *Adv. of T. J. Snodgrass* (1928) 26. *Drat the thing, I wish it were done* 1868 *Letters* (1917) I viii 151 (OED A vulgar form of imprecation. 1815.. So W S C U Wr T. A in B F DN.V; but cf. Cl: A peculiarly British form of objurgation)

draw, sb. [AB²] *An innocent little parlor game, commonly called "draw"* 1859 Letter in *New Orleans Daily Crescent*, May 8 (OEDS 1c. Short for *draw-poker*, *U.S. colloq.* 1876.. So Cl. Not A in W S. This sense not in C)

draw, sb. [?AB¹] *"I bleeve I could smoke this pipe all day, but he'd keel over just with two draws on a pipe"* 1876 TS xvi 138 (Wr: A puff at a pipe. *Scotch*. This sense not in OED W S C)

draw, v. [?AB³] *"I certainly held threes...but I drew and didn't fill. That's where I'm so often weak in the game"* 1904 "Bequest" (1906) iii 14 (To take cards from the dealer in place of cards discarded. OED 32. *absol. (Cards)*. 1870.. A in B Cl as a poker term. The *absol.* use not in W S C)

draw, v. [B¹] *The mesmerizer...began to "draw" me with the disk* 1907 "Chaps. from Autob" 6 (This use, of mesmeric attraction, not in OED W S C)

drawly, adv. [?AB¹] *They talked lazy and drawly* HF xxi 209 (The adv. use not in OED W S C; but cf. OED Drawly, a. *Scotch*. Characterized by drawling. 1825.. So W. Cf. also *long talk*, below)

drawn butter, sb. [?AB¹] See *slosh*, v. 1880 (W: Butter melted and, usually, mixed with flour and hot water for use as a sauce. So C. Not in OED S)

draw off, v. [?AB¹] *Next morning he got some big sheets of wrapping paper and some black paint, and drawed off some handbills* 1884 HF xxii 225 (This sense not in OED W S C)

draw out, v.intr. [?AB¹] *"I was just about to go and vote...but when they told me there was a state in this country where they'd let that nigger vote, I drawed out"* 1884 HF vi 43 (To withdraw. Cf. C: To move out or away. A in Th.III,1894. This intr. sense not in OED W S)

dray–horse, v. [B¹] *"You have been dray-horsing over the same tiresome ground for a year"* 1896 *Letters* (1917) II xxxv 637 (Verb-use not in OED W S C)

dray–pin, sb. [B¹] *In these strangely magnifying waters, one may count the scales on a trout (a trout of the large kind) at a depth of a hundred and eighty feet... might even count a paper of dray-pins* 1869 IA xx 204 (Comb. not in OED W S C. Presumably a linchpin for the axletree of a dray—or an ordinary pin magnified to the same size)

dreadful, adv. [?A] *"You are dreadful wet"* 1894 TET i 322 (OED. Now *vulgar*. 1682..1870. So W Wr. A in B F Cl T DN.III,V. Not in S C)

dream-failure, sb. [B¹] *The measure of the magnitude of a dream-failure is the measure of the disappointment* 1900 "My Boyhood Dreams" 255 (Comb. not in OED W S C)

dream-haze, sb. [B¹] *Over it all a mellow dream-haze of history* 1897 FE xxix 282 (Comb. not in OED W S C)

dream-life, sb. [B²] *Aleck, in her dream-life, went over to the Episcopal camp* 1904 "Bequest" (1906) 34 (OED Dream, sb. 4b. No ex. So W. Not in S C)

dream-people, sb. [B¹] *His dream-people were so fine* 1881 PP ii 30 (Comb. not in OED W S C)

dream-picture, sb. [B¹] *The play gave me the sense of the passage of a dimly connected procession of dream-pictures* 1898 "About Play Acting" (1900) 214 (Comb. not in OED W S C; but cf. OED Dream-image, no ex.)

dream-stuff, sb. [B¹] *The Egyptian, the Babylonian, and the Persian rose, filled the planet with sound and splendor, then faded to dream-stuff and passed away* 1899 "Concerning the Jews" (1900) 281 (Comb. not in OED W S C)

dream-thought, sb. [B¹] *You can't originate a dream-thought for it to work out* 1906 "WIM" (1917) 67 (Comb. not in OED W S C)

dreamy, v. [B¹] *The more you hear about a...noble thing or person, the more it kind of dreamies out, as you may say, and gets to be a big dim wavery figger* 1894 TSA xii 539 (Nonce use)

dream-yacht, sb. [B¹] *They were sailing the summer seas in their dream-yacht* 1904 "Bequest" (1906) 38 (Comb. not in OED W S C)

dreamy–eyed, a. [B²] *The other person is his only son and heir, a dreamy-eyed young fellow* 1892 AmCl i 17 (Given in OED W, no ex. Comb. not in S C)

drearinesses, sb. [B¹] See *attitudinizing* 1873 (This concrete sense not in OED W S C)

drench, sb. [?AB¹] *Eating it hot, along with some sugar and a drench of cream* 1897 *Autob* (1924) I 112 (A portion sufficient to cover. This use, of food, not in OED W S C)

dress–change, sb. [B¹] *The dress-changes of Oxford for twelve centuries stood revealed to the eye* 1907 "Chaps. from Autob" 171 (Comb. not in OED W S C)

dressed–stone, sb. [?AB¹] *He murdered them "in his splendid dressed-stone mansion"* 1870 SNO (1875) 244 (Comb. not in OED W S C; but cf. Dressed, ppl.a., A in Th.III,1526: Made ready for market or for immediate use)

dressing–bureau, sb. [?AB¹] *He noticed a bottle on his uncle's dressing-bureau* 1906 *Autob* (1924) I 342 (Comb. not in OED W S C; but cf. Bureau, above)

dress-pattern, sb. [AB¹] *He thought of buying three or four dress-patterns for presents* 1869 IA xiii 121 (Comb. not in OED W S C; but cf. OED Pattern, sb. 10. A sufficient quantity of material for making a dress; a dress-length, *U.S.* 1847. So W)

dress-reform, sb. [?AB²] *Another advantage achieved by the dress reform period* 1883 LM xxv 276 (OEDS A movement to make dress more practical. U.S. exs. 1889. Comb. not in W S C)

dried–apple–pie, sb. [?AB¹] *It seems curious that dried-apple-pie should have seemed such a great thing* 1906 "Helpless Situation" 116 (Comb. not in OED W S C. Cf. pie, below)

drift, sb. [?C] *At last, in the drift of time, Hadleyburg had the ill luck to offend a passing stranger* 1899 "MCH" (1900) 2 (OED 3. *fig.* Natural or unconscious course, progress, process (of action, argument, †time, etc.). 1575, only ex. of time. This use not in W S C)

drift, sb. [?C] *Tom watched with interest emphasized by anxiety. Too late he divined her "drift." The handle of the telltale teaspoon was visible under the bed-valance* 1876 TS xii 111 (OED 4. What one is 'driving at;' purpose, intention. Now *rare*, exc. in reference to speech or writing. 1526..1855. So W. Not *rare* in S C U)

drift, v. [AB²] *A week drifted by* 1873 GA ix 97. *A procession of villagers filed through Judge Thatcher's house...tried to speak but couldn't—and drifted out* 1876 TS xxxii 248. See *accommodations* 1880. *He got up and went drifting about* 1892 AmCl xviii 191. *A long wavering line of torches drifting down the main street* 1894 PW xi 556 (OEDS 1c. To move or pass passively or aimlessly. orig. *U.S.* 1884.. Not A in W S C U. A favorite word with M.T., probably because it is a *Naut.* metaphor)

drift-canoe, sb. [?AB¹] *It was a drift-canoe sure enough* 1884 HF vii 48 (Comb. not in OED W S C. Cf. drift-wood, below)

drift-log, sb. [?AB¹] *Drift-logs that went slipping along, black and still, hundreds of yards out from shore* 1884 HF vii 53 (Comb. not in OED W S C. Cf. drift-wood, below)

drift-wood, sb. [A] *The river was coming up pretty fast, and lots of driftwood going by on the rise* 1884 HF vii 50 (OEDS esp. wood carried down by a river. *U.S.* 1785.. Not A in W S C)

drinking–water, sb. [B²] *They used that tank to draw drinking-water from* 1869 IA xliv 459 (OEDS 1888, only ex. So W U. Comb. not in S C)

drink up, v. [?AB¹] *I ain't got no money, because it's likely pap's been back before now, and got it all away from Judge Thatcher and drunk it up* 1884 HF xliii 437 (To consume completely in drinking. The comb. *drink up* in this sense not in OED W S C; but cf. OED Drink, v. 8. To consume or spend in drinking, 1492.. 1765)

drippings, vbl.sb. [B¹] *We all love to get some of the drippings of Conspicuousness* 1902 "Does the Race Love a Lord?" 441 (This *fig* sense not in OED W S C)

drive, sb. [?AB¹] *She was making the honest best drive at it she could, and no fault of hers that she couldn't fetch the home plate* 1889 CY xxii 278 (A long hit in baseball; here *fig* for a strenuous effort, attempt, 'try.' This sense not in OED W S C; but cf. OED Drive, v. 8c. *Baseball.* To throw or hit a ball very swiftly. 1857..)

drive, v. [?AB³] *Harry told the Colonel that they must drive the thing through* 1873 GA xl 359 (OED 25b. *fig.* To work hard, 'go at' strenuously. *colloq.* Earliest ex. U.S. 1835.. Not A in W S C)

drive, v. to drive the center. [?AB¹] See *center* 1869, 1892. (To hit the bull's eye or center of the target. Phr. not in OED W S C. Cf. B: Driving the nail: A favorite amusement amongst cowboys. A stout nail is driven into a post about half-way up to the head; the riflemen fire at the nail, the object being to drive it home)

driveway, sb. [AB³] *The walks and driveways of the cemetery* 1883 LM xlii 431 (OEDS Chiefly *U.S.* A carriage drive. 1838.. So B F Cl Th T H. Not A in W S C)

drool, v. [AB³] *How would you like to have John Camden Hotten...drool two or three chapters on to the end of that book?* 1872 "To the Editor of *The Spectator*" (1911) 115 (OED *dial* and *U.S.* = Drivel, in var. senses. 1847.. So W S C Wr Th DN.II,V)

drop, sb. get the drop on. [AB³] *Only question was, which of them got the drop on the other* 1883 LM xxvi 286. *If he got the drop on me, I could name the corpse* 1889 CY xxxix 504 (OED 14. orig. *U.S.* OEDS 1869.. So W C F Cl Th T M H DN.IV. Not A in S)

drop, v. drop it. [?AB³] *"Drop it, boy, 'tis not wise, nor well"* 1881 PP xvii 217 (OED 25. *colloq* or *slang.* Have done! leave off! 1872.. So W S C)

drop on to, v. [?AB²] *"How did you happen to drop on to that idea in this curious fashion?"* 1892 AmCl xviii 182 (OEDS 9b. To come casually to knowledge of something. *colloq.* 1901. So W Wr. Not in S C)

drop out, v. [?AB²] *I asked him to hold my musket while I dropped out and got a drink* 1883 LM li 507 (OEDS 30. *intr.* To disappear from one's place. No ex. So W S C U)

drop over, v. [?AB¹] *"I only just dropped over to ask about the little madam"* 1893 "Californian's Tale" (1906) 109 (To come over unexpectedly, pay a casual visit. Phr. not in OED W S C; but cf. OED Drop in, 1667..; Drop across, 1862..)

drot, int. [AB³] *"Drot your pore broken heart"* 1884 HF xix 184 (OEDS *U.S.* variant of Drat. 1834. So DN.V. Not A in C Wr. Cf. Wr: 'drot' is seldomer used than 'drat' and carries a greater amount of emphasis with it. Not in W S)

drownded, ppl.a. [?AE] *"Somebody's drownded!"* 1876 TS xiv 125. See also *holler*, v. 1884 (OED Drowned. This form now *dial* and *vulgar*. A in M DN.III,V AS. XI.239. Not in W S C)

drowsing, ppl.a. [B²] *Over it and about it a drowsing air of repose* 1869 IA xliv 456 (OED 1881, only ex. So W S C)

drugged, ppl.a. [B¹] *"There's plenty land. Sahara's drugged with it"* 1904 "Bequest" (1906) vii 42 (Crammed, oversupplied. This sense not in OED W S C; but cf. OED Drug, sb. 2. A drug in the market. 1840)

drugstore, sb. [AB³] *"They can keep drug stores"* 1869 IA xxvi 269. *They carry a sun-struck man to the drug-store* 1889 CY x 135. *They fetched the drug-store and emptied it into him* 1901 "Two Little Tales" (1928) 202 (OEDS *U.S.* A druggist's shop. 1845.. So F Cl T M H AS.I.492. Not A in W. Comb. not in S C)

drummer, sb. [AB³] *Any experienced "drummer" will testify that, when you want to do business, there is no economy in ham and lemonade* 1899 "Diplomatic Pay" (1928) 236 (OED 2. *fig.* A commercial traveller. *U.S.* 1827.. So W S C U B F Cl Th T M H)

drum up, v. [?AB³] *They drummed up sixteen dollars* 1906 *Autob* (1924) II 280 (OED 6b. *colloq.* To obtain by canvassing. 1849.. So W S C. Cf. above)

drunk, sb. [?AB³] *Pap said he had enough whiskey there for two drunks and one delirium tremens* 1884 HF vi 45. *"Here comes old Boggs!—in from the country for his little old monthly drunk"* do. xxi 212. See also *solid* 1897 (OEDS 1. Earlier U.S. ex. 1839.. A in Wr B F Cl Th.III. Not A in W S C U T)

druther, sb. [AB¹] *"Any way you druther have it, that is the way I druther have it"—"There ain't any druthers about it, Huck Finn; nobody said anything about druthers."* 1896 TSD ix 523 (A in Cl: In the South often heard in the sense of choice, preference. So DN.I,III,IV AS.III.9, Ozarks. Not in OED W S C)

dry, a. [AB³] *He suddenly changed from a friendly attitude toward whiskey to uncompromising teetotalism, and went absolutely dry* 1906 *Autob* (1924) II 318 (OED 11 *U.S. political slang.* 1888.. So W S C U F Cl Th T M)

dry battery, sb. [B¹] *I told him that in theory a dry battery was just a curled darling* 1892 *AmCl* viii 80 (W: A battery of dry cells. So U. Not in OED S C)

dry goods, sb. [AB³] *The store had everything from anvils and dry goods...to fish* 1889 *CY* xxxi 401 (OEDS A name, chiefly in U.S., for the class of merchandise comprising textile fabrics. 1806.. So W Cl Th,1777 T M H. Not A in S C U)

dry-goods box, sb. [AB¹] *Two or three coatless young men sat in front of the store on a dry-goods box, and whittled it with their knives* 1873 *GA* v 56. *There were empty dry-goods boxes under the awnings* 1884 *HF* xxi 209 (Comb. not in OED W S C. Cf. above)

dry gripes, sb. [?AB¹] *Jokes that had given me the dry gripes* 1889 *CY* iv 53. *There has never been a time, from that day to this (forty years), that I have been able to look at even the outside of a theater without a spasm of the dry gripes, as "Uncle Remus" calls it* 1906 "Unpublished Chaps. from the Autob." (1922) 456 (A revulsion of feeling; a strong repugnance. Comb. not in OED W S C; but cf. OED Gripe, sb. 2b. An intermittent spasmodic pain in the bowels. Usually *pl.* 1601..)

dryness, sb. [AB²] *When the others drink I like to help; otherwise I remain dry. This dryness does not hurt me* 1905 *Speeches* (1910) 430 (OEDS 4. The condition of being 'dry' or without alcohol. *U.S.* 1920.. So S. This sense not in W C. Cf. dry, a., above)

dry up, v. [?AB³] See *walk*, sb. 1881. *"Dry up! I don't want to hear no more out of you!"* 1884 *HF* xxx 313 (OEDS 5d. To stop the flow of words, cease talking. Earlier U.S. exs. 1855.. A in B F Th T DN.III. Not A in W S C U)

duck, sb. *like a duck*. [?AB¹] *He took to it like a duck* 1889 *CY* x 120 (Eagerly, wholeheartedly. Phr. not in OED W S C; but cf. OED Duck, sb. 2. quot. 1894: "like a duck to water")

duck, sb. [AB²] See *gospel-mill* 1872. *"Up you go for misprision of treason—lucky duck if they don't hang you, too"* 1883 *LM* xxiv 269 (OEDS 4. A fellow, 'customer.' *U.S. slang.* 1889.. So M DN.II,V AS.II.49. Not A in W S. This sense not in C)

dude, sb. [AB³] *The remnant...was restricted to dudes and dudesses* 1889 *CY* viii 100. See *exequatur* 1904. *Nobody could tell me from a parson, a barber, a dude* 1905 "Czar's Soliloquy" 321 (OED *U.S.* A factitious slang term which came into vogue in New York about the beginning of 1883, in connexion with the 'aesthetic' craze of that day. A dandy, a 'swell.' 1883.. So W U F Cl Th T M DN.III. Cf. *Athenaeum* 1900 (II) 444. Not A in S C)

dudess, sb. [AB¹] See *dude* 1889 (Not in OED W S C. Cf. Dudine, A in Th,1883 M AS.IV.206; also Dudine, Dudeen, Dudette, A in AS.XII.161)

duds, sb. [?A] *The gentleman ought to be politely requested to bundle up his "duds" and make himself scarce* 1853 *Hannibal Journal*, May 23. See also *starchy* 1894 (OED 1. Clothes. *slang* or *colloq.* 1440.. So W S C U. A in Wr B F Cl DN.II,III,IV,V. Not A in M)

dueling-day, sb. [B¹] *The regular dueling-day of one of the corps approaches* 1880 *TA* v 52 (Comb. not in OED W S C. This and the other compounds with *dueling* entered below may have had German models)

dueling-house, sb. [B¹] *In the dueling-house, in the parks, on the street, and anywhere and everywhere that students go* 1880 *TA* vii 67 (Comb. not in OED W S C)

dueling-place, sb. [B¹] *My agent obtained permission to bring me to the student's dueling-place* 1880 *TA* v 15 (Comb. not in OED W S C)

dueling-room, sb. [B¹] *The ten men whose duels I had witnessed...mingled with the assemblage in the dueling-room* 1880 *TA* vii 63 (Comb. not in OED W S C)

duffer, sb. [B¹] *"This duffer, this scrub, this bilk!"* 1892 *AmCl* xv 156 (W: A sham or cheat. *English.* This gen. sense not in OED S C U; but cf. OED 1. One who sells trashy goods as valuable, upon false pretences. 1756.. So S C. *obs* in U)

duffer, sb. [B³] *"Duffers like us don't know what real thought is"* 1902 "DBDS" (1928) 326 (Considered by OED as a distinct word from the above. OED *colloq* and *slang.* 1. A stupid or foolish person. 1842.. So W S U)

duffy, a. [?AB¹] *They will bake you up a couple, burnt on one side, and flabby and "duffy" on the other* 1864 *SS* (1926) 137 (Wr: Of bread: doughy, half-baked, under-cooked. *Scotch.* Not in OED W S C; but cf. OED Duff, sb. Dough, paste, *dial.* 1847; OEDS Earlier U.S. ex. 1838; DN.II, a flour pudding)

dug-out, sb. [AB³] *We...borrowed a dug-out, and pulled back six miles to the upper camp* 1861 *Letters* (1917) I iii 58 (OED Chiefly *U.S.* 1. A canoe made by hollowing out the trunk of a tree. 1819.. So W B F Cl Th M DN.II,III. Not A in S C U)

dull, v. [C] *The king...dulled down to drowsiness* 1889 *CY* xxxiii 419 (OED 7. To become dull, grow weary. *obs.* 1220..1440. So C. Not *obs* in W S. Cf. Wr: Dull down, *fig.* to pass out of mind, be forgotten)

dulnesses, sb. [B¹] *The men were getting freshened up from the day's monotonies and dulnesses* 1897 *FE* ii 42 (This *concrete* sense not in OED W S C)

dumb, a. [AB³] *This Englishman...would jump to the conclusion that American girls were as dumb as himself* 1892 *AmCl* xxi 221. *"She's a good creature, but she's dull and dumb and illiterate"* 1894 *Letters* (1917) II xxxiv 606 (OEDS 7b. Foolish, stupid. *U.S. colloq.* 1823.. So W S C Th M H DN.IV AS.II.353, VIII.2.77)

dumb-waiter, sb. [AB³] *Dumb-waiters will carry the food down* 1870 "Curious Dream" (1872) 32 (OED 2. *U.S.* A movable frame, by which dishes, etc., are passed from one room or story of a house to another, OEDS 1856.. So T M H. Not A in W S C U)

dummy-whist, sb. [?AB³] *They played dummy whist with him till bedtime* 1899 "My Debut" (1900) 74 (OED 1843. So W S U. Cf. in same sense OED Dummy, sb. 2. 1736..; So C Wr; A in B F Cl Th)

dump, sb. [AB³] *Tasmania was a convict dump, in old times* 1897 *FE* xxix 279. *Rogers has only built one road...I saw that dump* 1909 *Speeches* (1910) 177 (OED 2. Chiefly *U.S.* A place where refuse material, esp. from a mine or quarry, is deposited. 1872.. So S C Cl Th.III DN.III. Not A in W U Wr)

dump, v. [AB³] *"Dump it on the doorstep, Jerry"* 1873 *GA* vii 76. *I took an old sack and put a lot of big rocks in it...and dragged it to the door and through the woods down to the river and dumped it in* 1884 *HF* vii 52 (OED 2. Chiefly *U.S.* 1828.. So W C Wr B F Cl Th T M DN.III AS.V.277. Not A in S U)

dump-pile, sb. [AB³] *She happened to fetch out a long word which had had its day weeks before and its prepared meanings gone to her dump-pile* 1903 "Dog's Tale" 12 (OED Chiefly *U.S.* 1844. Not A in W. Not in S C)

dumps, sb. [?A] *"What puts you in the dumps to-day?"* 1873 *GA* xxxi 280 (OED 2. A fit of depression; now only in pl. 1529.. So W S C U. A in F DN.II AS.II.353)

Dunkard, sb. [A] See *Adventist* 1907 (OED *U.S.* =Dunker; cf. below. 1784.. So W S C M AS.VIII.3.12)

Dunker-Baptist, sb. [AB¹] *Aunty Cord is a violent Methodist and Lewis an implacable Dunker-Baptist* 1877 *Letters* (1917) I xvii 308 (Comb. not in OED W S C; but cf. OEDS Dunker: A member of a body of German-American Baptists. 1751..)

dure, v. [C] *"Sir Gawaine's strength feebled and waxed passing faint, that unnethes he might dure any* *longer"* 1889 CY xv 181 (OED 2. To persist, 'hold out' in action. *obs.* 1297..1573. So W S C U Wr)

durian, sb. Spelled **dorian.** [E] *The dorian, if that is the name of it...was a most strange fruit, and incomparably delicious to the taste, but not to the smell. Its rind was said to exude a stench of so atrocious a nature that when a dorian was in the room even the presence of a polecat was a refreshment* 1897 FE I 478 (OED The fruit of a tree of the Indian Archipelago...of a strong civet odour, but agreeable taste. 1588..1887. So W S C U. OED gives the sp. *dorian* as 19th c., but has no ex. of it)

durn, sb. [AB²] *"I don't re'ly k'yer a durn"* 1880 TA xxiii 225 (OEDS *U.S.* variant of Darn, Dern. 1888.. So T. *Colloq* in W. Not in S C)

durn, v. [AB²] *"Durn him, he didn't come"* 1880 TA xx 193 (OEDS *U.S.* variant of Darn, Dern. No ex. So C B F T DN.V. Not A in W. Not in S)

dust, v. [?AC] *So she took and dusted us both with the hickry* 1884 HF xxxix 395 (OED †7a. To beat; to thrash. 1612, only ex. Not *obs* in C Wr. A in Cl. Not in W S; but cf. OED 6b. To dust one's jacket. *colloq.* 1690.. So W S C U; A in DN.III)

duster, sb. [AB³] *We found him in his working costume, with an old, short, linen duster on* 1885 Autob (1924) I 13 (OED 4. Dust-cloak. Chiefly *U.S.* 1864.. So B Cl T H. Not A in W S C)

dusting, vbl.sb. [B¹] *The distressful dustings and smokings and swelterings of the past weeks* 1897 FE i 25 (Sprinkling or covering with dust. This sense not in OED W S C; but cf. OED The action of the verb in various senses; usually, that of freeing from dust. 1623.. Here the sense is rather that of Dust, v. OED 3. To sprinkle with dust. 1592..)

dust–rag, sb. [B¹] *She was polishing around with a dust-rag* 1893 PW ii 237 (Comb. not in OED W S C)

dust–storm, sb. [B²] *That hot wind sweeps out Sydney sometimes, and brings with it what is called a "dust-storm"* 1897 FE ix 117 (Given in OED W S C. No ex. Cf. Washoe zephyr, below)

dusty, a. [?AB¹] *Although I am not a very dusty Christian myself, I take an absorbing interest in religious affairs* 1864 *Letters* (1917) I iv 96 (Exemplary; 'gilt-edged.' This sense not in OED W S C. Cf. OED 4b. Mean, worthless, vile; now only in slang phr. *not so dusty* = not so bad. 1893. So W U Wr. M.T.'s use may have been due to a misapprehension of the force of the British slang phrase *not so dusty*, although his sense is really just the opposite; or it may be an extension from *dust* in the sense of gold-dust, valuable ore)

dusty–looking, ppl.a. [B¹] *Commercial houses were as dusty-looking as ever* 1883 LM xli 424 (Comb. not in OED W S C)

Dutch, a. [AC] *Down here to St. Louis...in the parlor of my Dutch boarding house in Fourth street...I told the Dutchman (who is for all the world like other humans)...* 1856 *Adv. of T. J. Snodgrass* (1928) 3 (OED 1. Of or pertaining to the people of Germany; German; Teutonic. *Obs* exc...in some parts of the U.S. c1460..1884. So F Cl Th.III H DN.III AS.VII.13,XII.94. Not A in W)

Dutchman, sb. [AC] See *Dutch* 1856 (OED 1. A German. *Obs* exc. locally in *U.S.* 1387..1788. OEDS Later U.S. exs. 1807..1872. So S C F Th H DN.III. Not A in W)

duty–call, sb. [B²] *He had happened into Lakeside to pay a duty-call upon an obscure grandmother of his* 1904 "Bequest" (1906) viii 46 (Given in OED, no ex. Not in W S C)

duty–visit, sb. [B¹] *"They'll never see my face except when they pay their little duty-visits to me"* 1888 "Meisterschaft" 460 (Comb. not in OED W S C)

dynamite–can, sb. [B¹] *Bouncing a dynamite-can around to find out what was in it* 1880 "Taming the Bicycle" (1917) 291 (Comb. not in OED W S C)

dyspeptic, sb. [?AB³] *Among them were three confirmed dyspeptics* 1898 "At the Appetite Cure" (1900) 151 (OED A person suffering from dyspepsia, indigestion ...applied to various forms of disorder of the digestive organs, esp. the stomach. 1822.. So W S C U. A in Cl: Has long lost its *spec* meaning in the U.S., and is now used to denote all the various forms of weakness of the digestive organs)

eagernesses, sb. [B¹] *He exploited three hundred and sixty-five red-hot new eagernesses every year of his life* 1906 *Autob* (1924) II 269 (This *concrete* sense not in OED W S C)

eagle, sb. [AB²] *Backus started off with an eagle.. Wiley "saw it", and went ten dollars better* 1883 LM xxxvi 394 (OED 5. A gold coin of the U. S., value ten dollars. No ex. So W S C U B F Cl Th,1789 M DN.V)

eagle, sb. **to fly the eagle, fliers of the eagle.** [AB¹] *You won't mind a body bragging a little about his country on the Fourth of July. It is a fair and legitimate time to fly the eagle* 1872 *Speeches* (1910) 415. *A crowd of ten thousand proud, untamed democrats, horny-handed sons of toil and fliers of the eagle* 1902 "Does the Race Love a Lord?" 441 (These phrases not in OED W S C; but cf. OEDS 1. In U.S. allusive uses: *to make the eagle scream.* 1904)

ear, sb. **on the ear.** [AB¹] See *biscuit* 1880; *batter-cake* 1897 (OEDS b. ellipt. for ear of corn: a head of Indian corn. *U.S.* This phr. not in OED W S C)

ear-boxing, vbl.sb. [B¹] *"No—not ear-boxing, but genuine blows!"* 1898 "Stirring Times in Austria" (1900) 324 (Comb. not in OED W S C. Modeled after German *Ohrfeige*, a box on the ears?)

ear-drop, sb. [?AB²] *The smaller lakes..did not look like puddles, but like blue eardrops which had fallen and lodged in slight depressions* 1880 TA xxix 304 (OED 1. An ornamental pendant worn in the ears. No ex. So W S C Wr. A in DN.II)

earned run, sb. [AB¹] *These boys have played base-ball...I would envy them somewhat of the glories they have achieved..if it were fair; but, no, it was an earned run, and envy would be out of place* 1889 *Speeches* (1923) 149 (W: *Baseball.* A run scored without the aid of errors or passed balls. So S C. Not in OED)

ear-socket, sb. [B¹] *"I am homesick from ear-socket to crupper, and from crupper to hock-joint"* 1880 TA xx 194 (Comb. not in OED W S C. Cf. OED Eye-socket, 1841..)

ear-splitting, ppl.a. [B²] *The thunder-peals came now in ear-splitting explosive bursts* 1876 TS xvi 141. *The discordant, ear-splitting, metallic laugh common to his breed* 1883 LM xlviii 480 (OED 1884, only ex. So W S C)

earth, sb. **on earth.** [?AB¹] *"I've got the biggest scheme on earth—and I'll take you in!"* 1873 GA i 29 (Used as intensive phr. with superlatives. This use, suggestive of Barnum's slogan "Biggest Show on Earth," not in OED W S C; but cf. with dif. force OEDS 9c. *On earth,* used chiefly in negative and interrogative contexts, as "What on earth is the matter?" 1774.. So W)

earthquake, sb. [?AB¹] See *cocktail* 1869 (An American mixed drink. This sense not in OED W S C)

ease, v. trans. [?AB³] *You warm the end of your plank ..and then raise it aloft and ease it up gently against a slumbering chicken's foot* 1870 SNO (1875) 83. *The widow caught the limp form and eased it to the earth* do. 186. *"Ease this down for a fellow, will you?" I eased the gravestone down till it rested on the ground* do.192 (OEDS 7b. To lift or shift gently. U.S. exs. 1850..Not A in W S C Wr)

ease all, v. intr. [?AB³] *When the measurements indicate that the yawl is approaching the shoalest part of the reef, the command is given to 'Ease all!'* 1875 OTM 568 (OEDS 8b. To stop rowing. U.S. exs. 1863.. Phr. not in W S C)

eased–up, ppl.a. [?AB¹] *She set there..looking kind of happy and eased-up, like a person that's had a tooth pulled out* 1884 HF xxviii 282 (Comb. not in OED W S C. Cf. ease up, below)

easement, sb. [C] *"Give thy misgivings easement"* 1881 PP vi 84 (OED 1. Relief, alleviation. Now somewhat *rare.* 1386..1796. So U Wr. Not *rare* in W S C)

ease off, v. intr. [?AB²] *The slope eased off* 1880 TA xli 477 (OEDS 10e. To fall away with a gentle slope. 1925, only ex. So W. A in DN.IV. Not in S C)

ease up, v. intr. [?AB²] *When I got down nearly to her, I eased up and went slow and cautious* 1883 LM iii 44. *She worked me middling hard for about an hour, and then the widow made her ease up* 1884 HF i 4 (OEDS 8b. To relax or cease one's efforts. 1889, first ex. of *ease up* ... So W. Not in S C)

East, sb. [AB¹?C] *A young sprig from the East blustered up* [Philip is on his way from Philadelphia to western Pennsylvania] 1873 GA xxix 267 (W: Formerly the part of the U.S. east of the Allegheny Mountains, esp. the New England States, or all the Atlantic States; now, often, the region east of the Mississippi River, esp. that which is north of Maryland and the Ohio River. So S C, without indicating that the limited sense is *arch.* F restricts the term to the six New England States; so DN.III. Cf. H: A relative term as one traverses the Am. continent. Thus, when the California newspapers report that settlers from the East are locating in Glynn County, the far easterner is surprised to learn that the reference is to people coming from Dakota. M.T.'s restricted sense is not given in OED)

East, adv. [AB¹?C] *Before he came East* [to New York] 1895 *Letters* (1917) II xxv 457 (Cf. above)

east-by-east, adv. [B¹] *"How's she heading?" "Nor'-east-and-by-nor'—east-by-east, half-east, sir"* 1880 TA xvii 155 (Unless intended as nonsense, this is a misprint for "Nor'-east-and-by-nor', nor'-east-by-east". There is of course no such point of the compass as "east-by-east")

Eastern, a. [A] See *quit* 1873. (OEDS 1b. Situated in the north-eastern parts of the U.S. 1776.. So F AS.IV. 4. This sense not in W S C)

easy, adb. **to take it easy.** [?AB³] *They had learned that it was wisdom to take things easy and go along comfortably* 1869 IA lvii 611. *"I'd advise you to..take it easy"* 1880 TA xxvi 271 (OED 4. *colloq.* 1867. So W U Wr. Phrase not in S C)

easy game, sb. [AB¹] *So I disguised myself and came back and studied you. Yow were easy game* 1899 "MCH" (1900) 52 (A in DN.I,II,III. Comb. not in OED W S C; but cf. OED Easy, a. 12. Of persons..compliant, credulous. 1611..)

easy-going, ppl.a. [?A] *A far-sighted but easy-going journeyman printer wandered along* 1873 GA xxv 233. *He was deliciously easy-going and comfortable in the presence of age, official dignity, and even the most august wealth* 1875 OTM 722 (OED b. *fig.* Comfort-loving, indolent. 1674..1879. So W S C U. A in B, p.782)

easy water, sb. [?AB²] *He told me that the easy water was close ashore and the current outside* 1875 OTM 220. See *clip,* v. 1875. *He came a-swinging up shore in the easy water* 1884 HF vii 54 (OEDS 10c. Of water, etc.: Not rapid, 1883, OTM quot., wrongly dated...This use not in W S C)

easy-working, ppl.a. [?AB¹] *His easy-working jaw had told me everything* 1883 LM xxxvi 388 (Comb. not in OED W S C. Cf. easy-going, above)

eat, v. Past tense **et.** [?AE] See *dish-rag* 1873. *They all smoked and talked, and I eat and talked* 1884 HF xvii 151. *The person that et it would want to fetch a couple of kags of toothpicks along* do. xxxvii 384. *The Portyghee et twenty-two of them* 1899 "My Debut" (1900) 76 (OED This sp. 12th to 14th c., but the pron. so indicated still in standard use in England. So W S C U. Not in standard use in U S., but widespread *colloq;* so M DN.II,III,IV,V AS.I.233,III.3,V.202,XI.348,XII.322)

eating-room, sb. [?AC] *A hut for an eating-room for passengers* 1872 RI iv 41 (OED *obs* exc *arch.* 1613.. 1849. Cf. H: Am. eating hall = Eng. dining hall. Comb. not in W S C)

eating–station, sb. [?AB¹] *At eating-stations he sends luncheon out to you* 1880 TA xxxii 353 (Comb. not in OED W S C. Cf. above)

economize, v. [B³] *Truth is the most valuable thing we have. Let us economize it.—Pudd'nhead Wilson's New Calendar* 1897 FE vii (OED 3. To use sparingly; to effect a saving in. 1820.. So W S C)

ecstasy, sb. [B¹] *This is the ecstasy of crawling servility* [comment on Swift's verses to his patron] 1868-1910 Margins on "Swift" (1935) 37 (Extravagant or insane manifestations of any feeling or emotion. This sense not in OED W S C. Cf. OED 4. Now chiefly, Intense or rapturous delight; the expressions *ecstasy of woe, sorrow, despair*, etc. still occur, but are usually felt as *transferred*)

Eddyty, sb. [AB¹] *The book as we have it—now that the salaried polisher has holystoned all of the genuine Eddyties out of it* 1899 "Chr.Sc. and the Book" 593 (Hum. coinage)

Eddy-worship, sb. [AB¹] *Eddy-worship will be taught in the Sunday-schools and pulpits of the cult* 1903 "Chr. Sc." ii 2 (Hum. coinage)

Edisonially, adv. [AB¹] *Gulls do not rank high mentally, but this one had memory and the reasoning faculty...and applied them Edisonially* 1906 "WIM" (1917) vi 80 (Nonce formation. Cf. OEDS Edisonite, from the name of Thomas Alva Edison, American inventor, 1847-1931)

Edisonian, a. [AB¹] *Man's thought-machine works just like the other animals', but it is a better one and more Edisonian* 1906 "WIM" (1917) 78 (Not in OED W S C. Cf. above)

editor-critic, sb. [B¹] *This editor is a critic...It is too late to reorganize the editor-critic now; we will leave him as he is* 1899 "How to Make Hist. Dates Stick" (1917) 160 (Comb. not in OED W S C; but cf. OEDS Editor-manager, 1899)

editorial, sb. [?AB³] *"They think you are crazy. And well they might after reading your editorials"* 1870 SNO (1875) 237. See *steal*, sb. 1873. *They* [German newspapers] *contain no editorials whatever, no "personals", no funny-paragraph column* 1880 TA App. F 626 (OED A 'leader.' OEDS Earlier U.S. exs. 1844..A in F Cl T M H. Not A in W S C U)

effect, sb. [B¹] *It was one of the best effects I ever invented...I stood up on the platform...and slowly pronounced this ghastly word: "Constantinopolitanischerdudelsackspfeifenmachersgesellschafft!" Just as I was moaning out the closing hunks of that word, I touched off one of my electric connections, and all that murky world of people stood revealed in a hideous blue glare!... I lifted my hands and groaned out this word—as it were in agony:"Nihilistendynamittheaterkaestchenssprengungsattentaetsversuchungen!" —and turned on the red fire!... After sixty seconds I shouted: "Transvaaltruppentropentransporttrampelthiertreibertrauungsthraenentragoedie !" and lit up the green fire! After waiting only forty seconds this time, I spread my arms abroad and thundered out the devastating syllables of this word of words: "Mekkamuselmannenmassenmenchenmoerdermohrenmutter marmormonumentenmacher!" —and whirled on the purple glare!* 1889 CY xxiii 290 (W: A method or device for producing an impression. This *spec* sense not in, or at least not clearly defined in, OED S C. The four polysyllabic formulae which produced so spectacular an "effect" are supposititious German compounds with comparatively harmless meanings. No 1 may be translated: "The Bagpipe Manufacturers Company of Constantinople"; No. 2, "Outrageous attempts by Nihilists to blow up the strong-box of a theater with dynamite"; No. 3, "The lamentable tragedy of the marriage of a dromedary drover in the tropical transport service of the army of the Transvaal"; and No. 4, "A manufacturer of marble monuments commemorating the Moorish mother of the assassins who perpe-

trated the general massacre of Mohammedans at Mecca." These tongue-twisters are of a type familiar in elementary German textbooks of the period, and may have been "lifted" bodily by M.T. from some such manual as the one he calls the "Meisterschaft" (q.v.). It is more likely, however, that he tried to improve upon his originals, for he has made certain obvious mistakes in his German: e.g., in No. 1 he has inserted a superfluous *r* at the end of *Constantinopolitanische*, an unnecessary *s* after *dudelsack* and *macher*, and an extra *f* in *Gesellschaft*; in No. 2, beside the needless *s* after *kaestchen* and the mistaken umlaut in *Attentat*, he has put the wrong word altogether at the end, for he evidently intended *Versuche* (attempts) here instead of *Versuchungen*, which means "temptations"! All of these errors have been faithfully reproduced in all the editions of CY, as M.T. would doubtless have wished them to be. They reflect his fascinated but somewhat impressionistic interest in German, especially at this time of his life, and constitute perhaps the best of his many jokes on the language.)

effect–collecting, ppl.a. [B¹] *He made one of his effect-collecting pauses* 1894 PW xxi 239 (Comb. not in OED W S C. Cf. above)

effusion, sb. [B²] *The prize was delivered to Tom with as much effusion as the superintendent could pump up* 1876 TS iv 50. *I said, with effusion..*1893 "Esquimau Maiden's Romance" (1900) 139 (OED 3b. Effusiveness. 1878..So W S C U)

eftsoons, adv. [C] *"Belike thou'lt change thy note eftsoons"* 1881 PP x 117. *"That will I tell eftsoons"* 1889 CY xv 175 (OED *obs* or *arch*. 3. In mod. archaistic use, the sense is commonly 'forthwith, immediately'. 1297.. 1871. So W S C U)

egg, sb. **to have all your eggs in one basket.** [B²] *"What's the objection?" "All the eggs in one basket— that's the objection"* 1904 "Bequest" (1906) ii 8 (OED 4b. To risk all one's property on a single venture. No ex. So W S C U)

egg, sb. **to suck eggs.** [?AB¹] *"Any body that'll take a dare will suck eggs"* 1876 TS i 22 (The peculiarly derogatory significance of the phrase in America is probably due to the habit of the skunk or polecat. Cf. Egg-sucking, below. This sense not in OED W S C; but cf. OED 10. † *To suck the eggs of*: to extract the 'goodness' of, cause to be unproductive. 1576..1750)

egg-bread, sb. [AB³] See *biscuit* 1880 (OEDS U.S. Bread made of the meal of Indian corn, with eggs, etc. 1854..So Th M DN.II,III,VI. Not in W S C)

eggnog, sb. [?AB³] *Bottles wherein were once curious liquors: Rum-punch, Jinsling, Eggnog* 1869 IA xl 429 (OED A drink in which the white and yolk of eggs are stirred up with hot beer, cider, wine, or spirits. U.S. exs. 1825.. Cf. W: A drink consisting of eggs beaten up with sugar, milk, and, sometimes, wine. For wine S and C substitute spirits. No mixture with beer is recognized as eggnog in the U.S. A in F Cl DN.VI. Not A in W S C U)

egg on, v. [?A] *The spectator was "egged on" by his friends* 1904 "Italian without a Master" (1906) 184 (OED 2. To incite. 1566..1852. So W S C U Wr T. A in B Cl DN.II,III,VI)

egg-sucking, ppl.a. [?AB¹] *"You dash-dashed aigsuckin', sheep- stealin', one-eyed son of a stuffed monkeyi"* 1875 OTM 448 (Cf. suck-egg dog, A in DN.I. Cf. also eggs, to suck, above. Comb. not in OED W S C)

egod, int. [ACE] *"Egod! He didn't get left!"* 1885 Autob (1924) I 18 (OED Egad; this form 18th c. 1791, only ex. A in AS.V.268,VII.49: Ozarks and Southern lumber-camps, spelled *I-god*. Not in W S C)

Egyptian, a. [B¹] *It seemed to me that the outlook was dark; almost Egyptian, in fact* 1895 "What Bourget

Thinks" 49 (Intensely dark. This sense not in OED W S C; but cf. the comb. Egyptian darkness, OED 1641..)

eight, a. [E] *Look at Henry the Eight* 1884 HF xxiii 232 (Eighth. OED Eighth, a. From the 13c. the forms are often identical with those of the cardinal. So C. This form not in W S)

eighteens, sb. [B¹] *He left footprints in the solid stones. I should judge that he wore about eighteens* 1869 IA liv 579 (Not in OED W S C; but cf. OEDS Eight, sb. 4. A shoe of the eighth size. 1913)

elbow, sb. elbow to elbow. [B¹] *I had seen moonlight and daylight together before, but I had not seen daylight and black night elbow to elbow before* 1880 TA xliii 500 (Phr. not in OED W S C. Cf. OED At one's elbow, 1548..Cf. also M.T.'s Breast to breast with, above)

elbow-mate, sb. [?AB¹] *Everybody talked to his elbow-mate* 1907 "Chaps. from Autob" 8 (Comb. not in OED W S C. Cf. below)

elbow-neighbor, sb. [AB¹] *We could just sit and talk privately to our elbow-neighbors* 1875 SNO 181 (A in Th.III,1895. Comb. not in OED W S C)

elecampane, sb. Spelled allycum pain. [E] *We like to got a hornet's nest, but we didn't... Then we got allycum pain and rubbed on the places, and was pretty near all right again* 1844 HF xxxix 396 (OED 1. Formerly used as a tonic and stimulant. 1398..So W S C U Wr. OED gives 19th c. sps. alycompaine, alicompayne, allicampane)

elect, v. [?AB¹] *Calling yourself a lady doesn't elect you* 1892 AmCl xi 113 (Here: to give one status or position by any means. This sense not in OED W S C. Cf. DN.III,IV, Elect: to choose)

electing, vbl.sb. [?AB¹] *"Whose right is it to do the electing?"* 1892 AmCl xi 113 (Choosing. This sense not OED W S C. Cf. above)

electric call, sb. [?AB¹] See *bicycle* 1899 (Comb. not in OED W S C. Cf. OED Electric alarm; OEDS Electric bell, 1891)

electric car, sb. [?AB¹] *The merry electric car replaced the melancholy bus* 1899 "Chr.Sc. and the Book" 592 (Comb. not in OED W S C)

electric storm, sb. [?AB²] *The evoking of cyclones and other kinds of electric storms* 1892 AmCl xxv 272 (OEDS 2b. *Meteorol.* 1906.. So C. Comb. not in W S)

electroincandescently, adv. [B¹] *Any fine, large word would have answered just as well: psychosuperintangibly—electroincandescently—oligarcheologically—sanchrosynchrostereoptically—any of these would have answered, any of these would have filled the void* 1907 CS II ii 120 (Hum. coinage)

Electropath, sb. [B¹] See *Allopath* 1902 (S: A practitioner of the treatment of disease by electricity. So C. Not in OED W; but cf. OED Electropathy, 1882)

elegant, a. [?A] See *left-hander* 1873. *The good superintendent..gave me a beautiful Bible—a splendid, elegant Bible* 1876 TS iv 51 (OEDS 8. Vulgarly used for 'excellent, first-rate'. Earlier U.S. exs. 1772..A in F Cl Th,1765 DN.V AS.II.30,V.303,XI.303. Not A in W S C. This use is classed as Irish in P.W.Joyce's *English as We Speak It in Ireland*, p.254)

elephant-driver, sb. [B¹] *The occupation of elephant-driver is confined to Mohammedans* 1897 FE xlix 464 (Comb. not in OED W S C)

elephant-fight, sb. [B¹] *Entertain visiting rajahs and viceroys with tiger-fights, elephant-fights, illuminations* 1897 FE xlv 412 (Comb. not in OED W S C)

elephantinely, adv. [B¹] *Elephantinely jolly* 1883 LM iii 41 (Not in OED W S C)

elephant-legged, a. [B¹] *The drawers are loose elephant-legged and elephant-waisted things* 1897 FE xlix 459 (Comb. not in OED W S C. Cf. OED Elephant-headed, 1854)

elephant-waisted a. [B¹] See *elephant-legged* 1897 (Comb. not in OED W S C)

elevated road, sb. [AB³] *I was coming up in a car of the elevated road* 1900 *Speeches* (1910) 280 (OEDS *U.S.* 1890..So H. Not A in W S C)

elevator, sb. [?AB³] *He finally took a waiting position in the neighborhood of the elevator* 1892 AmCl vi 59. See *bicycle* 1899 (OEDS 3d. A lift. 1883..So W S C. A in U B F Cl Th.III,1873 M H AS.II.68)

elevator-load, sb. [?AB¹] *The elevator-load which had the suspect for fellow-passenger* 1892 AmCl vi 70 (Comb. not in OED W S C. Cf. above)

ell, sb. [AB²] *He was out of the window and creeping along the roof of the "ell" on all fours* 1876 TS ix 86 (OEDS *U.S.* A shed placed against a building. 1875, this quot...So Th T H. Not A in W S C Wr. Cf. L, below)

elocute, v. Spelled yellocute. [AB¹E] *Another time they tried a go at yellocution; but they didn't yellocute long till the audience got up..and made them skip out* 1884 HF xxxi 315 ((Hum. nonce-spelling. The verb is A in M DN.III,IV AS.I.246. W: To declaim. *Derisive*. Not in OED S C)

eloquence, sb. [B¹] See *adjective-piling* 1885. *The Southern author had a passion for "eloquence"* 1893 "Cure for the Blues" 79. See also *enthuse* 1906 (Windy and inflated language; false eloquence. This bad sense of the word not in OED W S C)

eloquent, a. [B¹] *Daniel Webster's..diffuse, conceited, "eloquent", bathotic..letters* 1880 *Letters* (1917) I xx 384 (Cf. *eloquence*, above)

embattled, ppl.a. [D] See *coat-of-arms* 1883 (OED 2. Having an edge or outline shaped like a battlement; crenellated; *spec* in Heraldry. c1386..1864—. So W S C U)

emergence, sb. [C] *"What is the custom and usage in this emergence?"* 1881 PP vii 91 (OED 3. Now replaced by Emergency. 1649..1849. *Obs* in W C. S: incorrect)

emery-bag, sb. [B²] *They* [the slaves] *would smouch provisions..or a brass thimble..or an emery-bag* 1893 PW ii 237 (OEDS Used for keeping needles bright and clean. 1895..So W S U. Not in C)

emeute, sb. [B¹] *"There's been an emute, as she calls it...There was a fuss between Major-General Tommy Drake and Lieutenant-Colonel Agnes Frisbie"* 1906 "Horse's Tale" 543 (Hum. nonce use. Cf. OED A popular rising or disturbance. 1862..; so W S C U)

emigrant, sb. [AB¹] *Among citizens of Salt Lake, we were well aware that these superior beings despised "emigrants"...Many a time in Nevada, afterward, we had occasion to remember with humiliation that we were "emigrants" and consequently a low and inferior sort of creatures...Poor thing! they are making fun of his hat, and the cut of his New York coat, and..looking down on him with a blighting compassion because he is an "emigrant" instead of that proudest and blessedest creature that exists on all the earth, a "Forty-Niner"* 1872 RI xvii 138. *Whatever the lagging, dragging journey* [from Tennessee to Missouri] *may have been to the rest of the emigrants, it was a wonder and delight to the children* 1873 GA iii 35 (A settler from the East. Cf. H: Emigrate, v., used in Am. not only of removal from one country to another but also of removal from one State in the Union to another. This sense not in OED W S C; cf. OED: One who removes from his own land to settle permanently in another. 1754..1856)

emigrant-train, sb. [AB¹] *We overtook a Mormon emigrant-train* 1872 RI xii 97 (A procession of settlers in wagons across the Plains. Not in OED W S C. The comb., in the sense of a railway train carrying emigrants from abroad, is given in OEDS 1883)

emit, v. [B¹] *There are eighteen doors to admit and emit 1,650 persons* 1891 "At the Shrine of St. Wagner" (1917) 211 (To discharge or let out persons. This sense not in OED W S C; cf. OED *trans*: Not used with personal object)

empering, vbl.sb. [B¹] *An Emperor..can hunt them, harry them, destroy them, just as he would so many rats if the accident of birth had furnished him a calling better suited to his capacities than empering* 1905 "Czar's Soliloquy" 322 (Hum. nonce coinage. Cf. OED Emperor, v. nonce-wd., 1855)

empocket, v. [B¹?C] *The individual empocketed the silver* ["Retranslated" from the French *empocher*; the original version of the "Jumping Frog" has *"The fellow took the money"*] 1875 SNO 33 (Hum. alienism. M.T. was hardly aware that the Eng. word once had the same meaning: OED *arch.* To put into one's pocket. 1728..1884. So S. Not *arch* in W. Not in C)

emprise, sb. [C] *He had started out on a high emprise* 1892 AmCl xv 153 (OED *arch.* 1. An enterprise, esp. one of an adventurous or chivalric nature. 1300..1871. So W S C U)

emptinesses, sb. [B³] *With the sillinesses and emptinesses..of a brainless society* 1883 LM xlvi 467 (OED 3b. Trifles, trivialities. 1843..This *concrete* sense not in W S C)

emptings, vbl.sb. **to run emptyings.** [AB²E] *Offers were made me for weekly literary contributions. I had known of no instance where a man had pumped himself out once a week and failed to run "emptyings" before the year was finished* 1887 *Letters* (1917) II xxvii 487 (OEDS To show signs of not holding out well. 1902, U.S. ex. A in B Cl Th.III,1881 DN.I,IV. Phr. not in W S C. Cf. OED Empting. In U.S., the pl. in the sense 'yeast' is pronounced *emptins* but often written *emptyings.* So W S C B F Th,1848 DN.II,III,IV)

encrusting, vbl.sb. [B¹] *I thought of the Taj, with its encrustings and inlayings of jewels* 1897 FE lix 578 (Encrustation. Not in OED W S C)

end–feather, sb. [B¹] *A vast hawk..with his wings spread wide and the blue of the vault showing through the fringe of their end-feathers* 1897 *Autob* (1924) I 110 (Comb. not in OED W S C)

endiometrical, a. [B¹] *Professor Snail..said:..."It is a dense vapor formed by the calorification of ascending moisture dephlogisticated by refraction. A few endiometrical experiments would confirm this"* 1875 SNO 128 (Nonsense coinage. A blend of *endiometral* and *diametrical?*)

endowment, a. [?AB²] *"It was effected on what the insurance companies call the 'endowment,' or the 'paid-up' plan, by which a policy is secured after a certain time without further payment"* 1873 GA xlviii 435 (OEDS 5. *attrib.* and *comb.* A form of life insurance. 1880.. So W S C)

endways, adv. [?A] *He was ready for the dog too, and knocked him endways with a rock* 1867 SNO (1875) 53 (OED 2b. End foremost. So W C. *Slang* in S. A in F)

energetic–looking, ppl.a. [B¹] *An energetic-looking man bustled in* 1892 AmCl iii 46 (Comb. not in OED W S C)

engame, v. [B¹] *"When a goat is ripe, his fur doth heat and sore engame his flesh"* 1889 CY xxxiii 438 (Nonce coinage: to make 'gamy'. Cf. OED Gamy, a. 3. Having the flavour of game that has been kept till it is 'high'. 1863..)

engine–bell, sb. [?AB¹] *He was boat and captain and engine-bells combined* 1876 TS ii 129. *We snatched our engine-bells out by the roots and piled on all the steam we had* 1875 OTM 449 (Comb. not in OED W S C)

engineer, sb. **mining engineer,** [B²] *The capital which has developed the mines came from England, the mining engineers from America* 1897 FE lxviii 687 (OED 3. Combinations, as *electric, gas, mining, railway, telegraphic engineer,* are used to designate those who devote themselves to special departments of engineering. No ex. So W C U. Not in S)

engineer, v. [AB³] *It required sixty priests to engineer the Jesuit church* 1869 IA xxv 174. *The weighty business of dressing began... The proper official poured the water,*

the proper official engineered the washing 1881 PP xiv 165 (OEDS 2b. *U.S.* to superintend, guide, or carry through any measure or enterprise. 1864..So F Th,1859 M DN.III,V. Not A in W S C)

engineer–in–chief, sb. [B¹] *A copper-plate card with "Engineer-in-Chief" on it* 1873 GA xxviii 250 (Comb. not in OED W C. Given in S)

engineer–in–general, sb. [B¹] *Harry had been constituted engineer-in-general, and he threw the full strength of his powers into his work* 1873 GA xxv 230 (Hum. nonce formation)

English, sb. [AB²] *You would infallibly put the "English" on the wrong side of the ball* 1869 IA xii 116 (W: In billiards, a spinning or rotary motion round the vertical axis given to the ball by striking it to the right or left of the center. *U.S.* Called *side* in English usage. So OEDS 7, no ex. So S C)

English–murdering, ppl.a. [B¹] *They had no English-murdering clerks* 1869 IA xv 147 (Comb. not in OED W S C)

Englishry, sb. [B³C] *The Norman Conqueror came over to divert the Englishry* 1897 *Autob* (1924) I 120 (OED 2b. *rare.* 1867, only ex. So W S C U)

engrailed, ppl.a. [D] See *coat-of-arms* 1883 (OED 1a. Heraldry. Of an ordinary: Having a series of curvilinear indentations in the edge. 1486..1871—. So W S C U)

enow, a. [C] *"Thy good Nan and Bet shall have raiment and lackeys enow"* 1881 PP iii 42. See also *bone-racking* 1881 (OED Now only *arch* and *dial.* ..1868. So W S C U Wr)

enthuse, v. [AB³] *There is a profound monotony about facts that baffles and defeats one's efforts to make them sparkle and enthuse* 1889 CY xxvi 341. *It did not enthuse over that crude Salvation Army eloquence* 1906 "WIM" (1917) iii 34. See also *ambition,* v. 1906 (OEDS *U.S.* 1859..So S U B F Cl T M DN.IV. Not A in W C)

entrails, sb. [C] *They would have dug his entrails out...to get at that tale and squelch it* 1889 CY iii 46 (OED † 4. The inward parts regarded as the seat of the emotions, thoughts, etc. 1374..1790. Not *arch* in W S C U)

entrance–door, sb. [B¹] *At the entrance-door upstairs we were halted by an official* 1880 TA xviii 168 (Comb. not in OED W S C; but cf. OED Entrance-way, 1883)

entreat, v. [C] *He had been so buffeted, so rudely entreated by his own kind* 1881 PP xviii 233 (OED 1. To treat. *obs exc. arch.* 1430..1864. So W S C U Wr)

Episcopal, a. [AB³] See *dream-life* 1904; *Adventist* 1907 (OED 3. Often *spec,* with initial capital, of the Anglican Church, of which in Scotland and the U.S. it is the ordinary designation. 1844. So W S C Th,1754)

Episcopalian, sb. [?AB³] See *Congregationalist* 1906 (OED b. One who belongs to an Episcopal church. 1884, first U.S. ex. So W S C. A in M. Cf. above)

equilibree, sb. [B¹] *Here are a few of the coquette variants which he has labelled: The Collector, The Equilibree, The Professional Beauty* 1895 "What Bourget Thinks" 53 (Nonce borrowing from French *équilibrée,* a well-poised woman; taken over from Bourget and used without explanation)

er, int. [B³] *"I only meant conventional piety, you know; er—shop piety"* 1904 "Bequest" (1906) iii 13 (OEDS Used to express the inarticulate sound of murmur made by a hesitant speaker. 1862..So W. Not in S C. See discussion of similar expressions by Otto Jesperson, "Linguistic Self-Criticism", *S.P.E. Tract* no. 48, 1937)

–er, –est, suffixes of comparison [?A?CE]

1856 *Adv. of T. J. Snodgrass* 1928) 44: *eternalist, confoundedist, damnationist, oneriest* (sic).

1876 TS: *more surer* xxiii 182; *foolishest, more lonesomer* xxv 195; *thankfullest* xix 167; *pleasantest* xxx 226; *lonesomest, awfulest* xxxv 274.

1880 TA: *solemnest* ii 37; *heavenliest* iii 39; *pizener, pizenest* xxiii 225; *livest-looking* xliii 499.

1883 LM: *seldomest* xxii 257; *dead-surest* xliii 438.

1884 HF: *certainer* vii 49; *ignorantest* ix 78; *carelessest, foolishest* x 84; *treacherousest* xii 104; *dad-fetchedest* xiv 121; *blessedest* xx 198; *best-naturedest* xxi 213; *pitifulest* xxii 220; *splendidest, most loveliest* xxii 221; *thrillingest* xxiii 226; *horriblest-looking, orneriest* xxiv 236; *glidingest* xxvii 272; *more nearer* xxviii 289; *pizenest* xxviii 294; *lovinger* xxx 313; *soberer* xxxi 322; *innocentest* xxxiii 339; *leveler* xxxvi 368; *faithfuler* xlii 426; *peacefuler* xlii 428; *mixed-upest-looking* xlii 432.

1889 CY: *killingest* viii 111; *sublimest* xviii 224; *troublesomest, tryingest* xx 247; *delightedest* xxi 256; *pleasanter* xxvi 471; *properer* xxvii 353; *restfulest* xxvii 354; *comfortablest* xxxix 498; *superbest* xxxix 503; *lowdownest* xxxix 504; *placidest* xli 523; *perfectest* xli 524; *awfuler* xliv 573.

1894 TET: *rippingest, rantingest* ii 333.

1894 TSA: *maliciousest* iv 120; *interestingest* vii 256.

1896 TSD: *levelest* i 345; *orneriest, lowdownest* iii 350; *blamedest, jambledest* xi 537.

1902 "DBDS" (1928) 356: *lowest-down*.

(OED *-er*, suffix. In mod. Eng. almost restricted to adjs. of one or two syls.; longer adjs., and also dissyllables containing any suffix other than -y or -ly, having the periphrastic comparison by means of the adv. *more*. Earlier writers, however, have *beautifuller, eminenter, slavisher*, etc.; a few modern writers, e.g. Carlyle, affect the same method.

This meager statement of Present Standard English usage is supplemented by H. Poutsma, *A Grammar of Modern English*, II (1914) i 474-491. To the list of dissyllabic adjs. permitting terminational comparison in -er and -est, Poutsma adds those ending in -al, -el, -er, -le (if preceded by a consonant), -on, -ow, in a less degree those ending in -ed, -et, -id, -ful, and -some, and also all dissyllables accented on the last syllable. But he notes that it is avoided or impossible with some adjs. having these terminations, such as *proper, eager, real*; with those ending in -le preceded by a vowel, as *agile, docile*; with participial adjs. in -ing or -ed when the -e- is silent, as *charming, pleased*; with dissyllables having the prefix a-, as *apart, awake*; and even with monosyllables ending in a harsh consonant group such as *just, lax, crisp*. See also H. E. Palmer, *A Grammar of Spoken English*, pp. 81-87, and O. Jespersen, *Essentials of English Grammar*, p. 222. No restrictions on the suffixes of comparison are mentioned in W S C.

For dialect usage cf. Wright, *English Dialect Grammar*, sect. 398: In the dialects the comparative suffix -er and the superlative -est are added to practically all adjs., polysyllabic as well as monosyllabic. *More* and *most* are as a rule used only to supplement or intensify the regular comparison, as *more beautifuller, most worst*.

M.T.'s usage is certainly not affected or archaistic like Carlyle's, but reflects rather a genuine survival in colloquial American speech, akin to that in the English dialects. Cf.M: The Am. vulgate boldly employs *more better*..In general, the -er and -est terminations are used instead of the *more* and *most* prefixes. So DN.V; as a special feature of the Ozark dialect, AS.III.8, V. 267, and of e. Texas, AS.XI.351. Cf. DN.III (under *fightingest*): The formation of superlative adjs. from present active participles is a common negroism. See also Dr. Louise Pound, "Notes on the Vernacular", *American Mercury*, Oct. 1924, for many additional illustrations.)

erect-haired, ppl.a. [B¹] *Into the midst of that peaceful scene burst that slim-shanked boy...wild-eyed, erect-haired, and shouting* 1880 TA x 96 (With hair on end. *Comb.* not in OED W S C)

errand, sb. [C] *He delivered his errand, and said the clans were already gathering* 1894 PW xi 556 (OED 1. A message. *obs.* 890..1754. So W. Not *obs* in S C Wr)

erst, adv. [C] *Still his strike he did maintain, And screamed as erst with might and main* 189 *Slovenly Peter*

(1935) 17 (OED 5. †b. Referring to a recent past: Not long ago. 1480..1791. So W S C U)

esquire, sb. [C] *"Knights of the Bath, each with a white lace on his sleeve; then their esquires"* 1881 PP ix 105 (OED 1a. A young man of gentle birth, who.. attended upon a knight. Now only *arch*. 1475..1852. So W S C)

establishment, sb. [B¹] *This mustang was clerking in a fruit establishment (he had the establishment along with him in a basket)* 1869 IA xxx 313. *"They wanted to know if I was from the same 'establishment' that you hailed from, did they? What did they mean by 'establishment'?"* ..."*They meant an asylum—an idiot asylum*" 1880 TA xxv 257. See also salary 1883. *This establishment's name is Hochberghaus. It is...a health resort* 1898 "At the Appetite Cure" (1900) 147 (A hum. extension of the sense in OED 10a. A public institution, a school, factory, house of business, etc. 1832.. So W S C U)

euchre, sb. [AB³] *"They got out a greasy old deck and went to playing euchre"* 1866 Speeches (1910) 5 (OEDS 1. A game of cards, of American origin. 1841..So B F Cl AS.VII.430, classed as "Gold-Rush English". Not A in W S C U)

euchre-party, sb. [AB¹] *At night there were gaps in the euchre-parties which could not be satisfactorily filled* 1869 IA xvii 160 (Comb. not in OED W S C. Cf. above)

European plan, sb. [AB³] *The "European plan"—pay for what you get* 1880 TA xxviii 300 (OEDS *U.S.* 1847.. So W S C Th T M H)

Evangelical, a. [AB¹] *Evangelical (two bodies); see Adventist* 1907 (W Evangelical Association: A religious body, Methodist in polity and doctrine, founded in 1800 by Jacob Albright in Pennsylvania; a division in 1891 resulted in the formation of the United Evangelical Church. Evangelical Protestant Church: A Christian body in America (German). So S C. Not in OED)

even, adv. Spelled e'en. [CE] *"E'en the grimmest penalty"* 1881 PP xxiv 291 (OED In literary use the contracted form now occurs only in verse. So U Wr. Not *arch* in W S C)

even, a. to get even. [?AB¹] *One should always "get even" in some way, else the sore place will go on hurting* 1880 TA xxv 257. *"I reckon it's only human to want to get even"* 1892 AmCl iv 38 (S: To retaliate. So C U. Phr. not in OED W; but cf. OED 10c. To be even with: to have one's revenge upon. 1589..1875)

even, a. to make even. [?AB¹] *It may be, as I have said, that I am among strangers, and sing the glories of a forgotten age to unfamiliar ears; so I will "make even" and stop* 1886 "The Old-Fashioned Printer" Speeches (1910) 185 (A *fig* use of the printer's sense in C: In type-setting, to space out a 'take' or piece of copy so as to make the last line full when it is not the end of a paragraph. So S. This sense not in OED W; but cf. OED 10b. To square accounts. *obs.* 1622..1661)

evening, sb. [AB³] *"He'll play hookey from school this evening"* [Footnote] *Southwestern for "afternoon"* 1876 TS i 19 (OEDS 2c. *dial* and *U.S.local*. 1836.. So W S C Wr B F Cl T DN.II,III,V,VI, in s.e.Mo., s.w.Mo., n.w.Ark., s.III., w.Ind., Ky., W.Va., e.Ala., and Newfoundland)

evening paper, sb. [B¹] *This society item in the evening paper* 1892 AmCl iv 56 (Comb. not in OED W S C)

ever-augmenting, ppl.a. [B¹] *The procession moved on...through ever-augmenting splendors and ever-augmenting tempests of welcome* 1881 PP xxxi 359 (Comb. not in OED W S C)

ever-glorious, a. [B¹] *Membership in our ever-glorious organization* 1894 PW xi 556 (Comb. not in OED W S C)

everlasting, adv. [AB³] *I have been so everlasting busy that I couldn't write* 1872 Letters (1917) I xii 201. *"You'll like the boys; they're everlasting sociable"* 1892 AmCl xi 106 (OED 5. quasi-adv. b. *U.S. slang.* Very, exceedingly, 18... So C B F Cl. Not A in S. This use not in W)

ever-progressing, ppl.a.[B¹] *A glacier is a stupendous, ever-progressing, resistless plow* 1880 TA xl 461 (Comb. not in OED W S C)

ever-vigilant, a. [B¹] *"The ever-vigilant and efficient officer"* 1870 SNO (1875) 120 (Comb. not in OED W S C)

every, a. **every last.** [?AB¹] *"I know it is with me—every last sentence of it"* 1888 "Meisterschaft" 460. *"I'se gwine as straight to yo' uncle as I k'n walk, en tell him every las' thing I knows 'bout you"* 1894 PW viii 339 (This idiom not in OED W S C. Nearest is OED Every, a. 1c. with a superl. adj. preceded by *the* interposed before the sb. *Obs.* or *arch.* 1620 Every the least remembrance ..1838. This would now be expressed by *even the least,* etc., treated as a parenthesis)

every, a. **every which way.** [AB³] *He put on the pack-saddle...and then wound a rope all over and about it and under it every which way* 1872 RI xxxvii 262. *There was pap looking wild, and skipping about every which way, and yelling about snakes* 1884 HF vi 45. See also *bulliness* 1884. *He got that big di'mond...and held it up and let it flash and blaze and squirt sunlight everwhichaway* 1896 TSD xi 537. *These cones turn bodily like pivot-guns and point every-which-way* 1897 FE lxv 645 (OEDS lf. U.S. 1840..So W S B F Cl T DN.III. Not in C)

everything, pron. **like everything.** [?AB¹] *The banks are caving and the shape of the shores changing like everything* 1875 OTM 284. See *come on* 1884. *It jolted her up like everything* 1884 HF xxviii 283 (Used as an adv. intensifier or superlative phrase. Cf. *like nothing,* below, which has, curiously, the same meaning. Not in OED W S C)

everything-in-which, sb. [B¹] *"Christian Science... proceeds directly from the All-in-all to the Everything-in-Which"* 1899 "Chr.Sc. and the Book" 589 (Nonsense comb.)

everywheres, adv. [?AB¹] See *lay over* 1865. *"He's been nearly to Coonville and most everywheres"* 1876 TS vi 66 (W: *dial* and *colloq.* A in DN.III. Not in OED S C. Cf. *anywheres,* above)

evidence, v. [?AC] *This sufficiently evidenced the great value of the chart* 1883 LM li 501 (OED 3. To demonstrate. *obs.* 1632..1807. Not *obs* in W S C U. A in Cl)

exaggeration-mill, sb. [B¹] *"That tale...that he will tell...every time he feeleth his exaggeration-mill a-working"* 1889 CY iii 45 (Nonce comb.)

exalted, ppl.a. [B¹] See *partake* 1875. *A burly watchman, considerably exalted with liquor* 1881 PP x 119 (Slightly intoxicated, 'elevated.' This sense not in OED W S C)

examination day, sb. [B¹] *The schoolmaster...wanted the school to make a good showing on "Examination" day* 1876 TS xxi 167 (Comb. not in OED W S C)

exception, sb. **to take exceptions to.** [?AC] *Many even took exceptions to the article* 1869 IA lxi 647 (OED 7e. *To take (an) excep'ion (†exceptions) to:* to find fault with. 1591..1662, last ex. pl. form. This form not in W S C)

exchange, sb. [?AB³] *We used to trade old newspapers (exchanges) for that brand* 1906 *Autob* (1924) II 101 (OEDS 7b. A newspaper sent to the office of another newspaper in exchange for the latter. Earlier U.S. exs. 1836.. A in Th T. Not A in W S C)

exclamation-point, sb. [AB³] *The newspaper...remarks, with ill-concealed exclamation points...* 1883 LM lx 583 (OED *U.S.* Note or point of exclamation. 1864, only ex. So H. Not A in W S C)

ex-Congressman, sb. [AB¹] *That is the ex-Congressman: the poor fellow whose life has been ruined by a two-year taste of glory and of fictitious consequence* 1902 *"Does the Race Love a Lord?"* 443 (Comb. not in OED W S C. Cf. Congressman)

ex-convict, sb. [B¹] *Out of the 359 persons present, 223 were ex-convicts* 1897 FE xxix 284 (Comb. not in OED. Given in W S C)

excursion, v.trans. [?AB¹] *He would excursion us in his flag-ship* 1895 *Letters* (1917) II xxxv 626 (The trans. sense not in OED W S C. Cf. OED v.intr. To go on an excursion, 1792.. Cf. also excursionist, below)

excursioning, vbl.sb. [?AB¹] *We concluded to try a bit of excursioning around on a steamboat* 1880 TA xxvii 273 (Not in OED W S C)

excursionist, sb. [?AB³] *I was provided with a receipt, and duly and officially accepted as an excursionist* 1869 IA i 24 (OED 1. One who goes upon a pleasure excursion. 1830.. So W S C U. A in B T M)

excursionize, v.intr. [?AB³] *The excursionizing tourists arriving and departing* 1880 TA xliv 512 (OED 2. To go on an excursion. 1866.. So W S C. Cf. excursionist, above)

ex-desperado, sb. [?AB¹] *Ex-desperado—nineteen scalps on his string* 1902 "DBDS" (1928) 354 (Comb. not in OED W S C. Cf. desperadoism, above)

executive family, sb. [?AB¹] *A member of the executive family of so fast and famous a boat* 1883 LM xviii 218 (The boat staff. A *fig* transfer from the political sense; cf. H (under *family*): in Am. the members of a Cabinet are often spoken of as the President's *official family.* Cf. also OED Executive, sb. 1b. The person or persons in whom the supreme executive magistracy of a country or state is vested. Chiefly *U.S.* 1787.. Comb. not in OED W S C)

executive session, sb. [AB²] *"Executive session of the Senate at 2 P.M.—got to get the appointment confirmed"* 1880 TA xxvi 265 (OED *U.S.* 1888, only ex. So W M H. Comb. not in S C)

exequatur, sb. [B¹] *"It is constructive nepotism to keep in office a 'Had' that can't come out when the wind is in the nor'-west—I won't have this dude on the payroll. Cancel his exequatur"* 1904 "Italian with Grammar" (1906) 196 (Hum. transf. use from the sense in OED 1. An official recognition of a consul by the government of the country to which he is accredited. 1788..)

ex-Governor, sb. [AB¹] See *Congress* 1873 (Comb. not in OED W S C. Cf. Governor, below)

exhibition, sb. [?AB¹] *He felt resentful toward all the three witnesses of his exhibition* 1894 PW xi 556 (U: Some thing or quality shown or manifested, which is absurd, grotesque, objectionable, contemptible. This sense not in OED W S C; but cf. the phr. in OED 5e. *To make an exhibition of oneself:* to behave so as to appear in a contemptible aspect. *colloq.* No ex.)

exhibition-ground, sb. [B¹] *The sun was well up when we got to the exhibition-ground* 1880 TA xxix 303 (Comb. not in OED W S C)

exhilaration, sb. [B¹] *The bar keeper...the vender of exhilaration* 1873 GA xiii 131 (The state of being intoxicated, 'merry,' 'mellow.' Cf. exalted, above. This euphemism not in OED W S C)

exhorter, sb. [?A] *He would be there...to bet on Parson Walker, which he judged to be the best exhorter about here* 1865 "Jumping Frog" (1875) 31 (OED 2. In various Christian churches, a person appointed to give religious exhortation. 1513..1772. OEDS Later U.S. exs. 1845..1871. Not A in W S C)

exhumer, sb. [B²] *The exhumers of Pompeii* 1869 IA xxxi 243 (OED 1872, this quot., wrongly dated... So W S. Not in C)

exitless, a. [B¹] *Lock the three up in a holeless, crackless, exitless prison-cell* 1909 ISD v 52 (Not in OED W S C)

ex-keelboatman, sb. [AB¹] *I remember...the ex-keelboatmen and their admiringly patronizing successors* 1883 LM iii 42 (Comb. not in OED W S C. Cf. keelboat, below)

ex-Member, sb. [AB¹] See *Congress* 1873 (Comb. not in OED W S C; but cf. OED Member, sb. 5. In full..in U.S., Member of Congress. 1774..)

ex-official, sb. [B¹] *The persecuted ex-officials* 1873 GA xxxiii 303 (Comb. not in OED W S C)

expect, v. [?A] *"Have you been questioned?...Well, I didn't expect you had"* 1889 CY xi 128 (OED 6. The misuse of the word as a synonym of *suppose*, without any notion of 'anticipating' or 'looking for,' is often cited as an Americanism, but is very common in dialectal, vulgar, or carelessly colloquial speech in England. 1592.. So W S U Wr T. A in C B F Cl M DN.II,III,V. Not A in AS.V.141)

expediting, ppl.a. [B¹] *Straightway she sounded "boots and saddles," that thrilling and most expediting call* 1906 "Horse's Tale" 547 (Not in OED W S C as adj.; but cf. OED Expedite, v. 2. To hasten the progress of. 1618..)

experience, v. *to experience religion.* [AB³] *Now George Benton experienced religion. The glad news flew all around* 1880 "Edward Mills" 229 (OEDS *U.S.* To be converted. 1837.. So S B F Cl Th. Not A in W C)

expert, sb. [?AB³] *The Expert came home with me to instruct me* 1880 "Taming the Bicycle" (1917) 285. *He gave orders that the remains of the late twins be embalmed by some St. Louis expert* 1892 AmCl iv 55 (OED 2. A specialist. 1825.. So W S C U. A in M)

expert accountant, sb. [B¹] *He offered his services now in the humble capacities of land surveyor and expert accountant* 1893 PW ii 235 (Comb. not in OED W S C)

express, sb. [?AB³] *In New Zealand, these fast expresses run twice a week* 1897 FE xxxi 290 (OED 2. Short for express train. 1848.. So W S C U. A in B T)

express, sb. [AB³] *It was his business to take care of the mails, baggage, express matter, and passengers* 1872 RI ii 25 (OEDS 3. *U.S.* An institution for the transmission of parcels; also attrib. 1839.. So C B F Cl Th T H. Not A in W S)

expressman, sb. [AB³] See *flat*, v. 1892 (OED An employé of one of the U.S. express companies. 1847.. So W C. Not A in S)

express train, sb. [?AB³] *The Pacific express-trains whiz through there now* 1872 RI xii 106. *We would go flying up the shore like a lightning express train* 1875 OTM 194 (OED 1841.. So W S C U. A in M)

express wagon, sb. [AB³] *"I do not refer to low people who come in a pine box mounted on an express wagon"* 1870 SNO (1875) 198 (OED *U.S.* 1860.. So C B F Th H DN.III,IV. Not A in W S)

ex-slave, sb. [B¹] *George—that peerless black ex-slave and children's idol* 1909 "Death of Jean" (1917) 119 (Comb. not in OED W S C)

extra, sb. [?AB³] *We got an extra issued by a Memphis paper* 1883 LM xx 237 (OEDS Earlier U.S. exs. 1849.. Not A in W S C)

extract, v. [B¹] *It was the first time I ever extracted a watermelon. That is exactly the word I want. Its use in dentistry connotes the delicate shade of meaning I am looking for* 1906 "Address at the University of Missouri" *Speeches* (1910) 228 (Hum. transfer from the sense in OED 3. Often with reference to dentistry. 1878. So W S C)

extradition, sb. [B¹] *"Extradition of the maxillaris superioris"* 1894 TET vii 408 (Malapropism for *extraction*)

extra-hazardous, a. [B¹] See *accidental insurance* 1869 (Comb. not in OED W. Given in S C)

extraordinariensis, a. [B¹] *"The most venerable creature that exists in the earth to-day—Ornithorhyncus Platypus Extraordinariensis!"* 1897 FE viii 106 (Nonce coinage)

eye, sb. *to get one's eye on.* [?AB¹] *He wished he could get his eye on a certain man* 1892 AmCl iii 31 (Phr. not in OED W S C; cf. OED *To give an eye to*, 1586)

eye, sb. *to keep an eye out for.* [?AB¹] *I moved away, at the same time keeping an eye out for any chance passenger in his right mind* 1889 CY ii 32 (Phr. not in OED W S C. Cf. OED *To keep an eye upon*, 1818)

eye, sb. *up to the eyes.* [?AB²] *She was immersed in the marvel up to her eyes* 1873 GA xxxii 292 (OED 2e. Deeply immersed or occupied. 1884.. So U. Not in W S C)

eye-contenting, ppl.a. [B¹] See *new-gold*, a. 1897 (Comb. not in OED W S C; but cf. OED Eye-delighting, 1757..; Eye-pleasing, 1580..)

eye-opener, sb. [AB³] See *cocktail* 1869 (OEDS *U.S.* A draught of strong liquor, esp. one taken in the morning. 1818.. So W S C F Cl M DN.I)

eye-witness, v. [B¹] *They seem to be always eye-witnessing the happenings* 1905 "King Leopold's Soliloquy" 14 (Not in OED S C as verb. Given in W)

F

facchino, sb. [B¹] *I told the facchino...I will explain that a facchino is a general utility domestic* 1904 "Italian with Grammar" (1906) 189 (Nonce borrowing from Italian)

fact-life, sb. [B¹] *In their sternly restricted Fact-life they remained as of old—plodding, diligent, careful, practical* 1904 "Bequest" (1906) vi 34 (Comb. not in OED W S C)

factory-girl, sb. [?AB³] *"If you call a factory-girl a young lady, what do you call the President's wife?"* 1892 AmCl xi 111 (OEDS Earlier U.S. exs. 1833.. Comb. not in W S C)

Faculty, sb. [AB³] *The Faculty's wives must flock over, one after the other* 1897 FE xxvi 254 (OEDS 9b. The whole teaching staff of a college or university. *U.S.* 1829.. So W M H. Not A in S C)

fad, sb. [?AB³] *One of his pet fads was palmistry* 1893 PW ii 235 (OED 1. A pet project, hobby. 1834.. So W S C U Wr. A in M)

fag, v.trans. [?AB³] *We fag ourselves out completely every day* 1863 *Letters* (1919) I iv 90 (OED 3. To tire, weary. 1826.. So W S C U. A in DN.III AS.IV.383)

Fair, sb. [?AB¹] *Last spring I went to Chicago to see the Fair* 1893 "Travelling with a Reformer" (1900) 248 (A in T: An exhibition, not primarily for making sales. Not A in W S. This sense not in OED C; OED has only 1. A periodical gathering of buyers and sellers ...in England they sometimes survive merely as gatherings for pleasure. c1330..)

fair, a. [C] See *marry,* int. 1889. *"Even so, fair my lord"* 1889 CY xix 230 (OED 1. †d. Used in courteous or respectful address. c1350..1588. So C. Not *obs* in W S)

fair, adv. **to say fair, ask fair.** [?AC] *"That's as fair as a man can say"* 1876 TS ix 91. *"I couldn't ask fairer than that"* 1892 AmCl xxiv 261 (OED 2. Now only in phr. *to speak fair.* 1000..1590, last ex. exc. with *speak.* Not *arch* in W S C)

fair and square, a. [?A] See *go back on* 1876. *It wouldn't be fair and square for the others* 1884 HF ii 14 (OED a. Honest, just. 1604.. So W S C. A in B. Not A in T)

fair daylight, sb. [?AC] *"It 'uz fair daylight when we passed our plantation"* 1894 PW xviii 19 (OED 12. b. Broad daylight. c1450..1605. Not *obs* in S W. A in H: In the sense of completely, fully, or clearly, distinctly, this word is now *obs* in Eng., exc. in certain dialects, but is still current in Am. Comb. not in W C)

fair field, sb. [B²] *For the first time in his life his talents had a fair field* 1873 GA xl 355 (OED 10b. Affording an equal chance of success. 1883, only ex. So S C. Comb. not in W)

fair grounds, sb. [?AB³] *There are ample fair-grounds, a well-kept park* 1883 LM lvii 556 (W: An enclosure where outdoor fairs, circuses, etc., are held; often pl. *U.S.* So S C. Not A in OED Fair, sb. 2. 1881. OEDS Earlier exs. 1741.. The only OEDS ex. of the pl. form, 1857, is U.S.)

fair-looking, ppl.a. [B¹] *Both threw away some tolerably fair-looking opportunities* 1880 PP xxii 274 (Comb. not in OED W S C)

fair-minded, ppl.a. [B²] *Fair-minded people declined to condemn her on mere suspicion* 1873 GA xxxiv 315 (OED 1874, only ex. So W S C)

fair-to-middling, a. [AB¹] *An inane dead-level of "fair-to-middling"* 1880 TA xlix 573. *We again had fair-to-middling views of the stupendous mountain* 1897 FE lvi 535 (DN.III: n.w.Ark., Fairly good. So S Wr. Doubtless *transf.* from the commercial sense in C: Moderately good; a term designating a specific grade in the market. Comb. not in OED W; but cf. OED Middling, a. 3. *Comm.* Used as the designation for the second of three grades of goods)

faith-curist, sb. [?AB³] So *moonshiner* 1895; *Allopath* 1902 (OED 1888. So W C. A in F Cl. Comb. not in S)

faith-doctor, sb. [?AB¹] *We had the "faith doctor," too, in those early days* 1897 Autob (1924) I 108. *When I was a boy, a farmer's wife who lived five miles from our village had great fame as a faith-doctor—that was what she called herself* 1899 "Chr. Sc. and the Book" 593 (S: var. of faith-healer. Comb. not in OED W C; but cf. OED Faith-healer, 1885)

faith-straining, ppl.a. [B¹] *Here are some faith-straining figures* 1897 FE xvii 172 (Comb. not in OED W S C)

faix, int. [B³CE] *"Faix an' is it Biddy Malone ye dare to be callin' names?"* 1869 SNO (1875) 69 (OED A var. of Fegs, which is a distortion of Fay, Faith; *obs* exc. *Sc.* and *dial.* 2. 1863, only ex. So W S C Wr. Cf. P. W. Joyce, *Eng. as We Speak It in Ireland,* p. 71: The use of the interjection *faith* is a sure mark of an Irishman all over the world...People who shrink from the plain word often soften it to *Faix*)

fake, sb. [?AB³] *When you throw up a feather it sails away on the air and goes out of sight; then you throw up a clod and it doesn't...I suppose it is an optical illusion. I mean, one of them is...I can only demonstrate that one or the other is a fake* 1905 "Eve's Diary" 31 (OED slang. 1. A trick, invention. 1827.. So S C U T. A in F Cl Th M. Not in W)

fall, sb. [AC] *Along in the fall the invitation came* 1873 GA xxx 275 (OED 2. In U.S. the ordinary name for autumn; in Eng. now rare. 1545..1864. So W S C U Wr B F Cl Th T M H DN.I,VI, AS.IV.475)

false start, sb. [B²] *The thirteen mules got away in a body, after a couple of false starts* 1883 LM xliv 464 (OED 6. A wrong start in a race. No ex. So U. Phr. not in W S C)

fames, sb. [B¹] *"It is not meet that you bare your head before the fleeting fames and dignities of a day"* 1896 JA II xiii 302. *Deriding our pride in our great heroes, our imperishable fames, our mighty kings* c1898 MS (1916) vi 55 (This *concrete* sense not in OED W S. Given in C: Rarely used in the pl.)

familywise, adv. [B¹] *Some of them married and experimenting familywise themselves* 1889 CY xviii 224 (Comb. not in OED W S C)

famine-breeder, sb. [B¹] *Shovel-hatted, long-robed, well-fed priests...they look like consummate famine-breeders* 1869 IA xvii 164 (Comb. not in OED W S C)

fancy, a. [?AB³] *This is not a fancy sketch. I got it from a clergyman...who vouched for its truth* 1891 "Luck" 407 (OED 4. Based upon or drawn from conceptions of the fancy. 1800.. So W S C U. A in Cl: fictitious, imaginary)

fancy-looking, a. [?AB¹] *A fancy-looking negro in Turkish costume* 1869 IA xxxviii 411 (Comb. not in OED W S C. Cf. Cl Fancy: applied to things and persons more ornamental than useful)

fancy-topped, a. [?AB¹] *She has two tall fancy-topped chimneys* 1875 OTM 70 (Comb. not in OED W S C. Cf. above)

fandango, sb. [AC] *He took him to circuses...and fandangoes* 1894 TET v 368. *He attended balls and fandangoes...every night* 1906 Autob (1924) II 125 (OED 2. A social assembly for dancing. Now only *U.S.* 1760..1785, last British ex. So S C B F Cl DN.I AS. VII.431. Not A in W T)

fan-distributor, sb. [B¹] *It* [i.e., a local Christian Science church] *can appoint its own fan-distributors, summers* 1907 CS II viii 235 (Comb. not in OED W S C; but cf. OED Fan-bearer, 1897)

fantastic, sb. [AB¹] *They were no whit behind the men for romps and noise and fantastics* 1895 JA II xii 543. *We had no fool ceremonies, no fantastics, no horse-play* 1897 FE iv 66 (S: A grotesquely dressed company that paraded the streets on the morning of Independence Day or some other holiday. Local *U.S.* So DN.III: A mummer..so called in the South just prior to the War. Not in OED W C)

fantasy, sb. [C] *"Yesternight toke Her Majestie, ye Queen, a fantasie such as she sometimes hath"* 1880 *Fireside Conversation, 1601* (OED 7. Inclination, liking, desire. *obs. c*1374..1618. So W S. Not *obs* in C)

fan-tods, sb. [?AB²] *Mush-and-milk journalism gives me the fan-tods* 1869 SNO (1875) 47. *"If a person starts in to jabber-jabber-jabber about scenery, and history, and pictures...I get the fan-tods mighty soon"* 1880 TA xxvii 283. *By and by I was close enough to have a look, and there laid a man on the ground. It most give me the fantods* 1884 HF viii 64. *These was all nice pictures, I reckon, but I didn't somehow seem to take to them, because if ever I was down a little they always give me the fan-tods* do xvii 155. See also *jimjams* 1896 (OEDS Variant of Fantad. 1884, quot. from HF. W: State of worry or excitement; fidgets. *slang.* So S C Wr)

fare, v. [C] *"Yes, thither will we fare"* 1881 PP xii 140 (OED 1. To journey. Now *arch* or *poet.* 971..1855. So S C U Wr. Not *arch* in W)

fare-ticket, sb. [?AB¹] *If you buy a fare-ticket and fail to use it, there is room thus made available for some one else* 1897 FE xlviii 447. *"Your luggage is rechecked, fare-ticket and sleeper changed"* 1902 *"Belated Russian Passport"* (1928) 178 (Comb. not in OED W S C)

farm, sb. *for a farm.* [?AB¹] *I wouldn't read another of those books for a farm* 1885 *Letters* (1917) II xxv 454 (For any consideration. This familiar phr. not in OED W S C)

farmacopia, sb. [B¹] *The first thing I did was to determine what manner of doctor I was to be. Being a Connecticut farmer, I naturally consulted my farmacopia* 1909 *Speeches* (1910) 335 (A pun, which suggests that M.T. grew up to pronounce the word "Phar'macopia" rather than the approved "Pharmacopoe'ia". Cf. OED Pharmacopoeia, 1621..)

farmeopath, sb. [B¹] *I at once decided to become a farmeopath* 1909 *Speeches* (1910) 335 (Hum. coinage. Cf. above)

farmer-class, sb. [B'] *He was born of good farmer-class parents who could not read* 1909 ISD iii 28 (Comb. not in OED W S C)

farmer-preacher, sb. [B¹] *He warn't only a farmer, he was a preacher, too, and had a little one-horse log church down back of his plantation...There was plenty other farmer-preachers like that, and done the same way, down South* 1884 HF xxxiii 339 (Comb. not in OED W S C)

farm-help, sb. [AB¹] *Everybody on the farm flocked to the arbor...the farm-help, the colored servants...* 1884 *Letters* (1917) II xxiv 444 (Comb. not in OED W S C. Cf. help, below, *U.S.* in this sense)

farm-land, sb. [?A] *The smooth levels of dainty green farm-land* 1880 TA xxix 304 (OEDS Farm, sb. 9. Earlier U.S. exs. 1638.. Comb. not in W S C)

far-receding, ppl.a. [B¹] See *cabin* 1883 (Comb. not in OED W S C)

far-sounding, ppl.a. [B¹] *Far-sounding cataclysms of uncreated space* 1892 AmCl xvi 169 (Comb. not in OED S C. Given in W)

Far West, sb. [AB³] *Showing their revolvers when they did not intend to use them—a thing which is considered bad judgment in the Far West* 1869 IA li 550. *An interesting episode in the history of the Far West* 1872 RI pref. *He would join the Indians, and hunt buffaloes... in the mountain ranges and trackless great plains of the Far West* 1876 TS viii 80. *The family's driftings to and fro in the Far West* 1892 AmCl iii 36. See also *South* 1904 (OEDS The western parts of the U.S. or of N. Am. 1830.. So W F AS.II.27. Comb. not in S C)

Far-Western, a. [AB³] *A little Far-Western girl of nine, equipped with an adult vocabulary* 1902 *"Chr.Sc."* 706 (OEDS *U.S.* 1845.. So W. Not in S C)

fash, sb. [B²E] *"He is a dear good soul, and all that; but invention isn't his fash"* 1888 *"Meisterschaft"* 458 (OEDS Fach, Ger. word: A line of work, department of activity, métier. 1930..M.T.'s spelling is his own attempt to naturalize the German pronunciation)

fashion-plate, sb. [B²] *Harry, with blue eyes, fresh complexion, silken whiskers, and curly chestnut hair, was as handsome as a fashion-plate* 1873 GA xiii 125. *Godey's Lady's Book, with painted fashion-plate of wax-figure women* 1883 LM xxxviii 400 (OED A pictorial design showing the prevailing style or new style of dress. No quot. So W S C U)

fast, a. [?C] *Hendon keeping a fast grip upon the prince's wrist* 1881 PP xii 133 (OED 6. Gripping, tenacious. *Obs* exc. in *Fast hold.* 1510..1724. Not *obs* in W S C U)

fat, sb. [B¹] *There's a good deal of "fat"...The "fat" is old pigeon-holed things, of the years gone by* 1906 *Letters* (1917) II xlv 796 (Matter exacting little or no labor on a writer's part. A nonce use, *transf.* from the sense in OED 5b. *Printing.* Short pages, light open matter, etc. 1796..1841. So S C. This sense not in W)

fat, a. [AB¹] See *incorporatorship* 1873. *"This ain't no fat thing, I reckon! If I ain't in luck!"* 1880 TA iii 39 (A in B, p. 782: Used of anything desirable. Not A in W S C U: Richly rewarding, desirable. This sense not in OED)

Father of his Country, sb. [AB¹] *Washington's disposition was born in him...the benignant disposition born to the Father of his Country* 1902 *"Defence of Gen. Funston"* 614 (Phr. not in OED C. Given in W S U)

fat up, v.trans. [B¹] *A battered little temple...with custom enough to fat-up a priest and keep him comfortable* 1897 FE xlix 461 (Hum. *transf.* to a person of the use in OED 3. To feed animals for use as food. 1561..1774. So U. Not in W S C)

fault, v. [C] *"Your majesty faulted thrice in your Greek"* 1881 PP xiv 171 (OED † 6. To make a mistake. 1530..1765. So W S C)

favor, sb. [C] *"The old Baron Morley, being mad, forgot the favor of his own countenance"* 1881 PP vi 83 (OED 9. Appearance. Now *arch* or *dial. c*1450..1863. So S C Wr. Not *arch* in W)

faze, v. Spelled **phase**. [AB³E] *She [the hen] could not "phase"those eggs, because they were nest eggs* 1870 *"Curious Dream"* (1872) 138. *"You might take and belt him over the head with a church and you couldn't phase him"* 1876 TS x 94. *It [a sarcastic remark] never fazed him; he didn't appear to know he was hurt* 1889 CY ii 33. *Lash and club and fist had done their work well; the king's body was a sight to see—and to weep over; but his spirit? why, it wasn't even phased* 1889 CY xxxv 457. *To her joy it [a confession] never phased him* 1892 AmCl xxii 230 (OED Phase, v. Erroneous spelling of Faze. 1889, quot. from CY...OEDS Faze, v. *U.S.* To discompose, disturb. 1843.. So W S C Wr B F Cl Th T M DN.I,II,III,IV. A favorite word with M.T.; but only once did he, or his printers, permit it to be spelled correctly)

fear, v.refl. [C] *I fear me the market price would advance* 1869 IA xviii 180 (OED 3. The refl. use *arch.* 1393..1859. So W. Not *arch* in S C)

fear-bound, a. [B¹] *Do not be afraid, or your limbs will be fear-bound* 1883 LM App. D 619 (Comb. not in OED W S C)

feather, sb. *in full feather.* [AB¹] *Lax court morals and the absurd chivalry business were in full feather* 1883 LM i 27. *The very same matter which is suppressed in one paper gets published in another in full feather and unmodified* 1898 *"Stirring Times in Austria"* (1900) 289 (S: In complete plumage; in good trim. A in Cl Th,1896 DN.VI. Phr. not in OED W C. Cf. OED In high feather, 1844; In fine feather, 1846)

feather-end, sb. [B¹] *A kind of bow-and-arrow arrangement, you see; the causeway the arrow, the boulevard at the feather-end of it* 1896 JA II xvii 444 (Comb. not in OED W S C)

Federal, a. [AB³] *Piloting a Federal gun-boat and shouting for the Union* 1885 "Private Hist. of Campaign" 193 (OED 3b. In the Am. Civil War: of or pertaining to the Northern or Union party. 1861.. So W S C F Th)

feeble, v. [C] See *dure*, v. 1889 (OED 1. To grow feeble. *obs.* 1225..1496. So W S C)

feeding-house, sb. [?AB¹] *I stuck by Harris's humble feeding-house* 1893 "Banknote" (1928) 117 (Eating-house, restaurant. This sense not in OED W S C. Cf. OED Feed, v. 3. To eat, of persons; now only *colloq*; Feeding-house (for animals), 1807)

feeding-place, sb. [?AB¹] *Another cheap feeding-place —the "Miners' Restaurant"* 1907 "Chaps. from Autob" 18 (This sense not in OED. Cf. OED Feeding-place (for animals), 1611. Comb. not in W S C)

feeler, sb. [?AB³] *I have "feelers" out in several directions, and have already asked for a hundred dollars from one source* 1856 *Letters* (1917) I ii 34. *Sellers threw a lot or two on the market, "as a feeler", and they sold well* 1873 GA xxv 231. *Sally had several times thrown out a feeler—that is, a hint* 1904 "Bequest" (1906) iv 17 (OED 4b. A proposal or hint put forth in order to ascertain the opinions of others. 1830.. So W S C U)

feel of, v. [AC] *"You come in here and feel of me if you don't believe me"* 1884 HF xxxiii 338 (OED 2a. Now only *dial* and *U.S.* with *of*. 1751..1878. So H. Not A in W S C)

fell, sb. [C] *Hjorleifshofdi* [in Iceland] *is a fell 640 feet in height* 1880 TA xl 466 (OED 1. A hill, mountain. *obs.* 1300..1610. So W S C)

fellow, sb. Spelled **feller**. [?AE] See *honest* 1876. *"When they're taking that feller away, you heave your cat after them"* 1876 TS vi 58 (OED This sp. used in renderings of dial and vulgar speech, 19th c. So W. A in M DN.II,III,IV,V. Not in S C)

fellow-barber, sb. [B¹] *He will wait for his fellow-barber's chair* 1871 SNO (1875) 258 (Comb. not in OED W S C)

fellow-conspirator, sb. [B¹] *He shall deceive his fellow-conspirators* 1899 "My First Lie" (1900) 160 (Comb. not in OED S C. Given in W)

fellow-pilot, sb. [B¹] *He was once a fellow-pilot for a trip or two with George Ealer* 1875 OTM 451 (Comb. not in OED W S C)

fellow-savant, sb. [B¹] *"This great marvel which we have just witnessed, fellow-savants, is nothing less than the transit of Venus!"* 1875 SNO 131 (Comb. not in OED W S C)

fellow-second, sb. [B¹] *My fellow-second and I paced off the thirty-five yards* 1880 TA viii 79 (Comb. not in OED W S C)

fellow-trader, sb. [B¹] *The most picturesque example in history of a trader's trust in his fellow-trader* 1899 "Concerning the Jews" (1900) 258 (Comb. not in OED W S C)

fellow-unfortunate, sb. [B¹] *The man who had been able to inspire a fellow-unfortunate to write such a tract* 1883 LM lii 517 (Comb. not in OED W S C)

fellow-villager, sb. [B¹] *He had made a good deal of a raid on his fellow-villagers a fortnight before* 1894 PW ix 550 (Comb. not in OED S C. Given in W)

female, sb. [?AC] *Now in one place he loses some "females"—as he always calls women—in the edge of a wood* 1895 "Cooper's Literary Offences" 4 (OED 2b. As a mere synonym for 'woman,' now commonly avoided by good writers, exc. with contemptuous implication. 1380..1801, last quot. not contemptuous. So W S U Wr. A in B Cl Th,1773 M AS.XII.121. This usage not in C)

fence, sb. [?AB³] *What is a U.S. custom house but a "fence?" That is all it is: a legalized trader in stolen goods* 1887 *Letters* (1917) II xxvi 480 (OED 8b. A receiving house for stolen goods. 1847.. So W S C U T. A in B Cl DN.V)

fence, v. [?AB¹] *We used to economize on the news... Most of the yearly ads were patent-medicine stereotypes, and we used to fence with them* 1886 *Speeches* (1910) 185 (To fill in with; to distribute according to convenience. This sense not in OED W S C; but cf. OED 11. To keep in position by a gauge or guide. *obs.* 1703)

fence-post, sb. [?AB³] *The mule's foot caved all the loose masonry and one of the fence-posts overboard* 1880 TA xxxv 386 (OEDS Earlier U.S. ex. 1853.. Not A in W. Comb. not in S C)

fence-rail, sb. [AB³] *We was both on our knees with our chins on a fence-rail and gazing* 1896 TSD v 355 (OEDS *U.S.* 1802.. So B. Not A in W. Comb. not in S C)

ferry-landing, sb. [?AB¹] *I heard people talking at the ferry-landing* 1884 HF vii 55 (Comb. not in OED W S C. Cf. Landing, below)

fesse, sb. Spelled **fess**. [DE] See *coat-of arms* 1883 (OED *Heraldry*. 1. An ordinary formed by two horizontal lines drawn across the middle of the field, and usually containing between them one-third of the escutcheon. 1486..1872—. So W S C U. The sp. *fess* not in OED. Given in W S C)

festival, sb. [AB¹] *I have heard shameless people say they were glad to get away from Ladies' Festivals where they were importuned to buy by bevies of lovely young ladies* 1869 IA lv 602 (S: *U.S.* An entertainment, often public, at which eatables are sold for some charitable object. This sense not in OED W C)

festoon, v.intr. [C] *Foliage and festooning vines* 1876 TS xiii 118 (OED 1. To hang in festoons. *obs.* 1789, only ex. Not *obs* in W. This intr. sense not in S C)

fetch, v. [?AC] *He flew down and got that acorn, and fetched it up and dropped it in* 1880 TA iii 39. *The drift of the canoe fetched me in at the bottom of the town* 1884 HF x 86. See also *dad-fetch* 1884. (OED 2. To cause to come...by a constraining force. Now *rare*. ..1862. So W. A in DN.II. This sense not in W S C)

fetch, v. [?A] *I have closed many and many a lecture, in many a city, with that. It always "fetches" them* 1866 *M.T. the Letter Writer* (1932) i 18. *I'll even "fetch" those Dutch Pennsylvanians with this lecture* 1872 *Letters* (1917) I xi 193 (OED 4. To move to interest or admiration. Not in dignified use. 1605.. So W S C U. A in F Cl)

fetch, v. [?AC] *"You couldn't fetch nothing for him to bet on but he'd match you"* 1865 *Jumping Frog* (1875) 32. *"Down he fetched a right bower"* 1877 *Speeches* (1910) 5. *The jury'll twaddle and twaddle and twaddle, and finally they'll fetch in a verdict* 1896 TSD vi 357. *She happened to fetch out a long word which had had its day weeks before* 1903 "Dog's Tale" 12 (OED 6. To draw, derive from a source, *esp.* from one more or less remote. Now *rare*. 1552..1871. C: *Obsolescent.* Not rare in W S U. DN.II: Common in Am. dialects)

fetch, v. [?A] *He fetched a prodigious "Whoosh!" to relieve his lungs* 1880 TA xx 194. *They all fetched a kind of Injun war-whoop* 1883 LM iii 44. *She would slip up behind a person and...fetch a war-whoop* 1906 *Autob* (1924) II 243 (OED 7. To utter, as a groan or scream. 1632.. So W S C U. A in F T DN.III)

fetch, v. [?AC] *He fetched the tub a rattling kick* 1884 HF vi 44. *She fetched first one and then another of them a clip* 1884 HF xxxii 330. *When somebody has fetched them a lifter* 1894 TSA ix 356 (OED 8. To deal, strike, as a blow. Now chiefly *colloq*. ..1888. So W Wr. Not *arch* in S C U. A in F Cl)

fetch, v. [?AC] *"Do you think I could venture to throw a rock here without hitting a captain of this ship?" "Well, sir, I don't know—I think likely you'd fetch the* *captain of the watch, maybe"* 1869 IA iii 37. See *haul off* 1870. *The inventor of the language can't talk grammatical: if the Dative didn't fetch him the Accusative would* 1888 "Meisterschaft" 465. See also *line-shot* 1906 (OED 8b. To 'have at,' reach, strike a person. *Obs.* . .1625. Not *obs.* in W S C)

fetch, v. [?AC] *You steer along. . .catch your breath, fetch a violent hitch this way and then that, and down you go again c*1880 "Taming the Bicycle" (1917) 289. *A brook that never goes straight for a minute. . .sometimes fetching a horseshoe three-quarters of a mile around* 1904 *Autob* (1924) I 237 (OED 9. To make or perform a movement; of a river, to make a turn, winding. *Obs* exc. *arch.* 1530. .1859. So W. Not *obs* in C. A in Cl. This sense not in S)

fetch, v. [?A] See *scoot* 1884. *"I'll fetch Goshen before daybreak"* 1884 HF xi 95. *No fault of hers that she couldn't fetch the home plate* 1889 CY xxii 279 (OED 10. *Naut.* To arrive at, come to, reach. 1556. .1880. So W S C Wr. The extension to baseball is American, at least)

fetch, v. [?AB¹C] *"Maybe that whack done for him!" "No, 'taint likely, Tom. He had liquor in him. . .When pap's full, you might take and belt him over the head with a church and you couldn't phase him. .But if a man was dead sober, I reckon maybe that whack might fetch him"* 1876 TS x 94 (To 'do for,' kill. Cf. C: To carry off. *Obs.* This sense not in OED W S; but cf. OED Fetch, v. 16b. Fetch off: To 'do' or 'do for;' to get the better of; to make an end of. *Obs.* 1597. .1653)

fetch around, v. [?AB¹] *"I persuaded myself this evening that I could fetch him around without any great amount of effort"* 1894 PW xiv 778 (To bring a person to one's own point of view. *trans.* This sense not in OED W S C)

fetch around, v. [?AB¹] *"They will leave tomorrow, letting on to go south, but they will fetch around north all in good time"* 1906 "Horse's Tale" vii 539. *Mrs. Eddy . .fetches around and comes forward and testifies again* 1907 CS II iv 141 (To take a roundabout course or method. *intr.* This sense not in OED W S C; but cf. OED Fetch about, 1551..)

fetch around, v. [?AB¹] *You feel strange. . .like somebody that has been struck by lightning and hasn't quite fetched around yet, and can't just get his bearings* 1889 CY x 135 (To recover consciousness. *intr.* So W Wr. Phrase not in S C. The *intr.* sense not in OED; but cf. OED Fetch, v. 2d. To restore to consciousness. *Obs.* 1621. .1744; also 12b. Fetch again, in same sense. *Obs.* 1601. .1669)

fetch away, v. [?AB¹] *He had fetched away a three-gallon jug of whiskey, too, that he found under a wagon* 1884 HF xx 200 (To steal or 'convey.' Phr. in this sense not in OED W S C; but cf. OED Fetch, v. 1c. To steal. *Obs.* 1377. .1622. So W Wr)

fetch up, v. [?AB³] See *neck* 1865. *"We fetches up dah right plum in de middle er de sermon"* 1883 LM lvi 554. *We cut along the path around the garden fence, and by and by fetched up on the steep top of the hill* 1884 HF ii 10 (OEDS 19i. *intr.* To 'pull up,' to stop. 1848. . So W S C Wr. A in B F Cl Th T H DN.III)

F.F.V., sb. [AB¹] See *caliber* 1893 (S: Abbreviation for "First Families of Virginia." So C B F Th,1847 T M. Not in OED W)

fickle-tempered, ppl.a. [B¹] *"That fickle-tempered, dissipated young goose"* 1894 PW xiii 775 (Comb. not in OED W S C; but cf. OED Fickle-minded, 1600)

fiddle, sb. [?AB¹] *The old ships offered the passenger no chance to smoke except in the place that was called the "fiddle." It was a repulsive den made of rough boards* 1893 "About All Kinds of Ships" 156 (Not in OED W S C)

fiddler, sb. [?A] *The drainage ditches were everywhere alive with little crabs—"fiddlers"* 1883 LM xlviii 479 (OED 4c. A small crab of the genus *Gelasimus.*

U.S. quots. 1714. . So U. A in W S C B F Cl Th DN.III)

fidgety, a. [?AB²C] *It's a mighty fidgety business to have to hold your hands still at such a time* 1884 HF xv 126 (OED 2. Producing fidgetiness. *Rare.* 1885, only ex. So W. This sense not in S C)

field, sb. [D] See *coat-of-arms* 1883 (OED 13a. *Heraldry.* The surface of an escutcheon or shield on which the 'charge' is displayed. c1400. .1859—. So W S C U)

fielding, vbl.sb. [AB³] *Inability. . .to work together harmoniously—not perhaps in fielding. . .but at least in the minor offices of keeping game and umpiring* 1906 "Amended Obituaries" 230 (OED 1c. *Baseball.* The action of stopping and recovering or returning the ball. 1859. . So C U. Not in W S)

fife-rail, sb. [B²] *Lay small object on fife-rail of mainmast* 1866 *Notebook* (1935) iv 29 (OED *Naut.* b. The rail around the main-mast. 1881, only quot. for this sense. So W S C U)

fifteen-ball pool, sb. [AB¹] *In the matter of fifteen-ball pool I never got Dolby's confidence wholly back* 1907 "Chaps. from Autob" 473 (S: So called from the number of balls used. Comb. not in OED W C; but cf. OED Pool, sb. 3. A game played on a billiard-table . . .in U.S., with balls numbered 1 to 15, the number of each ball a player pockets being added to his score. No ex. So W C)

fifteen-puzzle, sb. [B¹] *"He's the 15-puzzle, that cuss. And his boy's another one. I can't make them out"* 1902 "DBDS" (1928) 316 (Comb. not in OED W S C. Probably the designation of some temporarily popular conundrum or puzzle-toy; cf. "Pigs in Clover," below)

fight along, v. [?AB¹] *The portrait of Sellers, by Tracy, was fighting along day by day* 1892 AmCl xxiii 239 (To progress gradually against obstacles. This *fig* sense not in OED W S C)

fighting, ppl.a. [?AB¹] *"You're a fighting liar and dasn't take it up!"* 1876 TS i 23 (An extension of the use in the phr. *fighting word*, A in DN.V., s.w.Mo.: An epithet the use of which ordinarily induces a fight . . .The term applies usually to 'liar' and 'son-of-a-bitch.' This use not in OED W S C)

fig-leaf, v. [B²] *These ridiculous creatures have been thoughtfully and conscientiously fig-leaved by this fastidious generation* 1880 TA l 577 (OED To cover with a fig-leaf. 1880, this quot. . . So W. Not in S C)

fig-paste, sb. [B¹] *Some fig-paste from Constantinople* 1872 RI iii 36 (Comb. not in OED. Given in W S C)

figure-artist, sb. [B¹] *The figure-artist is a German shoemaker with an untaught passion for art* 1892 AmCl xvi 163 (Comb. not in OED W S C; but cf. OED Figure-carver, 1868; Figure-painting)

figure-drawing, vbl.sb. [B¹] *Vogel taught us figure-drawing* 1880 TA xi 100 (Comb. not in OED W S C; but cf. OED Figure-piece, 1873)

figure-head, sb. [B²] *Crowned heads in Europe. . .can never be gods again, but only figure-heads* 1883 LM xlvi 467 (OED 2. 1883. . So W S C U)

filch, sb. [B³?C] *There is no moral difference between a big filch and a little filch* 1901 "To My Missionary Critics" 530 (OED 4. The act of filching or stealing. 1877, only ex. So W C. *Obs* in S)

file, sb. [?AC] See *budge* 1881 (OED *obs.* A pickpocket. 1673. .1743. Not *obs* in W S C Wr. A in DN.V)

filibuster, sb. [?AB³] *A party of filibusters from Eschol captured the place* 1869 IA xlvi 479 (OED 2c. One who engages in unauthorized and irregular warfare against foreign states. 1860. . So U. A in W S C B F Cl Th,1857 M)

filibustering, vbl.sb. [?AB³] *He had fought all through that remarkable man's* [Walker's] *filibustering campaign in Central America* 1906 *Autob* (1924) I 351 (OED 1856. . A in W S C B F Cl Th.III)

filigree, v. Also **filagree.** [B³E] *Americans...who are not gilded and filigreed with the ineffable graces of the first society* 1867 *Speeches* (1923) 21. *A domed and filagreed white temple...burst upon us* 1869 IA xxxvii 395 (OED To ornament with jewel work. 1831.. The sp. *filagree* has been in use since the 17th c., the more correct *filigree* only since the 19th. So W S C U)

fill, v. [AB²] See *and* 1867. *"I certainly held threes— but I drew and didn't fill. That's where I'm so often weak in the game"* 1904 "Bequest" (1906) iii 14 (OEDS 1f. In Poker: to complete a 'full house,' flush, straight, etc., by drawing the necessary cards. 1882.. So W S C F Cl)

fill the bill, v.phr. [AB³] *I wanted a horse that could shy, and this one fills the bill* 1869 IA xlii 439. See *all-around* 1893 (OEDS 7c. *U.S.* 1860.. So S C Th M. Not A in W)

fill up, v. [AB¹] *They simply took your measure, and concluded to fill you up* 1880 TA xxv 256 (To hoax, 'stuff,' cram with misinformation. A in H: Am. fill up =Eng. stuff up. *Colloq* in W. This sense not in OED S C. Cf. freight up, load up, below)

find, sb. [?AB³] *Word had gone down to Ilium that coal had been found... The great "find" was nothing but a worthless seam* 1873 GA xlix 449. *Another time the expedition made a great "find"* 1875 SNO 145 (OED 1. A discovery, e.g. of minerals. *colloq.* 1825.. So W S C U. A in F Cl. Not A in T)

fine language, sb. [B¹] *A prevalent feature in these compositions was...a wasteful and opulent gush of "fine language"* 1876 TS xxi 71 (Comb. not in OED W S C; but cf. OED Fine, a. 18. Of speech, writing, etc.: Affectedly ornate or elegant. 1773..)

finger-ball, sb. [B¹] *"The patterns upon the finger-balls of the accused"* 1894 PW xxi 237 (Comb. not in OED W S C; but cf. OED Ball, sb. 15. Any rounded or protuberant part of the body; now chiefly applied to those at the base of the thumb and great toe. No ex. for the tip of the finger)

finger-board, sb. [AB³] *Guides are necessary* [in Switzerland], *for none but a native can read those finger-boards* 1880 TA xxxix 450. *A literary swamp which has so many misleading fingerboards as this book is furnished with* 1894 "Defence of Harriet Shelley" 245 (OEDS *U.S.* = Finger-post. 1845.. Not A in S. Not in W C)

finger-mark, sb. [B³C] *The right-hand thumb and finger-marks of that unknown murderer* 1883 LM xxxi 346. *The fad without a name was one which dealt with people's finger-marks* 1893 PW ii 236. *"Never mind; he'll make his mark some day—finger-mark, you know, he-he!"* 1894 PW xi 553 (OED 1840.. OEDS Now always Finger-print. Not *obs* in W S C U)

finger-print, sb. [B³] *"I reckon he wants to print de chillen's fingers"...Wilson took the finger-prints* 1893 PW iii 240. See also PW xx 184; xxi 188 (OED 1884.. So W S C U. M.T.'s hesitation between this compound and the one above offers an instructive case of linguistic rivalry. In fixing upon a name for what was then a novel means of criminal identification, he wavered at first between *finger-mark* and *finger-print,* using the older term *finger-mark* in the earlier chaps. of PW, but later settling upon the comb. that has since won general acceptance. The victory of *finger-print* is doubtless due to the greater suitability of its accompanying verb-forms *to print the fingers* and *to finger-print* (OEDS 1905..). To call the new process *marking the fingers,* or *fingermarking,* would necessarily have been ambiguous. For another possibility, considered but promptly discarded, see *grease-print,* below)

finisher, sb. [B¹] *We kind of liked them from the start, and traveling with them put on the finisher* 1894 TSA xi 397 (That which completes or perfects. This favorable sense not in OED W S C; cf. OED 2c. Something that finishes, discomfits, or 'does for' anyone; a settler. 1827..; so W S C)

finish up, v. [?AB³] *"They're finishing one* [picture] *up"* 1892 AmCl xvi 162 (OEDS 5. 1878.. So W U. A in M. Not in S C)

fip, sb. [AB²] *I paid my sixpence, or "fip," as these heathens* [in Philadelphia] *call it* 1853 Letter in *Iowa Journ. of Hist.* (1929) 411 (OED *U.S.* In Pennsylvania, and several of the Southern states, the vulgar name for the Spanish half-real. 1860.. Cf. B: Federal Currency. Spanish coins, including the half-real, one-sixteenth of a dollar, or 6¼ cents, were very common in the U.S. until the act of 1857. The half-real was called in New York a sixpence; in New England, fourpence ha'penny, or simply fourpence; in Pennsylvania, Maryland, and in Virginia, a fip, contracted from fippenny bit, or fivepence; and in Louisiana, a picayune. The different terms used in different parts of the U.S. go back to colonial days, and are explained by the depreciation of the paper currency, which took place at different rates. In 1750 the value of English paper currency was fixed about as follows: in New England, one Spanish dollar was worth six shillings, in New York eight shillings, in Pennsylvania 7s 6d; whereas in some Southern states it remained at about par, or 4s 6d. The half-real was accordingly worth in New York sixpence, but in Pennsylvania only a little over fivepence. So W S C F Cl Th,1822 T DN.III,IV)

fire-assay, sb. [?AB¹] *The "fire-assay"—a method used to determine the proportion of gold, silver, and base metals in the mass* 1872 RI xxxvi 255 (Comb. not in OED S C. Given in W. Cf. assay-office, above)

fire-auction, sb. [?AB¹] *Some fire-auction carpets which blaspheme the standards of color and art* 1904 *Autob* (1924) I 196 (An auction sale to dispose of goods damaged by fire; hence cheap, tawdry. Comb. not in OED W S C; but cf. fire-sale, given only in W)

fire-boy, sb. [?AB¹] *Then the fire-boys mounted to the hall and flooded it with water* 1894 PW xi 557 (Comb. not in OED W S C. Cf. fire-department, below)

fire-bug, sb. [AB³] *Wicklow coldly described him as a nigger-trader, horse-thief, and fire-bug* 1881 "Curious Experience" 46 (OED *U.S.* An incendiary. 1872.. So W S C U F Cl Th T M H)

fire-bug, sb. [A] See *lightning-bug* 1906 (OEDS *U.S.* The glow-worm. 1797.. So Th. U: firefly. This sense not in W S C; but cf. W Firefly: the wingless females and larvae are popularly termed *glowworms*)

fire-building, vbl.sb. [B¹] *The subject of sweeping appeared to weary him; fire-building failed to stir him* 1881 PP xix 241 (Comb. not in OED W S C; but cf. Fire-kindling, OED 1884)

firecracker, sb. [AB³] *Tom was literally rolling in wealth. He had...twelve marbles, a couple of tadpoles, six firecrackers...* 1876 TS ii 31. *A cigar with a fire-cracker in it* 1880 TA xxiii 226 (OEDS *U.S.* 1849.. Not A in W S C)

fire-department, sb. [AB³] *He was chief of the fire-department* 1873 GA xxxiii 301. See *hook-and-ladder* 1883. *I was training some horses and building some... fire-engines, with an eye to a paid fire-department by and by* 1889 CY xxx 381 (OED *U.S.* A body of firemen. 1855.. So W S C M H)

fire-eater, sb. [?AB³] *This wrinkled, smoldering old fire-eater occupying the other side* 1880 TA xxi 206 (OED 2. One who seeks occasion to quarrel or fight. 1864.. So W S C U. A in Th,1847 M DN.IV. Not A in T)

fire-faced, a. [?AB¹] *But he was sleeping, and sleeping very peaceful too; and pale, not fire-faced the way he was when he come* 1884 HF xlii 428 (Comb. not in OED W S C; but cf. OED Fire-mouthed, 1590)

fire-hued, a. [B¹] *The window-curtains were of red silk damask, and the walls were covered with the same fire-hued goods* 1880 TA xlvii 550 (Comb. not in OED W S C)

fire-new, a. [?C] *Mr. Foley began to do schoolboy poems in a fire-new and blood-curdling and criminal fashion of spelling* 1906 "Carnegie Spelling Reform" 488 (OED *arch.* 1594..1842. Not *arch* in W S C Wr)

fire out, v. [AB³] *I found the astronomer of the university gadding around after comets...I said I should have to fire him out* 1888 *Speeches* (1923) 144 (OED 16. *U.S. slang.* To turn anyone out of a place. 1885.. So S C Cl Th. Not A in W U T. Cf. Fire, v. in this sense, A in M H)

fire-red, a. [?AC] "*Cotton-velvet westcot, fire-red and yaller squares*" 1896 TSD v 356 (OED *obs* 1382..1626. Not *obs* in W S C)

fire-spouting, ppl.a. [B¹] *I ought not to need salves... even against fire-spouting dragons* 1889 CY x 133 (Comb. not in OED W S C; but cf. OED Fire-breathing, 1591..)

fire-water, sb. [AB³] *His flask of scientific fire-water* 1898 "Austrian Edison" (1900) 267 (OEDS 2. Any strong liquor or ardent spirits. Orig. *U.S.* 1817.. So W S C U B F Th.III M)

firm, sb. [B¹] *An image of Shiva...has three eyes. He is the only god in the firm that has three* 1897 FE li 491 (Cf. OED 2b. A commercial house. 1817.. So W S C U. Here, by hum. *transf.*, of the Hindu pantheon)

firmament-clogging, ppl.a. [B¹] *Firmament-clogging rottenness* 1880 *Fireside Conversation, 1601* (Comb. not in OED W S C)

firmament-obliterating, ppl.a. [B¹] *A firmament-obliterating irruption of profanity* 1883 LM xx 244 (Comb. not in OED W S C)

first-best, a. [B¹] *Carry this message to her first-best friend* 1901 "Two Little Tales" (1928) 209 (Comb. not in OED W S C)

first-class, a. [?AB²] *We cordially hailed it as a first-class curiosity* 1872 RI viii 72. *First-class magazines* 1873 GA xii 117. *First-class hotels* 1883 LM xxxviii 399 (OED 2b. Extremely good, 'first-rate.' *colloq.* 1879. So W S C U. A in B DN.III)

First Family, sb. [AB¹] See *high-toned* 1873. *The Tumble-Bug was content to be of the old first families. He was willing that the parvenus of these new times should find comfort where they might* 1875 SNO 139. "*He wuz the highest quality in dis whole town—ole Virginny stock. Fust famblies, he wuz*" 1894 PW ix 550 (Ellipt. for "First Families of Virginia." Cf. F.F.V., above. Comb. not in OED W S C)

First Member, sb. [AB¹] *The select body entitled First Members are the aristocracy of the* [Christian Science] *Mother-Church* 1907 CS II vii 166. See also *clincher* 1907 (Comb. not in OED W S C)

first-off, adv. [AB²] "*First-off, I thought it would certainly give me the botts*" 1880 TA xx 193. See also *foul*, v. 1908 (OEDS First, adv. 1f. In the first place. *U.S.* 1891.. So Wr DN.I. Not A in W. Not in S C)

first-rate, a. [?AB³] "*It's a first-rate imitation*" 1883 LM xxxix 413. *Pretty soon I was feeling first-rate* 1893 "Banknote" (1928) 113 (OED 2. Extremely good. 1812.. So W S C U. A in B T DN.III,IV)

first-rate, adv. [?AB³] *Henry holds out first-rate* 1866 "Forty-Three Days" 107. *We got along first-rate with the friar* 1869 IA xxv 261. "*Say, Roxy, how does yo' baby come on?*" "*Fust rate; how does you come on, Jasper?*" 1893 PW ii 236 (OED 4. *colloq.* Very well. 1844.. So W S U. A in B F Cl DN.III,IV. Not A in T. Not in C as adv.)

first-uttered, ppl.a. [B¹] *That sickening effect which first-uttered suspicions against one's idol always have* 1883 LM lii 518 (Comb. not in OED W S C; but cf. OED First-mentioned, 1877)

fish-belly, a. [B¹] *A tree-toad white, a fish-belly white* 1884 HF v 31 (Not in OED W S C as a color term. Cf. OED Fish-belly, used *attrib.*: Shaped like a fish's belly. 1888)

fish-bladder, sb. [B¹] *The other pretext was thin enough; it was tissue, tinfoil, fish-bladder* 1881 *Speeches* (1910) 18. *I wouldn't give a fish-bladder for the whole of it* 1893 "Esquimau Maiden's Romance" (1900) 141 (Comb. not in OED W S C)

fisher-loafer, sb. [B¹] *One may see the fisher-loafers just as...happy and patient* 1880 TA xxvi 271 (Nonce comb.)

fishing-things, sb. [?AB¹] *My blazer I give to brother Will, and my fishing-things and Bible* 1902 "Belated Russ. Passport" (1928) 187 (Comb. not in OED W S C. Cf. OED Fishing-gear, 1863; OEDS *U.S.*, 1839..)

fishing-worm, sb. [AB¹] *A hard piece of corn-crust...was shot across the table, and took one of the children in the eye, and curled him up like a fishing-worm* 1884 HF xxxvii 376 (A in DN.I,III: angle-worm; used in Ind., e.Ala., n.w.Ark. Not A in W. Comb. not in OED S C)

fish-interior, sb. [B¹] "*Candles!—and soap!—*" "*And fish-interiors!— slush...whale-blubber!*" *This vision of an ideal feast was too much for her* 1893 "Esquimau Maiden's Romance" (1900) 143 (Comb. not in OED W S C)

fish-line, sb. [?AB³] *Once I got a fish-line but no hooks* 1884 HF iii 17 (OEDS 1864, U.S. ex. Not A in W S C)

fitten, a. [?AC] "*It was fitten to make a body's heart break*" 1873 GA ii 32. "*I reckon I ain't dressed fitten for a pirate*" 1876 TS xiii 120. "*Clothes that ain't fitten for a hog*" 1884 HF vi 42 (OED *obs.* Suitable, fit. 1642, only ex. So W Wr. A in DN.II,IV,V, s.e.Mo., New Orleans; AS.VII.90, Ky. Not in S C)

five, sb. [AB¹] "*Out with another five, or here she stays*" 1876 TS ix 89 (W: a five-dollar bill. Not in OED S C; but cf. OED Fiver, in U.S., a five-dollar note, 1853)

five-center, a. [AB¹] *Jim always kept that five-center piece 'round his neck with a string* 1884 HF ii 10 (Not in OED W S C. Probably formed on the analogy of *five-dollar*)

fix, sb. **in a fix**. [AB³] *Plainly we were in an ugly fix* 1880 TA xxxvii 426. *If we get left on this wreck we are in a fix sure* 1884 HF xiii 109. "*Mother, we are in an awful fix*" 1894 PW xiv 780 (OEDS 1. orig. *U.S.* A tight place, a difficulty, a dilemma. 1833.. So B F Cl Th M DN.III,V. Not A in W S C U T)

fix, v. [A] *Fixing the concern so that the sails could be moved instead of the mill* 1869 IA vi 55. *I took the watch to another watchmaker...He fixed it* 1870 SNO (1875) 20. *He patiently fixed and refixed it until it was exactly right* 1880 TA ii 23. See also *rubbish* 1896 (OED 14b. In wider sense, chiefly *U.S. colloq*; To arrange, get ready, put in order. 1769.. So C U Wr B F Cl Th,1708 M H DN.V. Not A in W S T)

fix, v. [AB¹] *I'll close the door against them all—which will "fix" all of the lot except Twichell* 1874 *Letters* (1917) I xiii 216. "*I will fix you*" (meaning to kill him) 1880 *Letters* (1917) I xx 383. *They would put everything aside next day and go up to Boston and fix that boy* 1893 "Travelling with a Reformer" (1928) 362 (S: *colloq, U.S.*, to settle or do for a person. So Wr B F Cl Th,1800. Not A in W. This sense not in OED C)

fixed, ppl.a. [AB²] *He always went "fixed" to make things go along smoothly* 1872 RI vi 57. See *close-fit* 1884. *His scheme now was to prepare himself to speak... said he had been "fixed" for it* 1892 AmCl xxiv 252. *I had a million dollars to my credit...and Hastings was fixed in the same way* 1893 "Banknote" (1928) 131 (OEDS 10. In predicative use: Situated materially. *U.S.* 1873.. So Wr F Cl Th.III,1803 M DN.II. This sense not in W S C)

fixed, ppl.a. [?AB¹] "*Are you heeled—that is, fixed?*" 1894 PW xix 21 (Armed, equipped with a gun. This sense not in OED W S C)

fixings, vbl.sb. [AB³] See *homely* 1884. *Her clothes were the prettiest...as to decorative trimmings and fixings*

1892 AmCl v 60 (OEDS 2a. In pl. orig. *U.S.*: Apparatus, equipment, trimming of a dress. 1820.. So C U B F Cl T M H DN.III. Not A in W S)

fix up, v. [AB²] *You fix up for the drought* 1875 *Speeches* (1923) 55. *I made up my mind I would fix up some way to leave there* 1884 HF vi 39. See *coach-candle* 1890. *"I was fixing up a mourning-dress"* 1892 AmCl v 59 (OED 14b. To arrange, get ready. Chiefly *U.S. colloq.* 1882.. So C U Wr B F Cl Th.III,1861 M T H DN.II. This sense not A in W S)

fix up, v. [?AB¹] *The feud between the Darnells and the Wilsons...could have been fixed up, easy enough* 1883 LM xxvi 286. *We fixed up an agreement* 1889 CY pref. 21 (W: To arrange a settlement, *colloq.* So C U. This *spec.* sense not in OED S)

fizzle out, v. [AB³] *I explained to him how St. Louis would fizzle out if Keokuk got offended at her* 1856 *Adv. of T. J. Snodgrass* (1928) 8 (OED 3a. Chiefly *U.S. colloq.*: To fail. 1847.. So B F Th M DN.III,IV. Not A in W S C U)

flame-front, sb. [B¹] *That continental stretch of dry prairie which stood for his imagination was afire, and across it was marching a slanting flame-front that joined its wide horizons together* 1892 AmCl iii 41 (Comb. not in OED W S C)

flame-jet, sb. [B¹] *The flame-jets, the smoke, and the explosions were repeated* 1881 PP xxxi 354 (Comb. not in OED W S C)

flange, sb. [B¹] *What had first called my attention to her was my stepping on an outlying flange of her foot* 1880 TA xxxv 393 (Hum. *transf.* from the sense in OED 3. Any rim or projecting surface (of machinery). 1876.. Cf. Wr.: A projection or rim of any kind; the brim of a hat)

flank, v. [AB³] *We would flank the farm-house—go out around* 1885 "Private Hist. of Campaign" 195. *"A cow steps out and puts her head down to munch grass with her broadside to the battalion...they split apart to flank her"* 1906 "Horse's Tale" 340 (OEDS 5b. *U.S. slang.* To dodge, avoid, get around. 1866.. So Th. III,1865. This sense not in W S C)

flapdoodle, sb. [?AB³] *He gets up...and slobbers out a speech, all full of tears and flapdoodle* 1884 HF xxv 247 (OED 2a. Nonsense, 'bosh,' humbug. 1878.. So W S C U. A in B F Cl Th,1833 DN.III,IV)

flapjack, sb. [AC] *She was tossing flapjacks in a frying-pan* 1872 RI lvii 418 (OED 1a. Now *dial* or *U.S.* 1600..1641, last British quot. So Wr B F Cl Th M DN.I,III AS.II.86. Not A in W S C U)

flare up, v. [?AB³] *The girl was almost disarmed for a moment. Then she flared up again* 1892 AmCl xxiii 244 (OED 6b. 1840.. So W S C U. A in M DN.II,III)

flashy, a. [?AB³] *A small cell all bejeweled and bespangled with flashy ornamentation* 1880 TA liii 572 (OED 5. Showy, gaudy. 1801.. So W S C U. A in DN.IV)

flat, sb. [?AB²] See *gulch* 1865. *"Was he a-mining on the flat, he done it with a zest"* 1865 SNO (1875) 74. *A slick alkali flat which was surfaced like steel* 1902 "DBDS" (1928) 320 (Cf. OED 5c. *Australian*, a low even tract of land generally occurring where creeks unite...with the usual rich auriferous drift immediately overlying the bed-rock. 1869.. This sense not given as U.S. by the OED; but the dates indicate that it was borrowed by the Australian gold-miners from U.S. usage. Cf. S C: A low-lying plain near...a river, *U.S.* So B F Cl T H DN.III,VI AS.V.160. Not A in W U Wr)

flat, sb. [?A] *The wood being nearly all out of the flat* 1883 LM xx 238 (OED 9a. A broad, flat-bottomed boat. 1749.. So W S C U Wr. A in B F Cl Th H)

flat, sb. [?A] *"She [an actress] got burnt out in a fire and lost $30,000 worth of diamonds...given to her, no doubt, by spoony young flats and sappy old bald-heads"*

1892 AmCl ix 85 (OED 13. *slang.* A duffer, simpleton. 1762..1848. So W S C U Wr. A in B)

flat, v. [?C] *The old expressman went bustling around, humming "Sweet By and By," in a low tone, and flatting a good deal* 1892 "Invalid's Story" (1906) 314. See also *sharp*, v. 1895 (OED †7. *Music.* To lower a note by one semitone. 1674, 1685. Not *obs* in W S C)

flat-boat, sb. [AB³] *A flatboat was there moored by it* 1873 GA xvii 162 (OEDS 1b. *U.S.* A large roughly made boat formerly much used for floating goods, etc., down the Mississippi and other western rivers. 1801.. So S C B F Cl Th M AS.II.30. Not A in W U)

flatboatman, sb. [AB³] *That flatboatman would be sure to go into New Orleans* 1875 OTM 448 (OEDS A hand employed on a flat-boat. *U.S.* 1843.. So B F Cl. Comb. not in W S C)

flat broke, a. [AB¹] See *clean out* 1865 (A in B F Cl T. *Slang.* in W. Comb. not in OED S C; but cf. OED Flat, adv. 2. Entirely, fully, quite. Now *rare.* 1577.. 1859)

flat-footed, a. **to come out flat-footed.** [AB³] *"I don't mind coming out flatfooted and saying there ain't any way to improve on them"* 1881 *Speeches* (1910) 24. *Here was this nigger...coming right out flat-footed and saying he would steal his children* 1884 HF xvi 137 (OEDS 2. *U.S. colloq.* To make a bold or positive statement. 1828.. So W B F Cl Th T M H DN.II,III AS.II.354. Not A in W S C)

flathead, sb. [AB²] *"Greenhorns, flatheads!"* 1884 HF xxiii 229 (OEDS 1b. A fool. *U.S. slang.* 1889.. So DN.IV,V. Not A in W Wr. Not in S C)

flat out, v. [AB³] *There warn't no sense in the tale, to chop square off, that way, before it come to anything, but I warn't going to say so, because I could see Tom was souring up pretty fast over the way it flatted out* 1894 TSA vii 258 (OED 4b. *U.S. fig.* To prove a failure, to collapse. 1859. So C B F Cl T. Not A in W S)

flatting, vbl.sb. [?C] *When a person has a poor ear for words, the result is a literary flatting and sharping; you perceive what he is intending to say, but you also perceive that he doesn't say it* 1895 "Cooper's Literary Offences" 11 (OED 3. *Music. Obs.* 1674, only ex. Not *obs* in S C. Not in W. Cf. flat, v., above)

flea-pasture, sb. [B¹] *I saw a dog start to nibble at a flea...he looked sadly at his flea-pasture* 1869 IA xxxiv 371 (Hum. nonce comb.)

flesh, sb. **to make one's flesh crawl.** [B¹] *"It makes my flesh crawl to hear you"* 1876 TS vi 61 (S: To have a sensation as of crawling things on the body. So W C. Phr. not in OED; but cf. OED 1e. To make one's flesh creep, 1727..)

flesh-bulk, sb. [B¹] *The moral flesh-bulk (that is to say, character) was built and shaped around the skeleton by training, association, and circumstance* 1902 "Defence of Gen. Funston" 613 (Comb. not in OED W S C)

fleshy, a. [?A] See *cub* 1891. *The German was forty and a little fleshy* 1892 AmCl xvi 144 (OED 1. Fat, plump. 1369..1837. So W S C U. A in F Cl Th,1788)

fling, v. [?A] *"Why, Tom what do you mean? Has Rowena—" "Flung me? No, but the old man has"* 1894 PW xiii 775 (OED 12b. *Scotch,* to jilt. 1790.. So Wr. This sense not in W S C)

flint-arm, sb. [B¹] *Although the flint-arm has gone out and the forts have tumbled down, the decree hasn't been repealed* 1892 AmCl ii 32 (Comb. not in OED W S C; but cf. OED Flint-gun, 1849)

filint-picker, sb. [B¹] See *War Department* 1892 (Comb. not in OED W S C)

flip out, v. [?AB¹] *"You shouldn't flip out such a gigantic thing as this in that colorless kind of way"* 1892 AmCl xviii 183 (To ejaculate, utter carelessly or indifferently. This sense not in OED W S C)

flirk, sb. [B¹] See *kahkahponeeka* 1880 (Hum. invention).

floating, ppl.a. [?AB¹] *Borrowed from a floating news-paper item* 1870 SNO (1875) 61 (Widely circulated. This sense not in OED W S C)

flooding, vbl.sb. [B²] *There had been a hundred and seventy-five floodings of the earth!* 1875 SNO 138 (OED 1b. *pl.* Floods. No ex. of the literal sense. So W S C)

flood-time, sb. [B¹] *The scheme to relieve the river, in flood-time, by turning its surplus waters off into Lake Borgne* 1883 LM xxviii 307 (Comb. not in OED S C. Given in W)

flood-wasted, ppl.a. [B¹] *No other food for them in the flood-wasted land* 1883 LM xxx 326 (Comb. not in OED W S C)

floor, sb. [AB³] *"He's got the floor, as the sayin' is"* 1881 "Curious Experience" 37. *Tracy tried to break in, but she stopped him, and kept the floor herself* 1892 AmCl xxii 231 (OED 4. The right of speaking. Chiefly *U.S.* 1816.. So C U B F Th T M H DN.VI. Not A in W S)

flouring-mill, sb. [AB³] *Thirty flouring-mills turn out two million barrels of the very choicest flour every year* 1883 LM lx 588 (OEDS *U.S.* 1817.. So C B F Cl Th.III H AS.II.30. Not A in S. Not in W)

flower-harvest, sb. [B¹] *The queen-bee...must not lay more than are needed in a slim flower-harvest* 1902 "The Bee" (1917) 281 (Comb. not in OED W S C)

fluke, sb. [B³] See *scratch,* sb. 1907 (OED *colloq.* In *Billiards,* a successful stroke made by accident or chance. 1857.. So W S C U)

flume, sb. [A] *The big flume warn't finished when he first came to the camp* 1865 SNO (1875) 30 (OED 3. *U.S.* An artificial channel for a stream of water to be applied to some industrial use. 1784.. So W U F Cl Th T M AS.V.145;VII.427. Not A in S C)

flume, sb. **up the flume.** [AB²] *"One of the boys has gone up the flume"* 1872 RI xlvii 333. *"Well, then, that idea's up the flume. We got to think of something else"* 1882 "Invalid's Story" 97 (OED 3c. *U.S. slang.* To come to grief, to die. 1882, above quot. So S F Cl Th. This sense not in W C)

flummery, sb. [?AB¹] *The bridal chamber whose pretentious flummery was overawing* 1883 LM xxviii 406. *A baby gown, with its bright blue bows and dainty flummery of ruffles* 1893 PW iii 239 (Wr: Needless show or ostentation; personal or household adornment of a useless character. This sense, applied to dress and room-furnishing, not in OED W S C. Cf. OED 2. *fig.* Flattery, nonsense, empty trifling. 1749..)

flush, sb. [?A] See *and* 1867. *"Go in, boy, and play 'em a knock-down flush to their two pair 'n' a jack!"* 1902 "DBDS" (1928) 341 (OED 1. A hand consisting of cards all of one suit. 1529.. So W S C U T. A in M, as poker term)

flush, a. [?AB³] See *busted* 1865. *You know the flush times are past* 1866 Letters (1917) I vi 121. *The grand "flush times" of Silverland began* 1872 RI xliii 302. *The flush times of steamboating* 1883 LM iii 61 (OED 3c. Prosperous. 1840.. So W S C U Wr. A in T)

flush, v. [B¹] *"Oh, I've flushed an easy batch!"* [i.e., of German words to translate] 1888 "Meisterschaft" 463. *"After I had got outside of our astronomical system, I used to flush a comet occasionally"* 1907 "Capt. Stormfield" 41 (This *fig* sense not in OED W S C. Cf. OED 2. To cause birds to fly or take wing. 1450..)

flutter, sb. [?AB³] *"We'll try that good-bye business a flutter"* 1888 "Meisterschaft" 463 (OED 4. *slang.* An attempt or 'shy' at anything. 1874.. So W S U. This sense not in C)

flutter-mill, sb. [AB²] *"Her tongue's just a flutter-mill"* 1888 "Meisterschaft" 460 (OEDS *U.S.* A mill worked by a flutter-wheel. 1896.. So S Th.III DN. II,III, in s.e.Mo. Not in W C. Cf. Flutter-wheel, A in B F Cl T)

fly around, v. [AB³] *Sailors don't fly around worth a cent unless you swear at them* 1892 AmCl xvii 177 (OEDS *U.S. colloq.* To bestir oneself. 1833.. So W C B F Cl Th DN.III. Not A in S)

fly-blister, sb. [B²] *A Venus with a fly-blister on her breast* 1869 IA xvii 169 (OED A plaster made of cantharides. No quot. So W S C)

flyer, sb. [AB³] *"My refusal was a 'flyer'—the object being to bring about an increase of the amount"* 1865 SS (1926) 170. *The boys all took a flier at the Holy Grail now and then* 1889 CY ix 112 (OEDS *U.S.* A speculative investment. 1848.. So S C B Cl Th T. Not A in W)

fly light, v. [AB¹] *St. Jerome...always went flying light in the matter of baggage* 1869 IA xxiii 238 (A in F: To take things easily; to make oneself comfortable. This quot. So Cl. Cf. C: To sail, as a ship, with but little cargo or ballast. Phr. not in OED W S)

fly-specked, ppl.a. [B²] *There was only one cruet left, and that was a stopperless, fly-specked, broken-necked thing* 1872 RI ix 43. *The map of this region is fly-specked all over with islands* 1897 FE vii 91 (OED 1883, only ex. So W S C)

fly the track, v. [?AB²] *When he finds he is approaching one of those streams, his dread is so lively that he is disposed to fly the track and avoid the implacable foe* 1880 TA xliii 510 (OEDS 7f. To fly off, leave suddenly. All exs. U.S. 1909.. Phr. not in W S C)

focus, sb. **to get a focus on.** [?AB¹] *To see just what sort of focus the French people got upon it* 1894 "Private Hist. of the Jumping Frog Story" (1900) 383 (Phr. not in OED W S C. Cf. OED To bring to a focus, 1788)

fog-horn, sb. [?AB³] *Schönerer uplifts his fog-horn voice* 1898 "Stirring Times in Austria" (1900) 328 (OED 1858. So W S C U. A in B)

foin, sb. [C] *Arthur smote...Mordred with a foin of his spear* 1889 CY xlii 535 (OED 1. A thrust. *obs* or *arch.* 1450..1814. So W S C)

folderol, sb. [?AB¹] *There was a feast, and plenty of pleasant palaver and fol-de-rol* 1883 LM ii 35. *Every time the magic of fol-de-rol tried conclusions with the magic of science...fol-de-rol got left* (W: var. of Falderal: Nonsense. So S C U Wr. A in DN.II,III. This sense not in OED; cf. OED Falderal, folderol: A meaningless refrain in songs; a gewgaw, trifle. 1701..1864)

folks, sb. [?A] See *whoop-jamboree* 1873; *sarcasm,* sb. 1880. *Three or four lights twinkling, where there was sick folks maybe* 1884 HF ii 11. See *cow-boy* 1892; *working-people* 1892. *"White folks done it"* 1893 PW iii 239 (OED 3a. Men, people indefinitely...the pl. since 17th c. is the ordinary form, the sing. being *arch* or *dial.* The word is now chiefly *colloq,* being superseded in more formal use by *people.* 1413..1871. So W S C U Wr T. A in B F Cl Th DN.III AS.IV.7; VII.256)

foo-foo, sb. [AB¹] *A tinker shrieked out a suggestion: "Foo-foo the First, king of the Mooncalves!"* 1881 PP xvii 217 (W: A fool, a ninny. *Slang, U.S.* So S B F T. Not A in C. Not in OED)

fool, a. [?AC] *"I say it's a fool way, anyhow"* 1884 HF ii 15 (OED Foolish, silly. *Obs* exc. *Scotch* and *dial* and *vulgar.* 1225..1823. So C Wr. Not *obs* in W S. OEDS Frequent in U.S. 1805..1924. A in Th H DN.II,III,IV)

fool along, v. [?AB¹] *"You turn back and fool along slow, so as to get to the house about the time you ought to"* 1884 HF xxxiii 338. *The days do seem to fool along considerable slower than they used to* 1885 Letters (1917) II xxv 464 (Comb. not in OED W S C. Cf. OED Fool about, 1861)

fool around, v. [AB²] *"What did Abel come fooling around there for?"* 1870 Screamers (1871) 38. *Fooling around won't furnish the bread* 1892 AmCl xiv 147. *"With her [Joan of Arc] is no dilly-dallying and fooling around"* 1895 JA II iii 140 (OED 2a. *U.S.* To 'hang about' aimlessly. 1885.. So U F Cl. Comb. not in W S C)

foot, sb. [AB¹] *We have now got about 1,650 feet of mining ground—and if it proves good, Mr. Moffet's name will go in—if not, I can get "feet" for him in the Spring which will be good* 1861 *Letters* (1917) I iii 60 (S: In mining measurements...cf. U.S. quot. 1867: "A 'foot' is twelve inches in length on the vein, including its entire width, whether six inches or sixty feet, and its whole depth down toward the earth's center." This *spec* sense not in OED W C)

foot, sb. **to set one's foot down.** [AB¹] *"When you set your foot down once, it's there to stay"* 1892 AmCl xxi 215 (A in B Cl: To be very decided. Not A in W S U. Phr. not in OED C; but cf. OED 28 To put one's foot down: to take up a firm position; To put (set) one's foot down upon: to have nothing to do with, to repress firmly)

foot, v. **to foot it.** [?A] See *tight,* adv. 1884; *canoe,* v. 1884 (OED 2b. To go on foot. 1576..1893. So W S C U Wr. A in DN.III)

foot, v. [?AB³] *"He'll foot the bill"* 1884 HF xiii 115. See also *air-blast* 1890 (OEDS 9c. To pay or settle. Earlier U.S. ex. 1844.. A in C Th T. Not A in W S U)

foot-casing, sb. [?AB¹] *"Where coal is, limestone with these fossils in it is pretty certain to lie against its foot-casing"* 1873 GA lxii 561 (Comb. not in OED W S C. Cf. Footwall, below)

foot-hill, sb. [AB³] *I knocked at a miner's lonely log cabin in the foot-hills of the Sierras* 1877 *Speeches* (1910) 2 (OEDS orig. U.S. 1859.. So Th.III T M DN.VI. Not A in W S C U)

footing-up, sb. [?AB¹] *We may now make a final footing-up of Mrs. Eddy, and see what she is* 1907 CS II ix 259 (Comb. not in OED W S C; but cf. OED Footing, vbl.sb. 14. Sum total. 1855.. Cf. foot up, v., below)

footstool, sb. [AB³] *If there is one individual creature on all this footstool who is more thoroughly and uniformly and unceasingly happy than I am I defy the world to produce him* 1874 *Letters* (1917) I xiii 215 (OEDS 1c. U.S. *colloq.* The earth; cf. *Isaiah* lxvi 1. 1821.. So B Th H. Not A in S C Wr. This sense not in W)

foot up, v. [?AB³] *"Do you know what our crop is going to foot up?"* 1897 FE xiii 145 (OED 9d. 1867.. So W S C U. A in Th,1840 H)

foot-wall, sb. [?AB³] See *casing* 1872. *A huge arch of solid ice, worn through the foot-wall of the Gorner Glacier* 1880 TA xxxviii 440 (OED *Mining,* the wall under a vein or lode. 1869. So W S C. A in AS.V.145)

forasmuch, adv. [C] *Forasmuch as the late king had provided in his will for conferring the ducal degree* 1881 PP xiv 168 (OED Now somewhat formal or *arch.* 1297..1879. So U. Not *arch* in W S C)

force, sb. **no force.** [C] *"No force,"* said Merlin, *"hereby is a sword that shall be yours"* 1889 CY iii 47 (OED 20. No matter. *obs.* 1369..1669. So W S C)

fore-and-aft, a. [?AB¹] *The fore-and-aft shaft of the driving-wheel* 1872 SNO (1875) 289. *The plow looks like a fore-and-aft brace of a Hudson River steamer* 1883 LM xlviii 476 (Cf. OED Placed or directed in the line of the vessel's length. Of sails. 1820.. So W S C U. Here *transf.* of parts of the engine on a steamboat)

forecastable, a. [B¹] See *tiger-average* 1897 (Not in OED W S C)

foreground, v. [B¹] *"We could do a prodigious trade [in portrait-painting] with the women if we could foreground the things they like"* 1892 AmCl xvi 167 (Not as *verb* in OED W S C. Cf. OED Foreground, sb. 1. esp. as represented in a picture. 1695..

forehatch, sb. [B¹] *A nobby thing for duchesses... with ruffles down the forehatch and the running gear clewed up with a feather-stitch to leeward* 1889 CY xxii

280 (Hum. *transf.* from the *naut.* sense, OED 1840. A nonce usage)

foreignize, v. [B³?C] *We are getting foreignized rapidly* 1869 IA xi 98 (OED 2. 1832.. So W S C. U: *rare*)

foremanship, sb. [B²] *He ought to take the contract for getting out some weekly paper, if he cannot get a foremanship* 1853 *Letters* (1917) I i 24 (OED 1859, only ex. So W S C)

foresightedness, sb. [B¹] *You complimented Mr. Rogers on his foresightedness* 1909 *Speeches* (1910) 179 (Not in OED S C. Given in W)

foreslander, sb. [B¹] *She often throws out a Forefelt or a Foresplendor, or a Foreslander* 1907 CS II iii 132 (Not in OED W S C. Cf. OED Forefelt, ppl.a., 1580; Fore-splendour, sb., 1831)

forest-bordered, ppl.a. [B¹] See *dark,* a. 1875 (Comb. not in OED W S C; but cf. OED Forest-belted, 1875)

foretop, sb. [AB³] *Perch in the foretop with the driver* 1869 IA xii 106 (OED 5. *U.S.* The front seat on the top of a vehicle. 1850.. So W S. This sense not in C)

foretopmaststuddingsail, sb. [B¹] See *lively,* adv. 1876 (Comb. not in OED C. Given in W S. Cf. OED Foretopmaststaysail, 1858)

forevermore, adv. [AB³] *She would be independent ...thenceforth forevermore* 1894 PW viii 337 (OED Now chiefly *U.S.* 1837.. Not A in W S C)

forfend, v. [C] *"If ever thou shouldst know misfortune—which God forfend—may thy goodness to me this day be remembered and requited!"* 1881 PP xv 185 (OED 2. To avert. *arch.* 1382..1887. So W S C U Wr)

Forks, sb. [AB¹] *"He's come back to the Forks"* 1873 GA i 21 (A settlement located at the fork of a road or river. Common in Am. place-names. So M. This sense not in OED W S C. Cf. OED Fork, sb. 12c. The point at which a river divides. Chiefly *U.S.* 1753.. 12d. Of a road. 1839.. So B Cl T DN.III,V)

forlornities, sb. [?AB¹] *Munich did seem the most desolate place... Livy and Clara sat down forlorn, and cried... Last night the forlornities had all disappeared* 1878 *Letters* (1917) I xviii 341 (This *concrete* sense not in OED W S C. Cf. OEDS Forlornity, sb. Forlornness. 1904, only ex. So W. A in B)

forsooth, adv. [C] *"Sir Kay, forsooth!"* 1889 CY iii 43 (OED 1a. In truth. *Obs.* ..1880. Not *obs* in W S C U)

for that, conj. [C] *"Men fear him for that he hath storms and devils...at his beck and call"* 1889 CY iii 46 (OED 1. Because. *arch* ..1894. So C. Not *arch* in W S)

for to, prep. [?AC] *"Don't want anybody fur to learn the business, 't ain't likely?"* 1880 TA xxiii 225. *People that's always the most anxious for to hang a nigger* 1884 HF xlii 425. Very common in HF. (OED For. 11. Before an inf. Now *arch* or *vulgar.* a1175..1774. So W S C U. *Dial* in Wr. A in B: Still retained in the West. So DN.III,IV AS.V.268, Ozarks; VII.19, Penna.)

fortune-making, sb. [B¹] *He perfected his invention ...and saved it for exhibition and fortune-making* 1898 "Austrian Edison" (1900) 264 (Comb. not in OED W S C; but cf. OED Fortune-maker, 1616)

fortuning, vbl.sb. [B¹] *My head distraught by late adventured haps and fortunings* 1889 CY xix 234 (Not in OED W S C. Cf. Wr Fortune, v. To chance, happen)

Forty-Niner, sb. [AB²] *That proudest and blessedest creature that exists on all the earth, a "Forty-Niner"* 1872 RI xvii 140 (OEDS *U.S.* One of those who settled in California during the 'gold fever' about 1849. 1873.. So W S C F Cl Th AS.VII.430)

forty-niner, sb. [B¹] See *seller* 1869 (Here apparently: a woman forty-nine years of age, with punning allusion to sense above. Nonce coinage)

forty-rod, a. [AB¹] *Then he busted out and had another one of them forty-rod laughs of his'n* 1896 TSD ix

524 (Prodigious, violent. This sense not in OED W S C. Probably *transf.* from the meaning given below)

forty-rod whiskey, sb. [AB²] *Trading for forty-rod whiskey, to enable you to get drunk and happy* 1869 SNO (1875) 70. See also *time, to have a good* 1884 (OEDS *U.S. slang.* Whiskey of the most villainous description. 1871.. So F Cl Th.III,1862 M DN.II AS.VII.169;XII.115, with quot. 1858. Not in W S C)

forward, adv. **forward for.** [AB³] *Rained hard. The cattle purchased at Alexandria for beef ought to be shingled. Or else fattened. The water stands in deep puddles in the depressions forward of their after shoulders. Also here and there all over their backs* 1869 IA lix 636 (OED 3. *U.S.* In front of. 1852.. Not A in W. Phrase not in S C)

forward, a. Spelled **for'rard.** [E] "*When a cow's laying down, which end gets up first?*" "*The hind end, mum.*" "*Well, then, a horse?*" "*The for'rard end, mum*" 1884 HF xi 95 (OED This pron. *dial.* So W S C. Cf. U: The old received pron.; now *obs, provinc.,* or *vulgar* exc. in *naut.* use; cf. forrader. So Wr)

forwards, adv. [AC] *He* [the chameleon] *whirls one eye rearwards and the other forwards* 1879 FE lxv 645 (The dicts. are highly conflicting here. Cf. OED: In *U.S. forward* is now generally used, to the exclusion of *forwards,* which was stigmatized by Webster (1832) as 'a corruption.' A in M: Our usage allows the *s* in cases where English usage would certainly be against it. W: *Obs* exc. *Dial.* Not A or *obs* in S C U; cf. S: The original and proper distinction was that *forward* referred to motion, *forwards* to position or manner; but U: Used indifferently in many adv. phrases)

forwhy, adv. [?AC] "*I took No. 9. And I'll tell you for why*" 1877 "Some Rambling Notes" i 444. "*You may call a jay a bird...but he is just as much a human as you be. And I'll tell you for why*" 1880 TA ii 37 (OED *obs.* 2. As indirect *interrog.* For what reason. Used *ellipt.* 1710, only ex. So W S C U Wr)

foul, v. [?AB³] *He lounged lazily across my path, fouling my course* 1880 TA xlvii 544. *First off, I flew thirty yards, and then fouled an Irishman and brought him down* 1908 "Capt. Stormfield" 266 (OED 5. Chiefly *Naut.* c. transf. To run foul of, collide with. 1859.. So W S C U. A in AS.IV.382)

foul-witted, a. [B¹] *Reckless fellows, every one, elephantinely jolly, foul-witted, profane* 1883 LM iii 41 (Comb. not in OED W S C. Cf. OED Foul-spoken, 1588)

fountain, sb. [C] *The word fountain means one thing in Syria—freshwater springs* 1897 FE lix 581 (OED 1. A spring. Now *arch* or *poet.* 1450..1842. So U. Not *arch* in W S C)

fountain-jet, sb. [B¹] *The level strip of ground is... adorned at intervals with lofty and sparkling fountain-jets* 1880 TA xxi 196 (Comb. not in OED W S C)

four-ace, a. [AB¹] *We may depend on that with a four-ace confidence* 1907 CS II vii 195 (From "four aces," next to the highest hand in poker. Comb. not in OED W S C)

four-hour, a. [B¹] *That boat has gained ground or lost some during each four-hour stretch* 1875 OTM 192 (Comb. not in OED S C. Given in W)

Four Hundred, sb. [AB³] "*Then you went for the aristocracy...We would make a plunge at the Four Hundred*" 1904 "Bequest" (1906) vii 40 (OEDS *U.S.* "An exclusive association of people who represent the very best Society." 1889.. So W S Cl Th.III H. Not in C)

four prices, sb. [?AB¹] "*Negroes would have gone up to four prices*" 1873 GA i 27 (Cf. six figures, below. Phr. not in OED W S C)

four-story, a. [B²] *Ten vast four-story buildings* 1883 LM lviii 567 (OED 1888. So W. Comb. not in S C)

fourth dimension, sb. [B²] *Perfect grammar is the fourth dimension, so to speak; many have sought it, but none has found it* 1898 *Autob* (1924) I 173. "*Is he a mystery? Why, the fourth dimension's foolishness to him*" 1902 "DBDS" (1928) 316 (OEDS Fourth, a. C. A supposed or assumed dimension. 1904.. So W S C U. The OED evidence is surprisingly inadequate here. The term *fourth dimension* was used in English as early as 1685, in John Wallis's *Treatise of Algebra;* cf. quot. in F. Cajori, *A Hist. of Mathematics,* 2nd ed., 1922, p. 184)

Fourth of July, sb. [AB³] See *gorgeous* 1867. *The subject of this sketch appeared at intervals at Fourth-of-July celebrations* 1868 "Gen. Washington's Negro Body-Servant" (1906) 208. *One Fourth of July per year is now inadequate* 1894 PW xvii 821. *It was a little democracy which was full of liberty, equality, and Fourth of July* 1897-8 *Autob* (1924) I 120 (OEDS Fourth, a. 2b. *U.S.* 1807.. So W S C U H)

fourth-proof, a. [AB³] See *A No. 1* 1886 (OEDS. Fourth, a. C. *U.S.* Highly refined; of a high grade or quality 1828.. Comb. not in W S C)

fox-fire, sb. [AC] *What we must have was a lot of them rotten chunks that's called fox-fire, and just makes a soft kind of a glow when you lay them in a dark place* 1884 HF xxxv 356 (OED Now only *U.S.* The phosphorescent light emitted by decaying timber. 1483.. So Wr F Cl Th DN.I,III,VI. Not A in W S C T)

fox-hearted, a. [B¹] "*Oh, thou fox-hearted slave, I see it all!*" 1881 PP xxv 304 (Comb. not in OED W S C)

fox-squirrel, sb. [A] *A fox-squirrel, with his tail bent high like a shepherd's crook* 1912 "My Platonic Sweetheart" (1922) 288 (OEDS Fox, sb. 16b. A North American squirrel. 1688.. So W S C)

foxy, a. [?AB³] *The scarecrow, Dean, in foxy shoes, down at the heels* 1883 LM lvii 558. *He wore...foxy shoes, imitation patent leather* 1897 FE xxxvi 326 (OED 3. Used to denote various defects...specked, spotted, etc. 1805.. So W S C U Wr. A in Cl DN.V)

fragment-strewn, a. [B¹] *We walked out into the grass-grown, fragment-strewn court beyond the Parthenon* 1869 IA xxxii 347 (Comb. not in OED W S C)

frame, sb. [AC] *The "mansion"...was a rickety old two-story frame* 1892 AmCl ii 28 (OEDS 10b. A building; in later use, one composed chiefly or entirely of wood. *Obs* exc. *U.S.* 1425..1884. OEDS U.S. exs. 1732..1873. A in Th.III. Not A in W S C)

frame-house, sb. [A] *I smoked at every pore, like a frame house that is on fire on the inside* 1869 IA xxxiv 379. See *L,* sb. 1898 (OEDS *U.S.* 1796.. So W B F Cl Th T M H. Not A in S C U)

frame shop, sb. [A] *In each block two or three brick stores...towered above interjected bunches of little frame shops* 1893 PW i 234 (OEDS 1796, only ex. U.S. A in Th. Comb. not in W S C)

fraud, sb. [AB³] *They despised themselves as being dupes of a wily fraud* 1876 TS iv 50. See *soldier,* v. 1880. *We shall know which of these two frauds is entitled to wear the belt as being the first dishonest blatherskite ever bred in this town* 1899 "MCH" (1900) 38 (OED 4b. An impostor. *spec U.S.* 1850.. So C B F Cl. Not A in W S U T)

freak, sb. [AB³] "*Pockets*"...*the most curious freak Nature ever indulged in* 1891 *Letters* (1917) II xxxi 542. See *dime-museum* 1894. *I had seen a picture of a youthful Italian "freak"—or freaks...a combination consisting of two heads and four arms joined in a single body...I thought I would write a...story with this freak of nature for hero—or heroes* 1894 TET intro. 311 (OED 4b. More fully *freak of nature = lusus naturae:* a monstrosity, an abnormally developed individual of any species; in recent use (*esp.* U.S.), a living curiosity exhibited in a show. 1847.. So Cl. Not A in W S C U)

freckle, v. [B¹] *A friend drops in to swap compliments with you, and freckles me with bullet-holes* 1869 SNO (1875) 49. *There was a tin lantern freckling the floor with little spots of light* 1894 PW ix 549 (Nonce use. A hum. extension of the sense in OED 1. trans. To cover with freckles or spots. 1613..; so W S C)

free, a. **free to say.** [?AC] *"I'm free to say that if you don't mind telling us..."* 1894 PW xiii 777 (OED 20b. With inf., Ready to do something; eager, willing. *Obs* exc. in phr. *free to confess.* 1660..1874. OEDS Also *free to admit.* 1921. Not *obs* in Wr. A in B F. Phr. not in W S C)

free gold, sb. [?AB¹] *There was no way of getting anything out of such rock but the coarser-grained "free" gold; but the new cyanide process has changed all that* 1897 FE lxviii 687 (W: *Mining.* Gold that is not combined with another element; native gold. Comb. not in OED S C)

free list, sb. [?AB³] *Positively no Free List, Except Members of the Press* 1869 IA xxxi 332. *Whenever it is put on the stage it packs the house, and the free list is suspended* 1898 "About Play-Acting" 213. *We began the game—with a large and eager free-list to superintend it* 1907 "Chaps. from Autob" 474 (OEDS A list of persons from whom payment is not expected. 1855, only ex. of theatrical sense U.S. Not A in W S C)

freemasonry, sb. [B¹] *He said a man could learn how to correctly handle the subtleties and mysteries and freemasonries of any trade* 1909 ISD i 16 (Special craft-language or custom. This sense not in OED W S C)

free papers, sb. [?AB¹] *I have not deserted Mr. Blaine, for as regards him I got my free papers before he bought the property* 1884 *Speeches* (1923) 115 (Certificate of manumission; here *fig.* Comb. not in OED W S C)

free silver, sb. [?AB¹] *I am in favor of...the gold standard and free silver* 1900 *Speeches* (1910) 192 (W: *Econ.* The free coinage of silver at a fixed ratio with gold. A in S. Comb. not in OED C)

free soil, sb. [AB³] *How do you like "free-soil"?—I would like amazingly to see a good old-fashioned negro* 1853 *Letters* (1917) I i 29 (OED *U.S.* Territory in which slaveholding was prohibited. 1850. So W S C B F Cl)

Free State, sb. [AB³] *The negro will seek freedom in the heart of the free states* 1883 LM iii 43. *We would sell the raft and get on a steam-boat and go way up the Ohio amongst the free states* 1884 HF xv 125 (OED 2. *U.S.* Before the Civil War, a state in which slavery did not exist. 1820.. So W S C B F Cl)

free trade, sb. [?AB³] *A dispute over free trade and protection* 1883 LM xxxv 386. *They had the protection system..we were working along down toward free trade* 1889 CY xxxiii 419 (OEDS 2. Trade or commerce left to follow its natural course. Earlier U.S. ex. 1812.. Not A in W S C U)

Free-Will Baptist, sb. [AB³] *"He's ben the pizenest kind of a Free-Will Babtis' for forty year"* 1880 TA xxiii 225 (W: A U.S. division of the Baptist denomination originating in N.C. in 1729. So S C. Cf. OEDS Free Will, sb. 3b. 1823..)

freeze, v. [AB¹] *"I'm just a-freezin' for something fresh, anyway"* 1884 HF xx 194 (A in B: To become possessed of an intense longing for anything. So F Cl. This sense not in OED W S C. Cf. suffer, v. in the same sense, below)

freeze, v. [B¹] *There was an ancient billiard-table in the garret...Sometimes the balls would get scattered into difficult positions. Sometimes if I managed to keep them together, I would freeze; and always when I froze, and had to play away from the contact, there was sure to be nothing to play at but a wide and uninhabited vacancy* 1907 "Chaps. from Autob" 679 (W: *Billiards, Pool,* etc.: Of a ball, to come to rest in contact with another ball or with a cushion. So S. This sense not given in

OED C for the *verb;* but cf. OEDS Frozen, ppl.a. 1c. 1904)

freeze out, v. [AB²] *They would let that man go on and pay assessments...and then they would close in on him and freeze him out* 1867 "Inquiries about Insurances" 79 (OEDS 7b. *U.S.* To exclude by severe competition. 1867, this quot... So S C B F Cl Th T M. Not A in W U)

freeze to, v. [AB³] *He would grab that other dog jest by the j'int of his hind leg and freeze to it* 1865 "Jumping Frog" (1875) 32. *He sat down, took about the same position, and froze to it* 1879 *Letters* (1917) I xix 369. *Well, they froze to me for two hours* 1884 HF xxxii 336 (OED 3b. *U.S.* and *Australian.* To keep tight hold of. 1837.. So W C B F Cl M AS.II.354. Not A in S)

freight, sb. [AB²] *The high prices charged* [in Utah] *were eloquent of high freights and bewildering distances of freightage* 1872 RI xvii 137 (OED Now extended, esp. in U.S., to land-transit; also money paid for this. No clear ex. of Am. usage. So W C U Cl Th T M H. Not A in S)

freightage, sb. [AB²] See *freight,* sb. 1872 (OED Now extended, esp. in U.S., to land-transit. 3. 1886. So W C U Cl. Not A in S)

freight-car, sb. [AB³] *We brought sixty donkeys in the freight-cars* 1869 IA xl 418 (OEDS *U.S.* 1841.. So W S C U B F Cl Th M. Cf. H: Am. freight-car = Eng. goods wagon)

freight-cart, sb. [AB¹] *Private carriages, freight-carts and wagons* 1880 TA xxxi 329 (Comb. not in OED W S C. Cf. above)

freighting, vbl.sb. [AB³] *Western investments, through lines, the freighting business* 1873 GA xxii 203 (OED *attrib.* 1856, first quot. for Am. use of goods carried by land.. So S C Th.III H. Not in W)

freight-pile, sb. [B¹] *In New Orleans it was my privilege to watch the freight-piles from seven in the evening until seven in the morning* 1906 *Autob* (1924) I 309 (Here used of water-transit. Comb. not in OED W S C)

freight-rate, sb. [AB¹] *They can deliver incontrovertible judgments concerning...time-tables, and freight-rates, and summer resorts* 1903 "Chr.Sc." 175 (Here of land-transit. Comb. not in OED S C; but cf. Freight-money, 1755. Given in W)

freight up, v. [AB²] *How to freight up against probable fasts before starting* 1889 CY xiii 153 (OED 1c. *U.S. intr.* To take in a cargo. *fig.* 1889, this quot. Not in W S C)

freight up, v. [AB¹] *There was a conspiracy to freight him up with all the strange extravagances* 1895 "What Bourget Thinks" 54 (Here *trans.* To cram, 'stuff,' hoax. This sense not in OED W S C. Cf. M.T.'s use of *fill up* and *load up*)

Frenchy, a. [?AB³] *The coming and departing company, so mustached, so frisky, so affable, so fearfully and wonderfully Frenchy* 1869 IA xii 113 (OED 1826.. So W S C. A in T DN.II)

fresh, a. [AB³] *"Maybe we've been just a little too fresh, just a shade too 'previous'!"* 1892 AmCl xv 158 (OEDS orig. *U.S.* Forward, impertinent. 1848.. So C U B F Cl T M H DN.II,IV. Not A in W S)

fresh-crowned, ppl.a. [B¹] *The fresh-crowned hero fell without firing a shot* 1876 TS iii 35 (Comb. not in OED W S C)

freshet, sb. [?AB³] *I never saw such a freshet of loveliness before* 1869 IA xvii 116. *She was so mad she couldn't get the words out fast enough, and she gushed them out in one everlasting freshet* 1876 TSD vi 359 (OED 3. A flood. *transf* and *fig.* 1858.. A in B F Cl M AS.XI.290. The *fig* sense not in W S C)

freshness, sb. [AB²] *The mob began to take its revenge —for the discomfort...it had brought upon itself by its own too rash freshness* 1892 AmCl xv 160 (OEDS *U.S.* Forwardness, impertinence. 1901.. Not A in W S C)

fret, v. [C] *"Here a poor prisoner, forsook by the world and friends, fretted his sorrowful life"* 1884 HF xxxviii 387 (OED 3b. *fig.* To devour, consume. *Obs* exc. in *fret the heart.* 1200..1856. Not *obs* in W S C)

friend, sb. [?AB¹] *Friend Williams—Please see that no reports or synopses are made of my lecture* 1868 *M.T. the Letter Writer* (1932) i 15 (Cf. OED 1d. Used in subscribing a letter. 1529..1661. Here used in the salutation of a letter. Neither use mentioned in W S C)

frills, sb. [AB²] *"You put on as many frills and make as much fuss..."* 1865 SS (1926) 189. See also *considerable,* adv. 1884; *cuss,* v. 1884 (OEDS 1d. *U.S. colloq.* An affectation of dress or manners, an air. Usually *pl.* 1870.. So S C F Cl Th.III H. Not A in W U)

fringe off, v. [AB¹] *It was a town that was compacted together...Its outlying borders fringed off and thinned away among the cedar forest* 1877 "Some Rambling Notes" iii 591 (The intr. use with *off* not in OED W S C. Cf. below)

fringe out, v. [?AB²] *Do you see where the line fringes out at the upper end and begins to fade away?* 1875 OTM 286. *The hamlet's most rearward border fringed itself out* 1893 PW i 234. *I was fringed out with an electrical nimbus that flamed around for miles and miles* 1907 "Capt. Stormfield" 41 (OEDS 4. To spread like a fringe away, out, over. 1883, OTM quot., wrongly dated.. Phr. not in W S C)

frisket, sb. [B¹] See *comp,* sb. 1909 (Nonsense use. Cf. OED *Printing.* A thin iron frame...for keeping the sheet in position while printing. 1683..1884. So W S C U)

frivolishness, sb. [?AB¹] See *loud,* a. 1884 (Not in OED W S C)

frog, sb. [?AB¹] *He left him pretty well talked out, but grateful "clear down to his frogs," as he expressed it* 1880 TA xx 194 (The sole of the foot. This sense not in OED W S C. Apparently *transf* from the sense in OED: An elastic horny substance growing in the middle of the sole of a horse's hoof. 1610..)

frog-shaped, ppl.a. [B¹] *The saddles were the high, stuffy, frog-shaped things we had known in Epehsus and Smyrna* 1869 IA lviii 618 (Comb. not in OED W S C)

frog-span, sb. [B¹] *It was ten frog-spans in diameter* 1875 SNO 145 (Nonce comb.)

front, sb. [?AB²] *The clerk promptly calls out, "Front! show his lordship to four-eighty-two!"* 1892 AmCl vii 72 (OEDS 11c. As a command: To the front. 1907.. So W. A in S. This sense not in C)

frontier, sb. [AB³] *We were going in the overland stage from the Missouri frontier to Nevada* 1872 RI i 20 (OEDS 4b. *U.S.* That part of a country which forms the border of its settled or inhabited regions. 1803.. So W C H. Not A in S)

front-piece, sb. [B¹] *He was "magnificently habited in a doublet of white satin, with a front-piece of purple cloth-of-tissue"* 1881 PP ix 106 (Comb. not in OED S C. Given in W)

front-yard, sb. [AB³] *No weed-grown front-yards of the poor, no back-yards littered with tin cans and old boots* 1897 FE xxix 282 (OEDS *U.S.* 1835.. Comb. not in W S C)

frozen, ppl.a. [AB²] *What these gentlemen want for a book is the frozen truth* 1883 LM xxxiv 374 (OED 1b. *fig.*...Of facts, truth. *U.S.* 1884.. Not A in W. This sense not in S C)

fruit-cake, sb. [?AB³] *The natives of the interior of New England...prefer it to the gooseberry for the making of fruit-cake* 1870 SNO (1875) 235 (OEDS Fruit, sb. 9. Earlier U.S. ex. 1848. Not A in W S C U)

fruit-peddler, sb. [B¹] *An unbroken procession of fruit-peddlers and tourist carriages* 1880 TA xxxi 328 (Comb. not in OED S C. Given in W. Cf. OED Fruit-dealer, 1810)

fruit-wagon, sb. [B¹] *The farmer's fruit-wagons* 1894 PW iv 330 (Comb. not in OED W S C)

fry, sb. **minor fry.** [B¹] *Breakfast for us minor fry was waiting in our mess-room* 1895 JA II xvii 748 (Phr. not in OED W S C. A nonce variant of *small fry, lesser fry.* Cf. OED Fry, sb. 4b. A collective term for young or insignificant beings. 1577.. Cf. also small-fry, a., below)

full, a. [?AC] *"Every time he hath gotten his barrel full"* 1889 CY iii 45 (OED 4. Full of food. Now *arch* and *vulgar. c*1000..1875. Not *arch* in W S C U Wr)

full, sb. [AB¹] See *raise,* sb. 1859 (W: *Poker:* A full house. So S C. This sense not in OED. Cf. OED Full house. 2. *Poker.* 1887.. Here applied punningly to high water in the river)

full-blood, a. [?AB³] *"Even these poor Lathersers would have been bright if they had been Sellerses; I mean full blood"* 1892 AmCl v 59 (OEDS Earlier U.S. exs. 1812.. Not A in W S C U)

full-dress suit, sb. [B²] *You can get a full-dress suit for the same money* 1869 IA xxx 319 (OED 1879, only ex. So W. Comb. not in S C)

full-fledged, ppl.a. [B²] *I was a pilot now, full-fledged* 1883 LM xxi 246 (OED 1884.. So W S C U)

fulsome, a. [?AC] *Inveterate liars...the idea originated in their own fulsome brains—or rather in the settlings which they regard as brains* 1869 SNO (1875) 46 (OED 6b. Morally foul, filthy, obscene. *obs.* 1604..1726. So W U. This sense not in S C)

fumigating, vbl.sb. [B²] *The miserable outcasts called that "fumigating"* 1869 IA xx 200 (OED 1881, only ex. So W S C U)

fumigator, sb. [B²] *We feel no malice toward these fumigators* 1869 IA xxi 209 (OED 1872, this quot... So W S C U)

functionable, a. [B¹] *"Does she seem to be in full and functionable possession of her intellectual plant?"* 1899 "Chr.Sc. and the Book" 586 (Able to function or operate. Not in OED W S C)

funnel, v. [B¹] *One often sees a tourist funnel his hands at his wife's ear* 1880 TA xlviii 562 (This sense not in OED W S C)

funnel-topped, a. [B¹] *Funnel-topped buskins, long rapier, and all that* 1895 JA II vii 236 (Comb. not in OED W S C; but cf. OED Funnel-top, 1854)

funny, a. [?AB³] *By a funny circumstance he knew everybody that I ever knew in Hannibal and Palmyra* 1866 *Letters* (1917) I v 107 (OED 2. Curious, queer, odd, strange. *colloq* 1806.. So W S C U Wr. A in M)

funny-paragraph, sb. [?AB¹] See *editorial* 1880 (Comb. not in OED W S C. Cf. OEDS Funny column, orig. *U.S.* 1890)

fur, sb. **to make the fur fly.** [AB³] *Then we picked and shoveled, and made the fur fly* 1884 HF xxxvi 369 (OEDS 2b. *U.S. slang.* 1834.. B: To make a great commotion. So C F Cl Th M DN.III AS.II.47,354. Phrase not in W S)

furbish up, v. [C] *We arrived in time to furbish up and get to the English church* 1880 TA xxiv 223 (OED 2. To brush or clean up any thing...chiefly with *up.* b. intr. for *refl. Obs. rare.* 1697, only ex. Not *obs* in S. Phrase not in W C)

furnace-stoker, sb. [B¹] *It can appoint its own furnace-stoker, winters* 1907 CS II viii 235 (Comb. not in OED S C. Given in W. Cf. OED Furnace-feeder, a stoker or fireman. 1858)

furniture-mender, sb. [B¹] *And took it to Hawkins's Yankee furniture-mender* 1892 AmCl iv 55 (Comb. not in OED W S C)

furniture-scout, sb. [?AB¹] See *sofa-shifter* 1864 (Comb. not in OED W S C; but cf. OED Scout, sb. At Oxford, also at Yale and Harvard: A male college servant. 1708..)

furtivenesses, sb. pl. [B²] *I could say all my say without any furtivenesses and without embarassment* 1895 JA I vii 850 (OED 1896, only ex. *Concrete* sense not in W S C U)

fury, sb. **like fury.** [?AB³] *Directly it begun to rain, and it rained like all fury, too, and I never see the wind blow so* 1884 HF ix 74 (OED 3b. Furiously, 'like mad.' *colloq.* 1840, only ex. U.S. Phr. not in W S C)

fuss-and-feathers, sb. [?AB³] *Without the marring additions of human pow-wow and fuss-and-feathers and display* 1893 "Is He Living?" (1900) 241 (OED Bustle and display. 1891, only ex. A in Th.III,1864 DN.VI AS.IV. Phr. not in W S C)

fuss up. v. [?AB¹] *Nothing breaks up an author's progress like having to stop to fuss-up the weather* 1892 AmCl, pref. (To fuss over, take special pains with. Cf. Wr, suppl.: To furbish up, smarten, do up. *Norfolk.* This sense not in OED W S C; but cf. OED 2. To flatter, treat with fussy politeness. ?*dial.* 1816..)

fussy, a. [?AB³] *The Tale of Fussy-Philip* [German, Zappel-Philipp]...*"Philip, if 'twon't make you ill, Try to sit a minute still"* 1891 *Slovenly Peter* (1935) 18. *Its coming made the fussy human pack seem infinitely pitiful* 1898 "About Play-Acting" (1900) 216. *A noble solitude unvexed by the fussy world* 1898 "At the Appetite-Cure" (1900) 153. See also *nickel-plated* 1900 (W: Full of commotion; bustling. Chiefly *U.S.* Not A in OED 1. Habitually busy about trifles. 1831.. Not A in S C U Wr)

futures, sb. [?AB³] *In his reflective intervals he will always be speculating in "futures"* 1897 FE li 492 (OED 6. *Comm.* in *pl.* Goods and stocks sold on an agreement for future delivery. 1880.. So W S C U. A in Th.III)

fuzzle, v. [?AC] *"Why, with a person pecking at me that way, I should get that fuzzled and fuddled"* 1894 TET v 389 (OED *obs.* To intoxicate...confuse, muddle. 1621, 1632. So W C. A in AS.XII.91: Fuzl'd: drunk, from Franklin's "Drinker's Dictionary," 1737. Cf. Wr. Fuzzle, sb. Beverage, tipple. Not in S)

G

gabble, sb. [AB¹] *When they got to snoring we had a long gabble, and I told Jim everything* 1884 HF xxx 313 (An intimate or eager conversation. A in DN.III. This sense not in OED W S C)

Gaekwar, sb. Spelled **Gaikowar.** [B³E] "*It was given to Luigi by a great Indian prince, the Gaikowar of Baroda*" 1894 PW x 555 (OEDS The title of the native ruler of Baroda. 1854.. So W S C U. This sp. not cited in any dict.)

gag, v. [?AC] *Nobody likes to eat a ton of black paint* [i.e., to 'eat one's words']...*After long, long and bitter gagging, some millions of the common serfdom of the party worried down their ton apiece* 1884 *Speeches* (1923) 127 (OED 1b. To choke, *lit.* and *fig.* Also, to retch. *Obs* exc. *dial.* 1707..1883. Not *obs* in W S C)

gage, v. [B¹?C] "*I gage two-and-half that she will die all of same*" ["Retranslated" from the French "Je gage;" the original version of the "Jumping Frog" has "I'll risk"] 1875 SNO 40 (Hum. alienism. M.T. was hardly aware that the Eng. word once had the same meaning: OED 2. To stake, wager. *Obs* ..1814. So W S C Wr)

gage, v. [?AB¹] *He made his fatal remark the first day...and it "gaged" him* (1893 PW i 235 (Cf. OED Gauge, v. 4. *fig.* To 'take the measure' of a person. 1583..1888. Here: To give one's measure; to fix or establish one's social status. This sense not in OED W S C)

gaily, a. [?AE] See *gala,* below.

gain, v. [?AB¹] *My beautiful new watch had run eighteen months without losing or gaining* 1870 SNO (1875) 17 (This sense not in OED W S. Given in C. Cf. Lose, below)

gait, sb. [AB¹] "*Preachin' was his natural gait*" 1865 SNO (1875) 74 (A in F: One's walk in life, calling, trade, profession. So Cl. This sense not in OED W S C)

gal, sb. [?AE] "*I'm acquainted with a right smart chance of gals in Keokuk*" 1856 *Adv. of T. J. Snodgrass* (1928) 13. See also *high water* 1856 and *high-toned* 1873. "*What's the name of the gal?*" "*It ain't a gal at all—it's a girl.*" "*It's all the same, I reckon; some says gal, some says girl—both's right, like as not. Anyway, what's her name, Tom?*" 1876 TS xxv 195 (OEDS Vulgar or *dial* pron. of Girl. Earlier U.S. exs. 1796.. A in M DN.I,IV,V AS.V.207, Ozarks. Not A in W S C Wr)

gala, sb. Spelled **gaily.** [?AE] "*Friends wanted a silver door on the coffin...You know a fellow couldn't roust out such a gaily thing as that*" 1871 SNO (1875) 247 (OED 4. *attrib.* Festive, showy. 1762.. So W S C. This sp. not given in OED W S C. "Gaily" is given as A in M DN.II,IV,V, Missouri and N.C., with the meaning of lively, well, in good health. Also in AS.IV. 110, from Fithian's *Journal,* Va., 1774. Mencken (p. 467, n.) mistakes it for an adjective use of the adverb *gaily!*)

galingale, sb. Spelled **galangals.** [E] Se *afarabocca* 1894 (OED This form 16th-19th c. 1. The aromatic root of certain East Indian plants. *c*1000..1830. So W S C U)

galley-west, adv. to knock **galley-west.** [AB²] *Your verdict has knocked what little* [critical penetration] *I did have gally-west!* 1875 *Letters* (1917) I xv 250. "*Of course, that knocked the mystery galley-west in a second*" 1880 TA iii 41. "*Says enough to knock their little game galley-west, doesn't it?*" 1883 LM xxviii 303 (OEDS *U.S. colloq.* To bring to confusion; to knock out completely, dispose of finally. 1883.. So W DN.II,III. Not A in S C)

gallinipper, sb. [AB³] *The gallinipper sucking the tip-end of her nose* 1865 SS (1926) 185 (OEDS Chiefly *U.S.* A large mosquito. 1801.. So S C B F Cl Th DN.I,III. Not A in W T)

gallows, sb. Spelled **galluses.** [AE] *He had home-knit galluses* 1884 HF xix 182 (OED 6. 'Suspenders.' Now

dial, Scotch, and *U.S.,* in the form *gallowses.* 1730.. A in S Wr B Th DN.I,II,III,IV,V, Ky., Mo. AS.II. 355, W.Va.; V.120, Me. Not A in W C)

gallows, a. Spelled **gallus.** [?ACE] *Camels are not beautiful, and their long underlip gives them an exceedingly "gallus" expression* 1869 IA xlii 439. "*She has a 'gallus' way of going with her arms akimbo*" 1870 "Curious Dream" (1872) 14. *With an earl's coronet tilted just a wee bit to one side in a most gallus and winsome way* 1892 AmCl xxiii 240 (OED 1. Fit for the gallows, villainous, wicked. Now only *dial* in weaker sense: Impish, wild, mischievous. *c*1425..1892. So W S U Wr T. A in B DN.I,V. This sense not in C. Cf. OED Gallus, a. *Obs* form of Gallows. Not *obs* in W S C)

gallows-buckle, sb. Spelled **gallus-buckle.** [AB¹E] "*Some feller wanted his gallus-buckle*" 1896 TSD ix 524 (Comb. not in OED W S C; but cf. OED Gallows-button, 1836)

gallows-builder, sb. [B¹] *And always the muffled and uncanny hammering of the gallows-builders in the courtyard* 1898 "From the London Times of 1904" (1900) 137 (Comb. not in OED W S C; but cf. OED Gallows-maker, 1602)

gallowsly, adv. Spelled **gallusly.** [?AB¹E] *The marvelous stove-pipe hat...with its poor pathetic old stiff brim canted up "gallusly" in the wrong places* 1877 "Some Rambling Notes" ii 592 (Not in OED W S C. Cf. gallows, a., above)

galoot, sb. [AB³] *He could lam any galoot of his inches in America* 1872 RI xvii 336. *A raft sliding by, away off yonder, and maybe a galoot on it chopping* 1884 HF xix 179 (OED 2. *U.S.* An awkward or uncouth fellow. 1866.. So S C Wr B F Th M DN.III,IV,V. Not A in W T)

gamble-money, sb. [B¹] "*I believe they will even steal ostensible gamble-money*" 1899 "MCH" (1900) 64 (Money obtained by gambling. Comb. not in OED W S C)

gamble on, v. [?AB³] *Whatever is found in its company may be gambled on as being the petrified truth* 1883 LM l 498 (OED 1b. *slang.* Earliest ex. U.S. 1866.. Not A in W S C. A in DN.II,III)

gambling-den, sb. [B²] *They won't wink for cash at gambling-dens* 1892 AmCl iii 45 (OED Gambling, vbl.sb. No ex. Comb. not in W S C)

gambling-palace, sb. [B¹] *There were military companies, brass-bands, gambling-palaces* 1872 RI xliii 303 (Comb. not in OED W S C)

game, sb. The game. [?AB³] See *seven-up* 1869 (One of the six "points" that may be scored in the Am. game of seven-up. Cf. OED 8f. In certain card games: The possession, at the end of the game, of the largest number of pips, for which the player scores one or more points. 1830.. So W S C)

game-bag, sb. [B¹] *A big shell burst near her...and a piece of iron carried away her game-bag of false hair* 1883 LM xxxv 380 (Hum. nonce use)

game of chance, sb. [?AB¹] *At that time, in Kentucky, the law was very strict against what are termed "games of chance"* 1870 SNO (1875) 159 (W: All games in which chance is the sole or a considerable factor in determining the outcome. So S. Phr. not in OED C)

game-shop, sb. [B¹] *The man that keeps the game-shop* 1901 "Two Little Tales" (1928) 207 (Comb. not in OED W S C)

gamy, a. [?AB³] *Some with one eye out but a gamey look in the other* 1869 IA vi 57 (OED 2. Spirited, plucky. 1844.. So W S C. A in DN.III)

gang, sb. [?AC] See *cavort* 1868; *corned* 1872. *What a lively gang of young people we were!* 1880 M.T. the *Letter Writer* (1932) iii 48 (OED 10. Any band or company of persons who go about together...in mod. usage mainly associated with criminal societies. 1632.. 1677, last ex. of word used in good or harmless sense. This sense not *obs* in W S C Wr; A in H DN.III)

gangly, a. [?AB[1]] *"I should have shot that long gangly lubber they called Hank"* 1872 RI vii 61 (W: Gangling, lanky. *colloq* and *dial.* So S. A in Th. Not in OED C; but cf. OED Gangling, ppl.a. Of straggling growth; loosely built. 1808..)

gang-plank, sb. [AB[3]] *If the landsman should wish the gang-plank moved a foot farther forward*...1875 OTM 73 (OEDS *U.S.* A landing-plank; gang-board. 1848.. So C. Not A in W S U)

gap, sb. [A] *The post route Indian Gulch to Shakespeare Gap changed partly to the old Mormon Trail* 1868 CD (1872) 45 (OED 5. A pass or gorge; very common in the U.S. 1555.. A in C B DN.VI. Not A in W S U Wr AS.I.350)

gape, sb. Spelled **gap**. [?ACE] *I took a good gap and a stretch* 1884 HF vii 53 (OED 1. A yawn. 1535..1807. This sp. 18th c. The sp. *gap* not mentioned in W S C)

gape, v. Also **gap**. [?ACE] *We gaped and yawned and stretched* 1869 IA xii 117. *"Don't gap and stretch like that, Huckleberry—why don't you try to behave?"* 1884 HF i 4. *He gapped and stretched himself* 1884 HF viii 64 (OED 6. To yawn, esp. from weariness. Now *rare* in southern Eng. and in literature; common *colloq* in midland and northern districts. c1440..1729. A in DN.I,II,III. Not A in W S C U. This sp. not mentioned in OED W S C; but the pron. with short *a* thus indicated is allowed by W C)

garboard-strake, sb. [B[1]] *Poor man, it knocked him silly, and he fell over the garboard-strake and barked his shins on the cat-heads* 1904 "Bequest" (1906) vii 41. See also *mizen-yard* 1907 (Nonsense use. Cf. OED Garboard-strake = garboard, the first range of planks laid upon a ship's bottom, next to the keel. 1626.. 1834; so W S C U. Cf. *cat-head*, above)

garden-acre, sb. [?AB[1]] *She built and furnished a pretty and comfortable two-thousand-dollar house in the midst of her garden-acre* 1904 "Bequest" (1906) i 2 (Comb. not in OED W S C; but cf. OEDS Garden-spot, *U.S.* 1687..)

garden-truck, sb. [AB[3]] *A gentleman could kill a free commoner and pay for him—cash or garden-truck* 1889 CY xviii 217 (OEDS *U.S.* Market garden produce. 1878.. So W B Cl T. Not A in S C)

garlic-exterminator, sb. [B[1]] *Making her name a familiar word in every garlic-exterminator mouth in Italy* 1869 IA xix 184 (Nonce comb.)

garter, sb. [AB[3]] See *house-snake* 1884. *When they were "house snakes" or "garters," we carried them home* 1897 *Autob* (1924) I 103 (OED 6b. *U.S.* Garter-snake. 1880. This sense not in W S C)

garter-snake, sb. [A] *"We can get you some garter-snakes"* 1884 HF xxxviii 392 (OED *U.S.* The name of various grass or ribbon snakes. 1775.. So W S C U Th M)

gas, v. [AB[3]] See *American language* 1880 (OEDS 5b. orig. *U.S.* To indulge in empty talk. 1855.. So Cl Th DN.III. Not A in W S C U)

gas-bill, sb. [B[2]] See *gas-office* 1882 (OED Gas, sb. 7(b). No ex. Comb. not in W S C)

gashly, a. [?AC] *"Doan' look at his face—it's too gashly"* 1884 HF ix 77 (OED *obs* exc. *dial.* Ghastly, horrid. 1633..1880. So W S C Wr)

gas-illuminated, ppl.a. [B[1]] *Under its dull gas-illuminated glass canopy* 1873 GA xlvi 416 (Comb. not in OED W S C; but cf. OED Gas-lighted, 1862)

gas-office, sb. [B[1]] *Gas office broken open here, and three months' unpaid gas-bills taken* 1882 SWE 22 (Comb. not in OED W S C)

gate-guard, sb. [B[1]] *The gate-guard at the railway station passes me through unchallenged* 1902 "Does the Race Love a Lord?" 438 (Comb. not in OED W S C; but cf. OED Gate-keeper, 1572..; Gate-man, 1796..)

Gatling, sb. [AB[3]] *All Gatlings, all of the same calibre and delivery* 1904 "Italian with Grammar" (1906) 190 (OED A form of machine gun first used in the Am. Civil War. 1872.. So U. Not in W S C)

Gatling gun, sb. [AB[3]] *Gatling guns at fifteen paces would be a likely way to get a verdict on the field of honor* 1880 TA viii 721. *"But are you sure?" "Sure as guns— Gatling guns!"* 1888 "Meisterschaft" 458 (OED 1870.. So W S C U. Cf. above)

gaudinesses, sb.pl. [B[1]] *The majestic elephants, clothed in their Sunday best of gaudinesses* 1897 FE lx 596 (This concrete sense not in OED W S C)

gaudy, a. [?AB[1]] See *roust out* 1871; *man-of-war-like* 1875. *Tom, like the rest of the respectable boys, envied Huckleberry his gaudy outcast condition* 1876 TS vi 64. *We played it to a hundred guests in our library, and had a perfectly gaudy time* 1888 *M.T. the Letter Writer* (1932) 49. See also *base*, sb. 1888 (Good, fine, 'dandy.' This sense not in OED W S C. Cf. OED 3c. *slang.* In negative sentences: Very good. 1884..; but M.T. uses the word in this sense affirmatively, and frequently)

gaum, v. [?A] See *Digger* 1869. *His funeral, which consisted of him being burnt and the other Injuns gauming their faces with his ashes and howling like wildcats* 1907 "Capt. Stormfield" 46 (OED 2. To smear with a sticky substance. 1796.. So C. *Dial* in W S Wr. A in B F Cl DN.I,III,IV,V,VI AS.V.426, Ozarks; VIII.1.5)

gavel, sb. [AB[3]] *The sharp blows of the speaker's gavel rose above the din* 1873 GA xlv 410 (OED 4b. *U.S.* A president's mallet. 1866.. So W B T. Not A in S C U)

gawk, sb. [?AB[3]] *"Those gawks making themselves so facetious over it"* 1872 RI vii 162. *The gaping crowd of country gawks* 1881 PP iii 39. *"To have the news go back to the village and make those gawks stare!"* 1895 JA II x 464 (OED An awkward person, a simpleton. 1837.. So W S C U Wr. A in DN.IV,V)

gawk, v. [A] *He just wanted to see those green Tennesseans stare and gawk when they saw him come a-ripping along in a sulky* 1880 TA xxvi 268. *Hans was gawking at the sky* [German, Hans Guck-in-die-Luft] 1891 *Slovenly Peter* (1935) 21 (OED *dial* and *U.S.* To stare or gape stupidly. 1785.. So Th DN.V. Not A in W S C Wr)

gawky-looking, ppl.a. [?AB[1]] *"That gawky-looking person with Miss Hawkins?"* 1873 GA xxxviii 340 (Comb. not in OED W S C. Cf. Gawky, a., A in DN.V; not A in OED W S C)

gay, a. [?AC] *I am running on preachers now, altogether. I find them gay* 1866 *Letters* (1917) I vi 122. *"Dat's a mighty gay marvel* [marble], *I tell you!"* 1876 TS ii 27. *"Everything belongs to them." "Ain' dat gay?"* 1884 HF xiv 119. *"My business and your law practice ought to make a pretty gay team, Dave"* 1894 PW xi 553 (OED 6. Brilliantly good; excellent, fine. *obs.* c1470..1593. So W. Not *obs* in C Wr. This sense not in S)

gear, sb. [?C] *The rest of his gear was blue silk and dainty laces* 1889 CY ii 33 (OED 1. Apparel, attire. 1310..1879. So W S C Wr. *Arch* in U)

geewhillikins, int. [AB[2]] *"Wish to jeewhillikins I could forget her!"* 1857 *Adv. of T. J. Snodgrass* (1928) 45. *"Geewhillikins," I says, "but what does the rest of it mean?"* 1884 HF xxxviii 386 (OEDS *U.S.* Perhaps a fanciful substitute for *Jerusalem!* 1857.. So W F Th DN.III,V. Not in S C)

Gemini, sb. by **Jimminy, geeminy,** etc. [?A?CE] *"I wish to geeminy she'd stick to one or t'other"* 1876 TS i 21. *By Jimminy, away down through the texas-hall we see a light!* 1884 HF xii 103. *"Going on two years, by geeminy"* 1880 TA xx 192. *"Py chiminy, nur hören Sie einmal!"* 1892 AmCl xvi 167. See also *chain-lightning* 1902 (OED 4. A mild oath, of uncertain derivation, perhaps from the constellation. *Vulgar.* 1664.. So W S C Wr. *Obs* in U. A in M DN.III,IV,V AS.IX.258. The sp. *jimminy* 19th c. in OED)

General, sb. [AB[1]] *His title of "Squire,"*...*as his wealth and popularity augmented, by imperceptible* stages, grew up into "Judge;" indeed, it bade fair to swell into "General" by and by 1873 GA lvii 515. See also Colonel 1902 (This honorific sense A in M H AS.IX.205. Not in OED W S C. Cf. Colonel, Major, Squire, etc., above and below)

general, a. [?C] See organized 1881; good-by 1884 (OED 1b. Pertaining in common to various persons. obs. c1380..1667. Not obs in W S C U)

general-talk, sb. [B¹] He became familiar with generalship and general-ways and general-talk 1909 ISD iv 47 (Nonce comb.)

general-ways, sb. [B¹] See general-talk 1909 (Nonce comb.)

generosities, sb.pl. [C] They lacked his humanities and generosities 1897 FE i 34 (OED 4. pl. Instances of generosity. rare 1647..1833. Concrete sense not rare in W S C U)

genre, sb. Spelled **johnry.** [B³E] See foreground, v. 1892 (OED 2. A style of painting in which scenes and subjects of ordinary life are depicted. 1873.. So W S C U. This attempt at phonetic spelling seems original with M.T.)

gent, sb. [?A] See thoroughbrace 1872. "Think of it, ladies and gents, he's expecting a cablegram!" 1892 AmCl xv 156. "Don't it look that way to you, gents?" 1893 PW i 235. See also parlor 1904 (OED Now only vulgar. 1564..1885. So W S C U T. A in B DN.IV)

Gentile, sb. [AB³] "Gentiles" are people who are not Mormons 1872 RI xiii 108. See also admire 1872; Morisite 1872 (OED 1b. 1847.. So W S C B F Cl T H AS.VII.119,VIII.2.31)

gentle-flowing, ppl.a. [B¹] He never changed his voice from the gentle-flowing key 1865 "Jumping Frog" (1875) 30 (Comb. not in OED W S C; but cf. OED Gentle-gliding, 1612)

gentle-humored, ppl.a. [B¹] None were gentle-humored 1881 PP xviii 223 (Comb. not in OED W S C; but cf. Gentle-hearted, 1593)

gentleman-servant, sb. [B¹] Six gorgeous gentleman-servants sprung to their feet 1881 PP v 59 (Comb. not in OED W S C; but cf. OED Gentleman-farmer, 1749..)

gentlenesses, sb.pl. [B¹] He brought all his native sweetnesses and gentlenesses and simplicities with him 1898 Autob (1924) I 135 (This concrete sense not in OED W S C)

gentle-spirited, ppl.a. [B¹] He was a most kind and gentle-spirited man 1909 ISD ii 22 (Comb. not in OED W S C)

geologic, a. [B¹] I never stir from the house, except at geologic intervals 1909 Letters (1917) II xlvii 827 (Of prodigious length. This hum. transf. sense not in OED W S C)

Germanic, a. [B¹] That sentence is Germanic, and shows that I am acquiring mastery of the art and spirit of the language 1899 "Chr.Sc. and the Book" 585 (W: Of or pertaining to the...German language. This sense not in OED S C. Cf. OED 2. Of or pertaining to the Teutonic race, with reference to the language...as, Primitive Germanic. Here: characteristic of the modern German language)

Geschirr, sb. [B¹] "Your mental Geschirr is not arranged for light and airy conversations" 1899 "Chr.Sc. and the Book" 586 (Nonce borrowing: Ger. Geschirr = gear, trappings, machinery. Not in OED W S C)

get, v. Past participle **gotten.** [A?CE] See inaugurate 1869; toggery 1875. He was delighted to have gotten Appomatox accomplished once more in his mind 1885 Autob (1924) II 144. See also tableau 1889; tornado 1899; test-remark 1899; break up 1906 (OED Headnote: In England the form gotten is almost obsolete (exc. dial) being superseded by got; in U.S. literature gotten is still very common, although Webster 1864 gives it as 'obsolescent.' W 1935 gives gotten as 'esp. in U.S.' Not called either obs or A in S C. Wr: Scotch. A in F Th,1796

T M H DN.I,III,V AS.II.495; VI.315. See also Nation LIII (1891) 237,447)

get, v. [AB²] "I don't know that I quite get the bearings of your position" 1892 AmCl xiv 149 (OEDS 7d. To understand; to catch. orig. U.S. colloq. 1907.. So M H DN.III,IV. Not A in W U. This sense not in S C)

get, v. **to get religion.** [AB³] There had been a "revival," and everybody had "got religion" 1876 TS xxii 179. "I am one of the gang, but have got religgion and wish to quit it and lead an honest life" 1884 HF xxxix 402. In the colored Methodist church...she "got religion" 1893 PW ii 237 (OED 12d. U.S. vulgar. To be converted. 1857.. So W S C B F Th,1826 M DN.I,II,III AS.II. 355)

get, v. [AB²] "Well, I'll be dashed! If this don't get me! 1873 GA xvii 161. "What is your own religion?" "Well, boss, you've kind o' got me, thar—and yit you hain't got me so mighty much, nuther" 1880 TA xxiii 225. "Dat's de time I got you!" 1893 PW ii 236. A low murmur sifted through the house; its import was, "He's got them both!" 1899 "MCH" (1900) 41 (OEDS 21d. To exercise, worry. orig. U.S. colloq. 1884.. So Wr B Th.III M. Not A in W. This sense not in S C)

get, v. **to have got to.** [B²] "This has got to be learned" 1875 OTM 283. "What you learn here, you've got to know" 1880 TA xx 193. See also flume 1882 (OED 24. The perfect tense is used in familiar language in senses equivalent to those of the present tense of have. So colloq or vulgar in recent use To have got to = 'to have to,' to be obliged to. 1889, only ex. AS.VII.286 cites Lewis Carroll, 1865. So W S C U)

get, v. Past tense **gat.** [CE] Sir Launcelot took Sir Kay's horse and gat him away into distant lands 1889 CY iii 44. See also comradeship 1889 CY; whenas 1889 CY (OED Headnote: Pa.t. arch. gat. 27b refl. To betake oneself. Now only arch. 1513..1886. So W S C)

get, v. [AB³] He got me so nervous that I couldn't look at the view 1897 FE lii 504 (OEDS 29b. To succeed in making. U.S. colloq. 1891.. So H. Not A in W S. This sense not in C)

get, v. **git.** [AB²E] Then he says, "One—two—three—git!"...and the new frog hopped off lively 1865 "Jumping Frog" (1875) 19. Tom asked him why he didn't show the flag and command them to git, in the name of the United States 1894 TSA xii 542 (OEDS The form git 19th c. dial. 31d. U.S. colloq or slang, often in form git: To be off, 'clear out.' 1869.. So W S C B F Cl Th.III T M DN.I)

get after, v. [?AB¹] A little fort...If we were ever to get after it with one of our turreted monitors they would have to move it out in the country 1869 IA v 51 (To attack, assail, harass. This sense not in OED W S C)

get along, v. [?AB³] They say there is no word for "home" in the French language. Well, considering that they have the article itself in such an attractive aspect, they ought to manage to get along without the word 1869 IA xii 106. "All of us so put to it for to get along and families so large" 1873 GA ii 33. I would try to get along without the compliment 1880 TA xvi 146. A young journeyman tinner who was getting along all right till he fell sick and lost his job 1892 AmCl xii 126 (OEDS 53b. To get on, fare; to manage. Earlier U.S. exs. A in Cl: The Am. substitute for the Eng. phrase "to get on." Not A in W C U. Not in S)

get along, v. [?AB¹] There was the old man down the path a piece. When he got along I was hard at it taking up a "trot" line 1884 HF vii 48 (To come up, come alongside, arrive. Cf. Wr: To pass, go by. Not in OED W S C in this sense)

get around, v. **no getting around.** [AB²] "This has got to be learned; there isn't any getting around it" 1875 OTM 283. The clothes are right, there's no getting around it 1892 AmCl xix 192. "There's no getting around proof like that" 1894 TET iv 362 (OEDS 35. Get around = Get round, 42a, to evade. U.S. 1888. So F Cl Th,1849.

Not A in W S C. The common phrase *no getting around* =undeniable, inescapable, inevitable, is not given in OED W S C)

get at, v. [B²] *"Don't let the damp get at them"* 1892 AmCl iii 48 (OED 36d (a) To attack, assail. 1893. So W S C)

get at, v. [?AB¹] *"Get at it, oh, get at it right away"* 1892 AmCl viii 78 (To begin work on, get started at. This sense not in OED W S C)

get away with, v. [AB³] *That night* [1879] *I heard for the first time a slang expression which had already come into considerable vogue, but I had not myself heard it before...*"Here *in Illinois we think there can't nobody get away with Bob Ingersoll"* 1885 *Autob* (1924) I 16 (OEDS 54c. *U.S. slang.* To get the better of. 1878.. So Wr Th M H DN.III,VI. Not A in W S. Not in C)

get down to, v. [?AB²] *"You've got to get right down to it and amuse your mind"* 1892 AmCl xv 161 (OEDS 57c. To settle down to. 1903.. So U. A in DN.III,IV. Phrase not in W S C)

get in. v. [?AB¹] *The Atlantic custom of betting on the ship's run is not a custom here. I myself am wholly indifferent as to when we are going to "get in"* 1897 FE lxii 516 (To make port. This *spec* sense not in OED; but cf. in gen. sense OED 60a. To succeed in coming to a place, etc... 1553.. Given in W S C)

get into, v. [?AB¹] *All through supper his spirits were so high that his aunt wondered "what had got into the child"* 1876 TS iii 37 (To take effect on, affect noticeably. This sense not in OED W S C; but cf. OED 38f. Of liquor: to take effect on, render unsteady. 1834..)

get off, v. [?AB³] See *leather-headed* 1880. *All the time he was getting this off, he was shaking his head and looking fierce* 1883 LM iii 45 (OEDS 62i. To succeed in uttering. Earlier U.S. exs. 1849.. A in C B Th T M AS. II.355. Not A in W S)

get out, v. [?AB²] *"It ain't right and it ain't moral, and I wouldn't like it to get out"* 1884 HF xxxvi 368 (OED 64d. To leak out, become known. 1891. So W S C)

get-out, sb. **like all get-out.** [AB²] *"We got to dig in like all git-out"* 1884 HF xxxviii 386 (OEDS *U.S. colloq.* 1. Used to indicate a high degree of something. 1884, this quot. So C. Cf. Wr: Get out, v. Used in comparisons: "As mean, impudent as get out," N. Ireland. Phrase not in W)

get out of, v. [?AB²] *It looked as if they wanted to get out of paying for that beef* 1870 SNO (1875) 104. *"So at last I consented—no getting out of it, had to do it"* 1892 AmCl ii 31. *"My First Lie, and How I Got out of It"* (title) MCH (1900) 159 (OED 65d. 1885.. So S C. Not in W)

get over, v. [?A] *"You mispronounce words that's got a's in them...but you'll get over that"* 1892 AmCl xi 107 (OED 41a. To overcome, surmount a difficulty. 1687..1889. So W S C U. A in M)

get through, v. [?AB²] *The Senator favored the appropriation and would endeavor to get it through* 1873 GA xx 190 (OEDS 68c. Of a bill: To put through. 1873, this quot. Not in W S C)

get to, v. [?AB³] See *Mick* 1872. *There was a place on my ankle that got to itching, but I dasn't scratch it* 1884 HF ii 9. *The brothers happened to get to wondering* 1893 "Banknote" (1928) 108 (Classed by OED under 31b. To reach, attain, come to an end aimed at, or a condition towards which progress has been made. 1626.. OEDS Recent U.S. exs. with vbl.sb. 1884, this quot. It seems to belong rather under OED 44. Get to: To begin, settle down to. 1861.. So W S Wr. Not in C)

get up and, v. [AB¹] *"Git up and hump yourself, Jim!"* 1884 HF xi 96 (To bestir oneself, show energy or enterprise. This sense not in OED W S C. Perhaps an extension of OED 72g. Get up! *colloq.* As a command to a horse=Go! go ahead! 1887. Cf. OEDS Get-

up, sb. 4. Inclination to get up and be active; energy, enterprise. *U.S. colloq.* 1873.. Cf. also S: To get up and dig, to get up and dust. *Colloq., U.S.*; To get up and get. *Slang, U.S.* So C B F Cl DN.III,IV,V. Cf. also Wr: Get and. To go and, to set to work and)

ghost, sb. [C] *"The man is this minute delivering up the ghost"* 1881 PP x 118 (OED 1. The principle of life. *Obs* exc. in phr. *To give up the ghost.* Earlier, *to give, give away, yield up the,* or *one's ghost.* a900..1598, last quot. exc. for the one phr. mentioned. So W C U. Not *obs* in S)

ghost-bag, sb. [B¹] *It was Jake Dunlap's ghost!... "It had its bag along, I noticed that." "So did I. How can there be a ghost-bag, Tom?" "Sho! I wouldn't be as ignorant as that if I was you, Huck Finn. Whatever a ghost has, turns to ghost-stuff. You see, yourself, that its clothes was turned to ghost-stuff. Well, then, what's to hender its bag from turning, too?"* 1896 TSD v 356 (Nonce comb.)

ghost-stuff, sb. [B¹] See *ghost-bag* 1896 (Nonce comb.)

giant swing, sb. [?AB²] *He could do the giant swing in the gymnasium* 1873 GA xii 117 (OED A revolution at arm's length around a horizontal bar. 1889. Only quot. from Cent. Dict. Not A in W S C)

gift, sb. [AB¹] See *seven-up* 1869 (W: At [the American game of] seven-up, the point given to the eldest hand if he begs and the dealer refuses to run the cards. This sense not in OED S C)

Gilderoy's kite, sb. [AB¹] *Italy squandered millions of francs on a navy she did not need, and the first time she took her new toy into action she got it knocked higher than Gilderoy's kite—to use the language of the Pilgrims* 1869 IA xxv 256 (A in Th,1869, this quot. So in M. Not A in S: An allusion to a celebrated robber hanged in Edinburg in 1636 on an unusually high gallows. Phr. not in OED W C)

gills, sb. **to be blue about the gills.** [?AB²] *Tom he turned kinder blue around the gills* 1884 HF xxxvii 376 (OED 3b. To be white, blue, yellow about the gills: to look dejected or in ill health. No ex. of the phr. with *blue.* So C Wr. Here: To look frightened, startled; to turn pale with fright. Phr. not in W S)

gilt-edged, ppl.a. [?AB³] *Twenty-four hundred millions, and all safely planted in Good Things, gilt-edged and interest-bearing* 1904 "Bequest" (1906) vi 32 (OED Applied *fig* in commercial slang to securities of exceptionally high standing. 1892. So W S U. A in C Cl Th,1867)

gimcrack, sb. Spelled **jimcrack.** [?AE] See *brisken* 1884 (Both spellings given in OED W S C Wr. The sp. *jimcrack* is called 18th c. in OED; A in AS.VI.258)

gingerbread, sb. [?AB¹] *A fanciful pilot-house, all glass and "gingerbread"* 1875 OTM 70 (S: Gaudy or unnecessary ornament. So W C Wr. This *spec* sense not in OED; but cf. OED 2. *fig,* esp. as the type of something showy and unsubstantial. 1605..)

gin-mill, sb. [AB²] *Business mostly gin-mills—that is for soldiers* 1867 *Notebook* (1935) v 50. *A one-horse town composed of two gin-mills, a blacksmith shop, and that mustard-plaster of a newspaper!* 1869 SNO (1875) 46 (OED *U.S.* A drinking saloon. 1872, only ex. So W S C B F Th.III T)

ginner, sb. [?AB³] *2,000,000 as ginners of cotton* 1892 AmCl x 101 (OEDS Earlier U.S. exs. 1858.. Not A in W S C)

gin-sling, sb. [AB³] *Curious liquors...Rumpunch, Jinsling, Eggnog* 1869 IA xl 429 (OEDS *U.S.* An American cold drink. 1800.. So W Th. Not A in S C. Cf. *sling,* A in AS.IV.9,15: Freneau, 1809)

girl-soldier, sb. [B¹] *All the great lords and ladies of the Court began to flock there to see and listen to the wonderful girl-soldier* 1895 JA II v 232 (Comb. not in OED W S C; but cf. OED Girl-warrior, 1894)

girly-girly, a. [?AB²] *The very feature that keeps it* [i.e., Mardi Gras] *alive in the South—girly-girly romance* 1883 LM xlvi 467. *She* [Mrs. Eddy] *has the same soft, girly-girly places in her that the rest of us have* 1907 CS II i 106 (OEDS Girlish in an exaggerated or affected manner. Earliest ex. U.S. 1891.. Comb. not in W S C)

give, v. Past tense *give*. [AE] *I give her a turn with the paddle and brung her nose to the shore* 1884 HF viii 64. *Jim he grumbled a little, but give in* do. xii 103. So *passim* in HF (This form not in OED W S C. A in Wr M DN.I,II,III AS.I.233,236; III.3, Ozarks)

give, v. [?AB¹] *"What are you giving me? Get along back to your circus, or I'll report you"* 1889 CY pref. 21 (To offer an assertion for credence, give it to be believed; to 'hand out.' This sense not in OED W S C. Cf. OED 62. Give out: To utter, profess, give it to be believed that. *c*1340..)

give, v. **to give good day, good night.** [?AC] *He roused up, and gave me good day* 1865 "Jumping Frog" (1875) 30. *"Give you good day!"* 1869 IA xxi 213. *The professor gives a cordial good night* 1880 TA iv 48. See also *Sir* 1884 (OED 17. The ellipt. use of 3rd pers. subj. in complimentary wishes, as in *give you joy* for *God give you joy*, seems to have been interpreted as an ellipsis of the first person, so that *give* has the sense of "to wish." Now *obsolescent*. 1340..1855. Not *obsolescent* in W C. This use not in S)

give away, v. [?AB³] *I think that I would give myself away if I should go on* 1893 Speeches (1910) 312. *From the "Secret History of Eddypus, the World-Empire," written A.D. 2902...*"*Mark Twain, the Father of History, in his noble book written during the Rise of Christian Science...often quotes things that have been said about him; and not always with good discretion, since they 'give him away'—a curious phrase which he uses so frequently that we must suppose it was a common one in his time"* 1903 "Chr.Sc." 179. See also *authoress*, 1906. (OED 54d. To betray, expose. *slang*. 1878.. So W S C U. A in F Th,1862 T)

giveaway, sb. [?AB²] *The stock was for sale at a giveaway* 1889 CY xlii 531 (OEDS 2. Applied to low prices. 1905.. A in Th,1890 M. This sense not in W S C)

given name, sb. [AB³] *"Kings don't have any but a given name." "Well, if they like it, Tom, all right; but I don't want to be a king and have only just a given name, like a nigger"* 1876 TS xxv 193 (OEDS Chiefly *Scotch* and *U.S.* 1833.. So S B F Cl Th M H DN.III. Not A in W C. Wr (Suppl.): Cornwall)

give up, v. [AB¹] *"That was a perfect portrait of my father once. It was given up by all the family to be the best that had ever been made of him"* 1885 Autob (1924) I 67 (A in DN.V; To admit, concede, Ky. This sense not in OED W S C)

give-up, sb. [?AB¹] *There was no give-up to those English* 1895 JA II xxii 887 (Yielding; the spirit of surrender. Not in OED W S C)

give way, v. [?AB³] *"Starboard, give way! With a will, men!"* 1875 OTM 568 (OED 49j. Naut. The order to a crew to renew rowing, or to increase their exertions. 1802.. So W S C. A in T)

glacier-paved, ppl.a. [B¹] *A grand glacier-paved Alpine platform* 1880 TA xxxvi 407 (Comb. not in OED W S C)

glad, v. [C] *He would have missed not a stench that used to glad him two thousand years before* 1890 "Majestic Literary Fossil" 439 (OED 2. To make glad. *arch. c*825..1870. So W S C U)

glade-furrowed, ppl.a. [B¹] *A wide panorama of wooded mountains...with their glade-furrowed sides dimmed with purple shade* 1880 TA xxii 219 (Comb. not in OED W S C)

glass-eyed, ppl.a. [B¹] *Large glass cases which were filled with all sorts of birds and animals, glass-eyed, ably*

stuffed 1880 TA xvii 159 (Comb. not in OED. This sense not in W S C)

glass-inclosed, ppl.a. [B¹] *A series of glass-inclosed parlors clinging to the outside of the house* 1880 TA ii 27 (Comb. not in OED W S C; but cf. OED Glass-cased, 1901)

glass-smooth, a. [B¹] *The water is glass-smooth* 1883 LM xxx 331 (Comb. not in OED W S C; but cf. OED Glass-clear, 1890)

glimpse, v. [?A] *Some cocoa-palms, glimpsed here and there, gave the land a tropical aspect* 1877 "Some Rambling Notes" iii 718. *De Soto merely glimpsed the river, then died and was buried in it* 1883 LM i 29 (OED 5. To catch a glimpse of. 1779.. So W S C T. Th.III: Now chiefly Am. So B Cl)

globe-lamp, sb. [?AB²] *The costly globe-lamps from their drawing-rooms* 1869 IA xxii 220 (OED A lamp in which the light is protected by a globe. 1897, only ex. Comb. not in W S C. Globe, in the sense of lamp-fixture, is A in DN.I)

globe-shadowing, ppl.a. [B¹] *Able to expand a human cipher into a globe-shadowing portent* 1905 "Czar's Soliloquy" 326 (Comb. not in OED W S C; but cf. OED Globe-engirdling, 1622)

glorifier, sb. [?AB¹] *He next recommended some of "Smith's Hair Glorifier"* 1871 SNO (1875) 261 (Name for a hair tonic. This sense not in OED W S C)

glorify, v. [AB¹] *She jerked up the child again, a-sobbing and glorifying all the time* 1894 TSA vi 254 (To ejaculate "Glory!" Cf. OED Glory, sb. 4c. Used as a devout ejaculation, short for "Glory be to God," in the worship of various religious sects. Hence vulgarly as a mere exclamation of delight. 1816.. This sense of the verb not in OED W S C. Cf. B: To boast; to brag; to be elated)

glory-fire, sb. [B¹] *The lilacs and laburnums, lit with the glory-fires of autumn* 1902 "DBDS" (1928) 304 (Comb. not in OED W S C)

gmwkwllolp, sb. [B¹] See *kahkahponeeka* 1880 (Hum. invention.)

gnat-and-bull, a. [B¹] *The development was looked after, gnat-and-bull fashion, for years* 1895 JA II ii 89 (Comb. not in OED W S C)

gnillic, sb. [B¹] See *kahkahponeeka* 1880 (Hum. invention.)

go, v. **went**=gone. [?ACE] *The unpolished* [Southerners] *often use "went" for "gone." It is nearly as bad as the Northern "hadn't ought." This reminds me that a remark of a very peculiar nature was made here in my neighborhood* (in the North) *a few days ago: "He hadn't ought to have went." How is that? Isn't that a good deal of a triumph? One knows the orders combined in this half-breed's architecture without inquiring: one parent Northern, the other Southern* 1883 LM xliv 449. *"I'll tell Miss Susan to say you've went away for a few hours"* 1884 HF xxviii 288 (OED A.8b. *Obs.* 1642..1749. A in Wr B M DN.I AS.I.234,XI.350. This usage not mentioned in W S C)

go, v. [C] *The king was there three days, and then were his wounds well amended that he might both ride and go* 1889 CY iii 47 (OED 1. To walk. *Obs.* ..1836. So W S U. *Dial* in Wr. Not *obs* in C)

go, v. **to go or be gone with.** [?AB³] *"What is gone with that boy, I wonder? You Tom!"* 1876 TS i 17. *The Lohars of Oodeypore put a traveler in their charge* [i.e., in charge of the Thugs] *"for safety."...We know what went with the traveler* 1897 FE xlvi 434 (OED 18d. What has gone with = What has become of—? 1803.. So W. A in T. Phrase not in S C)

go, v. **from the word go.** [AB³] *"We turned out the whole thing—clean from the word go"* 1883 LM xxxix 414 (OEDS 22. From the start. *U.S. colloq.* 1838.. So S Th.III. Not A in C. Phrase not in S)

go, v. **to go security.** [?AC] *He did the friendly office of "going security" for Ira* 1870 Autob (1924) I 6 (OED

32f. Go with a complementary sb. *Obs.* exc. in *to go bail.* 1768, only ex. of *to go security.* Not *obs* in C. Phrase not in W S)

go, v. to go to. [AB¹] *Many of them* [Southerners] *say "I didn't go to do it," meaning "I didn't mean to do it"* 1883 LM xliv 449 (W: To intend, purpose; chiefly *dial.* S: *colloq.* A in Wr DN. II,III. This idiom not in OED C; but cf. with dif. sense OED 34c. 1752-1890.)

go, v.trans. [?AB³] *"There's one thing...which a person won't take in pine if he can go walnut; and won't take in walnut if he can go mahogany... That's a coffin"* 1883 LM xliii 438 (OED 35e. To go to the extent of; to venture as far as. All exs. U.S. 1855..1883, this quot. *Colloq* in W S C)

go, v.trans. to go better. [?AB³] *"I see that, and go you a hundred better"* 1883 LM xxxvi 394. *She sails in and goes the O'Shaughnessy about four hacks and an omnibus better* 1883 LM xliii 439 (OED 36. To outbid or outdo somebody else. 1878.. So W S C U. A in F Cl Th,1859 M)

go, v. to go it. [?AB³] *"Go it, don't mind me"* 1873 GA vii 80 (OED 46c. *colloq* and *slang.* To go along at great speed; to pursue one's actions with vigour. 1821.. So W S C U T. A in B F Cl DN.III)

go, v. to be going to, gwine to. [?AE] See *indeedy* 1873. *"You'll find you ain't gwyne to have no trouble"* 1894 PW xvi 821 (OED 47b. Used as a more colloquial synonym of *about to.* 1482..1890. So W S C U. The sp. *gwine* or *gwyne,* conventionally imitative of negro pron., is given as A in DN.I, and as *dial* in W S. Not given in OED C)

go, sb. [?A] *Have no fears. Your piece will be a Go. It will go out the back door on the first night* 1887 *Letters* (1917) II xxvi 477. *"Use Peterson's Tooth-Brush—All the Go"* 1889 CY xx 238 (OED 8b. The rage. 1793.. So W S C U. A in B Cl T)

go, sb. no go. [?AB³] *The lawyer said it was no go* 1862 *Letters* (1917) I iii 78 (OED 8a. *colloq.* Hopeless. 1825.. So W S C. A in AS.X.42)

goad-stick, sb. [AB³] *They banged the donkeys with their goad-sticks* 1869 IA vi 58 (OEDS *U.S.* 1825.. So Th. Not A in S. Not in W C)

go-ahead, a. [AB³] *One breathes a go-ahead atmosphere here* 1883 LM lvii 562 (OEDS *colloq.* orig. *U.S.* Forward and energetic. 1839.. So B F Cl Th DN.III. Not A in W S C U T)

go-ahead bell, sb. [AB¹] *Putting his hand on a go-ahead bell* 1883 LM xxiv 264 (Comb. not in OED W S C. Cf. above)

go-as-you-please, a. [?AB²] *Overthrow the Catholic church and set up on its ruins...a go-as-you-please one* 1889 CY xl 514 (OEDS Go, v. VIII. 1889.. So W S U. A in Th.III,1886. Comb. not in C)

goatee, sb. [?AB³] *The superintendent was a slim creature of thirty-five, with a sandy goatee* 1876 TS iv 47. *This morning struck into a region of full goatees* 1883 LM xxii 248 (OEDS Earlier U.S. exs. 1844.. A in F Cl Th T M. Not A in W S C U)

gob, sb. [?A] *"He'd flop down on the floor as solid as a gob of mud"* 1865 "Jumping Frog" (1875) 18 (OED 1b. A lump, clot. Now *dial* or *vulgar.* 1555..1872. So W S C. A in Wr Cl DN.I,III,VI)

go back on, v. [AB³] *"You've always been fair and square with me, Muff Potter, and I won't go back on you"* 1876 TS ix 91. *The very person he asked for advice might go back on him* 1893 TSA i 20 (OED 74d. To betray. *colloq. U.S.* 1868.. So B F Cl Th.III,1861 T M. Not A in W C U. Not in S)

gobble, v. [AB³] *Any private mine may be "gobbled"...if it has not been worked during five years previously* 1873 E&E (1923) 85 (OED 2. *U.S. slang.* To seize. 1825.. So S C B Th.III T. Not A in W)

go-cart, sb. [?AB³] *A rickety little go-cart hauled by a donkey not much bigger than a cat* 1867 IA xxx 318

(OED 4. A kind of light open carriage. 1828.. So W S C U. A in B F T)

God-a-mercy, int. [?AC] *"God-a-mercy!" exclaimed Canty* 1881 PP x 118 (OED *Obs.* ...1828. So W C Wr. Not *obs* in S. A in DN.V)

God-Bless-Our-Home, sb. [B¹] *You couldn't go into a room but you would find an insurance chromo, or at least a three-color God-Bless-Our-Home over the door* 1889 CY vii 83 (Nonce comb.)

Godspeed, v. [B¹] *No godspeeding a parting guest* 1883 LM xxv 376 (Not in OED S C as a verb. Given in W)

go for, v. [?AB³] *The lightning began to "go for" my house* 1870 SNO (1875) 25. See *clean,* v. 1872. *He went for me, too, for not stopping school* 1884 HF vi 37 (OEDS 58e. To assail, attack. Earlier U.S. exs. 1838.. A in C B F Cl Th T M. Not A in W S U)

go in for, v. [?AB³] *"I go in for having the best of a thing, even if it does cost a little more"* 1873 GA xi 111 (OEDS 81a. To make one's avowed object, one's usual style or fashion. Earlier U.S. exs. 1849.. A in B F Cl Th T DN.III. Not A in W S C U)

going on, prep.phr. [?AB¹] *"Been here going on two years"* 1880 TA xx 193 (Phrase not in OED W S C. Given as *dial* in Wr)

going-over, vbl.sb. [AB²] *I got a good going-over in the morning from old Miss Watson on account of my clothes* 1884 HF iii 17 (OEDS An overhauling; a talking-to. U.S. 1884, this quot... Comb. not in W S C)

Golconda, sb. [B²] See *bonanza* 1880 (OED The old name of Hyderabad, formerly celebrated for its diamonds; used as a synonym for a 'mine of wealth.' 1884.. So W S C U)

golden buck, sb. [?AB¹] *Luncheon: cold tongue... pickled pig's feet, grilled bones, golden buck* 1898 "At the Appetite Cure" (1900) 157 (W: Welsh rabbit with a poached egg upon it. Comb. not in OED S C)

gold-leaf, a. [?AB¹] See *kid-glove,* a. 1873, 1875; *chaw,* v. 1884 (Superlatively fine or excellent. This *fig* use not in OED W S C)

gold-miner, sb. [B¹] *A gold-miner in California* 1883 LM xxi 246 (Comb. not in OED; but cf. OED Gold-mining, 1852. Given in W S)

gold-pan, sb. [AB³] *To me, the other writers are miners working some of the gold washes over with the gold-pan of necessity* 1906 "Howells" (1917) 229 (OEDS *U.S.* 1875.. Not A in W. Comb. not in S C)

gold-sack, sb. [B¹] *Everybody ran to the bank to see the gold-sack* 1899 "MCH" (1900) 18 (Comb. not in OED W S C)

gold-strike, sb. [AB¹] *The first great gold-strike made in Australia* 1897 FE xxiv 231 (Comb. not in OED W S C. Cf. Strike, sb., below)

gone, ppl.a. [B³] *"I'mos' flopped down on de groun', I felt so gone"* 1894 PW xviii 19 (OED 1. A feeling of utter exhaustion. 1892.. So W S C U)

goner, sb. [?AB³] *"Lordy, Tom, we're goners! Can you pray?"* 1876 TS ix 88. See *nip,* v. 1876. *I thought I was a goner* 1884 HF xix 180 (OEDS *slang.* 1847.. So C U. A in S B F Cl Th T M DN.III,IV AS.II.355. Not in W)

good, a. [C] *"Ah, good your worship!"* 1881 PP iii 42 (OED 2b. As a conventional epithet in forms of address. *Obs* ...1742. So W. Not *obs* in S C)

good, a. to feel good. [AB³] *"Don't you feel good?"* 1892 AmCl xvii 172 (OEDS 3c. *U.S. colloq.* 1888.. So F Cl Th,1854 M H. Phrase not in W S C)

good, a. to make good. [AB³] *It was under these damaging conditions that he got up to "make good," as the vulgar say* 1907 "Chaps. from Autob" 488 (OEDS 22i. To succeed, orig. *U.S.* 1901.. So F Cl Th T M H. Not A in W S. Phrase not in C)

good, adv. [AB³] See *blood,* v.; *crawfish,* v.; *tan,* v., all 1884 HF. *I was tangled good now* 1884 HF xv 126.

The present author can do only a few ordinary trifling kinds of weather, and he cannot do those very good 1892 AmCl Pref. (OEDS Now *U.S.* 1834.. So Th M DN.III,V. Not A in W S C)

Good Book, sb. [?AB²] *"Spare the rod and spile the child, as the Good Book says"* 1876 TS i 19 (OED Good, a. 8b. The Bible. 1896.. So W S. Comb. not in C)

good-by, a. [?AB³] *They was through with the job, and was tapering off with a kind of general good-by cussing* 1884 HF xlii 425 (OED 2. *attrib.* Earliest ex. U.S. 1854.. Not A in S C. This use not in W)

good day, int. [?AB¹] *"Give it here—good day!—people will think I've robbed a nigger barber shop!"* 1892 AmCl iii 47 (Here used as an exclamation of surprise. This sense not in OED W S C)

good even, sb. **give good den.** [CE] *"Give ye good den, and God be with ye!"* 1881 PP vi 80 (OED *Obs* exc. *dial.* ..1651. So W S C Wr)

good gracious, int. [?AB³] *"Well, good gracious, why don't you come out and tell me what it is?"* 1892 AmCl ii 30 (OED Good, a. 6b. 1862.. So C. A in DN.V. Comb. not in W S)

good lack, int. [C] *"Good lack! how can he know so many dishes?"* 1881 PP xix 241 (OED Good, a. 6b. 1638. .1782. Cf. OED Lack, sb. ..1807. *Obs.* So W S C)

good licks, int. [?AB¹] *"Oh, good-licks, are you in real deadwood earnest, Tom?"* 1876 TS xxxv 272 (Comb. not in OED W S C. A corruption of *Good lack?*)

goodman, sb. [C] *"I will call him villein."* *"No, no; for he may be a free man."* *"Then peradventure I should call him goodman"* 1889 CY xxviii 363 (OED 1. Sometimes used as a respectful form of address. *Obs.* ..1400-50. So W S C. *Dial* in Wr)

Goodman, sb. [C] *He was playing, all alone, in the fair meadow called Goodman's Fields, when a dwarf appeared to him suddenly* 1881 PP xiv 162 (OED 1. *Obs. Scotch.* Applied euphemistically to the Devil. See quot. 1779. So Wr. This sense not in W S C)

goodness, int. [?AB²] *"So help me goodness, I couldn't help it"* 1875 OTM 195. *"That's the Lord's truth, goodness knows...But my goodness, he never plays them alike"* 1876 TS i 19. *"Goodness gracious! well, I never!"* 1892 AmCl iv 52. *"Praise goodness it wasn't a shingle nail"* 1892 AmCl xix 200. *"Chambers, you's a-jokin', ain't you?"* *"'Clah to goodness I ain't, mammy"* 1894 PW viii 337 (OED 5. In various exclamatory phrases ...not now in dignified use. 1613..1890. Of those used by M.T., only *Goodness gracious,* 1840, and *Goodness knows,* 1819, are illustrated in OED. So W S C. A in DN.V)

Good Place, sb. [?AB¹] See *Bad Place* 1884. (Wr: an expression used for Heaven; *Essex* and *Scotch.* Comb. not in OED W S C. Cf. *Bad Place,* above)

goods-box, sb. [AB¹] *A little bit of a goods-box of a barn* 1880 TA xix 178 (A in DN.II: for *dry goods box,* n.w.Ark. Comb. not in OED W S C)

good thing, sb. [B³] *It had what is technically called a "good thing" in financial circles, and knows a good thing when it sees it* 1898 "Austrian Edison" (1928) 266. See also *gilt-edged* 1904. (OED a. A successful act or speculation. 1820.. So W S. Not in C)

goodwife, sb. [C] *A sounding blow...sent him staggering into goodwife Canty's arms* 1881 PP x 113 (OED 2. Prefaced to surnames = Mrs. *Obs.* ..1691. So W. Not *obs* in S C Wr)

goodwilly, a. [C] *"I'll call at your house and drink a 'right gude willie waught' wi' you and Mrs. Carnegie"* 1897 *M.T. the Letter Writer* (1932) xiii 165 (OED *Scotch, obs.* c. Cordial. 1533..1788, Burns, the phrase quoted. Not *obs* in W S Wr. Not in C)

goody, int. [AB³] *"Goody!—No, Tom, that ain't it"* 1876 TS xxvii 210 (OEDS *U.S.* A childish exclamation denoting delight and satisfaction. 1853.. So B DN.I, III,IV,V. Not A in W Wr. Not in S C)

goody-goody, a. [?AB³] *Two or three goody-goody works* 1883 LM xxxviii 400. *No people in the world ever did achieve their freedom by goody-goody talk* 1889 CY xx 241 (OED a. Good in a weak or sentimental way. 1871.. So W S C U. A in DN.I,III,IV)

google, v. [E] *The duke he never let on he suspicioned what was up, but just went a goo-gooing around happy and satisfied, like a jug that's googling out buttermilk* 1884 HF xxix 295 (Not in OED W S C. A nonce spelling of *gurgle?*)

goo-goo, v. [?AB¹] See *google* 1884. *I could imagine the baby goo-gooing something in reply* 1889 CY xliii 549. *Tom said he warn't able to make anything out of deaf and dumb signs, and the same with goo-gooing* 1896 TSD viii 520 (Not in OED W S C)

go on, v. [AB³] *I didn't go much on clothes, nohow* 1884 HF xix 179 (OED Go, v. 61e. *U.S. colloq.* To care for. 1882.. So DN.I. This sense not in W S C)

goose-egg, sb. [AB³] *I beseech for these visitors a score bulletin barren of goose-eggs* 1888 Speeches (1910) 170 (OED *U.S.* In scoring at athletic contests: zero. 1886.. So S T DN.II,V. Not A in W C)

goose-milk, sb. [?AB¹] *"What's the good of a plan that ain't no more trouble than that? It's as mild as goose-milk"* 1884 HF xxxiv 348 (Comb. not in OED W S C)

go over, v. [AB²] *"According to the by-laws it must go over to the next regular meeting for action"* 1894 PW xi 556 (OED Go, v. 87h. To be postponed. *U.S.* 1911. Not A in W S. Not in C)

gopher, sb. [AB³] *A railroad is for the accommodation of the people and not for the benefit of gophers* 1873 GA xvi 152 (OED *U.S.* A burrowing rodent. 1812.. So W S C U B F Cl Th T M DN.II,III,IV AS.II.29,31)

gore, sb. [A] *"All along a line that's being surveyed, there's little dabs of land that they call gores"* 1883 LM xxxvi 390 (OED 1c. A small strip of land lying between larger divisions. Chiefly *U.S.* 1650.. So W Th H AS.VIII.3.79;XI.303. Not A in S C Wr)

gorge, sb. [AB²] *George and I cleared out again—found the channel first trial, but got caught in the gorge and drifted helplessly down the river. The Ocean Spray came along and started into the ice after us* 1858 Letters (1917) I ii 37 (OED 12. *U.S.* A mass choking up a narrow passage; esp. in *ice-gorge.* 1884.. Not A in W S C)

gorgeous, a. [?AB²] *Don't neglect to keep a gorgeous secretaryship or a high interpretership for me in your great embassy* 1866 M.T. the Letter Writer (1932) i 18. *Had gorgeous 4th of July jollification yesterday at sea* 1867 Letters (1917) I vii 131. *"Well, that's gorgis, ain't it?" said the Oracle* 1869 IA x 90 (OED 2. *colloq.* Used as an epithet of strong approbation. 1883.. So W U. This sense not in S C)

gorgeousnesses, sb.pl.[B¹] *The barbaric gorgeousnesses, for instance, and the princely titles* 1897 FE xxxix 357 (This *concr.* sense not in OED W S C)

gorilla, a. [?AB²] *"Who is that spider-legged gorilla with the sanctimonious countenance?"* 1869 IA iii 36 (OED b. *transf.* 1884. So W. This sense not in S C)

gospel-mill, sb. [?AB¹] *"Are you the duck that runs the gospel-mill next door?"* 1872 RI xlvii 331 (A church. Comb. not in OED W S C. Here *-mill* is probably to be taken in the same sense as in *gin-mill,* i.e., a place where people crowd or mill together)

gospel-sharp, sb. [AB²] *"What we want is a gospel-sharp." "A what?" "Gospel-sharp. Parson"* 1872 RI xlvii 333 (OEDS *Western U.S.* 1872, this quot. So F Cl. Comb. not in W S C)

gossipless, a. [B¹] *Leave that village voiceless and gossipless behind him* 1909 ISD vi 59 (Not in OED W S C)

go through, v. [AB¹] *Whenever they did come upon a man who was alone, they said, Behold, this person has the wherewithal—let us go through him. And they went* *through him* 1869 IA xl 426 (A in Th,1867: To plunder thoroughly. So F Cl T M. *Slang* in W S C. Not in OED)

gouge, v. [?AB³] *I could have gouged an office out of Bill Stewart for him* 1867 *Letters* (1917) I vi 128 (OED 3. *fig.* 1815.. A in B Th H. This sense not in W S C)

gouge, v. [?A] See *clinch* 1869. *He went through the motions of thrashing an imaginary boy—pummeling the air, and kicking and gouging* 1876 TS xviii 156. *We looked on while they rolled, and struggled, and gouged, and pounded* 1889 CY xxxiv 439 (OED 3b. 1785, to squeeze out a man's eye with the thumb, a cruel practice used by the Bostonians in America (Grose, *Dict. Vulg. Tongue*)...A in B Th DN.VI. Not A in W S C U Wr T. C is at pains to show that the practice was not distinctively American. Nevins (*British Travelers in America*) noted it as characteristic of the frontier South; so Freneau, 1809, cf. AS.IV.4,7,12. A current novelist locates it in tidewater Virginia (Hergesheimer's *Balisande*); so B Th. So are compliments bandied back and forth!)

gouge, v. [AB²] *Hotels gouge Californians—charge sailing passengers $8 a week for board, but steamer passengers ten* 1866 *Notebook* (1935) 15. "*They give the magistrate a poor little starvation salary, and then turn him loose on the public to gouge for fees*" 1877 "Some Rambling Notes" iii 723 (OED 4. *U.S.* To cheat, impose upon. 1875.. So W C B Th,1845 T H. Not A in S)

gouger, sb. [?A] *If one gouger had captured the general's book, here was evidence that he had only prevented another gouger from getting it* 1885 *Autob* (1924) I 55 (OEDS Earlier U.S. exs. 1790.. A in S C. This sense not in W)

go under, v. [?AB²] See *pile, go one's* 1867 (OED Go, v. 93. To fail, succumb, go to ruin. 1891, first ex. this sense. So W S U. A in C B F Cl Th,1849 T M DN.III)

go up, v. [?AB²] "*Negroes would have gone up to four prices*" 1873 GA i 27 (OED Go, v. 94e. To increase in price. 1883.. So W S. This sense not in C)

gourd, sb. [?AB¹] *He never got it through his gourd, That he was walking overboard* 1891 *Slovenly Peter* (1935) 22 (Head. Not in OED W S C in this sense)

gout-smitten, a. [B¹] *I am just back from a gout-smitten 3 weeks' visit to Clara* 1905 *M.T. the Letter Writer* (1932) 96 (Comb. not in OED W S C; but cf. OED Gout-tormented, 1711)

governess-German, sb. [B¹] *She has a good working use of governess-German and Italian* 1906 "Horse's Tale" ii 329 (Comb. not in OED W S C)

government bond, sb. [AB¹] *Forty-five tons best old dry government bonds* 1906 "Letter to Sec. of Treas." 229 (A in M = Eng. consols. Comb. not in OED W S C; but cf. OED Government-paper, 1802)

government-office, sb. [B²] *Polite as three-dollar clerks in government offices* 1880 TA xxi 197 (OED 1891, only ex. Comb. not in W S C)

governor, sb. [A] See *colonel* 1902. *They sat down to consider the Governor's son and the son of the Congressman* 1904 "Bequest" (1906) v 29 (OED 3. Now used as the official title of the executive head of each of the United States. 1683, Wm. Penn, Governor of Pennsylvania, only ex. So W S C)

gowkarak, sb. [B¹] See *kahkahponeeka* 1880 (Hum. invention)

grab for, v. [AB²] *Tom's hands itched to grab for it* 1876 TS v 56 (OED 3. *U.S.* for "grab at." 1885. So M Phr. not in W S C)

grace-of-God, a. [B¹] *Some little dancing was done by grandees belonging mainly to "grace-of-God" families* 1873 E&E (1923) 63 (Comb. not in OED W S C; but cf. OED Grace, sb. 6c. Phr. *by the grace of God*, appended to the formal statement of the titles of sovereigns. 1495..)

gracious, a. [?AB²] "*I hain't been doing a single thing, Aunt Sally, I hope to gracious if I have*" 1884 HF

xl 404. See also *buck*, sb. 1902 (OED 5b. ellipt. as a substitute for the name of God. This phr. 1893. So W S C U. A in B T DN.V)

grade, sb. [?AB³] *When a lady of any prominence comes to one of our cities...all the ladies of her grade favor her in turn with an initial call* 1873 GA xxxii 296 (OED 4a. A degree or position in the scale of rank, dignity, social position. 1808.. So W S C U T. A in Cl M DN.V,VI)

grade, sb. [?AB³] *He said, with a grade of injured dignity almost ducal...* 1892 AmCl xv 154 (OEDS 5a. In things: A degree of comparative quality or value. Earlier U.S. exs. 1807.. A in B Cl. Not A in W S C U)

grade, sb. [?AB³] *A long, smooth, narrow street, with a gradually descending grade* 1872 RI xii 106 (OED 10. Amount of inclination in a road or railway. *U.S.* 1835.. A in W C B Cl Th T H; cf. C: Am. grade = Eng. gradient. Not A in S U)

grade, sb. [AB³] *We went rumbling and thundering away, down a mountain "grade"* 1872 RI ix 77. See also *chock* 1897 (OEDS 10b. An inclined portion of a railway or road. *U.S.* 1850.. A in W C. Not A in S)

graded school, sb. [AB³] *I now had an admirable system of graded schools in full blast* 1889 CY x 117 (OEDS Chiefly *U.S.* 1852.. So M H. Not A in W S C U)

graduate, v.intr. [?AB³] *The reading continued; finally, the patient graduated and got his nickel* 1889 CY xxvi 336 (OED 3b. To qualify. 1829.. A in M H. This *transf.* sense not in W S C)

graft, sb. [AB³] *The exponents of conscienceless graft—colossal graft—in great municipalities* 1906 "Unpublished Chaps. from Autob." (1922) 456 (OEDS orig. *U.S. slang.* 1889.. So S C U Th T M H. Not A in W)

grafter, sb. [AB³] *A group of Goulds and Vanderbilts and other professional grafters* 1906 "Unpublished Chaps. from Autob." (1922) 457 (OEDS Chiefly *U.S. colloq.* 2. 1896.. So S C U Th.III H. Not A in W)

grail, v. [B¹] *The boys all took a flier at the Holy Grail now and then...Every year expeditions went out holy grailing...Sir Sagramor was still out grailing...Sir Bedivere was going grailing* 1889 CY ix,x,xi 112,121,134 (Hum. nonce word)

grain-elevator, sb. [AB²] *Pictures of wharves crowded with steamboats, and of huge grain-elevators on the bank* 1873 GA xxii 203 (OEDS *U.S.* 1873, this quot. Not A in W S. Comb. not in C. Cf. Elevator (for storing grain), A in Th,1795 H)

grain-sack, sb. [B²] "*I robbed de sugar hogsheads en grain-sacks on de wharf*" 1894 PW xviii 19. See also *sack-pile* 1897 (OED Grain, sb. 18a. No ex. So W. Comb. not in S C)

gramercy, int. [C] "*Gramercy, it is marvelous*" 1889 CY xxvii 351 (OED *obs* exc. *arch.* 2. 1607..1843. So W C U. Not *obs* in S)

grandam, sb. [C] See *overkind* 1881 (OED *arch.* 1. Grandmother. a1225..1871. Not *arch* in W S C U Wr)

grand-daddy-longlegs, sb. [AB¹] *The learned and aged Lord Grand-Daddy-Longlegs...had been sitting in deep study, with his slender limbs crossed and his stemmy arms folded* 1875 SNO 130 *The sun...flung the long shadders of the camels on the gold sand like a thousand grand-daddy-long-legses marching in procession* 1894 TSA xi 395 (A in Wr DN.I,III. Comb. not in OED W S C; but cf. OED Daddy-long-legs, above; also Grand-daddy, in same sense, 1808)

grandmother, int. [AB¹] "*Yes, sir, it's as true as the world. Pap he says—*" "*Oh, your grandmother!*" *They all laughed.* 1883 LM iii 60 (A in DN.V: used to express incredulity. This interjectional use not in OED W S C; but cf. OED 1b. Phr. *This beats my grandmother*: said of something that excites astonishment. 1883 Cf. *granny*, below)

Grand Old Party, sb. [AB³] *He is the last one that is left—a Grand Old Party all by himself* 1900 *Speeche*

(1910) 357 (OEDS *U.S. politics.* 2. The Republican party. 1888.. So W. Phr. not in S C)

grand-stand, sb. [?AB³] *The grand-stand was well filled with the beauty and the chivalry of New Orleans* 1883 LM xlv 459 See also *mammoth* 1889 (OED The principal stand for spectators. 1841.. So W S C U. A in DN.II)

granite, sb. Spelled **granita**. [AB²E] *People at small tables* [in Venice] *are smoking and taking granita, a first cousin to ice-cream* 1869 IA xxiii 232 (OED *U.S.* A kind of rough-grained water-ice or sherbet. Also called *rock-punch* and *rock ice-cream.* 1887.. Not A in W S C. M.T.'s spelling, which is not recorded in OED W S C, and the early date of his use apparently point to a time before the dish had been introduced into the U.S.)

granite-bound, a. [B¹] *You whirl your wheel away from the curb instead of toward it, and so you go sprawling on that granite-bound inhospitable shore* 1880 "Taming the Bicycle" (1917) 294 (Comb. not in OED W S C)

granite-hearted, ppl.a. [B¹] *This granite-hearted, bloody-jawed maniac of Russia* 1890 *Letters* (1917) II xxx 536 (Comb. not in OED W S C; but cf. OED Granite-headed, 1902)

granny, sb. [?AB²] *"You couldn't even fool one of these sleepy old syentiffic grannys from the Coledge"* 1875 SNO 143 (OED 3. *dial.* A stupid person. 1887.. So W S. A in DN.III. This sense not in C)

granny, int. [AB¹] *"Do they hop?"* *"Hop—your granny! No"* 1876 TS xxv 193. *"Mumps your granny! They don't set up with people that's got the mumps"* 1884 HF xxviii 291. *"Camels your granny; they're spiders"* 1894 TSA vi 252. *"Sick your granny; what's to make him sick?"* 1894 TET i 320 (A in DN.III: A mild expletive. This interjectional use, to express incredulity, not given in OED W S C. Cf. *grandmother,* above)

granulating-pipe, sb. [B¹] *Run it...through the granulating-pipe to condense it* 1883 LM xlviii 479 (Comb. not in OED W S C; but cf. OED Granulating machine, 1873)

grape-doctor, sb. [B¹] *Grapes being necessarys of life to certain invalids whom physicians cannot repair, and who only continue to exist by the grace of...grapes. One of these departed spirits...preserved from decomposition by the grape system, told me the grapes were of a peculiar breed, highly medicinal in their nature, and that they were counted out and administered by the grape-doctors* [at Interlaken, Switzerland] *as methodically as if they were pills* 1880 TA xxxiii 357 (Comb. not in OED W S C; but cf. OED Grape-cure; the treatment of disease by a diet consisting mainly of grapes. 1862)

grape-system, sb. [B¹] See *grape-doctor* 1880 (Comb. not in OED W S C)

grass, sb. **to go to grass.** [AB³] *"I thought we was right on the track of a slution, but it's gone to grass, partly"* 1884 HF xxix 302 (OED 9c. *U.S.* To die; to be ruined. 1848.. So C Th,1807 DN.III AS.II. Not A in W S T)

grass, sb. **to hunt grass.** [?AB²] *"When you get in with your left I hunt grass every time"* 1872 RI xlvii 334 (OED 9c. To be knocked down. 1872, this quot. A in F: To decamp. Phr. not in W S C)

grass-carpeted, ppl.a. [B²] *We followed a torrent of ice water up to its far source in a sort of little grass-carpeted parlor* 1880 TA xxxiii 361 (OED 1889, only ex. So W. Comb. not in S C)

grasshopper-soup, sb. [B¹] *Tahoe means grasshoppers. It means grasshopper-soup. It is Indian, and suggestive of Indians* 1869 IA xx 205 (Comb. not in OED W S C)

grass-widower, sb. [?AB³] *Whether he was bachelor, widower, or grass widower, remained his own secret* 1898 *Autob* (1924) I 145 (OEDS Earlier *U.S.* ex. 1862.. A in Th. Not A in W S C U)

gravel, v. [AB³] *It is just lightning poetry—a thing which it gravels me to say because my own efforts in that line have remained so persistently unrecognized* 1874 *Letters* (1917) I xiv 239. *It "gravels" me, to this day, to put my will in the weak shape of a request, instead of launching it in the crisp language of an order* 1875 OTM 721. *"He graveled the prophets of Baal every way he could think of. Says he...'Your god's asleep'"* 1877 "Some Rambling Notes" ii 590. *They gravel me, these stale and overworked stage directions* 1906 "Howells" (1917) 237 (OED 4b. *U.S.* To irritate; to go against the grain with. 1871.. So F Cl DN.V, s.w.Mo. Not A in W S C U Wr T)

gravel-train, sb. [AB²] *You find a gravel-train from Marseilles arriving* 1869 IA xiii 115. *I have not jumped at this conclusion; I have traveled to it per gravel-train, so to speak* 1880 TA xxxvi 411 (OED From Gravel, sb. sense 3, *U.S.* = Ballast. 1881, only ex. Not A in W. Comb. not in S C)

graveyard, sb. [?A] *"I reside in the shameful old graveyard a block or two above you here, in this street"* 1870 SNO (1875) 193. *Wading through the tall grass of the graveyard* 1876 TS ix 86. *If Napoleon the First had stood in the shoes of Louis XVI...there would be a well-stocked Communist graveyard in Paris* 1880 TA xxvi 261 (OEDS A burial ground. Earlier U.S.exs. 1773.. A in B Cl DN.III AS.I.150. Not A in W S C U Wr T)

graveyardy, a. [AB¹] *It was miserable quiet and still and night-breezy and graveyardy and scary* 1896 TSD v 355 (Not in OED W S C. Cf. above)

gravy, sb. [?A] See *corn-bread* 1873. *They ate and ate, till the gravy appeared in their eyes* 1892 AmCl v 59 (OED 2. The fat and juices which exude from flesh during and after the process of cooking. 1591.. So W S C U. A in B Cl T DN.III,IV)

Grayback from Wayback, sb. [?AB¹] *"He thinks he'a a Sheol of a farmer; thinks he's old Grayback from Wayback"* 1889 CY xxxi 401 (An 'old hand;' an expert. Phr. not in OED W S C. Cf. OED Greyback, sb. *U.S. colloq.* 1. A Confederate soldier, 1864; 2. A Confederate treasury note, 1897; 3. a louse, 1864)

grease-biscuit, sb. [?AB¹] *You shall see the frog turn in the air like a grease-biscuit* ["Retranslated" from the French *un beignet,* fritter; the original version of the "Jumping Frog" has "*You'd see that frog whirling in the air like a doughnut*"] 1875 SNO 41 (Comb. not in OED W S C)

grease-jet, sb. [B¹] *A great hall lighted by hundreds of grease-jets* 1889 CY xvii 201 (Comb. not in OED W S C)

grease-print, sb. [B¹] *Under this row of faint grease-prints* 1893 PW ii 236 (M.T.'s first attempt to find a name for the new means of criminal identification, for which the term finger-print later found general acceptation. See *finger-mark, finger-print,* above. Comb. not in OED W S C)

Greaser, sb. [AB³] *"Digger, Chinaman, Greaser, and American"* 1865 SS (1926) 161 (OED 2. *U.S. slang.* Orig. applied contemptuously by Americans in the s.w. U.S. to the Mexicans. 1849.. So W S C U B F Cl Th T M H DN.V AS.VI.12)

grease-wood, sb. [AB³] *Grease-wood is a perfect... imitation in miniature of a live oak tree* 1861 *Letters* (1917) I iii 54. *No vegetation but the endless sage-brush and grease-wood* 1872 RI xxi 157 (OEDS A name for various prickly shrubs...found in dry alkaline valleys of the w. U.S. 1845.. So W S C B F Th T)

greasy water, sb. [?AB¹] See *bald-headed* 1907 (Wr: muddy. This sense not in OED W S C)

great, a. [?AB³] *"The old man thinks he's great on sarcasm"* 1892 AmCl xii 126 (OED 16a. With on; Of considerable knowledge or skill in. 1878. So W. A in B F Th,1844. Cf. U: much interested in, keen on. This use not in S C)

great, a. [AB³] *"We've had great times here"* 1892 AmCl xxi 221 (OED 16b. Used as a more or less rapturous term of admiration. *U.S.* and *colloq.* 1809.. So B F Cl. Not A in W U. This sense not in S C)

Great Plains, sb. [AB¹] See *Far West* 1876; *buffalo-range* 1906 (W: *U.S.,* the prairie lands extending from North Dakota to Texas and from the Mississippi to the Rocky Mountains. Comb. not in OED S C)

Great Republic, sb. [AB¹] *You have wrought into enduring form the splendid story of the Great Republic* 1905 "Concerning Copyright" 5 (The United States. Comb. not in OED W S C)

Great Scott, int. [?AB³] *"Great Scott, look here!"* 1892 AmCl iii 45 (OED 1885.. So W. A in F M DN.V. Comb. not in S C)

Great-Scotting, vbl.sb. [?AB¹] *"Gr-reat Scott!"* *ejaculated the Major. "Why, what are you Great-Scotting about, Major?"* 1902 "Belated Russian Passport" (1928) 191 (Nonce comb.)

Great Waters, sb. [AB¹] See *pale-face* 1869 (A supposedly Indian term for the ocean. Used by Peck, 1834; see AS.II.27. Not in OED W S C)

greenback, sb. [AB³] *That would be about seventy-five dollars in greenbacks, wouldn't it?* 1864 *Letters* (1917) I v 100. *No, you are not obliged to take greenbacks at par* 1867 SNO (1875) 75. *The man was a New Englander, with a head full of crochets, and preferred greenbacks to gold or drafts* 1902 "DBDS" (1928) 298 (OED 1. The popular name for one of the legal-tender notes of the U.S., first issued in 1862. 1862.. So W S C U B F Cl Th T)

greens, sb. [AB¹] See *biscuit* 1880. *Jim he got out some pork and cabbage and greens* 1884 HF xviii 176. *Then they come and locked him up. I hoped they was going to say he...could have meat and greens with his bread and water* 1884 HF xlii 427 (Cf. OED 11c. Green vegetables such as are boiled for the table; the Am. dicts. refer to spinach and the leaves of dandelion and beet as examples of what would be called 'greens.' 1725.. So W S C U. Here, however, at least in the last quot., the term would seem to have the wider meaning given as A in Cl T: Vegetables in general; so commonly in the South. Tom would hardly have worried over Jim's being deprived merely of spinach)

green-spectacled, ppl.a. [B¹] See *Yank* 1869 (Comb. not in OED W S C)

grievous, a. [C] *"These be grievous times for the unfortunate"* 1881 PP xxiii 283 (OED 1. Oppressive. *obs.* 1382..1849. So W U. Not *obs* in S C)

grindstone, sb. **Gld Red Grindstone.** [B¹] *"All belonged to that remote geological epoch known to science as the Old Red Grindstone Post-Pleosaurian"* 1897 FE viii 106 (Hum. nonce comb.)

grip, sb. [AB³] *An old woman passed by, carrying a grip* 1902 "DBDS" (1928) 298 (OED 8. *U.S. colloq.* short for gripsack. 1883.. So W S C U F Cl T H DN.V)

grip, sb. [AB¹] *i saw the leather was a grip (easy to get)* [given as "thieves' argot"] 1883 LM lii 512 (A in F Cl. This sense not in OED W S C)

grip, sb. [?AB¹] *"You got a wrong start, that's the whole trouble. But you hold your grip, and we'll see what can be done"* 1892 "Switzerland" (1917) 206. *"Come, cheer up, old man; there's no use in losing your grip"* 1894 PW xx 234. *"Now hold your grip, hold your grip, I tell you, and I'll land him sure!"* 1894 TET vi 274 (U: Faculty of understanding a situation and of coping with it in a practical way; control. So C. A in Cl. This sense not in OED W S; cf. OED 2. *fig.* Now esp. associated with the idea of oppression or irresistible force. Here associated rather with the idea of courage and self-control)

gripsack, sb. [AB³] *"Take your gripsack and get along"* 1889 CY xxiii 286. *We pile gripsacks in a vacant seat to keep him from getting it* 1899 "Concerning the Jews" (1900) 278 (OED *U.S. colloq.* A traveller's handbag. 1883.. So W S C U F Th T M)

grisly, a. [C] *The grisly fate hanging over the heads of the condemned* 1881 PP xv 182. *Everybody crossed himself in a grisly fright* 1889 CY xvii 204 (OED Now only *arch* and *literary.* 1c. 1200..1892. Not *arch* in W S C U)

grist, sb. [AB³] *"Dunlop is a long sight richer than any of the others, and owns a whole grist of niggers"* 1896 TSD i 345. *"You know what a grist of years it took you to come here from the earth"* 1908 "Capt. Stormfield" 267 (OEDS 2d. *U.S.* A 'lot,' number, or quantity of. 1832.. So W B F Cl Th T H DN.II. Not A in S. This sense not in C)

grit, sb. [AB³] *The showman drummed up his grit and started in fresh* 1871 SNO (1875) 297. See *back-down,* sb. 1884. *A few men of character and grit woke up out of the nightmare of fear which had been stupefying their faculties* 1894 "Scrap of Curious History" (1917) 189 (OED 5. *colloq.* orig. *U.S. slang.* Spirit, pluck, stamina. 1843.. So W S C U B F Cl Th DN.III)

grit, sb. **to be grit.** [AB³] *Capt. says the boys were good grit—Henry's underlip never quivered but once* 1866 Notebook (1935) iv 26. *"Johnny's grit; give him a chance"* 1892 AmCl xiii 135 (OED 5. *colloq.* orig. *U.S. slang.* To be clear, hard, etc. grit; to have genuine spirit or pluck. 1825.. So B Cl Th. Not A in U T. Phr. not in W S C)

grit, v. [?A] *Lovers made pilgrimages to this shrine... to weep and wail and "grit" their teeth* 1869 IA xv 141. *You can hear it grit its Christian teeth* 1899 "Concerning the Jews" (1900) 280. *This muffled clicking and gritting and grinding and rasping continued* 1899 "Chr.Sc. and the Book" 590 (OEDS 4. To grind or grate. 1797.. So W S C U Wr T. A in F Th)

grizzly, a. Spelled **grisly.** [E] *A grisly elephantine patriarch* 1882 *Letters* (1917) I xxii 419 (OED This sp. 17th c. 1602..1626. Given as var. sp. in W S, not in C)

grizzly-headed, ppl.a. [B¹] *A grizzly-headed man gave me a sort of start as he passed me* 1883 LM li 506 (Comb. not in OED W S C)

groggery, sb. [AB³] *Dusenheim, standing in the door of his uninviting groggery* 1873 GA xxix 270 (OEDS *U.S.* A low drinking-place. 1822.. So W C B F Cl Th T M. Not A in S)

gros de laine, sb. [B¹] *A simple gros de laine...with overskirt of sacre bleu ventre saint gris, cut bias on the off-side* 1880 TA xxxii 340 (A nonsense comb., since the French term *gros* is always applied to fabrics of silk. Cf. OED Gros de Naples, 1828..; Gros de Tours, 1799; so W C)

ground-circuit, v. [?AB¹] *I had ground-circuited their wire* 1897 FE liii 511 (Not in OED W S C as verb; but cf. Ground-circuit, sb. in S: An electric circuit completed by the ground; an earth-circuit. So W. Cf. Ground-wire, below, A for Eng. earth-wire)

ground-connection, sb. [?AB¹] *The wires have no ground-connection outside the cave* 1889 CY xlii 540 (S: The connection of an electric circuit with the ground; an earth. Comb. not in OED W C; but cf. OED Earth, sb. 6. *Electr.* A communication with the earth. 1870. Cf. above)

ground-floor, sb. [AB³] *This stripe of prophet is always to be had in the market at ground-floor rates* 1903 "Chr.Sc." 173 (OED b. *fig. U.S.* On the same terms as the original promoters. 1864.. So F Th.III H. Not A in W S C U)

ground-wire, sb. [?AB²] *I have laid a groundwire to the school* 1889 CY xxiv 304 (OEDS A wire used to complete a ground-connexion in a circuit; = earth-wire. 1910.. So W S. A in M: Am. ground-wire = Eng. earth-wire. Comb. not in C)

grouper, sb. [B¹] See *deducer* 1895 (One who can group or associate ideas. Not in OED W S C)

grouty, a. [AB³] *A grouty Northern invalid* 1872 RI lxiv 462. *The planter remains grouty toward the former slave* 1883 LM xxxiii 368 (OED *U.S.* Sulky, cross.

1836.. So W Wr B F Cl Th T DN.I,III,IV. Not A in
S C)

grove-plumed, ppl.a. [B¹] *A grove-plumed promontory
juts far into the lake* 1869 IA xx 203 (Comb. not in
OED W S C)

grub, sb. [?A] *"You've fought a good fight...and if
we had grub to go on, I'm d—d if we wouldn't stand by
you"* 1873 GA lxii 562 (OED 6. *slang.* Food or pro-
vender of any kind. 1659..1889. So W S C U Wr.
A in M AS.VII.167)

gruel, sb. [B¹] *"Do you suppose my subscribers are
going to stand such gruel as that?"* 1869 SNO (1875) 45
(A *fig* name for "mush-and-milk" journalism, q.v.
This sense not in OED W S C)

guano, sb. [A] *A guano rock in the Straits of Sunda*
1892 AmCl ii 33 (OED 1. A natural manure found...
esp. on the islands about Peru. 1604.. So W S C U
B T)

guard, sb. [?AB³] *"Ladies, if you wish to enjoy a good
laugh, step out on the guards"...Every passenger in the
boat had by this time collected on the guards* 1852 "The
Dandy Frightening the Squatter" (1930) 447. *They
were holding the boat so close to the shore that the willows
swept the guards almost from stem to stern* 1873 GA iv
46. *Along comes a steamboat up the river...she bulged
out...with her monstrous bows and guards hanging right
over us* 1884 HF xvi 144. See also *paddle-box* 1894
(OEDS 16j. A lateral extension of the deck of a steamboat beyond the lines of the hull. Earliest exs. U.S.
1840.. A in Th.III. Not A in W S C. Ct. cabin-guard,
above)

guard-deep, a. [?AB¹] *A boat guard-deep with costly
freight* 1883 LM xix 232 (Comb. not in OED W S C.
Cf. above)

gubernatorial, a. [A] *The wife of the Governor was
going to deliver a gubernatorial laugh* 1906 *Speeches*
(1910) 222 (OED Chiefly *U.S.* 1734.. So S C B F Th
T M. Not A in W U)

guess, v. [A] *I guess I will bring you some of them*
1866 *Letters* (1917) I v 104. See *bulge*, sb. 1880. *The
Northern word "guess"—imported from England, where
it used to be common—is but little used among Southerners. They say "reckon".* 1883 LM xliv 450. *I guessed I
wouldn't stay in one place, but just tramp right across
the country* 1884 HF vi 41. *"I guess I hear them coming
now"* 1892 AmCl xvi 164. See also *dig*, sb. 1894 (OED
6. *I guess...colloq* in northern *U.S* = 'I am pretty
sure.' 1692.. So S U Wr B F Cl Th M H DN.I,II,III,
IV,V AS.I.159;IV.8,12. Not A in W C T)

guess out, v. [?AC] *"I'll live with them as being a
stranger, and the neighbors won't ever guess me out"*
1896 TSD ii 349 (OED 8. †To discover by conjecture.
1636, only ex. Comb. not in W S C. Cf. above)

guest-room, sb. [?AB¹] *Each proceeded upstairs toward the guest-room* 1894 PW v 333 (Comb. not in
OED. Given in W S C)

guideboard, sb. [?AB³] *A guideboard, upon which was
the legend "10 Miles to Hawkeye"* 1873 GA xvii 162
(OEDS Earliest exs. U.S. 1843.. A in Th.III. Not A
in W S C)

guide-English, sb. [B¹] *I give it as a specimen of
guide-English* 1869 IA xix 183 (Comb. not in OED
W S C)

guide-in-chief, sb. [B¹] *The Guide-in-Chief of the
Chamonix Guild of Guides* 1880 TA xliii 503 (Comb.
not in OED W S C)

gulch, sb. [AB³] *They all feel stirring within themselves souls too vast for confinement in narrow flats and
gulches* 1865 SS (1926) 178. See *gap*, sb. 1868. *There
were six log-cabins in the camp—strung pretty well
separated up the gulch from its mouth at the desert to
where the cabin was, at the divide* 1904 "A Helpless
Situation" (1906) 116 (OEDS 1. *U.S.* A narrow and
deep ravine. 1835.. So W S C U B F Cl Th T M
DN.III,VI)

gules, sb. [B¹D] See *coat-of-arms* 1883 (Hum. malapropism. When he inserted in his coat-of-arms "a
couple of gules for supporters," Tom Sawyer must
have had the word confused with *ghouls*. Cf. OED:
Red, as one of the heraldic colours. c1375..1856—. So
W S C U)

Gulf Stream, sb. [A] *The Milky Way, otherwise the
Gulf Stream of the skies* 1875 SNO 308 (OED A great
oceanic current that...runs parallel to the American
coast... 1775.. So W S C U)

gully-keeper, sb. [?AB¹] *They had an exhausting
time playing "hi-spy" and "gully-keeper"* 1876 TS xxix
217 (Not in OED W S C. Probably a local pron. of
the children's game still called in Missouri *goal-keeper*
or *goalie-keeper*, a variation of the very old game of
prisoner's base. Cf. OED Prisoner's bars, base, earlier
prison-bars and prison-base: A game played in a variety
of ways, chiefly by boys; the players are divided into
two parties, who occupy distinct demarcations, 'bars,'
'homes,' or 'dens,' the aim of each side being to make
prisoners by touching any player of the opposite side
who runs out from his enclosure. 1598.. So W S C.
In the Missouri game, the aim is rather to protect the
home-base or 'goal' from being captured, by touching,
or 'tagging,' players on the opposing side before they
can enter it)

gum, sb. [AB³] *A dense growth of ash, oak, gum, and
hickory* 1883 LM App. A 597 (OED 5. Short for
Gum-tree: various species of the N.American genus
Nyssa. 1802.. So W S C U B F Cl T)

gum-drop, sb. [AB³] *"Oh, gum-drops, gum-drops! But
I never allow them to eat striped candy"* 1880 "Telephonic Conversation" 842. *"Fetch along your doughnuts and your gum-drops"* 1889 CY xxxix 495 (OED
A confection. *U.S.* 1864.. Not A in W S C)

gumption, sb. [?A] *"See if you've got gumption enough
to round her to"* 1883 LM xviii 225. *"Anybody dat had
any gumption"* 1884 HF xiv 122 (OED 1. *colloq.*
Common sense. 1719.. So W S C U W. A in DN.II,
III,V,VI. On the exact meaning of the term see AS.
VII.452)

gun, sb. **great guns!** [?AB²] *"Great guns! Is he her
uncle?"* 1884 HF xiii 115. *"Why, great guns!"* 1889 CY
xi 132. *"Oh, great guns!"* 1892 AmCl viii 78 (OED 7d.
Used as an exclamation. 1895, only ex. So S C. A in
DN.III,IV,V. Comb. not in W)

gunny-sack, sb. [?AB³] *He would curl up on a gunny-
sack in the corner and go to sleep* 1871 *Screamers* 17
(OEDS b. Earliest exs. U.S. 1870.. A in DN.III.
Not A in W C U. Comb. not in S)

gurgly, a. [B³C] *The best word in that list, and the
most musical and gurgly, is Woolloomooloo* 1897 FE
xxxvi 330 (OED *rare.* 1894, only ex. So W S. Not in C.
Cf. google, v., for gurgle, above)

gush, v. [?AB³] *We were ashamed that we had "gushed"
so* 1872 RI xviii 143. *Gushing with apologies for not
being able to pay* 1875 OTM 195. *The New Orleans
editor...wastes no words, and does not gush* 1883 LM
xlv 459. See also *freshet* 1896 (OED 5. *colloq.* Earliest
citation from W. 1864.. A in C DN.III. Not A in
W S U)

gushy, a. [?AB²] *A mere rhythmical, gushy euphemism*
1880 TA App.D 613 (OED Earliest citation from C.
1889.. Not A in W S C U)

gut, v. [?AB¹] *Gutting a one-horse bank* 1892 AmCl
xix 195 (W: To plunder, destroy by removing the con-
tents of. So S C U. This sense not in OED)

guts, sb. [?C] See *quiffsplitter* 1880. *"Marse Sam, has
you ever seen a smoked herring?" "No...Anything peculiar about it?" "Yes, suh, you bet dey is. Dey eats 'em guts
and all!"* 1898 "Chaps. from Autob" (1906) 454. In this
passage as reproduced in the *Autob* (1924) I 127, Mr.
Paine has changed "smoked herring" to "dried herring"
and "guts" to "innards" (OED Gut, sb. 1. *collect.pl.*
The bowels; entrails. Formerly, but not now, in digni-

fied use with reference to man. *a*1000..1853. W: *Now Coarse*. S: *Vulgar*. C: *Low*. U: Not delicate. Cf. Mencken's remarks on the widespread taboo, in Hollywood and elsewhere, on this fine old English word. The feeling which led Mr. Paine to change the word is not shared by Professor Delancey Ferguson, who remarks indignantly, in his article entitled "The Uncollected Portions of Mark Twain's Autobiography," *American Literature* VIII (March, 1936) 46: "Mark Twain is a classic. As such, his text should be sacred. The reader has a right to be certain that what he is reading is what Mark Twain wrote, without expurgations or distortions...If it was some other hand than his which replaced 'guts' with 'innards,' Mark himself has expressed the inadequacy of comment: 'I get so damned short of profanity at a time like this'!" For other examples of Mr. Paine's "polishing" noted by Professor Ferguson, see *hollow*, *L*, *uncledom*. Further examples which are open to suspicion on the same count are noted under the words *beat* (beaten) *out, begattings, object-lesson, outlay, peach-bloomy*)

gutter-scum, sb. [?AB¹] *Tattered gutter-scum and ruffians* 1881 PP xvii 209 (Comb. not in OED W S C. Probably coined on the model of *gutter-snipe;* cf. below)

gutter-snipe, sb. [?AB³] "*Fall back, you gutter-snipes!*" 1902 "DBDS" (1928) 355 (OED 2b. One of the lowest class. 1882.. So U. *Slang* in W S C T. A in Cl Th.III,1871 AS.XII.115, quot. 1856)

guy, v. [?AB²] *Happy the Roman street boy who ate his peanuts and guyed the gladiators from the dizzy galleries* 1869 IA xxvi 278. *It guyed its poor victim, baited him, worried him* 1892 AmCl xv 160 (OED 2. To make an object of ridicule. 1872, quot. from IA... So W C U. A in S Th T M H AS.V.280)

gymnastic, sb. [B³C] *I introduced a new gymnastic— one that he had never seen before* 1907 "Chaps. from Autob" 4 (OED 4. A gymnastic feat. *rare*. 1860, only ex. So S. Not *rare* in W. This sense not in C)

H

haberdashery, sb. [B²?C] *The Bridge was a sort of town to itself; it had its inn, its beerhouses, its bakeries, its haberdasheries* 1881 PP xii 134 (OED 1813, only ex. So W. *Rare* in S C)

habit-sodden, ppl.a. [B¹] See *cipher*, v. 1909 (Comb. not in OED W S C. Cf. OED Habit-bound, no ex.)

haboolong, sb. [B¹] See *kahkahponeeka* 1880 (Hum. invention)

hack, sb. [A] *There were thousands of vehicles abroad ...there were very common hacks, with father and mother and all the children in them; conspicuous little open carriages...* 1869 IA xiv 137. *Mrs. O'Shaughnessy hired fifty-four dollars worth of hacks, and flung as much style into Dennis's funeral as if he had been a duke or an assassin* 1883 LM xlii 439 (OED 2. Now only *U.S.* 1704.. So S F Cl Th M H DN.II,III,IV. Not A in W C)

hack-driver, sb. [AB³] *Taken in by every hack-driver's son* 1892 AmCl xv 156 (OEDS Earlier U.S. exs. 1835.. A in Th. Comb. not in W S C)

hackful, sb. [AB¹] *This hackful of small reptiles was deemed necessary to fill a crack in the world's unnoted myriads* 1869 SNO (1875) 65 (Comb. not in OED W S C. Cf. above)

hack-grinding, vbl.sb. [B¹] *The editorial work is not hack-grinding, but literature* 1883 LM xli 428 (Comb. not in OED W S C. Cf. OED Hack-work, 1851..)

hackman, sb. [A] *There was no swaggering intrusion of services by rowdy hackmen* 1869 IA xii 112. *"When we land a passenger on the American side there's nothing betwixt him and the hotel but hell and the hackman"* 1895 *Speeches* (1910) 362 (OEDS *U.S.* 1796.. So C F Cl Th. Not A in W S)

hackman-general, sb. [AB¹] *A kind of hackman-general seemed to have the whole matter of transportation in his hands* 1869 IA xii 112 (Comb. not in OED W S C. Cf. above)

hackman-gondolier, sb. [AB¹] *We hear the cries of the hackman-gondoliers* 1869 IA xxiii 232 (Nonce comb. Cf. above)

had, sb. [B¹] *"This foolish discrimination...lets one Had go hadding in any kind of indefinite grammatical weather"* 1904 "Italian with Grammar" (1906) 195 (Nonce usage)

haddock, sb. [?AB¹] *"She was very fond of the late earl—idolized him, sir." "I idolized that smoked haddock?"* 1892 AmCl v 60 (*Dial* in Wr: A term of contempt. This sense not in OED W S C)

Hadji, sb. [B¹] *Hadjis are people who have made the pilgrimage...I, a fellow Hadji* 1869 IA "Valedictory" 642 (Nonce use for the "pilgrims" of the Quaker City party)

hail, sb. [?AB¹] *"That hail we had at Napoleon was Wash Hastings, wanting to come to Cairo"* 1873 GA iv 48. *"She's a big New Orleans boat, and I was afeard she mightn't stop there. When they're deep they won't stop for a hail"* 1884 HF xxiv 241 (A call to a passing steamboat by a prospective passenger. This *spec* sense not in OED W S C. Cf. the *gen.* sense in OED 2. A shout or call to attract attention. 1811..)

hail-barge, sb. [?AB¹] *The heavens are infested with old ramshackle comets which ought long ago to have been destroyed or turned into hail-barges* 1875 SNO 309 (Nonce coinage. Cf. the Am. use of *barge* and *coal-barge*, above)

Hail Columbia, sb. [AB¹] *The pride of country rose in his heart, Hail Columbia boomed up in his breast* 1902 "Belated Russian Passport" (1928) 190 (American patriotism. This sense not in OED W S C; but cf. *To give one Hail Columbia:* to scold, A in S Th,1854 DN.III,V)

hail from, v. [?AB³] *Our passengers hailed from fifteen states* 1869 IA ii 29. *St. Louis was a greater city, but its floating population did not hail from great distances* 1873 GA xxiv 217. See *establishment* 1880; Old

Virginia 1894. *The mere fact that a young man hailed from Hadleyburg was all the recommendation he needed* 1894 "MCH" (1900) 2 (OED 4b. *transf.* of a person: to come from. 1841.. So W S C U. A in B T DN.III)

hailstorm-discourager, sb. [B¹] *The hailstorm-discourager kept off the hailstorms, or explained why he failed* 1897 FE xlix 463 (Nonce comb.)

hair, sb. to have where the hair is short. [AB¹] *I've got it* [the German language] *where the hair's short, I think* 1880 TA xx 193 (A in AS.II.356: to have in a position in which one can be dictated to, W.Va. So DN.III, w.Ind. Phr. not in OED W S C; but cf. OED 8p. *To get by the short hairs:* to have complete control over. 1899..)

hair, sb. to be in one's hair. [?AB¹] *"What you learn here, you've got to know...or else you'll have one of these ...spectacled, ring-boned, knock-kneed old professors in your hair* 1880 TA xx 193 (Phr. not in OED W S C; but cf. OED *To comb one's hair:* to beat, give a 'dressing' to. 1596..)

hair-ball, sb. [?A] *Miss Watson's nigger, Jim, had a hair-ball as big as your fist, which had been took out of the fourth stomach of an ox, and he used to do magic with it* 1884 HF iv 27 (OED Masses of hair found in the stomachs of oxen. 1712..1753. So S C U. W: Often used, as by American negroes, in magic and divination)

hair-lifting, ppl.a. [B¹] *I flung out a hair-lifting, soul-scorching, thirteen-jointed insult* 1889 CY xxvii 354. *It gave the spies a hair-lifting but pleasurable thrill* 1902 "DBDS" (1928) 325 (Comb. not in OED W S C. Cf. OEDS Hair-raising, 1900)

hair-oil, sb. [B²] *They use up more hair-oil than any six men* 1867 SNO (1875) 252 (OED 1870, only ex. So C U. Comb. not in W S)

hair-spine, sb. [B¹] *"You haven't seen a kitten with the hair-spines on its tongue pointing to the front, have you?"* 1898 MS (1916) v 44 (Comb. not in OED W S C; but cf. OED Hair-shaft, 1906)

hair-trigger, sb. [?AB²] *I finally took my watch to another watch-maker...he said there appeared to be something the matter with the hair-trigger* 1870 SNO (1875) 20. *The inmates were asleep, but it was a sleep that was set on a hair-trigger, on account of the exciting episode of the night* 1876 TS xxx 226 (OED *fig.* 1894.. So W S C U. A in Th,1806)

half, a. [?A] *A half-dozen tents were pitched under the trees* 1873 GA xvi 157. *"De man dat think he kin settle a 'spute 'bout a whole chile wid a half a chile"* 1884 HF xiv 122. *"I haven't examined half a dozen hands in the last half-dozen years"* 1894 PW xi 554 (A in H: Am. *a half*=Eng. *half a.* This highly questionable dictum is not supported by OED W S C or any other authority. For another distinction see OED 1c. With sbs. denoting numbers, quantities...as *half a dozen...* when these are viewed as independent numbers, etc., *half* is preceded by *a, the,* etc., and hyphenated to the sb., as *a half-dozen...A half-crown* is the silver coin worth 2s. 6d.; *half a crown* includes the equivalent amount in any coins, e.g., in five sixpences. This ingenious and logical distinction is not supported by W S C, nor by the usage of M.T. Probably the only differentiation between the two forms in actual usage is one of rhythm)

half, adv. [B³] *Two leadsmen sprang to their posts, and in a moment their weird cries rose...."Half three!"* 1873 GA iv 46. See *twain* 1875. (OED 4c. *Naut.* In soundings *half* before a numeral adds half to it. 1809.. So W S. This sense not in C)

half-apologetic, a. [B¹] *The station-master became pleasant and even half-apologetic* 1893 "Traveling with a Reformer" (1900) 371 (Comb. not in OED W S C)

half-bank, sb. [B¹] *Drifting straight along like a river at half-bank with no reefs in it* 1906 Autob (1924) I 299

(Comb. not in OED W S C; but cf. OED Bank-high: swolien up to the bank, 1882)

half-breed, sb. [A] *A young half-breed with a compexion like a yellow-jacket* 1872 RI xvii 138. *"Yes," said Injun Joe..."Did you think I'd forget? The Injun blood ain't in me for nothing"... The half-breed saw his chance and drove the knife to the hilt in the young man's breast* 1876 TS ix 90. See also *Missourian,* a. 1909. (OED 2. In U.S., applied to the offspring of whites or negroes and American Indians. 1791.. So C T M; but cf. W: esp. in the U.S. of the Am. Indian and the white race; so U Th,1775. Not A in S)

half-breed, sb. [?AB¹] See *go, went=gone* 1883. *I happened to tell him a lie—a modified one, of course; a half-breed, a mulatto* 1899 "My First Lie" (1900) 164 (This *transf.* use not in OED W S C)

half-confession, sb. [B¹] *The hedging and half-confessions of over-haste and exaggerated resentment* 1893 "Traveling with a Reformer" (1900) 362 (Comb. not in OED W S C)

half-confidence, sb. [B¹] *Ruth fascinated him more than ever with her little demurenesses and half-confidences* 1873 GA xxii 212 (Comb. not in OED W S C)

half-consciousness, sb. [B¹] *His senses struggled to a half-consciousness* PP xvii 208 (Comb. not in OED W S C)

half-dime, sb. [A] *We had always been used to half-dimes and "five cents' worth"* 1872 RI xvii 137 (OED A coin of the U.S. 1796.. So W S C)

half-dollar, sb. [A] See *salting* 1869; *cent* 1889 (OED A silver coin of the U.S. 1786.. So W C. Comb. not in S)

half-doubt, sb. [B¹] *It left Prissy's half-doubts not a leg to stand on* 1881 PP xix 238 (Comb. not in OED W S C)

half-generation, sb. [B¹] *How the world had been using the Colonel during this half-generation* 1892 AmCl iii 36 (Comb. not in OED W S C)

half-god, sb. [?C] *That a commonplace person should become a god or a half-god or a quarter-god is nothing* 1907 CS II vi 152 (OED *Obs.* 1374..1895. So S C. Not *obs* in W, and apparently not so felt by M.T.)

half-intoxicated, a. [B¹] *A half-intoxicated guest rose up and threw something* 1873 GA lx 549 (Comb. not in OED S C. Given in W)

half-massacred, a. [B¹] *A half-massacred Indian may recover* 1872 SNO (1875) 265 (Comb. not in OED W S C)

half-minded, a. [B¹] *He was half-minded to resign* 1881 PP xix 162 (Comb. not in OED S C. Given in W)

half-petticoat, sb. [B¹] *The half-petticoat of steel which hangs down in front...is scolloped out behind* 1889 CY x 134 (Comb. not in OED W S C)

half-seas-over, a. [?A] *What a man can do, when he's "half seas over"* 1852 *Hannibal Journal* Sept. 9 (OED 2. Half-drunk. 1700.. So W S C U. A in AS.XII.92)

half shell, sb. [?AB¹] *Blue points on the half shell* 1880 TA xlix 574 (Comb. not in OED. Given in W S C)

half-sole, v. [?AB¹] *Part of the works* [of my watch] *needed half-soling* 1870 SNO (1875) 20. *He's going to half-sole some of our old Italian masterpieces* 1892 AmCl xix 199. *The revamping and half-soling of "Science and Health"* 1907 CS II viii 252 (Hum. nonce use. Cf. OEDS To furnish with new half-soles. All exs. U.S. 1844.. Not A in W S C)

half-stretch, sb. [B¹] See *trail,* sb. 1889 (Comb. not in OED W S C)

half-uttered, a. [B¹] *I heard muttered sentences, half-uttered screams that seemed smothered violently* 1870 SNO (1875) 217 (Comb. not in OED W S C)

half-wheel-deep, a. [B¹] *Coaches and carriages wallowing through these countries in mud and slush half-wheel-deep* 1880 TA xxxi 335 (Comb. not in OED W S C)

half-white, sb. [?AB¹] *I asked after "Billy" Ragsdale, interpreter to the Parliament in my time—a half-white* 1897 FE iii 63 (Comb. not in OED W S C. Cf. half-breed, above)

halidome, sb. [C] *The discarded and forgotten "steeds" and "halidomes" and similar stage-properties once so dear to our grandfathers* 1906 "Howells" (1917) 237 (OED *obs* or *arch* 3. Much used, down to the 16th c., in oaths and adjurations. c1000..1561. So W S C U)

Halifax, sb. [AB³] *"I was going after it, but I'd see you in Halifax, now, before I'd do it"* 1875 OTM 569 (OEDS Now regarded as a euphemism for *hell.* In U.S. with supposed allusion to Halifax, Nova Scotia. 1807.. So Wr Th.III AS.II.478. Cf. DN.I,II: The expression "Go to Halifax!" is a survival from Revolutionary times, and meant originally "You are a Tory; go where you belong." Not in W S C. Cf. Hannibal, below)

halt, a. [C] *And rake in the lame, the halt, and the blind* 1892 AmCl iii 40 (OED *arch* and *literary.* c893.. 1859. So U. Not *arch* in W S C)

halver, sb. [?AC] *No man can say he ever see him do anything by halvers* 1867 SNO (1875) 74 (OED *obs* exc. dial. 2. A half-share. 1517..1887. So W Wr. Not *obs* in S. A in F DN.II,III. Not in C)

ham-bone, sb. [B¹] *We have only left a lower end of a ham-bone* 1866 "Forty-Three Days" 111 (Comb. not in OED W S C)

ham-rag, sb. [B¹] *Ate the meat and rind of our ham-bone, and have the bone and the greasy cloth from around the ham left to eat to-morrow...The ham-rags are not quite all gone yet* 1866 "Forty-Three Days" 113 (Comb. not in OED W S C)

hand, sb. [?C] *A fly, calmly rubbing its hands together* 1876 TS v 56 (OED 1b. Applied formerly to the tarsus of the anterior leg in insects. 1535, only ex. So W C. This sense not in S. Apparently not felt by M.T as *arch*)

hand, sb. [?A] *On Monday the hands are paid off in sparkling gold* 1853 *Letters* (1917) I i 26 (OED 8. A workman. 1655.. So W S C U. A in DN.II,III,VI AS.IX.208)

hand, sb. **a man of his hands.** [C] *He is a passing good man of his hands* 1889 CY xv 177 (OED 30. A man of valour, skill, or practical ability. *arch.* 1513.. 1886. So W C. Phr. not in S)

hand, sb. **hand over fist.** [?AB³] *He was getting rich, hand over fist* 1889 CY xxxi 397 (OEDS 55a. *fig.* of the making of money. 1888.. So W S C Wr. A in Th DN.II,III)

hand, sb. **to have one's hand in.** [?AB¹] *I told, in patient belief-compelling detail, all about the finding of a petrified man...And then, my hand being "in," so to speak, I went on, with the same unflinching gravity, to state that...deceased came to his death from protracted exposure* 1870 SNO (1875) 240 (W: to be in practice in doing something. So S C U. Phr. not in OED)

hand, sb. **to take a hand.** [?AB¹] *They invited him... to take a hand* 1892 AmCl xiii 131 (U: to take part in. Phr. not in OED W S C. Cf. OED 3b. To have a hand in, 1597..)

hand, sb. **with one hand tied behind.** [?AB¹] *The editor of a newspaper cannot be independent, but must work with one hand tied behind him by party and patrons* 1875 OTM 721 (Phr. not in OED W S C; but cf. OED 36b. With both hands: with all one's might. 1611..)

hand-bag, sb. [?AB²] *He had gone out with a hand-bag, saying that he had to go to New York* 1873 GA xlvi 419 (OED 1880, only ex. So W S C U)

hand-car, sb. [AB³] *We changed to a little canvas-canopied hand-car for the 35-mile descent* 1897 FE lvi 535 (OED *U.S.* 1850.. So W Th M. Not A in S C)

hand-free, a. [B¹] *This left the prince hand-free for a second* 1881 PP x 120 (Comb. not in OED W S C; but cf. OED Hand-bound, 1600.

handkerchief-turban, sb. [?AB¹] *She took off her handkerchief-turban* 1893 PW iii 238 (Comb. not in OED W S C. Cf. turban, below)

handle, sb. **to fly off the handle**. [AB³] *George's voice was just "turning," and it was apt to fly off the handle* 1869 IA iv 45 (OEDS 1b. *U.S. colloq.* To be carried away by excitement; to lose control. 1825.. So B C F Cl Th. Not A in W S)

handle-bar, sb. [?AB²] *By this time you have learned ...to steer without wrenching the tiller out by the roots* (*I say tiller because it is a tiller; "handle-bar" is a lamely descriptive phrase*) c1880 "Taming the Bicycle" (1917) 289 (OEDS 1894.. So W S C U)

hand-painted, a. [B¹] *He closes his pamphlet with a grim Indictment which is as eloquent in its flowerless straightforward English as is the hand-painted rhapsody of the early prophet* 1897 FE vi 89 (Comb. not in OED W S C; but cf. OED Hand-coloured, no ex.)

hand-print, sb. [B¹] "*The hand-print of one twin is the same as the hand-print of the fellow twin*" 1894 PW xi 553 (Comb. not in OED S C. This sense not in W)

hand-shake, sb. [?AB³] *When we left he had a hand-shake all around* 1880 TA xxiii 240. See also *bone-mashing* 1902 (OED 1873.. So W S C U T. A in B F. Comb. not in S)

handspring, sb. [?AB²] *He would actually throw one handspring after another* 1872 RI vii 63. *I glanced at the list [of dishes], and my stomach threw a handspring* 1898 "At the Appetite-Cure" (1900) 150 (OED 1875.. So W S C U Wr. A in H)

handspring, v. [?AB¹] *He was below, handspringing across the back yard* 1877 "Some Rambling Notes" iv 14 (Not in OED W S C as verb. Cf. above)

hand-tooled, ppl.a. [B¹] *An illustrated, gilt-edged, tree-calf, hand-tooled, seven-dollar Friendship's Offering* 1895 "Cooper's Literary Offences" 2 (W: Tooled or lettered by hand. So S. Comb. not in OED C)

hand-write, sb. [A] *I most vividly see your hand-write in a square blue envelop* 1909 *Letters* (1917) II xlvii 830 (OEDS *Scotch* and *U.S.* Handwriting. 1617.. So Wr. A in B F Th T DN.II,III,IV,V. Not in W S)

hang, sb. **to get the hang of**. [AB³] *I do not seem to have just got the hang of this sort of thing* 1865 SS (1926) 206. *I practised around all day to get the hang of the things* 1884 HF x 85. (OED 3. *U.S. colloq.* 1845.. So B F Cl Th T DN.III,IV. Not A in W S C U)

hang, v. **hang fire**. [?AB³] *It appears to hang fire somewhere* 1880 TA xxix 302 (OED 6. *fig* to hesitate or be slow in acting. 1801.. So W S C U. A in DN.III)

hanging-bout, sb. [?AB¹] *She had found me at the hanging-bout* 1889 CY xli 522 (Comb. not in OED W S C. Wr: an execution. *Yorkshire*)

hanging-eve, sb. [B¹] *The hanging-eve history of a million rascals* 1894 PW xv 820 (Comb. not in OED W S C)

hanging wall, sb. [?AB²] See *casing* 1872 (OED The rock which hangs over the lode. 1875, only ex. So W S Wr. Comb. not in C)

hang out, v. [?AB³] "*You've got to camp at my house as long as you hang out here*" 1873 GA ii 34 (OED 26c. To reside, lodge. *colloq* or *slang*. 1811.. So W S C U Wr T. A in B Cl)

hang up, v. [?AB³] "*Italy cracked on such a rattling impost that cotton-seed olive-oil couldn't stand the raise; had to hang up and quit*" 1883 LM xxxix 413 (OEDS 28f. To suspend action. 1854.. So W S C U. A in Wr Cl Th DN.I)

hang up, v. [AB¹] *The Colonel muttered something to the barkeeper about "hanging it up"* 1873 GA xiii 131 (To debit to one's account. A in S F T. Dial in Wr. This sense not in OED W C)

hanker, v. [?AC] *There's plenty of boys that will come hankering and grovelling around you when you've got an apple* 1893 TSA i 23 (OED 1. To 'hang about;' to linger or loiter about with longing or expectation. Now *dial.* 1601..1858. So W Wr. Not *dial* in S. C: *colloq*)

Hannibal, sb. [AB¹] *Love Concealed; to Miss Katie of H—l* (title) 1853 *Hannibal Journal* May 6. *Mr. Editor: In your yesterday's paper I see a piece of poetry addressed "To Katie in H—l"* (*hell*). *Now, I've often seen pieces to "Mary in Heaven," or "Lucy in Heaven," or something of that sort, but "Katie in Hell," is carrying the matter too far.* do. May 7. *Read again—see if it is not "of" H—l* (*Hannibal*), *instead of "in" Hell.* do. May 9. *I merely glanced at your doggerel, and naturally supposing that you had friends in "H—l,"* (*or Hannibal, as you are pleased to interpret it*). do. May 10. *Tell me all that is going on in H—l* 1853 *Letters* (1917) I 28, Oct. 26. (M.T.'s youthful and irreverent use of the name of his boyhood town is recounted inaccurately by himself in "My First Literary Venture" 1870 SNO (1875) 94, and in Paine's *Biography*, 1912, I.90, III.1674. A full and accurate account of the episode is given by Dr. M. M. Brashear in her *Mark Twain, Son of Missouri*, 1933, 119-126. The innuendo was perhaps suggested by the similar use of Halifax, for which cf. above. Hannibal is at any rate typographically closer to Hell than Halifax is!)

hansom, sb. [B³?C] *A gentleman who was passing in a hansom* 1899 "My First Lie" (1900) 165 (OED A low-hung two-wheeled cabriolet. 1847.. So W S C. U: Now *obs*)

hap, sb. [?AC] "*I am going to bring that morning back again, every hap as it happened*" 1881 PP xxxii 377 (OED *arch.* 2. An event or occurrence. c1205.. 1849. So U. Not *arch* in W S C Wr. A in Th)

happen, sb. [B¹] *It was one of those happens that you can't guard against* 1892 AmCl xxiv 253 (Wr: An accident, occurrence. Not in OED W S C as sb.)

happen in, v. [AB³] *Just as we finished, Sir Bedivere happened in* 1889 CY xi 134 (OEDS Happen, v. 4d. To go or come in casually. *U.S.* 1838.. So B F Cl Th DN.III. W: *obs exc. dial.* Not A in S C Wr T)

happiness-machine, sb. [B¹] "*Every man is a suffering-machine and a happiness-machine combined*" 1898 MS (1916) vii 83 (Nonce comb.)

Happy-Land-of-Canaan, sb. [B¹] *The sergeant-at-arms very soon put a quietus upon the observations of the representative of the nation, and convinced him that he was not in the over-free atmosphere of his Happy-Land-of-Canaan* 1873 GA lix 539 (Nonce comb., from the familiar gospel hymn)

happy-looking, a. [B¹] *A most homelike and happy-looking region* 1883 LM xl 420 (Comb. not in OED W S C)

harbour, v. [C] "*I was moved to seek the kennel where I was born and bred...yet which harboreth my mother and sisters*" 1881 PP v 64 (OED 3b. Of a place, etc.: To afford accommodations or room for. *Obs.* 1362.. 1680. So W S C Wr)

hard-boil, v. [?AB¹] *No more time to decide it in than it takes to hard-boil an egg* 1895 JA II xxii 886 (Not in OED W S C as a verb. Cf. Hard-boiled, ppl.a., 1833)

hard-boiled, a. [AB²] *Hard-boiled, hide-bound grammar* 1886 *Speeches* (1923) 137 (OEDS Hardened, callous, hard-headed. orig. *U.S.* 1919.. So M H. Not A in W. This sense not in S C. The sense here is rather: Rigid, narrow, pedantic. Cf. DN.XII.258 for the Western use = 'tight wad,' dated as early as 1885, and its later development)

hard cash, sb. [?AB³] "*You'll get a clean solid eighty shillings bounty—hard cash, you know*" 1897 FE xiii 143 (OED Cash, sb. 2b. 1837. So W S C U. A in Th,1809. Not A in H)

hard-driven, ppl.a. [?AB¹] *The poor and hard-driven* 1902 CS II 762 (Comb. not in OED S C. Given in W)

hard-looking, ppl.a. [?AB¹] *A couple of mighty hard-looking strangers* 1884 HF xi 89 (Comb. not in OED

S C. Given in W. Cf. Hard, a. A in Cl: bad, worthless, tough)

hard lot, sb. [AB¹] *She tole...all about pap and what a hard lot he was, and what a hard lot I was* 1884 HF xl 88. *The Indian crow...is the hardest lot that wears feathers* 1897 FE xxxviii 353 (A in B Th. Comb. not in OED W S C; but cf. OED Hard case: a difficult case to deal with, manage; a 'bad. lot.' *U.S.* 1848..)

hardpan, sb. [AB³] *"It'll be pretty much all hardpan"* 1873 GA xiii 127 (OEDS 1. *U.S.* A firm subsoil; hard, unbroken ground. 1817.. So W S C U B Cl Th T DN.I)

hard-pushed, ppl.a. [?AB³] *"Poor old Uncle Silas— why, it's pitiful him trying to curry favor that way—so hard pushed and poor* 1896 TSD i 345 (OEDS In difficulties. 1834. So W Wr. A in B Cl DN.III. Comb. not in S C)

hard-tack, sb. [?AB³] *The hardest kind of hard-tack* 1864 SS (1926) 138 (OEDS Earlier U.S. exs. Ship-biscuit. 1836.. A in B Cl T AS.VII.168. Not A in W S C U)

hard up, a. [?AB³] *"An' say you'll sell me cheap 'ca'se you's hard up"* 1894 PW xvi 821 (OED 2. In want, esp. of money. 1821.. So W S C U. A in B DN.III. Explained as orig. a naut. phrase, AS.IV.381)

hardware, sb. [?A] *Most knights would have thought of getting his armor, but...he could keep his hardware for all of me* 1889 CY xii 143. See also *busted* 1889 (OED 1515..1844. So W S C U. A in Th M. H, under dry goods, says that hardware is now Eng.)

hardware store, sb. [A] *Two "highly connected" young Virginians, clerks in a hardware store* 1883 LM xl 420 (OEDS *U.S.* An ironmonger's shop. 1789.. Not A in W S. Comb. not in C)

hard-worked, ppl.a. [B²] *He was coarsely fed and hard-worked* 1894 PW iv 330 (OED Hard, adv. 8a. No ex. Comb. not in S C. Given in W)

hare-foot, sb. [B¹] *They [German students] call him "hare foot," which is the German equivalent for chick-en-hearted* 1880 TA vi 62 (Nonce borrowing, from German *Hasenfuss,* coward)

hare-lip, sb. [B¹] *"Joanna's about fourteen—that's the one that gives herself to good works and has a hare-lip" ...The king he spread his arms, and Mary Jane she jumped for them, and then the hare-lip jumped for the duke, and there they had it!* 1884 HF xxv 246. *Then Susan she waltzed in, and if you'll believe me, she did give Hare-lip hark from the tomb!* do. xxvi 263 (Nonce use, for a person with a hare-lip)

hark-from-the-tomb, sb. [?AB¹] See *hare-lip,* sb. 1884. *A newspaper...is hark from the tomb for a dead nation* 1889 CY ix 108. *"You will write him a letter and give him Hark from the Tomb?" "No, I shall write him a letter, but not in that spirit, I trust"* 1900 Autob (1924) I 179 (Something of a rousing nature, an invigorator. Comb. not in OED W S C. Cf. Hail Columbia, above)

harmonious, a. [AB¹] *The love of self-deification is really only the spiritual form of the material appetite for pie, and nothing could be more strikingly Christian-Scientifically "harmonious"* 1903 "Mrs. Eddy in Error" 514 (The *spec* Chr.Sc. meaning not in OED W S C)

harness, sb. [?AB¹] *At the Metropolitan in New York they sit in a glare, and wear their showiest harness* 1891 "At the Shrine of St. Wagner" (1917) 225 (C: Clothing, dress, garments. *Rare.* This sense not in OED W S)

harness, sb. **to work in harness.** [?AB¹] *"He and I are sworn brothers on that measure; we work in harness"* 1873 GA lxii 373 (To work together, in partnership. Phr. not in OED W S C. Cf. OED 4b. In harness: in the routine of daily work, 1841..; OEDS 4. Double harness: often *fig.* 1901. So W U)

harness, v. [?AB¹] *"Smiley always come out winner on that pup, till he harnessed a dog once that didn't have no hind legs"* 1865 "Jumping Frog" (1875) 32 (Apparently the meaning is: to challenge, to match with, or to attack, assail. No such use of the word is given in OED W S C. The French version shows that the meaning of this passage was not clearly understood: *"Smiley gagnait toujours avec cette bête-la; malheureusement ils ont fini par dresser un chien qui n'avait pas de pattes de derrière."* This is "retranslated" as: *"Unhappily they have finished by elevating a dog who no had not of feet of behind")*

Harrisite, sb. **Laurence Oliphant Harrisite.** [AB¹] See *Allopath* 1902 "Chr.Sc." 757 (Not in OED W S C. A follower of Thomas Lake Harris (1823-1906; see *Dict. of Amer. Biog.),* who founded a community of spiritualists in 1850. About 1865 he made a disciple of Laurence Oliphant (1829-1888; see *Dict. of Nat. Biog.),* a wealthy Englishman and member of Parliament. Oliphant turned over to him his entire fortune, which was used to purchase a home for the community at Brocton, or 'Salem-on-Erie,' N. Y., and became Harris's "spiritual slave." But in 1875 he became convinced that Harris was an impostor, broke with him, and sued to recover his land. Harris and his followers removed to Santa Rosa, Cal. From 1881 on, Oliphant was regarded as head of affairs at Brocton. In 1886 he published a book entitled *Masollam* giving his final judgment of the prophet. By "Laurence Oliphant Harrisite," M.T. apparently means a member of the faction that followed Oliphant after the split.)

harvest, v. [?AB¹] *After harvesting a good deal of very pleasant coaxing and petting and persuading, I forgave her* 1893 "Esquimau Maiden's Romance" (1928) 145. *She went harvesting among the kitchens every time she came to the village* 1894 PW x 552. *Joan had harvested a good many compliments* 1895 JA II iv 93. See also *lawyer-talk* 1909 (Cf. OED 2. *transf.* To gather and lay up in store; to 'reap,' to husband. 1888.. So W S C U. Here: to receive, obtain, be showered with, without any implication of gathering, husbanding, or storing up; a favorite word with M.T., used in a sense that seems peculiar to him)

has-been, sb. [?A] *She is not a Has Been, she is an Is—the Author of "Science and Health"* 1903 "Mrs. Eddy in Error" 507 (OED 1606..1827. OEDS Later dial and U.S. exs. 1853..1914. A in M H. Not A in W S C Wr)

hash, sb. [?AB¹] *I mean to ship "Pudd'nhead Wilson" to you—say, tomorrow. It'll furnish me hash for awhile, I reckon* 1893 Letters (1917) II xxxiii 592 (Subsistence, support. This sense not in OED W S C. Cf. S: Food in general, *slang.* A in Th,1807: One's business. Cf. Hash-house, A in Cl: a place where food of any sort may be procured)

hassock, sb. [?C] *She combs out some creditable Scots...naively explaining which Sir William Wallace it was, lest we get the wrong one by the hassock.* (Footnote: *I am in some doubt as to what a hassock is, but anyway it sounds good)* 1907 CS II i 107 (OED 1b. *transf.* A 'shock' of hair. 1785..1825. All exs. *Scotch.* So Wr S. Cf. C: The lock of wool that grows on the halse or throat of a sheep. This sense not in W)

hat, sb. **at the dropping of a hat.** [?AB¹] *There isn't a squaw...who doesn't stand ready at the dropping of a hat to desert to the buck with the biggest string of scalps* 1889 CY xv 177 (Cf. W: At the drop of the hat: as soon as the signal is given. Phr. not in OED S C)

hatchet, sb. **to bury the hatchet.** [A] *"Shall we bury the hatchet and be good friends?"* 1873 GA xlii 385 (OED 2. To cease from hostilities; phr. derived from the customs of the N.Am. Indians. 1794.. So W S C B F Th,1784 M DN.VI)

hate-inspiring, ppl.a. [B¹] *To human beings this is a much more hate-inspiring thing than is any detail connected with religion* 1899 "Concerning the Jews" (1900) 268 (Comb. not in OED W S C)

hat-rack, sb. [B²] *A sort of vestibule, where they used o keep the hat-rack* 1869 IA xxxi 330 (OED 1872, this quot. So W S C U)

haul, v. to haul down one's colors. [B¹] *You will haul down your colors and go to impoverishing yourself with fees* 1880 TA App.A. 585 (U: To surrender. Phr. not in OED W S C)

haul off, v. [?AB¹] *"Suppose he should take deliberate aim and 'haul off' and fetch me with the butt-end of the gun?"* 1870 CRG (1919) 45 (W: To draw back the arm so as to gain impetus for a blow. So S. This sense not in OED C)

haunt, v. to go ha'nting around. [?AB¹E] *He said a man that warn't buried was much more likely to go a-ha'nting around* 1884 HF x 80. *"After it [the ghost] started to go ha'nting around"* 1896 TSD vi 357 (C: intr., To reappear, as a disembodied spirit. A in DN.I,III. The *intr.* use not in OED W S. OED gives the form *hant* as 14th-17th c. This form given as A in F T AS.V.201, Ozarks)

Havana, sb. [AB³] *The brand offered did not suit him; he motioned the box away and asked for some particular Havanas, those in separate wrappers* 1873 GA xiii 130. *Nearly any cigar will do me, except a Havana c1893* "Concerning Tobacco" (1917) 277. See also *cabbage-leaf* 1907 (OED A cigar of a kind made at Havana or in Cuba. 1826.. So W S C U)

have, v. [?AB³] *"Put me down for California." I had him again, Peters! He puzzled a second* 1907 "Capt. Stormfield" 43 (OED 15b. To have caught; to have put into a fix or non-plus. *colloq.* 1820.. So W S C U Wr. A in B)

have, v. [?A] *"We can't have that: there's enough of us already"* 1909 ISD xii 137 (OED 18c. With a negative, sometimes: Not to allow, permit, bear, or suffer. 1583..1890. So W S C U. A in Cl)

have, v. [?AC] *"If he'd a chawed up all the men he's ben a-gwyne to chaw up in the last twenty years..."* 1884 HF xxi 212. *If I'd 'a' knowed what a trouble it was to make a book I wouldn't 'a' tackled it* 1884 HF xliii 438 (OED 26. In 15th and 16th c. occur many instances of redundant *have had*, in the compound tenses. 1442 ..1768. OEDS Later *U.S.* exs. 1816..1911. A in M DN.III. *Dial* in Wr. This use not in W S C)

have, v. hain't. [AE] *"I beg pardon...but hain't you forgot something?"* 1907 "Capt. Stormfield" 45 (This form not in OED W. A in Wr. Not A in S C)

have, v. [?AB¹] *The bride...said with arch severity: "Well, you would have me,—nothing else would do"* 1880 TA xxxi 333. *"Then you are the son of an earl, after all," said Sally, reproachfully. "Yes, I—." "Then I won't have you!"* 1892 AmCl xxv 267 (To marry. This sense not in OED W S C; but cf. in *gen.* sense OED 14. To accept, take. 1000..)

have, v. to have it. [?AB¹] See *hare-lip* 1884 (To have a time: to have a satisfactory, exciting, thrilling experience. This sense not in OED W S C. Cf. OED 14c. To have it: to gain the victory, to win the match. 1596.. 14d. To have it: to receive a drubbing, thrashing, reprimand. 1592..)

haw-haw, v. [?AB³] *They roared and clapped and stormed and haw-hawed till he come back and done it over again* 1884 HF xxiii 227 (OED To laugh loudly or boisterously. 1834.. So W S C U T. A in B DN.III,V)

hay-cutting, vbl.sb. [?AB¹] *Hay-cutting time was approaching* 1906 *Autob* (1924) II 48 (Comb. not in OED W S C)

hay-ride, sb. [?AB¹] *The remembrance of poor Susy's lost hay-ride still brings me a pang* 1906 *Autob* (1924) II 50 (A ride by a party of young people in a hay-wagon. Comb. not in OED W S C)

hay-scales, sb. [A] *If you wished to weigh one of their airiest little commonplace statements you would want the hay-scales* 1872 RI xiii 112 (OEDS Hay, sb. 5. *U.S.* 1773.. Not A in C. Comb. not in W S)

haze, v. [AB³] *"When we get hold of a man of a peculiarly sensitive nature, oh, but we do haze him!"* 1876 "Facts Concerning the Recent Carnival of Crime" 646 (OED 3. To subject to cruel horseplay, as practised by American students; to bully. *U.S.* 1850.. So W U B F Cl Th,1840 H DN.II. Not A in S C Wr)

he, sb. any he. [C] *"I will answer it to any he that desireth"* 1889 CY xxxix 504 (OED 6. Any person whatever. *arch* and *poet.* 1384..1682. So C. Not *arch* in W U Wr. This use not in S)

head, sb. full head, half-head. [?AB³] *I had my native shrewdness turned on 'full head,' as the engineers say* 1870 SNO (1875) 317. *The Pennsylvania was creeping along on a half-head of steam* 1883 LM xx 237. *In the room the gas was burning full head* 1892 AmCl vii 73. *My pipe was ready...I lit up at once, and by the time I had got a good head of reserved steam on, here they came* 1889 CY xiv 167 (OED 17b. The difference of pressure of a confined body of gas or vapour. 1862.. So W S C. A in Th.III DN.VI)

head, sb. [?AB¹] *A long, narrow, wooded island with a shallow bar at the head of it* 1876 TS xiii 114 (The upper end of a river island. This sense not in OED W S C)

head, sb. out of one's head. [AB³] *A one-armed man ...flying along one of the halls, apparently out of his head with fright* 1892 AmCl viii 78. *"He laid dah moanin' en cussin,' en all out of his head, you know"* 1894 PW xviii 18 (OEDS 36b. Out of one's mind. *U.S.* 1825.. Not A in W S C)

head, sb. to shut one's head. [AB¹] *The meek eyes of the pale young fellow...rested upon the old man's face a moment, and the meek mouth began to open. "Shet your head!" shouted the old mariner* 1877 "Some Rambling Notes" ii 587 (To be silent. Phr. not in OED W S C; but cf. OEDS Open one's head: To speak. *U.S. slang.* 1885..)

header, sb. [?AB¹] *They were curious things, those old high-wheel machines. You were perched away up in the air, with the feeling that you were likely at any moment to strike a pebble or something that would fling you forward with damaging results...The word "header" seems to have grown out of that early bicycling period. Perhaps Mark Twain invented it. He had enough experience to do it* 1912 Paine's *Biog.* 11 767, telling of the spring of 1884. (W: A fall or plunge headforemost, as while riding a bicycle. *colloq.* So S C U. Cf. OED 7. A plunge or dive head foremost. *colloq.* 1849.. All the OED quots. refer to deliberate and premeditated dives or plunges. It is very unlikely that M.T. invented this familiar Am. usage)

head-line, sb. [?AB²] See *spring-line* 1876 (OEDS 3b. A line fastening the head of a vessel to the shore. 1877. So C. This sense not in W S. On a steamboat the head-line is fastened to the forward bitts and runs upstream; cf. spring-line, below)

head-line, sb. [B¹] See *heart-line* 1894 (W: *Palmistry.* This sense of the comb. not in OED S C; but cf. OED Line, sb. 8b. *Palmistry...line of the head,* etc. No ex.)

head-mark, sb. [?AB¹] *The pilot can...give you such a lot of head-marks, stern-marks, and side-marks to guide you that you ought to be able to take the boat there and put her in that same spot again yourself* 1875 OTM 571 (Comb. not in OED W S C in this sense)

head off, v. [?AB³] *We took shipping for Beirut, calculating to head off the other vessel* 1870 SNO (1875) 103. *Hawkins went down and headed off the procession* 1892 AmCl xxiv 252 (OEDS 13b. 1841.. So S C U. A in F Cl Th.III T DN.III. Comb. not in W)

head-on, adv. [AB²] *I sat down in the stern-sheets and pointed her head-on to the shore* 1872 RI xxiii 177. *A huge log, lying deep in the water, would suddenly appear right under our bows, coming head-on* 1875 OTM 448 (OEDS orig. *U.S.* 1916.. Not A in W S C U)

head-piece, sb. [C] "*I believe thee, whether thy small head-piece be sound or cracked, my boy*" 1881 PP xii 136 (OED 3. The head. *arch.* 1579..1838. So Wr. Not *arch* in W S C U)

healer, sb. [AB[1]] *A healer has to have the Annex and the Scriptures, or he is not allowed to work the game... The exactions of the ordinary C.S. "healer" are not exorbitant* 1907 CS I vii 74, 79 (W: A Christian Science practitioner; not so called by the Christian Scientists themselves. S: *colloq.* So U. This sense not in OED C)

health-journal, sb. [B[1]] *Her health-journals of the current month upset everything they had recommended before* 1876 TS xii 108 (Comb. not in OED W S C)

healthy, a. [?A] *Philadelphia is one of the healthiest places in the Union* 1853 *Letters* (1917) I i 30 (OED 2. Conducive to health: healthful. 1552..1871. So W S C U. A in M)

heap, sb. [?A] "*Ten thousand. It is a heap of money*" 1883 LM xxxii 357 (OED 4. *colloq.* A great deal, a 'lot.' *a*1661..1884. So W S C U T. A in B DN.I,II, III,IV,V)

heap, adv. [?AB[3]] *Bob called him a heap rougher names* 1883 LM iii 47. *I got home a heap too quick for that length of trip* 1884 HF xxxiii 339. (OED 4c. *colloq.* 1834.. So C U Wr. A in B T DN.II, s.e.Mo.; III, n.w. Ark.; IV,V. The adv. use not in W S)

heap, adv. **heap much**. [AB[1]] "*Heap*" is "*Injun-English*" for "*very much*" 1872 RI xxxix 276. "*She heap much hungry*," explained *Injun Billy* 1902 "DBDS" (1928) v 323 (S: A locution commonly ascribed to American Indians speaking English; e.g. from an Indian orator: "He is a big man; heap big man." So M DN.V. The peculiarly Indian usage seems rather that of the comb. *heap much* or *heap big* than of the simple *heap* as adv., which is a common colloquialism; cf. above. This usage not in OED W C. Cf. OEDS 5f. *A heap sight. U.S.* 1874..)

hear, v. Past tense **hearn**. [AE] "*You all hearn me: he's crazy, s'I; everything shows it, s'I*" 1884 HF xli 416 (A in B F Cl M DN.II,III AS.I.233,V.264. This form not given in OED W S C)

hearably, adv. [B[1]] *His lips quivered, visibly but not hearably speaking* 1898 "Stirring Times" (1900) 299 (Not in OED W S C)

hearing-orifice, sb. [B[1]] *I close-reefed my ears—that is to say, I bent the flaps of them down and furled them into five or six folds and pressed them against the hearing-orifice* 1880 TA xiii 116 (Comb. not in OED W S C)

hearse-horse, sb. [B[1]] "*He warn't distressed any more than you be...just as ca'm and collected as a hearse-horse*" 1871 SNO (1875) 247. See also *dashed* 1875 (Comb. not in OED W S C)

heart-and-heart, a. [?AB[1]] *The chill that comes upon me sometimes when I feel that long absence has made me a stranger in my own home...I see them heart-and-heart with people I do not know a*1869 Letter in Clara Clemens, *My Father* (1931) 20 (Intimate, on affectionate terms with. Comb. not in OED W S C; but cf. OEDS 51c. *Heart-to-heart*. Used to denote conversation, etc., of real frankness and sincerity. Earliest ex. U. S. 1902..)

heart-lift, sb. [B[1]] *Oh, the heart-lift that was in those words!* 1893 "Esquimau Maiden's Romance" (1900) 155 (Comb. not in OED W S C)

heart-line, sb. [B[1]] *Wilson began to study Luigi's palm, tracing life lines, heart lines, head lines, and so on* 1894 PW xi 554 (W: *Palmistry*. Comb. not in OED S C. Cf. Head-line, above)

heart-secret, sb. [B[1]] *The heart-secrets that were revealed that night* 1900 "My Boyhood Dreams" 258 (Comb. not in OED W S C)

heart-sinking, a. [B[2]] *The heart-sinking misery of it* 1876 TS xxxi 244 (OED Heart, sb. 55a. 1879. Comb. not in W S C as adj.)

heart-torturing, a. [B[1]] *I should have carried to my grave a heart-torturing uncertainty* 1883 LM li 507 (Comb. not in OED W S C)

heat-lightning, sb. [B[2]] *The heat-lightning was squirting around low down in the sky* 1884 HF xx 191 (OED Heat, sb. 14d. 1890. So W S C U)

heat-shimmer, sb. [B[1]] *You could see the quivering heat-shimmer playing over it* 1894 TSA viii 349 (Comb. not in OED W S C)

heave, v. Past tense **hove**. [?ACE] "*I heaved a brick through his window—but don't you tell*" 1876 TS vi 67. *Pretty soon he gapped and stretched himself and hove off the blanket* 1884 HF viii 64. See also *bulliness* 1884; *mud-puddle* 1884. *They said: "Oh, what a guy!" and hove clods at us* 1889 CY xi 136 (OED 9. To throw, cast. Now only *Naut.* and *colloq.* 1592..1863. So W S C U T. A in B. The past tense *hove* is called 14th c. in OED, but A in B F Cl Th M DN.II AS.III.3)

heave, v. [CE] "*Ambitions did mildew a nature erst so white...whenso it hove with the shining multitudes*" 1889 CY xxi 254 (This may be OED 12. To be moved or agitated in mind; to feel vexation. *obs.* c1400; but it is more likely that the word M.T. had in mind was *Hove*, v. OED *obs.* 2. To tarry, dwell, remain. c1220..1595, in which case he should of course have written *hoved* here. So W S C)

heaves, sb. [?AB[3]] "*It gives me the heaves just to think of it*" 1906 "Horse's Tale" 341 (OED 3. pl. A disease of horses. 1828.. So W S C U. A in Th,1793)

heavy, a. [C] "*It grieveth me, my lord the king, to bear so heavy and unwelcome tidings*" 1881 PP viii 99 (OED 12. Serious, grave. Now *rare* or *obs.* 971..1890. Not *obs* in W S C U)

heavy weight, sb. [AB[2]] *The king looked puzzled—he wasn't a very heavy weight, intellectually* 1889 CY xxviii 363 (OED b. *fig.* 'A person of weight or importance.' *U.S. colloq.* No ex. So W. Not A in S C)

heel, v. **to heel it**. [AB[1]] *Children was heeling it ahead of the mob, screaming and trying to get out of the way* 1884 HF xxii 218. *We was scared anyway, and begun to heel it back to the balloon* 1894 TSA v 126 (This sense not in OED W S C. Wr: To run off, take to one's heels. *Scotch.* A in AS.II, W.Va.)

heel-blistered, a. [B[1]] *We straggled into New London, heel-blistered, fagged with our little march* 1885 "Priv. Hist. of Campaign" 195 (Comb. not in OED W S C)

heeled, ppl.a. [AB[3]] *Her stripling brought an armful of aged sheet-music from their room—for this bride went "heeled" as you might say* 1880 TA xxxii 341. *He comes back "heeled," rams his knife into the bear* 1883 LM lx 592. "*Are you heeled—that is, fixed?*" 1894 PW xix 21 (OEDS 2. Provided, equipped; armed. *U.S. slang* 1868.. So W S C F Cl Th T DN.I,II,III AS.X.16)

heeler, sb. [AB[3]] *Our consular service was largely in the hands of ignorant, vulgar, and incapable men who had been political heelers in America* 1906 *Autob* (1924) II 159 (OED 5. One who follows at the heels of a leader or 'boss.' *U.S.* 1877.. So W S C U B F Cl Th T M AS.X.17)

heft, sb. [A] *I would beg that all crates be of the same heft* c1880 M.T. *the Letter Writer* (1932) iii 43 (OED 1. Weight. *dial* and *U.S.* 1558.. So C Wr B Cl Th DN.I,III,V AS.V.151. Not A in W S)

heft, sb. [AB[3]] "*A little for Brigham...but the heft of it for the Indians*" 1872 RI ii 26 (OED 3. The bulk, mass, or main part. *U.S. colloq.* 1816.. So W S C B Th DN.V AS.V.419)

heft, v. [AB[3]] "*And he ketched Dan'l by the nap of the neck, and hefted him*" 1865 "Jumping Frog" (1875) 35 (OED *dial* and *U.S. colloq.* 2. To lift for the purpose of trying the weight. 1816.. So S U Wr B Cl Th M DN.I,III,V AS.V.151,419. Not A in W C)

hefty, a. [AB[2]] "*Time was when she was as likely a book as any in the State, and as hefty*" 1865 SS (1926)

159. *This contract was a shade too hefty for a novice* 1889 CY xxii 272 (OED *dial* and *U.S.* Weighty, heavy; hard, grievous. 1867.. So C B Cl Th M DN.I,III,V AS.III.121, IV.80. Not A in W S)

he-he, int. [?A] See *finger-mark* 1894 (OED He, int. Repeated, as *he, he.* c1000.. So W C. A in DN.V. Not in S)

heifer, sb. [AB¹] *On the hill where Ahab, King of Judah* [sic]*, lived with his awful heifer, Jezebel* 1867 *Notebook* (1935) viii 95. *"I've always ben kind of offish and pa'tic'lar for a gal that's raised in the woods...but I reckon I'm a pretty sociable heifer after all"* 1872 RI ii 28 (W: *U.S. slang.* A woman. F: A term which, in the West, does the same duty as the kindly, if rough, "old woman" of the English lower classes. So Cl. DN.VI, Ozarks: To call a hill woman a heifer is to call her a meddlesome gossip. AS.II.46, XI.280: A young woman. The Am. uses do not seem to be covered by the def. in OED 1c. *fig.* Wife. 1609, only ex. Not in S C)

heifer-paddock, sb. [?AB¹] *Australia has a slang of its own...At the moment I can call to mind only a few of the words and phrases ... This one is not without merit: "heifer-paddock"—young ladies' seminary* 1897 FE xxii 221 (Comb. not in OED W S C. No authority supports M.T.'s Australian ascription, and it sounds suspiciously like one of his own coinages. Cf. above)

hell, sb. [?A] *"They say he is hell when he gets started!" "Yes," I said, "I have heard that he is a great speaker."* 1885 *Autob* (1924) I 16. *"It's a charming town, with a hell of a hotel...It's the worst hotel in Australia"* 1897 FE xxxi 291 (OEDS 4d. Infernal; also exceedingly bad, great, loud, etc. 1778..1922. A in M AS.VI.434. This use not in W S C)

hell-bent, a. [AB³] *To use an expression which is commonly ignored in polite society, they were "hell-bent" on stealing some of the luscious-looking oranges* 1860 *Letters* (1917) I ii 47 (OEDS *U.S.* 'Fiendishly' determined. 1835.. So W C Th.III M H DN.III,IV AS.VI.434, VIII.1.81. Not in S)

hell-box, sb. [?AB²] See *comp* 1909 (OED A term for a box for holding damaged or broken type. No ex. So W S C. A in F: The counterpart of the "batter-slipper" of the English printing-offices. So Cl T M)

hell-brand, sb. [B¹] *"They came from Satan. I saw the hell-brand on them"* 1899 "MCH" (1900) 67 (Comb. not in OED W S C)

hellfired, a. [?A] *"He said it was the hellfiredest nightmare he ever struck!"* 1902 "Belated Russian Passport" (1928) 195 (OED 2. As an intensive: Damned. 1756, only ex. Not in W S C. Cf. all-fired, above)

hellion, sb. [AB³] *What a silky smooth hellion she was!* 1889 CY xvii 206. *This thundering rabble of new recruits at Blois...unspeakable hellions, every one* 1895 JA II xi 465 (OEDS *U.S. colloq.* A troublesome or disreputable person. 1845.. So S Wr B Cl Th T M DN.I,II,III AS.II.357, W.Va.;VIII.1.81, n.e.Mo. Said in AS.VI.435, VII.240 to have originated among the Mormons, which seems improbable. Not A in W. Not in C)

hell-matter, sb. [?AB²] *I put the good type in his case and the broken ones among the "hell-matter"* 1886 *Speeches* (1910) 182 (OED The broken or battered type in the 'hell-box.' This quot., only ex. So S C. A in F Cl. Comb. not in W. Cf. hell-box, above)

hello, int. [?AB¹] *Tom hailed the romantic outcast, "Hello, Huckleberry"* 1876 TS vi 64. *I used to wake and say, "Hello, Central"* 1889 CY xv 183 (C: A mere greeting between persons meeting. So W S. A in M. This familiar *colloq* Am. use does not seem to be covered by the def. in OED: An exclamation to call attention; also expressing some degree of surprise, as on meeting any one unexpectedly. 1883..)

hello-girl, sb. [AB¹] *The humblest hello-girl...could teach the highest duchess* 1889 CY xv 176 (S: *U.S.*

colloq. A young woman telephone operator. So M. Not A in W. Comb. not in OED C)

hell's-mint, sb. [AB¹] *"He's come back to the Forks with jist a hell's-mint o' whoop-jamboree notions"* 1873 GA i 21 (A in B: An immense quantity, *Tennessee.* Cf. Wr: *Hell-mint:* unnatural and unseasonable growth. Comb. not in OED W S C)

helm, sb. [C] *They bruised their helms and their hauberks* 1889 CY xv 181 (OED 1. A helmet. Now poet and arch. c725..1870. So W S C U)

helm-a-lee, int. [B²] *"Hellum-a-lee—hard a port! Stand by to meet her when she comes!"* 1876 TS xiii 116 (OED Helm, sb. 1c. The call of the helmsman when his helm is hard down in tacking. 1880, only ex. So W S C)

help, sb. [AB³] *If they had been hired "help"* 1872 RI xii 107. *The "help" are all natives; they talk Italian to me; I answer in English* 1904 "Italian without a Master" (1906) 171 (OED 3d. The body of servants belonging to a farm or household. *U.S.* 1817.. So W S C U B F Cl Th M H DN.I,III,V AS.IX.207)

help, v. Past tense **holp**, participle **holpen**. [?ACE] *"Of a truth I was right—he hath holpen in a kitchen!"* 1881 PP xix 241. *Then they holp up their father* 1889 CY xix 253 (OED These forms *arch.* So W S C U Wr. A in B F Cl DN.II AS.II.357, W.Va.; III.3,V.264, Ozarks)

help, v. **so help me!** [?AB¹] *"It's jes' de truth, en nothin' but de truth, so he'p me!"* 1894 PW ix 549 (C: A minced oath, for *so help me God.* This clipped form of the phr. not in OED W S)

hemp-colored, ppl.a. [B¹] *I shall recognize her by... the plaited tails of hemp-colored hair hanging down her back* 1880 TA xxii 208 (Comb. not in OED W S C)

herb-doctor, sb. [?AB¹] *An old slave, who was a sort of an herb doctor* 1901 "Osteopathy" (1910) 255 (W: One who cures or professes to cure by means of herbs. So S C Wr. Not in OED)

her-blam, int. [B¹] *Whoop! the tailor lands her-blam!* [German, *Bauz!*] 1891 *Slovenly Peter* (1935) 16 (Nonce comb. Cf. *ker-*, prefix, below)

heredities, sb.pl. [B¹] *Every man is made up of heredities* 1892 AmCl xix 193 (This *concrete* use not in OED S C; but cf. W: That which is derived by hereditary transmission)

hern, poss.pron. [?ACE] *When we got home Aunt Sally...give me one of them lickings of hern that don't amount to shucks* 1884 HF xli 416 (OED *obs* exc. southern and midland dials. 1340..1876. So W. S: *Prov. Eng.* and *U.S.* So C. A in Wr Th M DN.II, III,V AS.III.5,V.267, Ozarks; XI.351, e.Texas)

hero-heart, sb. [B¹] *Her hero-heart was a young girl's heart, too* 1895 JA II xviii 752 (Comb. not in OED W S C)

herumfrodite, sb. [?AB¹E] *One of the most trying defects which I find in these thugs, these herumfrodites, these blatherskites, is their spirit of irreverence* 1909 ISD xii 134 (Not in OED W S C. Cf. OED Hermaphrodite, sb. 1b. An effeminate man, a-catamite. 1594.. Also *erron.,* 15th and 16th c., hermofrodite. Wr: Morfreydite, morfradite, moffery, morfrey, etc. Cf. Morfrodite, A in B DN.I,III,V AS.III.5; Morphadyte, morphydyke, AS.XII.160. This particular deformation of the word, though not quite identical in spelling, was [perhaps suggested by Kipling; cf. his line "For he's a giddy harumfrodite," referring to the marine, in *Seven Seas,* 1896)

hic, int. [?AB²] *He now came reeling forward...saying "Nice ('ic!) nice old boy"* 1875 SNO 132 (OED An imitation of the sound of a hiccup, esp. as an interruption in the speech of a drunken person. 1898. So W S C Wr)

hickory, sb. [A] *A dense growth of ash, oak, gum, and hickory* 1883 LM App. A 597 (OED 1. A North American tree. 1653.. So W S C U B F Cl Th T M DN.I AS.IV.8)

hickory, sb. [AB³] *But by and by pap got too handy with his hick'ry, and I couldn't stand it* 1884 HF vi 38. See *dust* 1884. *"I lay I'll excuse you—with a hickory!"* 1896 TSD i 345 (OED 2b. A rod, stick, or the like made of this wood. 1805.. So W U Th DN.II,III,IV AS.V.18, Ozarks; XI.315. This sense not in S C)

hickory-bark, sb. [AB¹] *"A hickry-bark ladder don't cost nothing and don't waste nothing"* 1884 HF xxxv 360 (A in W S. Comb. not in OED C)

hickory-nut, sb. (A) *A bullet as big as a hickory nut* 1901 *Speeches* (1910) 142 (OED Hickory, sb. 4b. 1683.. So W S C B F Cl DN.IV. Cf. above)

hickory-tree, sb. [A] *In a corner of the front yard were a dozen lofty hickory trees* 1897-8 *Autob* (1924) I 99 (OED Hickory, sb. 1. 1682.. Comb. not in W S C. Cf. above)

hiding-quarters, sb. [B¹] *We slid the raft into hiding-quarters for the day* 1884 HF xx 193 (Comb. not in OED W S C)

hide up, v.trans. [?AB¹] *"It's reckoned he left three or four thousand in cash hid up som'ers"* 1884 HF xxiv 241 (Cf. OED 2b. *intr.* To conceal oneself. Also with *up.* 1872. Comb. not in OED W S C in *trans.* sense. Given in Wr)

hie, v. [C] *"Hie thee hither"* 1881 PP x 117 (OED 3b. *refl.* To hasten. *obs.* a1300..1649. So U Wr. Not *obs* in W S C)

hifalutin, sb. [AB³] *He made the minister...read his funeral sermon...making him scratch out every bit of brag about him, and all the hifalutin* 1871 SNO (1875) 248 (OED Highfalutin. orig. *U.S. slang.* A. sb. Absurdly pompous speech or writing; bombast. 1848.. So C Cl Th.III T M. Not A in W S U)

hifalutin, a. [AB²] *Somebody ripped out something hifalutin* 1856 *Adv. of T. J. Snodgrass* (1928) 12. *"Who told you you might meddle with such hifalutin foolishness?"* 1884 HF v 31. (OED Highfalutin. orig. *U.S. slang.* B. adj. Absurdly pompous or bombastic in style. 1857.. So C B F Cl Th,1854 T M DN.III,IV,V. Not A in W S U)

higgledy-piggledy, a. [?A] *Before I get to the higgledy-piggledy point, as Mr. Howells suggested I do, I want to thank you* 1902 *Speeches* (1910) 364 (OEDS Confused, jumbled. Earlier U.S. exs. 1662.. A in DN.IV. Not A in W S C U Wr)

high, sb. [AB³] See *seven-up* 1869 (One of the six "points" that may be scored in the Am. game of seven-up or high-low-jack. Cf. OEDS 3. *Cards.* The ace or highest trump out. 1814.. So W S C U)

high, sb. **how is that for high?** [AB³] *"Buck was always nifty himself, and so you bet his funeral ain't going to be no slouch,—solid silver door-plate on his coffin, six plumes on the hearse, and a nigger on the box in a biled shirt and a plug hat,—how's that for high?"* 1872 RI xlviii 334 (OEDS An exclamation inviting admiration; in allusion to the card called the high in the game of high-low-jack. *U.S. colloq.* 1871.. So B F Cl DN.III. Phr. not in W S C)

high, a. **high times.** [?AB³] *"High Times in the Valley of Holiness!"* 1889 CY xxvi 338 (OEDS 16. Earlier exs., all U.S., of the phrases *high old time* and *high time.* Elated, merry, hilarious. 1833.. Not A in W U. Phr. not in S C)

high-ceiled, a. [B¹] *They are like long, narrow, high-ceiled bird-cages hung against the building* 1880 TA ii 27 (Comb. not in OED S C. Given in W)

high-collared, a. [AB¹] *Grandpa and grandma... stiff, old-fashioned, high-collared, puff-sleeved* 1883 LM xxxviii 404 (A in DN.III. Not A in W. Comb. not in OED S C)

high-grade, a. [?AB²] *Only the few are educated up to a point where high-grade music gives pleasure* 1880 TA xxiv 237 (OED High, a. 22a. 1890. So W S C. A in Th.III)

high-keyed, a. [B²] *Explosion followed explosion... reports grew steadily sharper and higher-keyed* 1883 LM li 502 (OEDS High, adv. 10a. 1906. So W S C)

high-laced, a. [B¹] *These wore...hobnailed high-laced walking-shoes* 1880 TA xxxiv 368 (Comb. not in OED W S C)

high-light, sb. [?AB¹] *"There's a Brooklyn preacher by the name of Talmage...He says that the first thing he does when he gets to heaven will be to fling his arms around Abraham, Isaac, and Jacob, and kiss them and weep on them...They ain't any fonder of kissing the emotional high-lights of Brooklyn than you be"* 1908 "Capt. Stormfield" 268 (A person of prominence. This sense not in OED W S C; but cf. OEDS 2. *fig.* A 'bright,' prominent, or outstanding feature or characteristic. 1905..)

high-low-jack, sb. [?AB²] *"We went to playing high-low-jack for dimes"* 1896 TSD iv 352 (Another name for the Am. game of seven-up. So W S C. Defined in OED as = All-fours. No ex.)

high-mightiness, sb. [?AB¹] *"Do you suppose it would help your high-mightiness?"* 1881 *Speeches* (1910) 259 (Comb. not in OED W S C; but cf. OED Mightiness, sb. c. As an ironical title. 1700..1883)

high muck-a-muck, sb. [AB¹] *"High Muck-a-Mucks, the paleface from the land of the setting sun greets you!"* 1869 SNO (1875) 69. *"I am a magician myself—and the Supreme Grand High-yu-Muckamuck, and head of the tribe, at that"* 1889 CY v 64 (W: Person of importance. *Slang, U.S.* So S F Cl T DN.III. Not in OED C)

high-quarter, a. [AB¹] *High-quarter coarse shoes* 1880 TA xi 102 (Comb. not in OED W S C. Cf. Wr: High-quartered, of shoes: having the 'quarter' or back part of the shoe higher than the sides)

high-river, a. [?AB¹] *In high-river stage,...the water is up to the top of the inclosing levee-rim* 1883 LM xli 423 (Comb. not in OED W S C)

high strikes, sb. [?AB³] *It just give the poor old man the high strikes. It made him sick to listen to Tom* 1893 TSA i 20 (OEDS *jocular colloq.*, orig. *dial* or *vulgar.* Perverted form of Hysterics. 1838.. This form not in W S C)

hight, v. [C] *"He hath ado with a knight of yours, that hight Egglame"* 1889 CY iii 48 (OED 5. To...be called. The archaic pa.t. *hight*...from 14th to 18th c. extended to the pres.t. *c*1340..1643. So W S C U Wr)

high-tariff, a. [B¹] *They will have high-tariff cigars* 1893 "Concerning Tobacco" (1917) 277 (Comb. not in OED W S C)

high-toned, a. [AB²] *I quit the "Era" long ago. It wasn't high-toned enough* 1864 *Letters* (1917) I v 100. See *bug* 1869; *burial-case* 1870. *"Si Higgins he's ben over to Kaintuck 'n' married a high-toned gal thar, outen the fust families"* 1873 GA i 21. *"A robber is more high-toned than what a pirate is—as a general thing"* 1876 TS xxxiv 272. See also *pirate-book* 1884 (OEDS 3b. *U.S. colloq.* Stylish, 'grand,' 'swell.' 1888.. So W S C F Cl Th.III,1857 T M H. One of M.T.'s favorite words)

high-up, a. [?AB³] *He was a high-up Son of Temperance...and she was a W.C.T.U.* 1904 "Bequest" (1906) v 28. *She knew all the birds; she was high up in that lore* 1909 "Death of Jean" (1917) 120 (OEDS *colloq* orig. *dial.* Of high place or rank. 1868.. So W Wr. Comb. not in S C)

high water, sb. [?AB¹] *In 1775 the water did not rise so high by thirty feet...These were "high-water" years* 1859 Letter in *New Orleans Daily Crescent* (W: *spec.*, the water of...a river, at its ordinarily highest flow. So S. This river sense not in OED C. Cf. OED The state of the tide when the surface of the water is highest. 1626..)

high water, a. [?AB¹] *Then some soldiers with bob-tailed tin coats on—high water coats we used to call 'em in Keokuk—come in, then some gals, with high water* *dresses on* 1856 *Adv. of T. J. Snodgrass* (1928) 9 (Short, abbreviated. This sense not in OED W S C)

high-water-stained, ppl.a. [?AB¹] *A group of high-water-stained, tumble-down cabins* 1883 LM xxx 326 (Comb. not in OED W S C. Cf. above)

highway, sb. [B¹] *For the first time in many years I am on the Highway, i.e., the platform, giving readings from Huck Finn and other of my books* 1884 *M.T. the Letter Writer* (1932) i 24 (This sense not in OED W S C)

highwayman-term, sb. [B¹] See *hold-up* 1897 (Nonce comb.)

hill-city, sb. [B¹] *We used to plow past the lofty hill-city, Vicksburg, down-stream* 1883 LM xxxv 375 (Comb. not in OED W S C; but cf. OED Hill-town, 1887)

Himalayan, a. [?AB²] "*An officer of the U.S. government, of perfectly Himalayan official altitude*" 1873 GA xxviii 256 (OED 2. *fig.* Enormous, gigantic. Only ex. U.S. 1878. The *fig* sense not in W S C)

hinder, v. Spelled **hender**. [?AE] "*I would give anything if I could do that*"..."*And what's to hender?*" 1894 TET iv 354 (OED This sp. 14th and 15th c. Given as *dial.* in W Wr. A in DN.I,III,V. Not in S C)

hindquarters, sb. [B¹] "*Why, our headquarters would be in Constantinople and our hindquarters in Further India!*" 1873 GA viii 89 (Hum. nonce use)

hired girl, sb. [AB³] *Churches,—the kind that the poor Irish "hired girl" delights to erect* 1883 LM lx 585 (OED b. In U.S. commonly applied to free women engaged as servants. 1820.. So W S Th,1800 M H DN.III AS.VI.232 *Nation* LXII.157. Not in C)

hire out, v. [AB³] *If agreeable, I will hire out to you for some years in that line* 1864 SS (1926) 135 (OEDS 3b. *U.S.* and *Colonial.* 1833.. Not A in W S C)

his'n, poss.pron. [?AE] "*I think of that last fight of his'n*" 1865 "Jumping Frog" (1875) 17 (OED *dial.* 1410..1845. So W Wr. A in S C Th M DN.II,III,V AS.III.5; V.267, Ozarks; XI.351, e.Texas)

hi-spy, sb. [?A] *They had an exhausting good time playing "hi-spy"* 1876 TS xxix 217 (OED Hy-spy, I spy. A boy's game played in many parts of Great Britain and of the United States. 1777.. A in Cl DN.I,IV. Not A in W S C)

history-building, vbl.sb. [B¹] *In history-building a fact is better than a presumption* 1909 ISD 54 (Comb. not in OED W S C)

history-creating, ppl.a. [B¹] *Slade with his history-creating revolver* 1872 RI x 82 (Comb. not in OED W S C)

historyless, a. [B¹] *When we read the praises bestowed by Lord Penzance...and try to fit them to the historyless Stratford stage-manager, they sound wild, strange, incredible.* 1909 ISD ix 113 (Not in OED W S C)

history-making, a. [B²] *On Thanksgiving Day the setting was a history-making one* 1898 "Stirring Times" (1900) 333 (OED History, sb. 9. No ex. Comb. not in W S C)

history-mill, sb. [B¹] *Sir Kay...began to fire up on his history-mill with me for fuel* 1889 CY iv 54 (Nonce comb.)

history-sodden, a. [B¹] *We missed one of the most picturesque and gigantic and history-sodden masses of constellated medieval ruin that Europe can show* 1891 *Letters* (1917) II xxxi 555 (Comb. not in OED W S C)

history-tank, sb. [B¹] *When they get hold of a presumption-tadpole he is not going to stay tadpole in their history-tank* 1909 ISD ix 110 (Nonce comb.)

hitch, v. **to hitch teams together.** [AB¹] "*Give me your hand, my boy...We'll hitch teams together, you and I*" 1892 AmCl ii 35 (A in Th,1855: to go into partnership, agree to collaborate. Given in slightly dif. sense in OED 5d. To agree, get on well together. *U.S. colloq.* 1837.. So B DN.III. Phr. not in W S C)

hive, v. [?AB¹] *We used to go charging down on hog-drivers, but we never hived any of them* 1884 HF iii 19.

The boys come to be anxious for me to hive those ogres 1889 CY x 133. *Two men...With their hooks and sticks contrive The struggling dunderhead to hive, And soon they fish him out alive* 1891 *Slovenly Peter* (1935) 23 (To capture, secure, rescue. This sense not in OED W S C)

hi-yi, int. [AB¹] *The cracking of the driver's whip, and his "Hi-yi! g'lang!"* 1872 RI iii 31 (A in DN.III, sp. *hi-i*, s. Ind., n.w. Ark.; DN.V, sp. *high yi*. Not in OED W S C; but cf. OED Hi, int. *c*1475)

hock-joint, sb. [B¹] See *ear-socket* 1880 (Hum. *transf.* use for human ankle. For lit. sense cf. OED 1874. Comb. not in W S C)

hoe-cake, sb. [A] See *biscuit* 1880 (OED *U.S.* orig. cake baked on the broad thin blade of a cotton-field hoe. OEDS 1774.. So W S C B F Cl Th T M H DN.II,III)

hog, sb. **to go the whole hog.** [?AB³] *As long as I was in, and in for good, I might as well go the whole hog* 1884 HF xxxi 321 (OED 11b. To go all the way; to do the thing thoroughly. *slang.* 1830.. So W S C U. OED claims a British origin for the phr.; but cf. Th,1828: The phrase became current in the Andrew Jackson campaign. A in B M AS.II.48,355)

hog, sb. **hog and hominy.** [AB³] "*Madame, avez-vous du vin...horseradish, sour-crout, hog and hominy—anything, anything in the world that can stay a Christian stomach?*" 1869 IA x 94. *They kept him loaded up with hog and hominy* 1896 TSD ix 522 (OEDS 1c. *U.S.* Pork and Indian corn. 1816.. So W S B F Cl Th DN.II,III. Comb. not in C)

hog, v. [AB²] See *chaw,* v. 1884. "*So,*" says I, "*s'pose somebody has hogged that bag on the sly?*" 1884 HF xxvii 275. "*I says to myself, I'll hog them di'monds |the first chance I get*" 1896 TSD iii 350 (OED 5. To appropriate greedily or selfishly. *U.S. slang* 1887.. So S C F Cl Th M DN.II, IV,V. Not A in W U)

hog-chain, sb. [?AB²] *They ran races up and down the deck, "skinned the cat" on the hog-chains* 1873 GA iv 43 (OED A chain in the nature of a tension rod passing from stem to stern of a vessel. 1875, only ex. So W S. A in C: Used chiefly in American river- and lake-steamers)

hogglebumgullop, sb. [B¹] See *kahkahponeeka* 1880 (Hum. invention)

hog-wallow, sb. [?AB³] *By Fontainebleau and scores of other beautiful cities we swept, always noting the absence of hog-wallows, broken fences, cowlots, unpainted houses, and mud* 1869 IA xii 112. *Nowhere [in Bermuda] is there dirt or stench, puddle or hog-wallow...It is the tidiest country in the world* 1877 "Some Rambling Notes" iii 720 (OED 13. A hollow or ditch in which pigs wallow. OEDS Earlier U.S. exs. 1829.. A in W Th.III M DN.III. Cf. H: In Am. *hog* virtually takes the place of the Eng. *pig...*and Am. *hogpen*=Eng. *pigsty.* Not A in S. This sense not in C. Another sense is given in OED 13: Also, *spec.* in U.S., a natural depression having this appearance. 1840.. This *spec* sense is given as A in W S C B F Cl Th T M. But M.T. clearly has in mind here the artificial and not the natural hog-wallow)

hog-wash, sb. [?A] See *soul-butter* 1884. *A splendid literature charms us; but it doesn't charm me any more than its opposite does—"hog-wash" literature* 1906 *Autob* (1924) I 324 (OED b. Contemptuously applied to weak inferior liquor or any worthless stuff. 1712.. 1883. So W S C U. A in DN.III)

hoist, v. Spelled **hyste**. [?AB²E] "*Dan'l give a heave, and hysted up his shoulders*" 1865 "Jumping Frog" (1875) 19. See also *sofa-back* 1894. (OEDS 1. In later use freq. without implication of effort or of much elevation. 1873.. This sense not in W S C. The pron. indicated by the sp. *hyste*, not mentioned in OED S C, is given as A in M DN.I,II,III,IV,V AS.XI.35)

hoist, v. [?AB³?C] *"I lay I'll take and hyste some of them preachers out of here"* 1865 SS (1926) 179 (OEDS 1d. *fig.* U.S. exs. 1834.. A in B F M. *Obs* in W in the sense: To lift and bear off, remove. This sense not in S C)

hoist, sb. [?AB¹] *In next Galaxy I give Nasby's friend and mine from Philadelphia a "hyste"* 1870 *Letters* (1917) I x 173. *"Give Tommy another highst!"* [i.e., a kick] 1894 TET v 377 (W: A lift; a boost. *colloq.* So S. Cf. B: Hyst, a violent fall; so F T. This sense not in OED C)

hoisting-works, sb. [B¹] *Bendigo* [Australia] *does a great quartz-mining business...The town is full of towering chimney-stacks and hoisting-works, and looks like a petroleum-city* 1897 FE xxv 241 (Comb. not in OED W S C)

hold, v. Past participle **holden.** [?ACE] *He smote... Arthur with his sword holden in both his hands* 1889 CY xlii 536 (OED This form *arch. a*1240..1868. So W C U. Not *arch* in S. A in F Cl AS.V.265, Ozarks)

hold, v. [C] *"Hold, hold, good sir—prithee, wait a little!"* 1881 PP xxiv 291 (OED 27. As an exclamation: Stop! *arch.* 1589..1818. So U Wr. Not *arch* in W S C)

hold, sb. [?AB¹] *Mr. Barnum had them* [the Siamese twins] *and they were just fresh from Siam. The ligature was their best hold then* 1888 *Speeches* (1910) 168 (Attraction, title to attention or consideration. This sense not in OED W S C. An extension from OED 3. *fig.* A grasp which is not physical. *a*1300.. Cf. holt, below)

hold down, v. [AB³] *"You won't be holding the ash-barrel down"* 1892 AmCl vi 69 (OEDS 35c. To continue to occupy a place or post. *U.S. colloq.* 1891.. So H. Not A in W. This sense not in S C)

hold on, v. [?AB³] *"Hold on there, Evangeline; what are you going to do with them?"* 1877 *Speeches* (1910) 6. *"Hold on, hold on! Collar all these four men"* 1884 HF xxix 305. *"Hold on, I tell you, and let me finish"* 1894 PW xiv 780 (OEDS 40e. Stop! wait! *colloq.* 1846.. So W S C Wr. A in B T M DN.III, n.w.Ark.)

hold on, v. [?AB³] *She set her iron will...and said she would hold on for five points more if she died for it* 1904 "Bequest" (1906) viii 45 (OED 40c. *intr.* To keep one's hold or grasp on something; to cling on; also *fig.* 1830.. So W S C U Wr. Cf. To hold on like grim death, A in Th,1848)

hold on, v. [?AB¹] *"Jim, how did you run Plum Point, coming up?" "I started out...and held her on the cabin under Plum Point till I raised the reef, then straightened up for the middle bar"* 1875 OTM 221 (To hold or keep the course of a vessel on or in the direction of. This sense not in OED W S C)

hold over, v. [AB²] *"You ruther hold over me, pard. I reckon I can't call that hand"* 1872 RI xlvii 332 (OEDS 42c. *U.S. colloq.* from Poker. 1872, this quot. So F Cl T. This sense not in W S C)

hold up, v. [AB³] *"Bail up" and "stick up"—equivalent* [in Australia] *of our highwayman-term to "hold up" a stage-coach or a train* 1897 FE xxii 221 (OED 44e. *U.S.* 1887.. So S C U F Cl Th T M H. Not A in W)

hold up, v. [AB³] *She was quite tuckered out and had to hold up* 1896 TSD vi 359 (OED 44h. To check oneself. *U.S. colloq.* 1843.. This *intr.* use not in W S C)

holler, v. [A] *They "holler" fire sometimes* 1862 *Letters* (1917) I iii 67. *Through the fog of battle Tom appeared, seated astride the new boy, and pounding him with his fists. "Holler 'nuff!" said he* 1876 TS i 24. *"Pile it on and sock it to him—he won't even holler"* 1883 LM xliii 438. *The old man hollered and asked me whether I was asleep or drownded* 1884 HF vi 42 (OEDS *dial* and *U.S.* 1699.. So W Wr B Cl M DN.I,III,V AS. II.357. Not A in S C)

hollow, sb. [?A] *We used to go down the river three miles to the cave hollow* 1906 *Autob* (1924) II 215. As first published in 1907 "Chaps. from Autob" 165, there was added to the above in parentheses: *"Mis-*

sourian for valley." See Prof. Delancey Ferguson's comment on this and other omissions made by Mr. Paine, *Am.Lit.* VIII.43 (OED 2. *spec.* A valley, a basin. 1553..1885. So W S U. A in C: Used in many place-names in the U.S. So M DN.VI AS.V.162)

holophotal, a. [B¹] *"Considerations concerning the alleged subterranean holophotal extemporaneousness"* 1906 "Simplified Spelling" 220 (Nonsense use. Cf. OED: Reflecting or refracting all, or nearly all, the light. 1850..)

holt, sb. [AB³] *"He was the handyest man about takin' holt of anything that come along"* 1865 SNO (1875) 74. *Livy laid her japonica down to get a better "holt" for kissing* 1875 *Letters* (1917) I xv 252. *The man left me a-holt of the rope* 1884 HF xxxi 323 (OED An unexplained phonetic variant of Hold, sb. OEDS *U.S. dial.* 1825.. So S C Th M DN.I,III,IV,V. Not A in W)

holt, sb. [?AB¹] *"I've done considerable in the doctoring way in my time. Layin' on o' hands is my best holt"* 1884 HF xix 183 (Specialty, title to attention or consideration. This sense not in OED W S C. Cf. hold, sb., above)

holy, a. [?AE] *Pants "holy" at the knees* 1894 PW iv 330 (OED var. of Holey, 14-17th c. *Dial* in Wr. This form not in W S C. Cf. OED Holey: The *e* is retained, to distinguish it to the eye from Holy. A in DN.III)

holy grail, v. [B¹] See *grail,* v. 1889 (Hum. nonce use)

holystone, v. [B¹] See *Eddyty* 1899 (Hum. nonce use)

homage-payer, sb. [B¹] *Each has his group of homage-payers* 1902 "Does the Race of Man Love a Lord?" 436 (Comb. not in OED W S C)

homeful, a. [B¹] *The farm-houses looked snug and homeful* 1893 TSA ii 28 (Not in OED W S C)

home-guard, sb. [AB³] *He was captain of the home-guards in Hawkeye* 1873 GA xviii 170 (OEDS a. A member of a local volunteer force. *U.S.* 1862.. So Th.III. Not A in W. Comb. not in S C)

home-knit, a. [B¹] *He had home-knit galluses* 1884 HF xix 182 (Comb. not in OED W S C; but cf. OED Home-woven, 1888)

homely, a. [?A:C] *The king said it was all the more homely and more pleasanter for these fixings* 1884 HF xxvi 258 (OED 3. Characteristic of home as the place where one receives kind treatment. Now *rare* or *obs.* c1375..1867. Not *rare* or *obs* in W S C U. A in DN.III, e.Ala. AS.X.79, Okla.)

homely, a. [?A] *"She is not tall, she is short; she is not beautiful, she is homely"* 1869 IA I 531. *We should have seen the homely rag carpet turn to noble Brussels* 1904 "Bequest" (1906) iv 23 (OED 5. Not beautiful, 'plain,' uncomely. 1590..1886. So W S C T. A in U B Cl Th M H DN.III,IV AS.V.216)

home-mate, sb. [B¹] *"Has ever a poor soldier fallen in my sight, and I not felt the grief of his home-mates in my own heart?"* 1896 JA II xiii 304 (Comb. not in OED W S C)

home of the brave, sb. [AB¹] *"With the Desert's bulk you could cover up every last inch of the United States ...Yes, sir, you could hide the home of the brave...clean out of sight under the Great Sahara"* 1894 TSA ix 355 (Phr. not in OED W S C. Cf. *Hail Columbia* and *Hark from the tomb,* above)

home-place, sb. [A] *It brought all the peaceful beauty of our old humble home-place back* 1895 JA II xxi 884 (OEDS. *U.S.* 1741.. Comb. not in W S C)

home-plate, sb. [AB¹] *She couldn't fetch the home plate* 1889 CY xxii 279 (Comb. not in OED C. Given in W S. Cf. OEDS Plate, sb. 4j. *Baseball,* 1891..)

home-shot, sb. [B¹] *It was a home shot, and made him wince* 1889 CY xxiii 287 (Comb. not in OED W S C; but cf. OED Home-thrust, 1622..; Home-truth, 1711..)

homestead, sb. [A] *I was writing to the friends at home directing them to look up a handsome homestead* *for my mother* 1872 RI xli 286 (OED 3. *U.S.* A lot of land adequate for the residence and maintenance of a family. 1693.. So U H. Not A in W S C)

home-stretch, sb. [AB³] *The poodle went sailing up the aisle* [of the church]... *he flew down the other aisle; he crossed before the doors; he clamored up the home-stretch* 1876 TS v 58. *They approached the final short dash of the home-stretch* 1880 TA xliv 516 (OEDS *U.S.* The return-stretch of a race-course. Also *fig.* 1861.. So Th.III M. Not A in W S C)

home-trail, sb. [?AB¹] See *clean out* 1867 (Comb. not in OED W S C. Cf. trail, below)

hominy, sb. [A] *That unhappy squib has deluged me with letters about potatoes, and cabbages, and hominy* 1870 CRG (1919) 31. See also *biscuit* 1880 (OED Of Am. Indian origin: Maize or Indian corn hulled and ground more or less coarsely. 1629.. So W S C U B F Cl Th T M DN.II,III,V,VI AS.IV.475)

honest, adv. [AB²] *"Tell me, Joe,—honest, now, old feller—did I do it, Joe?"* 1876 TS ix 91. *"If you'll believe me, he just set up the rest of the night—he did, honest"* 1892 AmCl xi 107 (OEDS 5b. Used to emphasize the truth of a statement. orig. *U.S. colloq.* 1876, this quot. Not A in W. This use not in S C)

honey, sb. [?A] *"Now be comforted, honey, that's a good child"* 1892 AmCl xxiv 253 (OED 5. A term of endearment. Now chiefly *Irish, Scotch,* and *Northumberland.* 1350..1832. So Wr. Not *dial* in W S C U. A in DN.II,III,V AS.IX.153)

Honorable, a. [AB²] *The people... elected the two gentlemen to... the New York legislature... Mr. O'Riley, still bearing the legislative "Hon." attached to his name (for titles never die in America, although we do take a republican pride in poking fun at such trifles), sailed for Europe* 1873 GA xxxiii 304 (OED 2b. In the U.S. it is given to members of both Houses of Congress, and of State legislatures. No ex. of this use. So W S C U B F Th M H)

honor bright, int. [?AB³] *"Honor bright, your majesty, I'm telling you the truth"* 1884 HF xxvii 277 (OED 9g. *colloq.* 1819.. So W S C. A in DN.V)

honor-reward, sb. [B¹] *It is an honor-reward, a testimonial to purity of character* 1899 "MCH" (1900) 55 (Comb. not in OED W S C)

hoodlum, sb. [AB³] *I saw some hoodlums chasing and stoning a Chinaman* 1906 "Unpub. Chaps. from Autob."* (1922) 456 (OED *U.S. slang.* A youthful street rowdy. 1872.. So S C U B F Cl Th T M DN. IV,V. Not A in W)

hoof, v. [?A] *I have to hoof it to New Jersey* 1870 SNO (1875) 200 (OED 1. *intr.* 1685..1852. OEDS Later U.S. exs. 1877.. Not A in W S C U. A in Cl Wr DN.III AS.II.45)

hoo-hooing, vbl.sb. [B²] *The clamorous hoo-hooing of its cuckoo clocks* 1880 TA xxxi 339. *How dismal was the hoo-hooing of the owls* 1897 Autob (1924) I 113 (OED Hooing, vbl.sb. 1842.. 1880, this quot, only ex. of reduplicated form. Not in W S C)

hook, sb. **on one's own hook.** [?AB³] *The captain called up the quarter-boats and said one would have to go off on its own hook* 1866 "Forty-Three Days" 107 (OEDS 16. In dependence on oneself or one's own efforts. *colloq.* 1812.. So S C. A in W B Th T DN.III AS.II.361)

hook, v. [?A] See *doughnut* 1876. *Taking sweetmeats was only "hooking," while taking bacon and hams and such valuables was plain simple stealing* 1876 TS xiii 121. *"Didn't you have it in your mind to hook the money and hide it?"* 1884 HF xxx 312 (OED 6. To steal, pilfer. 1615.. So W S C U Wr. A in B DN.III)

hook-and-ladder, a. [AB³] *Davenport has a fire-department, consisting of six hook-and-ladder companies* 1883 LM lviii 566. See also *rummy* 1894 (OEDS *U.S.,* often *attrib.* in 'hook-and-ladder company.' 1851.. So Th. Not A in W S C)

hookey, sb. **to play hookey.** [AB³] *He would not play hookey, even when his sober judgment told him it was the most profitable thing he could do* 1870 SNO (1875) 56. *"He'll play hookey from school this evening"* 1876 TS i 19. *Whenever I got uncommon tired I played hookey* 1884 HF iv 24. *"As easy as playing hookey"* 1884 HF xxxiv 351 (OEDS 1. *U.S.* school slang. 1848.. So B Cl T DN.II,III. Not A in W S C)

hoop-pole, sb. [?AB³] *In plain English, the freight thus aggrandized was hoop-poles and pumpkins* 1875 OTM 448 (OED A smooth straight sapling of green wood for making hoops. 1807.. A in S C AS.V.419. Not in W)

hoop-skirt, sb. [?AB³] *Rude travesties upon waterfalls, hoop-skirts* 1869 IA xxxviii 404. See *kerosene-lamp* 1871. *Consider the hoop-skirt. When it intruded itself upon us fifty years ago it was odious to us* 1906 "Carnegie Spelling Reform" 488 (OEDS Hoop, sb. 13b. Earlier U.S. exs. 1865.. Not A in W S C)

hoop-snake, sb. [AB³] *When they were black snakes, or belonged to the fabled "hoop" breed, we fled, without shame* 1897 Autob (1924) I 103 (OED Hoop, sb. 13b. A snake fabled to take its tail in its mouth and roll along like a hoop, *spec* the harmless *Abastor erythrogrammus* of U.S. OEDS 1840. So W S C)

hop, v. [?AB¹] *"I don't know no kings, Tom"*...*"If you was to go to Europe you'd see a raft of 'em hopping around." "Do they hop?" 'Hop?—your granny! No!' "Well, what did you say they did, for?" "Shucks, I only meant you'd see 'em—not hopping, of course—what do they want to hop for?—but I mean you'd just see 'em—scattered around, you know, in a kind of a general way"* 1876 TS xxv 193 (Tom's "faded" sense of the word not in OED S C. Cf. W: Loosely, to go; as hop along, hop to it. *Slang*)

hopow, sb. [B¹] See *kahkahponeeka* 1880 (Hum. invention)

hopping, ppl.a. [AB¹] *"Oh, my lan', old Marse was jes a-hoppin'"* 1894 PW viii 338 (W: Angry enough to hop with rage. Chiefly *dial.* Not in OED S C in this sense. Elliptical for Hopping-mad, OED *dial* and *U.S.* 1675..; so S C Wr B F Cl Th DN.III)

horizon-rim, sb. [B¹] *You soon find your long-ago dreams of India rising in a sort of vague and luscious moonlight above the horizon-rim of your opaque consciousness* 1897 FE xxxix 357 (Comb. not in OED W S C; but cf. OED Horizon-line, 1877)

horizontal, sb. **to assume the horizontal.** [B¹] *The men would drop like so many ten-pins, while Brown assumed the horizontal in the bottom of the boat* 1858 Letters (1917) I ii 37 (High-flown for 'to lie down.' Phr. not in OED W S C)

horn, sb. **to blow one's horn.** [?AB²] *Permit me to "blow my horn"* 1859 Letters (1917) I ii 43 (OEDS 13b. To blow one's own trumpet, boast, brag. 1903, only ex. Phr. not in W S C)

horn, sb. **to toot one's horn.** [?AB¹] *"Just go in and toot your horn"* 1872 RI xlvii 334 (To say one's say, speak out. Phr. not in OED W S C. Cf. above)

horn, sb. [AB¹] *I was out prospecting with pick and pan and horn, and washing a hatful of dirt here and there* 1893 "Californian's Tale" (1906) 103 (Short for horn spoon, used in assaying; cf. Paine's *Biog.* I.193. This sense not in OED W S C. Cf. the phr. *By the Great Horn Spoon,* A in AS.IV.256)

horn-blow, sb. [?AB¹] *We had missed the morning horn-blow* 1880 TA xxviii 305 (A summons to breakfast used on the farm. Comb. not in OED W S C)

horrible-looking, a. [B¹] *Blamed if he warn't the horriblest-looking outrage I ever see* 1884 HF xxiv 236 (Comb. not in OED W S C)

horse, sb. [?A] *Buck looked about as old as me—thirteen or fourteen...* "Come along, old hoss," he says 1884 HF xvii 151 (OED 4. *fig.* Applied contemptuously or playfully to a man. 1500.. So W S. A in B F Cl Th M. This sense not in C)

horse, sb. [?A] See *arrastre* 1909 (OED 11. A fault or obstruction in the course of a vein of ore. 1789.. So W S C Wr. A in AS.V.145, Colo. Cf. *horseback* in same sense, A in AS.IV.372, Penna.)

horse, sb. [?AB¹] *"There is the hog speculation. That's the horse to put up money on"* 1873 GA viii 85 (Venture, speculative risk. This sense not in OED W S C; but cf. OED 25c. Phrases and proverbs. quot. 1897, where the word is used in much the same sense)

horseback-riding, vbl.sb. [AB³] *"Horseback-riding was what the doctor had always recommended"* 1880 TA xxvi 268 (OED Used chiefly in U.S; in England, *ride, riding* are understood to be on horseback, unless otherwise expressed or implied. 1878.. Comb. not in W S C)

horse bill, sb. [?AB¹] *I can see that printing office of prehistoric times yet, with its horse bills on the wall* 1886 *Speeches* (1910) 185 (Comb. not in OED W S C)

horse-billiards, sb. [?AB²] *Horse-billiards is a fine game* 1869 IA iv 39. *The short-voyage passenger gets his chief physical exercise out of "horse-billiards"—shovelboard* 1897 FE iv 66 (OED A game played on board ship with wooden disks. These two quots. only exs. given. Not A in W S. Not in C)

horse-bite, sb. [B¹] *The horse was always biting Bowers's legs...then Bowers, already irritated by the pain of the horse-bite, would resent the laughter* 1885 "Priv. Hist. of Campaign" 197 (Comb. not in OED W S C; but cf. OED Horse-bitten, 1677)

horse-blanket, sb. [?AB³] *There was an old horse-blanket nailed against the logs at the far end of the cabin behind the table, to keep the wind from blowing through the chinks and putting the candle out* 1884 HF vi 40. See *wickyup* 1902 (OEDS U.S. exs. 1820.. Comb. not in W S C)

horse-car, sb. [AB³] *Jimmy's father stopped him from driving imaginary horse-cars one Sunday* 1880 TA xlii 488. *Driving the horse-cars, and whitewashing fences* 1889 *Letters* (1917) II xxix 521. *Away late that night we were coming up-town in a horse-car* 1893 "Travelling with a Reformer" (1900) 352 (OED 1. A tramcar drawn by a horse or horses. U.S. 1864.. So W S C B F Cl Th T DN.VI)

horse-chestnut, sb. [?AB¹] *"There is every shade of complexion: ebony, old mahogany, horse-chestnut, sorrel"* 1897 FE lxii 622 (W: A color, reddish red-yellow in hue, of low saturation and very low brilliance. Not in OED S C as color-term)

horse-feed, sb. [?AB³] *Hicks is still helping...in Vermicelli's horse-feed shed* 1893 PW intro. 223 (OEDS U.S. exs. 1831.. Comb. not in W S C)

horse-holding, vbl.sb. [B¹] *The horse-holding legend ought to be strangled; it too formidably increases the historian's difficulty in accounting for the young Shakespeare's erudition* 1909 ISD iv 46 (Comb. not in OED W S C)

horse-laughter, sb. [B³?C] *Coarse jests...accompanied with bursts of horse-laughter* 1881 PP xviii 224. *A very lively conversation punctuated with horse-laughter* 1892 AmCl xiii 132. *Here the narrator bursts into explosion after explosion of thunderous horse-laughter* 1895 "How to Tell a Story" (1900) 228 (OED Nonce word. 1821, only ex. Not a nonce word in W S C, and certainly not in M.T.)

horse-post, sb. [?AB¹] *They dragged him to the horse-post, backed him against it, and chained him to it* 1902 "DBDS" (1928) 355 (W: A hitching post. So S C. This sense not in OED; but cf. OED Horse-block, 1713)

horseshoe, sb. [?AB¹] *The water cuts the alluvial banks of the "lower" river into deep horseshoe curves* 1875 OTM 192. *A brook that never goes straight for a minute ...sometimes fetching a horseshoe three-quarters of a*

mile around 1904 *Autob* (1924) I 237 (C: A looplike bend in a river. So S. This *spec* sense not in OED W)

horse-talk, sb. [B¹] *I can name the tribe every mocassin belongs to by the make of it. Name it in horse-talk* 1906 "Horse's Tale" 327 (The language of horses. Comb. not in OED W S C)

horse-thief, sb. [?A] *This hive of horse-thieves and assassins* 1872 RI x 83. See *fire-bug* 1881. *Robbers, horse-thieves, negro-stealers, and counterfeiters* 1883 LM xxix 311. See also *squaw-man* 1906 (OEDS 1772.. A in Th,1768. Comb. not in W S C)

horse-trade, sb. [AB³] *Recording in a sprawling, ignorant hand appointments, bets, horse-trades, and so on* 1892 AmCl vii 75 (OEDS *U.S.* 1846.. Comb. not in W S C)

horsy, a. [?AB¹] *A pungent horsy odor that was almost suffocatingly powerful* 1881 PP xviii 231. *In the matter of smell he was pretty aromatic, in fact, quite horsy* 1899 "Chr.Sc. and the Book" 590 (This sense, applied to smell, not in OED W. Given in S C)

hosanna, v. [B¹] *Millions were coming to the cloudbank all the time, happy and hosannahing* 1907 "Capt. Stormfield" 47 (This *intr.* use not in OED W. Cf. OED v.trans. 1697.. Not given as verb in S C)

hospital-bird, sb. [B¹] *A loafing consumptive hospital-bird* 1904 "Italian with Grammar" (1906) 196 (Comb. not in OED W S C)

hospitalities, sb.pl. [?AB³] *In his hospitalities, he kept up its traditions* 1893 PW i 234 (OED 1b with pl. An instance of the quality. Earliest ex. U.S. 1856.. Not A in S C. This *concrete* sense not in W)

hostile, sb. [AB³] *We were in a friendly land, with the hostiles all behind us* 1895 JA I iv 94 (OEDS A hostile person; *spec. U.S.* a N.Am. Indian unfriendly to the whites. 1855.. So W S C B H AS.VII.2)

hot, a. [?AB²] See *cold* 1876 (OEDS 8a. In a game or pursuit, near the discovery of something concealed. 1882.. So W S U. This sense not in C. Cf. under Cold, above)

hot, a. [?AB¹] *By George, it was a hot race!* 1872 RI vii 63. *Showing the white feather when matters grew hot and perilous around him* 1883 LM xxvi 281 (W: Pressing hard or close, as, a hot chase. So S C U. This sense not in OED, unless it be considered to belong under OED 7. Attended with feverish or violent exertion... intense, severe, keen, etc. a1000..)

hot air, sb. [AB²] *The most airy scheme inflated in the hot air of the Capital* 1873 GA xliv 399 (OEDS 2. *slang orig. U.S.* Vaporous or boastful talk. 1899.. So C M H. U: *colloq.* Phr. not in W S)

hot and heavy, adv. [?AB¹] *I took out after the raft, hot and heavy* 1884 HF xv 126 (C: Vigorously or violently. So S. Comb. not in OED W, although this quot. is used in OEDS Hot, adv. 3)

hot-box, sb. [AB³] *It seemed as if the train would never reach Baltimore. A hot box had to be cooled at Wilmington* 1873 GA xlvi 419 (OEDS *U.S.* An over-heated journal-box. 1855.. So Th M. Not A in W C. Comb. not in S)

hotel-car, sb. [AB³] *In the hotel-car...the Major called for broiled chicken* 1893 "Travelling with a Reformer" (1900) 372 (OED A dining-car. *U.S.* 1875. So S. Not A in C. Not in W)

hotel clerk, sb. [AB³] *It is the pride of the average hotel clerk to know nothing whatever* 1880 TA App.A 582 (OEDS Hotel, sb. 4. *U.S.* 1879. Comb. not in W S C)

hotel-devil, sb. [B¹] *The hotel-devils lazily deranged a breakfast for us* 1878 *Letters* (1917) I xviii 340 (Nonce comb.)

hotelward-bound, a. [B¹] *Tourists...hotelward-bound from wild adventures* 1880 TA xxxvi 411 (Nonce comb.)

hot wave, sb. [AB³] *We have heard of the hot wave every Wednesday, per the weekly paper* 1901 *Letters* (1917) II xl 711 (OEDS *U.S.* A heat wave. 1888, only ex. So C. Not A in W. Not in S)

House, sb. [AB¹] *Habitués of the House comprehended* 1873 GA xliii 394. See also *Senate* 1873; *Captain* 1873 (C: *spec.* in the U.S., the lower house or House of Representatives. So W S F. OED 4d gives only the gen. sense as any legislative or deliberative body or assembly. 1775, first Am. ex.)

house, sb. **like a house afire.** [?AB³] *The next minute he sprung up and dropped the bridle and stood! and the horse a-going like a house afire, too* 1884 HF xxii 224 (OED 18. *colloq.* Very fast or vigorously. 1809.. So W C Wr. A in DN.II. Phr. not in S)

house-cat, sb. [?A] *He returned an answer whose curtness, vapidity, and inadequacy would have discredited the house cat* 1900 *M.T. the Letter Writer* (1932) vii 105 (OEDS Later U.S. exs. 1785-1845. Not A in U. Comb. not in W S C)

house-corner, sb. [B¹] *A mighty cask...which is propped against the house-corner on stilts* 1883 LM xli 429 (Comb. not in OED W S C)

house-emptier, sb. [B¹] *For each house-filler allotted them they (the lyceums) must hire several of his house-emptiers...There were two women who should have been house-emptiers* 1898 *Autob* (1924) I 156 (Nonce comb.)

house-filler, sb. [B¹] See above. *Olive Logan and Kate Field were recognized house-fillers for certainly two years* 1898 *Autob* (1924) I 156 (Nonce comb.)

housekeeper, sb. [?AC] *I try to appear (to strangers) to be an old housekeeper* 1870 SNO (1875) 21 (OED 1. =Householder. Now *rare* or *obs.* 1440..1833. So W S. Not *rare* or *obs* in C, and app. not so felt by M.T.)

house-minion, sb. [B¹] *He saved his house-minions from going down the river* 1893 PW iii 238 (Comb. not in OED W S C)

house-porch, sb. [AB¹] *From the house-porch the grounds sloped gradually down to the lower fence* 1899 "How to Make Hist. Dates Stick" (1917) 144 (Comb. not in OED W S C. Cf. Porch, below)

house-snake, sb. [AB²] *We went for the snakes, and grabbed a couple of dozen garters and house-snakes* 1884 HF xxxix 396. See also *garter* 1897 (OED A large harmless snake...found in N.Am. No ex. So W S C)

house-thief, sb. [B¹] *"Why, they've stole everything they could lay their hands on...they stole flour, and candles, and candlesticks, and spoons..." "House-thieves as well?"* 1884 HF xli 419 (Comb. not in OED W S C)

housetop, sb. **on the housetop.** [B²] *Both parties prayed for the Irish cause on the housetop and blasphemed it in the cellar* 1892 AmCl xi 104 (OEDS b. *fig.* use, with allusion to Luke xii.3. 1899.. So S C. Phr. not in W)

how, interrog.adv. [AB³] *"What is that multitude of people gathered in the street for? How?—'looking at the lightning-rods!' Bless my life, did they never see any before?"* 1870 SNO (1875) 25. *"Did you mean to?" "How?" The widow was a little embarrassed again... "I thought it might be a mistake"* 1894 TET ii 338 (OED 4. In U.S. colloq. speech 'How?' is used in asking for the repetition of something not quite understood. 1846.. So B F Cl M DN.III AS.VIII.1.76, a quot. from N.Y., 1833. Not A in W S C T)

howdah, sb. [B¹] *I shall come escorted by a troop of native howdahs richly clad* 1895 *Letters* (1917) II xxxv 629 (Nonsense use. Cf. ayah, above)

howdah-house, sb. [B¹] *In the howdah-house there were many howdahs that were made of silver* 1897 FE xlv 411 (Comb. not in OED W S C)

howdy, sb. [?AC] *Tell Marie and Ete "howdy" for me* 1857 Letter in *Iowa Journ. of Hist.* (1929) 411. *"Children, it's your cousin Tom! tell him howdy"* 1884 HF xxxii 330 (OED Now *obs.* or *dial.* 2. 1575..1894. A in C: A colloq. greeting, now almost peculiar to the so. and w. U.S. So S B T DN.I,II,III,V, Ky., s.e.Mo., n.w.Ark. Not A in W)

howdy-do, sb. [?AB³] *"That would be a pretty howdy-do, wouldn't it!"* 1884 HF xxxv 360 (OED 3. A 'business;' an embarrassing or awkward state of things. 1835.. So W S C. A in DN.III)

howitzer, sb. [B¹] *He [the Canon] was nothing more than a kind of mountain howitzer, likely, because they had no heavy artillery in those days* 1869 IA xv 142 (Hum. nonce use. Cf. canon, sb., above)

howler, sb. [?AB¹] *He ran a bold tilt against total abstinence and the Red Ribbon fanatics...By the time my letter reached him, he was already winning laurels as a Red Ribbon Howler* 1879 "Pen-Picture of His Brother" (1917) 352 (A vociferous advocate or supporter. This sense not in OED W S C)

howling, ppl.a. [?AB¹] *"Le's all three slide out of here one of these nights and get an outfit, and go for howling adventures amongst the Indians"* 1884 HF, last chap. 437. *"It's just a howling outrage!"* 1892 AmCl xix 195 (W: Extreme, great. So S C U Wr. M.T.'s use is hardly covered by the def. in OED 3. *fig.* chiefly *slang.* Glaring, very pronounced, 'screaming.' 1865..)

howsoever, adv. [?AC] *I wish to lay before the nation what share, howsoever small, I have had in this matter* 1870 SNO (1875) 101 (OED *arch.* 2b. 1696, 1751. Not *arch* in W S C U)

hub, sb. **up to the hub.** [AB³] *"I'm in, up to the hub, for anything that will pay"* 1884 HF xx 194 (OEDS 2. In Am. use: deeply, to a great extent, inextricably involved. 1800.. So W Th. Not A in S. Phr. not in C)

huckleberry, sb. [AB¹] *The juvenile pariah of the village, Huckleberry Finn, son of the town drunkard* 1876 TS vi 63. *Huckleberry Finn* (title) 1884 HF. *"The Saracen...is no huckleberry"* 1889 CY xxvi 338 (Cf. OED *U.S.* A low berry-bearing shrub common in N.Am. 1670.. So W S C B F Th DN.I,III. Here used as a symbol or type of something worthless or disreputable. This sense not in OED W S C; but cf. OEDS Persimmon, sb. 3. *To be a huckleberry above one's persimmon*, 1833.. B: A quaint Southern phrase meaning that something apparently simple and easy is far above the ability of the person making the attempt. So F Cl Th)

huffy, a. [?A] *The duke stayed huffy a good while* 1884 HF xix 188 (OED 4b. Ready to take huff or offence. 1680..1890. So W S C U. A in Th DN.I,II, III,IV,V)

hula hula, sb. [AB²] *They dance the hula-hula* 1866 *Speeches* (1923) 15 (OEDS A Hawaiian women's dance. 1892.. So W S C)

hum, v. [?AB²] *"Didn't de line pull loose en de raf' go a-hummin' down de river?"* 1884 HF xv 131. *He lit into that horse with his whip and made him fairly hum* 1884 HF xxii 224. *"We'll make things hum"* 1892 AmCl ii 35 (OED 3. *colloq.* To be in a condition of busy activity, to be all astir. 1889..1898. OEDS Earlier and later U.S. exs. 1887..1914. A in C F Cl. Not A in W S U)

human, sb. [?AC] See *Dutch* 1856. *"I've never heard a jay use bad grammar but very seldom; but when they do, they are as ashamed as a human; they shut right down and leave...They got off as many leather-headed opinions as an average crowd of humans could have done"* 1880 TA ii 37. *The dogs were as still as the humans* 1884 HF xvii 149. Cf. also Clara Clemens, *My Father*, 1931, p.66: *"I remember long conversations Father and Susy used to have about the value or significance of certain words. In one instance my sister wished to use the word 'humans' for the sake of brevity in a poetic line, and Father said there was no such word"* (OED Formerly much used; now chiefly humorous or affected. 1533.. 1879. OEDS U.S. exs. 1830..1924. A in Wr B F Cl Th DN.I,II,III. Not A in W S C T)

human-beingship, sb. [B¹] *My confidence in her human-beingship is getting shaken* 1907 CS II viii 255 (Comb. not in OED W S C)

humor, sb. [D] *Humor is the saving thing, after all. The minute it crops up, all our hardnesses yield, all our resentments flit away* 1895 "What Bourget Thinks" 61. *The secret source of Humor is not joy but sorrow. There is no humor in heaven* 1897 FE x 119 (OED 7b. 1682.. 1887—. So W S C U)

humorism, sb. [B¹] *In a dream I have at last encountered a humorism that actually remained one after waking* 1897 *Notebook* (1935) 335. *His eloquent remarks were mistaken for humorisms* 1907 *Speeches* (1910) 38 (This *concrete* sense not in OED W S C. Cf. OED 2. The characteristics of a humorist; humorous style or manner. 1831)

humor-lover, sb. [B¹] *I think humor-lovers would enjoy the book* 1909 "A Capable Humorist" 13 (Comb. not in OED W S C; but cf. OED Humour-loving, 1897)

hump, v. [AB³] *I'll have to hump myself and not lose a moment* 1871 *Letters* (1917) I x 185. *Our party made this specimen "hump himself"* 1872 RI iii 32. See *pall-bearer* 1883. *"Git up and hump yourself, Jim!"* 1884 HF xi 96. *She* [Mrs. Eddy] *would have had the late proprietor on salary and humping himself, as the worldly say* 1907 CS II x 264 (OED 3. *refl.* To gather oneself together for an effort. *U.S. slang.* 1835.. So W S C Wr F Cl T DN.I,III,V)

hump, v. **to hump it.** [AB²] *I never hunted for no back streets, but humped it straight through the main one* 1884 HF xxix 307 (OEDS orig. *U.S. slang* 3b. To hurry. 1905. So W S DN.IV. This intr. use not in C)

hump up, v. [?AB¹] *I came down to help hump-up the binderies* 1885 *Letters* (1917) II xxv 465 (This *trans.* use not in OED W S C)

hunch, v. [AB³] *Then the king he hunched the duke private—I see him do it—and then he looked around* 1884 HF xxv 246 (OEDS 2c. To nudge. *U.S.* 1846.. So DN.II. Not A in W S C Wr)

hundred-faceted, a. [B¹] *Clear, cold, hard, rose-cut, hundred-faceted, diamond-flashing reasoning* 1909 ISD i 10 (Comb. not in OED W S C)

hunk, sb. [?AB³] *"Jist a hunk of brains—that is what he was"* 1871 SNO (1875) 25. *A hunk of maple-sugar* c1880 "Taming the Bicycle" (1917) 292. *"Pass me along another hunk of fish and some hot corn-bread"* 1884 HF ix 75. *An erudition he* [Shakespeare] *was acquiring hunk by hunk and chunk by chunk* 1909 ISD iv 46 (OED Known only in the 19th c. 1. A large piece cut off. 1813.. So W S C Wr T. A in B Cl DN.I,II,III,IV)

hunks, sb. [?A] *"You leave the damned hunks and come with me; don't you be afraid, I'll take care of him"* 1902 "DBDS" (1928) iv 309 (OED A surly, cross-grained old person, a 'bear.' 1602..1857. So W S C U Wr. A in DN.III,IV)

hunky, a. [AB³] *"We're all hunky, after all"* 1894 TET vii 418 (OEDS *U.S. slang.* Safe and sound. 1865.. So W C B F Cl Th.III M DN.IV. Not A in S)

hunterman, sb. [AB¹] *Behold the dreadful hunterman, In all his fateful glory stand!* [German, *Jägersmann*] 1891 *Slovenly Peter* (1935) 12 (A in AS.VIII.1.50: Hunter, Ozarks; one often sees this in country newspapers. Not in OED W S C)

hunting-ground, sb. [?A] *Does her sad spirit wander afar toward the hunting-grounds whither her brave...is gone?* 1869 SNO (1875) 69. *Every woman the avenger of her own wrongs, and all society the hunting-ground*

for her victims 1873 GA xlvi 420 (OEDS U.S. exs. 1721.. A in W. Not A in S C)

hurrah, sb. **to make a hooraw over.** [?AB¹E] See *lift the roof* 1894. *"There wasn't much of a hooraw made over you when you arrived—now was there?"* 1908 "Capt. Stormfield" 273 (To greet with enthusiasm, give a noisy reception to. Neither the phr. nor the sp. is found in OED W S C)

hurricane, sb. [A] See *burster* 1895 (OED From a Carib word. A name given primarily to the violent wind-storms of the West Indies...hence, any storm or tempest. 1588.. So W S C U B Th M AS.IV.8)

hurricane-deck, sb. [?AB³] *They sat by the hour in the shade of the pilot-house on the hurricane-deck* 1873 GA iv 41. See *boiler-deck* 1875. *A life-boat on the hurricane-deck* 1883 LM xlix 490 (OEDS A light upper deck or platform in some steamers. Earlier U.S. exs. 1835.. A in W S U B Th T. Not A in C)

husky, sb. [AB²] *That big husky had me by the wrist* 1884 HF xxix 305 (OEDS *U.S.* A strong, stoutly-built person. 1884, this quot. So S. C, Suppl.: An energetic fellow, a hustler. *Canadian Northwest.* Not A in W)

hustings, sb. [?AB³?C] *Teach one thing at the hearth-stone, the political hustings, and in a nation's press* 1886 "What American Authors Think About Copyright" 634 (OED 4. 1850.. So W S C. A in H: Now *rare* in England, because the thing it once denoted was abolished by the Ballot Act of 1872, but survives in Am. in the sense of a platform at a meeting held during a political campaign. So DN.III)

hybernian, sb. [B¹] *"It is a hybernian, for it hybernates"* 1897 FE viii 102 (Hum. nonce word)

hydraulic, sb. [?AB¹] *I don't believe you could have sluiced it out with a hydraulic* 1889 CY xi 130 (W: Short for hydraulic engine. This sense not in OED S C. Cf. OED Hydraulic mining: A method in which the force of a powerful jet of water is used to wear down a bed of auriferous gravel or earth, and to carry the debris to the sluices where the particles of gold are separated. 1873.. In quot. 1898 the engines used are called "monitors, huge squirts")

hydrocephalous, a. [B¹] *"The kangaroo and other Australian hydrocephalous invertebrates"* 1897 FE viii 106 (Nonsense use)

hyphenated name, sb. [B¹] *People of strange, hyphenated names—Six-Fingered Jake, Young-Man-Afraid-of-his-Shadow, and the like* 1892 AmCl vii 75 (Here merely any name written with a hyphen. Often used for names formed, according to a comparatively recent custom, by joining the family name of the mother and father. Comb. not in OED W S C; but cf. OED Hyphen, v., quot. 1891: "The Joneses, when their father was induced to remove from Shepherd's Bush to Kensington, showed their gratitude to their mother by hyphenating her name with their own: 'The Misses Robinson-Jones' ")

hypodermic, a. [B¹] *The past tense of the compound reflexive adverbial incandescent hypodermic irregular accusative Noun of Multitude* 1909 ISD ix 112 (Nonsense use)

hypothenuse, sb. [B¹] *He advanced the hypothenuse that the Milky Way was a detachment or corps of stars* 1895 "What Bourget Thinks" 60 (Hum. malapropism, for hypothesis)

I

ice, sb. on the ice. [?AB[1]] *"Having departed this life five days ago...he is on the ice yet, him and his brother ...I shall take immediate occasion to have their noble remains shipped to you"* 1892 AmCl i 23 (An undertaker's phrase: Preserved by refrigeration. Not in OED W S C)

ice, sb. on thin ice. [?AB[2]] *"How'd you get your breakfast so early on the boat?" It was kinder thin ice, but I says: "The captain see me standing around"* 1884 HF xxxii 333 (OED 3. In *fig.* expressions, with allusion to the slippery, cold, or brittle nature of ice. Only ex. of "thin ice" 1892. So W U. Phr. not in S C)

ice-arch, sb. [B[1]] *The great ice-arch where the mad Visp boils and surges out from under the foot of the great Gorner Glacier* 1880 TA xxxix 458 (Comb. not in OED W S C)

ice-barren, sb. [AB[1]] *The ice-barrens of Greenland* 1897 FE xlix 461 (Comb. not in OED W S C; but cf. OED Barren, sb. 3. spec. applied in N.Am. to tracts of barren land. 1784..)

ice-bead, sb. [B[1]] *Every one of the myriad ice-beads pendent from twig and branch is an individual gem* 1897 FE lix 580 (Comb. not in OED W S C)

ice-breaker, sb. [?AB[1]] *They closed up the inundation with a few words—having used it, evidently, as a mere ice-breaker and acquaintanceship-breeder—then they dropped into business* 1883 LM xxxix 412 (This *fig* sense not in OED W S C; but cf. OED Ice, sb. 2b. *To break the ice:* to break through cold reserve or stiffness. 1823.. The comb. is given in W S C only as a mechanical device for breaking ice)

ice-bridge, sb. [B[1]] *A young porter disengaged himself from the line and started across an ice-bridge which spanned a crevasse* 1880 TA xl 460 (Comb. not in OED S C. Given in W)

ice-cavern, sb. [B[1]] *The tourist should visit that ice-cavern* 1880 TA xlvi 531 (Comb. not in OED W S C; but cf. OEDS Ice-cave: a hollow in the ice at the lower end of a glacier. 1897)

ice-coated, a. [B[1]] *By and by they came to an ice-coated ridge* 1880 TA xxxiv 377 (Comb. not in OED W S C)

ice-cream, sb. [?A] See *granite* 1869. *We do not get ice-cream everywhere* [in Europe] *and when we do we are apt to dissipate* 1869 IA xxxvi 388 (OEDS Earlier U.S. exs. 1744.. A in Th. Not A in W S C U T. Cf. OED *Iced cream,* the earlier term. 1688..)

ice-crest, sb. [B[1]] *An isolated ice-crest* 1880 TA xliv 526 (Comb. not in OED W S C)

ice-factory, sb. [?AB[1]] *Like Vicksburg and New Orleans, she* [Natchez] *has her ice-factory; she makes thirty tons of ice a day* 1883 LM xxxix 410 (Comb. not in OED W S C)

ice-machine, sb. [?AB[2]] *The ice-machine has traveled all over the world, now, and brought ice within everybody's reach* 1897 FE iii 62 (OED Ice, sb. 8. A machine for the artificial production of ice. No ex. So W S C)

ice-man, sb. [AB[3]] *You have to keep a sharp eye on your ice-man* 1893 "Esquimau Maiden's Romance" (1900) 141 (OED 3. One engaged in the ice trade. U.S. 1864.. Not A in W S C)

ice-pitcher, sb. [?AB[2]] *"Take that ice-pitcher down to the texas-tender!"* 1883 LM xviii 221 (OED Ice, sb. 8. No ex. Comb. not in W. Given in S C. Cf. pitcher as A, below)

ice-storm, sb. [?AB[2]] *If we hadn't our bewitching autumn foliage* [in New England] *we should still have to credit the weather with one feature which compensates for all its bullying vagaries—the ice-storm: when a leafless tree is clothed with ice from the bottom to the top...and becomes a spraying fountain, a very explosion of dazzling jewels* 1877 "The Weather," *Speeches* (1910) 63. *Here in London the other night I was talking with some Scotch and English friends, and I mentioned the ice-storm, using it as a figure—a figure which failed, for none of them had ever even heard of the ice-storm... The oversight is strange, for in America the ice-storm is an event...The ice-storm is Nature's supremest achievement in the domain of the superb and the beautiful* 1897 FE lix 578-580 (OEDS 1886; only quot. calls the word Am. Not A in W S C)

ice-water, sb. [?A] See *sheet-bath* 1867. *America is healthier than Europe, notwithstanding her "deadly" indulgence in ice-water* 1880 TA xlvi 536. See *biscuit* 1880; *American* 1895. *Europe does not need ice-water...and yet, its word for it is better than ours...Europe calls it "iced" water. Our word describes water made from melted ice* 1897 *Autob* (1924) I 98 (OED Water cooled by ice; iced water. 1722..1797. OEDS Later U.S. exs. 1829..1906. A in M. Not A in W S C)

ice-wave, sb. [B[1]] *We crossed the Mer de Glace in safety...The huge round waves of ice were slippery and difficult to climb...A deep swale between two of the biggest of the ice-waves...* 1880 TA xlvi 535 (Comb. not in OED W S C)

ich-habe-gehabt-haben, sb. [B[1]] *"This book's Otto's grammar. It's a mighty good book to get the ich-habe-gehabt-haben's out of"* 1880 TA xxvii 281 (Nonce comb.)

identifier, sb. [B[1]] *"There was never a twin...that did not carry from birth to death a sure identifier"* 1894 PW xxi 237 (An identifying mark, in this case the finger-print. So W: One who or that which identifies. In OED S C only of a person; cf. OED One who identifies, 1889)

idiot-asylum, sb. [B[1]] *"They wanted to know if I was from the same 'establishment' that you hailed from, did they?...They meant an asylum—an idiot-asylum, do you understand?"* 1880 TA xxv 257 (Comb. not in OED W S C)

idiotcy, sb. [B[3]?C] *"You are talking nonsense—nonsense—lurid idiotcy!"* 1892 AmCl l 19 (OED irregular form = Idiocy. 1818.. So W. C: *Rare.* Not in S)

idiot-factory, sb. [B[1]] *Dilsberg is a quaint place... The seven hundred inhabitants are all blood-kin to each other...It has been said that for ages Dilsberg has been merely a thriving and diligent idiot-factory* 1880 TA xix 173 (Comb. not in OED W S C)

idlesse, sb. [C] *"I will repeat it anon in my idlesse"* 1889 CY xv 175 (OED arch. 1596..1873. So W S C)

idyllic, a. [B[1]] *The odic and idyllic forces* 1880 TA xliii 507 (Nonce use)

i'fegs, int. [C] *"Come, Kangaroo...foreshortened as to legs, And sack marsupial, i'fegs"* 1897 FE viii 107 (OED In faith. obs exc. dial. 1610..1853. So W Wr. Not in S C. Cf. Faix, above)

ignorant, a. [B[1]] *This fellow had...an ignorant silver watch and a showy brass watch-chain* 1875 OTM 71. *All over the walls was the ignorantest kind of words and pictures made with charcoal* 1884 HF ix 78. *It ought to be the ablest weather that can be had, not ignorant, poor-quality, amateur weather* 1892 AmCl, pref. (U: Of actions, conduct, etc: Springing from, due to, betokening ignorance. This *transf.* use, applied to material things, not in OED W S C)

illuminate, v. [?AB[1]] *For eight-and-forty hours no soul in all the barony but did dance and sing, carouse and illuminate, to celebrate the great event* 1871 SNO (1875) 176 (Possibly M.T. uses the word here in the sense: To get drunk, become intoxicated. So AS.IV.440, VII.88, *Am. slang.* This sense not in OED W S C; but cf. OED Lit, ppl.a. Slightly drunk, 1922)

illy, adv. [A] *It seemed to him that this fairness was but illy appreciated* 1873 GA xlv 410 (OEDS Chiefly U.S. 1549.. So B F Cl Th M H DN.V,VI AS.IV.473, V.303. Not A in W S C T)

imagination-manufactured, a. [B[1]] *The Science secures to him life-long immunity from imagination-manufactured disease* 1902 "Chr.Sc." 768 (Nonce comb.)

imagination-mill, sb. [B¹] *His imagination-mill was hard at work in a minute* 1899 "MCH" (1900) 26 (Nonce comb.)

imagination-stunning, a. [B¹] *The imagination-stunning material development of this century* 1892 AmCl x 101 (Comb. not in OED W S C; but cf. OED Imagination-stirring; no ex.)

immigrant, sb. [?A] *A solid deckload of immigrants and harvesters* 1883 LM lviii 571 (OEDS Earlier U.S. exs. *c*1787.. A in B Th AS.V.136 *Nation* LXX.10. Cf. Immigration, A in DN.VI. Not A in W S C U. Cf. Emigrant, above)

immortalities, sb.pl. [B¹] *"Give God thanks that you are father to this child, this dispenser of immortalities"* 1896 JA II xiii 302 (This *concrete* sense not in OED W S C)

immortelle, sb. [?AB¹] *A milder form of sorrow* [in the New Orleans cemeteries] *finds its inexpensive and lasting remembrancer in the coarse and ugly but indestructible "immortelle"—which is a wreath or cross or some such emblem, made of rosettes of black linen, with sometimes a yellow rosette at the junction of the cross's bars—kind of sorrowful breastpin, so to say* 1883 LM xlii 431 (This sense not in OED W S C, which know the word only as the name of a flower)

imperial, sb. [?AB³] *He cultivated a mustache and imperial, and did what else he could to suggest...that he resembled Louis Napoleon* 1869 IA xxiii 234 (OEDS 8. A small part of the beard left growing beneath the lower lip. Earlier U.S. exs. 1841.. Not A in W S C U)

Imperishable, sb. [B¹] *I am of the aristocracy of the Imperishables* 1898 MS (1916) iii 27 (Not in OED W S C as sb.)

Importance, sb. [B¹] *To place the Virgin first, the Saviour second, and Mrs. Eddy third, seems to...make it an ascending scale of Importances, with Mrs. Eddy ranking the other two and holding first place* 1907 CS II v 147 (W: A person of importance. *Humorous.* This concrete sense not in OED S C)

in, adv. [?AC] *As long as I was in, and in for good, I might as well go the whole hog* 1884 HF xxxi 321. *I couldn't venture it now; I was in too deep* 1893 "Banknote" (1928) 120 (OED 6b. Engaged, involved, entangled in an action. *obs.* 1588..1623. Not *obs* in W S C)

in, prep. **in it**. [AB¹] *They examine the historical earthquakes and cataclysms and volcanic eruptions: verdict, none of them "in it" with me* 1905 *King Leopold's Soliloquy* 26 (A in Th.III,1892: In the same class with. This sense not in OED W S C; but cf. OEDS 39b. *Nothing in it:* little or no difference between competitors, or any persons or things that are compared. orig. *Racing slang.* 1914..; so W S C)

inaugurate, v. [?AB³] *It would be well if such an excursion could be gotten up every year and the system regularly inaugurated* 1869 IA Concl. 650 (OED 4. To...initiate. Sometimes merely grandiose for 'begin.' 1851.. So W S C. OEDS: Later U.S. exs. 1905.. A in B T)

inboard, [?AB³] *The mule gave a violent lurch inboard to save himself* 1880 TA xxxv 386. *It was a long, low dog, with very short, strange legs—legs that curved inboard* 1897 FE xlv 413 (OEDS *Naut.* Towards the centre of the vessel. Earlier U.S. exs. 1830.. Not A in W S C)

inch-mark, sb. [B¹] *Having proved his trial candle's rate, he blew it out...and put his inch-marks on a fresh one* 1902 "DBDS" (1928) 343 (Comb. not in OED W S C)

incline, sb. [?AB²] *"Say you go down on it with a shaft, straight down, you know, or with what you call 'incline'"* 1872 SNO (1875) 284. See also *arrastre* 1909 (OED 2b. *Mining.* A shaft or opening into a mine having considerable inclination or slope. 1877.. So W S C)

inconsequentiality, sb. [B³?C] *You can't talk pale inconsequentialities when you've got a crimson fact* 1883 LM xlv 455. See *twin-monster* 1894 (OED 1. Inconsequence; an instance of inconclusiveness. 1832.. *Rare* in C. *Concr*. sense not in W S)

incorporatorship, sb. [AB²] *"It would be more money in my pocket, in the end, than my brother-in-law will get out of that incorporatorship, fat as it is"* 1873 GA xlii 387 (OEDS 1873, this quot. Not in W S C. Cf. OED Incorporator, *spec. U.S.* one of the original members of an incorporated body or company. 1883..)

indeedy, adv. [AB¹] See *shake*, v. 1872. *"An' d' you spec' he gwyne to let 'em off don't somebody ast him to do it? No indeedy!"* 1873 GA iii 39. *"Yes indeedy! If I ain't an American there ain't any Americans, that's all"* 1880 TA xx 192 (A in W Th,1856, DN.I,II. Not in OED S C)

indented, ppl.a. [D] See *coat-of-arms* 1883 (OED 2. *Heraldry.* Of an ordinary: Having a series of similar indentations or notches. *a*1400..1864—. So W S C)

Independence Day, sb. [AB³] *It was rung for the first time on "Independence Day"* 1853 Letter in *Iowa Journ. of History* (1929) 412 (OEDS 1841.. So W S C B Cl H)

independent, a. [?AB¹] *One is an old "independent" fireman* 1892 AmCl xvi 164 (Apparently means a volunteer fire-fighter, of the type in vogue before the days of organized "fire departments" or "hook-and-ladder companies." Cf. these expressions, above. This *spec* sense not in OED W S C)

Indian, sb. [A] See *buffalo* 1869, 1872; *tomahawk* 1870; *corn-field* 1871; *Far West* 1876; *buck*, sb. 1902 (OED 2. An American Indian. 1553.. So W S C U B F AS.IV.8)

Indian, sb. [A] See *grasshopper-soup* 1869 (OED 4. The language, or one of the languages, of the aborigines of America. 1714.. So W S. This sense not in C)

Indian corn, sb. [A] *An ear of green Indian corn* 1878 "Some Rambling Notes" iv 15 (OED Cultivated by the North American Indians. 1621.. So W S C U B F Cl Th T M DN.III,VI)

Indian doctor, sb. [AB¹] *Then there was the "Indian doctor;" a grave savage, remnant of his tribe, deeply read in the mysteries of nature and the secret properties of herbs* 1897 *Autob* (1924) I 107 (Comb. not in OED W S C)

Indian file, sb. [A] *We slid out, and stooped down, not breathing, and slipped towards the fence in Injun file* 1884 HF xl 408 (OEDS Indian, a. 4b. The same as *single file*, so called because the North American Indians usually march in this order. 1758.. So W S C U B F Cl Th T M)

Indian meal, sb. [A] *"Barley-corn, barley-corn, injun meal shorts; Spunk-water, spunk-water, swaller these warts"* 1876 TS vi 65. *Take a lot of water and add to it a lot of coarse Indian-meal* 1880 TA xlix 575 (OED Indian, a. 3. 1635.. So W S C U B F Cl M DN.III AS.IV.8,15,V.419)

Indian mound, sb. [AB³] *Troy...is situated on three large Indian mounds, circular in shape* 1883 LM App. A 600 (OEDS Indian, a. 4b. in the U.S.A. 1869. So W S C B F Cl)

Indian sign sb. [AB¹] *I know some of the Indian signs—the signs they make with their hands, and by signal-fires at night and columns of smoke by day* 1906 "Horse's Tale" 327 (Here: sign language. Not in OED W S C in this sense)

indication, sb. [?AB²] *We went and looked at the ledges, and both of them acknowledged that there was nothing in them but good "indications"* 1862 *Letters* (1917) I iii 80. *"Prospecting" is hunting for a "placer;" "indications" are signs of its presence* 1872 RI lxi 443 (OEDS 2b. *Mining.* Something which indicates the presence of valuable ore. 1873.. A in AS.V.146,Colo. This sense not in W S C)

indictive, a. [B²C] *Each sang his indictive narrative, in turn* 1880 TA ix 85 (OED 2. *rare*. Accusing; containing an indictment or charge. 1880, this ex. Not *rare* in W S. This sense not in C)

indoors, sb. [B¹] *Satisfied neither with the outdoors nor the indoors* 1873 GA xiv 132 (Not in OED W S C as sb.)

indorse, v. [AE] *"Now was the description set forth by our ancestors wonderfully indorsed and confirmed by the fossils before us"* 1875 SNO 142 (OED This form of *Endorse* is found in legal and statutory use, and in most political economists; it is also that approved in all American dictionaries. 1849.. So W S C M)

induction-talent, sb. [B¹] *Now and then, when Ealer stopped to cough, I pulled my induction-talents together and hove the controversial lead myself* 1909 ISD i 12 (Nonce comb.)

infant-schooly, a. [?AB¹] *"You can get up the infant-schooliest ways of going at a thing!"* 1884 HF xxxv 357 (Not in OED W S C. Cf. OED Infant-school, 1833)

infest, v. [?AB¹] *One may live in Vienna many months and not hear of this place; but having once heard of it and sampled it, the sampler will afterwards infest it* 1898 "At the Appetite Cure" (1900) 148 (To frequent assiduously. This sense, in which the subject may be sing., not in OED W S C. A hum. transfer from OED 2. To swarm in or about. 1602.. Cf. DN.VI: "A little cat infests us")

inflamed, ppl.a. [B¹] *A splendid flunkey, all in inflamed plush and buttons* 1892 AmCl i 22 (Hum. transferred sense: Red, scarlet. This sense not in OED W S C)

inflated, ppl.a. [?AB²] *Taking advantage of the inflated market, many operators are selling short* 1869 IA xxxviii 409 (OED 5. Raised in price by speculation. 1881.. So W S C U)

influence, sb. [?AB¹] *Nobody got in the least degree "under the influence," and we had a pleasant time* 1879 Letters (1917) I xix 367 (Here *spec*: influence of intoxicants. This sense not in OED W S C)

influential, sb. [?AB³C] *It was their official duty to entertain the influentials after some sort of fashion* 1899 "Diplomatic Pay" (1928) 235 (OED An influential person, *rare* 1831. Not in W S C. Cf. Influential, a. A in M)

ingot, sb. [B¹] *Tom Sawyer called the hogs "ingots" and he called the turnips and stuff "julery"* 1884 HF iii 19 (Hum. nonce usage)

ingrain, a. [AB³] *Ingrain carpet; mahogany center-table* 1883 LM xxxviii 400 (OED 1b. Applied, chiefly in U.S., to carpets...in which the pattern goes through and through and appears on both sides. 1863.. Not A in W S C U)

inhabit, v. [B¹] *These ladies had never inhabited such clothes before* 1899 "MCH" (1900) 32 (Hum. *transf.* use. Not in OED W S C)

inharmoniousnesses, sb.pl. [B¹] *We must not get impatient over these curious inharmoniousnesses and irreconcilabilities in Shelley's character* 1894 "In Defence of Harriet Shelley" 363 (This *concrete* sense not in OED W S C)

initiation fee, sb. [?AB²] *The initiation fee had been raised to fifty dollars* 1875 OTM 728 (OED 2b. 1890, only ex. A in H: In Am. clubs, initiation fee = Eng. entrance fee. Comb. not in W S C)

Injun, sb. [AB³E] *"That's Meredith Higgins...great-grandmother was an Injun"* 1870 SNO (1875) 199. *"The Injuns is powerful troublesome"* 1872 RI ii 26. See also *on*, prep. 1872; *land-dealer* 1873; *war-path* 1884; *Aztec* 1908 (OEDS *colloq* and dial *U.S.* form of Indian. 1812.. So W F M DN.II. This form not in S C)

Injun, sb. **honest Injun**. [AB²] *"Ben, I'd like to, honest Injun. But—"* 1876 TS ii 31. *"I said I wouldn't, and I'll stick to it. Honest injun, I will"* 1884 HF viii 67. *"Honest injun, now, hain't you been telling me a lot of lies?"* *"Honest injun,"* says I 1884 HF xxvi 262 (OEDS *colloq* and dial *U.S.* Honour bright: perhaps orig. an assurance of good faith extracted from Indians. 1876, this quot. So F DN.V. Not A in W! Comb. not in S C)

Injun-English, sb. [AB¹] *I will explain that "heap" is "Injun-English" for "very much"* 1872 RI xxxix 276 (Comb. not in OED W S C)

innards, sb. [?A] See *guts* 1898 (OED Inward, sb. 1b. pl. Now only in the *spec* sense: Entrails. a1300.. 1850. So C. *Dial* in W S Wr. This pron. in W U Wr; A in DN.III,IV, N.H. and s.e. Ohio. See note under *guts* on the change made in the wording of this passage)

inning, sb. [AB²] *Then Mary Jane she took another inning and went in sweet and lovely again—which was her way* 1884 HF xxvi 264. *The Boss scores on his first innings!* 1889 CY xxvi 338. *I saw Texas Tom make a string of seven points on a single inning!* 1907 "Chaps. from Autob" 333 (OED 4b. In Great Britain always in the pl. A turn. 1855..1885, only ex. of U.S. sing. form..So W S C. The sing. form A in M H)

inroader, sb. [?C] *They have to repudiate the inroad and stand by the inroader* 1897 FE lxvii 668 (OED Inroad, v. Now *rare*. Hence Inroader, 1611..1661. So S C. Not *rare* in W. More likely a hum. coinage in M.T. than a conscious archaism)

insanity plea, sb. [?AB¹] *We have an insanity plea that would have saved Cain* 1872 Speeches (1910) 414 (A form of criminal defence often used in the U.S. Comb. not in OED W S C; but cf. OED Insanity, sb. 3. *attrib* 1892..)

inside, prep. [?AB¹] *"You can go up inside the old sycamore snag, now."* [Footnote] *"Inside" means between the snag and the shore* 1875 OTM 284 (This *spec* sense not in OED W S C)

inside, sb. [?AB¹] *"I hear de gong ag'in. 'Come ahead on de inside,' I says. Gong ag'in. 'Stop de outside'"* 1894 PW xviii 19 (Of a river steamboat: The side-wheel nearer the shore. This *spec* sense not in OED W S C)

inside of, prep. [AB³] *I would boss the whole country inside of three months* 1889 CY ii 35 (OED C.3. In reference to time: Within the space of; before the end of. *U.S.* and *Colonial. colloq.* OEDS 1877.. So S C. *Colloq* in W)

inspiration-works, sb. [B¹] *I feel almost sure that Mrs. Eddy's inspiration-works are getting out of repair* 1903 "Mrs. Eddy in Error" 505 (Nonce comb.)

instalment plan, sb. [?AB²] *If they couldn't persuade a person to try a sewing machine on the instalment plan...they removed him and passed on* 1889 CY xl 512 (OEDS 1894.. All exs. U.S. A in S M, for the Eng. term *hire-purchase plan.* So H: "It may, or may not, be significant that this kind of business transaction is ordinarily regarded in Am. from the point of view of the seller, but in Eng. from that of the buyer." Not A in W C U)

institution, sb. [?AB³] *We visited the Thousand and One Columns...They said it was built for a reservoir ...I suppose he meant me to understand that the institution was there before the Turkish occupation* 1869 IA xxxiii 365 (OED 6b. *colloq.* Any well-established or familiar object. 1839.. So W S T. A in B: A flash word of recent introduction, as applied to any prevalent practice or thing. So Th: Much used during the long controversy about slavery, which was called the "peculiar institution." This sense not in C)

insurance-agency, sb. [?AB¹] *"Insurance-agency business, you know; mighty irregular"* 1883 LM xliii 436 (Comb. not in OED W S C; but cf. OEDS Insurance-agent, 1874; Insurance-man, 1879; earliest exs. all U.S.)

insurance-chromo, sb. [?AB¹] See *God-bless-our-home,* sb. 1889 (Comb. not in OED W S C. Cf. above, and cf. also chromo, above)

insurance-policy, sb. [?AB²] See *collect,* v. 1869 (OED Insurance, sb. 5; no ex. Cf. above. Not A in S C U. Comb. not in W!)

intellects, sb. [?AC] See *love,* v. 1896 (OED 3. pl. 'Wits,' 'senses.' Very common in 17-18th c. Now *arch* or *vulgar.* 1698..1839. So W S C. *Dial* in Wr)

Interior Department, sb. [AB²] *One baby can furnish more business than you and your whole Interior Department can attend to* 1879 *Speeches* (1910) 66 (OED Used in U.S. Corresponds to the Home Office in Great Britain. 1899, only ex. Comb. not in W S C; but C has Department of the Interior)

interject, v. [?C] See *frame shop* 1893 (OED 1c. †In *passive:* To be interposed or situated between. 1578.. 1752. Not *obs* in W S C, and app. not so felt by M.T.)

interlard, v. [?C] *Interlarding guesses as to the origin of the tragedy* 1902 "DBDS" (1928) 334 (OED 4. To interpolate. *obs.* 1545..1755. Not *obs* in W S C U)

interview, v. [?AB³] *All parties had been "interviewed"* 1873 GA xlvi 424. *"There is a reporter trying to interview me, as they call it"* [said by an Englishman] 1892 AmCl vii 72 (OED Earliest exs. U.S. 1869.. A in B Th.III M. Not A in W S C U T. Cf. *Nation* X 209)

interview, sb. [?AB³] *It originated as a variation of the inexpensive "interview"* 1887 *Letters* (1917) II xxvi 476 (OED 1c. *spec.* in recent use: A meeting between a representative of the press and some one from whom he seeks to obtain statements for publication. Earliest ex. U.S. 1869.. Not A in W S C U. Cf. above)

interviewer, sb. [?AB³] See *bath-tub* 1875; *bully* 1907 (OED *spec.* a journalist who interviews. Earliest exs. U.S. 1869.. Not A in W S C)

invalid-car, sb. [?AB¹] *We brought Mrs. Clemens through successfully in an invalid car* 1902 M.T. *the Letter Writer* (1932) vi 95 (Comb. not in OED W S C. Cf. below)

invalid-chair, sb. [?AB²] *I wished to recline in a cushioned invalid-chair* 1869 IA xii 113 (OED 1875, only ex. Comb. not in W S C)

invected, ppl.a. [D] See *coat-of-arms* 1883 (OED *spec.* in *Heraldry* = Invecked: bordered by or consisting of a series of small convex lobes. 1657..1864—. So W S C)

inventionless, a. [B³C] *"I would just like to see Howells...work his futile and inventionless subterfuges"* 1898 *Letters* (1917) II xxxvii 659 (OED *rare* 1887, only ex. Not *rare* in W S. Not in C)

inventor-tribe, sb. [B¹] *The Government can't seize ...the telegraph, the telephone, the air-brake, the Pullman car, and some others, the Shakespeares of the inventor-tribe, so to speak* 1905 "Concerning Copyright" 3 (Nonce comb.)

invoice, sb. [B¹] *With a full invoice of love from us all* 1889 *Letters* (1917) II xxix 509 (A *fig* nonce use)

involuted, ppl.a. [B¹] *Whatever moral you put into a speech gets diffused among those involuted sentences* 1905 *Speeches* (1910) 290 (Involved, entangled. So W S C. This *fig* sense not in OED, which has only 1.=Involute: spiral, curled up. 1816..)

Irish, sb. [AB³] *She'd got her Irish up now* 1856 *Adv. of T. J. Snodgrass* (1928) 21 (OEDS 5. Temper, passion. *U.S.* and *dial.* 1834.. So B DN.III. Not A in W S Wr. This sense not in C)

Irish potato, sb. [A] See *batter-cake* 1897 (OED Potato 3b. Now *U.S.* 1664.. So B F Cl T DN.IV,VI. Not A in W S C)

iron-armed, a. [B¹] *I sat down in one of the iron-armed compartments of an old sofa* 1871 SNO (1875) 258 (Comb. not in OED W S C)

iron-clad, sb. [AB³] *One of the teams wore chain-mail ulsters, and the other wore plate armor...When a man threw himself on his stomach to slide to his base, it was* like an ironclad coming into port 1889 CY xl 518. *The iron-clad banished romance from the war-marine* 1893 "About All Kinds of Ships" 180 (OED An iron-clad ship. Appears to have come into common use at first in the U.S. during the Civil War. 1862.. Not A in W S C U)

iron-clad, sb. [AB¹] *After the Tortoises came another long train of ironclads—stately and spacious Mud Turtles* 1875 SNO 127. *Out from his tent rode great Sir Sagramor, an imposing tower of iron...When I had snaked five men out, things began to look serious for the ironclads* 1889 CY xxxix 502 (An iron-clad warrior. This *fig* use not in OED W S C. Cf. above)

iron-clad, a. [?AB¹] *We reached Tabor safely, and considerably in advance of that iron-clad swindle of a guard* 1869 IA xlix 320 (Armed with iron weapons. This sense not in OED W S C. Cf. above)

iron-clad, sb. [AB¹] *Your long-vanished ancestors—the super-high-moral old iron-clads of Cape Cod* 1881 *Speeches* (1910) 24 (A person of rigid morality. This sense not in OED W S C; but cf. OED Iron-clad, a. 3. *fig.* chiefly *U.S.* Of an extremely strict or rigorous character. 1884..)

ironer, sb. [?AB³] See *washer* 1870 (OEDS 1. *spec.* One whose occupation it is to iron clothes. Earlier U.S. ex. 1835.. Not A in W S C)

iron horse, sb. [?AB³] *The "Iron Horse" will snort o'er his head, and the notes of its whistle upbraid him* 1852 *Hannibal Journal,* May 23. See *depot* 1856. *"Yes, this is the railroad, all but the rails and the iron-horse"* 1873 GA xvii 163 (OED A locomotive. 1874..1887. OEDS Earlier and later U.S. exs. 1846..1918. A in F Th M. Not A in W C. Not in S)

iron-jawed, a. [AB¹] See *corpse-maker* 1883. *A big iron-jawed man worked himself in there from outside* 1884 HF xxv 253 (A in M. Not A in W. Comb. not in OED S C; but cf. OED Iron-faced, *fig.,* 1677)

iron-molder, sb. [B²] *There wasn't any place for him but with the iron-molder* 1892 AmCl xi 107 (OED Iron, sb. 11b; no ex. So W S. Not in C)

iron-railed, a. [B²] *Long, iron-railed verandas running along the several stories* 1883 LM xliv 442 (OED Iron, a. 4. 1893. So W. Not in S C)

iron-rust, sb. [B¹] *"What'll we make the ink out of?" "Many* [prisoners] *makes it out of iron-rust and tears"* 1884 HF xxxv 361 (Comb. not in OED W. Given in S C)

irreconcilabilities, sb.pl. [B¹] See *inharmoniousnesses* 1894 (This *concrete* sense not in OED W S C)

irreverencer, sb. [B¹] *The Catholic Church says the most irreverent things about matters which are sacred to Protestants, and the Protestant Church retorts in kind ...then both of these irreverencers turn upon Thomas Paine and charge him with irreverence* 1909 ISD xii 138 (Nonce word)

irreverencies, sb.pl. [B¹] *I found myself unpleasantly affected by pert little irreverencies* 1889 CY xxvi 339 (Not in OED W S C; but cf. OED Irreverence, sb. 1b. with an and *pl.*: An instance of irreverence; an irreverent act or utterance. a1744..)

irruption, sb. [?AC] *A firmament-obliterating irruption of profanity* 1883 LM xx 244. *The very combination of colors which in a volcanic irruption would add beauty* 1892 AmCl v 62. *Her own volcanic irruption of infernal splendors* 1893 PW iii 239 (OED Confused with Eruption. *obs.* 1613..1811. So W. This sense not in S C. Cf. Irrupt, v., A in B; not A in T)

is, sb. [B¹] *She is not a Has Been, she is an Is* 1903 "Mrs. Eddy in Error" 507 (Nonce use)

it, pron. [?C] *"We'll let the cry-baby go home to its mother, won't we, Huck? Poor thing—does it want to see its mother? And so it shall"* 1876 TS xvi 137. *"It is a dear good lad, my Nick," she said* 1898 MS (1916) viii 103 (OED 2d. †Used where *he, she,* or *that* would now be preferred. 1596..1604. So Wr. Not *obs* in W S C)

item, sb. [?AB³] *Mr. Bloke's "Item"* (title)...*The paper had already gone to press, but knowing that our friend would consider the publication of this item important...we stopped the press at once* 1865 SNO (1875) 168. See also *floating* 1870; *scoop* 1902 (OED 2b. A detail of information or news, esp. one in a news-paper. 1819.. So W U. *Colloq* in S C. A in B F Cl T)

ivy-grown, ppl.a. [B¹] *The gilded and pillared splendors of her ambition, all crumbled to ruins and ivy-grown* 1873 GA lx 544 (Comb. not in OED W S C; but cf. OED Ivy-clad, 1875)

ivy-mailed, ppl.a. [B¹] *Heidelberg Castle, with its...ivy-mailed battlements* 1880 TA ii 27 (Comb. not in OED W S C; but cf. OED Ivy-mantled, 1750)

J

jab, v. [?AB³] *He never bit into nothing but what he jabbed his fork into it in three or four places first* 1884 HF xxxvi 372 (OED *colloq* or *dial*. To poke roughly, to stab. b. 1827.. So W S U Wr T. A in C B F Cl DN.I,III)

jabber-jabber-jabber, v. [B¹] See *fantods* 1880 (An intensive form of *jabber*, not in OED W S C. Cf. OED Jabber, v.intr. 1b. 1817..)

jabers, int. **be jabers**. [?AB¹] *"Sir Marhaus the king's son of Ireland talks like all the rest; you ought to give him a brogue, or at least a characterisic expletive ...It is a common literary device with the great authors. You should make him say, 'In this country, be jabers, came never knight since it was chrʻstened, but he found strange adventures, be jabers'."* 1889 CY xv 182 (Wr: Irish slang, a quasi-oath. So W S. Not in OED C. A in DN.V)

Jack, sb. [AB¹] See *seven-up* 1869 (One of the six "points" that may be scored in the Am. game of seven-up, or high-low-jack, q.v. It is scored by the player who wins the jack of trumps, either by saving it or capturing it. This sense not in OED W S C; but cf. OED 5. *Cards*. Name for the knave of trumps in the game of all-fours. 1674.. So W)

jackass, sb. [AB³] *Take a jackass, for example: a jackass...is valuable to this world because he is a jack-ass; but a nobleman is not valuable because he is a jackass* 1889 CY xv 182. *"Yes, sir, he's a dam fool." "Perfect jackass—yes."* 1893 PW i 235 (OED 2. A blockhead. 1823.. So W S C U. A in M AS.II.46)

jackass, a. [?AB²] *"It's one of the most jackass ideas I ever struck"* 1884 HF xxxvi 371 (OED attrib., in sense 2. 1884, only ex. This adj. use not in W S C)

jackassful, a. [?AB¹] *Rabbits as big as a dog, and such tall and noble jackassful ears that that is what they name them by* 1906 "Horse's Tale" 332 (Not in OED W S C. Cf. OED Jackassery, 1833; Jackassification, 1822; Jackassism, 1845,—all more or less nonce words)

jackass rabbit, sb. [AB³] See *coyote* 1861. *An animal known from Kansas clear to the Pacific Ocean as the "jackass rabbit"* 1872 RI iii 32 (OED The jack-rabbit: One of several species of large prairie-hares, with remarkably long ears and legs. *U.S.* 1851.. So S C B F Cl. Not in W)

jackass-voiced, a. [?AB¹] *"Some cursing and squawking parrots and a jackass-voiced macaw"* 1894 PW xix 21 (Comb. not in OED W S C; but cf. OED Jackass-headed, 1883)

Jack-at-all-science, sb. [?AB¹] *"Come, Dave, show the gentlemen what an inspired Jack-at-all-science we've got in this town"* 1894 PW xi 554 (Nonce comb. Cf. OED Jack at all trades, 1618.. A in DN.III)

jack-knife, sb. [A] *I illustrated it with cuts engraved on the bottoms of wooden type with a jack-knife* 1871 SNO (1875) 93 (OEDS 1. App. of U.S. origin. A large clasp-knife for the pocket. 1711.. Not A in W S C U)

jack-leg, sb. [AB³] *The reader...has been told many a time how the born-and-trained novelist works. Won't he let me round and complete his knowledge by telling him how the jack-leg does it?* 1894 TET intro. 311 (OEDS *U.S.* A term of contempt or depreciation. 1853.. So Th: A contemptuous term applied to an inferior lawyer, and less commonly to members of the other professions. So W F Cl DN.III,IV. Not in S C)

jack-legged, a. [AB³] *Jim was a kind of jack-legged tailor* 1894 TSA viii 354 (OEDS *U.S.*=prec. 1839. So Th. Not in W S C)

jack-pair, sb. [B¹] *"He drove that jack-pair around town and showed them the sights"* 1894 PW xii 776 (Nonce comb. for a pair of knaves or rascals)

jack-plane, v. [?AB²] *Surely the straight, smooth, pure white turnpikes are jack-planed and sand-papered every day* 1869 IA xii 76. *My Autobiography is pretty freely dictated, but my idea is to jack-plane it a little before I die* 1885 Letters (1917) II xxv 462 (OED To smooth with a jack-plane. 1872, quot. from IA, only ex. Not A in W Wr. Not in S C as a verb)

jack-pot, sb. [AB³] See *and* 1899 (OEDS In draw-poker, a pot or pool that has to accumulate till one of the players can open it with a pair of jacks or better. 1888.. So W S C U F Cl Th M)

Jackson, sb. **by Jackson**. [AB¹] *"By Jackson, he's got you"* 1894 PW xv 237. Cf. Clara Clemens, *My Father*, 1931, p. 26: *"Once, in the middle of a careful description of a very devout clergyman that Mother had been reading aloud, Father sprang to his feet and danced a kind of hornpipe while he sang, 'By the humping, jumping Jesus, what the hell is that to you?' Never shall I forget the strange sound that burst from Mother's lips. It contained mirth and horror...I noticed that the next time he repeated this gem from the literature of song, the words had been altered to 'By the humping, jumping Jackson, what the yell is that to you?' "* (A minced oath, from the name of President Andrew Jackson. Not in OED W S C)

Jacksonian, a. [AB²] *The distinguished visiting minister from the great town a hundred miles away—gray hair pushed up and back in the stern intellectual Jacksonian way* a1870 Letter in Clara Clemens, *My Father* (1931) 9 (OEDS Characteristic of Andrew Jackson. 1885, only ex. So W S C)

jail, sb. [AE] *The jailor...commanded that the prisoners be conducted to the jail yard* 1881 PP xxvii 325 (OED In U.S. the official spelling for Gaol. So M. Not A in W S C)

jake, sb. [AB²] *"These country jakes won't ever think of that"* 1884 HF xx 194 (OEDS *U.S.* slang. A rustic lout. 1884, this quot. So W Cl DN.I,III,IV. Not in S C)

jam, v. [?AB¹] *They swarmed up in front of Sherburn's palings as thick as they could jam together* 1884 HF xxii 218 (The *intr.* sense not in OED C. Given in W S)

jam, adv. [AB³] *That night the house was jam full of men in no time* 1884 HF xxiii 226. See also *Old Mistress* 1894 (OEDS orig. *U.S.* 2. Thoroughly, completely. 1835.. So DN.III. Not A in W Wr. The adv. use not in S C)

jamble, v. [AB¹?C] *He preached them the blamedest, jambledest, idiotic sermons you ever struck* 1896 TSD xi

537 (Apparently the same as Jambled=drunk, given in Franklin's "Drinkers' Dictionary," 1737, AS.XII.91. Cf. OED *obs* var. of Jangle, 1715..1726. Wr (Suppl.): To shake a liquid in order to mix it. Not in W S C. As M.T. uses it, the word was probably felt as a 'blend' of *jumble* and *jam*)

jammed, ppl.a. [?AB²] *Here is a packed and jammed city inclosed in a massive stone wall* 1869 IA xiv 85. *A splendid audience in Indianapolis last night—a perfectly jammed house* 1872 *Letters* (1917) I xi 193 (OED 5b. Blocked up. 1887. So W S C)

janders, sb. [?ACE] *"What's the matter with her?"* ..."*Well, measles...and yaller janders, and brain-fever, and I don't know what all"* 1884 HF xxviii 291 (OED *obs* form of Jaundice, also 19th c. *dial.* The ending of the word in *-s* led to its frequent treatment from the 15th c., and esp. in the 17th c., as a plural in *-ers*, as in other plural names of diseases, cf. *measles, mumps, glanders*. 1. Three varieties (yellow, black, and green) are recognized and distinguished according to the color of the skin in each case. 1303.. So W S C Wr. A in M DN.II,III,IV,V AS.V.201, Ozarks. Cf. DN.II: Two varieties of this disease are recognized by old-fashioned people, 'yaller janders' and 'black janders')

japanesic, a. [B¹] *Half a dozen naked branches full of elbows slant upward like artificial supports...the branches are japanesic* 1897 FE lxv 646 (Inclining to a Japanese character. Not in OED W S C; but for similar attempted coinages cf. OED Japanesque, 1883; Japannish, 1851; OEDS Japanesy, 1890)

jarred, ppl.a. [?AB²] *She was a good deal jarred up and jolted* 1883 LM lix 579 (OED 1892.. So W S C. A in H: As a trans. verb *jar* is now rare in Eng., but is still in constant use in Am., in both the *lit* and the *fig* sense)

jaw, v.intr. [?A] *He was a born boss, and loved to command, and to jaw and dispute with inferiors and harry them and bullyrag them* 1897 FE lx 588 (OED 2a. 1748.. So W S C. A in DN.III,V)

jaw, v.trans. [?AB¹] *They only scared us and jawed Greek at us* 1867 *Speeches* (1923) 25 (This trans. use not in OED W S C. Cf. above)

jay, sb. [AB³] *Then a shrill jay swept down, a flash of blue flame* 1876 TS xiv 122. See also *Congressman* 1880 (OED 1b. The Blue Jay of N.Am. 1838.. So W S C)

jayhawker, sb. [AB³] *They were constantly being hunted by the "jayhawkers," who were pro-slavery Missourians, guerillas, modern free lances* 1907 "Chaps. from Autob" 330 (OEDS *U.S.* A name given to members of the bands who carried on irregular warfare in and around eastern Kansas, in the free soil conflict and the early part of the Civil War, and who combined pillage with guerilla fighting. 1860.. So S C B Th,1849 T. M.T.'s surprising statement that the original jayhawkers were pro-slavery Missourians is supported by the quot. in Th,1862; also by usage in early Nebraska as reported in AS.VIII.4.50. But cf. W: Originally anti-slavery men, esp. in Kansas and Missouri; later natives or residents of Kansas. F: The Jayhawkers waged war against both parties alike... Their name is identified with Kansas, that state having been the scene of the thickest of the strife.)

jeans, sb. [AB²] *They were dressed in homespun "jeans," blue or yellow—there were no other varieties of it* 1873 GA i 19 (OED 2. Jean, sb. A twilled cotton cloth. The form *jeans* is used in U.S. b. Garments of this material. 1879, only ex. So W U Th,1743 AS.IV. 8,15. Not A in S C)

jeans, a. [AB²] *He had...ragged old blue jeans britches* 1884 HF xix 182 (OED Jean, sb. 2c. *attrib.* 1801..1885, first ex. of *jeans* so used. A in Th. Not A in T. The *attrib* use not in W S C)

jeans-clad, a. [AB²] See *chills-racked* 1875. *A loose-jointed, long-legged, tow-headed, jeans-clad, countrified cub of about sixteen* 1880 TA xxiii 224 (OED 1885, only ex. Comb. not in W S C)

jeff, v. [?AB³] See *comp* 1909 (OED *Printers' slang.* 'To throw or gamble with quadrats as with dice.' 1888, only ex. So W S C. A in B F Th,1837)

jerk, v. [?AB¹] *"Somebody to jerk a little chin-music for us"* 1872 RI xlvii 332 (*Slang*: to render, perform, utter. This sense not in OED W S C. Cf. OED 3. *fig.* To utter or throw out words or sounds abruptly, or sharply and shortly. 1602.. In M.T.'s use, no esp. abruptness is implied)

jerked, ppl.a. [A] *Biltong...is what our plainsmen call "jerked beef"* 1897 FE lxvii 684 (OED Corrupted from Am. Spanish: Cured, esp. beef, by cutting into long thin slices. 1712.. So W S C U B F Cl T M H AS.VII.426)

jew down, v. [?AB³] *"One thing in this world a person don't ever try to jew you down on—that's a coffin"* 1883 LM xliii 437 (OEDS With *down.* 1870.. So W S C Wr T. A in M Th.III DN.III)

jewel-box, sb. [B¹] *"D'ye mane to soy that Bridget O'Shaughnessy bought the mate to that joo-ul box to ship that dhrunken divil to Purgatory in?"* 1883 LM xlii 438 (Coffin; M.T.'s variation on casket, q.v. This sense not in OED W S C)

jewelry, sb. [B¹] See *ingot* 1884 (Nonce use)

Jewry, sb. [C] *Tom and his gallant procession... made a short march through the Old Jewry* 1881 PP xi 123 (OED 2. *obs* exc. *Hist.* a1225..1876. So C U. Not obs in W S)

jew's-harp, sb. Also **juice-harp** [?AE] *By him lay a new jewsharp, a new top...* 1880 TA xxiii 229. See *scoop*, v. 1884. *"You got anything to play music on?" "I ain't got nuffin but a coa'se comb en a piece o' paper, en a juice-harp"* 1884 HF xxxviii 392 (OED 1. 1595.. So W S C U. A in AS.VI.386. The form *juice-harp* is A in DN.IV,V)

jew's-harp, v. [?AB¹] *Jim found so much fault with jew's-harping the rats* 1884 HF xxxviii 394 (Not in OED W S C as verb. Cf. above)

jibe, v. [AB³] *"The piece you happened to be playing ...didn't seem to jibe in with the general gait of the picture that was passing at the time"* 1866 *Screamers* (1871) 146 (OEDS *U.S.* To chime in with; to be in harmony. 1813.. So W C B F Cl Th T M DN.III. Not A in S)

jig, sb. **the jig is up.** [?AB³] *"Behold, the jig is up—let us die"* 1869 IA xl 428 (OEDS 5. 'The game is up;' it is all over. Now *dial* or *slang*. 1800.. So W S. A in C B Th M DN.III)

jigger, v.intr. [?AB³] *They did not go jiggering up and down* 1872 RI xxiv 178. *The river lashed up white as milk as far as you could see for miles, and there was that bar'l jiggering along, same as ever* 1883 LM iii 54. *He jiggered...and joggled...and squirmed* [German, *Er gaukelt und schaukelt*] 1891 *Slovenly Peter* (1935) 18 (OED To make a succession of rapid jerks. 1867.. So W S C. A in F Cl: To move uneasily, to fidget; so used in the Southwest)

jigger, v.trans. [?AB¹] *The scream of the jiggered and tortured violin* 1873 GA xv 147 (To play monotonously or jiggingly. This trans. use not in OED W S C)

jigger, sb. [?AB¹] *"My tongue is doomed to wag forever to the jigger of that remorseless jingle"* 1878 "Punch, Brothers, Punch" (1882) 148 (A monotonous or jigging sound; transf. from the verb-sense above. This sense not in OED W S C)

jimjams, sb. [?AB²] *They gave me the jimjams and the fantods and caked up what brains I had* 1896 TSD xi 537 (OEDS 3b. The 'creeps;' the fidgets. 1904.. So S. A in W C B F Cl T)

jimpson-weed, sb. [AB³] *She looked out among the tomato vines and jimpson weeds that constituted the gar-*

den 1876 TS i 18. *A deserted garden...thickly grown with the bloomy and villainous "jimpson" weed* 1880 TA xxiii 226. See also *ash-pile* 1884 (OEDS = Jamestown-weed. *U.S.* The thorn-apple. 1832.. So W S C B F Th T M)

jing, sb. **by jings.** [?AB²C] *By jings! the postman will be here in a minute* 1881 *Letters* (1917) I xxi 412. *By jings, it was my old Jim* 1884 HF xviii 170 (OED *Scotch.* By jing! 1785. Rarely By jings! No ex. This form not in W S C. A in DN.V)

job-printing, sb. [AB³] *He printed the book through a job-printing house* 1906 "Chaps. from Autob" 451 (OEDS *U.S.* The printing of small pieces of work. 1832.. Not A in W S C)

job-office, sb. [?AB²] *I worked in that little job-office in Keokuk* 1906 *Autob* (1924) II 288 (OED *Printing.* An office at which only job-work is done. No ex. Not A in S C. Comb. not in W. Cf. above)

job-work, sb. [?AB¹] *How many subscribers has the Journal got? What does the job-work pay?* 1853 *Letters* (1917) I i 29 (C: In *printing, spec.* a class of miscellaneous work. The *spec. printing* sense not in OED W S, although the word is used in the OED def. of *job-office,* q.v.)

jockey, v. [?AB¹] *The two great steamers back into the stream, and lie there jockeying a moment* 1875 OTM 191 (W: To maneuver skilfully for a legitimate advantage, as in a yacht-race. So S. This *spec Naut.* sense not in OED C, although the word is so used in OED 1d. quot. 1899)

John, sb. [?AB²] See *mining-tax* 1870 (OEDS 1c. A Chinaman. All exs. U.S. 1873.. A in B F Cl Th T. *Slang* in W. This sense not in S C)

joint, sb. Spelled **jint.** [AE] *"A jint of stove-pipe"* 1884 HF vi 43 (This sp. A in M DN.III,IV. *Dial* in W. Not given in OED S C)

joker, sb. [?AB¹] *"I have entirely stopped using the typewriter...I don't want people to know I own this curiosity-breeding little joker"* [from a letter dated March 19, 1875] 1905 "First Writing-Machines" (1906) 166 (Jigger, thingumajig, doodad; indefinite term for an object of any kind. Cf. the list of such expressions in the article by Miss Louise Pound, AS.VI.257f. This sense not in OED W S C. Cf. OED 3a. Something used in playing a trick. 1858.. Cf. also Th.III,1858: A pea or small marble used in thimble-rigging; so AS.XII.115, 1856)

jokist, sb. [?AB²] *Here is "The Jokist's Own Treasury"* 1873 GA xxxvi 331 (OEDS A professed or habitual joker. 1873, this quot., only ex. So W S. Not in C)

jollification, sb. [?AB³] *Had gorgeous 4th of July jollification yesterday* 1867 *Letters* (1917) I vii 131 (OED *colloq.* A merrymaking. Earliest ex. from W. Irving. 1809.. Not A in W S C U)

jolt, sb. [?AB²] *I was scared now...but in a minute I see I was mistaken—that is, after the first jolt...he being so unexpected* 1884 HF v 30 (OEDS 2b. *fig.* A surprise; a shock which disturbs one's mental composure. U.S. exs. 1905.. A in H: Used *fig* in Am. much more commonly than in Eng. The *fig* sense not in W S C)

jolt, v. [?AB¹] *She would launch a slap at him that would have jolted a cow* 1872 RI ii 27. *I said I didn't know. "Don't know?" His manner jolted me* 1875 OTM 219. See *jarred* 1883. *"You shouldn't flip out such a gigantic thing in that colorless kind of way...You do jolt a person so"* 1892 AmCl xviii 183 (To give one a shock or surprise. Cf. W: To jar with a quick or hard blow. Not in OED S C in this sense as a verb. Cf. jolt, sb., above)

jolt, sb. [?AB¹] *"A mighty responsible old Webster-Unabridged...Coddington had her a week, and she was too much for him—he couldn't spell the words; next, Dyer, he tried it a jolt, but he couldn't pronounce 'em"*

1865 SS (1926) 159 (A while, time; a 'spell.' Cf. DN.V: A term in jail. This sense not in OED W S C)

jour, sb. [AB³] *I can see, also, the tramping "jour," who flitted by in the summer and tarried a day* 1886 *Speeches* (1910) 185 (OEDS *U.S. colloq* abbreviation of *Journeyman.* 1845.. So S C B F T M. Not in W)

journeyman, sb. [B¹] *The movement of the narrative ...skips forward and back and here and there and yonder, prentice-fashion. Many a journeyman has broken up his narrative and skipped about and rambled around, but he did it for a purpose, for an advantage* 1907 CS II iii 127 (Cf. OED 1. A qualified mechanic or artisan who works for another...Distinguished on one side from *apprentice,* on the other from *master.* 2. *fig.* Chiefly depreciatory, 1548..1817. So S. The *fig* use not in W C. Here the *fig* sense is complimentary to the journeyman)

jour printer, sb. [AB²] *"What's your line—mainly?" "Jour printer by trade"* 1884 HF xix 183. *I was for some years a traveling "jour" printer* 1891 *Letters* (1917) II xxxi 542 (OEDS *U.S.* 1884, this quot., only ex. So B F T. Not A in C. Comb. not in W S)

joy-flame, sb. [B¹] *The air was laden with music, the river-banks were beruffled with joy-flames* 1881 PP xi 123 (Bonfire. Comb. not in OED W S C)

joy-song, sb. [B¹] *The mysterious solemnity and silence of the dawn began to give place to the joy-songs of the birds* 1880 TA xiv 126 (Comb. not in OED W S C)

juba, sb. [AB³] See *break down,* v. 1873. *Next they got out an old fiddle, and one played, and another patted juba* 1883 LM iii 49 (OED *U.S.* A species of dance or breakdown practised by the plantation-negroes of the southern U.S. c1800.. So W S C B Th T M DN.II. Explained by Herbert Quick, *Mississippi Steamboatin',* 1926, p. 246, as originally "patting Juby or jubilee")

Jubiter, sb. [E] *"The sun's diramic combination with the lymphatic forces of the perihelion of Jubiter"* 1869 IA x 90. *"What a name—Jubiter! Where'd he get it?... The school-teacher seen a round brown moie the size of a dime on his left leg above his knee, and four little bits of moles around it, and he said it 'minded him of Jubiter and his moons"* 1896 TSD i 345 (OED Jupiter, sb. This form 13th-14th c. 1398, only ex. Not in W S C)

judge, v. [?A] *"Peters, do you ever read the Bible?" "Well—yes." "I judge it ain't often, by the way you say it"* 1877 "Some Rambling Notes" ii 589. *I judged I would saw out and leave that night if pap got drunk enough* 1884 HF vi 42. *He'd been to college, you see, and so he judged he was all right* 1892 AmCl xi 107. See also *calculate* 1907 (OED 11. with object clause: To form the opinion that; think, consider, suppose. 1297..1850. So W S C U. Wr: To suspect, *dial.* A in M AS.VII.299)

Judge, sb. [AB¹] See *General* 1873. *Titles of honor and dignity once acquired in a democracy...are as permanent here as eternity is in heaven...Once a justice of the peace for a week, always "judge" afterward* 1906 *Autob* (1924) II 350 (W: In both the U.S. and Great Britain, the term *judge* has become a general and often loose title. So S. A in M AS.IX.206. This use not in OED C)

judge, sb. **county judge.** [AB²] *The middle-aged man turned out to be the county judge* 1876 TS iv 49 (OED 1b. Local magistrate in U.S. 1889, only ex. So C. Comb. not in W S)

judge-advocate, sb. [AB¹] *Persons who have served ...on the staff of our multitudinous governors and have been...judge-advocates temporarily* 1902 "Does the Race of Man Love a Lord?" 442 (W: In the U.S., an officer appointed to act as prosecutor at a court-martial; in Great Britain he is legal adviser to the court, but does not act as prosecutor. The *spec* Am. sense not explained in OED S C)

jug, sb. [A] See *tin cup* 1883. *A four-gallon jug of whisky* 1884 HF vi 41. *Like a jug that's googling out buttermilk* 1884 HF xxix 295 (OED 1. A deep vessel ...in U. S. having a narrow neck or orifice, usually stopped by a cork. 1538.. So W S C H)

jug, v. [?AB³] *"I'm going to jug the other chaps"* 1872 RI 1 354. *"He was the justice of the peace that jugged me for a vagrant"* 1875 TS xxix 223 (OED 3. *slang.* To shut up in jail. 1841.. So W S C U. A in M DN.III)

jumbulacious, a. [B¹] *I will not go so far as to say it is a harum-scarum jumble, but...it is at least jumbulacious in places* 1907 CS II vii 184 (Hum. coinage)

jump, sb. **at one jump.** [B¹] *It was my idea to spread [that name] all over the world, now, at one jump* 1899 "My Debut" (1900) 70 (Phr. not in OED W S C; but cf. OED At the first jump, 1577; OEDS All of a jump, 1825)

jump, sb. **on the jump.** [?AB²] *My nigger had a monstrous easy time...but Buck's was on the jump most of the time* 1884 HF xviii 162. *We heard it coming— and coming on the jump, too* 1889 CY xxxiv 441 (OEDS 7. At great speed. U.S. ex. 1884, this quot. A in S C B. Not A in W)

jump, v. [AB³] *Man in San Francisco jumped lot and built house on it* 1865 *Notebook* (1935) i 8 (OEDS 9b. To take summary possession of a piece of land. Chiefly *U.S.* and Colonial. 1846.. So S C B F Cl Th,1839 M AS.IV.127,VII.429. Not A in W U T)

jumper, sb. [AB³] *Cal and I came wandering back into Esmeralda one night just in time to be too late to save our fortune from the jumpers* 1906 *Autob* (1924) II 254 (OED 4. One who jumps a claim. 1855.. So S. A in C B Cl AS.VII.9,430. This sense not in W. Cf. above)

jumping-off place, sb. [?AB³] *At the end of twenty steps the corridor ended in a "jumping-off place"* 1876 TS xxxi 245. *That blue quarter-deck runs the rest of the way aft to the jumping-off place* 1890 "Wonderful Pair of Slippers" 312 (OEDS b. A place at which one alights at the end of a journey, or from which one jumps off into the region beyond. Earlier U.S. exs. 1826.. A in F Cl Th T M DN.III. Not A in W S C)

June-bug, sb. [?AB³] *It is better to be a young June-bug than an old bird of paradise* 1894 PW viii 337 (OED A name for various beetles. 1862.. A in W S C Wr Th,1832 M DN.III)

junior, a. [?AB¹] *It was Junior England all the way to Christchurch [New Zealand]...And Christchurch is an English town* 1897 FE xxxii 297 (A *fig* extension of the sense described as Am. in H: Within an Am. household a son who bears the same name as his father is often addressed or designated as Junior instead of by his Christian name. Here, as applied to New Zealand: A younger copy or replica of. This sense not in OED W S C)

junketing, vbl.sb. [A] *Sometimes a stack of people would come there...and have such junketings round about and on the river* 1884 HF xviii 162 (OED Chiefly *U.S.* A going on a pleasure excursion, picnicking, 1555.. So W. Not A in S C U Wr)

junk-shop, sb. [?AB²] *We were out raiding the old junk-shops for disabled andirons and other antiquities* 1880 *M.T. the Letter Writer* (1932) iii 47 (OEDS The shop of a junk-dealer. U.S. quot. 1881, only ex. A in Th,1848. Not A in W S C U. Cf. OED Junk-dealer, U.S., a marine-store dealer. 1882.. So Cl)

justice, sb. **Chief Justice.** [AB²] *The Supreme Court of the United States was opened with the usual formalities, the nine judges appearing in their black robes, and the new chief justice presiding* 1898 "From the London Times of 1904" (1900) 144 (OED 9. The designation of the presiding judge in the U.S. Supreme Court. No ex. So S C. Not A in W)

justice of the peace, sb. [AB¹] *My father was a justice of the peace* 1875 OTM 70. See also *jug,* v. 1876; *judge,* sb. 1906 (W: In the U.S. his principal duties are to administer summary justice in minor cases and to commit for trial in a superior court; in Great Britain he also grants licenses and acts as judge at quarter session. The *spec* functions of the Am. justice of the peace are not distinguished in OED S C)

justifier, sb. [B²] *A setter and a justifier could turn out about 3,500 ems an hour on it...To add a justifying mechanism to that machine would take a few months... I agreed to add said justifier* a1888 *Autob* (1924) I 76 (OED 2a. A device in a type-setting machine to do the work of the workman who 'justifies' the type. 1888. The invention seems to have been first used on M.T.'s projected invention)

K

Kaet, sb. [B¹] *The chiefs of most of the bands* [of Thugs] *performed the religious ceremonies themselves; but the Kaets delegated them to certain official stranglers* (*Chaurs*). *The rites of the Kaets were so holy that no one but the Chaur was allowed to touch the vessels and other things used in them* 1897 FE xlvi 430 (Not in OED W S C. M.T.'s information about the Thugs was all derived, as he acknowledges in FE xlvi 426, from Major W. H. Sleeman's *Report on the Depredations Committed by the Thug Gangs,* Calcutta, 1840, which is still, according to the *Encyclopaedia Britannica,* the principal authority on the subject. For the words *Chaur* and *Kaet,* cf. Sleeman, Intro., pp.xli-xliii: "The Chaur is a strangler...We Kaets always have one if possible. Other castes have no Chaurs." M.T.'s word *bheel* is apparently the same as *bele,* explained in Sleeman, pp.xv-xvii, as "favorite places of murder," or "sporting places, known to all Thugs who are accustomed to hunt on the same ground." See also the curious map given by Sleeman, opposite p. 126, where 274 of the murder places (here spelled *Bail*) are marked off for the Kingdom of Oude alone.)

kahkahponeeka, sb. [B¹] *Official Report of a Visit to the Furka Region, by H. Harris, Agent: About seven o'clock in the morning, with perfectly fine weather, we started from Hospenthal...The want of variety in the scenery made the* kahkahponeeka *wearisome...Exactly in front of us, at a* hopow *of only fifteen miles, this magnificent mountain...No other prominent feature is visible from this* bong-a-bong...*We formed a large* xhvloj *as we descended...All felt the heat exceedingly in the climb up this very steep* bolwoggoly...*Posts set up to indicate the direction of the pass in the* owdawakk *of winter...The track which connects the Grimsel with the head of the Rhone* schnawp...*Down to the bank of the gloomy little* swosh-swosh...*A deluge of* haboolong *and hail...A pedestal of ice high enough to admit of our all creeping under it for* gowkarak. *A stream of* puckittypukk *had furrowed a course for itself in the ice...A very cold* bzzzzzzzzeeeee *accompanied the storm...An instantaneous clap of* yokky *sounding like a large gun...We sallied out to walk through a* haboolong *which was quite enough to give us a thorough soaking...Barren rocks which afford only scanty food for a herd of* gmwkwllolp ...*Next morning the* hogglebumgullop *still continued bad...Nor were we* nappersocket *in our expectation...I was much inclined to think that the whole story was a ruse to make us* slowwk...*The gap was certainly not larger than a* mmbglx *might cross with a very slight leap... A few steps cut in the* whoopjamboreehoo *enabled us to walk completely under it...The fine form of the Wellhorn looking down upon it completes the enchanting* bopple... *Before we arrived at the top the* gnillic *and mist became so thick we could not see one another at more than twenty* poopoo *distance...When I looked out I was surprised to find that the daylight was considerable, and that the* balragoomah *would evidently rise before long...The* wlgw *was very severe...The snow had fallen to the depth of a* flirk *during the past evening...There must have been at least twelve* dingblatter *of frost...*

I said: "You have done well, Harris: this report is... in many ways an excellent document. But it has a fault,— it is too learned. What is dingblatter?" "Dingblatter *is a Fiji word meaning degrees"..."What is* gnillic?" "*That is the Esquimaux term for snow." "What does* mmbglx *stand for?" "That is Zulu for pedestrian." "What is* bopple?" "Picture. It's Choctaw." "What is* schnawp?" "*Valley. That is Choctaw, also." "What is* bolwoggoly?" "*That is Chinese for hill." "Kahkahponeeka?" "Ascent. Choctaw." "What does* hogglebumgullup *mean?" "That is Chinese for weather."..."Why have you used all this Chinese and Choctaw and Zulu rubbish?"..."To adorn*

my page. They all do it. Everybody that writes elegantly" 1880 TA xxx 313 (Hum. invention. A dark suspicion that M.T. might possibly be telling the truth here, at least about his alleged "Choctaw" words, inasmuch as he has elsewhere shown a special interest in this Indian speech (see Choctaw, above), prompted a consultation of Cyrus Byington's *Dict. of the Choctaw Language,* ed. by John R. Swanton and Henry S. Halbert, Smithsonian Institution, Bureau of Am. Ethnology, Bulletin 46, 1915. But the suspicion proved an unworthy one. And yet the actual Choctaw words for picture, valley, and ascent, viz. *holba, okfa,* and *oiya,* might have served his purpose here, had he known them, quite as well as *bopple, schnawp,* and *kahkahponeeka!*)

Kanaka, sb. [?AB³] *He had played from his birth with the little Kanakas on his father's plantation* 1897 FE iii 57 (OED A native of the South Sea Islands. 1840.. So W S C U. A in B F Th)

kangaroo-chasing, a. [B¹] *The wanton slaughter of the kangaroo-chasing black innocents* 1897 FE xxix 281 (Comb. not in OED W S C; but cf. OED Kangaroo-hunting, 1894)

katydid, sb. [A] *A great band of Katy-dids and Crickets discoursed martial music* 1875 SNO 127 (OEDS *U.S.* A large green insect...which abounds in the central and eastern states of America. 1784.. So W S C U B F Cl Th T M)

kazark, sb. [B¹] *"Have we got enough brimstone?... How much have we got in cargo for Satan?" "Eighteen hundred thousand billion quintillions of kazarks." I found out, over there, that a kazark is exactly the bulk of a hundred and sixty-nine worlds like ours!* 1907 "Capt. Stormfield" 42 (Hum. coinage. Cf. *bezark,* AS.VII.329, Johns Hopkins slang for 'person')

k box, sb. [?AB¹] See *d box* 1886 (Not in OED W S C. Cf. note on *d box,* above)

keelboat, sb. [AB³] See *mule-power* 1880; *broad-horn* 1883; *break-down* 1883 (OEDS b. A large flat boat used on American rivers. 1801.. So W S C B F Cl Th,1801 AS.II.31,VI.240)

keelboating, vbl.sb. [AB¹] *Then keelboating died a permanent death* 1883 LM iii 41 (Not in OED W S C. Cf. above)

keelboatman, sb. [AB³] *The keelboatmen selling their boats in New Orleans* 1883 LM iii 41 (OEDS *U.S.* 1839.. So W. Not in S C)

keel over, v. [AB³] See *draw,* sb. 1876. *The nigger Nat...keeled over onto the floor amongst the dogs and begun to groan like he was dying* 1884 HF xxxvi 373 (OED 3b. To turn over; to fall over as if by shock. Orig. *U.S.* a1860.. So S C B F Cl DN.III AS.IV.383. Not A in W)

keep, sb. [?C] *The corridors are in guard and keep of men-at-arms* 1889 CY v 61 (OED 2. Care or heed, charge. a1300..1818. So Wr. *Obs* in W S C)

keep, sb. [?AB³] *The king...visited a distant noble whom he wished to bankrupt with the cost of his keep* 1889 CY xxv 315 (OED 6c. Maintenance, support. 1825.. So W S C U. A in B)

keep, v. [AB³] *I lead an easy life, though, and I don't care a cent whether school keeps or not* 1863 *Letters* (1917) I iv 92 (OEDS 38b. Of a school: To be held. *U.S.* 1845.. Not A in W S. This sense not in C)

keep door, v. [B¹] *You could keep door and peddle photographs* 1867 M.T. the Letter Writer (1932) I 16 (This phr. not in OED W S C. Cf. in gen. sense OED 16c. To have charge of. a1300..)

keep game, v. [?AB¹] *The minor offices of keeping game and umpiring* 1906 "Amended Obituaries" 230 (To manage or preside over a game as umpire or referee. Phr. not in OED W S C. Cf. in gen. sense OED 34. To carry on, conduct, as presiding officer or a chief actor, an assembly, court, fair, market, etc. 1432..)

keeps, sb. [AB¹] *They got their marbles and played "keeps"* 1876 TS xvi 135. See also *stake*, v. 1894 (W: A game played 'for keeps.' A in Th,1886 DN.IV,V. Not in OED S C)

keeps, sb. **for keeps.** [AB³] *Jean wanted to keep the MS for another reading-aloud, and for "keeps," too, I suspected* 1906 *Letters* (1917) II xlv 797 (OED Keep, sb. 7. For good. *U.S. colloq.* 1886.. So C Wr T H. Not A in W S U)

kennel-rat, sb. [B¹] *"I talk the language of these base kennel-rats like a very native"* 1881 PP xi 126 (Persons of low degree; slum-dwellers. Comb. not in OED W S C)

ker-, prefix. [AB¹,B²] *"Directly he come down ker-whop about ten foot off f'm where we stood"* 1872 RI lxi 442. *You'd see the ax flash and come down...and by the time it's above the man's head again you'd hear the k'chunk!* 1884 HF xix 179. *"Jes' den, 'long come de wind en slam it to, behine de chile, ker-blam!"* 1884 HF xxiii 234. *Bang! here goes the door ker-slam!* 1891 *Slovenly Peter* (1935) 16. *Whack! Ker-blim! and down they go* (Ger. Bauz! perdauz!—da liegen zwei) 1891 *Slovenly Peter* (1935) 21 (OED *U.S. vulgar.* The first element in numerous onomatopoeic or echoic formations intended to imitate the sound or the effect of the fall of some heavy body, as *kerchunk*, *kerslam*, *kerwhop*, etc. 1843..1885 *Ker-whop*..1899 *Ker-slam*. No ex. of *Ker-chunk*. *Ker-blam* and *Ker-blim* not mentioned. So S B F Th T M DN.III. Not A in W C. Cf. M: "Several of my correspondents suggest that it may have been suggested by the German prefix *ge-* —that it may represent a humorous attempt to make German words by analogy, e.g. *geflop*, *gesplash*, etc." Cf. the extensive list of *ker-* words in AS.VII.142)

kernel-sound, a. [B¹] *Young Kaspar he was kernel-sound* 1891 *Slovenly Peter* (1935) 17 (Comb. not in OED W S C. Nonce formation, after German *kerngesund*: sound to the core, hearty, hale)

kerosene-lamp, sb. [?AB²] *Perishing by kerosene-lamp and hoop-skirt conflagrations* 1871 *Screamers* 140. *The legation furniture consists of...a desk, three chairs, kerosene-lamp, a cat, a cuspidor* 1902 "Belated Russian Passport" (1928) 190 (OED 1879, only ex. A in B T. Comb. not in W S C)

keybox, sb. [?AB²] *I mean to hang a card to my keybox, inscribed "Gone out of the City for a week"* 1872 *Letters* (1917) I xii 199 (OEDS 1904. Comb. not in W S C)

kid, sb. [AB¹] *"I went to picnics and dances and parties with the fellows, and tried to carry on and talk nonsense with the girls, but it wasn't any use...When my work was done, I wanted to sit quiet and smoke and think—not tear around with a parcel of giddy young kids"* 1907 "Capt. Stormfield" 48 (A young person of either sex. This precise meaning is not provided by any dict. Cf. OED 5. *slang.* A child, esp. a young child. Originally low slang, but of late frequent in familiar speech. 1690..1894. So S C U T; A in Cl DN.I. Cf. also OEDS 5d. A young man, fellow. *U.S. slang.* 1896.. W: A child; a youngster. *Colloq.* S: *U.S.*, a young woman. DN.III: students of both sexes, n.w. Ark.)

kid-glove, a. [?AB¹] *"What he don't know about the river ain't worth knowing—a regular gold-leaf, kid-glove, diamond-breastpin pilot Wash Hastings is"* 1873 GA iv 48. *"He can do such gold-leaf, kid-glove, diamond-breastpin piloting!"* 1875 OTM 452 (This sense not in OED W S C. Cf. OED 2. Dainty or delicate in action or operation; avoiding real exertion or everyday work; free from roughness or harshness. Here the sense is an entirely different one: Supremely good, skilful, expert)

killing, ppl.a. [?AB²] *A lecturer...flooded an audience with the killingest jokes for an hour* 1889 CY viii 111 (OED 2e. 'Excruciatingly' funny; that makes one 'die' with laughing. *colloq.* No ex. So W U. A in S DN.I AS.XI.351. This sense not in C)

killing-grudge, sb. [?AB¹] *The only person in camp who had a killing-grudge against Flint Buckner* 1902 "DBDS" (1928) 337 (Comb. not in OED W S C)

killingly, adv. [?AB¹] *He made himself so killingly funny* 1881 PP xvii 219 (Excruciatingly; used as a humorous intensive. This sense not in OED W S C. Cf. killing, ppl.a., above)

kind, sb. **kind of**, or **kinder**, adv. [?A] *Then the feller says, kinder sad-like, "Well, I'm only a stranger here"* 1865 "Jumping Frog" (1875) 34. See *heifer* 1872; *gill* 1884; *cold* 1884. *The duke kind of soured on him* 1884 HF xix 188. *That made it kind of easy to ask help of him* 1892 AmCl iii 36. See also *finisher* 1894 (OEDS 14d. *colloq.* Used adverbially: In a way, as it were, to some extent. Earlier U.S. exs. 1796.. A in B Th M DN.III AS.XI.352. Not A in W S C U Wr T)

kindlings, sb. [AB²] *He got back barely in season to help Jim saw next day's wood and split the kindlings* 1876 TS i 3 (OED 2. In U.S. usually plural. 1878, only ex. Am. form. So B F Cl T. Not unknown in Eng., but *firewood* is much more usual. Not A in W S C U)

kindling-wood, sb. [?AB³] *He would have danced the furniture to kindling-wood* 1893 "Banknote" (1928) 130 (OED 1850.. So W S C U. A in Wr B. So H: In descriptions of the results of collisions and similar accidents, Am. *kindling-wood* = Eng. *matchwood*)

kinfolks, sb. [AB¹] *"No father, no mother, no kinfolks of no kind"* 1873 GA ii 33. *These people was mostly kinfolks of the family* 1884 HF xviii 162 (A in DN.II,III,V. *Dial* in W. This form not in OED S C. Cf. OED Kinsfolk, Kinsfolks, now *rare*, c1450..1855; both forms *dial* in Wr)

king-bee, sb. [?AC] *He was king-bee of the little village* 1895 JA II vii 236 (Supreme ruler, master, autocrat. A in DN.IV, from Va. This sense not in OED W S C. A *fig* use of the *obs* sense = Queen-bee, OED 1679; so W S C. Cf. OED King, sb. 8. Applied by earlier writers, after Latin, to the queen-bee. *obs.* c1386..1710)

king-bolt, sb. [?AB¹] *I took [my watch] to another watch-maker. He said the king-bolt was broken* 1870 SNO (1875) 19 (Hum. malapropism. Cf. W: A vertical bolt by which the forward axle and wheels of a vehicle or the trucks of a railroad car are connected with the other parts. So S C. A in B Cl T. This *spec* sense not in OED)

Kingdom, sb. [?AB¹] *"For a man that has been in the Kingdom as long as I reckon you have, you do seem to know powerful little about its customs." "Its customs!" says he. "Heaven is a large place, good friend"* 1909 "Capt. Stormfield" 45 (Heaven or Paradise; the next world; short for Kingdom-Come, q.v. This sense not in OED W S C)

Kingdom-Come, sb. [?A] *"Why, you'd think it was Christopher C'lumbus discovering Kingdom Come"* 1884 HF xii 103 (OED Kingdom, sb. 6a. Heaven or Paradise; the next world. *slang.* 1785.. So W S C U Wr. A in B DN.III)

king-feature, sb. [B¹] *It was a dog-show. There was a double-leaded column about the king-feature of this one, which was called a St. Bernard* 1897 FE xlv 415 (Comb. not in OED W S C)

kingfisher, sb. [A] See *West*, sb. 1864 (OED 1. The Belted Kingfisher of N.America. 1622.. So W S C)

king-parenthesis, sb. [B¹] *All the parentheses and reparentheses are massed together between a couple of king-parentheses* 1880 TA App.D 603 (Nonce comb.)

kings-and [AB¹] See *and* 1867 (A poker hand: probably "two pair", one of them being a pair of kings. See discussion under *and*, above. Comb. not in OED W S C)

kink, sb. [?AB³] "*I am going to show them some new kinks in the publishing business*" 1901 *Speeches* (1910) 344 (OED 2b. *fig.* A 'dodge', 'wrinkle'. Earliest exs. U.S. 1889.. A in B Th,1846. Not A in W. This sense not in S C)

kinky, a. [?AB³] See *after*, a. 1869 (OED 1. Said esp. of the hair of some races. OEDS Earliest exs. U.S. 1844.. A in F Th M. Not A in W S C)

kiss-the-Bible, sb. [B¹] "*I don't want nothing more out of you than just your word—I druther have it than another man's kiss-the-Bible*" 1884 HF xxxviii 283 (Sworn testimony. Phr. used as sb. not in OED W S C. Cf. OED Kiss, v. 6. To kiss the book. 1523..)

kit, sb. [?AB³] *When the boat touched the levee...she moved her kit ashore* 1894 PW viii 337. See also *swag* 1897 (OED 2b. Personal effects. 1833.. So W S C U Wr T. A in B)

kit, sb. **the whole kit and biling.** [AB³] "*Give a body a rest! Go 'long now, the whole kit and biling of ye*" 1884 HF xxxvii 378 (OEDS 3. *vulgar U.S.* 1869.. So B DN.I,III. Phr. not in W S C. Cf. Wr: The whole kit; The whole kit and boodle, *American*. Cf. also boiling, sb., above)

kitchen cabinet, sb. [AB¹] *Her master left a couple of dollars lying unprotected on his desk...She covered the tempter with a book, and another member of the kitchen cabinet got it* 1893 PW ii 237 (Cf. OEDS Kitchen, sb. 7. *U.S.* A group of friends and personal supporters of President Jackson who were alleged by his opponents to have more influence with him than his official Cabinet; hence, a private or unofficial group of advisers to any one holding a political office. So C B. Cf. Th.III: Afterwards extended to similar juntos, real or imaginary. Not in W S. Here, by *hum. transf.*, of rascally servants in a private household)

kite-line, sb. [B¹] *He took a kite-line from his pocket* 1876 TS xxxi 244 (Comb. not in OED W S C)

Klondike, sb. [AB³] *It was—materially—a sawdust mine when she got it, and she has turned it into a Klondike* 1907 CS II i 102 (OEDS 1. The name of a district in Yukon, N.W. Canada, the scene of a gold-rush in the years following 1896. Hence, *fig.*, a mine or quarry of valuable material. 1897, only ex. The *fig* sense not in W S; word not in C)

kneip, sb. [B²E] *Kneips are held, now and then* [at the University of Heidelberg], *to celebrate great occasions* 1880 TA iv 43 (OEDS Kneipe, pl. Kneipen. *German.* A convivial meeting of University students at a tavern or restaurant. 1924, only ex. So W S C. M.T.'s pl. *Kneips* not given in OED W S C)

knife, v. [AB³] *The shady devil who lives and lurks and hides and watches inside of human beings...had knifed her* 1892 AmCl xxii 235 (OED 1c. *U.S. slang.* To strike at secretly. 1888.. So W S C U F Cl Th M DN.III)

knife-sheath, sb. [B¹] *He reached for his prize and seized it, dropping his knife-sheath* 1894 PW xix 22 (Comb. not in OED W S C)

knight-stroke, sb. [B¹] "*Well then*," (*and gave him the knight-stroke*)... "*rise as knight*" 1880 TA i 21 (Act of knighting, after the German *Ritterschlag*. Comb. not in OED W S C)

knob, sb. [A] *The district was called the "knobs" of East Tennessee* 1873 GA i 17. *His boyhood was spent up there among the "knobs"—so called—of East Tennessee* 1906 *Autob* (1924) II 268 (OED 2. A prominent isolated rounded mound or hill...esp. in U.S. 1650..1791, first U.S. ex. So S C B F Cl Th M DN.VI AS.II.30. Cf. F: Primarily a Kentuckian term. Not A in W Wr T)

knob, v. [?AB³] *His skin satin, his rounded muscles knobbing it as if it had eggs under it* 1897 FE xxxviii 346 (OEDS 1. To form knobs upon. Earlier U.S. ex. 1849.. Not A in W S C)

knock around, v.intr.[AB¹] *I like this knocking around, loose and easy, and making acquaintances and talking* 1880 TA xxvii 278 (A in DN.II,III,IV: To wander about. Comb. not in OED W S C; but cf. OED Knock about: To wander or roam; OEDS Earlier U.S. exs., 1833.. Cf. also Knock round, A in B)

knock down, v. trans. [AB³] *They would "knock down" fares—I mean rob the company* 1889 CY xl 512 [OEDS 8i. *U.S. slang.* To appropriate or embezzle passengers' fares. 1860.. So W S C B F Cl Th T H DN.III)

knockdown, sb. [?AB³] See *dog-pelter* 1864 (OED 2. A stand-up or free fight. 1845, only ex. So W S. A in B Cl. Not in C as sb.)

knock-kneed, a. [?A] See *hair* 1880 (OED Having the legs bent inward. OEDS Earlier Am. exs. 1774.. A in B. Not A in W S C U T)

knock off, v.intr. [?A] "*I'm for knocking off and lighting out*" 1884 HF xxvi 266. See *barbecue* 1886. *I mean to try to knock off tomorrow, but it's doubtful if I do* 1888 *Letters* (1917) II xxviii 500. "*Do they knock off at noon?*" 1889 CY xxii 276 (OED 10c. To cease from one's work. 1649.. So W S C U Wr. A in B)

knock off, v.trans. [?AB³] *All the population had knocked off work* 1892 AmCl xxiv 250 (OED 10d. Earliest ex. U.S. 1840.. Not A in W S C U Wr)

knock off, v. trans. [?AB³] *I am not willing to antedate his crimes by fifteen hundred years. I must ask you to knock off part of that* 1894 "Private Hist. of the Jumping Frog Story" (1900) 375 (OED 10f. To deduct from an amount or sum. 1858.. So W S C U. A in B DN.III)

knock out, v.trans. [?AB³] "*I am clear knocked out by this new detail*" 1892 AmCl xix 199 (OED 12d. *fig.* To drive out of the contest, vanquish. 1883.. So W S C U. A in H: Used *fig*, as is *knock on the head* in England)

knock out, v.trans. [AB²] *The religious feature has been pretty well knocked out of it* [i.e., Mardi-Gras at New Orleans] 1883 LM xlvi 465. *Their appetites were weakening. I made them knock out a meal* 1898 "At the Appetite Cure" (1928) 164 (OEDS 12h. To eliminate, get rid of. *U.S.* 1889.. This sense not in W S C)

knock out, v.trans. [?AB¹] *It was the twins knocking out a classic four-handed piece on the piano in great style* 1894 PW vi 335 (To play, perform vigorously. This sense not in OED W S C. Cf. OED 12e. To make roughly or hastily, as a picture. *colloq.* 1856..)

knock out of, v.trans. [?AB²] *Here was the most beautiful young creature he had ever seen in his life... "She knocked everything out of me, you know—" "Wonderful girl, wonderful"* 1892 AmCl v 63 (OEDS 6e. 1931, only ex. Comb. not in W S C)

know-it-all, a. [?AB²] *Pathfinder said in that calm, indifferent, know-it-all way of his...* 1895 "Cooper's Literary Offences" 8 (OED U.S. quot. 1895, only ex. Not A in W S. Comb. not in C)

know on, v. [AB¹] "*Did you ever see us before?*" "*No, sah; not as I know on*" 1884 HF xxxiv 353 (A in Wr: To know of, *New England*. Comb. not in OED W S C. Cf. OED Know, v. 18c. *Not that I know of, colloq.* 1742..)

knucks, sb. [AB³] *They got their marbles and played at "knucks"* 1876 TS xvi 135 (A in Cl: A game at marbles in which the winner shoots at his adversary's knuckles. So OEDS *U.S.* 1840.. DN.I,III,IV,V. *Dial* in Wr: *Yorkshire*. Not in W S C)

kodak, v. [AB³] *Joseph is gone to Nice to educate himself in Kodacking—and to get the pictures mounted* 1892 *Letters* (1917) II xxxii 564. *We marched thence, very much hurrah'd and limitlessly kodak'd* 1907 "Chaps. from Autob" 169 (OED trans. and intr. 1891.. So W S U. Not in C. From Kodak, sb. OED Am. coinage, 1890.. So W S C M,1888 AS.II.70)

L

L, sb. [?AB²] *We were still living in Hannibal, Missouri, in the new "frame" house built by my father five years ago. That is, some of us lived in the new part, the rest in the old part back of it—the "L"* 1906 "Chaps. from Autob" 453 (OED 2. An extension of a building at right angles to the main block. 1879.. So W S C. A in Th H. Professor Delancey Ferguson, in *Am. Lit.* VIII.43, notes that in the transcript of this passage in *Autob* I 125, the word "L" has been "polished" away by Mr. Paine)

la, int. [?AC] *"La, sweet your worship, one may lightly answer that, I ween"* 1889 CY x 132 (OED Now only *dial, vulgar,* or *arch.* 1598..1881. So W S C U. A in Wr)

labor-dirt, sb. [B¹] *The old patrician brushed imaginary labor-dirt from his white hand* 1892 AmCl i 21 (Comb. not in OED W S C)

labored-out, ppl.a. [B¹] *This one detail will give you a better idea of Sammy's character than any labored-out description I could furnish* 1902 "DBDS" (1928) 303 (Comb. not in OED W S C; but cf. OEDS Laboured-at, 1876)

labor-union, sb. [?AB³] *By labor-union law the colazione must stop* 1904 "Italian with Grammar" (1906) 196 (OEDS Earliest exs. U.S. 1866..Not A in W S C)

labrick, sb. [AB¹] *As a rule, a knight is a lummox and sometimes even a labrick* 1889 CY xxx 381. *"He's a labrick—just a Simon-pure labrick, if ever there was one"* 1893 PW i 235 (C: A fool; an ass. U.S. (Missouri) slang, this quot. Not in OED W S)

lackaday, int. [C] *"Lackaday, sir, they be not of that breed"* 1889 CY xiv 168 (OED *Obs* or *arch.*. 1849. So W U. Not *obs* in W S)

lack for, v. [B²?C] *"Here's hoping he'll never lack for friends"* 1892 AmCl iii 40 (OEDS Lack, v. 4. 1899.. This construction not in W S C. Cf. U: intr. only in Pres. Part.: *nothing is lacking for your comfort*)

ladder railroad, sb. [B¹] *There isn't a mountain in Switzerland now that hasn't a ladder railroad or two up its back like suspenders* 1892 "Switzerland" (1917) 193 (A rack railway, one with a rack-rail or cogged rail. Comb. not in OED W S C; but cf. OED Rack railway, 1884. Perhaps a nonce term coined by M.T.; but cf. S Ladder rack: in a rack-railway, a rack of bars resembling a ladder)

ladder railway, sb. [B¹] *In that remote time there was only one ladder railway in the country* 1892 "Switzerland" (1917) 193 (Cf. above)

ladle in, v: [B¹] *He ladled in a few such Scriptural phrases* 1872 RI xvi 127 (Comb. with *in* not in OED W S C; but cf. OED Ladle, v. To lift out with a ladle; also with *out*, 1858; OEDS Also with *up*, 1851..)

lady, sb. [?A] *"You were about to enter the 'ladies' car' without knowing it"* 1873 GA xxiv 218. *"She's one of the boarders; young lady that works in the fact'ry." "In a shoe factory; and you call her a young lady?"* 1892 AmCl xi 111 (OED 4. Often used as a more courteous synonym for 'woman', without reference to the status of the person spoken of. 1205.. So W S C U. A in F Cl M AS.XII.117f. Cf. *Atlantic Monthly* LXXVI. 431 for an interesting discussion of the social implications involved in this usage)

lady, sb. [B³] *The child's manners were those of a little lady, and her clothes were daintier and finer than any Mrs. Hawkins had ever seen before* 1873 GA v 53. See also *elect* 1892; *working-people* 1892 (OED 5. A woman whose manners.. have the refinement characteristic of the higher ranks of society. 1861.. So W S C U)

lady-bug, sb. [A] *A brown spotted lady-bug climbed the dizzy height of a grass-blade, and Tom bent down close to it and said, "Lady-bug, lady-bug, fly away home, your house is on fire, your children's alone"* 1876 TS xiv 122 (OEDS *dial* and *U.S.*= Lady-bird. 1787.. So W C Th H. Not A in S Wr)

lady-finger, sb. [?A?C] *They will dish them up into crisp, delicate "lady-fingers"...suggestive of soft dalliance with pastry, ices, and sparkling Moselle* 1864 SS (1926) 138 (OED 2a. A kind of cake. *?Obs.* 1820..1828. OEDS Delete *?Obs* and add mod. exs. 1864, this quot... Not *obs* or A in W S C)

lager, sb. [AB³] *A giant refreshed with new lager beer* 1872 RI xlv 318. *Give an Irishman lager for a month, and he's a dead man* 1883 LM xxiii 260 (OED A light beer, consumed largely in Germany and America. 1853.. So S C B Th M AS.XII.115. Not A in W U)

lagniappe, sb. [AB³] *We picked up one excellent word—a word worth traveling to New Orleans to get..."Lagniappe". They pronounce it "lanny-yap". It is the equivalent of the thirteenth roll in a "baker's dozen". It is something thrown in, gratis, for good measure. The custom originated in the Spanish quarter of the city. When a child or a servant buys something in a shop.. he finishes the operation by saying: "Give me something for lagniappe".* (OEDS Local *U.S.* 1853.. So W S C B F Cl Th T M)

lake-front, sb. [?AB¹] *The lake-front is walled with masonry like a pier* 1880 TA xxv 245 (Comb. not in OED S C; but cf. OEDS Front, sb. The promenade of a seaside resort, 1904. Given in W)

lake-reservoir, sb. [B¹] *Some believed in the scheme of northern lake-reservoirs to replenish the Mississippi* 1883 LM xxviii 307 (Comb. not in OED W S C)

lam, v. [?A] See *galoot* 1872. *"Joe, you can be Friar Tuck and lam me with a quarter-staff"* 1876 TS viii 84. *He said he could lam any thief in the lot* 1883 LM iii 44 (OED 1. To beat soundly. Now *colloq* or *vulgar.* 1595.. So W S C U. A in Wr B F Cl DN.I,III,V)

lambrequin, sb. [AB²] See *boxing*, vbl.sb. 1883 (OED *U.S.* A short curtain or piece of drapery, with the lower edge either scalloped or straight. 1883.. So W. Not A in S C U)

lamellibranchiate, a. [B¹] *Professor Snail.. said: "This [protuberance] is lamellibranchiate in its formation"* 1875 SNO 145 (Nonsense use. Cf. OED *Zool.* term: Belonging to the group of molluscs having lamellate gills. 1855.. So W S C U)

lamp-lighting, vbl.sb. [?AB²] *We went out to a restaurant, just after lamp-lighting* 1869 IA xii 112 (OED 1872, this quot., only ex. Comb. not in W S C)

lanai, sb. [AB¹] *Nearly every house [in Honolulu] has what is called a lanai. It is a large apartment, roofed, floored, open on three sides, with a door or draped archway opening into the drawing-room* 1897 FE iii 61 (S: Hawaii: A portico or veranda. So M. Not in OED W C)

land, int. [AB³] *"Good land, duke, lemme hug you!"* 1884 HF xxv 251. *And moreover—but land, I reckon we are both tired by this time* 1887 *Letters* (1917) II xxvi 482 (OED 3e. *U.S.* Substituted euphemistically for Lord, in phrases *the land knows, Good land!* 1849.. So W DN.II,III,IV,V. This use not in S C)

land, int. **My land!** [AB²] *"My lan', what de reason 'tain't enough?"* 1894 PW xiv 778 (OEDS 3e. *U.S.* 1916, only ex. So DN.IV. Comb. not in W S C)

land, int. **land's sake**. [AB³] *"Oh for the land's sake! Give a body a rest!"* 1884 HF xxxvii 378 (OEDS 3e. *U.S.* 1848.. So B F Th,1846 DN.II,III,IV. Comb. not in W S C)

land, v. [?AB¹] See *lifter* 1894. *Mr. Phelps said with exulting indifference—"An ancestor of mine". I retorted with scathing languidness—"Ancestor of mine. But it is a small matter. I have others." It was not noble in me to do it. But it landed him. I wonder how he felt.* 1897 Autob (1924) I 85 (To give a quietus to; to 'settle', 'fetch', 'get'. This sense not in OED W S C. A *fig* extension of the sense in OED 2e. slang. To get a blow home. 1888..)

land, v. [?AB³] *"I can play him at my leisure and land him when I choose"* 1873 GA xxxvii 338 (OED 3. *Angling.* b. *fig.* To catch or get hold of a person. 1857, only ex. this sense. So W S U. Not in C. Cf. *play*, v., below)

land-boom, sb. [?AB³] *There was nothing to remind one of the humble capital of huts and sheds of the long-vanished day of the land-boom* 1897 FE xviii 181 (OED 1891, only ex. Comb. not in W S C .Cf. *boom,* above)

land-dealer, sb. [AB²] *"He's made the riffle on the Injun; great Injun pacificator and land-dealer"* 1873 GA xxxi 279 (OEDS Chiefly *U.S.* 1873, this quot., only ex. Comb. not in W S C)

land-dinner, sb. [B¹] *Everybody went ashore to have that luxury of luxuries to sea-voyagers—a land-dinner* 1897 FE vii 94 (Comb. not in OED W S C)

landing, sb. [?A] *We beached the boat at our own landing* 1872 RI xxii 172. *He understood from Colonel Sellers how the land lay at Stone's Landing* 1873 GA xvi 152 (OED 5. A landing-place. 1690..1793. OEDS Later U.S. exs. 1832.. A in AS.V.163. Not A in W S C)

landing-cabin, sb. [?AB¹] *They hail a steamboat and clear out. Sometimes there was a single lonely landing-cabin* 1883 LM xxx 326 (A cabin at the landing? Comb. not in OED W S C; but cf. OED Landing-pier, 1858)

landlord-apprentice, sb. [B¹] See *call-boy* 1880 (Comb. not in OED W S C)

land-office business, sb. [AB¹] *You can do such a land-office business on such a small capital* 1865 SS (1926) 167. *"The prophets of Baal took all the trade. Isaac..went a-prophesying around, letting on to be doing a land-office business, but it wan't any use"* 1877 "Some Rambling Notes" ii 590 (A in Th,1882: At a time when the land-offices were fully occupied, this phrase came to mean a rushing business. So W C. Phr. not in OED S, although OED has the 1882 quot. which illustrates it)

land of the free, sb. [AB¹] *"If you was to lay it* [the Sahara Desert] *down on top of the United States, it would cover the land of the free out of sight like a blanket"* 1894 TSA ix 355 (Phr. not in OED W S C. Cf. *Hail-Columbia, Happy-Land-of-Canaan,* etc., above)

landslide, sb. [AB³] *"Do you see that white place up yonder where there's been a landslide?"* 1876 TS xxxiii 257. *He had gone down like a landslide when I pronounced that fearful name* 1889 CY xxiii 293. *It would bring down a landslide of ridicule upon him* 1893 "Traveling with a Reformer" (1900) 353 (OEDS *U.S.*=Landslip. 1838.. So Th M H. Not A in W S C U)

land-speculator, sb. [A] *He might have been a "railroad man", or a politician, or a land-speculator* 1873 GA 1 456 (OEDS Chiefly *U.S.* 1798.. So AS.VII.9, Nebraska. Comb. not in W S C)

language, sb. **strong language.** [?AB¹] *She made a guarded remark which censured strong language* 1906 *Autob* (1924) II 88 (W: Language..unbecomingly forcible or vehement. This sense not in OED, which has only: Expressions indicative of violent or excited feeling; no ex. So S. Comb. not in C. Cf. OED Bad language: coarse or vulgar expressions. Cf. also Fine language, above)

languishy, adv. [?AB¹] *"You must say it soft and sick and languishy"* 1884 HF xxi 205 (Not in OED W S C)

languors, sb.pl. [B¹] *It mollified spite to see him so enjoy his imitation languors, and arts, and airs* 1897 FE xxxvi 326 (This *concrete* sense not in OED W S C. Given in U, with quot. from Swinburne: "The lilies and languors of virtue")

lanky, a. [?AC] *A long, cadaverous creature, with lanky locks hanging down to his shoulders* 1870 SNO (1875) 235 (OED Of hair: somewhat lank. *obs.* 1670, only ex. this use. Not *obs* in W S C)

lap, v. [C] *"The crowd lapped them up"* 1881 PP xiii 156 (OED 3b. To hem in, press close upon. *obs. c*1330.. 1552. So W. Not *obs* in S C)

lap-bred, a. [B¹] *A lap-bred, house-fed, uneducated, inexperienced kitten* 1909 ISD v 52 (Comb. not in OED W S C)

lap-robe, sb. [AB¹] See *cutter* 1904 (A in C Th.III M. Not A in W S. Not in OED)

larboard, sb. Spelled **labboard.** [?ACE] *He would speak of the "labboard" side of a horse in an easy natural way* 1875 OTM 71. *The term "larboard"...was always used on the river in my time* 1875 OTM 568. See *large,* adv. 1880. *"I'll hunt the labboard side, you hunt the stabboard"* 1884 HF xii 108 (OED *Naut.* The term has now been discarded in the navy and supplanted by *port.* 1583..1853. So W S C U. Cf. Quick, *Mississippi Steamboatin',* 1926, p.196: "The portside remained the larboard side throughout river days")

large, sb. **at large.** [A] *Colonel Mulberry Sellers, Perpetual Member-at-large of the Diplomatic Body* 1892 AmCl v 56 (OED 5l. *U.S.* Said of electors or elected who represent the whole of a State and not merely a district of it. 1741.. So W S C H)

large, adv. [?AB¹] *"What water have you got?" "Two foot large on the stabboard, two and a half scant on the labboard!"* 1880 TA xvii 156 (This *spec* sense, used in sounding, not in OED W S C; but cf. OED 7c. *Naut.* Wide of a particular course. 1670.. Cf. also OED Large, a. 5. Indicating the full or rather more than the full quantity. *obs.* 1377.. 1737; so W S C)

large-mouthed, a. [B¹] See *breast-board* 1883 (Comb. not in OED S C. Given in W)

largess, sb. [C] *Every now and then rose the cry, "A largess! a largess!"* 1881 PP xxxi 357 (OED *arch* and literary. 2c. A call for a gift of money. 1377..1825. So W S C. *Dial* in Wr)

lariat, sb. [?AB³] *"I cautiously unwound the lariat from the pommel of my saddle"* 1872 RI xii 64. See *saddle-horn* 1889 (OED A cord or rope with a noose used in catching wild cattle. 1835.. So W U. A in S C B F Cl Th.III M T)

lark, sb. [B³] *He set to work that very night to celebrate the event by a grand lark* 1880 TA App.C. 599 (OED *colloq.* A frolicsome adventure. 1811.. So S C U Wr. Not *colloq* in W)

lark, sb. **to play larks.** [?AB¹] *I was of a merry disposition, and chose to play larks on the public in the matter of dress* 1893 "Banknote" (1928) 110. *She was appointed one of a committee to draught By-Laws for its government. It may be observed that this was larks for her. She did all the draughting herself* 1907 CS II vii 161 (Neither the phr. nor the pl. use in OED W S C)

larrikin, sb. [B³] *He said that the only game-bird in Australia was the wombat, and the only song-bird the larrikin* 1897 FE viii 101. *In the larrikin, he will not be able to discover a new species, but only an old one.. variously called loafer, rough, tough, bummer, or blatherskite* 1897 FE xvi 164 (OED Chiefly *Austral.* A usually juvenile street rowdy. 1870.. So W S C U. Cf. Wr (Suppl): A mischievous or frolicsome youth; *Warwickshire, Worcestershire*)

lasso, sb. [AB³] See *donkey-voiced* 1870. *He swings this rope aloft like a lasso* 1880 TA xxxvi 413. *I was.. swinging the great loop of my lasso about my head* 1889 CY xxxix 500 (OED 1. A long rope of untanned hide,.. having at the end a noose to catch cattle and wild horses; used chiefly in Spanish America. 1808.. So S C U B F M AS.VII.432. Not A in W)

lasso, v. [AB³] *They used to go forth and lasso a poor wretch of a plebeian native* 1866 *Speeches* (1923) 8. *I lassoed Sir Lamorak..and Sir Galahad* 1889 CY xxxix 502 (OED 1807.. Cf. above. A in S C U B F M. Not in W)

last, sb. **to see the last of.** [?AB²] *Whenever the literary German dives into a sentence, that is the last you are going to see of him till he emerges on the other side of his Atlantic with his verb in his mouth* 1889 CY xxii 280 (OEDS 9h. 1910, only ex. Phr. not in W S C)

latch-string, sb. [?AB³] *I went in the back door—you only have to pull a buckskin latch-string, they don't fasten the doors* 1884 HF xxxiv 352 (OEDS Earlier U.S. ex. 1857.. A in H. Not A in W S C)

late-night, a. [B¹] *The damp, earthy, late-night smells* 1885 "Private Hist. of Campaign" 202 (Comb. not in OED W S C)

Latter-Day Saint, sb. [AB³] See *Destroying Angel* 1872; *Adventist* 1907 (OED The name by which the Mormons call themselves. 1842.. So W S C U B F T)

lattice-box, sb. [?AB²] *"Smiley kep' the beast in a little lattice box"* 1865 "Jumping Frog" (1875) 33 (OEDS 1865, this quot., only ex. Comb. not in W S C)

laugh, sb. [?AC] *He would be "so full of laugh" that he could hardly begin* 1875 OTM 572 (OED 1. The action of laughing.. or an inclination to laugh. *rare.* 1690..1891. A in DN.II,III. This sense not in W S C)

laughter-and-chatter, sb. [B¹] *The gay laughter-and-chatter fog of that dinner table* 1906 *Autob* (1924) II 134 (Nonce comb.)

law-dog, sb. [?AB¹] *A succession of baffling disguises.. was a protection from meddling law-dogs in Britain* 1889 CY xxxvii 481 (Comb. not in OED W S C. Cf. Sleuthhound, U.S., below)

law-equipment, sb. [B¹] *Shakespeare's multifarious craft-equipments...his law-equipment* 1909 ISD vii 67 (Comb. not in OED W S C)

lawing, vbl.sb. [?AC] *Four or five years of lawing has brought him $26* 1879 *Letters* (1917) I xix 355 (OED 1. Going to law; litigation. *obs exc. arch.* c1485..1891. Not *obs* or *arch* in W S C Wr. A in B: *Western.* So F. Not A in T)

law-office, sb. [AB²] *The clients stopped with this new clerk in the anteroom of the law-office* 1873 GA xii 117 (OEDS *U.S.* 1873, this quot... So W. Comb. not in S C)

laws, int. [?A?C] *"Laws! the idea!"* 1892 AmCl iii 39. *"But laws, what am I thinking about?"* 1892 AmCl xi 108 (OED In later use it has coalesced with *lor' = Lord* as an exclamation. Now *vulgar.* 1588..1887. So W Wr. Not *arch* in S C. A in B F)

laws-a-me, int. [AB¹] *"Laws-a-me! he's my own dead sister's boy"* 1876 TS i 19. *"Laws-a-me, I've been hungry for it"* 1884 HF xxxii 331 (A in B F. So DN.IV: Probable corruption of "Lord have mercy on me!" *Dial* in Wr. Not in OED W S C; but cf. OED Law, int. 1887, laws o' mercy)

laws goodness, int. [?AB¹] *"Laws goodness, you know what that would be like"* 1892 AmCl iii 41 (Comb. not in OED W S C. Cf. above)

lawsy, int. [?AB²] *A kind-hearted, well-meaning corpse was the Boston young man, but lawsy bless me, horribly dull company* 1880 *Letters* (1917) I xx 383. *"But lawsy, how you did fool 'em, Huck!"* 1884 HF xvi 142 (OEDS Var. of *laws,* int. U.S. quot. 1914, only ex. A in DN.II. IV. Not A in W. Not in S C)

lawyer-farmer, sb. [B¹] *This tract of land seemed an immense possible fortune to this New England lawyer-farmer* 1873 GA 1 460 (Comb. not in OED W S C)

lawyer-talk, sb. [B¹] *The kitten..could have attended cat-assizes on the shed-roof..and have harvested a knowledge of cat lawyer-talk* 1909 ISD v 53. See also *lawyer-way* 1909 (Comb. not in OED W S C)

lawyer-way, sb. [B¹] *The man who wrote them* [Shakespeare's plays] *was limitlessly familiar with the law.. and lawyer-talk, and lawyer-ways* 1909 ISD i 15 (Comb. not in OED W S C)

lay, v. trans. [?A] *"I lay I'll take and hyste some of them preachers out of here"* 1865 SS (1926) 179. See also *wallow,* v. 1876; *hickory* 1896 (OED 12b. To wager, bet. c1380..1889. So W S C U. A in Wr DN.I,III)

lay, v. trans. [?A] *I have already laid a timber claim on the borders of a lake* 1861 *Letters* (1917) I iii 59 (OED 26b. To present in legal form. Earliest ex. U.S. 1798.. Not A in W S C)

lay, v. intr. [?AC] *By and by I was close enough to have a look, and there laid a man on the ground* 1884 HF viii 64. So *passim* in HF and elsewhere (OED 43. In intransitive uses, coinciding with or resembling those of

lie. Now only *dial* or illiterate. c1300..1900. So W S C. A in Wr B M H DN.I,II,V)

lay, sb. [?AB³] *I only wanted to get the lay of the land* 1884 HF xxxi 322. *He took the "lay" of the place with a pocket-compass* 1902 "DBDS" (1928) 334 (OED 7. The position in which something lies; esp. said of country. 1819.. So W S C U W. A in B Th.III)

lay by, v. intr. [AB¹] *We resolved not to "lay by at Cottonwood"* 1872 RI ii 28 (Here used of stagecoach travel; so AS.VI.251, Nebraska. This sense not in OED W S C; but cf. OED 50e. *Naut.* =Lay to: To come to a stationary position. 1697..1741; so W S U)

lay for, v. trans. [?A] *He was always ready and laying for a chance* 1865 "Jumping Frog" (1875) 31. See *softy,* sb. 1872; *allow* 1876. *"Somebody tried to get in, so I was laying for him"* 1884 HF vii 47. See also *ark* 1895; *rock* 1904 (OED 18b. To lie in wait for. 1494..1893. So W S C. A in DN.I,II,III)

lay in, v. intr. [?AC] *"They had laid in together to ruin me with the people"* 1896 TSD xi 531 (OED 53d. To scheme or exert oneself to do something. *obs.* 1599.. 1681. So W. This sense not in S C)

lay into, v. trans. [?AB³] *He laid into his work like a nigger* 1880 TA iii 40 (OED 32d. To 'pitch into'. *slang* or *colloq.* 1838.. So W. A in Wr, this quot. This sense not in S C)

lay low, v. intr. [?AB³] *"If you had laid low and kept dark"* 1872 RI xxiv 182. *"Lay low and hold your breath, for I'm 'bout to turn myself loose"* 1883 LM iii 45. *"I'd better lay low and keep dark and not write at all"* 1884 HF xxvii 275 (OEDS 43=Lie low. U.S. exs, 1861.. A in B T. This use not in W S C)

lay off, v. trans. [?AC] See *overcoat* 1873. *He laid off his coat* 1894 PW xix 21 (OED 54a. †To take off. 1529.. 1727. OEDS Mod. U.S. ex. 1919. A in H. Not A in S C. This sense not in W)

lay off, v. intr. [AB³] See *sleep up* 1884. *Then when we had got pretty well stuffed, we laid off and lazied* 1884 HF viii 66 (OEDS 54f. *dial* and *U.S.* To take a rest. 1863.. So Th.III M H. Not A in W. This sense not in S C)

lay on, v. trans. [?A?C] *We can understand why Shelley's happiness in his home had been wounded, and no one can persuade us into laying it on Harriet* 1894 "In Defence of Harriet Shelley" 250 (OED 29. To bring forward as a charge or accusation; to impute, attribute, ascribe, something objectionable. Const. with...on. ?arch. 1690..1890. Not arch in W S C)

lay on the oars, v.phr. [B¹] *I will lay on my oars for awhile, and see how the wind sets* 1856 *Letters* (1917) I ii 34 (To suspend operations. This *fig* sense not in OED; but cf. OED 43b. *Naut.* To cease rowing. 1830.. Phr. not in W S C)

lay open, v.trans. [?AB¹] *The risk they ran of getting their heads laid open* 1894 PW iv 330 (To beat over the head, break, crack. So S C: To produce an open wound in. Phr. not in OED W)

lay out, v.trans. [?AB³] *"The old man he rode up and shot him down. But he didn't git much chance to enjoy his luck, for inside of a week our folks laid him out"* 1884 HF xviii 166. See *crusher* 1889. *A heavy bat on the jaw laid the lad out* 1902 "DBDS" (1928) iv 311 (OEDS 56b. *slang.* To 'do for'; *fig* to put 'hors de combat'. Earlier U.S. ex. 1829.. A in F Th T. Not A in W S C U)

lay out, v. trans. [?A?C] *It was beautiful to hear the lad lay out the science of war* 1889 CY xxv 320 (OED 56g. To set forth, expound. ?Now *rare.* 1440..1864. So C U. Not *rare* in W S. Wr: *Scotch.* A in Th T)

layout, sb. [AB²] *He must go back at once to the line and superintend the layout with reference to his contract* 1873 GA xix 177 (OED 1. Chiefly *U.S.* The laying out or disposition of land, streets, etc. 1888.. So B F Th.III. Not A in W S C U H)

layout, sb. [AB³] *"Everybody was a-movin' from the old buryin'-ground, and was for a new lay-out in the new* *simitery on the hill... We've bunched the departed...A little crowded towards the end of the lay-out, maybe"* 1877 "Some Rambling Notes" i 444. *Authorities agree that there is no such tremendous "layout" of snowy Alpine sublimity to be seen from any other accessible point* 1880 TA xxxviii 448. See *bust,* v. 1883. *"If I had capital and a theater, I wouldn't want a better lay-out than that"* 1884 HF xxvii 278 (OED Chiefly *U.S.* 2. Something laid out; a display, a 'spread'. 1869.. So B F Th,1817 T. Not A in W S C)

layout, sb. [AB²] *"He ca'mly bunched the hands and went to shuffling for a new layout"* 1877 *Speeches* (1910) 5 (OED Chiefly *U.S.* 3. *Cards.* 1889.. A in H. Not A in W S C)

lay over, v.intr. [AB¹] *"You git out at Cottonwood, you fellers, and lay over a couple of days"* 1872 RI ii 28 (W: *colloq. U.S.,* To stop over; to break a journey. So S. The intr. sense not in OED C; but cf. OED 57b. *U.S. colloq.* To allow to pass by, to postpone. 1885.. So DN.III)

lay over, v.trans. [AB²] *Fellers that had travelled and been everywheres all said he laid over any frog that ever they see* 1865 "Jumping Frog" (1875) 33. See *begin with* 1877; *pile it on* 1884. *The cussing he done then laid over anything he had done previous* 1884 HF vi 45. *"Why, Peters, I laid over the lot of them!"* 1907 "Capt. Stormfield" 41 (OED 57c. *U.S. Colloq.* To excel. 1869.. Not A in W S C)

lay preacher, sb. [B¹] See *lumber-camp* 1906 (Comb. not in OED W S C; but cf. OED Lay elder 1594..; Lay reader 1883..)

lay to, v.intr. [?AC] *There isn't any way to shorten sail...You could lay to, with your head to the wind* 1908 "Capt. Stormfield" 266 (OED †58c. *Naut.* To come to a stationary position, with the head towards the wind. 1798..1868. Not *obs* in W S C U)

lay tongue to, v. [?AB²] *And so he went on, calling Sherburn everything he could lay tongue to* 1884 HF xxxi 214 (OEDS 21f. To apply the tongue to some kind of utterance. 1893, only ex. So Wr. Phr. not in W S C)

lay up, v.intr. [?AB²] *A man that was running stumbled and fell and sprained his ankle so that he had to lay up* 1883 LM iii 53 (OED 60e. In recent *colloq* use: To take to one's bed. 1893.. The intr. use not in W S C)

lazy, v. [?AB²] *Just lazying a heavenly life out in their own private unpestered society* 1883 *Letters* (1917) I xxiii 427. *Afterwards we would watch the lonesomeness of the river, and kind of lazy along, and by and by lazy off to sleep...So we would put in the day, lazying around, listening to the stillness* 1884 HF xix 178. *We lazied the rest of the pleasant afternoon away* 1885 "Private Hist. of Campaign" 197 (OED 2. quasi-trans.=Laze, to enjoy oneself lazily. 1885, above quot... So W S C Wr. A favorite word)

lead, sb. [?AB³] *Each one was a well-defined lead by itself, and without a spur* 1869 IA xxxix 414 (OED 6a. A lode. 1812.. So W S. A in C Th)

lead, sb. **to lay in the leads** [?AB¹] *"What are you laying in the leads for?"* 1909 ISD i 4 (Phr. not in OED W S C; but cf. OED 10d. *Naut.* The direction in which running ropes lead fair, and come down to the deck. *c*1860.. The meaning is perhaps to set the helm or steering wheel on the fore-and-aft line, i.e. straight ahead. Cf. Amidships, adv., To set amidships, above)

leader, sb. [B³] *I wrote my "leader" in the forenoon* 1872 RI lv 400 (OED 12. Leading article. 1844.. So W S C U. Cf. editorial, above. The two rival substitutes for the clumsy term 'leading article" (OED 1807..1877) are first cited by the OED in the same year, 1844, 'leader' being first used in Great Britain by Disraeli, and 'editorial' in the U.S., where it has now almost driven 'leader' from the field. M.T.'s usage shows that 'leader' was then still in familiar use in Am. newspapers. Cf. leader-writer, below)

leader-writer, sb. [B³] *The Tribune was in its early home, at that time, and Hay was a leader-writer on its staff...I think it must have been 1870 or '71* 1905 "John Hay" 1530 (OED 1888, only ex. So W S C)

leadsman, sb. [?AB³] See *half* 1873. *Then came the leadsman's sepulchral cry—"Deep four! Mark three!"* 1875 OTM 574 (OED The man who 'heaves' the lead in taking soundings. 1857.. So W S C. Here *spec* of the river steamboat official so named)

lead up to, v. [?AB³] *Trying to "lead up" to this really apt and beautiful quotation* 1872 RI xviii 145. *When Jeff arrived Tom accosted him, and led up warily to opportunities for remark about Betty* 1876 TS xii 112 (OED 22b. To prepare gradually for. 1861.. So W S C U. M.T's use of quotation marks in the first ex. indicates that he had heard it used in *colloq* speech)

leaf tobacco, sb. [?A] *Every individual was either chewing natural leaf tobacco prepared on his own premises, or smoking the same in a corncob pipe* 1873 GA i 20 (OED 1600, 1851. So W C. Comb. not in S. Cf. tobacco, below)

league-long, a. [B²] *"You drag through league-long picture galleries"* 1880 TA xxxviii 441 (OED League, sb. b. 1883.. So W. Comb. not in S C)

league-striding, a. [B¹] *"You are only a dainty page, not a league-striding war-colossus"* 1896 JA II xiv 434 (Comb. not in OED W S C)

league-wide, a. [B¹] *Stretch their league-wide levels back to the dim forest walls* 1883 LM xxxix 419 (Comb. not in OED W S C)

leak, v. [?AB¹] *That was the boot that had a couple of his toes leaking out of the front end of it* 1884 HF vi 44 (To protrude. This hum. *transf.* sense not in OED W S C)

leak, v. [?AB¹] *They bust out a-crying.. I never see two men leak they way they done.. the place was that damp I never see anything like it* 1884 HF xxv 245 (To shed tears, weep. This hum. *transf.* sense not in OED W S C)

leaky, a. [?AB¹] *As a rule, the grammar was leaky* 1889 CY xxvi 341 (Defective, 'full of holes'. This hum. *fig* sense not in OED W S C)

leal, a. [C] *"All that be leal men and true"* 1881 PP x 119 (OED Now *Sc.* and in literary use derived from Scottish, 1a. *a*1300..1876. So W S C U Wr)

learn, v. [?AC] See *Sucker* 1853. *"He never done nothing but..learn that frog to jump"* 1865 "Jumping Frog" (1875) 32. *"When I say I'll learn a man the river I mean it".* [Footnote] *"Teach" is not in the river vocabulary* 1875 OTM 286. *"Can't learn an old dog new tricks"* 1876 TS i 19. *"Some of them learns people how to talk French"* 1884 HF xiv 123 (OED 4. To teach, in various constructions. Now *vulgar. c*1200..1889. So W S C Wr. A in M DN.I,II,III,V. Cf. *Mod.Lang.Notes* XVI (1901) 161)

learn, v. [?AB¹] *"Damn you, I'll learn you!"* 1873 GA xxix 266 [Wr: Freq. used ironically as a threat of punishment. This very common use not in OED W S C. The correct "teach" would never be used in this sense)

lease-roll, sb. [B¹] *A parish in London with two thousand houses on its lease-roll* 1892 AmCl i 17 (Comb. not in OED W S C)

least, adv. [?AB¹] *"Yes, least I reckon so"* 1876 TS vi 65 (Wr: At least; *Scotch* and *Yorkshire.* This use not in OED W S C)

leastways, adv. [?AB³] *"Leastways, I's suffered so much"* 1894 PW xviii 17 (OED b. At least. *dial* and *vulgar.* 1852.. So W S U Wr T. C: *obs.* A in B DN.III AS.XI.312, Ozarks)

leather, sb. [AB¹] *"I pulled off an old woman's leather"* (*robbed her of her pocket-book*) [Given as "thieves' argot"] 1883 LM lii 511 (A in F Cl DN.V AS.I.652, X.18. This sense not in OED W S C)

leather, sb. [?AB¹] *They play billiards; there are some cues, but no leathers* 1902 "DBDS" (1928) 308 (W: Billiard-cue tip. So U. This sense not in OED S C)

leather-face, a. [?AB¹] *"You ain't one of these leather-face people. I don't want no better book than what your face is"* 1884 HF xxviii 287 (Comb. not in OED W S C; but cf. OED Leather-skinned, 1655..)

leather-head, sb. [?A] *You leather-head, if I talk in Boston both afternoon and evening March 5, I'll have to go to Boston the 4th* 1873 *Letters* (1917) I xii 203 (OED slang. A blockhead. 1700.. So W S C Wr. A in Th,1888 DN.II,III,IV,V)

leather-headed, a. [?A] *They* [the jays] *got off as many leather-headed opinions about it as an average crowd of humans could have done* 1880 TA iii 41. *He was bright and not leather-headed* 1884 HF xxxiv 350 (OED Stupid. 1668, only ex. So W S Wr. Not in C. Cf. above)

leather-headedness, sb. [?AB²] *His* [the ant's] *leather-headedness is the point I make against him* 1880 TA xxii 215. *A case of monumental leatherheadedness* 1881 *Speeches* (1910) 18 (OED Stupidity. 1880, above quot., only ex. So S. Not in W C. Cf. above)

lecture-agent, sb. [?AB²] *"I am a business man. I am a lecture-agent"* 1873 GA lviii 527 (OEDS 1873, this quot., only ex. Comb. not in W S C)

lecture-double, sb. [B¹] *I had set the law after living lecture-doubles of mine a couple of times in America* 1897 FE xv 160 (Nonce comb.; cf. OED Double, sb. 2b. A counterpart.. of a person. 1818..)

lecture-hall, sb. [?AB³] *It provided for the erection of certain buildings for the university, dormitories, lecture-halls, museums, libraries* 1873 GA lxv 406 (OEDS 1870, 1873, U.S. exs. Comb. not in W S C)

lecture-raid, sb. [?AB¹] *I could not thank the "Alta" for bankrupting my lecture-raid* 1904 *Autob* (1924) I 245 (Nonce comb.; cf. Raid, sb., below: A predatory incursion. A in B F Cl)

lecture-season, sb. [?AB¹] *That was the easiest and pleasantest month of the four or five which constituted the "lecture season"* 1898 *Autob* (1924) I 156. (Comb. not in OED W S C. Cf. above)

lecture-skirmish, sb. [B¹] *My lecture-skirmish on the coast would have paid me ten thousand dollars* 1904 *Autob* (1924) I 244 (Nonce comb.)

lecture-tour, sb. [?AB²] *I had a curiosity to know about that man's lecture-tour and last moments* 1897 FE xv 160 (OEDS 1897, this quot., only ex. Comb. not in W S C)

lecturing-trip, sb. [?AB²] *The starting-point of this lecturing-trip around the world was Paris* 1897 FE i 25 (OEDS 1897, this quot., only ex. Comb. not in W S C)

ledge, sb. [?AB³] See *claim,* sb. 1869. *The ledge was as barren of silver as a curbstone* 1872 RI xxxv 250. See also *arrastre* 1909 (OED 5b. *Mining.* A stratum of metal-bearing rock. 1847.. So W S. A in C: a common name in the Cordilleran range for the lode...frequently used, as *reef* is in Australia, to designate a quartz-vein)

leech, sb. [C] See *waiting-woman* 1871. *An hermit who was a good man and a great leech* 1889 CY iii 47 (OED 1. A physician. Now arch. c900..1870. So W C U. Not arch in S Wr)

leeward, sb. Spelled **looard.** [E] *"Keep away, boy— keep to looard"* 1884 HF xvi 139. *I could see I was going considerable to looard of the bush* 1908 "Capt. Stormfield" 266 (This sp. not in OED W S C U, although the pron. is indicated)

left, ppl.a. **to get left.** [AB²] *"They have started in with big confidence...but they are going to get left"* 1883 LM xxviii 303. *I had never been accustomed to getting left* 1889 CY xiv 160. See also *folderol* 1889 (OEDS Leave, v. 7d. *colloq.* orig. *U.S.* To be left in the lurch, 1883.. So W S Th.III H. Not A in C U)

left-handed, a. [?A?C] See *sham-supplication* 1883. *The king he give me a left-handed look out of the corner of his eye, and so I knowed enough to talk on the right side*

1884 HF xxix 300 (OED 4. Sinister. ?Obs. 1609..1809 Not *obs* in W S C U Wr)

left-hander, sb. [?AB³] *That gentleman delivered the young aspirant for a muss one of his elegant little left-handers* 1873 GA xxix 267 (OED c. A blow delivered with the left hand. 1861.. So S C U. This sense not in W)

left-over, a. [?AB²] *Irish stew made of the potatoes and meat left over from a procession of previous meals* 1892 AmCl xii 119. *A job-lot of left-over standards and ideals* 1906 *Autob* (1924) II 305. See also *mesozoic* 1909 (OEDS 1. Not used up or disposed of. 1897.. So W S. A in H. Not in C)

leg, sb. **not a leg to stand on.** [?AB²] See *half-doubt* 1881 (OED 2c. No support whatever. 1889, only ex. So W S U Wr. A in B AS.III. Phr. not in C)

leggings, sb.pl. Spelled **leggins.** [?AE] *I came upon a gentle daughter of the aborigines in moccasins and leggins* 1869 SNO (1875) 68 (OED Chiefly pl. This sp. 18th and 19th c. 1763..1869. So W S C, but this sp. not in W. A in B T DN.VI AS.IV.474)

legislate, v. [?AB³] *The Jew is being legislated out of Russia* 1899 "Concerning the Jews" (1900) 263 (OED 3. quasi-trans. To drive by legislation *into* or *out of.* 1845.. So W S. A in C M)

Legislature, sb. [A] *"Our Congress and our fifty State Legislatures are members..of the Blessings-of-Civilization Trust"* 1901 "To the Person Sitting in Darkness" 175 (OED 1. *spec. U.S.* The legislative body of a State or Territory. 1783.. So W S C)

leg-power, sb. [B¹] *The leg-power passed from one to the other* [of the Siamese twins] 1894 TET v 391 (Nonce comb.)

leg-shop, sb. [AB¹] *"They're playing 'Undine' at the Opera House, and some folks call it the leg shop"* 1871 *Screamers* 144 (A in F: Theatre where stage dancing forms a prominent feature of the entertainment. So Cl. Comb. not in OED W S C)

leman, sb. [C] See *sheep-witted* 1889 (OED 2. An unlawful lover or mistress. In later archaistic use applied chiefly to the female sex. c1275..1871. So W C. Not *arch* in S U Wr)

lengthy, a. [A] *You will excuse me if this is not lengthy* 1853 *Letters* (1917) I i 30 (OED Before the 19th c. found only in Am. writers. a. Extending to great length; prolix, tedious. 1759.. A in B F Th T M DN.III,V,VI AS.IV.473, V.303, VI.301. Not A in W S C U. See other refs. in Kennedy, p. 319)

let, v. [C] *"Prithee do not let me." "Let you what?" "Hinder me, then, if the word please thee better"* 1889 CY ii 32 (OED 1. *arch.* To hinder. c888..1894. So W S C U. *Dial* in Wr)

let, sb. **let or hindrance.** [B³?C] *"None durst offer let or hindrance to my will"* 1881 PP xv 182 (OED Now *arch*; most common in the phr. *let or hindrance.* 1842.. Phr. not *arch* in W S C U)

let, v. **lemme, less** (for *let me, let us*) [?AE] *"Less see 'em"* 1876 TS iv 45. *"Lend a hand and less heave him overboard!"* 1883 LM iii 58. *"Lemme hug you!"* 1884 HF xxv 251 (These forms given in W Wr. A in M, sp. *les.* A in DN.I,III AS.XI.234. Not in OED S C)

let alone, v.phr. [?AB³] *"It's all I can do to tell t'other fum which, let alone his pappy"* (OED 18e. 'Not to mention'. 1816.. So W C U Wr. ?A in Th. Phr. not in S)

let down, v.trans. **let down softly.** [?AB³] *Then the teacher lets me down softly with the remark...* 1880 TA App.D 602 (OED 29g. To treat considerately, *colloq.* 1834.. A in B F. Phr. not in W S C)

let in for, v.trans. [?AB³] *He* [Washington] *had probably arranged to let his brother Edward in for the cherry-tree results* 1899 "My First Lie" (1900) 168 (OED 31e. To involve in. Earliest ex. U.S. 1837.. Not A in C. Phr. not in W S)

let into, v.trans. [?AB³] *He let into the camel-driver the hardest he knowed how* 1894 TSA x 394 (OEDS 7c. slang. To attack. Earlier U.S. ex. 1851.. Not A in S C Wr. Not in W)

let on, v.intr. [A] See *bullyrag* 1865. *"If I was as ignorant as you I wouldn't let on"* 1884 HF ii 15. *I hadn't an idea; but it would have been cruel to confess... so I never let on* 1889 CY xli 523 (OED 33. To reveal, disclose, betray, *dial* and *U.S.* 1725.. A in Wr B F Th T M DN.II,III,IV,V. Not A in W S C U)

let on, v.trans. [AB³] *The privilege of staying home from school when you let on that you are sick* 1865 *Jumping Frog* (1867) 165. *Benjamin Franklin would..sit up nights, and let on to be studying algebra by the light of a smouldering fire...In order to get a chance to fly his kite on Sunday, he used to hang a key on the string and let on to be fishing for lightning* 1870 SNO (1875) 276. *"Come now, you don't mean to let on that you like it?"* 1876 TS ii 30. *I let on to be interested—and I was, too* 1884 HF xi 90. See also *fetch around* 1906 (OEDS 33b. To pretend. *dial* and *U.S.* 1822.. So Wr Th DN.II,III,V. Not A in W S C)

let on, v.trans. [?AB¹] *"He being, as he says to me, a gentleman—which is pretty plain letting-on that the boys ain't"* 1892 AmCl xi 90 (To insinuate, allege, allow it to be understood. Apparently a distinct sense, not in OED W S C. Cf. DN.III: To talk to an ostensible purpose, n.w.Ark.)

let out, v.intr. [AB³] *Then school "let out"* 1898 "Austrian Edison" (1900) 267 (OED 34j. To end, break up. *U.S.* 1888.. So S C Th DN.III. Not A in W Wr)

let out, v.intr. [?AB³] *He let out with his left leg and kicked me across a ten-acre lot* 1866 *Letters* (1917) I v 105 (OED 34h. To strike out. 1840.. So W S C U. Here *spec* of a horse kicking; so AS.VIII.4.51, Nebraska)

let out, v.trans. [?AB¹] *"That lets you out, you know, you chowder-headed old clam. Go—get your money, and cut your stick!"* 1871 SNO (1875) 299. *I have written the Galaxy people that I will never furnish them another article, long or short...I hope that lets them out, for I will stick to that* 1871 *Letters* (1917) I x 185. *"They said he [the negro] could vote when he was at home. Well, that lets me out!"* 1884 HF vi 43 (To be enough for; to release from responsibility or concern. This sense not in OED W S C. An extension of the sense in OED 34a. To set free, liberate, release from confinement. 1154..)

letter-correspondence, sb. [B¹] *What can be found in a German daily?...telegrams, mainly about European national and international political movements; letter-correspondence about the same things...The average German daily is made up solely of correspondence,—a trifle of it by telegraph, the rest of it by mail* 1880 TA App.F 626 (News sent by mail. Comb. not in OED W S C)

letter-crossing, vbl.sb. [B¹] *The "crossing" of letters has been so frequent as to become monotonous...I have grown superstitious about this letter-crossing business* 1891 "Mental Telegraphy" 99 (Comb. not in OED W S C; but cf. OED Cross, v. 10b. Of two letters. 1793..)

letter-perfect, a. [B¹] *Tom's conduct had remained letter-perfect during two whole months* 1894 PW xvii 822. *The flexible and letter-perfect English of the "Venus and Adonis"* 1909 ISD iv 42 (Absolutely correct, above criticism, unexceptionable. This sense not in OED W S C. A *fig* extension of the theatrical sense in OED Letter, sb. 8a. Knowing one's part to the letter, 1885)

letter-sack, sb. [B¹] *We stirred up the hard leather letter-sacks* 1872 RI iv 37 (Comb. not in OED W S C; but cf. OED Letter-bag, 1809..)

let up on, v. [AB³] *When she [the steamboat's wheel] fights strong and the tiller slips a little..let up on her a trifle* 1875 OTM 287. *"I'll ask the widow to let up on you a little, Huck"* 1876 TS xxxv 272. *"Oh, let up on this cussed nonsense!"* 1884 HF xxx 311 (OEDS 35b. To cease to have to do with, talk of, interfere with, trouble, etc. *U.S.* 1857.. So Th H. This sense not in W S C)

levee, sb. [A] *He spilled it out on the levee* 1856 *Adv. of T.J.Snodgrass* (1928) 21. *Barrels and boxes were spinning athwart the levee* 1875 OTM 190. See also *crevasse* 1883; *kit* 1894 (OED *U.S.* An embankment to prevent the overflow of a river. 1718.. So W S C U B F Cl Th T M H DN.III)

levee, v. [AB³] *He ought to be damned—or leveed, I should say* 1869 IA xv 147 (OEDS *U.S.* To raise a levee. 1834.. So W S C B F. Here, of course, used punningly)

levee-rim, sb. [AB¹] See *high-river*, a. 1883 (Comb. not in OED W S C. Cf. above)

level, a. [AB²] *The wanderers were right, and the heads of the same were level* 1869 IA xl 426. See *bridgy* 1881. *A man of practical sense and level head* 1883 LM xxv 275. *"Your head gets leveler and leveler all the time, Tom Sawyer"* 1884 HF xxxvi 368. *Tom Sawyer was..the levelest head I ever see* 1896 TSD i 345 (OED 7b. Well balanced. orig. *U.S.* 1870.. So C B F Th. Not A in W S U)

level, a. **one's level best**, etc. [AB³] *"He done his level best"* 1867 SNO (1875) 74. *I only wish I could see her look her level best, once* 1874 *Letters* (1917) I xii 210. *An Indian chief who has taken off his last rag in order to appear at his level best* 1883 LM ii 34. *The old man he was on hand and looking his level pisonest* 1884 HF xxviii 294 (OEDS 9. orig. *U.S.* Similarly *level worst*, etc. 1851.. So C B F Cl Th. Not A in S U Wr. Phr. not in W)

level, a. [?AB¹] *I have worked at it for three level months* 1880 TA App.D 614. See also *blamed if* 1892 (Whole, entire, continuous. This sense not in OED W S C. Cf. *solid*, a., below, in same sense)

lewd, a. [C] *The poor devil..so laughed at for his silly claimantship by the lewd American scum around him* 1892 AmCl i 22 (OED 3. Belonging to the lower orders; common, low, vulgar, base. *obs*. c1380..1640. So W S C U)

libel suit, sb. [B¹] *Backed by threat of a libel suit* 1892 AmCl Pref. (Comb. not in OED W S C; but cf. OED libel summons, 1870)

liberation-party, sb. [B¹] *The objects of the several Russian liberation-parties* 1890 *Letters* (1917) II xxx 535 (Political parties working for freedom. Comb. not in OED W S C)

liberty-loving, ppl.a. [B²] *He would bend every energy to the task, limit as it might his liberty-loving life* 1894 PW xii 775 (OED 1897, only ex. Comb. not in W S C)

liberty-pole, sb. [?A] *Unionville consisted of eleven cabins and a liberty pole* 1872 RI xxviii 203 (OED A tall mast or staff with a Phrygian cap or other symbol of liberty on the top. 1775.. So W. A in C B F Th,1770 AS.IV.8. Comb. not in S)

lick, sb. [AB³] *"By George, she [his watch] is good on shore, but somehow she don't keep up her lick here on the water—gets seasick, maybe"* 1869 IA v 48. *If I keep up my present lick three weeks more...* 1871 *Letters* (1917) I x 188. *"This is Mongrel—and not a half-bad horse, either". "I've noticed he keeps up his lick first rate"* 1906 "Horse's Tale" 544 (OED 6. *dial*, *U.S.*, and *Australian*. Speed. 1847.. So S B Cl Th T DN.II,III. Not A in W C U)

lick, sb. [AB³] *He will not desert us now, after putting in four licks to our own one on this book all this time* 1885 *Letters* (1917) II xxv 463. *"Not another lick of work left in their old hides"* 1892 AmCl iii 39 (OEDS 6. A turn of work. Esp. with negatives. *U.S.* 1868.. So S B Cl Th. Not A in W C U)

lick, v. [?A] *That sheaf of green rods which the lictors used to carry before the Roman consuls to lick them with when they didn't behave* 1890 "Wonderful Pair of Slippers" 312 (OED 6. slang. To beat, thrash. 1535.. So W S C U. A in Cl DN.III. Here punningly)

lick, v. [?AB³] *"Johnny, which licked?" "You licked him!"* 1871 *Screamers* 158 (OED 6b. *slang*. To overcome, get the better of. 1800.. So W S C U. A in Cl DN.III)

lie in with, v. [?AB¹] *As I lay in with the livery stables, I didn't forget to mention that Mrs. O'Shaughnessy hired fifty-four dollars worth of hacks* 1883 LM xliii 439 (To be in league with; to be in the good graces of. Comb. not in OED W S C)

Lieutenant of the Tower, sb. [C] *Next he drew the beautiful sword, and bowed, by way of salute to the lieutenant of the Tower* 1881 PP v 57 (OED 1c. The acting commandant delegated by the Constable. Now only *Hist.* 1596, only ex. Not *arch* in S C. Not in W)

lieves, adv. [?AB³] *"I'd just as lieves be married to Niagara Falls, and done with it"* 1892 AmCl iii 41 (OEDS var. of *lief*: gladly, willingly. 1863, only ex. A in Wr B DN.I,III. Not in W S C)

life-day, sb. [?C] *I shall tackle Adam once more...I've been thinking out his first life-days to-day* 1893 *Letters* (1917) II xxxiii 592 (OED *obs* exc. *arch*. A day or some period of a man's life. 1375..1876. This sense not in W S C. A reinvention, after German *Lebenstag?*)

life-day, sb. [?C] *"In my life day haf I never heard so brecious worts"* 1892 AmCl xvi 167 (OED *obs* exc. *arch*. Life-time; all the days of one's life. Chiefly pl., occas. sing. 900..1538. So W S C. A reinvention, after German *Lebtage?*)

life-history, sb. [B¹] *Philosophers, burglars, high-waymen, journalists, physicians, surgeons—you can get the life-histories of all of them but one* [Shakespeare] 1909 ISD 141 (Biography. This sense not in OED W S C, which have the word only in its *biological* sense; cf. OED: The development of an organism from the egg to the adult stage, 1879..; so W, with better definition: "until its natural death." So S C)

life-line, sb. [B¹] See *heart-line* 1894 (Comb. in this sense not in OED C. Given in W S. Cf. OED Line, sb. 8b. *Line of life,* in *Palmistry,* 1596..

life policy, sb. [B¹] *"If I had taken out a life policy on this one the premiums would have bankrupted me long ago"* 1907 "Chaps. from Autob" 14 (Comb. not in OED W S C)

life-preserver, sb. [?AB³] *"It's like drowning with a life-preserver in my reach"* 1894 PW xiv 778. *A life-preserver—a big round canvas one, which would float after the scrap-iron was soaked out of it* 1906 *Speeches* (1910) 348 (OED 2. 1804.. So W S C. A in M)

life-stream, sb. [B¹] *She was drenched with blood to her feet, for bodies had poured their red life-streams over her* 1895 JA II xxii 886 (Comb. not in OED W S C)

lift, sb. [B³] *The top story consists of twenty bedrooms ...There would need to be a lift—not a European lift, with its mere stand-up space and its imperceptible movement* 1904 *Autob* (1924) I 199 (OED 10. An apparatus for raising or lowering persons or things from one floor or level to another. 1851.. So W S C U. Cf. *elevator,* above)

lift, v. [?AB³] *You "lifted" that word from further along—and with what valuable result? The next sentence has no meaning* 1900 *Autob* (1924) I 184. *It would not be honest in me to encourage by silence the inference that I composed the Horse's private bugle-call, for I did not. I lifted it, as Aristotle says. It is the opening strain in The Pizzicato in Sylvia, by Delibes* 1906 "Horse's Tale" 549 (OED 8. *slang*. To steal; *transf.* of plagiarism. 1885.. So W S C U. A in Wr DN.III,V)

lift the roof, v.phr. [?AB¹] *She was here to watch the trial, and was going to lift up just one "hooraw" over it... "When dat verdic' comes, I's gwyne to lif' dat roof, now, I tell you"* 1894 PW xx 233 (To shout loudly, make a vociferous demonstration. Phr. not in OED W S C)

lifter, sb. [?AB²] *"As long as I'm going to hit him at all, I'm going to hit him a lifter"* 1889 CY xxxii 425. *It was a sockdologer. It landed Tom Sawyer...All he said was..he'd just as soon have intellectual intercourse with*

a catfish. But anybody can say that—and I notice they always do, when somebody has fetched them a lifter 1894 TSA ix 356 (OED 2a. In mod. slang, a heavy blow. 1889, this quot., only ex. *Dial* in Wr. Not in W S C)

light-bread, sb. [AB¹] *Hot light-bread, Southern style;* see *biscuit* 1880 (A in B: Fermented bread of wheat flour; so called to distinguish it from corn-bread; *Southern* and *Western.* So W S Cl T DN.I,II,III,IV AS.II.359. Comb. not in OED C)

light into, v. [AB¹] *He lit into that horse with a whip* 1884 HF xxii 224 (W: To attack; to set upon. *slang, U.S.* So S. This sense not in OED C; but cf. OEDS Light, v. 5b. To join in a fight. U.S. exs. 1889..)

lightly, adv. [C] *"An he had seen you ye had not lightly departed"* 1889 CY iii 48 (OED 4. Easily, readily. *obs* exc. *arch.* c1175..1870. So W. Not *obs* in S C U Wr)

lightly, adv. [C] See *la,* int. 1889. *"I will well, and lightly will begin"* 1889 CY xv 175 (OED 5. †Quickly, swiftly, c1220..1632. Not *obs* in W S C U Wr)

lightning, a. [?AB²] *It is just lightning poetry!* 1874 *Letters* (1917) I xiv 239. *"By the Shadow of Death, but he's a lightning pilot!"* 1875 OTM 224. *Pilots are not all alike, and the smartest pilots will win the race. If one of the boats has a "lightning" pilot, whose "partner" is a trifle his inferior, you can tell which one is on watch by noting whether that boat has gained ground or lost* 1875 OTM 191. *"They say he is lightning!" "Yes, I have heard that he is a great speaker"* 1885 *Autob* (1924) I 16 (OEDS 3d. Acting with the rapidity of lightning. Only ex., 2nd quot. from OTM. In the light of the other quots. given above, a better definition would seem to be: Superlative, excellent, extremely good. This sense not in W S C. Cf. the *spec* sense in Th.III)

lightning-bug, sb. [?A] *It was Jack-o'-lanterns or lightning-bugs* 1884 HF xvi 135. See also *racing-mobile* 1904 (OEDS Earliest ex. U.S. 1797.. A in S C B F Cl Th T M DN.III. Cf. H (under Bug): Am. lightning-bug = Eng. fire-fly. Not A in W)

lightning express, sb. [AB³] See *express train* 1875. *A tramp stealing a ride on the lightning express* 1909 *Letters* (1917) II xlvii 833 (OED *U.S.* A designation given to certain very rapid trains. 1860. So F Cl Th. Comb. not in W S C)

lightning-heeled, a. [B¹] *"Fnobjectionbilltakuzhlcourssoreferred!" This long lightning-heeled word signified that if there was no objection, the bill would take the customary course of a measure of its nature, and be referred to the Committee* 1873 GA xliii 394 (Comb. not in OED W S C; but cf. OED Lightning-footed, 1870)

lightning-rod, sb. [B¹] See *camrod* 1870. *They constructed a lightning-rod and some wires* 1889 CY vii 87 (OED = Lightning conductor. 1790.. So W S C U. A in Th,1789 M)

lightning-shod, a. [B¹] *We are a race of lightning-shod Mercuries* 1890 "Majestic Literary Fossil" 439 (Comb. not in OED W S C)

lightning-vivid, a. [B¹] *Such a lightning-vivid picture of his mailed form and flaunting banners!* 1896 JA II xvi 439 (Comb. not in OED W S C)

light on, v. [AB¹] See *skyugle* 1865 (To attack; to set upon. Not in OED W S C in this sense; but cf. *light into,* above)

light out, v. [AB³] *When I couldn't stand it no longer I lit out* 1884 HF i 2. See also *knock off* 1884 (OEDS 5b. *U.S. slang.* To decamp, 'make tracks'. 1873.. So W S C B F Th T M DN.II,III)

light-ray, sb. [B¹] *In the "Legends of the Rhine", done into English by the wildly gifted Garnham..."Of Light-rays, was the Figure wove"* 1880 TA xvi 142 (Comb. not in OED W S C. After German *Lichtstrahl?*)

lights, sb. [?AC] *It most scared the liver and lights out of me* 1884 HF xxix 307 (OED Now applied only to the lungs of beasts. a1200..1671, last ex. of a human being. A in Wr DN.V AS.X.172. Not A in W S C U)

light-throwing, ppl.a. [B¹] *He asked questions that would have brought light-throwing answers* 1894 PW vii 336. *He furnished to us light-throwing examples of their behavior* 1895 "What Bourget Thinks" 53. *Macaulay has a light-throwing passage upon this matter* 1897 FE xliii 395 (Comb. not in OED W S C. A coinage of which M.T. was fond)

light-weight, a. [?AB²] *A silly young miss for heroine ...Rowena, the light-weight heroine* 1894 TET Intro. 312 (OED *fig.* 1809. So W S C U. A in Th. Cf. heavy-weight, above)

like, a. [C] *Claws like to a mole's but broader* 1875 SNO 141. *"Nan and Bet are like to her in this"* 1881 PP iii 42 (OED 1a. Const. with *to*...Now *arch.* a1300.. 1859. So W S. Not *arch* in C Wr)

like, a. [?C] *He so worked upon his feelings that he had to keep swallowing, he was so like to choke* 1876 TS iii 38. *"Give me thy hand...lord, I am like to die of very joy!"* 1881 PP xxv 300. *I was like to get fried in that stove* 1889 CY xii 143 (OED 9. predicatively, const. to with *inf.*: That may be reasonably expected to, likely to. Now somewhat *rare* in literary use; still common *colloq.* a1300 ..1896. So W C Wr. Not *arch* or *colloq* in S)

like, a. [?AC] *We like to got a hornet's nest, but we didn't* 1884 HF xxxix 396 (OED 9b. Formerly sometimes with ellipsis of the vb. substantive, so that *like* becomes='was, or were, like'. *Obs.* 1600..1709. OEDS. Addit. U.S. exs. of *like*=was like. 1884, this quot... A in Wr DN.I,III,IV,VI. This idiom not in W S C, which give only the phonetically almost indistinguishable use of *Like*, v. intr.=To be likely to, as in "He liked to have been too late". This usage is called "Now *dial* or *uncultivated*" in W, *colloq* in S, *rare* in C. S and C point out that it is used only in the past tense, as "He liked to have died of hunger". Whether we should write the idiom as "He liked to" or as "He like to" can hardly be determined from spoken English, although M.T.'s ear would seem to have been accurate in hearing no -d in actual *colloq* Am. pronunciation)

like, conj. [?AC] *A Southerner talks music...But there are some infelicities, such as "like" for "as"...I heard an educated gentleman say, "Like the flag-officer did". His cook or his butler would have said, "Like the flag-officer done"* 1883 LM xliv 449. See also *brisken, keel over* 1884 (OED 6. Used as conj.='like as', as. Now generally condemned as vulgar or slovenly, though examples may be found in many recent writers of standing. a. Introducing an unabridged clause. *c*1530..1886. So W S Wr. A in C: Never used in New England, but universal in the South and West. So B M DN.V. Not A in *Nation* LV.86. See other refs. in Kennedy, p.319)

like, conj. [?AC] *"A city, built up like the rod of Aladdin had touched it"* 1873 GA xvi 151. *"Skin for the raft like the dickens was after you!"* 1884 HF xxiii 229. See *mud-puddle* 1884. *She takes to any kind of romantic rubbish like she was born to it* 1892 AmCl iv 53 (OED 6e. As if, 'like as'. *Obs.* 1493, 1530. OEDS Modern U.S. exs. 1859.. A in B M DN.II,V AS.XI.352. Not A in W S C Wr.)

like, v. [C] *"It likes me not, my love"* 1881 PP vii 92 (OED 1. To please, be pleasing to, suit a person. Now only *arch* and *dial.* 971..1850. So W S C U)

like as if, conj. [?AC] *Goodson looked him over, like as if he was hunting for a place on him that he could despise the most* 1899 "MCH" (1900) 10 (OED Like, conj. 5. Now somewhat *rare.* 1609..1799. W: *dial.* Wr: *dial, Northern.* Comb. not in S C)

likely, a. [A] See *contraband* 1862; *hefty* 1865. *"Mighty likely boy, is Jerry"* 1873 GA vii 76 (OED 4b. Now chiefly *U.S.,* of young persons: promising, hopeful. 1454.. So B F Th M. Not A in W S C Wr T)

likely, a. [?AC] *"A verse from some likely hymn"* 1871 SNO (1875) 247 (OED 6. Seemly, appropriate. *Obs.* *c*1470..1742. Not *obs* in W S C U Wr. A in Th M)

limber, a. [?AC] *Pap was a-going on so he never noticed where his old limber legs was taking him to, so he went head over heels over the tub of salt pork and barked both shins* 1884 HF vi 44 (OED 1.†c. In unfavorable sense. Limp, flabby. 1592..1747. W: *obs exc. dial.* So Wr. This sense not in S C)

limber, adv. [?AB¹] *She'd...come up...scattering her legs around limber* 1865 "Jumping Frog" (1875) 31 (Wr: Nimble; also used adverbially. Not in OED W S C as adv.)

Limburger, a. [?AB²] *A package of peculiarly mature and capable Limburger cheese...*1882 "Invalid's Story" 96 (OEDS attrib. with *cheese.* Only ex. U.S. 1887. So W S C)

lime-town sb. [B¹] *"On a dairy-farm you never can get any milk for your coffee, and it is against sense to go to a lime-town to hunt for whitewash"* 1883 LM xxv 274 (Comb. not in OED W S C)

limitless-distance, sb. [B¹] *The improved "limitless-distance" telephone was presently introduced* 1898 "From the London *Times* of 1904" (1900) 131 (Comb. not in OED W S C)

limit-rope, sb. [AB¹] *Promptly hustled outside the limit-rope by the police* 1892 AmCl vii 73 (A in H: Limit is rarely used in Eng. but commonly in Am. of physical boundary. Comb. not in OED W S C; but cf. OED Limit-line, 1864)

line, sb. [?A] *Those steamboats belonging to the little Cairo line and the little Memphis line* 1893 PW i 234 (OED 22. A regular succession of public conveyances plying between certain places. OEDS Earlier exs., all U.S. 1786.. Not A in W S C U)

line, sb. [?C] *The father and founder of this proud old line was William the Conqueror his very self* 1892 AmCl i 17 (OED 25. Lineage, stock, race. ?Somewhat *arch.* *c*1330..1874. Not *arch* in W S C U)

line, sb. [?AB³] *We were building several lines of railway...and our line was in operation* 1889 CY xl 512 (OED 26b. Short for *railway line.* 1825.. So W S C U. A in B T. Not A in H (under *Road*): Am. *road,* as an abbreviation of *railroad,* often takes the place of the Eng. *line*)

line, sb. out of one's line. [B²] *You know a body always enjoys seeing himself attempting something out of his line* 1881 *M.T. the Letter Writer* (1932) iii 37 (OED 28b. Unsuited to one's capacity. No ex., but cf. *in one's line,* 1838.. So S. Phr. not in W C)

line, sb. [?AB²] *Radishes, onions, squashes—everything imaginable in the vegetable line* 1857 Letter in *Iowa Journ. of Hist.* 430. See *nobby* 1889. *Something had gone wrong in the millinery line* 1892 AmCl xx 184 (OED 30. Comm. The stock on hand of a particular class of goods. 1882.. Not in W S C U)

line, sb. [?AB¹] *"What's your line—mainly?" "Jour printer by trade...What's your lay?" "Preachin's my line, and workin' campmeetin's"* 1884 HF xix 183. See also *call,* v. 1889; *oils* 1892 (Specialty, special calling or trade. Not in OED W S C)

line out, v. [?AB²] *The preacher was lining out a hymn* 1884 HF xx 196 (OED 6. To read out...line by line for the congregation to sing. 1885.. So W S C Wr. A in DN.II,III,IV)

liner, sb. [?AB³] *The big Orleans liners stopped for hails only* 1893 PW i 234. *The legation furniture consists of...pictures of the American liners* 1902 "Belated Russ. Passport" (1928) 190 (OED 8a. A vessel, now usually a steam-ship, belonging to a 'line' of packets. 1838.. So W S C U. A in B T)

line shot, sb. [?AB¹] *He was longer than a rail and thinner. Nothing would ever fetch him but a line shot, and then like as not he would split the bullet* 1906 *Autob* (1924) I 357 (App. a shot hitting exactly upon the line of a target. Comb. not in OED W S C)

linsey-woolsey, sb. [?AB²] *An old dame in linsey-woolsey* 1873 GA i 22. *"We gwine to jump in de river,* *den de troubles o' dis worl' is all over...No, I ain't gwine to be fished out...in dis mis'able old linsey-woolsey"* 1893 PW iii 238 (OED lb. A garment woven from a mixture of wool and flax. 1894.. So W S C U. A in DN.III)

lint, sb. [?AB²] *In sixteen hundred pounds crude cotton, four hundred are lint, worth, say, ten cents a pound; and twelve hundred pounds of seed* 1883 LM xxxiii 367 (OEDS 3b. Raw cotton fibre. Only ex. U.S. 1887. So S: Southern U.S. Not A in W C Wr)

lip, sb. [?AB³] *"Don't you give me none of your lip",* says he 1884 HF v 31. *He didn't give me any lip* 1889 CY xxxi 397 (OED 3a. *slang.* Saucy talk, impudence. 1821.. So W S C U Wr. A in M DN.III)

liquid, a. [B¹] *Her eyes were brown and liquid* 1893 PW ii 236 (S: Limpid, clear, bright. So C U. This sense not in OED W. Cf. OED 1c. *occas.* of the eyes: Filled with tears, 1598..1873)

liquor-drinking, vbl.sb. [B¹] *She admonished me against liquor-drinking* 1870 SNO (1875) 271 (Comb. not in OED W S C)

liquorice, sb. Spelled **licorice, lickerish.** [?AE] *"What'll you give?" "Piece of lickerish and a fish-hook"* 1876 TS iv 45. *Give the child a bit of licorice-root* 1883 LM xliv 450 (OED The var. sp. *licorice* current since the 16th c.; *lickerish* 19th c. *dial.* So W. The sp. lickerish not in S C; given as A in DN.I,III AS.XI.251)

liquor saloon, sb. [?AB²] *He soon saved money enough to open quite a stylish liquor saloon* 1873 GA xxxiii 302 (OED U.S.ex. 1874. Comb. not in W S C. Cf. Saloon, A in this sense, below)

list, v. [C] *"List to thine handmaid"* 1889 CY xvi 196 (OED *arch. c*1000..1871. So W S C U. *Dial* in Wr)

listening-distance, sb. [B¹] See *blasting-powder* 1870 (Comb. not in OED W S C)

literally, adv. [?AB³] *Tom was literally rolling in wealth* 1876 TS ii 31 (OED 3b. Now often improperly used to indicate that some conventional metaphorical or hyperbolical phrase is to be taken in its strongest admissible sense. U.S. quot. 1863, only ex. of this "improper" sense. Cf. W S: Often used hyperbolically. This use not in C)

literary, a. Spelled **littery.** [E] *"I warn't used to the ways of littery swells"* 1866 *Speeches* (1910) 3 (W calls this pron. *esp. British.* Not so called in OED S C)

literature-preserver, sb. [B¹] *Margaret of Navarre was writing the "Heptameron" and some religious books—the first survives, the others are forgotten, wit and indelicacy being sometimes better literature-preservers than holiness* 1883 LM i 27 (Nonce comb.)

littered-up, ppl.a. [?AB²] *It was a dirty, littered-up place* 1884 HF xx 196 (OED 2. 1895, only ex. with *up.* Comb. not in W S C. A in DN.III)

live, v. **where one lives.** [AB³] *The compliment touched him where he lived* 1909 ISD i 13 (OEDS 12c. At the right or vital point. *U.S.slang.* 1860.. Phr. not in W S C)

lively, adv. [?AC] *"Lay out aloft there, half a dozen of ye—lively, now!"* 1876 TS xiii 116 (OED Now *rare.* 3. Actively, briskly. 1400..1883. *Arch* in S. Not *rare* or *arch* in W C)

live-looking, a. [AB¹] *It was altogether the livest-looking street we had seen in any village on the continent* 1880 TA xliii 499 (Comb. not in OED W S C; but cf. OED Live, a. 2b. Chiefly *U.S.* Full of energy and alertness; 'wide-awake', up-to-date. 1877.. So F Cl Th; 1857)

live-oak, sb. [A] *A gnarled and venerable live-oak tree* 1872 RI iii 33 (OED An American evergreen tree growing in the Southern Atlantic states. 1610.. So W S C B F Cl Th T M)

liver, sb. **to make one's liver curl.** [AB¹?C] *Two red-hot steamboats raging along, neck-and-neck, straining every nerve.. this is sport that makes a body's very liver curl with enjoyment* 1883 LM xlv 464 (A in F: To produce intense feeling, enjoyable or otherwise. Phr. not in

OED W S C; but cf. OED 2a. Formerly often mentioned *fig.* with allusion...to the ancient notion that it was the seat of love and of violent passion generally; now only *arch.* 1390.. 1897)

liver-sausage, sb. [B¹] *Link by link the liver-sausage disappears* [German, Leberwurst] 1891 *Slovenly Peter* (1935) 5 (Comb. not in OED W S C)

livery-flunkey, sb. [B¹] *"She's had her share of snubs from the livery-flunkey sort"* 1892 AmCl iv 55 (Comb. not in OED W S C; but cf. OED Livery-servant, 1702)

living-room, sb. [AB³] *We stepped into a small living-room* 1880 TA App.C 596 (OEDS 2. *U.S.* A sitting-room, usually occupied during the day. 1867.. A in S C B T M. Not A in W U)

lo, int. **lo and behold you.** [?AB³] *"Here I go over to Sereny Harper's, like an old softy, expecting I'm going to make her believe all that rubbage...when lo and behold you she'd found it all out from Joe"* 1876 TS xix 158 (OEDS b. Phr. freq. in mod. use, usually facetious. 1850.. Not in W S C)

loaden, v. [?AC] *He was just loadened down with chances...to make a name for himself* 1884 HF xxxviii 394. *Our plates was all loadened* 1896 TSD vi 358 (OED *obs* exc. *dial.* 1568..1889. So W S Wr. A in M AS.V.495. Not in C)

load up, v. [?AB¹] *I loaded them up with paregoric and put them to bed* 1880 TA xxxviii 435. *The Doctor loads him up with drugs* 1891 *Slovenly Peter* (1935) 5. *They kept him loaded up with hog and hominy* 1896 TSD ix 522 (Here *fig,* to feed, stuff with food, dose heavily. Comb. not in OED W S C in this sense; but cf. OED Load, v.I. To furnish with a cargo. Loaded down: weighted down with a load. 1847..)

load up, v. [?AB¹] *He said the cadets would "load me up"...They turned their whole attention to giving me military information* 1881 *Speeches* (1923) 99. *The pilot warmed to his opportunity, and proceeded to load me up in the good old-fashioned way* 1883 LM xxiv 266 (Here *fig,* to cram, 'stuff', hoax. Comb. in this sense not in OED W S C. Cf. Fill up, and Freight up, above. Cf. Load, A in DN.III, n.w.Ark., to deceive)

load up, v. [?AB¹] *We slid for the cellar cupboard and loaded up a good lunch* 1884 HF xl 403 (U: *colloq.,* to eat and drink copiously. Comb. not in OED W S C in this sense)

load up, v. [?AB¹] *He loads up the house with cripples and idiots* 1892 Am Cl iii 37. See also *certain-sure* 1901 (Here *fig,* to weigh down, clog, encumber. Comb. in this sense not in OED W S C; but cf. OED Load, v. 6, in this sense. 1526..1884)

loaf, v. [?AB³] *"He ain't no account...just fishes a little...and loafs around considerable"* 1876 TS xxiii 182. *Then we went loafing around town* 1884 HF xxi 209. See also *recess-time* 1896 (OED To spend time idly. Earliest ex. U.S. 1838.. A in B Cl T M DN.III. Not A in W S C U)

loafer, sb. [?AB³] *Myself some vast loafer from Brobdingnag* 1872 RI iii 32. See also *awning-post* 1884; *rowdy* 1894; *larrikin* 1897; *half-breed,* a. 1909 (OEDS Earlier U.S. exs. 1835.. A in B Cl T M DN.III AS.VIII.1.76, N.Y., 1833. Not A in W S C U)

loafing, ppl.a. [?AB³] See *potter,* v. 1896. *Jack Halliday..the loafing, good-natured, no-account, irreverent fisherman* 1899 "MCH" (1900) 18. See also *hospital-bird* 1904 (OED 1857.. So W U. Not in S C. Cf. above)

loafing-place, sb. [?AB³] *An occasional loafing-place of that erratic genius, Henry Clay Dean* 1883 LM lvii 566 (OED 1838.. A in M. Comb. not in W S C)

lobby, sb. [AB³] *He knew all the Senators and Representatives, and especially the lobby* 1873 GA xl 357 (OED 3b. *collective. U.S.* the persons who frequent the lobby of the house of legislature for the purpose of influencing its members. 1859.. So S C B F Cl T H. Not A in W)

lobbyist, sb. [AB³] *There was an undercurrent of suspicion in some quarters that she was one of that de-*

tested class known as "lobbyists" 1873 GA xxxiv 315. (OED Chiefly *U.S.* One who frequents the lobby; cf. above. 1863.. So W S C B F Cl M H AS.VIII.1.72)

local editor, sb. [?AB¹] *I took the position of local editor with joy* 1906 *Autob* (1924) I 271 (Comb. not in OED W S C; but cf. Local, sb. in S: A reporter who furnishes local items. *U.S.*)

local item, sb. [?AB¹] *No "local item" unveilings of what is happening in town* 1880 TA App.B 626. *He got in all the details, and that is a good thing in a local item* 1889 CY ix 108 (Comb. not in OED W S C; but cf. Local, sb. in W S C: *U.S.* An item of local interest in a newspaper)

localized, ppl.a. [?AB³] *The Killing of Julius Caesar Localized* (title) 1864 SNO (1875) 162 (OED Invested with local characteristics. 1816.. So U. A in Cl T. This sense not in W S C. Cf. B: Localize, v. To prepare for publication local items; so F Cl Th T)

locate, v. [AB²] *We located some timber-lands on its shores* 1872 RI xxii 168 (OED 2. To enter on or take possession of a land-claim, gold-mine, etc. *U.S.* 1877.. So W S C B F Th,1797 M DN.V)

locate, v. [AB³] *We located ourselves at the Jungfrau Hotel* 1880 TA xxxii 340 (OED 3. To fix or establish in a place. Chiefly *U.S.* 1807.. So B F Cl Th M DN.III,V. Not A in W S C U T H)

locate, v. [?AB³] *All I need to know is...how to locate his vitals* 1889 CY xx 244 (OED 7. To discover the exact locality of. 1882. So W S C U. A in F Th.III M T. Not A in H)

location, sb. [AB²] *The "locators" were obliged to do a reasonable amount of work within ten days after the date of the location* 1872 RI xl 284 (OED 5. *U.S. spec.* A mining claim. No ex. of *spec* sense. So W S C B F Cl H DN.V)

locator, sb. [AB³] *The "locators" or claimants of a ledge* 1872 RI xl 284. *He had an "option" to sell the Gould and Curry Extension for the "locators" of it* 1893 "Banknote" (1928) 129 (OED 2. *U.S.* One who takes up a grant of land, opens a mine, etc. 1817.. So W S C B F Cl Th AS.II.86, V.145. Not A in U Wr)

locked-hair, sb. [B¹] *In the "Legends of the Rhine", done into English by the wildly gifted Garnham... "To share its light, locked-hair strove"* 1880 TA xvi 142 (Hum. alienism. Prob. an attempt to render the German *Lockenhaar* or *Lockenkopf*, curly-head)

locker-bunk, sb. [B¹] *I made straight for my locker-bunk, and stretched myself out there* 1894 TSA vi 250 (Comb. not in OED W S C; but cf. OED Locker-seat, 1877)

locker-sofa, sb. [B¹] *Mrs. I., an invalid, had to sleep on the locker-sofa under her port* 1897 FE iv 73 (Comb. not in OED W S C)

lock-pick, sb. [B¹] *I could only get hold of a piece of iron which I could shape into a lock-pick* 1889 CY xxxvi 417 (Comb. not in OED W S C; but cf. OED Lock-picker, 1882; also Picklock, 2. An instrument for picking locks. 1591.. 1879)

locust, sb. [?AB²] See *pinch-bug* 1856 (Here probably OED 2b. The seventeen-year locust, *Cicada Septendecim.* 1899. A in W S C B)

locust-tree, sb. [A] *It looked just like an American city; locust-trees bordering the sidewalks* 1869 IA xxxvi 388. *The locust-trees were in bloom and the fragrance of the blossoms filled the air* 1876 TS ii 26 (OED 2. A well-known N. Am. tree, having thorny branches and dense clusters of white, heavily scented flowers. 1640.. So W S C B Th T M)

lodge, sb. [AB³] *A great shut-in meadow, full of Indian lodges and dogs and squaws* 1906 "Horse's Tale" 332 (OED 10. The tent of a N. Am. Indian. 1805.. So W S C U Th.III AS.VII.2)

lodging-money, sb. [B¹] *She needed the lodging-money for trifling luxuries* 1894 PW v 333 (Comb. not in OED W S C in this sense. Cf. OED An allowance

made to officers and soldiers for whom there is not sufficient accommodation in barracks. 1802. So S)

log, sb. **easy as rolling off a log.** [?AB²] *A man who could have elected himself Major-General Adam or anything else as easy as rolling off a log* c1880 *Speeches* (1923) 97 (OEDS U.S. quot, 1904. A in Th. Phr. not in W S C)

log cabin, sb. [?AB³] *"They came upon a log cabin in the woods"* 1873 GA ii 31. See also *foot-hill* 1877 (OED U.S. exs. 1850.. A in B F Cl M. Not A in W S C)

log raft, sb. [?AB¹] *Through a fog...a log raft would appear vaguely through the webby veil* 1875 OTM 449. *A log raft in the river invited him* 1876 TS ii 39 (Comb. not in OED W S C)

log-rolling, vbl.sb. [AB³] *A mutual aid which in a more vulgar body would be called "log-rolling"* 1873 GA xlvi 417 (OED 2. *U.S. slang.* Combination for mutual assistance in political or other action. 1823.. So W S C B F Cl Th T M H)

lone hand, sb. [?AB³] *"You had a lone hand up your sleeve"* 1904 "Bequest" (1906) 41 (OEDS In Euchre: a hand played without aid from a partner's cards; also *fig.* Earliest ex. U.S. 1879.. So S C. Not in W)

long, a. **to be long on.** [?AB³] *He was proud of her daring in exploiting worldly stocks;... she was always long on the others* 1904 "Bequest" (1906) 21 (OED 14. *Comm.* U.S. quot. 1859, only ex. A in B T. Not A in S. Phr. not in W C)

long-agone, a. [B¹C] *"We played together once, in long-agone days"* 1898 MS (1916) viii 115 (Comb. not in OED W S C. Cf. OED Agone, *arch.*.1846. So W)

long-coveted, a. [B¹] *The next moment I had my long-coveted desire* 1880 TA xix 182 (Comb. not in OED W S C)

long-departed, a. [B¹] *Their long-departed owners seemed to throng the gloomy cells* 1869 IA xi 102 (Comb. not in OED W S C)

long-descended, a. [B¹] *Every man is made up of heredities, long-descended atoms and particles of his ancestors* 1892 AmCl xix 193 (C: Of ancient lineage. Comb. not in OED W S)

long-discarded, a. [B¹] *She took up music again... and the other long-discarded delights of her maidenhood* 1902 "DBDS" (1928) 292 (Comb. not in OED W S C)

long-distance, sb. [?AB²] *Aleck's imaginary brokers were shouting frantically by imaginary long-distance, "Sell! sell!"* 1904 "Bequest" (1906) 44 (OEDS. *ellipt.* for long-distance telephone 1905. So W S C. A in M H = Eng. *trunk*)

long-liver, sb. [B¹] *An elective Papacy is a safe and wise system, and a long-liver* 1907 CS II xiv 281 (Comb. not in OED W S C; but cf. OED Long-lived, 1420..)

longly, adv. [B¹?C] *The individual retook the box, examined it...longly* ["Retranslated" from the French *longuement*; the original version of the "Jumping Frog" has: *"The feller took it and looked at it careful"*] 1875 SNO 42 (Hum. alienism. M.T. was hardly aware that the word once existed in English: OED 1. For a long while. *obs.* 1340..1605. So W S C)

long-nine, sb. [AB³] *"There is not a cigar in the house but those old Wheeling long nines". I had just come across those "long nines" a few days before. I hadn't seen a long nine for years. When I was a cub pilot on the Mississippi in the late '50s, I had had a great affection for them* 1906 *Autob* (1924) I 296 (OEDS *U.S.* A kind of cheap cigar. 1830.. So Th. Comb. not in S C. This sense not in W)

long-oval, a. [B¹] *Another shell—of the long-oval sort* 1883 LM xxxviii 404 (Comb. not in OED W S C)

long-pent, a. [B¹] *Ealer let his long-pent breath pour in a great relieving sigh* 1875 OTM 451 (Comb. not in OED W S C)

long-pent-up, a. [B¹] *The women could not restrain their long-pent-up emotions* 1873 GA lviii 522 (Comb. not in OED W S C)

longshoreman, sb. [?AB³] *A wretched tavern, down by the water, a resort of longshoremen* 1881 "Curious

Experience" 44 (OED 1800.. So S C U. A in W B T. Cf. H (under *shore*): Am. longshoreman = Eng. docker)

longside, prep. [?AB¹] *"A shiveree wasn't nothing longside it"* 1857 *Adv. of T. J. Snodgrass* (1928) 45 (Shortened from *alongside of*, q.v. Not in OED W S C)

long-speech, a. [B¹] *Breaking the long-speech record with Dr. Lecher's twelve-hour effort* 1898 "Stirring Times in Austria" (1900) 296 (Comb. not in OED W S C)

long spoon, sb. [B¹] *Extract from a letter of a British private:* "*The Boers begged for mercy. And we gave it them—with the long spoon"*. (Note) *The long spoon is the bayonet. See Lloyd's Weekly, London, of those days* 1901 "To the Person Sitting in Darkness" 167 (Comb. not in OED S. This sense not in W C)

long talk, sb. [?AB¹] *A commonplace remark, which his* (M.T.'s) *peculiar drawl made amusing...His mother always referred to his slow fashion of speaking as "Sammy's long talk". Her own speech was still more deliberate, but she seemed not to notice it* 1912 Paine's *Biog.* I 52 (Not in OED W S C)

long-talked-of, a. [B¹] *His long-talked-of Pacific coast mission* 1873 GA lviii 528 (Comb. not in OED W S C)

long term, sb. [?AB¹] *Her face was filled with a troubled surprise...*"*I may not part from thee"... "Elected for the long term", I sighed to myself* 1889 CY xxi 255 (Hum. transf. from the use of the phr. in Am. politics, where candidates are sometimes elected to the same office but for terms of different length. Phr. not in OED W S C)

long-vanished, ppl.a. [B¹] See *land-boom* 1897 (Comb. not in OED W S C)

look, v. **look-a-here**, **looky-here**. [AB¹E] "*Besides, look-a-here, maybe that whack done for him*" 1876 TS x 94. "*Looky here, Huck, what fools we're making of ourselves*" 1876 TS xxxiii 259. "*Why, looky-here, Dick Albright*" 1883 LM iii 52. "*Now looky here, you stop that putting on frills*" 1884 HF v 32 (A in DN.IV. These forms not in OED W S C; but cf. OED 4. Idiomatic uses of the imperative: In mod. *colloq* use often *look you* (in representations of vulgar speech written *look'ee*) = 'mind this'; also *look here*, a brusque mode of address. a1814. .)

look around, v. [?AB¹] "*I'll look around a little, and if I can't do better I'll come back and take it*" 1883 LM xliii 437 (To look further for an article one desires to purchase. Comb. not in OED W S C in this sense; cf. OED 30. To look in several directions; to take a comprehensive view of things. 1754..)

loom-work, sb. [?C] *An ingenious invention for applying photography to pattern-designing as used in the textile industries, whereby...to reduce the customary outlay of time, labor, and money expended on that department of loom-work to next to nothing* 1898 "Austrian Edison" (1900) 263 (OED † Weaving. 1598..1640. Comb. not in W S C)

loon, sb. **as drunk as a loon**. [?AB³] See *chain-lightning* 1865 (OEDS 1b. All exs. U.S. 1848.. A in B, p.807. Phr. not in W S C; but cf. *crazy as a loon*: A in W S C AS.II.55)

loop, sb. [B²] See *pattern* 1894 (OEDS 4g. A configuration in finger-prints. 1902, only ex. So W. This sense not in S C)

loop-engineering, sb. [B¹] *Far down the mountain we got out to look at a remarkable piece of loop-engineering* 1897 FE lvi 539 (Comb. not in OED W S C)

loot-basket, sb. [B¹] "*It is yet another Civilized Power, with its loot-basket and its butcher-knife*" 1901 "To the Person Sitting in Darkness" 169 (Comb. not in OED W S C)

lope, sb. [?AB³] *He comes down to a long, graceful "lope"* 1872 RI iii 32. *The lion was arriving, fetching a most ghastly roar with every lope...You could see them coming on the lope from every direction* 1893 TSA v 127 (OEDS 2. A long bounding stride. 1824.. So W S C U. A in B Cl Th DN.II,III)

lope, v. [?AB³] *White rabbits went loping about the place* 1880 TA xviii 161 (OED 3. To run with a bounding stride. 1825.. So W S C U. A in B F Cl Th DN.II III,V)

lope, v.˙[?AB³] *He come a-loping into Washington, and put up his horse* 1893 TSA i 22 (OED 3b. causative. To make (one's horse) to lope. 1885.. So W U. C: rare. A in S B)

lordy, int. [AB³] "*Oh lordy, lordy, lordy, I wisht I only had half your chance!*" 1876 TS x 97. "*Oh, lordy, that's one of them!*" 1896 TSD iii 349 (OEDS *U.S.* 1857.. So DN.II,III. Not in S C. This sense not in W)

lose, v. [?AB³] See *gain*, v. 1870 (Of a watch: To lose time, become 'slow'. This sense not in OED W S C)

Lost Cause, sb. [AB¹] *You testify by honoring two of us, once soldiers of the Lost Cause...* 1901 *Speeches* (1923) 231 (A in B: The Southern Confederacy. So W S C F Th T. Comb. not in OED)

lot, sb. [A] See *jump*, v. 1865; *clean*, v. 1872; *spot*, v. 1873. *A mechanic could buy ten town lots on tolerably long credit for ten months' savings out of his wages* 1895 "What Bourget Thinks" 57 (OED 6a. Now chiefly *U.S.* A plot or portion of land. 1633.. So Wr B F Cl Th T M H DN.V. Not A in W S C U)

lot, sb. **across lots**. [AB³] *Our idea is to strike across lots and reach St. Louis the 20th of April* 1882 *Letters* (1917) I xxii 417 (OEDS 6a. Across the lots or fields as a short cut. *U.S. colloq.* 1846.. So B F Cl Th T M DN.III. Not A in S C. Phr. not in W. Cf. Cross-lots, above)

lot, sb. [?AB³] *Lots of the boys here has seen that Smiley* 1865 "Jumping Frog" (1875) 31. *Take a lot of water and add to it a lot of coarse Indian-meal and about a quarter of a lot of salt* 1880 TA xlix 575. *He won a lot of money* 1894 PW x 552. See also *burn* 1907 (OED 9. *colloq.* A considerable number. Used both in sing. and plur. 1812.. So W S C U Wr. A in B T DN.III)

loud, a. [?AB³] *There warn't no frivolishness about him..and he warn't ever loud* 1884 HF xviii 161 (OED 4. Vulgarly obtrusive, flashy. 1849.. So W S C U. A in B)

loud, adv. [?AB¹] *He was a simpering coxcomb of the first water, and the "loudest" dressed man in the state* 1871 SNO (1875) 94 (Cf. above. The adv. not in OED W S C in this sense)

loudly, adv. [?AB³] *One loudly dressed mechanic in stately attitude* 1892 AmCl xvi 163 (OED c. 1849.. So W S C U. Cf. above)

louse-brat, sb. [B¹] "*Shut up, infamous louse-brat!*" 1898 "Stirring Times in Austria" (1900) 326 (Comb. not in OED W S C. After German *Lausbube?*)

love, v. [?AB¹] *They loved the old man's intellects back into him again, and he was as sound in his skull as ever he was* 1896 TSD xi 537 (To effect by the power of love. This sense not in OED W S C)

love, sb. [?AB³] *We had a perfect love of a sounding-boat* 1875 OTM 569. *She was eager to know what I thought of her jewel...*"*It is a love, now isn't it?* 1893 "Esquimau Maiden's Romance" (1928) 146 (OED 9e. A 'duck'. *colloq* 1814..So W S U. A in B. This sense not in C)

love-box, sb. [B¹] *She gave Neddy a love-box on the arm with her fan* 1880 TA xxxi 333 (Comb. not in OED W S C; but cf. OED Love-pat, 1876)

love-duel sb. [B¹] *This was not a love duel, but a "satisfaction" affair* 1880 TA vi 58 (Here: A duel in play, *i.e.*, not serious. Comb. not in OED W S C)

love-quarreling, vbl.sb. [B¹] *Dumb-show of love-quarrelings* 1888 "Meisterschaft" 466 (Comb. not in OED W S C; but cf. OED Love-quarrel, 1671)

love-sign, sb. [B¹] "*I will waft a vast sun-spot across the disk...and you will know it for my love-sign*" 1892 AmCl xxv 273 (Comb. not in OED W S C; but cf. OED Love-token, 1590..)

love-tap, sb. [B²] *"When I make up my mind to hit a man, I don't plan out a love-tap"* 1889 CY xxxiii 425 (OED Love, sb. 16. 1889, this quot. So S C. Comb. not in W)

low, sb. [AB³] See *seven-up* 1869 (One of the six "points" that may be scored in the Am. game of seven-up. Cf. OED 4. In All-fours: the deuce of trumps, or the lowest trump dealt. 1818.. So W S C.

'low, v. [AE] See *allow*.

low-down, a. [AB³] *I was so ignorant, and so kind of low-down and ornery* 1884 HF iii 18. See *corn-pone* 1884. *Merlin...smiling his low-downest smile of malicious gratification* 1889 CY xxxix 504. *Some low-down job that a good dog wouldn't have* 1892 AmCl xiv 149. *"Farming is business, just common low-down business"* 1893 TSA i 24. *"Me dat fetched sich a po' low-down ornery rabbit into de worl'!"* 1894 PW xiv 779. See *ornery* 1896. *The lowest-down coward there is* 1902 "DBDS" (1928) 356 (OEDS b. Chiefly *U.S.* Degraded. 1850.. So U Th T M DN.II,III,IV. Not A in W S C. One of M.T.'s favorite expressions)

lower river, sb. [AB¹] See *horseshoe* 1875; *token* 1875 (The lower part of the Mississippi. Comb. not in OED W S C)

low-grade, a. [?AB³] *I suppose the Fremersberg is very low-grade music* 1880 TA xxiv 236 (OED Low, a. 20. 1879. So W. A in Th III. Not in S C)

low-hung, a. [B¹] *We had not supposed there was anything behind that low-hung blanket of sable cloud but level valley* 1880 TA xxxiii 359 (Comb. not in OED S C. Given in W)

low-necked, a. [B²] *She passed on into the maelstrom of bejeweled and richly attired low-necked ladies* 1873 GA xxxii 290 (OED Low, a. 21. 1901. So W S C)

low-quarter, a. [AB¹] *He wore very low-quarter patent-leather shoes* 1880 TA xxvii 275 (A in DN.III. Comb. not in OED W S C; but cf. OED Quarter, sb. 20c. Part of a shoe. 1753.. Cf. also *high-quarter*, above)

low-rate, a. [?AB¹] See *race-aversion* 1897 (Comb. not in OED W S C; but cf. OED Low-class 1898)

low-water, a. [?AC] *During the low-water season* 1875 OTM 450. *Shaving the bank down to low-water mark* 1883 LM xxviii 302 (OED † In a river, a time when the stream is shallow. 1582, only ex. Not *obs* in W. This sense not in S C)

lubber, sb. [C] See *gangly* 1872. *This innocent vast lubber did not see any difference between the two* 1889 CY xix 239 (OED 1. A big, clumsy, stupid fellow; a lout. *obs* exc. *arch* or *dial*. 1362..1888. So Wr. Not *obs* in W S C U)

lucifer, sb. [?AB³?C] *"This thing of beauty likes painted German lucifers...but she prefers California matches"* 1867 SNO (1875) 79. See *paddle*, v. 1873. *"The paddle-wheel has ground the sounding boat to lucifer matches"* 1875 OTM 569. *"We want...some of these new-fangled things they call lucifer matches"* 1876 TS xxxiii 257 (OED 3. A friction match. 1831.. 1884. So W S C T. A in B AS.VII.427. *Arch* or *obs* in U B)

lumber-camp, sb. [AB³] *In the Adirondack woods... in the lumber-camps* 1906 "WIM" (1917) 31 (OED U.S.

quot. 1882, only ex. Cf. OED Lumber, sb. 3. *N.Amer*. Timber sawn into rough planks. 1662.. So B F Th M H. Comb. not in W S C)

lumberman, sb. [AB³] *The lumberman is fired with a desire to throw away his excellent worldly prospects* 1906 "WIM" (1917) 31 (OED *N.Amer*. 1817.. So W S C B F Th M H)

lumber-raft, sb. [AB³] See *coal-barge* 1883; *stern-wheeler* 1883. *One night we catched a little section of a lumber-raft—nice pine planks* 1884 HF ix 76 (OED *N.Amer*. 1837.. Comb. not in W S C)

lummox, sb. [AB³] See *labrick* 1889. *"In my opinion he hain't got any mind"..."Well, he's a lummox, anyway"* 1893 PW i 235 (OEDS *dial* and *U.S.* An ungainly or stupid lout. 1825.. So W S C Wr B F Cl Th DN.I,II,III,IV,V)

lump, v. [?AB³] See *reckon* 1875. *"You can lump that hat if you don't like it"* 1876 TS i 22 (OED 2. In antithesis with *like*: to be displeased with. *colloq*. 1833.. So W S C U. A in B Th T)

lunkhead, sb. [AB²] *The duke said these Arkansaw lunkheads couldn't come up to Shakespeare* 1884 HF xxii 225. *"Oh, shucks, Huck Finn, I never see such a lunkhead as you"* 1894 TSA vi 251 (OEDS *colloq U.S.* A blockhead. 1884, above quot...SoW S C B F Th T DN.II,III,IV,V)

luxury-loving, a. [B¹] *We are...the most luxury-loving people on the earth* 1899 "Diplomatic Pay" (1928) 240 (Comb. not in OED W S C)

lyceum, sb. [AB³] *By that verdict all the lyceums in the country determined the lecture's commercial value* 1898 *Autob* (1924) I 151 (OED 4. *U.S.* An institution in which popular lectures are delivered on literary and scientific subjects. 1820..So W S B F Cl H DN.III. Not A in C T)

lyceum system, sb. [AB³] *The "lyceum system" was in full flower in those days* 1898 *Autob* (1924) I 156 (OEDS *U.S.* 1843..Comb. not in W S C)

lymphatic, a. [B¹] See *Jubiter* 1869 (Nonsense use)

lynch, v. [AB³] *Demands for the villain Coddington, and threats to lynch him* 1865 SS (1926) 161. *"Before night they wanted to lynch him, but he was gone, you see"* 1884 HF xi 89. *The town broke into a fury of rage and swarmed toward the cooper-shop to lynch Hardy* 1894 "Scrap of Curious Hist." (1917) 184 (OED orig. *U.S.* To condemn and punish by lynch law. 1836..So W S C U Cl Th.III M. See also *Nation* LXXV.439,LXXVI.415)

lyncherdom, sb. [AB¹] *"The United States of Lyncherdom"* (title) E&E (1923) 239 (Not in OED W S C. Cf. above)

lynching, vbl.sb. [AB³] *It is always the way with lynchings: when they find out it is a mistake they too are sorry* 1902 "DBDS" (1928) 353 (OEDS 1836..So C U B Th. Not in W S. Cf. above)

lynch law, sb. [AB³] *Muriel escaped lynch law* 1883 LM xxix 315 (OED orig. *U.S.* 1817.. So W S C U B F Cl Th M. Not A in T)

M

ma, sb. [?AB³] *Tell Ma my promises are faithfully kept* 1853 *Letters* (1917) I i 22. See also *cob pipe* 1884 (OED A childish and colloquial shortening...now often ridiculed as *vulgar.* 1829.. So W S C U. A in M DN.I,II,III,IV,VI)

macedonian, sb. [B¹] See *afarabocca* 1894 (Hum. coinage? Cf. OED Macedonian parsley, 1707)

machete, sb. [AB³E] *He had furnished his recruits with gigantic bowie-knives, to be swung with the two hands, like the machetes of the Isthmus* 1885 "Private Hist. of Campaign" 203 (OED Matchet, sb. This form 19th c. A broad and heavy knife or cutlass used esp. in Central America and the West Indies 1854.. So W S C U M DN.I)

machine, sb. [?AB²] See *mounting-peg* 1880 (OED 4b. *spec* in recent use, often for a bicycle or tricycle. No ex. of bicycle. So W S C)

machine-expense, sb. [B¹] *$3,000 due for the last month's machine-expenses* 1890 *Letters* (1917) II xxx 530 (Nonce comb.: the expenses incurred by M.T. on his projected type-setting machine)

machine politics, sb. [AB²] *That curious invention of machine politics, an Established Church* 1892 *AmCl* x 97 (OED 1893, only ex. Comb. not in W S C. Cf. OED Machine, sb. 8. *U.S. politics:* The controlling organization of a political party. 1876.. So S C F Cl Th M H. Not A in W)

machine-shop, sb. [?AB³] *The distribution of work in a hive is as cleverly and elaborately specialized as it is in a vast American machine-shop or factory* 1902 "The Bee" (1917) 284 (OEDS 1845.. So W S C. A in M: here *shop* has its *spec* Am. meaning of 'factory')

machinist, sb. [B¹] *My machinist type-copied a book for me in 1874* 1905 "The First Writing Machines" (1906) 169 (Nonce word for typist, operator of the new "writing machine" or typewriter. Cf. typewriter copyist, below)

mad, a. [A] *And then he see how it was, and he was the maddest man* 1865 "Jumping Frog" (1875) 35. *The dog is only a short twenty feet behind the coyote...he begins to get aggravated, and it makes him madder and madder to see how gently the coyote glides along...and then that town-dog is mad in earnest* 1872 RI v 51. *Don't you be mad about this blunder,* Howells 1875 *Letters* (1917) I xv 257. See *muff* 1877. *They made fun of him till he got mad* 1883 LM iii 44. See also *freshet* 1896 (OED 5. 'Beside oneself' with anger. Now only *colloq.* In many dialects in Great Britain and the U.S. the ordinary word for 'angry.' 1300..1847. OEDS Later U.S. exs. 1887.. A in S B Th,1847 M H DN.I, II,III,IV,V,VI. Not A in W C U Wr T)

madam, sb. [AB³] *"I only just dropped over to ask about the little madam, and when is she coming home"* 1893 "Californian's Tale" (1906) 109 (OED 3b. The mistress of a house. Now only *U.S. vulgar.* 1824.. So W S C. *Dial* in Wr)

madhouse, sb. [?AC] *Thirty-six years in a madhouse* 1883 LM liii 528 (OED Now *rhetorical* or *derisive.* 1687..1901. *Arch* in S. Not *arch* in W C U)

magazine-agent, sb. [B¹] *You ought to let Osgood be your magazine-agent* 1882 *Letters* (1917) I xxii 418 (Comb. not in OED W S C; but cf. OED Magazine-editor, 1877)

magazining, vbl.sb. [B²] *What would France teach us?...Journalism? No. Magazining? No, that is our own specialty* 1895 "What Bourget Thinks" 49 (OED The conducting of a magazine. No ex. this sense. Not in W S C)

magnanimous-incident, a. [B¹] *All the readers of this article have in some sweet and gushing hour...played the role of Magnanimous-Incident hero* 1878 "About Magnanimous-Incident Literature" 619 (Nonce comb.)

magnify, v. [B¹] *The rats would bite some one's toe, and the person who owned the toe would start up and magnify his English and begin to throw corn in the dark*

1885 "Private Hist. of Campaign" 202 (Hum. nonce use: to embellish with profanity. Cf. OED 2. To render magnificent. *Obs*)

magnolia, sb. [?AB³] *The magnolia trees were lovely and fragrant* 1883 LM xl 416 (OED c. 1821.. A in W S C U B. Not A in H)

mail, v. [AB³] *Harris was for contributing him to the British Museum; but I was for mailing him to his widow* 1880 TA xxxv 390 (OED *U.S.* To send by post. 1828.. So W S U B F Cl H. Not A in C)

mailing, vbl.sb. [AB²] *During the first ten days following the mailing of the letter* 1892 AmCl xxiii 237 (OED *U.S.* 1900.. So W F Cl M. Not A in S C)

mail-matter, sb. [AB³] *Our printed mail-matter doesn't come here* 1906 *M.T. the Letter Writer* (1932) vi 97 (OEDS *U.S.* 1875.. So M H. Not A in C. Comb. not in W S)

mail-train, sb. [?AB³] *He could not wait for the papers themselves to crawl along down to Washington by a mail-train which has never run over a cow since the road was built* 1873 GA xliii 391 (OED A fast train which carries the mails. 1844. So S C. Comb. not in W. Not A in H. Cf. above)

main-brace, sb. to splice the main-brace. [B³] *"I thought I might...get acquainted with the grandees, anyway—not exactly splice the main-brace with them, you know, but shake hands and pass the time of day"* 1908 "Capt. Stormfield" 269 (OED b. *Naut. slang.* To serve out 'grog.' 1805.. So W S C U)

majesty, v. [B¹] *"I must humor the poor lad's madness; I must sire him, I must majesty him"* 1881 PP xii 142. *People always called him "Your Majesty"...So Jim and me set to majestying him* 1884 HF xix 188 (Not in OED W S C as verb)

Major, sb. [A] See *Captain* 1873 (Used in the U.S. as a mere title of courtesy, like Captain, Colonel, General, q.v. So M AS.IX.204. This use not in OED W S C)

make, v. **make it**. [?AB¹] *"Have you got that drink yet?"...He softened, and said make it a bottle of champagne* 1883 LM li 507 (Let it be: used in announcing one's decision as to a choice of drinks, etc. This use not in OED W S C; but cf. OED 51e. *Make it so:* Naut. phr., the order of a commander to confirm the time, etc., reported to him by the officer of the watch. 1835..)

make, v. **to make good time**. [?AB²] *Hopkins made the best time on record* 1870 SNO (1875) 103 (OED 66. To accomplish a distance in a short time. 1887.. So. W. A in Th,1842 T. Phr. not in S C)

make at, v. [C] *The prince picked himself out of the mud and made fiercely at the sentry* 1881 PP iii 45 (OED 77. To make a hostile movement towards. Now somewhat *arch.* 1637..1889. Not *arch* in W C Wr. This sense not in S)

make down, v. [A] *One county has gone into the river from the Missouri point, and the Cairo point has "made down" and added to its long point of territory correspondingly* 1883 LM xxv 280 (OED 73b. *U.S.* and *Colonial.* Of land: to extend in a certain direction. 1787.. So T. This use not in W S C)

make out, v. [A] *Only the experienced old hands made out to eat it* 1872 RI iv 43. *"He knows, if he can make out to put me off for a minute, or make me laugh...I can't hit him a lick"* 1876 TS i 19. See also *crossing* 1884 (OED 91c. To manage, make shift to do something. Chiefly *U.S.* 1609.. So Th M H DN.IV,V. Not A in W S C Wr)

make-up, sb. [?AB³] [Austria] *forever changing in its exact make-up* 1898 "Stirring Times in Austria" (1900) 286 (OED 1. Composition. 1821.. So W S C U. A in B, p.788: The whole as distinguished from the several parts composing it; the equivalent of the French *tout ensemble*)

make-up, sb. [?AB³] *The make-ups of illustrious historic personages seemed perfect, both as to portraiture and costume* 1907 "Chaps. from Autob" 171 (OED 2. Chiefly *Theatr.* An appearance assumed in order to impersonate a character. 1858.. So W S C U. A in B, p.788)

malison, sb. [C] *She lived, she throve—Heaven's malison upon her!* 1871 SNO (1875) 172 (OED *arch* and *dial.* A curse. *a*1300..1865. So S U Wr. Not *arch* in W C)

mamma, sb. Spelled **momma.** [AE] *Poppa and momma would take care of this* 1904 "Bequest" (1906) v 26 (OED In educated use, so far as is known, the stress has in England always been on the last syllable; in the U.S., however, stress on the first syllable is more usual; a prevailing U.S. pronunciation is represented by the spelling *momma*, occasionally used in novels. No ex. of *momma.* So Th,1808 M. W: *Illiterate.* This form not in S C)

mamma-partridge, sb. [?AB¹] *The mamma-partridge ...goes limping and scrambling away* 1906 "Hunting the Deceitful Turkey" 57 (Comb. not in OED W S C)

mamma-turkey, sb. [?AB¹] *A mamma-turkey...finds she has made a mistake* 1906 "Hunting the Deceitful Turkey" 57 (Comb. not in OED W S C)

mammoth, a. [AB³] *The mammoth grand-stand was clothed in flags, streamers, and rich tapestries* 1889 CY xxxix 497 (OEDS Huge, gigantic. Freq. in Am. use before 1850. 1802.. So Th. Not A in W S C U)

man-bird, sb. [B¹] *Near the double Man-Bird was found an ancient record of his* 1875 SNO 147 (Comb. not in OED S C. This sense not in W. Cf. OED Manbeast, 1633)

man-factory, sb. [B¹] *No bond-slave of pope or bishop can enter my man-factory* 1889 CY xiv 159 (Comb. not in OED W S C)

manhood, sb. [?C] *They really hadn't manhood enough* 1898 "At the Appetite-Cure" (1900) 164 (OED 3. Manliness, courage, valour. *arch.* 1377..1853. Not *arch* in W S C U), and app. not so felt by M.T.)

manhood-testing, a. [B¹] *A high enough compliment for a duke or any other man in those manhood-testing circumstances* 1899 "My Debut" (1900) 92 (Comb. not in OED W S C)

manifest, sb. [B¹] *The doctor is not done taking inventory. He will make out my manifest this evening* 1869 SNO (1875) 71 (Hum. *transf* use from the sense in OED 3. The list of a ship's cargo. 1706.. So W S C U)

manito, sb. [A] *Here our troubles will commence, for he* [a supernatural creature in the shape of a bear] *is a mishemokwa and a manito* 1883 LM App.D 615 (OED Among some Am. Indians, a spirit...also anything which is regarded as having supernatural power. 1698.. So W S C U B F Cl DN.VI AS.II.29)

man-mystery, sb. [B¹] *There were remarkable things about the stranger called the Man-Mystery* 1907 CS II 99 (Comb. not in OED W S C; but cf. OED Manmiracle, 1898)

man-of-war-like, a. [B¹] *It is so gaudy and man-of-war-like to sit up in the stern sheets and steer a swift yawl* 1875 OTM 568 (Comb. not in OED W S C)

manologist, sb. [B¹] *That school of scientists called manologists, whose specialty is the deciphering of the ancient records of the extinct bird termed Man* 1875 SNO 145 (Nonce coinage)

manor-house, sb. [AB¹] *A pillared and porticoed great manor-house* 1883 LM xxxix 420 (Here: the home of a plantation owner. So AS.V.163. This Am. sense not in OED W S C U; cf. OED The mansion of the lord of a manor. 1575..)

mansard roof, sb. [?AB³] *Foreign youth...go to the university to put a mansard roof on their whole general education* 1880 TA iv 50. *A swell house, with a mansard roof and all the modern inconveniences* 1883 LM xliii 350 (OED A form of curb-roof, in which each face of the roof has two slopes, the lower one steeper than the upper. 1842.. So W S C U T. A in F)

mansion-and-brewery, a. [B¹] *These* [New Orleans] *mansions stand in the center of large grounds...No houses could well be in better harmony with their surroundings...One even becomes reconciled to the cistern presently; this is a mighty cask, painted green, and sometimes a couple of stories high, which is propped against the house-corner on stilts. There is a mansion-and-brewery suggestion about the combination* 1883 LM xli 429 (Nonce comb.)

manure-pile, sb. [?AB¹] *They* [the children] *had mimic alpenstocks and ice-axes, and were climbing a meek and lowly manure-pile with a most blood-curdling amount of care and caution* 1880 TA xlii 486 (Comb. not in OED W S C; but cf. OED Manure-heap, 1887)

manzanita, sb. [AB³] *The fire seized upon a dense growth of dry manzanita chapparal* 1872 RI xxiii 176 (OEDS A berry-bearing shrub found in the U.S. 1848.. So W S C DN.I AS.VII.432)

maple sugar, sb. [A] *A boy, who was perched on a gate-post munching a hunk of maple sugar* c1880 "Taming the Bicycle" (1917) 292. See also *canned-goods* 1904 (OEDS *U.S.* 1720.. So W S C B F Cl)

maple-sugar camp, sb. [AB¹] *We occupied an old maple-sugar camp, whose half-rotted troughs were still propped against the trees* 1885 "Private Hist. of Campaign" 195 (Comb. not in OED W S C. Cf. above, and see *sugar-camp* below)

maple syrup, sb. [AB²] See *biscuit* 1880 (OEDS *U.S.* 1882.. So W S C B F)

mar, v. [C] *"Mar them* [i.e. these "mummeries"] *not till thou'st enjoyed them"* 1881 PP x 110. *"You are marring the game"* 1893 "Travelling with a Reformer" (1900) 366 (OED 1. *trans.* To hamper, hinder, interfere with. *obs.* c1000..1849. So W. *Dial* in Wr. This sense not in S C)

marble time, sb. [B¹] *It was getting closer and closer onto barefoot time every day; and next it would be marble time* 1896 TSD i 344 (Comb. not in OED W S C)

marble-topped, a. [B¹] *They never used a stove, but cooked their meals on a marble-topped table, just with the natural heat* 1886 *Letters* (1917) II xxvi 470 (Comb. not in OED S C. Given in W)

marble-visaged, a. [B¹] *In each of these lay several marble-visaged babes* 1883 LM xxxi 338 (Comb. not in OED W S C)

marble yard, sb. [B¹] *Littered up with chips...till the place looks like a marble yard* 1870 SNO (1875) 219 (Comb. not in OED W S C)

march-out, sb. [B¹] *He made a fine and picturesque thing of the march-out from the Audience* 1895 JA II vii 239 (Comb. not in OED W S C)

march-past, sb. [B¹] *The march-past and introductions began* 1894 PW vi 334 *Always before, in the march-past, the battalions had gone swinging by in a storm of cheers* 1896 JA II xii 297 (C: The march of a body of soldiers in front of a reviewing officer. So S. This sense not in OED W, which have only: A tune.. designed to accompany the marching of troops. 1896, only ex.)

margin, sb. [?AB³] *"Do you know what the margins would foot up, to buy it at sixty days?"* 1897 FE xiii 145. See also *margin,* v. 1904 (OEDS 2c. Stockbroking and Comm. (a) 1848.. So W S C U. A in B Th)

margin, v. [?AB³] *She was willing to go into the one on a margin, and take chances, but in the case of the other, "margin her no margins"—she wanted to cash in a hundred cents per dollar's-worth, and have the stock transferred on the books* 1904 "Bequest" (1906) iv 21 (OED 4. Stockbroking. To deposit a 'margin' upon stock. Earliest ex. U.S. 18—.. A in B. Not A in W S C)

margin-business, sb. [?AB¹] *Her anxieties were too great for further endurance—she being new to the margin-business and unhardened as yet* 1904 "Bequest" (1906) iv 22 (Comb. not in OED W S C. Cf. above)

mark, sb. [D] "*Mark three! Quarter less three! Half twain!*" [Footnote] "*Mark three*" is three fathoms 1875 OTM 284. See also *leadsman* 1875; *mark twain* 1873 and ff. (OED 12b. *Naut.* A measured notification on a hand lead-line. 1769, 1860—. So W S C)

mark, sb. **to make one's mark.** [?AB³] "*But never mind; he'll make his mark some day*" 1894 PW xi 553 (OEDS 13b. To attain distinction. Earliest exs. U.S. 1847.. Not A in S C. Phr. not in W)

mark, sb. **easy mark.** [AB³] *Whenever I wished to play billiards I went out to look for an easy mark* 1906 *Speeches* (1910) 269 (OEDS A person who is easily persuaded or deceived. *U.S.slang.* 1904, only ex. So C M H. Not A in W S)

mark, sb. **in, into her marks.** [?AB¹] *As the steamer swung into her (to me) utterly invisible marks...he would meet and fasten her there...After a pause, another subdued voice: "Her stern's coming down just exactly right, by George!" "Now she's in the marks!"...The marvellous precision required in laying the great steamer in her marks in that murky waste of water...*1875 OTM 222 (C: A guiding or indicative sign or token..which serves as an indication of place or direction; as, to guide a vessel by landmarks on the shore. This quot. This *Naut.* use not in OED W S)

market-report, sb. [?AB¹] *What can be found in a German daily?...telegrams...market reports* 1880 TA App.F 626 (Comb. not in OED W S C; but cf. OEDS Market-reporter: one who records the market rates of goods or stocks. U.S. quot. 1853, only ex.)

mark twain, sb. [?AB¹] *Just then—this was early in 1863—news came to him that the old pilot he had wounded by his satire, Isaiah Sellers, was dead. At once the pen-name of Captain Sellers recurred to him...He went up to Virginia City. "Joe," he said to Goodman, "I want to sign my articles...I want to sign them 'Mark Twain'. It is an old river term, a leadsman's call, signifying two fathoms—twelve feet. It has a richness about it; it was always a pleasant sound for a pilot to hear on a dark night; it meant safe water."...It was first signed to a Carson letter bearing date of February 2, 1863, and from that time was attached to all Samuel Clemens' work* Paine's Biog. I.221-2. "*Six feet!*" *Bang! She hit the bottom! George shouted through the tube: "Spread her wide open! Whale it at her!"...The boat ground and surged and trembled—and slid over into—"Mark twain!"...And away she went* 1873 GA iv 48. See other quots. under *twain*, 1875 and ff. *There are still findable..several deck-hands who used to heave the lead for me and send up on the still night air the "Six—feet—scant!" that made me shudder, and the "Mark—twain!" that took the shudder away* 1909 ISD vi 65 (Beside the *Naut.* meaning of two fathoms or twelve feet, the phr. has developed the *fig* sense of safety, relief, satisfaction, illustrated by the quots., and doubtless supplying the real inspiration for the pen-name. This *fig* sense not in OED W S C)

marriage-week, sb. [B¹] *He had begun in his marriage-week at four hundred dollars a year* 1904 "Bequest" (1906) i 1 (Comb. not in OED W S C; but cf. OED Marriage-day, 1594)

marry, int. [C] "*Marry*", *quoth the peasant...*1869 IA xxi 212. "*Marry, fair sir, me seemeth...*" 1889 CY ii 32 (OED *Obs* exc. *arch* or *dial.* Originally the name of the Virgin used as an oath. *c*1350.. 1855. So W U Wr. Not *obs* in S C)

Mars, Marse, sb. [AB²] "*Why, Mars Tom, I doan want no rats*" 1884 HF xxxviii 391. "*Marse Washington Hawkins, suh*" 1892 AmCl ii 29. "*Mars Tom, I reckon dey's a mistake about it somers*" 1893 TSA i 24 (OEDS Variant of *Mas*, shortening for *Master.* All exs. U.S. 1901.. Cf. S: A negro corruption. So W B DN.II,III. This form not in C)

marshall. sb. [A] *The man was arrested...by the marshall—large name for a constable, but that was his title* 1883 LM lvi 549 (OED 9a. *U.S.* A civil officer in each judicial district, answering to the sheriff of a county. 1793.. So W S C U B H)

mart, sb. [C] "*Then will we hie us to the mart by the Tabard inn*" 1881 PP xiii 154 (OED 2. Now *poet.* 1590.. 1882. So U. Not *poet.* or *arch* in W S C)

martin-box, sb. [AB³] *A little snowflake of a church, no bigger than a martin-box* 1869 IA xx 203 (OEDS A box or coop used in America for martins to build in. 1853.. Comb. not in W S C)

martyr-maker, sb. [B¹] *Geoffrey Clement the martyr-maker was an ancestor of mine* 1897 *Autob* (1924) I 84 (Cf. OED Martyr-maker: contemptuous name for the martyologist John Foxe. 1826. Here: one who subjects another to martyrdom. As M.T. goes on to explain, his ancestor was a member of the court of judges who tried Charles I and condemned him to execution. Comb. not in W S C)

marvel, sb. [AE] "*Jim, I'll give you a marvel. I'll give you a white alley!...And it's a bully taw*" 1876 TS ii 27 (OEDS Common Eng. and U.S. *dial* var. of Marble, sb. 1727.. So Wr B DN.III,IV AS.V.19, Ozarks. Not A in W. Not in S C)

marvel, v. [?C] *He marveled to find that this final change was not merely intellectual* 1892 AmCl xv 153 (OED Now only *literary.* 1d. constr. with inf. 1535..1582. Not *literary* or *arch* in any way in W S C U. The OED is surely wrong here)

mash, v. [B¹] See *wilt*, v. 1889 (To crush or overwhelm with embarrassment. This *fig* sense not in OED W S C)

mask-law, sb. [B¹] "*In Frankfort at the Romer was a great mask-ball, at the coronation festival...According to mask-law, each masked guest must make himself known*" 1880 TA i 19 (Comb. not in OED W S C. Perhaps after a German compound such as *Maskengesetz.* Cf. *Maskenfreiheit*, freedom of the masquerade or carnival)

massed, ppl.a. [B²] *The massed world on the river burst into a mighty roar of welcome* 1881 PP ix 106 (OED 1885.. So W S C)

mass-meeting, sb. [AB³] *A religious mass-meeting was assembled* 1856 Letter in *Iowa Journ. of Hist* (1929) 423. *In the middle of the town was a place for public auctions, horse trades, and mass-meetings* 1872 RI xxi 158. See also *Athenaeum* 1883; *range*, sb. 1902; *Republican* 1906 (OEDS orig. *U.S.* 1842.. So B F Th T M. Not A in W S C U)

massy, a. [?C] *It looks so massy, and carries one in imagination to the ruined piles of ancient Babylon* 1853 Letter in *Iowa Journ. of Hist.* (1929) 411. *Its furniture was all of massy gold* 1881 PP vii 89 (OED Formerly in common use; now *rhetorical* or *arch*; in ordinary prose superseded by 'massive' 1a. 1382..1877. Not *arch* in W S C U Wr)

matable, a. [B¹] *He* [Shakespeare] *was a genius without a mate, a prodigy not matable* 1909 ISD x 123 (Not in OED W S C)

materialization, sb. [?AB³] "*You have heard of materialization—materialization of departed spirits?*" 1892 AmCl iii 43 (OED 2. *Spiritualism.* The appearance of a spirit in bodily form. 1880.. So W S C U. A in F Cl)

materialize, v.trans. [?AB³] *One...comes out and materializes himself into anybody you want* 1892 AmCl iii 44. (OED 2a. *Spiritualism.* 1880.. So W S C U. A in F Cl Th DN.VI)

materialize, v.intr. [AB³] *The matter started as a joke, but it came somewhat near to materializing* 1906 "Monument to Adam" 234 (OED 2c. *transf.* To... become actual fact, to 'come off.' orig. *U.S.* in journalistic use. 1885.. So F Cl Th. Not A in W S C U T)

materializee, sb. [?AB¹] *The feeling...is not engendered by the mere conduct of the materializee* 1892 AmCl xvii 175 (The being or spirit materialized. A in Cl. Not A in W. Not in OED S C)

materializer, sb. [?AB²] *One learned...that the Colonel was a Materializer, a Hypnotizer* 1892 AmCl ii 28 (OED One who materializes. No ex. of the *Spiritualistic* sense. So W. Not in S C)

materializing, vbl.sb. [?AB³] *Meantime the materializing recipe would be perfected* 1892 AmCl v 65 (OED *Spiritualism*. 1882, only ex. So W S C. A in F)

matter, sb. **what is the matter of?** [AB¹] *I wouldn't give a dern to know what's the matter of Phillips, I says to myself* 1896 TSD ii 347 (A in DN.III, n.w.Ark. This phr. with *of* not in OED W S C; but cf. OED Matter, sb. 25b. What is the matter with? 1715..)

matteration, sb. [B¹] *"Another remarkable specialty to Christian Science—viz., ease and flow and lavishness of words." "Yes—God-all...non-Matter, Matteration, Spirit..."* 1899 "Chr. Sc. and the Book" 588 (Presumably means the state of being, becoming, or turning into matter. Not in OED W S C)

maunder, sb. [C] See *budge* 1881 (OED *Cant. Obs.* A beggar. 1609..1829. So W C. Not in S)

maxillaris superioris, sb. [B¹] *"This would be followed by ossification and extradition of the maxillaris superioris"* 1894 TET vii 408 (Nonsense comb. Cf. OED Superior maxilla: the upper jaw-bone. 1727..)

maxillary, sb. [B¹] *Deceased wiped his os frontis with his major maxillary* 1870 SNO (1875) 192 (Nonsense use. Cf. OED = maxillary bone, 1836..)

may, v. Past tense **mought**. [?AE] *"He tole Hanks he mought git to Obed's tomorrer"* 1873 GA i 21 (OED Now *dial*. This form had an extensive literary currency in the 16th and 17th c. A in Wr B F Cl Th,1821 DN.I,II,V,VI AS.V.203, Ozarks; VII.91, Cumberlands. *Dial* in W S C)

maybe, adv. [?A?C] *"Where you going to dig next?" "I reckon maybe we'll tackle the old tree that's over yonder on Cardiff Hill back of the widow's." "But won't the widow take it away from us, Tom? It's on her land." "She take it away! Maybe she'd like to try it once"* 1876 TS xxv 195. See also *galoot* 1884; *brash* 1892; *fresh* 1892; *must-have-been* 1909 (OED *a*1425..1871. So W S C. A in F H DN.II,III. Cf. H: In Eng. *maybe* has almost become an archaism and a *dial*. word, having been supplanted by *perhaps*. In Am. it is still in everyday use)

mayhap, adv. [?AC] *"Fathers be alike, mayhap"* 1881 PP iii 41 (OED Now *arch, rhetorical*, and *dial. a*1536..1900. So W. Not *arch* in S C. A in Wr)

Mayoritish, a. [B¹] *Many a memorial of the lost race was afterwards found—the "Mayoritish Stone"' being so called from the word "Mayor" in it* 1875 SNO 145 (Nonce coinage. Perhaps suggested by the "Moabite (or Moabitish) Stone")

mean, a. [?AC] *Mary Jane set at the head of the table ...and said how bad the biscuits was, and how mean the preserves was* 1884 HF xxvi 258 (OED 3. Poor in quality; of little value, inferior. *obs.* 1377..1770. Not *obs* in W S C Wr. A in B F Cl Th H DN.III. Not A in T)

mean, a. **to feel mean.** [AB³] *I would feel mean to lie abed and sleep, and leave her to watch and toil over our little patient* 1875 SNO 88. See *mother*, v. 1884. *"I could have saved him, and I hadn't the pluck to do it... I feel mean, ever so mean"* 1899 "MCH" (1900) 9 (OED 5b. *U.S. colloq*. To feel ashamed of one's conduct. 1839.. So W S F Th M. Not A in C)

mean, a. [AB³] *I do more mean things...than ever I can get forgiveness for* 1867 Letters (1917) I vi 126. See *sour on*, v. 1876. *Troubles we was going to get into with quarrelsome people and all kinds of mean folks* 1884 HF xv 132. *"It was mean and base of me, I know"* 1894 PW xviii 17. *"They take a mean pleasure in saying 'Your friend Burgess', because they know it pesters me"* 1899 "MCH" (1900) 9 (OEDS 5b(a). *U.S. colloq*. Disobliging; pettily offensive or unaccommodating. 1848.. So W Wr Cl Th,1808 T DN.I,III. Not A in S C)

mean, a. [?AB³] *"I'll give it to you, because there ain't anything mean about me"* 1876 TS xii 107. *The government will be able to find excuses for continuing its diplomatic salaries at the present mean figure* 1899 "Diplomatic Pay" (1928) 238 (OED 6. Penurious, 'stingy'. Earliest exs. U.S. 1860.. Not A in W S C U)

mean, v. [?AB²] *"I didn't know I was doing any harm; I didn't mean to do any harm"* 1880 TA xxv 257. *Now if you mean it, old man—if you are in earnest—proceed* 1884 Letters (1917) II xxiv 442 (OED 1. In mod. *colloq* use sometimes: To intend with determined purpose. 1904, only ex. of this emphasized sense. This sense not in W S C)

meander, v. [?AB¹] *"If you'll just give me a lift," said the undertaker, "we'll skeet him into the hearse and meander along"* 1871 SNO (1875) 248 (Cf. OED 2. To wander deviously or aimlessly. 1831.. So W S C. Here merely: To proceed, to be on one's way. So AS.IV.57, Ozarks. This more generalized *slang* use not in OED W S C)

measly, a. [?AB³] *Once they were a frank and manly race, now they are measly hypocrites* 1893 "Esquimau Maiden's Romance" (1900) 149 (OEDS 4. *slang*. Contemptible. 1864.. So W S C U Wr. A in DN.II,III, IV,V)

measurably, adv. [A] *The ground ought to be measurably sacred by this time* 1869 IA xiv 131 (OED 3. To some extent; 'in a measure'. *U.S.* 1756.. So H DN.V. Not A in W S C U)

measure-defying, a. [B¹] *Stretching away on every hand into dim, measure-defying distance* 1883 LM xxii 253 (Comb. not in OED W S C)

meat, sb. **to be one's meat.** [AB²] *"Come along—you're my meat now, my lad"* 1872 RI l 357. *He is "my meat"*, *as they say in the mines* 1880 TA xxvi 263. See *chaw up* 1883. *"She's my meat...I'm on her track"* 1894 PW xv 818 (OED 3d. *U.S.* One's quarry or prey. *transf*. 1882, only ex. *fig* sense. So Th.III DN.IV. Not A in W. Phr. not in S C)

meat-feast, sb. [B¹] *He had been blowing and bragging about his grand meat-feast* 1889 CY xxxii 414 (Comb. not in OED W S C)

medicine-man, sb. [AB³] *The medicine-man of that day, like the medicine-man of our Indian tribes, did what he could to meet the requirements* 1890 "Majestic Literary Fossil" 441. *From the beginning of time, the sorcerer, the quack, the wild medicine-man, have made use of the client's imagination to help them in their work* 1899 "Chr. Sc. and the Book" 593 (OED Medicine, sb. 6b. A magician among the American Indians and other savages. 1817.. So B W C M AS.VII.2. Not A in S U)

medicine-sack, sb. [AB¹] *See my medicine-sack and my war club tied to it* 1883 LM App.D. 613 (Comb. not in OED W S C; but cf. OED Medicine-bag, 1809; Medicine-pouch, 1855, from Medicine 4. Used to represent the terms applied in their native languages by North American Indians to denote any object or ceremony supposed by them to possess a magical influence. 1805..)

medieval, a. Spelled **meedyevil**. [E] *He got out two or three curtain-calico suits, which he said was meedyevil armor for Richard III* 1884 HF xx 194 (The pron. indicated, with the first syllable long, is given by OED as a permissible alternative, and is preferred in W S C. M.T. apparently imagined it to be *dial* or *colloq*.)

meditation-breeding, a. [B¹] *Its meditation-breeding air of repose and dignity* 1907 "Chaps. from Autob" 171 (Comb. not in OED W S C)

medium, sb. [?AB³] *Receiving a letter from a deceased relative through a New York spiritualistic medium* 1883 LM xlviii 481 (OED 8b. *Spiritualism*. A person supposed to be the organ of communication from departed spirits. 1853.. So W S C U. A in B F T)

meeky, v. [?AB¹] *He warn't a boy to meeky along up that yard like a sheep; no, he come ca'm and important,* *like the ram* 1884 HF xxxiii 340 (To skulk, sneak along; to proceed with an air of guilt. Not in OED W S C. Cf. OED Meek, v. *obs.* 3. intr. To become meek, to be meek. *a*1300..1400; also OED Meeken, v. 2. To submit meekly, 1844.. Cf. also Wr Meeking, ppl.a. Ailing, lacking energy, drooping, *Shropshire;* A in DN.I, N.Y: Descriptive of the guilty appearance of one caught pilfering. Even closer in sense is OED Meech, Miche, v. Now *dial.* 2. To lurk out of sight; to skulk. 1558..; so W S C; A in Wr Th. Huck Finn's word is probably a descendant, or at least a close relative, of Shakespeare's mysterious "miching mal-lecho")

meet, sb. [?AB¹] *We'll manage a meet yet* 1889 *Letters* (1917) II xxix 512 (W: Act of meeting, as of two trains. So U. This sense not in OED S C)

meet, a. [C] *"My lord, it is not meet that they sit in thy presence"* 1881 PP vi 73. See also *fame* 1896 (OED Now *arch.* 3b. Fitting, proper. *a*1300..1846. So U. Not *arch* in W S C Wr)

meet, v. [?AB³] *"Now then!—meet her! meet her! snatch her!"* 1873 GA ii 47. See *helm-a-lee* 1876. *"You going to hold her all day? Let her go—meet her! meet her!" Then he would snatch the wheel from me and meet her himself* 1883 LM xviii 223. See also *crowd,* v. 1909 (OEDS 2g. *Naut.* In bringing a ship on to a desired course, to turn the helm or rudder in the other direction before the ship reaches the desired course, to prevent its going round too far. Early exs. U.S. 1815.. Not A in W S C)

meeting-house, sb. [AC] See *thunderation* 1856 (OEDS 2. A place of worship: in the general sense, now only *U.S.* 1633..1896. So W S C B F Cl DN.III AS.I.194,V.120,419,VII.91,VIII.4.49. Cf. Wr: A Non-Conformist chapel; so T)

meet up with, v. [AB³] *Sir Lancelot met up with old King Agrivance of Ireland unexpectedly last week* 1889 CY xxvi 339. *I "met up" with that charming Colonel Chapman* 1910 *Letters* (1917) II xlviii 838 (OEDS 13. To overtake or fall in with. *U.S. colloq.* 1837.. So S C B F DN.I,II,III,IV,V. Comb. not in W)

megalophonous, a. [B³?C] *"Let the megalophonous grasshopper sound a blast"* 1875 SNO 145 (OED *Burlesque nonce-wd.* Having a great voice. 1819, Shelley's *Peter Bell,* only ex. Not a nonce word in W S C)

Meisterschaft, sb. [B¹] *"I hate Meisterschaft!... Neither Annie nor I can put two words together, except as they are put together for us in Meisterschaft or that idiotic Ollendorf!"...We knock the German Meisterschaft sentences out of the first scene, and replace them with sentences from the French Meisterschaft* 1888 *Meisterschaft* 457. See also *trowel-in* 1888 (A phrasebook or language manual. Nonce borrowing from the German title of a popular series of handbooks. Not in OED W S C)

Mekkamuselmannenmassenmenchenmoerdermoh-renmuttermarmormonumentenmacher, sb. [B¹] See *effect* 1889 (Hum. coinage)

mellow, a. [?A] *The king sneaked into the wigwam and took to his bottle for comfort, and before long the duke tackled his bottle...They both got powerful mellow* 1884 HF xxx 313 (OED 6. Affected with liquor. 1611.. So W S C. A in AS.XII.91)

melodeon, sb. Also **melodeum**. [AB³] *Our parlor organ and our melodeon were to be the best instruments of the kind* 1869 IA ii 26. *They had borrowed a melodeum—a sick one; and when everything was ready a young woman set down and worked it, and it was pretty skreeky and colicky* 1884 HF xxvii 272 (OED 1. An earlier form of the 'American organ'. OEDS Earlier U.S. ex. 1849.. So U. Not A in W S C)

melon-rind, sb. [B¹] *Chambers did his stealing, and got the peach-stones, apple-cores, and melon-rinds for his share* 1894 PW iv 330 (Comb. not in OED W S C)

memento, sb. [?AB¹] *Blucher...gathers mementoes with perfect recklessness, mixes them all up together, and then serenely labels them without any regard to truth, or even plausibility* 1869 IA xxxv 385 (C: *spec,* a souvenir. So S. This sense not in OED W)

memento-factory, sb. [?AB¹] *It was a memento-factory, and the stock was large, cheap, and varied* 1880 TA xlvi 539 (Comb. not in OED W S C. Cf. above)

memento-magazine, sb. [?AB¹] *We lounged into an apartment where there was a great crowd, to see what was going on. It was a memento-magazine. The tourists were eagerly buying paper-cutters marked "Souvenir of the Rigi"* 1880 TA xxviii 295 (Comb. not in OED W S C. Cf. above)

memento-seeker, sb. [?AB¹] *One of the irrepressible memento-seekers...was pecking at the venerable sarcophagous* 1869 IA lviii 626 (Comb. not in OED W S C. Cf. above)

Memnon, sb. [B¹] *"Try to conceive of Darwin feeling flattered by the notice of a princess...Yet that Memnon was flattered by the notice of that statuette"* 1892 AmCl xi 116 (Here *fig:* A man of colossal greatness. Not in OED W S C in this sense)

memorial-spoon, sb. [B¹] *Already whatever she [Mrs. Eddy] puts her trade-mark on, though it be only a memorial-spoon, is holy and is eagerly bought* 1903 "Chr. Sc." ii 2 (Comb. not in OED W S C; but cf. OED Memorial Day, *U.S.,* 1836)

memory-exhibition, sb. [B¹] *Among the shows offered ...for his entertainment was a memory-exhibition* 1897 FE ii 36 (Comb. not in OED W S C)

memory-expert, sb. [B¹] *The memory-expert, a high-caste Brahmin, was brought in* 1897 FE ii 36 (Comb. not in OED W S C; but cf. OED Memory-man: a professor of mnemonics, 1815)

Mental Science, sb. [AB¹] See *prayer-cure* 1899 (W: A system of mental healing, also known as New Thought or Divine Science. In England known as Higher Thought. So C. Not in OED S)

Mental Scientist, sb. [AB¹] See *Allopath* 1902 (Comb. not in OED W S C. Cf. above)

mental telegraphic, a. [B¹] *An extraordinary experience of mine in the mental telegraphic line* 1891 "Mental Telegraphy" 95 (Comb. not in OED W S C. Cf. below)

mental telegraphist, sb. [B¹] *Inanimate objects every now and then give the mental telegraphist a lift* 1891 "Mental Telegraphy" 102 (Comb. not in OED W S C. Cf. below)

mental telegraphy, [B¹] sb. *The discovery that certain sorts of things which, from the beginning of the world, had always been regarded as merely "curious coincidences" —that is to say, accidents—were no more accidental than is the sending and receiving of a telegram an accident... I made this discovery sixteen or seventeen years ago and gave it a name—"Mental Telegraphy"* 1891 "Mental Telegraphy" 95. See *mind-transference* 1897. *If I had invented my story I should say that it was all mental telegraphy* 1900 *M.T. the Letter Writer* (1932) vii 109 (Comb. not in OED W S C. M.T.'s claim to have invented the term about 1875 is confirmed by Paine, *Biog.* I.543)

mercy sakes, int. [?AB¹] *"We had to send in spoons and things...in your apron pocket!" "Mercy sakes!"* 1884 HF xlii 429 (Cf. Mercy sakes alive, A in B DN.III. Phr. not in OED W S C; but cf. OED Mercy, sb. 4. For mercy's sake, 1860)

meretricious, a. [B¹] See *technical* 1872 (Hum. malapropism)

meseems, v. [C] *"Meseemeth I could forego the crown"* 1881 PP iii 44 (OED *arch. c*1400..1876. So W S U. Not *arch* in C)

mesozoic, a. [B¹] *I never stir from home, except at geologic intervals, to fill left-over engagements in mesozoic times when I was younger* 1909 *Letters* (1917) II xlvii 827 (Hum. nonce use. Cf. OED *Geol.* 1840..; so W S C U)

messenger-splendor, sb. [B¹] *The messenger splendors of the coming sun* 1880 TA xxviii 292 (Comb. not in OED W S C; but cf. OED Messenger-authority, 1711; messenger-bird, 1869; messenger-wind, 1898, etc.)

Metaphysical, a. [AB¹] *Mrs. Eddy is president of the Trust's Metaphysical College in Boston, where the student of C. S. healing learns the game by a three weeks' course* 1907 CS I vii 70 (The *spec* Christian Science meaning of "metaphysical," whatever it may be, is not given in OED W S C)

meteor-flight, sb. [B¹] *The marvellous child's meteor-flight across the war-firmament of France* 1895 JA I i 683 (Comb. not in OED W S C)

Methodist, sb. [A] See *Adventist* 1907 (OED 4a. In England...Wesleyan-Methodist. In the U.S., the most influential body of Methodists is the Methodist Episcopal Church...There are also several other bodies in the U.S. that adopt the name as part of their official designation. 1733.. So W S C)

Methusalem-numskull, sb. [?AB¹CE] *"I lay you'll be the Methusalem-numbskull of creation before ever I ask you"* 1884 HF xxxiii 343 (Comb. not in OED W S C. Cf. OED Methusaleh: the sp. Methusalem 17th-18th c. This corruption, after Jerusalem, still survives in vulgar use. 1647, 1711. W calls the form *obs* exc. *lit.*; S says it is the French form of the name. Not in C. Evidently it survived into the 19th c. in Missouri)

Mexicanized, ppl.a. [AB²] *Mexicans, Californians, and Mexicanized Americans* 1872 RI xxiv 178 (OED 1887, only ex. So W S C Th.III)

miaow, v. Spelled **meow, maow, me-yow, me-yo.** [E] *"Will you meow?" "Yes—and you meow back if you get a chance. Las' time, you kep' me a-meowing around till old Hays went to throwing rocks at me and says, 'Dern that cat!'"* 1876 TS vi 67. *"All you got to do is to trot up Hooper Street a block and maow—and if I'm asleep, you throw some gravel at the window"* 1876 TS xxviii 215. *Mintz and Mountz, the catties..."Me-yow! Me-yo! Me-Yow! Me-Yo!"* [German, Miau! Mio!] 1891 *Slovenly Peter* (1935) 6 (OED 1632.. These forms not in OED C. W and S have meow. The sp. *meow* is called A in DN.V)

Mick, sb. [?AB²] *"The Micks got to throwing stones through the Methodist Sunday-school windows"* 1872 RI xlvii 336 (OEDS Shortened form of *Michael*, applied jocularly to an Irishman. 1872, this quot. So W C. A in S F T M DN.I,IV)

mid-Atlantic, sb. [B¹] *Two shipments would meet and part in mid-Atlantic* 1892 AmCl v 65 (Comb. not in OED S C. Given in W)

middle name, sb. [B¹] *He had all the look of an American person who would be likely to begin his signature with an initial, and spell his middle name out. He introduced himself, smiling a smirky smile borrowed from the courtiers of the stage* 1880 TA xxxviii 440 (Comb. not in OED W S C)

Middle States, sb.pl. [A] *He checked off what to-day's weather is going to be on the Pacific, down South, in the Middle States* 1879 *Speeches* (1910) 61 (OEDS Middle, a. 6. 1784.. So W S C F)

middling, adv. [?AB³] *"Oh, I'se middlin'; hain't got nothin' to complain of"* 1893 PW ii 236 (OED *colloq* and *dial.* 2. Fairly well in health. 1810.. So W S C U Wr. A in B DN.V)

mid-movement, sb. [B¹] *It is like a sea whose long, rolling swells have been caught in mid-movement* 1880 TA xlvi 532 (Comb. not in OED W S C)

mid-nothingness, sb. [B¹] *The sense of floating high aloft in mid-nothingness* 1872 RI xxiii 175 (Comb. not in OED W S C)

Midway, sb. [AB³] See *chain-gang* 1898 (OEDS 3. *U.S.* An avenue in the middle of an exhibition or fair. Also *attrib.* The use originated in the inclusion of the 'Midway Plaisance' of Chicago in the grounds of the exposition held there in 1893. 1891.. So W C H. This use not in S)

Might-Have-Beener, sb. [B¹] *I had only a warm desire to laugh at...the Might-Have-Beeners* 1909 ISD ii 24 (Comb. not in OED W S C)

mightily, adv. [?AC] *I mightily wanted to speak to him* 1870 SNO (1875) 192. *They were mightily looked up to* 1875 OTM 722. *Mightily enjoying each other's narratives* 1881 PP xxv 296 (OED 3. Now somewhat rare; very common in 17th-18th c. 1593..1886. Not rare in W. *Obs* in Wr. *Colloq* in S C U. A in DN.II)

mighty, a. [?A] See *airy* 1869. *"Sometimes I've got a mighty notion to just leave the country for good and all"* 1884 HF vi 42 (OED Very great. In later use, chiefly *colloq* or *familiar.* 1586..1871. So W U Wr. This *colloq* use not in S C. A in DN.II,III,V)

mighty, adv. [?A] *"Mighty likely boy, is Jerry"* 1873 GA vii 96. See *swan*, v. 1877. *"You hain't got me so mighty much, nuther"* 1880 TA xxiii 225 (OED Now *colloq* or *familiar*, often with ironical implication = 'vastly', 'precious.' a1300..1883. So W S C U. A in Wr B Th.III M H)

Milam, a. [AB¹] *"Here's a big Milum apple I've been saving for you, Tom, if you was ever found again"* 1876 TS xviii 152 (Not in OED W S C. Cf. S. A. Beach, *The Apples of New York*, 1905, I. 209: "Milam...A medium-sized dessert apple...formerly quite popular in some portions of the Middle West. Origin uncertain")

mile, sb. [?ACE] *We unhitched a skiff and pulled down the river two mile and a half* 1884 HF ii 12. So *passim* in HF. See also *Big House* 1894 (OED 1. The use of the sing. form with a pl. numeral is now only *vulgar* or *dial.* c1290..1850. So Wr. A in B M DN.III AS.III.10, Ozarks. This use not mentioned in W S C)

mileage, sb. [A] *In ten days more I hope to be able to collect little dabs of mileage* 1867 M.T. the Letter Writer (1932) i 16. *They did as any honorable, high-minded men would naturally do—declined to receive the mileage tendered them by the government* 1873 GA xxx 275 (OED 1. A travelling allowance at a fixed rate per mile; *spec. U.S.*, the allowance made to a member of Congress. 1754.. So S C B F Cl Th T M H DN.VI. Not A in W)

mile-posted, ppl. a. [B¹] *The road was mile-posted with English fortresses* 1896 JA II xi 294 (Comb. not in OED W S C; but cf. OEDS Mile-post, sb. 1768..)

milestone, v. [?AB²] *Other effects had been milestoning the course of the Fosters' splendid financial march* 1904 "Bequest" (1906) vi 33. *You could look back over that speech and you'd find it dimly milestoned along with those commas* 1906 Autob (1924) I 299 (OEDS To mark stages on a road by milestones; also *fig.* 1921, first *fig* ex. So W. Not in S C as verb)

mile-wide, a. [B¹] *The magnificent Mississippi, rolling its mile-wide tide along* 1875 OTM 70 (Comb. not in OED W S C; but cf. OED Mile-deep, 1903; Mile-long, 1834)

milk-route, sb. [?AB²] *The vested rights...are frequently the subject of sale or mortgage, just like a milk-route* 1897 FE xlix 464 (OEDS A route on which a milk-dealer regularly supplies milk to his customers. 1897, this quot., only ex. Not A in W C. Comb. not in S)

mill, sb. [A] See *cent* 1889 (OEDS A money of account in the U.S., one-tenth of a cent. 1786.. So W S C U F Cl Th T M H)

mill, sb. [?AB¹] *I hadn't minded her mill that morning* 1889 CY xii 146 (Chattering, loquacity. This sense not in OED W S C)

miller-gun, sb. [B¹] *The miller-gun was a little invention of my own, and I had officially ordered that every shopkeeper in the kingdom keep them on hand* 1889 CY xxxi 402. *The miller-gun was a little double-barreled tube of toughened glass, with a neat little trick of a spring* *to it, which upon pressure would let a shot escape...In the gun were two sizes—wee mustard-seed shot, and another sort that were several times larger. They were money. The mustard-seed shot represented milrays, the larger ones mills. So the gun was a purse...I made them of several sizes—one size so large that it would carry the equivalent of a dollar.* do. xxxiv 437 (Comb. not in OED W S C. Apparently both the device and the word were of M.T's own invention, the product of his unquenchable interest in all sorts of new mechanical contrivances. The suggestion for this one came perhaps from one form of that contemporary Am. invention the cash register, with his new coins the 'mill' and the 'milray' (q.v. below) taking the place of the usual Am. small change. Cf. OEDS Cash register, orig. *U.S.*, 1886..)

Millerite, sb. [AB³] See *ascensionist* 1869; *Allopath* 1902; *Congregationalist* 1906 (OED *U.S.* A believer in the doctrines of William Miller (*died* 1849), an American preacher who interpreted the Scriptures as foretelling the early coming of Christ. 1846.. So W S C U B F Th.III,1844 DN.VI)

millinerize, v. [B¹] *She couldn't design or millinerize* 1892 AmCl xxi 209 (To perform the functions of a milliner. Not in OED W S C)

millinerizing, vbl.sb. [B¹] *Never before had millinerizing seemed so void of interest to her* 1892 AmCl xxi 209 (Not in OED W S C; but cf. OED Millinering, vbl.sb.: a milliner's work, 1886..)

millionaire, sb. [?AB³] *"One of these days it will be the rich Miss Emily Hawkins, and Gov. Henry Clay Hawkins, millionaire"* 1873 GA v 55. See *nobility* 1892. *"He can't tell a millionaire from a tramp"* 1893 "Banknote" (1928) 116. See also *squatter*, 1897; *multimillionaire* 1899 (OED A person possessed of a 'million' of money', as a million pounds, dollars, francs, etc. 1826.. So W S C U. In M.T.'s usage the word always means the possessor of a million dollars; the owner of a million pounds he calls a 'million-pounder', q.v., below)

millionaire, sb. **hundred-millionaire**. [?AB¹] *John Mackay developed suddenly into the first of the hundred-millionaires* 1906 Autob (1924) I 272 (Owner of a hundred million dollars. Comb. not in OED W S C)

million-pound, a, [B¹] *"The £1,000,000 Banknote"* (title) 1893 (Comb. not in OED W S C)

million-pounder, sb. [B¹] *You could not take up a newspaper...without finding in it one or more references to the "vest-pocket million-pounder"* 1893 "Banknote" (1928) 118 (Comb. not in OED W S C)

million-voiced, a. [B¹] *The two sat unconscious of the million-voiced music of the mosquitoes* 1894 TET i 322 (Comb. not in OED W S C; but cf. OED Million-handed, 1847)

mill-saw, sb. [?AB²] *Everybody was a bobbin up and down like a mill-saw* 1856 Adv. of T. J. Snodgrass (1928) 25 (OED A saw for use in a saw-mill. 1897, only ex. So W S C)

milray, sb. [B¹] See *cent* 1889; *miller-gun* 1889 (Here M.T. has coined a new monetary term, evidently meaning a tenth of a mill. Perhaps the Portuguese *milreis* was in his mind; but if so, he must have mistakenly recollected it as a thousandth part of a *real*, instead of a thousand *reis*, as it really is. Cf. OED Milreis (also milrey, milleray, etc.): a Portuguese gold coin and money of account equal to 1,000 Reis, and of the value of 4s. 5¼d. English money. 1589.. Cf. also M.T.'s experience with Portuguese money in the Azores: *"The Portuguese pennies or reis (pronounced rays) are prodigious...It takes one thousand reis to make a dollar"* 1869 IA v 52)

mind, v. [?AC] *"Here is the stump to keep me minded of it"* 1881 PP xvii 214 (OED 1. To remind. Now *rare*. 1340..1890. So W S. Not *rare* in C Wr. A in B T DN.II,III,V)

mind-cure, sb. [?AB³] *The Colonel was...a Mind-Cure dabbler* 1892 AmCl ii 28. *"What do you attribute this strange miracle to?" "Mind-cure—simply mind-cure"* 1894 Letters (1917) II xxxiv 606. See also *prayer-cure* 1899 (OED U.S. quot. 1885, only ex. Not A in W S C)

mind-curist, sb. [?AB²] *A patient had actually been killed by a mind-curist* 1894 Letters (1917) II xxxiv 606. See also *regular*, sb. 1894; *Allopath* 1902 (OEDS U.S. quot. 1904, only ex. Not A in W S C)

mind-extinguished, a. [B¹] *Four men—all bent, and wrinkled, and mind-extinguished patriarchs* 1889 CY xviii 224 (Comb. not in OED W S C)

mind-sect, sb. [B¹] *I believe it might be shown that all the "mind" sects except Christian Science have lucid intervals* 1899 "Chr. Sc. and the Book" 594 (Comb. not in OED W S C. Cf. mind-cure, Mental Science, etc., above)

mind-telegraphing, vbl.sb. [B¹] *I laid the manuscript aside, purposing to add to it instances of mind-telegraphing from time to time* 1891 "Mental Telegraphy" 99 (Comb. not in OED W S C. Cf. Mental Telegraphy, above)

mind-transference, sb. [B¹] *Here was a clear case of mental telegraphy; of mind-transference* 1897 FE xxxiv 317 (Comb. not in OED W. Given in S C)

mining-broker, sb. [?AB¹] *I was a mining-broker's clerk in San Francisco* 1893 "Banknote" (1928) 106 (Comb. not in OED W S C)

mining-camp, sb. [?AB²] *The dilapidated tavern in the decayed mining camp of Angel's* 1865 "Jumping Frog" (1875) 30. *"Don't you put on any exclusiveness in a mining-camp"* 1902 "DBDS" (1928) 332 (Given in OED, no ex. So S C. Comb. not in W)

mining-tax, sb. [?AB¹] *California imposes an unlawful mining-tax upon John the foreigner, and allows Patrick the foreigner to dig gold for nothing* 1870 SNO (1875) 117 (Comb. not in OED W S C)

minstrel, sb. [AB³] *He was worse than the minstrels, worse than the clown in the circus* 1889 CY iv 53 (OED 4. The designation assumed by certain public entertainers in the U.S. and subsequently also in England. 1864.. So W S C U)

miracle-factory, sb. [B¹] *The church would have set up a miracle-factory there* 1880 TA xxi 206 (Comb. not in OED W S C)

miracle-performance, sb. [B¹] *These miracle-performances are simply compensation* 1883 LM xli 433 (Comb. not in OED W S C)

miscall, v. [?AB³] See *wonderly* 1889 (OED 1b. To misread, mispronounce. *dial.* 1853.. So W S C U Wr)

miscarry, v. [?AC] See *overthwart and endlong* 1889. *My defects had a large chance for display...As soon as the guests were out of the house, I saw that I had been miscarrying again* 1906 Autob (1924) II 156 (OED 2. *intr* and *refl.* To behave amiss, do wrong, misbehave. *Obs.* 1325..1732. So W. This sense not in S C. App. not felt as *obs.* by M.T.)

misery, sb. [B¹] *"She is well better, grace to the infinite misery—grace à l' infinie misericorde"* 1875 SNO 39 (Hum. nonce rendering)

mishemokwa, sb. [B¹] See *manito* 1883 (Not in OED W S C. An Indian term for a supernatural creature of some sort)

mislike, v. [C] *"That would I not mislike"* 1881 PP iii 44 (OED Now chiefly *literary* or *dial.* 3. To dislike. 1513..1878. So Wr. Not *lit.* or *dial* in W S C U)

Miss, sb. for **Mrs.** [AB³E] *Just then the nigger woman steps onto the passage, and says: "Missus, dey's a sheet gone"..."Where's it gone, Lize?" "Clah to goodness, I hain't no notion, Miss' Sally"* [i.e., "Aunt Sally," or Mrs. Sally Phelps] 1884 HF xxxvii 378 (OED 5. *dial* and *U.S.* Cf. C: Mrs. is commonly abbreviated in rustic use in New England and among the Southern negroes to Miss, often printed Mis'. *Dial* in W. S: *Southern U.S.*, the mistress of the house; used by the former slaves. So B Th,1790 DN.II, s.e.Mo., n.w.Ark.; DN.III, e.Ala., w.N.Y. In DN.III it is pointed out that in Southern use when meant for *Mrs.* the word is always pronounced *Miz* and clearly distinguished from *Miss*, the last letter of which is never voiced. Doubtless M.T.'s ear deceived him here when he wrote *Miss'* instead of *Miz.* Dr. Belden suggest that the slaves may have said "Miss Sally" but "Miz Phelps"; but M.T. never uses the form *Miz* anywhere, and if he was responsible for the apostrophe here, he certainly meant his *Miss'* as a shortened form of *Miz.*)

mission, sb. **foreign missions**. [?AB²] *An absence of any "whatnots" in the corners with Hindu gods and Chinese idols...might be taken as denoting a languidness in the family concerning foreign missions* 1873 GA xxi 197 (OED 5a. esp. pl. The organized effort involved in the preparation and equipment of persons sent out by a religious community into foreign lands for the conversion of the heathen. 1888, only ex. So W S C)

missionary, v. [?AB³] *In Canada, the French were schooling them in a rudimentary way, missionarying among them* 1883 LM i 30 (OEDS a. intr. To act as a missionary. 1862, only ex. So W. A in B F. Not in S C)

missionarying, vbl.sb. [AB¹] *"Preachin's my line, too, and workin' camp-meetin's and missionaryin' around"* 1884 HF xix 183. *Missionarying was a better thing in those days than it is in ours* 1892 "Switzerland" (1917) 198 (A in B F: Performing missionary work. Not in OED W S C)

mission school, sb. [?AB³] *"I forgot to tell you of my mission school, Sunday School class...I went out two Sunday afternoons, and picked up seven kids and got them to come in"* 1883 LM lii 515 (OED A school for children who do not regularly attend a church. 1879.. *U.S.* in W. Cf. B: The Am. term for what the English denote by 'ragged school.' So F Cl T. Not A in S C)

Missouri, a. [AB³] See *Missourian,* a. 1885 (OEDS 2. *attrib.* 1805.. This use not in W S C)

Missourian, sb. [AB³] See *jay-hawker* 1907 (OEDS A native or inhabitant of the State of Missouri. 1820.. So W S C)

Missourian, sb. [AB¹] *I wanted Tom to...git somebody that knowed the town and could talk Missourian* 1894 TSA xiii 545 (This sense not in OED W S C)

Missourian, a. [AB¹] *The Masons gave us a Missouri country breakfast, in Missourian abundance* 1885 "Private Hist. of Campaign" 201. *I have the strange sense of being thrust back into that Missourian village and of reliving stirring days* 1894 "Scrap of Curious History" (1917) 182. *Isn't it curious that two "town drunkards" and one half-breed loafer should leave behind them, in a remote Missourian village, a fame a hundred times greater?* 1909 ISD xiii 150 (W: Of or pertaining to Missouri. So S C DN.V. Not in OED)

mist-dimmed, a. [B¹] See *atomy* 1880 (Comb. not in OED W S C; but cf. OED Mist-blurred, 1880)

mitten, sb. **to give one the mitten**. [?AB³] *"Is ole Miss Cooper's Nancy done give you de mitten?"* 1893 PW ii 236 (OED 3. *Slang* or *colloq.* To reject. 1848.. So W S C. A in Wr B F Cl Th T DN.III,V)

mixed-up-looking, a. [B¹] *Aunt Sally she was one of the mixed-upest-looking persons I ever see* 1884 HF xlii 432 (Comb. not in OED W S C)

mix up, v. [?AB³] *"I didn't want to be mixed up in this business"* 1883 LM xix 227. *"It's the most mixed-up thing I ever see!"* 1893 TSA i 24 (OED Mix, v. 6b. Now only with unfavorable implications: To associate unsuitably or confusingly. 1806.. So W S C U. A in B DN.II,III)

mizen-yard, sb. [B¹] *"It was lashed to the garboard-strake of the main-to'gallant mizzen-yard"* 1907 "Chaps. from Autob" 18 (OED *Naut.* 1485..1786. So C. Comb. not in W S. Here, of course, nonsense use. Cf. cat-head and garboard-strake, above)

mmbglx, sb. [B¹] See *kahkahponeeka* 1880 (Hum. invention.

mob-tide, sb. [B¹] *The mob-tide...dashed itself against the champion* 1881 PP xi 127 (Comb. not in OED W S C)

moccasin, sb. [A] *I found the shops at Niagara Falls full of dainty Indian beadwork, and stunning moccasins* 1869 SNO (1875) 67. See also *Blackfoot* 1906 (OED 1. A kind of foot-gear...worn by the Indians of North America. 1612.. So W S C U B F Cl Th M DN.VI)

moccasined, ppl.a. [AB³] *A favorite [device] was to make a moccasined person tread in the tracks of the moccasined enemy* 1895 "Cooper's Literary Offences" 3 (OEDS 1829.. So W S C. Cf. above)

mocker, sb. [A] See *catbird* 1876 (OED 3. A mocking-bird. 1773.. Cf. OED Mocking-bird. 1. An Am. song-bird of the genus *Mimus.* The "Northern mocker", here referred to, is *Mimus Caroliniensis.* So W S C DN.III)

mock trial, sb. [?AB¹] *We also had a mock trial on board* 1869 IA iv 43 (A fictitious trial; a performance under the guise of a court trial given for entertainment or amusement; sometimes used by law students as a sort of test of proficiency. This familiar Am. sense not in OED, which has only Mock, a. 1b. Of a thing that deceptively resembles that which the sb. properly denotes; sham, counterfeit; cf. quot. 1844 Thirlwall *Greece* VIII. 361 "A mock trial in which their enemies were judges." Comb. not in W S C)

modern-born, a. [B¹] *The modern-born disposition on the part of men to believe that a new idea can have value* 1890 "Majestic Literary Fossil" 439 (Comb. not in OED W S C; but cf. OED Modern-bred, 1808)

modern-style, a. [B¹] *Inviting modern-style pleasure resorts* 1883 LM xli 427 (Comb. not in OED W S C; but cf. OED Modern-dress, a. 1885)

modest-salaried, a. [B¹] *The modest-salaried operator in our telegraph office* 1885 "Private Hist. of Campaign" 201 (Comb. not in OED W S C)

modify, v.intr. [?AB¹] *I would give the pain a chance to modify before I should see him in the evening* 1896 JA III xi 378 (W: To undergo modification; to change. This intr. sense not in OED S C)

mogul, sb. **great** or **grand mogul**. [?AB¹] *A brave knight...tried conclusions once with no less a Mogul than Sir Gaheris himself* 1889 CY xx 239. *"My old friend, the great mogul—the station-master, you know"* 1902 "Belated Russian Passport" (1928) 178. *A brace of such grand moguls [in Heaven!] as Moses and Esau* 1908 "Capt. Stormfield" 276 (S: Humorously, for any important personage. This hum. or *slang* use of the comb. not in OED 4. *U.S.* A negro. 1871.. So Cl T M DN.I AS.VIII.4.52. Not A in W S C)

molasses, sb. [AC] See *coonskin* 1873; *clarifying-tank* 1883; *saucer* 1884. *Preserves and New Orleans molasses* 1892 AmCl xii 119 (OED 1. Now *rare* in British use, but in the U.S. commonly used. 1582..1864. A in B F Cl M Th,1705 DN.I,VI AS.IV.4,8. Not A in W S C U T)

molasses candy, sb. [AB³] *It recalls your lost boyhood and the Parthenons done in molasses candy which made it blest and beautiful* 1873 GA xxiv 221 (OED 1809.. Comb. not in W S C. Cf. above, and cf. also candy, above)

moldy, a. [AE] *Out of the moldy past* 1883 LM liv 530 (Cf. OED Mould, sb.: the sp. *mold* now *U.S.* So C. Not A in W S)

Mondays, adv. [?AB¹] See *rehash* 1880 (This adv. use not in OED W S C. See *-s*, suffix, below)

money, sb. **There is money in—**. [?AB²] See *incorporatorship* 1873. *"There's money in oleomargarine; why, you can't imagine the business we do"* 1883 LM xxxix 412. See also *patent-right* 1893 (OED 6d. Money can be made out of it. 1887, only ex. So W S C)

money-loss, sb. [B¹] *Our feeling has its source in the money-loss involved* 1892 AmCl xvii 175 (Comb. not in OED W S C; but cf. OEDS Money-losing, 1870)

money-necessity, sb. [B¹] *Not even money-necessity was able to overcome me* 1909 *Letters* (1917) II xxvii 487 (Comb. not in OED W S C)

money-sack, sb. [?C] *Millions of people were discussing the stranger and his money-sack* 1899 "MCH" (1900) 17 (OED Money, sb. 7a. †1603. Comb. not in W S C. App. not felt as *arch* by M.T.)

monitor, sb. [AB³] *We landed under the walls of a little fort... If we were ever to get after it with one of our turreted monitors...* 1869 IA v 51 (OED 6. An ironclad...built on the model of the vessel invented by Captain Ericsson in 1862. 1862.. So W S C U B F Cl Th.III T)

monkey-shines, sb. [AB³] *Here it is a solemnity, there it is monkey-shines* 1907 "Chaps. from Autob" 13 (OEDS *U.S. slang.* 1847. Cf. H: Am. *monkey-shines* = Eng. *capers.* So W S C B F Cl Th T AS.II.50)

monotonies, sb.pl. [B¹] See *dullnesses* 1897 (The *concrete* sense not in OED W S C)

monstrous, adv. [?AC] *Smiley was monstrous proud of his frog* 1865 "Jumping Frog" (1875) 33. See *Union* 1874. *Behind a monstrous long raft* 1884 HF xvi 134. See also *jump, on the* 1884 (OED 8b. Exceedingly, wonderfully, 'mighty.' Now *rare* or *obs.* 1590..1840. So U. OEDS U.S. ex. 1848. A in DN.II,III,V. Not A or *obs* in S C U. This use not in W)

monthly, sb. [?AB³] See *daily*, sb. 1883 (OEDS Earlier ex., U.S. 1833.. Not A in W S C U. Cf. daily, above, and weekly, below)

moon, sb. [AB²] *I spent my last 10 cents for a moon (large round sea-biscuit)* 1883 LM lii 513 (OED 5(b). *U.S. slang.* 1883, this quot., only ex. So F. Not in W S C)

moonshiner, sb. [AB³] *The Faith-Curists, the train-robbers, the White Caps, the Moonshiners* 1895 "What Bourget Thinks" 52 (OED *U.S.* An illicit distiller. 1860.. So S C B F Cl Th.III. Not A in W U)

moonshiny, a. [?AB¹] *The same old scheming, generous, goodhearted, moonshiny, hopeful, no-account failure he always was* 1892 AmCl iii 36 (Moony, credulous, dreamy. This sense not in OED W S C; cf. OED 3. Of the nature of moonshine: vain, unreal. 1880.. So W S C)

moral, sb. [B¹?C] *I hadn't a single moral. Yes, I started like that—the world before me, not a moral in the slot* 1905 *Speeches* (1910) 432 (OED 6. *sing.* A person's moral principles or practice. *Obs.* 1688.. 1820. So W C. Not in S. As used by M. T. it is more likely a hum. nonce-variation of the current *pl.* form than a survival)

morganatic, a. [B¹] *A dozen direct censures are easier to bear than one morganatic compliment* 1897 FE iv 65 (Ironical, 'left-handed'. This hum. *transf.* sense not in OED W S C. Cf. U: Morganatic marriage...also styled a *left-handed marriage*)

morgue, sb.[AB³] *Next we visited the Morgue* [in Paris], *that horrible receptacle for the dead who die mysteriously* 1869 IA xiv 132. *When they arrived at the scene of the fire, the poor old earl took one glimpse at the melancholy morgue* 1892 AmCl ix 86 (OED The name given to a building in Paris, in which the bodies of those found dead are exposed...Hence, esp. in the U.S., any building or room used for the same purpose. 1821.. Not A in W S C U)

moribund, a. [B¹] *"I can't live without seeing Margaret...I should die if I tried to hold out longer—and you are as moribund to see Annie as I am to see Margaret"* 1888 "Meisterschaft" 461 (Desperately anxious, 'dying'. This hum. *transf.* sense not in OED W S C)

Morisite, sb. [AB¹] *It is a luscious country for thrilling evening stories about assassinations of intractable Gentiles.*

I cannot easily conceive of anything more cozy than the night in Salt Lake which we spent in a Gentile den, smoking pipes and listening to tales of how Burton galloped in among the pleading and defenseless "Morisites" and shot them down, men and women, like so many dogs 1872 RI xv 119 (Not in OED W S C. The word is more properly "Morrisite", and M.T. was mistaken in calling them "Gentiles". The Morrisites were followers of Joseph Morris, a native of Manchester, England, who was converted to Mormonism and came to Utah, where he received a revelation assuring him that he was a prophet and the true successor to Joseph Smith. On Feb. 11, 1861, he instituted a schismatic movement against the rule of Brigham Young, on which account he was formally excommunicated, but established a separate community in the Weber River valley. On June 12, 1862, his camp was besieged by a force under the command of Robert T. Burton, the Mormon sheriff of Salt Lake County. The Morrisites were forced to surrender, and Morris and a number of his followers were killed. It is charged, but denied, that they were shot down in cold blood by Burton himself. For a full account of this episode of Mormon history see J. H. Beadle, *Life in Utah,* 1870, pp. 413-427)

Mormon, sb. [AB³] *I dread the idea of appearing before those miners of Montana. Or those Mormons of Salt Lake* 1867 *M.T. the Letter Writer* (1932) i 16. See also *admire* 1872; *Allopath* 1902; *Congregationalist* 1906 (OEDS 1. A member of a religious body...founded in 1830 at Manchester, N.Y. 1837.. So W S C U B F Cl M AS.II.30)

Mormon, a. [AB³] *The old Mormon trail* 1868 CD (1872) 45. *A Mormon preacher* 1872 RI xx 153 (OED 2. *attrib.* passing into *adj.* 1842.. So W C. The adj. use not in S)

Mormondom, sb. [AB³] *Like portraying Mormondom and leaving out polygamy* 1872 RI xlviii 343 (OED 1860.. So W S C B F Cl)

morning-glory, sb. [AB³] *Blue morning-glories of great size* 1877 "Some Rambling Notes" iii 720 (OED 1. An Am. plant...1836.. Not A in W S C U)

mornings, adv. [?AC] See *organize* 1881. *Mornings before daylight I slipped into cornfields* 1884 HF xii 101 (OED Morning, sb. 3c. Now *rare* or *dial.* 1620..1893. So W Wr. A in S. Not in C. Cf. *-s*, suffix, below)

morning-suit, sb. [B²] *He was giving orders for dress-suits, morning-suits* 1893 "Banknote" 341 (OED 1896, only ex. Comb. not in W S C)

morocco-covered, a. [B¹] *A very official chair behind a long green morocco-covered table* 1873 GA xxviii 250. (Comb. not in OED W S C; but cf. OED Morocco-bound, 1820)

morrow, sb. [C] *"This very morrow shall he be installed in his princely dignity"* 1881 PP v 66 (OED Now only *literary* and *dial.* c1290..1878. So W U. This sense not in S C)

mort, sb. [C] See *budge* 1881 (OED *Cant.* b. A harlot, loose woman. 1567..1812. So W C. Not in S)

mortal, a. mortal mind. [AB¹] See *claim* 1903 (S: Christian Science. Nothing, claiming to have existence falsely, since real mind is immortal; error generating further error; subjective error by way of the material senses; idolatry, sickness, and death. This *spec* Chr.Sc. sense not in OED W C. The very full and sympathetic definitions given in S to all terms connected with Christian Science form one of its distinctive features)

mortal, adv. [?AC] *And mortal heavy grew his gun* 1891 *Slovenly Peter* (1935) 12 (OED 10. Now only *dial.* or *vulgar.* c1407..1867. So W U. *Colloq* in S C T. A in Wr B)

mortar-boarded, ppl.a. [B¹] *We marched thence* [at the University of Oxford] *gowned, mortar-boarded, and in double file* 1907 "Chaps. from Autob" 169 (Comb. not in OED W S C; but cf. OED Mortar-board, sb. 1854..)

moschata, sb. [C] See *afarabocca* 1894 (OED *obs.rare.* 2. The nutmeg. 1587..1823. Not in W S C)

Moses, int. [?AB³] *"The suffering Moses!—there ain't enough money in the ship to pay that bill"* 1869 IA v 52 (OED Used as an oath or expletive. 1855.. A in DN. III. This use not in W S C)

mosey, v. [AB²] *"I got to mosey along"* 1870 CRG (1919) 57. *"De way dey made dem sojers mosey roun!"* 1874 SNO (1875) 204. *"Tomorrow I'll be up bright and early...and mosey off to Tennessee"* 1880 TA xxvi 269 (OED 2. *slang U.S.* To jog along. 1877.. So W S C B F Cl Th, 1836 T M DN.I,III,IV,V,VI)

mosque, sb. [B¹] *In the Christian Science Mosque in Boston she noticed some things..* 1902 "Chr. Sc." 759 (This *transf.* use not in OED W S C)

mosquito, sb. [?A] *"Here I've sot a-bustin' muskeeters"* 1872 RI ii 27. *They passed the mouth of the Ohio; they passed the canebrakes; they fought mosquitoes* 1883 LM ii 35. See also *soft* 1883; *bar*, sb. 1894 (OED 1. 1583.. So W S C U. A in F Cl M)

mosquito-bar, sb. [AB³] *The climate of San Francisco is mild and singularly equable...You sleep under one or two light blankets summer and winter, and never use a mosquito-bar* 1872 RI lvi 410. *Some natives arranged the mosquito-bar* 1897 FE xxxviii 352 (OEDS *U.S.* 1809.. So B F Cl Th DN.IV AS.X.196. Not A in W S C)

moss, v. [?AB¹] *Why is that compliment to that old gentlewoman intruded?...It was her other self that was there...in those early sweet times before antiquity had cooled her off and mossed her back* 1894 "Defence of Harriet Shelley" 117 (This sense not in OED W S C. An adaptation from Moss-back, sb.; cf. OED 2b. One attached to antiquated notions. 1885..; so Th, 1850 T M)

moss-backed, ppl.a. [AB²] *Still mouthing empty reverence for those moss-backed frauds* 1889 *Letters* (1917) II xxix 520 (OED *U.S.* 1900, only ex. So W. Not A in S C. Cf. above)

moss-bearded, ppl.a. [B¹] See *cypress-top* 1883 (Comb not in OED W S C; but cf. OED Moss-clad, 1747)

moss-hung, ppl.a. [B¹] *Look down upon these moss-hung ruins* 1869 IA xl 421 (Comb. not in OED W S C)

most, adv. [AC] *"Well, it does seem most too good to be true"* 1873 GA v 57. *"Every time I hit him my old heart most breaks"* 1876 TS i 19. See *fantods* 1884, and *passim* in HF. *"They quarrel together pretty much all the time—'most always about religion"* 1892 AmCl iii 40 (OED 4. Almost, nearly. *obs exc. dial.* ..1874. OEDS For '*obs exc. dial*', read 'Now *dial* and *U.S.*' 1775.. A in S Wr B Th T M H DN.III. Not A in W C T)

mote-magnifying, ppl.a. [B¹] *A fault-finding, mote-magnifying tyrant* 1883 LM xviii 217 (Comb. not in OED W S C)

mother, sb. **my sainted mother!** [B¹] *"Twenty-five cigars, at 100 reis, 2500 reis! Oh, my sainted mother!"* 1869 IA v 52 (No interjectional use in OED W S C)

mother, v. [?AB³] *She tucked me in and mothered me so good I felt mean* 1884 HF xlv 421 (OED 2. To take care of as a mother. Earliest exs. U.S. 1863.. Not A in W S C U Wr)

Mother-Church, sb. [AB¹] *Mrs. Eddy is herself the Mother Church* 1903 "Mrs. Eddy in Error" 506. See also *bargain-counter* 1903; *First Member* 1907 (Here *spec* of Christian Science. This sense not in OED W S C; but cf. OED 2. The church of which another church is a "daughter" or offshoot. 1574..)

mother-heart, sb. [B²] *Her mother-heart was touched, and she was ashamed* 1893 PW iii 239 (OED Mother, sb. 14a. No ex. Comb. not in W S C)

mother-instinct, sb. [B¹] *Her sharp mother-instinct seemed to detect it* 1881 PP x 114 (Comb. not in OED W S C)

mother-title, sb. [B¹] *That Mother-title would not be offered to her until five years later* 1903 "Mrs. Eddy in Error" 507 (Comb. not in OED W S C)

motif, sb. [B²] *The original intention or motif is apt to get abolished* 1894 TET intro. 310 (OED 1b. In literary composition. 1897.. So W S C U)

motor-car, sb. [B³] *A Republican simplicity has invented...the best motor-cars* 1899 "Diplomatic Pay" (1928) 239 (OED 1895.. So W S C U. M.T.'s claim for Am. priority is quite unfounded, either for the word or for the thing. Cf. H: In Am., *automobile* is commonly preferred to *motor-car*, the term which is in general use in Eng. So AS.V.273)

Mound City, sb. [AB³] *Saint Louis—the Mound City, as they call it* 1856 Adv. of T. J. Snodgrass (1928) 3 (OEDS *U.S.* So called from the Indian mounds that occupied the site on which the city was built. 1854.. So W S B F Cl Th.III. Term not in C)

mount, v. [B¹] *Everybody else had "mounted" the train, as they say in these regions* [Geneva, Switzerland] 1893 "Playing Courier" 203 (An alienism, from the French *monter*, to board, enter a vehicle. This sense not in OED W S C)

mountain-cabbage, sb. [A] *We saw* [in Bermuda] *five or six mountain-cabbage palms (atrocious name!)...not the largest or the tallest trees I have ever seen, but they were the stateliest, the most majestic* 1876 "Some Rambling Notes" iv 15 (OED A West Indian palm tree. 1681..1796. Not A in W. Not in S C)

mountain-climber, sb. [B¹] *We were in the home of the mountain-climbers* 1880 TA xxxvi 411 (Comb. not in OED W S C; but cf. OED Mountain-climbing, 1872)

mountain-railway, sb. [B²] *We had never seen a mountain-railway yet* 1880 TA xxviii 287 (OED 1898, only ex. So W. Comb. not in S C)

mounting-peg, sb. [?AB¹] *When you have reached the point in bicycling where you can balance the machine... you hop along behind it on your right foot, resting the other on the mounting-peg* c1880 "Taming the Bicycle" (1917) 288 (Comb. not in OED W S C)

mourner, sb. [AB³] *He goes through the camp-meetings and puts them on the mourner's bench* 1864 SS (1926) 129. *Folks got up...and worked their way to the mourners' bench, with the tears running down their faces; and when all the mourners had got up there to the front benches in a crowd, they sung and shouted* 1884 HF xx 173 (OEDS 1d. A person on the 'anxious seat' at a 'revival' meeting; i.e., one who is mourning for his sins. *U.S.* 1845.. So W S C B F T M DN.I,II,III,IV AS.II.361)

moustached, a. Spelled **mustached**. [AE] *The coming and departing company so mustached, so Frenchy!* 1869 IA xii 113 (Cf. OED Moustache, sb. In present British use the unaltered Fr. spelling greatly predominates, but...all the American Dicts. prefer the semi-Anglicized form *mustache*. So W S C M. W points out that the dif. in sp. corresponds to a dif. between Am. and British pron. for the vowel of the first syllable)

mph, int. [B¹] *"What would people say? Why, they'd say 'Mph! Tom Sawyer's gang! pretty low characters in it!'"* 1876 TS xxxv 272 (This s p. not in OED W S C. Cf. Umf, below)

much, a. [?AC] *"In this country a doctor ain't so very much"* 1892 AmCl xi 107 (OED 16. With reference to ...importance, or eminence. *Obs.* c1205..1450. So W S C. A in B F Cl)

much-nicked, a. [B¹] *Upon the table was the usual service, the heavy, much-nicked stone ware* 1873 GA xxix 271 (Comb. not in OED W S C)

mucilage, sb. [AB²] *If he uses mucilage, it mingles with the ink and next year he can't read his scraps* c1880 M.T. the Letter Writer (1932) iii 52 (OED 1c. Chiefly *U.S.* In England commonly called 'gum'. 1888.. So Th.III,1879 M H. Not A in W S C U)

mucilage-bottle, sb. [AB²] *There is a mucilage-bottle broken* 1870 SNO (1875) 237 (OEDS 1877, only ex. Comb. not in W S C. Cf. above)

muck, sb. [?AB²] *"It's a prime comfort to see faces that's friendly when a body's in such a muck of trouble"* 1876 TS xxiii 183 (OED 4. *colloq* or *vulgar*. Also *fig.* 1876, this quot., only *fig* ex. This sense not in W S C. A in DN.II,III)

mud, sb. **to fling mud.** [?AB²] *These people fling mud at that elegant Englishman...and make fun of him* 1880 TA xx 187 (OED 3. To make disgraceful imputations. 1884. Phrase not in W S C. Cf. mud-slinger, A in DN.IV: a slanderer)

mud, sb. **to sell for the mud.** [?AB¹] *Dennis waited for the million, but he never got a cent. His holding was sold for the "mud"—so that he came out without anything* 1906 *Autob* (1924) I 276 (Phr. not in OED W S C; but cf. OED 2. *fig.* a. As a type of what is worthless. 1563..)

mud-cat, sb. [AB³] *He didn't really catch anything but only just one small useless mud-cat* 1883 LM liv 532. *He warn't no more quality than a mudcat himself* 1884 HF xviii 160. *I fished from the platform and landed mud-cats that outweighed me* 1907 "Chaps. from Autob" 6 (OED *U.S.* name given to several species of catfish. 1882, only ex. So W S C F Cl DN.III)

mud-clerk, sb. [AB³] *The doctor's and postmaster's sons became "mud-clerks"* 1875 OTM 71. *He had served as "mud clerk", that is, subordinate purser, on certain of the packet-boats* 1881 "Curious Experience" 46. *Mud-clerks received no salary, but they were in the line of promotion* 1906 *Autob* (1924) I 307 (OEDS *U.S.* 1872.. Cf. DN.II: The second clerk of a river steamer; so called because it was his duty to go on shore, often at a mere mud-bank, to receive or check off freight. Comb. not in W S C)

mud-cure, sb. [B¹] See *bath-cure* 1898 (Comb. not in OED W S C; but cf. OED Mud-bath: a medicinal bath of heated mud. 1843)

muddle, sb. [?AB³] *"It's all a muddle; I can't make head or tail of it"* 1893 "Travelling with a Reformer" (1900) 368 (OED 1. 1818.. So W U T. *Colloq* in S C. A in B)

mud-dobber, sb. [AB¹E] *The old mud-dobber tackled the piano, and ran his fingers up and down once or twice* 1866 SNO (1875) 297 (A disparaging epithet for a nomadic workman or tramp; *transf* from the name of a wasp. Not in OED W S C; but cf. OED Mud-dauber: a wasp that builds its nest of mud. So known popularly in America. 1856, only ex. A in W S C Th DN.III. Cf. Dob, for daub, above)

Muddy, sb. [AB²] *When it was daylight, here was the clear Ohio water inshore, sure enough, and outside was the old regular Muddy!* 1884 HF xvi 143 (OEDS 1c. The Missouri or Mississippi. 1884, this quot., only ex. for the Mississippi. This sense not in W S C or any other authority, all of which agree that the name 'Muddy' or 'Big Muddy' applies only to the Missouri. What M.T. was thinking about, however, was the color of the water, which in this section of the Mississippi, below Cairo, and of course far below the mouth of the Missouri, is indistinguishable from that of its mighty tributary)

muddy-water, a. [B¹] See *clear-water* 1875 (Comb. not in OED W S C)

mud-puddle, sb. [?AB²] *The nigger kind of smiled around gradduly over his face, like when you heave a brickbat in a mud-puddle* 1884 HF xxxiv 352 (OEDS 1884, this quot., only ex. Not A in W. Comb. not in S C)

mud-sill, sb. [AB³] *He said that the Republicans of the North—no, the "mudsills" of the North—had swept away the old aristocracy of the South* 1877 *Autob* (1924) I 87. *"A mudsill like me trying to push in and help receive an awful grandee?"* 1908 "Capt. Stormfield"

271 (OED The lowest sill of a structure, usually embedded in the soil; hence, *U.S.* a person of the lowest class of society. 1858.. So W S C B F Cl Th DN.III, IV,VI)

mud-stripe, sb. [?AB¹] *Big double log house for the white folks—hewed logs with the chinks stopped up with mud or mortar, and these mud-stripes been whitewashed some time or another* 1884 HF xxxii 329 (Comb. not in OED W S C; but cf. OED Mud, sb. 1d. *Mud and stud, dial*: posts and laths filled in with mud, as a material of which cottages are built. 1839..)

mud-turkle, sb. [AB¹E] *"And so you ain't had no meat nor bread to eat all this time? Why didn't you get mud-turkles?"* 1884 HF viii 69 (A in DN.III: this pron. chiefly among the negroes. Cf. S: Turkle, *Southern U.S.* Not in OED W C)

mud-turtle, sb. [A] *Throwing a clod at a mud-turtle which was sunning itself on a small log in the brook* 1869 IA xlvii 490. See also *iron-clad*, sb. 1875; dashed 1875 (OEDS *U.S.* A turtle which lives in the mud or muddy water. 1796.. So W S C B F Cl Th,1801 DN.III)

mud-turtle, sb. [AB¹] *"He's in that pilot-house now, showing those mud-turtles how to hunt for easy water"* 1873 GA iv 48. *"A mud-turtle of a back-settlement lawyer"* 1896 TSD xi 527 (A disparaging epithet for a person. This *transf* use not in OED W S C)

mud-turtle-shaped, ppl. a. [AB¹] See *pickaninny* 1871 (Nonce comb.)

mud-valve, sb. [?AB²] *The awful thunder of a mud-valve suddenly burst forth* 1873 GA iii 38 (OED A valve by which mud is discharged from a steam-boiler. 1875. So S C. Comb. not in W)

mud-wagon, sb. [?AB¹] *We had to change our stage-coach for a less sumptuous affair, called a "mud-wagon"* 1872 RI vii 60 (Comb. not in OED W S C)

muff, sb. [?AB³] *"Don't you fool away any sympathy on the poor mariner's dangers and privations and sufferings. Leave that to the poetry muffs...If there's one thing that can make me madder than another, it's this sappy, damned maritime poetry!"* 1877 "Some Rambling Notes" ii 588 (OED 1. A 'duffer'. 1837.. So W S C U. A in DN.IV)

muggins, sb. [?AB³] *Any muggins can write about Old Times on the Miss.* 1874 *Letters* (1917) I xiv 236. *"Why, you talk like a muggins"* 1884 HF xxviii 292. *"You don't know how to value it, you little provincial muggins"* 1893 "Esquimau Maiden's Romance" (1900) 141 (OEDS 1. *slang*. A fool, simpleton. Earlier U.S. ex., from Bret Harte. 1873.. Not A in W S U Wr. This sense not in C)

muggins, sb. [?AB²] *I have been playing the noble game of "Muggins"* 1864 SS (1926) 123 (OEDS 2a. A children's game of cards. 1865.. So W S C U. A in DN.III)

mugwump, sb. [AB²] *The life-long loyalist scoffs at the Independent—or, as he calls him, with cutting irony, the Mugwump* 1884 Speeches (1923) 130. *All the Republicans are insane, but only the Democrats and Mugwumps can perceive it* 1902 "Chr. Sc." 757. See also *Allopath* 1902 (OED *U.S.* One who holds more or less aloof from party-politics. 1884.. A better definition in W: A bolter from the Republican party in the national election of 1884; hence, an independent in politics. So S C U F Cl Th T M DN.I,IV,VI AS.II.137, V.220)

mulatto, sb. [?A] *"There was a free nigger there from Ohio—a mulatter, most as white as a white man"* 1884 HF vi 43 (OED 1. The offspring of a European and a Negro. 1595.. So W S C U T. A in B F Cl AS.IX.208)

mule-headed, a. [?AB²] *That mule-headed old fool wouldn't give in then!* 1884 HF xxix 302 (OEDS Stubborn. 1884, this quot. Comb. not in W S C) mule-hoof, sb. [B[1]] *We found the masonry slightly crumbled, and marked by mule-hoofs* 1880 TA xlii 486 (Comb. not in OED W S C)

mule-meat, sb. [?AB[3]] *Descending portions of mule-meat, frozen solid* 1880 TA xxxvii 429 (OEDS Earliest exs. U.S. 1846.. Comb. not in W S C)

mule-mounted, a, [B[1]] *An endless double procession of mule-mounted tourists filed past us* 1880 TA xxxiv 368 (Comb. not in OED W S C)

mule-path, sb. [B[1]] *We were soon tramping leisurely up the leafy mule-path* 1880 TA xxviii 284 (Comb. not in OED W S C)

mule-power, sb. [B[1]] *Big keel-boats on their way up, using sails, mule power, and profanity* 1880 TA xv 131 (Comb. not in OED W S C)

mule-race, sb. [?AB[2]] *The ladies of New Orleans attend so humble an orgy as a mule-race* 1883 LM xlv 462 (OEDS U.S. quot. 1888, only ex. Comb. not in W S C)

mule-road, sb. [B[1]] *We followed the mule-road, a zig-zag course* 1880 TA xxxviii 445 (Comb. not in OED W S C)

mule-rush, sb. [?AB[1]] *The most enjoyable of all races is a steamboat race; but, next to that, I prefer the gay and joyous mule-rush* 1883 LM xlv 464 (Comb. not in OED W S C. Cf. mule-race, above)

mull, v. [AB[3]] *Old Probabilities doesn't know what the weather is going to be in New England...Well, he mulls over it, and by and by he gets out something about like this...* c1879 *Speeches* (1910) 62. *It is not like studying German, where you mull along for thirty years* c1880 "Taming the Bicycle" (1917) 288 (OED 2. *U.S. colloq.* 1879.. Cf. H: In Eng. the word means to make a mess of...in Am., usually with *over*, to cogitate, ruminate, without any suggestion of failure. So B F Cl Th DN.I,V. Not A in W S C)

mullen-stalk, sb. [AE] "*One er dem big cat-tail-lookin' mullen-stalks would grow in heah*" 1884 HF xxxviii 373 (Cf. OED Mullein. The form *mullen* 18th-19th c., *U.S.* So W S C)

mullet-headed, a. [?AB[2]] "*They're so confiding and mullet-headed they don't take notice of nothing at all*" 1884 HF xxxix 399. "*It's enough to make a body sick, such mullet-headed ignorance!*" 1893 TSA i 24 (OEDS Stupid, dull, 1884, this quot., only ex. Not in W S C. Cf. Mullet-head, A in DN.III,IV: A stupid or ignorant person)

multi-billionaire, sb. [?AB[1]] *There would not be any multi-billionaire alive, perhaps, who would be able to buy a full set* 1906 "Chaps. from Autob" 322 (Comb. not in OED W S C. Cf. Billionaire, above)

multi-millionaire, sb. [?AB[3]] *A millionaire commands respect...a multi-millionaire the deepest deeps of adoration* 1899 "Concerning the Jews" (1900) 269 (OED 2. 1858, only ex. So W S C U. A in Th.III)

mum, a. [?AC] "*Hucky, you sure you can keep mum?*" 1876 TS x 94 (OED *colloq.* now somewhat *arch* exc. *dial.* 1521..1894. Not arch in W S C U. A in Wr)

mumble-the-peg, sb. Spelled mumble-peg, mumbletypeg. [AE] *If anybody caught him [Benjamin Franklin] playing 'mumble-peg' by himself...he would immediately appear to be ciphering out how the grass grew* 1870 SNO (1875) 277. *Next it would be marble-time, and next mumbletypeg* 1896 TSA i 344 (OED Now *U.S.* 1627..1895. The forms *mumble-peg* 19th c., and *mumblety-peg* 17th and 19th c. A in Wr DN.I,III, with the form *mumbletepeg* reported from Ill., Ia., Minn., N.Y. Not A in W S C T)

mummery, sb. Spelled mommarye. [CE] "*Next came in a mommarye. Then the minstrels danced*" 1881 PP xi 125 (OED A performance of mummers. 1530..1820. This sp. 16th c. So C. This sp. not in W S)

murrey, sb. [C] *Doublets of murrey and blue cloth* 1881 PP ix 105. See also *coat-of-arms* 1884 (OED Now

only *Hist.* and *arch*. The popular name for the colour heraldically termed *sanguine*. c1412..1834. So U. Not *arch* in W S C Wr)

murther, v. [CE] "*These murthered the baron and fired the house*" 1889 CY xxx 386 (OED *obs* form of Murder, 13th-18th c., *dial* in 19th c. So W C. Not *obs* in S Wr)

muscle-training, ppl.a. [B[1]] *Who shall say it is not muscle-training pastime, climbing the Pyramids?* 1869 IA lviii 622 (Comb. not in OED W S C)

mush-and-milk, a. [AB[1]] *Mush-and-milk journalism gives me the fantods* 1869 SNO (1875) 47 (Insipid, weakly sentimental. Not in OED W S C; but cf. OED Mush, sb. *N.American*. A kind of porridge made of meal. 1671.. So Th,1775 T M DN.III,V,VI AS.I.150, IV.475. OEDS Mush and milk, 1817. Cf. also OED Mush, sb. 3c. *transf* and *fig.* 1841.. W S: Weak sentimental drivel or writing)

mushily, adv. [AB[2]] *The column of inert mortality sank mushily to the ground* 1896 JA II xi 296 (OEDS 1910, only ex. From mush; cf. above. So W. Not in S C)

mush up, v. [AB[1]] *The Freethinkers and the Baptist Bible class use the same room over the Market house, but...they don't mush up together and use it at the same time* 1894 TET iv 355 (To mix, unite in a common mass, like mush; cf. above. Not in OED W S C as verb in this sense. Clearly not the sense in OEDS Mush, v. To travel on foot through the snow. 1903..)

mushy, a. [AB[2]] "*Mushy, slushy early spring roads*" 1880 TA xxvi 267 (OED Soft, pulpy. 1883. From mush; cf. above. So W S C U)

music-room, sb. [B[2]] See *card-room* 1875 (OED A room in which music is performed. No ex. of this mod. sense. So W. Not in S C)

musketry-clatter, sb. [B[1]] *Their talk is a curious and funny musketry-clatter of little words* 1906 *Autob* (1924) II 52 (Comb. not in OED W S C)

muskmelon, sb. Spelled mushmelon. [?AE] See *cantelope* 1884. *Mornings before daylight I slipped into corn-fields and borrowed a water-melon or a mushmelon* 1884 HF xii 101 (OED This sp. 19th c. 1884, only ex. *Dial* in W. A in S F M DN.I,III,V AS.V.206, Ozarks; XII.107)

muss, sb. [AB[3]] See *left-hander* 1873 (OEDS 4. *dial* and *U.S.* A disturbance, row. 1840.. So W S C U Wr B F Cl Th M. Not A in T)

mustang, sb. [AB[3]] *Once I crossed the plains and deserts and mountains of the West, in a stage-coach... It was worth a lifetime of city toiling and moiling to perch in the foretop with the driver and see the six mustangs scamper under the sharp snapping of a whip that never touched them* 1869 IA xii 106 (OED 1. The wild or half-wild horse of the Am. plains. 1808.. So W S C U B F Cl Th T M AS.IV.129)

mustang, sb. [AB[1]] *A vagabond who was eating his dinner on the curbstone...I found that this mustang was clerking in a fruit establishment* 1869 IA xxx 313 (A young fellow, chap, 'bloke'. This *transf.* sense not in OED W S C)

mustard-plaster, sb. [B[1]] *That mustard-plaster of a newspaper* 1869 SNO (1875) 46 (Hum. nonce use, perhaps suggested by the yellow color of mustard; cf. M.T.'s use of yellow journalism, yellow-covered novel, below)

must-have-been, sb. [B[1]] *We set down the "conjectures," and "suppositions", and "may-bes", and "must-have-beens"* 1909 ISD ii 23 (Nonce comb.)

Must-Have-Beener, sb. [B[1]] See *Perhapser* 1909 (Nonce comb.)

mutual, a. [?AC] *Cairo and New Orleans will then have joined their streets together, and be plodding along under a single mayor and a mutual board of aldermen* 1875 OTM 193 (OED 4a. Of things, actions, senti-

ments: common. Now regarded as incorrect. 1591..
1882. So W U. Defended as still in good use by S C)

my, int. [A] *He said, "Oh, my!" and then staggered
away* 1869 IA iii 33. *Panting and red-faced, Stephen
would begin: "My, what a race I've had!"* 1875 OTM
193 (OED 3. Common, esp. *U.S.,* as a mild exclamation of surprise. 1849.. So U Wr DN.V. Not A in
W S. The int. use not in C)

myriad-accomplished, a. [B¹] *The man who wrote the
plays was not merely myriad-minded, but also myriad-accomplished* 1909 ISD vii 67 (Comb. not in OED W
S C; but cf. OED Myriad-minded, 1817, Coleridge's
epithet for Shakespeare)

mystery, sb. [C] *A good blacksmith...offered to
teach him the trade—or 'mystery'* 1889 CY xxxii 409
(OED 2. Handicraft, art, trade, profession, or calling.
Now *arch.* 1375..1872. So W S C U)

mystery-dispelling, ppl.a. [B¹] *"All honor to the
mystery-dispelling eye of godlike Science!"* 1875 SNO
147 (Comb. not in OED W S C)

N

na, adv. [C] *"He was a brave heart—na—na, I mean he hath the look of it"* 1881 PP xv 184 (OED *obs North. and Scotch* form of No. c888..c1350. So W S C)

nail, v. [?AC] *"Nailing an alibi where it can't be budged"* 1902 "DBDS" (1928) 332 (OED 5b. To clench, prove. *rare.* 1785, only ex. Not *rare* in W S C U Wr)

nail-file, sb. [B²] *She took from her dressing-table several small articles...a nail-file* 1902 "DBDS" (1928) 290 (OEDS 1922, only ex. So S C. Comb. not in W)

nail-grab, sb. [?AB¹] *"Thar he sot", his "nail-grabs" grasping a pew like grim death* 1852 *Hannibal Journal* Sept. 16 (Hands? Not in OED W S C)

nail-kag, sb. [AB²] *"They [Americans] wear a conical hat termed a 'nail-kag' "* 1869 IA xxvi 269 (OED *U.S.* A hat. 1872, this quot., only ex. So DN.V. Comb. not in W S C)

nail-keg, sb. [?AB²] *A helmet on his head the size of a nail-keg with slits in it* 1889 CY intro. 20 (OED A small barrel containing nails. 1889, this quot., only ex. So S. Not in W C)

naivety, sb. [E] *They make their awful statements with a frankness and a child-like naivety, indeed, which is enchanting* 1885 *Letters* (1917) II xxv 459 (OED Anglicized form of Naiveté. 1708..1898. So W S C U)

name, sb. **no name for it.** [?AB¹] *"Cap'n, ain't you pretty physically tired?" Says I: "Sam, it ain't any name for it! I'm dog-tired"* 1907 "Capt. Stormfield" 47 (Used for a word or expression that seems inadequate. Phr. not in OED W S C)

nap of the neck, sb. [AE] *And he ketched Dan'l by the nap of the neck* 1865 "Jumping Frog" (1875) 34 (W: The pron. *nap* for *nape* is very common in the U.S.; generally regarded as *colloq* or *dial.* So DN.III. This form not in OED S C; but cf. OED Nape of the neck, 1440..)

nappersocket, a. [B¹] See *kahkahponeeka* 1880 (Hum. invention)

nary, a. [AB³] *"There's three dozen steamboats and nary barge or raft"* 1883 LM xxviii 307. See also *pale*, sb. 1884 (OEDS *U.S.* and *dial* var. of *ne'er a.* Not a. 1821.. So Wr B F Cl T M DN.I,II,III,V AS.II.361, III.8,140, V.268, Ozarks. Not A in W S)

natheless, adv. [C] *Natheless, God send you good success* 1889 CY xxii 276 (OED Nevertheless. Now only *arch.* c900..1867. So W S C)

nation, sb. [AB³] See *throw off* 1865; *beat one's time* 1869. *Where in the nation can I get that portrait?* 1872 *Letters* (1917) I xi 195. *And the wind a-blowing like the very nation* 1875 OTM 723. *"Oh, that's all very fine to say, Tom Sawyer, but how in the nation are these fellows going to be ransomed if we don't know how to do it to them?"* 1884 HF ii 14 (OED *dial* and *U.S.* A euphemistic abbreviation of *Damnation.* 1842.. So Wr B Th DN.VI AS.V.427, Ozarks. Not A in W. Not in S C as sb. in this sense)

nation, sb. [A] *No.I reads a nation sight better in print than it did in MS.* 1877 *Letters* (1917) I xvii 299. (OEDS Very large, very great, etc. *dial* and *U.S.* 1765.. So Wr B Th. Not A in W. Not as adj. in S C)

nation, adv. [A] *"It's so nation dark"* 1872 RI iii 30. *"I'm nation sorry for you"* 1884 HF xix 186 (OED *dial* and *U.S.* Very, extremely, etc. 1785.. So C Wr B Th DN.V. Not A in W S)

Nationalism, sb. [?AB³] *To whom does Bellamy's "Nationalism" appeal? Necessarily to the few: people who...are compassionate and troubled for the poor and hard-driven* 1902 CS 762 (OED 3. A form of socialism. based on the nationalizing of all industry. 1892. So S C. A in W)

Nationalist, sb. [?A?B¹] See *Allopath* 1902 (A believer in Bellamy's Nationalism, as defined above? This sense not in OED W S C. More probably, however, the sense here is that in OED 2. *Theol.* A believer in nationalism, the doctrine that certain nations are the object of divine election. 1846, only ex. So S C. Not in W. The position of the name in M.T.'s list favors the theological meaning)

nattily, adv. [?AB³] *All were well and neatly dressed, many of them nattily, a few of them very stylishly* 1877 "Some Rambling Notes" iii 719 (OED 1849.. So W S C. Cf. below)

natty, a. [?AB³] *A body would find it considerable better to attract attention by a picturesque moral character than a natty burial-case* 1871 SNO (1875) 247. See *chirk*, a, 1877. *A natty blue naval uniform with brass buttons* 1883 LM xxv 276 (OED 1b. Neatly smart; spruce, trim. 1801.. So W S C U Wr. A in DN.IV AS.III.124,IV.80)

natural, a. **to come natural to.** [?AB²] *The doctor asks the questions, generally, because he can keep his countenance...It comes natural to him* 1869 IA xxvii 290 (OED 9c. To be a natural action for. 1890, only ex. Phr. not in W S C)

naught, sb. [C] *"He shall show naught of unrest to the curious that look on"* 1881 PP vi 74 (OED A1. Now *arch.* c888..1894. So U. Not *arch* in W S C Wr)

navigate, v. [?AB¹] *They tucked the old man in a beautiful room...When they come to look at that spare room they had to take soundings before they could navigate it* 1884 HF v 36 (A in DN.III,IV: To move about in. This sense not in OED W S C. A hum. transf. from the sense in OED 2. To sail over, on, or through the sea. 1646..)

navigate, v. [B¹] *No donkeys ever existed that were as hard to navigate as those* 1869 IA xl 419 (Hum. nonce use, by transf. from the sense in OED 3. To sail, direct, or manage a ship. 1670..)

navy, sb. [?AB²] *She turned on that smirking Spanish fool like a wild cat, and out with a 'navy' and shot him dead in open court* 1870 SNO (1875) 140. See also *six-shooter* 1906 (OEDS 5c. A navy revolver. All exs. U.S. 1875, this quot. This sense not in W S C)

navy revolver, sb. [?AB²] See *belt*, sb. 1869. *The man wore a great long "navy" revolver* 1872 RI iv 42 (OEDS Earliest ex. U.S. 1861.. Comb. not in W S C)

navy yard, sb. [A] *The caulker and the blacksmith that work in the navy yard* 1892 AmCl xi 107 (OEDS Now *U.S.* A government dockyard. 1771..1886. So S C Th.III M H. Not A in W)

nay, sb. **to say one nay.** [C] *"Thou canst order matters as thou wilt, with none to say thee nay"* 1881 PP xiv 172 (OED Now *arch* or *dial.* 2b. 1390..1878. So U Wr. Not *arch* or *dial* in W S C)

near, adv. [AC] *I mighty near stepped on a good-sized snake* 1884 HF viii 61 (OED 5a. Now usually expressed by Nearly. c1200..1891. W: *Obs exc. dial.* Not *obs* in S C Wr. A in M)

near-by, a. [AB³] *The Englishmen seated themselves at a near-by table* 1902 "Belated Russian Passport" (1928) 189 (OED Chiefly *U.S.* 1858.. So C M H DN.III. Not A in W S U Wr)

neck, sb. [?AB¹] *"She'd always fetch up at the stand just about a neck ahead"* 1865 "Jumping Frog" (1875) 32 (Not in OED W S C as a racing term; but cf. C: To win by a neck: to be first by a head and neck)

neck-and-neck, a. [?AB³] See *dead-heat* 1880. *Two red-hot steamboats raging along, neck-and-neck* 1883 LM xlv 464 (OED Neck, sb. 9. Keeping abreast. 1837.. So W S C. A in AS.II.45. Not A in H; see under *nip and tuck*, below)

need, v. [?AB¹] *"I killed the man for good reasons ...He needed killing"* 1894 PW xi 555 (To require, deserve, by a sort of moral necessity. This sense not in OED W S C. Perhaps a development of the impersonal construction in OED 1. It needs: it is needful or necessary that. *obs.* c960..1765. Cf. *owing*, below)

ne'er-do-well, sb. Spelled **ne'er-do-weel.** [E] *"In-jun Joe", "Jimmy Finn", and "General Gaines" were prominent and very intemperate ne'er-do-weels in Hanni-*

bal two generations ago 1909 ISD xiii 150 (OED The word being of northern and Scottish origin, the form *-weel* is freq. employed even by southern writers. So W S C Wr)

neglects, sb.pl. [C] *"You must try to overlook these little things, Mr. Bunker, these little neglects on my part"* 1892 AmCl xii 122 (OED 2b. An instance of negligence. Now *rare*. 1638..1845. So W. Not *rare* in S C)

negotiate, v. [?AC] *I negotiated for a box of them and took them away with me* 1910 *Speeches* 268 (OED 1. *intr.* b. To trade; to traffic. *Obs* ..1759. Not *obs* in W S C U)

negro minstrel, sb. [?AB³] See *suffer* 1875. *The first of all the negro minstrel shows came to town, and made a sensation* 1876 TS xxii 178. *When a personage talks like an illustrated, gilt-edged...Friendship's Offering in the beginning of a paragraph, he should not talk like a negro minstrel in the end of it* 1895 "Cooper's Literary Offences" 2 (OED Negro, sb. 3. quot. from DeVere's *Americanisms*. 1864.. So W S C B)

negro-stealer, sb. [?AB³] *Robbers, negro-stealers, and counterfeiters* 1883 LM xxix 311 (OEDS 1827. Comb. not in W S C)

negro-trader, sb. [?AB¹] See *uncle* 1873 (Comb. not in OED W S C. Cf. nigger-trader, below)

neighborhood, sb. **in the neighborhood of.** [?AB³] *I can "bank" in the neighborhood of $100 a month* 1859 *Letters* (1917) I ii 43. See *annex* 1898 (OED 3b. Somewhere about. 1857.. So W U. A in S C B F Cl T DN.III. Cf. H: Described by H. W. Fowler in *Modern Eng. Usage* as 'a repulsive combination of polysyllabic humour and periphrasis', until recently this expression has been peculiar to Am., where it has been in common use since the beginning of the present century, at any rate. Mr. Horwill might have learned, both from the OED and from M.T., that the usage is far older than 1900)

nerve, sb. [?AB³] *"I know I can go through the whole, clinics, dissecting-room and all. Does thee think I lack nerve?"* 1873 GA xiv 135. *If I had the nerve, I would kill it* 1892 AmCl xxii 120. Courage or coolness. 1809.. So W S C U. A in Th T)

nerve-web, sb. [B¹] *I feel my nerve-web tingle with a new thrill of wonder and delight* 1897 FE xxxix 358 (Comb. not in OED W S C; but cf. OEDS Nerve-net, 1927)

neutralities, sb.pl. [B¹] *The dull neutralities of undecorated speech* 1877 "Some Rambling Notes" ii 589 (This *concrete* sense not in OED W S C)

Nevadian, a, [AB¹] *I had just succeeded in stirring up a little Nevadian literary puddle myself* 1877 *Speeches* (1910) 1 (Not in OED W S C; but cf. C: Nevadan, a.)

never-diminishing, a. [B¹] *The war of epithets crashes along with never-diminishing energy for a couple of hours* 1898 "Stirring Times" (1900) 326 (Comb. not in OED W S C)

never-never, v. [B¹] *He swears he wishes he may never-never if he's got a cent in the world* 1906 *Speeches* (1910) 110 (A euphemism for "never escape damnation" or the like. Not in OED W S C. Cf. OED Never, adv. 1c. Repeated for the sake of emphasis, 1605..)

Never-Never Country, sb. [B³] *Australia has a slang of its own...The wide, sterile, unpeopled deserts have created eloquent phrases like "No Man's Land" and the "Never-Never Country"—also this felicitous form: "She lives in the Never-Never Country"—that is, she is an old maid* 1897 FE xxii 221 (OED Never, adv. 9. Northern Queensland, Australia. 1884.. So W S U. Not in C)

Never-Never Country, sb. **to live in the Never-Never Country.** [B¹] See above, 1897 (Phr. not in OED W S C)

new chum, sb. [B³] See *tenderfoot* 1897 (OED Now *colloq*. In Australia: a fresh immigrant. 1886. So W S C)

new deal, sb. [AB¹] *The air was full of rumors of a new deal* 1894 PW xvii 822 (Here *fig*: a fresh beginning, with better conditions implied. A in H (under *deal*) AS.VIII.1.20. Phr. not in OED W S C)

New Englander, sb. [A] *The man was a New Englander, with a head full of crochets* 1902 "DBDS" (1928) 298 (OED 1637.. So W S C Cl)

new-gold, a. [B¹] *Great green expanses of rolling pasture-land, bisected by eye-contenting hedges of commingled new-gold and old-gold gorse* 1897 FE xxiv 230 (Comb. not in OED W S C)

new-paint, v. [B¹] *It's been new-painted* 1875 OTM 569. *Consider his "little book"...which reconstructs and new-paints the Bible* 1902 "Chr. Sc." 759 (Comb. not in OED W S C)

new-time, a. [B¹] *Any other old-time or new-time palace on the continent of Europe* 1904 *Autob* (1924) I 198 (Comb. not in OED W S C)

newspaper-bag, sb. [B¹] *"Here is the very direction which is wrote on all the newspaper-bags"* 1872 RI ii 18 (Comb. not in OED W S C)

newspaper-clipping, sb. [B²] *Perhaps I have been affected by these depressing newspaper-clippings* 1905 "Czar's Soliloquy" 325 (OEDS 1907, only ex. So W S C)

newspaper-hawking, sb. [B¹] *He took to boot-polishing and newspaper-hawking* 1873 GA liv 487 (Comb. not in OED W S C)

newspaperless, a. [B¹] *This was a newspaperless globe* 1889 *Speeches* (1923) 152 (Not in OED W S C)

newspaper-office, sb. [?AB²] *The drudgery of the newspaper-office was too distasteful* 1873 GA xii 116 (OEDS All exs.U.S. 1873, this quot.. Comb. not in W S C)

newspaper-picture, sb. [B¹] *He would be proud to appear in a newspaper-picture in his company* 1902 "Does the Race of Man Love a Lord?" 441 (Comb. not in OED W S C)

newspaper reporter, sb. [?AB²] *Philip learned that Harry and Laura had both been taken to the city prison, and he went there; but he was not admitted. Not being a newspaper reporter, he could not see either of them that night* 1873 GA xlvi 422. *I became a silver miner in Nevada; next, a newspaper reporter* 1883 LM xxi 246 (OEDS Newspaper, sb. b. 1873, above quot., only ex. Not A in U. Comb. not in W S C)

news-scrap, sb. [B¹] *There is a great and peculiar charm about reading news-scraps in a language which you are not acquainted with* 1904 "Italian Without a Master" (1906) 180 (Comb. not in OED W S C)

New Yorker, sb. [A] *There is a godless grace and snap and style about a born and bred New Yorker* 1883 LM xxii 248. *My pilot-mate was a New Yorker* 1885 "Priv. Hist. of Campaign" 193 (OED 1765.. So W C M. Comb. not in S)

next-to-impossible, a. [B¹] *Using next-to-impossible French names* 1883 LM xlvii 472 (Comb. not in OED. Given in W S C)

Niagara, sb. [AB³] *The torrent cooled in the winds from the sea—a petrified Niagara* 1872 RI lxxiii 530. *Cyclones of frantic joy, and whole Niagaras of happy tears* 1889 CY xviii 223 (OED 1861.. So W S. Not in C)

nice, a. [?AB²] *"Who cares?" said Tom. "Nobody wants you to. Go 'long home and get laughed at. Oh, you're a nice pirate"* 1876 TS xvi 137. See also *bilk*, sb. 1902 (OED 15d. In ironical use. 1846.. So U. A in AS.X.236. This use not in W S C)

nick, sb. **in the nick of time.** [?AC] *It came into my mind, in the nick of time, how Columbus...played an eclipse as a saving trump once* 1889 CY v 65 (OED 10b. At the critical moment. *obs*. 1642..1724. Not *obs* in W S C U)

nickel, sb. [AB³] See *cent* 1889 (OED 2. *U.S.* b. 1883.. So W S C U B F Cl Th T H DN.III)

nickel-clad, a. [B¹] *Suddenly the nickel-clad horse takes the bit in its mouth and goes slanting for the curbstone* c1880 "Taming the Bicycle" (1917) 294 (Comb. not in OED W S C. Coined on the model of *ironclad?*)

nickeled, ppl.a. [B¹] *For every nickeled joy, marred and brief, We pay some day its weight in golden grief* 1900 "My Boyhood Dreams" (1928) 259 (Here *fig:* Sham, counterfeit, 'brummagem'. This disparaging use not in OED W S C. Cf. OED, in literal sense, 1885..; so W S C. Cf. also OED Brass 3c. *fig.* Debased yet pretentious, 1586..; Copper 9c. Spurious, pretentious, worthless. *obs.* 1603..1799; Tin 4b. Mean, petty, worthless, counterfeit. 1886.. Cf. tin, a., below. M.T. would seem to have discovered a new metal to use as a type of shoddy imitation. Cf. below)

nickel-plate, sb. [B¹] *The main part of that* [civilization] *was nickel plate and tinsel* 1889 Speeches (1923) 151. *Reverence for nickel plate and brummagem* 1892 AmCl x 99 (Cf. for literal sense OED Nickel, sb. 3a. 1875. Here *fig,* cf. above. The sb. use not in W S C)

nickel-plated, a. [B¹] *He had some pathetic little nickel-plated aristocratic instincts* 1885 "Priv. Hist. of Campaign" 194. *It is curious and interesting to notice what an attraction a fussy, nickel-plated, artificial word has for you* 1900 Autob (1924) I 183 (For literal sense see OEDS Nickel, sb. 3a. 1884.. Here *fig,* cf. above. *Fig* use not in OED W S C)

nifty, a. [AB³] *"He was always nifty himself, and so you bet his funeral ain't going to be no slouch"* 1872 RI xlviii 334 (OED *U.S. slang.* Smart, fine, splendid. 1868.. So W S F Th.III T M DN.IV AS.III.119, IV.80. Not A in C)

nigger, sb. [?A] *He laid into his work like a nigger* 1880 TA iii 40. *"Good gracious! anybody hurt?" "No'm. Killed a nigger". "Well, it's lucky; because sometimes people do get hurt"* 1884 HF xxxii 333. See also *mud-puddle* 1884; *jump, on the* 1884; *good-day!* 1892; *loafer* 1894; *outen* 1894. *"It's de nigger in you, dat's what it is. Thirty-one parts o' you is white, en on'y one part nigger, en dat po' little one part is yo' soul"* 1894 PW xiv 779 (OED 1. *colloq* and usually contemptuous. 1786.. So W S C U Wr. A in B F Th M DN.II,III AS.XI.11. Not A in T. Cf. also OEDS 1d. *To work like a nigger:* To work very hard. 1909.. Wr: Nigger: A hard worker, an adept, *Scotch*)

nigger, sb. [B³] *"Those 'niggers' spare their wounded, and the Americans massacre theirs!"...Read the letter of an American soldier-lad in the Philippines* 1901 "To the Person Sitting in Darkness" 174 (OED 1b. Loosely or incorrectly applied to members of other dark-skinned races. 1857.. So W S C U)

nigger-bill, sb. [?AB¹] *"He 'uz talkin' to de man en givin' him some bills—nigger-bills, I reckon, en I'se de nigger"* 1894 PW xviii 19 (Hand-bills advertising runaway negro slaves. Comb. not in OED W S C)

nigger-corner, sb. [?AB¹] *In the "nigger corner" sat Chambers* 1894 PW xxi 233 (Comb. not in OED W S C)

nigger-gallery, sb. [?AB¹] *It usurped the place of pious thought in the "nigger gallery"* 1894 TET viii 420 (Comb. not in OED W S C; but cf. S: *Nigger-heaven,* in same sense. A in DN.II,III,IV)

nigger-head, sb. [?AB²] *"You borry'd store tobacker and paid back nigger-head"* 1884 HF xxi 211 (OEDS 3. A strong plug tobacco of a black colour. 1884, this quot. So W S C. A in B F Cl T)

niggerkin, sb. [?AB¹] *Black as sin—blacker than that niggerkin* 1891 Slovenly Peter (1935) 11 (Not in OED W S C. A nonce formation after German *Negerchen?* Cf. OED Niggerling, 1842)

nigger-minstrel, sb. [?AB³] *Then there was a nigger-minstrel show, of the genuine old sort* 1898 Letters (1917) II xxxvii 670 (OED 6a. 1873. So U. Comb. not in W S C)

nigger-show, sb. [?AB¹] *"They never go to the circus, nor theater, nor 'nigger' shows, nor nowheres"* 1884 HF xxvi 261. *The nigger-show was always a passion of mine* 1898 Letters (1917) II xxxvii 670. See *clog-dancing* 1898. *Billy Rice was a joy to me, and so were the other stars of the nigger-show* 1907 "Chaps. from Autob" 247 (Negro minstrel entertainment. Comb. not in OED W S C)

nigger-stealer, sb. [?AB³] *I couldn't believe it. Tom Sawyer a nigger-stealer!* 1884 HF xxxiii 339 (OEDS 1840.. Comb. not in W S C)

nigger-trader, sb. [?AB³] See *fire-bug* 1881; *rascal-nest* 1881. *"I noticed dey was a nigger trader roun' de place considerable lately, en I begin to git oneasy"* 1884 HF viii 67. *The "nigger trader" was loathed by everybody* 1898 Autob (1924) I 124 (OEDS 1853.. Comb. not in W S C)

nigh, prep. [?AC] *Those who stood nigh his Grace* 1881 PP xxxi 355 (OED *Near* has taken the place of *nigh* exc. in *arch* or *dial* use. 2. In prep. use. a900.. 1826. So W U Wr. Not *arch* in S C. A in T DN.II, III,V)

night-breezy, a. [B¹] See *graveyardy* 1896 (Not in OED W S C; but cf. OED Night-breeze, 1774..)

night-garment, sb. [B¹] *Mr. X pranced in, in his long night-garment, with a candle* 1880 TA xiii 121 (Comb. not in OED W S C; but cf. OED Night-gown. 3. A light garment worn in bed. 1822, Byron...; Night-shirt, 1857..)

night-hawk, sb. [A] *An hour after supper the moon came up...A spark appeared, close to the water, several miles down the river. The pilot took his glass and looked at it steadily for a moment, and said, chiefly to himself: "It can't be the 'Blue Wing'. She couldn't pick us up this way. It's the 'Amaranth', sure."... "Don't appear to be any night hawk on the jack-staff—it's the 'Amaranth', dead sure!"* 1873 GA iv 44 (The meaning of the passage is not entirely clear. Probably we are to understand that the 'Blue Wing' carried a figure of the Am. bird as an ensign or symbol of the line. An eagle is so carried on the jackstaff of many steamboats today. Cf. C: The common night-hawk of the U.S., also called *bullbat*...a bird of powerful flight. So W S OEDS 1b. 1793..)

night-hawk, sb. [?AB¹] *Charley Langdon, Jack Van Nostrand, Dan, and I (all Quaker City night-hawks) had a blow-out at Dan's home* 1868 Letters (1917) I viii 142 (W: One who is habitually up or abroad at night. So C U Wr. In S only of cab-drivers. This sense not in OED)

night-key, sb. [?AB³] *It caused his friends all the more anguish to see him shake hands with the pump and try to wind his watch with his night-key* 1869 SNO (1875) 212 (OED U.S. exs. 1860.. Cf. F: The Am. equivalent for *latch-key.* A in Cl T. Not A in W S C)

night-marching, vbl.sb. [B¹] *"Night-marching in sleet and wind"* 1895 JA II iv 93 (Comb. not in OED W S C; but cf. OED Night-march, 1806..)

night-owl, sb. [?AB¹] *"He calculated to be off before night-owls like me turned out of bed"* 1880 TA xxvi 270 (W: One who keeps late hours at night. *Colloq.* So S: *slang.* Comb. not in OED C)

nights, adv. [A] *"You let a cat get to pulling fur with another cat on a shed, nights"* 1880 TA ii 37. *He always locked the door and put the key under his head nights* 1884 HF vi 38. See also *K box* 1886 (OEDS Now *dial* and *U.S.* 1786.. So W S C Wr Th. See *-s,* suffix, below)

night-times, adv. [?AB¹] *Just tramp right across the country, mostly night-times* 1884 HF vi 41 (Wr: *Somerset* and *Devon.* Comb. not in OED W S C. See *-s,* suffix, below)

Nihilistendynamittheaterkaestchenssprengungsat-tentaetsversuchungen, sb. [B¹] See *effect* 1889 (Hum. coinage)

nine, sb. [?AB³] *This experiment was baseball. I chose my nines by rank* 1889 CY xl 518 (OED 2b. A set of nine...players. 1860.. This *Baseball* use is A in W S C H)

nine-log, a. [B¹] See *bow-end* 1880 (Comb. not in OED W S C)

Nineteener, sb. [B¹] *He would have liked to be a Nineteener; but such was not for him* 1899 "MCH" (1900) 37 (An "ad hoc" coinage, with ref. to the nineteen "aristocratic" families of Hadleyburg)

nip, v. [?AB¹C]*"Whoever nipped the whiskey... nipped the money, too, I reckon—anyways it's a goner for us, Tom"* 1876 TS xxxiii 256 (S: To steal, pilfer. *obs* and *cant.* So C. U: *colloq* and *slang.* Wr: *dial.* This sense not in OED W)

nip and tuck, sb. [AB³] *"So they had it, nip and tuck, for five mile or more"* 1884 HF xviii 166. *It was nip and tuck with us, and I knew it. If I spent the eleventh shot without convincing these people, the twelfth man would kill me, sure* 1889 CY xxxix 507 (OEDS *U.S.* Neck and neck. 1832.. So W S C Wr B F Cl Th T DN.III, n.w.Ark. Cf. H: Am. nip and tuck=Eng. neck and neck, a close thing. Cf. nuck and tip, below)

no, adv. [AB¹] *"What hotel are you stopping at?" "Schweitzerhof." "No! is that so?"* 1880 TA xxvii 276 (This use given as current in Iowa and Florida, AS.V. 257. Not in OED W S C. Cf. OED 1c. Used interrogatively. 1374..1884; but in all the OED quots. the interrogative *No* is used after negative statements, e.g. *c*1374 Chaucer, *Troilus* II.1162: "Trewely I nil no lettre wryte". "No? than wol I", quod he. In the M.T. ex., used after a positive statement, it app. has the *spec* sense of surprise, doubt, incredulity)

no-account, a. [AB³] See *moonshiny* 1892 (OEDS *U.S.* Worthless. 1845.. So W S C B F Th T M DN.II, III,IV,V AS.VII.94)

no-account, sb. [AB²] See *loafing* 1899. *"Who ever had anything agin that poor trifling no-account?"* 1896 TSD ix 523 (OEDS *U.S.* A 'no-account' person. 1922.. So Th DN.II,III,IV. Not in W S C)

nobbily, adv. [?AB²] *Two hundred Bermudians, half of them black, half of them white, and all of them nobbily dressed, as the poet says* 1877 "Some Rambling Notes" ii 591 (OEDS 1880, only ex. So S. *Slang* in W C C. Cf. below)

nobby, a. [?AB³] See *rig,* sb. 1872. *"We'll play Robin Hood—it's nobby fun"* 1876 TS xxvi 200. *"Undertaking is the dead-surest business in Christendom, and the nobbiest"* 1883 LM xlii 438. *"A line of goods suitable for kings, and a nobby thing for duchesses"* 1889 CY xxii 280. *"It's the very thing—plain, rich, modest, and just ducally nobby"* 1893 "Banknote" (1928) 116. *A fact saunters forth in this nobby outfit* 1894 "In Defence of Harriet Shelley" 109 (OED *slang.* Extremely smart or elegant. b. Of places and things. 1844.. So W S C U Wr. A in B. Not A in T. One of M. T's favorite words)

nobilities, sb. pl. [B³] *"I thought you were opposed to nobilities?" "Transmissible ones, yes. But that's nothing. I'm opposed to millionaires, but it would be dangerous to offer me the position"* 1892 AmCl xiv 149. See *back-alley* 1894. *Now and then these kings and nobilities got caught out after the gates were locked* 1904 *Autob* (1924) I 201. (OED 4b. One belonging to the noble class. 1840, only ex., from Carlyle. This *concrete* use not in W S C)

noble, a. [?AC] See *back-log* 1881. *"These be noble large stitches"* 1881 PP xiii 154. *They are noble boulders* 1897 FE xxiii 229. See also *divinity-circuit* 1903; *jack-assful* 1906 (OED 8b. Notable, very great. *obs. rare.* 1604, 1694. Not *obs* in W S C U Wr)

noble, adv. [?AB¹] *It just worked noble* 1884 HF xxxvi 372 (This adv. use not in OED W S C)

noble-episode, a. [B¹] *He had struck something fresh in the noble-episode line* 1878 "About Magnanimous-Incident Literature" 617 (Nonce comb.)

nohow, adv. [?AB³] *"I saw it wasn't no good, nohow"* 1883 LM lii 511. See *go on* 1884. *We couldn't get sleepy nohow and noway* 1896 TSD vii 360 (OEDS Earlier U.S. ex. 1833.. A in B F Th M DN.III. Not A in W S C U T)

No Man's Land, sb. [B¹] See *Never-Never Country* 1897 (This *spec* Australian sense not in OED W S C. For other senses cf. AS.V.380)

nombril, a. [B¹] See *coat-of-arms* 1883 (Nonsense use, since of course there cannot be more than one "nombril point". Cf. OED *Heraldry.* That point on an escutcheon which lies midway between the Fesse Point and the Base Point. 1562..1868. So W S C)

non-association, a. [B¹] *Every day some outraged captain discharged a non-association pilot* 1875 OTM 726 (Nonce word, for a non-member of the "Pilots' Benevolent Association")

non-associationist, sb. [B¹] *In a very little while non-associationists began to be pretty plenty* 1875 OTM 726 (Nonce word; cf. above)

non-committal, a. [AB³] *"I told you to write a non-committal letter...an ambiguous letter"* 1868 SNO (1875) 150 (OEDS orig. *U.S.* 1829.. So W S C U B Th T M)

non-conforming, ppl.a. [B¹] *Worn officially, our non-conforming swallow-tail is a declaration of ungracious independence* 1897 "Diplomatic Pay" (1928) 228 (W S C U: Failing or refusing to conform. This *general* sense not in OED, which has only the ecclesiastical use of the word)

non-cultivation, sb. [B¹] *In my then uneducated state, that went home to my non-cultivation* 1880 TA xxiv 238 (Comb. not in OED S C. Given in W, without definition)

nonesuch, sb. [?AC] *The bills said: "The King's Cameleopard or The Royal Nonesuch!!!"* 1884 HF xxii 225 (OED 2. An unmatched or unrivalled thing. 1590..1745. So W. S C: Formerly so used. OEDS Later U.S. exs. 1821..1927. A in Wr)

non-necessity, sb. [B¹] *Sally had seldom known what it was to be privileged to squander a dime on non-necessities* 1904 "Bequest" (1906) 5 (This *concr.* sense not in OED W S C; but cf. OED Necessity, sb. 9b. An indispensable or necessary thing. 1481..also Non-necessary, sb. 1754.)

nonpareil, sb. [AB²] *I saw our newest cub set...2,150 ems of solid nonpareil in an hour* 1889 *Letters* (1917) II xxix 517. *I was to furnish one column of leaded nonpareil every day* 1906 *Autob* (1924) I 271 (OED 2. Printing. A size of type intermediate,...in America, between minion and agate. No ex. Am. sense. So C. Not A in W S)

non-participant, sb. [B¹] *Could you come nearer to reproducing it [the siege of Vicksburg] to the imagination of a non-participant?* 1883 LM xxxv 379. *The Jews have no party; they are non-participants* 1899 "Concerning the Jews" (1900) 269 (Comb. not in OED S C. Given in W, without definition)

non-progressionist, sb. [B¹] See *China,* a. 1885 (Comb. not in OED W S C)

noon, v. [AB³] *We nooned an hour at the celebrated Balaam's Ass Fountains* 1869 IA xliv 454 (OED *U.S.* 1806.. So W AS.VI.251. Not A in S C Wr)

nooning, sb. [AB³] *It was another thirteen hour stretch, including an hour's "nooning"* 1869 IA xliv 454. *She said she would look at pictures all through the nooning* 1876 TS xviii 157. *I stopped for an hour's nooning, to rest my horse and myself* 1887 *Letters* (1917) II xxvi 478 (OED 3b. *U.S.* An interval in the middle of the day, esp. for rest or food. 1865.. So W Wr B F Cl AS.V.419, VII.429. Not A in S C T)

nor, conj. [C] *"A doll, that hath nor brains nor hands to help itself withal"* 1881 PP xiv 167 (OED 2b. Introducing both alternatives. Chiefly *poet.* 1576..1852. So W S C U)

nor, conj. [?A] *"I don't see no pints about that thar frog more nor about any other frog in partickler"* 1865

"Jumping Frog" (1875) 34 (OED *Scotch* and *dial.* Than. *c*1400 .. 1883. So C. W: *dial.* S: *Prov. Eng.*)

North, sb. [A] See *mud-sill* 1877; *go, went = gone* 1883; *batter-cake* 1897; *Civil War* 1899 (OEDS 2c. *U.S.* The northern States...bounded on the south by Maryland, the Ohio River, and Missouri. 1796.. So W S C B F. U has this amazing bit of information: North and South America (U.S.A.), as divided by Mason and Dixon's line!)

norther, sb. [AB³] See *burster* 1895 (OEDS A strong north wind...which blows, during the autumn and winter months, over Texas, Florida, and the Gulf of Mexico. 1827.. So W S C U B F Cl Th T DN.V)

Northern, a. [AB³] *They found people sitting on the doorsteps of their dwellings, in a manner not usual in a Northern city* 1873 GA xiii 125. *A Northern or Southern literary periodical of forty or fifty years ago* 1883 LM xlvi 469. See also *guess* 1883; *batter-cake* 1897 (OED lb. *U.S.* 1836.. So W U. The *spec* Am. sense not in S C)

Northerner, sb. [AB³] See *American,* sb. 1880 (OEDS *U.S.* 1831.. So W S C U B F Th T)

note-booking, vbl.sb. [B¹] *My last voyage's note-booking was but a confusion of meaningless names* 1875 OTM 57 (Comb. not in OED W S C)

nothing, sb. **like nothing.** [?AB¹] *"A calf that et apples and just chawed up dishrags like nothing!"* 1873 GA vii 81. *"Done it just as slick as nothing at all!"* 1884 HF xl 410 (To a superlative degree; used as an adv. intensifier. Cf. *like everything,* above, which has, oddly enough, the same meaning. Not in OED W S C; but cf. OEDS 1g. *like nothing on earth,* 1927)

nothing, adv. [C] *"I was therein nothing blameful"* 1881 PP v 63 (OED 2. Now *arch. a*1050..1867. So W. Not *arch* in S C U Wr)

notice, sb. [?AB¹] *The conferring upon the editor of a present and begging a "notice" of it* 1870 Screamers 109. *The puzzle of the absence of Tilbury's death notice... On its way to the standing-galley Tilbury's notice got pied* 1904 "Bequest" (1906) iii 15 (An item of personal news or mention in a newspaper. This *spec* sense not in OED W S C; but for gen. sense cf. OED 8a. A brief mention in writing, a review. 1841..)

notice, sb. [?AB¹] See *Bible-class* 1870. *The Rev. Mr. Sprague turned himself into a bulletin-board, and read off "notices" of meetings* 1876 TS v 55. *The reading from the pulpit of a tedious list of "notices"* 1880 TA xxxvi 402 (An announcement read from the pulpit. This *spec* sense not in OED W S C)

notice, sb. [AB¹] *We liked the appearance of the place, and so we claimed some three hundred acres of it and stuck our notices on a tree* 1872 RI xxii 171 (A in F: An announcement of a claim being taken up. So Cl. This *spec* sense not in OED W S C)

nougat-peddler, sb. [B¹] *"We are not at home even to nougat-peddlers"* 1888 "Meisterschaft" 459 (Comb. not in OED W S C)

nous, sb. [?A] *"Archy would have learnt something if he'd had the nous to stand by and take notice"* 1902 "DBDS" (1928) vii 335 (OED 2. *colloq* or *slang.* Intelligence, common sense, gumption. Common in 19th c. 1706..1884. So W S C U Wr. Cf. Nouse-box, A in F: The head)

nowheres, adv. [AB¹] *"I hain't been nowheres"* 1884 HF xli 415 (A in W M DN.III AS.XI.352. This var. form of Nowhere not in OED S C. Cf. Anywheres and Somewheres)

Now-I-lay-me-down-to-sleep, a. [B¹] *I just run over my little old "ich habe gehabt, du hast gehabt"...kind of "Now-I-lay-me-down-to-sleep" fashion* 1880 TA xxvii 281 (Nonce phrase: by rote)

Noyoudont, sb. [?AB¹] *"Try Noyoudont."* This was a toothwash I was introducing 1889 CY xx 239 (Nonce coinage. Cf. B F: An exclamation of dissent frequently heard in the North. This application of it was probably suggested by Sozodont, q.v. below)

nub, sb. [AB³] *The French newspapers have a strange fashion of telling a perfectly straight story till you get to the "nub" of it, and then a word drops in that no man can translate, and that story is ruined* 1869 IA xi 99. *The "nub" or moral of the burlesque escapes notice* 1870 CRG (1917) 32. *When the nub was sprung, the assemblage let go with a horse-laugh* 1889 CY xvii 203. *He told them a good many humorous ancedotes, and always forgot the nub* 1894 PW vii 336. See also *snapper* 1895 (OEDS 3. *U.S.* The point or gist of a story. 1834.. So W S B F Th.III T. Cf. H: In Eng. a lump or protuberance; in Am. the core, kernel, or central point of an affair. Not A in C)

nuck and tip, sb. [?AB¹] *"It was nuck and tip whether the beaver would catch the dog"* 1871 Screamers 131 (Not in OED W S C; but cf. OEDS Nip and tuck, and the var. forms there cited: Rip and tuck, 1832; nip and tack, 1846; nip and chuck, 1846)

nugget, sb. [?AB³] See *brain-plow* 1869; *slug,* sb. 1872. *A random remark...brought this nugget of information out of him* 1883 LM xxii 260. *Ballarat was a great region for "nuggets"...In fact, the Ballarat region has yielded the largest ones known to history* 1897 FE xxiv 232 (OED 1. A rough lump of native gold. Also *transf.* 1852.. So W S C U. A in AS.V.145)

number, sb. **to take one's number.** [?AB²] *I felt obliged to take his number and report him* 1888 Speeches (1923) 143 (To make a note of the identifying mark or number of an employee or officer. OEDS 4. 1908, only ex. of this sense. Not in W S C)

number, sb. **to take one's number.** [?AB²] *That was the sort of master we had. I took his number* 1889 CY xxxv 458 (To size up, form a correct estimate of. A *fig* extension of the above. OEDS 4. All exs. U.S. 1912.. *Colloq* in W. Not in S C)

numberable, a. [C] *Merely the numerable packages of meat* 1892 AmCl xi 101 (OED *rare.* 1. Capable of being numbered. 1340..1839. Not in W S C)

numskull, sb. [?A] *He was an old numskull, a magician who believed in his own magic* 1889 CY xxii 273. See also *sentimentals* 1892 (OED 1. A dull-witted or stupid person. 1728.. So W S C U. A in DN.II,III,IV,V)

nut, sb. **nuts to, for.** [?A] *"Ain't it gay?" said Joe. "It's nuts!" said Tom* 1876 TS xiii 118. *Tom had his store clothes on, and an audience—and that was always nuts for Tom Sawyer* 1884 HF xxxiii 340. *It would be nuts for him, being a mystery, and he'd make an adventure out of it, and be perfectly satisfied* 1884 HF xlii 432. *The combination was nuts for the Ornithorhyncus, if I may use a term like that without offence* 1897 FE viii 103. *"Say, wouldn't it 'a' been nuts if he'd a-been here last night?"* 1902 "DBDS" (1928) 227 (OED 5a. A source of pleasure or delight to one. Now *slang.* 1617..1891. So S C U. A in B M. This use not in W. Mencken says this slang use of *nuts* came into popularity in the U.S. c.1920, but reports a "rumor" to the effect that M.T. had previously used it in FE. As the exs. above show, the phr. was a favorite with M.T. from a far earlier period)

nuther, adv. [?ACE] See *get* 1880. *"I don't want it at all—nor the six thousand, nuther"* 1884 HF iv 27. See also *common* 1893 (OED *dial* var. of Nother, conj. *obs exc. dial.* 1873, 1886. A in Wr DN.II,V. This form not in W S C)

nutritiousness, sb. [B²] *Their testimony to its nutritiousness is worth nothing* 1872 RI iii 35 (OED 1877, only ex. So W S C)

nutshell, v. [B²] *The clerk nutshelled the contrast between the former time and the present, thus...* 1883 LM lviii 570 (OED To state concisely. 1892.. So W S. Not in C)

nutting-expedition, sb. [?AB²] *Parties, picnics, rowing matches, moonlight strolls, nutting expeditions in the October woods* 1873 GA xxi 200 (OEDS All exs. U.S. 1873, this quot...Comb. not in W S C)

O

oar-handle, sb. [B¹] *One of the quarter-boats had an oar-handle stove through her* 1866 "Forty-Three Days" 107 (Comb. not in OED W S C)

obituarial, a. [?AB¹] *"I scribbled off a sort of a little obituarial send-off for him"* 1904 "Bequest" (1906) viii 48 (Not in OED W S C; but cf. OED Obituarize, 1891; Obituarily, 1864, U.S. ex.)

object, sb. **no object.** [?A] *That garrulous attention to minor detail which is born of secluded farm life or life at sea on long voyages, where there is little to do and time no object* 1877 "Some Rambling Notes" ii 587 (OEDS 5b. Frequently misused of distance, expense, etc., not taken into account or forming no obstacle. 1782.. The earliest ex. of the "misuse" is 1796, an Am. quot. Phr. not in W S C. Cf. the discussion of the origin of this phr. in "Distance No Object", by C. T. Onions, *S.P.E. Tract* no. 36, 1931, pp.531-4; here the earliest quot. for the sense "no obstacle; a matter of no importance; not a consideration" is 1800)

object-lesson, sb. [?AB²] *In the time of which we are writing, the Bridge furnished "object-lessons" in English history* 1881 PP xi 135. *Judge North was anxious to have some object-lessons for that law* 1906 "Chaps. from Autob" 1223. In the reproduction of this passage in *Autob* (1924) I 359, the word *object-lessons* has been "improved" to *victims.* Cf. *guts,* above (OED *fig* Something that furnishes instruction by exemplifying some principle in a concrete form. 1896, only ex. *fig* sense. So W S C)

oblique, a. [B¹] See *antiphonal* 1906 (Nonsense use)

obscene, a. [?C] *The obscene Tumble-Bug* 1875 SNO 148 (OED 1. Offensive to the senses, or to taste or refinement; disgusting, repulsive. Now somewhat *arch.* 1593..1869. So S U. Not *arch* in W C)

observance, sb. [C] *But the tramp gave them* [the emperor's daughters] *no observance* 1880 TA xvii 152 (OED 3. The observing of due respect or deference to. *arch.* c1374..1859. So W S C U)

occasional, sb. [?AB²] *I am on the N.Y. Tribune staff here as an "occasional"* 1867 *Letters* (1917) I vii 142 (OED 2. *colloq.* An occasional workman; a casual. 1892, only ex. Here an occasional printer or typesetter. This sense not in W S C)

occasion of state, sb. [B¹] *She thought it a pity that they had to be such changed and dreary creatures on occasions of state* 1873 GA xxxiii 300 (Comb. not in OED W S C. Cf. OED Occasion, 9b. A special ceremony, a 'function'. Chiefly *colloq.* 1860..)

odds, sb. **What's the odds?** [?AB²] *"It's bound to come out sooner or later, so what's the odds?"* 1873 GA xi 111 (OED 2c. *colloq.* What difference does it make? 1886, only ex. So W S C U. Cf. OEDS 4. To ask no odds. *U.S.* 1806..; so Th.III)

odic, a. [B¹] *The refrangibility of the earth's surface would impact the odic and idyllic forces together* 1880 TA xliii 507 (Hum. nonsense use. Cf. OED Of or pertaining to the hypothetical force called Od, a force held by Baron von Reichenbach (1788-1869) to pervade all nature. 1850..; so W S C)

'Od's bodikins, int. [C] *'Obsbodikins, it was but a dull lie* 1889 CY vi 72 (OED 2. The possessive *'od's* occurs like *God's* in many asseverative or exclamatory formulae...now mostly *obs* or *dial.* 1709..1834. So W S C U Wr AS.IX.256)

'Od's body, int. [C] *"Ods body! I seem to be in evil case"* 1881 PP xxiv 291 (OED 2. Now *obs* or *arch.* No ex. So W S C U)

'Od's my life, int. Spelled **Odds my life.** [CE] *"Odds my life, a strange boon!"* 1881 PP xv 184 (OED 2b. The origin of *Od's* being forgotten, it was freq. written as *Odds*...In such phrases *'s* is perhaps for *save.* 1600.. 1823. So W S C U Wr)

oesophagus, sb. [B¹] *Far in the empty sky a solitary oesophagus slept upon motionless wing* 1902 "DBDS" (1928) 304 (Hum. nonce use. Cf. AS.I.296, where it is

noted that M.T.'s celebrated joke is imitated in a recent editorial: *"Many wonderful oesophagi, resting-places of great kings, have been unearthed in ancient Egypt"*)

of, prep. [?AC] *Was he a-leading of the choir—He done his level best* 1867 SNO (1875) 74 (OED 32. After what was formerly a verbal sb. governed by *in* or *a,* but is now identified with the present participle. Now *dial* or *vulgar.* 1523..1749. So W S C Wr. A in B T DN.IV, Virginia)

of, prep. [C] *Know that I have sent him of an errand* 1881 PP xxi 261 (OED 55. In sense of *on. Obs, colloq,* or *vulgar.* c1380..1777. So W C Wr. Not *obs* in S)

of, prep. [?AC] *"What can be the matter of him, do you reckon?"* 1896 TSD i 346 (OED 61. In sense of *with.* Mostly *obs.* 1523..1843. So W. Not *obs* in S C. A in Wr DN.IV)

of, v. var. form for **have.** [AB³E] *"I'd of liked to run up to town"* 1884 HF xlii 426 (OEDS *U.S. dial* or *vulgar.* 1847.. So M. This form not in W S C)

off, adv. [?AC] *He is off, far off, in his mathematics* 1908 *Speeches* (1910) 41 (OED 2c. *fig.* Distant or remote in fact, nature, character, feeling, thought, etc. *Obs* or *arch* (in Great Britain). 1555..1887. OEDS Further U.S.exs. 1809..1902. Not A in W S C U)

offal, sb. [?A] *"If thou do but touch him, thou animated offal, I will spit thee like a goose"* 1881 PP xii 136 (OED 5. *fig.* 1581..1828. So W S C U. A in Wr F Cl T M)

off-color, a. (AB³) *Their pronunciation was sufficiently off-color to be very interesting* 1888 *M.T. the Letter Writer* (1932) iii 49. (OEDS 1. Of questionable taste. *U.S.* 1875.. Called *Slang, U.S.* in W 1911, but not in W 1935. Not A in S C. A in Wr F Cl, c1870)

offen, prep. Also **off'n.** [AB³] *He'd snake a fly off'n the counter* 1865 "Jumping Frog" (1875) 32. See *bounce* 1876 (OEDS *Dial,* also *U.S.* Off from; from off. 1828.. So B F M. Not A in W. Not in S C)

office-seeker, sb. [AB³] *There are now some 60,000 future office-seekers* 1879 *Speeches* (1910) 68 (OEDS Chiefly *U.S.* 1813.. So S Th H. Not A in W C)

offish, a. [?AB³] See *heifer* 1872; *rag-tag-and-bobtail* 1872. *"Do not be offish and unsociable"* 1873 GA xlii 377 (OED 1842.. OEDS Earlier U.S. ex. 1830. A in Wr B Th T. Not A in W S C U)

off of, prep. [?AC] *Every now and then I'd borrow two or three dollars off of the judge for him* 1884 HF vi 37. See also *cowhiding* 1884. (OED 7. In all cases, *off* may be followed by *from;* formerly, and still *dial,* by *of.* 1593..1875. So W. Not *arch* in S C. A in M H)

offset, v. [A] See *sort of* 1889. *You offset these discreditable features by the creditable ones* 1899 "Concerning the Jews" (1900) 260 (OED Chiefly *U.S.* 1. 1792.. So B F Cl. Cf.M: Am. *Offset* = Brit. *Set off.* Not A in W S C U)

off-watch, sb. [?AB¹] *The off-watch was just turning in* 1875 OTM 218. *How good a time I might have been having with the off-watch below* 1883 LM xviii 217. *The "on" watch could not be depended upon to call the "off" watch* 1906 *Autob* (1924) II 114 (Comb. not in OED W S C)

oil, sb. **to strike oil.** [AB³] *To be vested with enormous authority is a fine thing...I couldn't help thinking about it, just as one does who has struck oil* 1889 CY viii 95. *"About the marriage business...first, we turned down the dentist and the lawyer...Then you went for the aristocracy; and I thought we had struck oil at last"* 1904 "Bequest" (1906) vii 40 (OED 3f. *U.S. fig. colloq.* To hit upon a source of rapid profit and affluence. 1866.. So W S B F Cl Th DN.III. Not A in U. The *fig* sense not in C)

oil-derrick, sb. [?AB²] *"That long, lank cadaver, old oil-derrick out of a job"* 1902 *Speeches* (1910) 367 (OED A frame used in boring for oil. No ex. So W S C. Here *fig* as hum. epithet)

oil-region, sb. [?AB³] *This youth from the oil-regions* 1909 *Speeches* (1910) 177 (OEDS U.S.exs. 1862.. Comb. not in W S C. Cf. Oil-belt, A in Th.III, 1894)

oil-stench, sb. [B¹] See *stencher* 1893 (Comb. not in OED W S C)

Oklahoma, sb. [AB¹] *They placed Twichell and me in a most colossal bedroom. There were six chairs in that Oklahoma* 1906 *Speeches* (1910) 330 (This *fig* use not in OED W S C. Cf. the river use of Texas, q.v., for the largest 'stateroom' on a steamer)

old-comradeship, sb. [B¹] *Thus simply did she take the sense of old-comradeship out of him and transform him into a stranger and a guest* 1881 PP xxvi 312 (Comb. not in OED W S C. Cf. OED Old-bachelor-ship, 1832)

Old Dominion, sb. [AB³] *"He is of the best blood of the Old Dominion"* 1894 PW xii 773 (OEDS Dominion sb. 2b. 1808.. So W S C F Cl Th,1812)

oldest-alumnus, a. [B¹] *Weary yearly marvels...of the Oldest-Alumnus sort* 1883 LM lx 584 (Nonce comb.)

Old-English, a. [B¹] *Her prized and precious old-English sugar bowl* 1906 *Autob* (1924) II 93 (Here applied to china-ware of some early period. This sense not in OED W S C. The only senses of Old-English in the OED, strangely enough, are the linguistic sense, OED English 1b, and 6b. *Printing*, a form of "Black Letter")

old-gold, a. [B¹] See *new-gold* 1897 (W: A dull,slightly metallic, and generally yellow color, supposed to resemble dull gold. So C. Comb. not in OED S)

old lady, sb. [?AB²] *"You make yourself perfectly comfortable, old lady"* 1873 GA xxvii 245 (OEDS Old, a. 8a. A woman, one's wife or mother. 1873, this quot... This use not in W S C)

old-maidy, a. [?AB²] *"Who ever heard of getting a prisoner loose in such an old-maidy way as that?"* 1884 HF xxxv 357 (OEDS 1923. Comb. not in W S C)

old man, sb. (?AB³] *The "old man" was the captain— he is always so, on steamboats and ships* 1873 GA iv 44 (OEDS 1b. 1845..1873, this quot. So W S C U. A in F)

old man, sb. [B³] *"The old man [proprietor of a boarding-house] thinks he's great on sarcasm"* 1892 AmCl xii 126 (OEDS 1d. A master, overseer, foreman, or superintendent. 1844.. So W S C U)

old man, sb. [AB³] *"Old man Bolton's behind him"* 1873 GA xl 359 (OEDS 1e. U.S. local. Substituted familiarly for 'old Mr.—'. 1843.. So B F Th DN.III. This usage not in W S C)

old man, sb. [?AB²] *I can make the money without lecturing. Therefore, old man, count me out* 1870 *Letters* (1917) I x 172. See also *double-team*, v. 1884 (OED Old, a. 8. Used as an expression of familiarity in addressing persons with whom one has an acquaintance of some standing. *colloq.* 1885.. So W S. This use not in C)

old master, sb. [B¹] *Who painted these things? Why, Titian, Tintoretto, Paul Veronese, Raphael—none other than the world's idols, the "old masters"* 1869 IA xxv 260. *Manure is the Black-Forester's main treasure—his pride, his Old Master* 1880 TA xxii 210. *There will be money in her altar-canvases—a thousand times as much as the Popes and their Church ever spent on the Old Masters* 1902 "Chr.Sc." 760 (W: Distinguished painters who lived before the modern period. So C. Comb. not in OED S)

Old Master, sb. **Ole Marster**, **Old Marse**, etc. [?AB¹E] *"En Ole Marster tell me"* 1892 AmCl viii 81. *"Old Marse was jes' a hoppin'!"* 1894 PW viii 338 (Slave's name for the master or slave-owner in the Southern U.S. Not in OED W S C. The prons. indicated are noted as So.U.S. in Wr M)

Old Mistress, sb. **Ole Missus**, **Missis**. [?AB¹E] See *broke* 1874. *"I dasn't, Mars Tom. Ole missis she'd take an' tar de head off'n me"* 1876 TS ii 27. *The slave woman exclaimed: "Ole Missus, de house is plum jam full o' people"* 1894 PW vi 334 (Used by slaves for their mistress. Not in OED W S C)

Old Probabilities, sb. [AB³] *Old Probabilities has a mighty reputation for accurate prophecy* c1879 *Speeches* (1910) 61 (OED Probability, sb. 2b. A humorous name for the chief signal-officer of the U.S. Signal Service Bureau. 1875. So W C B F Cl Th. III,1874. Not in S)

Old-School Baptist, sb. [?AB²] *"She was an Old-School Baptist"* 1873 GA vii 60 (OEDS 1b. *Theol.* Adhering to established or traditional views or interpretation of doctrine: old-school Presbyterian 1837.. Old-School Baptist 1873, this quot...All exs. U.S. Not A in W S C)

old sledge, sb. [?AB³] *Playing "seven-up" or "old sledge" for money* 1870 SNO (1875) 159 (OED Old, a. D.4. 1837. So W S C. A in B F Cl Th T)

old soldier, sb. [AB³] *A wooden box of sand, sprinkled with cigar stubs and "old soldiers"* 1869 SNO (1875) 45 (OEDS Old, a. D.4. U.S. slang. The remaining part of a smoked cigar or a chewed quid. 1845.. So B F Cl H AS.XI.304. Not A in W. This sense not in S C)

old-time, a. [?AB²] *As the weeks wore away, Conrad's color came back to his cheeks, and his old-time vivacity to his eye* 1871 SNO (1875) 176. See *breezy* 1873; *city-capture* 1883. *Half a dozen old-time steamboats* 1883 LM xxiv 269. See also *new-time* 1904 (OED 1888.. So W S C U)

old-timer, sb. [AB³] *Did Mrs. Eddy borrow from Quimby the Great Idea, or only the little one, the old-timer, the ordinary mental healing?* 1907 CS II xv 282 (OED An old-fashioned person or thing. Chiefly *U.S.* 1882... So H. Not A in W S C)

Old Virginia, sb. [AB¹] See *First Family* 1894. *These two had been boys together in Virginia when that state still ranked as the chief and most imposing member of the Union, and they still coupled..."old" with her name... In Missouri a recognized superiority attached to any person who hailed from Old Virginia* 1894 PW xii 772 (Comb. not in OED W S C; but cf. OEDS Old Dominion, 1808..)

old woman, sb. [?AB³] See *snort* 1867 (OED 1b. Among the vulgar = Wife. OEDS 1834.. All exs. U.S. A in Wr. Th DN.I,II,III,VI. Not A in W S U. Not in C)

Old World, sb. [?AB³] See *bicycle* 1899 (OED Old, a. 12b. The Eastern Hemisphere, as opposed to the New World of America. U.S. exs. 1837.. So W S C U)

oleomargarine, sb. [AB³] *"It's oleomargarine. You can't tell it from butter"* 1883 LM xxxix 412. *Christian Science literary oleomargarine is a monopoly of the Mother Church Headquarters Factory in Boston* 1903 "Chr.Sc." ii 3 (OED Now legally called in Great Britain *margarine*. In U.S. *oleomargarine* is the recognized name of the commercial product. 1873.. So W S C U B F DN.III,V)

oligarcheologically, adv. [B¹] See *electroincandescently* 1907 (Nonsense coinage.A blend of oligarchy and archeology)

ombra, sb. [B¹] *I found Mr. Beals hard at work in the rain with his decorations...Piles of still-bundled flags clutter up the ombra* 1880, Oct.16 Letter from the home in Hartford, Paine's *Biog.* II 692. *The large window which opened into the ombra at the rear of the house was standing wide* 1906 *Autob* (1924) II 81. (Not in OED W S C. Apparently a family coinage for 'veranda'; cf. Paine I 523, speaking of the Hartford home: A wide, covered veranda, the "ombra" as they called it, secluded from the public eye—a favorite family gathering-place on pleasant days)

on, prep. **on the river**. [?AB¹] *When I was a boy, there was but one permanent ambition among my comrades... that was, to be a steamboatman...Boy after boy managed to get on the river...Some of us were left disconsolate. We could not get on the river—at least our parents would not let us* 1875 OTM 71 (Cf. OED 1g(c). Employed on. Cf. quot. 1882 *"A leading writer on the press"*; 1890 *"Speaking of their several avocations, I learned that So-and-so was 'on the pigs', another 'on the kitchen', and a third 'on* *the table'*." No ex. of 'on the river'. This use not in W S C)

on, prep. [?A] "*The thing I'm on now is to roust out somebody to jerk a little chin-music for us*" 1872 RI xlvii 332 (OED 10b. Engaged in, occupied with. 1768. OEDS Later exs., all U.S., 1849, 1889. A in F. Not A in W S C)

on, prep. **to be on it.** [AB²] "*But pard, he was a rustler! You ought to seen him get started once...Pard, he was on it! He was on it bigger than an Injun!*" "*On it? On what?*" "*On the shoot. On the shoulder. On the fight, you understand. He didn't give a continental for anybody.*" 1872 RI xlvii 334 (OEDS 10c. To be ready or prepared for, to be skilled in, something. *U.S.colloq.* 1872, this quot... So F Cl. Phrase not in W S C)

on, prep. [?AB¹] *Those horses were the hardest lot I ever did come across...One brute had a neck on him like a bowsprit* 1869 IA xli 434. *Tom told him to work till the rest of his candle quit on him* 1884 HF xxxviii 389 (This use of *on*, as the 'ethical dative" would be used in Latin, is not clearly recognized in any dict. Nearest is W. 10: Indicating cost or disadvantage; specif., chiefly *colloq.* a. To the disadvantage, detriment, or discomfiture of; as, *the fire went out on him.* Less applicable is OEDS 21b. *U.S.* Against (a person). 1901 "*Oh, wasn't that one on me!*"... 1916 "*The joke is sure on us*"... 1927 "*I had nothing on her*". No use resembling it in S C. But cf. P. W. Joyce, *English as We Speak It in Ireland*, p. 31: "'*She had a nose on her*', i. e., looked sour, out of humor. '*They never asked had I a mouth on me*': universally understood and often used in Ireland, and meaning 'They never offered me anything to eat and drink'. I find Mark Twain using the same idiom [above quot. from IA] but there I think Mark shows a touch of the Gaelic brush, wherever he got it")

once, adv. Spelled **wunst.** [?AB³E] "*Wunst I had fo'teen dollars*" 1884 HF viii 70 (OEDS This sp. 19th c. Earliest ex. U.S. 1840. . A in Wr B F. Not A in W T. Not given in S C. Cf. the sp. *oncet, onct*, given as A in M DN.I,II,III,IV,V AS.XI.239. The variation is of course merely orthographical, both spellings being attempts to indicate the pron. with the adherent *t*. Cf. Twice, sp. *twiste*, below)

one-horse, a. [AB³] *It would take them one-hoss fiddlers down a peg* 1856 Adv. of T. J. Snodgrass (1928) 6. See *gin-mill* 1869; *farmer-preacher* 1884; *round-log* a. 1884. *One-horse kings with a defective title* 1889 CY xi 133. *Gutting a one-horse bank* 1892 AmCl xix 195. "*One of them bayous or one-horse rivers down Louisiana way*" 1896 TSD ii 346 (OED 2. Petty; of limited resources or capacity. *U.S.colloq.* OEDS 1854. . So B F Cl Th M DN.III, e.Ala.; IV, V, Conn., N.Y. AS.I.45; IX.319. Not A in W S C U)

one-hundred-millionaire, sb. [?AB¹] *The annual cost to the one-hundred-millionaire and to the sucking child of the day laborer was precisely the same* 1889 CY xxvi 335 (Cf. *millionaire, hundred-millionaire*, above. Comb. not in OED W S C)

one-limbed, a. [B¹] See *cottonwood* 1875 (Comb. not in OED W S C)

one-liner, sb. [?AB¹] *There were headings—one-liners and two-liners* 1904 "Italian without a Master" (1906) 173 (A head-line consisting of one line of print only. Comb. not in OED W S C)

one-pounder, sb. [B¹] *They find they've given a tramp a million-pound bill when they thought it was a one-pounder* 1893 "Banknote" (1928) 111 (Comb. not in OED W S C in this sense. Cf. *five-center*, above)

one while, adv. [AB²] *It all came of the World's Fair and the Congress of Religions. If India knows about nothing else American, she knows about those, and will keep them in mind one while* 1897 FE liii 511 (OEDS One, a. 33. *U.S.* For some time. 1897, this quot., only ex. Comb. not in W S C)

onion, sb. [B¹] *The onion is the pride and joy of Bermuda...In Bermudian metaphor it stands for perfection,—perfection absolute. The Bermudian weeping over the departed exhausts praise when he says, "He was an onion!"...The Bermudian setting his son upon the stage of life...comprehends all ambition when he says, "Be an onion!"* 1877 "Some Rambling Notes" iii 716 (Hum. nonce use)

onto, prep. [?AB³] See *dob* 1871; *drool* 1872. "*To see him climb onto the bed*" 1873 GA ii 32. See *clip*, v. 1884; *keel*, v. 1884. *I tossed four dollars onto the table* 1889 CY xxxi 415. "*You get a little too much costumery onto your statements*" 1883 LM xxxiv 374. See also *drop*, v. 1892; *marble-time* 1896 (OED To a position on or upon. 1819. .1900. OEDS U.S. exs. 1905..1911. A in B F Cl Th DN.VI. Not A in W S C Wr)

Oolitic, a. [B¹] *In the Old Oolitic Silurian Period, just a million years ago next November* 1875 OTM 193. *The cave bear, primeval man, and the other Oolitics of the old Silurian family* 1880 TA xxxix 457 (Nonsense use. Cf. OED 2. *Geol.* 1832..; so W S C U. Cf. M.T.'s use of Silurian, below)

opera-house, sb. [?AB¹] *An opera-house has lately been built there which is in strong contrast with the shabby dens which usually do duty as theaters in cities of Burlington's size* 1883 LM lvii 562 (W: Loosely, in small towns, a theater. So S. A in DN.II,III, n.w.Ark. This sense not in OED C; cf. OED A theatre for the performance of operas. 1720)

operation, sb. [AB³] "*I've got some prodigious operations on foot*" 1873 GA viii 84 (OED 5b. A business transaction, esp. one of speculative character. Orig. *U.S.* OEDS 1832. . Not A in S U. This sense not in W C)

operator, sb. [?AB³] See *inflated* 1869. *The two young men went down to the Wall Street office of Henry's uncle and had a talk with that wily operator* 1873 GA xii 120 (OED 4. One who carries on financial operations in stocks, shares, or commodities. 1828. . So W S C U. Cf. above)

opossum, sb. [A] *In the woods were found the coon, the opossum...* 1873 GA xlv 407 (OED Small marsupial mammal of the Am. family *Didelphyidae*. 1610. . So W S C U B F Cl Th M DN.II)

or, sb. [D] See *coat-of arms* 1883 (OED *Heraldry*. The tincture gold or yellow in armorial bearings. 1562..1875—. So W S C U)

or, conj. [C] "*Would God I had died or I saw this day*" 1889 CY iii 46 (OED *arch* and *dial*. C. 1b. *c*1220. . 1886. So W S C U. *Dial* in Wr)

orator of the day. [?AB¹] *We passed the Fourth of July on board the "Quaker City" in mid-ocean...The President piped the Orator of the Day to quarters and he made the same old speech about our national greatness* 1869 IA x 92 (Phr. not in OED W S C)

orchestrelle, sb. [?AB¹] *Paine began playing on the orchestrelle Schubert's "Impromptu"* 1909 "Death of Jean" (1917) 124 (The "Aeolian Orchestrelle", a mechanical instrument installed by M. T. in 1904 in his home at 21 Fifth Avenue, N.Y., and thence removed to "Stormfield" in 1908; presented after his death to the Library of the State Historical Society at Columbia, Missouri; now in the Mark Twain Museum at Hannibal. See Paine's *Biog.* III 1227, 1446. Not in OED W S C; but cf. OED Orchestrina. b. A mechanical instrument intended to imitate the effect of an orchestra. 1838..)

order-book, sb. (?AB²) "*We are doing a ripping trade, too, as I could easily show you by my order-book for this trip* 1883 LM xxxix 414 (OED d. In business, a book in which the orders of customers are entered. 1893, only ex. So S C. Comb. not in W)

orderly sergeant, sb. [?AC] *He was made orderly sergeant* 1885 "Private Hist. of Campaign" 195 (OED 4. *Mil.* † The first sergeant of a company, whose duties formerly included the conveyance of orders. So W S. Not *obs* in C)

order-maker, sb. [B¹] *An official called an "Ordner"... a sergeant-at-arms... The weary President threatened to summon the dread order-maker* 1898 "Stirring Times in Austria" (1900) 306 (A nonce translation of German *Ordner.* Comb. not in OED W S C)

order-restoring, ppl.a. [B¹] *The President dispatches the Ordner...on his order-restoring mission* 1898 "Stirring Times in Austria" (1900) 307 (Comb. not in OED W S C)

organic, a. [B¹] See *technical* 1872 (Hum. malapropism)

Organic Act, sb. [AB³] *"We're not even a Territory, there's no Organic Act"* 1892 AmCl ii 35 (W: An act of Congress conferring powers of government upon the Territories. So S B OED Organic, a. 6b. 1883. Cf. Organic Law, A in OEDS 1849..; so Th T H. Comb. not in C)

organize, v. [?AB¹] *Some bundles of ancient and dirty straw...these could not rightly be called beds, for they were not organized; they were kicked into a general pile, mornings, and selections made from the mass at night* 1881 PP ii 28. *"I'll get you organized in no time'* 1892 AmCl ii 35. *"When we organize, we'll get three shares for one"* 1904 "Bequest" (1906) ii 7 (U: To give structural, systematic shape or form to; to arrange, group. This *spec* sense not in OED W S C; cf. OED 2. *gen.* To form into a whole with mutually connected and dependent parts. Cf. reorganize, below.)

organ-tone, sb. [B²] *There was nothing weak in the deep organ tones that responded* 1894 PW xii 773 (OED 1901, only ex. Comb. not in W S C)

orgy, sb. [B¹] *"We'll hold our orgies there, too. It's an awful snug place for orgies." "What's orgies?" "I dono. But robbers always have orgies, and of course we've got to have them, too"* 1876 TS xxxiii 258. See *mule-race* 1883." *So it's fitten that his funeral orgies sh'd be public... I say orgies, not because it's the common term, because it ain't—obsequies bein' the common term—but because orgies is the right term. Obsequies ain't used in England no more now—it's gone out. We say orgies now in England...It's a word that's made up of the Greek 'orgo', outside, open, abroad; and the Hebrew 'jeesum', to plant, cover up; hence inter. So you see, funeral orgies is an open or public funeral"* 1884 HF xxv 254. *It was a sort of mad orgy of joy* 1898 "From the London Times of 1904" (1900) 141. (W: *pl.* Humorously misused for *obsequies* by Mark Twain. These malapropisms not noted by OED S C. One of M.T.'s favorite words)

originating, vbl.sb. [B¹] *His mind had done the originating and telegraphing, and mine the receiving* 1891 "Mental Telegraphy" 98 (Not in OED W S C as vbl.sb.)

ornery, a. [AB³] *He warn't worth a cent but to set around and look ornery* 1865 "Jumping Frog" (1875) 32. *"I got to go to church and sweat and sweat...I hate them ornery sermons"* 1876 TS xxxv 270. *"I proved by eleven witnesses that the cat was of a low character and very ornery"* 1877 "Some Rambling Notes" iii 723. See *lowdown* 1884. *It was the orneriest, low-downest thing he ever heard of* 1896 TSD iii 350 (OEDS *U.S. colloq.* Poor in quality; mean, low. 1816.. So W S C U Wr B F Cl Th M DN.I,II,III,IV,V AS.II.361; reported from Mass., Conn., W.Va., Ky., Ohio, Ind., Ill., Iowa, Mo., and Texas. In AS.IX.276, Mr. A. W. Read states that the word formerly carried an indecent implication; but there seems to be no trace of this in M.T.'s usage)

ornithologer, sb. [?C] *I could have been an ornithologer myself, because I always loved birds* 1893 TSA v 124 (OED Ornithologist. *rare.* 1661, only ex. Not in W S C. More likely a fresh coinage by M.T. than a survival)

ornithorhyncus, sb. [B¹] *That curious combination of bird, fish, amphibian, burrower, crawler, quadruped, and Christian called the Ornithorhyncus* 1897 FE viii 102.

See also *anisodactylous* 1906; *superimbrication* 1906 (Nonsense use. Cf. OED An aquatic mammal of Australia. 1800..; so W S C)

os frontis, sb. [B¹] See *maxillary* 1870 (Frontal bone or forehead. The Latin term not in OED W S C)

osteopath, sb. [?AB³] See *osteopathy* 1900 (OED U.S. ex. 1897.. Not A in W S C. Cf. below)

osteopathic, a. [?AB³] See *osteopathy* 1900 (OED U.S. quot. 1899, only ex. Not A in W S C. Cf. below)

osteopathy, sb. [?AB²] *I do not believe there is any difference between Kellgren's science and osteopathy; but I am sending to America to find out* 1899 Letter quoted in Paine's *Biog.* II 1087, as written in the summer of 1899. *Dr. Still, in the middle of Kansas, began to experiment in 1874, only five years after Kellgren began the same work obscurely in the village of Gotha, in Germany... This new science was well known in America under the name of Osteopathy...It has established 20 Osteophathic schools and colleges...Presently the Osteopath will come over here from America* 1900 *Letters* (1917) II xxxix 689. *I was born in Missouri. Osteopathy was born in the same State* 1901 "Osteopathy" *Speeches* (1910) 255 (OED 2. A theory of disease and method of cure founded on the assumption that deformation of some part of the skeleton and consequent interference with the adjacent nerves and blood-vessels are the cause of most diseases. 1899, quot. from *Brit. Med. Journ.* Mar. 11: *"Dr. A. T. Still...was, in 1889...delivered of a new system, the name of which was called 'osteopathy' "*. Not A in W S C U. There would seem to be no room for doubt that M.T. was correct about the Am. origin of the word, however much conflict may exist about priority in the theory)

Other Place, sb. [B¹] *Washington was alternately in paradise or the other place just as it happened that Louise was gracious to him or seemingly indifferent* 1873 GA xi 108. *We only had one brief little season of heaven during all this diligent and acrimonious reproduction of the other place* 1880 TA ix 86 (Euphemism for 'Hell'. This usage not in OED W S C)

Other Side, sb. [B¹] *It is my desire that such journals as have obituaries of me lying in their pigeon-holes will... kindly send me a marked copy...I will correct them... striking out such clauses as could have a deleterious influence on the Other Side, and replacing them with clauses of a more judicious character* 1906 "Amended Obituaries" 232 (Comb. not in OED W S C; but cf. W The other world: the world beyond the grave)

other thing, sb. **to do the other thing.** [?AB²] *Senator Jones would have examined the machine and approved, or done the other thing* 1890 *Letters* (1917) II xxx 530 (OEDS Other, a. 2. *colloq.* The contrary, opposite, or reverse. 1929. Phrase not in W S C)

ouch, int. [?AB³] *He stuck a pin in another boy to hear him say "Ouch!"* 1876 TS iv 46. *If a door banged, Aunt Sally she jumped and said "ouch!"* 1884 HF xxxix 400. *"En bang-bang went de pistols, en de twin he say, 'Ouch!'—hit him on de hand dis time"* 1894 PW xiv 780. *I put my finger in, to feel it, and said ouch!* 1905 "Eve's Diary" 28 (OEDS An exclamation expressing pain or annoyance. 1837.. So W S C. A in Wr B F Cl Th M DN.I,II,III)

ought, v. **hadn't ought.** [?AB³E] See *go,* v. 1883 (OED IV.7. c. *Hadn't ought*=ought not to have. Vulgar Eng., earliest ex. U.S. 1836.. A in Wr B M DN.III,V. Not A in W. This usage not in S C)

ourn, poss.pron. [?AE] *They've got all their own money back, and all of ourn but a shekel or two"* 1884 HF xxx 313 (OED *dial.* These *-n* forms are midland and southern. c1380..1861. W: *Obs* exc. *dial.* A in S C Wr M DN.II,III,V AS.III,5; V.267, Ozarks; XI.351, e. Texas. Cf. hern, and his'n, above)

out, adv. **from this out.** [AB²] *I think I can behave myself from this out* 1884 *Speeches* (1923) 1. *"You's young Marse Tom fum dis out"* 1893 PW iii 239 (OEDS

3c. Henceforth. *U.S.* 1905. Not A in C. Phrase not in W S)

out, adv. [?AB¹] *There was a flush out agin him, and naterally...he went under* 1867 SNO (1875) 74 (*Poker.* In play; among the cards or hands competing. This sense not in OED W S C)

out, sb. [?A] *He had left out a couple of words in a thin-spaced page of solid matter...In the line in which the "out" had been made...*1906 *Autob* (1924) II 281 (OED 5. *Printing.* An omission. 1784..1864. So W S C. A in H)

out, v. to out with. [?AB³] *"Quicker than lightning I out with the Allen and let him have it"* 1872 RI vii 66. *Then you'll out with the pipes* 1876 TS ii 14. See *five*, sb. 1876. *"He outs with a match"* 1877 "Some Rambling Notes" ii 591. See *coal-oil* 1883. *Then I out with my saw and went to work on that log again* 1884 HF vii 50 (OED 4b. *colloq.* 1802.. So Wr W C. Phrase not in S. When uninflected, the word is to be interpreted rather as OED Out, adv. 13b. *c*1205..)

out-and-out, a. [?AB³] See *book-talk* 1880; *blister* 1884. *"I ain't got no disposition to throw anything in the way of a fair, open, out-and-out investigation"* 1884 HF xxix 299 (OED Complete, thorough-going. 1813.. So W S C. A in DN.III,IV, Virginia)

out back, adv. [?AB¹] *There was a message now from out back* 1892 AmCl iii 36 (From the back or rear part of the house. This sense not in OED W S C)

out-cabin, sb. [?AB¹] *He slept in an out-cabin near Flint's* 1902 "DBDS" (1928) 309 (Comb. not in OED W S C; but cf. OED Outhouse, 1533.. Out-hut, 1856)

outcropping, vbl.sb. [B³] See *arrastre* 1909 (OED *Mining.* The part of a stratum that crops out. 1872.. So S. Not in W C)

outdoors, sb. [?AB¹] See *indoors*, sb. 1873 (Not in OED W S C as sb. Cf. OEDS Outdoors, adv. 1817.. A in DN.III)

outen, prep. [?AC] *He'd yank a sinner outen Hades* 1867 SNO (1875) 74. See *white-oak* 1873. *"Her husban' was a nigger king outen Africa—en yit here you is, a-slinkin' outen a duel!"* 1894 PW xiv 779. *"A Yank outen New England"* 1894 PW xviii 18. *"Here's de biggest giant outen de 'Rabian Nights a comin' for us!"* 1894 TSA xii 540 (OED *obs* exc. *dial.* B.1. Without, outside, away from. *c*1250, only ex. So W S. The Am. use is better defined in C: Out; out of; out from. A in Wr B DN.II,III AS.III.11, Ozarks)

out-engineer, v. [B¹] *"Jeff Thompson can out-engineer any civil engineer that ever sighted through an aneroid"* 1873 GA xxvii 246 (Not in OED W S C; but cf. OED Out- in comb. 23a. 1601..; e.g. to out-bishop the bishop, 1781; to out-saint the saint, 1612)

outer-border, sb. [B¹] *No clutter on the sidewalks, no outer-borders fraying out into dirty lanes and tin-patched huts* 1897 FE xxix 282 (Comb. not in OED W S C; but cf. OED Outer edge, 1902; Outer line, 1530)

outfit, sb. [AB³] *Livy, dear, I have bought full wedding outfit today a*1870 Letter in Clara Clemens, *My Father* (1931) 18. *In that day, all explorers traveled with an outfit of priests* 1883 LM ii 31. *Around her head she wore a hoop of flame-red poppies. It was as sweet an outfit as ever I saw* 1889 CY ii 26. See also *nobby* 1894 (OEDS 3. A set of things for any purpose. *U.S. colloq.* 1869.. Cf. Th: In the far West, everything is an outfit, from a railway train to a pocket-knife. A in B F Cl T M H DN.III AS.VI.257; VII.5. Not A in W S U. This sense not in C)

outfit, v. [AB³] *"A scheme for getting rich by selling it at famine prices to the crowned heads over in Europe to outfit their palaces with"* 1894 PW xi 553 (OED From prec. sb.: To provide with an outfit; to fit out. 1848.. Cf. above. So W S C U. A in B F Cl)

outlander, sb. [?AC] *To my mind, one relative or neighbor mixed up in a scandal is more interesting than a whole Sodom and Gomorrah of outlanders gone rotten*

1906 "Italian without a Master" 174 (OED A man of foreign nationality; a stranger. Now *poetic*, or a literary revival. 1605..1887. So S. Not *arch* in W C U Wr, and app. not so felt by M.T.)

outlandish, a. [?A] *Outlandish names of streets and courts and byways* 1873 *Letters* (1917) I xii 208 (OED 2. Foreign-looking, odd, bizarre. 1596..1885. So W S C U. A in Wr DN.III,IV,V)

outlaw, v. trans. [A] *A debt outlawed by the statute of limitations* 1873 LM xlii 433 (OED 2. To deprive of legal force. Now only in U.S. 1647..1864. So W Th T. Not A in S C U)

outlaw, v. intr. [?AB²] *Honour is a harder master than the law. It cannot compromise for less than a hundred cents on the dollar, and its debts never outlaw* 1895, quoted in Paine's *Biog.* II 1007, from M.T.'s 1895 statement to the press relative to his bankruptcy (OED 2b. *intr.* for *refl.* 1895, this quot. The *intr.* sense not in W S C)

outlay, sb. [?AB¹] *He could play billiards tolerably well. I said: "Take a ball and begin, Mr. Dalton. How many can you run with an outlay like that?"* 1907 "Chaps. from Autob" 679 (Layout, 'set-up', 'spread'. No *billiards* sense in OED W S C. Doubtless *layout* was the word that M.T. actually used, and its replacement by *outlay* here is another example of Mr. Paine's "polishing". For other exs. see under *guts*, above)

output, sb. [B¹] *The tiger's annual output of slaughtered human beings in India* 1897 FE lvii 545. *The little newspaper was a Thursday sheet. Tilbury's letter had started in plenty of time to make connection for the next output* 1904 "Bequest" (1906) 12 (Hum. twist of meaning from OED: The product of any industry or exertion, viewed quantitatively.. orig. a technical or local term of iron-works, coal-mines, etc. 1858.. So W S C U)

outrage, sb. [B¹] *"Who is that smooth-faced, animated outrage yonder in the fine clothes?"* 1869 IA iii 35. See also *bracketed* 1883; *horrible-looking* 1884 (Hum. *transf.* use, not in OED W S C)

outside, adv. [?AB²] *Outside we could see that there was a tremendous sea on* 1869 IA ii 29 (OED C.1.In the open sea beyond the harbour. 1872, this quot., wrongly dated. So S C. This sense not in W)

outside, adv. [?AB¹] *Here was the clear Ohio water inshore...and outside was the old regular Muddy* 1884 HF xvi 143 (In the direction away from the nearer river bank; an extension of the sense above. This *spec* river sense not in OED W S C. Cf. *inside*, above)

outside, adv. [?AB¹] *"Come ahead on the stabboard! Stop her! Let your outside turn over slow"* 1876 TS ii 29. *"Set her back on de outside...Come ahead on de inside"* 1894 PW xviii 19 (Of a river steamboat: The sidewheel farther from the shore. This *spec* sense not in OED W S C)

outstart, sb. [?AB³] *I judged they had our gang in a pretty tight place right at the outstart* 1884 HF xxix 299 (OED 1866.. So W. Rare in S. A in Th.III. Not in C as sb.)

out-superintend, v. [B¹] *Tom superintended. He could out-superintend any boy I ever see* 1884 HF xxxviii 388 (Not in OED W S C; but cf. OED Out- in comb. 22. Out-general, 1767; out-captain, etc.)

outvote, v. [B¹] *Roxy was as white as anybody, but the one-sixteenth of her which was black outvoted the other fifteen parts and made her a negro* 1893 PW ii 236 (Here *fig*, to outweigh, overbalance. This sense not in OED W S C. Cf. OED To outnumber in voting. 1647..)

overalls, sb. [A] *We were dressed alike; blue army shirts, blue overalls* 1880 TA xi 102 (OED 2a. orig. *U.S.* 1782.. So H DN.II. Not A in W S C U)

overcoat, sb. [?AB³] *"Lay off your overcoat, Washington, and draw up to the stove"* 1873 GA vii 78 (OED A great-coat, top-coat. 1848.. So W S C U. A in Th T M)

over-conspicuous, a. [B¹] *"We have as much talent as other nations, but we are discouraged from making it over-conspicuous"* 1898 "Stirring Times" (1900) 291

(Comb. not in OED W S C; but cf. OED Over-famous, a1800)

over-described, ppl.a. [B¹] *I consider that that person is over-described* 1880 TA App.D 608 (Comb. not in OED W S C; but cf. OED Over-instructed, 1841)

over-description, sb. [B¹] *Under-description is bad enough, but over-description is surely worse* 1880 TA App. D 608 (Comb. not in OED W S C; but cf. OED Over-imitation, 1655)

overdo, v. [?AC] *I have been a dramatist for thirty years. I have had an ambition to overdo the work of the Spaniard who said he left behind him four hundred dramas when he died. I leave behind me four hundred and fifteen* 1900 Speeches (1910) 162 (OED 6. To surpass or exceed in performance; to outdo, excel. *arch. a*1625..1859. So W S. Not *arch* in C Wr, and app. not so felt by M.T.)

over-express, v. [B²] *Terms which did not over-express the admiration with which the people viewed them* 1883 LM xxxviii 399 (Given in OED Over- in comb. 27. *a*1900. No ex. So W. Not in S C)

over-flatter, v. [B¹] *It would not have surprised me, nor even over-flattered me* 1898 Autob (1924) I 133 (Comb. not in OED W S C))

overflow-meeting, sb. [?AB³] *When Rowena had at last done all her duty by the people in the parlor, she went upstairs to satisfy the longings of an overflow-meeting there* 1894 PW vi 335 (OED 1880, only ex. So S. A in Th.III. Comb. not in W C)

over-fondle, v. [B¹] *The number of compositions in which the word "beauteous" was overfondled* 1876 TS xxi 173 (To cultivate or employ to excess. This *fig* use not in OED W S C. The *lit.* use in OED 1714; so W)

over-gently, adv. [B¹] *The gang might not deal over-gently with an unpopular member* 1881 PP xxii 273 (Given in W. Not in OED S C)

over-kind, a. [B²] *"Then is thy grandam not overkind to thee, I take it"* 1881 PP iii 40 (OED 1899, only ex. So W S C)

overland, a. [AB²] *We were going in the overland stage from the Missouri frontier* 1872 RI i 20. See also *clear,* v. 1906 (OED (2) In America, any route westward from the Atlantic to the Pacific across the continent. No ex. Not A in W S C U)

over-patient, a. [B²] *"I like not much bandying of words, being not overpatient in my nature"* 1881 PP xii 137 (OED *a*1900, no ex. So W S. Comb. not in C)

over-plump, a. [B¹] *Others would have thought her a trifle over-plump* 1893 "Esquimau Maiden's Romance" (1900) 136 (Comb. not in OED S C; but cf. OED Over-fat, *c*1050. Given in W)

over-sentimental, a. [B¹] *He seemed over-sentimental* 1875 OTM 73 (Comb. not in OED S C; but cf. OED Over-sad, 1633. Given in W)

oversize, v. [?AC] *There is not any name among the world's nationalities that can oversize that one* [Ameri-

can] 1880 *M.T. the Letter Writer* (1932) iii 43. *Two or three thousand feet below us...were a lot of black and white sheep which looked merely like oversized worms* 1880 TA xxxv 385. *That list would oversize nearly anybody's geographical knowledge* 1887 "English as She Is Taught" (1917) 241. *"That one oversizes my hand. Gimme five cards"* 1904 "Italian without a Master" (1906) 177 (OED *obs.* 1. trans. To exceed in size. 1615, only ex. *Rare* in W C. This sense not in S. Obviously not felt as *obs* by M.T.)

overskirt, sb. [?AB²] See *gros de laine* 1880 (OED A second skirt, worn over the skirt of a dress. All exs. U.S. 1883.. Not A in W S C)

overtasked, ppl.a. [B²] *Relief for overtasked eyes and brain from study and sight-seeing* 1869 IA xxvii 289 (OED 1895, only ex. So W S C)

overterseness, sb. [B¹] *Baedeker, with his customary overterseness* 1880 TA xxxv 388 (Comb. not in OED W S C; but cf. OED Overdiffuseness, 1870)

overthwart, prep. [C] See *random*, v. 1889 (OED Now *obs* or *rare exc. dial*. 1. Across, athwart. *c*1380..1892. So S C. Not *obs* in W)

overthwart and endlong, adv. [C] *"My mind miscarrieth...in such sort that the words do seem to come endlong and overthwart"* 1889 CY xix 234 (OED Crosswise and lengthwise. *obs* or *rare*. 1340..1460; for this order cf. quot. 1417. Not *obs* in Wr. Phr. not in W S C)

owdawakk, sb. [B¹] See *kahkahponeeka* 1880 (Hum. invention)

owing, ppl.a. [?AB¹] *When I laid down my editorial pen I had four horsewhippings and two duels owing to me* 1906 Autob (1924) I 360 (Intended for, planned, threatening. This sense not in OED W S C. A hum. extension of the sense in OED 2. Owed, due. 1411.. Cf. need, v., above)

owing to, adv. phr. [B³] *Being crushed by a log at a smoke-house-raising, owing to carelessness on the part of all present* 1892 AmCl i 23 (OED 3b. On account of, because of. 1814.. So W S U. This use not in C. It is odd that this adv. use of *owing to* is held perfectly respectable by all authorities, whereas precisely the same use of *due to* is widely condemned)

own up, v. [?AB²] See *tuckered out* 1877. *The wise way would have been to frankly own up* 1880 TA xxv 249. *It was Dick Allbright's baby; he owned up and said so* 1883 LM iii 55. (OED 5c. To confess frankly. *colloq.* 1880.. So W S C U Wr. A in B Th,1862 T)

Oxford-trained, a. [B¹] *Oxford-trained aristocrats* 1892 AmCl x 102 (Comb. not in OED W S C)

oyster-supper, sb. [?AB³] *It is simply absurd to suppose that he* [Noah] *did not know any more than to feed the beasts on oyster suppers* 1869 IA xxxix 415 (OEDS 1835, 1856, both exs. U.S. A in M: The Englishman never goes to oyster-suppers. Comb. not in W S C)

P

pa, sb. [?AB³] *"But when he saw it was his pa, He changed his mind again, aha!"* 1891 *Slovenly Peter* (1935) 14 (OED A childish short form of 'papa.' 1811.. So W S C U. A in M DN.I,II,III,IV,VI)

pachydermata, sb.pl. [B¹] *He told me a great deal about worms, and the kangaroo, and other coleoptera, and said he knew the history and ways of all such pachydermata* 1897 FE viii 101 (Nonsense use)

Pacific-coaster, sb. [AB¹] *The men present were old gray Pacific-coasters* 1893 *Letters* (1917) II xxxiii 597 (Residents on the Pacific coast. Comb. not in OED W S C)

pack-mule, sb. [AB³] *The burdens of the pack-mules* 1880 TA xxxvii 421 (OEDS *U.S.* A mule used for carrying packs. 1839.. Not A in S C. Comb. not in W)

pack-train, sb. [AB³] *Shortly after six, our pack-train arrived* 1869 IA xli 435 (OEDS *U.S.* A train of pack-animals. 1856.. Not A in S C. Comb. not in W)

paddle-box, sb. [?AB³] See *rapids* 1869. *The paddle-boxes are gorgeous with a picture or with gilded rays above the boat's name* 1875 OTM 70. *She stood on the lower guard abaft the paddle-box* 1894 PW xvi 821 (OED The casing which encloses the upper part of a steamer's paddle-wheel. 1837.. So W S C U)

paid-up, a. [?AB¹] *"What the insurance companies call the 'endowment,' or the 'paid-up' plan, by which a policy is secured after a certain time without further payment"* 1873 GA xlviii 435 (So W, under Life Insurance. This insurance sense not in OED S C)

paingiving, a. [B¹] *The executioner...was a good painstaking and paingiving official* 1889 CY xviii 215 (Comb. not in OED W S C; cf. OED Painstaking, 1866..)

pain-killer, sb. [AB³] *Now she heard of Pain-killer for the first time. She ordered a lot at once* 1876 TS xii 109 (OEDS *U.S.* A medicine for relieving or abolishing pain. 1855.. So B: A nostrum made at Providence, R.I., which has a world-wide fame. Not A in W U. Comb. not in S C)

pain-proof, a. [B¹] *No Christian Science family would consider itself pain-proof without an Annex* 1903 "Chr. Sc." 3 (Comb. not in OED W S C; but cf. OED Pain-free, 1628)

palace-bordered, a. [B¹] *Along the palace-bordered canals of Venice* 1893 PW i 234 (Comb. not in OED W S C; but cf. OED Palace-covered, 1865)

palace-car, sb. [?AB³C] See *bicycle* 1899 (OEDS A railway carriage fitted up in luxurious style. Early exs. U.S. 1869.. A in S C B F Th.III T M. Cf. M: Now extinct. Not A or *obs* in W U)

palace-hotel, sb. [?AB²] See *bicycle* 1899 (OED A hotel of palatial splendour. 1900, only ex. Cf. OED Palatial hotel, 1884. Comb. not in W S C)

palace-shop, sb. [?AB¹] *In Broadway...when one is walking cityward, and has before him the long lines of palace-shops* 1873 GA xii 114 (Comb. not in OED W S C. Cf. above)

paladin, sb. [B²] *All France, except a couple of dozen moral paladins, lay under the smother of the silent-assertion lie* 1899 "My First Lie" (1928) 161 (OED *fig.* A knightly hero. No ex. *fig* use. So S C U. The *fig* sense not in W)

palatial car, sb. [AB¹] *"As the down noon express was leaving H— yesterday a lady...attempted to force herself into the already full palatial car"* 1873 GA xxix 267 (A in F. Comb. not in OED W S C. Cf. palace-car and -hotel, above, and parlor-car below. The dates suggest an interesting linguistic rivalry, in which the clumsy and pretentious 'palatial car' was superseded by the merely pretentious 'palace-car,' and both in turn replaced by the more modest 'parlor-car,' and later still by the current 'Pullman car' or 'first-class carriage')

palaver, sb. [?AB¹] *I have been a quartz miner...and know all the palaver of that business* 1909 ISD vii 74

(Lingo, jargon, special trade vocabulary. This sense not in OED W S C)

pale, sb. [B¹] *I reckoned they'd turn pale. But no, nary a pale did they turn* 1884 HF xxix 295 (Hum. nonce use)

pale-face, sb. [AB³] *"Noble Red Men...the pale-face from beyond the great waters greets you all"* 1869 SNO (1875) 69 (OED A name for a white man attributed to the N. Am. Indians or 'red men.' 1822.. So W S C U B F Th T M AS.VII.1)

palings, sb. pl. [?AB³] *They swarmed up in front of Sherburn's palings as thick as they could jam together. It was a little twenty-foot yard* 1884 HF xxii 218. See *smoke-house* 1897. *"Iron fence?" "No, palings."* 1902 "Belated Russ. Passport" (1928) 193 (OED 3c. 1834.. So W S C U. A in DN.II,III)

paling fence, sb. [?AB³] *Hawkins put up the first "paling" fence that had ever adorned the village* 1873 GA v 60. *Then quite a group of boys and girls came by, and stood looking over the paling fence* 1876 TS xvii 145. *Large grassy yard, with paling fence painted white* 1883 LM xxxviii 400. (OED 1805. OEDS Later *U.S.* exs. 1843..1901. Comb. not in W S C)

pall-bearer, sb. [AB¹] *"Hump yourselves, you petrifactions, snail-bellies, pall-bearers!"* 1883 LM xx 244 (Hum. *fig* nonce use as a disparaging epithet)

palmetto, sb. [A] See *pawpaw* 1883 (OED Name of several smaller species of palms...of the South-eastern U.S. 1624, first Am. quot...So W S C U)

palmiste, sb. [B¹] *Another dish, called palmiste* [in Mauritius] *is like raw turnip-shavings and tastes like green almonds. Costs the life of a palm tree, for it is the pith* 1897 FE lxiii 627 (Not in OED W S C)

pan, sb. [?AB²] *We got many good "prospects," but when the gold gave out in the pan and we dug down, hoping and longing, we found only emptiness...At last we shouldered our pans and shovels and struck out over the hills to try new localities* 1872 RI lxi 443. See also *horn* 1893 (OED 2e. A circular sheet-iron dish in which gold is separated from gravel, crushed quartz, etc., by agitation and washing. 1875.. So W S C. A in AS.VII. 427)

pan, v.trans. [?AB³] *He never could altogether understand that eternal sinkin' of a shaft an' never pannin' out anything* 1872 RI lxi 441 (OED 1. To separate by washing in a pan. 1872, this quot... OEDS 1859. So W S C U. A in B AS.II.86)

pan, v.intr. [?AB³] *Out there on the hillside while you and dear old Stoker panned and washed* 1870 *Letters* (1917) i ix 170. *We had panned up and down the hillsides till they looked plowed like a field* 1872 RI lxi 443 (OED 1b. To search or try for gold with the pan. 1872, quot. from RI. OEDS 1850. So W C. A in S B AS.II.86)

Panama hat, sb. [AB³] *They dressed in white linen and wore broad Panama hats* 1884 HF xviii 162 (OED A misnomer for a hat made from the undeveloped leaves of the stemless screwpine of tropical S. America. 1833.. So W S U. Comb. not in U)

panegyrics, sb. [B¹] *When writers try to distribute their gratitude here and there and yonder by detail they run across difficulties...and when they appear we know that man has got the panegyrics* 1897 FE xi 125 (Nonce use, on the model of 'hysterics')

panful, sb. [?AB²] See *prospect,* sb. 1872 (OED U.S. exs. 1874.. Not A in W C U. Not in S)

panning out, vbl.sb. [?AB¹] *"Panning out" refers to the washing process by which the grains of gold are separated from the dirt* 1872 RI lxi 443 (A in T. Comb. not in OED W S C; but cf. OED Panning, vbl.sb., 1870)

panoply, v. [B²] *It would be judicious to send her forth well panoplied. So he had added new and still richer costumes, and costly jewelry* 1873 GA xxxii 290. See also *walking-costume* 1880 (OED b. *fig.* To array with something brilliant. 1895, only ex. So W S. This sense not in C)

panoramist, sb. [B¹] *The Scriptural Panoramist* (title) 1871 SNO (1875) 296 (The manager of a panorama exhibition or show. Given in OED W S only as: A painter of panoramas. 1881.. Not in C)

pan out, v. [?AB³] *"How'd the old thing pan out this time, duke?"* 1884 HF xxiii 229 (OED 4b. *fig.* To yield results, succeed. 1871.. So W C U. A in S F Cl Th T M DN.III)

pantalettes, sb.pl. [AB³] *He saw a new girl in the garden...with white summer frock and embroidered pantalettes* 1876 TS iii 35. *Children in slippers and scalloped pantalettes* 1883 LM xxxviii 403 (OED Worn by young girls *c*1825-53. Chiefly *U.S.* OEDS 1834.. So T. Not A in W S C U)

pantaloons, sb.pl. [AB³] See *buckskin-seated* 1869. *My money was with my pantaloons, and my pantaloons were with the Indians* 1869 SNO (1875) 71. See also *country-woven* 1872 (OED 3d. Trousers generally, esp. in U.S. 1804.. So Th AS.II.31. Not A in W S C U)

panther, sb. [A] *A huge panther had been killed* 1873 GA xxix 270 (OED 2. Applied in America to the puma or cougar. 1730.. So W S C U Cl)

pantograph, sb. [B¹] *"Take the third pantograph marked B"* 1894 PW xxi 239 (A drawing made by means of a pantograph. This sense not in OED W S C, which refer only to the instrument itself, OED 1803..)

pants, sb.pl. [AB³] *The chief editor had a long-tailed black cloth frock-coat on, and white linen pants* 1869 SNO (1875) 45. *Pants "holy" at the knees* 1894 PW iv 330 (OED 1a. A vulgar abbreviation of Pantaloons. Chiefly *U.S.* OEDS 1842.. So B F Cl Th M DN.IV AS.V.286. Not A in W S C U)

pap, sb. [AB³] *"She witched pap. Pap says so his own self"* 1876 TS vi 66. *"Pap's so po' he can't run me no mo'"* 1880 TA xxiii 225. *Pap he hadn't been seen for more than a year* 1884 HF iii 18. So *passim* in TS and HF (OEDS *U.S.* 1844.. So C F DN.II,III,V, s.e.Mo., n.w.Ark., s.Ind. Not A in W S)

paper-collar, sb. [?AB¹] See *breech-clout* 1899 (Comb. not in OED W S C; but cf. OED Paper-collared, no ex. A cheap collar made of paper with glazed surface, to be used but once and then discarded. This Am. invention has now gone out of use)

paper-overlaid, ppl.a. [B¹] *He was wheezing the music of "Camptown Races" out of a paper-overlaid comb which he was pressing against his mouth* 1880 TA xxiii 229 (Comb. not in OED W S C; but cf. OED Paper-covered, 1872..)

paper-stock, sb. [B²] *A scheme to plant a swamp with cane to grow paper-stock* 1873 GA xv 40 (OED Raw material from which paper is made. 1875, only ex. So S C. Comb. not in W)

pappoose, sb. [A] *"Is he satisfied to make bead reticules for the pappooses of the paleface?"* 1869 SNO (1875) 68 (OED A N.Am. Indian young child. 1634.. So W S C U B F Cl T M DN.III,IV AS.II.29)

pappy, sb. [?AC] *"Oh, pappy, how could you!"* 1892 AmCl xv 159 (OED A child's pet name for 'father.' Now *rare.* 1763..1897. Not *rare* in W C. A in DN.III, IV,V. Not in S)

paralyze, v. [?AB³] *Both were so paralyzed with joy* 1892 AmCl xii 125 (OED 2. *fig.* To deprive of power of action. 1805.. So W S C U. A in Th.III)

parcel, sb. Spelled **passel.** [?AE] *"I begin to reckon you was a passel of sickly fools"* 1872 RI ii 27. *"I don't mind a passel of guests"* 1877 Speeches (1910) 4. *Smiling and bobbing their heads like a passel of sapheads* 1884 HF xxv 248. See also *kid* 1907 (OED 6b. In depreciative or contemptuous use: A 'lot,' 'set,' 'pack.' 1607.. 1881. This form 19th c. *dial.* So W S C. A in Wr M DN.II,III,V AS.V.201, Ozarks)

pard, sb. [AB²] See *cheese it, chip in, raise out, rustler,* all 1872 RI. *"Here now, don't you hit my pard!"* 1876 TS ix 89. *"One of my pards was a man named Dick Allbright"* 1883 LM iii 50. *I said I was an officer in disguise, and my pard was yonder at the door* 1889 CY xxxvii 481 (OED *slang,* chiefly *U.S.* 1872, quot. from RI.. So W S C UB F Th T M DN.III,IV)

pardy, int. [C] *"Pardy, the woman's case is rotten at the source"* 1889 CY xxv 318 (OED *arch.* Verily, certainly. *c*1290..1842. So W S C Wr)

paregoric, v. [B¹] *I paregoricked the men, established the watch, and went to bed* 1880 TA xxxix 454 (Not in OED W S C as verb)

parenthesis disease, sb. [B¹] *We have the Parenthesis disease in our literature, too; and one may see cases of it every day in our books and newspapers* 1880 TA App.D 604 (Comb. not in OED W S C)

parenthesis-mark, sb. [B¹] *In the original there are no parenthesis-marks or hyphens* 1880 TA App. D 603 (Comb. not in OED W S C. Cf. exclamation-point, above)

parent-honoring, a. [B¹] *So he went away with the parent-honoring student* 1880 TA xx 194 (Comb. not in OED W S C)

Paris, sb. Spelled **Pairree, Parry.** [E] *He called Paris "Pairree" in ordinary English conversation* 1869 IA xxiii 234. *"It's real pitiful the way the children pine for Parry"* 1873 GA xxxiii 305 (W: Humorously often so pronounced, approximately the French pron. This pron. not mentioned in OED S C)

parlor, sb. [AB³] *A gratis quart of strawberry water-ice arrived from Hostetter's Ladies' and Gents' Ice-Cream Parlors* 1904 "Bequest" (1906) iii 15 (OED 4. *U.S.* Commercial cant. 1890. So W S C U Cl H DN.II)

parlor-car, sb. [AB³?C] *The smoking-compartment in the parlor-car was full* 1893 "Travelling with a Reformer" (1900) 355 (OED *U.S.* A luxuriously fitted railway carriage. 1882.. So W C U M H. Not A in S. M: Now elbowed out by *Pullman.*)

parlor-desperado, sb. [?AB¹] *"Drop your hand, you parlor-desperado"* 1902 "DBDS" (1928) 355 (Comb. not in OED W S C. Cf. desperadoism, above)

parlor-magic, sb. [B²] *Merlin is a very passable artist in the parlor-magic line* 1889 CY xxii 276 (OED Feats of legerdemain performed in or suited to a parlor. No ex. Comb. not in W S C)

parlous, a. [C] *"Sir, it is parlous news I bring"* 1889 CY xxi 264 (OED *arch* and *dial.* A syncopated form of Perilous. *a*1400.. 1892. So W C U. Not *arch* in S Wr)

part, sb. [AB²] *He brushed his hair with elaborate care, accomplishing an accurate 'part' behind* 1871 SNO (1875) 260 (OED 17. The parting of the hair. *U.S.* 1890.. So W S C)

particle, sb. [C] *Now began a movement of the gorgeous particles of that official group* 1881 PP xxxii 374 (OED 1. A small part, portion, or division of a whole. Now rare or obs. 1380..1836. This sense not in W S C)

particular, a. [B³] See *heifer* 1872. *"Aunt Polly's awful particular about this fence; it's got to be done very careful"* 1876 TS ii 30. *All I wanted was a change, I warn't particular* 1884 HF i 4. *"Much diff'rence dat make! White folks ain't particular"* 1894 PW xvi 821. See *cantankerously* 1894. *I have never married a Clemens myself, and should think twice before I ventured such a thing; still, less particular people have taken the risk* 1899 M.T. the Letter Writer (1932) vi 90 (OED 10. Exacting in regard to details, nice in taste, fastidious. 1814.. So W S C U Wr. A favorite word with M.T.)

partner, sb. [AB¹] *Mr. Bixby's partner grounded the boat* 1875 OTM 222. *"Partner" is technical for "the other pilot"* do. 284 (This *spec* sense not in OED W S C)

partridge, sb. [A] See *batter-cake* 1897 (OED 1b. In U.S. popularly applied to several birds of the Grouse Family and the Pheasant Family. 1634.. So W S C U M DN.II,III,IV AS.II.30)

party, sb. [?AC] *They can't appreciate a party's efforts* 1868 SNO (1875) 152. *"In the saloon playing poker with that long-haired party with the striped trousers"* 1873 GA xiii 123 (OED 14. Now shoppy, vulgar, or jocular, the proper word being 'person.' *c*1460..1888. So W S C U)

party-collar, sb. [?AB¹] *In America if you know which party-collar a voter wears, you know what his associations are* 1906 "WIM" (1917) iv 44 (Comb. not in OED W S C; but cf. OED Collar, sb. 5. A band of iron.. worn as a badge of servitude. 1480.. Cf. also tax-collar, below)

pass, sb. [AB¹] *The width* [of the Mississippi] *steadily diminishes until, at the "Passes," above the mouth, it is but little over half a mile* 1883 LM i 22 (C: One of the channels in the delta of a river; as, the passes of the Mississippi. *Southern U.S.* This *spec* Mississippi sense not in OED W S)

pass, v. [AB²] *I shall never want another Turkish lunch...The fellow took a mass of sausage-meat and... laid it aside and a dog walked sadly in and nipped it... The cook took it away from him and laid it before us. Jack said, "I pass"—he plays euchre sometimes—and we all passed in turn* 1869 IA xxxiv 375 (OED 26b. In euchre: To decline or voluntarily forego one's opportunity. 1884, only ex. So W S C)

pass, v. **to pass the time of day.** [?AB³] See *mainbrace, to splice* 1908 (OED 52c. To exchange salutations. Earliest exs. U.S. 1836.. *Colloq* in W C. Phr. not in S)

passenger-bear, sb. [B¹] See *verge stay* 1873 (Nonce comb.)

passenger-car, sb. [?AB²] *There were two passenger-cars* 1880 TA xxix 305 (OED Passenger, sb. 7. 1881. So W S. A in C)

passenger coach, sb. [?AB³] *There are gentlemen in England who drive four-horse passenger coaches twenty or thirty miles on a daily line* 1876 TS ii 32 (OED 1841.. Comb. not in W S C. A in M)

passenger-dog, sb. [B¹] *They made friends with the passenger-dog chained under the life-boat* 1873 GA iv 43 (Nonce comb.)

passenger-kennel, sb. [B¹] *"That train from Maryborough will consist of eighteen freight cars and two passenger-kennels"* 1897 FE xxxi 295 (Nonce comb.)

passenger-list, sb. [B¹] *We had the whole passenger list for company* 1869 IA xx 199 (Comb. not in OED S C. Given in W)

passenger-packet, sb. [B¹] *He was once fellow-pilot with George Ealer, on a great New Orleans passenger-packet* 1875 OTM 451 (Comb. not in OED W S C)

passing, adv. [C] *Sir Arthur looked on the sword and liked it passing well* 1889 CY iii 48 (OED Exceedingly, very. Now somewhat *arch.* 1387..1891. So S U. Not *obs* in W C)

paster, sb. [AB³] *"They'll change the tickets and baggage pasters for me"* 1902 "Belated Russ. Passport" (1928) 175 (OEDS 2. *U.S.* 1885.. So W S C F Th.III, 1870)

pastorate, sb. [B¹] *For five-and-twenty years I was under the Rev. Mr. Twichell's tuition, I was in his pastorate, occupying a pew in his church* 1902 Speeches (1910) 372 (Parish, congregation. This sense not in OED W S C)

pastor emeritus, sb. [?AB¹] *She appointed herself Pastor Emeritus...It advertises her as being a merely honorary official. The Czar of Russia is Emperor Emeritus on the same terms* 1907 CS II vii 162 (Comb. not in OED W S C. A *spec* Christian Science use)

patch-eyed a. [B¹] *"I've had dreams enough all night —with that patch-eyed Spanish devil going for me"* 1876 TS xxvii 209 (Comb. not in OED W S C; but cf. OED Patch, sb. 1c. A pad or piece of cloth worn to protect an injured eye. 1598..)

patent-leathers, sb.pl. [?AB¹] *He began to check off the luxuries which he should earliest wish to secure. "Horse—buggy—lap-robe—patent-leathers—dog—plug hat"* 1904 "Bequest" (1906) ii 9 (Shoes or boots made of patent leather. This sense not in OED W S C)

patent-medicine, sb. [?AB²] *Kanakas will lie—lie like patent-medicine advertisements* 1866 Speeches (1923) 7. See *rock-cutting* 1873; *fence,* v. 1886. *It is probably the old original first patent-medicine* 1890 "Majestic Literary Fossil" 444 (OEDS In popular use incorrectly applied to any proprietary medicine. 1899.. So W S C U. A in DN.III)

patent-right, sb. [?AB³] *"If it's a patent-right, there's no money in it"* 1893 TSA i 23 (OED The exclusive right conferred by letters patent. 1825.. So W S C. A in B F)

Patrick, sb. [?AB¹] See *mining-tax* 1870 (An Irishman. This sense not in OED W S C; but cf. OED Pat: a nickname for an Irishman, 1825..; so Paddy, 1780..)

patriotisms, sb. pl. [B¹] See *shabbinesses* 1895 (*Concr.* sense not in OED W S C)

patriot-maker, sb. [B¹] *O illustrious company of the Builders, Defenders, and Patriot-Makers of the grateful Republic!* 1905 "Concerning Copyright" 5 (Comb. not in OED W S C)

pattern, sb. [B¹] *He made each individual line of the bewildering maze of whorls or curves or loops which constituted the "pattern" of a "record" stand out bold and black by reenforcing it with ink* 1894 PW xxi 235. See also *finger-ball* 1894 (The convolutions in a finger-print. This *spec* sense not in OED W S C; but cf. in gen. sense OED 8b. Applied to a style of figuring or marking of natural or fortuitous origin. 1849..)

pattie, sb. [?AB¹] *Mintz and Mountz, the catties, Lift up their little patties* [German: "Und Minz und Maunz, die Katzen, Erheben ihre Tatzen, Sie drohen mit den Pfoten"] 1891 *Slovenly Peter* (1935) 6 (Hands, paws. Not in OED W S C)

pauperize, v. [B¹] *He did not propose to pauperize his farm by applying his personal ignorance to working it* 1883 LM xlix 487 (To impoverish, make poor, exhaust the fertility or richness of. This *transf.* sense not in OED W S C)

paupershod, a. [B¹] *The poor devil...so threadbare and paupershod as to raiment* 1892 AmCl i 6 (Comb. not in OED W S C; but cf. OED Pauperfed, 1845)

paust, sb. [?AB¹E] *Tramping miners dumped their paust shovels by the threshold* 1872 RI lxi 443 (Not in OED W S C in this form. Possibly the same as OED Post, sb.⁵ 2. *Metallurgy.* A batch of ore for smelting at one time. 1839, only ex. So W S. This word is from German *Posten,* parcel, lot, batch of ore, which is of course pronounced with a short or open *o.* M.T.'s sp. with *au* may be his attempt to render the sound of a word which he knew only in the spoken language of the miners)

paw, v. [B¹] *I don't care to have the critics paw the book at all* 1889 Letters (1917) II xxix 513 (To subject to crude or impertinent criticism. This sense not in OED W S C. A *fig* extension of OED 3a. To handle, esp. coarsely or rudely, *colloq.* 1604..)

paw-mark, sb. [B¹] *"Are you going to ornament the royal palaces with nigger paw-marks?"* 1894 PW xx 234 (A disparaging name for a finger-print. Comb. not in OED W S C)

Pawnee, sb. [AB¹] *The oldest Americans are the Pawnees* 1901 "To the Person Sitting in Darkness" 163. See also *Blackfoot* 1906 (S: One of a tribe of N. Am. Indians of Caddoan stock, formerly in Nebraska and Kansas. So W C. Not in OED)

pawpaw, sb. [A] *The abundant growth of the pawpaw, palmetto, and orange* [at Natchez, Mississippi] 1883 LM xxxix 409. *I remember the pawpaws, the hazelnuts, and the persimmons* 1897-8 *Autob* (1924) I 110 (OED 2. Name in U.S. for a small N. Am. tree, *Asimina triloba* ...or for its oblong edible fruit. 1760.. So W S C U B F Cl Th,1613 M AS.II,29,IV.9)

paynim, sb. [C] *"A crusade is a war to recover the Holy Land from the paynims"* 1893 TSA i 23 (OED 2. *arch* and *poetic.* 1382..1848. So W S C U)

pay-rock, sb. [?AB²] *We'll have a mill-site, water-power, and pay-rock, all handy* 1862 *Letters* (1917) I iii 64. See also *prospector* 1891 (OED *Mining.* Rock containing precious metal in sufficient quantity to be profitably worked. No ex. So S C. A in W: *Western U.S.* So B F Cl Th)

peace, sb. **to hold one's peace.** [?C] *I was carrying about as many short answers as my cargo room would admit of, so I held my peace* 1875 OTM 219. *He held his peace and said nothing* 1892 AmCl xii 101 (OED 12. *arch.* a1310..1890. Not *arch* in W S C, and app. not so telt by M.T.)

peace, v. [C] *"Peace! Sheriff, name the day the deed was done!"* 1881 PP xv 186 (OED 1. Be silent. *arch.* c1386..1847. Not *arch* in W S C)

peach, sb. [AB³] *She was a peach* 1906 *Speeches* (1910) 234 (OEDS 1b. *slang* orig. *U.S.* A person or thing of superlative merit...a pretty or attractive young woman. 1870.. So S Th T DN.II,IV. Not A in W C U)

peach-bloomy, a. [B¹] *She was dainty and sweet, peach-bloomy and exquisite* 1906 "Chaps. from Autob" 455. Changed in *Autob* (1924) I 129 to *peach-blooming* (Comb. not in OED W S C. For other exs. of "polishing" see under *guts*, above)

peach-vine, sb. [B¹] *Not a solitary individual who could tell a watermelon-tree from a peach-vine* 1870 SNO (1875) 238 (Nonsense comb.)

peanut, sb. [AB³] *The Roman street boy who ate his peanuts and guyed the gladiators* 1869 IA xxvi 278 (OED The fruit of *Arachis hypogaea*, a native of the West Indies. OEDS 1807.. So W S C U B F Cl Th T M H)

peanut-boy, sb. [AB¹] *"In the cars, you know, the peanut-boy always reassures you with his eye, and hands you out a book of murders if you are fond of theology"* 1873 GA xxxvi 333 (A peddler of peanuts and other wares in railroad trains. Comb. not in OED W S C. Cf. above)

peanut-commerce, sb. [AB¹] *"Even to the peanut-commerce of weighing baggage"* 1897 FE xxxi 296 (Comb. not in OED W S C; but cf. OED Peanut-politics: underhand and secret tactics. *U.S.slang*, 1887. Cf. also W: Peanut, a. Small, mean, petty. *Slang, U.S.*; so Th.III,1892 H)

peanut-peddler, sb. [AB¹] *Avery Kicks, peanut-peddler* 1873 GA liv 492. *He said they were peanut-peddlers masquerading as gentlemen* 1894 PW xiv 822 (Comb. not in OED W S C. Cf. peanut-boy, above)

peart, a. [A] *"Don't you git too peart"* 1884 HF x 81 (OED var. of Pert. *dial* and *U.S.* 4. Saucy, uppish. 1515, only ex. this form. So Wr B F Cl Th M DN.II, III, s.e.Mo., e.Ala. AS.II.361; V.203, Ozarks; IX.320, Ind. Not A in W S C U)

pebble-splash, sb. [B¹] *The raindrops struck the river with such force that they knocked up the water like pebble-splashes* 1897 FE lv 527 (Comb. not in W S C)

Peculiar People, sb. [B³] See *Allopath* 1902 (OED A modern religious sect founded in 1838, and most numerous about London. 1875.. So W S C U)

peddle, v.intr. [?A] *Little trading-scows, peddling along from farm to farm* 1883 LM xxviii 298 (OED 1.-1532.. So W S C U. A in T)

peddle, v.trans. [AB³] *I had to peddle my own poetry* 1870 SNO (1875) 278. *"We would...peddle banks like lucifer matches!"* 1873 GA viii 87. See also *bargain-counter* 1903 (OED 2. To carry about and offer for sale. Chiefly *U.S.* 1837.. So Wr Cl Th T. Not A in W S C U)

peek, v. [?A] *I peeked through the little peek-holes they have in theatre curtains* 1906 *Speeches* (1910) 222 (OED To peer, peep, c1374.. So W S C. A in B Th M H)

peek-a-boo waist, sb. [AB¹] *Why not adopt some of the women's styles? Take the peek-a-boo waist, for instance* 1908 *Speeches* (1910) 87 (S: *Colloq U.S.* Waist decorated with openwork or lacework. So Th M H. Comb. not in OED W C)

peek-hole, sb. [?AB²] See *peek* 1906 (OEDS Peep-hole. *U.S.* quot. 1927, only ex. Comb. not in W S C)

peeled, ppl.a. [?A?C] *"If Juliet's such a young gal, duke, my peeled head and my white whiskers is goin' to look oncommon odd on her, maybe"* 1884 HF xx 194 (OED 2. Bald. c1470..1653. *Obs* in C. This sense not in W S)

peeled, ppl.a. **to keep one's eyes peeled.** [AB³] *When I come to the farm-houses...I kept my eyes peeled, but didn't see nobody around* 1884 HF xxxi 322 (OEDS 4b. *fig. U.S. colloq.* 1853.. So S F DN.V AS.II. Not A in W. Phr. not in C)

peel off, v. [B¹] *He peeled off one of his bulliest old-time blessings, with as many layers to it as an onion* 1896 TSD vi 358 (Hum. *fig* use, not in OED W S C. Cf. OED 3b. To strip off or pare off. 1573..1897)

peg, v. [?AB³] *I will stay here and peg away as long as it lasts* 1871 *Letters* (1917) I x 187. *"You've got to peg and peg, and there just ain't any let-up"* 1880 TA xx 193 (OED 10. To work on persistently; esp. *peg away.* 1805.. So W S C U Wr. A in B T Th)

pemmican, sb. [AB³] *Where does he get* [in his literary style] *its pemmican quality of compression?* 1906 "Howells" (1917) 230 (OED A preparation made by certain N. Am. Indians of lean meat, dried, pounded, and pressed into cakes; hence b. *fig* Extremely condensed thought; c. *attrib.* 1831.. So W S C U B F Cl Th.III T M)

penitentiary, sb. [AB³] *"You will be sent to Congress. Next to the penitentiary"* 1872 SNO (1875) 184. *A United States law making it a penitentiary offence to strike a pilot* 1883 LM xviii 223 (OED 7. *U.S.* 1816.. So W S U H AS.II.31. Not A in C)

pensioner, sb. [C] *"His guard of honor, his fifty Gentlemen Pensioners"* 1881 PP xv 197 (OED 2. *spec.* One of a body of gentlemen instituted by Henry VIII in 1509...Originally called *Spearmen*, in 1539 *Pensioners*, later *Gentlemen-Pensioners. Obs.* a1548..1737. So W S C)

pepper away, v. [?AB²] *The Grangerfords peppered away at him* 1884 HF xviii 167 (OED 4b. To discharge shot *at* something. 1890, only ex. So W S C U)

pepper-box, sb. [AB¹] *An old original "Allen" revolver, such as irreverent people called a "pepper-box"* 1872 RI ii 23. *He put his old pepper-box revolver under his head* 1893 TSA ii 28 (W: A popular name for a pistol invented by Ethan Allen about the time of the Am. Revolution. This sense not in OED S C)

peradventure, adv. [C] *"Peradventure I mistook"* 1881 PP v 64 (OED *arch.* 3. Perhaps, belike. 1297.. 1859. So W U. Not *arch* in S C)

perchance, adv. [C] *"Perchance he is but mad upon this one strain"* 1881 PP v 65 (OED *arch.* 3c. Maybe, haply. c1400..1858. So W S C U)

perfecting press, sb. [AB³] *Jacquard looms, perfecting presses, Arkwright's frames—all mere toys, simplicities!* 1889 *Letters* (1917) I xxix 508 (OED *U.S.* A printing machine on which the sheet is printed first on one side and then on the other. 1858, only ex. Not A in W S C)

perfuse, v. [B¹] *"The Goddess Flora sitting. Behind her a fertile valley perfused by a river"* 1880 TA xvi 148 (Hum. alienism)

perhaps, adv. Spelled **praps**. [E] *There was a report got around that praps he was murdered* 1896 TSD ix 522 (OED Used in vulgar or careless speech. 1835.. W rashly calls this pron. *British*. U: *colloq.* Not in S C)

perhapsedly, adv. [B¹] *The last three* [years], *spent by the little Stratford lad at Stratford school supposedly, and perhapsedly, and maybe, and by inference* 1909 ISD ix 109 (Hum. coinage)

Perhapser, sb. [B¹] *I had only a warm desire to laugh at the Supposers, the Perhapsers, the Could-Have-Beeners, the Must-Have-Beeners, the Without-a-Shadow-of-Doubters, the We-Are-Warranted-in-Believingers... He said the Satanic Traditioners and Perhapsers and Con-*

ecturers were themselves Sacred! 1909 ISD ii 24 (Nonce word)

period, sb. **the period.** [?AB³] *The moment I appeared in a hat of the period I noticed a change* 1892 AmCl xii 109 (OED 4d. esp. the present day. 1868.. So W S U. A in B. This use not in C)

perscontation, sb. [B¹] *"The result of my perlustration and perscontation of this protuberance"* 1875 SNO 145 (Hum. coinage. Perhaps a blend of *percontation*, OED *rare* 1623..1821, and *perscrutation*, OED 1603..1843, both of which mean 'inquiry, scrutiny, examination')

persimmon, sb. [A] *The p'simmons wouldn't be ripe for two or three months yet* 1884 HF xii 102. See also *pawpaw* 1897 (OED 1. The Am. Date-plum. 1612.. So W S C U B F Cl Th T M DN.II AS.II.32)

personal, sb. [AB³] See *editorial* 1880. *Put a personal in the Baltimore Sun* 1892 AmCl iii 33 (OEDS 2c. *U.S.* Paragraph in a newspaper relating to an individual person. 1873.. So W. Not A in S C)

personal-assault, sb. [B¹] *"He finds friends pretty scarce today, likely, after the disgrace of carrying a personal-assault case into a law-court"* 1894 PW xiii 775 (Comb. not in OED W S C; but Cf. OED Personal injury, 1882)

personal-gossip, sb. [B¹] *I was at the bottom of the personal-gossip column* 1893 "Banknote" (1928) 118 (Comb. not in OED W S C)

persuader, sb. [B¹] *I also comforted him with a whiskey; gave him another...After a fourth persuader...* 1889 CY ii 19 [Here: Something used to induce or persuade; an incentive. This sense not in OED W S C. Cf. OED b. Something used to compel submission or obedience, as a weapon, spurs, etc. *slang.* 1796.. So W S)

perturbate, v. [B¹] *These recent perturbations are considered remarkable because they perturbate through three seconds of arc* 1909 "New Planet" 13 (Nonce use in *Astron.* sense; cf. OED Perturbation, sb. 2b. *Astron.* The deviation of a heavenly body from its theoretically regular orbit. 1812..; so W S C U)

pesky, a. [AB³] *It was most pesky tedious hard work, and slow* 1884 HF xxxviii 388 (OEDS *U.S. colloq.* Plaguy, disagreeable. 1830.. So W S C U Wr B F Th T M DN.II,III,IV,V. See also *Anglia Beiblatt*, 1920, XXXI.67)

pestiferous, a. [AB¹] *The pestiferous New England climate* 1906 *Autob* (1924) I 316 (W: *colloq.*, pestering; plaguy; troublesome. So C. A in DN.III. This softened sense of the orig. meaning 'pestilential, noxious, plague-bearing' not in OED S)

pest-ridden, a. [B¹] *The railway train flies by the pest-ridden city* 1883 LM xxix 322 (Comb. not in OED S C. Given in W)

pet aversion, sb. [B²] *For years my pet aversion has been the cuckoo clock* 1880 TA xxvi 262 (OED 1890.. So W U. Comb. not in S C)

petrifaction, sb. [B¹] See *pall-bearer* 1883 (A term of abuse for a slow or lazy person. This sense not in OED W S C)

petrified, ppl.a. [B¹] *I do not state this as a petrified fact* 1869 IA xlvi 481. *"Here, here, you petrified fool"* 1870 SNO (1875) 219. *An unimaginative devotion to petrified facts* 1871 SNO (1875) 154. See also *gamble on* 1883 (Absolute, exact; perhaps an extension from the phr. 'cold fact.' This use of the word not in OED W S C. A favorite with M.T.)

petroleum-city, sb. [?AB¹] *The town is full of towering chimney-stacks and hoisting-works, and looks like a petroleum-city* 1897 FE xxv 241 (Comb. not in OED W S C. Cf. oil-region, above)

petting, ppl.a. [B²] *They had very petting ways* 1896 TSD vii 359 (OED That pets. No ex. So W S C)

pettings, sb.pl. [B¹] *Alfred did what he could to respond with some show of heart to the Major's kindly pettings and reassurings* 1902 "Belated Russian Passport" (1928) 182

(This *concrete* sense not in OED W S C. Cf. OED Petting, vbl.sb. Indulgence, fondling. 1873..; so W S C)

phantom, sb. [B¹] *Then this New Jersey phantom rose up and bowed and begged pardon* 1869 IA xv 149. See also *waltzing* 1875 (An oddity, queer person. This sense not in OED W S C. Cf. M.T.'s use of specter and sprite, below)

pheasant, sb. [A] See *batter-cake* 1897 (OED 1b. Locally applied to the Ruffed Grouse of the U.S. 1637.. So W S C B F Cl H)

phew, int. Spelled **pfew-few.** [E] *"To have to confess such an origin—pfew-few!"* 1892 AmCl v 42 (OED Also *pfew* in 17th c. A vocal gesture expressing impatience, disgust, discomfort, or weariness. 1604..1892. This form not in W S C U. Wr gives the form *Pheuch*)

philippina, sb. Spelled **philopena, phillipene.** [?AB¹E] *"Boys, I move that he keeps still and lets this human philopena snip you out a speech"* 1894 PW xi 557. *"Ugh, it was awful—just the mere look of that phillipene!"* 1894 TET i 323 (Here applied *fig* to the "Twins." This sense not in OED W S C; but cf. OED A custom or game reputed to be of German origin...also applied to the double nut or kernel. OEDS 1839.. So W S C U. A in B F Th AS.X.187. OED cites the sps. *philopena, phillipine, fillipeen,* but not *phillipene*)

phit, int. [?AB²] *"The dog had almost caught him, when phit! the beaver skun up a tree"* 1871 *Screamers* 131 (OED An imitation of various sounds, esp. that made by a rifle-bullet. Earliest ex. U.S. 1894.. Not A in W S. Not in C)

phiz, sb. [?A] *Their faces are more like the "phiz" of an orang-outang* 1853 *Hannibal Journal*, Sept. 8 (OED *hum. colloq.* Face, countenance. 1688..1868. So W S C U. A in DN.IV)

phlox, sb. [A] See *prairie* 1873 (OED A N.Am. genus of herbaceous plants. 1601.. So W S C U)

phonetics, sb. Spelled **fonetics.** [E] *There isn't a waste letter in it anywhere. It reduces the fonetics to the last gasp* 1906 *Speeches* (1910) 209 (Cf. OED 1841.. So W S C U. This sp. mentioned only in S)

phonograph, sb. [AB³] See *cotton-gin* 1889. *The telegraph...the phonograph...were working their way into favor* 1889 CY xl 513. *Talk into a phonograph in an ordinary conversation-voice* 1891 *Letters* (1917) II xxxi 543. *It was as if some eavesdropping phonograph had treasured up his words* 1892 AmCl xiv 125 (OED 3. An instrument invented by Thomas A. Edison. 1877.. So W S C U. Cf. M: Am. phonograph = Eng. gramophone)

phonographer, sb. [?AB²] *I was proposing to acknowledge the receipt of the play and the little book per phonograph...I believe it could teach one to dictate literature to a phonographer* 1891 *Letters* (1917) II xxxi 545 (A pun on the sense, One who uses the phonograph, OED 3. *rare,* no ex.; and the sense, One skilled in phonography, a shorthand writer, OED 2. 1845.. Both senses in W S C; only the latter in U)

photo, sb. [?AB³] *My secretary will choose a photo which will go handily in the mail* 1907 M.T. *the Letter Writer* (1932) vii 107 (OED 1. *colloq* abbrev. of Photograph. 1860.. So W S C U. A in M DN.IV)

photograph-album, sb. [B²] *Gwendolen was sitting on the sofa...absorbed in examining a photograph album* 1892 AmCl xxi 201 (Given in OED, no ex. Comb. not in W S C)

phrase-family, sb. [B¹] *These great officials are of the phrase-family of the Church-Without-a-Creed...that is to say, of the family of Large-Names-Which-Mean-Nothing* 1907 CS II vii 163 (Comb. not in OED W S C)

phrase-juggler, sb. [B¹] *Colonel Ralls, the practiced politician and phrase-juggler* 1885 "Private Hist. of Campaign" 195 (Comb. not in A in M DN.III; but cf. OED Phrase-coiner, 1901)

phrenophone, sb. [B¹] *This age has one important contract on its hands yet— the invention of the phreno- phone: that is to say, a method whereby the communication of mind with mind may be brought under command and reduced to certainty and system* 1891 "Mental Teleg- raphy" 101 (Nonce coinage)

piazza, sb. [A] *A wooden house with a dirty piazza (unroofed) in front* 1873 GA xxix 269. *Sugar planters, whose showy houses, gray piazzas, trig gardens...gave an exceedingly thriving air* 1883 LM xl 420 (OED 2b. Chiefly *U.S.* The verandah of a house. OEDS 1771.. So W S U Th T H DN.II,VI AS.V.124. Not A in C. See also *Nation* LXVIII.416)

Picciola, sb. Spelled **Pitchiola**. [B¹E] "*Could you raise a flower here, do you reckon?... And call it pitchiola— that's its right name when it's in a prison. And you want to water it with your tears*" 1884 HF xxxviii 373 (Tom Sawyer, or his creator, must have read the sentimental romance *Picciola*, written in 1836 by Joseph-Xavier Boniface (1798-1865), better known by his pen-name Saintine. *Picciola* is the story of the comte de Charney, a political prisoner in Piedmont, whose reason was saved by his cult of a tiny flower growing between the paving-stones of his prison yard. A masterpiece of the sentimental kind, the tale was awarded the Montyon Prize by the French Academy, was translated into all the languages of Europe, and has maintained its pop- ularity to the present day. Saintine says nothing, however, about the prisoner's watering his flower with his tears. This detail is a piece of added embroidery by M.T. Not in OED W S C)

pick, v, to pick a fuss. [?AB¹] "*De dog he went for de shell, gwine to pick a fuss wid it*" 1883 LM xxxv 385 [Phr. not in OED W S C; but cf. OED 8. To pick a quarrel, *c*1449)

pick and shovel, v. [B¹] *Then we picked and shoveled, and made the fur fly* 1884 HF xxxvi 369 (Comb. not in OED W S C; but cf. OEDS Pick-and-shovel, a. 1907..)

pickaninny, a. [AB²] "*A pickaninny, mud-turtle- shaped craft of a schooner*" 1871 *Screamers* 132 (OED A West Indian Negro term for a little one, a child. B. adj. Very small. 1876.. So W DN.II.VI. This sense not in S C)

picket-watch, sb. [B¹] *They always kept a picket- watch outside the town* 1883 LM xxxi 348 (Comb. not in OED W S C; but cf. OED Picket-guard, 1703)

Pickwickian, a. in a Pickwickian sense. [B³] *What the President has to say about the guest of the evening has to be taken in a Pickwickian sense* 1909 *Speeches at the Lotos Club* (1911) 409 (OED *humorous.* In a con- veniently idiosyncratic or esoteric sense. 1837.. So W S C U)

picnic, sb. [?AB³] *As soon as the vessel entered sum- mer weather, the voyage became a holiday picnic* 1899 "My Debut" (1900) 74 (OED 1c. *transf.* and *fig.* 1887.. So W U. A in S: *Slang, U.S.*, an easy or agree- able time. So Th.III. This sense not in C)

picnicking, vbl.sb. [B²] *Picnicking, berrying, and circusing* 1880 "Edward Mills" 226 (OED 1883.. So W S C)

pictorial paper, sb. [?AB¹] *The pictorial papers cari- catured its friends* 1873 GA xliii 394 (Comb. not in OED W S C; but cf. OED Pictorial, sb. A journal of which pictures are the main feature. 1880..; so W S; A in Th.III,1872. A new departure in journalism, which apparently started in America and promptly simplified its name from a comb. to a single word)

picture-proclamation, sb. [B¹] *Afterwards a picture- proclamation* [to the natives, in Tasmania] *was issued. It was painted upon boards, and these were nailed to trees in the forest* 1897 FE xxvii 259 (Comb. not in OED W S C; but cf. OED Picture-story, 1895)

picturesque, a. [B¹] *Why does he mix such elaborate and picturesque drinks for the nigger hands on the boat?*

1883 LM xxxiii 369 (This application is hardly covered by any of the labored definitions in the dicts. Cf. OED 1. Possessing pleasing and interesting qualities of form and color. 1703..1877; W: That combines what is un- usual and charming; S: Having the kind of beauty in which the diversity is more prominent than the unity, the component elements being often bold, striking, or irregular; C: Picture-like...the word does not imply the presence of the highest beauty or of sublimity. As used by M.T. of American drinks, the term prob. means merely: Unusual, startling, attractively strange)

picturesquenesses, sb.pl. [B¹] *Repetition of pet poetic picturesquenesses* 1907 CS II iii 130 (This *concrete* use not in OED W S C)

pie, sb. [?A] *Peach pie. American mince pie. Pump- kin pie.* See *biscuit* 1880; also *batter-cake* 1897 (These combs. not in OED W S C, but cf. OED Pie, sb. b. With defining word, as apple-pie, etc. 1602.. A in F M. Cf. H: Am. pie = Eng. tart)

pie, sb. [AB²] *They want to send me abroad, as a Consul or a Minister. I said I didn't want any of the pie* 1868 *Letters* (1917) I viii 147. "*It's the last you hear of him. He wouldn't come back for pie*" 1883 LM xxiv 268 (OED 4. *fig.* Something to be eagerly appropriated; a prize, a treat, a bribe. *U.S.slang.* OEDS 1888.. So Th.III. This sense not in W S C)

pie, sb. [AB¹] "*Tom Sawyer, you're just old pie, 'longside o' what I am*" 1876 TS x 97. "*Mr. Longfellow smiles as sweet as pie*" 1877 *Speeches* (1910) 5. "*You're always as polite as pie to them*" 1884 HF ii 15. *So he took him to his own house and dressed him up clean and nice...and was just old pie to him, so to speak* 1884 HF v 34 (The essence of goodness or amiability; the per- sonification of kindness. This sense not in OED W S C)

pie, sb. Spelled **pi**. [AE] *In our country printing- offices the apprentice learns to sort "pi"* 1880 TA App.A 586. *I put the good type in his case...and if he wasn't there to see, I dumped it all with the "pi" on the imposing stone* 1886 *Speeches* (1910) 182. *In their galleys "live" matter is immortal, unless a pi accident intervenes* 1904 "Bequest" (1906) iii 16 (OED *Printing.* This sp. *U.S.* 1659..1771, Franklin's *Autob.*, first ex. sp. *pi.* So W U. Not A in S C)

piece, sb. to go all to pieces. [AB¹] See *chromo* 1891. *The hackman will just go all to pieces when he sees that* 1892 AmCl xvii 153 (To be completely overwhelmed, 'flabbergasted.' Cf. OEDS 1c. All to pieces: Completely, through and through. *U.S.* 1839.. So C Wr B Cl Th. Not A in W. Phr. not in OED S)

piece, sb. [?A] *Down the road a piece* 1880 TA xxxiii 356. *I took the gun and went up a piece into the woods* 1884 HF vii 51. *Down a piece, abreast the house, stood a little log cabin* 1897 *Autob* (1924) I 99 (OED 14c. A portion of the way between two points; a short distance. *dial.* 1612..1852. So W Wr. A in DN.II,III,IV,V, reported from Me. to La. AS.II.361, VII.20. This sense not in S C)

pied, ppl.a. [?A?C] *A thing that gets pied is dead; its chance of seeing print is gone* 1904 "Bequest" (1906) iii 16 (OED *rare.* Converted into printers' pie. 1870, only ex. Not *rare* in W S C U)

pie-plant, sb. [AB³] "*You are the loser by this rupture, not me, Pie-plant*" 1870 *Screamers* 58 (OED *U.S.* Garden rhubarb. 1847. So W S C B F Cl T DN.III. Here used as a hum. epithet)

piety-hive, sb. [B¹] *We went to Benares and inspected that strange and fascinating piety-hive* 1897 FE lvii 548 (Comb. not in OED W S C; but cf. OED Piety-shop, 1893)

pig, sb. [?AC] See *arrastre* 1909 (Here of silver- mining. Cf. OED 7. An oblong mass of metal, as obtained from the smelting-furnace. Not now of gold or silver. 1630..1683, last ex. for silver. So W S. This sense not in C)

pigeon, sb. [AB³] *I remember the pigeon seasons, when the birds would come in millions and cover the trees* 1897 *Autob* (1924) I 114 (OED 1b. Passenger-pigeon: the 'Wild Pigeon' of N. Am., noted formerly for the countless numbers in which it passed from place to place. 1802.. So W S C)

pigeon-hole, v. [?AB³] *I reckon it would ruin the book—that is, make it necessary to pigeon-hole it* 1885 *Letters* (1917) II xxv 463 (OED 1. To shelve for the present. 1861.. So W S C U. A in B, p.791)

Pigs in Clover, sb. [?AB²] *A toy puzzle called Pigs in Clover had come into sudden favor* 1892 AmCl xxiv 250 (OED A game which consists in rolling a number of marbles into a recess or pocket in a board by tilting the board itself. 1900.. So W C. C give 1895 as the date of the game's popularity; evidently it was a few years earlier. Cf. Th: An emblem of contentment, 1813. Comb. not in S)

pike, sb. [C] *"Boots with pykes"—points a foot long* 1881 PP xi 125 (OED 4a. The long point or peak of a shoe, such as was fashionable in 14th-15th c. *Obs* exc. *Hist.* c1380..1834. So S C. Not in W)

pile, sb. **to go one's pile**. [AB¹] *See and* 1867 (To risk one's entire fortune. A in F Cl. Phr. not in OED W S C; but cf. OED Pile, sb. 3h. ellipt. for 'pile of wealth.' A fortune accumulated or heaped up. Chiefly in colloq. phr. *to make one's pile*. 1741..; so W; A in S C U B F Cl Th T DN.III AS.VII.424. Dr. H.M.Belden suggests that, whatever may be sense of *pile* in *to make one's pile*, its use in *to go one's pile* is more likely a *fig* extension of the Poker sense, i.e., the 'pile of chips.' One 'goes one's pile' by shoving into the pot all the chips one has. This gambler's sense for *pile* is given in W S, not in OED C)

pile down, v. [AB²] *A lot of men begun to pile down off of the benches and swarm toward the ring* 1884 HF xxii 222 (OEDS 3c. To climb down; to come out of in crowds. *U.S.* 1884, this ex. Comb. not in W S C)

pile in, v. [AB³] *Here comes a couple of the hounds in from under Jim's bed; and they kept on piling in till there was eleven of them* 1884 HF xxxvi 373 (OEDS 3b. To climb into, enter in crowds. Orig. *U.S.* 1854.. So DN.II,III,IV, n.w.Ark. Not A in W S C)

pile it on, v. [?AB²] *See holler* 1883. *I reckon that was sort of piling it on, maybe* 1884 HF vi 45. *"Too much color"..."Well, yes, he does pile it on pretty loud"* 1892 AmCl xvi 147 (OEDS 2b. To prolong and intensify the effect of anything by adding fresh details. 1884, quot. from HF, only ex. A in W Th,1839. Not A in U. Not in S C)

pile-driving, ppl.a. [B¹] *The title came upon them as a kind of pile-driving surprise* 1894 PW vi 335 (Crushing, overwhelming. This *fig* use not in OED W S C. For literal sense cf. OED 1809..)

pilgrim, sb. [C] *These pilgrims from New England* 1869 IA iv 38 (OED 1. A wayfarer; a traveler. Now *poet.* or *rhet.* c1200..1850. *Arch* in U. Not *arch* in any way in W S C)

Pilgrim, sb. [A] *You are celebrating the landing of the Pilgrims* 1881 *Speeches* (1910) 18 (OED 4. *Amer. Hist.* 1630.. So W S C U)

pillow-fight, sb. [?AB²] *They generally wound up with a pillow-fight, in which they banged each other over the head, and threw the pillows in all directions* 1892 AmCl xiii 112 (OED 1904, only ex. So W. Comb. not in S C)

pilot, sb. [AB¹] *"There's only one way to be a pilot, and that is to get this entire river by heart"* 1875 OTM 219. *A pilot, in those days, was the only unfettered and entirely independent human being that lived in the earth do.* 721. See also *penitentiary* 1883 (Strangely enough, no dict. gives a definition that fits the *spec* sense of a Mississippi River pilot. Cf. OED 1. One who steers or directs the course of a ship; *spec.* a person duly qualified to steer ships into and out of a harbor. 1530..1847; so W S C U)

pilot-apprentice, sb. [AB¹] *I steered for him a good many months—as was the humble duty of the pilot-apprentice* 1909 ISD i 4 (Comb. not in OED W S C)

pilot-farmer, sb. [AB¹] *The pilot-farmer disappears from the river annually about the breaking of spring, and is seen no more until frost. Then he appears again... combs the hayseed out of his hair, and takes a pilot-house berth for the winter* 1883 LM xlix 486 (Comb. not in OED W S C)

pilot-house, sb. [?AB³] See *hurricane-deck* 1873; *gingerbread* 1875; *rattletrap* 1875; *breast-board* 1883; *texas* 1884. *A pilot-house that is perched forty feet above the water* 1909 ISD i 8 (OEDS Wheel-house. All exs. U.S. 1849.. A in Th. Not A in W S C)

piloting, vbl.sb. [?A] *Verily, all is vanity and little worth—save piloting* 1866 *Letters* (1917) I v 101. See *kid-glove* 1875. *He could throw a sort of splendor around a bit of devil-may-care piloting* 1875 OTM 723. *The marvelous science of piloting* 1883 LM iii 61 (OED Earliest ex. U.S. 1716.. Not A in W S C)

pin, sb. **on pins and needles**. [?AB²] *I was on pins and needles during that little while* 1889 CY vi 74 (OED 3d. In a state of excessive uneasiness. 1897, only ex. of this phr. So W S C Wr)

pinch-bug, sb. [AB²] *A tenor and bass duet by thirty-two thousand locusts and ninety-seven thousand pinch bugs was sung* 1856 Letter in *Iowa Journ. of Hist.* (1929) 423. *A large black beetle with formidable jaws—a "pinch bug" he [Tom Sawyer] called it* 1876 TS v 57 (OEDS A species of stag-beetle found in the southern states of N. Am. 1870.. So W S Cl Th.III. Comb. not in C)

pine, sb. **white pine**. [A] *White-pine cot-bedsteads* 1872 RI xxi 162 (OED 2. The Norway pine or spruce of N. Am. 1785..So W S C)

pine, sb. **yellow pine**. [AB³] *"There are thousands of acres of the finest yellow-pine timber in America"* 1870 *Autob* (1924) I 4. *It was yellow-pine timberland* 1872 RI xxii 171 (W: Any of various Am. pines or their timber, as...the Georgia pine, the pitch-pine; in the w. U.S., the bull- pine; also the Arizona pine. So OED 2. 1822; so S C)

pine-grown, a. [B¹] *Some pine-grown summits behind the town* 1880 TA xxxv 397 (Comb. not in OED W S C)

pine-knot, sb. [A] *The mud-clerk had to continue his labors into the night, by the light of pine-knot torches* 1906 *Autob* (1924) I 307 (OEDS *U.S.* A knot of pine-wood burned for illumination. 1670.. So C B F Cl Th M. Not A in S. Comb. not in W)

pinery, sb. [?AB³] *"There is no end to the tar, pitch, and turpentine which these vast pineries will yield"* 1870 *Autob* (1924) I 4 (OEDS 2. A grove of pine trees. Earliest ex. U.S. 1822.. A in C B F Cl Th T DN.II AS.VIII.1.51, Ozarks. Not A in W S U)

pipe of peace, sb. [A] *Dreamily smoking the pipe of peace...where all was repose and contentment* 1869 IA xii 106. *The pipe of peace did the same office for La Salle. The white man and the red man struck hands* 1883 LM ii 36 (OED The Calumet, or peace-pipe of the Am. Indians; also used allusively. 1722.. So W S U B F M. Comb. not in C)

piper, sb. **drunk as a piper**. [?AC] *He came home drunk as a piper* 1865 SS (1926) 205 (OED 1b. †Quite drunk. 1770, 1772, only exs. Not *obs* in C Wr. Phr. not in W S)

pipe up, v.intr. [?AB²] *Then a bird pipes up* 1883 LM xxx 331. *As the guard laid a hand upon me, she piped up with the tranquillest confidence..."It is the Boss!"* 1889 CY xvi 196 (OED 9b. To raise the voice, speak up. 1889, above quot...)

pirate-book, sb. [B¹] *Everybody said it was a real beautiful oath, and asked Tom if he got it out of his own head. He said some of it, but the rest was out of pirate-*

books and robber-books 1884 HF ii 13 (Comb. not in OED W S C)

pirogue, sb. [A] *A pirogue sometimes flits from the bushes and across the Red River on its way out to the Mississippi* 1883 LM App. A 595 (OED Probably from the Carib dialect of Cayenne. 1. A long narrow canoe hollowed from the trunk of a single tree. 1609.. So W S C U B F Cl Th DN.IV, New Orleans)

pistol-case, sb. [B¹] *The pistol-case was opened and the long slim tubes taken out* 1894 TET vi 398 (Comb. not in OED W S C; but cf. OED Pistol-bag, 1701)

pit, v. [B¹] *Some time before daylight, passed near another place where Joseph's brethren pitted him* 1867 *Notebook* (1935) viii 96 (Not of a person in OED W S C. Cf. OED 1. To put or cast into a pit, esp. roots, vegetables, etc., for storage. 1546..; so W S C)

pitcher, sb. [AC] *In the corner a washstand, with real china-ware bowl and pitcher* 1893 "Californian's Tale" (1906) 106 (OED Now somewhat of a literary archaism ... in U. S. applied to a bedroom jug or ewer. *c*1290.. 1897. So W F M T H. Not A in S C U)

pitcher-bearer, sb. [AB¹] *The commonest of village sights was lacking here—the public pump, with its group of gossiping pitcher-bearers* 1880 TA xix 174 (Comb. not in OED W S C. Cf. above.

pitch in, v. [AB³] *The priest pitched in and broke it all up* 1883 LM xliii 439 (OED 23a. To set to work vigorously. *colloq.* Chiefly *U.S.* 1847.. Not A in W S C)

pitch-pine, sb. [A] *Volumes of the blackest smoke are created with a bit of pitch-pine* 1875 OTM 70 (OED The *Pinus rigida* of N. Am. OEDS 1676.. So W S C U Th M)

pity, sb. **more's the pity**. [?AB²] *A chance to get acquainted with a youth who had taken deck passage—more's the pity, for he easily borrowed six dollars of me* 1875 OTM 217 (OED 3. 1890, only ex. of this phr. So W C U. Phr. not in S)

Piute, sb. [AB¹] *It is Indian; they say it is Piute* 1869 IA xx 205. *"It was a Pi Ute Injun I used to know in Tulare County"* 1907 "Capt. Stormfield" 46 (W: Var. of Paiute. An Indian of Shoshonean stock. So S. Not in OED C)

place, v. [AB³] *"You don't know me, John!"* ... *The ancient passenger scanned him perplexedly ... with a hesitation that indicated strong internal effort to "place" the gentle old apparition* 1877 "Some Rambling Notes" ii 591. *You hear things "placed" as having happened since the war* 1883 LM xlv 454. *One letter was in a hand which seemed dimly familiar to me. I could not "place" it at first, but presently I succeeded* 1891 "Mental Telegraphy" 97 (OEDS 5e. To determine who or what a particular person or thing is; to identify or recognize. *U.S.* 1855.. So B F Cl Th T. Not A in W S U. This sense not in C)

placer, sb. [AB³] *"Prospecting" is hunting for a "placer"* 1872 RI lxi 443 (OED *Mining.* Chiefly *U.S.* A deposit containing gold. 1848.. So W S C U B F Cl Th T M AS.VII.424)

placer-diggings, sb. [AB³] *In "placer-diggings," the gold is scattered all through the surface dirt* 1872 RI lxi 443 (OED Surface-diggings. 1868, only ex. So B F Cl. Comb. not in W S C)

plagued, ppl.a. [?A] *"I don't know anything about your plagued French"* 1869 IA x 94 (OED 3. 'Confounded,' 'cursed,' 'plaguy.' 1728.. So plegged in *U.S.dial.*, quot. 1887. This sp., from *Free Joe* by J. C. Harris, merely indicates the usual Am. pron., whereas it is pronounced with a long *a* in Eng., acc. to the OED. A in W Wr DN.I. This sense not in S C)

plague-sore, sb. [B¹] *"St. Rochus sitting in a landscape with an angel who looks at his plague-sore"* 1880 TA xvi 148 (Comb. not in OED W. Given in S C)

Plains, sb. [A] *I dread the idea of appearing before those miners of Montana ... Perhaps you can make it appear that the children of the Plains are crying for me*

1867 *M.T. the Letter Writer* (1932) i 17. *"You've never been to the Rocky Mountains?" "No." "You've never been out on the plains?"* 1892 AmCl xii 107 (OED 1b. In colonial and U.S. use applied to level treeless tracts of country; prairie. 1779.. W: With *the*, the territory extending from N.D. to Texas and from the Mississippi River to the Rocky Mountains. So S C DN.VI)

plainsman, sb. [?AB³] *Biltong .. is what our plainsmen call "jerked beef"* 1897 FE lxvii 684 (OEDS Earlier exs., all U.S.,1870.. A in DN.VI. Not A in W S C U)

plank, sb. [AB³] *They cannot put a plank into any candidate's platform* 1899 "Concerning the Jews" (1900) 277 (OED 5. An article in a political program. Orig. and chiefly *U.S.* 1848.. So B F Cl Th T M H. Not A in W S C U)

plank, v. [AB³] *"Up she goes," says I, planking the cash* 1877 "Some Rambling Notes" i 445. *"I plank out your share of the dollars regular"* 1883 LM xxxvi 389. *"You gits fifty dollahs a month; you's gwine to han' over half of it to yo' ma. Plank it out!"* 1894 PW ix 550 (OED 2b. To table or lay down money. *colloq.* OEDS 1824.. So W B Cl Th T M. Not A in S C U)

planked, ppl.a. [AB¹] *The trade-mark of the richest and freest and mightiest republic of all the ages: the pine disk, with the planked eagle spread upon it, his head and shoulders among the stars, and his claws full of out-of-date war material* 1902 "Belated Russian Passport" (1928) 190 (Cf. OED 2. Of fish: Cooked by being split, fastened on a board, and held to the fire. *U.S.* OEDS 1855.. So S C B F Cl Th.III M H. Not A in W. Here, by an irreverent extension, of the "spread eagle")

plank fencing, sb. [B¹] *Every few hundred yards one came across a panel or so of plank fencing* 1880 TA xxxv 386 (Comb. not in OED W S C)

plank sidewalk, sb. [?AB¹] *Plank sidewalks on stilts four feet high* 1883 LM xxx 336 (Comb. not in OED W S C; but cf. OED Plank-road, *U.S.*, 1853..; so B F)

plant, sb. [B³] See *functionable* 1899. *Each of the Protestant sects is represented and has a plant of its own* 1904 "Bequest" (1906) i 1 (OED 6b. *fig.* The instrumentalities employed in carrying on spiritual or intellectual work. 1861.. So W S. This sense not in C. This passage is twice cited by Mr. Stephen Leacock, *Humor*, 1935, pp. 37, 124, as a typical example of M.T.'s distinctive method of twisting the meaning of words. But the transfer of this particular term from factory to church had already, as the OED quots. show, been made repeatedly on the other side of the Atlantic)

plant, v. [AB²] *He died. There was not a dry eye in the crowd when they planted him* 1867 Jumping Frog 163. *"Now if we can get you to help plant him—" "Preach the funeral discourse? Assist at the obsequies?" "Obs'- quies is good. Yes"* 1872 RI xlvii 334. *Jim said a man that warn't buried was more likely to go a-ha'nting around than one that was planted and comfortable* 1884 HF x 80 (OEDS *slang.* 11. *U.S.* To bury. 1867.. So W F Th.III T AS.XI.199. Not A in S. This sense not in C)

plant, v. [?AB¹] See *gilt-edged* 1904 (To invest. This sense not in OED W S C)

plantain, sb. [A] *Oranges, lemons, plantains, watermelons, plums, and various other fruits were to be seen on one table* 1857 Letter in *Iowa Journ. of Hist.* (1929) 430. (OED A tropical plant closely allied to the Banana... In the West Indies the name is given to those with larger and coarser fruit. 1555.. So W S C U B F Cl T AS.IV.9)

plantain-patch, sb. [AB¹] *Rob a poor widow and her helpless family of a meager plantain-patch* 1870 SNO (1875) 312 (A in Cl: A potato-grant; in the West Indies, a patch of land for growing vegetables, allotted to resident laborers on estates. Comb. not in OED W S C; but cf. OED Plantain-garden, 1697)

plantation, sb. [A] *I have been clattering around among the plantations for three weeks* 1866 Letters (1917) I v 105. See *clean out* 1873. *"We've got to land at Jones's* *plantation, sir"* 1875 OTM 218. See also *farmer-preacher* 1884; *fair daylight* 1894; *Kanaka* 1897 (OED 5. A spot of ground in America for the planting of tobacco, sugar-canes, etc. 1706.. So W C B F Cl T H DN.I,II. Not A in S U)

plantation hymn, sb. [AB¹] *They play and sing plantation hymns together* 1892 AmCl iii 23 (Comb. not in OED W S C; but cf. OED Plantation song: a song of the kind sung by negroes on the Am. plantations. 1871..)

planter, sb. [A] *We had conversations with rivermen, planters...* 1883 LM xxviii 307. See also *Cotton State* 1899 (OED 4. The proprietor of a plantation... orig. in the W.Indies and southern colonies of N. Am. 1647.. So W C B F Cl H DN.I AS.IV.9. Not A in S U)

plant-root, sb. [B¹] *To glut the earth and the plant-roots and the air with disease germs* 1883 LM xlii 432 (Comb. not in OED W S C)

plant out, v. [B¹] *They would often plant out eleven columns of new ads on a standing galley* 1906 *Autob* (1924) I 274 (This *Printer's* use not in OED W S C. Cf. OED Plant, v.1c. *Plant out,* to transfer from a pot or frame to the open ground. 1793..)

plate, sb. [B¹] *He hunted out the plate containing the finger-prints made by Tom when he was twelve years old* 1894 PW xx 235 (A thin sheet of metal or glass on which finger-prints are taken and preserved. This *spec* sense not in OED W S C; but cf. OED 5c. *Photogr.* 1840..)

platform, sb. [AB³] *They cannot put a plank into any candidate's platform* 1899 "Concerning the Jews" (1900) 277 (OED 9b. *spec* in U.S. politics. OEDS 1803.. So S C B F Cl Th M H. Not A in W U)

platform, sb. [?AB¹] *For the first time in many years I am on the Highway, i.e., the platform, giving readings from "Huck Finn" and other of my books* 1884 *M.T. the Letter Writer* (1932) i 24 (The lecture platform, the activity of public lecturing. This *spec* sense not in OED W S C)

platform-business, sb. [?AB¹] *We started westward from New York in mid-summer, with Major Pond to manage the platform-business as far as the Pacific* 1897 FE i 25 (Comb. not in OED W S C; but cf. OED Platform oratory, 1879)

play, v. [?AB³] *"Playing us for Chinamen because we are strangers!"* 1869 IA xxvii 294. See *land,* v. 1873. *He said he never intended to sign the Fairchild contract—he was only playing Fairchild* 1893 *Notebook* (1935) xxi 232. *"Do you reckon he's playing us?"* 1896 TSD iii 351 (OED 6e. To give play to a fish. Also *fig.* 1856, first *fig* ex... So W S C U. A in Th.III)

play, v. [?AB²] *"He played it on the prophets of Baal"* 1877 "Some Rambling Notes" ii 589. *Nothing would do Tom but he must crawl to where Jim was, and play something on him* 1884 HF ii 10 (OED 9. To practise or perform a trick, prank, joke; const. *on, upon,* or with simple dative. *c* 1391.. but no ex. with *on.* So W S C U. A in F)

play, v. [?AB¹] *That was the order I wanted, and that was the one I played for* 1884 HF xxxi 326 (To scheme or plan craftily for. This *fig* sense not in OED W S C; but cf. OED 17b. *spec.* To play for stakes, esp. for the sake of gain. 1511..1832)

play, v. [?AB²] *One thing at a time...and just play that thing for all it is worth* 1889 CY ii 35 (OED 22b. *Cards...Also fig.* To deal with a thing for one's own advantage. No ex. of *fig* sense, exc. in phr. *to play one's cards,* 1753..; so W S C)

play, v. [?AB¹] *"You could have played him on a stranger for an effigy"* 1879 *Letters* (1917) I xix 369. *"Trying to play yourself for a stranger and an innocent"* 1883 LM xxiv 271. *You could have played the gathering on a stranger for a prayer-meeting* 1883 LM xlv 457. See *cowboy* 1892. *Human nature has tried, from the Creation down, to play itself upon its possessor as a boon* 1898 "About Play Acting" (1928) 219 (To present a person or thing falsely as something which it is not; to pass

off as; const. with *on* of the person deluded, and with *for* or *as* of object counterfeited. This sense not in OED W S C; but cf. OED 18d. *To play it on:* to play a trick upon, take in, cheat. 1871..)

play-acting, sb. [?AB³?C] *"I don't know nothing about play-actin'"* 1884 HF xx 194. *The actual Death—not a play-acting artificiality* 1898 "About Play-Acting" (1928) 216. *Then three pretty full years follow. Full of play-acting* 1909 ISD iii 30. See also *call-boying* 1909 (OED Dramatic performance. 1873.. So W C. S: *arch* or usually derogatory. A in Wr. Cf. B *play-actorin',* given as A in this sense)

played, ppl.a. [?AB¹] *"That used to be, but that's all played now"* 1883 LM xliii 439 (Played out, come to an end. This sense not in OED W S C)

played out, ppl.a. [?AB²] *That sort of thing is "played out," you know* 1862 *Letters* (1917) I iii 65. *"The fact is, Laura, our romance is played out"* 1873 GA xviii 175. *Bottles and rags, and played-out tinware* 1884 HF xxi 209. *In a few years from now we shall have nothing but played-out kings and dukes on the police force* 1889 *Letters* (1917) II xxix 521 (OED Play, v. 32c. Finished, used up, worn out. 1863.. So W S C U. A in B Cl Th T M)

plaza, sb. [?A] *The "plaza" is native to all towns beyond the Rocky Mountains* 1872 RI xxi 99 (OED In a Spanish-speaking country, a market-place, square. 1683.. So W U. A in S C B F Th M DN.I)

pleasant-spoken, a. [?AB²] *Senator Dilworthy was:.. a pleasant-spoken man, a popular man with the people* 1873 GA xx 187 (OED 1896, only ex. So W. A in B T. Comb. not in S C)

please-it-you, v.phr. [C] *"With never a by-your-leave or so-please-it-you, or anything of the sort"* 1881 PP xii 138 (OED Please, v. 3b.† May it please you. 1388.. 1602. Phr. not in W S C)

pleasure-resort, sb. [?AB²] *Modern-style pleasure resorts* 1883 LM xli 427 (OED Pleasure, sb. 6a. 1891. Comb. not in W S C)

pleasure-walk, sb. [B¹] *When a pleasure-walk is planned* [German, Spaziergehn] 1891 *Slovenly Peter* (1935) 1 (Walking for pleasure. This sense not in OED, but cf. in dif. sense quot. 1763: "The ground is agreeably laid out in pleasure-walks." Comb. not in W S C)

pleasuring, vbl.sb. [?AB²] *A pleasuring party of entirely respectable gentlemen and ladies* 1869 IA xli 430 (OED 3. *attrib.* designating things designed for pleasure. 1869.. So W S C. A in Wr)

plenty, sb. **a-plenty.** [A] *The bag of bread and meat.. lasted me all the way, and I had a-plenty* 1884 HF xi 93 (OED 2b. with *a.* Now chiefly *U.S.* 1627..1857. So W S Wr. This form not in C)

plenty, a. [?AB³] *I've noticed that thing plenty times since* 1884 HF ii 9. See also *corn-cob pipe* 1884; *farmer-preacher* 1884; *drugged* 1904 (OED 1c. Preceding a substantive: "plenty of." *dial.* 1878, only ex. So W S C. A in Th.III,1874 H)

plenty, adv. [AB³] *There is plenty good enough material for a republic in the most degraded people that ever existed* 1889 CY xx 389. *He was plenty good enough Spaniard as it was* 1892 AmCl xii 102. *It was granted that this was plenty good enough circumstantial evidence* 1894 PW xiii 776. *It is plenty strong enough as concerns Austria* 1899 "Concerning the Jews" (1900) 272 (OED III. Abundantly. Common *colloq* throughout Gt. Britain, also in U.S. 1842.. So Wr. Not A in W S U. This use not in C)

plesiosaurian, sb. [B¹] See *anisodactylous* 1906 (Non-sense use)

plotting-place, sb. [B¹] *Plotting-places for discontented revolution-breeders* 1869 IA xvi 157 (Comb. not in OED W S C; but cf. OED Plotting-school, 1861)

plow, v. [AE] *They plowed through the fields of floating ice* 1883 LM ii 35 (OED The sp. *plough* became usual in Eng. during the 18th c., when sb. and vb. were levelled in form; in U.S. they have both become *plow*. So W S C U M)

pluck, v. [C] *"Pluck the lad from him!"* 1881 PP xi 126 (OED 2. To snatch. *arch*. 1377..1877. Not *arch* in W S C)

plug, sb. [?A] See *dog-leg* 1884. *Store tobacco is flat black plug* 1884 HF xxi 210. *In the pockets...small bills and silver. Plug of tobacco* 1892 AmCl vii 57 (OED 4b. A piece of cake or twist tobacco. 1728..1844. So W S C. A in B AS.II.32)

plug, sb. [AB²] *The Kanaka, without spur or whip, sailed by us on the old plug* 1866 Speeches (1923) 13. *We bought two sorry-looking Mexican 'plugs'* 1869 IA xxvii 208. See *simon-pure* 1872. *"You are not a Mexican Plug, you are a gentleman...Buffalo Bill's horse!"* 1906 "Horse's Tale" 338 (OED *U.S.* and *Colonial slang*. Explained in Amer. dicts. as 'a horse past his prime.' 1872, quot. from IA... So W B F Cl T H DN.I,IV AS.II.362,IV.129,XII.103. Not A in S C)

plug, v. [?AB³] *"He could take his yew bow and plug a ten-cent piece every time, a mile and a half"* 1876 TS xxvi 200. See also *center* 1892 (OEDS 2. To put a bullet into, to shoot. *slang*. 1875.. So W U. A in S C)

plug, v. [AB¹] *I know how to tell when a watermelon is ripe without "plugging" it* 1897 Autob (1924) I 111 (S: *Local U.S.* To cut into and take out a plug; as, to plug a melon. So W C. This sense not in OED)

plug hat, sb. [AB²] *Plug hat, broad gold band* 1866 Letters (1917) I v 111. See *boiled shirt* 1872. *He was in the gentlemen's furnishing line and his specialty was plug hats* 1889 CY xxi 263. *English grooms in plug hats and tight-buttoned coats* 1892 AmCl iv 37. *Indians in rabbit-skin robes, battered plug hats, and tin-can necklaces* 1902 "DBDS" (1928) 307. See also *patent-leathers* 1904; *trot out* 1910 ((OEDS *U.S.slang*. A 'chimney-pot' hat. 1873.. So W B F Cl Th.III T H DN.I,III. Not A in S C)

plug tile, sb. [AB¹] *Kid gloves, plug tile, hair parted behind* 1883 LM lviii 570 (Comb. not in OED W S C. Cf. above, and see tile, below)

plum, sb. [?AB³] *A literary plum, snatched from my very mouth at the instant it was ready to drop into it* 1880 TA xxxvi 406. (OED 4d. *fig*. A 'good thing'; one of the 'prizes' of life. 1825.. So W S C U. A in H)

plumb, adv. Also *plum*. [A] *I could see plumb back into the kitchen* 1856 Adv. of T. J. Snodgrass (1928) 14. See *town-site* 1873. *"They prayed an hour—two hours—three hours—and so on, plumb till noon"* 1877 "Some Rambling Notes" ii 590. See *fetch up* 1883. *The place was plum full of farmers and farmers' wives* 1884 HF xli 416 (OED 2c. Entirely, quite. Chiefly *U.S. slang*. 1587..1897. So W C B F Cl Th M DN.I,II,III,V AS. V.427, Ozarks. Not A in S)

plunder, sb. [AB³] *"Shoulder this plunder and follow me"* 1873 GA vii 76 (OED 3. Luggage, baggage. *U.S. local*. 1817.. So W S C B F Cl Th,1815 M DN.II AS. IX.320. Not A in U)

plunk, v. [AB³] *"Fog! he's got an eye 't can plunk through it like a bullet"* 1902 "DBDS" (1928) 318 (OEDS 6. *U.S. slang*. To shoot. 1891.. So C DN.II. This sense not in W S)

plunk, int. plunkety-plunk, plunk-plunk-plunk. [?AB¹] *I hear a plunkety-plunk, plunkety-plunk, and says to myself, horses coming* 1884 HF viii 63. *"Feel my pulse: plunk-plunk-plunk"* 1892 AmCl xix 175 (These doubled forms not in OED W C. Given in S. Cf. OED Plunk, int. 1895..)

ply, v. [?A] *Passage to Albany (160 miles) on the finest steamers that ply the Hudson is now 25 cents* 1853 Letters (1917) I 125 (OED 7b. To traverse (a river, ferry, etc.). Earliest exs. U.S. 1700..1897. A in B. Not A in W S. This sense not in C)

Plymouth Brethren, sb. [B³] See *Allopath* 1902 (OED A religious body...which arose at Plymouth *c*1830. 1842.. So W S C U)

pocket, sb. [?AB³] *Went out to the "pocket" claim* 1865 Notebook (1935) i 6. See *strike*, v. 1872. *I've done "pocket-mining" during three months in the one little patch of ground in the whole globe where Nature conceals gold in pockets* 1891 Letters (1917) II xxxi 542 (OED 7a. Mining. A cavity in the earth filled with gold or other ore. Earliest ex. U.S. 1850.. A in B F Cl T AS. II.86. Not A in W S C U)

pocket, sb. [?AB¹] *The house which Tom's father lived in was up a foul little pocket called Offal Court* 1881 PP ii 27. See also *alley* 1892 (W: A blind alley. This sense not in OED S C)

pocket-miner, sb. [AB¹] *I have been a "pocket" miner—a sort of gold mining not findable in any but one little spot in the world, so far as I know. I know how to find the compact little nest of yellow metal reposing in its secret home under the ground* 1909 ISD vii 75 (A in B. Comb. not in OED W S C)

pocket-mining, sb. [AB¹] *In that one little corner of California is found a species of mining which is seldom or never mentioned in print. It is called pocket-mining* 1872 RI lx 436. See also *pocket* 1891 (Cf. above. Comb. not in OED W S C)

pocket-pup, sb. [?AB¹] *From pocket-pup to mastiff* 1903 "Dog's Tale" 11 (A very small or 'pocket-sized' dog. Comb. not in OED W S C)

poetastical, a. [?AB²] *I say "daughter of Eve," meaning it as kinder figurative or poetastical like* 1857 Adv. of T. J. Snodgrass (1928) 41 (OED Erroneously for *poetastrical*. *U.S.* quot. 1858, only ex. Not in W S C)

poet lariat, sb. [B¹] *"Maybe the poet lariat ain't satisfied with them deductions?"* 1869 IA x 91 (Hum. malapropism)

poet-laureatic, a. [B¹] *A poet-laureatic explosion of colored fireworks* 1897 FE lxvi 666 (Comb. not in OED W S C)

poet-orator, sb. [B¹] *Two poet-orators who...had MS. funeral orations projecting from their breast pockets* 1880 TA viii 76 (Comb. not in OED W S C; but cf. OED Poet-actor, 1867; Poet-humorist. 1897, etc.)

poi, sb. [AB³] *They brought us water, poi, bananas* 1866 "Forty-Three Days" 112. *Eat their poi and raw fish and welcome* 1866 "Sandwich Islands" Speeches (1923) 9 (OED A dish made in Hawaii.. 1840.. So W S C U)

point, sb. Spelled **pint**. [?AE] *"I don't see no pints about that frog more nor about any other frog in partickler"* 1865 "Jumping Frog" (1875) 34 (OED A 26b. *spec*. A physical feature in an animal, esp. one by which excellence or purity of breed is judged. 1546.. So W S C U. A in F Cl. Cf. also OED Head-note: The occasional sp. *pynt*, *pyntte*, prob. indicate a pron. formerly prevalent and still *dial* of *oi* as a 'long i', *point* being pronounced like *pint*. This pron. A in DN.III,IV AS. VIII.1.24, heard in sections of N.C., Tenn., Va., W. Va., and Ky. Not mentioned in W S C U)

point, sb. [AB¹] *The point at Cairo, which has not even been moistened by the river since 1813, is now entirely under water* 1859 Letter in New Orleans Daily Crescent. See *river-glimpse* 1875; *make down* 1883. *The big raft was away out of sight around the point* 1883 LM iii 61 (A in Th: A cape formed by the devious course of the Mississippi River, 1826. Not A in W S U. This sense, of a river, not in OED C; but cf. OED B 2b. *spec* a tapering promontory running into the sea)

point, sb. [?AB¹] *He said it would be necessary to know how many "points" I wanted put up, what parts of the house I wanted them on, and what quality rod I preferred* 1870 SNO (1875) 21 (The metallic end of a lightning-rod. This *spec* sense not in W S C; but cf. OED B 3e. *Electr*. A metallic point at which electricity is discharged or collected. 1836..)

point, v. [?AB¹] See *cold*, a. 1876. *"I am but now come from the Valley of Holiness, please you sir."* *"I am pointed for that place myself"* 1889 CY xxi 264 (To direct or set on one's way. This sense, of human beings, not in OED W S C; but cf. OEDS 17. *U.S.* To turn, guide, or deflect cattle in a particular direction. 1903..)

point-blank, adv. Spelled **pine-blank**. [AE] "*They told him pine blank and once for all, he couldn't*" 1896 TSD i 345 (This form A in AS.VII.94, VIII.1.24. Cf. *pint-blank* in DN.II, s.e.Mo. Not in OED W S C)

pointer, sb. [AB³] *The king would ask for . . . a pointer or two as to locality of castle, best route to it, and so on* 1889 CY xi 126 (OED 3f. *U.S. colloq.* A piece of information. 1884.. So W Wr F Cl Th M H. Not A in S C)

poison, a. Spelled **pison, pizen**. [?ACE] "*He's been the pizenest kind of a Free-Will Babtis' for forty year. They ain't no pizener ones 'n what he is*" 1880 TA xxiii 225. *The old man was . . looking his level pisonest* 1884 HF xxviii 294 (OED Envenomed. *Obs*, exc. as coinciding with the attrib. use of the sb. 1530..1897. Not *obs* in W. The adj. use not in S C. W gives *pizen* as *dial* var. This pron. A in M; not mentioned in OED S C)

poison, adv. [AB¹E] *The funeral sermon was very good, but pison long and tiresome* 1884 HF xxix 275. '*You's got to be pison good*" 1894 PW xiv 780 (Used as a mere intensive: extremely, excessively. This sense not in OED W S C. A in DN.II,III AS.XI.35)

poison, v. [?AB¹E] *Do you reckon Tom Sawyer was satisfied after all them adventures? . . . No, he wasn't. It only just p'isoned him for more* 1893 TSA i 20 (To urge on, whet, increase one's desire. This sense not in OED W S C. Perhaps a hum. transf. from the sense in OED 3a. *fig.* To corrupt, pervert morally, influence perversely. 1395..)

poison-swilling, a. [?AB¹] *The immemorial mile of cheap, foul doggeries [along the St. Louis river-front] remained, but business was dull with them; the multitudes of poison-swilling Irishmen had departed* 1883 LM xxii 256 (The use of 'poison' as a synonym for alcohol has been widespread among U.S. supporters of prohibition. Neither this sense nor the comb. are given in OED W S C)

poke fun at, v.phr. [?AB³] "*Titles never die in America, although we do take a republican pride in poking fun at such trifles*" 1873 GA xxxiii 304. "*Please to don't poke fun at a poor girl like me, mum*" 1884 HF xi 92 (OED 5b. 1840.. So W S C U. A in B)

poker, sb. [AB³] "*Poker and seven-up . . have depleted your purses*" 1869 SNO (1875) 69. See *party* 1873 (OED Chiefly *U.S.* A card game, popular in America, a variety of Brag. OEDS 1836.. So W S C U B F Cl T M)

poker-clergy, sb. [AB¹] *He "held the age," as the poker-clergy say* 1907 "Chaps. from Autob" 569 (Poker experts; those 'learned' in poker lore. Hum. coinage; not in any dict. Perhaps M.T. was thinking of the *arch* meaning of the word *clergy*, OED 5. Clerkly skill, learning, scholarship. a1225..1822)

pole, v. [?A] *They floated and sailed from the upper rivers to New Orleans, changed cargoes there, and were tediously warped and poled back by hand* 1883 LM iii 41. (OED 6. To propel a boat or raft with a pole. 1774.. So W S C U A in Th)

polecat, sb. [A] "*You recommend the domestication of the polecat on account of its playfulness and its excellence as a ratter!*" 1870 SNO (1875) 237. See *durian* 1897. *He is a timid, sneaking, human polecat* 1898 "Memorable Assassination" (1917) 170 (OED 1b. In U.S., the skunk. 1688.. So W S C U DN.II,III AS IV.15)

police, sb. [?AB¹] *He was a police* 1856 *Adv. of T.J. Snodgrass* (1928) 8 (A policeman. This sing. use not in OED W S C)

police-parade, sb. [B¹] *The king, class G, is happy in the cold collation and the police-parade provided for him by the king, class B* 1902 "Does the Race of Man Love a Lord?" 437 (Comb. not in OED W S C)

policy business, sb. [B¹] *Dull policy business till next fire* 1883 LM xliii 437 (Comb. not in OED W S C; but cf. OED Policy-holder, 1906)

policy-Christian, sb. [B¹] *Any Christian who was not a policy-Christian had that healing power* 1907 CS II xv 284 (A Christian for profit or expediency. Comb. not in OED W S C)

polish off, v. [?AB¹] *After that he polished off with a kind of general cuss all round* 1884 HF vi 40 (To conclude, come to an end. This *intr.* use not in OED W S C; but cf. OED 4. To finish off quickly, *colloq.* orig. *Pugilistic* slang. 1829..)

polite-letter, a. [B¹] *I gradually got myself cooled down to a polite-letter temperature* 1901 "Two Little Tales" (1928) 200 (Comb. not in OED W S C)

polls, sb. [?AB³] *He had seen them around the polls "canvassing"* 1883 LM xxxiv 373. *Twenty thousand would-be exclusives come up to the polls* 1892 AmCl xi 95. (W: Usually in the *pl.* in the U.S. So S C AS.II. 29. This Am. *pl.* use not in OED U; cf. OED Poll, sb. 7b. 1832.. But the only U.S. quot. given in OED, 1860, from Emerson, uses the pl. form)

polling-day, sb. [B²] "*I will fling a hint at it from the stump on the polling day*" 1894 PW xv 820 (Given in OED, no ex. Comb. not in W S C)

polytechnique, sb. [B¹] "*Don't you think he is just a trifle overstrong in technique?*" "*Technique—technique —polytechnique—pyrotechnique; that's it, likely—fire works—too much color*" 1892 AmCl xvi 147 (Hum. nonce word)

pompano, sb. [AB³] *We had dinner [in New Orleans] —the chief dish the renowned fish called pompano, delicious as the less criminal forms of sin* 1883 LM xliv 445 (OED 1. One of various N. Am. fishes, highly esteemed for the table. 1863.. So W S C U DN.I)

pone, sb. [A] *Knead into the form of a pone* 1880 TA xlix 575 (OED Now, in southern U.S., a cake or loaf made of maize. 1796.. So W S C U B F Cl Th,1634 T M DN.I,II,VI, s.e.Mo. AS.IV.4,9; VII.168)

pool, sb. [?AB²] *No pools permitted on the run of the comet—no gambling of any kind* 1875 SNO 340 (OED 4b. *Betting.* The collective stakes of a number of persons . . in a contest, the proceeds being divided among the backers of the winner. 1881, only ex. So W S U. A in Cl Th.III,1872. This sense not in C)

pool, sb. [AB³] See *check* (to pass in one's checks) 1889 (OED 6. An arrangement by which rates or prices are fixed, and business or receipts divided, in order to do away with mutually injurious competition; orig. *U.S.* 1881.. So B Cl Th.III,1875 T. Not A in W S C U)

pool, v. [AB³] *Gillette and I pooled intellects on this proposition* 1890 "Wonderful Pair of Slippers" 309 (OED From the above: To throw into a common stock. 1879.. A in F Cl Th.III,1878 T. Not A in W S C U)

poopoo, sb. [B¹] See *kahkahponeeka* 1880 (Hum invention)

poorhouse, sb. [?A] *This wandering wench hadn't any more trouble to get access to the king in his palace than she would have had to get into the poorhouse in my day and country* 1889 CY xi 132 (OED 1782.. So W S C U. A in Wr. So M: Am. *poorhouse* = Eng. *workhouse*)

poor mouth, to put up a, v. phr. [AB¹] *Any selfish tramp . . can come and put up a poor mouth* 1892 AmCl iii 37 (A in DN.III, e.Ala. Phr. not in OED W S C; but cf. OED Mouth 3m. To make a poor mouth: to plead poverty. 1822.. ; A in Th DN.VI)

poor-quality, a. [B¹] *Ignorant, poor-quality, amateur weather* 1892 AmCl intro. 1 (Comb. not in OED W S C)

pop, sb. [?AB²] *I am simply lecturing for societies, at $100 a pop* 1868 *Letters* (1917) I ix 156 (OEDS 2d. A turn at doing something. 1904. This sense not in W S C)

pop-corn, sb. [AB³] *"Ten minutes for refreshments.. b'nanners, sand'ches, pop-corn!"* 1889 CY xv 182 (OED *U.S.* 1858.. So W S C U B F Cl Th M H)

pop-eye, sb. [?AB³] *He was inordinately good—and he had pop-eyes—and I would have drowned him if I had had a chance* 1906 *Autob* (1924) II 179 (OEDS 1828.. So W S. A in C B F Cl T H DN.II)

poppa, sb. [AB³] See *mamma* 1904 (OED *U.S. colloq.* = Papa. 1902.. So W. Not in S C)

poppy, sb. [?AB¹] *"He's cabled over to his poppy to send it"* 1892 AmCl xv 136 (Pap, pappy. Not in OED W S C)

populo, sb. [B¹] *"This will be followed by... the consequent embrocation of the bicuspid redax populo referendum rotulorum"* 1894 TET vii 409 (Nonsense word)

porcelaintype, sb. [B¹] *I have bundled up Livy's picture, and will try and recollect to mail it tomorrow. It is a porcelaintype* 1869 *Letters* (1917) I ix 160 (From a letter written to M.T.'s sister in St. Louis, on Aug. 20, 1869, from Buffalo, N. Y. Comb. not in OED W S C. This variety of photograph, produced on a sensitized porcelain plate or "opal" glass, was formerly popular and is still occasionally made, but is now known in the trade simply as a "porcelain" or an "opal". It was often retinted by hand.)

porch, sb. [AB³] *Crowds of people gathered on the porches and pressed their noses against the windows to look and marvel, but the bravest never ventured in* 1880 TA xxxii 345 See *baby-wagon* 1894; *cunning*, a. 1899 (OED 3b. A verandah. *U.S.* 1840.. So W S C H DN.II AS.I.150, V.21)

porch-roof, sb. [AB¹] *This porch-roof is composed of tremendous slabs of stones* 1869 IA xlii 448. See *time, to have a good* 1884 (Comb. not in OED W S C)

pork-house, sb. [?AB³] *Some gentlemen entered the pork house of Mr. Brittingham and helped themselves to two hams* 1853 *Hannibal Journal*, Apr.29 (OEDS A business house trading in pork. U.S. exs. 1831.. Comb. not in W S C)

pork-millionaire, sb. [?AB¹] *"Yesterday a visiting party of American pork-millionaires had a picnic in Westminster Abbey"* 1897 FE liii 515 (Comb. not in OED W S C. Cf. *millionaire*, above)

pork-packer, sb. [?AB³] *They discussed the son of the pork-packer and the son of the village banker* 1904 "Bequest" (1906) v 28 (OED Earliest exs. U.S. 1884.. Not A in W. Comb. not in S C)

pork-packing, sb. [?AB³] *He worked in the big cooper shop belonging to the great pork-packing establishment* 1894 "Scrap of Curious Hist." (1917)184 (OEDS Earliest exs. U.S. 1867.. Not A in W. Comb. not in S C)

porte-monnaie, sb. Also **port-monnaie, port-money**. [?AB³E] *"I've left my portmoney in the grocery"* 1857 *Adv. of T. J. Snodgrass* (1928) 42. *"Where the mischief is that port-monnaie?"* 1873 GA vii 76. *She was dripping portmonnaies and keys* 1906 *Autob* (1924) I 287 (OED A pocketbook. 1855.. So W S C U. A in DN.III. The first OED ex. of sp. *portmoney* is a U.S. quot., from Bret Harte)

porter-house steak, sb. [AB³] *"A mutton roast today, or will you have a nice porterhouse steak?"* 1869 IA xiii 126. *Blucher watched the men stow away porterhouse steaks* 1872 RI liv 434. See also *archipelagoed* 1880; *biscuit* 1880 (OEDS *U.S.* 1843.. So W S C Cl Th T M. Not A in U)

Portygee, sb. [?AE] *"Oh, he Christian—Portygee; live in Goa; mother not Portygee, mother native"* 1897 FE xxxix 362. *Four sick sailors...among them a "Portyghee"* 1899 "My Debut" (1900) 75 (OED Portuguese, sb. In modern times, a *sing.* has arisen in vulgar use, esp. among sailors. 1878. So W. A in M DN.II,III. This form not in S C)

possessed, ppl.a. **like all possessed.** [AB³] *The women certainly act like all possessed* 1889 CY xv 177 (OEDS

2d. With great vehemence or spirit. *U.S.* 1834.. So W S B Cl Th,1833 T DN.IV. Phr. not in C)

possum, sb. [A] *"He put the other eye to the hole like a possum looking down a jug"* 1880 TA iii 38. See also *coon* 1898 (OED Aphetic form of *opossum.* 1613.. So W S C U B F Cl Th T M DN.II,III,IV,VI)

post, v. [?C] *The editor... swoops down upon a correspondent who posted him as a Radical* 1869 SNO (1875) 44 (OED 5b. To expose to ignominy by advertising or bringing before the public. Now *rare.* 1642..1884. Not *rare* in W S C U, and app. not so felt by M.T.)

post, v. [AB³] *He was a man who was always "posted"* 1870 E&E (1923) 19. *He was shrewd, prompt, posted, and punctual* 1880 TA xxxii 354. *Tom perceived that here was someone whom his keepers ought to have posted him about* 1881 PP xiv 169. *"Well, I've been posting myself a good while"* 1892 AmCl xviii 163 (OED 9. orig. *U.S. colloq.* To supply with full information. 1847.. So B Cl Th T DN.III. Not A in W S C U)

postal currency, sb. [AB³] *25 and 50 cent postal currency* 1906 "Letter to the Sec. of the Treasury" 229 (OED *U.S.* A paper currency of denominations less than a dollar, issued by the U.S. in 1862. 1862.. So W S B F Cl T. Comb. not in C)

postal service, sb. [B¹] See *back number* 1895 (Comb. not in OED W S C, although the term is used in the OED definition of Postage)

poster, sb. [?AB³] *The tall van, plastered with fanciful bills and posters, that follows the band-wagon* 1869 IA xvii 167. *He put up posters promising to devote his whole paper to matters connected with the great event* 1894 "Scrap of Curious Hist." (1917) 186 (OED 2. A placard displayed in a public place. 1838.. So W S C U. A in Th.III)

poster-fence, sb. [?AB¹] *There are no poster-fences* 1893 "The German Chicago" 217 (Comb. not in OED W S C. Cf. above)

post-college, a. [?AB¹] *He had finished a post-college course in an Eastern law school* 1893 PW i 235 (Comb. not in OED W S C; but cf. OED Post-graduate, orig. *U.S.,* 1858..)

Postmaster-General, sb. [AB³] See *Speaker* 1880 (OED The administrative head of the postal service ..in the U.S. always a member of the cabinet. 1872. So S C. Not A in W)

post-mortuary, a. [?AB²] *No more comprehensive program of farewells, post-mortuary general orders, etc., could be framed* 1870 "Post-Mortem Poetry" (1906) 249 (OED Post-mortem. U.S. quot. 1893, only ex. Not A in W S C)

post-Pleosaurian, a. [B¹] *"That remote geological epoch known to Science as the Old Red Grindstone Post-Pleosaurian"* 1897 FE viii 106 (Nonsense comb., by error for Plesiosaurian, which of course means a reptile, not an epoch)

post up, v. [AB¹] *"We must suck the maps and cyclopedias dry. And while we posted up in this way..."* 1897 FE xxvi 254 (To inform oneself, acquire full information. This intr. use not in OED W S C; but cf. OED 9. *Post up:* To supply with full information. orig. *U.S. colloq.* 1847..)

pot, sb. [AB¹] *What is still more irregular, the man that loses a game gets the pot* 1889 *Speeches* (1923) 147 (W: A pool. So S C. A in Th M. This sense not in OED. Cf. *pool*, sb., above)

potato, sb. [A] See *biscuit* 1880 (OED The plant *Solanum tuberosum*, a native of the Pacific slopes of South America. 1597.. So W S C U B F AS.IV.9)

potato-gun, sb. [?AB¹] *Out comes a little potato-gun of a revolver* 1869 IA li 540 (C: A special form of powder gun for dusting potato-plants with an insecticide. Not in OED W S)

potato-patch, sb. [AB³] See *high-altitude*, a. 1892 (OEDS *U.S.* 1807.. Comb. not in W S C)

Potomac, sb. **All quiet on the Potomac!** [AB¹] *"Order, gentlemen!" All quiet on the Potomac, you bet!* 1877 *Speeches* (1910) 6 (A Civil War phr. for a condition of tranquility. A in F Cl. Not in OED W S C)

pot-shaped, a. [B²] *This track was perforated by huge pot-shaped holes in the bed-rock* 1880 TA xxvii 272 (OED 1893, only ex. Comb. not in W S C)

potter, v. [?AB³] *"The lazy cuss slid out because he wanted a loafing spell. He'll come pottering back in a couple of weeks"* 1896 TSD ix 524 (OED 5b. To saunter, dawdle. 1829.. So S W C U Wr. A in B; but cf. F Cl: Potter Eng. = Putter Am. Cf. putter, v., below)

poultry-raising, sb. [B²] *From early youth I have taken an especial interest in the subject of poultry-raising* 1870 SNO (1875) 81 (Given in OED W, no ex. Comb. not in S C)

pounce, v. [C] *A mantle of white cloth-of-gold, pounced with the triple-feather crest* 1881 PP ix 106 (OED 2. To ornament by cutting or punching eyelet-holes, figures, etc. *Obs* exc. *Hist.* c1386..1840. Not *obs* in W C U. This sense not in S)

poundiferous, a. [?AB¹] *A long, poundiferous, and vitreous jingling of applause announces the conclusion* 1871 *Letters* (1917) I x 183 (Accompanied by pounding; an onomatopoetic coinage. Not in OED W S C)

pourpoint, sb. [C] *"Twelve French gentlemen in splendid habiliments, consisting of pourpoints of white damask barred with gold"* 1881 PP ix 105 (OED *obs* exc. *Hist.* A doublet, stuffed and quilted, worn by men in the 14th and 15th c. 1426..1876. So W S C)

poursuivant, sb. [C] *Guétin had sent a messenger through our lines...Of course this poursuivant had arrived ahead of us* 1895 JA II vi 150 (OED 2b. Messenger. *obs.* c1530..1631. So W S C)

poverties, sb.pl. [?C] *The household poverties...had been made to blossom like the rose* 1892 AmCl v 60 (OED 1 † b. Formerly also in *pl.* a1533..1574. So S. This *concrete* use not in W C. Not felt as *arch* by M.T.)

powder-can, sb. [B¹] *The pair carried fuse, drills, and the powder-can to the shaft* 1902 "DBDS" (1928) 311 (Comb. not in OED W S C)

powder-keg, sb. [B¹] *An empty powder-keg* 1876 TS xxxiii 260 (Comb. not in OED W S C; but cf. OED Powder-barrel, 1769..)

power, sb. [?A] *"I'd give the whole world to believe that—it would cover up a power of sins, Tom"* 1876 TS xix 167. *Here she was finding a power of fault with me for doing a thing that had some good in it* 1884 HF i 3. *There was a power of excitement on board the comet* 1907 "Capt.Stormfield" 42 (OED 10b. An abundance, a great deal, a 'lot'. Now *dial* or *vulgar colloq.* 1671.. So W C U Wr. A in DN.II,III,IV,V, Ky., Me., N.H., Mo., Ga. This sense not in S)

powerful, adv. [?AB³] *You hit powerful hard, but Lord, I can forgive* 1867 M.T. *the Letter Writer* (1932) i 16. *"The Injuns is powerful troublesome"* 1872 RI ii 26. *"Powerful warm, warn't it?"* 1876 TS i 20. *Church music mixed up with a bombardment is a powerful queer combination* 1883 LM xxxv 382. *We are powerful glad you are all back* 1883 *Letters* (1917) I xviii 434. *So also time, to have a good* 1884; *strong* 1894; *comb.* sb. 1896 (OED Very, exceedingly. *dial* and *vulgar.* 1835.. So W S. A in C Wr B Th,1833 T M DN.I,II,III, Ill., Ind., Mo., Ala., Conn. AS.IV.292, VIII.1.23)

powwow, sb. [AB³] *The powwow about the completion of the Pacific Railroad* 1869 CRG (1919) 129. *It was a perfect powwow for a while* 1883 LM iii 48. *The powwow and racket were prodigious* 1889 CY xxiv 445 (OED 3. *transf.* Applied to any meeting compared to an Indian conference; a merry-making; a 'palaver' of any kind. Chiefly *U.S.* 1812.. So W S C U B F Cl Th,1768 T M AS.VII.3)

powwow, sb. [AB¹] See *fuss-and-feathers* 1893. *It all helps to augment the general sense of swiftness and energy and confusion and powwow* 1897 FE xxxviii 346 (Cf.

above. Here extended to the quality of noisiness and confusion, rather than a concrete example of it. This abstract sense not in OED W S C)

powwow, v. [A] *"I'm keeping quiet...Your old hand don't go around powwowing and letting everybody see his k'yards and find out his little game"* 1873 GA viii 76. *We would go to the cave and powwow over what we had done* 1884 HF iii 19 (OED 1b. *transf.* To confer, discuss, talk. Chiefly *U. S.* 1780.. So W S C U B F Cl Th)

prairie, sb. [A] *The prairie, with its new grass and unending acres of brilliant flowers—chiefly the innumerable varieties of phlox—bore the look of years of cultivation, and the occasional open groves of white oaks gave it a parklike appearance* 1873 GA xvi 156. *We marched to a shady piece of woods on the border of the far-reaching expanses of a flowery prairie* 1885 "Private Hist. of Campaign" 195. See *continental* 1892.. (OED Applied chiefly to the grassy plains of North America. 1773.. So W S C U B F Cl Th T M DN.II,IV,V,VI AS.II.32)

prairie-chicken, sb. [AB³] See *batter-cake* 1897 (OED The Pinnated Grouse, a gallinaceous bird of N. America. Also applied to the Sharp-tailed Grouse. (OEDS 1847. So W S C U)

prairie-dog, sb. [AB³] *He would see buffaloes and Indians, and prairie-dogs* 1872 RI i 19. *Apparently these people were sufficiently sentimental... Shelley moved to Bracknell purposely to be near this unwholesome prairie-dogs' nest* 1894 "In Defence of Harriet Shelley" 115 (OED A N. American rodent animal. 1807.. So W S C U B F Cl Th,1805 M)

prairie-farm, sb. [AB³] See *bottom*, sb. 1884 (OEDS b. 1838. Comb. not in W S C)

prairie-fire, sb. [AB³] *I beckoned her to come—which she did..with the rush of a prairie fire* 1889 CY xx 245. *We was racing along like a prairie fire* 1893 TSA iv 120 (OEDS 1836.. Comb. not in W S C)

prairie-hen, sb. [AB³] See *biscuit* 1880 (OED = Prairie-chicken. 1805.. So W S C U B F Cl Th M DN.IV)

prairie-land, sb. [AB³] *Level prairie lands, holding in their lap the beautiful Wabasha* 1883 LM lix 576 (OED 1807. So Th. Comb. not in W S C)

prairie-pink, sb. [AB¹] *One emerged abruptly upon a level great prairie which was vividly starred with prairie pinks* 1897 *Autob* (1924) I 106 (Comb. not in OED W S C)

prairie-rattlesnake, sb. [AB³] *They were a perfect protection against prairie-rattlesnakes, which never strike above the knee* 1873 GA xiii 125 (OEDS 1831.. So W C. Comb. not in S)

pray, v. [B¹] *I went to church last Sunday and came mighty near getting prayed to death* 1866 *Speeches* (1923) 10 (Hum. nonce use)

prayer cure, sb. [?AB²] *Within the last quarter of a century in America, several sects of cures have appeared.. There are the Mind Cure, the Faith Cure, the Prayer Cure, the Mental Science Cure, and the Christian Science Cure* 1899 "Chr. Sc. and the Book" 594 (OED A cure wrought by means of 'the prayer of faith' (Jas. v. 15), a faith-cure. No ex. So S. Comb. not in W C)

precious, adv. [?AB³] *Precious soon they had occasion to reconsider that motion* 1869 IA xiv 131 (OED b. With intensive force: very. *colloq.* 1837.. So W S C U. A in Th)

preempt, v. [AB³] *So the old man went in and preempted a county or two* 1867 *Notebook* (1935) ix 105 (OED Chiefly *U.S.* To occupy public land so as to establish a pre-emptive title. 1837.. So W S C B F Cl Th.III T H. Not A in U)

preforeordestination, sb. [B¹] *Everybody has such a powerful lot to say about faith and good works and free grace and preforeordestination* 1884 HF xviii 167 (**Hum.** nonce word: a blend of predestination and foreordination)

pregeological, a. [B¹] *Other works of art, conceived and committed on the premises, by the young ladies...landscapes, mostly...petrified clouds, pregeological trees, anthracite precipice; name of criminal conspicuous in the orner* 1883 LM xxxviii 403 (Hum. nonce use; cf. M.T.'s use of 'geologic,' above. For literal sense cf. S: Antedating the evidence of reliable records of geology. So OED 1882 W C)

prehistoric, a. [B¹] *I can see that printing office of prehistoric times yet* 1886 *Speeches* (1910) 185 (Hum. nonce use; cf. above. For literal sense cf. OED: Of the period antecedent to history. 1851.. So W S C U)

prentice, sb. [C] *"We lads of Offal Court do strive against each other with the cudgel, like to the fashion of the 'prentices"* 1881 PP iii 44. *"You're a runaway 'prentice, that's all"* 1884 HF xi 193 (OED Now arch or dial. 1. Apprentice. c1300..1857. So W S C U Wr. M.T.'s use of the word in HF indicates that it was not *arch* in Missouri in his boyhood)

prentice-fashion, sb. [B¹C] *The movement of the narrative rambles around, 'prentice-fashion* 1907 CS II iii 127 (Comb. not in OED W S C; but cf. OED Prentice-like, 1594)

prentice-hand, sb. [C] *They seem to me to prove the presence of the 'prentice hand* 1907 CS II iii 127 (OED 1784. So Wr. Comb. not in W S C. Cf. above)

prentice-work, sb. [C] *His frantic and lubberly 'prentice-work found but a poor market for itself* 1881 PP xxii 269. *All the music that they had ever heard before seemed spiritless prentice-work* 1894 PW vi 335 (OED 1860. Comb. not in W S C. Cf. above)

presentee, sb. [B¹] *There was an absentee who ought to be a presentee—a word which she meant to look out in the dictionary* 1892 AmCl xxi 189 (Hum. coinage for one who is present)

President, sb. [A] *"Nobody goes there, Miss Hawkins, —at least, only persons of no position in society. And the President"* 1873 GA xxiii 299 (OED 4. The officer in whom the executive power is vested in a modern republic. Used first in the United States of America. 1793.. So W S C B M H. Not A in U)

presidential, a. [?A] *Pewter presidential campaign medal* 1883 LM xxxviii 404 (OED Pertaining to a president. 1603..; first Am. use, 1785. A in B M. Not A in W S C)

press-notice, sb. [B¹] *I thank you ever so much for not forgetting to remember to send me the press notice* 1888 *M.T. the Letter Writer* (1932) iii 49 (Comb. not in OED W S C; but cf. OED Press-noticed, 1906)

presumption-tadpole, sb. [B¹] See *history-tank* 1909 (Hum. nonce comb.)

pretty, a. [?AC] *"Try how pretty you can be Till I come again," said she. "Docile be, and good and mild."* [German, Sei hübsch] 1891 *Slovenly Peter* (1935) 15 (OED 3. Excellent, admirable, commendable. a. Of persons. Now arch. 1400..1886. Not arch in W S C. Dial in Wr. A in B Th; cf. Th. quot. 1827: "When the Yankee says 'pretty,' he does not mean handsome but agreeable")

pretzel, sb. [AB³] *Kaspar flew to join the band, His toothsome pretzel in his hand* [German, Brezel] 1891 *Slovenly Peter* (1935) 8 (OED *U.S.* A crisp biscuit baked in the form of a knot. 1879.. So B F Cl Th T M AS.X.169. Not A in W S C)

previous, a. [AB³] See *fresh* 1892 (OED 3. *slang* or *colloq.* orig. *U.S.* Hasty, premature. 1885.. So Th M. Not A in W S U. This sense not in C)

previous-engagement, a. [B¹] *The previous-engagement pleas...you can lay aside forever* 1905 *Speeches* (1910) 434 (Comb. not in OED W S C)

price-raiser, sb. [B¹] *"That congregation's real estate stands at a low figure. What they are anxious to have now ...is a price-raiser"* 1906 *Autob* (1924) II 24 (Comb. not in OED W S C)

primary, sb. [AB¹] *These powers went to the "primaries" in strong force* 1870 CRG (1919) i 2. *They continued to sit comfortably at home and leave the true source of our political power, the "primaries," in the hands of saloon-keepers* 1873 GA lix 530. *They allow the scum of the country to assemble at the "primaries," name the candidates for office from their own vile ranks, and elect them* 1873 E&E (1923) 27 (W: *U.S.* short for primary election. So S. Only the earlier sense of primary assembly, caucus, in OEDS 6. *U.S.* 1861.. A in C U F Th,1821 T M H)

printing-house, sb. [?AC] *Orion severed his connection with the printing house in St. Louis* 1906 *Autob* (1924) II 285 (OED Now only *Hist.* A printing-office. 1576..1856. Not *arch* in S C. Comb. not in W)

prism, sb. [B¹] *The pet of the house, a very prism in her cheap but ravishing Sunday rig, blew him a kiss* 1892 AmCl xv 139 (A glittering object. This sense not in OED W S C)

prism-fringed, a. [B¹] *She* [a steamboat] *glittered with no end of prism-fringed chandeliers* 1875 OTM 220 (Comb. not in OED W S C)

prithee, int.phr. [C] *"And prithee, why not?"* 1881 PP iii 42. *"Prithee do not let me"* 1889 CY ii 32 (OED Archaic colloquialism for 'I pray thee'. 1577.. 1875. So W U Wr. Not *obs* in S C)

privacy, sb. [C] *It gave him the painful sense of being an intruder upon a sacred privacy* 1892 AmCl xxi 190 (OED 4. A private matter, a secret. Now rare. 1591.. 1759. So W. This *concrete* sense is not rare in S C, and app. not so felt by M.T.)

private, adv. [?AC] See *bust, v.* 1876. *They all drunk more than usual—not together, but each man sidled off and took it private, by himself* 1883 LM iii 54 (OED 16. Privately, secretly. *obs* 1590..1704. So W. This use not in S C)

privileged sex, sb. [B¹] *The colored waiters filled the plates and glasses, and the male guests moved hither and thither conveying them to the privileged sex* 1873 GA xxxii 293 (Phr. not in OED W S C. Cf. Privilege, sb. 4. quot. 1840 from Longfellow: "Beautiful almost beyond the privilege of woman!")

privilege of the floor, sb. [?AB¹] *The ex-Congressman clings piteously to the one little shred that is left of his departed distinction—the "privilege of the floor"* 1902 "Does the Race of Man Love a Lord?" 443 (Right of admission to the Congress chamber. Phr. not in OED W S C)

proceed, v. [B¹] *B said, "I'll kill you!" and proceeded for him with his revolver* 1883 LM xxx 389 (To 'go for,' attack. This grandiloquent use not in OED W S C)

processionally, adv. [B¹] *There were now three bullets in that one hole—three bullets imbedded processionally* 1895 "Cooper's Literary Offences" 10 (Successively, in succession. This sense not in OED W S C; but cf. OED Processional, a. c. *humorously*, forming a long series or 'string,' e.g. of words. 1905)

procrastinated, ppl.a. [C] *I have no sort of moral right to let that ancient and procrastinated contract hamper you in any way* 1885 *Letters* (1917) II xxv 463 (OED Procrastinate, v. 1. trans. To postpone, defer. Now rare. 1588..1871; Procrastinated, ppl.a. 1789, only ex. So W. Not *rare* in S C)

procrastinaturalist, sb. [B¹] *I am as prompt as a clock if I only know the day a thing is wanted—otherwise I am a natural procrastinaturalist* 1874 *Letters* (1917) I xiv 237 (Hum. nonce coinage: a blend of procrastinator and naturalist)

product, sb. [B¹C] *The infant son of the eldest product grew up* 1892 AmCl i 6 (C: Offspring. rare. This sense not in OED W S)

profanity, sb. [A] *The old Admiral...a roaring, terrific combination of wind and lightning and thunder, and earnest, whole-souled profanity* 1872 RI lxii 444. *He wove a glittering streak of profanity through his garrulous fabric that was refreshing to a spirit weary of the* *dull neutralities of undecorated speech* 1877 "Some Rambling Notes" ii 589. See also *mule-power* 1880; *tobacco-smoke* 1883; *firmament-obliterating* 1883; *crash-word* 1889; *anti* 1909 (OED More common in U.S. than in England, where *profaneness* was the usual word down to 1800. 1607.. A in B. Not A in W S C. An indispensable part of M.T.'s vocabulary)

profanity-mill, sb. [?AB¹] *A mate in the olden times could have got his profanity-mill adjusted* 1883 LM xxiii 261 (Comb. not in OED W S C. Cf. above)

professor, sb. [AC] *She was not a professor of religion* 1873 GA xxxii 293. *The people...wondered if the baptizing would really happen, or if the twin who was not a "professor" would stand out and prevent it* 1894 TET viii 421 (OED 3b. *spec.* One who makes open profession of religion; a professing Christian. Now chiefly *Scotch* and *U.S.* 1597.. So Wr B F Cl Th T M DN.V. *Arch* in W. Not A or *arch* in S C U)

professor, sb. [?AB³] *An ample crop of "Professors" of various kinds* 1869 IA i 26. *My subject is the mesmerizer now...Straightway came the professor and made passes over my head* 1907 "Chaps. from Autob" 6 (OED 5b. Assumed as a grandiose title by professional teachers and exponents of various popular arts and sciences. 1864.. So W S C U B F Cl)

profile paper, sb. [?AB²] *He plotted the line on the profile paper* 1873 GA xvii 160 (OED Paper ruled with equidistant vertical and horizontal lines for convenience in drawing to scale. 1892, only ex. So W S C)

prohibition, sb. [?AB³] *If they couldn't persuade a person to try a prohibition journal, they removed him and passed on* 1889 CY xl 513. See also *anti* 1909 (OED 4. *spec.* The forbidding by law of the manufacture and sale of intoxicating drinks. All exs. U.S. 1851.. A in S B F Cl T AS.II.138. Not A in W C U)

prohibitionist, sb. [?AB³] *Told them my first wife was a Free Will Baptist, and her grandfather was a Prohibitionist, and I used to know a man who had two thumbs on each hand* 1889 CY xxxi 397. *He was a relentless prohibitionist and head of the order in the District of Columbia* 1892 AmCl xx 184. *He was a prohibitionist and had never drunk a drop in his life* 1894 TET intro. 312. *The multitudinous hot toddies that were circulating began to exert a powerful influence upon the new prohibitionists* 1906 *Autob* (1924) II 177 (OED One who advocates or favors prohibition. Earliest exs. U.S. 1846.. A in S B F Cl. Not A in W C U)

proof-reading, sb. [?AB³] *The proof-reading on the P and P cost me the last rags of my religion* 1884 *Letters* (1917) II xxiv 443. *It was good enough Arkansas proof-reading* 1889 CY xxvi 41 (OEDS 1881.. So W S C U. But cf. OED Proof-reader, sb. quot. 1907: "Thomas Bailey Aldrich entered literature as a 'proof-reader'...That is the American equivalent of our 'corrector to the press' or 'printer's reader'")

prophecy-enthusiast, sb. [B¹] *Some infatuated prophecy-enthusiast blundered along and said..."In sooth, here is astounding fulfillment of prophecy"* 1869 IA xxxviii 409 (Comb. not in OED W S C; but cf. OED Prophecy-monger, 1655..)

prophecy-gun, sb. [B¹] *A man who goes around with a prophecy-gun ought never to get discouraged* 1897 *Autob* (1924) I 89 (Comb. not in OED W S C)

prophecy-savan, sb. [B¹E] *The cruelest habit these modern prophecy-savans have is that of fitting the prophetic shirt on the wrong man* 1869 IA xxxviii 408 (Comb. not in OED W S C; but cf. OED Savant, sb. incorrect form Savan, 1765, 1864)

prosecuting attorney, sb. [?AB³] *The courtroom was crowded at an early hour... There was a little stir when the prosecuting attorney, with two assistants, made his way in* 1873 GA liv 486 (OEDS U.S. exs. 1832.. Not A in W C. Comb. not in S)

pro-slavery, a. [?AB³] *They were pro-slavery Missourians* 1907 "Chaps. from Autob" 330 (OED U.S. quot. 1843, only ex. A in W S C B F Th)

prospect, sb. [?AB³] *A "prospect" is what one finds in the first panful of dirt* 1872 RI lxi 443. See also *pan* 1872 (OEDS 10c. *Mining.* A sample of ore or 'dirt' for testing. Earliest ex. U.S. 1852.. A in B F Cl AS.II.86. Not A in W S C U)

prospect, v. [AB³] *"What—sure that it's coal?" "Most of the indications were there, but not all of them. So we thought we'd prospect a bit"* 1873 GA xlix 444. See *horn* 1893. *He has a shanty and goes out prospecting daily* 1902 "DBDS" (1928) 299 (OED *Mining.* orig. *U.S.* 4. To explore a region for gold or other minerals. 1848.. So C B F Cl Th,1845 T. Not A in W S U)

prospect, v. [AB³] *"You can get that book and prospect her"* 1865 SS (1926) 159. *Those donkeys didn't prospect these liars for details* 1889 CY xi 130. *"I'll prospect the hotel"* 1892 AmCl vi 53 (OED *Mining.* orig. *U.S.* 5c. *fig.* To survey as to prospects. 1864.. So C B F Cl Th T. Not A in W S U)

prospecting, vbl.sb. [AB³] *"Prospecting" is hunting for a "placer"* 1872 RI lxi 443 (OEDS *Mining.* From Prospect, v., above. 1850.. A in C B Th. Not A in W S)

prospector, sb. [AB³] *I've been a prospector, and know pay rock from poor when I find it* 1891 *Letters* (1917) II xxxi 542 (OED From Prospect, v., above. One who explores a region for gold or the like. 1857.. A in C B Th.III AS.II.86. Not A in W S U)

prostrating, ppl.a. [?AB²] *It was all so sudden and prostrating* 1893 "Esquimau Maiden's Romance" (1900) 145 (OED Reducing to helplessness. 1890. So W S C. A in AS.VII.427)

Protestant Episcopal, sb. [A] See *Adventist* 1907 (OED Official style of the church in the U.S. descended from and in communion with the Church of England. 1780. So W S C M)

protoplasm, sb. (B²) *I told him to make perfectly free with any idea of mine that struck him as being good protoplasm for poetry* 1879 *Speeches* (1910) 58 (OED *Biol. fig.* 1894.. The *fig* use not in W S C)

proud, a. **to do one proud**. [?AB³] *I take off my hat to my life-long friend and comrade, and...say, in the language of Alabama, "You do me proud"* 1906 "Entertaining Article" 225 (OED 10b. To gratify highly. *colloq.* 1819.. So W S C U. A in M)

prove, v. [C] *He seized Miles by the arm, dragged him to the window, and began to devour him from head to foot...stepping briskly around him and about him to prove him from all points of view* 1881 PP xxv 300 (OED 1. To try, test. *arch.* c1200..1867. So Wr. Not *arch* in W S C)

prove, v. **to prove title**. [B¹] *A home without a cat may be a perfect home, perhaps, but how can it prove title?* 1893 PW i 233 (Phr. not in OED W S C; but cf. OED 7b. *spec.* To prove a will, 1439..)

provision-basket, sb. (B²) *The gay throng filed up the main street laden with provision-baskets* 1876 TS xxix 218 (Given in OED, no ex. Comb. not in W S C)

pry, v. [AB³] *They pried off the lid with the shovels* 1876 TS ix 89 (OED *dial.* and *U.S.* Shortened from Prize. To force up. 1823.. So Wr B F Cl M. Not A in W S C U)

psychologizer, sb. [B¹] *The Observer of Peoples has to be a Classifier, a Grouper, a Deducer, a Generalizer, a Psychologizer* 1895 "What Bourget Thinks" 49 (Not in OED W S C)

psychosuperintangibly, adv. [B¹] See *electroincandescently* 1907 (Nonsense coinage)

public school, sb. [A] *He could get the monthly public school report* 1872 RI xliii 299. *The public-school pupil wrestles with the potential features of the Great Republic* 1887 "English as She Is Taught" (1917) 251 (OED 3. In Scotland, British colonies and dominions, and

U.S.A.. A school provided at the public expense and managed by public authority for the use of the community of a defined district. The term has been used in N.E. and Pa. from the 17th c., and has been adopted in all States of the Am. Union. 1644.. So W S C U M)

puckittypukk, sb. [B¹] See *kahkahponeeka* 1880 (Hum. invention)

puddinghead, sb. Spelled **pudd'nhead**. [?AB²E] *Perfect jackass—yes, and it ain't going too far to say he's a pudd'nhead* 1893 PW i 235. *"We went ahead and done it, like a couple of pudd'nheads"* 1896 TSD iii 352. *We know that 9 in 10 of the species are pudd'nheads* 1900 *Letters* (1917) II xxxix 690 (OED A stupid person. No ex. So W S C U Wr. A in DN.IV. OED gives the forms *pudden, puddin*, as 19th c. *dial* and *vulgar*)

puff-adder, sb. [AB¹] *When they were rattlesnakes or puff-adders, we killed them* 1897 *Autob* (1924) I 103 (S: A puffing-adder, or hognose-snake, a N. Am. colubrine snake with flattened head and prominent snout. This sense not in OED W C, which know the Am. snake only as the *puffing-adder*)

puff-sleeved, ppl.a. [B¹] See *high-collared* 1883 (Comb. not in OED W S C; but cf. OEDS Puff-sleeve, sb. 1932)

pull, sb. [AB¹] *All the way down the Lower Mississippi without having to change steam-boats at St. Louis; not so very much short of a thousand miles at one pull* 1896 TSD ii 346 (A continuous voyage; an unbroken portion of a journey. This sense not in OED W S C. An extension of the sense in OED 2c. A pull at an oar; hence, a short spell at rowing; a journey in a rowing-boat. 1793..)

pull, v. [AB³] *"When they happened to meet, they pulled and began. Men would shoot boys, boys would shoot men"* 1883 LM xxvi 286 (OEDS 7h. To draw and fire a gun or pistol. *U.S. absol.* 1841, only ex. *absol.* use. So W Cl. This sense not in S C)

pull, v. [?AB³] *If I were going to advise San Francisco as to the best strategy to employ in order to secure the whaling trade, I should say, "Cripple your facilities for 'pulling' sea captains on any pretense that sailors can trump up"* 1866 *Letters* (1917) I v 112 (OED 16. To arrest. *slang.* 1811.. So W S C. A in Cl)

pull, v. to pull one's words. [?AB¹] *"What makes you pull your words that way?"* ("pulling" being the river term for drawling) *Bixby asked him... "You'll have to ask my mother"*, he [M.T.] said, more slowly than ever. *"She pulls hers, too."* 1912 Paine's *Biog.* I. 118, conversation ascribed to 1857 (This idiom not in OED W S C)

pull, v. [?AB¹] *"Them odds and ends have got 'ir little old secret, and they think there ain't anybody can pull it; but, land! when he [Sherlock Holmes] sets his grip there, they've got to squeal"* 1902 "DBDS (1928) 335 (To extract, discover, elucidate. This sense not in OED W S C)

pull down, v. [?AB¹] See *shove up* 1883. *Brown was steering; I was "pulling down"* 1883 LM xix 227. See also *bald-headed* 1909 (To exert a downward pressure on the spokes of the steering-wheel. This *Naut.* usage not in OED W S C)

pull off, v. [?AB¹] *"I pulled off an old woman's leather"* (*robbed her of her pocketbook*) [Given as "thieves' argot"] 1883 LM lii 511 (This sense not in OED W S C)

pull on, v. [?AB¹] *Living in a house and sleeping in a bed pulled on me pretty tight mostly* 1884 HF iv 25 (To wear upon, put a strain on. This sense not in OED W S C)

pull out, v. [AB²] *We got under way and pulled out for the summit again* 1880 TA xxviii 287. *Sir Charolais... will pull out today for home* 1889 CY xxvi 340. *He pulls out for the tavern* 1902 "DBDS" (1928) 329 (OED 28d. To go away, take one's departure. Chiefly *U.S.* 1884.. So U F Cl Th DN.III,IV. This sense not in W S C)

pull through, v. trans. [?AB³] *"I pulled it through, Colonel, but it was a tough job"* 1873 GA xxv 238. *This is an attempt to pull a book through without weather* 1892 AmCl intro. 2 (OED 29b. To bring to a successful issue. 1856.. So W S C U. A in B T)

pull through, v.intr. [?AB³] *His invention always stood the strain and he pulled through all right* 1883 LM xxiv 265. See *calculate* 1889. *I have been a long time pulling through with... my very first attempt at art* 1890 "Wonderful Pair of Slippers" 309. *"I'm at your back, and we'll pull through"* 1892 AmCl xvi 149. *Sunday.—Pulled through. This day is getting to be more and more trying* 1893 "Extracts from Adam's Diary" (1901) 762 (OED 29c. To get through with effort and difficulty. 1852.. So W S C U. A in B T)

Pullman, a. [AB³] *The Pullman conductor and the train conductor capitulated* 1906 *Speeches* (1910) 137 (OED From the name of the designer, George M. Pullman of Chicago. b. *attrib.* 1885.. So W S C U B Cl M)

Pullman car, sb. [AB³] See *inventor-tribe* 1905 (OED 1874.. So W C B F. Comb. not in S. Cf. above)

pulpit, sb. [?AB¹] *The judge stood up in his pulpit* 1896 TSD xi 537. See also *bowie* 1896 (The bench, or judge's seat. This sense not in OED W S C; but cf. W S: A desk or platform for a public speaker, a reader, or the like; *rare*)

pulu, sb. [?AB¹] *"Pulu" or "Tuler", or whatever they call it—a species of unpoetical willow that grows on the banks of the Carson* 1861 *Letters* (1917) I iii 54 (See Tule, below. Cf. OED Pulu, sb. *Hawaiian.* A fine vegetable wool obtained from the base of the leaf stalks of the Hawaiian tree-ferns. 1858.. Apparently M.T. confused the name of the Nevada bulrush 'tule' with the tree-fern of Hawaii, which at this time (1861) he had not yet visited)

pump-house, sb. [?AB²] *I passed along the pavement by the pump-house* [of a water-works] 1853 Letter in *Iowa Journ. of Hist.* (1929) 411 (OED (c) A pumping-station. 1863, only ex. So W S. This sense not in C)

pumpkin, sb. Spelled **punkin**. [AE] *Concerning the pumpkin. This berry is a favorite with the natives of the interior of New England... It is now generally conceded that the pumpkin as a shade tree is a failure* 1870 SNO (1875) 235. See *hoop-pole* 1875. *Mornings before daylight I slipped into corn-fields and borrowed... a punkin* 1884 HF xii 101 (OED In U.S. the *m* is often assimilated to the *k*...and the word spelled *punkin*. 1. In U.S. applied *spec* to particular varieties in distinction from the squash. 1647.. So W S C U F M DN.I,IV AS.XI. 238, XII.107)

pumpkin-head, sb. [AB²] *"Ef we hadn' ben sich punkin-heads, as de sayin' is, we'd a seed de raf'"* 1884 HF xviii 170 (OED *U.S. colloq.* d. A stupid fellow, a dolt. No ex. So W S C DN.IV,V)

pumpkin-pie, sb. [AB³] See *biscuit* 1880; *batter-cake* 1897 (OED In U.S., considered especially appropriate to Thanksgiving Day. 1817.. Comb. not in W S C)

pumpkin-show, sb. [AB¹] *Going down to Carson to report horse-races and pumpkin-shows* 1872 RI lv 398 (An agricultural exhibit. Comb. not in OED W S C)

pumpkin-vine, sb. [AB³] See *simlin* 1897 (OED 1840. So S C. Comb. not in W. Cf. above)

punch, sb. Santa Cruz Punch. [AB¹] See *cocktail* 1869 (Given in F as an American drink. Not in OED W S C)

punch, v. [?AB¹] *I have disinvited the boys I thought I was going to punch billards with* 1889 *Letters* (1917) II xxix 519 (No *billiards* sense in OED W S C. Perhaps an extension from the sense in OED 2. In U.S. and Colonial use: To drive cattle. 1886..)

puncheon floor, sb. [AB³] *A puncheon floor is made of logs whose upper surfaces have been chipped flat with the adz* 1877 *Autob* (1924) I 7. *Hogs likes a puncheon floor in summer-time because it's cool* 1884 HF xviii 168

(OEDS *U.S.* 1838.. So W S C B F Th,1790 T H DN.II, s.e.Mo.)

pungle, v. [AB¹] *"I'll ask him; and I'll make him pungle, too, or I'll know the reason why". Next day...he went to Judge Thatcher's and bullyragged him and tried to make him give up the money* 1884 HF v 33 (W: To pay or contribute money. *dial. U.S.* So Th.III,1854. Not in OED S C)

pure-white, a. [B¹] *The last one helped the pure-white slave over the door-sill* 1894 PW viii 338 (Comb. not in OED W S C)

purfle, v. [C] *"The Lord High Chancellor of England, in a robe of scarlet, open before, and purfled with minever"* 1881 PP ix 105 (OED 1. To border. *arch. c*1325..1840. So U Wr. Not *arch* in W S C)

purple-plumed, a. [B¹] *He was a gracious figure in his mantle...and purple-plumed cap* 1881 PP xiv 165 (Comb. not in OED W S C; but cf. OED Purple-topped, 1759)

purse-reach, sb. [B¹] *Within the purse-reach of none but kings and successful brewers* 1878 *Notebook* (1935) xiv 140 (Purchasing power. Comb. not in OED W S C)

push along, v. [B¹] *"Push along, cabby, push along— no great lot of time to spare, now"* 1902 "Belated Russian Passport" (1928) 178 (Comb. not in OED W S C; but cf. OED 7. Push on: To press forward)

put, v. [AC] *I took up the river road as hard as I could put* 1884 HF xviii 172 (OED 8b. *obs* exc. *U.S. colloq.* To make off, be off. 1400..1897. So S B F Cl. This sense not in W C)

put-in, sb. [?AB¹] *Never speak when it's not your "put-in"* 1853 *Hannibal Journal,* May 25 (Turn or place to speak. This sense not in OED W S C; but cf. OED Put in, v. 44g. To interpose a word or remark. 1693..)

put in, v. to put in the time. [?AB³] *I put in the time for a while, reading the framed advertisements of all sorts of quack nostrums* 1871 SNO (1875) 258. *I went and set on the bank and listened to the current swashing along, and counted the stars and drift-logs and rafts that come down, and then went to bed; there ain't no better way to put in time when you are lonesome* 1884 HF viii 61. *I couldn't do anything with the letters after I had written them. But it put in the time* 1889 CY xliii 549 (OED 44k. *colloq.* To pass, spend, use up a portion or period of time. 1863.. So S. A in F, under Time, M.T. quot. Phr. not in W C)

putrefied, ppl. a.[AB¹] *He was just fairly putrefied with astonishment* 1896 TSD xi 536 (Hum. malapropism for *petrified.* Given as an early Western usage in AS.xiii.91)

putrid, a. [?AB²] *La Salle drew from these simple children of the forest acknowledgments of fealty to Louis the Putrid, over the water* 1883 LM ii 37 (OEDS 3b. *slang.* Worthless, 'beastly', 'rotten'. 1902.. So W. This sense not in S C)

putter, v. [AB³] *'The matters ye are puttering over are of no consequence!'* 1895 JA II viii 458 (OED *dial* and *U.S.* var. of Potter, v. To dawdle, loiter. 1882.. So W B F Cl. Not A in S C. Cf. Potter, above)

puttering, vbl.sb. [AB²] *Mementoes of Pudd'nhead's old-time childish "puttering" and folly* 1894 PW xix 234. *Her work was the uncalculated puttering of a novice* 1907 CS II iii 128 (OED *U.S.* 1894, only ex. So W Wr B F Cl. Not A in S C)

put through, v. [AB³] *The community was in good shape to make a night of it; so we...put it through on that line* 1889 CY xxii 272 (OED 50b. To carry out, bring to a finish. Chiefly *U.S.* 1852.. So W B Th,1847. Not A in S C U Wr)

put to, v. [?AC] *It may interest the reader to know how they "put horses to" on the continent* 1880 TA xxxi 329 (OED 51c (c). *obs.* To attach to a vehicle. 1768.. 1862. Not *obs* in W S. This sense not in C)

putty-hearted, a.[B¹] *"In a word, the great putty-hearted public loves to 'gush' "* 1873 GA xliii 393 (Sentimental, soft-hearted. This sense not in OED W; but cf. OEDS: Lacking in courage, cowardly, 1927. Comb. not in S C)

put up, v. [AB²] *And so the feller...put up his forty dollars along with Smiley's* 1865 "Jumping Frog" (1875) 34. See *horse* 1873. *This was a plain case of "put up or shut up"* 1889 CY xl 512. *Aleck "put up" as long as she could, but at last there came a call which she was powerless to meet, and her imaginary brokers sold her out* 1904 "Be-quest" (1906) viii 45 (OED 53n(e). To stake a sum of money; to pay up. Also *absol. U.S.* and *Colonial.* 1884.. So S Cl F Th.III T. Not A in W. This sense not in C)

put up, v. [?AB³] *"i just got down on my nees & thanked the Lord for the job & to help me to square it, & to bless you for putting me up to it"* 1883 LM lii 544 (OED 53q(b). To stir up, incite, persuade. Earliest ex. U.S. 1824.. A in T. Not A in W S C U)

put up, v. [?AB³] *He'd see if he couldn't put up something on that Arkansaw village* 1884 HF xxiv 236. *Any American can tell him. It was "put up" on him, as we say. It was a jest—to be plain, it was a series of frauds* 1895 "What Bourget Thinks" 54. *"He put up that scheme on us"* 1896 TSD iii 352 (OED 53t. To concoct or plan in combination with others; to prearrange, preconcert. orig. and chiefly *Thieves' slang.* 1810..So W S U. A in Th.III T. This sense not in C)

put up, v. [?AB¹] *Exhibitions of unspoken suggestion became a favorite with the public. In case I failed to guess what the professor* [i.e., the mesmerizer for whom M.T. was acting as assistant] *might be willing me to do, I could count on putting up something that would answer just as well* 1907 "Chaps. from Autob" 8 (To devise or concoct *without* prearrangement or preconcert. This sense not in OED W S C. An extension of the sense above?)

put up, v. [?AB²] *"Would you like to have me explain that thing to you?...Now, this was the way I put it up"* 1877 "Some Rambling Notes" ii 589. *"Didn't I put you up right?" "Oh, yes." "Sho! I spotted you for my kind the minute I heard your clack"* 1880 TA xx 192. See *damfool* 1893. *"Blake, what do you think of this matter?" "Well, Pudd'nhead, I'm bound to say I put it up the way Tom does"* 1894 PW xv 819 (OEDS 53u. To look upon, regard, or interpret in a particular way. U.S. quot. 1895, only ex. This sense not in W S C)

put-up, ppl. a. [?AB³] *"It was a put-up convenience between those twins"* 1894 TET vi 403 (OED 1. Arranged. or concocted beforehand; preconcerted. 1810.. So W C. A in S: *colloq. U.S.* So B, p.792. So Th.III T)

puzzled-up, ppl. a. [?AB¹] *Tom says, in a puzzled-up kind of way: "Well, that's mighty curious"* 1884 HF xxxiv 353 (Comb. not in OED W S C)

puzzlesome, a. [?AB¹] *"You remember about that puzzlesome little screwdriver?"* 1896 TSD iii 352 (Not in OED W S C)

pyjamas, sb.pl. Also **pajamas.** [?AB³E] *That was on account of pyjamas. This foolish nightdress consists of jacket and drawers* 1897 FE xlix 459. *Yours in the hope of a hereafter for both of us where the asbestos pajamas you have been spending large money on will not be needed* 1910 *M.T. the Letter Writer* (1932) xiii 169 (OED Loose drawers or trousers...worn by both sexes among the Mohammedans...in England often inaccurately applied to a sleeping suit of loose trousers and jacket. 1800..1893, first ex. English use.. So W S C U. The sp. *pyjamas* is called *chiefly British* in W; so M)

pyrotechnique, sb. [E] See *polytechnique* 1892 (Hum. nonce spelling. Cf. OED Pyrotechnic, sb. 2b. 1840..)

Q

quail-shot, sb. [AB²] *He got the frog out and prized his mouth open and took a teaspoon and filled him full of quail-shot* 1865 "Jumping Frog" (1875) 34 (OEDS 1865, this quot., only ex. Comb. not in W S C. Cf. OED Quail, sb. 3. One of several Am. gallinaceous birds resembling the European quail. 1817.. So W S C AS.I.31)

quaint, a. [C] *This quaint lie was most simply told* 1889 CY iv 52 (OED 2. Of actions, schemes, devices, etc.: Marked by ingenuity, cleverness, or cunning. *obs. a*1225..1641. So W S C. Not *obs* in U)

Quaker, sb. [B¹] *They wanted me to play the game of "Quaker" with them. ....The pattern of it was this: they had a pile of Mexican dollars on the table; twelve of them were of even date, fifty of them were of odd dates. The bankers were to separate a coin from the pile and hide it under a hand, and I must guess "odd" or "even". If I guessed correctly, the coin would be mine; if incorrectly, I lost a dollar* 1907 "Chaps. from Autob" 473 (This sense not in OED W S C)

Quaker City, sb. [AB¹] *The very beautiful and substantial side-wheel steamship Quaker City has been chartered for the occasion* 1869 IA 1 23 (A transf. from the sobriquet of the Am. city. Cf. OEDS *U.S.* Philadelphia. 1903, only ex.; so W S C B F Cl Th,1844 M H)

quality, sb. [C] *My quality travels ahead of me* 1892 AmCl vii 72 (OED 4. Nobility, high birth or rank, good social position. Now *arch.* 1579..1871. So W S C. Not *arch* in Wr)

quality, sb. [?AC] *If you are with the quality, or at a funeral...if you are anywheres where it won't do for you to scratch, why you will itch all over in upward of a thousand places* 1884 HF ii 9. See also *corn-pone* 1884; *mud-cat* 1884; *First Family* 1894 (OED 4b. *concrete.* People of good social position. Now *arch* or *vulgar* and *dial.* 1693..1889. So W S C Wr. Not *arch* in U. A in DN.II, III, s.Ill., n.w.Ark.)

quarantine-blockade, sb. [?AB¹] *These people... didn't know that we were quarantine-blockade runners* 1867 Speeches (1923) 25 (Comb. not in OED W S C. Cf. blockade, to run, ?A, above)

quarantine-term, sb. [B¹] *To do it would cost us a quarantine-term in Sidney* 1897 FE iii 58 (Comb. not in OED W S C)

quarter, sb. [D] *"Mark three! Quarter less three!"* 1875 OTM 574. See also *twain,* 1875, 1906 (OED 7b. *Naut.* The fourth part of a fathom. 1769, 1855—. Cf. quot. 1769: "If he judges it to be a quarter...more than any particular number, he calls, 'And a quarter five!' At four fathoms and 3-quarters he calls, 'A quarter less five!' " So W. This sense not in S C)

quarter, sb. [A] See *cent* 1889. *"A half a dollar if you git me to the Capitol in half an hour, and a quarter extra if you do it in twenty minutes!"* 1893 TSA i 22 (OEDS 9b. *U.S.* 1783.. So W S C U B F Cl Th.III T H DN.III AS.I.152)

quarter, v. [?AB²] *I see a black something floating on the water away off to stabboard and quartering behind us* 1883 LM iii 51 (OED 10d. To move in a slanting direction. 1894,1895, U.S. exs. Not A in W S C)

quarter-civilization, sb. [B¹] *Modify their savagery to a semi-civilization—or at least to a quarter-civilization* 1897 FE xxxv 319 (Comb. not in OED W S C)

quarter-god, sb. [B¹] See *half-god* 1907 (Comb. not in OED W S C)

quarter-horse, sb. [AB³] *I broke for home like a quarter-horse* 1857 Adv. of T. J. Snodgrass (1928) 44 (OEDS *U.S.* A horse specially trained to run quarter-mile races. 1845.. So W S C Cl Th DN.I,II AS.II.45. S and C call this comb. *Southern U.S.*)

quarter-hour, a. [B¹] *My uneasy spirit kept dragging me back at quarter-hour intervals* 1883 LM xxxvi 392 (Comb. not in OED W S C; but cf. OED Quarter, sb. 8c. A fourth part of an hour. 1617..; OEDS Quarter-hourly, a. 1929)

quarters, sb.pl. [A] *The unpretending sort of thing I have seen in the negro quarters of Arkansas* 1869 IA xxxiv 378 (OEDS 15c. *U.S. South.* The cabins in which the negroes on a plantation live. 1745.. So W S C U B F Cl Th DN.II,III, s.e.Mo., n.w.Ark., e.Ala.)

quartz-mill, sb. [?AB²] See *tailings* 1891; *arrastre* 1909 (OEDS *Mining.* 1908, only ex. So W S C)

quartz-milling, vbl.sb. [?AB¹] *He is in the quartz-milling business in Virginia City* 1864 SS (1926) 128. See also *arrastre* 1909 (Comb. not in OED W S C)

quartz-miner, sb. [B¹] *"He is a quartz-miner in Colorado, and well-to-do"* 1902 "DBDS" (1928) 293. See also *arrastre* 1909 (Comb. not in OED W S C; but cf. OED Quartz-mining, 1872)

quick-motioned, a. [?AB¹] *Not quick-motioned enough for a Californian* 1866 Speeches (1923) 9 (Comb. not in OED W S C. Cf. Slow-motioned, below)

quiet, sb. **on the quiet.** [?AB²] *"The other day he let me into a little secret, strictly on the quiet"* 1873 GA xi 112 (OEDS 4c. Secretly, covertly. 1903,1909, U.S. exs. Not A in W S C)

quiffsplitter, sb. [?AB¹] *"Ye guts of them that doe quiffsplitters bear stand comely stiff and round"* 1880 Fireside Conversation, 1601 (Comb. not in OED W S C. Cf. OEDS Quiff, *U.S.* and *dial* variant of Whiff, sb.; OED Whiff, sb. 3. A wave or waft of (usually unsavoury) odour. 1688..1884. Cf. also AS.VI.440, "Convicts' Jargon:" quiff, a cheap prostitute. The comb. is doubtless a hum. coinage of M.T.'s)

quintessential, sb. [B¹] *These are the very quint-essentials of good citizenship* 1899 "Concerning the Jews" (1900) 257 (Not in OED W S C U as sb.)

quit, v. [A] See *high-toned* 1864. *"Well, do you know, they've quit burning wood in some places in the Eastern states"* 1873 GA i 25. See also *cross, shake the,* 1883 (OED 6. To cease. stop, discontinue doing something Now *U.S.* 1754..1882. So W Wr B Th T H DN.I,II AS.I.153. Not A in S C U)

quit, v. [?A] See *tuckered out* 1877. *They couldn't stand the raise; had to hang up and quit* 1883 LM xxxix 413. *Tom told him to work till the rest of his candle quit on him* 1884 HF xxxviii 389. See also *curl up* 1889; *day, call it a* 1889 (OED 6b. *absol.* Also *U.S.* with *off.* So W S C. A in Th.III H)

quivery, a. [B³C] *The headlines sent a quivery little cold wave through me* 1889 CY xxiv 338 (OED *rare.* 1877, only ex. Not *rare* in W. Not in S C)

quoth, v. [C] *"Marry,"* quoth the peasant, *"an it please your worship.."* 1869 IA xxi 212 (OED Now *arch* or *dial. c*1250.. 1884. So W S C Wr. U: *Sham archaic*)

R

rabbit, sb. [AB¹] See *batter-cake* 1897 (C: The common gray rabbit or wood-rabbit of the U.S., *Lepus sylvaticus*. So W S M. The Am. species is not mentioned in OED)

rabbit, sb. [B¹] *A peasant's house which was occupied by the family and a lot of cows and calves—also several rabbits.* (Editor's note: *His word for fleas*) 1891 *Letters* (1917) II xxxi 551 (Nonce meaning. Cf. chamois, above)

rabid, a. [B³] *Orion's wife has followed him into the outer darkness, after 30 years' rabid membership in the Presbyterian Church* 1879 *Letters* (1917) I xix 362. *He was a rabid Protestant* 1880 TA xxxvi 403. *Even the rabid republican* 1892 AmCl xv 153 (OED 1c. Of persons: Having some quality, feeling, view, etc., in a violent degree. 1820.. So W S C U. This is one of those hum. twists of meaning that M.T. would infallibly have invented, if it had not already been invented before him,—in this case used first by Lamb, later by Emerson and others. Cf. plant, above)

race-aversion, sb. [B¹] *It must have been race-aversion that put upon them a good deal of the low-rate intellectual reputation which they bear* 1897 FE xxi 185 (Comb. not in OED W S C; but cf. OED Race-hatred, 1882)

race-prejudice, sb. [B¹] *That will probably keep the race-prejudice against you alive* 1899 "Concerning the Jews" (1900) 279 (Comb. not in OED W S C; but cf. OEDS Race-feeling, 1907)

racer, sb. [AB³] *When they were black snakes, or racers, we fled without shame* 1897 *Autob* (1924) I 103 (OED 2b. *spec* as the name of several species of American snakes. 1864. So W S C)

raceway, sb. [AB³] *The first pin-block projected its third pin as the first word came traveling along the raceway* 1889 *Letters* (1917) II xxix 507 (OED *U.S.* 2. A course or passage for a shuttle. 1875. So W S C. Here, a passage for type)

racing-mobile, sb. [AB¹] "*The radium in 20,000 lightning bugs would run a racing-mobile forever*" 1904 E&E (1923) 335 (Comb. not in OED W S C; but cf. W: Mobile, sb. An automobile, esp. one propelled by steam. *Colloq.U.S.* So S)

racing-pressure, sb. [B¹] *He was full of steam—racing pressure—one could almost hear his gauge-cocks sing* 1902 "Belated Russ. Passport" (1928) 173 (Comb. not in OED W S C)

racket, sb. [?AB³] *I meant to work this racket more and more* 1889 CY x 119 (OED 3. *slang*. A trick, dodge, scheme, game, line of business or action. 1812.. So W C U. A in S Th.III H)

racket, sb. to **stand the racket**. [?AB³] "*All you've got to do is just be ca'm and stack it up—they'll stand the racket*" 1883 LM xliv 440 (OED 4 (b.) To face the consequences. 1823.. So W C U. A in S)

rack-heap, sb. [?AB¹] *There was only one boat advertised...a Grand Tower packet...She was a venerable rack-heap, and a fraud to boot* 1883 LM xxiii 259. *Fridolin entered...with a tall skeleton stalking in his rear...The testimony of this wandering rack-heap of unidentified bones...* 1892 "Switzerland" 200. *When the Pennsylvania blew up and became a drifting rack-heap freighted with wounded and dying* 1909 ISD i 18 (Comb. not in OED W S C; but cf. OED Rack, sb. 2a. A wrecked ship; *obs.rare*. a1658; Wrack, sb. 1b. Remnants of a wrecked vessel. 1428.. Cf. also Rack and ruin, OED 1599..; A in B T)

radiator, sb. [?AB¹] *The German stove...is lovely, compared with any "radiator" that has yet been intruded upon the world—that odious gilded skeleton!* 1891 E&E (1923) 178 (W: A nest of pipes or the like containing circulating steam, hot water, etc., for heating a room. So S C. This is hardly covered by the def. in OED b. A small chamber or compartment heated by means of steam or hot air, and radiating warmth into a room; OEDS Earlier U.S. ex., 1851..)

raffle off, v.trans. [?AB¹] "*I shan't know what to do with them, unless I raffle them off*" 1889 CY xv 176 (W: To dispose of by means of a kind of lottery; often with *off*. So S C. The constr. with *off* not in OED)

raft, sb. [?A] *I have traveled by canal-boat, ox-wagon, raft* 1880 TA xxxviii 457. See also *coal-flat* 1883; *wigwam* 1884; and *passim* in HF (OED 3. 1590.. So W S C. A in B F Cl in ref. to the distinctive log rafts of the Mississippi)

raft, sb. [AB³] "*He had me measure him and take a whole raft of directions*" 1870 CRG (1919) ix 56. See *hop*, v. 1876. "*You can see Millport from here, and...a raft o' farms*" 1877 "Some Rambling Notes" i 444. *I have since prepared and delivered a lecture for charity—it cost me a raft of time* 1899 *M.T. the Letter Writer* (1932) ii 28. *When it fell, it wiped out a considerable raft of stars* 1907 "Capt.Stormfield" 42 (OED *dial* and *U.S.* A large collection; a lot. Used disparagingly. 1833.. So S C Wr B F Cl Th T H DN.III, n.w.Ark., e.Ala. Not A in W)

rafting, vbl.sb. [?A] *Then he worked all day, getting all ready to quit rafting* 1884 HF xvi 142 (OED Earliest exs. U.S. 1753.. A in B F Cl. Not A in W S C)

raftsman, sb. [?A] *Those dialect-speaking raftsmen* 1880 TA xviii 164. See *rawhide*, v. 1883 (OED 1776.. So W S C U. A in B F)

raft-voyage, sb. [?AB¹] *A pedestrian tour in Europe doesn't begin with a raft-voyage for hilarity and wild adventure* 1891 *Letters* (1917) II xxxi 558 (Comb. not in OED W S C. Cf. above)

rag, sb. [?AB¹] *I stood and up shook my rags off and jumped into the river* 1883 LM iii 43 (W: Used jocularly of any attire. So S U. This use not in OED C)

rag, sb. to **drop the rag**. [?AB¹] "*I've got to stay here, till the old man drops the rag and gives the word—yes, sir, right here in this country I've got to linger till the old man says Come!*" 1880 TA xx 194 (To give the signal, to give notice. Phr. not in OED W S C; but cf. OED Handkerchief, sb. *To drop or throw the handkerchief*, i.e., in young people's games, in which he or she to whom it is thrown runs after and tries to catch the other; no exs.)

rag, sb. to **knock all to rags**. [?AB¹] *The blow came crashing down and knocked him all to rags* 1889 CY xxxiii 432 (To shatter, knock out completely. Phr. not in OED W S C)

rag-baby, sb. [?AB³] "*He looks as helpless as a rag-baby*" 1873 GA xxxviii 340 (OEDS A doll made of rags. All exs. U.S. 1809.. Not A in W S C)

rag carpet, sb. [AB³] *Bedrooms with rag carpets* 1883 LM xxxviii 405. See also *homely* 1904 (OEDS *U.S.* 1837.. So S C B F Cl. Comb. not in W)

rag carpeting, vbl.sb. [AB³] *The other rooms were clothed in the "rag" carpeting of the country* 1873 GA v 60. *The boys played circus for three days afterward in tents made of rag carpeting* 1876 TS xxii 178 (OEDS *U.S.* 1813.. Comb. not in W)

rag dollar, sb. [?AB¹] "*Yo' po' little old rag dollah... you ain't got no money*" 1894 PW viii 339 (Comb. not in OED W S C; but cf. OED Rag-money: contemptuously, of paper-money. Earliest exs. U.S. 1878..; A in B Cl Th.III AS.VIII.4.49, Neb., 1858; X.19)

ragged edge, sb. [AB¹] *He was always on the ragged edge of apprehension* 1889 CY xvi 196. *It was away out in the ragged edge of Washington* 1892 AmCl ii 28 (A in T. Not in OED W S C; but cf. W: *on the ragged edge*: on the verge of losing or being without means, health, etc.)

ragged-filagree, a. [B¹] *The muzzle was eaten by rust of centuries into a ragged-filagree work* 1869 IA xlix 517 (Comb. not in OED W S C. Cf. filigree, filagree, above)

ragged-looking, a. [B²] "*And t'other one was a rusty, ragged-looking devil*" 1876 TS xxx 229 (OED 1884, only ex. Comb. not in W S C)

ragged-topped, a. [B¹] *Some ragged-topped cocoa-palms* 1877 "Some Rambling Notes" iii 718 (Comb. not in OED W S C)

raggedy, a. [B²] *A raggedy white patch between the shoulders...looked like somebody had hit him with a snow-ball* 1896 TSD vi 358 (OED 1899, only ex. So W S C)

raging, ppl.a. [?AB¹] *He was doing a raging business* 1889 CY xxxi 398. *A raging lot of sand* 1894 TSA xi 400 (Tremendous, enormous. This sense not in OED W S C)

rag-lamp, sb. [B¹] *He had reinstituted the ancient rag-lamp* 1889 CY xlii 531. *The house was shut up tight and the rag-lamps lighted* 1893 "Esquimau Maiden's Romance" (1900) 150 (Comb. not in OED W S C; but cf. OEDS Rag-torch, 1923)

rag-store, sb. [AB¹] *Filthy dens on first floors, with rag stores in them* 1869 IA xvi 157 (Comb. not in OED W S C; but cf. OED Rag shop: a shop for rags and old stores. 1851.. See also the *U.S.* use of store, below)

rag-tag and bob-tail, sb. [?AB²] See *rough-scruff* 1865. "*I am offish with the rag-tag and bob-tail*" 1872 RI ii 28. "*I want you to work privately among the rag-tag and bob-tail*" 1894 PW xv 820 (OED 2. The rabble. 1820.. So W S C U. A in DN.III AS.II.362)

raid, sb. [?AB¹] "*It's stolen. There has been another raid on the town*" 1894 PW xiii 776 (A series of simultaneous thefts or robberies. This sense not in OED W S C. Cf. B: A predatory incursion. So A in F Cl)

raid, v. [?AB¹] "*It's perfectly plain that the thief took advantage of the reception...to raid the vacant houses undisturbed...It's the same old raider*" 1894 PW xiii 776 (To make a series of thefts or robberies. This sense not in OED W S C. Cf. above)

raid, v. [B¹] *In my fancy, he is quicksilver raiding down a riffle—no grain of the metal stands much chance of eluding him* 1906 "Howells" (1917) 229 (This sense not in OED W S C. A *fig* extension of the sense above?)

raider, sb. [?AB¹] See *raid,* v. 1894. (One who makes a series of thefts. This sense not in OED W S C. Cf. above)

rail, sb. **by rail.** [B²] *They can by rail go on to Florence* 1869 IA i 21. *Sometimes traveling by rail* 1886 Speeches (1910) 154 (OED 5. 1872, only ex. of phr. So W S C)

rail, v. **to rail it.** [?AB³] *We shall rail it through on that day to Ouchy* 1891 Letters (1917) II xxxi 555 (OED 6. To travel by rail. Also with *it.* 1853. So W S. A in B F Cl. Not in C)

railbed, sb. [?AB¹] *There was no level ground at the Kaltbad station; the railbed was as steep as a roof* 1880 TA xxix 306 (Comb. not in OED W S C. App. means the roadbed or permanent way of a railroad. Cf. George H. McKnight, *English Words and Their Background,* 1923, p. 34: "English *permanent way* =American *road-bed*")

rail-fence, sb. [A] See *chills-racked* 1875. *Lanes with rail fences and cornfields on either side* 1877 Autob (1924) I 7 (OEDS *U.S.* A fence made of wooden posts and rails. 1649.. So Th.III. Not A in S. Comb. not in W C)

railroad, sb. [A] *I came here from New York by way of the Camden and Amboy railroad* 1853 Letter in *Iowa Journ. of Hist.* (1929) 413. See *air-line* 1856. *There was no Pacific railroad in those fine times* 1872 RI i 20. See also *gopher* 1873; *towboat* 1883; *cotton-gin* 1889 (OED Now chiefly *U.S.*, the usual term in Great Britain being Railway. 1775.. Cf. W: *Railroad* in this sense is usually limited to roads for heavy steam transportation and also to steam roads partially or wholly electrified or roads for heavy traffic designed originally for electric traction. The lighter electric street-car lines and the like are usually termed *railways*. In Great Britain and the British colonies, exc. Canada, all such roads, whether for heavy or light traffic, are usually called railways. So S C U N F Cl T M H DN.II,III)

railroad, sb. [AB¹] *I was astonished at the way that railroad was a gittin over the ground* 1856 Adv. of T.J.

Snodgrass (1928) 26. See also *iron horse* 1873 (Railroad train, locomotive. This sense not in OED W S C. Cf. above)

railroad-building, vbl.sb. [AB¹] *Philip devoted himself day and night...to the science of railroad-building* 1873 GA xxiii 216 (Comb. not in OED W S C. Cf. above)

railroading, vbl.sb. [AB³] *It is hard to make railroading pleasant in any country* 1869 IA xii 106. *I couldn't do the railroading I am proposing to do* 1891 Letters (1917) II xxxi 557 (OED Chiefly *U.S.* 1. Travelling by rail. 1855.. So S H. This sense not in W C)

railroading, vbl.sb. [AB³] *France knows nothing valuable about railroading* 1895 "What Bourget Thinks" 49. *Knowledge of the commercial, railroading, financial, and international banking relations* 1898 "Stirring Times" (1900) 309 (OED Chiefly *U.S.* 2. The business of making or working railroads. 1882.. So C M. Not A in W S)

railroad man, sb. [AB³] See *land speculator* 1873 (OEDS 1863. A in M. Comb. not in W S C. Cf. above)

railroad president, sb. [AB¹] *A lawyer, doctor, editor, author, tinker, loafer, railroad president, saint* 1892 AmCl xiv 149 (Comb. not in OED W S C. Cf. above)

railroad-train, sb. [AB³] *Each and every word a seventeen-jointed vestibuled railroad train* 1906 Speeches (1910) 206 (OED Railroad, sb. 3a. 1836. So S. Comb. not in W C. Cf. railroad, above)

rails, sb. [?AB²] *Three miles...were ready for the rails, and also ready and ripe for manipulation in the stock-market* 1889 CY xlii 532 (App. M.T. has in mind the sense in OED 5. On the Stock Exchange in pl. =railway shares. 1893, only ex. So S U. A in W. This sense not in C)

railway-center, sb. [B¹] *Louisiana, Missouri...a brisk railway-center now* 1883 LM liii 523 (Comb. not in OED W S C)

railway official, sb. [B¹] *The railway officials...are not aware that there are any kind of insults except spoken ones* 1893 "Traveling with a Reformer" (1900) 357 (Comb. not in OED W S C)

raiment, sb. [C] "*Fetch raiment of another sort; clothe him like a prince!*" 1889 CY vi 76 (OED Now *rhet.* c1440..1868. So S C. Not *rhet.* or *arch* in W U)

rain, sb. **to come in out of the rain.** [?AB¹] See *bkac,* by the 1884. *Furnish this country with a Congress that knows enough to come in out of the rain* 1892 AmCl iii 46 (Phr. not in OED W S C. Cf. below)

rain, v. **to come in when it rains.** [AB²] *I suppose he don't know enough to come in when it rains* 1867 Jumping Frog 124. "*I give you my word he doesn't know enough to come in when it rains*" 1900 Autob (1924) I 177 (OEDS 1. To exercise ordinary prudence. *U.S.* 1867, this quot... Phr. not in W S C)

rain, v. **to rain brickbats.** [?AB¹] *Every time Merlin prophesied fair weather it rained brickbats* 1889 CY xxiii 286 (Cf. W Rain cats and dogs, rain pitchforks: To rain very heavily. *colloq.* So S C. None of these phrases in OED)

rain-dog., sb. [?AB¹] *What the sailors call "rain-dogs"—little patches of rainbow—often are seen drifting about the heavens* 1872 RI lxxi 361 (Comb. not in OED W S C; but cf. OED Dog, sb. 10a. Fog-dog; cf. quot. 1867: "the lower part of a rainbow visible towards the horizon, and betokening squally weather...On the banks of Newfoundland they are considered precursors of clearer weather")

raise, sb. [?A] See *crack on* 1883. "*De dream say let Balum inves' de ten cents en he'd make a raise for me*" 1884 HF viii 72 (OEDS 5. An increase in price, salary, wages, etc. Earliest ex. U.S. 1728.. A in H. Not A in W. This sense not in S C)

raise, sb. [?AB¹] *As we say in an innocent little parlor game, commonly called "draw," if they can only "stand the raise" this time, they may enjoy the comfortable assurance that the old river's banks will never hold a "full"* *again* 1859 Letter in *New Orleans Daily Crescent*, May 17 (Here used in the sense of Rise, OED 13. An increase in the height of the sea, streams, etc.; with punning allusion to Raise in sense given in OEDS 5. An increase of stakes at poker, 1921. The former sense is not in OED W S C)

raise, v. [A] See *heifer* 1872. *"A man's own son, which he has had all the trouble and all the anxiety and all the expense of raising"* 1884 HF vi 42. *I was raised in the country and have always lived there* 1893 "Petition to the Queen" (1928) 359 (OED 10. To rear, bring up, a person. Now chiefly *U.S.* 1744.. So W S U Wr B F Cl Th,1601 T M H DN.II,V AS.I.152, VII.20, VIII.3.12. Not A in C)

raise, v. [?A] *The principal crop is corn, and they raise it and grind it just as their great-great-great-grandfathers did* 1869 IA vi 55. See also *ash-pile* 1884 (OED 10c. To grow plants. 1669.. So W S C U. A in B F Cl Th T M H DN.IV,V)

raise, v. to raise the mischief. [?AB²] *The head editor has been in here raising the mischief, and tearing his hair and kicking the furniture about, and abusing me like a pickpocket* 1865 SNO (1875) 168. *Such a general raising of the mischief was never seen in the ship before!* 1869 IA xli 431 (OED 20b. To make a disagreeable disturbance. 1865, above quot., only ex. So W S C. A in Th,1803 DN.I,II,III,IV,V)

raise, v. [?AB¹] *Just before we came to Joseph's Pit, we "raised" a hill, and there, a few miles before us, lay the Sea of Galillee* 1869 IA xlvii 350. *I "raised the hill" overlooking the town* 1872 RI xli 287 (To come in sight of land. This sense not in OED W S C. An extension to land travel of the *Naut.* sense in OED 23a. To come in sight of another ship, etc. 1556..; so W S C U)

raise, v. [?AC] *He raised up two or three times and looked away off and around on the water* 1883 LM iii 51 (OED 35. intr. To rise. *obs.* 1470..1761. OEDS Later U.S. exs. 1770..1911. A in S. Not A in W. This sense not in C)

raise out, v. [?AB²] *"I have to pass. You've raised me out, pard"* 1872 RI xlvii 332 (OED 32. To cause a player to withdraw from a game by making the stake too high for him. 1894, only ex. Comb. not in W S C)

rake, sb. [B¹] *She wore a pink satin dress, plain in front but with a good deal of rake to it—to the train, I mean—it was said to be two or three yards long* 1870 SNO (1875) 153 (Hum. nonce use, by extension from the *Naut.* sense in OED 1a. The projection of the upper part of a ship's hull at stem and stern beyond the corresponding extremities of the keel. 1626..; so W S C)

rake, sb. [B¹] *The first rake of his razor loosened the very hide from my face* 1869 IA xii 114 (The act of raking or scraping. This sense not in OED W S C)

rake and scrape, v. [?AB¹] *"I've raked and scraped and saved a considerable many years, and I've got it all here"* 1883 LM xxxvi 389 (W: To seek gain by small acquisitions and petty savings. Comb. not in OED S C)

rampage, sb. to ride a rampage. [?AB¹] *"The raven... sets on her shoulder often when she rides her breakneck rampages"* 1906 "Horse's Tale" 335 (Phr. not in OED W S C. Cf. OED orig. *Scotch*: A state of excitement or violent passion...esp. in phr. *on the rampage.* 1861.. This phr. A in B)

rampant, a. [B¹] See *coat-of-arms* 1883 (Cf. OED 1b. *Heraldry.* Standing on the sinister hind-leg, with both forelegs elevated. 1562..1814. So W S C. Here, of course, nonsense use, as applied to the "nombril points"!)

ramshackle, a [?AB³] See *hail-barge* 1875; *trap* 1892; *slander-mill* 1895. *It seems as though Austria was too ramshackle to go on holding together any length of time* 1898 "Stirring Times" (1900) 286 (OED 1. Loose and shaky, as if ready to fall to pieces. 1830.. So W S C U Wr. A in DN.III,IV)

ramshackly, a. [?AB³] *Decayed, ramshackly old steamboats* 1883 LM xlviii 475 (OED 1857.. So W S C. Cf. above)

ranch, sb. [AB³] *The Secretary and I took quarters in the "ranch" of a worthy French lady by the name of Bridget O'Flannigan...a Carson boarding-house* 1872 RI xxi 161 (OED *U.S.* 1 A hut or house in the country. 1808.. So C B F Th T. This sense not in W S)

ranch, sb. [AB²] *There are "ranches," or farms, where they say hay grows* 1861 *Letters* (1917) I iii 55. *I have a ranch of unknown extent* 1865 SS (1926) 190. See also *vamose*, v. 1866; *cattle-pen* 1899 (OED *U.S.* 2. A cattle-breeding establishment, farm, or estate. 1872.. So W S C U B F Cl Th.III,1867 T M DN.II,VI AS.I.152)

ranch, v. [AB²] *He had been ranching in Washoe District* 1872 RI xxiv 242 (OED *U.S.* To conduct a ranch. 1890. So W S C U F Cl M)

ranch-life, sb. [AB¹] *It told me where to begin to talk ranch-life in Carson Valley* 1899 "How to Make Hist. Dates Stick" (1917) 143 (Comb. not in OED S C. Given in W. Cf. above)

ranchman, sb. [AB³] *Ranchmen and farmers had come with their families from five miles around* 1873 GA liii 479 (OED *U.S.* 1872.. So W S C U B F Cl M)

rancid, a. [B¹] *He couldn't get his breath at first. When he did get it, it came rancid with sarcasm* 1892 AmCl xv 156 (Embittered, sour, "rank." This *fig* use of the sound of a voice not in OED W S C. For a slightly different *fig* use cf. OED 2. Nasty, disagreeable, odious. 1883..; so W)

random, sb. with great random. [C] *Two knights came together with great random* 1889 CY xv 180 (OED 1. Impetuosity, force, or violence. *obs. c*1450..1611. So W C U. This sense not in S)

random, v. [C] *And rightso a thought came randoming overthwart this majestic dream* 1889 CY xxvii 349 (OED *obs. rare.* 2. To fly at random. 1602, 1605. So W. Not in S C as verb)

range, sb. [AB³] See *Far West* 1876. *"Poking around all over the sage-brush range"* 1902 "DBDS" (1928) 329 (OED 6. *U.S.* An extensive stretch of gazing or hunting ground. 1808.. So W C B F Cl M DN.VI AS.IV.129. Not A in S T)

ranger-saddle, sb. [AB¹] *My horse...was a beauty, glossy as silk, and naked as he was when he was born, except for bridle and ranger-saddle* 1889 CY xxxix 499 (Comb. not in OED W S C. Cf. OED Ranger, sb. 3. pl. A body of mounted troops...employed in ranging over a tract of country. Chiefly *U.S.* 1742..; so W S C)

rank, v. [AB³] *In the gossip column I ranked all dukes not royal* 1892 "Banknote" (1928) 124. *The work wrought by Joan of Arc may fairly be regarded as ranking any recorded in history* 1895 JA Pref. 680. See also *Importance* 1907 (OEDS 5. *U.S.* To take precedence of. 1841.. So S C Th T H. Not A in W)

ransom, v. [B¹] *"Keep them till they're ransomed." "Ransomed? What's that?" "I don't know...But per'aps it means that we keep them till they're dead"..."Why can't a body take a club and ransom them as soon as they get here?"* 1884 HF ii 15 (Hum. nonce use)

ranting, ppl.a. [AB¹] *"'Bob Ridley' is a common rackety slambang secular song, one of the rippingest and rantingest and noisiest there is"* 1894 TET ii 333 (Wr: Romping, roistering. *Scotch* and *N. Eng.* This sense not in OED W S C)

rap, sb. [AB¹] *"When I suggested theft about the watch...I got such a rap"* 1894 PW xiii 776 (A rebuke, rebuff, scolding. This *fig* sense not in OED W S C; but cf. OEDS Rap, v. 1c. To criticize, rebuke. *U.S.* 1906.. So H. Cf. also W Rap, sb. An adverse criticism; a "knock." *slang*)

rapids, sb. [A] *He saw the little steamer, Maid of the Mist, descend the fearful rapids...first one paddle-box was out of sight behind the raging billows and then the other* 1869 SNO (1875) 64 (OED Orig. *U.S.* 1776.. So B T M. Not A in W S C U)

rapscallion, sb. [?A] *Whisky-drinking, breakdown-dancing rapscallions* 1883 LM xviii 571. See *dead-beat* 1884. *"But, Huck, dese kings o' ourn is regular rapscallions; dat's jist what dey is; dey's regular rapscallions"* 1884 HF xxiii 230 (OED A rascal, scamp. 1699..1885. So W S C U. A in Wr DN.II,IV)

rare, a. [?AC] *A small piece of the fatted calf—rare and no gravy* 1869 *Letters* (1917) I ix 165 (OED b. Of meat: Underdone. Now often regarded as an Americanism, but current in many English dialects, and used by English writers in the first half of the 19th c. 1784.. A in W S C U Cl Th,1655 H. Cf. also *Academy* XX.493; XXI.10)

rascal-nest, sb. [B¹] *A nigger-trader and fire-bug from the most notorious rascal-nest in Galveston* 1881 "Curious Experience" 46 (Comb. not in OED W S C)

rasp, v. [?AB³] *Then he flung himself on the sofa again, and rasped out the remark...* 1894 PW viii 338 (OED 4. To utter with a grating sound. 1843. So W C U. A in Wr. This use not in S)

raspberry, sb. Spelled **razberry.** [?AE] *I found plenty strawberries, ripe and prime; and green summer grapes, and green razberries* 1884 HF viii 61 (This form A in DN.II. The sp. is not given in OED W S C, though the pron. so indicated is found in all dicts.)

rat, sb. [?AB³] *"My men wouldn't stay with me if I should employ a 'scab' or 'rat,' or whatever the phrase was"* 1892 AmCl xiii 130 (OEDS 4d. A workman who refuses to strike along with others; also one who works for lower wages than the ordinary rate. 1855.. So W S C U. A in B F Cl Th,1824. Here merely one who does not belong to the union)

rather, adv. Spelled **ruther, druther.** [AE] *Feeling rested and ruther comfortable* 1884 HF viii 57. *He said he'd druther not take a child away from its father* 1884 HF v 34 (These prons. not recorded in OED W S C. A in M DN.III,IV,V)

ration, v. [B³?C] *The milk and sugar supply was not left at the discretion of the boarders, but was rationed out at headquarters* 1892 AmCl xii 119 (OED 2. To serve out in fixed quantities. 1870.. So W U. *Rare* in S C)

rats, sb.pl. [AB²] *"You may write a blistering article on the police—give the Chief Inspector rats"* 1869 SNO (1875) 48 (OED *slang* orig. *U.S.* Used ironically in pl. 1890.. A in F: Contemptuous sarcasm. So Cl. Not A in W S. This use not in C)

ratsbane, sb. [?AC] *"What was that cat's name that eat a keg of ratsbane by mistake over at Hooper's?"* 1877 "Some Rambling Notes" iii 723 (OED 1. Rat-poison; *spec.* arsenic. Now only literary. 1523..1820. So W. Not *arch* in S C U)

rat's nest, sb. [?AB¹] *He stood there in the red glare for'ard...his hair all rat's nests and one suspender hanging* 1907 "Capt. Stormfield" 42 (Tangled, uncombed. This sense not in OED W S C)

rat terrier, sb. [?AB³] See *chicken-cock* 1865 (OED 1851.. So S C. A in DN.I. Comb. not in W)

rattle, sb. [A] *He had kicked his string of rattlesnake rattles off his ankle* 1876 TS xvi 135 (OED 2a. A set of horny, loosely connected rings forming the termination of the tail in the rattlesnake. 1624.. So W S C U. Cf. rattlesnake, below)

rattle, v. [AB³] *The earl was rattled, thrown off his bearings, his head was in a whirl* 1892 AmCl xviii 189 (OEDS 11. *U.S.* 1869.. So F Cl Th M H. Not A in W S C U)

rattler, sb. [?AB¹] *"The Cyclone was a rattler to go, and the sweetest thing to steer that ever walked the waters"* 1883 LM xxiv 271. *It was a rattler, that caravan, and a mighty fine sight to look at* 1894 TSA xi 395 (W: Anything remarkable of its kind. *slang.* So S U. This sense not in OED C; but cf. OED 2b. *slang.* A (rattling) coach)

rattler, sb. [?AB²] *One of them rattlers with a clatter of syllables as long as a string of sluice boxes* 1865 SS (1926) 159 (OEDS 3d. A long resounding word. 1865, this quot., only ex. This sense not in W S C)

rattlesnake, sb. [A] See *rattle* 1876; *alligator* 1883. *I went to the cavern...and found a rattlesnake in there* 1884 HF x 81. See also *puff adder* 1897 (OED A venomous Am. snake. 1630.. So W S C U B F T DN.II)

rattletrap, sb. [?AB³] *The old rattletrap of a brick store* 1876 TS xxvii 210. *The pilot-house was a dingy, battered rattle-trap* 1875 OTM 220 (OED 3. Any rickety or shaky thing. 1833.. So W S C U. A in DN.IV)

rattling, adv. [?AB³] See *book-talk* 1880. *"A rattling bully pleasure tramp through the summer woods"* 1880 TA xxvi 269. *It appears to me it is a rattling-good idea* 1881 *Speeches* (1923) 101. *The Committee...have given us a rattling tip-top puff* 1885 *Letters* (1917) II xxv 452 (OED 4c. 1829.. So W S C U Wr. A in DN.IV)

rat-trap, sb. [?AB¹] *"It wouldn't have occurred to anybody else to name this poor old rat-trap Rossmore Towers"* 1892 AmCl iv 56 (Rattletrap. This sense not in OED W S C)

ratty, a. [?AB²] *Village of Bethany. It is fearfully ratty—some houses—mud* 1867 *Notebook* (1935) viii 99. *We got a ratty old bedquilt off the bed* 1884 HF ix 78. *Displayed in profusion about the little ratty studio* 1892 AmCl xvii 172. *He overhauled a pile of rejected suits, and selected the rattiest one for me* 1893 "Banknote" (1928) 114 (OED 2. Wretched, mean, nasty. *slang.* Earliest ex. U.S. 1885.. Not A in W S C)

ratty-looking, a. [?AB¹] *"Both of them had big, fat, ratty-looking carpet-bags"* 1884 HF xix 182 (Comb. not in OED W S C. Cf. above)

raven, sb. [B¹] *The raven croaked again. If he had spoken in English he would not have said any more plainly than he did say in raven, "Well, what do you want here?"* 1880 TA ii 32 (Nonce meaning: the language of ravens)

rawhide, v. [?AB¹] *"Some raftsmen would rawhide you until you were black and blue"* 1883 LM iii 61 (W: To whip. *colloq.* So S. Not in OED C as verb; but cf. OEDS Rawhiding, a beating with a rawhide whip, U.S. ex., 1848. Rawhide, sb. is A in F Cl Th,1829 T)

rayed, ppl.a. [C] *"A thick, rayed cloth or carpet was then unfolded"* 1881 PP ix 105 (OED *obs* exc. *Hist.* Striped, streaked. c1369..1866. So W S C)

reach, sb. [?A] *A "reach" is a piece of straight river* 1875 OTM 192 (OED 13a. That portion of a river that lies between two bends. 1536.. So W S C U. A in DN.I,VI)

reader, sb. [?AB¹] *Then the President, throned behind the cable-locker with a national flag spread over it, announced the "Reader," who rose up and read the same old Declaration of Independence* 1869 IA x 92. *The public reciter or "reader" who goes around trying to imitate the various sorts of bells with his voice* 1880 TA xxxvi 402 (W: A professional reciter of selections, etc.; an elocutionist. So S C. This *spec* sense not in OED; but cf. reading, vbl.sb., below)

Reader, sb. [AB¹] *In every C.S. church, two "Readers," a man and a woman. No talkers, no preachers in any Church—readers only. Readers of the Bible and her books—no others* 1903 "Mrs. Eddy in Error" 511. *Readers are a feature of first importance in the church-machinery of Christian Science... They occupy the pulpit. They hold the place that the preacher holds in other Christian churches* 1907 CS II vii 169. See also *Annex-polisher* 1907 (This *spec* Christian Science use not in OED W S C; but cf. OED 3. *spec.* One who reads the lessons or other parts of the service in a place of worship. c961..)

reading, vbl.sb. [?AB³] *I think that was the first exploitation of a new and devilish invention—the thing*

called an *Author's Reading* 1906 *Autob* (1924) II 147
(OED 2e. A social or public entertainment at which the
audience listens to a reader. 1858, 1869. So W S C U.
Of the two quots. in OED, the first is from Dickens, the
other is U.S. The custom seems to have arisen in England, but later to have become a distinctive Am.
institution)

reading-matter, sb. [?AB²] *The reading matter in my
copy of the Munich journal consists of a total of 1,654
words...One fourth of the first page is taken up with the
heading of the journal...The rest of the first page...and
all the second page is reading matter; the other six pages
are devoted to advertisements...A single issue of the
bulkiest daily newspaper in the world—the London
Times—often contains 100,000 words of reading matter*
1880 TA App.F 628 (Given in OED without definition.
Cf. the only quot.: 1884 Grant Allen *Philistia* "To
supply the reading matter, the letterpress I think you
call it." The two terms are clearly differentiated in W:
Reading matter, regular news or editorial or contributed
matter as distinguished from paid advertising matter
(*Cant*); Letter-press, reading matter in distinction from
the illustrations. So S C. Obviously M.T.'s use agrees
with the Am. dicts. It seems likely that this distinctive
sense of reading matter is *U.S.*, the term being apparently little used in England)

read up, v. [?AB²] *I shall throttle down my emotions
hereafter about this sort of people, until I have read them
up* 1869 IA xv 147. "*I am better read up in most sciences,
maybe, than the general run of professional men*" 1873
GA xi 112. *I am not so ignorant about glacier movement
now as I was...I have "read up" since* 1880 TA xl 459
(OED 15c. To collect information by reading. U.S.
quot. 1889, only ex. Not A in W S C U)

ready, sb. **a good ready.** [?AB²] *He climbed out with
nothing on but his socks and a shirt...He said, "I could
have ketched them cats if I had had on a good ready"*
1867 "Jim Wolfe" (1872) 76. *We backed out and
"straightened up" for the start—the boat pausing for a
"good ready" in the old-fashioned way* 1883 LM li 500
(OEDS 4. A period or process of preparation. All exs.
U.S. 1883, above quot... A in AS.XII.115, quot.
1855. Not A in W C. This use not in S)

ready-bell, sb. [?AB¹] "*In about an hour I heard de
ready-bell, en den de racket begin*" 1894 PW xviii 18
(The signal for the steamboat to start. Comb. not in
OED W S C)

real, adv. [A] "*Sometimes it's real pitiful the way the
children pine for Parry*" 1873 GA xxxiii 305. So *passim*
in TS, HF, etc. (OED In later use, chiefly *Scotch* and
U.S.: Very, extremely. 1658..1887. So S C U B Cl
Th M H AS.III.235. Not A in W T AS.VIII.1.60)

real estate, sb. [AB³] *An extraordinary year there in
real estate matters* 1883 LM lvii 556 (OEDS *U.S.* attrib.
Connected with or dealing in landed property. 1849..
So U F Cl M DN.II. Cf. H: In Eng. a legal term only;
in Am. an everyday business term also. Not A in W S C)

realizing, ppl.a. [A] "*That will give you a realizing
idea of what our house is*" 1892 AmCl v 63 (OED *U.S.*
1768.. So C Th.III. Not A in W S)

rear, sb. [?AB¹] *Jim bent over the toe with absorbing
interest...In another moment he was flying down the
street with his pail and a tingling rear...and Aunt
Polly was retiring from the field with a slipper in her
hand* 1876 TS ii 28 (U: *colloq* or *vulgar*. The buttocks,
rump. This sense not in OED W S C. The omission of
this familiar and harmless usage from all dicts. exc. the
Universal is a glaring instance of that Victorian
squeamishness of our lexicographers of which Mr. A. W.
Read remarks in his article "An Obscenity Symbol,"
AS.IX.274: "It is to the lasting shame of Murray and
Bradley that their linguistic sense was not strong
enough so that they could dissociate themselves from
the warped outlook of their age")

rear-skirts, sb. [B¹] *We shall let go our obsequious hold
on the rear-skirts of the sceptered land-thieves of Europe*
1902 "Defence of General Funston" 616 (Comb. not in
OED W S C)

rearwards, adv. [?AB²] See *forwards,* adv. 1897 (OED
1897, only ex. So W S U. Not in C. Cf. under forwards,
above)

reassurings, sb.pl. [B¹] *Alfred did what he could to
respond with some show of heart to the Major's kindly
pettings and reassurings* 1902 "Belated Russian Passport" (1928) 182 (Not as vbl.sb. in OED S C. Given in
W. Here *concrete*)

Rebel, sb. [AB¹] *I was a rebel, and the son of a man
who owned slaves* 1885 "Private Hist. of Campaign"
193. See also *reconstruct* 1901 (A derogatory name for
an adherent of the Confederate cause in the Civil War.
So M AS.IV.344,VIII.4.50. This sense not in OED
W S C; but cf. Reb in C)

receipt, v. [AB³] *The prince strode to his throne with...
the sternness of a Julius Caesar coming to receive and
receipt for a back-country kingdom* 1897 FE xli 384
(OED 3. *U.S.* To give a receipt *for.* 1880.. So W. Not
A in S C U)

recess-time, sb. [?AB³] *We loafed along, allowing to
strike the school about recess time* 1896 TSD viii 521
(OED U.S. quot. 1885, only ex. A in M. Comb. not in
W S C)

recheck, v. [AB¹] See *fare-ticket* 1902 (Not in OED
S C. Given in W. Cf. Check, v., above)

reciprocate, v.intr. [?AC] *He had loved one "too fair
for earth," and she had reciprocated* 1883 LM lv 542
(OED 3.
Now *rare* or *obs.* 1626..1781. Not *rare* or *obs* in W S C U)

reckon, v. [A] *I will shake this laziness off soon, I
reckon* 1853 *Letters* (1917) I i 29. See *buck,* pass the 1872.
"*I'm no more conceited than most people, I reckon*"
1873 GA vii 82. "*If Jones don't like it, he'll have to lump
it, I reckon*" 1875 OTM 219. "*I reckon it wouldn't
hardly do, Ben. You see, Aunt Polly's awful particular
about this sense*" 1876 TS ii 30. See also *chance,* v. 1880;
guess, v. 1883; *double-team, hide up, suggest,* all 1884;
break, v. 1892; *poison,* v. 1893; *shad* 1894 (OED 6b. To
think, suppose, be of opinion. Current in the Southern
States. 1603.. So S C Wr B F Cl Th,1811 T M DN.II,
III,IV,V, Mo. and Ga. AS.V.19,428, Ozarks. Not A in
W U)

reconcentrado, a. [AB¹] *It was Funston's report that
made us copy Weyler's reconcentrado horror* 1902 "Defence of General Funston" 624 (W: In Cuba, Philippines, etc. one of the rural non-combatants subjected
to the policy of being concentrated in or about towns for
convenience of military administration. So S C. Not in
OED)

record, sb. **of record.** [?AC] "*That verdict is of record,
and holds good to this day*" 1870 SNO (1875) 161
(OED 2.† *c*1386..1588. Phr. not *obs* in W S C)

record, sb. [B¹] *The strips...now took their place
among what Wilson called his "records"* 1893 PW ii 236
(The preserved tracing of a finger-print. This *spec* sense
not in OED W S C; but cf. OED 5. Also, in recent use,
a tracing or series of marks made by a recording instrument; no exs.)

recreation-time, sb. [B¹] *It seriously shortened his...
recreation-time* 1909 ISD iv 45 (Comb. not in OED
W S C)

recruit, v. [B¹] *It was forbidden by law to "recruit" a
native without his consent* 1897 FE v 81 (Used euphemistically of impressment or forced labor in the South
Seas. This *spec* sense not in OED W S C)

recruiting, vbl.sb. [B¹] *They make "Recruiting" as he
calls it ("Slave-Catching," as they call it in their frank
way) a trouble* 1897 FE vi 83 (This sense not in OED
W S C. Cf. Recruit, v., above)

red, sb. [AB³] *Smiley would ante up money on him
as long as he had a red* 1865 "Jumping Frog" (1875) 33

(OEDS 7. *U.S.* A red cent. 1861.. So W S C B F Cl Th,1857 T DN.I AS.XII.116, quot. 1856)

red-hot, a. [?AB¹] *Suddenly a red-hot new idea came whistling down into my camp* 1891 "Mental Telegraphy" 97. See also *break down,* v. 1894; *eagernesses* 1906 (W: Fresh, up to the minute, as, red-hot news. This sense not in OED S C)

Red Man, sb. [A] *The noble Red Man has always been a friend of mine* 1869 SNO (1875) 67 (OED 2. The N. Am. Indian. 1744.. So W S C U B F AS.VII.1)

redoubt, sb. [B¹] *I got this from a high officer at the Point, who told me he used to be a redoubt on General Grant's staff* 1881 Speeches (1923) 100 (Hum. malapropism)

redoubtable, a. [C] "*So redoubtable was he that our English knights refused to measure weapons with him*" 1881 PP xii 147 (OED Now *rhet.* Formidable. c1374.. 1889. So W. Not *arch* in S C U)

red rag to a bull, phr. [B²] "*What do you suppose I told you the names of those points for?*" "*Well, to—to be entertaining, I thought.*" *This was a red rag to a bull* 1875 OTM 219 (OED 1885.. So W S U. Phr. not in C)

Red Ribbon, sb. [AB¹] *He couched his lance and ran a bold tilt against total abstinence and the Red Ribbon fanatics* 1879 Letters (1917) I xix 355 (Red and blue ribbons, worn in coat lapels, were badges of influential temperance movements in the '40s and later decades; see Mark Sullivan, *Our Times,* 1927, II.113. This *spec* use not in OED W S C)

Reds, sb.pl. [AB³] *It is a restful chapter in any book of his when somebody doesn't step on a dry twig and alarm all the reds and whites for two hundred yards around* 1895 "Cooper's Literary Offences" 4 (OED 6a. pl. Red Men. 1804.. So W. This sense not in S C)

Redskin, sb. [A] *A redskin does not like to be ridiculed* 1895 "What Bourget Thinks" 55 (OED A N. Am. Indian. 1699.. So W S C U B F AS.VI.243, VII.1)

red-tape, sb. [?A] *They put their representatives to a deal of red-tape circumlocution* 1869 IA ix 87 (OED b. Excessive formality. Early exs. U.S. 1696.. A in Cl. Not A in W S C U)

redwood, sb. [AB³] *A Californian forest is best at a distance: redwood, pine, spruce, fir* 1872 RI lvi 408 (OED 2. A tall Californian timber-tree. 1819.. So W S C U)

re-dying, ppl.a. [B¹] *The affirmative nod of the re-dying rascal* 1883 LM xxxi 353 (Dying a second time. Comb. not in OED W S C)

reef, sb. [?AB¹] *I lit out and shook the reefs out of my hind legs* 1884 HF xxxi 316 (This sense not in OED W S C. A *Naut.* metaphor; cf. OED 1. Freq. in phr. *to take in a reef*; also in *fig* context. 1885)

reef-bench, sb. [B¹] *A mouldering ship perched high up on a reef-bench* 1897 FE vii 92 (Comb. not in OED W S C; but cf, OED Reef-platform, 1904)

reel off, v. [?AB¹] *The hands [of my watch] would straightway begin to spin round and round...She would reel off the next twenty-four hours in six or seven minutes* 1870 SNO (1875) 20. *We reeled off ten or twelve miles* 1872 RI iv 46. *Reeling off his tranquil spool of lies* 1883 LM xxiv 265 (Cf. OED 2b. *transf.* To rattle off a story, song, etc., without pause or effort. 1837.. So W S C U. Here, by extension, of any rapid and incessant action)

refix, v. [AB¹] See *fix,* v. 1880 (Not in OED W S C in this Am. sense; cf. fix, v., above)

reflush, v. [B¹] *The tints remained during several minutes...paling almost away for a moment, then reflushing—a shifting, restless, unstable succession of soft opalescent gleams* 1880 TA xlii 495 (Not in OED C. Given in W S)

reform-compelling, ppl.a. [B¹] *A severe and reform-compelling punishment* 1907 "Chaps. from Autob" 115 (Comb. not in OED W S C)

Reformed, a. [AB²] *Reformed (3 bodies);* see *Adventist* 1907 (See C for a full description of all three American denominations: the Reformed (Dutch), the Reformed (German), and the Reformed Episcopal Churches. So W S. Cf. OED Part of the *spec* names of various churches and religious bodies in different countries. No ex. for the Am. denominations)

refragability, sb. [B¹] See *diramic* 1869 (Nonsense use)

refrangibility, sb. [B¹] See *odic* 1880 (Nonsense use)

refreshment-peddler, sb. [B¹] *The road was simply paved with refreshment-peddlers* 1880 TA xxxi 335 (Comb. not in OED W S C)

refresh up, v. [?AB¹] "*It refreshes me up so—don't it you?*" 1880 TA xxvii 282 (Comb. not in OED W S C. A blend of *to refresh* and *to freshen up?*)

regular, a. [?AB³] See *kid-glove* 1873. *It put him in a regular passion* 1894 PW xiii 779 (OED 6c. *colloq.* Thorough, absolute. 1821.. So W S C U. A in Wr)

regular, sb. [?AC] *When the mind-curist is done with you, you have to call in a "regular"* 1894 Letters (1917) II xxxiv 606 (OED 4b. A regular practitioner. *obs.* 1764.. 1795. So W. This sense not in S C)

regular, sb. [?AB²] "*Regulars*" *are permanent sources of news* 1872 RI xliii 299. *All the courts came under the head of "regulars." They were sources of reportorial information which never failed* 1906 "Unpublished Chaps. from Autob" (1922) 455 (OED 4c. A regular customer, contributor, etc. 1898.. A in Cl. This sense not in W S C)

rehash, sb. [?AB³] *German newspapers contain no religious columns Saturdays, no rehash of cold sermons Mondays* 1880 TA App. F 626 (OED A mere restatement. 1849.. So W S C U. A in B)

rehash, v. [?AB³] *I am going to talk...again here if I have time to rehash the lecture* 1866 Letters (1917) I vi 121 (OED To restate in new language. 1822.. So W S C U. ?A in T)

rejump, v. [AB¹] *The lot was rejumped by its proper owners early in the morning* 1865 Notebook (1935) i 8 (Not in OED W S C. Cf. jump, above)

relevancy, sb. [B¹] *Conversations consisted mainly of irrelevances, with here and there a relevancy with an embarrassed look, as not being able to explain how it got there* 1895 "Cooper's Literary Offences" 10 (A relevant remark or speech. This *concrete* sense not in OED W S C. Cf. OED: The quality or fact of being relevant. 1561..)

relic, sb. [B¹] *I came upon a noble Son of the Forest sitting under a tree, diligently at work on a bead reticule... I addressed the noble relic as follows...* 1869 SNO (1875) 67. "*How much of it can you two undertake?*" "*All of it!*" *burst from both ladies at once.* "*You do ring true, you brave old relics!*" 1902 "Was It Heaven?" (1906) 81 (Here *transf.,* of a person. This sense not in OED W S C)

relic-peddler, sb. [B¹] *We got away from Bethlehem and its troops of beggars and relic-peddlers in the afternoon* 1869 IA lv 601 (Comb. not in OED W S C; but cf. OED Relic-vender, 1848)

relict, sb. [?AC] *Things that was valuable on account of them being relicts* 1884 HF xxxvii 384 (OED 1. Relic. Now *rare* or *obs.* 1535..1827. So W S C. In Huck Finn's mouth, this use is more likely an Am. survival than a conscious archaism)

relief-steamer, sb. [B¹] *The Times-Democrat sent a relief-steamer up one of the bayous* 1883 LM xlv 459 (Comb. not in OED W S C; but cf. OED Relief-boat, 1897)

relieve, v. [?AB¹] *He was "relieved" from duty when the boat got to New Orleans. Somebody expressed surprise at the discharge* 1875 OTM 723 (A euphemism for 'discharge,' 'dismiss.' This sense not in OED W S C)

religiouswise, adv. [B¹C] *142,550 persons respected the day religiouswise* 1883 LM li 508 (Religiously, in religious fashion. Not in OED W S C. Cf. OED Wise, sb. II.1b. With general adjs., often forming an equivalent of *-ly*. The free use, apart from the established simple forms, is now only *arch.* So humble-wise, despiteful-wise. *a*1300..1903)

relocatable, a. [AB¹] *At midnight the ledge would be "relocatable"* 1872 RI xli 290 (Not in OED W S C; but cf. OED Relocate, v. *U.S.* 1a. To allocate or assign afresh. 1847..; so Th.III)

remainders, sb.pl. [?AB¹] *"There'll be a double-barreled inquest here...and your remainders will go home in a couple of baskets"* 1872 RI 1 357. *I was having a good enough time seeing them hunt for my remainders* 1884 HF viii 58 (Remains, corpse. This sense not in OED W S C)

remember, v.refl. [C] *"I remember me of a small house that standeth over against the fish-market"* 1881 PP xiv 167 (OED 5. To bethink oneself. The refl. use now *rare*. *c*1386..1891. So W S C DN.III)

reminiscing, vbl.sb. [?AB²] *A deal of pretty jolly reminiscing was done* 1906 *Autob* (1924) II 204 (OEDS 1929, only ex. Not in W S C)

remotenesses, sb.pl. [B¹] *Switzerland and many other regions which were unvisited and unknown remotenesses a hundred years ago* 1880 TA xxxii 345 (This *concrete* sense not in OED W S C)

reorganize, v. [B¹] *The rude impact of the thought of these people upon his reorganized condition of mind* 1892 AmCl xiv 144. *I have conceived the stupendous idea of reorganizing the climates of the earth* 1892 AmCl xxv 247 (For this *spec* sense cf. M.T.'s use of the verb 'organize,' above. This sense not in OED W S C. Cf. OEDS Reorganized, ppl.a., 1929, only ex.)

reparenthesis, sb. [B¹] See *king-parenthesis* 1880 (Not in OED W S C)

repeater, sb. [?AB³] *Shooting him with...a repeater* 1873 GA liv 489 (OED 3c. A repeating fire-arm. Earliest ex. U.S. 1868.. Not A in W S C U)

repent, v.refl. [C] *Repenting him of charging them with burning the cabins* 1871 SNO (1875) 114 (OED 1. To affect oneself with contrition. Now *arch* in refl. use. *c*1290..1842. So W S C U)

repentancies, sb.pl. [B¹] *Humiliations which keep on persecuting me regardless of my repentancies* 1877 *Letters* (1917) I xvii 316 (Word not in OED W S C. Here *concrete*)

repetitious, a. [A] *All manner of wordy, repetitious, and wearisome papers* 1881 PP xiv 168 (OED Tiresomely iterative. Common in recent Am. use. 1675.. 1860. So S C U B F Th.III. Not A in W T)

repetitiousness, sb. [AB³] *To disguise repetitiousness of fact under variety of form* 1889 CY xxvi 340 (OED *U.S.* as above. 1882, only ex. So S C B. Not A in W U)

reporter-material, sb. [B¹] *It was my purpose...to start a newspaper...So I wanted to...be finding out what sort of reporter-material I might be able to rake together* 1889 CY ix 108 (Comb. not in OED W S C. Cf. OEDS Reporter, 1798..)

reportorial, a. [?AB³] *From mere reportorial instinct, I noted the time of day* 1872 RI lvii 422 (OED Irreg. formation from Reporter. Earliest exs. U.S. 1860.. A in B F Cl Th.III T. Not A in W S C)

Representative, sb. [A] *I disposed my feet on the table like a representative* 1872 SNO (1875) 268. *Names headed by all the Senators and Representatives from the state* 1873 GA xix 180. See also *dead-head* 1873 (OED 2. *U.S.* 1789.. So W S C U)

Republican, sb. [AB³] *The majority of the republicans are going to vote for Blaine* 1884 *Letters* (1917) II xxiv 446. See *Allopath* and *mugwump*, 1902. *He was a Republican, and upon invitation he agreed to make a campaign speech at the Republican mass-meeting* 1906 *Autob* (1924) II 330 (OED 3. *U.S.* politics, applied to the party founded in 1854. 1866.. So W S C U B F Cl DN.II)

Republican, a. [AB³] See *corruptible* 1873. *He made a rousing Republican campaign speech* 1906 *Autob* (1924) II 330 (OED *U.S.*, as above. 1862.. So W S C U B)

repudiation, sb. [AB³] *Repudiation has begun! the nation is lost* 1872 SNO (1875) 269 (S: First used in the sense of rejecting a bonded debt by a State in Mississippi in 1841. So OED 2b. 1843.. So W C U Th.III)

repulsivenesses, sb.pl. [B¹] *A patient stood forward to have his repulsivenesses stroked* 1889 CY xxvi 337 (This *concrete* sense not in OED W S C)

reputation, sb. Spelled **ruputation**. [?AE] *"If he'd a chawed up all the men he's ben a-gwyne to chaw up in the last twenty year he'd have considerable ruputation now"* 1884 HF xxi 212 (This form not mentioned in OED W S C)

re-renounce, v. [B¹] See *shore up* 1892 (Not in OED W S C)

resanctification, sb. [B¹] *The Fort was built three centuries ago by a Mohammedan Emperor—a resanctification of the place in the interest of that religion* 1897 FE xlix 473 (Not in OED W S C; but cf. OED Resanctify, v. 1675..)

residenter, sb. [A] *"When I tell the old residenters that..."* 1873 GA xxv 238 (OED 2. *Scotch* and *U.S.* A resident, inhabitant. 1678..1875. So W C Th DN.II, III. Not A in S T)

resin-colored, a. [B¹] *A gaunt, shackly country lout... in old resin-colored breeches* 1897 FE lxviii 694 (Comb. not in OED W S C)

respectworthy, a. [?AB²] *They were about all that was useful, or worth saving, or respectworthy* 1889 CY xiii 153. *I find him destitute of morals and not respectworthy* 1905 *Letters* (1917) II xliv 766. *There is no shred of respectworthy evidence that anything of the kind happened* 1909 ISD iv 39 (OEDS 1915, only ex. So W. Not in S C)

restaurant, sb. [?AB³] *Then we went out to a restaurant* 1869 IA xii 113. See also *stand-up*, sb. 1897; *feeding-place* 1907 (OED Earliest exs. U.S. 1827.. A in M DN.II. Not A in W S C U)

rest up, v. [AB²] *He could not rest up from his fatigue when he got worn out* 1895 JA II viii 458 (OEDS 2f. To recover one's strength by resting. *U.S.* 1911.. Not A in W. This constr. not in W)

resurrect, v. [?AB³] *She was bending down and punching under the bed with the broom...She resurrected nothing but the cat* 1876 TS i 18 (OED 1. To restore to life or to view again. c. *fig*, with ref. to things. 1863.. So W S C. A in B, this quot. So F Cl Th M AS.I.247)

retire, v.trans. [?AB²] *He was so awkward at this service that she retired him from it* 1881 PP xix 244 (OED 11b. To withdraw from the usual sphere of activity; to take off. All exs. U.S. 1883.. A in B. Not A in W S C U)

retire upon, v. [B¹] *When I retired from the rebel army in '61, I retired upon Louisiana in good order* 1883 LM liii 523 (Cf. OED 2. Of an army: To fall back, retreat; also const. with *to, into* (a place), *from* (an enemy, etc.). The const. with *upon* not in OED W S C)

return-entertaining, vbl.sb. [B¹] *You can judge what sort of return-entertaining she has done* 1899 "Diplomatic Pay" (1928) 234 (Comb. not in OED W S C)

retying, vbl.sb. [B¹] *It is become old and frayed out and damaged by a dozen annual retyings of its remains* 1884 *Speeches* (1923) 1 (Not in OED S C. Given in W. Cf. OED Retie, v. 1711..)

revamping, vbl.sb. [?AB³] See *half-sole*, v. 1907 (OED Patching up again. All exs. U.S. 1859.. A in B F Cl T. Not A in W S C)

reverence, sb. **to make reverence**. [C] *The Lord St. John made reverence and stood aside* 1881 PP vi 74 (OED 1d. † To show respect for by some action. *c*1400, *c*1489. So W C. Not *obs* in S)

Reverend, sb. [?A] *The Reverend said he would go, too: a good man, one of the best of men, although a clergyman* 1877 "Some Rambling Notes" i 443. *The Reverend was a man of strict veracity* 1891 "Luck" 407 (OED 2d. A clergyman. 1608..1894. So W S Wr. A in DN.II. This use not in C)

revolution-breeder, sb. [B¹] See *plotting-place* 1869 (Comb. not in OED W S C)

revolver, sb. [?AB³] See *Far West* 1869. *He snatched a navy revolver from his belt and fired* 1869 SNO (1875) 46. *A dragoon revolver* 1889 CY xxxix 506 (OED 1. A pistol provided with mechanism by which a set of loaded barrels is revolved. Earliest ex. U.S. 1835.. A in B DN.II. Not A in W S C U)

revolveration, sb. [B¹] "*Revolveration in Theatre*" 1904 "Italian without a Master" (1906) 184 (Humalienism, for revolver-shooting)

reward, sb. **to go to one's reward.** [B¹] *He went to his reward, whatever it was, two years ago* 1883 LM li 503 (To die. Phr. not in OED W S C)

rheum ponticum, sb. [B¹] See *afarabocca* 1894 {Ingredient in nonsense prescription. *Rheum rhaponticum*, or *Rha Ponticum*, is the common garden rhubarb; so W S C. Not in OED)

rheums, sb.pl. [C] "*How like a man it was to let him lie here uncovered and fill his body with deadly rheums*" 1881 PP xii 138 (OED Now *arch*. 2. *spec*. A cold in the head; catarrh. Chiefly pl. 1377..1864. Not *arch* in W S C Wr)

rhyme-jingle. sb. [B¹] *At some time or other you have been captivated by a ridiculous rhyme-jingle?* 1906 "WIM" (1917) v 66 (Comb. not in OED W S C)

riata, sb. [AB³] *We saddled our horses, hitched them with their long riatas* 1872 RI xxxvii 261 (OEDS Lariat. All exs. U.S. 1848.. A in W S C B F T DN.I)

riband, sb. [C] *The vague riband of trees on the further shore* 1873 GA iii 35 (OED Now *arch*. 4a. An object resembling a ribbon in form. 1801..1890. So C. Not *arch* in W S U)

riband, v. [C] "*A cloak of crimson satin flowered with gold, and ribanded with nets of silver*" 1881 PP ix 106 (OED Now *arch*. To adorn or trim with ribands. 1362..1840. So C U. Not in W S as verb)

ribby, a. [B³C] *A tall skeleton...clad in a tattered and moldy shroud, whose shreds were flapping about the ribby latticework of his person* 1870 SNO (1875) 193. See also *scrawny* 1872 (OED *rare*. Having prominent ribs. 1849, only ex. Not *rare* in W. Not in S C)

rice Christian, sb. [B³] "*Rice-Christians, occupationless incapables who join the church for revenue only*" 1897 FE lxv 652. *The "rice Christian" of the Orient... goes for rice, and remains to worship* 1909 ISD i 12 (OED A Hindu convert. 1816.. Comb. not in W S C)

richen, v. [?AB¹] "*A Cincinnati corpse don't richen a soil any*" 1883 LM iii 50 (To manure, render fertile. This sense not in OED W S C)

riddle, v. [?AB²] *I dosed him with bad jokes, and riddled him with good ones* 1872 SNO (1875) 96. *There was a booming roar, a thundering crash, and the riddled Amaranth dropped loose from her hold* 1873 GA iv 49. *Take notice how the Frenchman has riddled the grammar* 1875 SNO 29. See also *steamboatful* 1909 (OED 2. To pierce with holes like those of a riddle, shatter with missiles. *fig*. 1888, only *fig* ex. So C U. The *fig* use not in W S)

ride on a rail, v.phr. [AB²] *A "ride on a rail" would be "mob law"* 1853 *Hannibal Journal*, May 26. See *tar and feather* 1853, 1876, 1884. "*They rode him on a rail about the village, and everybody followed along, beating tin pans and yelling*" 1908 "Capt.Stormfield" 270 (OEDS 21. All exs. U.S. 1855.. A in S F Th,1854. Phr. not in W C)

riffle, sb. **to try, make the riffle.** [AB³] "*You think the prospect is pretty poor?*" "*We'll try it a riffle, first*" 1872 RI xxviii 206. "*He's made the riffle on the Injun; great Injun pacificator and land-dealer*" 1873 GA xxxi 279 (OEDS 3b. *To make the riffle*: To be successful in an attempt or undertaking. 1859.. So S C. A in Th AS. IV.342. Phr. not in W. The numbering in OEDS ap-

parently connects the phr. with the sense in OED 3. In card-sharping: the shuffle in which the thumbs 'riffle' or bend up the corners of the cards. 1894. It is more probably derived from the sense in OED 4. *U.S.* A rocky obstruction in the bed of a river, a rapid. 1796.. So AS.VI.230. *To try*, or, *to make the riffle*, would thus signify originally to attempt such a difficult passage in a stream)

riffle, sb. [AB³] *Quicksilver raiding down a riffle* 1906 "Howells" (1917) 229 (OED *U.S.* 5. In gold-washing. b. A groove or channel across the bottom of a cradle or sluice. 1875.. So W S C Cl)

riffraff, sb. [?AC] *Some hundreds of riffraff sarcastically called nobles* 1888 *Notebook* (1935) xx 195 (OED 1c. A collection of worthless persons. *obs*. 1570..1600. This collective sense not in W S C)

rifle-match, sb. [B¹] *They* [German newspapers] *contain no information about prize-fights...yachting-contests, rifle-matches, or other sporting matters* 1880 TA App. F 626 (Comb. not in OED W S C)

rifle-pistol, sb. [B¹] "*I rose and drew an elegant rifle pistol on him*" 1883 LM xxix 317 (Comb. not in OED W S C; but cf. OED Rifle-musket, 1841..)

rig, sb. [?AB³] *Her cheap but ravishing Sunday rig* 1892 AmCl xv 139. *I thought what a figure I should cut stepping out amongst the redeemed in such a rig* 1907 "Capt.Stormfield" 44 (OED 2. *colloq*. Costume, outfit. 1857.. So W S C U Wr. A in AS.XII.116, quot. 1856)

rig, sb. [AB²] "*I've heard tell of carriages all my life, and now...I mean to have the nobbiest rig that's going*" 1872 RI xlvi 325 (OED 3. *U.S.* b. An equipage, vehicle. 1885.. So C Th T H DN.III,V. Not A in W S)

Riggs' Disease, sb. [AB¹] *If you don't know what Riggs's Disease of the Teeth is, the dentist will tell you* 1900 "My Boyhood Dreams" (1928) 261 (W: After J.M.Riggs, Am. dentist (1810-85): Pyorrhea alveolaris. So C. Not in OED S)

right, adv. [AB³] "*They shut right down and leave*" 1880 TA ii 37 (OED 3c. *U.S.* Straight, with temporal connotation. 1849.. So W B F Cl T M AS.V.428, Ozarks. Not A in S U. This sense not in C)

right, adv. [?AC] *I did not feel right comfortable for some time afterward* 1869 IA xiv 134 (OED 5. Quite, altogether, to the full. Now *dial* or *arch*. c893..1854. Not *arch* in W S C. Cf. W: Now chiefly *colloq*. A in B F Cl M)

right, adv. [C] *They were waved aside with a right royal gesture* 1881 PP iii 40 (OED 9b. Very. Now *arch*. c1200..1877. So W U. Not *arch* in S. This sense not in C)

right, sb. [?AB¹] "*If you've done wrong, Si Hawkins, it's a wrong that will shine brighter at the Judgment Day than the rights that many a man has done before you*" 1873 GA ii 34 (A right action; a good deed. This sense not in OED W S C. Cf. the widespread Am. phrase *to have a right to* = to have a duty or moral obligation to, ought, should; AS.VIII.3.78, IX.317, X.77,153. This is listed as an Irish idiom in P.W.Joyce's *English as We Speak It in Ireland*, p.21)

right along, adv. [?AB²] *We tore right along* 1880 TA xlii 497 (OED Right, adv. 2. No ex. A in W S B F Cl T M H. Not in C)

right and left, adv. [?AB²] "*You begin to squander a fortune right and left*" 1873 GA xxxiv 319 (OED 1b. 1893. So W S C)

right away, adv. [AB³] *His face lit up right away* 1876 TS iii 36. *He would be famous—right away* 1899 "My Debut" (1900) 70 (OED Right, adv. 3b. Orig. *U.S.* 1818.. So W S C Wr B F Cl Th T M H DN.II,III)

right-down, adv. [?A] *It was right down awkward* 1884 HF xxvii 273. *We had a right down good sociable time* 1884 HF xxxvi 372 (OED 2. Thoroughly; out and out 1648..1888. So C. W: Now *colloq*; so U. Wr: In gen. *colloq* use, and Am. A in DN.III. Not in S)

right-feeling, a. [?AB²] *Any right-feeling reptile would do that* 1883 LM xlii 432 (OED Right, adv. 16b. No ex. Comb. not in W S C)

right-fielder, sb. [AB¹] *What a handy right-fielder he was!* 1889 CY xlii 533 (W: *Baseball,* Comb. not in OED S C)

right-hearted, a. [?AB²] *She got up right-hearted and happy* 1893 PW iii 239 (OEDS Right, a. 5b. 1908. So S C. Comb. not in W)

right off, adv. [A] *He wanted to know all about it right off* 1884 HF xxxiii 338. See also *familiarity* 1892 (OED 3b. Orig. *U.S.* 1790.. A in S C B F T M DN.III. Not A in W)

right so, adv. [C] See *random,* v. 1889 (OED Right, adv. 8b. Qualifying *as* or *so* in various constructions. Now *arch.* c1175..1871. So Wr. Not in W S C)

rigidify, v. [B³C] *He was toward fifty years old, with a slight stoop—a stoop rigidified by long habit* 1897 FE xxxix 362 (OED *rare.* To make rigid. 1842, 1879. OEDS 1911. Not *rare* in W. Not in S C)

rig up, v. [AB³] *I rigged up my pile-driver* 1889 CY xxxiii 420 (OED 6b. To fit up. 1841.. So W S C U. A in DN.II,III)

rile, v. [AB³] *"I says dat word, too, when I's riled"* 1874 SNO (1875) 242 (OED Chiefly *U.S.* and *colloq.* 2. To vex, annoy. 1825.. So W B F Cl Th M DN.I, III,V AS.V.204, Ozarks. Not A in S C U)

ring in with, v. [?AB¹] *"I tried to ring in with the old people"* 1907 "Capt. Stormfield" 48 (To make friends with. Phr. not in OED W S C)

ring-streaked-and-striped, ppl.a. [AB¹] *He was painted all over, ring-streaked-and-striped* 1884 HF xxiii 227. *"Our young saints wear wings all the time—gold, and variegated, and rainbowed, and ring-streaked-and-striped ones"* 1908 "Capt.Stormfield" 267 (Comb. derived by faulty memory from the Bible phr. *ring-straked and spotted,* Gen.xxx.35. Given as A in DN.III, e.Ala. Comb. not in OED W S C)

riot, sb. **to read the riot act.** [?AB²] *All the children chimed in now, with one general Babel of information—nobody offering to read the riot act or seeming to discountenance the insurrection or disapprove of it in any way* 1873 GA vii 80 (OEDS 4c. transf. To announce or declare that some course of action or conduct must cease. All exs. of the *transf* sense U.S. 1916.. Not A in W S C U Wr)

rip, sb. [?AC] *"A cat by the name of Yelverton...a troublesome old rip, with no more principle than an Injun"* 1877 "Some Rambling Notes" iii 722. *"What does the old rip want with me?...Send her in!"* 1894 PW viii 338 (OED 2. A worthless, dissolute fellow. b. Applied to a woman; somewhat *rare.* 1791..1900. This use not in W S C. A in B T)

rip, v. [AB³] *"What was that thing that ripped by here?"* 1875 SNO 146. See *gawk,* v. 1880. *The storm ripped and roared around all night* 1883 LM iii 54 (OEDS 7. To rush along with violence or at great speed. Orig. *U.S.* 1853.. So B F Cl. Not A in W S C)

rip, adv. [?AB¹] *Then rip comes another flash and another sockdologer* 1884 HF xx 192 (This use not in OED S C; but cf. OEDS Rip, sb. 4. *Like rips:* To an excessive degree, violently. *U.S. colloq.* 1901.. Cf. also W: *rip-.* A combining form used as a vague intensive, as in rip-roaring. A in Th)

rip and tear, v. [AB¹] *"A man wants rest, a man wants peace—a man don't want to rip and tear around all the time"* 1873 GA xxvii 249. *It was perfectly lovely the way he would rip and tear* 1884 HF xxi 207 (A in B F DN. III,IV. S: To scold and rage furiously. *colloq.* So C. Phrase not in OED W)

rip out, v. [?AB³] *Somebody ripped out something hifalutin* 1856 *Adv. of T. J. Snodgrass* (1928) 12. *He ripped out something brisk and said let him alone* 1884 HF vii 55 (OED 6c. To utter with violence. 1828.. So W C Wr. A in B F Cl T DN.II,III. Comb. not in S)

ripper, sb. [?AB³] *"If I get to be a regular ripper of a robber, I reckon she'll be proud"* 1876 TS xxxv 274. *The waves warn't running so high now...But all of a sudden along comes a regular ripper* 1884 HF xx 193 (OED 3. *slang.* a.1851.. So W S C U Wr. A in B)

rise, sb. [B³] See *broad-horn* 1875. *The June rise used to be always lucky for me; because as soon as that rise begins here comes cordwood floating down* 1884 HF vii 48 (OED 13. An increase in height of the sea, streams, or water, by tides, floods, etc. 1847, first ex. used *spec* of a river.. So W C. This sense not in S)

risk, v. [?AB¹] *"Maybe you don't want to bet you will, Tom?"...Says I, "Do you want to risk two and a half that I won't do it?" "Make it a V," says he. "Done," says I* 1877 "Some Rambling Notes" i 435 (To bet, wager. This sense not in OED W S C)

risky, a. [?AB³] *I was not anxious to try the experiment in any risky way* 1880 TA xxxix 453 (OED 1. Dangerous. Earliest ex. U.S. 1827.. A in B T. Not A in W S C U)

River Brethren, sb. [AB¹] See *Adventist* 1907 (W: A denomination of Christians formed about 1807 in Pennsylvania. So S C. Not in OED)

river-edge, sb. [B¹] *St.Louis is a great city; but the river-edge of it seems dead* 1883 LM xxii 256 (Comb. not in OED W S C; but cf. OED River-frontage, 1865)

river-front, sb. [?AB¹] *The pavements along the river-front were bad* 1883 LM xxii 256 (W: The land or area along a river, esp. in a city. Comb. not in OED S C)

river-glimpse, sb. [B¹] *The "point" above the town, and the "point" below, bounding the river-glimpse and turning it into a sort of sea* 1875 OTM 70 (Comb. not in OED W S C)

river-inspector, sb. [?AB¹] *We had a fine company of those river-inspectors along, this trip* 1875 OTM 221 (Comb. not in OED W S C)

river-pilot, sb. [?AB¹] *Two or three river-pilots...saw me do creditable things in those ancient days* 1909 ISD vi 65 (Comb. not in OED W S C. Cf. pilot, above)

river road, sb. [B¹] *I was stretching up the river road at a five-mile gait* 1896 TSD iv 353 (Comb. not in OED S C. Given in W)

roach, v. [AB³] *The Judge roached his gray hair up with his fingers* 1894 TET v 393 (OED 2. *U.S.* OEDS 2b. Of persons. Also with *up.* 1854.. So W S C Th)

roached-backed, ppl.a. [AB¹] *Roached-backed animals that he said was hyenas* 1894 TSA ix 355 (Comb. not in OED W S C; but cf. OEDS Roached, ppl.a. *U.S.* Having an upward curve. 1776..; also W: Roach-back, sb. An arched back. *Western U.S.,* a grizzly bear)

road, sb. [AB³] *"Report such things to me instead of blackguarding the road"* 1893 "Travelling with a Reformer" (1900) 359. *It is a narrow-gauge road to the frontier, and a broader gauge thence to Melbourne* 1897 FE xiv 153 (OED 4c. *U.S.* A railroad. 1837.. So M H. Not A in W S C)

road-pegging, vbl.sb. [B¹] *A carriage-road wound through the grounds and up the hill. I staked it out with the English monarchs, beginning with the Conqueror...If the road-pegging scheme had not succeeded, I should have lodged the kings in the children's heads by means of pictures* 1899 "How to Make Hist. Dates Stick" (1917) 149 (Comb. not in OED W S C)

road-straggler, sb. [B¹] *One of those ragged road-stragglers* 1895 JA I iv 693 (Comb. not in OED W S C; but cf. OED Road-pilgrim, 1890)

roast, v. [B¹] *In all cases the Jew had to roast, no matter which side he was on* 1898 "Stirring Times in Austria" (1900) 340 (To suffer persecution or ignominy. This milder *fig* meaning not in OED W S C. Cf. OED 6. To undergo the process of being cooked, tortured, etc. 1300..)

robber-book, sb. [B¹] See *pirate-book* 1884 (Comb. not in OED W S C)

rock, sb. [AB³] See *bounce* 1876; *miaow* 1876. *Italian laborers were blasting away the frontage of the hills to make room for a new railway...We raised our sun-umbrellas and waited the results. No harm done; none of the stones fell in the water. Another blast followed...It appeared certain that we must perish, but...the bitterest thought was the bizarre wording of the resulting obituary: "Shot with a rock, on a raft"* 1880 TA xvii 154. See also *dump,* v. 1884 (OED 1b. *U.S.* and *Australian.* A stone of any size. 1838.. So W S C B F Cl Th,1712 T M H DN.I,II,III, IV,V)

rock, sb. [AB³] *A girl that was laying for a title, or a title that was laying for rocks* 1904 "Italian with Grammar" (1906) 189 (OED 2e. *U.S. slang.* A piece of money. 1848.. So W S C B F Th T H AS.IV.357, X.19)

rock-cutting, sb. [B¹] *Long rock-cuttings, devoted to the advertisement of patent medicines* 1873 GA xlvi 419 (Comb. not in OED W S C; but cf. OED Cutting, sb. 8. An open excavation. 1836..)

rocker, sb. [AB³] *Cane-seat chairs, splint-bottomed rocker* 1883 LM xxviii 406 (OED 4b. *U.S.* A rocking-chair. 1857.. So S F Cl Th,1855 T. Not A in W C)

rocking-chair, sb. [?AB³] *The rocking-chairs and sofas were not present* 1872 RI iv 42 (OED A chair mounted on rockers. Not called *U.S.,* but early quots. indicate Am. origin for the thing. 1832.. A in B, p.793. Not A in W S C U)

rocky, a. [?AB³] *Most of the folks that shook farming to go crusading had a mighty rocky time of it* 1893 TSA i 25 (OED b. *slang,* in vaguely depreciative sense. 1883.. A in Th.III, 1875: Difficult. This vague sense not in W S C, which all define the *U.S.slang* use as: Unsteady, giddy, tipsy, or dizzy; so Cl)

Rocky Mountains, sb. [AB³] *The "plaza" is native to all towns beyond the Rocky Mountains* 1872 RI xxi 158. See also *buffalo-range* 1908 (OED 1b. 1805.. So W S C)

roger, v. [B¹] *"Was not Her Grace of Bilgewater rogered by four lords before she had a husband?"* 1880 *Fireside Conversation 1601* (The obscene sense is fully explained in Farmer and Henley, *Slang and Its Analogues,* with quots. 1750..1885. Not in OED W S C; but cf. OED Roger, sb. 3a. 1653..1719)

roll, v. [?AB¹] *In our country printing-offices the apprentice learns to "roll"* 1880 TA App.A 586 (W: To ink with a roller, *Printing.* So S. This sense not in OED C)

rolling, ppl.a. [AB³] *Just here the land was rolling—regular elevations and depressions as far as the eye could reach* 1872 RI ii 25 (OED 5. Of prairie-land: Undulating. orig. *U.S.* 1819.. So W B Cl Th,1818 T M AS.II. 31. Not A in S C U)

romance-literature, sb. [B¹] *You have made the American home beautiful with your noble romance-literature* 1902 "Concerning Copyright" 5 (Comb. not in OED W S C; but cf. OED Romance-novel, 1820)

romance-reading, vbl.sb. [B¹] *There was no romance-reading that night* 1904 "Bequest" (1906) ii 5 (Comb. not in OED W S C; but cf. OED Romance-writing, 1829)

romance-tinge, sb. [B¹] *The names betray the latest romance-tinge in the parental blood* 1904 "Bequest" (1906) i 3 (Comb. not in OED W S C)

Roman-looking, a. [B¹] *We came to a noble Roman-looking ruin* 1869 IA xlviii 505 (Comb. not in OED W S C)

romaunt, sb. [C] *"It hath wrought this curious romaunt"* 1881 PP xii 144 (OED *arch.* 1. A romantic tale. 1530..1884. So W S C)

roof-clustered, ppl.a. [B¹] *A hill...with its roof-clustered cap of architecture* 1880 TA xix 171 (Comb. not in OED W S C)

roost, sb. [?AB³] *It is a pity he* [i.e., Mohammed] *could not judge the world from some roost of his own in Mecca, without trespassing on our holy ground* 1869 IA liv 584 (OED 1d. *fig.* A resting-place. Early exs. U.S. 1858.. Not A in W S C)

roost, v. [?AB³] *I found him roosting on the bitts forward* 1884 HF xiii 112 (OED 1b. Of persons: To seat oneself, perch. *colloq.* All exs. exc. the earliest U.S. 1816.. Not A in W S C Wr)

rooster, sb. [AB³] See *donkey-voiced* 1870 (OEDS Chiefly *U.S.* and *dial.* A cock. 1802.. So W C Wr B F Cl Th T M H DN.III, V,VI. AS.IX.277. Not A in S U T)

roosterish, a. [AB¹] *He stands vast and conspicuous... self-satisfied and roosterish* 1898 "Stirring Times" (1900) 326 (Cocky, pert, jaunty. Not in OED W S C; but cf. OED Rooster, sb. 1b. *transf.* of persons. 1871..)

rope in, v. [AB³] *"Let the rest of the town get roped in"* 1884 HF xxiii 229 (OED 4b. To draw into some enterprise; to ensnare. Orig. *U.S.* 1848.. So W S C B F Cl Th.III T M DN.III. Not A in U)

rose-leafy, a. [B¹] *Every lady's rose-leafy dress flapping soft and silky* 1884 HF xxii 222 (Comb. not in OED W S C)

rose-tinted, ppl.a. [B¹] *He sold me $10,000 worth of another rose-tinted stock* 1885 *Letters* (1917) II xxv 452 (Over-estimated, regarded or described with undue optimism. This *fig* use not in OED W S C; but cf. OED Rose-coloured, a. 3. *fig.* Characterized by a tendency to regard matters in a highly favourable or attractive light. 1861..)

Ross, v. [B¹] *We shall run over to the Ross's* [sic] *frequently...We shall go Rossing* 1892 *Letters* (1917) II xxxii 571 (Hum. nonce use)

roster, sb. [?AB³] *Every single diplomatic post in the roster of this government* 1892 AmCl ii 33 (OED 2. A list or table of persons. 1858.. So W S C U. A in B T)

rot, sb. [?AB³] *All the "rot" they* [health periodicals] *contained about ventilation...was all "gospel" to her* 1876 TS xii 108. *All that kind of rot, the way women always do for to force out compliments* 1884 HF xxvi 258 (OED 5. *slang.* Trash, bosh. 1848.. So W S C U. A in DN.IV)

rotten, adv. [?AB¹] *"I'm most rotten certain 'bout that"* 1880 TA xxiii 226. *There ain't nothing more to write about, and I am rotten glad of it* 1884 HF "Chapter the Last" 438 (This adv. use not in OED W S C; but cf. OED Rotten, a. 8b. *slang,* as a mere expletive. 1892; so W)

rough, sb. [?AB³] See *bone-yard* 1873. *The pirate is only a seedy, unfantastic "rough"* 1873 GA vii 76. *Three boisterous roughs got aboard* 1893 "Travelling with a Reformer" (1900) 352. *Some brutal roughs from Daly's gorge had Holmes in their grip* 1902 "DBDS" (1928) 354 (OED 7. A rowdy. 1837.. So W S C U. A in B T)

rough, a. [?AB²] *Another devilish thing is that the Alta copyrighted the letters—that was rough* 1867 *M.T. the Letter Writer* (1932) i 16. *It was rough living in the house all the time, considering how dismal regular and decent the widow was in all her ways* 1884 HF i 2. *One of the roughest Sundays I had run across yet* 1884 HF xviii 167 (OED 9. *colloq.* a. Bearing or falling hardly on a person. Earliest quot. from Bret Harte. 1870.. A in B T. Not A in W C. This sense not in S)

rough, a. [?AB²] *"I spent my last 10 cents for... cheese & i felt pretty rough"* 1883 LM lii 513 (OED 10. *dial.* Unwell, sick, ill. a1893, only ex. So Wr. This sense not in W S C)

rough, v. **to rough it.** [?A] *Roughing It* (title) 1872 RI (OED 4. To face or submit to hardships. 1768.. So W S C. A in AS.VII.426)

Rough-Rider, sb. [AB¹] *We have tried for governor an illustrious Rough Rider* 1900 *Speeches* 1910 (355) (W: An officer or enlisted man in the 1st U.S. Volunteer Cavalry...largely organized by Theodore Roosevelt. So S C H. This *spec* sense not in OED; but cf. OED Rough-riding, vbl.sb. 1844..)

rough-scruff, sb. [AB¹] *"The ruff-scruff and rag-tag-and-bob-tail of noble old Calaveras"* 1865 SS (1926) 161 (Not in OED W S C. A var. form of Rough-scuff, OED *U.S.* The rabble. 1859..; so W S C B F T DN.III)

roundabout, sb. [AB³] *He wore a "roundabout"* 1872 RI viii 70. *To seize a small boy by the slack of his roundabout* 1876 TS i 18 (OEDS 2b. *U.S.* A short jacket. 1818.. So Cl Th T H DN.I. Not A in W S C)

round-log, a. [?AB¹] *Phelps's was one of these little one-horse cotton plantations...round-log kitchen* 1884 HF xxxii 329 (Comb. not in OED W S C)

round out, v. [?AB³] *"We've got to round out our territory"* 1873 GA xxxviii 343 (OED 8a. To complete, fill out. Earliest ex. from Hawthorne. 1856.. Not A in W S C)

roundsman, sb. [AB²] *The rank of constable or even roundsman* 1870 CRG (1919) 63. *As easy as a burglar knows a roundsman* 1883 LM xxiv 269 (OED 2. *U.S.* A police officer. 1883.. So W S C Th.III H)

round to, v. [?AB¹] *When we wanted to land we sent a ine ashore and "rounded her to" with a yoke of oxen* 1859 Letter in *New Orleans Daily Crescent*, May 17. *The other night I was about to round to for a storm* 1859 *Letters* (1917) I ii 43 (Not in OED W S C as an operation performed by a river steamboat. Cf. for a sailing vessel OED 13d. *Naut.* To come to the wind and heave to. 1830..; so W S C)

round trip, sb. [AB³] *I sailed round and round it forty-four times...each round trip a half mile* 1869 SNO (1875) 70. See *back-pay* 1874. *A great reduction will be made where parties wish to make the round trip* 1875 SNO 309. *Thirteen hundred miles of river four times traversed in every thirty-five days—the time required by that swift boat to achieve two round trips* 1909 ISD i 8 (OEDS 2. *U.S.* A circular trip; an outward and return journey. 1868.. So Th.III M H. Not A in W. Comb. not in S C)

round-up, sb. [AB³] *Young Barker...looks much improved by his vacation round-up* 1889 CY xxvi 341 (OEDS 2b. *U.S.* A meeting or social gathering. 1880.. So W S F Cl Th M H. Not A in S C)

round up, v. [AB³] *One doesn't know...how near it came to being complete, nor what was still wanting to round it up and make it so* 1893 "Cure for the Blues" 82 (OED 5e. To collect cattle. Orig. *U.S.* and *Australian.* transf. 1889.. So W Cl T H. Not A in C. This sense not in S)

rouser, sb. [?AB³] *"Drink his health! Give him a rouser!"...Everybody bellowed forth in song* 1894 PW xi 556 (OED 3. A noisy song. 1893, only ex. So W S C U. A in B F Cl T)

roustabout, sb. [AB³] *Deck-hands, firemen, and roustabouts* 1875 OTM 220. *"Do you mean the Roman army—those six sandaled roustabouts in nightshirts?"* 1883 LM li 505. *Several roustabouts and mates* 1909 ISD vi 65 (OED 1. *U.S.* A wharf labourer or deck hand. 1868.. So W S C B F Cl Th T M)

roust out, v. [A] *"A fellow couldn't roust out such a gaudy thing as that in a little country-town like this"* 1871 SNO (1875) 298. See *chin-music* 1872. *"As long as they can roust out something wonderful to tell"* 1883 LM xxiv 268. *"Why didn't you roust me out?"* 1884 HF vii 47 (OED *dial* and *U.S.* To rout out. 1658..1890. So Wr DN.III,V. Not A in W S C)

rowdy, sb. [AB³] *If a drunken rowdy should get in* 1869 IA xii 107. *He found the "nigger" in him...giving the road to the white rowdy and loafer* 1894 PW x 551 (OED Of Am. origin: a rough, disorderly person. 1819.. So B Cl Th T M DN.III AS.VIII.1.76. Not A in W S C U)

rowdy, a. [AB³] *Intrusion of services by rowdy hackmen* 1869 IA xii 112 (OED Of Am. origin. 1. 1819.. So U B Cl Th T M DN.III,V. Not A in W S C)

royalty, sb. [?AB²] *We have sold 40,000 copies, which gives £3,000 royalty to be divided between the authors*

1874 *Letters* (1917) I xiii 215. See also *Comanche* 1885 (OED 6e. A payment made to an author. Earliest ex. U.S. 1880.. Not A in W S C U)

rubbish, sb. Spelled **rubbage**. [?AE] *"Rubbage! I don't believe it"* 1876 TS vi 62. *"Ain't you had anything but that kind of rubbage to eat?"* 1884 HF viii 65. *"What kind of a lie are you fixing your mouth to contribit to this mess of rubbage?"* 1896 TSD vi 358 (OED This form *obs* or *dial.* So W S C. A in DN.III,V, s.e.Mo.)

rubbish-pile, sb. [B¹] See *wore-out* 1884. *Just a rubbish-pile of battered corpses* 1889 CY xix 235 (Comb. not in OED W S C; but cf. OED Rubbish-heap, *c*1887)

ruck, sb. [AB²] *Flowers and general ruck sent to him by Tom, Dick, and Harry from everywhere* 1885 *Letters* (1917) II xxv 460 (OED 5. *U.S. colloq.* Nonsense, rubbish. 1890, only ex. So S. Not A in W C U)

ruffle-cuffed, ppl.a. [B¹] *I did not get back the same drawers I sent down...I got a pair on a new plan. They were merely a pair of white ruffle-cuffed absurdities, hitched together at the top with a narrow band* 1880 TA xxxv 399 (Comb. not in OED W S C)

ruffler, sb. [C] See *budge* 1881. *As to yonder base rufflers, think ye not they have not their fill* 1889 CY xiv 170 (OED 1. One of a class of vagabonds prevalent in the 16th c. *obs.* 1535..1818. So W S C U)

rugged, a. [AB³] *Restore it to rugged health* 1892 AmCl xxiii 236 (OED 9. *U.S.* Strong, robust, vigorous. 1848.. So S C B T DN.III. Not A in W)

rule out, v. [?AB²] *Apocryphal writings have been ruled out of our Bible* 1869 IA li 539. *The mule-race... has brought some pretty fast mules to the front. One of these had to be ruled out, because he was so fast that he turned the thing into a one-mule contest* 1883 LM xlv 463. *They was going to rule me out* 1884 HF ii 13 (OED 8d. To shut or put out by formal decision. 1890, 1893. OEDS Further exs. 1925, 1928. So W S U. This const. not in C)

rum, sb. [AB³] *There was a strong rum party and a strong anti-rum party* 1894 PW xi 556 (OED 1c. *U.S.* Used generically as a hostile name for intoxicating liquors. 1858, only ex. So W U B F Cl Th M DN.IV. Not A in S C)

rum-hole, sb. [AB³] *Gambling dens and unlicensed rum-holes* 1892 AmCl iii 45 (OED *U.S.* A grog-shop; used in N.Y. 1859, only ex. So S C B F Cl Th T. Comb. not in W)

rummage around, v. [B¹] *He came rummaging around in the dark among the shingle bundles* 1883 LM iii 58 (Comb. not in OED W S C; but cf. OED 8b. Rummage about. 1867..)

rum-mill, sb. [AB¹] *I sent down to the rum-mill on the corner* 1870 SNO (1875) 387. *Mr. O'Riley kept his first rum-mill* 1873 GA xxxiii 307 (A in B: A low tavern or groggery, 1859. So S F T. Comb. not in OED W C)

rummy, sb. [AB³] *"I'd been runnin' a little temperance revival...makin' it mighty warm for the rummies"* 1884 HF xix 182. See also *anti* 1894 (OED *U.S.* The political opponents of the temperance party. 1860.. So W S C DN.III,IV)

rum-shop, sb. [AB¹] *Industry and economy soon enabled him to start a low rum shop in a foul locality, and this gave him political influence* 1873 GA xxxiii 301. See also *almshouse* 1883 (W: A saloon, *U.S.* So C. Comb. not in OED S)

run, sb. **to keep the run of.** [AB³] *"That child has worked, and kep' the run of the med'cin, and the times of giving it"* 1873 GA ii 32. *"Sometimes she sews it with white, and sometimes she sews it with black. I wish to geeminy she'd stick to one or t'other—I can't keep the run of 'em"* 1876 TS i 21 (OED 30b. To keep in touch with; to keep oneself informed about. *U.S.* 1862.. Not A in W C. Phr. not in S C)

run, v.intr. [AB³] *Buckstone and the constable had come to ask him to run for mayor* 1894 PW xiii 777 (OEDS 7b. To stand as a candidate for. Orig. *U.S.* 1851.. So W B F Cl M H. Not A in S C)

run, v.trans. **to run the blockade**. [?AB²] *Inquired about chances to run the blockade and visit the Alhambra* 1869 IA lix 636 (OED 40b. Earliest ex. U.S. 1869.. Not A in W S C)

run, v.trans. [AB³] "*I should like to run the Treasury Department about six months*" 1873 GA xl 357. See *rummy* 1884. "*If I was running this shop I'd make him say something*" 1902 "DBDS" (1928) 316 (OEDS 51c. To direct, conduct, carry on (a business, etc). Orig. *U.S.* 1827.. So W S C B F Cl Th T. Not A in U)

run, v.trans. [?AB¹] *I had...turnips enough to run the family for two years!* 1871 SNO (1875) 95. "*Pap's so po' he cain't run me no mo', so I want to git a show somers if I kin. I don't turn my back on no kind of work*" 1880 TA xxiii 225 (To provide for, support. This sense not in OED W S C. Perhaps an extension from the sense above, the term for operating a business being transf. to supporting a family, much as plant (q.v.) is extended from factory to church)

run across, v. [?AB²] "*If I don't run across you in Italy, you hunt me up in London before you sail*" 1880 TA xxi 202. *I had run across that camp-fire* 1884 HF viii 64 (OED 59. To meet or fall in with. U.S. quot. 1887, only ex. Not A in W C U. Comb. not in S)

runaway-nigger, sb. [?AB¹] See *coat-of-arms* 1883. "*Dey sticks up runaway-nigger bills*" 1894 PW xviii 19 (Comb. not in OED W S C)

run down, v. [?AB³] *She had run down and down and down and had at last reached a point where medicines no longer had any helpful effect upon her* 1897 FE i 32 (OED 73b(b). To fall off in vigour or health: of persons. Earliest ex. U.S. 1846.. Not A in W S C U)

run on, v. [?A] *I am running on preachers, now, altogether* 1866 *Letters* (1917) I vi 122 (OED 65c. To show a marked demand or preference for. 1683, 1895. This seems to be a transf. sense from the printing idiom *to run on sorts*, to require an unusual or disproportionate quantity of one or more characters of type. The printing phr. is illustrated in the OED quot. 1683, and is given in W S C. The transf. use, exemplified above and in OED quot. 1895, is not found in W S C)

run to, v. [?AB¹] "*Dr. Spooner runs so much to emetics...that we changed off and took Dr. Leathers*" 1873 GA xxxiii 307. *In my nature I have always run to pie, whilst in his nature he has always run to mystery* 1896 TSD ii 346 (To be addicted to, show a preference for. This sense not in OED W S C)

run-to-cover, sb. [B¹] "*It is the nature of women to ask trivial, irrelevant, and pursuing questions—questions that pursue you from a beginning in nothing to a run-to-cover in nowhere*" 1877 "Some Rambling Notes" ii 586 (Nonce comb.)

rural-looking, a. [B¹] *I caught a glimpse of two young rural-looking men* 1870 SNO (1875) 234 (Comb. not in OED W S C)

rush, sb. **in a rush**. [?AB¹] *He is always in such a rush that he never thinks of anything* 1876 TS xviii 149 (In a great hurry, in great haste. Phr. not in OED W S C; but cf. OED 5b. *With a rush:* in a sweeping or rapid manner; earliest ex. U.S. 1859..)

rush through, v. [?AB¹] *Where was the use in rushing this whole globe through in six days?* 1883 LM li 503 (Cf. OED 4. To force at an unusual or excessive pace or speed; also with *on, up.* 1850.. This constr. with *through* not in OED W S C)

rustle, v. [AB³] *The sneeze started those scoundrels a-rustling to get out of the path* 1876 TS xxx 227. "*We'll rustle around and gather up whatever pickin's we've overlooked*" 1884 HF xii 106 (OED 4. *U.S. colloq.* To bestir oneself. 1872.. So W S C F Cl T H DN.I, III AS.I.150)

rustler, sb. [AB²] "*But, pard, he was a rustler! You ought to seen him get started once*" 1872 RI xlvii 333. *What a rustler he was!* 1897 FE xxxix 365 (OED 2a. *U.S.* An energetic or bustling man. 1872.. So W S C F Cl Th.III H)

rusty, a. [?AB¹] *It was after sun-up now...The king and the duke turned out by and by looking pretty rusty* 1884 HF xxi 204. *We began to feel rusty and stretchy, and first we knowed we was all asleep* 1893 TSA ii 29 (Tired, sleepy, inclined to stretch. This sense not in OED W S C. Cf. OED 1. Of horses: Restive. 1562.. Cf. also DN.IV: out of date, dull; DN.V, s.w.Mo.: Old, uncouth, unkempt, shaggy, unshaven)

rye, sb. [AB³] *There was a long row of bottles with Old Rye in them* 1864 SS (1926) 126 (OEDS 3. Ryewhisky. *U.S.colloq.* 1836.. So W S C B F Cl AS.IV. 385. Not A in U)

S

-s, suffix. **Mondays, mornings, nights, night-times, Saturdays, summers, winters,** q.v. [?A] (OED Originally *-es*, identical with the suffix of the genitive singular of many neuter and masculine sbs. A favorite formation of M.T.'s, probably reflecting its extended use in Am. speech. Of those listed above, only *mornings* and *nights* are given in any dict. *Mornings* is called A in S, and *nights* in OED W S C Wr Th)

Sabbath-school, sb. [?AB³] *He always learned his book, and was never late at Sabbath-school* 1870 SNO (1875) 56. See *vacation* 1876. *The van-leader of civilization is never the Sabbath-school* 1883 LM lx 586 (OED 1845. OEDS Earlier U.S.ex. 1822. Another earlier U.S. ex., 1837, noted in AS.II.30. Not A in W S C)

sable, a. [D] See *coat-of-arms* 1883 (OED 1. *Heraldry.* Black. 1470..1875—. So W S C U)

sachem, sb. [A] *"Does the mighty Sachem yearn to drink the blood of his enemies?"* 1869 SNO (1875) 67. *"No, No! by the great Sachem, No!"* 1876 TS xxvi 206 (OED 1. The supreme head or chief of some American Indian tribes. 1622.. So W S C U B F Cl Th M DN.VI AS.IV.9)

sack, sb. [?AB³] *A cowboy hat, and below it a plaided sack of rather loud pattern* 1892 AmCl vi 70 (OED 2. A loose-fitting coat. 1847.. So W C U. A in S Cl)

sack-pile, sb. [B¹] *He saw a white linen figure stretched in slumber upon a pile of grain-sacks... The form whirled itself from the sack-pile* 1897 FE xxviii 273 (Comb. not in OED W S C)

sacre bleu, int. [B¹] *"Is, ah...is he dead?" "Oh, sacre bleu, been dead three thousan' year"* 1869 IA xxvii 294. See also *gros de laine* 1880 (Alienism, not in OED W S C)

saddle-bag, v. **saddle-baggs**. [AB²E] *"They lost their steering-oar, and swung around and went a-floating down, stern first, about two mile, and saddle-baggsed on the wreck"* 1884 HF xiii 114 (OEDS *U.S.* To catch on an obstruction and double round it. 1905. So W C DN.II. Not in S. No dict. gives this sp.)

saddle-blanket, sb. [AB²] *The Syrian saddle-blanket is a quilted mattress two or three inches thick* 1869 IA xlv 477 (OED *U.S.* 1885. So C DN.II. Not A in W S)

saddle-colored, a. [?AB²] *I saw long-haired, saddle-colored Sandwich Island maidens* 1872 RI lxiii 456 (OEDS 1900. Comb. not in W S C)

saddle-horn, sb. [?AB³] *I coiled my lariat and hung it on my saddle-horn* 1889 CY xxxix 502 (OED 1890. OEDS Earlier U.S. ex.1856. Comb. not in W S C)

sadful, a. [?AC] *She could write about anything... just so it was sadful* 1884 HF xvii 158 (OED *Obs. rare.* Sorrowful. 1658. Not in W S C. Certainly not a conscious archaism here. Probably to be classed as an American survival)

sad-visaged, ppl.a. [B¹] *I never saw such utterly wretched, starving, sad-visaged, broken-hearted looking curs in my life* 1869 IA xxxiv 370 (Comb. not in OED W S C; but cf. OED sad-avised, 1878; sad-faced, 1588)

safe, a. [?AB¹] *"He is distinguished for being, in pilot phrase, 'close', as well as superhumanly 'safe'"* 1859 Letter in *New Orleans Daily Crescent* (Of a river pilot: Skilful in avoiding accident. This *spec* sense, evidently felt as a localism by M.T., not in OED W S C; but cf. OED 11a. Sure in procedure trustworthy. 1604..1678)

safe, sb. [?AB³] See *combination* 1880. *His plan was to steal the safe-key...and then go back and rob the safe* 1894 PW xix 22 (OEDS 1b. Earlier U.S. ex. 1820.. A in T. Not A in W S C)

safe-deposit, sb. [A] *I have in a safe deposit box the manuscript of an unfinished work of mine* c1890 *M.T. the Letter-Writer* (1932) vi 82 (OED orig. *U.S.* A place in which valuables are stored.1783.. So in W S C U)

safe-door, sb. [?AB¹] *The safe-door was open* 1894 PW xix 22 (Cf. Safe, sb., above. Not A in W. Comb. not in OED S C)

safe-key, sb. [?AB¹] See *safe*, sb. 1894 (Cf. above. Comb. not in OED W S C)

safeness, sb. [?AB¹] *"His method of accomplishing this feat proves what we have just said of his 'safeness'—he sounded the chute first"* 1859 Letter in *New Orleans Daily Crescent* (For *spec* sense cf. Safe, a., above. Not in OED W S C)

safety-box, sb. [B¹] *"I hold in my fingers a burnt Swedish match—the kind one rubs on a safety-box"* 1902 "DBDS" (1928) 340 (A box with a prepared surface on which safety-matches may be ignited. Comb. not in OED W S C; but cf. OED Safety-match, 1863)

sag, v. [A] *I awoke, and found myself lying with my head out of bed and "sagging" downward considerably* 1870 SNO (1875) 201 (OED 2. To hang to a lower level, through lack of strength or effort. Chiefly *fig.* Common in U.S. 1508.. So Wr F Cl. Not A in W S C U)

sagamore, sb. [A] *The Weekly Sagamore arrived* 1904 "Bequest" (1906) iii 12 (OED = Sachem. 1613.. So W S C U B F Cl M. Here, a newspaper so named)

sage-brush, sb. [AB²] *On the plains, sage-brush and grease-wood grow about twice as large as the common geranium* 1861 Letters (1917) I iii 54. See *grease-wood* 1872; *range*, sb. 1902. *Before them stretched the sage-brush plain, dim, vast, and vague* 1902 "DBDS" (1928) 320 (OED Sage, sb. 5b. Any one of various shrubby species of *Artemisia*, growing in elevated plains of the Western U.S. 1872.. OEDS also *attrib.* 1904.. So W S C U B F Cl T)

sage-bush, sb. [AB³] *He has crouched behind a sage-bush* 1872 RI iii 32. See *sand-wave* 1902. (OED Sage, sb. As above. 1807. So in W C. Not in S)

sail, v. [?AB³] See *wench* 1874; *home-stretch* 1876. *See him sail along in the joy and pride of his power* 1876 *Speeches* (1910) 61. *You could see dogs sailing over fences and around corners everywheres* 1884 HF xxxii 330 (OED 5b. To move or go in a stately or dignified manner. Occas. of an animal. 1841.. OEDS Earlier U.S. ex. 1836.. Not A in W S C U. A in DN.II. M.T's use of the word connotes rapidity rather than dignity)

sail, v. [?AB²] See *plug* 1866. *As our coach rattled up to each station, six harnessed mules stepped gaily from the stable...In the night we sailed by a most notable curiosity...a natural ice-house* 1872 RI xii 98 (OED 4. Of a vehicle: To move smoothly. 1902.. Cf. above. This sense not differentiated by other dicts.)

sail-boat, sb. [?AB³?C] *The steamboats skimming along under the precipices were diminished by distance to the daintiest little toys, the sailboats and rowboats to shallops proper for fairies* 1880 TA xxviii 288 (OED Sail, sb. 10. *?rare.* 1835, 1888. A in H: "Am. sailboat = Eng. sailing-vessel". Neither A nor *rare* in W S C U)

sail in, v. (?AB²) *Old General Pillow, mounted on a white horse, sailed in, too* 1883 LM xxvi 283. *"Then serve it all up in a slush-bucket, and invite the neighbors and sail in!"* 1893 "Esquimau Maiden's Romance" (1900) 143 (OED Sail, v. 5c. *slang.* To proceed boldly to action. 1889.. OEDS Earlier U.S. ex. 1883, this quot. A in B Th AS.XII.116. Not A in W S C U)

sailor-knot, sb. [?AB²] *Black-silk neck-cloth tied with a sailor-knot* 1872 RI lxii 447 (OED 1882. W S U have only sailor's knot. Not in C)

sailor-people, sb. [B¹] See *soldier-people* 1909 (Comb. not in OED W S C; but cf. OED Sailor-boy, 1855; Sailor-man, in uneducated and jocular use, 1790)

sailor-talk, sb. [B¹] *It is my conviction that Shakespeare's sailor-talk would be Choctaw to the captain of any sailing vessel of our time* 1909 ISD vii 72 (Comb. not in OED W S C; but cf. OED Sailor-phrase, 1812)

sailor-way, sb. [B¹] *He became familiar with seamanship and sailor-ways* 1909 ISD iv 47 (Comb. not in OED W S C)

saint, v. [?C] *It would have been enough merely to have forgiven Swift in this paragraph—not sainted him* 1868-1910 *Margins on "Swift"* (1935) 47 (OED 2. To reckon among the saints. b. *fig. Obs.* 1597..1728. Not *obs* in W S U, and app. not so felt by M.T. This sense not in C)

St. Louis, sb. **St. Looy.** [AE] *He was always talking about "St.Looy", like an old citizen* 1875 OTM 71 (Not in OED C. This pron. mentioned in W S DN.I)

sake, sb. **sakes alive.** [AB³] *"Sakes alive, it's mos' enough to buy a tol'able good second-hand nigger wid"* 1894 PW viii 338 (OED 10. A vulgar exclamation expressing surprise. *dial* and *U.S.* 1846.. So B Th T DN.II,III,IV. Not A in Wr S. Not in W C)

salary, sb. **on salary.** [?AB¹] *They furnish the liquors from their own establishment and hire the bar keepers "on salary"* 1883 LM xxxiii 370 (Phrase not in OED W S C. Cf. share, sb., on shares,below)

saleratus, sb. [AB³] *The Mormons often came there from Great Salt Lake City to haul away saleratus* 1872 RI xii 98 (OEDS *U.S.* An impure bicarbonate of potash. 1837. So B T AS.VII.427. Not A in W S C U)

saloon, sb. [B³] *The boys came down into the main saloon of the Boreas* 1873 GA iv 51 (OED 4a. A large cabin in a passenger-boat for the common use of passengers. 1842.. So W S C U)

saloon, sb. [B³] *Our pack-train arrived...five stately circus-tents were up...And soon the bell rang, and we were invited to "the saloon". I had thought before that we had a tent or so too many, but now here was one, at least, provided for; it was to be used for nothing but an eating saloon* 1869 IA xli 436. *It* [Alexandria, Egypt] *was a sort of reminiscence of Paris. But finally Jack found an ice-cream saloon* 1869 IA lvii 612 (OED 5. An apartment to which the public may resort for a specified purpose, as *billiard, boxing, dancing, shaving saloon,* etc. 1852.. So W S C U. Cf. H: The use of *saloon* in such combs. is peculiar to Eng. In Am. *hall* or *parlour* takes its place)

saloon, sb. [AB³] See *corned* 1872. *A gentleman who had kept the principal "saloon" and sold the best whiskey* 1873 GA xxxiii 300. *The principal saloons were always populous with rivermen* 1883 LM xxii 251 (OED 6. *U.S.* A place where intoxicating liquors are sold and consumed. 1884.. OEDS 1848.. So W S C U F Cl Th T M H)

saloon-keeper, sb. (AB²) *Leave the true source of our political power in the hands of saloon-keepers* 1873 GA lix 530 (OED Saloon, sb. 7. *U.S.* 1879. So W S C Th M H)

salt, v. [?AB³] *One plan of acquiring sudden wealth was to "salt" a wildcat claim* 1872 RI xlv 311 (OED 9. *Mining slang.* To make a mine appear to be a paying one by sprinkling gold dust in it. 1864.. So W S C U. A in Th AS.V.145)

salt-horse, sb. [AB¹] *We stepped into the Revere House, thinking we would chance the salt-horse in that big dining-room* 1877 "Some Rambling Notes" i 445 (Not in OED. F: The nickname given in the United States army to the salted beef supplied in their rations. So B Cl. *Slang* in W S C U)

salting, vbl.sb. [?AB²] *When it was discovered that those lumps were melted half dollars and hardly melted at that, a painful case of "salting" was apparent* 1869 *Letters* (1917) I ix 164 (OED 2. 1887, only ex. So W S. Cf. salt, v., above. A in AS.V.147. Not in C)

saltire, sb. [D] See *coat-of-arms* 1883 (OED *Heraldry.* An ordinary in the form of a St. Andrew's cross, formed by a bend and a bend sinister, crossing each other. *a*1400..1864—. So W S C)

salt-warehouse, sb. [B¹] *The old brick salt-warehouses clustered at the upper end of the city* 1883 LM xli 423 (Comb. not in OED W S C)

salutatory, sb. [AB²] *Your new editor feels called upon to write a "salutatory" at once* 1869 "Salutatory" (1923) 15 (OED 2. *U.S.* a. An address or greeting to the reader of the first number of a newspaper or magazine. 1880.. So W. Not in S C)

salvage, sb. [CE] *They were always prepared, as one of the quaint chronicles of the time phrased it, to "explain hell to the salvages"* 1883 LM ii 31 (OED This form of Savage now *arch.* So C U Wr. Not in W S)

salvation-notion, sb. [B¹] *These salvation-notions that were whirlwinding through my head* 1894 *Letters* (1917) II xxxiv 617 (Nonce comb.)

Salvation Warrior, sb. [B¹] See *Congregationalist* (Nonce comb. for a member of the Salvation Army)

same, adv. [?AB²C] *Strange niggers would...look him all over, same as if he was a wonder* 1884 HF ii 10. *The eclipse...started a revival, same as it always does* 1893 TSA i 23 (OED C. 1a. In the same manner. Now *rare* in lit. use, common *dial,* often with omission of *the.* No ex. with *the* om. Not in W S C)

Sam Hill, sb. [AB¹] *Hateful people...giving me Sam Hill because I shirked* 1894 TSA vii 258 (A in Th,1839: A euphemism for the devil. So W B T DN.II,III,IV. Not in OED S C)

samite, sb. [C] *Arthur was ware of an arm clothed in white samite* 1889 CY iii 47 (OED *Obs* exc. *Hist.* A rich silk fabric. *a*1366..1847. So W S C. Not *obs* in U)

sample-grain, sb. [B¹] *Whole mountain-ranges from single sample-grains of sand* 1894 AmCl xxi 221 (Comb. not in OED W S C; but cf. OED Sample-blade, 1820; Sample-bottle, 1849)

sample-room, sb. [AB³] *You feel as happy, and groggy, and satisfied, with your quart of mixed metaphor aboard, as you would if it had been mixed in a sample-room, and delivered from a jug* 1893 "Cure for the Blues" 88 (OED *U.S. slang,* a place where liquor is sold by the glass. 1874. So W S C B F T M)

sanchrosynchrostereoptically, adv. [B¹] See *electro-incandescently* 1907 (Nonsense coinage)

sand, sb. [AB³] *I warn't feeling very brash, there warn't much sand in my craw* 1884 HF viii 62. *No more pride than a tramp, no more sand than a rabbit* 1890 *Autob* (1924) I 75. (OEDS 7b. Chiefly *U.S. slang.* Pluck, stamina. 1875.. So S C U F Cl Th T H DN.III. W: *slang*)

sandbar, sb. [?AB³] *That fast packet started down the river, but she run clean up on top of a sand bar* 1856 *Adv. of T. J. Snodgrass* (1928) 21. *A very interesting time we had on that barren sandbar for the next four hours* 1858 *Letters* (1917) I ii 37. See *bluff,* sb. 1873; *snag* 1881. *Its whole river-frontage is now occupied by a vast sand-bar* 1883 LM xxxix 408. See also *towhead* 1884 (OEDS A sand bank in a river. 1802.. So W S C. A in AS.II.31)

sand-mound, sb. [B¹] *He climbs the nearest sand-mound and gazes into the distance* 1872 RI v 51 (Comb. not in OED W S C; but cf. OED Sand-heap, 1602)

sand-quarry, sb. [B¹] *"A sheet of iced oil-cloth to step on in the morning when you get out of the sand-quarry"* [i.e., out of a bed filled with sand] 1897 FE xxxi 291 (Nonce comb.)

sand-reef, sb. [?AB¹] *You can tell a sand-reef—that's all easy* 1883 LM xxiv 267 (W: A low ridge of sand built up by waves or currents. Comb. not in OED S C)

sand-wave, sb. [?AB¹] *He started on a run, racing in and out among the sage bushes a matter of three hundred yards, and disappeared over a sand-wave* 1902 "DBDS" (1928) 322 (A desert formation resembling a wave. Given in OED 1819, in dif. sense. Comb. not in W S C)

Sanhedrim, sb. [?AB¹] *"Fetlock Jones, by the great Sanhedrim!" roared the crowd* 1902 "DBDS" (1928) 347 (Not in OED W S C as an oath)

Santa Claus, sb. [AB³] *This was the children's friend, Santa Claus, or St. Nicholas* 1880 TA xxxi 325 (OED Orig. *U.S.* 1828.. So W S U M. Not in C)

saphead, sb. [?A] *"You don't seem to know anything somehow—perfect saphead"* 1884 HF iii 23 (OEDS Earlier U.S. ex. 1796.. A in F Th DN.II,III,IV,V. *Colloq* or *slang* in W S C U Wr)

sapheaded, a. [?A] *"Of all the sap-headed milksops!"* 1902 "DBDS" (1928) 311 (OED Foolish, stupid. 1665.. A in AS.XI.296. Colloq in W S C Wr)

sappy, a. [?A] See *muff* 1877. *He was much better company than the sappy literature he was selling* 1883 LM xxiii 261. *Sappy inanities illustrated in die-away mezzotints* do. xxxviii 400. See also *flat* 1892 (OED 7. Foolish. 1670.. A in F T DN.IV. Not A in W S C U Wr, suppl.)

Saratoga potatoes, sb. [AB¹] See *biscuit* 1880 (Comb. not in OED W S C; but cf. W Saratoga chips: Thin slices of raw potato fried crisp in deep fat)

Saratoga trunk, sb. [AB²] *Blocks of marble as large as a Saratoga trunk* 1869 IA x 424 (OEDS *U.S.* A large kind of trunk much used by ladies. 1869, this quot. So W S C U B F Cl Th T)

sarcasm, sb. [B¹] *These folks in this canton leave a road to make itself, and then fine you three francs if you 'trot' over it—as if a horse could trot over such a sarcasm of a road* 1880 TA xxxvi 404 (This sense not in OED W S C)

sarcasm, v. [B¹] *When it comes to sarcasming, I reckon I know how to keep my end up* 1889 CY xxiv 309 (Not in OED W S C as a verb)

sarcastified, a. [?AB¹] *That's a kind of a sarcastified remark* 1856 *Adv. of T. J. Snodgrass* (1928) 31 (Not in OED W S C)

sarsaparilla, sb. Spelled **sassaparilla**. [AE] *"Next is the sassaparilla region"* 1873 GA xxvii 247 (OED 1. A plant belonging to any of the species of the order *Smilaceae*, indigenous to tropical America from Mexico to Peru. 1577.. So W S C U B M)

sasshay, v. [AB³] *"They keep her sasshaying around from shanty to shanty"* 1865 SS (1926) vii 159 (OED Sashy, Sashay, or Sasshay. *U.S. vulgar.* To move to and fro. 1860.. So W S M DN.II,III,V AS.IX.213. Not in C)

satin-clad, a. [B¹] *Satin-clad officials are flitting and glinting everywhere* 1881 PP xxxii 367 (Comb. not in OED W S C)

Saturdays, adv. [?AB¹] See *rehash* 1880; *board*, sb. 1893 (This use not in OED W S C. See *-s*, suffix, above)

sauce, sb. Spelled **sass**. [?AB³E] See *bounce* 1876. *"I'm a-standing about all I can now, so don't gim'me no sass"* 1884 HF v 33. See also *slang* 1891 (OED 6b. Sauciness, impertinence. *colloq* and *dial.* 1835.. This sp. called 19th c. *vulgar.* So W Wr. A in S C B Cl T M DN.I,III,IV)

sauce, v. Spelled **sass**. [?AB³E] *"I don't want to sass such famous littery people"* 1866 *Speeches* (1910) 4. *You ought never to "sass" old people* 1867 SNO (1875) 96. *What did he want to sass back for?* 1893 TSA ii 26 (OED 4d. To speak impertinently to. 1864.. This sp. called 19th c. *vulgar.* So W U Wr. A in S C B M)

saucer, sb. Spelled **sasser**. [?AE] *"Pass that-air sasser o' m'lasses, won't ye?"* 1884 HF xli 417 (OED calls this sp. *obs* and 16th c. So Wr. Not in W S C)

saucy, a. Spelled **sassy**. [?AE] *She had an easy, independent carriage—when she was among her own caste—and a high and "sassy" way withal* 1893 PW ii 236 (OED 2. Now chiefly *colloq.* 1530.. So S U. A in W M DN.I,IV. Not in C. OED gives sp. *sassy* as *vulgar* in the 18th c.)

sausage-stuffing, sb. [B¹] *You just trade off the earldom...and stick to the sausage-stuffing* 1892 AmCl xiv 152 (Comb. not in OED W S C; but cf. OED Sausage-stuffer, 1875)

sausage-wreath, sb. [B¹] *"I'm making a study of a sausage-wreath to hang on the cannon"* [i.e., as a feature of a painting] 1892 AmCl xvi 168 (Nonce comb.)

sawbones, sb. [B³] *"They say that Ruth Bolton is really going to be a sawbones; attends lectures, cuts up bodies, and all that"* 1873 GA xv 145 (OED Slang. A surgeon. 1837.. So W S C U. Cf. AS.IV.344)

saw-buck, sb. [AB³] *A sort of saw-buck, with a small mattress on it...this furniture covered about half the donkey* 1869 IA vi 58. *He put on the saddle, a thing like a sawbuck* 1872 RI xxxvii 262 (OED Buck, sb. 5d. A rest for pieces of wood while being cross-cut. OEDS *U.S.* 1855.. So W S C B F T DN.I,II,III)

sawdust-mine, sb. [?AB¹] *It was—materially—a sawdust mine when she got it, and she has turned it into a Klondike* 1907 CS II i 102 (App. means a worthless mine; perhaps as if one yielding sawdust instead of gold-dust? Cf. Wr Sawdust, *fig.*: Nonsense. Phrase not in OED W S C)

saw-log, sb. [AB³] *A slab bench is made of the outside cut of a saw-log, with the bark side down* 1877 *Autob* (1924) I 8. *We could see saw-logs go by in the daylight sometimes* 1884 HF ix 76. See also *dog-iron* 1884 (OEDS *U.S.* 1831. So B F Cl DN.I,II,III. Not A in W S C)

saw-saw-quan, sb. [AB¹] *He gave the saw-saw-quan, and struck a tree with his war-club* 1883 LM App.D 614 (M.T.'s note: War-whoop. Not in OED W S C)

sawyer, sb. [A] See *bar*, sb. 1883 (OED 3. *U.S.* Large trunks of trees brought down by the force of the current. 1797.. So W S C Wr B F Cl Th T DN.II, V,VI AS.II.31)

say, s'I, s'e, sh-she (for *said I, said he, said she*). [AB¹E] *"She'll tell you so herself. Sh-she, look at that-air rag-ladder, sh-she; 'n' s'I, yes, look at it, s'I...It's jist as I was a-sayin' to Brer Phelps, his own self. S'e, what do you think of it, Sister Hotchkiss? s'e. Think of what, Brer Phelps? s'I"* 1884 HF xli 417 (These forms are used by M.T. only in chap. xli of HF, in his reproduction of the conversation of a group of Louisiana farmers and farmers' wives. They are evidently intended to represent what he calls in the "Prefatory Note" to HF "the extremest form of the backwoods Southwestern dialect." They are also found in New England: cf. DN.II, Cape Cod; AS.II.235,V.131, by old persons in Maine when telling stories. They are not given in OED W S C; but cf. OED 3b: The 3rd sing. pres. is often substituted *colloq* for the pa.t. *said.* Hence, in vulgar speech or jocular imitations of it, *says I, says you* = 'said I,' 'said you.' In uneducated use often with repetition. 1682..1852. So W)

say, v. [AB³] *"Now, say—my friend—don't you know any better?"* 1869 IA iii 14. See also *bounce* 1876; *first-rate* 1893 (OED 6c. *absol.* The U.S. colloquial *say* seems, when introducing a question, to be a shortening of *I say* (12b). 1857.. So S B T H AS.VII.256. W: illiterate or careless. Not in C)

say-so, sb. [AC] See *back-up*, v. 1883. *I reckon the best way to get a sure thing is to go and examine for yourself, and not take anybody's say-so* 1893 TSA ii 26 (OED Now *dial* and *U.S.* A person's mere word or dictum. 1637.. A in Th T H DN.III,V. Not A in W S C)

scab, sb. [AB³] *"My men wouldn't stay with me if I should employ a 'scab'"* 1892 AmCl xiii 130 (OEDS 4b. orig. *U.S.* A workman who refuses to join an organized movement in behalf of his trade. 1806.. So B F Cl Th T M H AS.IV.344. Not A in W S C U)

scaffolding, sb. [?AC] *We saw a tall wooden scaffolding on the very peak of the summit* 1880 TA xxviii 296 (OED b. A wooden platform or framework. *Obs.* 1537..1789. Not *obs* in W S C U. App. an Am. survival)

scalliwag, sb. [AB³E] *A dinner given by a lot of newspaper Editors and literary scalliwags* 1868 *Letters* (1917) I viii 148 (OED *slang* or *colloq*, orig. *U.S.* 1. 1848.. So S U B F Cl Th T M DN.IV. Not A in W C. W S C give only the forms *scalawag* and *scallawag*)

scalp, sb. [A] *The buck with the biggest string of scalps* 1889 CY xv 177 (OED 3. Prized by American Indians as a battle trophy. 1601.. So W S C U)

scalp, v. [A] *I have camped with Indians...I have roamed with them, scalped them, had them for breakfast* 1869 IA xx 205. *He was tomahawked and scalped* 1870 SNO (1875) 19. *I was as glad as a person is when he is* *calped* 1889 CY xi 128 (OED 1. *trans.* Chiefly said of N.Am. Indians. 1676.. So W S C U F Cl T M DN.VI)

scalp-dance, sb. [AB³] *He reproduced in his theatrical war-dances, scalp-dances, and so on, incidents which he had seen in real life* 1906 "WIM" (1917) v 72 (OEDS Scalp, sb. 6c. Earlier U.S. ex. 1837. So W S. Not in C)

scalp-lock, sb. [AB³] See *after*, a. 1869. "*You were now but an incoherent series of compound fractures extending from your scalp-lock to your heels*" 1889 "Chr. Sc. and the Book" 585 (OED Scalp, sb. 6c. A long lock of hair left on the head, the rest being shaved, by North American Indians as a challenge to their enemies. 1827.. So W S C B Cl)

scalp-plant, sb. [B¹] *There was a ten-foot reed with a flowing suit of what looked like yellow hair hanging from its upper end. I do not know its name, but if there is such a thing as a scalp-plant, this is it* 1897 FE xxxiv 316 (Nonce comb.)

scant, adv. [?AB¹C] See *large* 1880; *mark twain* 1909 (Here *spec Naut.*, qualifying a report of depth in sounding; cf. *large*, above. This sense not in OED W S C; but cf. OED 1b. Qualifying a numeral, which sometimes precedes. Now *arch* (?U.S.). c1400..1867)

scantling, sb. [?A?C] *About two hundred yards off . . . we built a pen of scantlings* 1889 CY xxiii 288 (OED 7s. A small beam or piece of wood. 1663.. So W S C Wr. U: Rarely used in any sense. A in DN.II)

scar, sb. [?AB¹] *So we unhitched a skiff and pulled down the river two mile and a half to the big scar on the hillside, and went ashore* 1884 HF ii 12 (A bare place on the side of a hill; quite different from the sense in OED 2. A lofty, steep face of rock upon a mountainside; a precipice, cliff. 1673.. So W S C U. M.T.'s use is doubtless influenced by a confusion with the other word *scar*, a white mark on the skin)

scare, v. pron. *skyer*. [?AE] "*Oh, it's de dad-blame witches, sah...dey do mos' kill me, dey sk'yers me so*" 1884 HF xxxiv 354 (OED calls the pron. *skear* or *skeer* 19th c. *dial* and *U.S. vulgar*. So C B F Cl Th,1799 DN.I,II,III. Not A in W S. M.T.'s spelling may indicate the same pron., but more probably is meant for the Virginia "breaking," as in *cart* and *garden*)

scare at, v. [?AC] *This creature has scared at everything he has seen today* 1869 IA xlii 440 (OED 2. *Obs*. ..1731. So S. Not *obs* in W C. An Am. survival?)

scare-head, sb. [?AB³] *A glance at the telegraphic page filled me with encouragement. There were no scareheads* 1904 "Italian without a Master" (1906) 173 (OED Scare, sb. 4. 1888.. A in W S. Not in C)

scare up, v. [AB³] "*Scare up all the men you can, and put them to work at once*" 1873 GA xxv 229 (OED Scare, v. *U.S.* To bring to light, to discover. 1853.. So B F Cl T DN.III. Not A in W S C)

scat, int. (?AB³) "*Oh, scat! I can't ever do it, Berry*" 1892 AmCl iv 53 (OED *colloq.* Begone! 1869.. So W S C U. A in F Cl T DN.V)

scat, int. like scat. [?AB¹] *But the scheme fell through like scat* 1889 CY xxxvii 481 (Phrase not in OED W S C. Cf. OEDS phr. *quicker than scat.* 1902.. So W S C U. A in F Cl)

scatter, v. [?AB¹] "*I was just in the act of sliding out when I ran across you. I told you I would scatter out with you*" 1884 HF xix 182. "*Go along with the rest of the dream! Scatter!*" 1889 CY v 57 (Here used of a single individual. This sense not in OED W S C. Cf. M.T.'s similar use of deploy and infest)

scatteration, sb. [?AB¹C] *I saw a raft wrecked. It hit the pier in the center and went all to smash and scatteration like a box of matches struck by lightning* 1880 TA xix 183 (W: Scattered condition. OED has only: *Rare.* The action of scattering. 1776.. So S C; but not *rare* in W S C. A in DN.I,III,IV)

scattering, ppl.a. [A] *Its sentinel rank of scattering trees standing on either bank* 1872 RI vii 60. *He fought too scattering* 1872 SNO (1875) 265 (OED 1b. Now

chiefly U.S. 1610.. So Th T DN.V AS.VII.30. Not A in W S C)

scepter-wielding, a. [B¹] *Charles the Second's scepter-wielding drabs* 1889 CY viii 95 (Comb. not in OED W S C)

schedule, sb. [AB³] *He had died to schedule* 1904 "Bequest" (1906) iii 15 (OED 4. A time-table. Chiefly U.S. Also *transf.* 1873.. So H. Not A in W S C)

schedule time, sb. [AB³] "*When he frowns, the shadow of it falls as far as Rome, and the chickens go to roost an hour before schedule-time*" 1896 JA II xvi 439 (OEDS orig. U.S. 1881.. Comb. not in W S C)

Schlag, sb. [B¹] See *bag*, v. 1880 (Nonce borrowing, with allusion to the multifarious senses of German *Schlag*, blow, stroke, etc.)

schnawp, sb. [B¹] See *kahkahponeeka* 1880 (Hum. invention)

school board, sb. [B³] *In the first place God made idiots. This was for practice. Then he made School Boards* 1897 FE lxi 597 (OED 1870.. So W S C)

school-bully, sb. [B¹] *I had a quarrel with a big boy who was the school-bully* 1907 "Chaps. from Autob" 7 (Comb. not in OED W S C)

school-knapsack, sb. [B¹] *Half a dozen little boys . . . stood in a row across the pavement, some with their schoolknapsacks on their backs* 1880 TA ii 23 (Comb. not in OED W S C)

school-slate, sb. [B¹] *Looking glass on wall, schoolslate size* 1883 LM xxxviii 405 (Comb. not in OED S C. Given in W)

schottische, sb. (?AB³) *She was horrified at the Schottische as performed by Miss Castle and myself* 1860 Letters (1917) I ii 47 (OEDS Earlier U.S. exs. 1855. Not A in W S C U)

schottische, v. [?AB²] *I polked and schottisched with a step peculiar to myself and the kangaroo* 1872 RI lvii 419 (OED 1872, this quot. See above. Not A in W. Not in S C)

science, sb. [B¹] See *chance*, sb. 1870 (Nonce use, applied to those who believe old sledge a game of science, not chance. Cf.W: A system based, or purporting to be based, on scientific principles; so S. This sense not in OED C)

Science, sb. [AB²] *Does the Science kill a patient here and there?* 1902 "Chr.Sc" 768. See also *Annex-polisher* 1902; *slang* 1902 (OEDS 5d. Christian Science. 1915. This sense not in W S C)

Science Pope, sb. [AB¹] *Mary Baker G. Eddy is the only Infallible that will ever occupy the Science throne. Many a Science Pope will succeed her, but she has closed their mouths* 1907 CS II vii 197 (Comb. not in OED W S C)

scientifics, sb. [?AB³] "*Here they don't give a shuck for his scientifics*" 1894 PW xi 553 (OED 2. Scientific matters. Nonce use, or *vulgar*. 1842. So W S. Not in C)

scientist, sb. [?AB³] See *manologist* 1875 (OED Man of science. 1840.. So W S C. U: The word is disliked and avoided by many, who prefer *man of science.* A in B F; so AS.II.68: "Not in good standing in England.. Their objection is that the word is hybrid, and that it is used loosely for *Christian Scientist*." For other discussions see refs. in Kennedy, p. 322)

Scientist, sb. [AB¹] *Where can you purchase that frame of mind, in any Church or out of it, except the Scientist's?* 1902 "Chr.Sc." 763. *The Scientist hastened to Concord and told Mrs. Eddy what a disastrous mistake had been made* 1903 "Mrs. Eddy in Error" 509 (A Christian Scientist; so W S. This sense not in OED C)

Scientist-Church, sb. [AB¹] *That is a detail which is a Scientist-Church specialty* 1902 "Chr.Sc." 765 (Comb. not in OED W S C)

scoff, v. [AC] *They jeered him and scoffed him...unmercifully* 1881 PP ii 39 (OED 2. *trans.* ?*Obs* exc. U.S. 1579.. 1892. *Rare* in S C. Not *obs* or A in W.)

scoffing, vbl.sb. [C] *People were full of scoffings when we begged them to believe really we had told only the truth*

1898 MS (1916) v 40 (OED *obs.* A scoff; an expression of mockery. 1530. Not in W S C in this sense)

scollop, v. [?AB¹] "*I reckon it ain't going to suffer none for lack of paint when you start in to scollop the facts*" 1896 TSD vi 356 (To embroider, embellish. This *fig.* sense not in OED W S C)

scoop, sb. [AB³] *They only laughed in their jolly fashion and said...it was a grand "scoop"* 1899 "My Début" (1900) 73. *If I could get a "scoop" on the other newspapers I could get a job* 1901 *Speeches* (1910) 141. *He accomplished what the profession call a "scoop"— that is, he got a valuable item and saw to it that no other paper got it* 1902 "DBDS" (1928) 297 (OED 3b. *U.S.* 1886.. So Cl T DN.I. Not A in W S C U)

scoop, v. [AB²] "*The alligators were not simply dredged; the most of the scoopful were scooped aboard*" 1883 LM xxiv 268 (OED 2c. *U.S.* To take with a dredge. 1891. So S. Not A in W C)

scoop, v. (?AB²) "*He wants to let on that if he had a chance to scoop an earldom he wouldn't do it*" 1892 AmCl xiv 150. *He was only "playing" Fairchild. He meant to scoop some money out of him, and he did. That is not his exact expression. I cannot recall the words, but they were still more conscienceless and atrocious than this* 1893 *Notebook* (1935) xxi 232 (OEDS 5. *slang.* a. To take... to appropriate. 1901.. So W S C)

scoop, v. [AB¹] "*It ain't no use. They've scooped him.*" "*Scooped him?*" "*Yes—death has*" 1872 RI xlvii 333. "*You want to set on your bed nights before you go to sleep, and early in the mornings, and play your jew's-harp; play 'The Last Link is Broken'—that's the thing that'll scoop a rat quicker'n anything else*" 1884 HF xxxviii 372 (This meaning not in OED W S C. DN.II,V: To beat, defeat. So F Th.III,1876)

scoopful, sb. [?AB¹] See *scoop,* v. 1883 (Not in OED S C. Given in W)

scoop in, v. [?AB³] "*Leave eight or nine thous'n' dollars worth o' property layin' around jest sufferin' to be scooped in?*" 1884 HF xxvi 266 (OED Scoop, v. 5. *slang.* a...Chiefly *to scoop in.* 1882.. So W S C)

scoop-shovel, a. [?AB¹] *One was a woman in a slim black dress...and a large scoop-shovel bonnet* 1884 HF xvii 154 (Comb. not in OED W S C. Cf. OEDS Scoop, sb. Scoop-bonnet. 1897. So W Wr. A in Th T)

scoot, v. [AB³] *I fetched the shore a half a mile above the village, and then went scooting along the bluff bank in the easy water* 1884 HF xxiv 237 (OED 3. *slang* or *colloq.* To go suddenly and swiftly, to dart. App. imported into general British usage from the U.S. 1847.. So S C Wr B F Cl Th T M DN.I,III. *Colloq.* in W)

scorch, v. [C] "*An I tell him this, he will scorch thee finely for it*" 1881 PP xviii 225 (OED *Obs.* To flay. c1430.. 1450. So W. Not in S C)

scorch, v. [B¹] *It hadn't ever come home to me before, what this thing was that I was doing. But now it did, and it stayed with me, and scorched me more and more* 1884 HF xvi 135 (To torment with remorse. This sense not in OED W S C)

scorcher, sb. [?AB²] *They read me a scorcher of a lecture* 1869 IA xliii 453. *What a scorcher I got, next mail! Such irony!* 1886-7 *Letters* (1917) II xxvi 474 (OED 3. *slang.* a. 1888.. So W S C. A in DN.IV)

scorpion bile, sb. [?AB¹] See *chain-lightning* 1865 (A brand of esp. potent liquor. Not in OED W S C)

Scotch, sb. [B³] *If I had previously overheated my imagination by drinking too much pestilential literary hot Scotch, I should have suffered disappointment* 1897 FE lix 570. *He had not a single vice, unless you call it a vice in a Scot to love Scotch* 1907 *Speeches* (1910) 394 (OED 3. Often elliptically, for Scotch whiskey. 1823.. So W S C U)

Scott, int. [B¹] "*Scott, what a head!*" 1904 "Bequest" (1906) ii 10 (Not in OED W S C. Cf. Great Scott, OED 1885..)

scour, v. [?AB²] "*Scour and scan me to thy content*" 1881 PP xxv 300 (OED 2b. To run over in the mind, with the eye, etc. 1883.. So W S C)

scourge, sb. [C] *He picked up the scourge from the ground* 1881 PP xxviii 337 (OED 1. A whip, lash. Now only *rhetorical.* a1225..1871. So Wr. Not *arch* in W S C)

scourge, v. [C] "*He always scourgeth me*" 1881 PP xiv 171 (OED 1. *trans.* Now *rhetorical.* 1297..1903. Not *arch* in W S C)

scout, sb. [?AB¹] *We are back at Fort Paxton once more, after a forty-day scout, away up as far as the Big Horn* 1906 "Horse's Tale" 328 (S: a scouting expedition. This sense not in OED W C)

scow, sb. [A] *A dozen rude scows were scattered about, lying aground wherever they happened to have been when the waters drained off* 1883 LM xxx 335. See *ark* 1895 (OED *U.S.* 1. A large flat bottomed lighter or punt. 1780.. So S B F Cl Th M DN.I,V. Not A in W C U)

scrabble, v. [?AB³?C] *We found a couple of shingle-nails that Tom said would be handy for a prisoner to scrabble his name and sorrows on the dungeon walls with* 1884 HF xxxvii 375 (OED 1b. *trans.* To write or depict something in a scrawling manner. 1856.. So W S C Wr. U: *arch* or Biblical, after 1 Sam. xxi. 13. A in DN.V)

scrabble, v. [?AC] *We scrabbled along forwards on the skylight* 1884 HF xiii 109. *She would have gone in the early scrabbling days for much less than an earl* 1907 CS II vii 202 (OED 3. *intr.* To scramble along on hands and feet; to stumble or struggle along, *lit.* and *fig.* Now somewhat *rare.* 1638..1900. So S C U Wr. Not *rare* in W. A in Th DN.I,II. Cf. Hardscrabble, widely used in Missouri as a mocking place-name)

scrap-book, sb. [B³] *Make a scrap-book with leaves veneered* 1872 *Letters* (1917) I xi 196. *When the average man...wants to put something in his scrap-book, he can't find his scrap-book, he can't find his paste* c1880 *M.T. the Letter Writer* (1932) iii 52 (Used with ref. to the "Mark Twain Scrap-Book" invented by the author in 1872: "a self-pasting scrap-book with the gum laid on in narrow strips, requiring only to be dampened with a sponge or other moist substance to be ready for the clipping"; see Paine's *Biog.* I. 457. OED 1825.. So W S C U)

scrap-book, v. [B²] *Put the enclosed scraps in the drawer and I will scrap-book them* 1879 *Letters* (1917) I xix 369. *I scrap-booked these reports* 1880 TA xlvi 537 (OED To place in a scrap-book. 1881, quot. from TA. So W. Not in S C)

scrap-booking, vbl.sb. [B¹] *He usually postponed the scrap-booking until Sunday* 1898 *Autob* (1924) I 139 (Not in OED W S C)

scrape, sb. [?A] *That would help us out of our scrape* 1889 CY xxxvii 480 (OED 7. An embarrassing or awkward predicament or situation. 1709.. So W S C U. A in Th M DN.IV)

scrape, v. [?AC] *Mr. Bixby made for the shore and soon was scraping it* 1875 OTM 219 (OED 7c. *trans.* To pass very closely along. *Obs.* 1603. Not in W S C. An Am. survival?)

scrape-up, sb. [B¹] *Once you absorb a Bayreuth-restaurant meal, it is your possession...I think a "Hermitage" scrape-up at eight in the evening...is the quietest thing you can lay on your keelson except gravel* 1891 "At the Shrine of St. Wagner" (1917) 223 (Comb. not in OED W S C)

scratch, sb. [?AB¹] *It is a hard scratch and a long six hundred and fifty miles* 1866 "Forty-Three Days" 109 (Not in OED S C. W: Test, trial, or proof of courage. Wr: A hard struggle)

scratch, sb. [AB¹] *We had played billiards on an ancient table that made the balls perform feats in the way of almost impossible "scratches"* 1869 IA xii 116. *I saw billiard champions of world-wide fame...I saw Texas Tom make a string of seven points on a single inning!—al*

calculated shots, and not a fluke or a scratch among them 1907 "Chaps. from Autob" 333 (W: Lucky stroke or fluke at billiards, *U.S.* So S C B T. This sense not in OED)

scratch, v. [AB²] *"I've got to scratch to starboard in a hurry, or I'll bang this boat against a rock"* 1875 OTM 285 (OEDS 5c. To move, make off. *U.S.* 1876, this quot. Wr: To hurry; to do anything in a hasty, scrambling way. This sense not in W S C)

scrawny, a. [AB³] *He is so scrawny, and ribby, and coarse-haired* 1872 RI v 49 (OED *U.S.* Lean, scraggy. 1833.. So W B F. Not A in S C)

screak, v. [?AC] *Sometimes you could hear a sweep screaking* 1884 HF xix 177. *The screaking of the wood-work* 1896 TSD ii 347 (OED Now chiefly *dial.* 1c. Of things such as an ungreased hinge or axle. 1565..1904. So C. Not *arch* or *dial* in W S. A in Wr)

screaky, a. Spelled **skreeky**. [?AB²CE] See *melodeon* 1884 (OED *rare*. Apt to screak. Earliest ex. U.S. 1892.. Cf. Wr Skrieky: creaky, *Amer*. Not *rare* or A in W. Not in S C. OED gives only the spellings *screaky, screeky, skrieky*. W S have *skreek* as *dial var*. of screak)

screech, v. [B³C] *The noise a nail makes when you screech it across a window-pane* 1880 TA x 91 (OED 3. To cause to utter a shrill, squeaking noise. 1862.. W: *Rare*. Not in S C)

screed, sb. [?A] *He was pretty sure to deliver you the entire screed from memory* 1875 OTM 572 (OED 2. *fig.* 1789.. So W S C U Wr. A in Th T Mait)

screw, sb. **a screw loose**. [?AB³] *In his case there was a screw loose somewhere, and it all happened just the other way* 1870 SNO (1875) 58 (OED 3b. *fig.* Something wrong in the condition of things. 1810.. So W S C U. A in B DN.V AS.II.363;III.140)

screw-shape, sb. [B¹] *The Hero wrenched this column into its present screw-shape with his hands* 1880 TA xviii 162 (Comb. not in OED W S C)

scrimp, v. [?AB³] *"Even if I have to scrimp to do it, I will put up a tombstone over that lone sufferer's grave"* 1871 SNO (1875) 151. *"I'd druther scrimp along on ten thousand dollars a year there, than suffer and worry here on a real decent income"* 1873 GA xxxiii 305 (OED 3. *intr*. To economize. 1848.. So W S C U. A in Wr M DN.III)

scrimping, vbl.sb. [?AB³] *The closest scrimping is necessary to get him through to the end of the twelve months debtless* 1883 LM xlii 435 (OED Scrimp, v. 1855.. Not in W S C. A in M DN.III)

scrimp-nosed, a. [B¹] *Yonder is that scrimp-nosed little doll trying to make herself agreeable* 1867 Notebook (1935) vi 59 (Comb. not in OED W S C. Sharp-nosed, 'nosy,' disagreeable?)

scrip, sb. [C] *I slipped it into my scrip* 1889 CY xxvii 354 (OED *arch*. A small bag, wallet, or satchel, *esp*. one carried by a pilgrim. a1300..1870. So W S. Not *obs* in C U)

scrooch, scrouch, v. [AB²] *I feel myself "scrooching,"* *as the children say* 1869 IA xxiii 229. *We scrouched down and laid still* 1884 HF ii 8 (OEDS *dial* and *U.S.* intr. To crouch, cower. 1884.. So S Wr B Cl Th Mait DN.I,III,IV,V AS.VII.30. Not A in W S. Not in C)

scrouge, v. [?AB³] *Well, pretty soon the whole town was there, squirming and scrouging and pushing and shoving to get at the window* 1884 HF xxi 216 (OED *colloq* or *vulgar*. 1b. To crowd. 1821.. So W S. A in C Wr B Cl Th,1798 DN.I,II,III,V)

scruffy, a. [?AB²] *He'd git the blues, and feel kind o' scruffy, aggravated and disgusted* 1871 *Screamers* ii 16 (OEDS b. 1925.. So W C. Not in S)

scrunch, v. [?AB¹] *Miss Watson would say, "Don't scrunch up like that, Huckleberry—set up straight"* 1884 HF i 4. *"The surgeon began to sew it up; it had to have a lot of stitches, and each one made her scrunch a little"* 1906 "Horse's Tale" 335 (To squeeze oneself into

compact shape; to quiver, wince. *intr*. for *refl*. So W: *colloq* and *dial*. This *intr*. use not in OED S C)

scuffle, sb. [?AC] *The Bacon-Shakespeare scuffle* 1909 ISD i 10 (OED 1b. A heated controversy. Now *rare*. 1641..1770. Not in W S C in this sense)

scurry, v. [?AB³] *Scurrying around the breezy hills and through the beautiful cañons* 1869 IA vi 60 (OED 2. To go rapidly, move hurriedly. 1810.. So W S C U Wr. A in B DN.III)

scutcheon, sb. [D] See *coat-of-arms* 1883 (OED Aphetic var. of Escutcheon. a1366..1820—. So W S C U)

scuttle, sb. [AC] *There was a garret above, pierced with a scuttle over his head* 1876 TS xxi 174 (OED 2. An opening in the roof of a building closed with a shutter or lid. Now only *U.S.* 1707..1902. So W. Not A or *obs* in S C U)

sealing, vbl.sb. [?AB³] *We went sealing together* 1893 "Esquimau Maiden's Romance" (1900) 137 (OED The hunting of the seal. OEDS Earlier U.S. exs. 1835.. Not A in W S C U)

sea-otter, sb. [A] See *silver-gray fox* 1893 (OED A marine otter of the shores of the North Pacific. 1664.. So W S C U)

searching-expedition, sb. [B¹] *Zermatt would send out searching-expeditions and we should be saved* 1880 TA xxxvii 426 (Comb. not in OED W S C)

seat-back, sb. [B¹] *The conductor bent all the seat-backs down* 1872 RI iii 30 (Comb. not in OED C. Given in W S)

sea-wonder, sb. [B¹] *Large schools of Portuguese men-of-war were added to the regular list of sea-wonders* 1869 IA v 48 (Comb. not in OED W S C)

secession, a. [AB³] *Representing Mr. Davis signing a secession act* 1869 IA xix 195. *The secession atmosphere had considerably thickened on the Lower Mississippi* 1885 "Private Hist. of Campaign" 193 (OED 6. *attrib*, quasi-adj. b. Favoring the cause of secession from the U.S. 1838.. Not in W S C as adj.)

secessionist, sb. [AB³] *He ran up the Confederate colors, and from that time till the end was a rampant and inexorable secessionist* 1872 RI lxii 446 (OED *U.S. Hist*. 1860. So W S C B F Cl)

second clerk, sb. [?AB¹] *Bimeby the second clerk came a-staggerin in hollerin "Tickets"* 1865 *Adv. of T. J. Snodgrass* (1928) 26. *Captain, chief mate, second mate, and second and third clerk* 1883 LM xxxviii 397 (Comb. not in OED W S C)

second-counting, ppl.a. [B¹] *Looking at it in a waiting, second-counting, but deeply grateful kind of way* 1892 AmCl xxi 224 (Comb. not in OED W S C)

second floor, sb. [AB¹] *He saw Sid just starting up the outside stairway that led to the back rooms on the second floor* 1876 TS iii 34 (W: In the U.S., the floor or story next above the ground floor. So M. This sense not in OED S C. Cf. OED Second, a. 7. The floor next but one above the ground floor. 1821. But the Am. sense is implied in OED First-floor 2. A ground-floor; now only *U.S.* 1663..1860. So S C U Th M H)

second-hand, a. [?A] *He sold the old carriage and bought a cheap second-hand buggy* 1880 TA xxvi 267 (OED 2. 1673.. So W S C U. A in M)

second-hander, sb. [B¹] *"I see him buy a red flannel shirt and some old ragged clothes...I seen our other pal lay in his stock of old rusty second-handers"* 1896 TSD iii 350 (Comb. not in OED W S C)

second-story, a. [AB¹] *Its broad second-story verandas crowded with gentlemen* 1883 LM xli 424 (Cf. Second floor, above. The Am. sense not in OED S C. Given in W B F)

Secretary of State, sb. [AB²] *He has been ambassador, brilliant orator, competent and admirable Secretary of State* 1906 *Autob* (1924) I 236 (OED In the U.S., the Secretary of State corresponds approximately to the British Foreign Secretary. No ex. So W S C U)

section, sb. [AB³] *The first negro minstrel show that ever came to our section* 1875 OTM 69 (OED 2e (*c*). Chiefly *U.S.* A district or portion of a town or country exhibiting uniform characteristics and considered as divided from the rest on account of such characteristics. 1816.. So B F Cl T M H DN.III,V. Not A in W S C U)

section, sb. [AB³] *The conductor had reserved a section for us* 1893 "Travelling with a Reformer" (1900) 370 (OED 2j. *U.S.* A portion of a sleeping-car containing two berths. 1874.. So H. Not A in W S C U)

sedition, sb. [B¹] *They took me to the guard house and searched me, but they found no sedition on me* 1869 IA xxiv 249 (Hum. nonce use)

see, v. [AB³] *Mr. Bolton knew very well what "seeing" a Pennsylvania legislature meant* 1873 GA xv 141 (OEDS 12b. *U.S. colloq:* To interview or consult in order to influence, esp. improperly. 1871, first ex. of Am. sense. So W C H. Not A in S)

see, v. [AB²] *Backus started off with an eagle now. Wiley hesitated a moment, then "saw it," and went ten dollars better* 1883 LM xxxvi 394 (OED 13. *Gaming.* To meet a bet...Now chiefly in *Poker.* 1599..1885, first quot. for Poker. So W S C F M)

seed, sb. [C] *"Seed of the Church's spoiler, close thy perishing eyes"* 1881 PP xxi 260 (OED 4. Offspring, progeny. Now *rare* exc. in Biblical phraseology. c825.. 1864. So C. Not *rare* in W S U)

seed-leaf, sb. [AB³] *I bought what was called a seed-leaf cigar with a Connecticut wrapper* 1910 *Speeches* 267 (OEDS A kind of tobacco grown in the northern U.S., used chiefly for wrapping cigars. 1888. So W S. Not in C)

seedy, a. [?AB³] *I was dazed, dreamy, wretched, seedy, unrefreshed* 1880 TA xliii 508 (OED 2b. Unwell, poorly, 'not up to the mark.' 1858.. So W S C. A in DN.II,IV,V)

seepage, sb. [AB³] *The flood, or possibly the seepage, had lately been ravaging it* 1883 LM xxx 336 (OED *U.S.* Percolation of water, leakage. 1825.. So W. Not A in S C. Cf. Seep, v. A in F Cl T DN.I,III,IV)

see through, v. [?AB¹] *Thirty camel-loads of treasures was enough to see a dervish through, because they live very simple* 1894 TSA x 393 (To suffice for one's material needs, supply adequately. This sense not in OED W S C; cf. OED 28. To take care that a person comes successfully through his difficulties. 1872. So W C. Here *transf.* from personal support to material sufficiency)

seldom, a. [?AC] *The seldomest spectacle on the Mississippi to-day is a wood-pile* 1883 LM xxii 257 (OED b. Rare, infrequent. *Obs.* 1483..1797. So W S C. A in Cl)

self-acquittal, sb. [B¹] *You can't get the best of all verdicts: self-acquittal* 1892 AmCl xiv 147 (Comb. not in OED W S C; but cf. OED Self-approval, 1812)

self-binder, sb. [AB³] *No harvesters below—there's a patent self-binder now* 1883 LM lviii 571 (OED orig. *U.S.* A reaping-machine which has an apparatus for binding the corn into sheaves automatically. 1882.. Not A in W S C U)

self-communion, sb. [B¹] *Days given to solitude, rest, self-communion* 1873 GA lx 543 (Not in OED C. Given in W S U)

self-conferred, ppl.a. [B¹] *Those foreign barbers who flit over here now and then with a self-conferred title of nobility* 1873 GA xxxiv 316 (Comb. not in OED W S C)

self-deification, sb. [B¹] *She is a faithful and untiring worshipper of herlef, and has carried self-deification to a length which has not before been ventured in ages* 1903 "Mrs. Eddy in Error" 510. See also *harmonious* 1903 (Comb. not in OED W S C)

self-made man, sb. [AB³] *The selection of the beds is given to some hearty, strong-backed, self-made man*

1897 FE lxiv 630 (OEDS orig. *U.S.* 1832.. Not A in W S C U)

self-pasting, ppl.a. [B¹] *A self-pasting scrap-book* 1872 *Letters* (1917) I xi 196. *This can all be saved... simply by substituting my self-pasting scrap book for the old-fashioned one* 1886 M.T. *the Letter Writer* (1932) iii 52 (Comb. not in OED W S C. M.T. probably invented the word as well as the thing)

self-poise, sb. [AB³] *She would not have entered a drawing-room with more self-poise, nor a church with more haughty humility* 1873 GA liv 488 (OED *U.S.* 1854.. So W. Not in S C)

self-upbraiding, vbl.sb. [B¹] *She confessed it with tears and self-upbraidings* 1902 "Was It Heaven?" (1906) 70 (Comb. not in OED C. Given in W S)

seller, sb. **seller ten.** [?AB²] See *short*, adv. 1864· *Sales of one lot of Circassians, prime to good, 1852-1854, at 240 @ 242½, buyer 30; one forty-niner—damaged— at 23, seller ten, no deposit* 1869 IA xxxiv 368 (OEDS 1c. *Stock Exchange.* Seller four, ten, twenty...a form of contract in which the seller has the right to effect delivery within the specified number of days. No ex. So W S C. Cf buyer, above)

semi-civilization, sb. [?AB¹] *These modify their savagery to a semi-civilization* 1897 FE xxxv 319 (Comb. not in OED C; given in W S. Under *semi*- H makes the questionable statement: "This prefix is in much more frequent use in Am. than in Eng. In Am. one never comes across the word *half-yearly*, for *semi-annual* invariably takes its place"!)

Senate, sb. [A] *"There are other men in the Senate and the House"* 1872 GA xlii 379 (OED 1f. The official name for the upper branch of the legislature in the U.S. 1780.. So W S C B F M)

Senator, sb. [A] *I do write too good a hand for a Senator* 1867 M.T. *the Letter Writer* (1932) i 16. See *Congressional, deadhead, lobby, spitball,* all 1873 GA. *General Hawkins, our new Senator—Senator from the latest and grandest addition to the radiant galaxy of sovereign states* 1892 AmCl xviii 189 (OED 1f. In the U.S., Senator prefixed to the surname denotes a member of the federal Senate, not of the Senate of a particular state. 1788.. So W S C F M)

send-off, sb. [AB²] *"We want to give him a good send-off"* [i.e., funeral] 1872 RI xlvii 332. See also *obituarial* 1904 (OED 1. orig. *U.S.* 1872, this quot... So F Th. Not A in W S C U)

send up, v. [?AB²] *The war news sent up the price* 1883 LM xli 424 (OED *transf.* of prices. 1895. Not in W S C in this sense)

sensation-preacher, sb. [B¹] *A crazy sensation-preacher preparing his next season's heroic attacks on the dance, the theater* 1882 SWE i 28 (Comb. not in OED W S C)

sensation-story, sb. [B¹] See *dime-novel* 1881 (Comb. not in OED W S C; but cf. OED Sensation-drama, 1861)

sense, v. [AB³] *One may sense the interval...in this way: after De Soto glimpsed the river, a fraction short of a quarter of a century elapsed, and then Shakespeare was born* 1883 LM i 29 (OED 4. To understand, grasp, 'take in.' Chiefly *U.S.* and *dial.* 1860.. So W S C U Wr B F Cl Th,1849 T DN.I,II)

sentimentals, sb. [?AB¹] *"When his sentimentals are up, he's a numskull"* 1892 AmCl ix 88 (Emotions, feelings, sentimental faculties. This sense not in OED W S C; but cf. OED Sentimental, a. 1b. *absol.* nonce use as sb., sentimental persons. 1749)

sentimenter, v. [?AB¹] *It warn't no time to be sentimentering* 1884 HF xiii 109 (W: To sentimentalize. Humorous. Not in OED S C)

sepulture, sb. [C] *We had lived to see his dust in honored sepulture* 1869 IA xxiv 245 (OED 2. Now only arch. a1375..1868. Not *arch* in W S C U)

sequoia gigantea, sb. [AB¹] *Before exhibiting the matured sequoia gigantea, I believe it will be best to exhibit the sprout from which it sprang* 1907 CS II i 103 (W: *Sequoia gigantea*, the "big tree," or giant sequoia, of California. C: *Sequoia gigantea*, by some formerly separated as a genus, *Washingtonia* (Winslow, 1854) and the *Wellingtonia* of English gardens. This name not in OED S. Cf. S: *S. washingtonia*; OED: A genus of large Am. coniferous trees belonging to the *Abietinae*...popularly often called *Wellingtonia*, the name given by Lindley, 1853. Here used *fig*)

serape, sb. [AB³] *The Spaniard was wrapped in a serape* 1876 TS xxvi 202 (OEDS A shawl or plaid worn by Spanish Americans. 1834.. So W S C U B F Cl Th T M DN.I)

serfdom, sb. [B¹] *Some millions of the common serfdom of the party* 1884 *Speeches* (1923) 127 (The body of serfs or slaves collectively; serfage. This sense not in OED W S C. Cf. OED Serfdom: the state or condition of a serf, bondage. 1850..)

sergeant-at-arms, sb. [AB²] See *Happy-Land-of-Canaan* 1873; *order-maker* 1898 (OED Sergeant, sb. 5. An officer in the U.S. Senate and House of Representatives, and other legislative assemblies. No Am. ex. So C. Not A in W S)

servant-tipping, sb. [B¹] *Take the case of servant-tipping in Europe* 1906 "WIM" (1917) iii 35 (Comb. not in OED W S C)

service, sb. [B¹] *He was engaged in the process of skinning the client. "Services" is the term used in that craft for operations of that kind* 1901 *Speeches* (1910) 152 (Nonce use. Cf. OED 19c. *collect.pl.* Friendly or professional assistance. 1832.. So W S C)

servilities, sb.pl. [B¹] *The trivialities, the servilities of our poor human race* 1905 *Speeches* (1910) 243 (Not in OED W S C in this concrete sense)

serving-man, sb. [C] *They were all dressed alike, and in the fashion which in that day prevailed among serving-men and 'prentices* 1881 PP iv 50 (OED Now *arch.* 1303..1888. So W U Wr. Not *arch* in S C)

servitor, sb. [C] *A silk-and-velvet servitor...offered it to him on a golden salver* 1881 PP vi 81 (OED 1. Now *arch.* c1330..1877. So W U Wr. Not *arch* in S C)

set, sb. [?AB¹] *Her sister, Miss Watson, a tolerable slim old maid, with goggles on, had just come to live with her, and took a set at me now with a spelling-book* 1884 HF i 3 (W:=*dead set*, a pointed attack; a determined onslaught. So Wr. Not in OED S C in this sense. Cf. *dead set* above)

set, ¹v. [?A] *"His name is Asy Allen and here he sets!"* 1875 SNO 299. See also *at* 1883; *mean*, a. 1884; *bowie* 1896; *rampage* 1906 (OED 5. *intr.* To sit, be seated. Now *dial.* or *vulgar.* c1205.. So W S C Wr. A in M DN.III,IV,V)

set, v. pa.ppl. **sot**. [?ACE] *I have not sot down here to answer your letter* 1879 *Letters* (1917) I xix 357 (OED This form *obs* and *dial.* So W S C Wr. A in Th,1776: Used in the U.S. in a more or less ludicrous way. So B F Cl T M DN.I,II,III,IV,V)

set back, v. [?AB¹] *The nigger was set back considerable, because he reckoned it was all done with witchcraft* 1884 HF viii 66. *"I judge he thought he could have any girl he wanted, just for the asking, and it must have set him back a good deal when he found he couldn't get Benny"* 1896 TSD i 345 (To surprise unpleasantly, astound, take aback. This sense not in OED W S C. But *set-back*, sb. is A in F Cl Th T in the sense: reverse, discomfiture)

set back, v. [?AB¹] *"Set her back on the stabboard!"* 1876 TS ii 29. *I crept over to the starboard side to pull the bell to set her back* 1883 LM xxvi 283. See *back water* 1884. *"I heard de ready-bell jingle...Pretty soon I hear de gong strike. 'Set her back on de outside,' I says to myself"* PW xviii 19 (*Naut.* Apparently means to

put or set a boat into reverse. The *Naut.* use is not given in OED W S C)

setting-room, sb. [AB¹] *As we were passing through the setting-room, the old man...laid it on the mantel shelf.* 1884 HF xxxvii 379. *"You just march into that setting-room"* do. xl 405 (Wr: a sitting-room, Berkshire and *Amer.* A in F. Not in OED W S C)

settle, v. [B³] *This quiet snub dropped on the boaster and "settled" him* 1875 OTM 222 (OED 21c. To silence, nonplus. 1850. So W S C U Wr)

settlement, sb. [AB³] *In the back settlements of the Mississippi Valley* 1899 "Concerning the Jews" (1900) 263 (OED 15. A small village or collection of houses, in the outlying districts of America and the colonies. 1827.. So C DN.II,III,IV,V AS.II.31. Not A in W S U)

set up, v. [?A] *You did write once, though, Annie, and that rather "set me up"* 1857 Letter in *Iowa J. of Hist.* (July, 1929) 429 (OED 154k. To make a person elated, proud, or vain. 1526.. So W S C Wr. A in B F Cl)

set up, v. [AB³] *They play billiards; and the man who can score six on a single break can set up the drinks at the bar's expense* 1902 "DBDS" (1928) 308 (OED 154m. *U.S.* To 'treat' to drinks or cigars. 1884.. So Cl DN.II. Not A in W S. This sense not in C)

seven-shooter, sb. [?AB²] *Armed with a seven-shooter* 1872 RI ii 23 (OED 1890. So W S C. A in B Th.III,1875)

seven-stepped, a. [B¹] *The falls rise in a seven-stepped stairway of foamy and glittering cascades* 1880 TA xxii 220 (Nonce comb.)

seventeen-jointed, a. [B¹] See *railroad-train* 1906 (Nonce comb.)

seventh-rate, a. [B¹] *The seventh-rate people have always figured as the aristocracies* 1889 CY viii 97 (Comb. not in OED W S C)

seventy-four-gun, a. [B¹] *That woman rose up till she appeared to be as tall and grand as a seventy-four-gun ship* 1870 SNO (1875) 122 (Comb. not in OED W S C as adj.; but cf. OED Seventy-four: a ship carrying seventy-four guns. Now *Hist.* 1797. So W S C)

seven-up, sb. [AB³] *Swapping knives and playing "seven up" with the Indians* 1859 Letter in *New Orleans Daily Crescent*. *The game of Seven-up did cease in Ephesus...Trumps, Gift, High and Low, Jack, and The Game* 1869 IA xl 428. See *old sledge* 1870. *The king got out an old ratty deck of cards...and him and the duke played seven-up awhile, five cents a game* 1884 HF xx 193 (OED *U.S.* The game of all-fours when played for seven 'chalks'. 1845.. So B F Cl Th T. Not A in W S C)

several-barreled, a. [B¹] *There was a pause, then a several-barreled sigh of disappointment* 1902 "DBDS" (1928) 322 (Nonce comb.)

sewing machine, sb. [?AB³] *England adopts our sewing-machines, without claiming the invention as usual* 1872 *Speeches* (1910) 413. See also *cotton-gin* 1889; *instalment plan* 1889 (OED 1. 1847.. So W S C U. Cf. C: First culminating practically in the machine invented by Elias Howe, 1846. A in B, p.794)

sewing-society, sb. [?AB³] See *Bible-class* 1870 (OED Only ex. U.S. 1842. Not A in W S C)

sex, sb. **the sex**. [C] *The customers applauded, the sex began to flock in* 1892 AmCl xvii 173 (OED 1e. The female sex. Now *rare*. 1589..1863. Not *rare* in W S C)

shabbinesses, sb.pl. [B¹] *Its prosperities and reverses, its shows and shabbinesses, its deep patriotisms* 1895 "What Bourget Thinks" 51 (Concrete sense not in OED W S C)

shackly, a. [AB³] *The country people were already beginning to come in all kinds of old shackly wagons* 1884 HF xxi 208 (OEDS *U.S.* and *dial.* Shaky, rickety, ramshackle. 1843.. So S C B F T DN.II,III. Not A in W)

shad, sb. **Connecticut shad.** [AB²] See *biscuit* 1880 (OED *U.S.* No ex. So W S C)

shad, sb. [?AC] *"Spiders in a desert, you shad?... You don't ever reflect, Huck Finn, and I reckon you really haven't got anything to reflect with"* 1894 TSA vi 252. *It cost me something to restrain myself and say these smooth things to this immeasurable idiot...It is higher and nobler to be kind to even a shad like him than just* 1900 *Autob* (1924) I 189 (OED 3. As a term of abuse. *Obs. rare.* 1610. Not in W S C in this sense)

shadbelly, sb. [AB¹] *When Halliday found the duplicate ecstasy in the face of "Shadbelly" Billson (village nickname), he was sure some neighbor of Billson's had broken his leg* 1899 *"MCH"* (1900) 29. *"Come to a vote, men!" This from one of the Daly gang, Shadbelly Higgins* 1902 *"DBDS"* (1928) 355 (Cf. OED *U.S.* A Quaker coat, so called from its shape, hence a Quaker. 1842.. OEDS 1829. So W S B F Cl Th T DN.I. Not in C. Here used as a nickname)

shade, v. [B¹] *The naturalist...is able to group these creatures into families...by nice shadings of differences observable in their characters. Then he labels all those shaded bugs and things with nicely descriptive group names...and he intimately knows every bug and shade of a bug there* 1895 "What Bourget Thinks" 49 (This meaning not in OED W S C)

shade-tree, sb. [?AB³] *That superb avenue bordered with patrician mansions and noble shade-trees* 1869 IA xi 100. See *pumpkin* 1870. *Shade-trees hung with Spanish moss* 1883 LM xxxiv 372 (OED Shade, sb. 13. 1806.. So S C. A in B Th H. Not in W)

shady, a. [B³] *My hands are full of business on account of my lecture for the 6th instant, and everything looks shady, at least, if not dark* 1867 *Letters* (1917) I vi 124 (OED 5. *colloq.* a. Of questionable merits or prospects of success. 1848.. So S. This sense not in W C)

shady, a. [?AB³] *The shady devil who lives and lurks and hides and watches inside of human beings* 1892 AmCl xxii 235 (OED 5b. Disreputable. 1862.. So W S C U. ?A in Th III)

shady, a. **to keep shady.** [?AB¹] *"So I kept shady, and watched"* 1896 TSD iii 350 (W: To keep out of sight, quiet, or hidden. *Slang.* So S C. A in B T. This sense not in OED)

shaft, sb. [B¹] *Mr. McLeod must get one of these American pens—the "Stylographic" or the "Mackinnan." The shaft of it holds ink enough to last for three weeks* 1881 *M.T. the Letter Writer* (1932) iii 37 (W: A long, slender part, esp. when cylindrical; handle of certain instruments. This sense not in OED S C)

shag, v. [?AB¹] *A ram will top above a hundred ewes 'twixt sun and sun, and then, if he have no more to shag...* 1880 *Fireside Conversation, 1601* (Not in OED W S C in this sense. Cf. Farmer and Henley, *Slang and its Analogues*: Shag, v. To copulate. A familiar colloquialism in the Ozarks; cf.AS.XI. 317)

shake, sb. **to be no great shakes.** [?AB³] *The Ohio River was friz to the bottom,—which warn't no great shakes in the freezing line* 1857 *Adv. of T. J. Snodgrass* (1928) 38 (OED 7. To be nothing extraordinary. 1819.. So W S C. A in Th T DN.I,III,IV)

shake, sb. **cold shake.** [AB¹] *But none of them herded with Dick Allbright. They all give him the cold shake* 1883 LM iii 54. *If we ever got the least show we would give them the cold shake and clear out and leave them behind* 1884 HF xxxi 315 (DN.III: Dismissal, act of getting rid of; the slip. Cf. *shake* in this sense in W S, but not *cold shake.* Phr. not in OED C)

shake, sb. **shake of a sheep's tail.** [AB¹] *I says to myself, spos'n he can't fix that leg just in three shakes of a sheep's tail, as the saying is? spos'n it takes him three or four days?* 1884 HF xli 414 (DN.I: "I will be there in three shakes of a dead sheep's tail," i.e. directly. Ky. C: *in the shake of a lamb's tail.* A brief moment; an instant. *Slang.* So S AS.II.48. Cf. OED *Shake,* sb. II 2b.

colloq or *slang.* Used as the type of instantaneous action, esp. in the phr. *in a shake.* Phrase not in W)

shake, v. [AB²] *"He never shook his mother...No indeedy...he looked after her and took care of her"* 1872 RI xlvii 336. *His father died, and his mother seized the property and "shook" him, as he phrased it* 1875 OTM 73. *"When I got him home late last night and found the raft gone, we said, 'That little rascal has stole our raft and shook us, and run off down the river'"* 1884 HF xxxi 323. See *rocky* 1893. *Brace wanted to marry Benny, and she shook him* 1896 TSD ii 347 (OED 13c. *U.S.* To get rid of, cast off a person. 1873.. So W S C F Cl Th.III. Cf. also DN.I: To jilt)

shake-down, sb. [AB³] *The pestiferous New England climate furnishes those regions a shake-down just in the way of experiment and to get its hand in for business when the proper time comes, which is* December 1906 *Autob* (1924) I 316 (Perhaps the meaning here is that in OEDS 2b. A forced contribution; an exaction. *U.S.* 1903. So W. This sense not in S C. Or possibly a metaphor from *shake-down* = a makeshift bed, OED 1730.., with the sense of trial, sample)

Shaker, sb. [A] See *Allopath* 1902 (OED 4b. One of an American religious sect. 1784.. So W S C U B F Cl T)

Shakespeare, sb. [B¹] *The telegraph, the telephone... the Pullman car...the Shakespeares of the inventor-tribe, so to speak* 1905 "Concerning Copyright" 3 (Nonce use: A thing of outstanding or surpassing merit or fame)

Shakespeare-adoring, ppl.a. [B¹] *Did he have something to say—this Shakespeare-adoring Mississippi pilot—anent Delia Bacon's book?* 1909 ISD i 300 (Nonce comb.)

Shakespeare-law, sb. [B¹] *The master of that wonderful trade has competent ways of knowing whether Shakespeare-law is good law or not* 1909 ISD vii 69 (Nonce comb.)

Shakespearite, sb. [B¹] *Two of these cults are known as the Shakespearites and the Baconians...The Shakespearite knows that Shakespeare wrote Shakespeare's works* 1909 ISD v 50. See also *cipher* 1909 (Not in OED W S C; but cf. OED Shakespearian, 1837; Shaksperolater, a worshipper of Shakespeare, 1875)

Shakesperiod, sb. [B¹] *One of the most trying defects which I find in these Stratfordolaters, these Shakesperiods ...is their spirit of irreverence* 1909 ISD xii 134 (Hum. nonce word)

shake up, v. [?AB²] *He said people allowed there'd be another trial to get me away from him and give me to the widow for my guardian, and they guessed it would win this time. This shook me up considerable, because I didn't want to go back to the widow's any more* 1884 HF vi 40. *"I do hate to have my nerves shook up so"* 1892 AmCl xix 200. *"I'm so shook up with what we've been through"* 1894 TET i 326 (OED 21g. To upset the nerves of, agitate, 1897, only ex. So W S C. A in B)

shake up, v. [?AB¹] *"Below there, ahoy! Shake her up, shake her up!"* 1907 "Capt. Stormfield" 41 (Here evidently a steamboat term: To redouble one's exertions, make more speed or progress. This sense not in OED W S C)

shake-up, sb. [?AB¹] *My nerves had hardly grown quiet after this affair when they got another shake-up— one which utterly unmanned me for a moment* 1880 TA xxxviii 438 (W: Agitation; disturbance. *Colloq.* So C. This sense not in OED S. Cf. Shake up, v., above)

shaky, a. [?AB³] *His confidence was beginning to get mighty shaky* 1871 SNO (1875) 298 (OED 5b. Unsettled, 1853.. So W S C. A in B T DN.III)

shaky, a. [?AB³] *Worry does the rest, and his mind gets shaky* 1892 AmCl xvi 170 (OED 5c. Not completely sound in health. 1844.. So W S C. A in T)

sham-duel, sb. [B¹] *Witnessing those playful sham-duels [at the German universities]* 1880 TA vii 68

(Comb. not in OED W S C. Perhaps after the German *das Scheingefecht, der Scheinkampf*)

sham-supplication, sb. [B[1]] *Sorrowing recollections and left-handed sham-supplications* 1883 LM liv 532 (Comb. not in OED W S C. Cf. German *die Schein-andacht, die Scheinbusse*)

shanty, sb. [AB[3]] See *sasshay* 1865. *Quite a settlement of board and log shanties had gone up* 1873 GA xlviii 440. *A man and a family of pigs were actually living here in some shanties* 1880 TA xxxiv 369. *A small old wooden shanty which had once been occupied by some humble negro family* 1892 AmCl iv 50 (OED 1. Chiefly *U.S.* and *Canada.* 1820.. So B F Cl Th T M DN.V AS.VII. 166,426. On its origin, probably as a loan-word from Am. French, see *Archiv* CVII (1901) 112-114. Not A in W S C U)

share, sb. **sheer.** [AE] "*Now you just take my sheer of it along with yourn*" 1876 TS xxxv 271 (This pron. called A in DN.I,II,III. Not given in OED W S C)

share, sb. **on shares.** [?A] *He put the farm into the hands of an agricultural expert to be worked on shares* 1883 LM xlix 487. See also *Cotton State* 1899 (OEDS Earlier Amer. ex. 1656.. A in Th DN.III,IV,V. Not A in W. Phrase not in S C)

shark-fisher, sb. [B[1]] *He was passing by a nodding shark-fisher* 1897 FE xiii 142 (Comb. not in OED W S C; but cf. OED Shark-fishing, 1852)

Shark God, sb. [B[1]] *The great Shark God seems to have been the most potent personage in their idolatrous mythology* [i.e., of the Sandwich Islanders] 1866 *Speeches* (1923) 8 (Comb. not in OED W S C)

sharp, sb. [?AB[2]] *No correspondence is good enough for the hypercritical notions of the Californian sharps* 1865 SS (1926) x 185 (OED 1. colloq. An expert, connoisseur. 1865.. So W C. A in S T H)

sharp, adv. [?AB[3]] "*Meet me on the Tarpeian Rock tomorrow evening, dear, at sharp seven*" 1869 IA xxvi 279. *My idea was...to begin at eleven twenty-five sharp* 1889 CY xxiii 289 (OED 1c. Punctually, precisely. 1840.. So W S C U. A in B F T)

sharp, v. [?C] *When a person has a poor ear for music, he will flat and sharp right along without knowing it* 1895 "Cooper's Literary Offences" 11 (OED 5c. Music. Obs. 1662..1746. Not obs in W S C U)

shave, sb. **a close shave.** [?AB[3]] *He had just swindled a coroner by the closest kind of a shave* 1880 TA xxxv 387 (OED 5. A narrow escape. 1856. So W S C U. A in B T)

shaving-cup, sb. [?AB[2]] *I read the names and noted the numbers on the private shaving-cups in the pigeon-holes* 1871 SNO (1875) 258 (OED 1875.. Not A in W S C)

she, pron. [AB[1]] *He was personating a steamboat...* "*Stop her, sir!...Set her back on the stabboard!*" 1876 TS ii 29. "*Say, Billy, got a yaller ticket? What'll you take for her?*" do. iv 45. "*That helps the blood to draw the wart, and pretty soon off she comes*" do. vi 66. "*The bluejay fetched another acorn and dropped it in...then he says, 'Confound it, I don't seem to understand this thing, no way; however, I'll tackle her again'*" 1880 TA iii 39. *The Awful German Language...Every noun has a gender, and there is no sense or system in the distribution...I translate this from a conversation in one of the best German Sunday-School books;* "*Wilhelm, where is the turnip?*" "*She has gone to the kitchen.*" "*Where is the beautiful English maiden?*" "*It has gone to the opera*"..."*Hear the Rain, how he pours...the Lightning has struck the Fishbasket; he sets him on fire; see the Flame, how she licks the doomed Utensil with her red and angry Tongue*" 1880 TA App. D 607 (As a matter of fact, some of M.T.'s satire on the irrational distribution of German genders might be retorted on his own Missouri dialect. See DN.VI.7 and AS. III. 83: "The Use of the Personal Gender for Inanimate Things," by T. H. Svartengren; here quots. from 1884 HF are given in which *she* is used of a loaf of bread

(viii 58), a clock (xvii 153), a fence (xxii 218), a lightning-rod (xxxiv 351), a bed-leg (xxxv 357), a sheet (xxxvii 378), a warming-pan (xxxvii 384), a grindstone (xxxviii 387), and money (xliii 437). Mr. Svartengren demonstrates that the frequent ascription of gender, predominantly feminine, to inanimate things is a distinctively Am. phenomenon, of native Am. growth, which cannot be restricted to any particular categories or classes of objects; in short, that the function of *she* in Am. Eng. is purely emotional. Cf. also DN.IV: In Va., *she* is used of boats, guns, pistols, rivers, and weather. This Am. extension in the use of *she* is not mentioned in OED W S C. Cf. OED 2a. Of a ship, or boat. Also (now chiefly in *colloq* and *dial* use) often said of a carriage, a cannon or gun, a tool or utensil of any kind; occas. of other things. So W)

shebang, sb. [AB[2]] "*You're welcome to ride here as long as you please, but this shebang's chartered*" (of an omnibus) 1872 RI xlvi 327. "*We've got a shebang* (i.e., a pulpit) *fixed up for you to stand behind*" 1872 RI xlvii 334 (OED *U.S.* slang. The former of these quots. is used by OED as its earliest under 1b. Applied to a vehicle, 1872.. The latter is given under OED 1. A hut, shed; one's dwelling, quarters. 1867.. Both quots. seem rather to belong under OED 2. 'More widely, almost any matter of present concern; thing; business; as, tired of the whole shebang.' Def. quoted from S; no ex. With S agree W C DN.III AS.V.75; VII.336. For the sense hut, shed, dwelling, cf. B F Cl Th T M DN.V. Any spec. meaning of vehicle for the word must be considered extremely doubtful)

she-brew, a. [B[1]] "*'Sides, don't it call 'em de he-brew chil'en? If dey was gals, wouldn't dey be de she-brew chil'en?*" 1873 GA iii 39 (Hum. nonce word)

she-college, sb. [B[1]] *Female college sounds well enough; but...it seems to me that she-college would have been still better* 1883 LM xl 418 (Comb. not in OED W S C)

shed, v.trans. [?AB[1]] *The duke shed his coat and said he was all right now* 1884 HF xx 196 (U: To take off, divest oneself of. Not in OED W S C in this sense)

shed, v.intr. [?AB[1]?C] *Behold, his flesh began to shed...Observe him now, how thin and weak!* [German: Da war er schon viel magerer] 1891 *Slovenly Peter* (1935) 11 (Not in OED W S C in this sense; but cf. OED 11. intr. for refl. a. Of the hair: To fall off. Obs)

shed-roof, sb. [?A] See *lawyer-talk* 1909 (OEDS Earlier Amer. ex. 1736.. Not A in W S C)

sheep-drover, sb. [B[1]] *They were expecting some sheep-drovers and their flocks* 1872 RI xxxiii 240 (Comb. not in OED W S C; but cf. OED Drover, sb. 1. One who drives cattle, sheep, etc., esp. to distant markets. c1425..)

sheep-head, sb. [AB[3]E] *We ate sheep-head, fish with mushrooms, shrimps and oysters* 1860 *Letters* (1917) I ii 48. *Sheephead and croakers from New Orleans* 1880 TA xlix 574 (OED 3b. A freshwater fish of the Mississippi and the Great Lakes. 1836.. So W S C B F Cl T. All dicts. give *sheepshead* as alternative form, usually preferred)

sheep-run, sb. [B[3]] *The "sundowner"...always times himself to arrive at a sheep-run just at sundown* 1897 FE viii 101 (OED orig. *Australian.* 1826.. So W S U. Not in C)

sheep-signal, sb. [B[1]] *Others was trying to get them to hold on and wait for the sheep-signal* 1884 HF xl 406 (Nonce comb. Cf. p. 373: "I will *ba* like a sheep")

sheep-witted, a. [B[2]] *The sheep-witted earl who could claim long descent from a king's leman* 1889 CY viii 101 (OED 10b. 1889, this quot., only ex. So W. Comb. not in C)

sheet-bath, sb. [B[1]] *A sheet-bath was recommended. A sheet soaked in ice-water was wound around me* 1867 SNO (1875) lxiii 303 (Comb. not in OED W S C)

sheet-music, sb. [?AB²] *A well-gnawed slab of ginger-bread as big and as thick as a volume of sheet-music* 1880 TA xxiii 229. See also *heeled* 1880 (OEDS |Music published in sheet-form as opposed to book-form. 1881.. Comb. not in W S C)

shekel, sb. [?AB³] *"They've got all their own money back, and all of ourn but a shekel or two besides"* 1884 HF xxx 313 (OED 2. *fig.* Coin, money. *Colloq.* 1823.. So W S C U. A in F DN.II,III AS.IV.257)

shell, v. [?A] See *corn-sheller* 1867 (OED 1. To remove (a seed) from its shell, husk, or pod. 1562..1860, first ex. of *To shell corn.* So W C U Wr T. A in S B Cl DN.III)

shell, sb. **to shut up one's shell.** [?AB¹] *If we got to asking questions, he would get suspicious and shet up his shell* 1896 TSD iii 127 (Phrase not in OED W S C; but cf. OED 9b. To creep into one's shell. 1853.. Cf. also in M.T.: *Tracy had shrunk promptly into his English shell* 1892 AmCl xi 114)

shell road, sb. [AB³] *We drove a few miles across a swamp, along a raised shell road* 1883 LM xliv 444 (OED *U.S.* A road having a bed or layer of shells. 1844.. So B Th M DN.II. Not A in W. Comb. not in S C)

shell-shower, sb. [B¹] *When she was running for the holes one morning, through a shell-shower, a big shell burst near her* 1883 LM xxxv 380 (Comb. not in OED W S C)

shenanigan, sb. [AB²] *Consider them all guilty of "shenanigan" until they are proved innocent* 1862 *Letters* (1917) I iii 77 (OEDS *U.S.* Chaff, nonsense, humbug, esp. to cover up some trickery. 1871.. So B F Cl Th.III T DN.I,III,V AS.II.488. Not A in W S C)

Sheol, sb. [?AB²] *The Round Table would think it was scandalous and maybe raise Sheol about it* 1889 CY xii 143. See also *grayback* 1889 (OED In recent slang sometimes jocularly substituted for 'hell.' No ex. So W S C U)

sheriff, sb. [AB³] *The sheriff proclaimed the opening of court* 1876 TS xxiii 185 (OED d. *U.S.* 1828.. So S C U H AS.IV.9. W does not distinguish the very different functions of the sheriff in Eng. and the U.S.)

sheriff's sale, sb. [?AB¹] *Those are forced terms—sheriff's sale prices* 1869 IA xx 204 (S: Public sale of property seized on a writ of execution by the sheriff. Not in OED W C. Cf. *sheriff*, above)

shifty, a. [?AB²C] *The average* [number of fleas] *was forty-five to a young person...the average for older people was shifty and indeterminable* 1880 TA ix 88 (OED 3. Changeable. *Rare.* 1882.., with punning allusion to OED 4. Changing or shifting in position. *Rare.* 1884.. So C. Not *rare* in S. Sense 3 is marked *rare* in W, but not sense 4. A in Th,1783 T)

shin, v. [AB³] *"Shin around, John, and get the gentleman a chair* 1869 CRG (1919) 136. *"I would have made him shin out of Galilee quicker than any turtle ever did yet"* 1869 IA xlvii 492. *"I shinned down the tree and shot for home"* 1872 RI vii 66. *"Shin for the raft like the dickens was after you"* 1884 HF xxiii 229. *"Hitch your rope ladder to the battlements and shin down it"* 1884 HF xxxv 358 (One of M.T.'s favorite words. OED 2. *U.S.* To use one's legs; to move quickly. 1845.. So W B F Cl Th M DN.V. Not A in S C T)

shindy, sb. [AB³] *They would have the same disposition to get up shindies with other royal cats* 1889 CY xl 514 (OEDS A row, commotion. *U.S.* 3. 1829.. So B F Cl T DN.III,IV AS.II.364. Not A in W S C U)

shines, sb. [AB³] *It would make a cow laugh to see the shines that old idiot cut* 1884 HF xxiii 227 (OED 3. *pl.* Capers, tricks. *U.S.* 1830.. So S C B F Th T DN.III AS.X.42. Not A in W U)

shingle, sb. [?A] *I got in among some bundles of shingles on the weather side of the fire* 1883 LM iii 43 (OED 1. A house-tile. c1200..1886. So W S C U T. A in F Cl Th,1705 M DN.VI)

shingle, v. [?A] See *forward* of 1869 (OED 1. *trans.* To cover, roof with shingles. 1562..1865. So W S C U. A in Th)

shingle-bundle, sb. [?AB¹] *The roaring of the wind through the shingle-bundles* 1880 TA xvii 156 (Comb. not in OED W S C)

shingle-nail, sb. [?AB³] See *scrabble*, v. 1884 (OED 1867. So S C. Not in W)

shining, ppl.a. [?AC] *"Everybody likes him just as well as if he was the shiningest success"* 1892 AmCl iii 36 (OED 3. With ref. to intellectual or moral qualities: Eminent, brilliant. Now *rare.* c900..1881. Not *rare* in W S C. A in F T)

shin-plaster, sb. [AB³] *In the South he got fifty dollars payable in Confederate shin-plasters worth a dollar a bushel* 1889 CY xxxi 395 (OED *U.S.* A piece of paper money...depreciated in value. 1824.. So W S C B F Cl Th T DN.III AS.VIII.4.49)

shin up, v. [?AB³] *Tom got the ladder and shinned up it a piece* 1893 TSA v 127 (OED 1b. *trans.* To climb up. 1891.. So W S C U. A in B F Cl Th,1852 M DN.III)

ship, sb. **to give up the ship.** [?AB³] *"We'll not give up the ship yet"* 1892 AmCl xv 161 (OED 3. In *fig* and allusive phrases, as...to give up the ship. 1816.. The earliest OED quot. for this phr. is from Jefferson, in allusion to Captain James Lawrence's famous dying words, "Don't give up the ship," at the taking of the Chesapeake, June 1, 1813. Phr. not in W S C)

ship, v. [AB³] See *jewel-box* 1883. *"Ship him to St. Louis"* 1883 LM liii 527. *I mean to ship "Pudd'nhead Wilson" to you soon* 1893 *Letters* (1917) II xxxiii 592 (OEDS 7. To transport goods by rail. *U.S.* 1872.. So W Th T H. Not A in S C U)

ship, v. [B³] *"Why d'n't you say you was petrified in your hind legs before you shipped?"* 1883 LM xxv 276 (OED 12b. To engage to serve on a ship. 1829.. So W S C U)

ship-going, ppl.a. [B¹] *How curiously unanecdotal the Colonials and ship-going English are!* 1896 *Notebook* (1935) xxiii 267 (Comb. not in OED W S C. Formed after the model of Sea-going OED 1860.., Shore-going OED 1895, Church-going OED 1712..)

ship-house, sb. [B¹] *Sometimes one of these monster precipices had the slight inclination of the huge ship houses in dockyards* 1880 TA xxvii 274 (Buildings to house ships? Nonce comb.)

ship of war, sb. [?C] *He went back there last week in a couple of ships of war* 1870 SNO (1875) 125 (OED ?Now *rare.* 1479..1876. Not *rare* in W. Comb. not in S C)

shipping, vbl.sb. **to take shipping.** [C] *So anxious were they to "take shipping" and sail upon the waters that had borne the vessels of the Apostles* 1869 IA xlvii 495 (OED 1a. To embark. Now *arch.* 1471..1852. So S C. Phrase not in W)

ship-talk, sb. [B¹] *The changes in ships and ship-talk that have taken place...in the last three hundred years* 1909 ISD vii 72 (Comb. not in OED W S C. Nonce formation for Sea-language, OED 1728)

ship-time, sb. [?AB²] *Young Mr. Blucher was a good deal worried by the constantly changing "ship time"* 1869 IA v 48 (OED 1891. So W S. Not in C)

ship up, v. [?AB¹] *"Ship up to back! Ting-a-ling-ling!"* 1876 TS ii 29. *"Ship up to back! set her back!"* 1875 OTM 287 (To stop both sidewheels and get ready to reverse them, in order to back the steamboat into her slip or place at the wharf. Phr. not in OED W S C)

shirt-bosom, sb. [AB³] *Shirt-bosom open* 1883 LM lvii 558 (OEDS Now *U.S.* 1833.. Comb. not in W S C)

shivaree, sb. [AB³] *"Sich a yell—shucks, a shiveree* [sic] *wasn't nothing longside it"* 1857 *Adv. of T. J. Snodgrass* (1928) 45. *I started such a rattling "shivaree"* *down below as never had astounded an engineer in this world before* 1875 OTM 287. *She turned on all the horrors of the "Battle of Prague," that venerable shivaree, and waded chin-deep in the blood of the slain* 1880 TA xxxii 341 (OEDS *U.S.* 1843.. Corrupt form of Charivari. So W S C F DN.I,II,III AS.I.152;VIII. 2.22f., XI.250)

sho, int. [AB³] *"You licked him! Sho! Really?"* 1871 *Screamers* xxxi 158. *"Why, sho! You don't mean to say you haven't caught her?"* 1894 PW xv 817. *"Do you reckon anybody reads them? Sho! not a single one"* 1901 "Two Little Tales" (1928) 206 (OED *dial* and *U.S.* An exclamation indicating impatient or contemptuous rejection of a statement. Cf. Shoo, Pshaw. 1845.. So C Th,1825 DN.IV,V. Not in W S)

shoal-mark, sb. [?AB²] *Began to work her warily into the next system of shoal-marks* 1875 OTM 451 (OED 1883, this quot. So S C. Comb. not in W)

shoal up, v. [?AB¹] *Gradually the water shoaled up* 1875 OTM 569 (Comb. not in OED W S C)

shoal water, sb. [B¹] *It jolted her up like everything, of course, but I was over the shoal water now, so I went right along...and told her every blame thing* 1884 HF xxviii 283 (*Fig* sense not in OED W S C)

shoe, sb. **to drop into the shoes of.** [?AB¹] *Always freshly posted and therefore ready to drop into the shoes of some reputable pilot* 1875 OTM 221 (This phr. not in OED W S C; but cf. OED 2k. To step into the shoes of. No ex.)

shoe, sb. **until (someone's) shoes are vacant.** [?AB¹] *He preferred to be supported by his uncle until his uncle's shoes should become vacant* 1894 PW v 332 (This phr' not in OED W S C; but cf. OED 2k. To wait for dead men's shoes, 1546)

shooter, sb. [?AB³] *He began to feel for his shooter* 1873 GA xxix 267 (OED *Colloq* or *slang*. A revolver. 1840.. So W S C. A in B T DN.III)

shooting, vbl.sb. [?AB¹] *Similar murders and shootings* 1873 GA xlvi 425 (W: The wounding or killing with a fire arm. This sense not in OED S C)

shop, a. [B¹] *"I only meant conventional piety, you know; er—shop piety"* 1904 "Bequest" (1906) iii 13 (This sense not in OED W S C. Cf. OED Shopkeeper, sb. 1b. A nation of shopkeepers: applied disparagingly to a nation whose chief interest and concern lies in commerce; now often, to England. 1776)

shop-right, sb. [?AB¹] *"I shall hope and expect to sell shop-rights to the minor countries at a reasonable figure"* 1892 AmCl xxv 272 (W: *Law.* A license from a patentee for the use of the patented device or process. Comb. not in OED S C)

shore up, v. [?AC] *This prop shored him up and kept him from floundering back into democracy and re-renouncing aristocracy* 1892 AmCl xxii 234 (OED 1. Now rarely *fig.* 1581..1773. So Wr. *Fig* sense not in W S C)

short, sb. [?AB³] *He was just getting ready to squeeze the shorts to-day* 1889 CY xl 516 (OED 5. *Commercial.* A broker who sells more stock than he has in his hands at the time of sale. 1881. OEDS Earlier U.S. ex. 1857. A in T Th.III. Not A in W S C U)

short, a. [?AB¹] *"Who's 'everybody?' Out with their names, or there'll be an idiot short"* 1884 HF xxxiii 342 (Missing, absent, removed. Not in OED W S C in this sense)

short, adv. **to sell short.** [?AB²] *One of these adventurous "seller thirty's" "selling short," at thirty dollars a foot* 1864 SS (1926) 149. See also *inflated* 1869 (OEDS 11. Earlier U.S. ex. 1872.. A in B T. Not A in W S C U)

short, adv. **to go short on.** [?AB¹] *She often went short on worldly futures* 1904 "Bequest" (1906) iv 21 (C: To go short: On the stock-exchange, to sell largely, expecting to buy later. Phr. not in OED W S. Cf. above)

short-stop, sb. [AB²] *The Expert took up the position of short-stop* c1880 "Taming the Bicycle" (1917) 286

(OED Short, a. 26d. In *Base-ball.* 1874.. So W S C)

Shoshone, sb. [AB³] See *Blackfoot* 1906 (OEDS One of a tribe of N.Am. Indians of Wyoming, Idaho, and n.Nevada. 1830.. So W S. Not in C)

shot-gun, sb. [AB³] *Shooting him with a shot-gun* 1873 GA liv 489. *A small single-barrelled shotgun* 1906 "Hunting the Deceitful Turkey" 57 (OED orig. *U.S.* 1828.. So B Cl Th,1820 M. Not A in W S C U)

shout, v. **Now you're shouting.** [AB³] *The driver was so glad he couldn't hardly hold in, and says, "Now you're shouting"* 1894 TSA x 392 (OEDS 1g. *U.S. slang.* Now you are speaking to the purpose. 1876.. So W S. Not in C)

shouting, ppl.a. [B¹] *Some shouting stupidity or other* 1891 "Luck" 409 (This *fig* use not in OED W S C)

shoutingly, adv. [B¹] *The new lodger, rather shoutingly dressed* 1894 TET ii 335 (Not in OED W S C in this sense: loudly, showily)

shouting Methodist, sb. [?AB³] *"Jinny's a shouting Methodist"* 1892 AmCl iii 40 (OEDS *U.S. ex.* 1876. A in S B F Cl AS.VII.30. Not in W C)

shove, v.trans. [B²] *The king he smiled eager, and shoved out his flapper* 1884 HF xxv 254 (OEDS 4e. To put down, up, etc. *slang.* 1902.. So W. U: *Colloq* and coarse. This sense not in S C)

shove, v.intr. [AB²] *I shoved out for the Massasawit House* 1856 Adv. of T. J. Snodgrass (1928) 31. *Second Mate and four deck hands took the sounding boat and shoved out in the ice to hunt the channel* 1858 *Letters* (1917) I ii 26. *I then took what small change he had and 'shoved'* 1867 SNO (1875) 274. *Every fellow just whipped out a sudden "See you again, gents!" and shoved* 1883 LM xxv 381. *We shoved for the town* 1884 HF xxxiii 345. *We just unfurled our heels and shoved* 1884 HF xl 409. *So then we shoved for home* 1894 TSA xiii 548. *"So he...tuck his lantern and shoved out thoo de storm"* 1895 "How to Tell a Story" (1900) 232 (OED 10d. *U.S.* To set out for home. No ex. W: To push onward, move onward by pushing or thrusting. So S C. Not A in W S C. Neither def. fits exactly M.T.'s use of this favorite word, which is rather merely: To decamp, depart, go away)

shovel, sb. **to put in one's shovel.** [?AB¹] *"Who told the widow she could put in her shovel about a thing that ain't none of her business?"* 1884 HF v 31 (Phrase not in OED W S C. An Am. variation on *To put in one's oar*, OED 1779..?)

shove up, v. [?AB¹] *Brown was at one side of the wheel, steering; I was at the other, standing by to "pull down" or "shove up"* 1883 LM xviii 225 (To push upward on the spokes of the steering-wheel. This *Naut.* sense not in OED W S C)

show, sb. [AB²] *Give him another show* 1864 SS (1926) iv 141. *"We must not give up the mine so long as we have any show"* 1873 GA xlix 450. *"I'm always kept down; I don't get no show"* 1884 HF xvii 150. *I lean a little his way, on account of his not having a fair show* 1899 "Concerning the Jews" (1900) 254 (OED 3c. Now *U.S.* and *Australian*. An opportunity. OEDS 1866.. So S C F Cl Th.III T. Not A in W)

show, v. **to show a pair of heels.** [?AB²] *Showing the rival boat a two-hundred-and-fifty-dollar pair of heels* 1875 OTM 724 (OED 9c. transf. of a ship. 1887. *Naut.* sense not in W S C)

shower, sb. [?AB²] *Hot foot-baths at night and cold showers in the morning* 1873 GA xxxiii 308 (OEDS 2c. 1873, this quot. So W S. Not in C)

show off, v. [?A] *A village fire-company does not often get a chance to show off* 1894 PW xi 557. *Boys are always "showing off"* 1898 "Memorable Assassination" (1917) 171 (OED 33d. 1793.. So W S C U. A in B T)

show-people, sb. [?AB¹] *These were not show-people. Alas, deformity is too common to attract attention* 1869 IA xx 199 (Comb. not in OED W S C. Cf. Side-show, below)

show up, v. [?AB¹] *"Come now, Eddy...show up; you must 'a' kept a part of that bar'l to prove the thing by"* 1883 LM iii 57 (W: To display or present for examination. This sense not in OED S C. A in M)

show-up, sb. [?AB¹] *"You've brought it to a show-up, I think, with your insanities"* 1902 "Was it Heaven?" 13 (Revelation, exposure; the act of being exposed. Only the active sense of the word is given in OED Show, v. 39. Show-up: The act of 'showing up' or exposing to ridicule, censure, or the like. 1830.. So W S C. Cf. above)

shredding, ppl.a. [B²] *Spectral trees, dimly glimpsed through the shredding fog* 1883 LM li 406 (OED Breaking up into shreds. 1904. Not in W S C)

shrimp-colored, a. [B¹] *A boy in shrimp-colored tights* 1889 CY ii 33 (Comb. not in OED W S C)

shrinkage, sb. [B²] *They invariably allowed a half for shrinkage in his statements* 1873 GA xliv 397 (OED 3. Of immaterial things. 1879.. So W S C)

shrunk-up, ppl.a. [?AC] See *wilt*, v. 1889. *All previous days had been but shrunk-up little things by comparison* 1897 FE iv 75 (OED 1b. Now somewhat *rare*. 1609, 1631. Not in W S C)

shuck, v. [AB¹] *He didn't try no more to win the fight, and he got shucked out bad* 1865 "Jumping Frog" (1875) 32 (To defeat, eliminate from a contest. Cf. OED 2. *U.S. transf.* and *fig.* To remove, get rid of. 1848.. So Th M. Not A in W. Not in S C)

shuck-mattress, sb. [AB³] *He tossed all night upon a shuck-mattress that was full of attentive and interesting corn-cobs* 1907 "Chaps. from Autob" 11 (OED Shuck, sb. Chiefly *dial* and *U.S.* 4. 1860. So Th DN.III. Comb. not in W S C)

shucks, sb. [AB³] *"Church ain't shucks to a circus"* 1876 TS vii 75. *Trees won't grow worth shucks in a Cincinnati graveyard* 1883 LM iii 50. See *hern* 1884. *He said he wouldn't give shucks to be a traveler now* 1893 TSA v 126 (OED Chiefly *dial* and *U.S.* 2. As a type of something worthless. b. in negative phrases. 1847.. So W S C B F Cl Th DN.II,III AS.V.129,IX.320)

shucks, int. [AB²] See *shivaree* 1856. *"Shucks!"* says the king, very sarcastic 1884 HF xxx 311. *"Shucks, Colonel, I haven't even a vote"* 1892 AmCl ii 35. See also *lunkhead* 1894 (OED Chiefly *dial* and *U.S.* 3. *pl.* As an interjection of contempt or indifference. 1885.. So W S C Wr B F Th DN.II,III,V)

shuck tick, sb. [AB²] *My bed was a straw tick—better than Jim's, which was a cornshuck tick; there's always cobs around about in a shuck tick* 1884 HF xx 168 (OED Chiefly *dial* and *U.S.* 4. 1885, this quot. Cf. *husk tick*, AS.VII.169, Neb. Comb. not in W S C)

shudder, v.trans. [B³] *They have dry towels in the hotels now, instead of the pulpy-damp rag of former days, which shuddered you up like a cold poultice* 1883 Notebook (1935) xvii 172 (OED 4. To cause to shudder. *nonce use.* c1801-3, Blake's *Auguries of Innocence.* So W. The *trans.* sense not in S C)

shut, v. **shet**. [?AE] *"You wouldn't shet me out!"* 1876 TS xxxv 272 (OED 19th c. *dial.* So W S C Wr. A in DN.I,II,III,IV,V AS.V.205, Ozarks)

shut, v. **to get shut of**. [?A] *I wished I hadn't ever come ashore that night to see such things. I ain't never going to get shut of them* 1884 HF xviii 174 (OED 11. *Obs* exc. in passive (*dial* and *colloq*). To be rid of, free from. 1500.. So W S Wr. A in C B Th Mait DN.II, III,IV,V)

shut down, v.intr. [?AB²] *We got to Heidelberg before the night shut down* 1880 TA xix 182. *"It shut down black and still, and then the wind began to moan around"* 1883 LM iii 52 (OED Shut, v. 13. Of fog, night. 1891.. So W. This sense not in S C)

shut down, v.trans. [AB¹] See *blimblammin'* 1884. *The train conductor arrived, and was going to shut down the game* 1893 "Travelling with a Reformer" (1900) 370. *"I jumped up and shut down the proceedings"* 1896

TSD xi 535 (Cf. OED 13c. To close (a manufactory). So W S C U Wr. Here: To stop, close, make to cease (any activity). This wider sense is given as A in Th, 1856)

shut down, v.intr. [?AB¹] See *human*, sb. 1880 (To shut up, shut one's mouth, stop talking. This sense not in OED W S C)

shut off, v.trans. [?AB¹] *I was ashamed by that time and shut him off* 1892 AmCl iii 39 (W: To stop one's course of conversation. *Colloq.* This sense not in OED S C)

shut off, v.intr. [?AB¹] *"Now who—"* He shut off sudden 1896 TSD x 526 (This intr. sense not in OED W S C)

shut up, v.intr. [?AB³] *Livy says, I have said enough bad things, and better...shut up* 1892 Letters (1917) II xxxii 569. *This was a plain case of "put up or shut up"* 1889 CY xl 512 (OED 19m. *colloq* or *slang.* 1853.. So W S C U. A in B DN.III)

shy, sb. [?AB³] *I was about to try a shy at the weather* 1880 TA xxv 252 (OED *colloq.* 2b. A trial; a 'shot,' a 'go.' 1848.. So W S C U. A in DN.II)

shy, v. [?AB³] *"I'll shy your lean carcass over the cataract"* 1869 SNO (1875) 69. *He shied his helmet into the corner* 1889 CY xl 516 (OED 2. 1828.. So W S C U. A in B DN.III)

shyster, sb. [AB³] *A lawyer of "shyster" calibre* 1872 RI lxvii 487 (OED *U.S. slang.* 1856.. So W S C U B F Cl Th T M DN.III AS.XII.116)

sick, a. [A] *Parson Walker's wife laid very sick once* 1865 "Jumping Frog" (1875) 31. *I have got back sick—went to bed as soon as I arrived* 1866 Letters (1917) I v 106. *The excursionists, if sick, will be surrounded by kind friends* 1869 IA i 22. *We looked away down into the village and could see three or four lights twinkling, where there was sick folks, maybe* 1884 HF ii 11 (OED 1. Suffering from illness of any kind. Now chiefly literary and *U.S.* 888.. So S U B F Cl Th,1778 M H DN.III AS.XI.305. Not A in W C T)

sick, a. [B³] *And how sick I was, to see how she had fooled me* 1880 TA xlvii 549 (OED 4b. *slang.* Disgusted, mortified, chagrined. 1853.. So W S U. This sense not in C)

sick, a. [?AB¹] See *melodeon* 1884. *"We will keep still till their cheap thing is over, then we will give one that will make it sick"* 1899 "MCH" (1900) 30 (Cheap, paltry, contemptible; here used of things instead of persons. This sense not in OED W S C)

sick, v. [?AB³] *You'd see a muddy sow and a litter of pigs come lazying along the street...and she'd stretch out and shut her eyes...and pretty soon you'd hear a loafer sing out, "Hi! so boy! sick him, Tige!" and away the sow would go with a dog or two swinging to each ear* 1884 HF xxi 211 (OED 1. Of a dog: To set upon, attack (an animal). Chiefly in imperative. OEDS Earlier U.S. ex. 1845.. So DN.I,III. Not A in S C. *Dial* in W)

sickheartedness, sb. [B¹] *Ward don't know what sickheartedness is—but he is in a way to find out* 1893 Letters (1917) II xxxiii 594 (Not in OED W S C)

sick-list, sb. [B¹] *Which one numbered the biggest sick-list?* 1883 LM xxviii 309 (Not in OED. Given in W S C)

side, sb. **to be on the good side of**. [?AB¹] *"I reckon he's somebody they think they better be on the good side of"* 1896 TSD i 345 (To be in favor with, in the good graces of, on the right side of. Strangely enough this familiar phrase seems to have gone unnoted in OED W S C. Cf. OED Right, a. 10d. On the right side of: in favor with. 1889, first quot. for this sense)

side, a. [B²] *"I'm down here now with reference to a little operation—a little side thing merely"* 1873 GA xiii 130 (OED 24d. 1873.. So W S C)

side drift, sb. [?AB¹] *He disappeared in the gloom of a "side drift" just as a head appeared in the mouth of the shaft* 1872 RI xl 279 (Not in OED W S C)

side-gaze, sb. [B¹] *He bent an injured and accusing side-gaze upon that unconscious old lady* 1880 TA xxxv 392 (Not in OED W S C)

side-glimpse, sb. [B¹] *One must steal side-glimpses of the artist* 1890 *Letters* (1917) II xxx 529 (Not in OED W S C)

side-mark, sb. [?AB¹] See *head-mark* 1875 (This meaning not in OED W S C)

side remark, sb. [B¹] *He was treated to many side remarks by his fellows* 1894 "Scrap of Curious Hist." (1917) 184 (Comb. not in OED W S C. Cf. OED Side speech, etc. 1809..)

side-show, sb. [?AB²] *And so I close my chapter on the Church of the Holy Sepulcher...With all its claptrap side-shows and unseemly impostures of every kind, it is still grand, reverend, venerable* 1869 IA liii 573 (OED *fig.* 1884.. So W S C U. A in Th.III,1876 DN.V)

side-show, sb. [?AB³] *I begged him to take a very small hall, and reduce the rates to side-show prices* 1906 *Autob* (1924) II 352 (OED *attrib* 1894. So W S C. A in DN.V)

side-table, sb. [?AB²] *A dozen children were propped up at side-tables in the same room* 1876 TS xxxiv 265 (OED 1888. So W S C U)

side-track, v. [?AB³] *The book was finished, she was side-tracked, and there was no possible way of crowding her in anywhere* 1894 TET Intro. 313 (OED Orig. U.S. 1. *trans.* Also *fig.* to push or set aside. 1881.. So S F Cl Th M H. Not A in W C U)

sidewalk, sb. [A] *No sidewalks worth mentioning* 1869 IA xxii 220. *Tom appeared on the sidewalk with a bucket of whitewash* 1876 TS ii 26. *The streets were narrow and roughly paved, and there was not a sidewalk or street-lamp anywhere* 1880 TA xii 112. *Plank sidewalks on stilts four feet high were still standing* 1883 LM xxx 336. See *outer-border* 1897; *flush,* a. 1902 (OED 2. A footway or pavement. Now *U.S.* 1739.. So W S C B F Cl Th T M H. Not A in U)

side-wheel, sb. [AB³] See *Quaker City* 1869. *See a steamboat coughing along up-stream, so far off towards the other side you couldn't tell nothing about her only whether she was a stern-wheel or side-wheel* 1884 HF xix 179 (OEDS Side, sb. 27. Of steamers having paddle-wheels at the sides. *U.S.* 1857.. So H. Not A in W S C)

side-whiskers, sb. [B³] *One of these waitresses, a woman of forty, had side-whiskers reaching half-way down her jaw* 1880 TA xxxii 340 (OEDS Side, sb. 27. 1867.. So W S C)

sight, v. [?A] *He [the surveyor] ran merrily along, sighting from the top of one divide to the top of another* 1873 GA xvii 160. See also *out-engineer* 1873 (OEDS 3. Earlier U.S. ex. 1787.. Not A in W S C U)

sight, adv. [?AB³] *"Them other fellows is a consarned sight meaner'n him"* 1856 *Adv. of T. J. Snodgrass* (1928) 11. *"I'd druther they was devils a dern sight"* 1876 TS ix 84. See *nation,* a. 1877; *dern,* a. 1884. *It seemed a sight longer than that* 1884 HF ii 9. See also *grist* 1896 (OED Sight, sb. 2b. used adverbially. *colloq* or *slang.* 1836.. So W S Wr. A in B Cl DN.III. Not in C)

sight, sb. **not by a long (considerable) sight.** [?AB²] *I asked her if she reckoned Tom Sawyer would go there, and she said not by a considerable sight* 1884 HF i 5. *"It ain't on'y jist Essex blood dat's in you, not by a long sight!"* 1894 PW xiv 779 (OEDS 2b. 1896, U.S. ex. A in DN.I,II AS.II. Not A in W U. Not in S C)

sighting-iron, sb. [?AB¹] *"Get out your sighting-iron and see if you can find old Sellers's town"* 1873 GA xvii 161 (Here used of a surveyor's level and telescope. Comb. not in OED W S C)

sightly, a. [AB¹] *"The University up there, on rising ground; sightly place—see the river for miles"* 1873 GA

xvii 165 (AS.X.236: Having a view; a rare sense, reported from N.Y. This sense not in OED W S C. Cf. OED b. *U.S.* Of places: Open to the view; so W S Cl)

signal-lantern, sb. [?AB¹] *The vessel's signal-lantern rising out of the curve of the sea* 1899 "My Debut" (1900) 83 (Comb. not in OED W S C. Given in W S C)

signation, sb. [B¹] *Attributed to Raphael but the signation is false* 1880 TA xvi 149 (Hum. malapropism, for signature, autograph)

sign-name, sb. [B¹] *The sign-names of castes were still in vogue* 1892 AmCl xi 115 (Comb. not in OED W S C)

silent-assertion, a. [B¹] *Ostensible civilizations working the silent-assertion lie* 1899 "My First Lie" (1900) 161 (Nonce comb.)

silk-and-velvet, a. [B¹] *A silk-and-velvet servitor* 1881 PP vi 81 (Comb. not in OED W S C)

silken-clad, a. [B¹] *Beautiful silken-clad French dolls* 1883 LM xxxix 410 (Comb. not in OED W S C)

silk-spinner, sb. [B¹] *This old dried-up reservoir is occupied by a few ghostly silk-spinners now* 1869 IA xxxiii 365 (Here: spider. W S C: An insect that spins silk. Comb. not in OED)

Silurian, a. [B¹] See *Oolitic* 1875, 1880. *It used to roam the earth in the Old Silurian times* 1899 "How to Make History Dates Stick" (1917) 155. *Galen, Hippocrates, and other debris of the Old Silurian period of medicine* 1890 "A Majestic Literary Fossil" 440 (Here *fig* for any early period; a favorite word with Mark Twain. Cf. OED 2. *Geol* 1835.. So W S C U)

silver-bowed, ppl.a. [B¹] *The Judge laid aside his silver-bowed spectacles* 1894 TET v 393 (Comb. not in OED W S C)

silver-claim, sb. [?AB¹] *His silver-claim was at the other end of the village* 1902 "DBDS" (1928) 308 (Comb. not in OED W S C. Cf. *claim,* sb.)

silver-gray fox, sb. [AB¹] *"All kinds of furs—seal, sea-otter, silver-gray fox"* 1893 "Esquimau Maiden's Romance" (1928) 138 (Cf. OED *silver fox,* a North American variety. This comb. in W C. Not in OED S)

silverite, sb. [AB³] *McKinley was a silverite* 1904 *Letters* (1917) II xliii 762 (OED Chiefly *U.S.* An advocate of a silver monetary standard. 1886.. So S C Th.III. Not A in W)

Silverland, sb. [?AB¹] *"You have been here in Silverland—here in Nevada—two or three years"* 1871 "My First Interview with Artemus Ward" (1872) 97. See also *flush,* a. 1873 (Comb. not in OED W S C)

silver-miner, sb. [B²] *To speak after the fashion of the silver-miners* 1869 IA vi 57 (OED 1875. So W. Not in S C)

silver-mining, vbl.sb. [B²] *The silver-mining fever in Nevada* 1872 RI Pref. (OED 1877. So W. Not in S C)

silver-tipped, ppl.a. [B¹] *Thirty-one silver-tipped points* 1870 SNO (1875) 27 (Comb. not in OED S C. Given in W)

silvery, a. [B¹] *His silvery tongue began to wag, and in a very little while Yates's two hundred and fifty dollars changed hands* 1875 OTM 195 (Here: persuasive, eloquent, cajoling. Not in OED W S C in this sense. Cf. OED *Silver* 13b. and *Silver-tongued*)

simlin, simblin, sb. [AE] *I know how a prize water-melon looks when it is sunning its fat rotundity among pumpkin-vines and "simblins"* 1897 *Autob* (1924) I 111 (OED 1. *U.S.* A species of squash having a scalloped edge. 1794.. So W S C B F Cl T DN.II,III. OED cites the sp. *simblin* as 19th c.)

simon-pure, a. [?AB²] *Soon the bell—a genuine, simon-pure bell—rang* 1869 IA xli 436. *"He is a simon-pure, out-and-out genuine Mexican plug"* 1872 RI xxiv 181. *An actual simon-pure table-cloth* 1889 CY xxxii 412. See *labrick* 1893 (OED b. Real, genuine. 1889.. So W S C. A in DN.III)

simple-natured, a. [B¹] *Good-hearted, simple-natured young Yates* 1875 OTM 195 (Comb. not in OED W S C)

Simplified Speller, sb. [?AB¹] See *hands down* 1899. *I myself am a Simplified Speller* 1899 "A Simplified Alphabet" (1917) 262 (Comb. not in OED W S C)

Simplified Spelling, sb. [?AB¹] *I have had a kindly feeling toward Simplified Spelling from the beginning of the movement three years ago* 1899 "A Simplified Alphabet" (1917) 256. *"In 1883, when the simplified spelling movement first tried to make a noise, I was indifferent to it"* 1906 "Simplified Spelling" 220 (Comb. not in OED S C. Given in W)

simultane, v. [B¹] *They did them all, but only in turn, not simultaneously. In the nature of things they could not be made to simultane* 1897 FE xlvii 668 (Hum. nonce word)

sin, sb. **like sin.** [?AB¹] *I have been working like sin all night to get a lecture written* 1868 *Letters* (1917) I vii 143 (U: *colloq.* Vigorously, vehemently, in earnest. So S. Phrase not in OED W C)

sinful, a. [B³] *They 'skirmish,' as Jack terms it, in his sinful, slangy way* 1869 IA ix 86 (OED 2b. Highly reprehensible. 1863.. OEDS Later U.S. ex. 1869, this quot. So S C. This sense not in W)

sinfully, adv. [?AB²] *So sinfully ugly that she couldn't smile after ten o'clock Saturday night without breaking the Sabbath* 1869 IA xlv 475 (OED 2. 1888.. So S C. This sense not in W)

singed cat, sb. [AB³] *"I reckon you're kind of a singed cat, as the saying is—better'n you look"* 1876 TS i 21. (OED b. In allusive use. *U.S.* 1847. So B DN.III,V AS.II.47,VII.343,X.42. Not A in W S C)

singing-geography, sb. [?AB¹] *"Teach singing-geography school for a change"* 1884 HF xix 183 (Comb. not in OED W S C)

single-barrelled, ppl.a. [B¹] See *double-barrelled* 1880. *The possibility of a single-barrelled speech which would occupy the entire time-limit* 1898 "Stirring Times" (1900) 309 (Here *fig* sense, not in any dict. Cf. the lit. sense in OED Single, a. 19. 1850. So W. Not in S C)

sing out, v. [?AB³] *He sings out: "Why, Huck!"* 1884 HF xxxiv 353 (OED Sing, v. 12d. 1833.. So W S C U Wr. A in B T DN.II AS.VI.57)

sink, sb. [A] *They end in various lakes or sinks* 1872 RI xx 151 (OED 7. A flat, low-lying area where waters collect and form a bog, marsh, or pool. Now *U.S.* 1596.. So B Th T. Not A in W S C)

sinon, sb. [B¹] See *afarabocca* 1894 (Hum. coinage)

Sioux, sb. [AB³] See *Blackfoot* 1906 (OEDS An important group of N.Am. Indians. 1815.. So W S C U)

siphon-squirting, vbl.sb. [B¹] *A tavern scene where siphon-squirting played a prominent and humorous part* 1898 "Stirring Times in Austria" (1900) 319 (Nonce comb.)

Sir, sb. **Yes, Sir. No, Sir.** [?A?C] *They* [Southerners] *have the pleasant custom—long ago fallen into decay in the North—of frequently employing the respectful "Sir." Instead of the curt Yes, and the abrupt No, they say "Yes, suh"; "No, suh"* 1883 LM xliv 449. *Col. Grangerford was a gentleman...When him and the old lady come down in the morning all the family got up out of their chairs and give them good day...Then Tom and Bob* [their sons] *went to the sideboard and mixed a glass of bitters and handed it to him...and then they bowed and said, "Our duty to you, sir, and madam"* 1884 HF xviii 161. *Tom turns to Jim and says; "Did you sing out?" "No, sah," says Jim; "I hain't said nothing, sah"* do. xxxiv 353. *"Marse Washington Hawkins, suh"* 1892 AmCl ii 29 (Th 1861: Now almost an Americanism, although it was once as common in England. In the U.S. it is still rather common among half-educated people...It is also used in an old-fashioned way, in talking to persons of dignified position. So AS.VII.255.

S: Gradually dropping into disuse. U: *Obs* as polite form in addressing a friend or equal. Not *arch* or A in OED W C; cf. OED 7. Used as a respectful term of address to a superior, or, in later use, an equal. 1320 ..1873)

Sir, sb. **Fair Sir.** [C] *"Fair Sir, will ye just?"* 1889 CY Intro. 20 (OED 7. With additions, as fair. *obs.* c1375, only ex. This use not in W S C)

Sire, sb. [C] *"It jumpeth with mine own conviction, Sire"* 1881 PP v 66 (OED 3. Now only *arch.* a1225.. 1845. Not *arch* in this sense in W S C U)

sire, v. [B¹] See *majesty,* v. 1881 (To address as "Sire." Nonce use)

sirocco, sb. [B¹] *The rococo, the sirocco, and the Byzantine schools* 1880 TA xlviii 566 (Hum. nonce usage)

Sirrah, sb. [C] *"Silence, Sirrah!" from the Court* 1889 CY xxxvii 476 (OED Now *arch.* 1. 1598..1855. So W S C U)

Sirrah, sb. [C] *"No more of this, sirrah Tumble-Bug!"* 1875 SNO 132 (OED Now *arch.* 1b. Used attributively with proper names. 1588..1860. So W S C)

Sirree-bob, int. [AB¹] *"No-sirree-bob, they ain't no trouble 'bout that speculation, you bet you"* 1884 HF xxxi 318 (Comb. not in OED W S C. Given as A in B F Cl Th,1857 DN.III,IV. Cf. OED Sirree. *dial* and *U.S.* 1823.. So W F Cl Th M)

sit, sb. [?AB²] *I shall look out for a sit* 1853 *Hannibal Journal,* Sept. 8 (OED *Printers' Slang.* Situation. 1888.. So S. A in B, p.796. Not in W C)

sith, conj. [C] *"Let others do this happy office sith 'tis denied to me"* 1881 PP viii 97 (OED 2. Now *arch* or *poet.* c1380..1872. So W S C U)

sitting-room, sb. [?A] *When he entered the sitting-room he noticed that the old haircloth sofa was absent* 1873 GA viii 84 (OEDS Earlier Amer. ex. 1771.. A in M DN.III. Not A in W S C U)

sitting-room, sb. [B²] *Trying to find sitting-room in the galleries* 1881 PP xxxii 365 (OED 2. Room or space in which to sit. 1882. So W C U. This sense not in S)

six figures, sb. [?AB¹] *Harry...always talked in six figures* 1873 GA xiii 123 (Largely, extravagantly; in hundreds of thousands. Cf. *four prices,* above. Phrase not in OED W S C)

six-fingered, a. [?AB¹] *Six-fingered Jake* 1892 AmCl vii 75 (Comb. not in OED S C. Given in W)

sixpence, sb. [AB³C] *I paid my sixpence, or "fip," as these heathens* [in Philadelphia] *call it* 1853 Letter in *Iowa J. of Hist.*(1929) 411 (OED 2b. Applied to Spanish coins. In later use *U.S.* for the Spanish half-real. OEDS 1818.. So W S C B. *Obs* in C. Cf. under *fip* for Bartlett's full explanation of these terms. The New York name of *sixpence* for the half-real or 6¼ cents was apparently also the one familiar to M.T. in Missouri)

six-shooter, sb. [?AB³] *The Major made Joe cock his navy six-shooter* 1906 Autob (1924) I 353 (OED 1856.. So W C U. A in S B F Th,1854 M DN.III AS.V.59)

sizable, a. [?AB¹] *The stories were pretty sizable* 1883 LM xxxiv 373 (Exaggerated, 'tall'. Not in OED W S C in this sense)

size, sb. **the size of.** [?AB²] *"Bloodshed!" "That's about the size of it",* I *said* 1880 TA viii 71 (OEDS 10f. What a thing amounts to or signifies. *colloq.* 1886.. So W U Wr. Phrase not in S C)

size, v. [AB²] *Somehow, it seemed to "size" the country* 1877 "Some Rambling Notes" iii 724 (OED 7a. Orig. and still chiefly *U.S.* To take the size or measure of. 1884.. So Wr B Cl Th T DN.III. Not A in W. Not in S C)

size up, v. [AB³] *Father stares in consternation, Can't size up the situation* 1891 *Slovenly Peter* (1935) 19. *"For sizing-up a stranger, he's got the most sudden and accurate judgment"* 1897 FE xx 200 (OED 7a. *U.S.* 1884.. So S C Wr F Cl Th T. Not A in W U)

sizzle, v.intr. [?AB³] *I sizzled...being slowly fried to death in my own blushes* 1880 TA xxv 253 (OED 2. *fig.* 1859.. So W S C U Wr. A in B F Cl T DN.III)

skaddle, v. [AB¹] *As soon as the mob would get nearly to them they would break and skaddle back out of reach* 1884 HF xxii 218 (W: short for *skedaddle, U.S.* Not in OED S C. A better derivation is suggested by Wr: *scaddle,* To run off in a fright)

skeet, v. [?AB¹] See *meander* 1871 (C: a *dial* form of *scoot;* eject with force, squirt. So Wr. A in DN.III.37 in sense *squirt;* in DN.IV in sense *skate, slide.* Not in OED W S in either sense)

skeleton, v. [B²] *The true Black Forest novel will be skeletoned somewhat in this way* 1880 TA xxii 210 (OED 2. 1880, this quot.. So S. Not in W C in this sense)

skeletonize, v. [B³] *In skeletonizing a list of the qualities which have carried her to the dizzy summit which she occupies* 1907 CS II xiii 278 (OED 2. 1865.. So S: To draft in outline. This sense not in W C)

skid, sb. [?AB³] *A pile of "skids" on the slope of the stone-paved wharf* 1875 OTM 70 (OED 2c. A plank or roller on which a heavy thing may be pushed along. 1846.. So W S C Mait. A in B T)

skill, v. [C] *"Whatsoever be his breed, it skills not"* 1889 CY xxi 260 (OED *arch* 2b. *impers.* To matter. 1460..1861. So W S C U Wr)

skill, v. [C] *"And wit you also that to know it skills not of itself, but ye must likewise pronounce it?"* 1889 CY xxiii 287 (OED 2c. *impers.* To avail, help. Now *arch* 1528..1880. So W S C U Wr)

skillet, sb. [?A] *I took...the skillet and the coffee-pot* 1884 HF vii 50 (OED 1. A cooking-utensil usually having three or four feet and a long handle; a saucepan, stew-pan. *a*1403.. So W C U Wr. A in DN.I,III. Huck's skillet may have been of the other type, without legs and with a short handle, often so called in the U.S.; cf. S: Any small frying-pan; so DN.II, s.e.Mo.: A shallow iron vessel with iron cover, used for cooking or baking at a fire-place)

skim, sb. [AB²] *It never has even a thin skim of ice upon its surface* 1869 IA xx 206 (OED 1c. *Amer.* A thin layer of ice. 1897. Not in W S C in this sense)

skin, v. **to skin the cat.** [AB³] See *hog-chain* 1873 (OEDS 4d. *U.S.* 1845.. So DN.I,III. Not A in W S C)

skin, v. [?AB³] *"These annual bills!...I was skinned by last year's lot"* 1875 SNO 62. *Then came the procession of robbers to levy their blackmail...after which the skinned freeman had liberty to bestow the remnant in his barn* 1889 CY xiii 156. *He was engaged in the process of skinning the client* 1901 *Speeches* (1910) 152 (OED 7b. *slang.* To strip of money. OEDS Earlier U.S. exs. 1839.. A in C F Cl T M DN.V. Not A in W S U Wr)

skin, v. [AB³] *"I'll skin this Meisterschaft to the last sentence in it...I'll have the whole fifteen by heart"* 1888 "Meisterschaft" 458 (OED 9a. *U.S. slang.* To copy or crib. 1849.. So W B F Th,1837 DN.II. Not A in S C)

skin, v. Past tense **skun.** [AB²E] *"The beaver skun up a tree"* 1871 Screamers xxiv 131 (OED 9b. *U.S. slang.* To abscond, make off. 1876.. So DN.III. This sense not in W S C. This form for the pa.t. not mentioned in OED W S C)

skip, v. [A] *It wasn't dark enough, and he was afeard to skip* 1896 TSD iv 354 (OED 2b. To abscond, make off. Now *U.S. colloq.* 1338.. So F Cl DN.II AS.IV.9. Not A in W S C U)

skip-jack, sb. [AB¹] *In his maw we found a flying-fish and two skip-jacks* 1899 "My Debut" (1900) 84 (A in B F Cl. Not A in W S C: Any of various fishes that jump above, or play at, the surface of the water. Not in OED)

skipper, sb. [AB³] *It is like dislodging skippers from cheese with artillery* 1890 "Majestic Literary Fossil" 444 (OED 2d. *dial* and *U.S.* A cheese-maggot. 1828.. So B F Cl T DN.II,III. Not in W S C Wr)

skip out, v. [AB¹] *Then he skipped out* 1876 TS iii 34. See *elocute* 1884. *"Skip out for the coast some night"* 1902 "DBDS" (1928) 309. (Cf. skip, above. Comb. not in OED S C. Not A in W)

skirmish, v. [?AB²] See *skirmisher* 1864. *When the commissary department fails, they "skirmish," as Jack terms it in his sinful, slangy way* 1869 IA ix 86 (OEDS 1c. To scout around in search of something. 1894. A in F. Not in W S C in this sense)

skirmisher, sb. [?AB³] *His cousin is a skirmisher and is with the parson—he goes through the camp-meetings and skirmishes for converts* 1864 SS (1926) ii 129 (OED 2. So W S C. Cf. above)

skunk, sb. [AB³] *"A mean skunk!"* 1884 HF xii 104. *A prominent citizen (who has two skunk friends on the School Board) had at last succeeded in getting the light moved from the Gillette Street corner* 1888 *Notebook* (1935) xx 203 (OED Of Algonquian origin. 2. *colloq.* A thoroughly mean or contemptible person. 1841.. So W S C B F Cl M DN.I,III,IV,V)

sky-blues, sb. [B¹] *We have all had the "blues"—the mere skyblues—but mine were indigo, now* 1872 RI xl 278 (Hum. coinage)

skylark, v. [?AB³] *The merry proprietors of the room came shouting and skylarking in* 1892 AmCl xi 116 (OED 1. *intr.* To frolic. 1809.. So W S C U. A in B T DN.III)

skylarking, vbl.sb. [?AB³] *The skylarking went on* 1893 "Travelling with a Reformer" (1900) 350 (OED 1809.. So S. A in B T DN.III. Not in W C)

sky-piercing, ppl.a. [B¹] *Those sky-piercing fingers or pinnacles of bare rock* 1880 TA xliii 500. *His vanity stands alone, sky-piercing, as sharp of outline as an Egyptian monolith* 1890 *Autob* (1924) I 72 (Comb. not in OED W S C)

sky-scraper, sb. [?A?C] *"Send two hundred thousand million men aloft to shake out royals and skyscrapers!" "Ay-ay, sir!"* 1907 "Capt. Stormfield" 42 (OED 1. *Naut.* A triangular sky-sail. 1794..1883. So S C U. W: *Rare.* A in F)

sky-scraper, sb. [AB³] *The foreigner is more impressed at first by our sky-scrapers* 1900 *Speeches* (1910) 124. See also *chimneyfied* 1900 (OED 4. A high building of many stories, esp. one of those characteristic of American cities. 1891.. So U F Cl Th.III M. Not A in W S C)

sky-towering, ppl.a. [B¹] *He spoke of me as this sky-towering monster* 1889 CY iv 54 (Comb. not in OED W S C)

skyugle, v. [AB¹] *Tom Maguire, Roused to ire, Lighted on McDougal; Tore his coat, Clutched his throat, And split him in the bugle. For shame! oh, fie! Maguire, why Will you thus skyugle? Why curse and swear, And rip and tear The innocent McDougal?* 1865, "poem" quoted in Paine's *Biog.* I 275 (App. means: To misbehave, 'cut up,' 'carry on.' A in B: A queer word that originated with the Union soldiers during the Civil War. It has any meaning that one chooses to attach to it. So F T. The sense here is clearly not the one given in W: To steal, *Slang;* so S. Not in OED C)

slab, sb. [?AB²] *A well-gnawed slab of gingerbread* 1880 TA xxiii 229 (OEDS 1b. A large piece or mass of cake. No ex. So W U. A in Wr: used esp, of anything edible. This sense not in S C)

slab, sb. [AB¹] *He hired a wooden-headed old slab* 1866 Screamers (1871) xxix 146 (F: A shaky or worthless character. So Cl. This sense not in OED W S C)

slack, sb. [?AB³] *Each dog took a soldier by the slack of his trousers* 1885 "Priv. Hist. of Campaign" 199. *His old man, losing all patience, caught him by the scuff of the neck and the slack of his pants* 1890 *M.T. the Letter Writer* (1932) vi 83 (OED 4b. *colloq.* The seat of a pair of trousers. 1848.. Earliest ex. U.S., from Lowell. Not A in Wr. This sense not in W S C)

slack water, sb. [?AB³] *Twelve or thirteen miles was the best our boat could do, even in tolerably slack water* 1875 OTM 194 (OED 3. A part of a river lying outside of the current. 1867.. So W S C. Earlier U.S. ex., 1837, noted in AS.II.30)

slam, v. [?AB²] *"I can't...slam around money the way he does"* 1884 HF xiii 113 (OED 2c. *fig.* 1899. The *fig* use not in W S C)

slam-bang, v. [?AB³] *Slam-banging with his desk board* 1898 "Stirring Times in Austria" (1900) 305 (OED 1. intr. 1837.. So W S C. Cf. slam-bang, adv., A in DN.III)

slander-mill, sb. [B¹] *"This ramshackle slander-mill has been doing its best to destroy my character for years"* 1895 JA II v 227 (Nonce comb.)

slang, sb. [B³] *He calls it his "claim"...which is Christian Science slang for "ailment"* 1902 "Chr. Sc." 764. *Those verbs which in the slang of the grammar are called Regular* 1904 "Italian with Grammar" 187 (OED 1b. The special vocabulary or phraseology of a particular calling or profession. 1802.. So W S C U)

slang, sb. [B³] *Slang was the language of Nevada* 1872 RI xlvii 330. *I never use slang to an interviewer* 1907 *Speeches* (1910) 388 (OED 1c. Language of a highly colloquial type, considered as below the level of standard educated speech, and consisting either of new words or of current words employed in some special sense. 1818.. So W S C U. Cf. other definitions collected in AS.I.216)

slang, sb. [?AB³] *The Senator frowned and said he did not like to hear that kind of newspaper slang* 1873 GA xxxviii 347. *The mighty Nicholas, Who hates rude ways and slang and sass* 1891 *Slovenly Peter* (1935) 9 (OED 1d. Abuse, impertinence. 1825. So S Wr. A in Th. This sense not in W C)

slangy, a. [B²] *They "skirmish," as Jack terms it in his sinful, slangy way* 1869 IA ix 86 (OED 2b. 1864.. So W S C U)

slap, v. [C] *She would slap down a line* 1884 HF xvii 158 (OED 2. To write or jot *down* quickly or smartly. *Obs* 1672, 1673. Not *obs* in W S C U Wr)

slap, v. [B³] *We kept a galley of deep philosophical stuff standing, and kept on slapping the same old batches of it in* 1886 *Speeches* (1910) 184 (OED 3b. To put or place *on* or *into*, with a slap or clap. 1836.. So W S C)

slapjack, sb. [AB³] *Boiled beans and slapjacks* 1892 AmCl ii 30 (OEDS 1. *U.S.* A griddle-cake. 1809.. So W S C B F T DN.III AS.VII.426,X.288,XI.102)

slash out, v. [?AB¹] See *blow-out*, sb. 1889. (This sense not in OED S C. W: To dash, as water or other liquid; to splash; to slosh)

slat, v. [?AB²] *I couldn't seem to stand that shield slatting and banging about my breast* 1889 CY xii 144. *Slatting the floor with their tails* 1903 "Dog's Tale" 12 (OED 4b. To flap or slap. 1889, these quots., only exs. So W S C U Wr. A in B)

slather, v. [?AB¹] *You have slathered too many frivolous sentimental tales into your paper* 1866 SS (1926) xvii 210. *The partialities of Providence do seem to me to be slathered around (as one may say)* 1875 *Letters* (1917) I xv 247 (W: To use in large quantities. *Colloq.* Wr: *dial.* This trans. use not in OED S C. Cf. *slathers*, sb., below)

slathers, sb. [AB²] *"And they got slathers of money— most a dollar a day"* 1876 TS vii 75 (OEDS *U.S. colloq.* Usually *pl.* A large amount. 1876, this quot. So W B F Cl DN.III,V. Not A in S C)

slaughter-pen, sb. [B¹] *He made this valley, so quiet now, a reeking slaughter-pen* 1869 IA xlvi 484 (Comb. not in OED S C. Given in W)

slave auction, sb. [B¹] *I have no recollection of ever seeing a slave auction in that town* 1898 *Autob* (1924) I 124 (Comb. not in OED W S C)

slave-lethargy, sb. [B¹] *My throne is in real peril and the nation waking up from its immemorial slave-lethargy* 1905 "Czar's Soliloquy" 324 (Comb. not in OED W S C)

slave-lord, sb. [AB¹] See *white, poor* 1889 (Comb. not in OED W S C. A in B F)

slave state, sb. [AB³] *I was born and reared in a slave state* 1901 *Speeches* (1923) 229 (OED Slave, sb. 9. One or other of the southern United States of America. 1812.. So W S C U B F)

slave-tyrant, sb. [B¹] *He fired the train, shouting "Down with all slave-tyrants!"* 1894 "Scrap of Curious Hist." (1917) 191 (Comb not in OED W S C)

slave-wench, sb. [B¹] *The slave-wench Nancy stood petrified and staring* 1894 TET i 321 (Comb. not in OED W S C)

slave-worked, ppl.a. [B¹] *A rich slave-worked grain and pork country* 1893 PW i 234 (Comb. not in OED W S C)

slazy, a. [?AB³E] *A raspy, scratchy, slazy woolen material* 1897 FE xlix 459 (OED Sleazy, a. 19th c. *dial.* 2. Thin or flimsy. 1825, only ex. W S C: Var. of *Sleazy.* Wr: *Sleezy, slazy, dial* and *Amer.* A in Th,1820 T, DN.I,II,III,V AS.V.130)

sledding, vbl.sb. [AB³] *"Luck has come our way at last, after all the hard sledding"* 1904 *Bequest* (1906) 10 (OED *U.S.* b. *fig.* Work or progress in any sphere of action. 1839.. So H DN.II,V AS.V.75. Not A in W S. Not in C)

sleeper, sb. [?AB²] *I must change cars there and take the sleeper train* 1881 *Speeches* (1910) 258. *The Major secured and paid for a state-room in a sleeper* 1893 "Travelling with a Reformer" (1900) 369. See also *fare-ticket* 1902 (OED 5. A railway sleeping-car. 1882.. So W U. A in S C B F Cl Th.III,1879 M H. Although not called U.S. in OED, all the exs. given are Am.)

sleeping-bench, sb. [B¹] *The ice-block sleeping-benches along the wall* 1893 "Esquimau Maiden's Romance" (1900) 138 (Comb. not in OED W S C)

sleeping-car, sb. [AB³] *England imported one of our sleeping-cars the other day* 1872 *Speeches* (1910) 413. *He feels as if he had spent his nights in a sleeping-car* 1880 TA xliii 509. See also *bicycle* 1899; *coach-candle* 1890 (OEDS *U.S.* 1839.. So C B F T. Not A in W S U)

sleeping-mixture, sb. [B¹] *"There ain't even a dog to give a sleeping-mixture to"* 1884 HF xxxv 357 (Comb. not in OED W S C)

sleeping-section, sb. [AB¹] See *ticket-office* 1881 (Comb. not in OED W S C. Cf. *section* in R.R. sense)

sleep up, v. [AB²] *We laid off after breakfast to sleep up, both of us being about wore out* 1884 HF vii 49 (OEDS 1g. To sleep late. *dial* and *U.S.* 1931.. Not in W S C)

sleigh-runner, sb. [AB³] *His boot-toes were turned sharply up, in the fashion of the day, like sleigh-runners* 1876 TS iv 47 (OED Chiefly *U.S.* and *Canada* 1824.. So B T M DN.V. Comb. not in W S C)

sleuth-hound, sb. [AB³] *There was no rest for her with those sleuth-hounds on her track* 1896 JA III x 663 (OED 2. *U.S.* a detective. 1856.. Not A in W U. Not in S C in this sense)

slew, v. [?AB³] *"Six of them haven't got quite backbone enough to slew around and come right out for you on the first ballot"* 1873 GA liii 483 (OED 2. intr. To swing round. Earliest ex. U.S. 1840.. A in Th AS.VI.57. Not A in W S C U Wr.)

slick, a. [AB¹] *The lines and circles in the slick water over yonder are a warning* 1875 OTM 289 (Cf. OED Slick, sb. 3a. *U.S.* A smooth place or streak on the surface of water, usually caused by the presence of some oily or greasy substance. 1849.. So B Cl Th.III. The adjective not in OED in this sense. Given in W C. Not in S)

slick, adv. [AB³] *"We'd 'a' whooped him over the border—and done it just as slick as nothing at all, too"* 1884 HF xl 410 (OED orig.*U.S.* 1. Smartly, cleverly; easily, quickly. 1818.. So Wr B F Th M DN.III. Not A in W S C)

slick up, v. [?A] *"Come down when you are slicked up enough"* 1876 TS xxxiii 263. *The English of the Annex [to Science and Health] has been slicked up by a very industrious and painstaking hand* 1897 "Chr.Sc.and the Book" 592 (OED 1b. To make elegant. 1340.. So W S. A in B F Cl Th M H DN.III. This sense not in C)

slide, v. [AB³] *I got a chance to slide ashore* 1883 LM xix 332. *"I stayed about one night longer than I ought to, and was just in the act of sliding out"* 1884 HF xix 182. See *load up* 1884. *He laid for a chance to slide* 1896 TSD iv 354 (OED 4b. *colloq.* To make off. orig.*U.S.* 1859.. So Wr B F Cl T. Not A in W S C)

slide, v. **to let slide.** [?AB³] *So I went to talking about other kings, and let Solomon slide* 1884 HF xiv 122 (OEDS 5b. Earlier U.S.ex. 1847.. A in B F. Not A in W S C)

slide, v. [AB¹] *When a man was running, and threw himself...to slide to his base, it was like an iron-clad coming into port* 1889 CY xl 518 (S: *Baseball.* To make a slide. This sense not in OED W C; but cf. OED Slide, sb.1d. 1912..)

slightually, adv. [?AB¹] *The Hooverville Patriot and Clarion had this "item": Slightually Overboard* 1873 GA xxix 266 (Hum. nonce word)

slim, a. [?AB³] *There was a slim chance at least that he reached the shore* 1869 IA lx 642. *A slim oatmeal diet* 1876 TS xii 109. See also *goatee* 1876; *flower-harvest* 1902. (OED 1d. 1852.. So W S C U.. A in Th,1809 M. Cf.H: now *obs* in England; in Am. still not unusual)

slim Jim, sb. [?AB¹] *One brave voice flung out...a word for me: "Go it, slim Jim!"* 1889 CY xxxix 499 (W: slim-jim, a very slim person. Not in OED S C)

slim-legged, a. [?AB¹] *A long, slim-legged boy* 1880 TA x 95 (Comb. not in OED W S C)

slim-shanked, a. [?AB¹] See *erect-haired* 1880 (Comb. not in OED S C. Given in W)

slobber, v. [B³] See *flapdoodle* 1884 (OED 3. To utter thickly and indistinctly. 1860.. So W S. This sense not in C)

slobber over, v. [B¹] *They treat you as a tramp until they find out you're a Congressman, and then they slobber all over you* 1892 AmCl xiii 139 (W: To gush, blubber. So U Wr. Not in OED S C)

slogan, sb. [B¹] *One time sent a boy to run about town with a blazing stick which he called a slogan, which was the sign for the gang to get together* 1884 HF iii 19 (Used by error for "fiery cross," ancient Scotch war-signal. In OED W S C only as: A war-cry or battle-cry)

slope, v. [?AB³] *"Tom, we can slope, if we can find a rope"* 1876 TS xxxiv 281 (OED 1. To make off, decamp. 1839.. So W S C U. A in B F T DN.V AS.IV.344, X.20)

sloppy, a. [?AB²] *The sloppy twaddle in the way of answers furnished by Manchester* 1883 LM xlviii 482. *An era of sentimentality and sloppy romantics* 1903 Letters (1917) II xlii 738 (OEDS 6. Weakly sentimental. *colloq* 1896.. So W U. This sense not in S C)

slop-shop, sb. [B³] *He wore slop-shop clothing* 1872 AmCl xi 113 (OED A shop where cheap or inferior clothing is sold. *attrib.* 1853.. So W S C U)

slop-shop, sb. [B¹] *It was nothing but an ordinary suit of fifteen-dollar slop-shops* 1889 CY iv 54 (Ready-made or inferior garments. This sense, obviously *transf.* from the above, is not given in OED W S C)

slop-tub, sb. [B¹] *Then you will proceed toward the window and sit down in that slop-tub* 1867 SNO (1875) 251. *"Then the slop-tubs! We have two in the parlor"* 1893 "Esquimau Maiden's Romance" (1900) 139 (Comb. not in OED W S C; but cf. OED Slop-barrel, Slop-bucket, 1856)

slosh, v. [AB³] *"They started her [the Dictionary] sloshing around the camps before I ever got a chance to read her myself"* 1865 SS (1926) 159. *"Devils don't slosh around much of a Sunday, I reckon"* 1876 TS vi 67. *It's awful undermining to the intellect, German is...Your* brains all run together, and you feel them sloshing around in your head same as so much drawn butter 1880 TA xxvii 281 (OED 2. *U.S.* To move aimlessly. 1854.. So W S C B F Cl Th. A favorite word with Mark Twain)

slouch, sb. [AB³] *"It ain't no slouch of a journal"* 1869 IA iv 42. *I said apocryphal was no slouch of a word* 1870 SNO (1875) 21. See *nifty* 1872. *I think that is no slouch of a compliment* 1874 Letters (1917) I xiii 228. *"Well, you would be a nice old slouch of a hermit"* 1876 TS xiii 119. *He done it pretty well, too, for a slouch* 1884 HF xxiv 242. *"It ain't no slouch of a name to spell right off without studying"* 1884 HF xvii 152 (OED 1b. *U.S.* slang A poor, indifferent, or inefficient thing, place, person, etc. Chiefly in the negative phrase. 1869.. OEDS 1840.. So Wr B F Th,1823 T M DN.I,IV. Not A in W S C)

slouchy, a. [A] See *pantaloons* 1873. *He is still in the slouchy garb of the old generation of mates* 1883 LM xxv 276. *"I am a very indifferent amateur, a slouchy dabster"* 1892 AmCl xvii 172. (OED Slouching, slovenly, untidy. Freq. in recent U.S. usage. 1693.. Not A in W S C)

slough, sb. [AB³] *There was a slough or a creek leading out of it on the other side* 1884 HF vii 52. *On the Rhone... Joseph and I got out and struck through a willow swamp along a dim path, and by and by came out on the steep bank of a slough or inlet or something* 1891 Letters (1917) II xxxi 552 (OED 4. *U.S.* and *Canada.* A marshy or reedy pool, pond, small lake, backwater, or inlet. 1817.. So W S C B C B F Cl Th DN.I,II,III,VI AS.II.30)

slow, a. [B³] *"It's awful slow, going around alone—don't you think so?"* 1880 TA xxvii 276 (OED 8 *colloq.* b. Dull or tedious. 1841.. So W S C U)

slow-dragging, ppl.a. [B¹] *The slow-dragging ages* 1876 TS xxxi 237 (Comb. not in OED W S C)

slow-drifting, ppl.a. [B¹] *It would not have stayed in my memory all these slow-drifting years* 1897 Autob (1924) I 101 (Comb. not in OED W S C)

slow-motioned, ppl.a. [B¹] *They are either excessively slow-motioned or very lazy* 1856 Letters (1917) I ii 33 (Comb. not in OED W S C. Cf. quick-motioned, above)

slowwk, v. [B¹] See *kahkahponeeka* 1880 (Hum. invention)

slue, sb. [A] *This indomitable engineer had carried his moving caravan over slues and branches* 1873 GA xvii 161 (OED 1. *U.S.* and *Canada* 1708.. So W S C T DN.VI. This sp. of *slough* indicates the customary Missouri pron.)

slug, sb. [?AB²] *Pailfuls of shining slugs and nuggets of gold and silver* 1872 RI i 19 (OED 3a. 1891. So W S C)

slug, sb. [AB¹] *The Moors have some small silver coins, and also some silver slugs worth a dollar each* 1869 IA viii 81 (AS.IV.358: current American slang for a dollar. Cf. OED 4c. *U.S.* A heavy gold piece privately coined in California in 1849, subsequently prohibited. 1890. So W S C Cl Th,1853 H)

sluice, sb. [?AB¹] *The lightning let go a perfect sluice of white glare* 1884 HF xxix 306 (W: *fig* A reserve store; a pent-up flood. So Wr. A in AS.VII.426. Not in OED S C in this *fig* sense)

sluice, v. [?A] *I don't believe you could have sluiced it out with a hydraulic* 1889 CY xi 130 (OED 4. To scour with a rush of water. 1755.. So W S C U. A in B F Cl)

sluice-box, sb. [?AB²] *"A clatter of syllables as long as a string of sluice-boxes"* 1865 SS (1926) vii 159 (OED One of the long troughs of which a gold-washing sluice is composed. 1874.. So W S AS.V.145,VII.427. Not in C. Cf. *sluice*)

slum, sb. [AB²] *Chili-beans and dish-water three times today as usual, and some kind of "slum" which the Frenchman called "hash"* 1865 Notebook (1935) i 6 (OEDS abbrev. of *Slumgullion.* 1909.. Cf. OED *Slumgullion* 2c. A kind of hash or stew. *U.S.* 1904. So S AS.I.652; IV.345: Used in Amer. hobo lingo. Not A in W. Not in C)

slumgullion, sb. [?AB²] *He poured for us a beverage which he called "slumgullion"* 1872 RI iv 44 (OED 1. *Slang*. Any cheap, nasty, washy beverage. 1874. So W S C. A in F M)

slump, v. [AB²] *I most slumped through the floor* 1884 HF xxxii 335. *We see him slump down flat an' soft in the bottom and lay still* 1893 TSA ii 28 (OED Chiefly *dial* and *U.S.* 2b. To plump down. 1884.. So B Cl Th,1804. Not A in W S C U Wr)

slung-shot, sb. [AB³] *It charged Laura with killing him with a slung-shot* 1873 GA liv 489 (OED *U.S.* 1848.. So B Cl Th,1842 T DN.III. Not A in W S C U)

slurring, ppl.a. [B²] *I never allow myself to do things in a slurring, slipshod way* 1880 TA xxx 311 (OED 2. 1880, this quot., only ex. Not in W S C)

slush, sb. [?AB²] *"He'll grind out about four reams of the awfullest slush"* 1869 IA x 91 (OED 4. Rubbishy discourse or literature. 1896. So W S U. This sense not in C)

slush–boy, sb. [B¹] *"Did you ever ask the slush-boy to come up in the cabin and take dinner with you?"* 1908 "Capt. Stormfield" 270 (Comb. not in OED W S C. Cf. OED Slush 2. *Naut*. The refuse fat or grease obtained from meat boiled on board ship. 1756..)

slush-bucket, sb. [B³] See *sail in* 1893 (OED Slush sb. 6. 1867. So C. Not in W S)

slush-plastered, ppl.a. [B¹] *The mock consul, a slush-plastered deck-sweep* 1869 IA xxxviii 404 (Nonce comb.)

small baggage, sb. [?AB¹] See *swag* 1897 (Baggage carried in the hand or on the arm. Comb. not in OED W S C; but cf. W small arms: arms carried on the person. So small wares, etc.)

small-fry, a. [?AB²] *"Dey wa'n't no small-fry officers, mine you; dey was de biggest dey is"* 1875 SNO 204. See also *rise*, sb. 1875 (OED Small, a. 22a. 1897.. So W S C U. A in DN.III,IV,V)

small-poxed, ppl.a. [B¹] *Water small-poxed with rain-splashes* 1901 *Letters* (1917) II xl 711 (Cf. OED Marked by or suffering from small-pox. 1774.. So W. Here *fig*. Not in S C)

smallpox-pitted, ppl.a. [B¹] *Saharas of sand, small-pox-pitted with footprints* 1897 FE xlix 465 (Nonce comb.)

smart, a. [A] *"You think you're mighty smart, don't you?"* 1876 TS i 22. *I told him the whole thing and he said it was smart* 1884 HF vii 66 (OED 10. Clever, capable. In later use chiefly *U.S.* 1628.. So B F Cl Th T. Not A in W S C U)

smart, a. **right smart**. [AB³] *"They must 'a' cost right smart,"* *referring to the boots* 1873 GA xvii 159 (OED 7a. Chiefly *dial* and *U.S.* 1856.. So C Wr B F Th,1842 DN.II,III. Not A in W S)

smart, adv. [AB³] *She was considerable better and coming on so smart* 1865 "Jumping Frog" (1875) 31 (OED 7a. Chiefly *dial* and *U.S.* 1839. Not A in W S C)

smartness, sb. [AB³] *The smartness of the hero, Jim Smiley, in taking the stranger in* 1894 "Priv.Hist. of Jumping Frog Story" (1900) 376 (OED 6. Chiefly *U.S.* 1842.. So B F Cl. Not A in W S C U)

smarty, sb. [AB²] *"Smarty! You think you're some, now"* 1876 TS i 22. See also *right away* 1880 (OED *U.S.* A would-be smart or witty person. 1880.. So W Th. III,1874 DN.III,IV,V. Not A in S C)

smarty, a. [?AB¹] *The barkeeper was gay and smarty and talky* 1883 LM xxxiii 370 (W: smart, smart-alecky. Not in OED S C as adj.)

smasher, sb. [?AB³] *"Oh, I tell you it was a smasher. You ought to have seen them go to pieces"* 1889 CY xxxiii 431 (OED 2a. *colloq*. A crushing reply. 1828.. So U. A in B. Not in W S C in this sense)

smell, v. [?AB²] *The boat had "smelt" the bar in good earnest* 1875 OTM 287. See *crowd*, v. 1909 (OED 2.'As sailors say of the ship that slackens speed as the water shallows under her'. 1875.. Not in W S C in this sense)

smile, v. Past tense **smole**. [?AE] *Then he smole a smile that spread around and covered the whole Sahara* 1894 TSA xi 400 (This form not given in OED W S C)

smile, v. **I should smile**. [?AB²] *"Well, I should smile"* 1889 CY ix 112 (OED 1c. Used to ridicule an idea. 1891.. S: *slang, U.S.* So F. Phr. not in W C)

smily, a. [?AB³] *Plump and smily young girls* 1897 FE vii 94 (OED 1848.. W: *dial*. A in DN.IV,V. Not in S C)

smirchless, a. [B¹] *My idea was to make liars and thieves of nearly half a hundred smirchless men and women* 1899 "MCH" (1900) 53 (Not in OED S C. Given in W)

smirky, a. [A] See *middle name* 1880 (OED *U.S.* Simpering. 1700.. So W. Not A in S C)

smokable, sb. [B¹] *There are people who deprive themselves of each and every drinkable and smokable* 1897 *Autob* (1924) I 98 (OED only in *pl*. 1849.. So W. Not in S C as sb. Here in *sing*.)

smoke, v. [C] *"You don't smoke me and I don't smoke you"* 1872 RI xlvii 332 (OED 8. To smell or suspect (a plot, etc.). Now *arch*. 1608..1886. So U. Not *arch* in W S C. F: English detective slang; so Cl)

smoke-charged, ppl.a. [B¹] *I found myself again amusing a child with smoke-charged soap-bubbles* 1907 "Chaps. from Autob" 3 (Comb. not in OED W S C)

smoke-house, sb. [A] *Log smokehouse back of the kitchen* 1884 HF xxxii 329. *Against these palings stood the smokehouse* 1897 *Autob* (1924) I 98 (OEDS Earlier U.S. exs. 1767. Not A in W S C)

smoke-house raising, vbl.sb. [?AB¹] *Crushed by a log at a smoke-house raising* 1892 AmCl i 23 (Comb. not in any dict. Cf. OED *House-raising*. *U.S.* So Cl)

smoke-mark, sb. [B¹] *Holding their candles aloft and reading the tangled web-work of names...with which the rocky walls [of the cave] had been frescoed (in candle-smoke)...They made a smoke-mark for future guidance* 1876 TS xxxi 237 (Comb. not in OED W S C)

smoker, sb. [?AB³] *We went into the regular smoker* 1893 "Travelling with a Reformer" (1900) 350 (OED 4a. A railway carriage...for the use of those travellers who wish to smoke. 1882.. So W S U. A in C Th.III M)

smoke-stack, sb. [AB³] *Read novels and poetry in the shade of the smoke-stacks* 1869 IA i 19 (OED 1a. *U.S.* The funnel of a steamboat. 1862. So B F Cl Th,1844 T. Not A in U. Not in W S C in this sense)

smoking-car, sb. [?AB³] *I went back to the Mississippi Valley, sitting upright in the smoking-car two or three days and nights* 1906 *Autob* (1924) II 288 (OEDS 1864.. So W S. A in C)

smoking-compartment, sb. [?AB¹] See *parlor-car* 1893 (Comb. not in OED W S C)

smoking-party, sb. [B¹] *This smoking-party had been gathered together partly for business* 1898 "From the London Times of 1904" (1900) 129 (Comb. not in OED W S C)

smooth-bore, a. [?A] *Canon Fulbert...the old smooth-bore* 1869 IA xv 146. *Some gentle old-fashioned flint-lock, smooth-bore, double-barrelled thing* 1904 "Italian with Grammar" (1906) 189. See *globe-sighted* 1907 (OED 2a. 1859.. OEDS Earlier U.S. ex. 1799. Not A in W S C U)

smooth-surfaced, ppl.a. [B¹] *The Devil's Tea-Table ...a great smooth-surfaced mass of rock* 1883 LM xxv 274 (Comb. not in OED S C. Given in W)

smouch, v. Spelled **smooch**. [AB³E] *I can almost tell...what they will say—because I have the books they will "smouch" their ideas from* 1869 IA xlviii 364. *"He used to smouch oysters from unguarded beds"* 1871 *Screamers* xxv 132. *The Mormon Bible is rather stupid and tiresome to read...Its code of morals is "smouched" from the New Testament, and no credit given* 1872 RI xvi 135. *Stole his gun and smooched his specs* 1891 *Slovenly Peter* (1935) 12. See *emery-bag* 1893. *Ours is a mongrel language which now consists of words smouched from every unwatched language under the sun* 1907

"Chaps. from Autob" 245 (OED Now *U.S.* 1. *trans.* To pilfer. 1826.. So S C B F Cl Th.III T DN.I,III,V. Not A in W. A favorite word of Mark Twain's. The spelling in *Slovenly Peter* prob. indicates his usual pron. *Smooch* is given as an alternative pron. in W S DN.III,V; but OED and C give only *smouch*, with diphthong *au*)

smouching, vbl.sb. [AB¹] *Always a streaming flood of brown people clothed in smouchings from the rainbow* 1897 FE lx 594 (Things taken or pilfered. Not in OED W S C. Cf. above)

snaffle, v. [B³] *Whenever anybody offers me a letter to a preacher, now, I snaffle it on the spot* 1866 *Letters* (1907) I vi 122 (OED 2. *slang.* To seize. 1860.. So W S C U. Cf. Wr: To steal, pilfer)

snag, sb. [AB³] *A confused jumble of savage-looking snags* 1872 RI i 21. *"Raised the second reef abreast the big snag in the bend"* 1875 OTM 221. See *blind reef* 1875; *break,* sb. 1875, 1894; *sand-bar* 1881; *bar,* sb. 1883. *A lot of snags that fairly roared, the current was tearing by them so swift* 1884 HF xv 127 (OED 1b. A trunk or large branch of a tree imbedded in the bottom of a river, with one end directed upwards. Orig.*U.S.* 1807.. So S Wr B F Cl Th DN.II,III,VI AS.II.31. Not A in W C U)

snag, sb. [AB³] *Snags and sand-bars grew less and less frequent, and Tom grew more and more at his ease* 1881 PP vi 78. *Wales read the proof, and presently was aghast, for he had struck a snag* 1906 *Autob* (1924) II 281 (OED orig. *U.S.* 1c. *fig.* 1830.. So Cl M AS.VI.121. Not A in W S C U)

snag-boat, sb. [AB³] *The government's snag-boats go patrolling up and down* 1883 LM xxviii 300 (OED orig. *U.S.* 4. A steam-boat fitted with an apparatus for removing snags. 1858. So W S C Wr B F Cl Th,1843 DN.II,III AS.II.27,Peck,1837)

snagging, vbl.sb. [AB²] *Impending snaggings and explosions* 1880 TA x 95 (OED 2. Chiefly *U.S.* and esp. of river steamers.1880 this quote. Not in W S C)

snail-belly, sb. [?AB¹] See *pall-bearer* 1883 (Comb. not in OED W S C)

snake, v. [AB³] *"He'd spring straight up and snake a fly off'n the counter"* 1865 "Jumping Frog" (1875) 32. *"For two cents I'd go out and snake them cats off that chimney"* 1867 "Jim Wolfe" (1872) 75. *"Snake him out, boys. Snatch him out by the heels"* 1883 LM iii 59. *"You ain't the only person that's ben snaked down wrongfully out'n a high place"* 1884 HF xix 186. See also *ironclad,* sb. 1889 (OED 5. *U.S.* To drag, pull, or draw forcibly. *fig.* 1833.. OEDS 1829. So W S C Wr B Cl Th T DN.II)

snake-charming, vbl.sb. [B¹] *The girls went through a performance which represented snake-charming* 1897 FE xlii 388 (Comb. not in OED W; but cf. OED Snakecharmer,1836. Given in S C U)

snap, sb. [AB³] See *New Yorker* 1883. *After the address, the prince responded with snap and brevity* 1897 FE xli 385 (OED 11. Alertness, energy, 'go.' Orig. *U.S.* 1872.. So B Cl Th.III H DN.III. Not A in W S C U)

snap, sb. [?AB³] *"I don't care a snap for that—go on!"* 1892 AmCl xxiv 255 (OEDS 15b. In negative phrases. Earlier U.S. exs. 1834.. Not A in W S C)

snap, v. [?AB¹] *He held up his di'monds this way and that; they seemed to snap fire out all around* 1896 TSD iv 354 (W: To emit sparks or flashes.. to sparkle; to scintillate. So S C. This sense not in OED)

snapper, sb. [AB³] *A humorous story finishes with a nub, point, snapper, or whatever you like to call it* 1895 "How to Tell a Story" (1900) 226 (OED 2e.*U.S.*1857.. Not A in C. Not in W S)

snapping-turtle, sb. [A] *Families of snapping-turtles used to congregate and drowse in the sun* 1907 "Chaps. from Autob" 246 (OED One of the N.Am. freshwater tortoises. OEDS 1784.. So W S C U B F Cl DN.III)

snappy, a. [?AB²] *They were snappy, able men* 1872 RI vi 57 (OED 6. Cleverly smart, full of 'go,' brisk. 1873. So W U Wr. A in S C)

snappy, a. [?AB²] *A snappy footnote* 1871 SNO (1875) 94. *It will be a starchy book, and should be full of snappy pictures* 1871 *Letters* (1917) I x 188 (OED 6b. Neat and elegant; smart, 'natty.' 1881.. So W U Wr. A in S C AS.III.126; IV.81; VII.236)

snatch, v. [AB¹] *"Snatch her!" The wheel flew to port so fast that the spokes melted into a spider web—the swing of the boat subsided—she steadied herself* 1873 GA ii 47. *We touched bottom...Mr. Bixby shouted through the tube..."Snatch her! snatch her!"* 1875 OTM 223. *"Now cramp her down! Snatch her!"* 1875 OTM 286. See *baldheaded* 1909 (*Naut.* sense, not in OED W S C. The meaning seems to be merely to make haste with whatever operation is indicated, act quickly, work fast. Cf. *snatched,* hurried, in DN.II,IV AS.II.364. Clearly *not* the sense in OED *Snatch,* v. 9. *Naut.* To place (a line) in a snatch-block. 1769..)

snatch on, v. [B¹] *"Quick, Huck, snatch on your clothes"* 1896 TSD ix 522 (Comb. not in OED W S C. Apparently a correlative of *snatch off*)

snicker, sb. [?AB³] *There was a smothered burst of snickers from behind the screen* 1898 *Autob* (1924) I 127 (OED 1857.. OEDS Earlier U.S. ex. 1836. Not A in W S C U. A in Wr M)

snifter, sb. [?AB³] *"I bleeve I could smoke this pipe all day," said Joe. "I don't feel sick"..."But I bet you Jeff Thatcher couldn't...Just one little snifter would fetch him"* 1876 TS xvi 138 (OED 3. A sniff. Chiefly dial 1835.. So W S C Wr. Cf. DN.V: *snifter,* a cocaine fiend)

snip out, v. [?AB¹] See *philippina* 1894 (Not in OED W S C. The meaning seems to be: to speak affectedly or with over-refinement. Cf. F: *Snip,* sb., An overdressed man; a coxcomb; so DN.III,IV)

snoop, v. [AB³] *They always put in the long absence snooping around...though none of them had any idea where the Holy Grail really was* 1889 CY ix 112. *There was twenty people there, snooping around and examining* 1893 TSA ii 26 (OEDS *U.S.* 2. 1832.. So W U F Cl Th M DN.I,III AS.V.420. Not A in S C)

snort, sb. [?AB³] *The rest of it brought a snort or two out of him* 1892 AmCl xxiii 237 (OED 2b. To express contempt, disdain. 1865.. So W S C U. A in F Cl)

snort, v. [?AB³] *He ate that jam...and observed 'that the old woman would get up and snort' when she found out* 1867 SNO (1875) 52 (OED 5. Of persons. a. To express contempt or indignation by a snorting sound. 1818.. So W S C U. A in Cl)

snow-block, sb. [B¹] *This great mansion of frozen snow-blocks* 1893 "Esquimau Maiden's Romance" (1900) 138 (Comb. not in OED W S C)

snow-drive, sb. [B¹] *It was like a storm at sea, for boom and crash and roar and furious snow-drive* 1906 *Autob* (1924) I 316 (Nonce comb.)

snow-hooded, ppl.a. [B¹] *The stately border of snow-hooded mountain peaks* 1880 TA xxv 245 (Comb. not in OED W S C)

snow in, v. [AB²] *Appalled at the imminent danger of being "snowed in," we pushed on* 1869 IA xxvii 286 (OEDS 6d. Snow, v. With *in.* Usually in pa.pple. *U.S.* 1869, this quot.. Not A in W C U. Comb. not in S)

snow-shoe, sb. [A] *Feet like snow-shoes* 1869 IA xxxiii 362 (OED 1a. A kind of foot-gear.. used by the Indians and others in North America. 1674.. Not A in W S C U)

snow-storm, sb. [B²] *A thrashing snow-storm of waving handkerchiefs* 1883 LM lvii 561 (OED *fig.* 1893.. Fig. sense not in W S C)

snow-summit, sb. [B¹] *The intellectual snow-summits built by Shakespeare and those others* 1898 "About Play Acting" (1900) 225 (Not in OED W S C)

snow under, v. [AB³] *They looked partly petrified, partly drunk, and wholly caught out and snowed under*

1889 CY xxv 322 (OED Snow 6b. With *under...fig.* to submerge, overwhelm, overpower, etc. Orig. *U.S.* 1880.. So M H. Not A in W C U. This sense not in S)

snow-wreathed, ppl.a. [B¹] *This magnificent mountain lifts its snow-wreathed precipices into the deep blue sky* 1880 TA xxx 312 (Comb. not in OED W S C)

snub, v. [AB³] *"Snub up your boat"* 1872 RI li 370 (OED 2b. *Naut.* and *U.S.* To fasten or tie up. 1841.. So B F Cl Th T. Not A in W S C U)

snuffle, v. [?AB¹] *Joe's spirits had gone down. The tears lay very near the surface...Joe snuffled a little* 1876 TS xvi 137 (To whimper, snivel; used of muffled or suppressed sobbing. So S. What S calls the lacrimose sense of the word is not given in OED W C U)

snuffy, a. [?AB¹] *Snuffy feather-bed—not aired often enough* 1883 LM xxxviii 405 (Not in OED W S C in this sense)

snuggery, sb. [B³] *Barnum and Jamrach were in Jamrach's little private snuggery...refreshing themselves after an arduous stroke of business* 1897 FE lxiv 639 (OED b. *spec.* The bar-parlor of an inn or public-house. 1837.. So W S C)

snuggle, sb. [B¹] *On cold winter mornings a snuggle of children occupying the hearthstone* 1897 *Autob* (1924) I 103 (Nonce use: A snuggling group; a huddle. Cf. OED Snuggle, sb. *rare.* An act of snuggling. 1901. So W. Not in S C as sb.)

sny, sb. [AB¹] *"Ef we slips acrost de river* [at Hannibal] *to-night arter de moon's gone down, en kills dat sick fam'ly dat's over on de Sny..."* 1893 TSA i 24 (Not given in any dict. A localism in use along the Mississippi and Missouri Rivers, signifying a narrow passage between an island and the shore. The word is Missouri French, derived from *chenal,* channel. The reference in TSA is to the passage in the Mississippi bottom opposite Hannibal, locally known as "The Sni." Cf. "Snicarty" (from *chenal écarté*) and "Sni levée" in Pike County, Illinois; "Sny Magill" in Iowa; and esp. "Sniabar" in the Missouri River, in Lafayette County, near Lexington, the derivation of which has been discussed in detail on pp. 32-36 of *An Introduction to a Survey of Missouri Place-Names,* by R. L. Ramsay, A. W. Read, and Esther Gladys Leech, University of Missouri Studies IX.1., Jan. 1, 1934)

so, conj.adv. **so as, so's.** [?ACE] *Anyway, just so's he got a bet he was satisfied* 1865 "Jumping Frog" (1875) 31. *"It keeps me in a sweat, constant, so's I want to hide som'ers"* 1876 TS xxiii 182 (OED 29. *So as:* in such a way that, so that. Now *dial.* 1523..1905. 30. *So as:* provided that. 1585..1853. Cf. OED *As,* conj.adv. 19. With finite verb. *Obs* and replaced by *that.* A. *So... as:* in such a manner, to such a degree...that. *c*1460.. 1777. Called *obs* in W; not *obs* in S C; *dial* in Wr; A in DN.III. The contracted form *so's* is not mentioned in any dict.)

so, conj.adv. **so as that, so'st.** [?ACE] *I would God I were in my room in the new house in Fairhaven, so'st I could have one good solid night's sleep* 1894 *Notebook* (1935) xxi 238 (OED 29c. *So as that*=so as, in such a way that, so that, 1583..1817. Cf. OED *As,* conj.adv. 21b. The transition from *so as* to *so that* gave the intervening *so as that,* arch. 1772..1784. The comb. *so as that* is not given in W S C. The contracted form *so'st* is not mentioned in any dict.)

soak, v. [?AB³] *I took it to a pawnshop and soaked it for a revolver* 1906 Speeches (1910) 348 (OED 7d. To put in pawn. *colloq* or *slang.* 1882. So W S C. A in F T AS.X.20)

soap-and-candle, a. [B¹] *There were various soap-and-candle boxes* 1894 PW ix 549 (Comb. not in OED W S C)

soap-fat, sb. [AB³] *"Our soap-fat carts will visit the corner designated"* 1864 SS (1926) i 122 (OED The refuse of kitchens, used in making soap. 1879. OEDS *U.S.* Earlier ex.1839.. Not A in W S C)

soary, a. [AB¹?C] *I am as soary and as flighty as a rocket, to-day* 1880 *Letters* (1917) I xx 375 (A in B F T. W: Soaring; exalted. *Rare.* Not in OED S C)

sober-colored, a. [B¹] *He drops into the studio as sober-colored as anything you ever see* 1892 AmCl xvi 168 (Comb. not in OED W S C)

sobrieties, sb.pl. [B³] *The children will resume their customary sobrieties until he comes in August* 1898 "Austrian Edison" (1900) 267 (OED 2b. In *plural.* 1826. This concrete sense not in W S C)

so boy, int. [AB¹] See *sick,* v.1884 (Given as *suboi, subuoy,* DN.I,III: Used in driving hogs; w.Ind. The comb. not in OED W S C; but cf. OED *Soh,* int. Var.of *So,* adv. 2. Used in soothing or quieting a restive horse,=Gently! Softly! Easy! 1820.. So W. Cf. also S: *So,* int. Stand as you are; stand still; be quiet; stop: said to horses and cows, and often spelled *soh.* So C. Wr: *dial* and *Am.* So DN.I)

sociable, sb. [AB³] *At church "sociables" he was called upon to read poetry* 1876 TS v 55 (OED 3. *U.S.* An informal evening party; esp. a social church meeting. 1826.. So W S C B F Cl Th H DN.III)

socialist-hated, ppl.a. [B¹] *It ought also to moderate that talk about French duelists and socialist-hated monarchs being the only people who are immortal* 1880 TA viii 69 (Comb. not in OED W S C)

society, sb. [AB³] *"I had a visit yesterday from the society's committee by way of discipline, because we have a piano in the house, which is against the rules"* 1873 GA xiv 133 (OED 10c. *U.S.* Congregation. 1828.. So W S C Cl. Here a distinctively Quaker usage; cf. AS.I.194; also II.32)

society item, sb. [?AB¹] *This society item in the evening paper* 1892 AmCl iv 56 (Comb. not in OED W S C. Cf. item, above)

sock, v. [?AB³] *"Pile it on and sock it to him"* 1883 LM xliii 438 (OEDS 1c. To 'give it' to one. Earlier U.S. exs. 1845.. A in Wr B F Cl DN.I,IV,V. Not A in W S C U)

sockdologer, sb. [AB³] *The thunder would go rumbling and grumbling away...and then rip comes another flash and another sockdologer* 1884 HF xx 192. See also *lifter* 1894 (OEDS *U.S. slang.* 3. Something exceptional in any respect. 1830.. So W S C U B F Cl Th T M DN.III,V AS.III.436. See also *Dial* XXXIII (1902) 86)

soda-squirt, sb. [B¹] *The undersigned desires an invitation to the next soda-squirt* 1898 "Stirring Times in Austria" (1900) 319 (Hum. nonce use for a social entertainment)

soda-squirter, sb. [?AB¹] *Hurrah for the soda-squirter!* 1898 "Stirring Times in Austria" (1900) 319 (Comb. not in OED W S C. Cf. *soda-squirt* in DN.V: one who works at a soda-fountain; so *squirt* in AS.XI.45)

sofa-back, sb. [B¹] *Tom hoisted a leg over the sofa-back* 1894 PW viii 338 (Comb. not in OED W S C)

sofa-shifter, sb. [B¹] *The accomplished furniture-scout and sofa-shifter performed his part* 1864 SS (1926) 132 (Hum. nonce term for scene-shifter)

sofa-skirmisher, sb. [B¹] *The furniture-scout and sofa-skirmisher was called before the curtain* 1864 SS (1926) 134 (Cf. above)

soft, a. **to be soft on.** [?AB¹] *He said that Arkansas had been injured and kept back by generations of exaggerations concerning the mosquitoes there... But if he was soft on the Arkansas mosquitoes, he was hard enough on the mosquitoes of Lake Providence to make up for it— "those Lake Providence colossi," as he finely called them* 1883 LM xxxiv 373 (To be partial to, lenient, favorable; opposite of 'hard on.' This sense not in OED W S C. An extension of OED 13c. To be in love with; to regard amorously or sentimentally.1840..)

soft-footed, ppl.a. [B¹] *He strikes a long, soft-footed trot through the sage brush* 1872 RI v 49 (Comb. not in OED S C. Given in W Wr)

softly, int. [B¹?C] *"What a leather-headed idea!"* exclaimed the constable..."*Softly, softly!" said Wilson to Blake* 1894 PW xii 777 (W: Softly, interj.=soft, interj. An exclamation urging silence or less haste; be quiet! not so fast! *Archaic.* Not *arch* in S: Sometimes an int., meaning "go easy." Not in OED or C as int.)

soft-shell crab, sb. [AB³] See *biscuit* 1880. *Small soft-shell crabs of a most superior breed* 1883 LM xliv 446 (OEDS Soft-shell, a. *U.S.* 1847.. So W S C B F)

soft-soaper, sb. [?AB²] *He was narrowly watching this soft-soaper of Democratic rascality* 1852 *Hannibal Journal*, Sept.16 (OEDS One who flatters or 'soft sawders.' Earlier U.S. ex. 1852, this quot. A in B. Not A in W. Not in S C. Cf. *soft-soap*, v., listed as A in DN.III,IV,V AS.II.365; IV.345; VII.336)

softy, sb. [?AB³] *"Any softy would know they would be laying for him"* 1872 RI ix 78. See *lo* 1876 (OED A weak-minded or silly person. 1863.. So W S C Wr. A in DN.V)

softy, a. [?AB²] *When the place was packed full the undertaker he slid around in his black gloves with his softy soothering ways* 1884 HF xxvii 272 (OEDS 1884, this quot. So W. Not in S C)

soggy, a. [AB³] *Soggy rolls, crackers, salt fish* 1898 "At the Appetite-Cure" (1900) 157 (OED 3. Of bread: Sodden, heavy. 1868.. Chiefly *dial* and *U.S.* Not A in W S C U)

solar sister, sb. [B¹] *He said that she—his ship—couldn't any more get out of order than the solar sister* 1893 TSA ii 27 (Hum. malapropism. Cf. OED Solar, a. 7. Solar system. 1704)

soldier, v. [?AB³] *A fraud who pretended to be cutting steps was "soldiering"* 1880 TA xliv 219. "*The Portyghee et twenty-two of them while he was soldiering there and nobody noticing"* 1899 "My Debut" (1900) 76 (OED 1d. To make a mere show of working. 1840.. So W S C. A in Cl T DN.I,III)

soldier-camp, sb. [B¹] *"There's a soldier-camp"* 1901 "Two Little Tales" (1928) 204 (Comb. not in OED W S C)

soldier-cap, sb. [B¹] *Small, stiff-brimmed soldier-cap hung on a corner of the bump* 1883 LM lvii 558 (Comb. not in OED W S C)

soldier-people, sb. [B¹] *He had to acquire a knowledge of war at the same time; and a knowledge of soldier-people and sailor-people* 1909 ISD iv 46 (Comb. not in OED W S C)

soldier-plume, sb. [B¹] *I knowed it was the king and the duke, though they was all over tar and feathers, and didn't look like nothing in the world that was human—just looked like a couple of monstrous big soldier-plumes* 1884 HF xxxiii 345 (Comb. not in OED W S C)

soldier-shoe, sb. [B¹] *"Why, to make soldier-shoes out of their hide"* 1883 LM xxiv 268 (Comb. not in OED W S C)

soldier-talk, sb. [B¹] *He became familiar with soldier-ship and soldier-ways and soldier-talk* 1909 ISD iv 47 (Comb. not in OED W S C)

soldier-way, sb. [B¹] See *soldier-talk*, 1909; *soldier-wile*, 1909 (Comb. not in OED W S C)

soldier-wile, sb. [B¹] *It could have gone soldiering with a war-tribe when no one was noticing, and learned soldier-wiles and soldier-ways* 1909 ISD v 53 (Comb. not in OED W S C)

solid, a. [AB³] *The mad multitude stood upon their feet in a solid body* 1883 LM lvii 561 (OED 8b. Unanimous, undivided; united in approval or opposition. Orig.*U.S.* 1884.. OEDS 1878.. So C F Cl. Not A in W S U)

solid, a. [?A] *One good solid night's sleep* 1894 *Notebook* (1935) xxi 238. *I think we may consider the business settled for ten solid years* 1899 *Speeches* (1910) 53 (OED 9b. Of a day, hour, etc.: Whole, entire, complete. Now *colloq.* 1718.. So W Wr. Not in S C in this sense)

solid, a. [?AB²] *Solid blackness—a crackless bank of it* 1883 LM lviii 571 (OED 10b. Of colour: of the same tone or shade throughout; uniform. Earliest ex. U.S. 1883.. A in T. Not A in W S C. Cf. Solid-colored, A in Cl)

solid, a. [A] *They bore themselves with a dignity proper to men of solid means and prodigious reputation as pilots* 1875 OTM 221 (OED 12d. *U.S.* and *dial.* Financially sound or reliable. 1788.. So F Cl Th M. Not A in W S C U)

solid, a. [?AC] See *bonanza* 1880. *"We might borrow something worth having out of the captain's stateroom. Seegars, I bet you—and cost five cents apiece, solid cash. Steamboat captains is always rich...and don't care a cent what a thing costs"* 1884 HF xii 103. *His drunk was still portentously solid next morning* 1897 FE lx 590 (OED 13. Well founded or established; of real value or importance; substantial. Freq. in the 17th and 18th centuries. a1601..1869. Not *arch* in W S C Wr)

solid matter, sb. [B³] See *nonpareil* 1889. *He had left out a couple of words in a thin-spaced page of solid matter, and there wasn't another breakline for two or three pages ahead. What in the world was to be done? Overrun all those pages in order to get in the two missing words?* 1906 *Autob* (1924) II 281 (OED 1c. *Typog.*...type composed without leads; also applied to type with but few quadrats in. 1888. The latter part of the OED def. applies here, where the meaning is clearly 'without paragraph-breaks or break-lines.' Only the sense 'without leads' given in W S C)

some, a. [AB³] *"Smarty! You think you're some, now, don't you?"* 1876 TS i 22 (OEDS 4e. *U.S.* In predicative use: Of some account; deserving consideration. 1845. So W B F Cl Th H DN.I AS.IV.122. Not A in S U Wr. Not in C in this sense)

some, adv. [AB³] *"We've thought some of the Hot Springs"* 1873 GA xxxiii 307. See also *bowie* 1884 (OED 2b. *U.S.* To some extent. 1825.. So S C B F Th,1785 T H DN.III. Not A in W Wr)

somers, adv. [?AB¹E] *"It keeps me in a sweat constant, so's I want to hide som'ers"* 1876 TS xxiii 182. See *hide up* 1884; *marse* 1893. *Aunt Polly wouldn't let him go traipsing off somers wasting time* 1896 TSD i 344 (W Somewhere, *Dial.* A in B DN.III. This form not in OED S C]

somewheres, adv. [?AB²] *He said he would go "somewheres" and steal a lamp* 1869 IA lvii 616 (OED *dial* or *vulg.* 1859.. So W. A in B M DN.III,IV AS.XI. 352. This form not in S C]

Son of the Forest, sb. [AB¹] See *bead-reticule* 1869; *putrid* 1883 (An Indian. Cf. Forest-born, above. Phrase not in OED W S C)

son of toil, sb. [B¹] See *eagle* 1902 (A workingman. Phr. not in OED W S C; but cf. OED 7, quots. for Son of Pride, Son of Liberty, Son of wax=shoemaker, U.S. ex.)

soon as, conj. [?AC] *Soon as I could get Buck down by the corn-crib, I says...*1884 HF xviii 164 (OED 42. Now *poet.* c1375..1894. Not in W S C)

soot-blackened, ppl.a. [B¹] *It rained all day... apparently trying its best to wash that soot-blackened town white* 1894 PW xviii 17 (Comb. not in OED W S C)

sooth, sb. sooth to say. [C] *"He smiteth with a heavy hand, yet spareth me; he spareth me not always with the tongue, though, sooth to say"* 1881 PP iii 42 (OED; Now *arch.* 1b. c1320..1855. So W S C U)

sooth, a. [C] *"Come—really, is that 'sooth'—as you people say?"* 1889 CY xiv 170 (OED Now *arch.* 2.True. c825..1879. So W S C)

sooth, adv. [C] *"Above forty witnesses have proved the storm; and sooth one might have had a thousand, for all had reason to remember it"* 1881 PP xv 189 (OED Now *arch* and *rare.* Truly. c1000..c1470. So W C Wr. Not in S as adverb)

soothering, ppl.a. [?AB¹] See *softy* 1884 (Not in OED W S C. Cf. Wr: flattering, coaxing, affectionate, used in *Ireland* and *Cumberland*)

soothing-syrup, sb. [?AB²] *"Soothing-syrup! Teething-rings!"* 1872 RI xv 125. *He called for soothing-syrup* 1879 *Speeches* (1910) 65 (OEDS Earlier U.S. ex. 1872, this quot... Comb. not in W S C)

sophomore, sb. [A] *Six Sophomores and a Freshman from the Gladiatorial College* 1869 IA xxvi 280 (OED 1. Now *U.S.* A student of the second year, 1726.. So S C U B Cl Th M. DN.II. Not A in W)

sophomoric, a. [AB³] *Their make-up is a complacent and pretentious outpour of false figures and fine writing, in the sophomoric style* 1907 CS II ii 115 (OED Chiefly *U.S.* 1837...So S C Th.III. Not A in W)

sore, adv. [C] *The cares of state do tax him sore* 1871 SNO (1875) 172. *All did laugh full sore* 1880 *Fireside Conversation, 1601*. *It "smote them sore with fear and dread"* 1889 CY xiv 170 (OED Now chiefly *arch* and *dial*. 10. *c*1440..1812 So W S C U Wr)

sore-back, a. [?AB¹] *They have always got a sore-back horse lying around somewhere to sell to the stranger* 1866 *Speeches* (1923) 9 (Comb. not in OED W S C)

sore-faced, a. [B¹] *There were three sore-faced babies* 1881 PP xvii 209 (Comb. not in OED W S C)

sorrow-sowing, ppl. a. [B¹] *Domremy has long ago forgotten what that dreaded sorrow-sowing apparition is like* 1896 JA II xii 301 (Comb. not in OED W S C)

sorry, a. [C] *"Hast been minded to cozen me with a sorry jest?"* 1881 PP v 62 (OED 4. Dismal. *obs.* *a*1225..1605. So U. Not *obs* in W S C)

sorry-looking, ppl.a. [?AB²] *The coyote is a sorry-looking skeleton* 1872 RI v 48 (OED 7. 1903. So W. Comb. not in S C. *Sorry* in this sense, i.e., vile, worthless, mean, is A in DN.III,IV,V; not A in OED W S C)

sort of, adv. [?AB³] *I sort of hoped you might decide to drop in* 1867 *M.T. the Letter Writer* (1932) i 17. *I was getting sort of used to the widow's ways* 1884 HF iv 25. *The farmers were bound to throw in something, to sort of offset my liberality* 1889 CY xiv 65 (OED Sort, sb. 8c. In a way; to some extent. Chiefly *dial* and *colloq*. 1833.. So W S C U. A in Th DN.II,III,V AS.XI.352)

sot, a. [AB³] *"When Tom Quartz was sot once, he was always sot"* 1871 *Screamers* ii 19. *"People dat's sot stays sot"* 1884 HF xxxiv 354 (OED 6b. Of persons: Obstinate. *dial* and *U.S.* 1848.. So Wr B F M DN.III,IV,V,VI. Not A in W S C T)

soul, sb. my souls! [?AB¹] *"My souls, but she's a stunner!"* 1892 AmCl xvii 173 (Cf. OED 10. Used in various asseverative phrases, or as an exclamation, as...*my soul!* 1824. So Wr. But no ex. of the curious *plural* form. Phrase not in W S C)

soul-blistering, ppl.a. [B¹] *Renounce these soul-blistering saturnalia!* 1881 *Speeches* (1910) 24 (Comb. not in OED W S C)

soul-butter, sb. [B¹] *Music is a good thing, and after all that soul-butter and hogwash I never see it freshen up things so, and sound so honest and bully* 1884 HF xxv 248 (Comb. not in OED W S C; but cf. OED Butter, sb. 1f. *fig*. Unctuous flattery. colloq. 1823..)

soul-capture, sb. [B¹] *But it could be argued that if he saved a hundred souls in New York—Not a solitary soul-capture was sure* 1906 "WIM" (1917) iii 33 (Comb. not in OED W S C)

soulful, a. [?AB³] *This piece is just one long, soulful, sardonic laugh at human life* 1898 "About Play Acting" (1900) 219 (OED 1. Full of soul or feeling. Common in recent use. 1863.. So W S C U. A in Th.III, 1872)

soul-scorching, ppl.a. [B¹] See *hair-lifting* 1889 (Comb. not in OED W S C)

soul-staining, ppl.a. [B¹] *"Is this a theater?...Is it some other vain, brilliant, beautiful temple of soul-staining amusement and hilarity?"* 1873 GA liii 481 (Comb. not in OED W S C)

sounding, vbl.sb. [?AB²] See *navigate* 1884 (OED 1. *transf*. 1891. So W S C U)

sounding-barge, sb. [?AB¹] *If there were serious doubts he would stop the steamer and man the sounding-barge and go down and sound the several crossings* 1906 "Carl Schurz, Pilot" 727 (Comb. not in OED W S C)

sounding-boat, sb. [?AB¹] See *shove*, v. 1858. *The boat has not that rare luxury, a regularly devised "sounding-boat"* 1875 OTM 567 (Comb. not in OED W S C; but cf. OED Sounding-ship, 1832)

sounding-pole, sb. [?AB¹] *"You can go up and get the sounding-pole"* 1875 OTM 569 (Comb. not in OED W S C)

sounding-yawl, sb. [?AB¹] *The next moment the sounding-yawl swept aft to the wheel* 1875 OTM 569 (Comb. not in OED W S C)

soup-and-bouille, sb. [B³E] *We have left a can of "soup-and-bouille"* 1866 "Forty-Three Days in an Open Boat" 109 (OED Soup, sb. 3b. *soup-and-bully*. 1862. Not in W S C)

sour-crout, sb. [?AE] *"Madame, avez-vous...horseradish, sour-crout, hog and hominy—anything, anything in the world that can stay a Christian stomach?"* 1869 IA x 94 [In most subsequent editions, the word is changed to sauer-kraut] (OED Anglicized form of Sauerkraut. 1775.. So W C T. A in B Cl Th M AS.IV.10, X.169. This sp. not in S)

sour-mash, sb. [?AB¹] *Over-confidence and gaiety induced by over-plus of sour-mash* 1892 AmCl i 23 (S: Brewing: mash in which fermentation is started by mixing in fermenting mash. The comb. not in OED W C)

sour on, v. [AB³] *"I reckon Injun Joe's left friends behind him, and I don't want 'em souring on me and doing mean tricks"* 1876 TS xxxiii 256. *But the duke kind of soured on him* 1884 HF xix 188. *To use a common expression, his congregation "soured" on him, and he found small pleasure in the exercise of his clerical office* 1906 *Autob* (1924) II 21 (OED 1c. To take a dislike to. Orig. *U.S.* 1862.. So S F Cl Th T DN.II,V. Not A in W. This sense not in C)

sour on, v. [?AB¹] *I would give him* [Merlin] *a lift when his poor little parlor-magic soured on him* 1889 CY vii 90 (To fail, go wrong. This sense not in OED W S C. An extension of the sense above?)

sour up, v. [?AB¹] See *flat out*, v. 1894. (Comb. not in OED W S C; but cf. OED Sour, v. To become embittered, morose, or peevish.1748..)

South, sb. [A] *Pilgrims from New England, the South, and the Mississippi valley* 1869 IA iv 38. See *mudsill* 1877; *War* 1883; *shinplaster* 1889; *Colonel* 1892; *chicken-coop* 1904. *Lakeside was a pleasant little town of five or six thousand inhabitants...It had church accommodations for 35,000, which is the way of the Far West and the South* 1904 "Bequest" (1906) i 1 (OED 2c. The southern States of America. [The erratic capitalization in OED of South, Southern, and State in their Am. senses has been preserved here and below.] Orig. *U.S.* 1779.. So W S C B F AS.IV.10)

South, sb. down South. [AB³] See *Middle States* 1879; *farmer-preacher* 1884; *Spanish moss* 1884. *"Dat overseer wuz a Yank, too, outen New Englan', en anybody down South kin tell you what dat mean"* 1894 PW xviii 18 (OED Down,adv. 29. down South: In the U.S., down the Mississippi; into or in the Southern states. 1852.. So S C. Phr. not in W!)

south, a. [B¹] *They are just like so many mothers, the rough mining-camp boys are, when you wake up the south side of their hearts* 1902 "DBDS" (1928) 352 (This sense not in OED W S C. Apparently original with M.T.)

South, adv. [AB²] *"I wish I could go West or South, or somewhere"* 1873 GA xiv 137. *Miss Watson would sell him South, sure* 1884 HF xiv 102 (OEDS 1b. In or into the southern States, *U.S.* 1885, quot. from HF. Not in W S C)

South Carolinian, sb. [AB¹] *We got in company with a young South Carolinian* 1883 LM xxix 318 (Not in OED S. Given in W C)

south end, sb. [?AB¹] *He bent stooping forward, with his back sagged and his south end sticking out far* 1883 LM ii 46 (Phr. not in OED W S C)

Southern, a. [AB³] See *go*, v.1883. *A brief dispute followed as to whether the difference between Northern and Southern moonlight really existed* 1883 LM xlv 456. *"We won't let you walk—it wouldn't be Southern hospitality to do it"* 1884 HF xxxiii 340. *The Southern author had a passion for "eloquence"* 1893 "Cure for the Blues" 79. See also *batter-cake* 1897 (OED 1b. *U.S.* Belonging to the Southern States. 1839.. So W S C U AS.IV.4, Freneau, 1809)

Southerner, sb. [AB³] *"A very agreeable man...a real Southerner"* 1873 GA xxxviii 348. See *American*, sb. 1880; *guess*, v. 1883; *Southron* 1883; at 1883; *like* 1883. *They said she talked like a Southerner* 1902 "DBDS" (1928) 289 (OED 2. One belonging to the southern States. 1836.. So W S C U B F Th.III T)

Southern-looking, ppl.a. [AB¹] *Lake Providence, Louisiana...is the first distinctly Southern-looking town you come to* 1883 LM xxxiv 372 (Comb. not in OED W S C)

Southern-style, sb. [AB¹] *Hot wheat-bread, Southern-style* 1880 TA xlix 574 (Comb. not in OED W S C)

Southron, sb. [AB³?C] *The Southerner—or Southron, according to Sir Walter's starchier way of phrasing it* 1883 LM xlvi 468 (OED 2b. *U.S.* Southerner. 1848.. So B F T. S: *Rare*. C: An affected use. Not in W)

sovereign, sb. [AB¹] *"I am a free-born sovereign, sir, an American"* 1869 IA xi 100 (A in B: One of the people of the United States; a voter. So F. This sense not in OED W S C)

Sovereign State, sb. [AB¹] *The radiant galaxy of Sovereign States* 1892 AmCl xviii 189 (S: A political community possessed of supreme authority in ordering its civil affairs and the administration of its government; sometimes limited in a union of states. Cf. on the other hand W: One exercising the usual powers of self-government and of declaring peace and war without outside control. C: The claim that each State possessed a separate sovereignty was one of the elements of controversy involved in the Civil War. This burning American issue about the meaning of the term is not mentioned in OED)

sozodont, sb. [AB¹] *Whiskey, brandy, beer, cologne, sozodont, tobacco* 1872 RI xx 155 (Name coined for a tooth-wash. A in B. Not in OED W S C)

space-annihilating, ppl.a. [B¹] *It is curious—the space-annihilating power of thought* 1897 FE xxxviii 352 (Comb. not in OED W S C)

Spanish moss, sb. [AB³] See *shade-tree* 1883. *Down south...we begun to come to trees with Spanish moss on them, hanging down from the limbs like long gray beards* 1884 HF xxxi 314 (OED *U.S.* 1833.. So W S C DN.IV)

spar, v. [AB²] *After three days labor, we finally succeeded in sparring her off with a capstan bar* 1859 Letter in *New Orleans Daily Crescent. Maybe she "strikes and swings." Then she has to while away several hours (or days) sparring herself off* 1875 OTM 568 (OED 2. *Naut.* and *U.S.* To aid a vessel over a shallow bar by the use of spars and tackles. 1883. So C. Not A in S U. Not in W)

spark, v. [AB³] *They won't spark the scullery maids* 1892 AmCl iii 45 (OED 2. *U.S.* To play the suitor. 1807.. So W U B F Cl T DN.I,III,IV,V AS.III.231. Not A in S C)

spat, sb. [AB³] *The Coxes too had completed their spat and their reconciliation* 1899 "MCH" (1900) 17 (OED 1. A tiff or dispute. orig. *U.S.* 1804.. So C Wr B F Cl Th T H DN.III AS.III.137. Not A in W S)

speak, v. Past tense **spake**. [?ACE] *The battery of guns spake not* 1869 IA ii 29 (OED Now *arch., poet,* or

dial...1848. So W S C Wr. A in B: This antiquated word is still heard occasionally from pulpit as well as in conversation (Pickering). So DN.III)

Speaker, sb.[A] *He could have been postmaster general, speaker of.the house* 1880 Speeches (1923) 96 (OED 3d. 1789, only ex. Am. sense. So W S C U H)

speaker-list, sb. [B¹] *Put me in the speaker-list about No. 3—can't you?* 1901 M.T. the Letter Writer (1932) xiii 167 (Comb. not in OED W S C)

speaking-tube, sb. [B³] *I flew to the speaking-tube and shouted to the engineer* 1875 OTM 574. *George reported it to us through the speaking-tube* 1906 Autob (1924) II 16 (OED 1. 1833.. So W S C U)

special, sb. [?AB¹] *People used to wonder where the "Specials" got that remarkable information with which they every morning surprised the country* 1873 GA xl 358 (W S U: A newspaper extra. Not in OED C in this sense)

special-brand, a. [B¹] *"He had a handful of special-brand cigars lying on the table"* 1902 "Does the Race of Man Love a Lord?" 440 (Comb. not in OED W S C)

specialty, sb. [?AB³] *The people in these old lands seem to make churches their specialty* 1869 IA xvii 164. *His specialty is a wonderful knack in the way of deciphering atrocious penmanship* 1875 SNO 279. *Advertisements inviting everybody to buy his specialty, which was a three-dollar shoe* 1892 AmCl xxi 212 (OED 8. A special line of work or business; an article specially dealt in or stocked. 1860.. So W S C U. A in M: *Specialty*, in America, is always accented on the first syllable; *speciality*, in England, on the third. The result is two distinct words, though their meaning is identical)

specs, sb. [?AB³] *The specs he set across his nose* 1891 Slovenly Peter (1935) 13 (OED *dial* or *colloq.* 1826.. So W S C. A in B T DN.III,IV)

specter, sb. [B¹] *Such a long-legged, lantern-jawed, unprepossessing-looking specter as he* 1869 IA xv 149 (Oddity, queer person. Cf. M.T.'s use of *phantom* and *sprite*. This sense not in OED W S C)

specter-earl, sb. [B¹] *"The specter-knight of the Kingdom of Dreams and Shadows is become a specter-earl!"* 1881 PP xxviii 337 (Comb. not in OED W S C)

specter-knight, sb. [B¹] See above (Comb. not in OED W S C)

spectral, a. [B¹] *Must he go down in his spectra, nightdress?* 1892 AmCl vii 73 (Odd, queer, eccentric. Cf. *specter*, above. This sense not in OED W S C)

speech-vehicle, sb. [B¹] *He is so hampered by his imperfect speech-vehicle that he seldom succeeds in saying exactly what he is trying to say* 1909 "A Capable Humorist" 13 (Comb. not in OED W S C)

spell, sb. [AB³] *"Gents, you'll have to turn out a spell"* 1872 RI iii 30 (OED 4d. For a time. In U.S., without prep. 1834.. So B Th.III. Not A in W S C)

spell, sb. for a spell. [?AB²] *I put up for a spell* 1856 Adv. of T. J. Snodgrass (1928) 31. *He held in for a spell* 1880 TA iii 39 (OED 4d. 1862.. A in DN.III AS.II.365. Phrase not in W S C)

spell, v. [A?C] *It was my watch, so I had to stay by the works...Then Tom came up and spelled me, and me and Jim had a swim* 1894 TSA viii 353 (OED 1. To take the place of a person at some work. Now *U.S.* 1595.. So B T H DN.II,III,IV,V,VI AS.III.365. W: *Obs* exc. *Cant.* U: *rare*. Not A or *obs* in S C)

spell down, v. [AB³] *The Friday-afternoon session always closed with spelling down* 1906 Autob (1924) II 68 (OEDS 3e. To put a person down in spelling. *U.S.* 1853.. So W. Comb. not in S C)

spelling-fight, sb. [?AB¹] *There were reading exercises and a spelling-fight* 1876 TS xxi 170 (Comb. not in OED W S C)

spick-and-span, a. [?AB³] *A spick-and-span new blue cloth uniform* 1880 TA ii 22 (OED 2b. 1857.. So W S C U. A in DN.III AS.V.128)

spider-strand, sb. [B¹] *The Schnurrtobel Bridge... swings its gossamer frame down through the dizzy air, over a gorge, like a vagrant spider-strand* 1880 TA xxix 308 (Comb. not in OED W S C)

spider's web, sb. [B¹] *They liked a touch of mystery along with their medicine in the olden time... A dying woman... was forced to swallow several wads of "Spiders-web"* 1890 "Majestic Literary Fossil" 442 (This *spec* medical use not mentioned in OED W S C; but cf. OED Cobweb-pill, quot. 1809 *Med. Jrnl.* XXI 355, "I immediately gave him a cobweb pill, for cobweb pills were among the hospital formulae")

spider-webby, a. [B¹] *The rain would thrash along by so thick that the trees off a little ways looked dim and spider-webby* 1884 HF ix 74 (Comb. not in OED W S C)

spignel, sb. [C] See *afarabocca* 1894 (OED The aromatic root of the umbelliferous plant *Meum athamanticum,* used, when dried and ground, in medicine as a carminative or stimulant. *Obs.* 1502..1718. Not *obs* in W S C)

spike-tailed coat, sb. [AB¹] *Would we not miss a spike-tailed coat and kids?* 1870 CRG (1919) iv 26 (W Spiketail coat, *slang, U.S.* So Cl Th.III, 1880. Not A in S. Comb. not in OED C)

spin, v. [?C] *He took his game-bag, powder, gun, And fiercely to the fields he spun* [German, Und lief hinaus ins Feld geschwind.] Footnote on *spun:* "Baby, you must take note of this awkward form of speech and never use it, except in translating. M.T." 1891 *Slovenly Peter* (1935) 12 (OED 9. To run quickly. 1400.. W: *obs* in this sense. S C: *colloq.*)

spinning-stick, sb. [?AB¹] *Here comes the white woman running from the house, her spinning stick in her hand* 1884 HF xxxii 330 (Comb. not in OED W S C. Apparently another name for *spindle,* defined in W as follows: In hand spinning, a round stick tapering toward each end, with a notch or catch at one end to hold the yarn. In using, the spindle is twirled around, usually by a movement against the right leg, to twist the yarn)

spiral-shaped, ppl.a. [B¹] *It was a spiral-shaped fossil* 1880 TA xlix 568 (Comb. not in OED W S C)

spiral twist, sb. [B¹] *He noticed that I needed some lightning-rods.. He said he could furnish "zinc-plated spiral twist" at 30 cents* 1870 SNO (1875) 21. *He called the Department of Biblical Exegesis the Spiral Twist "for short." He said it was always difficult to drive a straight text through an unaccommodating cork, but that if you twisted it it would go* 1907 CS II vii 197 (Comb. not in OED W S C. But it was earlier used by Poe in the 1831 version of "Fairyland")

spirit-contenting, ppl.a. [B¹] *It is no matter about the bad boy's act. Whatever it was, he had a spirit-contenting reason for it* 1906 "WIM" (1917) ii 24 (Comb. not in OED W S C)

Spiritualism, sb. [?AB³] *To whom does Spiritualism appeal?* 1902 "Chr.Sc." 762 (OED 3. 1855.. So W U. S: Usually considered to have begun about 1848, in the United States; so C)

spiritualist, sb. [?AB³] *A pilot whom I used to steer for is become a spiritualist* 1883 LM xlviii 480. *A crowd was as bad for a magician's miracle in that day as it is for a spiritualist's miracle in mine* 1889 CY xxii 271. *Mr. Myers, President of the London Psychical Research Society,... was a spiritualist* 1901 *Letters* (1917) II xl 707. See also *Allopath* 1902; *Congregationalist* 1906; *Adventist* 1907 (OED 4. A believer in the modern spiritualism. 1859.. So W U. A in S C B F)

spiritualistic, a. [?AB³] See *medium* 1883 [OED 2. 1865.. So W S C U. Cf. above)

spiritualize, v. [B²] *About it a drowsing air of repose to spiritualize it* 1869 IA xliv 456 (OED 1c. 1889. So W S C U)

spit, sb. **the spit and image of.** [?AB³] *"You're the spit'n image of Jubiter"* 1896 TSD ii 347 (OED 3b. The exact counterpart. 1869.. So W Wr. Cf. also Wr,

spitten image, and the Irish phrase "William is the spit out of his father's mouth," cited in P. W. Joyce, *Eng. as We Speak It in Ireland,* p.142. A in DN.I,III, IV,V,VI AS.V.86,125,209,496. Phr. not in S C)

spit-ball, sb. [AB³] *Six boys... with secret spit-ball designs on the bald-headed man dozing below c*1870 Letter in Clara Clemens's *My Father* (1931) 10. *So awed were they by the presence of a living United States Senator, that during three minutes not a "spit-ball" was thrown* 1873 GA liii 479 (OEDS *U.S.* 1.1846.. So B T H. Not A in W S C)

spittoon, sb. [?AB³] *The darky boy who purifies the Department spittoons... represents Political Influence* 1873 GA xxiv 223 (OED 1840.. So W S C U. A in Th T M)

splattery, a. [?AB¹] *"I knowed him by his old green baize work-gown with a splattery white patch in the middle of the back"* 1896 TSD xi 530 (Not in OED W S C)

splint-bottom, a. [AB²] *The master, throned on high in his great splint-bottom arm chair, was dozing* 1876 TS vi 68. *I had been confined... by day to a splint-bottom chair* 1906 *Autob* (1924) II 124 (OEDS *U.S.* 1876, quot. from TS... Not A in W. Comb. not in S C)

splint-bottomed, ppl.a. [AB³] *Their splint-bottomed chairs tilted back against the wall* 1875 OTM 70. (OEDS *U.S.* 1850.. So DN.II. Not A in W S C)

split, v. [?AB¹] See *skyugle* 1865 (Apparently, to strike a rending or splitting blow; to 'tear into.' This obviously *slang* use not in OED W S C)

split, sb. [?AB¹] *"You dash-dashed split between a tired mud-turtle and a crippled hearse-horse!"* 1875 OTM 73 (This sense not in OED W S C. Perhaps a *fig* use of *split* in the sense of mixed drink, half-and-half; cf. DN.III,IV)

split-bottom, a. [AB³] *I got the old split-bottom chair* 1884 HF vi 46 (OED *U.S.* OEDS 1838.. So DN.III, n.w.Ark.: Home-made chair with a cane bottom. Not A in W S. Comb. not in C)

split-bottomed, ppl.a. [AB³] *"Split"-bottomed chairs here and there, some with rockers* 1897 *Autob* (1924) I 103 (OED *U.S.* OEDS 1843.. Not A in S C. Comb. not in W)

spoil, v. **to be spoiling (spiling) for.** [AB³E] *"Dey's jes a-spi'lin' to see de gen'lemen!"* 1894 PW vi 333 (OED 14b. To long for, desire ardently. Orig.*U.S.* 1865.. Not A in W S C U. The pron. *spile* is called 19th c. *dial* in OED. So W S C Wr. Used in Am. dialects, AS.XI.35)

spondulicks, sb. [AB³] *"I'm derned if I'd live two mile out o' town... not for all his spondulicks"* 1884 HF xiii 113 (OED *slang* orig.*U.S.* Money, cash. 1857.. So W S C U B F Th T M DN.III AS.IV.357)

sponge, sb. **to throw up the sponge.** [?AB³] *He would hang on till they throwed up the sponge, if it was a year* 1865 "Jumping Frog" (1875) 32. *Says I to myself, now he'll throw up the sponge—there ain't no more use* 1884 HF xxix 303. *I throw up the sponge. I pull down the flag. Let us begin on the debts* 1897 *Letters* (1917) II xxxvi 653 (OED 1c. To abandon a contest or struggle. *colloq.* 1860.. So W S C U. A in B)

sponge, sb. **to throw up the sponge.** [?AB¹] *"One of the boys has gone up the flume... throwed up the sponge ... kicked the bucket... he's dead"* 1872 RI xlvii 333 (To die; an extension of the above. This sense not in OED W S C)

spook, v. [?AB³] *The court's persistent fashion of coming back to that subject every little while and spooking around it and prying into it was not to pass the time* 1896 JA III viii 300 (OED 2. *intr.* 1890.. So W S C. *Spook,* sb., is A in F Cl Th T DN.III,V AS.X.171)

spool, sb. **spool of thread.** [AB¹] *"It takes her a week to buy a spool of thread and trade a hank of yarn"* 1873 GA i 29. *Reeling off his tranquil spool of lies* 1883 LM xxiv 265 (H: In Am. the term *spool of thread* is used to denote what in Eng. is called a *reel of cotton.* So Th M. Comb. not in OED W S C)

spoon vittles, sb. [?AB³] *"Meat first, and spoon vittles to top off on"* 1884 HF xxi 213 (OED Spoon, sb. 9a. 1880. So W S C Wr. A in B DN.III,IV,V)

spoony, a. [?AB³] See *flat,* sb. 1892 (OED 2. Sentimentally or foolishly amorous. 1836.. So W S C U. A in DN.III)

spot, sb. **to knock the spots out of.** [AB³] *He howled and spread around and swelled up his chest, and just knocked the spots out of any acting ever I see before* 1884 HF xxi 206 (OED 4c. To beat thoroughly, surpass, excel. Orig.*U.S.* 1867.. So S C Th,1861. Cf. Th: The phrase may have originated in the practice of using cards as targets in pistol-shooting. Phr. not in W)

spot, v. [?AB³] *"We lay out a line, spot the good land, enter it up, know where the stations are to be, spot them, buy lots"* 1873 GA xii 120. See *put up* 1880. *"Why, I spotted you for a boy when you was threading the needle"* 1884 HF xi 96 (OED 9b. *colloq.* To mark or note; to recognize or detect. 1860.. So W S C U. A in B M DN.II,III)

spot cash, sb. [?AB²] *Please deliver with all convenient dispatch at my house in Riverdale at lowest rates for spot cash* 1906 *"Letter to Sec. of Treasury"* 229 (OEDS Commercial. Cash down, ready money. 1907.. So W S U. A in Th.III,1900. Phr. not in C)

spout, sb, **up the spout.** [B³] *The king "put it up the spout." (From the Greek...meaning "pawned it")* 1897 FE lxix 700 (OED 4b. 1812.. So W S C U. Evidently British slang; had the phrase been an Americanism, M.T. would not have felt it needed explanation)

spread, sb. [?AB³] *That spread laid everything in the shade that ever that crowd had seen before* 1889 CY xxxii 411 (OED 7. A banquet, feast. 1822.. So W S C U. A in B T DN.II)

spread, v. [AB²] See *spot,* sb. 1884. *"We see Jubiter Dunlap here spreading around in the very same disguise Jake told us he was going to wear"* 1896 TSD xi 534 (OED 7b. *absol. U.S.* To make a display, show off. 1897.. So Wr B F Th T. This sense not in W S C)

spread, v. [?AB¹] *"Bow your necks and spread, for the pet Child of Calamity's a-coming!"* 1883 LM iii 46 (Scatter, disperse. This sense not in OED W S C)

spread-eagle, a. [AB³] *The duke got out his book and read the parts over in the most splendid spread-eagle way, prancing around and acting at the same time* 1884 HF xx 194 (OED 4b. *U.S.* Bombastic, extravagant. 1858.. So W S U B F Cl Th M. See *Academy* 1908, LXXV 474. Not A in C)

spread oneself, v. [AB³] See *walk,* sb. 1871. *The superintendent had always made the boy come out and "spread himself"* 1876 TS iv 46. *Nobody could spread himself like Tom Sawyer in such a thing as that* 1884 HF vii 52 (OED 7b. *refl. U.S.* To exert oneself. 1857.. So W S C Wr B F Cl Th T M DN.II,III)

spread open, v. [?AB¹] See *mark twain* 1873 (Steamboat term: To push the engines to their utmost. An extension of the sense above? Not in OED W S C)

spree, sb. [?AB³] *They all got on a spree* 1872 RI xvi 130. *They would be calculating to go ashore for a spree* 1883 LM iii 43 (OED Chiefly *colloq.* 2. 1808.. So W S C U Wr. A in Th T DN.III)

spree, v.trans. [?AB²] *It was the remittance-man's custom to...spree away the rest of his money in a single night* 1897 FE i 33 (OEDS 1928. The trans. sense not in W S C)

spreeing, vbl.sb. [?AB²] *The drunkenness (and sometimes pretty reckless spreeing) ceased before he came East* 1885 *Letters* (1917) II xxv 457 (OED 1890. Not in W S C)

spring, v. [?AB²] *"Old Mr. Jones is going to try to spring something on the people here to-night"* 1876 TS xxxiv 265. See *nub* 1889. *It is not like studying German, where you mull along, in a groping, uncertain way, for thirty years; and at last, just as you think you've got it, they spring the subjunctive on you, and there you are c*1880 *"Taming the Bicycle"* (1917) 288 (OED 21d. To bring an announcement, etc. suddenly upon a person. 1884.. So W S C U)

spring-book, sb. [B¹] *Your suggestion that my new spring-book bear that name arrives too late* 1892 *Letters* (1917) II xxxii 573 (A book issued in the spring. Nonce comb.)

spring chicken, sb. [AB¹] *Spring chickens thirteen hundred years old* 1889 CY xi 130. *My remotest ancestors are but spring chickens compared with these robed and stately antiques* 1893 PW Intro. 233 (Young or inexperienced person. So S DN.III,V AS.II.365; V.128. Not in OED W C in *fig* sense)

spring fever, sb. [?AB³] *I had the "spring fever" and wanted a change* 1872 RI lv 398. *Me and Tom Sawyer had the spring fever* 1896 TSD i 344 (The listless feeling caused by the first sudden increase of temperature in the spring. So OED *Spring,* sb. 7a. 1859. So W S. A in C B DN.III)

spring-line, sb. [?AB¹] *"Come ahead on the stabboard! Get out that headline! Come—out with your spring-line! ...Take a turn round that stump with the bight of it!"* 1876 TS ii 29 (When the steamboat approaches a landing, ropes are run out from the forward bitts or cleats to the shore or dock to hold the boat steady. Of these the head-line runs from the head of the boat forward or up-stream, the breast-line at right angles, and the spring-line aft. The last-named is so called because it takes up or checks the tendency of the boat to "spring" or drift off. This sense not in OED W S C)

spring-mattress, sb. [?AB²] *Our guide fidgeted about as if he had swallowed a spring-mattress* 1869 IA xxvii 290 (OED Spring, sb. 25a. 1875. So W C U. Not in S)

spring step, sb. [B¹] *The same slender figure, the same tight curls, the same spring step* 1883 LM xlviii 475 (Comb. not in OED W S C)

sprint, sb. [?AB³] *All followed the sprint she made for the wickiup* 1902 *"DBDS"* 322 (OED 2. 1865.. So W S C U. Called A in Wr, this quot.)

sprite, sb. [B¹] *The officer saluted and fell back. The New Jersey sprite bowed in return* 1869 IA xv 149 (Not in OED W S C in this sense: oddity, queer person, 'freak.' Cf. Mark Twain's use of *phantom, specter*)

spry, a. [A] *"They're young and spry, and k'n easy earn a livin'"* 1884 HF xxvi 267. *"I always had an idea that in heaven we would all be young, and bright, and spry"* 1907 *"Capt. Stormfield"* 48 (OED Current in Eng. dials., but more familiar as an Americanism. 1.1789.. So C Wr B Cl Th M DN.III,IV,V,VI AS.V. 303,VI.301. Not A in W S U)

spume-spray, sb. [B¹] *Shedding foam-flakes like the spume-spray that drives before a typhoon* 1872 RI xxiv 182 (Comb. not in OED W S C)

spunk-water, sb. [AB¹] *"He took and dipped his hand in a rotten stump where the rain-water was...trying to cure warts with spunk-water...You've got to go all by yourself, to the middle of the woods, where you know there's a spunk-water stump"* 1876 TS vi 65 (This term is explained by Mr. Vance Randolph, AS.VIII.1.52, as used in the Ozarks: "Rain water which remains in cavities of trees or stumps, used in removing warts, etc.". Comb. not in OED W S C. Cf. OED Spunk, sb. 3. One or other of various fungoid growths on trees. 1665.. Spunk is defined in DN.I as "punk," and in DN.V, s.w.Mo., as "rotten wood")

spur, sb. [B³] See *lead,* sb. 1869; *arrastre* 1909 (OED 11c. A branch of a lode, railway, etc. 1833. So W S C)

squally, a. [AB³] *It was rather squally times, but any port in a storm* 1883 LM xxix 319. *Things looked squally* 1889 CY xxxix 507 (OED 3. *fig* Chiefly *U.S.* 1814.. Not A in W S C U)

squalmish, a. [AB¹E] *I am very tired of being seasick... All I take an interest in is being squalmish and getting* *to shore again* 1867 *Notebook* (1935) vi 59 (Wr: squeamish, *dial* and *Amer.* So B. Cl: *Squawmish*, in parts of New England, said for queasy; so DN.I. Cf. also DN.V: *Squamish*=nauseating or squeamish; so AS.V.126. Word not in OED W S C. Cf. OED Squeamish: 16-17c. *Squamish, north. dial.* Cf. W Squeamish: Perhaps confused with *qualmish;* so C. This form not in S)

square, sb. [A] *It was a handsome mansion on the square opposite the President's house* 1873 GA xxxix 349 (OED 12b. *U.S.* A block of buildings bounded by streets. 1700.. So S B Cl Th T M. Not A in W C U)

square, adv. [AB²] *He shot the dragon square in the center of his cavernous mouth* 1880 TA xvii 152. *Tom rose square up in bed* 1884 HF xlii 431. See *flat out* 1894 (OEDS 3b. *U.S.* 1902.. Not A in W C. Not in S as adv.)

square, v. [?AB³] *I have been up to Sacramento and squared accounts with the Union* 1866 *Letters* (1917) I v 119. *He wanted to pay his little bill...*"*I'll square it next time I'm in Berlin*" 1902 "Belated Russian Passport" (1928) 178 (OED 5c. *colloq.* To put a matter straight; to settle satisfactorily. 1853.. So W S C U. A in Cl)

square away, v. [?AB¹] *I didn't waste any time...but squared away for business* 1889 CY xxxvii 479 (Not in any dict. in this *fig* sense: To make ready, put oneself in condition. A *transf.* use from the *Naut.* sense in OED Square, v. 12c. To sail away with the yards squared. 1887.. Cf. AS.IV.382: "A ship was squared away when her direction was changed to that of the prevailing wind. The yards were then turned to a direction at right angles with the deck, i.e. squared, and under approximately such conditions most ships could be counted upon to show their best speed.")

square crossing, sb. [?AB¹] "*Square crossing, ain't it?*" "*Yes, but the upper bar's working down fast*" 1875 OTM 221 (*Naut.* phrase, not in OED W S C. A "crossing" at approximately right angles to the river. Cf. *crossing,* above)

square deal, sb. [AB²] *I thought I had better give him a square deal* 1883 LM lii 514 (OEDS Square, a. 8a. orig. *U.S.* 1895.. So in AS.I.2. Not A in W S. Not in C)

squarely, adv. [AB³] "*Tom, tell me squarely—didn't he find any fault?*" 1894 PW xii 776 (OED 5c. *fig.* Plainly.. *U.S.* 1860.. So Th. Not A in W S C U)

square meal, sb. [AB³] *They wanted what they term in California "a square meal"* 1869 IA xxxiv 377 (OED Square, a. 10f. Orig. *U.S.* 1868.. So B Cl Th,1867 M. Not A in W S C U F)

square off, v. [AB²] *I ran against another man and he squared off for a fight* 1864 SS (1926) 155 (OEDS Square, v. 11. To put oneself into a position of defence. *U.S.* 1864, this quot. So AS.XII.156, quot. 1856. Not A in W S C)

square oneself, v. [?AB¹] *Caesar...squared himself to receive his assailants* 1864 SNO (1875) 165 (To square off, square up to. Cf. above, also OED Square, v.intr. 11. This refl. use not in OED W S C)

square up, v. [?AB²] "*When he squared up, there warn't nothing left but sixteen dollars*" 1884 HF xx 190 (OED 5d. *absol.* To settle a debt, etc. 1904, only ex. So W S C)

squash, sb. [A] See *biscuit* (OED From Am. Indian. A fruit of the bush gourd. 1. 1643.. So W S C U B F Cl Th T M)

squatter, sb. [A] *Hannibal was but a "wood-yard" surrounded by a few huts belonging to some hardy "squatters"* 1852 "The Dandy Frightening the Squatter" (1930) 447. *In America you take off your hat to no squatter...the word indicates the possessor of few acres and a doubtful title* 1897 FE xi 126 (OED 1. *U.S.* A settler having no formal or legal title. 1788.. So C B F Cl Th T M H DN.V,VI AS.VII.9. Not A in W S)

squatter, sb. [B³] *In Australia when you speak of a squatter you are supposed to be speaking of a millionaire* 1897 FE xi 126 (OED 2. *Austr.* One occupying a tract of pastoral land as a tenant of the crown; a grazier or sheep-farmer, esp. on a large scale. 1840.. So W S C U)

squaw, sb. [A] *The New England Indians and their squaws looked on in wondering silence* 1883 LM xxvii 296. See also *hat* 1889; *buck,* sb. 1906 (OED 1. A North American Indian woman or wife. 1634.. So W S C U B Cl F M DN.VI)

squaw-man, sb. [AB³] "*He is a bad sort. Trap-robber, horse-thief, squaw-man, renegado*" 1906 "Horse's Tale" 336 (OEDS A white who marries a North American Indian woman. 1866.. So W S C U F Cl M DN.I,IV AS.VII.3)

squeal, v. [?AB³] See *pull,* v. 1902 (OED 3. *slang.* To turn informer. 1865.. So W S C U Wr. A in B F Cl T DN.III,IV)

squeeze, v. [AB¹] *He was just getting ready to squeeze the shorts to-day* 1889 CY xl 516 (W: *squeeze the shorts. Exchanges.* To force parties who have sold short to pay high prices for covering their deliveries. This sense not in OED S C. A in Cl)

squelch, v. [?AB³] See *entrails* 1889. *I am hoping to eternally and everlastingly squelch your vanity* 1899 "MCH" (1900) 53. (OED 1b. *fig.* To suppress. 1864.. So W S C U Wr. A in F Cl DN.III)

squench, v. [?A] "*I squench the thunder when I speak!*" 1883 LM iii 45 (OED Now *dial.* To suppress, quell. 1577..1610. OEDS Now *dial.* and *colloq.* 1865.. So W S C. Wr: *dial* and *Amer.* So DN.I,V)

squire, sb. [?A] "*Squire*" *Hawkins got his title from being postmaster of Obedstown* 1873 GA i 17. See *General* 1873 (OED 5a. Any lawer or prominent citizen; loosely and generally as a title. 1645.. So W. A in S C F Cl Th H)

squire, sb. [AB³] *Squire Oliver Montague, a lawyer* 1873 GA xxi 196 (OED 6. *U.S.* A lawyer or judge. 1817.. So W S C B F Cl Th M DN.V)

squirm, v. [A] *To charge the editor of a neighboring country paper with a piece of gratuitous rascality and "see him squirm"* 1871 SNO (1875) 94. *He joggled and boggled On his chair and squirmed* [German, Er trappelt und zappelt] 1891 *Slovenly Peter* (1935) 18 (OED 1. *intr.* Chiefly *U.S.* and *dial* 1691.. So B F Cl Th,1804 DN.III,V. Not A in W S C U)

squirm, v. [?AB¹] *An effort was made to squirm it into some aspect or other that the moral and religious could contemplate with edification* 1876 TS xxi 171. See *cream-yellow* 1897 (An extension of the *intr.* sense illustrated above. This *trans.* meaning not in OED W S C)

sqush, v. [AB¹] *He'd 'a' squshed down like a bluff bank that the river has cut under* 1884 HF xxix 303 (Here *intr.*: to collapse, fall into a pulpy mass. This sense not in any dict. An extension of the *trans.* sense in W: To squash, mash. *dial.* A in B F T DN.III,IV. Cf. Wr: *Squish,* to squash to a pulpy mass. Not in OED S C)

stack, sb. [?AB²] "*Never saw such a stack of them in one establishment*" 1870 SNO (1875) 25. See *water-moccasin* 1884. *Stacks of money had been placed in the bank for him* 1892 AmClm xxiv 253 (OED 1b. A quantity, a 'pile.' 1894.. OEDS Often in *pl.*='heaps.' *slang.* 1903.. So W S C. A in DN.III)

stack up, v. [?AB²] *My billiards table is stacked up with books relating to the Sandwich Islands* 1884 *Letters* (1917) II xxiv 440 (OED Stack, v. 4. To pile materials on. 1892. So S. This sense not in W C)

staff, sb. [C] *Their halberd staves were covered with crimson velvet* 1881 PP ix 105 (OED 3c. *Obs* 1515.. 1708. Not *obs* in W S C)

stage, sb. [AB³] *The stumps there are out of water at this stage* 1875 OTM 219 (OED 1j. *U.S.* A level of water. 1814.. So W AS.II.31. Not in S C)

stage, sb. [?A] *There were no stages out, and we could not get on the pier from the ship* 1869 IA x 93. *The broad stage is run far out over the port bow* 1875 OTM 70 (OED 4g. A landing stage. 1773... So W S C. A in AS.VI.57)

stage, sb. [AB²] *I went to the Exchange yesterday and deposited myself in a Fairmount stage* 1853 Letter in

Iowa Journal of History (July, 1929) 411. *The Phila. bus drivers cannot cheat. In the front of the stage is a thing like an office clock* 1853 *Letters* (1917) I i 28. See also *frontier* 1872 (OED 9c. *U.S.* An omnibus. No ex. So S C. Not A in W U)

stage-carpentering, vbl.sb. [B¹] *He had to retire from his profession of stage-carpentering* 1899 "Chr.Sc. and the Book" 593 (Comb. not in OED W S C)

stage-coaching, vbl.sb. [B³] *It is hard work to make railroading pleasant in any country...Stage-coaching is infinitely more delightful* 1869 IA xii 106. *It was fascinating—that old Overland stage-coaching* 1872 RI iv 39 (OED 1844.. So W S. Not in C)

stage-courtier, sb. [B¹] *He bent his body forward three times at the hips, as the stage-courtier does* 1880 TA xxxviii 440 (Comb. not in OED W S C)

stage-direction, sb. [B¹] *His "stage-directions"— those artifices which authors employ to throw a kind of human naturalness around a scene and a conversation* 1906 "Howells" (1917) 235 (Not in any dict. in this sense. Cf. OED Stage, sb. 13. A direction in a written or printed play. 1790.. So W S C U. Here *transf.* to corresponding passages in a novel)

stage-fright, sb. [B²] *A ghastly stage-fright seized him* 1876 TS xxi 169 (OED 1878.. So W S C U)

stage-office, sb. [AB¹] *The first thing we did was to hunt up the stage-office, and pay...for tickets per overland coach* 1872 RI ii 22 (Comb. not in OED W S C. Cf. Stage = omnibus, above)

stage-plank, sb. [?AB¹] *The deck-hand who stood on the end of the stage-plank with the coil of rope in his hand* 1875 OTM 70 (Comb. not in OED W S C. Cf. Stage = landing-stage, above)

stage-whispering, ppl.a. [B¹] *"The captain's voice!" said the stage-whispering ruffian* 1883 LM xxxi 341 (Comb. not in OED W S C)

stagger, sb. [?AB²] *He would make one more stagger at it anyway* 1866 *Screamers* (1871) xxix 149 (OED 3. dial and slang. An attempt. 1880.. So W. A in S Wr DN.II. Not in C)

stair-step, sb. [?AB³] *"De sta'r-steps is broke down"* 1894 PW viii 340 (OED 1833.. So W. A in DN.I,III. Comb. not in S C)

stake, sb. **to pull up stakes.** [AB³] *I always intended to be so situated that I can "pull up stakes" and clear out whenever I feel like it* 1861 *Letters* (1917) I iii 62 (OED 1e. *U.S.* To move one's habitation. 1830..So W B F Cl Th M. Not A in S. Phr. not in C)

stake, sb. [?AB³] *Leave a stake of turnips and such or Millet to live on for a few days* 1893 "Is He Living?" (1900) 248 (OED 4. *slang.* 1812.. So W S U. A in DN.V. Not in C)

stake, v. [AB³] *Tom staked him with marbles to play "keeps" with* 1894 PW iv 330. *"Run over him; we'll stake you"* 1902 "DBDS" (1928) 309 (OEDS 5. To furnish with money or supplies. *U.S.* a1889.. So DN.III AS.X.21. Not A in W S C U. Not in C)

stale, a. [?AB¹] *I know the art of searching for a trail, and I know the stale track form the fresh* 1906 "Horse's Tale" 327 (W: Not new; not freshly made. This sense not in OED S C)

stall, v. [AC] *It seemed a prompt good way of weeding out people that had got stalled* 1894 TET Intro. 314 (OED 11b. esp. in *pass.* To become stuck. Now only *U.S.* or *dial.* c1460..1821. So Wr B F Cl Th H DN.II, III, IV, V. Not A in W S C U)

stampede, sb. [AB³] *A terrific hubbub and wild stampede* 1869 IA xiv 137. See *panic* 1869 (OED b. Orig. *U.S.* transf. 1846.. So B Th T M DN.III. Not A in W S C U)

stand, sb. [?AB²] See *well,* a. 1889. *Edwin Booth made a one-night stand there with his troupe* 1906 *Autob* (1924) I 329 (OED 2e. *Theatr.* 1896.. So W S C U)

stand, sb. [A] *We can resume Business at the old stand* 1901 "To the Person Sitting in Darkness" 176

(OED 16a. *U.S.* A position, site, or building for a business. 1787.. So S B F Cl Th H AS.II.27. Not A in W S C)

Standard Oil Trust, sb. [AB¹] *We had nine barrels of cod-liver oil and it lasted me nine years...I was the first Standard Oil Trust. I had it all* 1905 *Speeches* (1910) 431 (Nonce use)

stand-by, sb. [?AB³] *"A Frenchman's got his little stand-by for a dull time, too"* 1895 "What Bourget Thinks" 62 (OEDS 3. A chief resource. Earlier U.S.ex. 1819.. A in DN.III. Not A in W S C U)

stand from under, v. [AB³] *You make up your mind that the earthquake is due; you stand from under, and take hold of something to steady yourself* 1879 *Speeches* (1910) 62. *There warn't nothing to do but just hold still and try and be ready to stand from under when the lightning struck* 1884 HF xxxii 334 (OEDS *fig.* To escape, get into a place of safety. *U.S.* 1857.. So W S C)

standing-galley, sb. [?AB¹] *On its way to the standing-galley Tilbury's notice got pied* 1904 "Bequest" (1906) iii 15. See also *plant out* 1906; *comp* 1909 (C: An immovable inclined plane, fitted with cleats, on which type is kept standing. Comb. not in OED W S)

stand-off, sb. [AB²] *It was about a stand-off; so both of them had to whoop up their dangerous adventures, and try to get ahead that way* 1893 TSA i 21 (OED *U.S.* 3. A draw or tie, as in a game. 1895.. So DN.II,III. Not A in W S C)

stand pat, v. [AB³] *"I drew and didn't fill. That's where I'm so often weak in the game. If I had stood pat— but I didn't"* 1904 "Bequest" (1906) iii 14 (OED 14. *U.S.* In Poker, to play one's hand just as it has been dealt. 1882.. So W S Th T M H DN.II. Phr. not in C)

standpoint, sb. [?AB³] *The draftsmen were set to making views of the Monument from different standpoints* 1875 SNO 146 (OED 1. 1829.. So W S C U. A in M)

stand a show, v. [AB¹] *A poor chap would stand considerable show with the widow's Providence* 1884 HF iii 18 (A in B: To have a chance. Not A in W. Phrase not in OED S C)

stand-up, sb. [?AB²] *He halted a moment in front of the best restaurant, then glanced at his clothes and passed on, and got his breakfast at a "stand-up"* 1897 FE xiii 143 (OEDS 2. 1920. This sense not in W S C)

star, sb. [?AB¹] *He had been around among the star pupils inquiring* 1876 TS iv 50. *They realized that they had had the star time of their trip* 1906 *Autob* (1924) II 225 (Cf. OED 5. *fig.* b. Chiefly *colloq.* One who "shines." 1850.. So W S C U. Here used *attrib,* and, by extension, of experiences as well as of persons. A in Th DN.II)

starboard, a. Spelled **stabboard.** [E] See *wheel,* sb. 1869; *outside,* sb.1876; *set back* 1876, 1883; *large,* a.1880; *larboard* 1884. *I was on watch and boss of the stabboard oar* 1883 LM iii 50 (OED 1495.. This sp. not mentioned in OED W S C)

starchy, a. [?AB¹] See *snappy* 1871; *Southron* 1883. *"Starchy clothes—very. You think you're a good deal of a big-bug, don't you?"* 1884 HF v 31. *We got ourselves up in the very starchiest of the Professor's duds for the blow-out* 1894 TSA xi 397. *Tom waves his hand, oh, ever so fine and starchy* 1896 TSD xi 531 (Cf. OED 4. *fig.* Of a person: Stiff, formal, precise. 1828.. So W S C U. Here, by extension: Pretentious, 'high-toned,' would-be impressive. A favorite word with Mark Twain)

Stars and Stripes, sb. [A] *She swept superbly by and flung the Stars and Stripes to the breeze* 1869 IA vii 64. *They ran up the Stars and Stripes and steered for California* 1870 SNO (1875) 156 (OED 6b. 1782.. So W S C U B F Cl AS.IV.10)

star-spangled banner, sb. [AB¹] *A robe...that was a very star-spangled banner of curved and sinuous bars of black and white* 1869 IA xlix 366. *It had bought them of the star-spangled banner Master-thief* 1887 *Letters* (1917)

II xxvi 480 (Cf. OED Star-spangled. 1814 F. S. Key, title of song.. So W S C U B F Cl. Here *fig*)

star-stuff, sb. [B²] *"Look what billions and billions of stars there is. How does it come that there was just exactly enough star-stuff?"* 1894 TSA ix 356 (OED Star, sb. 16b. 1902. Comb. not in W S C)

start, v. [?AB¹] *You couldn't start a face in that town that I didn't know* 1884 HF x 86 (Bring forward, present, introduce. This sense not in OED W S C)

starter, sb. [AB³] *He would begin to groan, as a "starter," as he called it* 1876 TS vi 61. *For a starter I would go to work and steal Jim out of slavery again* 1884 HF xxxi 321 (OEDS 7. *colloq U.S.* 1873. Not A in W S C)

start in, v. [AB²] *"So when some roughs jumped the Catholic bone-yard and started in to stake out town lots in it, he went for 'em"* 1872 RI xlvii 334. See *fantods* 1880. *He would start in to do it, too* 1892 AmCl xxi 214 (OED 12d. *U.S.* 1872, this quot.. So C M H. Not A in W U. Not in S)

start out, v. [?AB²] *He had started out on a high emprise* 1892 AmCl xv 153 (OED 12d. 1897, only ex. A in F Cl M H. Not A in S C. Not in W)

State, sb. [A] *I have only seen two or three bank bills since I have been in the State* 1853 Letters (1917) I i 26. See also *hail from* 1869; *water-supply* 1883; *Senator* 1892 (OED 31c. One of...the United States of America. 1774.. So W S C U B F Th)

State, sb. **the States.** [?A] *From thence back to San Francisco—and then, doubtless, to the States* 1866 Letters (1917) I v 105 (OED 31d. The United States of America. 1777.. So W. A in B F Th AS.IV.10. But S C call it an Anglicism)

state-prison, sb. [AB³] *Serving a nine-year term in a certain state prison for burglary* 1883 LM lii 510 (OED State, sb. 41b. *U.S.* 1828.. So W DN.II. Comb. not in S C)

state-room, sb. [AB³] *I rejoiced to know that a few vacant state-rooms* [on the S.S. Quaker City] *were left* 1869 IA i 24. *On May 26, 1836, he completed the steamer 'Prairie'...the first steamer with a stateroom cabin ever seen at St. Louis* 1883 LM 1 494 (OED 3. *U.S.* A sleeping apartment on a passenger steamer. 1837.. So F Cl T. Not A in W S C)

state-room, sb. [AB³] See *sleeper* 1893. *I picked out a state-room on a train* 1906 Speeches (1910) 137 (OED 3b. *U.S.* A private compartment in a railway train. 1867.. So C F Cl. Not A in W S U)

station-boss, sb. [AB²] *The station-boss stopped dead still* 1872 RI iv 45 (OED 1872, this quot. From OED Station, sb. 19. *U.S.* A place on a coach route. 1797.. Comb. not in W S C)

station-house, sb. [?AB³] *He came home drunk as a piper, and got into the station-house the first thing* 1865 SS (1926) 205 (OED 2.The lock-up attached to a police-station. 1836.. So W S C U. A in B T H)

station-man, sb. [AB¹] See *country-woven* 1872 (Attendant at a place on a coach route. Cf. Station-boss, above. Comb. not in OED W S C)

statistic, sb. [?AB¹] *There is not a statistic wanting* 1880 TA xvi 148. *I began the chapter with this statistic* 1894 TET 313. *The wary Boston h.c. had thoughtfully concealed that statistic* 1902 Letters (1917) II xli 72. *I am uncertain, and I can't manage a statistic* 1906 Speeches (1910) 324 (On this form OED makes the astonishing statement (Statistic, sb. 1b): "The alleged sense 'a statistical statement' (*Cent.Dict.*), 'any statistical element' (Webster 1911) seems to be merely inferred from the plural use in *Statistics*." The quots. cited above, however, show the singular form in actual use. It seems, indeed, to have been rather a favorite with Mark Twain. W and C are supported on this point by S)

statistics, sb. [B³] *This must be the list of statistics* 1873 GA xlii 381. *Marred in the matter of statistics by*

inaccuracies 1883 LM xxvii 295 (OED 2. 1837.. So W S C U)

statue-rigid, a. [B¹] *Flinging his statue-rigid reflection upon the still water* 1883 LM xliv 445 (Comb. not in OED W S C)

stave, v. [AB³] *Other pedestrians went staving by us with vigorous strides* 1880 TA xxxiv 368 (OED 10. To go with a rush or a dash. *Scotch* and *U.S.* 1819..So B Th T DN.III. Not A in W S C Wr)

staving, ppl.a. [AB³] *You are running it in staving, tip-top, first-class style* 1870 Letters (1917) I ix 169. *"But this one was a staving dream"* 1884 HF xv 132 (OED 2. *U.S.colloq.* As an intensive. 1850.. So B F Cl T DN.I, II,III. Not A in W S. Not in C in this sense)

stay, v. [C] *I was moved to comfort and stay him* 1889 CY xvi 193. *He does need me by him to stay his footsteps* 1892 AmCl xiii 139 (OED 1b. To support, sustain, strengthen, comfort. Now *arch.* 1526..1913. So S. Not *arch* in W C U)

stay, v. [AB²] *"Anything in the world that can stay a Christian stomach!"* 1869 IA x 94. *All the revolting dishes that ever famishing men had stayed their hunger with* 1898 "At the Appetite Cure" (1900) 155 (OED 5b. *U.S.colloq* 1894, first U.S. quot. So B. Not A in W S C U Wr)

stay, v. [C] *"I may not stay ye, being powerless"* 1881 PP xxxii 377 (OED 23. To prevent, hinder, check, restrain. Now *rare* or *poet.* 1560..1852. Not *rare* in W S C U Wr)

stay, v. **stay one's hand.** [C] *"There be times when she stayeth her hand"* 1881 PP iii 41 (OED 23c. Now somewhat *arch.* 1560..1880. Not *arch* in C U. Phr. not in W S)

staying capacity, sb. [B¹] *Resolution and staying capacity.* 1892 AmCl xxi 214 (This comb. not in OED W S C. Cf. OED Staying, ppl.a. 3. *attrib.* and *Comb.,* as...*staying power...staying qualities,* etc.)

stead, sb. **in his stead.** [?C] *A spurious Prince of Wales was being feasted by the city in his stead* 1881 PP x 120 (OED 12d. *In his stead* (c) As a substitute in the place occupied by him (*obs*)...1823. Cf. OED 12d. (d) Instead of him (not called *obs*). The fine distinction drawn by the OED is not observed by W S C U, which do not call the phr. *obs* in any sense)

stead, v. [C] *"An thou would save thy neck, nothing but flight may stead thee"* 1880 PP x 118 (OED 1a. Now *arch.*.1879. So S. Not *arch* in W C)

stead of, prep. [?AC] See *close-fit* 1884 (OED Instead of. Now only *dial.* 1430..1818. *Obs* in C. A in Wr. Not in W S)

steal, sb. [AB²] *An editorial justifying the salary steal on the ground that Congressmen were not paid enough* 1873 Speeches (1923) 47 (OED 1b. *U.S.* and *colonial.* A piece of dishonesty or fraud on a large scale. 1884.. So M. Not A in W S C)

steal a base, v.phr. [AB²] *The boys who ploughed a new equator round the globe stealing bases!* 1889 Speeches (1923) 149. *Then he stole a base—as he called it—that is, slipped from the presence, to keep from getting brayed in his wife's discussion-mill* 1904 "Bequest" (1906) iv 17 (OED 5g. *Baseball.* 1891.. So W S C. Here *fig*)

stealing-raid, sb. [?AB¹] *Wilson tried to connect her with the stealing-raid* 1894 PW xix 24 (Cf. Raid, above. Comb. not in OED W S C)

steamboat, sb. [?A] *"Nancy, you've heard of steamboats, and maybe you believed in them—of course you did"* 1873 GA i 24. See also *nary* 1883; *cough,* v. 1884; *cub* 1909 (OED 1787.. So W C U. A in S: First successfully operated in the U.S. in 1790. A in B T M AS. II.29)

steamboat-boiler, sb. [?AB¹] *It was flaked with rust like an old steamboat-boiler* 1869 IA xlix 517 (Cf. above. Comb. not in OED W S C)

steamboatful, a. [?AB[1]] *I wrote out a passage from Shakespeare—and riddled it with his wild steamboatful interlardings* 1909 ISD i 13 (Characteristic of or associated with steamboats. Not in OED W S C)

steamboating, vbl.sb. [?AB[3]] *He was a great personage in the old steamboating days* 1875 OTM 721. *If there was anything...better than steamboating, it was the glory to be got by telling about it* 1894 PW viii 337 (OED a. 1834.. So W S C. A in B Cl)

steamboat-landing, sb. [?AB[1]] *The Shepherdsons and Grangerfords used the same steamboat-landing* 1884 HF xviii 162 (Comb. not in OED W S C. Cf. Steamboat)

steamboatman, sb. [?AB[1]] *When I was a boy, there was but one permanent ambition among my comrades in our village on the west bank of the Mississippi River. That was, to be a steamboatman* 1875 OTM 69 (Not in OED S C. Given in W. Cf. Steamboat)

steamboat-owner, sb. [?AB[1]] *Steamboat-owners would have to submit* 1875 OTM 729 (Comb. not in OED W S C. Cf. Steamboat)

steamer, sb. [B[3]] *Passage to Albany on the finest steamers that ply the Hudson is now 25 cents* 1853 Letters (1917) I i 25. See also *biscuit* 1880; *state-room* 1883; *sounding-barge* 1906 (OED 1825.. So W S C U. Cf. AS.V. 281)

steam-ferry, sb. [B[1]] *"Go for the steam-ferry"* 1884 HF xiii 114 (Comb. not in OED W S C)

steam-ferryboat, sb. [B[1]] *The old steam-ferryboat was chartered* 1876 TS xxix 218 (Comb. not in OED W S C)

steam-sawmill, sb. [B[1]] *A little steam-sawmill was on the bank* 1884 HF xxxi 322 (Comb. not in OED W S C)

steamship, sb. [?AB[3]] *The participants were to sail away in a great steamship* 1869 IA i 19. See also *cotton-gin* 1889 (OED 1819.. So W S C U. In Am. use restricted to lake and ocean steamers; river steamers being known as steamboats: so AS.II.29)

steamshipping, vbl.sb. [B[1]] *Steamshipping? France has no superiorities over us in that matter* 1895 "What Bourget Thinks" 49 (Not in OED W S C)

steed, sb. [C] See *halidome* 1906 (OED From the 16th c. used only *poet.* or *rhet.* a900..1894. So W S C U)

steel, a. [?AB[2]] *The best picture I have had yet is the steel frontispiece to my new book* 1880 *M.T. the Letter Writer* (1932) iii 48 (OED 14. Engraved on steel. 1884. This sense not in W S C)

steel pen, sb. [B[1]] *Steel pens on his table with the ink-bottle* 1892 AmCl vii 71 (So W. Comb. not in OED S C)

steel-pen-coated, a. [B[1]] *She passed on into the maelstrom of...white-kid-gloved and steel-pen-coated gentlemen* 1873 GA xxxii 290 (Nonce comb.)

steel plate, sb. [?AB[1]] *Steel plates—Trumbull's "Battle of Bunker Hill," and the "Sally from Gibraltar"* 1883 LM xxxviii 403 (The engraving produced from a steel plate. This sense not in OED W S C)

steel ship, sb. [B[1]] See *cotton-gin* 1889 (Comb. not in OED W S C)

steer clear of, v.phr. [?A] *Foreign youth steer clear of the gymnasium* 1880 TA iv 50 (OED 2f. Chiefly *fig.* To avoid completely. 1723.. So W S C U. A in DN.II, III,V)

stem-winder, sb. [AB[3]] *He began to check off the luxuries which he should earliest wish to secure: "Horse—buggy—stem-winder—new teeth"* 1904 "Bequest" (1906) ii 9 (OED *U.S.* A keyless watch. 1875 .. So B F Cl T M H. Not A in W S C U)

stencher, sb. [B[1]] *Columbus's ship was small and very old...suffocating with oil-stench...He turned in, in his little coffin-bunk, and blew out his flickering stencher* 1893 "About All Kinds of Ships" 175 (Nonce word for an ill-smelling lamp)

step out, v. [AB[1]] *I thought what a figure I should cut stepping out amongst the redeemed in such a rig* 1907 "Capt. Stormfield" 44 (To take part in social activities, go into company or "society". Inappropriate to

M.T.'s use here is the def. in W: To indulge in unwonted gaiety, display, extravagance, etc.; hence, to dissipate; to live fast. Neither sense is given in OED S C)

step over, v. [?AB[1]] *He would promptly take ship for America...Yes, he would step over and take a hand in this matter himself* 1892 AmCl xxiii 237 (To cross the ocean, esp. the Atlantic. This sense not in OED W S C)

step-papa, sb. [B[1]] *"Yes, he's my step-papa, and the dearest one that ever was"* 1893 "Bank-Note" (1928) 134 (Comb. not in OED W S C)

stern-countenanced, a. [B[1]] *This stern-countenanced invalid was the dread Henry VIII* 1881 PP v 62 (Comb. not in OED W S C)

stern-line, sb. [?AB[2]] *"Lay her in shore and stand by to jump with the stern-line"* 1880 TA xvii 157 (OED *Naut.* Rope by which a vessel's stern is moored. 1898, only ex. So W S. Not in C)

stern-mark, sb. [?AB[1]] See *head-mark* 1875. *I vaingloriously turned my back and inspected the stern-marks* 1875 OTM 287 (Comb. not in OED W S C)

stern-wheel, a. [?AB[3]] See *side-wheel,* a. 1884 (OED 1856.. So W. A in B F. Not in S C)

sternwheeler, sb. [?AB[3]] *We met lumber-rafts shoved by a powerful stern-wheeler* 1883 LM lviii 571. *We got a chance in a stern-wheeler from away North* 1896 TSD ii 346 (OED 1859.. So C. A in W S U B F Cl AS.VI. 240)

stick, v. [?AC] *You never saw a narrow-minded, self-conceited, almighty mean man in your life but he had stuck in one place ever since he was born* 1867 Speeches (1923) 30. *"He expects everybody to stick at that age—stand stock still—and expects them to enjoy it!"* 1907 "Capt.Stormfield" 49 (OED 6. To remain persistently in a place. Now only *colloq.* 888..1882. Not *arch* in W S C U)

stick, v. [?AB[1]] *The captain of the raft...was as full of history as he could stick* 1880 TA xvii 150 (Not in OED W S C in this sense: To contain, hold, accommodate)

stick, v. to be stuck after. [?AB[1]] *"She untied the raven and fetched him home...In two days she had him so stuck after her that she—well, you know how he follows her everywhere"* 1906 "Horse's Tale" 335 (To have one's mind or fancy set upon. Phr. not in OED W S C. A variation of OED 23d: To be stuck on. *U.S.slang.* 1886..)

stick down, v. [B[1]] *"Stick your head down lower—there, that'll do; you can't be seen now"* 1884 HF xxxii 333 (S: Thrust in any direction. This comb. not in OED W C)

stick it out, v. [?AB[2]] *I have promised Osgood, and must stick it out* 1882 Letters (1917) I xxii 419. *The proprieties required me to stick it out* 1889 CY xxvi 334 (OED 32c. *colloq.* 1901, only ex. So W S C U Wr. A in B F Cl)

stick through, v. [?AB[1]] *"I meant to stick the trip through, for pride's sake"* 1902 "Belated Russian Passport" (1928) 172 (Comb. not in OED W S C. Cf. Stick it out, above)

stick up, v. [B[3]] See *hold up* 1897 (OED 34k. *Australian.* 1846.. So W C U. Comb. not in S)

stiff-brim, a. [B[1]] See *stove-pipe,* 1896 (Comb. not in OED W S C)

stiff-jointed, a. [B[1]] *They felt rusty and stiff-jointed* 1876 TS xiv 142 (Comb. not in OED S C. Given in W)

stiff-standing, ppl.a. [B[1]] *A stiff-standing sentinel at every door* 1889 CY xxxix 497 (Comb. not in OED W S C)

still-hunt, sb. [?AB[3]] *"The professional detective when he has got his clues together and is out on his still-hunt"* 1894 PW xv 818 (OED 2. *transf.* The pursuit of any object quietly or cautiously. 1890.. So S C. A in W F Cl T H)

stock, sb. **to take stock in.** [AB²] *The "chance" theory is calculated to inflict pecuniary loss upon any community that takes stock in it* 1870 SNO (1875) 161 (OEDS 56. To have regard for. Orig. *U.S.* 1874.. So Mait H. Not A in W S C Wr)

stock, v. [?AB¹] *I stocked the business and unloaded* 1889 CY xxii 281. *"Your idea is to sell a part of him... Now mine is...stock him—of course...I'll get up the company and issue the stock, all in good time"* 1892 AmCl xix 197 (To incorporate as a stock company; to issue stock in. Not in OED W S C in this sense)

stock-board, sb. [?AB¹] *He was president of the stock-board* 1889 CY xl 516 (Comb. not in OED W S C in this sense. Cf. Stockholder)

stockholder, sb. [A] *The same stockholders increased the capital* 1883 LM xxxix 411 (OED Now *U.S.* Shareholder. 1753.. So M H. Not A in W S C U)

stogy, a. [AB³] *Each of us put on a rough, heavy suit of clothing, "stogy" boots included* 1872 RI ii 22 (OED a. *U.S.* The distinctive epithet of a rough heavy kind of boots or shoes. 1847.. So F Cl Th T M DN.I,III. Not A in W S C)

stogy, sb. [AB³] See *change off* 1910 (OED b. *U.S.* A long, slender, roughly made cigar. 1892.. So S F Cl Th T. Not A in W C. F has the curious definition: A short, thick cigar)

stomp, v. [?AE] *The woods were full of teams and wagons...stomping to keep off the flies* 1884 HF xx 196 (OED dial pron. of Stamp. So W S C. A in B: To stamp; the pron. *stomp* is almost universal in the U.S. So F T M DN.II,III,IV,V AS.IV.475)

stone-benched, ppl.a. [B¹] *We all stood in the stone-benched amphitheater* 1869 IA xl 420 (Nonce comb.)

stone-breaker, sb. [B¹] See *bung-starter* 1897 (One of M.T.'s invented names for the coppersmith bird, or crimson-breasted barbet of India)

stone-fence, sb. [AB³] See *cocktail* 1869 (OED *U.S.* slang. A name for various intoxicating drinks. 1809.. So W U Th M DN.II,V. Not in S C)

stonemason, sb. [?A] *My class-teacher, Mr. Barclay, the stonemason* 1909 ISD ii 20 (OEDS Earlier Amer. exs. 1758.. Not A in W S C U)

stoop, sb. [A] *The work about the doors, stoops, etc... was composed of this pretty marble* 1853 Letter in *Iowa Journal of Hist* (1929) 411. *We see visiting young ladies stand on the stoop* 1869 IA xxiii 230 (OEDS *U.S.* and *Canada* 1755.. So W S C U B F Cl Th,1749 T M H DN.I,II,III AS.VIII.1.76)

stop, v. [?AB³] *At every hotel we stop at we always have to send out for soap* 1869 IA xix 189 (OED 36. To remain. 1801.. So W S C U Wr. A in B T DN.III)

stop over, v. [AB³] *You renewed your ticket after stopping over in Baltimore* 1873 GA xxiv 218 (OEDS 35b. To make a halt and proceed by a later conveyance. *U.S.* 1857.. So W M H. Not A in S C)

stopper, sb. [B³] *He was shouting with laughter... before he could put on a stopper* 1901 "Two Little Tales" (1928) 204 (OED 2b. *fig.* 1852. So W S C)

store, sb. [A] *By the muddy roadside stood a new log-cabin, one story high—the store* 1873 GA v 56. See *concern* 1884; *frame shop* 1893. *Saladin Foster was book-keeper in the principal store* 1904 "Bequest" (1906) i 1 (OED 12 a. The usual *U.S.* and *colonial* equivalent for Shop. 1740.. So W S C U B F Cl Th T M H DN.V AS.I.492,IV.10)

store, sb. **to keep store.** [A] *He "kept store" there several years* 1870 *Autob* (1924) I 6 (OED 12a. Chiefly *U.S.* 1752.. So Th. Phr. not in W S C)

store, a. [AB³] *Hawkins fitted out his house with "store" furniture from St. Louis* 1873 GA v 60. *Five pounds of "store" candy* 1880 TA xxiii 229. See *nigger-head* 1884; *plug* 1884. *"I made you a white gen'l'man en rich, wid store clothes on"* 1893 PW ix 550 (OED 13d. *U.S.* and *colonial.* In sense of 'purchased or purchasable at a store' 1822.. So W S C B F Cl Th M H DN.II,III)

storiette, sb. [?AB³] *In substance the storiette was as follows* 1897 FE ii 42 (OED 1889.. So W S U. Not in C. A in F)

storm-buffeted, a. [B¹] *We felt a great gladness, like storm-buffeted birds that have found their nest again* 1875 SNO 88 (Comb. not in OED W S C)

storm-gloom, sb. [B¹] *The constantly deepening storm-gloom* 1896 JA III ix 661 (Comb. not in OED W S C)

storm-quarters, sb. [B¹] *Three or four wigwams scattered about the raft's level space for storm-quarters* 1883 LM iii 42 (Comb. not in OED W S C)

storm-rack, sb. [B¹] *The storm-racks were on the table all the way over* 1893 "About All Kinds of Ships" 172 (Comb. not in OED W S C)

storm-scarred, ppl.a. [B¹] *Several lofty storm-scarred towers* 1880 TA xxxv 397 (Comb. not in OED W S C)

storm-wash, sb. [B¹] *A receding of tides, a quieting of the storm-wash to a murmurous surf-beat* 1873 GA lx 543 (Comb. not in OED W S C)

stout, a. [?AC] *"Your word 'stout' means 'fleshy'; our word 'stout' usually means 'strong'"* 1882 "Concerning the American Language" 269 (OED 6. Strong in body. *obs.* c1386..1842. A in Cl: in New England often used for strong; so DN.I,II,III,IV. Neither A nor *obs* in W S C)

stove-lid, sb. [B¹] *She could have seen through a pair of stove-lids just as well* 1876 TS i 18 (Comb. not in OED W S C)

stove-pipe, sb. [?AB³] *Like the end of a burnt-out stove-pipe* 1869 IA xlix 517. *"It ain't rightly a hat at all, but more like my head was shoved up through a jint o' stove-pipe"* 1884 HF vi 43 (OED 2. 1858.. So W S C U. A in T; cf. discussion in DN.II)

stove-pipe, sb. [AB³] *It was the first season anybody wore that kind—a black stiff-brim stove-pipe* 1896 TSD v 356 (OED 3a. A tall hat of cylindrical shape. Orig. *U.S.* 1883.. So W C U B Th,1861 DN.III. Not A in S)

stove-pipe hat, sb. [AB³] See *boiled rag* 1872. *A big white fur stovepipe hat on the back of his head* 1884 HF xxi 217. *He wore a shiny stove-pipe hat* 1889 CY xxi 263 (OED Stove-pipe, sb. Also stove-pipe hat. Orig. *U.S.* 1851.. So W C U B Th T DN.III,V. Not A in S)

stove-polish, v. [B¹] *He said he was after the stove-polish man..."An I do not stove-polish him an I may find him, leave it to me"* 1889 CY xx 241 (Nonce use as verb)

stove-wood, sb. [?AB¹] *Men charged three or four dollars for sawing up stove-wood* 1872 RI xxv 122 (Comb. not in OED S C. Given in W)

straddle, v. [?AB³] *"She'd come cavorting and straddling up"* 1865 "Jumping Frog" (1875) 31 (OED 2. dial. 1825.. So W S C U Wr)

straddle, v. [AB²] See *blind,* sb. 1872 (OED 7. Poker. To double, of a stake, bet. 1882.. So W S C U; also F, under Blind)

straddle-bug, sb. [AB³] *He would follow that straddle-bug to Mexico* 1865 "Jumping Frog" (1875) 31 (OED *U.S.* A long-legged beetle. 1839... So W S C B Th T)

straight, a. [?AB³] *"Come, now, tell a straight story"* 1883 LM iii 59 (OED 6. Of conduct: Frank, honest. 1864.. So W S C U Wr. A in B Cl T)

straight, a. [AB³] *Calaveras possesses "straight" whiskey that will throw a man a double somerset* 1865 SS (1926) 163. *"You'll take whiskey straight or you'll go dry"* 1877 *Speeches* (1910) 4 (OED 9. *U.S.* a. Unmixed, undiluted; of spirits, 'neat.' 1856.. So B F Cl T M H DN.III. Not A in W S C)

straight, a. **to vote the straight ticket.** [AB³] *I have never voted a straight ticket from that day to this* 1906 *Autob* (1924) II 15 (OED 9. *U.S.* a. To vote for all the official candidates of one's party. 1862. So W S F Cl Th M. Not A in C)

straight, adv. [C] *"It was your worship's will that the boy come to you straight"* 1881 PP xiii 155 (OED 2.

Immediately. Now *poet* or *arch*..1871. So W U Wr. Not *arch* in S C)

straight along, adv. [?AB¹] *"I've been getting more heavy-hearted and doubtful straight along ever since"* 1894 PW xiv 778. *It went on looking better and better, straight along* 1899 "MCH" (1900) 25 (Continuously, all the time. Comb. not in OED W S C)

straighten down, v. [?AB¹] *The boat had backed out from St. Louis and was "straightening down"* 1883 LM xviii 218 (*Naut.* sense, not in OED W S C. To turn (the boat) so as to proceed straight down-stream)

straighten out, v. [?AB²] *Now and then a merchant got him to straighten out his books* 1893 PW ii 235 (OEDS Straighten, v. 4. Also with *out*. 1911.. So W S C)

straighten up, v. [?AB¹] *The pilot was lucky if he managed to "straighten her up" before she drove her nose into the opposite bank* 1873 GA iv 42. See *hold on* 1875; *ready*, sb. 1883 (*Naut.* sense, not in OED W S C. To turn (the boat) so as to proceed straight upstream)

straightening-out, vbl.sb. [?AB¹] *With this straightening-out and classification of the dreamer's position to help us* 1900 "My Boyhood Dreams" 255 (Comb. not in OED W S C. Cf. *Straighten out*, v.)

straight flush, sb. [AB³] *Some day you will see a pair of jacks beat a straight flush* 1889 Speeches (1923) 148. See *and* 1899 (OED Straight, a. 9. *U.S.* b. 1882. So C F Cl. Comb. not in W S U)

straight-off, adv. [B²] See *square away* 1889 (OED 2. Immediately. 1873.. So U. Comb. not in W S C)

straight-out, a. [AB³] *"Buying committees for straight-out cash on delivery"* 1873 GA xxv 228. (OEDS *U.S.* Unrestrained, going all lengths. 1848.. So W S C B Th DN.III. The sense here is rather: Unqualified, immediate, absolute)

straight-up-and-down, a. [AB¹] *The peak we had to climb looked almost too straight-up-and-down* 1869 IA xxx 323 (Precipitous, perpendicular. A in Wr B F Cl AS.VII.94. Given by W in *fig* sense only. Comb. not in OED S C)

strange-shaped, ppl.a. [B¹] *His strange-shaped knapsack* 1880 TA xvii 151 (Comb. not in OED W S C)

strangling-cloth, sb. [B¹] *The sword and the strangling-cloth were sacred emblems* [to the Thugs] 1897 FE xlvi 430 (Comb. not in OED W S C)

strangulated sorosis, sb. [B¹] *"This will be followed by compound strangulated sorosis"* 1894 TET vii 408 (Nonsense comb.)

strap, v. [?AC] *This outlaw strapped his razor on his boot* 1869 IA xii 114 (OED 3. To strop, sharpen. Now rare or *obs* 1785..1856. Not *obs* or *rare* in W S C U)

Stratfordian, sb. [B¹] *Stratfordians who were not Stratfordians of Shakespeare's day, but later comers* 1909 ISD vi 58 (Inhabitant of Stratford. Not in OED W S C in this sense)

Stratfordian, sb. [B³] *It has been evolved out of the fertile imaginations of embarrassed Stratfordians, seeking for some explanation of the Stratford rustic's marvellous acquaintance with law and legal terms* 1909 ISD viii 91 (OEDS A supporter of the view that William Shakespeare of Stratford-on-Avon was the author of the plays generally attributed to him. 1908.. Not in W S C U)

Stratfordian, a. [B¹] *This is a charming specimen of Stratfordian argument* 1909 ISD viii 90 (Derived from the above. Not in OED S C as adjective. W has *Stratfordian*, a. pertaining to Stratford, but not the sense here)

Stratfordolater, sb. [B¹] *Defects which I find in these Stratfordolaters* 1909 ISD xii 133 (Nonce word: opprobrious name for the Stratfordians as idolatrous or credulous believers in Shakespeare's authorship. Cf. OED Shaksperolator: a worshiper of Shakespeare, 1875)

straw bail, sb. [?AB³] *He was always on hand at the police courts to give straw bail for his customers* 1873 GA xxxiii 302 (OED Straw, sb. 14. Worthless bail. 1853. So W S C. A in B Cl T)

strawberry, v. [?AB¹] *I said if I caught him strawberrying around after any more asteroids, especially, I should have to fire him out* 1888 Speeches (1923) 144 (Not in OED S C as verb. W: to gather or seek strawberries, usually in the form *strawberrying*. Here *fig*.)

stray cat, sb. [?AB¹] *"He loads up the house with cripple and idiots and stray cats and all the different kinds of poor wrecks that other people don't want"* 1892 AmCl iii 38 (Comb. not in OED W S C in this sense: a waif, vagabond)

streak, v. [?AB³] *His long gray form "streaking it" through the low sage-brush* 1872 RI iii 32. *Pretty soon she made the cold chills streak all down my back* 1884 HF xxxii 333 (OED 5b. To go or advance quickly. Now *dial* and *U.S.* 1833.. But OEDS says: Delete 'Now *dial* and *U.S.*' Not A in W S. C: *obs* or *prov. Eng.* and *U.S.* A in B F Cl Th T)

streaky, a. [?AB²] *Blissful emotion quivered in a succession of streaky thrills down my backbone* 1864 SS (1926) iv 136 (OED 3. Variable, uneven, changeable. *colloq.* 1898. So W S C Wr. A in B F Cl)

street Arab, sb. [?AB³] *He had, in fact, descended so far and so low that he found himself, when a boy, a sort of street Arab in that city* 1873 GA liv 487. See *at* 1883 (OED Street, sb. 4e. 1865.. So W S C U. A in B T)

street-car, sb. [AB³] *Taking a street-car he rode away to the northern part of the city* 1873 GA lxiii 570. See *band-box* 1880. *Several processions of hurrying street-cars* 1883 LM xli 424 (OED *U.S.* 1862.. So W S C Cl AS. V.21)

street-crossing, sb. [B¹] *Go on until you know every street-crossing* 1875 OTM 571 (Comb. not in OED W S C)

street-lamp, sb. [B²] *There are no street-lamps there* 1869 IA xliv 458 (OED Street, sb. 4b. 1870.. Comb. not in W S C)

stretch, v. [?A] *Doubtless Mr. B. was stretching* 1876 OTM 29. *There was things which he stretched, but mainly he told the truth* 1884 HF i 1 (OED 22d. *fig.* To exaggerate in narrative. *colloq.* 1674..1884, quot. from HF. All 19th c. exs. U.S. Not A in W S C Wr)

stretchy, a. [?AB²] *In the night the pup would get stretchy* 1872 RI xxvii 151. See also *rusty* 1893 (OED *colloq* 2. Inclined to stretch oneself. 1872. So W S C)

strike, sb. [?AB³] *Aleck made a wonderful strike which swelled her imaginary hundred thousand to four hundred thousand* 1904 "Bequest" (1906) v 28 (OED 11. *fig.* A stroke of success. 1883.. So W S. A in B F Cl T H DN.II. This sense not in C)

strike, v. [A] *He struck the home trail* 1865 SNO (1875) 74 (OED 68a. To come upon, reach a hill, river, path, etc. Chiefly *U.S.* and *colonial.* 1798.. So Cl Th. Not A in W S C U)

strike, v. [AB³] See *beatenest* 1884; *recess-time* 1896. *"I'd never struck a comet before that could lay over me"* 1907 "Capt.Stormfield" 42 (OED 68c. To come across, meet with, encounter. Chiefly *U.S.* 1851.. So Cl Th, 1798 H DN.I. Not A in W S C U)

strike, v. [?AB³] *At the end of two months we had never "struck" a pocket* 1872 RI lxi 443 (OED 68d. To come upon, find, in prospecting, boring, etc. 1864.. So W S C U)

strike, v. strike one's average. [?AB¹] *He did not understand me. I turned and twisted my question around and about, trying to strike that man's average, but failed* 1880 TA xviii 163 (To size up, estimate. Phr. not in OED W S C)

strike, v. strike bottom. [?AB¹] *Within thirty minutes he struck bottom; grief, misery, fright, despair could go no lower* 1902 "Belated Russian Passport" (1928) 186 (To fail or sink utterly. Phr. not in OED W S C)

strike, v. strike it lucky. [?AB¹] *We struck it mighty lucky* 1884 HF xxi 208 (To meet with good fortune.

Phr. not in OED W S C. Cf. F: To strike luck, to make a successful venture)

strike, v. strike it rich. [?AB²] *Well, if you haven't "struck it rich"*— 1862 *Letters* (1917) I iii 76 (OED 68d. To find a rich mineral deposit. 1885. So W S C. A in F M AS.V.146, VII.428)

striker, sb. [AB²] *He turned up as apprentice engineer or "striker" on a steamboat* 1875 OTM 70 (OED 3b. *U.S.* A green hand who works at low wages, but is one of the crew of a vessel. 1891. So C B F Cl DN.V. This sense not in W S)

striker, sb. [AB³] *Murel's gang of robbers...was composed of two classes...The active agents were termed strikers* 1883 LM xxix 315 (OEDS 6c. *U.S.* A hired ruffian. 1836.. So C B Cl. This sense not in W S)

string, sb. [AB³] See *scratch,* sb. 1907 (OED 12c. *Billiards. U.S.* The number of points made in a game. 1879.. So W. Not A in S C)

string, sb.[?AB¹]*"You've banked your ball clean outside the string"* [i.e., missed the point, misunderstood completely] 1872 RI xlvii 336 (S: *Billiards.* The string-line: a line drawn across the table through the light-red spot: used in stringing for lead. Cf. also S: *String, v.*: To drive the cue-ball from within the string against the farther cushion and back, the player whose ball stops nearest the cushion at the head of the table having the choice of order in playing. W and C have similar definition, not so clear or detailed. Neither *string* nor *string-line* is called *U.S.* in W S C. This sense not in OED; but cf. OED String 32. *String-line* (b) *Billiards, U.S.,* the baulk-line. 1897, only ex. Here, of course, *fig.* a wild play used for a complete misapprehension)

string, sb. **on a string.** [?AB²] *It is considered very bad policy to fee a servant while you are still to remain longer in the hotel...Keep his expectations "on a string"* 1880 TA App.A 584 (OED 1f. To have under control, be able to do what one likes with. 1894, first ex. of this phrase.. So W S. Not in C)

string, sb. **at one's string's end.** [?AB³] *"Well, I'm at the end of my string now"* 1880 TA viii 72 (OED 1m. *dial* 1854.. So Wr. Phr. not in W S C)

string along, v. [?AB¹] *"Isaac knelt down and began to pray: he strung along, and strung along...till everybody had got tired"* 1877 "Some Rambling Notes" ii 590. *They held the auction in the public square along towards the end of the afternoon, and it strung along, and strung along* 1884 HF xxviii 294. *"Well, the time strung along and along, and that fellow never come!"* 1896 TSD iii 351 (To delay, stretch out, be prolonged. This sense not in OED W S C)

string-bean, sb. [A] See *biscuit* 1880; also *batter-cake* 1897 (OEDS String, sb. 32. *U.S.* 1789.. So B F H. Not A in W S C)

string out, v. [?AB¹] *What is the use of stringing out your lives to a lean and withered old age?* 1867 SNO (1875) 73. *There is no use in stringing out the details* 1889 CY xxxiv 449. *It* (i.e., the story) *is not strung out as I have strung it out, but it is all there* 1894 "Private History of the 'Jumping Frog' Story" (1900) 375 (W: To extend or stretch in a line, often with *out.* So S. This sense not in OED C)

strip, v. [C] *The pickpockets had stripped him of his last farthing* 1881 PP xxxiii 385 (OED 3b. To plunder; to spoil. Now *rare.* 1594..1769. Not *rare* in W S C U)

stripe, sb. [C] *He would take the stripes* 1881 PP xxviii 335 (OED 2. A stroke or lash with a whip or scourge. Now *arch,* chiefly in *pl.* c1485..1887. So C. Not *arch* in W S U)

stripe, sb. [AB³] *"You'll not find many of your stripe in there"* 1864 SS (1926) v 150. See *Swinburnian* 1890. *This prompt and all-competent stripe of prophet* 1903 "Chr.Sc." 173 (OED 8a. *U.S.* A sort, class, type. 1853.. So B F Cl Th T H. Not A in W S C)

stroll, v.trans. [?AC] *The young men read, strolled the ample deck* 1899 "My Debut" (1900) 74 (OED 3. *obs.* 1693..1810. Not *obs* in W S. The trans. sense not in C)

strong, a. **strong suit.** [?AB¹] *Jumping on a dead level was his strong suit* 1865 "Jumping Frog" (1875) 33 (Special excellence, forte. This *fig* sense not in OED W S C. Given in *lit.* sense in OED 24. Of a hand or suit: Composed of commanding cards. 1862.. So W)

strong, a. **to be strong with.** [?AB¹] *"She's pow'ful strong wid de 'Jedge"* 1894 PW xiv 780 (To be influential with, in favor with. This sense not in OED W S C)

stub, sb. [?AB³] *You cannot throw an old cigar "stub" down anywhere, but some vagabond will pounce upon it on the instant* 1869 IA xvii 162 (OEDS 9. Earlier U.S. ex. 1855.. Not A in W S C)

stub, v. [AB³] *"Fix me so I can eat for two and only stub toes for one"* 1894 TET i 327 (OED 9. Chiefly *U.S.* 1848.. So S C B F Cl T DN.III. Not A in W U)

stub-hunter, sb. [?AB¹] *One of these stub-hunters calculating how long my cigar will be likely to last* 1869 IA xvii 162 (Comb. not in OED W S C; but cf. Stub, sb., above)

stuck, ppl.a. [?AB²] See *cold,* a. 1876 (OED Unable to go further. 1885.. So W S C. A in B DN.III)

stuck-up, a. [AB³] *The two heroes were not long in becoming insufferably "stuck-up"* 1876 TS xvii 153. *He got stuck up on account of having seen the devil* 1884 HF ii 11 (OED *colloq.* 1829.. So W S C U. A in B T DN. III,IV,V)

student-corps, sb. [B¹] *I had the idea, once, in Heidelberg, to find out all about those five student-corps* 1880 TA xviii 165 (Comb. not in OED W S C. Cf. German *Studentenkorps*)

study, v. [AC] *The fellow studied a minute, and then says..."I ain't got no frog"* 1865 "Jumping Frog" (1875) 34. *Says I to myself, I can explain better how we come to not be in that room this morning if I go out to one side and study over it a little* 1884 HF xli 420 (OED 2. To think intently; to reflect. *Obs exc. dial* and *U.S. colloq.* 1340.. So C Wr DN.I,II,III,V,VI AS.IV.57, Ozarks. U: *arch.* Neither A nor *obs* in W S)

study up, v. [?AB²] *Studying up the subject of Alpine climbing* 1880 TA xxxvi 412. See also *deviltry* 1884 (OED 7b. No ex. Not A in S C. Comb. not in W)

stuff, sb. [?AB²] *It was a good pup...for the stuff was in him...it don't stand to reason that a dog could make such a fight under them circumstances if he hadn't no talent* 1865 "Jumping Frog" (1875) 32. (OED 7d. Fighting material. *colloq.* 1883.. So W. This sense not in S C)

stuffing, vbl.sb. **to knock the stuffing out of.** [?AB³] *I seem to have knocked the stuffing all out of them* 1889 CY xxxiii 422 (OED 2d. *colloq.* 1887.. So U. A in B. Phr. not in W S C)

stump, sb. [AB³] See *polling-day* 1894 (OED 14b. orig.*U.S.* A place or an occasion for political oratory. 1816.. So W S C B F Cl Th T M. Not A in U)

stump, sb. **up a stump.** [AB³] See *reader* 1880. *I see I was up a stump* 1884 HF xxvi 259 (OEDS 2. 'Up a tree.' *U.S.slang.* 1829.. So W S. Not A in C)

stump, v. [B³] *A dervish was stumping it along through the desert, on foot* 1894 TSA x 392 (OED 2b. *slang* 'To go on foot'; also *stump it.* 1841.. So W S C U Wr)

stump, v. [AB³] *"A body might stump his toe"* 1884 HF xxviii 291 (OED 13. *U.S. colloq* 1828.. So B M DN.III AS.VII.31. Not A in W S U)

stump, v. [AB³] *"Now, there's that business with the prophets of Baal; like enough that stumped you?...Own up, now; it stumped you"* 1877 "Some Rambling Notes" ii 590. *Well, nobody could think of anything to do—everybody was stumped* 1884 HF ii 14 (OED 14. Orig.*U.S.* To cause to be at a loss. 1807.. So W C B Th,1800 T M DN.I,III,V. Not A in S U)

stump, v. [AB³] *He was out stumping the State at the time* 1897 *Autob* (1924) I 86 (OED 16. Chiefly *U.S.* b.

trans. To travel over a district making stump speeches. 1856.. So W S C B Th. Not A in U)

stump-tail, a. [?AB¹] *"Merlin's sort—stump-tail prophets, as we call them in the profession"* 1889 CY xxvii 353 (Inferior, second-rate. This *fig* sense not in OED W S C. Cf. OED Stump-tail, sb. A stump-tailed dog, 1902. Cf. also Stump-tailed, ppl.a., A in B F Cl)

stump-toed, a. [?AB¹] *He moved along the side-walk in his shiny, stump-toed boots* 1872 RI xlviii 343 (Comb. not in OED W S C)

stumpy, a. [AB³] *We were shaving stumpy shores* 1875 OTM 449 (OED 3. Of ground: Full of stumps. *U.S.* 1838.. So W. Not A in S C)

stunner, sb. [?AB³] *"My souls, but she's a stunner!"* 1892 AmCl xvii 173 (OED 2. *colloq.* 1848.. So W S C U. A in B T DN.IV)

stunning, ppl.a. [?AB³] *Indian beadwork and stunning moccasins* 1869 SNO (1875) 67. *Now came great news! Stunning news! joyous news, in fact* 1904 "Bequest" (1906) ii 4 (OED 2. *colloq.* Excellent. 1849.. So W S C U. A in B T DN.IV)

stylographic, a. [?AB³] *Must get one of these American pens—the "Stylographic"* 1881 *M.T. the Letter Writer* (1932) iii 37 (OED 2. A variety of fountain pen. 1880.. So W S C U. M.T. himself is a witness that the word was orig. *U.S.*)

styrax calamita, sb. [D] See *afarabocca* 1894 (OED An aromatic gum, the resin of the tree now known as *Styrax officinalis.* 1558. Comb. not in W S C)

sub, sb. [AB³] *I worked three months as a "sub" on the "Inquirer" and the "Public Ledger"* 1906 *Autob* (1924) II 287 (OED 4. *U.S.* esp. of substitute printers. 1830.. So B M. Not A in W S. Not in C)

sub, v. [AB²] *I am subbing at the "Inquirer" office* 1853 *Letters* (1917) I i 26 (OED 2. To work as a printer's substitute. 1879, U.S.ex. A in B. Not A in W S. Not in C)

subbing, vbl.sb. [AB²] *If I want it, I can get subbing every night of the week* 1853 *Letters* (1917) I i 26 (OED No ex. Not A in S. Not in W C)

subjectry, sb. [B¹] *When he returned, he abused his whole subjectry for liars* 1909 "A Fable" 71 (Subjects, subject people. Nonce word, formed on the model of citizenry, Englishry, etc.)

sublimity, sb. [?AB¹] *The sublimity of the young loafer's cheek* 1892 AmCl xv 156 (S: Acme, climax, quintessence. So C. This ironical use not in OED W; but cf. OED Sublime, a. 5b. *colloq.* with ironical force. No ex.)

subscriber, sb. [?AB¹] *Had an immense house tonight ...It is hard to make Albany Dutchmen laugh and applaud but the subscriber did it* c1870 Letter in Clara Clemens, *My Father* (1931) 209. *In an hour and twenty-five minutes I would be two weeks old...My mother said..."Let us have Abraham for one of his names." I said, "Abraham suits the subscriber."* 1870 Screamers (1871) 42 ("me." Cf. S: *Colloq,* the one who writes his name at the end; said by the writer of an article or the signer of a document in speaking of himself. So C. A in DN.V. Not in OED W in this sense. Cf. *yours truly,* below)

subscription, sb. [AB³] *In the profane subscription-trade, it costs the publisher heavily to canvass a three-dollar book* 1907 CS II 253 (OED 9. Book-trade. e. *U.S.* The house-to-house sale of books by canvassers. Freq. attrib. 1880.. Not A in W S C)

succotash, sb. [A] See *biscuit* 1880; also *batter-cake* 1897 (OEDS A dish of N.Am. Indian origin. 1751.. So W S C U B F Cl Th M DN.III,V,VI)

suck, v. to suck one's fingers. [?AB¹] *I can "bank" in the neighborhood of $100 a month...and that will satisfy me for the present (principally because the other youngsters are sucking their fingers)* 1859 *Letters* (1917) I ii 43 (To be idle, unemployed. Phrase not in OED W S C)

suck back, v. [B¹] *The front wall of the crowd begins to roll in like a wave...The racket stopped, and the wave sucked back* 1884 HF xxii 219 (Not in OED W S C in this intr. sense)

Sucker, sb. [AB³] *The McDonough (Ill.) Independent has copied the article contributed to this paper by "B.H.W."...without giving the credit. It's a hard matter to learn you "Suckers" manners* 1853 Hannibal Journal, May 23 (OED 6b. *U.S.* An inhabitant of the state of Illinois. 1833.. So W S C B F Cl Th T DN.V AS. VII.389)

sudden death, sb. [?AB¹] See *chain-lightning* 1865 (A brand of esp. potent liquor. Not in OED W S C in this sense; but cf. OED Sudden death, *slang* in other senses. 1834..)

sufa, sb. [B¹] *"It was a sufa." I understood. It was the dream-word for "part of a continent"* 1912 "My Platonic Sweetheart" (1922) 297 (A pure invention)

suffer, v. [?AB¹] *The first negro minstrel show that ever came to our section left us all suffering to try that kind of life* 1875 OTM 69. *"Eight or nine thous'n' dollars worth o' property layin' around jest sufferin' to be scooped in"* 1884 HF xxvi 266 (To long, desire intensely, 'ache' to do something. Cf. ache, v., above. This sense not in OED W S C)

suffering-machine, sb. [B¹] See *happiness-machine* 1916 (Nonce comb.)

suffrage, sb. [A] *Austria opens the suffrage to him on fairly liberal terms* 1899 "Concerning the Jews" (1900) 272 (OED 11. orig. *U.S.* 1789.. Not A in W S C U)

sugar-bowl, sb. [AB³] *The sugar-bowls with the zinc teaspoons sticking up in them* 1873 GA xxix 271 (OED 1834.. So W. A in M. Comb. not in S C)

sugar-bush, sb. [AB³] *The sun had again set on the "sugar-bush"* 1883 LM lx 590 (OED 1. A grove or plantation of sugar-maples. 1823.. OEDS 1. *U.S.* So C B F Cl Th DN.II,IV AS.V.166; VI.99. Not A in W S)

sugar-camp, sb. [A] *Our first afternoon in the sugar-camp* 1885 "Priv. Hist. of Campaign" 197 (OED *U.S.* A place in a maple forest or plantation where the sap is collected and boiled for sugar. OEDS 1788.. So C B F Cl Th DN.II.IV. Not A in W S)

sugar-coated, ppl.a. [B¹] *Stephens sweetened him up and put him off a week...He called then...and came away sugar-coated again* 1875 OTM 195 (Deluded by "sweet" flattery. This *fig* sense not in any dict. Cf. for literal meaning OED Sugar, sb. 4c.1870.. So W S C)

sugar-hogshead, sb. [B¹] *I got into my old rags and my sugar-hogshead again, and felt free and satisfied* 1884 HF i 2 (Sugar-barrel. Comb. not in OED W S C)

sugar-plantation, sb. [?AB¹] See *Coast* 1883 (Cf.OED 1714.. Here *spec* of a 'plantation' in the Southern sense, devoted to the raising of sugar-cane. Cf. plantation, above. Comb. not in W S C)

sugar-rag, sb. [?AB¹] *"Somebody fetch this sick doll a sugar-rag"* 1895 JA II i 136 (A 'pacifier' for babies. Comb. not in OED W S C)

sugar-shovel, sb. [?AB¹] *A remarkable zinc thing like a sugar-shovel* 1897 FE iv 73 (A sugar-spoon, table utensil for serving sugar. Comb. not in OED W S C)

sugar-trough, sb. [?AB¹] *The sugar-troughs came very handy as horse-troughs* 1885 "Priv. Hist. of Campaign" 197 (Troughs used for collecting sap and making maple-sugar. Comb. not in OED W S C. Cf. sugar-bush and sugar-camp, above)

suggest, v. Pron. sejest. [E] *"I should 'a' reckoned the difference in rank would 'a' sejested to you that a corn-shuck bed warn't just fitten for me to sleep on"* 1884 HF xx 191 (This pron. is the only one recognized in OED S C U. W gives it as the prevailing British pron., but states that in the U.S. the hard g is usually retained. Mark Twain evidently thought the omission of the hard g incorrect)

suggester, sb. [B¹] *It [a story] may have been a suggester, though* 1898 *Letters* (1917) II xxxvii 666 (Cf.

OED 2. One who suggests or prompts. 1671.. So W. Here *transf* of a suggestive thing or incident; cf. S C: That which suggests)

suicide-average, sb. [B¹] See *tiger-average* 1897 (Comb. not in OED W S C)

suit, sb. **suit of hair**. [AB¹] *She had a heavy suit of fine soft hair* 1893 PW ii 236. *A flowing suit of what looked like yellow hair* 1897 FE xxxiv 316 (S C: *Suit of hair*, Local *U.S.* So B F Th,1854 T. Phr. not in OED W)

sulky, sb. [A] *"He sold the buggy and bought the remains of an old sulky"* 1880 TA xxvi 267 (OED 1. A light two-wheeled carriage...for one person; now used principally in America. 1756.. So B F Cl T H AS.V.135; VIII.4.51; XI.305. Not A in W S C U)

sultry, a. [?AB²] *It was getting pretty sultry for me* 1880 TA xxv 250. *"The first dishonest blatherskite ever bred in this town—which will be a sultry place for him from now out!"* 1899 "MCH" (1900) 38 (OED 2b. *colloq* or *slang*. 'Hot,' 'warm,' lively. 1899.. Not A in W S C U)

sumac-berry, sb. [A] See *autumn-butter* 1906 (OED Sumac, sb. 3. 1655, only ex. Comb. not in W S C. For the species of Am. Sumac which M.T. had in mind see under autumn-butter, above)

sumach-tobacco, sb. [AB¹] *She charged a couple of church-wardens with willow-bark and sumach-tobacco for us, and told us to smoke* 1889 CY xl 517 (Comb. not in OED W S C. The leaves of the American species of Sumac or Sumach, *Rhus glabra*, were a regular ingredient of Indian tobacco or *kinnikinic*, together with the bark of Red Willow or Silky Cornel. Cf. OED Kinnikinic 1. 1797.. So W S C. Just why the Connecticut Yankee and Sir Lancelot should have conceived the idea of smoking the Indian substitute for tobacco, and how they procured these Missouri ingredients in Arthurian England, is not revealed by Mark Twain)

summer, v. [A] *When you and your father start summering around, don't pass us by* 1897 M.T. the Letter Writer (1932) vi 89 (OED 1. intr. Now chiefly Scotch and *U.S.* 1440.. So F. Not A in W S C U)

summer-grape, sb. [AB³] See *raspberry* 1884 (OED Summer, sb. 5b. A N. Am. wild grape, 1814. So W S C DN.III, n.w.Ark.)

summer-resort, sb. [AB³] *Hotels of the usual light summer-resort pattern* 1883 LM xliv 445. *This park* [Eden] *would make a tidy summer-resort* 1893 "Extracts from Adam's Diary" (1906) 416 (OED orig. *U.S.* A locality where summer holidays are spent. 1857.. Not A in W. Comb. not in S C)

summer-resorter, sb. [AB¹] *They respected these elegant summer-resorters* 1907 "Chaps. from Autob" 327 (Comb. not in OED W S C. Cf. summer-resort)

summers, adv. [?AB¹] See *fan-distributer* 1907 (Not in OED W S C. Cf. *-s*, suffix, above)

sumpter, sb. Spelled **sumter**. [E] *Over a thousand "sumter" mules* 1884 HF iii 19 (OED 4b. Sumpter mule = pack-mule. 1707. The sp. *sumter* 18th c. This sp. not in W S C)

sun-bonnet, sb. [?AB³] *There was...a sun-bonnet hanging against the wall* 1884 HF ix 28 (OED Sun, sb. 13. 1860. OEDS Earlier U.S.exs. 1837.. A in B T. Not A in W S C U)

Sunday best, sb. [?AB³] *They walk by sedately...in their Sunday-best* 1894 "Defense of Harriet Shelley" 109. See also *gaudinesses* 1897 (OEDS Earlier U.S. ex. 1849.. Not A in W S C U)

Sunday-dressed, ppl.a. [B¹] *Tom accosted a Sunday-dressed comrade* 1876 TS iv 45 (Comb. not in OED W S C)

Sundays, sb. [?AB¹] *Tommy was...not in his Sundays, but in his dreadful work-clothes* 1901 "Two Little Tales" (1928) 203 (Not in OED W S C in this sense. Cf. OED Sunday clothes. 1642..)

Sunday-school, a. [B³] See *Bible-class* 1873; *gush* 1873. *When I was a Sunday-school scholar, something*

more than sixty years ago, I became interested in Satan 1909 ISD ii 20 (OED *attrib*.1836.. So W S C U. Cf. Sabbath-school, above)

Sunday-school-book, a. [?AB¹] *The most unpleasant feature about being a Sunday-school-book boy* 1870 SNO (1875) 58 (Comb. not in OED W S C)

Sunday-service, sb. [B¹] *The threadbare costume of venerable fashion that had done Sunday-service no man knows how many years* 1877 "Some Rambling Notes" ii 591 (Comb. not in OED W S C)

sundown, sb. [A] See *tuckered out* 1877. *Bad luck... if you shook the table-cloth after sundown* 1884 HF viii 69. *It was so close to sundown when we got home that we never stopped in our road* 1896 TSD v 355 (OED 1. Chiefly *U.S.* and *dial.* 1620.. So Wr B F Cl Th H DN.I, II,III. Not A in W S C U)

sundowner, sb. [B³] *Sundowner was merely the Australian equivalent of our word, tramp* 1897 FE viii 101 (OED *Australian colloq.* 1875.. So W S C U)

sunflower, sb. [A] See *ashpile* 1884 (OED 2. Chiefly natives of N.America. 1597.. So W S C)

sun-perch, sb. [AB³] *They were back again with a couple of sun-perch and a small catfish* 1876 TS xiv 123 (OED 13b. Am. fish. 1825. So W S C)

sun-umbrella, sb. [?AB²] *Each man carried a sun-umbrella* 1880 TA xi 102 (OED 1904. Comb. not in W S C)

sun-up, sb. [AB³] See *check* 1870; *weaken down* 1884 (OED Chiefly *U.S.* 1847.. So S C U Wr B F Cl Th, 1843 T H DN.I,II,III AS.V.74,VII.94. Not A in W)

supe, sb. [?AB³] *The supes started the panorama grinding along again* 1871 SNO (1875) 298 (OED *slang*. Short for Super, sb. 1824.. So W S C. A in DN.IV)

super-high-moral, a. [B¹] See *iron-clad*, sb. 1881 (Nonce comb.)

superhonorable, a. [B¹] *My superhonorable loyalty to the public* 1886 *Letters* (1917) II xxvi 474 (Comb. not in OED W S C)

superimbrication, sb. [B¹] *"Considerations concerning ...the extemporaneousness of the conchyliaceous superimbrication of the ornithorhyncus"* 1906 "Simplified Spelling" 220 (Nonsense word)

superscription, sb. [?AC] *No two of the superscriptions were in the same hand* 1899 "MCH" (1900) 28 (OED 3. The address or direction on a letter. *obs* or *arch* 1518..1840. Not *obs* or *arch* in W S C)

superstition-monger, sb. [B¹] *A knight is open to pretty poor arguments when they come glibly from a superstition-monger* 1889 CY xxx 381 (Comb. not in OED W S C)

supper, sb. [AB³] *"I had no supper yesterday"* 1869 SNO (1875) 225. See also *word* 1884 (OEDS 1c. *U.S.* Tea called supper in America. 1817.. So F M DN.III. Not A in W S C U)

supper-bell, sb. [A] *Presently the supper-bell began to ring* 1892 AmCl xii 118 (OEDS *U.S.* 1770.. So Wr. Comb. not in W S C)

supper-table, sb. [A] *She sat at the supper-table with her parents* 1870 SNO (1875) 190 (OED *U.S.* 1794.. Comb. not in W S C)

supper-time, sb. [?A] *It was dark, and past supper-time* 1894 PW xii 773 (OED 1362.. Not A in W C. Comb. not in S. Cf. Supper, above)

supplication-mill, sb. [B¹] *"Prayin', sir. When he once gets his supplication-mill agoin', there just simply ain't any let-up to him"* 1881 "Curious Experience" 137 (Nonce comb.)

supporter, sb. [D] See *coat-of-arms* 1883 (OED 4. Heraldry. A figure of an animal, mythical creature, human being, etc., represented as holding up or standing beside the shield. 1572..1868—. So W S C U)

supposably, adv. [AB³] *Over in the vacant lots was Jasper...at work, supposably* 1893 PW ii 236. *He was supposably storing up Latin for literary use* 1909 ISD

iv 42 (OED Chiefly *U.S.* 1881..1893, quot. from PW..
Not A in W S C U)

suppress, v. [?AB¹] *"Suppress that hat!"* 1892 AmCl
xii 124 (Discard, cease to wear. This *slang* use not in
OED W S C)

supremacy-bell, sb. [B¹] *"It takes both of them together to ring the supremacy-bell"* 1897 FE ix 113
(Nonce comb.)

sure, adv. [AB³] *"They're coming, sure"* 1876 TS iv
83. See *fix,* sb. 1884 (OEDS 3. Now *poet.,* exc. *dial
(Irish)* and *U.S.* 1861.. So B M AS.VIII.1.60. Not A in
W S C U Wr)

sure, adv. **sure as guns.** [B¹] *"But are you sure?"
"Sure as guns—Gatling guns!"* 1888 "Meisterschaft"
458 (A characteristic variation of OED 4a. As sure as
a gun. 1859. So S C Wr. Phr. not in W)

sure-enough, a. [AB³] *The knife would not cut anything, but it was a "sure-enough"* Barlow 1876 TS iv
43. See *bull-pup* 1876. *They all come riding in...looking
just like a gang of real sure-enough queens* 1884 HF xxii
221. *There was the sure-enough water right under us—
clear, and blue, and cool, and deep* 1894 TSA viii 353
(OEDS *U.S.* 1846.. So W S B F Cl DN.II,III. Not A
in C U)

sure thing, sb. [AB²] See *say-so,* sb. 1893. *I am betting
on what is termed "a sure thing"* 1906 "Entertaining
Article" 225 (OEDS Sure, a. 9a. *Sure thing,* orig. *U.S.*
1896.. Not A in W S C)

surety, sb. **of a surety.** [C] *"Of a surety thou must
remember me, my lord"* 1881 PP xiv 169 (OED 4c. For
certain. *arch.* 1535..1816. So S U. Not *arch* in C. Phr.
not in W)

surface line, sb. [AB²] See *conductor* 1906 (OEDS
6d. *U.S.* A line on which surface cars run. No ex. Comb.
not in W S C)

surface-miner, sb. [B¹] *I have been a surface miner—
gold—and I know all its mysteries* 1909 ISD vii 75
(Comb. not in OED W S C; but cf. OED Surface-
mine, 1877)

surf-beat, sb. [B¹] See *storm-wash* 1873 (Comb. not
in OED W S C)

surf-wave, sb. [B¹] *As soon as he...was aware of the
surf-waves...he begged permission to land* 1880 TA xvi
142 (Comb. not in OED W S C)

surgery-practice, sb. [B¹] *The application of anesthesia
to surgery-practice* 1899 "Letter to Whitman" (1926) 174
(Comb. not in OED W S C)

suspenders, sb. [AB³] *The man wore no suspenders*
1872 RI iv 42. *All wore one suspender and sometimes two*
1873 GA i 19. *He wore a leather belt and used no suspenders* 1875 OTM 71 (OED 4. Chiefly *U.S.* 1810..
So W U B F Cl Th T M H AS.V.21. Not A in S C)

suspicion, v. [AB³] *I begun to suspicion something*
1884 HF xvi 142. See *google* 1884 (OEDS *U.S.* To suspect. 1820.. So Wr B F Cl Th T M DN.II,III. Not A
in W S C)

suspicion-point, sb. [B¹] *If modified below the suspicion-point it was flat and meaningless* 1892 AmCl v 64
(Comb. not in OED W S C)

Susquehannian, a. [AB¹] *Are you serious when you
propose to pay my expence—if that is the Susquehannian
way of spelling it?* 1887 *Letters* (1917) II xxvi 477
(Nonce coinage, from the Susquehanna River)

swab, sb. [?AB²] See *Columbiad,* sb. 1867 (OED 1c.
1874.. So W S C)

swab, v. [?AB¹] *Every woman...went off sobbing and
swabbing* 1884 HF xxv 246 (W: To wipe with or as with
a mop or swab, as..to swab up the tears in one's eyes.
So S Wr. Not in OED C in this sense)

swag, sb. [?AB³] *Bret Harte...asked me to help him
write a play and divide the swag* 1876 *Letters* (1917) I
xvi 287. *Whoever could ravish a column from a pagan
temple, did it and contributed his swag to this Christian
one* 1880 TA xlix 568. See also *camp* 1894; *allow* 1896;
Congressional 1897 (OED 9. A thief's plunder. *slang*
1812.. So W S C U. A in AS.IV.345; X. 21)

swag, sb. [?AB³] *A "swag" is a kit, a pack, small
baggage* 1897 FE xxxiii 306 (OED 10. *Austral.* 1864..
So W S C Wr. Used in same sense in the Am. under-
world: AS.X.21)

swale, sb. [A] See *ice-wave* 1880. *The storming party
crossed the swale and began to climb up the steeps* 1897
FE lxvii 673 (OED *U.S.,* a moist or marshy depression
in a tract of land, esp. in the midst of rolling prairie.
1584.. So C Wr B F Cl Th DN.I,V,VI. Not A in W S)

swallow off, v. [B¹] *He swallows off into his real
impromptu speech* 1884 *Speeches* (1923) 6 (Nonce use)

swallow-tail, sb. [?AB³] *I suppose we shall have to be
gotten up regardless of expense, in swallow-tails, white
kids, and everything* 1867 *Letters* (1917) I vi 126. *Our
representative appears in a black swallow-tail* 1899
"Diplomatic Pay and Clothes" (1928) 227 (OED 8.
colloq 1835.. So W S C U. A in DN.III)

swamp, sb. [A] *Gliding by the waters of the bordering
swamp* 1883 LM ii 35 (OED 1. Orig. and in early use
only in the N. American colonies. 1624.. So C Th M
DN.IV AS.IV.10; X.30f. Not A in W S U)

swamp, v. [?AB³] *She was already nearly swamped
with work* 1892 AmCl vi 67 (OED 4. *fig* 1818..So W S
C U. A in B T DN.III,IV)

swamp, v. [?AB³] *He had "swamped the bank"* 1869
IA viii 81 (OED 4b. To ruin financially. 1864.. So C.
This sense not in W S)

swan, v. [AB³] *"I swan you've took me mighty unexpected, William"* 1877 "Some Rambling Notes" i
444 (OED *U.S.slang* I declare. 1823.. So W S C B F
T DN.II,III,IV,V AS.V.20,124)

swap, v. [?A] *I want to swap lies and business both
with you* 1867 *M.T. the Letter Writer* (1932) I 16. *A
friend drops in to swap compliments with you* 1869 SNO
(1875) 49. *"I was calculating to swap a little gossip with
them"* 1908 "Capt.Stormfield" 273 (OED 8. Chiefly,
now only, *slang* or *colloq.* 1594.. So W S C. A in Wr
B Th,1742 DN.III,V AS.IV.474)

swap, v. **to swap knives.** [?AB¹] *It was no time to
swap knives* 1875 OTM 728. *By jingo, I most slumped
through the floor! But there warn't no time to swap knives*
1884 HF xxxii 335 (To change tactics, alter one's plans.
Phr. not in any dict. Cf. the phr. *To swap horses while
crossing a stream)*

swap about, v. [?A] *There was freckled places on the
ground where the light sifted down through the leaves, and
the freckled places swapped about a little, showing there
was a little breeze* 1884 HF viii 57 (OED 4b. To flap or
beat up and down. 1520..1884, this quot. This sense
not in W S C; but cf. *Swap around* in S, below)

swap around, round, v. [?A] *"Percy'll die if he don't
have a change; and so I'm going to swap round a little
and see what can be done"* 1873 GA xxxiii 307. *So the
chat would swap around to some other subject* 1892
AmCl xv 205 (S: Local *U.S.* To change from one place
to another. Not in OED W C)

sway-backed, a. [?AB²] *These rambling, sway-backed
tunnels are very attractive things* 1880 TA xxvi 263
(OED *transf.* 1880, this quot. So W S C U. A in DN.III)

swearing, adv. [?AB¹] *He was swearing mad about
something or other* 1880 TA xxviii 287 (Not in OED
W S C as adv.)

swearing-off, ppl.a. [?AB¹] *They never miss swearing-
off day* 1906 *Speeches* (1910) 110 (Not in OED W S C.
Cf. *swear off* below)

swear off, v. [?AB¹] *I swore off my taxes like the most
conscienceless of the lot* 1906 "Chaps. from Autob"
(1922) 457 (To escape payment by making a sworn
statement of non-liability. Not in OED S C in this
sense. Cf. W: To get rid of with an oath)

sweat, sb. **in a sweat.** [A] See *somers* 1876. *If he
hadn't been in such a sweat to play his witless practical
joke on me* 1883 LM xxx 331. *I was in a sweat to get
away* 1884 HF ii 10. *He didn't sleep much, he was in
such a sweat to get in there* 1896 TSD ii 346 (OED 10.

A state of impatience. Chiefly *Scotch* and *U.S.* 1715.. So Wr B DN.I. Not A in S. Not in W C in this sense)

sweat, v. [?AC] *He was done with his sweating and worrying* 1889 CY xxxv 456 (OED 9. To fume, rage. Now *rare* or *obs.* 1400..1846. Not *rare* in S. A in B. Not in W C in this sense)

sweat, v. [AB¹] *It seems a piteous thing to sweat this poor devil for a burglary he hadn't the least hand in* 1892 AmCl xix 194 (W: To give a prisoner the "third degree." So S. A in H DN.V. Not in OED C in this sense; but cf. OED Sweat, sb. 11. *sweat-box, U.S.*, a compartment in which a prisoner is interrogated by the police. 1904..)

sweeper-out, sb. [B¹] *He had moved along so briskly, from sweeper-out, up through the several grades, that he was now on the editorial staff* 1906 *Autob* (1924) II 346 (Comb. not in OED W S C; but cf. OED Sweeper, sb. 2. 1657..)

sweet, a. [C] *"Go to thy rest, sweet sir—leave me to my sorrow"* 1881 PP xiv 161 (OED 8b. In forms of address, now *arch.* a1225..1875. So W S C)

sweeten, v. [?AC] See *sugar-coated* 1875. *"You's got to be pison good...en you's got to sweeten around old Aunt Pratt, too"* 1894 PW xiv 780 (OED 7. To persuade by flattery or gifts; to cajole. Now only *slang* or *dial* 1594..1872. W: Now *Rare.* This sense not in S C. Cf. Wr: *sweeten*, to bribe)

sweetnesses, sb.pl. [B¹] *All his native sweetnesses and gentlenesses* 1890 *Autob* (1924) I 135 (Not in OED W S C in *concrete* sense)

sweet-potato, sb. [A] See *biscuit* 1880; also *batter-cake* 1897 (OED Potato 3a. 1775.. So W S C U Th M AS.II.32)

Sweet Singer, sb. [?AB¹] *The Sweet Singer of Michigan, Mrs. Julia Moore* 1897 FE viii 107 (W: A poet. Cf. OEDS 2. A religious poet. 1892.. But the term as commonly applied in America suggests sickly sentimentality rather than piety. Not in S C)

swell, sb. [?AB³] *"I warn't used to the ways of littery swells"* 1866 *Speeches* (1910) 23. *He had need of all the resources of his wardrobe to keep even with the young swells of the town* 1873 GA xiii 126 (OED 9. *colloq* 1804.. So W S C U. A in DN.IV.)

swell, a. [?AB³] See *bulliness* 1883; *mansard roof* 1883. *The king's duds was all black, and he did look real swell and starchy* 1884 HF xxiv 237. See *working-people* 1892. *In the swell room of the house* 1893 PW Intro. 233 (OED *colloq.* a. 1810.. So W S C U. A in Wr M DN.IV)

swell, v. [AB¹] *How these complacent bald heads would swell* 1893 LM 1 496 (An adaptation from the phr. *swelled head.* Cf. OED Swell-head, *U.S.* 1845.. So B Th.III DN.IV,V. Not A in W S U. The verb Swell in this sense not in any dict.)

swill-room, sb. [B¹] *All the cabins were full...Every inch of floor and table in the swill-room was packed with sleeping men, and remained so until the place was required for breakfast* 1897 FE xxxii 302 (An opprobrious name for the dining-saloon of a dirty, disreputable boat. Comb. not in OED W S C)

Swinburnian, sb. [B¹] *If I am a Swinburnian...I hold human nature in sufficient honor to believe there are eighty million mute Russians that are of the same stripe* 1890 *Letters* (1917) II xxx 538 (Here: A violent republican or revolutionary. Not in OED W S C in this sense. Cf. OEDS Swinburnian, a. Of, pertaining to, imitative, or characteristic of the poet. 1867.. So W)

swindle, sb. [?AB²] *"I knowed it was all a swindle"* 1852 *Hannibal Journal,* Sept.16. *The whole project was a blackmailing swindle* 1887 *Letters* (1917) II xxvii 485. *Those transparent swindles, transmissible nobility and kingship* 1889 CY xxviii 366. See also *car* 1894; *trust* 1906 (OED 1. An act of swindling. 1852.. So W S C U. A favorite word of Mark Twain's)

swindle, v. [B³] *I shan't swindle you if I can keep nature down* 1867 *M.T. the Letter Writer* (1932) i 16 (OED 2. trans. 1803.. So W S C U)

swing, v. [AB²] *"We can swing a two-thirds vote"* 1873 GA xlv 405 (OEDS 14. To direct or control the action of. *U.S.* 1873, this quot. So H. This sense not in W S C)

swing, sb. [B¹] *Some of these old American words do have a kind of bully swing to them; a man can express himself with 'em* 1880 TA xx 194 (Cf. OED 10. A steady vigorous rhythm or movement characterizing a verse or musical composition. 1829.. So W S C. M.T. has extended the meaning from verse-rhythm to word-rhythm; or he may have in mind what he considers the free swing or untrammeled gait of the American imagination)

swing round, v. [?AB¹] *I swung round to his view of the matter* 1883 LM lvii 563 (This *fig* sense not in OED W S C)

switchback, sb. [?AB²] *"There will be a branch track built, and 'switchback' up the hill"* 1873 GA xlix 445 (OEDS Applied to a form of railroad used on steep slopes. 1873, this quot. So W S C U. A in M)

switchman, sb. [?AB³] *A switchman of two years' experience was negligent once and threw a train off the track and killed several people* 1893 "Travelling with a Reformer" (1900) 361 (OED 1843.. So W S C U. A in M H: Am. *switchman* = Eng. *pointsman*)

switch off, v. [AB²] *Our train ran back half a mile and switched off another track, and stopped* 1853 Letter in Iowa Journal of Hist (July, 1929) 413. *We intended to switch off at Baalbec* 1869 IA xli 432 (OEDS 6. intr. *U.S.* 1861.. So W S C B Cl Th T M. Not A in U.)

swivel, sb. [B¹] *The good old swivel ̲aw here a rare opportunity.* 1869 IA xv 142 (Hum. nonce use: pun on *swivel-gun* for *canon*)

swoon, sb. [B¹] *There was that swoon in the air which one associates with the tropics, and that smother of heat* 1897 FE xxxvii 339 (A state or condition conducive to swooning. Not in OED S C in this sense. Cf. W: A spell, fit, attack, suggestive of a swoon)

sword-play, sb. [?AB²] *It was not merely under the excitement of the sword-play* 1880 TA vi 61 (OED 1b. 1889.. So W S C U)

sworn-off, ppl.a. [?AB¹] *It is money filched from the sworn-off personal tax* 1905 "Humane Word from Satan" (1906) 238 (For the *spec* sense here, see *swear off* and *swearing-off*, above. This sense not in OED W S C; but cf. OED Sworn, ppla. 3b. 1869)

swosh-swosh, sb. [B¹] See *kahkahponeeka* 1880 (Hum. invention)

swush, v. [B¹] *It got awful dark, and the rain started, and the wind swished and swushed along* 1884 HF xxix 306 (Nonce word. Cf. OED Swish, v. 1756..)

sycamore, sb. [AB²] See *inside*, prep. 1875. *He said he would wait for us in a little bunch of sycamores* 1896 TSD iv 355 (OED 3a. In N.America, a plane or tree of the genus *Platanus,* esp. the buttonwood. 1814.. So W S C B M AS.II.30)

syndicate, sb. [?AB³] *We did meet in Washington in 1867. We became the originators of what is a common feature in the newspaper world now—the syndicate. We had twelve journals on our list* 1907 "Chaps. from Autob" 490 (OED 3. A combination for the acquisition of articles, etc., and their simultaneous publication in a number of periodicals. 1889.. So W S C U. Note M.T's claim for American priority)

syndicating, vbl.sb. [?AB²] *The amount of matter is but 3,000 words short of the "American Claimant," for which the syndicate paid $12,000...I don't want any more syndicating* 1893 *Letters* (1917) II xxxiii 591 (OED 1893. Cf. Syndicate, above. Not in W S C)

synopsize, v. [AB³] *Synopsized, it amounted to this* 1893 "Banknote" (1928) 129. *He has synopsized Bacon's history—a thing which cannot be done for the Stratford Shakespeare, for he hasn't any history to synopsize* 1909 ISD ix 106 (OED trans. *U.S.* To epitomize. 1882.. Not A in W. Not in S C)

T

tabard, sb. [C] *"The Garter king-at-arms, in his tabard"* 1881 PP ix 105 (OED 2. A short surcoat. Now only *Hist.* c1450..1843. So W S C U)

table, sb. *to set a good table*. [B¹] *Boats that had an established reputation for setting good tables* 1875 OTM 221 (Given in W U. Phr. not in OED S C; but cf. OED 6c. Provision of food for meals, fare. c1400..)

table-fare, sb. [B¹] *The table-fare was of the regulation pattern of the day* 1898 "At the Appetite Cure" (1900) 157 (Comb. not in OED W S C)

table-room, sb. [?AC] *"There is table-room for only half the passengers"* 1894 TET ii 339 (OED† Room or place at table. 1607, only ex. So S C. Comb. not in W)

tack-hammer, sb. [?AB²] *Egyptian granite has nothing to fear from the tack-hammers of ignorant excursionists* 1869 IA lviii 630 (OED A light hammer for driving tacks. Earliest ex. U.S. 1889.. Not A in S C. Comb. not in W)

tackle, v. [?AB³] *A dog might tackle him* 1865 "Jumping Frog" (1875) 32 (OED 4a. *colloq.* To grip, lay hold of, encounter (a person or animal) physically. 1828.. So W S C U Wr. A in B DN.III)

tackle, v. [?AB³] *"The fellows have all tackled the old Oracle, as they say, but the old man's most too many for them"* 1869 IA x 91 (OED 4b. *colloq.* To enter into a discussion with. 1840.. So W S C U Wr. A in DN.III)

tackle, v. [?AB³] *"If I should conclude to tackle science for a regular business..."* 1864 SS (1926) 156. See *mud-dobber* 1866. *"If you was to tackle this fence and anything was to happen to it..."* 1876 TS ii 31. *"Do you ever read the Bible?...Now, you tackle it in dead earnest once, and you'll find it'll pay"* 1877 "Some Rambling Notes" ii 589. *If I'd a knowed what a trouble it was to make a book, I wouldn't 'a' tackled it* 1884 HF xliii 437 (OED 4c. To grapple with, to try to deal with (a task, a difficulty, etc.) 1847.. So W S U. A in C B DN.III. A favorite word with M.T.)

tackle, v. [?AB²] *So the king sneaked into the wigwam and took to his bottle for comfort, and before long the duke tackled his bottle* 1884 HF xxx 313 (OED 4d. To fall upon, begin to eat or drink. 1889.. So W. A in DN.I,II. This sense not in S C)

tadpole, v. [B¹] *We all start as moon-faced fools, then later we tadpole along into horse-faced marvels of intellect and character* 1892 AmCl xxi 213 (Nonce use)

tael, sb. [B¹] *Taels I win, Heads you lose* [M.T.'s comment on news reports that Protestant missionaries were collecting 300 taels indemnity for each Chinese Christian murdered in the Boxer Rebellion, while the Catholics were demanding, in addition, head for head] 1901 "To the Person Sitting in Darkness" 163 (Hum. nonce use)

taffy, sb. [AB³] *Above my judgment I prefer yours. I mean this—it is not taffy* 1892 Letters (1917) II xxxii 573 (OED 2. *U.S.slang.* Crude or vulgar compliment or flattery. 1879.. So S C Cl Th.III M. Not A in W. Cf. trade-taffy, below)

Tahoe, sb. [B¹] *People say that Tahoe means "Silver Lake"* 1869 IA xx 205 (C: A lake in w.Nevada and e. California. So W S. Not in OED)

tailings, vbl.sb. [?AB³] *One could always "screen tailings"* 1872 RI xxxvi 254. *I have shoveled silver tailings in a quartz-mill a couple of weeks* 1891 Letters (1917) II xxxi 542. See also *arrastre* 1909 (OED 2b. *Mining.* The residuum after most of the valuable ore has been extracted. 1864.. So W S C U. A in B Cl Th,1860 T AS.VII.429)

tailing-pile, sb. [?AB¹] *The gold fields of the world now deliver up fifty million dollars worth of gold per year which would have gone into the tailing-pile under the former conditions* 1897 FE lxviii 687 (Comb. not in OED W S C. Cf. above)

tailor-man, sb. [B²] *"Noble large stitches...that do cause these small stingy ones of the tailor-man to look mighty paltry"* 1881 PP xiii 154 (OED 1899, only ex. *Dial* in Wr. Not in W S C)

take, sb. [?AB²] *When one gets a good agate take, he is sure to make money* 1853 Letters (1917) I i 26. *When I took a "take," foremen were in the habit of suggesting that it would be wanted "some time during the year"* 1872 RI xlii 293. See also *comp* 1909 (OED 7. *Printing.* A portion of copy taken at one time by a compositor to be set up in type. 1864.. So W S C U. A in Cl T)

take and, v.intr. [AB³] See *hoist*, v. 1865; *bounce*, v. 1876; *faze* 1876; *blimblamin'* 1884; *dust*, v.1884. *"En bimeby she died, en he tuk en toted her way out dah on de prairie en buried her"* 1895 "How to Tell a Story" (1928) 232. *"I'll take and wring your neck for you one of these days"* 1895 JA II i 135 (OEDS 24d. To proceed to. U.S. 1836.. So Wr. Not A in W S. This const. not in C)

take down, v.trans. [?AB¹] *I enlisted a poet for company, and a stenographer to "take him down"* 1883 LM xxii 247 (To take dictation from. Not in OED W S C with person as object. Cf. OED 80e. To write down, take a written report of. 1712..)

take hold, v.intr. [AB³] *Miss Watson would take hold and knock it all down again* 1884 HF iii 18 (OED 69e. To apply oneself to action; to set to. *dial* and *U.S.* 1868.. So Wr Th,1830. This sense not in W S C)

take hold of, v.trans. [?AB³] *"It can take a-hold of a prowling, thieving, infernal, white-shirted free nigger"* 1884 HF vi 43 (OED 69c. With *of:* To take possession of, take under control. ?U.S. Not A in W S C)

take in, v.trans. [AB²] *"An owl that came from Nova Scotia to visit the Yo Semite took this thing in on his way back"* 1880 TA iii 42 (OED 82k. To include in a journey or visit. U.S. 1883, only ex. So H. Not A in W C. This sense not in S)

take in, v.trans. *to take in one's sign*. [?AB¹] *"If a jay ain't human, he better take in his sign"* 1880 TA ii 37 (To resign, retire from business. Phr. not in OED W S C)

take in, v.intr. [AB¹] *She could hardly wait for school to "take in"* 1876 TS xx 162 (W: *Southern U.S.* To open or commence, as a church service. So DN.II, III. This sense not in OED S C)

take-off, sb. [?AB³] *Observe his nice take-off of Middle-Age art-dinner-table scene* 1889 Letters (1917) II xxix 513 (OEDS 2. A caricature. Earlier U.S. ex. 1846.. Not A in W S C)

take on, v.intr. [?A] See *dang* 1884. *I never see a person take on so* 1893 TSA ii 27 (OED 84j. To rage, rave. Now *colloq* or *dial.* 1430..1852. So W S C U Wr. A in B DN.I,III,IV,V)

take out, v.intr. [AB¹] *"I tuck out up the river road"* 1884 HF viii 68. See *hot and heavy*, adv. 1884; *tight*, adv. 1894. *Out jumps four men and took out up the road as tight as they could go* 1896 TSD v 355 (A in Wr: To go, depart. So DN.III,IV. Not in OED W S C in this sense)

taker, sb. [B¹] *A youth staked out a claim and tried to sell half of it for £5; no takers* 1897 FE xxxvii 333 (One who accepts a business offer. This sense not in OED W S C; but cf. OED 2f. One who accepts a bet. 1810..)

take up, v.trans. [AB²] *This dear young thing in the theater had been sitting there unconsciously taking up a collection* 1880 TA ix 88. *They take up a collection and bury him* 1892 AmCl ii 31 (OED 90d (d). To make (a collection). *Scotch* and *U.S.* 1892, above quot...So C. Not A in W. This sense not in S)

take up, v.intr. [?AB²] *The bell for school to "take up" tinkled faintly* 1876 TS xiii 113 (OED 90r. *absol.* To begin, commence. *dial.* U.S. quot. 1876, only ex. this use. A in B DN.III,IV AS.II.365. This sense not in W S C)

take up, v.trans. [?AB¹] *"You're a fighting liar and dasn't take it up!"* 1876 TS i 23 (To accept, as a challenge; to resent an insult, etc., actively. This sense not in OED W S C)

taking, ppl.a. [B¹] *"I have noticed, in such literary experiences as I have had, that one of the most taking things to do is to conceal your meaning when you are trying to conceal it; whereas, if you go at literature with a free conscience and nothing to conceal, you can turn out a book, every time, that the very elect can't understand"* 1892 AmCl v 64 (Exacting, difficult, requiring effort. This sense not in OED W S C)

takings, vbl.sb. [B¹] *He added several of the valuables of that house to his takings* 1893 PW x 552 (Thefts, things stolen. This sense not in OED W S C; but cf. OED 5a. Receipts or earnings of merchants. 1632..)

takings, vbl.sb. [B¹] *He took this trio of finger-marks again. He liked to have a "series", two or three "takings" at intervals* 1893 PW ii 237. (Fingerprint records. This sense not in OED W S C. Cf. OED Take, v. 33b. To obtain by drawing; to obtain or make a figure of. 1607..)

talk back, v. [AB²] *There was no "talking back", no dissatisfaction* 1869 IA xi 112. *"When dey talk back at her, she up and she says, 'Look-a-heah!'* " 1874 SNO (1875) 203 (OEDS 3e. To answer back; to indulge in 'back-chat.' U.S.colloq. c1870, quot. from SNO, wrongly dated... So Th. Not A in W S. Not in C)

talking-walk, sb. [B¹] *He soon returned, and the talking-walk was resumed* 1902 "DBDS" (1928) 331 (Nonce comb.)

talk-machinery, sb. [B¹] *It took some little work to get the talk-machinery to running smoothly again after this derangement* 1877 "Some Rambling Notes" i 445 (Comb. not in OED W S C)

talk off, v. [?AB¹] *Books couldn't teach a student a multitude of pilot-phrases so thoroughly and perfectly that he could talk them off in book and play and conversation and make no mistake* 1909 ISD i 11 (To utter readily, rattle off. Comb. not in OED W S C)

talk out, v. **to be talked out.** [?AB¹] *He left him pretty well talked out, but grateful* 1880 TA xx 194 (S: To have used up one's thoughts; to have no more to say. So C. This sense not in OED W. Cf. W: To talk out: to carry on the debate of a bill until adjournment of a session in order to prevent its being voted upon. *Eng.* So OED 1873. But M.T.'s sense is illustrated in the OED quot. 1903: "Give Mr. Chamberlain time to talk himself out")

talky-talk, sb. [?AB²] *All that kind of humbug talky-talk, just the way people always does at a supper, you know* 1884 HF xxvi 258 (OEDS Trivial conversation, talk for talking's sake. Earliest ex. U.S. 1902.. So W. Comb. not in S C)

tallow-dip, sb. [?AB³] *Tom, all undressed for bed, was surveying his drenched garments by the light of a tallow dip* 1876 TS iv 45 (OED A candle made by dipping a wick repeatedly into melted tallow. 1835, only ex. So W S. A in B T. Comb. not in C)

tallow-drip, sb. [?AB¹] *He stood about five minutes, picking tallow-drip off of his candle and thinking* 1884 HF xxxvii 379 (The drippings of tallow from a candle. Comb. not in OED W S C)

tally-keeper, sb. [B²] *The tally-keeper tallied one for the opposition in his book* 1880 TA v 55 (OED 1883, only ex. Comb. not in W S C)

talonlike, a. [B²] *His hand was talonlike, it was so bony and long-fingered* 1883 LM xxxi 339 (OED Like the claws of a bird or beast. 1897, only ex. Not in W S C)

talons, sb.pl. [B¹] *On his fingers...Scissors seldom come. Lets his talons grow a year...* [German, *seine Nägel*] 1891 *Slovenly Peter* (1935) 2 (Here *spec*, fingernails. So U. This sense not in OED W S C; cf. OED 2c. Applied allusively to the grasping hands or fingers of human beings. 1588..; so W S)

Tammany, sb. [AB¹] *Great Britain had a Tammany and a Croker a good while ago* 1901 *Speeches* (1910) 114 (Any corrupt political organization. This *gen.* sense not in OED W S C; but cf. OED The name of the central

organization of the Democratic party in the City of New York, esp. associated with political and municipal corruption. 1787..; so W B F Cl Th M)

tamp, v. [?AB³] *"Put in some dirt! Put in some gravel! Tamp it down!"* 1902 "DBDS" (1928) 311 (OED 1. *Mining.* To stop up with clay, sand, etc., rammed in. 1819.. So W S C U. A in AS.II.87)

tan, v. [?AB²] *"If I catch you about that school I'll tan you good"* 1884 HF v 32 (OED 3. To thrash soundly; *slang* or *colloq* 1890.. So W S C U. A in DN.V)

tangle, v. [?AC] *I was tangled good now. That was somebody else's whoop, or else I was turned around* 1884 HF xv 126 (OED † 1. To confuse the brain, mind, etc. a1340..1671. So U. This sense not in W S C)

tanglefoot, a. [AB³] *He could hold more tanglefoot whisky than any man in seventeen counties* 1872 RI xlvii 336 (OED *U.S. slang.* An intoxicating beverage. 1860.. So S C B F Th.III T M DN.III. *Slang* in W)

tangle-headed, a. [?AB²] *"I think you're a tangle-headed old fool, Jim"* 1884 HF xv 131 (OED Tangle, sb. 3. 1908. Here *fig.* So W. Comb. not in S C)

tap, sb. **on tap.** [?AB³] *Hot and cold water on tap* 1899 "Diplomatic Pay" (1928) 239 (OED 1c. Ready for immediate consumption or use; *lit.* and *fig.* U.S. quot. 1862, only ex. Not in W S C U)

tapadero, sb. Spelled **tapidaro.** [AB²E] *It was a Spanish saddle, with ponderous tapidaros* 1872 RI xxiv 178 (OED Tapadero. Also *tapidero*. A heavy leather housing for the front of the stirrup, used in California. 1891.. OEDS 1872, this quot. So W S F Cl. Spelled *tapadera* in C DN.I. M.T.'s sp. seems to be original with him)

taps, sb. [AB³] *Then the bugle sang "Taps"...Taps is the soldier's nightly release from duty and farewell* 1906 "Horse's Tale" 547 (OED 2. *U.S. Milit.* A signal...at which all lights in the soldiers' quarters are to be extinguished. 1862.. So F Cl T H DN.III. Not A in W S C U)

tar and feather, v. [A] *The gentleman ought to be ridden on a rail, tarred and feathered* 1853 Hannibal *Journal,* May 23. *They felt compelled to give him a friendly admonition for his own good, and so tarred and feathered him* 1870 SNO (1875) 312. *The villagers had a strong desire to tar-and-feather Injun Joe and ride him on a rail, for body-snatching* 1876 TS xi 106 (OED A punishment sometimes inflicted by a mob, esp. in U.S. OEDS 1769.. So S C Th. Not A in W U)

tarantula, sb. [A] *Prodigious hairy spiders—tarantulas* 1872 RI xxi 164 (OED 1b. The great hairy spiders of the genus *Mygale,* natives of the warmer parts of America. 1794.. So W S C U)

tar-baby, sb. [?AB³] *Mr. Joel Chandler Harris... deeply disappointed a number of children who had flocked eagerly to get a glimpse of the oracle of the nation's nurseries...They said: "Why, he's white!"...To console them, the book was brought that they might hear Uncle Remus's Tar-Baby story from the lips of Uncle Remus himself* 1883 LM xlvii 471. *For two years the 'Courant' had been making a "tar baby" of Mr. Blaine, and adding tar every day—and now they were called upon to praise him, and urge their well-instructed clientele to elevate the "tar baby" to the Chief Magistracy of the nation* 1906 *Autob* (1924) II 18. *Whenever we have been furnished with a tar baby ostensibly stuffed with jewels, and warned that it will be dishonorable and irreverent to disembowel it and test the jewels, we keep our sacrilegious hands off it... Disbelief* [sic; M. T. evidently meant "belief"] *in a healthy and deeply-loved tar baby has never been known to disintegrate quickly* 1909 ISD xi 129 (OED quot. from "Uncle Remus" 1881, only ex. The term is not defined in OED. M.T.'s *fig* use of it in the two latter quots. has little relevance with Harris's familiar version of the story. In the quot. from the *Autob,* it seems to mean 'scapegoat,' object of abuse, 'cockshy,'—perhaps with a confused reminiscence of the phr. 'to tar and feather.' As M.T. uses it in ISD, on the other hand, it apparently means 'idol,' object of veneration, fetish. Can it be that M.T. had in mind some quite different version of the folk-tale, perhaps one heard in his youth long before he had made the acquaintance of Uncle Remus in person? M.T.'s use not in W. Comb. not in S C)

tarry, v. [?AC] *"But why not tarry yet a little?"* 1881 PP v 64 (OED 4b. To abide, sojourn. *arch* exc. in U.S. 1432..1877. Not *arch* in W S C Wr. A in F Cl Th,1778.. 1892. App. M.T. felt it as *arch* rather than Am.)

ta-ta, int. [?AB³] *"Ta-ta! ta-ta! Any word to send to your family?"* 1907 "Capt. Stormfield" 42 (OED A nursery expression for 'Good-bye.' 1837..So W S C U. A in DN.I,IV,V)

tattoo-mark, sb. [B²] *His horny hands and wrists were covered with tattoo-marks* 1892 AmCl xvi 164 (OED 1899, only ex. Comb. not in W S C)

tavern, sb. [AB¹?C] *"Number two...maybe it's the number of a room—in a tavern, you know!"...He found that in the best tavern, No. 2 had long been occupied by a young lawyer* 1876 TS xxvii 210 (W: Often used, esp. in rural districts of the U.S., practically as synonymous with 'hotel.' So B T M. C calls this use now *rare.* Not in OED S)

tavern-keeper, sb. [AB¹?C] *The tavern-keeper's son said No. 2 was kept locked all the time* 1876 TS xxvii 210 (Hotel owner, innkeeper. Given in C. This sense not in OED S. Comb. not in W. Cf. above)

tavernward, adv. [AB¹?C] *New friends carried Pudd'n-head off tavernward* 1894 TET v 395 (Not in OED W S C; but cf. OED Tavernwards, adv. 1892; so W. For sense cf. above)

tax-collar, sb. [B¹] *"I do not know what the word ['scientist'] means, but my mother would know how to use it and get effects. She would know how to depress a rat terrier with it and make a lap-dog look sorry he came. But that is not the best one; the best one is 'laboratory'. My mother could organize a Trust on that one that would skin the tax-collars off the whole herd"* 1903 "Dog's Tale" 14 (Hum. nonce comb. The point of the joke is obscure; perhaps M.T. alludes to the supposed ability of the "Trusts" to escape their just taxes. Cf. party-collar, above)

tax-gatherer, sb. [?AC] *He found out that a respectable number of the tax-gatherers...collect the tax twice* 1870 SNO (1875) 117 (OED *arch.* A collector of taxes. 1693.. 1904. So U. Not *arch* in W S C)

taxpayer, sb. [AB³] *The pavements were not repaired! ...Ruts five and even ten inches deep are worn into the thick flagstones by the chariot wheels of swindled taxpayers* 1869 IA xxxi 328 (OED In U.S., including local rate-payers. 1853, only ex. Am. sense. So M. The Am. use not given in W S C)

tax-return, sb. [?AB²] *A wicked tax-return—a string of impertinent questions about my private affairs...calculated to make a man report about four times his actual income to keep from swearing to a falsehood* 1870 SNO (1875) 319 (A sworn statement of taxable property. OED 1888, only ex., used of U.S. procedure. Not A in W. Comb. not in S C)

td, abbrev. [?AB¹C] *We marked the ads, but we seldom paid any attention to the marks afterward; so the life of a "td" ad and a "tf" ad was equally eternal* 1886 Speeches (1910) 184 (In former Am. newspaper usage, the notation "td" on an advertisement meant "to-day" only; whereas "tf" signified that the advertisement was to run "till forbid." These abbreviations not in OED W S C)

teacher-factory, sb. [B¹] *I had started a teacher-factory and a lot of Sunday-schools* 1889 CY x 117 (Nonce comb.: hum. name for a normal school)

tea-grounds, sb. [B¹] *There is even a brand of European smoking-tobacco that I like. It is loose and dry and black and looks like tea-grounds* 1893 "Concerning Tobacco" (1917) 279 (Comb. not in OED W S C; but cf. OED Tea-dregs, no ex; Coffee-grounds, 1764)

tea-group, sb. [B¹] *I stop work... and join the tea-group to wonder and exclaim* 1892 Letters (1917) II xxxii 573 (Nonce comb.: a group at tea)

team, sb. [?AB³] *One of the teams wore chain-mail ulsters, and the other wore plate-armor* 1889 CY xl 518 (OED 4b. *transf...* now *esp* a definite number...forming a side in a match. 1885.. So W S C U. A in Cl T DN.II)

tea-planting, vbl.sb. [B¹] *Tea-planting is the great business in Ceylon now* 1897 FE lxii 611 (Comb. not in OED S C; but cf. OED Tea-plantation, 1842. Given in W)

tear around, v. [AB¹] See *kid* 1907 (W: To go about in excited haste. *Colloq.* So S C. A in B F Cl T DN.III. Comb. not in OED)

tear-jug, sb. [B¹] *A Pisan antiquarian gave me an ancient tear-jug* 1869 IA xxv 252 (Comb. not in OED W S C; but cf. OED Tear-bottle: lachrymatory; applied to small bottles or phials, found in ancient tombs, supposed, with doubtful correctness, to contain tears shed for the deceased. 1658..)

technical, a. [B¹] *Mr. Ballou, through whose iron-clad earnestness no sarcasm could pierce, said...the horses were "bituminous from long deprivation." The reader will excuse me from translating. What Mr. Ballou customarily meant, when he used a long word, was a secret between himself and his Maker...The old gentleman said the dog was "so meretricious in his movements and so organic in his emotions"...We tried to use the strong alkaline water of the Sink... The coffee we made of this water was the meanest compound man has invented. Mr. Ballou drank a half cup, but finally threw out the remainder, and said frankly it was "too technical for him"* 1872 RI xxvii 222 (Hum. malapropism)

tedious, a. [?AC] *That remark was too tedious for him—he couldn't stand it* 1907 "Capt. Stormfield" 42 (OED 2. Wearisome in general; annoying, irksome, troublesome, disagreeable. *obs* exc. *dial.* 1454..1871. So S. Not *obs* in W Wr. This sense not in C)

teething-ring, sb. [?AB¹] See *soothing-syrup* 1872 (Comb. not in OED S C. Given in W: A ring, usually of bone, ivory, or composition, for a teething infant to bite on)

teetotaler, sb. [?AB³] See *anti-* 1894. *He had been a hard drinker at sea, but after his conversion he became a firm and outspoken teetotaler* 1902 "Was It Heaven?" 12 (OED 1834.. So W S C U. A in B M DN.V)

teetotalism, sb. [?AB³] See *dry,* a. 1906 (OED 1834.. So W S C U. Cf. above)

telegram, sb. [?AB³] *The latest news follows, under the head-line "Telegrams"* 1880 TA 629 (OED 1852.. So W S C U. Cf. below)

telegraph, sb. [?A] See *cotton-gin* 1889; *calculator* 1889; *inventor-tribe* 1905 (OED 2. In full, electric or magnetic telegraph. 1797.. So U. A in W: The electric telegraph, of which the form still in most common use is the Morse telegraph, first used publicly [in the U.S.] in 1844. So S C B F T M)

telegraph, sb. [?AC] *Coming down the street like half a dozen telegraphs* 1852 Hannibal Journal, Sept. 16 (OED 3. A message sent by telegraph; a telegram. *obs.* Earliest ex. U.S. 1850..1862. C: *Rare.* Not *obs* or A in W S)

telegraph-pole, sb. [?AB²] See *dead-wall* 1864. *A pile of telegraph-poles half as high as a church* 1872 RI xxiv 182 (OED 1869.. So W S C U)

telelectrophonoscope, sb. [B¹] *The telelectrophonoscopes of the globe were put to service now, and for many hours the kings and queens of many realms...talked with S.* 1898 "From the London 'Times' of 1904" (1900) 142

(Coinage for an imaginary instrument supposed to reproduce both voice and visual image at a distance. Cf. OED Telephonograph, 1878; Telelectroscope, below)

telelectroscope, sb. [B²] *The youthful inventor of the "telelectroscope" for seeing at great distances* 1898 "Austrian Edison" (1900) 263 (OED 1898. So W S C)

telephone, sb. [?AB³] *The telephone is everywhere* 1883 LM xli 427. *In a corner of the drawing-room was a telephone hanging on a transmitter* 1892 AmCl iv 55. See also *inventor-tribe* 1905 (OED 2b. Applied to the 'Electrical Speaking Telephone' of Alex. Graham Bell, introduced in 1876. So W S C U. Since Bell's work was done in America, and his new instrument first given to the world at the Philadelphia Exposition, it may be claimed as orig. *U.S.* So B F T M. Strangely enough, however, it is not expressly included by M.T. in his exultant list of things which "a Republican simplicity has invented and exported to the Old World" (see bicycle, above) where he speaks merely of "the best and smartest systems of electric calls and telephonic aids to laziness and comfort")

telephone, v. [?AB³] *Telephone me when you are coming* 1907 *M.T. the Letter Writer* (1932) ix 131 (OED 1c. 1889.. So W S C U. A in F)

telephone-station, sb. [?AB¹] *The connection was made with the international telephone-station* 1898 "From the London 'Times' of 1904" (1900) 135 (Here M.T. was dreaming of a future "World Central" or exchange. Comb. not in OED W S C. Cf. above)

telephone-wire, sb. [?AB¹] *In one place the telephone wire running along six inches above the comb [of the roof] is covered* 1881 *M.T. the Letter Writer* (1932) iii 36 (Comb. not in OED S C. Given in W. Cf. above)

telescoper, sb. [B¹] *I wanted to stand with a party on the summit of Mt.Blanc...and I believed the telescope could set me within seven feet of the uppermost man. The telescoper assured me that it could* 1880 TA xliv 515 (Hum. coinage; cf. OED Telescopist, 1870)

telescopulariat, sb. [B¹] *The telescopulist—or the telescopulariat—I do not know which is right—said a party were making a grand ascent* 1880 TA xliv 515 (Hum. coinage)

telescopulist, sb. [B¹] See above, 1880 (Hum. coinage)

temperance, sb. [?AB³] *Temperance tracts* 1872 RI xxiv 184. *Great temperance meetings* 1873 GA lii 474. See *anti-* 1882. *A temperance lecture* 1892 AmCl xxiv 251 (OED 2. Now often applied to the practice or principle of total abstinence; teetotalism. Earliest ex. with Am. ref. 1826.. b. attrib. 1836.. Not A in W S C U. A in DN.II)

Temple, sb. **Friends of the Temple.** [?AB¹] See *Adventist* 1907 (W: Hoffmanites, followers of Christoph Hoffmann of Germany, who established in Palestine (1868 to his death in 1885) small colonies, German Temple Communities, with a government modeled on the Mosaic Law. Called also, *U.S.*, Temple Societies. Not in OED S C)

tend, v. [AB²] *Tending bar and reporting for the newspapers* 1871 SNO (1875) 155 (OED 3b. To have the care and oversight of; said also (now *dial* and *U.S.*) of a shop, etc. 1889, only ex. U.S. sense. So F Cl Th.III, 1764 T M. Not A in W S. This sense not in C)

ten-day, a. [B²] *A ten-day trip by steamer* 1883 LM lx 582 (OED 1898, only ex. So W. Comb. not in S C)

tenderfoot, sb. [AB³] *"New-chum" is the* [Australian] *equivalent of our "tenderfoot"—new arrival* 1897 FE xxii 221 (OED *U.S.* and *Colonial*. 1881.. So W S C U F Cl Th T M DN. IV,V AS.VII.424)

tenderfooted, ppl.a. [AB³] *Immediately after the War of 1812 tourists began to come to America, from England ...Each tourist went home and published a book which was usually calm, truthful, reasonable, kind, but which seemed just the reverse to our tender-footed progenitors* 1883 LM xxvii 292 (OED From the prec.: Cautious,

timid. *fig.* 1854. So Th. Not A in W C. Comb. not in S. The meaning here is rather: Sensitive, thin-skinned)

tenderloin, sb. [AB³] *The long white bone which divides the sirloin from the tenderloin* 1880 TA xlix 572 (OED *U.S.* 1. The tenderest or most juicy part of the loin. 1828.. So U Th T M H. Not A in W S C)

tending, vbl.sb. [AB¹] *The government...pays ten or fifteen dollars a month for the lighting and tending [of the beacon lights]* 1883 LM xxx 326 (Oversight. Not in this sense in OED. Not in W S C. Cf. tend, v., above)

tenement-house, sb. [AB³] *The windows looked out on a little alley in the rear of some tenement-houses* 1880 TA xi 106 (OED orig. *U.S.* A house let in flats or sets of apartments. OEDS 1861.. So F Cl T. Not A in W S C U. Cf. W: Often, esp. in ref. to large cities, such a building occupied as dwellings by the poorer classes)

Tennessean, a. [AB²] *The fervent spirit of Tennessean journalism* 1869 SNO (1875) 50. *The proposition was that the Tennessean gentleman should sell that land* 1906 *Autob* (1924) II 321 (OEDS 1869, above quot., only ex. So W S C)

ten-ounce, a. [B¹] *The little whining ten-ounce black-and-tan reptile* 1873 GA xxxiii 310 (Comb. not in OED W S C)

ten-pins, sb. [AB³] See *horizontal* 1858. *Setting up ten-pins* 1871 SNO (1875) 155 (OED Chiefly *U.S.* Called in England 'American bowls.' 1807.. So W S B F Th T M H. Not A in C)

ten-pound, a. [B²] *A ten pound lump of coal* 1883 LM xix 228 (Given in OED; no ex. So W. Comb. not in S C)

ten-strike, sb. [AB³] *Mrs. Rose Terry Cooke's story was a ten-strike* 1877 *Letters* (1917) I xvii 298. *The office staff adjourned to a great bowling establishment... The player who scored the fewest ten-strikes in the hour would have to provide oysters* 1907 "Chaps. from Autob" 471 (OED In the U.S. game of ten-pins, a throw which bowls over all the pins. 1850.. So W S C B F Cl Th,1844 T H DN.II)

terrace-like, a. [B¹] *This pile of stone...comes down out of the clouds in a succession of rounded, colossal, terracelike projections—a stairway for the gods* 1880 TA xxxv 397 (Comb. not in OED W S C)

terrapin, sb. [AB³] See *biscuit* 1880 (OED A N. Am. turtle. b. The flesh of this animal used as food. 1867.. So W S C U B F Cl Th.III,1613 T M DN.II,IV)

Territorial, a. [AB³] *Governor Nye liked to run down to San Francisco every little while and enjoy a rest from Territorial civilization* 1906 *Autob* (1924) II 308 (OED 3. Of or belonging to one of the 'territories' of the U.S. 1812.. So W S C)

Territory, sb. [A] *In the new territories, when a man puts his hand on a weapon, he knows that he must use it* 1869 IA li 550. See *come in* 1873; *water-supply* 1883; *Organic Act* 1892. *The Government of the new Territory of Nevada was an interesting menagerie* 1906 *Autob* (1924) II 305 (OED 4. In the U.S., one of certain regions not yet admitted as a state. 1799.. So W S C B F Th.III H)

terror, sb. [B¹] See *crime* 1892 (C: Often used in hum. exaggeration. This sense not in OED W S)

test-remark, sb. [B¹] *There was no other way by which you could have gotten hold of the test-remark* 1899 "MCH" (1900) 35 (Comb. not in OED W S C; but cf. OED Test question, 1867)

texas, sb. [AB³] *"There ain't nothing to watch but the texas and the pilot-house"* 1884 HF xii 103 (OED 1. *Western U.S.* The uppermost structure of a river-steamer, containing the pilot-house and officers' quarters. OEDS 1857.. So W S C B F Cl Th T. Cf. W: On Mississippi steamboats were the staterooms were named after the states, and the officers' rooms were the largest)

texas-deck, sb. [AB²] See *boiler-deck* 1875. *She has a fanciful pilot-house perched on top of the "texas" deck* 1875 OTM 70 (OED Texas, sb. 1. 1883, this quot. So Th. Comb. not in W S C)

texas-hall, sb. [AB[1]] *Away down through the texas-hall we see a light!* 1884 HF xii 103 (Comb. not in OED W S C)

texas-tender, sb. [AB[2]] *A tidy, white-aproned, black "texas-tender"* 1875 OTM 220. See also *ice-pitcher* 1883 (OED The waiter on the texas or upper deck. 1889, only ex. So B F Cl. Comb. not in W S C)

text-meaning, sb. [B[1]] See *Adventist* 1907 (Comb. not in OED W S C; but cf. OED Text-monger, 1883)

tf, abbrev. [?AB[1]C] See *td* 1886 (Not in OED W S C. Cf. under td, above)

thank goodness, v.phr. [?AB[3]] *"You're all right, thank goodness"* 1892 AmCl xvi 170 (OED Thank, v. 3g. Ejaculatory phr. 1811.. A in DN.V. Phr. not in W S C)

Thanksgiving, sb. [A] *Roast turkey, Thanksgiving style* 1880 TA xlix 575 (OED 1b. *spec* in *U.S.* for Thanksgiving Day. 1760.. So W S C H)

that, dem.pron. **at that**. [AB[3]] *It was all down-hill, too, and very muddy at that* 1880 TA xlii 489 (OED 5c. orig. *U.S.colloq* or slang. 'Into the bargain.' 1855.. So B F Cl Th T DN.III. Not A in W S. Phr. not in C)

that, dem.adv. [?AC] See *fuzzle*, v. 1894. *"You were looking pale, too." "Pale? I was that pale that if—why, you just compare it with this lap-robe"* 1897 FE ii 44. *"Now I've come up again, and I'm that distracted and scared and heart-broke"* 1902 "DBDS" (1928) 319 (OED III. To that extent or degree; so much. Now only *dial* and *Scotch. c*1450..1902. So W S C U Wr. A in B T)

that-air, dem.adj. [AB[3]E] *"Pass that-air sasser o' m'lasses, won't ye?"* 1884 HF xli 417 (OED That, dem. adj. II.2b. Strengthened by *there*, abbrev. 'air. Cf. There, adv. 2c. *dial* and *vulgar*. 1825, only ex. A in M. This form not in W S C. Cf. this-here, below)

that-away, adv. [AB[3]] *"Lots of 'em's talkin' that-away down thar"* 1873 GA i 21. *"It is a pity if Huck is to be talked to that away"* 1896 TSD vi 358 (OEDS *dial* and *U.S.* In that manner. 1839.. So S M DN.I,II,III,IV,V AS.II.366. Not A in W Wr. Comb. not in C. Cf. this-away, below)

that-is-ing, vbl.sb. [B[1]] *"Well, yes—it does. That is—that is—" "Why so much that-is-ing?"* 1899 "MCH" (1900) 8. (Nonce comb.)

that-settles-it, a. [B[1]] *With a that-settles-it toss of the head* 1898 "Stirring Times" (1900) 326 (Nonce comb.)

the, def.art. [B[1]] *"I don't forget to mention that Mrs. O'Shaughnessy...flung as much style into Dennis's funeral as if he had been a duke or an assassin. And of course she [Mrs. O'Flaherty] sails in and goes the O'Shaughnessy about four hacks and an omnibus better"* 1883 LM xliii 439 (Cf. OED 10b. With the surnames of some Irish and Scottish chiefs of clans. 1561..1910. So W S C U. Here, hum. extension to an Irish woman of humble rank)

the, def.art. [?AB[1]] *"You [English] say 'out of window'; we always put in a 'the'"* 1882 "Concerning the American Language" 265 (Perhaps M.T. had in mind the usage of the article mentioned in W 2e: Chiefly *dial*. Limiting to the individual thing, part, or supply thought of as at hand; with names of commodities or appurtenances of daily life; as, *the* sugar is cheap; tired from lying in *the* bed; too fond of *the* booze. So Wr. This *spec* usage is not distinguished in OED S C, and is not called American in any dictionary, though M.T.'s remark is cited in M)

the, sb. [B[1]] *There were very few The's, and I was one of them. If you spoke of the duke, or the earl, or the bishop, how could anybody tell which one you meant? But if you spoke of The King or The Queen or The Boss, it was different* 1889 CY viii 102. *"The."* *I uncover to that imperial word. It lifts the Mother-Church away up in the sky and fellowships it with the rare and select and exclusive company of the The's of deathless glory—The Saviour...The Bible...and now The First Church, Scientist* 1907 CS II viii 238-9 (Nonce use as sb. Cf. OED 11 *spec*. Used emphatically, in the sense of 'the

pre-eminent'...*the* being often stressed in speech, and printed in italics. 1824..; so W S C U. M.T. was fond of playing about with the definite article)

theater-actor, sb. [B[1]] *It* [Shakespeare's death] *made no more stir in England than the death of any other forgotten theater-actor would have made* 1909 ISD iii 35 (Comb. not in OED W S C)

thee, pron. [?AE] *"Mother, thee knows I couldn't stand it at Westfield"* 1873 GA xiv 133. *"Has thee consulted thy mother about a career?"* do. xiv 138. See also *world's people* 1873 (OED 3. Used as nominative, instead of *thou*...in recent times, usually by Quakers. *c*1375.. 1687, first Quaker ex... So W S Wr. A in M. The usage of Am. Friends is fully discussed in AS.I.194, 638; IV.359,361; VIII.1.13. This usage not in C U)

theft-raid, sb. [B[1]] *The theft-raid which he had made upon the village* 1894 PW x 552 (Comb. not in OED W S C. Cf. raid, above)

theirn, poss.a. [?AB[2]E] *"I hain't ever seen eyes bug out the way theirn did"* 1896 TSD xi 532 (OED A midland and southern *dial* form. No ex. So W. A in Wr M DN.II,III AS.III.5; V.267, Ozarks; XI.351. This form not in S C)

there, dem.adv. **to be all there**. [?AB[3]] *These four of us are all good men. There is Bill Ferguson...Bill is there in every respect* 1909 Speeches (1910) 335 (OED 12b. *colloq*. To be smart or on the alert. 1864.. So W S C. A in B F)

there, dem.adv. **there you are**. [?AB[2]] *The immortelle requires no attention: you just hang it up, and there you are* 1883 LM xlii 431 (OED 16b. *colloq*. There it is for you; there you have it. 1907, only ex. Phr. not in W S C)

thesaurus, sb. [B[1]] *Tautological repetition which has no justifiable object, but merely exposes the fact that the writer's balance at the vocabulary bank has run short and that he is too lazy to replenish it from the thesaurus* 1898 *Autob* (1924) I 172 (Here *spec* of a dictionary of ideas designed to assist in finding words for them, such as Roget's *Thesaurus*. This *spec* sense not in OED W S C. Cf. in *gen*. sense OED 2. A " treasury" or "storehouse" of knowledge, as a dictionary, encyclopedia, or the like; so W S C U)

they, adv. [?AB[1]E] *"Dey wa'nt no small-fry officers, mine you; dey was de biggest dey is"* 1875 SNO 204. *"Huck, they couldn't anybody get you to tell, could they?"* 1876 TS xxiii 182. *"They's a mighty short cut that they don't anybody know about"* 1876 TS xxxiii 257. See also *wood-flat* 1884; *marse* 1893 (Used to represent the *colloq* unstressed pronunciation of the unemphatic or introductory *there*. This form not in OED W S C. An ex. in Am. use in M, p.424; cf. also DN.IV)

thick-fingered, a. [B[1]] *I am so thick-fingered that I miss the keys* 1874 Letters (1917) I xiii 238 (Comb. not in OED S C. Given in W)

thick-legged, a. [B[2]] *Propped on its long row of low, thick-legged columns* 1880 TA xlix 567 (Given in OED, no ex. So W C. Comb. not in S)

thin, a. [?A] *"Oh, come, this is too thin!"* 1888 "Meisterschaft" 466. See also *fish-bladder* 1881 (OED 1d. *fig*. Easily 'seen through,' transparent, flimsy. 1613..1904. So W S C U. A in B F Th T)

think, v. Past tense **thunk**. [?AE] *We just sat there and "thunk," as Jim calls it, and said never a word* 1893 TSA iv 120 (This form not in OED W S C)

think, sb. [B[3]C] *Think by think his thoughts dream on* 1891 *Slovenly Peter* (1935) 5 (OED *dial* or *colloq*. 1b. An idea, a thought. *nonce* use. 1886, 1887. Not a *nonce* use in W S C; W Chiefly *slang*; S *colloq*)

thinker, sb. [B[3]C] *When a person joins Mrs.Eddy's Church, he must leave his thinker at home* 1907 CS II vii 206 (OED 3. Thinking faculty, mind. *nonce* use. 1835.. W: *slang*. This use not in S C)

thinkful, a. [B²C] "*I like it—it is so sad and thinkful*" 1864 SS (1926) 123 (OED Thoughtful. *rare*. 1910, only ex. So W. Not in S C)

think up, v. [AB³] *They can't think up anything to freshen up the old moss-grown dulness of the language lesson* 1904 "Italian with Grammar" (1906) 188 (OEDS 17. To make up or compose by thinking. *U.S.* 1855.. So W. *Dial* in Wr: To arrange, plan, originate. *Yorkshire*. Comb. not in S C)

think-works, sb. [B¹] "*His think-works is just a-grinding now*" 1902 "DBDS" (1928) 326 (Nonce comb.: brains, intellectual machinery. Cf. Thought-machine, below)

thin-spaced, a. [B¹] See *solid matter* 1906 (Comb. not in OED W S C; but cf. OEDS Thin space, *Typog.*, a space used for separating words, cast five to an em of its own body. 1683..)

third clerk, sb. [?AB¹] See *second clerk* 1883 (An official on a steamboat, ranking just below second clerk. Not in OED W S C)

third degree, sb. [B¹] *She was...a widow in the third degree* 1899 "Chr.Sc. and the Book" 586 (Hum. nonce use: having three deceased husbands. Cf. OED Third, a. 5. quot. 1901: "In the third degree in Free Masonry a skull and cross-bones are employed")

Third House, sb. [AB²] *I am responsible to the Third House only* 1864 *Letters* (1917) I iv 96 (OED 5. *U.S. political slang*, the lobby. 1889, only quot. from F. So W S C. M.T.'s Nevada "Third House" was rather an organization of newspaper men and political correspondents than a lobby; cf. Paine's *Biog.* I.244: "The two Houses of the last territorial legislature of Nevada assembled *January* 12, 1864. *A few days later a* 'Third House' *was organized—an institution quite in keeping with the happy atmosphere of that day and locality, for it was a burlesque organization, and Mark Twain was selected as its* 'Governor' ")

third-quality, a. [B¹] *Bright Improvement has arrived, with her civilization, and her Waterbury, and her umbrella, and her third-quality profanity* 1897 FE vi 89 (Comb. not in OED W S C)

third-rate, sb. [B¹] *It is mainly the repetition over and over again, by the third-rates, of worn and commonplace and juiceless forms that makes their novels such a weariness* 1906 "Howells" (1917) 238 (A third-rate person. This sense not in OED W S C; but cf. OED Third-rater, 1816)

thirteen-jointed, a. [B¹] See *hair-lifting* 1889 (Nonce comb.)

thirty-cord, a. [B¹] *Those boats will never halt...except to hitch thirty-cord wood-boats alongside* 1875 OTM 191 (Nonce comb.)

this-away, adv. [AB¹] "*Why, how did that happen?*" "*Happened dis-away*" 1894 PW xiv 780 (In this manner. A in Wr M DN.II,III,V AS.II.366. Not A in W. Comb. not in OED S C. Cf. that-away, above)

this-here, dem.adj. Spelled **thish-yer**, **this h-yere**. [?AE] "*Thish-yer Smiley had rat-terriers*" 1865 "Jumping Frog" (1875) 33. "*Pap would come back to thish yer town some day*" 1876 TS xxv 194. "*We got to be together a blamed long time on this h-yere raft*" 1884 HF xix 188 (OED This, dem.adj. II.1.i. Strengthened by *here* immediately following. Now *dial* or *vulgar. c*1380..1872. So W S C. A in Wr B M DN.I,III,V AS.III.7, XI.352, Ozarks, e.Texas. Cf. that-air, above)

this-worldly, a. [B²] *The guests were always this-worldly, and often profane* 1883 LM xlviii 480 (OEDS Concerned with this world. 1883, this quot... So W. Comb. not in S C)

thoroughbrace, sb. [AB³] "*Gents, you'll have to turn out a spell. Thoroughbrace is broke*" 1872 RI iii 30 (OED *U.S.* Each of a pair of strong braces...supporting the body of a coach. 1837.. Not A in W S C)

thought-machine, sb. [B¹] *Man's thought-machine works just like the other animals'* 1906 "WIM" (1917) vi 78 (Comb. not in OED W S C)

thought-machinery, sb. [B¹] "*Dumb*" *beast suggests an animal that has no thought-machinery* 1906 "WIM" (1917) vi 83 (Comb. not in OED W S C)

Thou-hast-wounded-the-spirit-that-loved-thee, a. [B¹] *Album full of original* "*poetry*" *of the Thou-hast-wounded-the-spirit-that-loved-thee breed* 1883 LM xxxviii 400 (Hum. nonce comb.)

thousand-mile, a. [B²] *The thousand-mile wall of dense forest* 1875 OTM 450 (OED Thousand, a. 5. No ex. So W. Comb. not in S C)

thousand-times-offered, a. [B¹] *Wolf withdrew his thousand-times-offered motion* 1898 "Stirring Times" (1900) 311 (Nonce comb.)

thrash around, v. [AB¹] *He didn't go to sleep, but was uneasy. He groaned and moaned and thrashed around this way and that* 1884 HF vi 45. *He got to thrashing around with his arms like a windmill* 1889 CY vii 89. *He does more thinking and reading on that subject...thrashes around over the whole field* 1892 AmCl iii 42 (A in Th, 1846 T. Comb. not in OED W S C; but cf. OED Thrash, v. 8. intr. To make wild movements; to throw oneself to and fro with violence; to toss, plunge. 1850..)

thread-spinner, sb. [B¹] *In 1840 our population was 17,000,000...2,000,000 (women) as thread-spinners... Today the work of the 2,000,000 thread-spinners is done by 1,000 girls* 1892 AmCl x 102 (Given in W, without def. Comb. not in OED S C; but cf. OED Spinning, vbl. sb. 1. The operation of converting fibres into thread or yarn by hand-labour or by machinery)

three-ball game, sb. [B¹] *We adjourned to a café* [in Milan] *and played billiards an hour, and I made six or seven points by the doctor pocketing his ball, and he made as many by my pocketing my ball... The table was of the usual European style... The natives play only a sort of pool on them. We have never seen anybody playing the French three-ball game yet, and I doubt if there is any such game known in France* 1869 IA xix 186. [Cf. also M.T.'s bitter account of Parisian billiards in IA xii] (Comb. not in OED W S C. But cf. C, under *Billiards*: Formerly in the U.S. the game was played with four balls on a table having six pockets... This is nearly the present *English game*. Since, however, expert players could continue an inning at the game thus played almost without limit, the pockets were dispensed with and counting was made to depend entirely upon caroms. Later, professional players adopted what is known as the *French game*, in which only three balls are used. According to the *Encyc.Brit.*, the French game became the accepted one in the U.S. about 1870. M.T. is evidence that it was known in the U.S. in the preceding decade, and also that the English game, or pocket-billiards, was still played on the Continent)

three-carat, a. [B¹] *That meek idolater of provincial three-carat royalty* 1892 AmCl x 99 (A cheap alloy, three-twenty-fourths fine or pure gold. Comb. not in OED W S C)

three-children-born-at-a-birth, a. [B¹] *Weary yearly marvels of the Three-Children-Born-at-a-Birth sort* 1883 LM lx 584 (Hum. nonce comb.)

three-dollar, a. [AB¹] *Inviting everybody to buy his specialty, which was a three-dollar shoe* 1892 AmCl xxi 212 (Comb. not in OED W S C. Cf. dollar, above)

three-leggedly, adv. [B¹] *I limped three-leggedly along* 1903 "Dog's Tale" 19 (Comb. not in OED W S C)

three-log, a. [B¹] See *bow-end* 1880 (Nonce comb.)

three-month, a. [B²] *That three-month pleasure excursion* 1872 RI i 20 (Given in OED, no ex. So W. Comb. not in S C)

threes, sb. [AB¹] "*I certainly held threes—but I drew and didn't fill*" 1904 "Bequest" (1906) iii 14 (W: A set of three cards of one denomination, as in poker, etc. So S. This sense not in OED C)

three-word, a. [B¹] *A few beggarly little three-word phrases* 1880 TA xxx 321 (Comb. not in OED W S C)

three-year-older, sb. [B¹] *The three-year-older's wound was of a formidable sort* 1907 "Chaps. from Autob" 562 (Comb. not in OED W S C)

throttle down, v. [B¹] *I shall throttle down my emotions hereafter* 1869 IA xv 147 (To suppress, hold in check. This *fig* sense not in OED W S C; but cf. OED Throttle, v. 4. To check or stop by means of a valve; to regulate the supply of steam to an engine. 1875..)

through-freight, a. [AB¹] *The railroads have killed the steamboat passenger traffic...and the towing fleets have killed the through-freight traffic* 1883 LM xxii 256 (Comb. not in OED W S C. Cf. freight, above)

through-line, sb. [?AB¹] *Harry had a way of casually mentioning Western investments, through lines, the freighting businss* 1873 GA xxii 203 (Comb. not in OED W S C; but cf. OED Through, a. 1b. through ticket, 1845; through train, 1846, all exs. U.S.)

throw, v. **to throw a card.** [?AB¹] *"I do solemnly swear that I will not throw a card or drink a drop of liquor while I am gone"* 1853 *Letters* (1917) I i 22 (Here used *absol*=to play cards. This sense not in OED W S C. Cf. OED 10b. To play (a card) out of one's hand; esp., to discard. 1879..; so W S C)

throw off, v. [?AB¹] *Smiley says, "I do wonder what in the nation that frog throw'd off for?"* 1865 "Jumping Frog" (1875) 34 (To give up, fail to make an effort. This sense not in OED W S C)

throw off on, v. [AB¹] *"Just you gimme the hundred dollars and I don't want no di'monds." "All right. But I bet you I ain't going to throw off on di'monds"* 1876 TS xxv 193 (To abandon, renounce. A in DN.IV. This sense not in OED W S C. Perhaps to be identified with the use above)

throw up, v. [?AB¹] *"One was for going one way, one another, so we throwed up, heads or tails, and the Upper Mississippi won"* 1896 TSD iii 350 (To toss a coin. The const. with *up* in this sense not in OED W S C; but cf. OED Throw, v. 10. To cast dice; also *absol*. 1587..)

throw up, v. [?AB¹] *All other boys might...have Benjamin Franklin thrown up to them* 1870 SNO (1875) 276. *The boys all hated him, he was so good. And besides, he had been "thrown up" to them so much* 1876 TS v 54 (To hold up before one as an example. This sense not in OED W S C. Cf. OED 48h. To cast in one's teeth, upbraid one with. 1890, only ex.; so W S Wr)

throw up, v. [?AB¹] *"I have here the natal autographs of the two children—thrown up to ten times the natural size by the pantograph"* 1894 PW xxi 238 (To enlarge, magnify. This sense not in OED W S C)

thug, sb. [AB³] *"This dismal place, in almost any other country, would swarm with thugs"* 1878 SWE (1882) 80. See also *herumfrodite* 1909 (OED b. transf. A cutthroat, ruffian, rough. Now *U.S.* 1839.. So Th.III H. Not A in W S C U)

thug-book, sb. [B¹] *I learned of an official Thug-book the other day...I am allowed the temporary use of it... The Report was made in 1839 by Major Sleeman, of the Indian Service, and was printed in Calcutta in 1840* 1897 FE xliv 400 (A book about the Thugs, an association of professional robbers and murders in India. Comb. not in OED W S C. Cf. Kaet, above)

thug-chief, sb. [B¹] *Major Sleeman captured...the Thug-chief, and got him to turn King's evidence* 1897 FE xlvi 427 (Comb. not in OED W S C)

thumbkin, sb. [B¹] *He's got his thumbkin in his mouth!* 1891 *Slovenly Peter* (1935) 15 (Modeled on German Däumchen or Daumlein. Not in OED W S C in this sense. Cf. W S C: Thumbkin, a thumbscrew)

thumb-sucker, sb. [B¹] *Story of the Thumb-Sucker* [German, *Daumen-Lutscher*] 1891 *Slovenly Peter* (1935) 15 (Not in OED W S C; but cf. OED Thumb-sucking. 1897, only ex.; so W)

thunder-and-lightning, a. [B¹] *Take What's-her-name, that plays those sensational thunder-and-lightning parts* 1892 AmCl ix 84 (Blood-and-thunder, melodramatic. This sense not in OED W S C; but cf. OED 3b. Applied to articles of apparel of a 'loud' or flashy style. 1837..; so W S C)

thunderation, int. [AB³] *Thunderation! It wasn't no more like a hoss than a meetin house* 1856 *Adv. of T.J. Snodgrass* (1928) 23 (OEDS *U.S.* Used as a vague expletive. 1845.. So W S C)

Thunder-Bird, sb. [?AB³] *In forty-eight hours the Indian encampment was here, illustrious old Thunder-Bird and all* 1906 "Horse's Tale" 330 (OED A mythical bird thought by some savage tribes to cause thunder. 1827.. So S C. A in Th.III. Comb. not in W. Here, transf. as an Indian personal name)

thunder-burst, sb. [B¹] *I can remember those awful thunder-bursts* 1906 *Autob* (1924) II 176 (Thundercrash. Comb. not in OED C. Given in W S)

thunder-gust, sb. [A] *"You, Devourer of Mountains—you, Roaring Thundergust —the paleface greets you all!"* 1869 SNO (1875) 69. *A thundergust of humiliating laughter* 1875 OTM 574. *"If I had room for such a thundergust..."* 1880 *Fireside Conversation of 1601* (OED Chiefly U.S. A strong gust of wind accompanying a thunderstorm. 1748.. So AS.VI.466; VII.312; X.172. Not A in W S C)

thundering, a. [A] *"It's a thundering lie!"* 1894 PW ix 549 (OED 4. As a mere intensive. *colloq* or *slang*. 1618..1900. So W S C. A in B Th)

thundering, adv. [?AB³] *A thundering poor success* 1889 CY xxvii 349 (OEDS 4b. Earliest quot. U.S, 1807 .. A in B Th. Not A in W S U. This use not in C)

thunder-tramp, sb. [B¹] *The procession...with its muffled thunder-tramp* 1881 PP xii 135 (Comb. not in OED W S C)

thwartships, adv. Spelled **thortships.** [E] *The puppy stands up behind the saddle, "thortships," as a sailor would say* 1866 *Speeches* (1923) 11. *A saddle that slips fore-and-aft, and "thortships," and every way* 1869 IA xliii 453 (OED *Naut*. From side to side of the ship. 1625, 1718. This sp. not given. So W S C)

tick, sb. [?AB²] See *shuck tick* 1884 (OED b. Used for the bed or bolster itself, instead of merely the case or cover. 1887. So W. A in AS.VII.169, Neb. This sense not in S C)

ticket, sb. [A] *He votes for a thief..on his own party's ticket, and against an honest man on the other ticket* 1906 "WIM" (1917) 42 (OED 8. In U.S. politics: The list of candidates nominated by a party. 1711.. So W S C B F Cl Th T M. Not A in U)

ticket, sb. [?AB³] *"Well," she says, "I'll run down to breakfast now, and then I'll start straight for Mr. Lathrop's." "'Deed, that ain't the ticket, Miss Mary Jane,"* I says 1884 HF xxviii 286. *"Quick! is it hang, or shoot?" "Neither...burning's the only permanency for him." The gangs...closed around him, shouting, "Fire! fire's the ticket!"* 1902 "DBDS" 355 (OED 9b. *slang*. The program or plan of action; that which is to be done. 1842.. So W S C. A in Wr)

ticket-money, sb. [B²] *The man could not get back the ticket-money* 1902 "Belated Russian Passport" (1928) 176 (Given in OED, no ex. Comb. not in W S C)

ticket-office, sb. [?AB²] *I asked the young man in the ticket-office if I could have a sleeping-section* 1881 *Speeches* (1910) 258 (Given in OED, no ex. So W. A in M, for Eng. 'booking-office.' Comb. not in S C)

ticket-taker, sb. [B¹] *At the hall I tried to press in, but was stopped by the ticket-taker* 1898 *Autob* (1924) I 161 (Comb. not in OED S C. Given in W)

tick-running, vbl.sb. [B¹] *"Tick-running and a Heart-break"* [chapter-title, not added till the 1910 edition] 1910 TS vii 72 (Nonce comb., for a game with a tick on a desk. Tom explains: *"Now as long as he is on your side of the line, you can stir him up and I'll let* *him alone; but if you let him get away and get on my side, you're to leave him alone as long as I can keep him from crossing over"*)

tidal wave, sb. [?AB²] *A great tidal wave of grief swept over us all* 1875 SNO 213 (OED 1b(b). *fig.* A great manifestation of feeling, etc. Earliest exs. U.S. 1884.. Not A in W S C U)

tide, v. [C] *"Tide me death, betide me life," saith the king* 1889 CY xlii 536 (OED † 2. To fall as a lot or portion. 955..1386. So W S C)

tide-water, sb. [A] *The turtles left for tide-water in disorderly procession* 1873 GA xxv 230 (OEDS 2. *U.S,* Tidal water. 1789.. So U H AS.II.30. Not A in W S C)

tidy, sb. [?AB³] *Wall-paper and framed lithographs, and bright-colored tidies and lamp-mats* 1893 "Californian's Tale" (1906) 105 (OED b. An ornamental loose covering for the back of a chair or the like. Earliest ex. U.S. 1850.. So B F Cl Th T. |Not A in W S C U)

tidy up, v. [?AB³] *The Commission will have the old thing all reorganized, and dredged out, and fenced, and tidied up* 1883 LM xxviii 307 (OED chiefly *colloq.* To put in order. 1821.. So W S C U. A in B T)

tie, sb. [AB³] *We took to the railway ties to keep from getting lost* 1880 TA xxviii 292 (OED 7b. *U.S.* A transverse railway sleeper. 1857.. So W Th T M H. Not A in S C)

tie up, v. [?AB³] *The boat ties up at the shore* 1875 OTM 567. *The captain wanted to tie up* 1880 TA xvii 156 (OED 11d. To moor a ship or boat; also *absol.* or *intr.* for *pass.* 1853.. So S. A in B Th.III. This sense not in W C)

tiger, sb. [AB³] *They sent up three rousing cheers and a tiger* 1872 RI lvii 417. *They finished up with a rousing three-times-three and a tiger* 1899 "MCH" (1900) 46. *"Hurrah! hurrah! hurrah! Tiger!"* 1902 "DBDS" (1928) 331 (OED 8. *U.S.* slang. A shriek or howl terminating a...cheer. 1856.. So S B F Cl Th T H. Not A in W C U)

tiger, sb. [AB³] *Hunting the "tiger," or some kindred game* 1869 *Curious Dream* (1872) vii 83 (OED 9a. The game of faro. *U.S. slang.* 1851.. So W B F Cl Th T. This sense not in S C)

tiger-average, sb. [B¹] *In India, the annual man-killings by snakes are...as forecastable as are the tiger-average and the suicide-average* 1897 FE lvii 546 (Comb. not in OED W S C)

tiger-fight, sb. [B¹] See *elephant-fight* 1897 (Comb. not in OED W S C)

tiger-persuader, sb. [B¹] *The other two established servants were the tiger-persuader and the hailstorm discourager. The one kept away the tigers if he could, and collected the wages anyway* 1897 FE xlix 463 (Comb. not in OED W S C)

tight, a. [?AB³] *Soaked banana and plantain in brandy, and got the monkey tight* 1867 *Notebook* (1935) v 52. See also *bullyrag* 1884 (OEDS 7. Drunk, tipsy. Earlier U.S. ex. 1843.. A in B T DN.III. Not A in W S C U)

tight, a. [AB³] *The old man and her had a mighty tight race of it* 1856 *Adv. of T.J.Snodgrass* (1928) 22 (OED 10a. Said of a contest in which the combatants are evenly matched; close. Orig. *U.S.* 1828.. Not A in W. This sense not in S C)

tight, adv. [A] See *pull on* 1884. *Here comes a couple of men tearing up the path as tight as they could foot it* 1884 HF xix 180. *"I jumped on his hoss en took out for de river as tight as I could go"* 1894 PW xviii 18. See also *take out* 1896 (OED 1. Now *dial* and *U.S.* 1790.. So C Wr DN.IV. *Dial* in W S. W S C consider *tight* in this sense as a var. sp. of *tite*, quickly, nimbly; but this identification is denied in OED)

tight-buttoned, a. [B¹] *Grooms in...tight-buttoned coats* 1892 AmCl iv 54 (Comb. not in OED W S C)

tight-legged, a. [B¹] *Blue cotton, tight-legged pants, tied close round the ankles* 1870 SNO (1875) 232 (Comb. not in OED W S C)

tight place, sb. [?AB³] *Truly this was the tightest place I was ever in* 1880 TA xxv 248. See also *outstart* 1884 (OED A position of difficulty. *colloq.* Only ex. called U.S. 1864. A in B Th,1856 DN.III. Not A in W S. Phr. not in C)

tight tongue, sb. [?AB¹] *"Don't you do any gabbling by the way. Just keep a tight tongue in your head"* 1884 HF xxxii 326 (The opposite of a 'loose tongue.' Phr. not in OED W S C)

tile, sb. [?AB³] *"Kid gloves, plug tile, hair parted behind"* 1883 LM lviii 570 (OED 3. *slang.* A hat. 1823.. So W S C U. A in B T)

timber, sb. [?A] *Being approached by a serpent, would...break for the nearest timber* 1909 ISD ii 21 (OED 4. Applied...collectively to trees; woods. 1634.. So C. This sense A in W S. Cf. B: Throughout the South and West applied to woodland. So F Cl T)

timber-front, sb. [?AB¹] *They are felling the timber-front for fifty yards back, with the purpose of shaving the bank down to low-water mark* 1883 LM xxviii 302 (The wooded bank of the river. Comb. not in OED W S C. Cf. above)

timber-land, sb. [AB³] *Located some timber-lands on its shores* 1872 RI xxii 168 (OEDS *U.S.* 1807.. So B. Not A in W S C)

timber-raft, sb. [?AB³] *Down came a swarm of timber-rafts* 1875 OTM 448 (OED 1853. Comb. not in W S C. Cf. raft, above)

timbrel, sb. [C] *She* [Mrs.Eddy] *begins to tune up on her fine-writing timbrel* 1907 CS II ii 125 (OED Now chiefly *biblical.* 1500..1850. Not *arch* in any way in W S C U)

time, sb. **to have a good time.** [A] *"You'll have a good time finding Mr. Jones's plantation such a night as this"* 1875 OTM 218. *In the night some time he got powerful thirsty and...traded his new coat for a jug of forty-rod... and had a good old time* 1884 HF v 36 (OED 6. *U.S. colloq.* A time of enjoyment. Common in Eng. from 1650 to 1688; it was app. retained in Am., whence readopted in Britain in 19th c. 1529..1902. So S C B F Cl Th,1843 T DN.IV. Not A in W U)

time, sb. **to have a time.** [AB¹] *She does not receive the lost sheep with glad emotion and set up the fatted calf and invite the neighbors and have a time* 1907 CS II vii 176 (To have a good time; cf. above. Phr. without *good* not in OED S C. Cf. B: Time, a spree. Not A in W)

time, sb. **to beat one's time.** [?AB¹] *"I swear it beats my time. ...See if you can't find out what in the very nation he wants"* 1869 IA lvii 616 (To pass one's comprehension, to overwhelm. A *fig* extension from time = rate of speed in a race? Phr. not in OED W S C; but cf. OED Time. 8b. Period in which a given course of action is completed. 1894. OEDS Earlier U.S. ex. 1842.)

time being, adv. [?AB¹] *"It's human nature—human nature in grief. It don't reason, you see. Time being, it don't care a d——n"* 1883 LM xliii 440 (Meanwhile. This ellipt. use not in OED W S C; but cf. OED Time, sb. 2. *For the time being:* during the period under consideration. 1486, only ex.)

time-passer, sb. [B¹] *We had one game in the ship which was a good time-passer* 1897 FE ii 41 (A pastime, amusement. Comb. not in OED W S C)

tin, a. [B³] *An archangel in a tin halo* 1899 "Diplomatic Pay" (1928) 239. *It pitilessly exposes him as a tin hero* 1907 CS II i 104 (OED 4b. *fig* in reference to tin as a base metal. 1886.. So W. This use not in S C. Cf. nickel, above)

tin-can, a. [?A] *A dozen Indians in rabbit-skin robes and tin-can necklaces* 1902 "DBDS" (1928) 307 (OEDS Earlier Amer. exs. 1770.. Not A in W Wr. Comb. not in S C)

tinct, v. [C] *They are all in the same image and tincted with the same color* 1889 CY xi 129 (OED *obs.* 1. To tinge, tint. 1594..1686. So W S C U)

tin cup, sb. [?AB[1]] *They had a jug, and tin cups, and they kept the jug moving* 1883 LM iii 44 (Comb. not in OED S C. Given in W)

tin-monger, sb. [?AB[1]] *The chief tin-monger's noisy notice to the world* 1893 PW i 234 (A tinman, dealer in tin-ware. Comb. not in OED W S C)

tin-patched, ppl.a. [B[1]] See *outer-border*, sb. 1897 (Comb. not in OED W S C)

tintype, sb. [?AB[3]] *They work these things up from twenty-five cent tintypes* 1892 AmCl xvi 163 (OED *Photogr.* A photograph taken as a positive on a thin tin plate. 1875.. So W C. A in S)

tin-ware, sb. [?A] *The scant pile of household goods... some bedticks, chests, tinware, stools...* 1883 LM xxx 326 (OEDS Earlier Amer. exs. 1758.. Not A in W S C)

tipple, sb. [?A] *This young woman had never moistened the selvedge edge of her soul with a less plebeian* [more plebeian?] *tipple than champagne* 1880 TA xxxi 333 (OED *colloq* or *slang*. Drink, liquor for drinking. 1581.. So W S C U. A in B F Cl T H)

'tisn't-anything-I-can-do-it-any-time-I-want-to, sb. [B[1]] *Such a complacent air of 'tisn't-anything,-I can-do-it-any-time-I-want-to* 1883 LM lix 574 (Hum. nonce comb.)

tissue, sb. [C] *A front-piece of purple cloth of tissue, powdered with diamonds* 1881 PP ix 106 (OED 1a. A rich kind of cloth, often interwoven with gold or silver. *Obs* exc. *Hist.* a1366..1785. So W S C. Not *obs* in U)

to, prep. [AC] *I jest want to tell you how they do things down here to Saint Louis* 1856 *Adv. of T.J.Snodgrass* (1928) 3. *The President was up to the Capitol* 1893 TSA i 22 (OED 4. Expressing simple position: At, in a place. Cf.Ger. *zu Berlin, zu hause.* Now only *dial* and *U.S. colloq.* 925..1901. So Wr B DN.III,V AS.X.315. Not A in W C T. This use not in S)

to, prep. [AB[2]] *An agonized voice, with the backwoods "whang" to it* 1875 OTM 448. *"There's more to a bluejay than any other creature"* 1880 TA ii 36. *Some of these old American words do have a kind of jolly swing to them* 1880 TA xx 194. *The steamboat shoved out up the creek. That was all there was "to it"* 1883 LM xlv 461. *There warn't a window to it* [the cabin] *big enough for a dog to get through* 1884 HF vi 39. *Training is all there is to a person* 1889 CY xviii 216. *There was no give-up to those English* 1895 JA II xxii 887 (OEDS 8d. Included, contained, or involved in; chiefly in phr. *That is all there is to it.* orig.*U.S.* 1886.. So H. Not A in W C. This use not in S. M.T.'s fondness for this usage proves that it is by no means confined to the phr. mentioned)

to, prep. **to home.** [AB[3]] *He told us to find out if Brace and Jubiter was to home* 1896 TSD iv 355 (OEDS Home, sb. 13. *dial*; also *U.S.* 1833.. So B F. Not A in W. Not in S C)

to, prep. **to a fraction.** [?AB[1]] *This was another Magdala, to a fraction, frescoes and all* 1869 IA li 545 (Phr. not in OED W S C; but cf. OED 13. to a hair, to a man, to an inch, etc.)

to, prep. **to not to.** [?AB[1]] *"It's all right, I've got that one." I wanted to offer to bet two dollars she hadn't, but I reckoned maybe it was just as safe to not to. So I never said nothing* 1884 HF xlii 433 (Used redundantly as a substitute for the verb. This use not in OED W S C. An extension of the use in OED 21. Absol. at the end of a clause, with ellipsis of the infinitive, which is to be supplied from the preceding clause; *rare* before 19th c.; now a frequent colloquialism. 1300..1909. So W S C U)

tobacco, sb. [A] *A strapping girl...asked me if I "used tobacco"—meaning did I chew* 1897 *Autob* (1924) I 109 (OED 1. The leaves of the tobacco-plant...a native of tropical America. 1588.. So W S C U B M AS.IV.10f.)

tobacco-chewing, vbl.sb. [AB[3]] *By and by we entered the tobacco-chewing region* 1883 LM xxii 249 (OED 1878. So W AS.IV.10. Comb. not in S C. Cf. above)

tobacco-commerce, sb. [AB[1]] *The convergence of that huge tobacco-commerce towards Memphis* 1897 FE xxviii 272 (Cf. above. Comb. not in OED W S C)

tobacco-curing, vbl.sb. [AB[1]] *The woody hill fell sharply away, past the barns, the corn-crib, the stables and the tobacco-curing house* 1897 *Autob* (1924) I 99 (Cf. above. Comb. not in OED W S C)

tobacco-field, sb. [AB[1]] *He would wait for us in a little bunch of sycamores right back of Tom's uncle Silas's tobacker-field* 1896 TSD iv 355 (Cf. above. Comb. not in OED W S C)

tobacco-juice, sb. [AB[3]] *One after another of the several chewers expressed a charge of tobacco-juice* 1873 GA i 21 (OED 1833. Comb. not in W S C)

tobacco-lover, sb. [AB[1]] *All the tobacco-lovers in the world could not elect a standard which would be binding upon me* c1893 "Concerning Tobacco" (1917) 275. (Cf. above. Comb. not in OED W S C)

tobacco-smoke, sb. [A] *Let out the surplus tobacco-smoke and profanity* 1883 LM xxxvi 387 (OED 1597. So W. Comb. not in S C)

tobacco-stemmer, sb. [AB[1]] *Henry Taylor, twenty-four, tobacco-stemmer* 1894 "Scrap of Curious Hist." (1917) 188 (This comb. not in OED W S C; but cf. OED Stemmer, sb. The workman who 'stems' tobacco-leaf; a stripper. 1895. Cf. also OED Tobacco-stripper, 1725)

toboggan-slide, sb. [AB[3]] *The road fell sharply down in front of us...suggesting nothing so uncomfortably as a crooked toboggan slide with no end to it* 1897 FE lvi 536 (OED Adaptation of a Canadian Indian name of a sleigh or sledge. 3. *toboggan-slide*, A steep incline for tobogganing 1887, O.W. Holmes. So W S C)

toby, sb. [AB[3]] See *change off* 1910 (OED 5. An inferior kind of cigar. *U.S. slang* 1896.. So W S C)

toe-hold, sb. [?AB[1]] *One man's toe-hold broke, and he fell!* 1880 TA xxxiv 379 (W: A place of support for the toes, as in climbing. So S. Comb. not in OED C)

toe-ring, sb. [B[2]] *All the females among them* [Hindoos] *bejeweled with cheap and showy nose-rings, toe-rings, leglets, and armlets* 1897 FE xliv 403 (OED 1905, only ex. So W S C)

toggery, sb. [?AB[3]] *I hurried toward the engine-room, picturesquely gotten up in storm toggery* 1875 OTM 569 (OED *slang* or *colloq*. 1. Garments. 1812.. So W S C U. A in M)

toilet, sb. [B[3]?C] *I was not acquainted with anybody... who wore twelve-hundred-dollar toilets to go fishing in* 1893 "Esquimau Maiden's Romance" (1900) 139 (OED 6. A dress or costume. 1821..1889. So S C U. W: *Now Rare*)

toilet article, sb. [B[1]] *He could have the use of mirror and toilet articles* 1894 PW x 552 (Given in W. Comb. not in OED S C; but cf. OED Toilet set, 1858)

token, sb. **by the same token.** [?C] *By the same token any person can see that seven hundred and forty-two years from now the Lower Mississippi will be only a mile and three-quarters long* 1875 OTM 193 (OED 15a(b). Since 1500, 'the proof of this being that'; introducing a corroborating circumstance, often weakened down to a mere associated fact. *arch* or *dial.* 1463..1907. Not *arch* in W S C U, and app. not so felt by M.T.)

tolerable, adv. [?AC] *A tolerable slim old maid* 1884 HF i 2. See also *sake* 1894 (OED 5a. Tolerably, moderately, fairly. After 1750 chiefly in inferior writers and *dial.* 1673..1823. OEDS Later U.S. exs. 1850..1884, above quot. A in Wr DN.I,II. *Dial* in W. Not in S C as adv.)

toll-road, sb. [AB[3]] *The legislature passed private toll-road franchises all the time* 1872 RI xxv 192. *Everybody had a toll-road franchise but no toll-road* 1906 *Autob* (1924) II 308 (OED A turnpike road. *Scotch* and *U.S.* 1825.. Not A in W. Comb. not in S C)

tomahawk, sb. [A] *I shall visit Paris again some day, and then let the guides beware! I shall go in my war-paint —I shall carry my tomahawk* 1869 IA xiii 124. *"You* *must produce the Indian and the tomahawk*" 1870 SNO (1875) 107 (OED 1. The ax of the N.Am. Indians. 1612.. So W S C U B F Cl M AS.IV.10)

tomahawk, sb. [AB³] *This editor is a critic. He has pulled out his carving-knife and his tomahawk and is starting after a book* 1899 "How to Make Hist. Dates Stick" (1917) 159 (OED 1e. *fig* 1805.. Fig. sense not in W S C)

tomahawk, v. [A] See *scalp,* v. 1870. "*Who tomahawked him?*" 1870 SNO (1875) 106. "*He has come over here to tomahawk papa*" 1892 AmCl xxv 262 (OED 1. 1755.. Cf. above. So W S C M)

tomato, sb. [A] See *bunch,* v. 1873. *A Boston newspaper reporter went and took a look at* [Turner's picture] "*The Slave Ship*"...*and said it reminded him of a tortoise-shell cat having a fit in a platter of tomatoes* 1880 TA xxiv 238. See also *batter-cake* 1897 (OED *U.S.* 1604 .. So W S C U B Th M DN.I,II,III)

tomato-vine, sb. [AB¹] See *jimpson-weed* 1876 (Comb. not in OED W S C. Cf. above)

tomb-desecrator, sb. [B¹] *The next detachment of image-breakers and tomb-desecrators arrives* 1869 IA xlvii 493 (Comb. not in OED W S C)

tomb-lantern, sb. [B¹] *More than a hundred tomb-lanterns* 1899 "Concerning the Jews" (1900) 279 (Comb. not in OED W S C)

Tom o' Bedlam, sb. [C] "*Gone stark mad as any Tom o' Bedlam!*" 1881 PP iv 53 (OED A madman...discharged from Bedlam and licensed to beg. *obs.* 1605.. 1880. So W Wr. Not in S C)

tongue-lashing, vbl.sb. [B²] *She promptly brought the king out of his dreams with a brisk and cordial tongue-lashing* 1881 PP xix 242 (OED 1885. So W S C)

tonnage, sb. [B³] *A dignitary of that tonnage* 1869 IA ii 27 (OED 4b. *fig.* 1806..1869, this quot. So W. The *fig* sense not in S C)

tony, a. [AB³] *He was the toniest aristocrat on the boat* 1883 LM xxxiii 370 (OEDS *U.S. colloq.* High-toned, stylish, 'swell.' 1880.. So W S C F Cl M DN.IV)

toothsomely, adv. [B²] *Gossip of any kind and about anybody is one of the most toothsomely Christian dishes I know* 1871 Letter in Clara Clemens, *My Father* (1931) 53 (OED 1880, only ex. So W)

tooth-wash, sb. [?AB²] See *atrocity,* 1871; *Noyoudont* 1889 (OEDS A liquid dentrifice. 1895, only ex. So W S. Comb. not in C)

top, v. [C] *A ram...will top above a hundred ewes 'twixt sun and sun* 1880 *Fireside Conversation of 1601* (OED 11. To 'cover.' *obs. rare.* 1604, 1633. So W. Not *obs* in S C)

top-buggy, sb. [AB³] *Cap. Phillips was there with his "turnout," as he calls his top-buggy that Cap. Cook brought here* [to the Sandwich Islands] *in 1778, and a horse that was here when Cap. Cook came* 1866 *Letters* (1917) I v 112. *I hired a two-horse top-buggy for the first third of the journey* 1880 TA xxxiii 358 (OEDS A buggy fitted with a top. *U.S.* 1849.. So Th.III DN.III. Not A in C. Comb. not in W S)

torch-basket, sb. [?AB¹] *It was inspiring to hear the crews sing, especially if the time were nightfall, and the forecastle lit up with the red glare of the torch-baskets* 1875 OTM 191. *Jake slipped down aft with his hand-bag... and walked ashore...and we see him pass out of the light of the torch-basket* 1896 TSD iv 354 (A steamboat means of illumination. Comb. not in OED W S C)

torch-lighted, ppl.a. [B¹] *We find the torch-lighted galleries already filling up with people* 1881 PP xxxii 365. *He sent us back to Courdray Castle torch-lighted and in state* 1895 JA II vi 235 (Comb. not in OED S C. Given in W)

torch-light procession, sb. [?AB²] *Does he want to get up a torch-light procession?* 1869 IA lvii 616. *Spots of light attended the monster like a torchlight procession* 1873 GA iii 37. *And they brought me home with a torch-light procession* 1892 AmCl ii 33. See *Democrat* 1906."*He*

expects to be received with a torchlight procession" 1908 "Capt.Stormfield" 267 (OED c. *attrib* 1876.. So W U. A in S: Especially in the U.S....a procession by uniformed organizations. Comb. not in C)

torch-plant, sb. [B¹] *Afterward in South Africa I saw another splendid effect made by red flowers. This flower was probably called the torchplant—should have been so named, anyway...From its top stood up a single tongue of flame* 1897 FE lvi 539 (Nonce comb. Cf. OED Torch sb. 1. *torch-plant* = *Torch-thistle,* a name for a columnar cactus of the genus *Cereus.* 1696. This is obviously an entirely different plant)

tornado, sb. [AB³] *There was a brief tornado of murky blasphemy* 1869 SNO (1875) 48. *The house had gotten itself all ready to burst into the proper tornado of applause* 1899 "MCH" (1900) 34 (OED 2b. In the Mississippi region of U.S., a destructive rotatory storm. c. *fig* 1818.. So W S C U M)

torpedo, sb. [AB³] *When an oilwell ceased to flow, they used to dynamite it out with a dynamite torpedo* 1889 CY xxii 275 (OED 3c. A cartridge exploded in an oil-well to cause a renewal or increase of the flow. *U.S.* 1877. Not A in W S C U)

tory, sb. [A] *We raised not a stone to mark where we buried a tory* 1853 *Hannibal Journal,* May 23 (OED 4. *U.S. Hist.* A member of the British party during the Revolutionary period. 1775.. So W S C B F Cl H AS.IV.4,10)

tote, v. [A] "*I tote water for Uncle Jake*" 1876 TS xxviii 216. "*You've got to admire men that can tote ideas of that size*" 1883 LM xxviii 304. *His friends toted him home on a shutter* 1889 CY xl 519. "*Tain't wuth totin' out on a shovel en throwin' in de gutter*" 1894 PW xiv 779. See *take* and 1895. *The meals was always toted in there by the waiters* 1896 TSD ii 346 (OED *U.S. colloq.* To carry as a burden or load. 1676..1896. So W S C U B F Cl Th T M DN.II, s.e.Mo.; III,IV,V,VI AS.I.149, IV.11,475, V.429, Ozarks; VI.230, VIII.1.23. See additional refs. in Kennedy, p. 324)

totem-post, sb. [AB³] *The totem-posts were there* [New Zealand] *ancestor above ancestor...grotesque and ugly devils, every one* 1897 FE xxxii 297 (OED A post carved and painted with totem figures, erected by the Indians of N. Am. in front of their houses. 1891, only ex. So W S C F Th.III. No dict. mentions their use among the Maoris)

t'other, pron. *to tell t'other from which.* [?AB²] "*Dog my cats if it ain't all I kin do to tell t'other fum which*" 1893 PW iii 239 (OEDS Jocular variant of *to tell one from the other.* 1914, only ex. A in DN.III. Phr. not in W S C)

t'other, a. [?A] "*Never saw t'other man*" 1876 TS xxv 202 (OED 1. The other of two. 1300..1816. So W S C U. A in Wr DN.I,II,III AS.V.207, Ozarks)

touch off, v. [?AB²] *His chance comes and he touches off his pet sentence* 1884 *Speeches* (1923) 6 (OED 32b. To fire off. 1907, only ex. So W S C)

touch up, v. [?AB³] *Him and the feller touched up the frogs from behind* 1865 "Jumping Frog" (1875) 34. *I might as well touch him up a little at the same time and make him ridiculous* 1870 SNO (1875) 240 (OED 34. To stimulate by striking lightly or sharply, as with a whip; hence *fig* to remind, 'to gently jog the memory' (Farmer). 1810.. No ex. of *fig* use. So W S C U. A in F)

tough, a. [?AB³] "*You read the Bible. Don't you worry about the tough places. They ain't tough when you come to think them out and throw light on them*" 1877 "Some Rambling Notes" ii 590 (OED 6b. Hard to believe or understand; taxing credulity or comprehension. Earliest ex. U.S. 1820.. S: *colloq.* This sense not in W C)

tough, a. [AB²] "*Yes, there is talk, always will be about a pretty woman so much in public as she is. Tough stories come to me, but I put 'em aside. 'Tain't likely one of Si Hawkins's children would do that*" 1873 GA xliv 400.

Each in his degree was tough, and there were three degrees—tough, tougher, toughest. They were just illustrious official brigands 1895 JA II xiii 547 (OED 7. *U.S.* Of criminal or vicious proclivities. 1884.. So W F H. Not A in S. This sense not in C)

tough nut, sb. [?AB¹] *His father was a rather tough nut* 1892 AmCl xxv 263 (Comb. not in OED W S C)

tourbillon, sb. [B¹?C] *We shot the Bridge of the Holy Spirit* [on the Rhone, above Arles]...*We were allowed to go through the wrong arch, which brought us into a tourbillon below, which tried to make this old scow stand on its head* 1891 *Letters* (1917) II xxxi 557 (A whirlpool or eddy in a river. Cf. OED 1. A whirlwind. *obs.* c1477..1819. W: Whirlwind or whirlpool, not *obs.* This sense not in S C)

tourist-book, sb. [B¹] *A glance at these tourist-books shows us... that the Mississippi has undergone no change* 1883 LM xxvii 226 (Comb. not in OED W S C)

tourist-resort, sb. [B¹] *Mr. Richmond had become possessed of Tom Sawyer's cave in the hills three miles from town, and had made a tourist-resort of it* 1906 *Autob* (1924) II 215 (Comb. not in OED W S C)

toward, a. [C] *"Defend thee, lord!...peril of life is toward!"* 1889 CY xiv 167 (OED 2b. Approaching, imminent, impending. Now *rare* or *obs.* c890..1877. So W S C U Wr)

tower of silence, sb. [B²] *Those grim receptacles of the Parsee dead, the Towers of Silence. There is something stately about that name...the hush of death is in it* 1897 FE xl 371 (OED 1910, only ex. So S C. Phr. not in W)

towboat, sb. [?AB³] *The towboat and the railroad had done their work* 1883 LM xxii 255 (OED A small vessel built for towing others, a tug. Earliest ex. U.S. 1815.. A in B F Cl DN.II,III. Not A in W S C)

towhead, sb. [AB³] *Hold open to right of high trees on towhead till close enough to go up shore of towhead* 1856 *Notebook* (1935) i 4. *A large town which lay shut in behind a towhead* (i.e., *new island*) 1883 LM xxiii 262. *A towhead is a sand-bar that has cottonwoods on it as thick as harrow-teeth* 1884 HF xii 99 (OEDS *U.S.* A slight obstruction in a stream causing a white ripple or foam at the surface. 1829..1883, above quot. So S C. A better def. in F: A small recently formed island. So W B Cl)

tow-head, sb. [?AB²] *On his tow-head musty Scissors seldom come* 1891 *Slovenly Peter* (1935) 2 (OED 4c. A light-colored head of hair; also an unkempt or tousled head. No ex. So W. A in B. Not in S C in this sense)

tow-headed, ppl.a. [?AB²] *A tow-headed, countrified cub of about sixteen* 1880 TA xxiii 224 (OED Having whitish or tousled hair. 1884, only ex. So W S C. A in DN.IV)

tow-linen, sb. [A] *Some of the children didn't have on any clothes but just a tow-linen shirt* 1884 HF xx 196. *I can still see her bare feet, her bare head, her brown face, and her short tow-linen frock* 1909 ISD xiii 149 (Coarsespun linen cloth. OEDS *U.S.* 1792..1884, above quot. Comb. not in W S C)

town-dog, sb. [B¹] See *mad* 1872 (Comb. not in OED W S C)

town drunkard, sb. [B¹] *Frank's father was at one time Town Drunkard, an exceedingly well-defined and unofficial office of those days* 1906 *Autob* (1924) II 174. See *half-breed*, a. 1909 (Comb. not in OED W S C)

township, sb. [A] See *county* 1865. *The raiment of Marco resembled township maps, being made up of patches which had been added township by township* 1889 CY xxxi 400. *The same thing was done when I was a boy on the Mississippi River. There was a proposition in a township there to discontinue public schools* 1900 *Speeches* (1910) 146 (OED 5. *U.S.* and Canada. A division of a county having certain corporate powers of local administration. 1685.. So W S C U B F Cl Th.III,1639 T H DN.II)

town-site, sb. [AB³] *He* [the surveyor] *ran merrily along, sighting from the top of one divide to the top of another, and striking "plumb" every town-site and big plantation within twenty or thirty miles of his route* 1873 GA xvii 160 (OED Town, sb. 10. ...*spec* in *U.S.* and Canada, a tract of land set apart by legal authority to be occupied by a town. 1872.. So C. Not A in W S)

tow-path, sb. [?A] *A wire rope led from the foretopmast to the file of mules on the tow-path a hundred yards ahead* 1880 TA xv 131 (OEDS Earlier U.S. exs. 1788) Not A in W S C U)

track, sb. *off the track*. [AB³] *Mr. Bright was in error, and clear off the track* 1887 "Petition to the Queen" (1928) 363 (OED 6a. Now *U.S.* Off the line or rails, derailed; also *fig.* 1875, only ex. So B F Cl. Not A in W S C U)

track, sb. *in one's tracks*. [AB³] *"It happened just so sure as I am sitting in these very tracks"* 1876 TS xviii 151. *"Wish I may die in my tracks"* 1883 LM lvi 552. See also *up-stream*, v. 1884 (OED 9. *U.S.* On the spot where one is at the moment. 1843.. So F Cl Th T. Not A in W S C)

trade, sb. [A] *In a trade, the Yankee was held to be about five times the match of the Westerner* 1899 "Concerning the Jews" (1900) 263 (OEDS 9. An act of trading, a transaction. orig. *U.S. slang.* 1772.. So W S F Cl Th T. This sense not in C)

trade, sb. [B¹] *She said, with a pious two-per-cent trade joyousness: "Let us be humbly thankful"* 1904 "Bequest" (1906) iii 13 (Here used *attrib*= Commercial, mercenary. This sense not in OED W S C)

trade, v. [A] See *forty-rod whiskey* 1869; *coonskin* 1873. *Tom had traded the next chance to Billy Fisher for a kite, in good repair* 1876 TS ii 31. See *time, have a good* 1884 (OED 9. To acquire or dispose of by barter. *U.S.* 1628.. So F Cl Th T. Not A in W S C U)

trade-form, sb. [B¹] *The moment he departs, by even a shade, from a common trade-form, the reader who has served that trade will know the writer hasn't* 1909 ISD i 15 (A technical idiom, technicality. Comb. not in OED W S C)

trade-mark, sb. [B²] *We see other monks looking tranquilly up to heaven, but having no trade-mark* 1870 *Screamers* (1871) 94 (OED b. *fig* A distinctive mark or token. 1873.. *Fig* sense not in W S C)

trade off, v. [A] See *sausage-stuffing* 1892 (OEDS 9. *U.S.* To barter, exchange. 1793.. So Th M. Not A in W. Not in S C)

trade-phrasing, sb. [B¹] *He will make mistakes; he will not, and cannot, get the trade-phrasings precisely and exactly right* 1909 ISD i 15 (Comb. not in OED W S C. Cf. trade-form, above)

trade-taffy, sb. [AB¹] *"We should throw in a little trade-taffy about the Blessings of Civilization"* 1901 "To the Person Sitting in Darkness" 172 (Cf. taffy in U.S. sense, above. Comb. not in OED W S C)

trading-post, sb. [A] *There's not a fort nor a trading-post in the whole sweep of the Rocky Mountains that we don't know* 1906 "Horse's Tale" 327 (OED *U.S.* 1796.. Not A in W S. Comb. not in C)

trading-scow, sb. [AB¹] *He ran over the steering-oar of a trading-scow* 1875 OTM 219. See *peddle* 1883. *About an hour after dark we come along down in our trading-scow* 1884 HF xiii 114 (Comb. not in OED W S C; but cf. OEDS Trading-boat, *U.S.* 1738..; cf. also scow in U.S. sense, above)

traditioner, sb. [?C] See *Perhapser* 1909 (OED *rare.* 2. Traditionist. 1882, only ex. Not *rare* in W S C)

trail, sb. [AB³] *"Are you going to see if you can work up another half-stretch on the trail of the cowboys?"* 1889 CY xix 231. See also *stale*, a. 1906 (OED 9. A path or track. Chiefly *U.S.* and Canada. 1807.. So B F Cl Th M DN.VI. Not A in W S C U T)

train-boy, sb. [AB³] See *Western* 1876. *Cheap histories of him were for sale by train-boys* 1883 LM xxix 312. *The* *train-boy came shouting in with an armful of literature* 1893 "Traveling with a Reformer" (1900) 361 (OED 22b. *U.S.* and *Canada*, a boy who sells newspapers, etc. on a railway train. OEDS 1872.. So W S C M. Cf. peanut-peddler, above)

train-time, sb. [B²] *It was train-time* 1880 TA xliii 499 (OED Train, sb. 22b. 1892. So W. Comb. not in S C)

train with, v. [?AB¹] *"Have you been training with that a ss again?"* 1892 AmCl i 21. *Buckstone was training with the rum party* 1894 PW xi 556. *The Republican was an aristocratic party and it was not becoming in the descendant of a regicide to train with that kind of animals* 1897 *Autob* (1924) I 123 (W: To associate; to be on familiar terms with. *Colloq.* So S C. A in H. Not in OED. Cf. OED 9. intr. † a. To walk in a person's train or retinue. *Obs. rare.* 1633.)

tramp, sb. [?AB³] *He is at last rescued by some old whisky-soaked, profane, and blasphemous infidel of a tramp captain* 1904 *Autob* (1924) I 209 (OED 5. In full, *Ocean tramp*: a cargo vessel which does not trade regularly between fixed ports. 1880.. So W S C U. A in Th.III)

tramp, v. Pronounced **tromp.** [AE] *Everybody had to clear the way or get run over and tromped to mush* 1884 HF xxii 218 (W: *dial. variant.* A in DN.I,II,III,IV,V This pron. not given in OED S C)

trample, v. Pronounced **tromple.** [AE] *She said she had "put shoes on one bar'footed nigger to tromple on her with," and that one mistake like that was enough* 1894 PW viii 337 (W: *dial. variant.* A in DN.I,III,IV This pron. not in OED S C)

transboreal, a. [B¹] *The finest example of Chinese art now in existence...from the Chung-a-Lung-Fung dynasty...The main preciousness of this piece lies in its color; that old sensuous, pervading, ramifying, interpolating, transboreal blue which is the despair of modern art* 1880 TA xx 187 (Nonsense coinage)

transcontinental, a. [?AB³] *He got upon the subject of transcontinental travel* 1872 RI xx 152. *Whenever she got...fairly started on one of those horizonless transcontinental sentences of hers, it was borne in upon me that I was standing in the awful presence of the Mother of the German Language* 1889 CY xxii 278 (OED Earliest exs. U.S. 1869.. Not A in W S C U)

transient, sb. [?AB¹] *The big Orleans liners stopped for hails only, or to land passengers or freight; and this was the case also with the great flotilla of transients* 1893 PW i 234 (A tramp steamboat, one not belonging to a regular line or having a fixed route. This sense not in OED W S C)

transom, sb. [AB³] *I looked out through the open transom* 1883 LM xxxix 412 (OED 2b. A small window above the lintel of a door. *U.S. colloq.* 1844.. So W C M H. Not A in S)

transom, sb. [?AC] *"Land aboard the starboard transom!" "Saved!" cried the captain* 1880 TA xvii 158 (OED 4. A crossbeam in the frame of a ship. *obs.* 1545.. 1871. Not *obs* in W S C U)

transpire, v. [AB³] *All the marvels that were transpiring far and wide* 1869 IA liii 567. *This is your birthday, darling...the anniversary of an event which was happening when I was a giddy schoolboy a thousand miles away...unconscious that an event had just transpired so tremendous, that without it all my future life had been a sullen pilgrimage* 1870 Letter in Clara Clemens's *My Father* (1931) 19 (OED 4b. Misused for: To occur, happen. App. begun in U.S. about 1800. 1802.. So B T. Not A in W S C U)

Transvaaltruppentropentransporttrampelthiertreiber-trauungsthraenentragoedie, sb. [B¹] See *effect* 1889 (Hum. coinage)

trap, sb. [AB³] *The place was a plain, unaffected, ramshackle old trap* 1892 AmCl vi 67 (Wr: A contemptuous term applied to anything old or worn out. *Amer.* S: *colloq.* This sense not in OED W C)

trap-robber, sb. [?AB¹] See *squaw-man* 1906 (One who steals game caught in other hunters' traps. Comb. not in OED W S C)

traps, sb. [?AB³] *I gathered up the traps and broke for home* 1857 *Adv. of T.J.Snodgrass* (1928) 44. *Liveried footmen and waiting maids who held the wraps and traps of their masters and mistresses on their arms* 1880 TA x 95. *I got my traps out of the canoe and made me a nice camp in the thick woods* 1884 HF viii 60 (OED A modern word of *colloq* origin; app. shortened from *trappings.* Some take it as pl. of *Trap*, sb., referring to the outfit of a trapper. Portable articles for dress; personal effects; belongings. 1813.. So W S C U Wr. A in B)

trapse, v. Also **traipse.** [?AE] *"So now I got to go and trapse all the way down the river, eleven hundred mile"* 1884 HF xlii 432. *Aunt Polly wouldn't let him go traipsing off somers wasting time* 1896 TSD i 344 (OED Trapes, also traipse, 18th-19th c. *dial* trapse. 1. To walk about aimlessly. 1647.. So W S C U Wr. A in B: To wander, gad about. So DN.I,III,V. Cf. DN.III: To move with purpose, but not so fast as to "hike," nor so slowly as to saunter; e. Ala.)

trash-dust, sb. [B¹] *Every man and woman and child is an influence...some contributing gold-dust, some contributing trash-dust* 1902 "Defence of Gen. Funston" 615 (Comb. not in OED W S C)

traveling-bag, sb. [?AB³] *Harry was cordially asked to bring his traveling-bag* 1873 GA xxxi 279 (OEDS Earlier U.S. exs. 1838.. Not A in W S C)

tree, v. [?A] *"I had the Unabridged and I was ciphering around in the back end, hoping I might tree her among the pictures"* 1875 "Encounter with an Interviewer" 28. *They couldn't 'a' treed me because I didn't breathe* 1884 HF xii 106. *The distant bay of an experienced dog announced that the game was treed* 1897 *Autob* (1924) I 114 (OED 2. To drive up a tree; to cause to take refuge in a tree, as a hunted animal; also *fig.* a1700.. So W S C. A in B F Cl Th.III T)

tree-box, sb. [?AB²] *Tom sat down on the tree-box, discouraged* 1876 TS ii 27 (OEDS A wooden casing used to protect a tree-trunk. All exs. U.S. 1876, this quot.. Not A in S. Comb. not in W C. Cf. boxing, above)

tree-toad, sb. [A] *A tree-toad white, a fish-belly white* 1884 HF v 31 (OED Found chiefly in tropical America. 1778.. W: The common species of the eastern U.S. (*Hyla versicolor*) is mottled gray or green. So S C Th)

trembly, a. [?AB³] *Jim said it made him all over trembly and feverish to be so close to freedom* 1884 HF xvi 135 (OED *colloq.* 1848.. So W S C. Wr: *American*)

trencher, sb. [C] *Wooden spoons and trenchers* 1881 PP xix 243 (OED 2. A flat piece of wood on which meat was served and cut up. *Arch* and *Hist.* c1308..1895. So W S C U Wr)

trial-time, sb. [B¹] *He begun to come out plain and square towards trial-time and acknowledge that he tried to kill the man* 1896 TSD xi 527 (Comb. not in OED W S C)

tribute, sb. [?AB¹] *Every time a man died, or a woman died, or a child died, she would be on hand with her "tribute"* 1884 HF xvii 158 (W: An encomium. This sense not in OED S C)

trick, sb. [?C] *One must try to divine the trick of her felicitous brush* 1890 *Letters* (1917) II xxx 529 (OED 4. The art, knack, or faculty of doing something skilfully or successfully. ?arch. 1611..1897. Not *arch* in W S C)

trick, sb. **a trick worth six of that.** [B¹] *"Our firm knows a trick worth six of that"* 1883 LM xxxix 414 (A characteristic M.T. variation on OED 12. *A trick worth two of that.* 1596..; so W S C)

trig, a. [?A] See *Coast* 1883; *piazza* 1883. *A trig and rather hilarious new edifice* 1883 LM liv 537 (OED 3. Trim, neat. Chiefly *Scotch* and *dial.* 1513..1889. So W S C U Wr. A in F Cl DN.II,III,IV,V)

trigness, sb. [?AB³] *The "trigness" of the houses* 1883 LM xl 421 (OED 1821.. So W S C. A in F Cl)

trim-built, a. [?AB¹?C] *He was tall, trim-built, muscular* 1881 PP xi 126 (Comb. not in OED W S C; but cf. OED Trim, a. 2c. Elegantly shaped, well-made, handsome. *obs.* 1568..1649)

trim-chiselled, a. [B¹] *That kind of trim-chiselled face that just seems to glint and sparkle with frosty intellectuality* 1903 "Dog's Tale" 14 (Comb. not in OED W S C)

trimmings, sb. [?A] *If a woman bought a few yards of calico she was entitled to a spool of thread in addition to the usual gratis "trimmin's"* 1877 *Autob* (1924) I 9 (OED 2. Any ornamental addition to the bare fabric of a dress. a1654..1906. So W S C U. A in F Cl Th)

trip, sb. **to get a trip.** [?AB¹] *This calm craft would go as advertised, "if she got her trip;" if she didn't get it, she would wait for it* 1883 LM xxiii 259 (To obtain a consignment or booking sufficient to justify a run. Phr. not in OED W S C; but cf. OED Trip, sb. 3. A short voyage or journey; a 'run.' App. originally a sailor's term. 1691..)

triple-lock, v. [B¹] *"I had its big door sheathed with boiler-iron and triple-locked"* 1876 TS xxxii 251 (Not in OED W S C; but cf. OED Triple-lock, a. 1895)

trolley, sb. [AB³] *A Republican simplicity invented... the electric trolley* 1899 "Diplomatic Pay" (1928) 239 (OED 3b. *U.S.* An electric car driven by means of a trolley. 1891.. So Cl H. Not A in W S C U)

tropical, a. [B¹] *Your people made it tropical for them* 1881 *Speeches* (1910) 22 (Hum. nonce use: 'hot,' 'warm,' dangerous)

tropics, sb. [B¹] *The moribund's progress toward the everlasting tropics* 1904 "Bequest" (1906) ii 4 (Hum. nonce use: Hell)

troth, sb. **in troth.** [C] *"In troth I might go yet farther"* 1881 PP xii 143 (OED 4b. *arch.* Truly, verily. a1380.. 1789. So W S C)

trot-line, sb. [?AB³] *I was hard at it taking up a "trot" line* 1884 HF vii 48. *Catching catfish with a "trot-line"* 1909 ISD iv 44 (OED *Fishing.* A trawl-line. U.S. quot. 1858, only ex. A in S C DN.II,III. Not A in W)

trot out, v. [?AB³] *"Trot out Mr. Allen, somebody"* 1892 AmCl xv 155. *They trotted out a plug-hat for me to wear* 1910 *Speeches* 87 (OED 4b. *fig.* To bring forward. *colloq.* 1838.. So W S C U. A in B T)

trouble-weighted, a. [B¹] *"I may not bear his burden on mine own trouble-weighted shoulders"* 1881 PP viii 99 (Comb. not in OED W S C)

troublous, a. [C] *"Troublous dreams! Mine end is now at hand"* 1881 PP viii 97 (OED 3b. Expressing or indicating trouble or grief. *obs. rare.*1535, 1590. Not *obs* in W S C)

trout, sb. [AB³] *Brook-trout, from Sierra Nevadas. Lake-trout, from Tahoe* (see under *biscuit* 1880) (OED 3. several U.S. varieties, 1868.. The species which M.T. had in mind are best identified in C: Brook-trout, *Salmo irideus,* or rainbow trout, native of streams west of the Sierra Nevadas; Lake-trout, *Salmo purpuratus,* also known as Rocky Mountain brook-trout, or Yellowstone trout, found in the Yellowstone and upper Missouri regions, the Great Basin of Utah, in Colorado, etc. W and S mention only the brook-trout and lake-trout of eastern N.Am., namely *Salvelinus fontinalis* or common Am. char, and *Salvelinus namaycush,* Mackinaw trout, or great lake-trout, found esp. in the Great Lakes)

trow, v. [C] *"I trow he cannot speak"* 1881 PP vi 77 (OED *arch.* 4. To believe, think. c1000..1872. So W S C U Wr)

trowel in, v. [B¹] *"I'll trowel-in a layer of Oilendorff mush between every couple of courses of Meisterschaft bricks"* 1888 "Meisterschaft" 459 (Comb. not in OED W S C; but cf. OED Trowel, v. 2. To lay on with a trowel; often *fig* of flattery or laudation. 1772..1898)

truck, sb. [A] *They say hay grows, and grass, and beets and onions, and turnips and other "truck"* 1861 *Letters* (1917) I iii 55. *"What's de use er makin' up de camp-fire*

to cook strawbries en sich truck?" 1884 HF viii 65 (OED 4c. *U.S.* Market-garden produce. 1784.. So W S C B F Cl Th T H DN.II,III,V)

trump, sb. [?A] *Columbus played an eclipse as a saving trump once* 1889 CY v 65 (OED 2. *fig.* 1595.. So W S C U. A in B)

Trumps, sb. [AB¹] See *seven-up* 1869 (One of the six "points" that may be scored in the Am. game of seven-up. It is "made" by the dealer if he turns up a jack or knave of any suit, which thereupon becomes trumps. This sense not in OED W S C)

trunk-lie, sb. [B¹] *Out of these trunk-lies spring many branch ones* 1906 *Autob* (1924) II 8 (Nonce comb. Cf. below)

trunk-line, sb. [?AB³] *Five trunk-lines of railway* 1883 LM xxix 323 (OED The main line of a railway. 1858.. So C U. W: Chiefly *U.S.* and *Canada.* So M Th.III H. Comb. not in S)

trunks, sb. [?C] *His mantle and trunks of purple satin* 1881 PP xiv 165 (OED 17. Trunk-hose. *obs.* 1583..1672. Not *obs* in W S C U)

truss, v. [C] *"Straightway trussed on his rags and went with the youth"* 1881 PP xii 155 (OED 5. To put on clothing. Now *rare.* a1225..1813. So W S C)

truss point, sb. [B¹] *He at last saw his long silken hose begin the journey down the line...till they finally reached the hands of the Chief Equerry in waiting, who... hoarsely whispered, "Body of my life, a tag gone from a truss point!"...after which, fresh hose, without any damaged strings to them, were brought* 1881 PP xiv 165 (Comb. not in OED W S C. Cf. OED Truss, sb. †3b. pl. Close-fitting breeches or drawers. 1592..1631; so W S C. Cf. also OED Point, sb. B.5. A tagged lace or cord for attaching the hose to the doublet. Now *arch* or *Hist.* 1390..1819; so W S. The comb. seems to be M.T.'s own invention)

Trust, sb. [?AB³] See *Legislature* 1901. *No member, young or old, of a Christian-Scientist church can retain that membership unless he pay "capitation tax" to the Boston Trust every year* 1903 "Chr.Sc." 3. *About the year 1870...ingenious men massed together a multitude of small and unprofitable oil-industries under the control of able managers—and that was the first Trust* 1903 "Chr.Sc." 181. *The most titanic and death-dealing swindle of them all, the Beef Trust* 1906 "Unpublished Chaps. from Autob" (1922) 456. See also *Metaphysical* 1907 (OED 7b. *spec* A combination of commercial or industrial companies, with a central governing body of trustees which holds a majority of the stock of each of the combining firms, thus having a controlling vote in the conduct and operation of each. OEDS Earlier U.S. ex. 1877.. A in F Cl Th.III T. Not A in W S C U)

truth-monger, sb. [B¹] *One of the heartless truth-mongers* 1899 "My First Lie" (1900) 166 (A fanatical believer in telling the truth at all costs. Comb. not in OED W S C)

Tube, sb. [B²] *There is just one good system of rapid transit in London—the "Tube"* 1900 *Speeches* (1910) 126 (OED 7b. Short for tube-railway. *colloq.* 1900.. So W C U. This sense not in S)

tuck, sb. **to take the tuck out of.** [?AB²] *Would it have taken some of the tuck out of that smirk?* 1878 *Notebook* (1935) xiv 140. *I would have taken the tuck somewhat out of your joyousness* 1882 *Letters* (1917) I xxii 426. *"I judge I've got the stuff here that'll take the tuck out of him"* 1882 "Invalid's Story" 102. *I judged it would take the tuck out of scrofula as handy as a nobler coin* 1889 CY xxvi 335. See also *war-whooping* 1907 (OEDS 1. *fig.* 1882, M.T. quot...A in W Wr DN.IV. Phr. not in S C)

tuck down, v. [B¹] *When you got to the table you couldn't go right to eating, but you had to wait for the widow to tuck down her head and grumble a little over the victuals* 1884 HF i 2 (To bow, incline the head. This sense not in OED W S C. Cf. OED 8. To thrust into a place where it is snugly held. 1587. .)

tuckered out, ppl.a. [AB³] *"About sundown, they were all tuckered out, and they owned up and quit"* 1877 "Some Rambling Notes" ii 590. *At last he could hardly flap his wings, he was so tuckered out* 1880 TA iii 40. *It was beautiful to hear that clock tick; and sometimes she would start in and strike a hundred and fifty times before she got tuckered out* 1884 HF xvii 153. See also *hold up* 1896 (OED *New Eng. colloq.* Exhausted. 1840. . So W S C B F Cl Th T DN.I,III,IV AS.II.366,VI.100)

tug-load, sb. [B¹] *Said he "wouldn't give a d— for a tug-load of such rot"* 1883 LM xlviii 480 (Comb. not in OED W S C)

tule, sb. Spelled **tuler**. [AB³E] See *pulu* 1861 (OED *U.S.* Also sp. *tula*. Either of two species of bulrush abundant in low lands along river-sides in California. OEDS 1845. . So W S C B F Cl Th. M.T.'s spelling not given in OED W S C; but cf. B: Tular, a marsh in which Tule abounds; so F DN.VI)

tumble, v. [?AB³] *She tumbled (discovered) her leather was gone* 1883 LM lii 512 (OED 10b. To understand, perceive, apprehend. *slang.* 1851. . So W S C. A in B T DN.I)

tumble-bug, sb. [AB³] *Ants and Tumble-Bugs to fetch and carry and delve* 1875 SNO 127. See *First Family* 1875. *A tumble-bug came next, heaving sturdily at its ball, and Tom touched the creature, to see it shut its legs against its body and pretend to be dead* 1876 TS xiv 122. *"Him a lion-heart!—that tumble-bug!"* 1895 JA II ii 89 (OEDS 1. Name in U.S. for a scarabaeid beetle. 1805. . So W S C B F Cl Th T DN.III)

tumbling-bug, sb. [AB¹] *He could not be insulted by Ursula any more than the king could be insulted by a tumbling-bug* 1898 MS (1916) v 40 (A var. form of the above. Comb. not in OED W S C)

tune, sb. **the tune the old cow died on**. [?AB³] *It was kind of poor, and one of them said it was the tune the old cow died on* 1883 LM iii 44 (OED 2e. Humorously applied to a grotesque or unmusical succession of sounds. 1836. So S. A in DN.III. Phr. not in W C)

tunnel-like, a. [B²] *One of the shows of the place was a tunnel-like cavern, which had been hewn in the glacier* 1880 TA xlvi 530 (OED 1885. Comb. not in W S C)

turban, sb. [AB³] *"Dey went to smilin' at my big red turban"* 1874 SNO (1875) 206 (OED 3. A bright-coloured cloth worn as a headdress by negroes, esp. women, in the West Indies and southern U.S. 1839. . So W S C)

turkey, sb. [A] *Roast turkey, Thanksgiving style;* see *biscuit* 1880. *Tame turkey;* see *batter-cake* 1897 (OED 2. All species are American; esp. *Meleagris gallopavo,* which was found domesticated in Mexico in 1518. 1555. . So W S C)

turkey sb. **wild turkey**. [A] See *biscuit* 1880; *batter-cake* 1897. *I remember the squirrel-hunts and the wild-turkey hunts* 1897-8 *Autob* (1924) I 114 (OED 2b. The wild original of the domestic fowl; commonly applied to the N. Am. bird, *Meleagris americana.* 1613. . So W S C DN.II AS.IV.11)

turkey-call, sb. [AB³] *The hunter concealed himself and imitated the turkey-call by sucking the air through the leg-bone of a turkey* 1906 "Hunting the Deceitful Turkey" 57 (OED The gobbling sound characteristic of the turkey-cock. 1873. So W S C. Cf. above)

turkeylet, sb. [AB¹] *She goes flitting along again, and. . .as soon as she has led you far enough away from her turkeylet she takes to a tree* 1907 CS II ii 122 (Not in OED W S C. Cf. above)

turkey-wing, sb. [AB³] *There was a couple of big wild-turkey-wing fans* 1884 HF xvii 153 (OEDS 1871. . Comb. not in W S C. Cf. above)

turn, v. [?AB¹] *George's voice was just "turning"* 1869 IA v 45 (To change in register. This sense not in OED W S C)

turn, v. **not to turn a feather**. [?AB¹] *It didn't disturb Sandy, didn't turn a feather* 1889 CY xv 181 (To ruffle, annoy, disturb. Phr. not in OED W S C. Cf. OED Hair, sb. 8n. *Not to turn a hair:* not to show any sign of being discomposed. 1798. .)

turn, sb. **turn of noon**. [?AB¹] *We got under way about the turn of noon* 1880 TA xxviii 287 (The exact moment of noonday. Phr. not in OED W S C. Cf. *turn of night,* A in DN.II)

turn down, v. [AB³] *"We turned down the Congressman's son and the Governor's"* 1904 "Bequest" (1906) vii 40 (OED 71d. *U.S. slang.* To reject, refuse to accept. 1891. . So C M Th.III H. Not A in W S U)

turned-around, ppl.a. [AB¹] *I could see the dim blur of the windows, but in my turned-around condition they were exactly where they ought not to be* 1880 TA xiii 119. See also *tangle* 1884 (A in F: In doubt as to one's whereabouts. Comb. not in OED W S C)

turn in, v. [?A] *"I was just turning in"* 1873 GA iv 44. *Tom turned in without the added vexation of prayers* 1876 TS iii 41. *When the watch changed, the off watch stayed up, 'stead of turning in* 1883 LM iii 54 (OED 72f. orig. *Naut.* To go to bed. *colloq.* 1695. . So W S C U. A in DN.III AS.IV. 383)

turn in, v. [AB¹] *We turned in and soothed him down and told him we would plan for him* 1896 TSD iv 354 (S: To help unitedly. *colloq.* A in DN.I. This sense not in OED W C)

turning-room, sb. [B¹] *No turning-room for anybody* 1883 LM xxxv 382 (Room to turn. Comb. not in OED W S C)

turnip, sb. [AB³] *He looked at his silver turnip, and then at the clock* 1893 TSA iii 118 (OED 3b. Slang term for an old-fashioned thick silver watch. 1840. . So W S U. A in B. This sense not in C)

turnip-barrel, sb. [B¹] *I laid it across the turnip-barrel* 1884 HF vi 46 (Comb. not in OED W S C)

turnip-shaving, sb. [B¹] See *palmiste* 1897 (Comb. not in OED W S C)

turn on, v. [?AB²] *There was a good deal of honest snickering turned on this time* 1866 Screamers (1871) 149 (OED 74a. To induce a flow of water, etc., by turning a tap; also *fig.* 1892, first *fig* ex. So W S. The *fig* use not in C)

turn out, v. [?AB³] *The fellows turned out of their tents, rubbing their eyes, and stared about them* 1873 GA xvii 161. *I turned out at six* 1883 LM xxiii 261. *"Turn out—the house is on fire!"* 1892 AmCl vii 73 (OED 75p. To get out of bed. *colloq.* 1805. . So W S C U. A in AS. IV.383: orig. *Naut.*)

turn over, v. [?AB¹] *"Come ahead on the stabboard! Stop her! Let your outside turn over slow"* 1876 TS ii 29 (Of the sidewheel of a steamboat. This sense not in OED W S C. Cf. OEDS 77l. Of the motor of an aeroplane. 1929)

turn over, v. [?AB¹] *To make up for short matter we would "turn over ads"—turn over the whole page and duplicate it* 1886 *Speeches* (1910) 184 (This sense not in OED W S C)

turn to, v. [?AB³] *"We will turn to and have a reg'lar good time"* 1886 *Speeches* (1910) 155 (OED 79a. To apply oneself, set to work. 1813. . So W S C U. A in AS.IV.383: orig. *Naut.*)

turtle, sb. [?AB¹] *He was reading out of the Bible. . . about the voice of the turtle being heard in the land. . . "But I sat there and watched that turtle nearly an hour to-day, and. . .I never heard him sing. . .If I had any sense I might have known a cursed mud-turtle couldn't sing"* 1869 IA xlvii 490. *After the Tortoises came another long train of ironclads—stately and spacious Mud Turtles* 1875 SNO 127 (W: Any species of tortoise in the widest sense. The restriction to marine tortoise is not warranted by modern usage. So S C. A in B. The OED has only 1. Any species of marine tortoise. 1657. .1870.

The mud-turtles with which M.T. was familiar in Missouri were certainly not marine tortoises!)

tush, sb. [?AC] *The great seas...crushed her to splinters and rubbish upon the rock tushes at the base of the precipice* 1897 FE ix 111 (OED 1. Tusk. Now chiefly *arch* or *dial.* c725..1848. Not *arch* in W S C Wr. A in AS.V.206, Ozarks; XI.238, e.Texas)

tush, int. [?AC] *"Tush, he must be the prince!"* 1881 PP vi 84 (OED *arch.* An exclamation of impatient contempt. c1440..1891. So S U. Not *arch* in W C. A in DN.V)

twain, a. [?AB¹C] See *mark twain* 1873, 1909. *"Had quarter twain with the lower lead and mark twain with the other."* [Footnote] *Quarter twain is 2¼ fathoms, 13½ feet. Mark twain is two fathoms* 1875 OTM 284. *"Half twain! Quarter twain! Mark twain! Quarter less twain!"* 1875 OTM 574. *The sleek and inviting dead stretch that promised quarter-less-twain and couldn't furnish six feet* [Footnote] *Leadsman's cries: "Quarter-less-twain," 10½ feet of water* 1906 "Carl Schurz, Pilot" 727 (This *Naut.* use not in OED W S C. Cf. OED An archaic and poetic synom of *two.* 2. *absol.* with ellipsis of sb. c1000 1881. So W S C U)

Twainiana, sb. pl. [B¹] *Today a Hannibal* Courier-Post *of recent date has reached me...I will make an extract from it..."The volume of 'Twainiana' is already considerable and growing in proportion as the 'old timers' drop away and the stories are retold second and third hand by their descendants"* 1909 ISD xiii 374 (Not in OED W S C; but cf. OED Ana, suffix. Appended to proper names with the sense of...anecdotes of...as *Shake-speariana, Burnsiana.* 1666..; so W S C U)

twenty, sb. [AB¹] *"I'll put a twenty-dollar gold piece on this board, and you get it when it floats by"..."Here's a twenty to put on the board for me"* 1884 HF xvi 140. See also *cent* 1889 (A twenty-dollar coin or bill; a double-eagle. This sense not in OED W S C)

twenty-dollar, a. [AB¹] See *twenty,* sb. 1884; *cent* 1889 (Comb. not in OED S C. Given in W)

twice, a. twiste. [?AB³E] *"We seen it twiste, en dat's proof"* 1894 TSA viii 351 (OED This sp. 19th c. *dial.* Only ex. U.S. 1888. Wr: *dial* and *U.S.* Not A in W. This form not in S C. Cf. the spellings *twicet, twict, twist,* etc., given as A in B F DN.I,II,III,IV AS.VI.100, XI.239. Cf. Once, sp. *Wunst,* above)

twilight, v. [?AB³] *The church was twilighted with yellow tallow candles in tin sconces hung against the walls* 1877 *Autob* (1924) I 8 (OED *trans.* To light imperfectly or dimly. Earliest quot. from Howells, from whom M.T. may have picked the word up. 1866.. Not A in W C. Not in S as verb)

twin-monster, sb. [B¹] *The twin-monster and the heroine had dwindled to inconsequentialities* 1894 TET 432 (Nonce comb., for M.T.'s Siamese-twin heroes)

twin-screw, sb. [B¹] *Five more books by Mrs.Eddy... some of them in "pebbled cloth," with divinity circuit, compensation balance, twin screw, and the other modern improvements* 1903 "Chr. Sc." 3 (Hum. nonsense use. Cf. OED *spec* of a steamer, having two screw propellers on separate shafts. 1864..; so W S C)

two-acre, a. [B¹] *"I am but a sheriff after all, a poor, shabby two-acre sheriff"* 1895 JA II xxiii 892 (Comb. not in OED W S C)

two-hour, a. [B²] *A two-hour pedestrian excursion* 1880 TA xix 171 (OED 1900, only ex. So W. Comb. not in S C)

two-liner, sb. [B¹] See *one-liner* 1904 (A two-line heading in a newspaper. Comb. not in OED W S C)

two-millionaire, sb. [?AB¹] *He long ago observed that a millionaire commands respect, a two-millionaire homage* 1899 "Concerning the Jews" (1900) 269 (Nonce comb. Cf. millionaire, above)

two-story, a. [B²] *A two-story public house* 1880 TA v 51. *"What kind of house was it?" "Brick—two-story"* 1902 "Belated Russian Passport" (1928) 193 (OED 1880, only ex. So W. Comb. not in S C)

two-taps-and-one, sb.phr. [?AB¹] *Whenever I have doubted my own competency to choose the right course, I have struck my two-taps-and-one ("get out the port and starboard leads"), and followed him through without hesitancy* 1906 "Carl Schurz, Pilot" 727 (A signal to take soundings on both sides of the boat. Comb. not in OED W S C)

type-channel, sb. [B¹] *The machine...began its work of its own accord when the type-channels needed filling* 1890 *Autob* (1924) I 71 (A furrow or groove holding the type in a typesetting machine. Comb. not in OED W S C. Cf. raceway, above)

type-copy, v. [B¹] *Three days later Mr. X brought my introduction to me, neatly typecopied* 1900 *Autob* (1924) I 177. *My machinist type-copied a book for me in '74* 1905 "The First Writing-Machines" (1906) 169 (To make a typewritten copy of. Comb. not in OED W S C)

type-girl, sb. [B¹] *He put his type-girl to work, and we timed her by the watch* 1905 "The First Writing-Machines" (1906) 167 (Typewriter girl, girl typist. Comb. not in OED W S C)

type-machine, sb. [B¹] *I saw a type-machine for the first time in—what year? I suppose it was 1873* 1905 "The First Writing-Machines" (1906) 167 (A typewriter. Comb. not in OED W S C)

type-setter, sb. [B²] *The type-setter goes on forever— at $3,000 a month* 1887 *Letters* (1917) II xxvii 494 (OED A composing machine. 1888.. So W S C)

typewriter copyist, sb. [B¹] *He had all the earmarks of a typewriter copyist, if you leave out the disposition to contribute uninvited emendations of your grammar and punctuation* 1889 CY xxv 326 (App. means merely typist, one who does typewriting. Comb. not in OED W S C. Cf. in same sense OED Typewriter, 1884..; Typist, 1885.. A case of linguistic rivalry between terms for the operator of the new "writing-machine;" for another unsuccessful candidate cf. M.T.'s nonce use of "machinist," above)

type-writer, v. [B¹] *Have these type-writered and keep the original* 1891 *Letters* (1917) II xxxi 560 (A nonce rival for the successful verb *typewrite,* OED 1887.. For another unsuccessful candidate for this function, cf. "type-copy," v., above)

typewriter-table, sb. [B¹] *She took from the drawer of the typewriter-table several squares of paper* 1902 "DBDS" (1928) 294 (Comb. not in OED S C. Given in W)

Tyrolese warbling, sb. [?AB¹] *We recognized that we were hearing for the first time the famous Alpine 'jodel' in its own native wilds. And we recognized, also, that it was that sort of quaint commingling of baritone and falsetto which at home we call "Tyrolese warbling"* 1880 TA xxviii 289 (This expression not in OED W S C. Cf. yodel, below)

U

ugh, int. [?AB³] *Ugh! ejaculated I, as I looked to see if Mr. C's bones were all safe* 1853 Letter in *Iowa Journ. of History* (1929) 413 (OED 2. An interjection expressive of disgust. 1837.. So W S C U. A in DN.V)

ugly customer, sb. [?AB³] *In about a second I begun to see I'd woke up a pretty ugly customer* 1907 "Capt. Stormfield" 42 (OED Ugly, a. 7d. A person who is likely to cause trouble. 1811.. *Colloq* in W S C. A in B)

ultimate, a. [B¹] *"It's one of them Pillows of Herkewls, I should say— and there's the ultimate one alongside of it." "The ultimate one—that is a good word"* 1869 IA vii 70 (Hum. malapropism)

ultramarine, a. [B¹] *"There's something divine about his art...vague-murmuring to the spirit out of ultra-marine distances"* 1892 AmCl xvi 169 (Nonsense use)

ultra-pious, a. [B¹] *A stove which I thought might possibly be a church...so imposing is it for size and so richly adorned with basso relievos of an ultra-pious sort* 1904 *Autob* (1924) I 196 (Comb. not in OED S C. Given in W)

umbrella–drippings, sb.pl. [B¹] *A man held one [a little girl] in his arms for an hour, with umbrella-drippings soaking into her clothing all the time* 1880 TA App.B 589 (Comb. not in OED W S C)

umf, int. Also **mph**. [?AE] *"Umf! Well, you didn't get a lick amiss, I reckon"* 1876 TS iii 38. *"What would people say? Why, they'd say 'Mph! Tom Sawyer's gang! pretty low characters in it!'"* 1876 TS xxxv 272 (OED Umph. Also *umff* in 16th c. Cf. *humph, umh, um*. An inarticulate sound, expressive of hesitation, doubt, or dissatisfaction. *a*1568.. 1894. So W. A in Wr. Not in S C)

un, prep. [?ACE] *"I wouldn't give a dern for a million un um"* 1884 HF xiv 122 (OED *Obs* form of On, prep. This form not in W S C. Cf. OED On, prep. 27. In senses now expressed by Of; common in lit. use to *c*1750.. still widespread in Eng. dialects. 1258..1828. W: *dial.* S: *obs.* C: *obs* or *vulgar*)

Unabridged, sb. [AB³] *Per overland coach to Carson City, Nevada...all we could take was twenty-five pounds ...My brother, the Secretary, took along...six pounds of Unabridged Dictionary* 1872 RI ii 23. See *avalanche*, v. 1872. *"I had the Unabridged and I was ciphering around in the back end"* 1875 "Encounter with an Interviewer" 28. *There are not enough words in the unabridged to describe it* 1893 "Banknote" (1928) 135 (OED ppl.a. b. *absol.* A copy of the 'unabridged edition' of Webster's Dictionary. 1860.. This sense not in W(!) S C U)

un-American, a. [AB³] *Showy rubbish and un-American pretentiousness* 1892 Am Cl iv 54. *It is un-English; it is un-American; it is French* 1899 "Concerning the Jews" (1900) 254 (OED Not in consonance with American characteristics. 1818.. So W S C U)

unanecdotical, a. [B¹] *How curiously unanecdotical the Colonials and ship-going English are. I believe I haven't told an anecdote or heard one since I left America* 1896 *Notebook* (1935) xxiii 267 (Not in OED W S C)

unbeknownst, a. Spelled **unbeknowens**. [?AB³E] *"There is things which you have done which is unbeknowens to anybody but me"* 1870 SNO (1875) 314 (OED *colloq* and *dial.* Unknown. 1854.. S: *provincial* or *obs.* So W C U Wr. A in DN.III,IV,V. OED gives the var. form *unbeknowns*, no ex.; this form not in W S C)

unbrahminically, adv. [B¹] *At a first glance it looks most unbrahminically uncommercial* 1897 FE xlix 470 (Not in OED W S C. Cf. OED Un-Brahminical, a., 1833)

uncashable, a. [B¹] *I don't know what Dick got, but it was probably only un-cashable promises* 1906 *Autob* (1924) II 288 (Not in OED W S C)

uncheapened, ppl.a. [B¹] *This testimony is so un-cheapened, unwatered by guesses, that it quite convinces me* 1909 ISD viii 101 (Not in OED W S C)

Uncle, sb. [AB¹] *The Hawkins hearts had been torn to see Uncle Dan'l and his wife pass from the auction-block into the hands of a negro trader* 1873 GA vii 78. *"He lets me, and so does his pap's nigger man, Uncle Jake"* 1876 TS xxviii 216. *An old darky did not notice what steamer it was...."Why, uncle, that was the Eclipse"* 1883 LM xxx 328. *We had a faithful and affectionate good friend, ally, and adviser in "Uncle Dan'l," a middle-aged slave whose head was the best one in the negro quarters* 1897 *Autob* (1924) I 100 (A in W: Used, esp. in the southern U.S., for a worthy old negro. So S C U B F Th,1835 T. This *spec* usage of negroes is not clearly distinguished in OED; cf. OED 2b. *local* and *U.S.* Used as a form of address to non-relatives, esp. to elderly men. 1793.. 1859)

uncledom, sb. [B¹] *I have lost his answer. I could better have afforded to lose an uncle. That letter was beyond price, beyond uncledom, and unsparable* 1907 "Chaps. from Autob" 467. In this passage as reproduced in *Autob* I 241, the word "uncledom," as has been noted by Professor Ferguson in *Am.Lit.* VIII.44, has been "polished" away by Mr. Paine; for other exs. see under "guts," above (Given in W. Not in OED S C; but cf. OED Unclehood, 1846)

unclodded, ppl.a. [B¹] *I'm not writing for critics, and I don't care to have them paw the book at all. It's my swan-song...and I wish to pass to the cemetery unclodded* 1889 *Letters* (1917) II xxix 573 (Unpelted by stupid criticism. Not in OED W S C; but cf. OED Clod, v. 5. To pelt with clods. 1755..)

un-college-bred, a. [B¹] *Those humble, un-college-bred inventors* 1892 AmCl x 102 (Not in OED W S C; but cf. OED Uncollegian, a. 1826)

uncommon, adv. Also **oncommon**. [?AE] *This drownded man was just his size and was ragged, and had uncommon long hair* 1884 HF iii 18. *"My peeled head and my white whiskers is goin' to look oncommon odd"* 1884 HF xx 194 (OED 6. As adv. = uncommonly. *colloq* or *dial.* 1784..1891. So W S C U Wr. Cf. OED On-, prefix, frequent ME., early mod.E., and dial. variant of Un-)

uncomplimentarily, adv. [B¹] *It would grieve me to know that any one could think so injuriously of me, so uncomplimentarily, so unadmiringly* 1909 ISD xi 127 (Not in OED W S C; but cf. OED Uncomplimentary, a. 1846..)

unconcreted, ppl.a. [B¹] *Pictures can be remembered ...much better than unconcreted facts* 1906 *Autob* (1924) I 314 (Given in W S, without def. Not in OED C. Cf. concreted = concrete, above)

unconsciousnesses, sb.pl. [B¹] See *brain-territory* 1880 (This *concrete* sense not in OED W S C)

uncover, v. [B¹] *He had a little small bull pup...As soon as money was up on him, his teeth would uncover and shine savage like the furnaces* 1865 "Jumping Frog" (1875) 32 (Here *absol*: To be exposed, allow (itself) to be seen uncovered. This sense not in OED W S C. Cf. OED 4. To remove the hat. 1607..)

underbrush, sb. [A] *They tramped along, over decaying logs, through tangled underbrush* 1876 TS xiv 123 (OED Shrubs and small trees forming the undergrowth in a forest. Orig. and chiefly *U.S.* OEDS 1775 .. So M. Not A in W S C U)

under-clerk, sb. [?AB¹] *My younger brother appeared on the hurricane-deck, and shouted to Brown to stop at some landing or other. Brown gave no intimation that he had heard anything. But that was his way: he never condescended to take notice of an under-clerk* 1883 LM xix 227. *George Black, Mr. Wood, and my brother, clerks, were asleep* 1883 LM xx 237 (One of the subordinate 'clerks' on a steamboat; cf. clerk, above. This *Naut.* sense not in OED W S C; cf. in gen. sense OED 1393..1841)

under-description, sb. [B¹] See *over-description* 1880 (Comb. not in OED W S C)

underhanded, a. [?AB³] *There were plenty who would not hesitate to say he had used underhanded means to get the appointment* 1880 TA xxxix 452 (OED 1. = Underhand, a.; clandestine, surreptitious. 1806.. So W S C U. A in M)

undertaker-eye, sb. [B¹] *The head waiter picked up the bottle, cast his undertaker-eye on it* 1880 TA xii 111 (Comb. not in OED W S C)

undertaker-furniture, sb. [B¹] *That woman's majestic coffin-clad feet...her undertaker-furniture* 1880 TA xlvii 548 (Hum. nonce comb.)

undertaker-looking, a. [B¹] *There was always an undertaker-looking servant along* 1869 IA xvii 163 (Comb. not in OED W S C)

undertaker-outfit, sb. [?AB¹] *Our representative appears in a plain black swallow-tail...a dress which makes him glaringly conspicuous; that is what his present undertaker-outfit does when it appears, with its dismal smudge, in the midst of the butterfly splendors of a Continental court* 1899 "Diplomatic Pay and Clothes" (1928) 230 (Nonce comb. Cf. outfit, above)

under-waiter, sb. [B¹] See *call-boy* 1880 (A subordinate waiter. Comb. not in OED W S C)

undictionarial, a. [B¹] *If I had a phrase-book of a really satisfactory sort I would study it, and not give all my free time to undictionarial readings* 1904 "Italian without a Master" (1906) 185 (Not in OED W S C; but cf. OED Dictionarial, a. *rare*. Of, pertaining to, or characteristic of a dictionary; lexicographical. 1750, only ex.)

undigestible, a. [?AC] *We had et up the sawdust, and it gave us a most amazing stomach-ache...It was the most undigestible sawdust I ever see* 1884 HF xxxix 398 (OED *obs. rare* for Indigestible. 1611, 1613. So W. Not *rare* in S C. Cf. Mr. Vance Randolph's remarks in AS.V.269 about the prevalent Ozark use of the prefix *un-* in cases where modern usage calls for *in-*, as in *unconstant, unpossible, unperfect;* and cf. also M.T.'s *undisposed, unregular,* and *unreverent,* below)

undiscredited, ppl.a. [B¹] *The town's pride in the purity of its one undiscredited citizen* 1899 "MCH" (1900) 67 (Not in OED C. Given in W S)

undisposed, ppl.a. [?A?C] See *double-team,* v. 1884 (OED 6. Not inclined or willing; indisposed. 1590.. 1650. So W U. *Obs* in S C. Cf. undigestible, above)

unendurableness, sb. [B¹] *We...was thirsty clean to unendurableness* 1894 TSA viii 351 (Not in OED W S C; but cf. OED Unendurability. 1858..)

unfloatable, a. [B²] See *cable-chain* 1880 (OED 1880, this quot... So W. Not in S C)

unfurl, v. [B¹] *"Who's that? Answer, or I'll shoot!" But we didn't answer; we just unfurled over heels and shoved* 1884 HF xl 409 (Hum. nonce use for the familiar phr. 'to show one's heels')

ungenuine, a. [?C] *Materials all ungenuine within and without* 1883 LM xl 417. *It seemed that the quality must be ungenuine* 1892 AmCl xi 115 (OED *rare.* 1665.. 1883. Not *rare* in W S C)

ungetaroundable, a. [B¹] *The ungetaroundable fact that...no people...ever did achieve their freedom by goody-goody talk and moral suasion* 1889 CY xx 242 (Not in OED W S C; but cf. OED Ungetatable. 1862..)

unhand, v. [C] *"Unhand me, thou foolish creature"* 1881 PP xxii 275 (OED To take the hand off. Chiefly *arch* in the imperative. 1602..1860. Not *arch* in W S C U)

unhandkerchief, v. [B¹] *Mrs. O'Flaherty comes in—widow——wiping her eyes— unhandkerchiefs one eye* 1883 LM xliii 438 (Not in OED W S C)

unhitch, v. [?AB³] *We unhitched a skiff* 1884 HF ii 12 (OED 3. To detach or unfasten (a thing). 1876.. So W S C U. A in DN.I,III)

unholpen, ppl. a. [CE] *"She did climb to that eminence by her own unholpen merit"* 1889 CY xxv 327 (OED Now *arch* 1382..1870. So W. Not *arch* in S. Not in C)

Union, sb. [A] *It was made up of the families of public men from nearly every state in the Union* 1873 GA xxxiii 311. *Other nations have been called thin-skinned, but the citizens of the Union have, apparently, no skins at all* 1883 LM App.C 609. See also *best-lighted* 1883. *South Carolina had gone out of the Union* 1885 "Private Hist. of Campaign" 193 (OED 7c. The U.S.A. 1775.. So W S C B F Cl M H)

Union, sb. [AB³] *"Enlisting as soldiers in the Union army"* 1881 "Curious Experience" 39. See also *Federal* 1885 (OED 7c. Sometimes in Am. use restricted to the Northern states which adhered to the Union in...the Civil War of 1861-5. 1865.. So W S C)

Union, sb. [AB¹] *"When de Unions took dat town..."* 1874 SNO (1875) 204 (Union soldier, Unionist. This use not in OED W S C)

Unionism, sb. [AB³] *He went on decrying my Unionism* 1885 "Private Hist. of Campaign" 193 (OED b. *U.S.* Attachment or adherence to a legislative union between states. 1864.. So W S C)

Unionist, sb. [AB³] See *cold shoulder, Confederate, bushwhacker,* all 1873 (OED 1b. *U.S.* A supporter or advocate of the Federal Union. 1830.. So W S C H)

unirrigated, ppl.a. [B¹] *When he emerged from the towel, he was not yet satisfactory, for the clean territory stopped short at his chin. Below there was a dark expanse of unirrigated soil* 1876 TS iv 44 (Hum. nonce use for 'unwashed.' Cf. for *lit.* sense OED 1878..)

Universalist, sb. [AB³] See *Adventist* 1907 (OED 1. *Theol. spec* in *U.S.* A member of a sect or Church holding the doctrine of universal salvation. 1861, only Am. ex. So W. Not A in C)

unkinship, sb. [B¹] *Its air of repose and dignity and unkinship with the noise and fret and bustle of these modern days* 1907 "Chaps. from Autob" 171 (Not in OED W S C; but cf. OED Unkinlike, 1869; Unkinsman, 1606)

unlimber, v. [B¹] *Every man...carried his alpenstock in his left hand, his umbrella (closed) in his right...I gave the order,—"Unlimber—make ready—HOIST!"—and with one impulse up went my half mile of umbrellas* 1880 TA xxxvii 422 (Hum. nonce use. Cf. OED 1. *Mil.* To free a gun from the limber...preparatory to bringing it into action. 1802..; so W S C U)

unload, v. [?AB³] *I stocked the business and unloaded, taking Sir Bors...into camp financially* 1889 CY xxii 281 (OEDS 6. *Stock Exchange.* To get rid of, sell out. Earliest exs. U.S. 1870.. A in W B Th. Not A in S C U)

unloaden, v. [?AC] *"She ain't unloadened yit"* 1883 LM xxiii 259 (OED *obs* exc. *dial.* 1567, 1663. Not *obs* in W. Not in S C)

unnethes, adv. [CE] See *dure* 1889 (OED Uneaths. *obs.* Not easily; with difficulty. This form 1520, 1530. So W S C)

unprepossessing-looking, a. [B¹] See *specter* 1869 (Comb. not in OED W S C)

unregular, a. [?AC] *It's so kind of strange and unregular. I never see nothing like it* 1884 HF xxviii 282 (OED Chiefly *dial.* 1602..1884, this quot. So W S. Wr: *American.* Not in C. Cf. undigestible, above)

unreinstatable, a. [B¹] *India is the Land of the Unreinstatable Widow* 1897 FE xlix 466 (Not in OED W S C. Cf. W Unreinstated)

unreverent, a. [?AC] *He was snatched roughly along by the officers, and got an occasional cuff, besides, for his unreverent conduct* 1881 PP xxviii 333 (OED Now *rare.* 1. Irreverent. 1388..1858. So S. Not *rare* in W C. Cf. undigestible, above)

unrisky, a. [B¹] *When an unrisky opportunity offered.. and he was feeling good, I showed it to him* 1909 ISD i 13 (Not OED S C. Given in W)

unsagacious, a. [B¹] *The unsagacious judges go on swearing such witnesses on the Scriptures* 1866 Speeches (1923) 8 (Not in OED C. Given in W S)

unseatable, a. [B¹] *He was given up for dead and his titles and estates turned over to his younger brother, usurper and personally responsible for the perverse and unseatable usurpers of our day* 1897 *Autob* (1924) I 122 (Without legal right to a seat or estate. Not in OED W S C)

unsneezed, ppl.a. [B¹] *I wanted to sneeze, but it seemed to me that I would rather go unsneezed than attract attention to myself* 1895 JA II xvi 746 (Not in OED W S C)

unswell, v. trans. [?AB¹] *"I had had my boots off to unswell my feet"* 1896 TSD iii 352 (This use not in OED W S C. Cf. OED intr. To recover from a swollen state. c1374..1778)

until, prep. [C] *The king and Merlin went until an hermit* 1889 CY iii 47 (OED Latterly *Scotch* and *North.* 1. To, unto. 1200..1824. So W S C)

untoughened, ppl.a. [B¹] *Very taxing on untoughened moral sinews* 1892 AmCl x 77 (Not in OED W S C)

unwatered, ppl.a. [B¹] *See uncheapened* 1909 (Undiluted, reliable, straightforward. This sense not in OED W S C. Given in U)

up, adv. [?AB³] *He saw something was up* 1883 LM lii 514. *"Hello, what's up? Don't cry, bub"* 1884 HF xiii 112 (OED 11d. *colloq.* Occurring (as a special, unusual, or undesirable event); taking place, going on. 1849.. So W S C U Wr. A in B)

up, prep. [AB³] *Up garret was a little cubby with a pallet in it* 1884 HF xxvi 237 (OEDS 6b. *U.S.* Up in. 1845, 1884, this quot. Not A in W. This use not in S C)

up, v.[?AB³] *Smiley up and asked him how she was* 1865 "Jumping Frog" (1875) 31. *All of a sudden the doctor ups and turns on them* 1884 HF xxv 254 (OED 5b. *colloq* and *dial.* To start up, come forward, begin abruptly or boldly to say or do something. Usually followed by *and.* 1831.. So W S C U Wr. A in DN.II. Cf. *down,* v., above)

up-anchor, v. [?AB²] *I was all complete and ready to up anchor and get to sea* 1889 CY xi 136 (OED To weigh or heave up the anchor. 1897, only ex. So W. Comb. not in S C)

up and around, a. [?AB¹] *She was up and around the same day* 1893 PW i 234. *She does not know that she is not expected to be up and around for months* 1902 *M.T. the Letter Writer* (1932) vi 96 (Convalescent, well enough to rise from bed and walk around. Phr. not in OED W S C)

up and doing, a. [?AB²] *Yes, the nation was excited, but Senator Dilworthy was calm—calm and up and doing* 1873 GA lix 531 (OED 19. 1901, only ex. So S U. *Colloq* in W: Enterprisingly active. Phr. not in C)

up-bound, a. [?AB¹] *Up-bound steamboats fight the big river in the middle* 1884 HF xii 99 (Bound upstream. Comb. not in OED S C. Given in W)

up-country, sb. [AB³] *A chap out of the Illinois River...accosts a couple of ornate and gilded Missouri River pilots: "Gentlemen, I've got a pretty good trip for the up-country"* 1875 OTM 722 (OED The general 19th c. use originated partly in India and partly in the U.S. 1b(b). The inland part of a country. OEDS 1817.. So B F Cl. Not A in W S C U)

up-country, a. [AB³] *The conversation in Roxy's presence was all about the man's "up-country" farm* 1894 PW xvi 821 (Cf. above. OEDS 1810.. A in B Cl. Not A in W S C U)

up-country, adv. [AB³] *I was up country trapping on the North Shore of the Erie* 1893 "Extracts from Adam's Diary" (1906) 422 (Cf. above. OED 3. 1864.. A in B. Not A in W C U. The adv. use not in S)

up-ended, ppl.a. [?AB²] *Propping them with her up-ended valise* 1880 TA xlvii 547. *A stile made out of logs sawed off and up-ended in steps, like barrels of different lengths* 1884 HF xxxii 328 (OED orig. *dial.* Set on end. 1880, above quot... Not in W S C)

upholster, v. [AB²] *It had cost something to upholster those women* 1873 GA xxxiii 300. *The bar-keeper had*

been barbered and upholstered at incredible cost 1875 OTM 221. *Women and girls upholstered in bright new clothes* 1883 LM xxx 336 (OED Back-formation from Upholstery; orig. *U.S.* 2b. *fig.* To furnish or trim with, or as with, upholstery. 1877, quot from OTM... The *fig* use not in W S C)

uplift, sb. [?AB³] *The thought of it gave him an immense uplift* 1892 AmCl xiii 141. *It brought a sort of uplift to the youth's despondent spirits* 1902 "Belated Russian Passport" (1928) 173 (OED 2. *fig.* An elevating influence. 1873.. So W S C. A in U M H)

upper bench, sb. [?AB¹] *"You are as solemn as the upper bench in Meeting"* 1873 GA xxxi 280 (The occupants of the most prominent position in a meeting of the Society of Friends. This sense not in OED W S C)

upper river, sb. [?AB¹] *What is called the "upper river"—the two hundred miles between St.Louis and Cairo, where the Ohio comes in—was low* 1875 OTM 221. *We was four days getting out of the "upper river"* 1896 TSD ii 346. See also *throw up* 1896 (As the account in TSD shows, the "upper river" includes all of the Mississippi above St.Louis, as well as the part between St.Louis and Cairo. The term not in OED W S C)

upper-river, a. [?AB¹] *In all these Upper-River towns* 1883 LM lvii 562 (Cf. above. Comb. not in OED W S C)

uppish, a. [?AC] *"Ain't the company good enough for you?" says the bald-head, pretty pert and uppish* 1884 HF xix 183 (OED 2c. Ready to take offence. Now *dial* or *obs.* 1778..1863. A in Wr M DN.IV,V. Not *obs* or A in W S C U)

up-river, a. [?AB³] *"I hid my things aboard the up-river boat"* 1896 TSD iii 350 (OEDS 1b. Directed toward the source of a river. Earliest ex. U.S. 1836.. A in B. Not A in W. Not in S C)

up-river, adv. [?AB³] *I had to go five miles upriver* 1907 *Speeches* (1910) 406 (OEDS 3. All exs. U.S. 1887.. A in B. The adv. use not in W S C)

up-steam, v. [?AB¹] *When they got pretty close onto us we dodged into the bush and let them go by...and then we up-steam again, and whizzed along after them* 1884 HF xl 409 (To make a fresh start, redouble speed. A steamboat metaphor. Not in OED W S C)

up-stream, a. [?AB³] *The steamers did all of the up-stream business* 1883 LM iii 41 (OED 2. Directed or taking place up-stream. Earliest ex. U.S., from Cooper. 1826.. Not A in W C U. Not in S as adj.)

upstreaming, vbl.sb. [?AB¹] *I resolved to be a downstream pilot and leave the up-streaming to people dead to prudence* 1875 OTM 218 (The up-stream business or activity. Not in OED W S C)

up-town, adv. [AB³] *They had to send far up-town* 1869 IA xix 188. *He went up-town to hunt a house* 1873 GA xxxiii 302. *He hadn't been up-town at all* 1884 HF xxiii 229 (OED 1. In, to, or into the higher or upper part of a town, or (*U.S.*) the residential portion. OEDS 1836.. So W S C F M H)

up-town, a. [AB³] *The Church of St.George the Martyr, up town* 1865 SS (1926) 171 (OED 2. Situated in the upper or (*U.S.*) residential part of a town or city. 1838.. So W S C F M H)

urgingly, adv. [B²] *I say it beseechingly, urgingly* 1882 *Speeches* (1923) 104 (OED 1893. So W. Not in S C)

use, a. [AB¹] *A strapping girl...asked me if I "used" tobacco—meaning did I chew it* 1897 *Autob* (1924) I 109 (This sense called A in B. Not in OED W S C)

use, v. **used to was.** [AB¹] *Then she got to talking about...her relations down the river, and about how much better off they used to was* 1884 HF xi 88. *"He ain't as popular now as he used to was"* 1896 TSD i 120 (A in M DN.II, N.Y. Wr: *dial* and *colloq.* Cf. *Used to could,* A in DN.I,II,III,IV,V, Mo., N.Y., n.w.Ark., e.Ala., Colo. AS.II.485, Cooper's *Pioneers*; VI.273, Ky.; XI.353, e.Texas. This usage not given in OED W S C; but cf. OED Use, v. 20. With *to* and inf.: To be accustomed *to* do something. Now only in pa.t. *used to*, with pronunc. *yust tu, yustu.* 1303..1884)

use around, v. [A] *He got to hanging around the widow's too much, and so she told him at last that if he didn't quit using around there she would make trouble for him* 1884 HF vi 38 (OED 22. *intr.* To frequent or haunt a place. Latterly *dial* and *U.S.* 1470..1884, this quot. So Wr Cl DN.I,II,III,V, s.e.Mo., Ozarks, Ky., La. AS.V.429, Ozarks. Not A in W S C)

used up, ppl.a. [?AB[3]] *"When mother got there she was so used up with anxiety that she had to go to bed and have the doctor"* 1873 GA xxxiii 308. *"I was sick and used up"* 1883 LM xxvi 284. *They came wandering back, worn out and used up* 1892 AmCl iii 38 (OED 5. *slang* or *colloq.*

Thoroughly exhausted. Earliest ex. U.S. 1840.. A in B Th,1833 T. Not A in W S C)

utilize, v. [?AB[3]] *"This grand new idea of mine—the sublimest I have ever conceived...is to utilize the spots on the sun—get control of them, you understand, and apply the stupendous energies which they wield to beneficent purposes"* 1892 AmCl xxv 272 (OED 1. To make or render useful, turn to account. Earliest ex. U.S., from Barlow's *Columbiad.* 1807.. A in M. Not A in W S C U)

utterance-point, sb. [B[1]] *He frames a German sentence in his mind...and then works up his courage to the utterance-point* 1880 TA App.D 608 (Comb. not in OED W S C)

V

V, sb. [AB[3]] *"I don't mind going a V on it, mate"—planking the cash* 1877 "Some Rambling Notes" i 445 (OED 4b. A five-dollar note. *U.S.* 1837.. So W S B Th. This sense not in C)

vacate, v. [?C] *In the 'Deerslayer' tale this rule is vacated* 1895 "Cooper's Literary Offences" 3 (OED 1b. To deprive of force; to render inoperative. Now *obs* or *rare.* 1655..1827. So W. Not *obs* or *rare* in S C, and app. not so felt by M.T.)

vacation, sb. [AB[2]] *There was no Sabbath-school during day-school vacation* 1876 TS xxx 232 (OED 2c. A holiday. Chiefly *U.S.* 1878.. So M H. Not A in W S C U)

vacuum-pan, sb. [?AB[3]] *The process of making sugar is exceedingly interesting. First, you heave your cane into the centrifugals...then run it through the evaporating-pan to extract the fiber...then through the vacuum-pan to extract the vacuum* 1883 LM xlviii 479 (OED 1839.. S: A steam-jacketed vessel for evaporating sirups.. through the formation of a partial vacuum. So W C. A in AS. VI.13)

vagabond, sb. [?C] *As early as '93 he* [Shakespeare] *became a "vagabond"—the law's ungentle term for an unlisted actor* 1909 ISD iv 47 (OED 1. *spec.* One who wanders about from place to place without regular occupation or obvious means of support. 1495..1706, first and last exs. of *spec* sense. So W S. This sense not in C)

vague-murmuring, ppl.a. [B[1]] See *ultramarine* 1892 (Comb. not in OED W S C; but cf. OED Vague-hovering, 1871)

valise, sb. [A] *Bimeby my vallis made its appearance, with shirts and cravats hanging out at one end* 1856 *Adv. of T.J.Snodgrass* (1928) 31. *Happy youth, that is ready to pack its valise and start for Cathay on an hour's notice* 1873 GA xii 121. *I packed my valise and took passage on an ancient tub called the Paul Jones* 1875 OTM 72 (OED 1. A travelling case or portmanteau. Now chiefly *U.S.* 1633..1884. So S H DN.II. Not A in W C U. W gives the pron. *valèz* as *esp.* British)

Valley, sb. [AB[1]] *It would not be fair to exact grammatical perfection from the peoples of the Valley* 1883 LM xxvi 289 (Short for the Mississippi Valley. This use not in OED W S C; but cf. OED 1d. The extensive stretch of flattish country drained or watered by one or other of the larger river-systems of the world. 1790..)

valley tan, sb. [AB[3]] *Valley tan is a kind of whisky or first cousin to it; it is of Mormon invention and is manufactured only in Utah* 1872 RI xiii 109 (OEDS *U.S.* 1868.. Comb. not in W S C)

valleywards, adv. [B[2]] *He went swinging along valleywards again* 1880 TA xxxv 387 (OED 1894, only ex. Not in W S C)

valor-breeding, ppl.a. [B[1]] *The Church was able to blight the valor-breeding inspiration of her name* 1896 JA III i 585 (Comb. not in OED W S C)

vamose, v. **vamose the ranch.** [AB[3]] *"Go to the door-keeper and get your money, and cut your stick—vamose the ranch!"* 1866 SNO (1875) 299. *"Adieu, adieu—vamose the ranch!"* 1869 IA xxxviii 405. *"If I was running this shop I'd make him say something, some time or other, or vamos the ranch"* 1902 "DBDS" (1928) 316 (OED *U.S.colloq.* 2. To decamp; to quit hurriedly. Freq. in phr. *to vamose the ranch.* 1852.. So S C U B F Cl Th,1848 T M DN.I,II,III, Texas, s.e.Mo., n.ᵥ.Ark, AS.VIII.1.32. *Slang* in W)

vanish, sb. [?AC] *A speed which can only be described as a flash and a vanish!* 1872 RI iii 33 (OED 1. Disappearance; vanishment. 1650, only ex. OEDS Mod. ex. 1872, this quot. So W. This sense not in S C)

vanity, sb. [C] *The claim that the knife had been stolen was a vanity and a fraud* 1894 PW xxi 236 (OED 4b. An idle tale; a statement of a worthless or unfounded nature. *obs.* 1340..1660. So W. This sense not in S C)

vanity-snubbing, ppl.a. [B[1]] *Then came one of those vanity-snubbing astronomical reports from the Observatory-people* 1897 FE Concl. 712 (Comb. not in OED W S C)

van-leader, sb. [B[1]] *The van-leader of civilization is always whisky* 1883 LM lx 586 (Comb. not in OED W S C. Cf. OED Van, sb. 2b. *fig.* To lead the van. a1661..)

vaporously, adv. [B[2]] *Talking largely and vaporously of old-time experiences on the river* 1883 LM i 495 (OED 1887, only ex. So S C. Rare in W. Cf. OED Vaporous, a. 4c. *fig.* Fanciful, idle, unsubstantial. 1605..1876)

variety store, sb. [AB[3]] *We looked at the dainty trifles in variety stores* 1869 IA xii 113 (OED One in which small goods of various kinds are sold; a general store. *U.S.* 1824, only ex. So F Th. Not A in W S. Comb. not in C)

varlet, sb. [C] *The stage-driver was a hero to the human underlings...when he uttered his one jest, the varlets roared* 1872 RI iv 40 (OED 1. A menial, a groom. Now rare. 1456..1853. So W S C)

varmint, sb. [AB[3]] *I went to the cavern and found a rattlesnake in there... The first thing the light showed was the varmint curled up and ready for another spring* 1884 HF x 81 (OED *dial* and *U.S.* 1b. An animal of a noxious or objectionable kind. 1829.. So Wr B Cl Th,1820 DN.I,II,III,IV AS.II.366; V.202, Ozarks; VI.230. *Dial* in W S C)

'vast, int. [?AB[3]] *I begun to cry, and that sort of worked on Davy and he says: "'Vast there. He's nothing but a cub"* 1883 LM iii 59 (OED Aphetic form of Avast. An order to stop. Earliest exs. *U.S.* 1841.. Not A in W. Not in S C)

velocipede, sb. [B³C] *"Pilot-town," which stands on stilts in the water...where the littlest boys and girls are as handy with the oar as unamphibious children are with the velocipede* 1883 LM xlviii 479 (OED 2. An early form of the bicycle or tricycle. Now *rare.* 1849..1886. So W S C U)

velvet-head, sb. [B¹] *Your little velvet-head intimated that nothing suited him like exercise and noise* 1879 "The Babies," *Speeches* (1910) 66 (A very young baby. This sense not in OED W S C. Cf. OED 2. Applied contemptuously (to an old man). *obs.* 1630, only ex.)

vengeance-hungry, a. [B¹] *The appeasing of her vengeance-hungry heart* 1894 PW iv 331 (Comb. not in OED W S C; but cf. OED Vengeance-crying, 1617)

vengeance-prompted, ppl.a. [B¹] *The surmised vengeance-prompted satire upon the magistrate in the play* 1909 ISD iv 40 (Comb. not in OED W S C)

ventre saint gris, sb. [B¹] See *gros de laine* 1880 (Nonce borrowing, and nonsense use)

Verbarium, sb. [?AB¹] *The game of Verbarium...was brand new at the time...A text word was chosen...The player could begin with the first letter of that text word and build words out of the text word during two minutes by the watch* 1906 *Autob* (1924) II 58 (S: A game in which the players try to form the largest possible number of words from the letters of a given word called the head-word; sometimes called 'dictionary.' So W C. Not in OED)

verdigris, sb. Spelled **verdigrease.** [E] *"A pin's brass. It might have verdigrease on it"* 1876 TS x 96 (OED This sp. 16th-19th c. U: The second element is popularly associated with the word 'grease.' This popular etymology not in W S C)

verge-staff, sb. [?AB¹] *They tried to make friends with a passenger-bear fastened to the verge-staff* 1873 GA iv 43. *Every outward-bound boat had its flag flying at the jack-staff, and sometimes a duplicate on the verge-staff* 1875 OTM 190 (Comb. not in OED W S C. The term is not used on present-day steamboats. Capt. Heckmann thinks it must have been what is now called the forward jack-staff, on which the insignia of the line are carried. Cf. OED Verge, sb. 4a. A rod or wand carried as an emblem of authority or symbol of office. 1494..1894)

vermifuginous, a. [B¹] *It is carnivorous...and vermifuginous, for it digs worms out of the mud and devours them* 1897 FE viii 102 (Nonsense coinage, for vermivorous, feeding on worms, OED 1704.. Cf. OED Vermifugous, expelling worms, *obs. rare.* 1726)

vermin-tortured, a. [B¹] *How the vermin-tortured vagabonds did swarm* 1869 IA xlviii 504 (Comb. not in OED W S C)

vert, a. [D] See *coat-of-arms* 1883 (OED 5. *spec.* in Heraldry. The tincture green. Also as adj. *c*1507.. *c*1828—. So W S C U)

vestibuled, ppl.a. [AB³] See *railroad train* 1906 (OED orig. *U.S.* 1890.. So S: vestibuled train: in Eng. corridor train. So C H AS.XI.305. Not A in W)

vest-pocket, sb. [?AB³] See *crank* 1893 (OED 1823.. Earliest ex. U.S. A in Th H. Cf. H: Am. *vest*=Eng. *waistcoat,* a sense of the word which is unknown in Eng. use exc. in tailors' advts. So AS.IV.11. Not A in W. Comb. not in S C)

vest-pocket, a. [?AB²] See *million-pounder* 1893. *Toy peaks, and a dainty little vest-pocket Matterhorn* 1897 FE lxiii 629 (OEDS *attrib.* 1912.. So W. Comb. not in S C. Cf. above)

victory-flush, sb. [B¹] *The victory-flush of Patay glowing in our faces* 1896 JA II xvii 442 (Comb. not in OED W S C)

victual, sb. **vittles.** [?AE] See *bullet-hole* 1872. *"Grub comes too easy—I don't take no interest in vittles"* 1876 TS xxxv 270. See *tuck down* 1884. *"Meat first, and spoon vittles to top off on"* 1884 HF xxi 213 (OED This sp. *obs* or *dial* in 18th and 19th c. 2. *plural.* 1554..1892. A in Wr DN.V. Not A in W S C)

vigilance committee, sb. [AB³] *This coroner's jury is going to turn out to be a vigilance committee in disguise, who will hear testimony for an hour and then hang the murderer on the spot* 1873 GA xlv 404 (OED *U.S.* A self-appointed committee for the maintenance of justice and order in an imperfectly organized community. 1858.. So W S C U B F Cl T H)

villain-looking, a. [B¹] *There was a villain-looking pedlar with his pack* 1881 PP xvii 209 (Comb. not in OED W S C; but cf. OED Villain-like, 1605)

vine-embowered, a. [B¹] *The vine-embowered home of his boyhood* 1867 SNO (1875) 55 (Comb. not in OED W S C; but cf. OED Vine-clad, 1854..)

vinegarishly, adv. [B¹] *My companion said vinegarishly, "Well, well! What do you say now?"* 1890 *Speeches* (1910) 261 (Not in OED W S C. Cf. OED Vinegarish, a. *fig.* 1845)

Virginia, sb. Spelled **Virginny.** [AB¹E] *"Ole Virginny stock"* 1894 PW ix 550 (B: The common negro appellation of the State of Virginia. So DN.IV. This sp. not in OED W S C)

Virginian, sb. [A] *Two "highly connected" young Virginians* 1883 LM xl 420. *Presently along would come a letter from some red-hot Virginian* 1898 *Autob* (1924) I 123 (OEDS b. 1654.. So W S C U)

Virginia reel, sb. [AB³] *The Virginia reel as performed on board the Quaker City had more genuine reel about it than any reel I ever saw before* 1869 IA iv 43 (OED A country dance. 1859.. So W C. A in B F Cl. Comb. not in S)

vision-seer, sb. [B¹] *One of their commonest inquiries of a dreamer or a vision-seer is, "Are you sure you were awake at the time?"* 1891 "Mental Telegraphy" 103 (Comb. not in OED W S C; but cf. OED Vision-seeing, 1827)

vivandière, sb. [B¹] *Wellington opened a tremendous fire upon him from a monster battery of vivandières* 1881 *Speeches* (1923) 102 (Hum. malapropism. Cf. OED A female sutler, no ex.; so W S C)

vodka-jug, sb. [B¹] *The hired girl squeezed herself into the corner by the vodka-jug* 1902 "Belated Russian Passport" (1928) 191 (Comb. not in OED W S C; but cf. OED Vodka-flask, 1876)

voided, ppl.a. [C] See *cannel-bone* 1881 (OED 2b. Of a garment: Cut so as to show the skin or another garment beneath. *Obs. rare.* a1548, a1623. This sense not in W S C)

volcanic, a. [B¹] *The hatchments were unnecessarily volcanic as to variety and violence of color* 1892 AmCl ix 90 (Offensively vivid or strong; 'loud.' This use, of colors, not in OED W S C)

volcano, sb. [B¹] *Keeping on the 'qui vive' for the general irruption of the Congressional volcano that must come when the time was ripe for it* 1873 GA xlv 409 (A noisy debate. This *fig* use not in OED W S C)

voyageur, sb. [AB³] *A little girl...paddled out in the smallest little canoe and handled it with all the deftness of an old voyageur* 1883 LM App. A 597 (OED A Canadian boatman. 1809.. So W S C B F Cl M)

W

wabbles, sb. [?AB¹] *The bicycle had what is called the "wabbles," and had them very badly* c1880 "Taming the Bicycle" (1917) 287 (A state of nerves; a tremulous, shaky condition. Not in OED W S C; but cf. OED b. *Australian.* A disease in cattle caused by eating the leaves of the palm-tree. 1855)

waddle, v.trans. [B¹] *If you take a great long low dog like that and waddle it along the street anywhere in the world...people will stop and look* 1897 FE xlv 414 (To make or cause to waddle. This use not in OED W S C)

waffle-iron, sb. [A] *One of the commonest decorations of the nation was the waffle-iron face* [from smallpox] 1889 CY xxx 384 (OEDS *U.S.* 1744.. So Wr Th T M. Not A in W S C U)

waffle-mould, sb. [AB²] *When he recovered from his illness his face was pitted like a waffle-mould* 1864 SNO (1875) 254 (OEDS *U.S.* 1864, this quot., only ex. Comb. not in W S C)

wagon, sb. [AB³] *"I'm going to buy a wagon and team and put you and the children in it and start"* 1873 GA i 23. See also *freight-cart* 1880; *alongside* 1884 (OED 6. *U.S.* A light four-wheeled vehicle. 1837.. So M H DN.I,II. Not A in W S C U)

waiting-parlor, sb. [B¹] *They had made those latecomers wait in the comfortable waiting-parlor* 1880 TA x 94 (Comb. not in OED W S C; but cf. OED Waiting-room, 1683..; Waiting-chamber, a1562..)

waiting-woman, sb. [C] *"Only the leech, the nurse, and six waiting-women"* 1871 SNO (1875) 172 (OED Now *arch.* 1565..1831. Not *arch* in W S C)

wake, sb. [B³C] *Marking his long wake across the level plain* 1872 RI v 50 (OED 2d. A track or trail on land. *rare.* 1851,1888. This sense not in W S C)

Waldenstromian, sb. [AB¹] *Swedish Evangelical Miss. Covenant (Waldenstromians);* see *Adventist* 1907 (Not in OED W S C. According to the *New Schaff-Herzog Encyc. of Religious Knowledge,* vol. 12 (1912), the followers of Peter Paul Waldenstroem, born in Sweden in 1838, leader of the Free Church movement in that country. He separated from the State Church in 1878. A large portion of his adherents removed to America in 1885 and settled along the northern border of the U.S., where they number about 33,000. They prefer to call themselves the Evangelical Mission Covenant)

walk, sb. **to take a walk.** [AB¹] See *block* 1869. *The first time he opened his mouth and was just going to spread himself, his breath took a walk* 1871 SNO (1875) 248. *They sing out, "Oh, dry up!" "Give us a rest!" "Shoot him!" "Oh, take a walk!"* 1881 "Curious Experience" 37. *Their position was turned, and they had to take a walk* 1892 AmCl xviii 184 (A in Cl: To be dismissed; to receive one's walking papers. So F: A euphemism signifying dismissal. The phr., in its *fig* or *slang* sense, not in OED W S C)

walk, v. [B²] See *rattler* 1883. *My duty was to hold the boat steadily on her calamitous course. Just as we were walking into the stern of a steamboat...*1883 LM xlix 487 (OED 3h. *Naut.* Of a ship: To make progress. 1884.. *Naut.* sense not in W S C)

walk, v. **to walk on air.** [B²] *The passion possessed her whole being, and lifted her up, till she seemed to walk on air* 1873 GA xviii 173 (OED 5l. To be in an exultant state of mind. 1887, only ex. So W. Phr. not in S C)

walking-costume, sb. [B¹] *I and my agent panoplied ourselves in walking-costume* 1880 TA xxviii 284 (Comb. not in OED W S C; but cf. OEDS Walking-dress, 1753..)

walking delegate, sb. [B²] *Fridolin...started a labor-union, the first one in history...In Germany and Switzerland, where St. Fridolin is revered and honored, the peasantry speak of him affectionately as the first walking delegate* 1891 "Switzerland, the Cradle of Liberty" (1917) 198 (OED Walking, ppl.a. 1c. A trades-union official who visits sick members, interviews employers, etc. 1892.. So W S C)

walking-suit, sb. [B¹] *The knapsacks, the rough walking-suits, and the stout walking-shoes which we had ordered* 1880 TA xi 102 (Comb. not in OED W S C. Cf. walking-costume, above, and OED Walking-shoe, 1839)

wall, v. [A] *The ladies would lift up their hands... and "wall" their eyes, and shake their heads* 1876 TS v 55 (OED To roll the eyes. Now only *U.S.* c1480.. 1883. So W DN.V. This sense not in S C)

Wallachian, a. [AB¹] *That harmless cataclysm in... Wallace, Indiana, excited not a person in Europe but me...You notice what a rich gloom...that word sheds all over the whole Wallachian tragedy* 1906 "Italian without a Master" 184 (Hum. nonce use. Cf. OED Of or pertaining to Wallachia, one of the two principalities which united to form the kingdom of Rumania. 1791..)

wallet, sb. [AB³] *"What have I done with that wallet?"* 1892 AmCl iii 46 (OED 3a. A pocket-book for holding paper money without folding, or documents. Orig. *U.S.* 1845.. Not A in W S C U)

wallop, v. Spelled **whollop.** [E] *You'd see a muddy sow and a litter of pigs come lazying along the street and whollop herself right down in the way* 1884 HF xxi 211 (OED 4a. To flounder, plunge. 1715.. OED cites sp. *whallup* in 19th c. This form not in W S C)

wallow, v. [?AB²] *"But if ever I get off this time, I lay I'll just waller in Sunday-schools"* 1876 TS x 97. *It was beautiful to hear the lad...wallow in details of battle and siege* 1889 CY xxv 320 (OED 6d. *jocular.* To give oneself up unrestrainedly to enjoyment; to revel in. 1887.. So W S C U)

wall-paper, sb. [?AB³] *I could not have believed that ...there could be such solace to the soul in wall-paper and framed lithographs* 1893 "Californian's Tale" (1906) 105 (OEDS Earlier exs., all U.S. 1827.. A in B T. Not A in W S C U)

Wall Street, sb. [AB²] *As to the railroad, Philip had made up his mind that it was merely kept on foot for speculative purposes in Wall Street* 1873 GA xxvi 239. *The devastating crash, when the bottom fell out of Wall Street* 1904 "Bequest" (1906) viii 45 (OED Street, sb. 2f. In mod. use primarily *U.S.*...the money market. 1883.. So W S U F Cl. Not in C)

walnut, sb. **black walnut.** [A] *In a corner of the front yard were a dozen lofty hickory trees and a dozen black-walnuts* 1897-8 *Autob* (1924) I 99. *I went to the little black-walnut bracket on the farther wall* 1893 "Californian's Tale" (1906) 107 (OED 2b. Black Walnut, the Am. species, *Juglans nigra.* OEDS 1714.. So W S C)

walnut, sb. **English walnut.** [AB²] *Perfectly round white things a trifle smaller than an English walnut* 1876 TS xvi 134 (OED 2b. Common Walnut, in British use, *Juglans regia,* called in the U.S. English Walnut. 1882, only ex. So W S C H)

walnut-hull, sb. [AB¹] *I know the stain of walnut hulls, and how little it minds soap and water* 1897 *Autob* (1924) I 110 (Comb. not in OED W S C. Obviously the Am. species is intended)

waltz, v.intr. [?AB³] *"He'd waltz in again...and do his level best"* 1867 SNO (1875) 74. *"You see it's booming right along in our direction...and within three months it will be just waltzing through this land like a whirlwind!"* 1873 GA xi 112. *"I've got to waltz to larboard again, or I'll have a misunderstanding with a snag"* 1875 OTM 286. See *hare-lip,* sb. 1884. *The dogs...were now waltzing up and down the shores trying to pick up the trail again* 1889 CY xxxiv 442 (OED b. *transf.* To move lightly or nimbly. Chiefly *slang.* All exs. but the earliest U.S. 1862.. Not A in W S C U. A favorite word with M.T.)

waltz, v.trans. [AB²] *"They've got to waltz that palace around over the country wherever you want it"* 1884 HF iii 22 (OEDS d. To transport or convey (anything heavy or clumsy). *U.S.* 1884, this quot... Not A in W. This sense not in S C)

waltzing, ppl.a. [?AB¹] *The black phantom...steadied the waltzing steamer with a turn or two* 1875 OTM 451

(OED 1811.., but no ex. of this *transf.* sense. Cf. *waltz*, v.intr., above. Not in W S C)

waly, int. [?C] "*O waly me!*" 1891 *Slovenly Peter* (1935) 2 (OED *Scotch* and *north.* An exclamation of sorrow. 1724..1894. So W S Wr. C: *obs* or *Scotch*)

wampum, sb. [A] *I came upon a camp* [of Indians] *gathered in the shade of a great tree, making wampum and moccasins* 1869 SNO (1875) 69 (OED Cylindrical beads ...serving as currency for the N. Am. Indians. 1636.. So W S C U B F Cl Th M AS.IV.11)

want of, v. [?AB³] "*What do we want of a saw?*" 1884 HF xxxv 357 (OED 5e. ?*dial* const. with *of*. 1828.. OEDS U.S.exs. 1858.. A in H. *Obs* in W. This const. not in S C)

War, sb. *befo' the War.* [AB¹] *Mention of the War will wake up a dull company and set their tongues going, when nearly any other topic would fail. In the South, the War is what A.D. is elsewhere; they date from it. All day long you hear things 'placed' as having happened since the War; or 'du'in' the War,' or 'befo' the War,' or 'right aftah the War'* 1883 LM xlv 454 (Used with *spec* ref. to the Am. Civil War. So F. This use not in OED W S C; but cf. OEDS Ante-bellum in same sense. 1879..; so W S C Th.III H)

warble, v. [?AB¹] *And so he warmed up and went warbling right along till he was actuly beginning to believe what he was saying himself* 1884 HF xxix 302 (Hum. substitute for talk, chatter. This use not in OED W S C; but cf. OED 2. Often merely as a jocose substitute for Sing. 1594..)

warbly, a. [?AB¹] *Your little talk sounded...fine and warbly* 1880 *Speeches* (1923) 85 (First-rate; cf. the vague complimentary use of 'bird', above. Given in W, without def. Not in OED S C)

war-canoe, sb. [?AB³] *Close at hand the carved and finely ornamented war-canoe* 1897 FE xxxii 298 (OED 1882, only ex. Comb. not in W S C. Cf. canoe, above)

war-colossus, sb. [B¹] See *league-striding* 1896 (Nonce comb.)

war-correspondence, sb. [?AB¹] "*We have started something fresh since you left—our paper has.*" "*No? What is that?*" "*War correspondence!...I will finish that battle by reading you what one of the boys says:* [Clarence reads a battle story from the *Morte d' Arthur*]" "*That is a good piece of war correspondence, Clarence; you are a first-rate newspaper man*" 1889 CY xlii 535 (Comb. not in OED W S C. Cf. below)

war-correspondent, sb. [?AB²] "*I had war correspondents on both sides*" 1889 CY xlii 535 (OED 1891, only ex. The OED quot., from Kipling, speaks of "*the New and Honorable Fraternity of War-Correspondents.*" Whether or not the new development in journalism originated in America, M.T. has a clear priority with the name. Comb. not in W S C)

War Department, sb. [A] *The bottom office in the gift of the Government of the United States—Flint-Picker in the cellars of the War Department* 1892 AmCl ii 32 (The department of the U.S. Government presided over by the Secretary of War. The corresponding department in Great Britain is usually referred to as the War Office. OED U.S. refs. 1797.. So W S. Comb. not in C)

warder, sb. [?C] *If I could find out something about a castle before ringing the door-bell—I mean hailing the warders—it was sensible to do so* 1889 CY xvi 189 (OED 1. A soldier or other person set to guard an entrance. c1400..1853. So W S C. *Obs* in U, and app. so felt by M.T.)

ware, a. [C] *And in the midst of the lake Arthur was ware of an arm* 1889 CY iii 47 (OED 1. Cognizant. *Obs* exc. *arch* c1000..1886. So W S C U)

ware, v. [C] "*Ware thy tongue, friend, belike he is dangerous!*" 1881 PP xi 126 (OED 3. Look out for. *arch* a900..1878. So W S C Wr)

war-ethics, sb. [B¹] *Our war-ethics permitted the purchase of our lives, or any mere military advantage...by*

deception 1895 JA II iv 94 (Comb. not in OED W S C)

war-firmament, sb. [B¹] See *meteor-flight* 1895 (Nonce comb.)

war-fleet, sb. [B¹] *Active service in the Mississippi war-fleet* 1883 LM xxvi 281 (Comb. not in OED W S C; but cf. OED War-galley, 1826; War-boat, 1836)

war-footing, sb. [?AB²] *We were reduced to a war-footing* 1872 RI ii 22 (OED 1894, only ex. W: A war-time basis; the status or condition of being at war or ready to go to war. Comb. not in S C)

warm, a. *to make it warm for.* [?A] *I hope to be permitted to make it exceedingly warm for that body* 1864 *Letters* (1917) I iv 96. *The old man...said he was boss of his son, and he'd make it warm for him* 1884 HF v 34. See also *rummy* 1884 (OED 9. To attack or 'go for.' Earliest ex. from a letter of Geo. Washington. 1793.. Not A in W S. Phr. not in C)

warm-blooded, a. [B¹] *The comical thing is that the fig-leaf is confined to cold and pallid marble, whereas warm-blooded paintings which do really need it have in no case been furnished with it* 1880 TA 1 577 (Voluptuous, tending to rouse amorous or sexual feeling. This sense not in OED W S C. An extension from the *fig* sense in OED b. Ardent, fervent, passionate. 1831, only ex.)

warming-pan, sb. [?AC] *Uncle Silas he had a noble brass warming-pan which he thought considerable of, because it belonged to one of his ancestors* 1884 HF xxxvii 384 (OED 1. A long-handled covered pan of metal... (usually of brass) to contain live coals, etc., formerly in common use. 1573..1840. So W U. Not *arch* in S C)

warm shoulder, sb. [B¹] *She was humanly grateful to have the warm shoulder turned to her and be smiled upon by her friends* 1898 MS (1916) vi 66 (Phr. not in OED W S C. A nonce variation of *cold shoulder*, q.v. above)

warm up, v. [?AC] See *camp-meeting* 1875. "*I'll just go over there and warm up that House of Lords*" 1892 AmCl xxiv 254 (OED 2b. To rouse from indifference. Now *rare.* c1580..1857. This sense not in W S C)

warm-up, sb. [?AB¹] *The song didn't seem to have much warm-up in it, somehow* 1883 LM iii 52 (Warmth, stirring or exciting quality. Cf. above. Comb. not in OED W S C)

war-paint, sb. [AB³] See *tomahawk* 1869. "*All the blackguards in the country arrive in their war-paint*" 1869 SNO (1875) 50 (OED 1. Among N. Am. Indians: Paint applied to the face and body before going into battle. 1826.. So W S C M AS.VII.2)

war-party, sb. [AB¹] *The Judge and his second found the rest of the war-party at the further end of the vacant ground* 1894 TET vi 396 (Nonce use for a duelling party, *transf.* from the sense in OED 2. A body of Indian 'braves' banded together for war. OEDS 1800..; so W S. Comb. not in C)

war-path, sb. [A] *to be on the war-path.* [A] See *buffalo* 1869; *battery* 1906 (OEDS Among N. Am. Indians: to go to war, be out for scalps. 1768.. So W S C U Cl M AS.VII.2)

war-path, sb. *to be on the war-path.* [AB²] *She was on the war-path all the evening* 1880 TA xxxii 345. *Boggs comes a-tearing along on his horse, whooping and yelling like an Injun, and singing out: "Cler the track, thar. I'm on the waw-path"* 1884 HF xxi 212 (OED b. *transf.* and *fig.* 1888.. So W S U B F Cl. The *fig* sense not in C)

war-plume, sb. [?AB¹] "*All my medicines, and my war-plumes, and my paints of all colors*" 1883 LM App. D 613 (Used of an Indian. Comb. not in OED W S C)

war-price, sb. [B¹] *Also we have Mrs. Eddy's and the Angel's little Bible-Annex in eight styles of binding at eight kinds of war-prices* 1903 "Chr.Sc." II 2 (Comb. not in OED W S C. Cf. OEDS War-profiteer, 1920)

warrant, v. *I warrant me.* [B³C] "*Out at this time of night again, and hast not brought a farthing home, I warrant me!*" 1881 PP iv 53 (OED 5b. orig. quasi-*arch*

='I warrant,' 'I ll be bound.' 1825 Scott *Talisman*, only ex. This refl. use not in W S C)

war-telegram, sb. [B¹] *It will be well to boast a little of our war-work...Of course, we must read the war-telegrams* 1901 "To the Person Sitting in Darkness" 173 (Comb. not in OED W S C)

war-tempest, sb. [B¹] *When the war-tempest breaks forth once more* 1883 LM xxxv 378 (Comb. not in OED W S C)

war-tiger, sb. [B¹] *Stopping before that old war-tiger, she put her small hand above his head* 1895 JA II vi 148 (Comb. not in OED W S C)

war-tribe, sb. [B¹] *Soldiering with a war-tribe* 1909 ISD v 53 (Comb. not in OED W S C)

war-whoop, sb. [A] See *wigwam* 1870. *Let a cry out of him the size of a war-whoop* 1884 HF xxxvii 376 (OEDS The Indian cry of war. 1739.. So W S C U B)

war-whooping, vbl.sb. [AB¹] *There was such a lot of Indjun tribes, and they kept up such another war-whooping that they kind of took the tuck out of the music in Heaven* 1907 "Capt.Stormfield" 46 (Not in OED W S C. Cf. above)

war-whooping, ppl.a. [AB¹] *A tribe of war-whooping savages swarmed out to meet and murder them* 1883 LM ii 35 (Not in OED W S C. Cf. above)

wash, sb. [?AB³] *We struggled out through a perfect wash of humanity* 1894 *Letters* (1917) II xxxiv 604 (OED 6b. A surge raised in the sea or other piece of water by the passage of a vessel. Earliest exs. U.S. 1883.. So W S C. Here *fig*)

wash, v. [?AB²] *Tides upon tides of rainbow-costumed natives swept along..and washed up to the long trains* 1897 FE xliv 403 (OED 12b. Of waves: To break or surge against; also *transf.* 1920, only ex. *transf.* sense So W. This use not in S C)

wash-basin, sb. [AB³] *By the door was a tin wash-basin* 1872 RI iv 41 (OED Now chiefly *U.S.* A wash-hand basin. 1812.. Not A in W S C U. Mencken calls the word Am. on p. 231, but on p. 236 he says it is English, for the Am. 'wash-bowl')

washboard, sb. [AB³] *A little girl passed by balancing a wash-board on her head* c1880 "Taming the Bicycle" (1917) 293. *"Dey knows how to work a nigger to death, en...whale 'em till dey backs is welted like a washboard"* 1894 PW xviii 18 (OEDS 3b. *U.S.* A hardwood board with a fluted surface, on which washerwomen rub clothes. 1851.. So H. Not A in W S C U)

wash-bowl, sb. [?AB³] *A sink with a wash-bowl* 1869 IA ii 29. *A chipped and cracked white wash-bowl* 1892 AmCl xi 113 (OEDS 2. 1816.. So W S C U. A in M H)

washer, sb. [?AC] *She was a washer and ironer, and knew enough by hard experience to keep money when she got it* 1870 SNO (1875) 166 (OED 3b. A laundress. *Obs.* 1530..1775. So Wr. Not *obs* in W S C U)

washerman, sb. [AB³] *The camp has about two hundred miners,...several Chinese washermen* 1902 "DBDS" (1928) 307 (OED...Chiefly designating the Chinese laundryman of the U.S. 1888, only ex. U.S. use. Not A in W S C)

washing, vbl.sb. **to take in washing**. [?AB¹] *A girl one hundred and two years old, who still takes in washing* 1872 SNO (1875) 158 (To receive and wash the soiled clothing of other households at one's own home. Phr. not in OED W S C; but cf. OED 1e. *spec.* The washing of clothes, esp. as one of the regular requirements of a household. 1480..)

washing-around, vbl.sb. [B¹] *This track was perforated by huge pot-shaped holes in the bed-rock, formed by the furious washing-around in them of boulders by the turbulent torrent which flows beneath all glaciers* 1880 TA xxvii 272 (Comb. not in OED W S C)

Washingtonian, a. [AB¹] *The Washingtonian character would not have been built* 1902 "Defence of Gen. Funston" 614 (S: Of or pertaining to George Washington, first President of the United States. So W C. Not in OED)

Washoe, sb. [AB¹] *Washoe is a pet nickname for Nevada* 1872 RI xxi 160. See also *ranch*, v. 1872 (So F Cl. Not in OED W S C)

Washoe Zephyr, sb. [AB¹] *According to custom the daily "Washoe Zephyr" set in; a soaring dust-drift about the size of the United States set up edgewise came with it, and the capital of Nevada Territory disappeared from view... The "Washoe Zephyr" comes right over the mountains from the West...Its office-hours are from two in the afternoon till two the next morning* 1872 RI xxi 160 (So F Cl. Not in OED W S C. This seems to have been the ancestor of our modern 'dust-storm', q.v. above)

washpan, sb. [?AB²] *We scratched around and found an old tin washpan* 1884 HF xxxvii 375 (OEDS A pan for heating water for washing. 1884, this quot., only ex. This sense not in S. Comb. not in W C)

wash-sink, sb. [?AB³] *It was a small room, with a wash-sink in one corner* 1873 GA xxix 270 (OEDS A sink used for washing. All exs. U.S. 1857, 1873, this quot. Comb. not in W S C)

washstand, sb. [?AB³] See *pitcher* 1853 (OED 1. A wash-hand stand. 1839.. So W S C U. A in M DN.II)

wash-up, sb. [?AB³] *In the dirt of the Kimberley streets there is much hidden wealth. Some time ago the people were granted the privilege of a free wash-up* 1897 FE lxix 704 (OED 2. *Mining.* The washing of a collected quantity of ore. 1890.. This *spec* sense not in W S C)

waste, v. [?C] *The afternoon wasted away* 1881 PP xvii 208 (OED 14. Of time: To pass away, be spent. *?Obs* c1385..1847. Not *obs* in W S C U)

waste, a. [?C] *To my mind there isn't a waste line in it* 1885 *Letters* (1917) II xxv 454 (OED 6. Superfluous, needless. *obs.* c1380..1618. So W S C. Not *obs* in U. In spite of the majority verdict of the dicts., this use of *waste* sounds thoroughly familiar and current. It was certainly not felt as *obs.* by M.T.)

waste-basket, sb. [AB³] *She was an embarrassing secretary, for she fished my correspondence out of the waste-basket and answered the letters* 1909 "Death of Jean" (1917) 120 (OED Now chiefly *U.S.*=Waste-paper basket. 1850.. Not A in W S C U)

waste-basket, v. [AB²] *Send me the pages with your corrections on them, and waste-basket the rest* 1889 *Letters* (1917) II xxix 514 (OED *U.S.* To put in the waste-paper basket. 1900, only ex. Not A in W. Not in S C)

waste-paper-littered, ppl.a. [B¹] *The dust, waste-paper-littered, was still deep in the streets* 1883 LM xli 424 (Comb. not in OED W S C)

watch, sb. **to go off watch**. [B¹] *I see the moon go off watch, and the darkness begin to blanket the river* 1884 HF viii 64 (This *fig* use not in OED W S C. Cf. OED 17. *To be off the watch*: to be off duty. 1848)

watch-and-watch, sb. [B²] *Sir Launcelot...stood watch-and-watch with me, right straight through, for three days and nights till the child was out of danger* 1889 CY xl 523 (OED Watch, sb. 18b. The arrangement by which the two halves of a ship's crew take duty alternately every four hours; also *transf.* 1889, this quot., only ex. *transf.* sense. So W S. Phr. not in C)

watch below, sb. [B¹] *The sailors in the forecastle amused themselves by burlesquing our visit to royalty ...The visiting "watch below," transformed into graceless ladies and uncouth pilgrims...moved solemnly up the companionway* 1869 IA xxxviii 404 (The men of the watch who are off duty. This sense not in OED W S C. Cf. OED 17. The time one is off duty. 1850, only ex.)

watch-out, sb. [?AB²] *I never tried to do anything, but just poked along low-spirited and on the watch-out*

1884 HF iv 25 (OED The action of watching or looking out for something. 1884, this quot., only ex. Comb. not in W S C. Cf. OED Watch, v. 4g. *To watch out. U.S.colloq.* a1888..; so W S B F Cl H)

watch-room, sb. [B¹] *One of the two establishments where the government keeps and watches corpses until the doctors decide that they are permanantly dead...a watch-room, where a watchman sits always alert* 1883 LM xxxi 338 (Guard-room in a morgue. Comb. not in OED W S C)

watch-tinker, sb. [B¹] *When your watch gets out of order...take it to the watch-tinker* 1897 FE lxiv 631 (A disparaging term for a mender of watches. Comb. not in OED W S C)

water, v. [?AB³] *I do not approve of watering stock, but...of course, you can water a gift as much as you want* 1889 CY xxvi 335. *"When it comes to judiciousness in watering a stock...I don't give in that you need any outside amateur help"* 1904 *"Bequest"* (1906) iv 19 (OED 7e. *Commercial.* To increase in nominal amount by the creation of fictitious stock. Earliest ex. U.S. 1870.. A in B Cl M. Not A in W S C U)

Waterbury, sb. [AB¹] *Bright Improvement has arrived, with her civilization, and her Waterbury* 1897 FE vi 89 (A cheap watch; from a well-known American trade-name. Not in OED W S C)

water-canteen, sb. [B¹] *We placed the water-canteen and pistols where we could find them in the dark* 1872 RI iv 37 (Comb. not in OED W S C)

water-career, sb. [B¹] *Great fleets plied the big river in the beginning of my water-career* 1909 ISD vi 64 (Nonce comb.)

water-cure, sb. [AB¹] *The torturing of Filipinos by the awful "water-cure," for instance, to make them confess* 1902 "Defence of Gen. Funston" 623 (W: A form of torture consisting of forcing a person to drink large quantities of water in a short time. *slang.* A in DN.IV. This sense not in OED S C. Doubtless *transf.* from the sense in OED: A method of medical treatment originated by Pastor Kneipp of Bavaria. 1842..; so W S C U)

water-drip, sb. [B¹] *It was the treasure-box, sure enough, occupying a snug little cavern, and some other rubbish well soaked with the water-drip* 1876 TS xxxiii 260 (The dripping of water. Comb. not in OED W. Given in S C, but only in the sense: A receptacle for the drip from faucets)

watered, ppl.a. [?AB²] *Everybody took in all this bosh...and never seemed to notice any discrepancy between these watered statistics and me* 1889 CY iv 54 (OED 4b. *fig.* Weakened in character or force by alteration or addition. 1897.. So W U. A in M. This *fig* sense not in S C)

watered, ppl.a. [?AB³] *We do not need any more, the stock is watered enough, just as it is* 1909 ISD xii 137 (OED 4c. Of the capital of a trading company. 1899.. So W S C. Cf. water, v., above)

waterfall, sb. [AB³] *The charming Miss B. appeared in a thrilling waterfall, whose exceeding grace and beauty compelled the homage of pioneers and emigrants alike* 1867 SNO (1875) 256. *I was glad to observe she wore her own hair...instead of the uncomely thing they call a waterfall, which is as much like a waterfall as a canvas-covered ham is like a cataract* 1869 IA xxxvii 394. *Half the children I had known were now wearing whiskers or waterfalls* 1872 RI lxxix 570 (OED 6. A chignon; also, a wave of hair falling down the back. Orig. *U.S.* 1866.. *Colloq.* in W S C)

water-glimpse, sb. [B¹] *The splendor of the sunlight, the charm of the water-glimpses!* 1897 FE xxix 281 (Comb. not in OED W S C)

watering-depot, sb. [?AB¹] *It was nothing but a watering-depot in the midst of the stretch of sixty-eight*

miles 1872 RI xviii 142 (A station for watering the stage-coach horses. Comb. not in OED W S C. Cf. depot, above)

water-lot, sb. [?AB¹] *"This memorial* [from San Francisco] *praying that the city's right to the water-lots upon the city front might be established by law of Congress"* 1868 SNO (1875) 150 (S: A town or city lot contiguous to water, as on a river or harbor. This sense not in OED W C. Cf. OED †Water-lot: *U.S.* A lot of ground covered with water, but capable of being filled in and converted into building land. 1777..1877; so W S C B Cl Th)

watermelon-tree, sb. [B¹] See *peach-vine* 1870 (Nonsense comb.)

water-moccasin, sb. [AB³] *"If you'll come down into de swamp, I'll show you a whole stack o' water-moccasins"* 1884 HF xviii 169 (OEDS *U.S.* A venomous crotaline snake, native of the Southern U.S. 1821..1884, this quot. So W S C U)

water-paint, sb. [?AB¹] *There was a big fireplace that was bricked on the bottom, and the bricks was kept clean and red...sometimes they wash them over with red water-paint that they call Spanish-brown* 1884 HF xvii 153 (A wash used for walls or pavements, made by mixing powdered pigment with water; calcimine. So W: Paint in which water is the vehicle. Comb. not in OED S C)

water-reading, vbl.sb. [?AB¹] *Mr. Bixby seemed to think me far enough advanced to have a lesson in water-reading...The face of the water, in time, became a wonderful book—a book that was a dead language to the uneducated passenger, but which told its mind to me without reserve* 1875 OTM 286. *The other two depended on genius and almost inspirational water-reading to pick out the lowest place on the reef* 1906 "Carl Schurz, Pilot" 727 (Comb. not in OED W S C)

water-spout, sb. [?AB¹] *Draw a picture of a whale... Make him spout his water forward...If you like, you may make merely the whale's head and water-spout* 1899 "How to Make Hist. Dates Stick" (1917) 152 (The column of spray thrown into the air by a whale when it "blows." This sense not in OED W S C; but cf. OED Spout, sb. 7d. in same sense. Earliest exs. U.S. 1824..)

water-supply, sb. [?AB²] See *doctor* 1875. *The Mississippi...draws its water-supply from twenty-eight states and territories* 1883 LM i 22. *A measure which is to furnish a water-supply to the city of New York* 1901 *Speeches* (1910) 257 (OED Pertaining to the storage and distribution of water. 1885, only ex. So W S C U)

water-turkey, sb. [AB¹] *A water-turkey now and again rises and flies ahead into the long avenue of silence* 1883 LM App.A 595 (W: The American snakebird. So S C. Comb. not in OED)

wawhawp, sb. [B¹] *Knives and other metal things are found in the eggs of the wawhawp—so the children often hunt for the nests of this imaginary bird* 1883 *Notebook* (1935) xvii 170 (Hum. coinage)

wax, v. [C] See *dure,* v. 1889 (OED Now *lit.* and somewhat *arch.* 9a. To become, grow. c1220..1880. So U. Not *arch* in W S C)

wax-white, a. [B²] *All of them with wax-white, rigid faces* 1883 LM xxxi 338 (OED 1890, Kipling, only ex. So W. Comb. not in S C)

way, sb. **down...way.** [?AB²] *"A vessel built away down Maine-way"* 1877 "Some Rambling Notes" ii 587. *"One of them bayous down Louisiana way"* 1896 TSD ii 346 (OED 9. In mod. colloq. and esp. rustic speech. 1902, only ex. A in AS.VI.100. This use not in W S C)

way, sb. **a ways.** [?AC] *I see a bunch of smoke laying on the water a long ways up* 1884 HF viii 58. See also *spider-webby* 1884; *wood-rank* 1884 (OED 23c. Used as a singular. Now only *dial.* 1588..1907. So W S C Wr. A in B H DN.III)

way, adv. [AB³C] *We would...go way up the Ohio amongst the free states* 1884 HF xv 125 (OED *Obs* exc. Scotch, north., and *U.S.* 2a. with preps. 1849..1901. So B F Th M H DN.IV. W: Now *dial* or *colloq.* So S C)

way-back, sb. from **way-back**. [AB²] *"He thinks he's a Sheol of a farmer; thinks he's old Grayback from Wayback"* 1889 CY xxxi 401. *"I tell you, he's an artist from way back!"..."Unquestionably your confederate —I mean your fellow-craftsman—is a great colorist"* 1892 AmCl xvi 167 (OEDS *U.S.* slang. From a remote or rural district. 1889, above quot... So Th DN.IV. The OED def. misses the force of the slang phr., which implies not rusticity but high ability: from the ground up, from start to finish, thorough, complete. Phr. not in W S C)

way-freight, sb. [AB²] *No way-freights and no way-passengers were allowed, for the racers would stop only at the largest towns* 1875 OTM 191 (OEDS *U.S.* Freight that is picked up or set down at intermediate stations. 1883, this quot., only ex. So W S Th,1799. Comb. not in C)

way-passenger, sb. [A] See above, 1875 (OED *U.S.* 1799.. So W S C Th T)

way-place, sb. [AB¹] *She got out of the cars at a way-place* 1883 LM lii 512 (Comb. not in OED W S C; but cf. OED Way-point, *U.S.* A wayside stopping-point. 1902)

way-port, sb. [AB¹] *A good many of us got ashore at the first way-port to seek another ship* 1897 FE xxxii 303 (Comb. not in OED W S C. Cf. above)

way-station, sb. [AB³] *A Mormon preacher got in with us at a way-station* 1872 RI xx 153. *The hack stopped at a way-station* 1902 "DBDS" (1928) 298 (OED *U.S.* A wayside station. 1856.. So W C Th T M H. Not A in S)

way-traffic, sb. [AB¹] *Freight and passenger way-traffic remains to the steamers* 1883 LM xxii 256 (A in W: Local traffic. So Th. Not A in S. Not in OED C)

way-train, sb. [AB²] *He descended, sleepy and sore, from a way-train* 1873 GA xxix 269 (OEDS *U.S.* A train which stops at intermediate stations. 1878, this quot... So W C T H. Not A in S)

weaken, v. [AB²] *"Don't you ever weaken, Huck, and I won't"* 1876 TS xxvii 211 (OED 12b. orig. *U.S.* To take a less firm attitude; to give way. 1876, this quot... So F Cl. Not A in W S U. This sense not in S C)

weaken down, v. [?AB¹] *And he said if a man owned a beehive and that man died, the bees must be told about it before sun-up next morning, or else the bees would all weaken down and quit work and die* 1884 HF viii 69 (To lose strength or vicality. Comb. not in OED W S C. Cf. above)

we-all, pron. [AB¹] *We-all send love to you-all* 1875 Letters (1917) I xv 268 (A in W: We. *colloq,* Southern *U.S.* So DN.V, Mo. AS.III.5, Ozarks. Comb. not in OED S C)

wear, v. [?A] *Then I said aloud, in a firm voice, "Father, I cannot wear the name of Samuel"* 1870 Screamers (1871) 42 (OED 8. To bear a name, title. 1777.. A in F. This sense not in W S C)

We-Are-Warranted-in-Believinger, sb. [B¹] See *Perhaper* 1909 (Hum. nonce comb.)

weather, sb. [D] *There is a sumptuous variety about New England weather that compels the stranger's admiration—and regret...In the Spring I have counted one hundred and thirty-six different kinds of weather inside of twenty-four hours* 1876 "The Weather," Speeches (1910) 59. *No weather will be found in this book. This is an attempt to pull a book through without weather ...the first attempt of the kind in fictitious literature* 1892 AmCl Intro. 1. [Not included here is perhaps the most familiar and most frequently used of all Mark Twain quotations: *"Everybody talks about the weather, but nobody does anything about it,"*—because unfortunately M.T. did not write it. Nothing he wrote is more

characteristic of him than this remark which he absentmindedly neglected to make. It belongs instead to his friend Charles Dudley Warner, who put it into an editorial for the Hartford *Courant* about 1890. Cf. Burton Stevenson's *Home Book of Quotations* (3rd ed., 1937), p. 2128, where Charles Hopkins Clark, editor of the *Courant,* is cited as declaring despondently: "I guess it's no use; they still believe Mark said it, despite all my assurances that it was Warner"](OED The condition of the atmosphere regarded as subject to vicissitudes. c725..1890—. So W S C U)

weather-clerk, sb. [B²] *I think it must be raw apprentices in the weather-clerk's factory who experiment and learn how, in New England* 1876 Speeches (1910) 59 (OEDS 1898, only ex.; but cf. OED Clerk of the Weather: An imaginary functionary humorously supposed to control the state of the weather. OEDS 1831.. Comb. not in W S C)

weather-defying, ppl.a. [B¹] *When we...plant a "We think we may assume," we expect it to grow up into a strong and hardy and weather-defying "There isn't a shadow of a doubt" at last* 1909 ISD v 54 (Comb. not in OED W S C; but cf. OED Weather-braving, 1800)

weather-failure, sb. [B¹] *Merlin...was the worst weather-failure in the kingdom* 1889 CY xxiii 287 (A failure at predicting and controlling the weather. Comb. not in OED W S C)

weather-gasket, sb. [B¹] *The standing rigging forward of the weather-gaskets* 1889 CY xxii 280 (Ropes to the weather-sail. Comb. not in OED W S C; but cf. OED Weather-bowline, 1669..; Weather-sheet, a1625..)

weave, v. [?AC] *"I went a-weaving down the river"* 1883 LM xxiv 271. *The preacher...begun in earnest too, and went weaving first to one side of the platform and then the other* 1884 HF xx 197 (OED 1. To move repeatedly from side to side; †to toss to and fro; to sway the body alternately to one side or another. Later quots. U.S. 1596..1898. Not obs in W. This sense not in S C)

Webster-Unabridged, sb. [AB¹] *"A mighty responsible old Webster-Unabridged"* 1865 SS (1926) 159 (Cf. AS.IV.90: "We use *Webster* (in America) colloquially as synonymous with *dictionary.*" Not in OED W(!) S C. Cf. also M.T.'s use of *Unabridged,* above; also his use of *Waterbury.*)

weekly, sb. [?AB³] See *daily,* sb. 1883; *cab* 1886 (OEDS Earlier U.S. ex. 1833.. Not A in W S C U. Cf. daily and monthly, above)

ween, v. [CE] *"One may lightly answer that, I ween"* 1889 CY xi 132. *"I wend thou knewest me better"* 1889 CY xvii 211 (OED *obs* exc. *arch.* Past tense, wend, 13th-16th c. 1. To think. 971..1848. So W S C U)

weet-weeter, sb. [B¹] *The "weet-weet"...roughly described, is a fat wooden cigar with its butt-end fastened to a flexible twig...An expert aboriginal has sent it a measured distance of two hundred and twenty yards... There must have been a large distribution of acuteness among those naked, skinny aboriginals, or they couldn't have been such unapproachable trackers and boomerangers and weet-weeters* 1897 FE xxi 207 (Nonce coinage. Cf. OED Weet-weet: An Australian toy, capable of being thrown to a great distance. 1878..; so W S C)

well, a. [C] *He is well enough for the provinces—one-night stands and that sort of thing* 1889 CY v 63 (OED 8c. Good. Now *arch* or *obs.* 1661..1803. So S. Not *arch* in W C U)

well-a-well, int. [?ACE] *"Well-a-well, man that is born of woman is of few days and full of trouble, as the Scripture says"* 1876 TS i 19 (OED Wella, int. *obs,* from OE *wella.* c888..c1205. Also Wellaway, Welladay, etc., but this form not given. Not in W S C. Perhaps an Am. survival)

well-gnawed, a. [B¹] See *slab* 1880 (Comb. not in OED W S C)

well-sustained, a. [B¹] *Her enchanting and well-sustained smile* 1867 SNO (1875) 256 (Comb. not in OED S C. Given in W)

well-tanned, a. [B¹] *He had a well-tanned complexion* 1892 AmCl xvi 164 (Comb. not in OED S C. Given in W)

wench, sb. [A] " *'Long comes such a spruce young nigger a-sailin' down de room wid a yaller wench*" 1874 SNO (1875) 206. See also *buck* 1884 (OED 3b. *U.S.* In America, a black or colored female servant; a negress. 1765.. So W S C B F Cl Th DN.I,II)

wend, v. [C] *As Tom wended to school after breakfast, he was the envy of every boy he met* 1876 TS vi 63. "*Certain witnesses did see them wending thither*" 1881 PP xv 189 (OED 13. To journey, travel. Now *arch.* ..1850. So W U. Not *arch* in S C)

West, sb. [AB³] "*A certain bird which has blue feathers and is mostly found in the West is the Kingfisher*" 1864 SS (1926) 129. *It was settled that they would start with the rest of the company next morning for the West* [i.e., from New York for Missouri] 1873 GA xii 120. *Our travellers stopped in Chicago...but the West was more attractive... They took railroad to Alton and the steamboat to St.Louis* 1873 GA xiii 123. *A cousin Mary gave what they called a candy-pulling in those days in the West* [i.e., in Missouri] 1874 *Speeches* (1910) 262 (OED 3b. The western states of North America. Formerly the country west of the original thirteen states, now usually taken to mean the country west (or north-west) of the Mississippi River. Sometimes limited, as *The Far, Middle West.* OEDS 1818.. So W S C U B F H. M.T.'s West is extended to include Missouri and contiguous territory, but not as yet Nevada or California, which he prefers to call the Far West (q.v.). He never uses the terms Middle West or Midwest)

West, sb. **out West.** [AB¹] *A minister of the Gospel living out West is sometimes chased around considerable by the bushwhackers* 1864 SS (1926) 129. "*The big delegate to Congress from out West...will ante his way right into the United States Senate when his territory comes in*" 1873 GA xiii 124 (A in H. Phrase not in OED W S C. Cf. *down South,* above)

West, adv. [AB³] "*I wish I could go West, or South, or somewhere*" 1873 GA xiv 137 (OED 1b (*b*). To the Western States. 1839.. So W. This adv. sense not in S C)

Western, a. [A] *In the Western venture* [i.e., in Missouri] 1873 GA xii 120. *Western investments, through lines, the freighting business* 1873 GA xxii 203. *Presently the train-boy would be back (as on all those Western roads)* 1876 *Letters* (1917) I xvi 286. *A grazier or farmer from the backwoods of some western State—doubtless Ohio* 1883 LM xxxvi 387 (OED 5b. Of or belonging to the Western States. OEDS 1713.. So W S C)

Westerner, sb. [AB³] *In a trade, the Yankee was held to be about five times the match of the Westerner* 1899 "Concerning the Jews" (1900) 263 (OED 1. An inhabitant or native of the Western States of America. 1837.. So W S C U B F)

West-Pointer, sb. [AB³] *He was a West-Pointer and, I think, had served in the Mexican War* 1906 *Autob* (1924) I 304 (OEDS *U.S.* An officer trained at the U.S. military academy at West Point. 1863.. So W S B F Cl Th. Not in C)

wet down, v. [AB¹] "*Wet them down! Wet them down! Give them a drink!*" 1894 PW xi 556 (A in B: To treat. This sense of the comb. not in OED W S C; but cf. OED Wet, v. 8. To celebrate by drinking...to wet a commission, deal, etc. *a*1687..)

whack, sb. [AB¹] "*I'll stay if you will.*" "*Good—that's a whack*" 1876 TS vi 70 (An agreement, 'bargain.' A in AS.V.21, Ozarks. Cf. whiz, below. This sense not in OED W S C)

whack, v. [?A] *All of a sudden he heaves all the tea in Boston Harbor overboard, and whacks out a declaration of independence, and dares them to come on* 1884 HF xxiii 231 (OED 2. *transf.* and *fig.* Substituted for 'put,' 'bring,' 'get,' etc., with implication of vigorous or violent action. Earlier exs. U.S. 1719..1903. This use not in W S C)

whack, v. [?AB¹] "*If everybody don't go just so, he whacks their heads off*" 1884 HF xiv 119 (Cf. Wr: To slash, esp. with a sharp instrument. This sense not in OED W S C)

whale, v. [A] "*And then didn't Jim get whaled!*" 1867 SNO (1875) 53. *He used to always whale me when he was sober and could get his hands on me* 1884 HF iii 18. See also *wash-board* 1894 (OED 1. Now *U.S. colloq.* To beat, flog, thrash. 1790..1884, above quot. So W S C Wr B T DN.III)

whale, v. [AB³] *The boat hit the bottom. George shouted through the tube*: "*Spread her wide open! Whale it at her!*" 1873 GA iv 47 (OED 2. Now *U.S. colloq.* To do something implied by the context continuously or vehemently. OEDS 1846.. So W. Here, to drive the boat hard, push the engines to the top of their capacity. This use not in S C)

whale-backed, a. [B²] *We can see the long, whale-backed ridge of Mt.Hermon projecting above the eastern hills* 1869 IA xlii 441 (OEDS 1869, this quot.. So W S C)

whang, sb. [AB²] *An agonized voice, with the backwoods "whang" to it, would wail out, "Whar'n the — you goin' to!"* 1875 OTM 448. "*It's got a business whang to it that's almost American*" 1888 "Meisterschaft" 461 (OED 2. *U.S.* A twang. 1883, quot. from OTM, only ex. So DN.II. This sense not in W S C)

wharf-boat, sb. [AB³] *There was a "wharf-boat" to land at* 1875 OTM 726. "*The boat landed just at daylight, and I left my baggage on the wharf-boat*" 1884 HF xxxii 332 (OED *U.S.* A boat used as a wharf. 1849.. So W S C B F Cl)

wharf-rat, sb. [?AB³] *His clothes differed in no respect from a "wharf-rat's," except that they were raggeder* 1883 LM lvii 557 (OED *slang.* A man or boy who loafs about wharfs, often with the intention of stealing. OEDS 1823.. So W S C. A in B DN.IV)

what, pron. Spelled **phwat.** [E] "*Phwat do yez want?*" *c*1890 *Speeches* (1910) 81 (An imitation of Anglo-Irish pronunciation. This form not in OED W S C)

what, v. [B¹] "*You, Tom!*" "*Well—what?*" *he says, kind of pettish.* "*Don't you what me, you impudent thing!*" 1884 HF xlii 433 (Nonce use)

what-have-I-done, a. [B¹] *Gwendolyn's face began to take on a sort of apprehensive, What-have-I-done expression* 1892 AmCl xxi 216 (Nonce phrase-word)

whatnot, sb. [B³?C] "*Whatnots*" *in the corners with rows of cheerful shells, and Hindu gods, and Chinese idols, and nests of useless boxes of lacquered wood* 1873 GA xxi 197. See *alum-basket* 1883. *Varnished whatnots, with seashells and books and china vases on them* 1893 "Californian's Tale" (1906) 105 (OED 2. An open stand with shelves one above another, for keeping or displaying ornaments, curiosities, books, etc. 1808.. So S C U. W: Used in 19th-century parlors)

wheat, sb. **good as wheat.** [AB¹] "*If I'm asleep, you throw some gravel at the window.*" "*Agreed, and good as wheat*" 1876 TS xxviii 215. "*Will you go in there with me and help get it out?*" "*I bet I will!...Good as wheat!*" 1876 TS xxxiii 256 (A in B: Good as gold. Phr. not in OED W S C; but cf. OEDS, quot. 1877: "Surprised that he took it all for wheat, and in the innocence of his heart was about to carry it into effect," *N.Y. Tribune.* Cf. also B, *All for corn:* Honest, well-meant, sincere. "He took it all for corn," i.e. he believed it to be true. *All for wheat* is also heard. So OEDS 1b. 1877, quot. from B. Cf. Wr, *As clean as wheat,* Yorkshire: said when a point in discussion is cleared up)

wheat-bread, sb. [AB¹?C] *Hot wheat-bread, Southern style;* see under *biscuit* 1880. *The Masons gave us a Missouri country breakfast: hot biscuit; hot "wheat-bread," prettily criss-crossed in a lattice pattern on top . . .* 1885 "Private Hist. of Campaign" 201. *Biscuits, hot batter-cakes, hot buckwheat cakes, hot "wheat bread," hot rolls, hot corn pone . . . The way that these things were cooked was perhaps the main splendor* 1897-8 *Autob* (1924) I 97 (This triumph of the culinary art is still remembered by elderly Missourians: it was made of biscuit-dough, shortened and sweetened, and cooked in a Dutch oven on the hearth, with hot coals on top, the crust being criss-crossed before serving to facilitate breaking off pieces of the delicious product. Comb. in OED 1377.., but only in the gen. sense of any bread made of wheat. Not in W S C)

wheel, sb. [?AB³] *We selected a stateroom forward of the wheel, on the starboard side, "below decks"* [the "Quaker City" was a sidewheel steamer] 1869 IA ii 29 (OED 3i. Paddle-wheel. 1842, only quot., from Dickens, with Am. reference. So S. This sense not in W C)

wheel-house, sb. [?AB³] *The Amaranth drew steadily up till her jack-staff breasted the Boreas's wheelhouse* 1873 GA iv 49. *"Rush astern to one of the life-boats lashed aft at the wheel-house"* 1906 *Autob* (1924) I 310 (OED The paddle-box of a steam-boat. U.S. quot. 1850, only ex. So W S. OEDS is clearly mistaken in citing the above quot. from GA as an ex. of the sense 'pilot-house.' The pilot-house encloses the steering-wheel and is placed forward on the upper deck, whereas the paddle-box, or wheel-house as the term is used by M.T., is over the paddle-wheel, at the stern in a stern-wheel steamboat, or at the sides in a side-wheel. In both the quots. above it was evidently at the stern. C has only the meaning 'pilot-house' for the word)

wheelman, sb. [?AB³] *I have been asked to tell, briefly, what bicycling is like . . . This is for the instruction of the guests who are not wheelmen* 1884 *Speeches* (1923) 109 (OED 2. A male cyclist. 1881.. So S C U. A in H. This sense not in W)

whenas, adv. [C] *They were . . . sixteen whenas I got me from Camelot* 1889 CY xxi 264 (OED *arch* 1. When. 1423.. 1904. So W S C)

whereat, adv. [C] *"Name thy wish" . . . whereat De Courcy made answer . . .* 1881 PP xii 147 (OED Now *formal* or *arch.* 2b. 1535..1897. So U. Not *arch* in W S C)

wherefore, adv. [C] *A timely touch upon his arm . . . saved him this indiscretion; wherefore he gave the royal assent* 1881 PP xiv 168 (OED 4. As a result of which. *arch. c*1250..1829. So W. Not *arch* in S C U)

whereso, conj. [C] *"Whereso if ye be minded . . . it is in the east"* 1889 CY xi 129 (OED *arch.* 4. Where. *c*1350, only ex. So W. Not *arch* in S C)

whereunto, adv. [C] *"These pomps and splendors whereunto I am not used"* 1881 PP v 64 (OED Now *formal* or *arch.* 2. Unto which. 1490..1871. So W S. Not *arch* in C U)

wherewithal, sb. [?AB³] *"Behold, this person hath the wherewithal—let us go through him"* 1869 IA xl 426. *"The inn is paid, and there is wherewithal left to buy a couple of donkeys"* 1881 PP xiii 153. *"I sent Brady out for the wherewithal before you finished breakfast"* 1892 AmCl xv 161 (OED 2c. Means, resources, supplies. 1809.. So W S C U. A in AS.IV.357. OED W S C all agree that the word in this sense is always preceded by the definite (rarely the indefinite) article, which qualifies the omitted or implied antecedent; but M.T. in the quot. from PP supplies one ex. without any article at all)

whet up, v.intr. [?AB¹] *"You see 'em begin to whet up whenever they smell argument in the air"* 1877 "Some Rambling Notes" ii 586. *I whet up now and then and flirt out a minor prophecy* 1889 CY xxvii 353. *The people were still in the drawing-room, whetting up for dinner*

1893 "Banknote" (1928) 121 (To sharpen one's wits or appetite. This intr. sense not in OED W S C. Cf. the trans. use in OED 3. *a*1400..1861; A in AS.V.420)

which, pron. [?AB³] *"Fair sir, will ye just?" said this fellow. "Will I which?"* 1889 CY pref. 20 (OED 2b. As a general interrogative, *obs* exc. as a humorous substitute for *what.* 1848, 1891. This use not in W S C)

which, pron. [?AC] *Parson Walker, which he judged to be the best exhorter about here* 1865 "Jumping Frog" (1875) 31 (OED 9. As a relative: Used of persons. Now only *dial.* U.S. exs. *a*1300..1899. Not A in W S C)

Whig, a. [AB³] *Of course they asked if that was the new stranger yonder . . . and which communion was he, Babtis' or Methodis', and which politics, Whig or Democrat* 1896 TSD viii 520 (OED 5. *Amer. Hist.* b. Party formed in 1834, succeeded in 1856 by the Republican party. 1839..1905. So W S C B F Cl Th,1837 H)

whilst, adv. [C] *They ate . . . whilst they chatted, disputed, and laughed* 1880 TA vi 58. *"Whilst I bide with the living"* 1881 PP xii 144 (OED 1a. *obs* exc. *dial.* 1613..1895. So S. Not *obs* in W C U)

whimper, v. [B¹] *The lightning kept whimpering* 1884 HF xiii 111 (To flicker, flash feebly. This *fig* sense not in OED W S C. Cf. OED 3. Of running water or the wind. 1795..)

whip, v. [A] *Both times Felder whipped him with his fists* 1870 SNO (1875) 188. *You can't tell one fight from another, nor who whipped* 1889 CY xv 180 (OED 12. To overcome, vanquish. Now *U.S.colloq.* 1571..1901; first U.S. ex. 1834. So S F Cl Th,1815 T DN.VI. Not A in W C U)

whipping-boy, sb. [C] *"Of a surety thou must remember me, my lord, I am thy whipping-boy"* 1881 PP xiv 169 (OED A boy educated together with a young prince or royal person, and flogged in his stead. Now only *allusively.* 1647..1914. So W S C U)

whip-poor-will, sb. Also **whippowill.** [AE] *A whippoor-will come and lit on the bannisters and sung* 1876 TS x 99. *I heard . . . a whippowill and a dog crying about somebody that was going to die* 1884 HF i 5 (OED Popular name in U.S. and Canada for a species of goat-suckers. 1747..1884, above quot. The sp. whippowill used in 19th c. So W S C U F Cl Th T AS.IV.3,11, Freneau, 1809, with sp. whipperwill)

whip-stroke, sb. [B¹] *A precaution had been suggested by the whip-stroke that had fallen to my share* 1889 CY xxvii 353 (Comb. not in OED W S C; but cf. OED Whiplash, 1573..)

whirl, sb. [?AB¹] *"Knight-errantry is a most chuckle-headed trade . . . No sound and legitimate business can be established on a basis of speculation. A successful whirl in the knight-errantry line . . . it's just a corner in pork, that's all, and you can't make anything else out of it"* 1889 CY xix 234 (A risky investment, speculation. This sense not in OED W S C)

whirlwind, v. [B²C] See *salvation-notion* 1894 (OED *Nonce-word*, intr. To rush impetuously like a whirlwind. 1895, only ex. Not *rare* in W. Not in S C)

whisky, sb. [?AB²] *Three hot whiskies did the rest* 1877 *Speeches* (1910) 2 (OED With *a* and *pl.* A drink of whisky. 1884.. So W. This use not in S C)

whisky-drinking, vbl.sb. [?AB²] *There was considerable whisky-drinking going on, and I saw three fights* 1884 HF xxi 212 (OED 1891, U.S. quot., only ex. Comb. not in W S C as vbl.sb.)

whisky-drinking, ppl.a. [?AB²] *Whisky-drinking, breakdown-dancing rapscallions* 1887 LM lviii 571 (Given in OED, no ex. So W. Not in S C. Cf. above)

whisky-habit, sb. [B¹] *Eradicating the whisky-habit* 1897 FE xxxiii 308 (Comb. not in OED W S C)

whisky-jug, sb. [?AB¹] *Jim grabbed pap's whisky-jug* 1884 HF x 81 (Comb. not in OED W S C. Cf. jug, above)

whisky-mill, sb. [AB¹] *He had fine horses and carriages, now, and closed up his whisky-mill* 1873 GA xxxiii 303 (A in B: A grog-shop. So F Cl. Comb. not in OED W S C)

whisky-shelf, sb. [?AB¹] *A man who kept a little whisky-shelf at the station* 1872 RI x 85 (Presumably, a bar consisting of a single shelf. Comb. not in OED W S C)

whisky-soaked, ppl.a. [?AB¹] *Some old whisky-soaked, profane, and blasphemous infidel of a tramp captain* 1904 *Autob* (1924) I 209 (Comb. not in OED W S C. Cf. whisky-sodden, below)

whiskey-sodden, a. [?AB²] *A harmless whisky-sodden tramp* 1883 LM lvi 548 (OED 1891, only ex. So W. A in B. Not in S C)

whisky-straight, sb. [AB²] See *cocktail* 1869 (OED *U.S.slang*. Whisky without water. 1872, only ex. So B. Comb. not in W S C)

whistle, v. [B²] *A large passenger train came round a bend in the road, and whistled past us like lightning* 1853 Letter in *Iowa Journal of Hist.* (July, 1929) 413 (OED 6c. To make one's way with whistling. 1853..So W S C)

whistle-lever, sb. [?AB¹] *"This one,"* indicating the *whistle-lever, "is to call the captain"—and so he went on…reeling off his tranquil spool of lies* 1883 LM xxiv 265 (Means, of course, the lever by which the whistle of the steamboat is sounded. Not in OED W S C; but cf. OED Whistle-line, 1898; Whistle-pull, 1892)

whit, sb. [C] *"The babe unborn is no whit more blameless"* 1881 PP xiii 157 (OED Now *arch* or *literary*. 2b. With negative. 1523…1893. Not *arch* in W S C U)

white, a. [AB²] *"The parson was one among the whitest men I ever see"* 1865 SNO (1875) 74. *He* [Rogers] *is the whitest man I have ever known* 1909 *Speeches* (1910) 181 (OEDS 4b. orig. *U.S.* Honourable, square-dealing. 1865, above quot… So W S C F Cl. Not A in U)

white, a. low white. [AB¹] *They enjoyed my defeat as much as any low white people could have done* 1880 TA ii 35 (A in F: Term applied, esp. by negroes, to white people of the lowest class in the South. Phr. not in OED W S C. Cf. *poor white,* below)

white, sb. poor white. [AB²] *The "poor whites" of our South were always despised and frequently insulted by the slave-lords around them* 1889 CY xxx 386 (OED *Poor whites = poor white folks* or *trash:* a contemptuous name given in America by negroes to white people of no substance. No ex. So W C B F Th,1836. The use of the term is of course not confined to negroes, as OED and W seem to think. Comb. not in S)

white-aproned, a. [B¹] *Everywhere were white-aproned waiters* 1902 *"Belated Russian Passport"* (1928) 171 (Comb. not in OED W S C)

white-ash, sb. [?AB³] *Each boat took to the "white-ash"—that is, to the oars* 1866 *"Forty-Three Days"* 105 (OED *colloq* for oar. Earliest ex. from Melville 1851.. Not A in W S C)

whitebait, sb. [AB²] *Deviled whitebait; also shrimps of choice quality…The other dishes were what one might get at Delmonico's or Buckingham Palace; those I have spoken of can be had in similar perfection in New Orleans only* 1883 LM xliv 446 (OED c. Applied to various N. Am. species of silversides. No ex. So W S. This use not in C)

White Cap, sb. [AB³] See *moonshiner* 1895 (OED 4. *spec.* One of a self-constituted body in the U.S. who commit outrages upon persons under the pretense of regulating public morals. 1891.. So W S C F Cl)

White House, sb. [AB³] *The servant at the White House door did not seem disposed to make way for me* 1872 SNO (1875) 267. *We reached the White House and I was shaking hands with the President* 1906 *Autob* (1924) II 153 (OED Popular name for the official residence of the President of the U.S. at Washington. 1833. So W S C U F H)

white-kid-gloved, a. [B¹] *She passed on into the maelstrom of bejeweled and richly attired ladies and white-kid-gloved and steel-pen-coated gentlemen* 1873 GA xxxii 290 (Comb. not in OED W S C. Cf. OED White-gloved, 1712)

white-oak, sb. [A] *"I reckon you kin git all the rails you want outen my white-oak timber over thar"* 1873 GA xvii 163 (OED A large Am. tree, sometimes called in England Quebec oak. OEDS *U.S.* 1635.. So W S C)

white-shuttered, a. [B¹] *The white-shuttered houses stared at the hot thoroughfares like closed bakers' ovens* 1873 GA lxiii 570 (Comb. not in OED W S C)

white-sleeve badge, sb. [B¹] *Jacob Fuller, the bridegroom…is of an old but unconsidered family which had by compulsion emigrated from Sedgemoor, and for King James's purse's profit, so everybody said…The bride is immeasurably proud of her Cavalier blood…"The things your father said of me…among others that my character was written in my face; that I was treacherous, a dissembler, a coward, and a brute without sense of pity or compassion: the 'Sedgemoor trade-mark,' he called it— and 'white-sleeve badge.' Any other man in my place would have gone to his house and shot him down like a dog"* 1902 *"DBDS"* (1928) 286 (Comb. not in OED W S C. What connection a "white-sleeve badge" had with the battle of Sedgemoor or with the rebels who were sold into indentured servitude after it has not been discovered. It might be suggested, as a counsel of despair, that the phrase be amended to "white-slave badge;" cf. OED White, adj. 11e, quot. 1840: "Like many thousands of 'white slaves,' that is German subjects, who were then sold by their princes to the Dutch or English, [he] had been shipped for the colonies." But all the editions of "DBDS" read "white-sleeve badge;" and it is hard to see why even a typesetter should have been perverse enough to change the plain and obvious "white-slave" to "white-sleeve," or how, if he did so, he could have escaped M.T.'s vengeance)

whitewash, v. [AB²] *The other side had got whitewashed* 1877 *"Some Rambling Notes"* ii 591 (OED 3. To beat the opponents so that they fail to score. *U.S. colloq.* 1884. So W S C)

white-wooled, a. [?AB¹] *An aged white-wooled negro coachman on the box and a younger darky beside him* 1873 GA xxxiii 297 (Comb. not in OED W S C. Cf. OED White-haired, c1400.., and Wool 2c. The short crisp curly hair of a negro. 1697..)

whither, adv. [C] *"Knowest thou whither they went?"* 1881 PP xvii 206 (OED Now, in all senses, only *arch* or *literary*; replaced in ordinary use by *where.* 1a. c1000..1884. So W. Not *arch* in S C U)

whiz, sb. [AB²] *Each of the seven lifted up his voice and said, It is a whiz* 1869 IA xl 426. *"If we don't find it, I'll agree to give you my drum and everything I've got." "All right—it's a whiz"* 1876 TS xxxiii 256 (OED 2. *U.S.slang.* An agreement, 'bargain'. 1869, 1876, these quots…So W. Cf. whack, above. This sense not in S C)

whole cloth, sb. out of whole cloth. [AB³] *Emotions are among the toughest things in the world to manufacture out of whole cloth* 1883 LM xxvii 293 (OED b. *U.S. colloq* or *slang.* Now esp. of a statement wholly fabricated or false. 1843.. So B F Cl Th H AS.II.360. Not A in W S C)

whole-hearted, a. [AB³] *"Oh, I saw Senator Balloon." "He will help us, I suppose? Balloon is a whole-hearted fellow"* 1873 GA xxxv 323. *The sort of whole-hearted peal of laughter which God has vouchsafed to the black slave* 1894 PW xiv 779 (OED orig. and chiefly *U.S.* Having one's whole heart in something, thoroughly earnest and sincere. 1840. So F. Not A in W S U. Comb. not in C)

whoo, v. who-whoo. [B¹] *I heard an owl, away off, who-whooing about somebody that was dead* 1884 HF i 5

(This form not in OED W S C; but cf. OED Whoo, v. 2. 1872.. and Whoo, int. Also repeated. 1770..)

whoop, v. [?AB¹] *"I wish we'd 'a' had the handling of Louis XVI...we'd 'a' whooped him over the border"* 1884 HF xl 410. *Won't you see if they won't call a sudden convention and whoop the thing through?* 1884 *Letters* (1917) II xxiv 447. *"Whoop along, cabby, whoop along; don't let them go to sleep!"* 1902 "Belated Russian Passport" (1928) 178 (C: To hurry or stir matters up. So W. A in H. This sense not in OED S. Cf. Whoop up, below)

whoop, sb. [?AB¹] *This report lacked whoop and crash and lurid description* 1889 CY ix 109 (The quality that would cause enthusiasm or excitement. Not in OED W S C as sb. Cf. above)

whoopee, sb. [AB²] *Then I propped myself against M. Gambetta's back, and raised a rousing "Whoop-ee!"* From "The Great French Duel" 1880 TA viii 80 (OEDS *U.S.* 1928. So M: first used by M.T. in this quot. Cf. DN.V AS.V.327, VI.234, 394. Not A in W. Not in S C. In spite of M.T.'s clear priority, credit for the invention of this epoch-making word has been unblushingly claimed (see AS.VII.44,313) by Mr. Walter Winchell!)

whooping, ppl.a. [?AB¹] *The first few days we came at a whooping gait* 1866 *Letters* (1917) I v 115 (W: immense, whopping. *Slang.* So S. Not in OED C. Cf. above)

whoop-jamboree, a. [AB¹] See *hell's mint* 1873 (Cf. OED Jamboree, sb. *U.S.slang.* A noisy revel, a carousal or spree. 1872.. So W S C B F Th DN.IV. This comb. not in OED W S C)

whoop-jamboreehoo, sb. [AB¹] See *kahkahponeeka* 1880. *"Don't do any thing but just the way I am telling you; if you do, they will suspicion something and raise whoop-jamboreehoo"* 1884 HF xxix 402. *Me and Jim went all to pieces with joy, and began to shout whoopjamboreehoo* 1894 TSA xi 399 (Comb. not in OED W S C. Cf. above)

whoop up, v. [AB³] *Any little thing that you heave in to whoop up the effect* 1892 AmCl xvi 167. See *stand-off* 1893. *He said that when it took a whole basketful of sesquipedalian adjectives to whoop up a thing of beauty, it was time for suspicion* 1909 "A Fable" 70 (OED 1a. To act or work in a stirring or rousing way. *U.S. slang.* 1884.. So S H. Not A in W C)

whoosh, sb. [?AB²] *He fetched a prodigious "Whoosh!" to relieve his lungs* 1880 TA xx 194 (OED A dull soft sibilant sound. 1906.. So W. A in B. Not in S C)

whoso, pron. [C] *"Whoso would shame him or do him hurt, may order his shroud"* 1881 PP xii 138 (OED *arch.* 1. Whoever. 1154..1891. So S U. Not *arch* in W C)

wicked, a. [?C] *The sea was very wicked—the waves broken and dangerous* 1866 "Forty-Three Days" 105 (OED 2b. Actually or potentially harmful, destructive, disastrous. 1340..1903. So W. *Obs* in S C)

wicket, sb. [?AC] *For two minutes we had been standing at a telegraph wicket* 1893 "Travelling with a Reformer" (1900) 350 (OED 2. A loophole, grill, or the like. *obs.* 1296..1797. So C. Not *obs* in W S U)

wickyup, sb. Spelled **wickiup, wickieup.** [AB³E] *Ten steps away was a little wickiup* [sp. *wickieup* when first published, in Harper's CIV.270], *a dim and formless shelter of rags and old horse-blankets* 1902 "DBDS" (1928) 322 (OED Also wickieup, wickiup, etc. *U.S.* Hut used by nomadic tribes in the West and Southwest. 1857.. So W S C Th DN.V AS.VII.2)

wide-awake, a. [?AB³] *"Life in some such...intelligent, wide-awake, and patriotic place as Hawkeye"* 1873 GA xx 189. *We can glance briefly at its* [the Mississippi's] *slumbrous first epoch in a couple of short chapters; at its second and wider awake epoch in a couple more; at its flushest and widest awake epoch in a good many succeeding chapters* 1883 LM i 25 (OED 2. *colloq,*

orig. *slang.* On the alert, sharp-witted, knowing. 1833.. So W S C U. A in B T)

wideawake, sb. [?AB³] *"Well," said the vice-president, crossing his legs, pulling his wideawake down over his forehead...*1873 GA xvi 154 (OED 3. Applied jocularly to a soft felt hat with a broad brim and low crown. 1841.. So W S C. A in B F Cl T. *Obs* in U)

wigwam, sb. [A] *Gentlemen who do not know a wigwam from a war-whoop* 1870 *Screamers* (1871) 57 (OED A lodge or hut of the N. Am. Indian tribes. 1628.. So W S C U B F Cl Th M AS.IV.11, VII.2)

wigwam, sb. [AB³] See *storm-quarters* 1883. *Jim took up some of the top planks of the raft and built a snug wigwam* 1884 HF xii 99 (OED c. Applied to a house or dwelling in general. 1818. So W. This use not in S C)

wild-brained, a. [B²] *Wild-brained martyrdom was succeeded by uprising and organization* 1894 "Scrap of Curious History" (1917) 192 (Given in OED, no ex. Comb. not in W S C)

wild cat, sb. [A] *All things have their uses...in Nature's economy: the ducks eat the flies—the flies eat the worms—the Indians eat all three—the wildcats eat the Indians—the white folks eat the wildcats—and thus all things are lovely* 1872 RI xxxviii 268 (OED 1. Applied in U.S. to species of lynx. 1682.. So W S C B F Cl)

wild cat, sb. [AB²] *"Wild cat" isn't worth ten cents* 1861 *Letters* (1917) I iii 54 (OED 3b. A note of a 'wildcat bank.' Orig. and chiefly *U.S. colloq.* 1883.. So B F Cl Th T. This sense not in W S C)

wild cat, a. [AB³] See *salt,* v. 1872. *Not a wildcat mine yielded a ton of rock worth crushing* 1872 RI xliv 307. *"They want me to go in with them on the sly...and buy up a hundred and thirteen wildcat banks in Ohio, Kentucky, Illinois, and Missouri"* 1873 GA viii 86. *An untraveled native of the wilds of Illinois, who had absorbed wildcat literature* 1875 OTM v 73. *He held out the wildcat bill* 1894 PW viii 339. *It is bad economy to employ a wildcat agency* 1907 CS II viii 258 (OED 4b. Applied to banks in the western U.S....also to illicit businesses or their products. 1838.. So W S C B F Cl Th T M AS.II.52, VIII.4.49)

wild goose, sb. [AB³] *George returned with his dreadful wild-goose stop turned on* 1869 IA x 92 (OED 1. In America, the Canadian goose. 1845. So W S C)

Wild West, sb. [AB¹] *A man who could hunt flies with a rifle and command a ducal salary in a Wild West show* 1895 "Cooper's Literary Offences" 8. (W: The Western U.S. in its frontier and lawless period; often used attributively. So F. Comb. not in OED S C)

wilt, v. [AB³] *Dowley was a good deal wilted, and shrunk up, and collapsed* 1889 CY xxxii 416 (OED Of *dial.* origin, in early 19th c. largely *U.S.* 2. To cause to become limp; to deprive of vigour or spirit. 1809.. So Wr B Th M. Not A in W S C U)

winded, ppl.a. [?AB²] *They couldn't keep that up very long without getting winded* 1883 LM iii 49. *When I struck the head of the island, I never waited to blow, though I was most winded* 1884 HF xi 96 (OED 3. Breathless, 'blown.' Earliest ex. U.S. 1897.. Not A in W S. Not in C)

window-box, sb. [B²] *A watering-pot in her hand and window-boxes of red flowers under its spout* 1895 JA II iv 144 (OED A box placed outside a window, in which ornamental flowers are cultivated. 1899, only ex. So W S U. Comb. not in C in this sense)

window-hole, sb. [B²] *When we got to the cabin we took a look...and on the north side we found a square window-hole* 1884 HF xxxiv 351 (An aperture for a window. OED 1897, only ex. Comb. not in W S C)

window-shade, sb. [?AB³] *Window-shades of oil stuff* 1883 LM xxxviii 404 (OED 1810, only ex. So W C. A in M, for Eng. *blind.* Comb. not in S)

window-slit, sb. [B¹] *The Castle of Chillon...has romantic window-slits that let in generous bars of light* 1880 TA xlii 490 (Comb. not in OED W S C)

wind-reef, sb. [?AB¹] "*It wasn't a bluff reef...It wasn't anything but a wind reef. The wind does that*" 1875 OTM 288. "*You can tell a wind-reef, straight off, by the look of it*" 1883 LM xxiv 267. *Bixby could read the faint and fleeting signs upon the Mississippi's face—the ostentatious wind-reef that had nothing under it* 1906 "Carl Schurz, Pilot" 727 (An appearance on the surface of the river like that of a reef, but really caused merely by the wind. Comb. not in OED W S C)

windrow, sb. Spelled **winrow**. [?AB³E] *Roland lay dying, all alone, with his face to the field and to his slain, lying there in heaps and winrows* 1895 JA I iv 695 (OED b. transf., of various thing resembling rows of mown grass set up to be dried by exposure to the wind. Earliest exs. of *fig* use U.S. 1868.. This use A in B AS.XII.107. Not A in W S C. The sp. *winrow* given as 18th-19th c. in OED. So W S C. This form not in W)

wind up, v. [?AB³] *Now the way that the book winds up is this...* 1884 HF i 1 (OED 22d. To come to a close. 1825.. So W S C. A in B)

wind-up, a. [?AB³] *We had a wind-up champagne supper that night* 1893 "Is He Living?" (1900) 153 (OED 2. Concluding, closing. 1843.. So W S C. Cf. above)

wine-bag, sb. [B¹] *The wine-bags also fell to my lot to carry* 1880 TA xli 473 (W: A wine-skin. So S C U. Comb. not in OED)

Winebrennarian, sb. [AB¹] See *Church of God* 1907 (W: A member of the Church of God in North America, q.v. So S C. Not in OED)

wine-sipper, sb. [B¹] *Among the wine-sippers were many familiar faces* 1895 JA II vii 238 (Comb. not in OED W S C. Cf. OED Wine-taster, 1632)

wing-dam, sb. [?AB³] *They are building wing-dams here and there to deflect the current* 1883 LM xxviii 302 (OEDS A dam or barrier built into a stream to deflect the current. Early exs. U.S. 1808.. A in B. Not A in W S C)

winters, adv. [?AB¹] See *furnace-stoker* 1907 (See *-s*, suffix, above. This use not in OED W S C)

wire, sb. by wire. [?AB³] *Break the news by wire or post* 1892 AmCl iv 52 (OED 3. By means of a telegraphic message. 1859.. So W S C U. A in F T)

wire-worker, sb. [AB³C] *The wire workers know they are not obliged to put up the fittest man for the office* 1884 *Speeches* (1923) 126 (OED 2b. *U.S.* An earlier synonym of *Wire-Puller*. 1835..1842. So B Cl Th. Not A or *obs* in W S C)

wise-drawn, a. [B¹] *He was willing that the parvenus of these new times should find what comfort they might in their wise-drawn* [sic] *theories* 1875 SNO 138 (Comb. not in OED W S C. A misprint for *wire-drawn*?)

wisht, v. [AB¹E] "*Cracky, I wisht I was*" 1876 TS xxvi 200 (W: To wish. *dial* and *illit*. A in M DN.III,V AS.XI.234. This form not in OED S C. It is obviously a *colloq* contraction of *wish that*)

wish-you-didn't-have-to-try, a. [B¹] *You didn't feel shy, you know, or have that wish-you-didn't-have-to-try feeling that you have with other people* 1892 Am Cl iii 37 (Nonce phrase-word)

wit, sb. [C] "*The law doth not permit a child to make or meddle in any weighty matter...holding that its callow wit unfitteth it to cope with the riper wit...of them that are its elders*" 1881 PP xv 190 (OED 2. Mental capacity. *arch. c*1230..1879. So W Wr. Not *arch* in S C U)

wit, v. [C] "*Wit ye well, I saw it done*" 1889 CY pref. 17 (OED *arch* exc. in legal use. 1a. 971..1821. So W S C U)

witch, v. [?A] "*She witched pap. Pap says so his own self*" 1876 TS vi 66. *He said the witches was pestering him awful these nights, and making him see all kinds of strange things...and he didn't believe he was ever witched so long, before, in his life* 1884 HF xxxiv 352 (OED 2. To put a spell upon, bewitch. *c*1350..1884, above quot. So W S C U. A in Wr)

witch-business, sb. [B¹] "*She thinks there's some deviltry, some witch business, somewhere*" 1894 PW iv 332 (Comb. not in OED W S C)

witch-cat, sb. [B¹] "*I have not seen this kind of a cat before*"...*In her heart she probably believed it was a witch-cat and an agent of the Devil* 1898 MS (1916) v 47 (Comb. not in OED W S C)

witch-commissioner, sb. [B¹] *The commission knew just what questions to ask, they being all written down for the use of witch-commissioners two centuries before* 1898 MS (1916) vi 62 (Comb. not in OED W S C)

witch-dread, sb. [B¹] *These were not ordinary times—on account of the witch-dread* 1898 MS (1916) vi 68 (Comb. not in OED W S C)

witch-hazel professor, sb. [AB¹] *The landlord at Ilium endeavored to persuade Philip to hire the services of a witch-hazel professor of that region, who could walk over the land with his wand and tell him infallibly whether it contained coal, and exactly where the strata ran* 1873 GA xxix 272 (Comb. not in OED W S C. Cf. OED Witch hazel, sb. A N.Am. shrub. 1760.. So W S C. Cf. S: The small branches have been used as divining-rods; so U)

witch pie, sb. [?AB¹] "*What makes the witches come here just at this runaway nigger's breakfast-time? It's because they're hungry; that's the reason. You make them a witch pie; that's the thing for you to do*"...*That pie was a job; we had no end of trouble with that pie...You see, we didn't want nothing but a crust...We took* [the washpan] *and lined her with dough, and set her in the coals, and loaded her up with rag-rope, and put on a dough roof* 1884 HF xxxvi 374, 384 (Comb. not in OED W S C)

witch-terror, sb. [B¹] *The witch-terror had risen higher during the past year than it had ever reached in the memory of the oldest villagers* 1898 MS (1916) vi 61 (Comb. not in OED W S C)

withal, prep. [C] "*I sleep in a neglected grave with invading vermin that gnaw my shroud to build their nests withal!*" 1870 SNO (1875) 195 (OED *arch*. Substituted for *With*, prep. *a*1300...1884. So W S C U Wr)

without, conj. [?AC] *You don't know about me without you have read a book by the name of 'The Adventures of Tom Sawyer'* 1884 HF i 1 (OED 2. If not, except, unless. Formerly common in lit. use...later *colloq* or *arch*, and now chiefly *illit*. 1393..1887. So S C U. W: Now chiefly *dial*. Wr: in gen. *colloq* use, and *Amer*. A in DN.III)

Without-a-Shadow-of-Doubter, sb. [B¹] See *Perhapser* 1909 (Nonce phrase-word)

wit-mechanism, sb. [B¹] *Take a "flash of wit"—repartee...Where there is a wit-mechanism it is automatic in its action and needs no help* 1906 "WIM" (1917) v 71 (Comb. not in OED W S C)

witness-stand, sb. [AB²] *If counsel for the defense chose to let the statement stand so, he would not call him to the witness-stand* 1894 PW xx 233 (OED *U.S.* The place where a witness is stationed while giving evidence. 1896, only ex. So M: used in Am. for Eng. *witness-box*. Not A in W S C)

wlgw, sb. [B¹] See *kahkahponeeka* 1880 (Hum. invention)

woe, sb. woe is me. [C] "*Alack, it was but a dream. Woe is me*" 1881 PP xii 140 (OED 3b. I am distressed, afflicted. Now only *arch* and *dial*. *c*1205..1892. So W S C U)

woman, sb. [AC] "*Just come whenever you can, and come as often as you can...You can't please us any better than that, Washington; the little woman will tell you so herself*" 1873 GA xi 109 (OED 4. A wife. Now only *dial* and *U.S. c*1450..1897. So DN.II. W: *Familiar*. S: *obs*. This use not in C)

Woman's Rights, sb. [?AB³] *Miss Lucy Stone is lecturing on Woman's Rights in Philadelphia* 1853 *Hannibal Journal*, May 25. *The woman's rights movement began in 1848* 1897 FE xxxii 300 (OED The rights claimed for women of equal privileges and opportunities with men. 1840.. So W. A in B: This movement began in the U.S. in the middle of the century. S has only *Women's rights*. Comb. not in C)

women-assemblage, sb. [B¹] *Hurrah for the Christian-Social work among the women-assemblages!* 1898 "Stirring Times in Austria" (1900) 319 (Comb. not in OED W S C)

womenfolks, sb. [?AB²] *"I trusted to the womenfolks to set that basket in the wagon"* 1873 GA xvii 166 (OED dial. b. The women of a household. 1877.. So W S. A in B. Comb. not in C)

wombat, sb. [B¹] *He said that the only game-bird in Australia was the wombat* 1897 FE viii 101 (Nonsense use. Cf. OED A burrowing marsupial of South Australia and Tasmania. 1728..)

wonder-dream, sb. [B¹] *A realization of their rosiest wonder-dreams* 1873 GA iv 41 (Comb. not in OED W S C)

wonderly, a. [C] *"An I miscall not the wonderly word, this being the first time it hath been granted me to hear it..."* 1889 CY xxxiii 422 (OED Wonderful. obs. c893..1533. So W S C)

wont, sb. [C] *"Let them not perceive that thou art changed from thy wont"* 1881 PP vi 76 (OED arch. 1530..1906. Not arch in W S C U)

wonted, pa.ppl. [AC] *The poor little ash-cat was already...wonted to his strange garret* 1881 PP xvi 195. *We are getting wonted* 1892 *Letters* (1917) II xxxii 572. *A couple of trips made her wonted and easy-going at the work* 1894 PW viii 337 (OED 2b. absol. Made familiar with one's environment. Now *U.S.* 1610..1874. So W. Not A in S C)

wonted, ppl.a. [AC] *The letter did its wonted work* 1883 LM lii 517 (OED Accustomed, customary, usual. Now *arch* or *U.S.* 1408..1860. Not *arch* or *U.S.* in W S C U)

wood, v. [?A] *We wooded off the top of the big bluff above Selma—the only dry land visible* 1859 Letter in *New Orleans Daily Crescent*, May 17 (OED 3b. To procure or take in a supply of wood for fuel. 1630..1921. So W S C. A in Th,1833. Cf. *to wood up* in this sense, A in B F Cl)

wood-and-water-station, sb. [?AB¹] *If Ilium had gained anything by being made a wood-and-water-station of the new railroad, it was only a new sort of grime and rawness* 1873 GA xxix 270 (Comb. not in OED W S C. Cf. Wooding-place, A in B F Cl; Wooding-station, A in Th, 1829)

wood-boat, sb. [?AB²] *Those boats never halt a moment...except...to hitch thirty-cord wood-boats alongside* 1875 OTM 191. *I tucked myself in among some wood-boats* 1884 HF xiii 115 (OED 1883, quot. from OTM, wrongly dated, only ex. Comb. not in W S C. Cf. wood-flat, below)

woodcock, sb. [AB³] See *biscuit* 1880 (OED The *Philohela minor* of N. Am., allied to the Old World woodcock. 1872, only ex. So W S C)

wooden-shuttered, a. [B¹] *The houses were dimly lighted by wooden-shuttered windows* 1895 JA I iii 685 (Comb. not in OED W S C)

wood-flat, sb. [A] *The few farm-animals were huddled together in an empty wood-flat riding at her moorings close by* 1875 OTM 449. *The 'Pennsylvania' was creeping along...towing a wood-flat which was fast being emptied* 1883 LM xx 237 (OEDS *U.S.* A raft or flat-bottomed boat used for transporting wood. 1785, 1883, above quot. Comb. not in W S C)

wood-pheasant, sb. [?AB¹] *The muffled drumming of wood-pheasants in the remoteness of the forest* 1897 *Autob* (1924) I 110 (Doubtless another name for the Am. wood-grouse or Canada grouse, or spruce-partridge, *Tetrao canadensis*. Given by OED only for the Old-World wood-grouse or capercailye, *Tetrao urogallus*. Comb. not in W S C)

wood-rank, sb. [AB¹] *There was a wood-rank four feet high a little ways in front of the tree* 1884 HF xviii 172 (Comb. not in OED W S C. Cf. Wood-rick, A in B: a pile of wood. Cf. also Rank, A in DN.II: a pile of anything regularly and evenly laid up; so DN.III: Half a cord, n.w.Ark.; DN.V, Mo.)

woods, sb. in the woods. [?AB¹] *"I've always ben kind of offish and pa'tic'lar for a gal that's raised in the woods"* 1872 RI ii 38. *"You have lived in the woods and lost much by it"* 1889 CY xxiv 309 (Remote from civilization or cultivation; 'in the backwoods.' Phr. not in OED W S C)

woods, sb. out of the woods. [AB³] *"En I's outer de woods en ain't got to drown myself at all!"* 1894 PW xviii 19 (OED 5b. *U.S.* 1801.. *Colloq* in W: Escaped from a situation of peril or difficulty. Phr. not in S C)

woods, sb. to take to the woods. [?AB¹] *Negroes and farmers' wives took to the woods when the buggy came upon them suddenly* 1894 TET iii 348 (Cf. *break for the nearest timber*, under break, v., above. To flee, run away in panic, hide oneself. Phr. not in OED W S C)

wood-sawing, ppl.a. [B¹] *He invented a wood-sawing machine* 1906 *Autob* (1924) II 329 (Comb. not in OED W S C)

wood-sawyer, sb. independent as a wood-sawyer's clerk. [AB¹] *I shall ask favors from no one, and endeavor to be (and shall be) as "independent as a wood-sawyer's clerk"* 1853 *Letters* (1917) I i 24 (Phr. not in OED W S C. A in AS.IV.155, VII.391: explained by a quot. from *Appleton's Journal* July 9, 1870, p.44: "The wood-sawyer, whose independence became proverbial, was the pit-sawyer who spent the greater part of his life in the forests, and was thus removed from the restraints and conventionalities of life." Used by R. H. Dana in his *Two Years before the Mast*, 1840, and widely current along the river in the late 19th c.—The explanation suggested seems doubtful. The phr. is not "independent as a wood-sawyer," but "as a wood-sawyer's clerk." A dealer in wood who employs a clerk would hardly have been chosen as the type of one "removed from the restraints and conventionalities of life." The true explanation is probably to be found in the pressing demand for wood in the days of early steamboat travel, so well described by M.T. in chap. xxii of LM, and the consequent advantageous and strategic position occupied by the wood-sawyer, which was naturally reflected in the attitude of his clerk.)

woodsy, a. [AB³] *The Ship Island region was as woodsy and tenantless as ever* 1883 LM xxx 326. *It drowsed in peace in the deep privacy of a hilly and woodsy solitude* 1898 MS (1916) i 1 (OED *U.S.* Sylvan. 1861.. So W S C)

word, sb. [?AC] *After supper pap took the jug, and said he had enough whisky there for two drunks and one delirium tremens. That was always his word* 1884 HF vi 45 (OED 2. A speech or utterance. arch. c1000..1871. This sense not in W S C)

word-musician, sb. [B¹] *This is Cooper. He was not a word-musician. His ear was not satisfied with the approximate word* 1895 "Cooper's Literary Offences" 11 (Comb. not in OED W S C; but cf. OED Word-music, no ex.)

word-of-honor-breaker, sb. [B¹] *"You leave the Christian Socialists alone, you word-of-honor-breaker!"* 1898 "Stirring Times in Austria" (1900) 322 (Nonce rendering of German *Ehrenwortbrüchige* or the like)

word-sense, sb. [B¹] *Cooper's word-sense was singularly dull* 1895 "Cooper's Literary Offences" 11 (Comb. not in OED W S C)

wore-out, a. [?AE] *The rubbage-pile in the backyard, where they keep the old boots, and rags, and wore-out tin things, and all such truck* 1884 HF xxxvii 375 (This form of worn-out not given in OED W S C; but cf. OED Wear, v. pa.pple. wore, 19th c. dial)

work, v. Pastparticiple **wrought.** [CE] See *romaunt* 1881 (OED This form *arch.* 10. *c*1250..1877. So S. Not *arch* in W C)

work, v. [AB²] *"Preachin's my line, too, and workin' camp-meetin's"* 1884 HF xix 183. *She was the Presbyterian parson's wife, and was working the Fosters for a charity* 1904 "Bequest" (1906) iii 12 (OED 14d. To practise on, hoax, cheat, 'do.' U.S. 1892.. So W S Wr DN.III, n.w.Ark. AS.X.23. Not A in C)

work, v. [?AB¹] See *racket* 1889. *"The thing for you to do is to go home and work the weather, John W. Merlin."* It was a home-shot, and made him wince; for *he was the worst weather-failure in the kingdom* 1889 CY xxiii 287. *In 1861 this deadly book* [Dictionary of Medicine] *was still working the cemeteries down in Virginia... enriching the earth with its slain* 1890 "Majestic Literary Fossil" 439 (Cf. OED 20b. In *fig* or allusive phrases expressing cunning management or manoeuvring, as, *to work the oracle, the ropes, one's ticket.* 1859.. Here extended beyond the *spec* phrases mentioned to gen. use. So W S C)

work-animal, sb. [?AB¹] *One side of the house was given up to the work animals, some twelve head* 1883 LM App.A 602 (Comb. not in OED W S C; but cf. work-mule, and work-stock, below, and OED Work-beast, 1380; Work-horse, 1543)

work-clothes, sb. [?AB¹] *Tommy was... in his dreadful work-clothes* 1901 "Two Little Tales" (1928) 203 (Comb. not in OED W S C; but cf. OED Working-clothes, 1892)

work down, v. [?AB¹] *"The upper bar's working down fast"* 1875 OTM 221 (S: To make progress or pass gradually... with *down.* So C. Comb. not in OED W. Cf. make down, above)

worked-out, ppl.a. [?AB²] *We admire his judgment in selling out of a worked-out mine* 1864 SS (1926) 143. See also *bounce,* v. 1892 (OED 5. Earliest ex. U.S. 1882.. Not A in W S C)

worker, sb. [AB²] *In Washington he was a clerk of the House Committees, a "worker" in politics* 1873 GA xliv 399 (OED 2e. *U.S. Politics.* One of a class of political agents. 1888, only ex. Not A in W. This sense not in S C)

work-gown, sb. [?AB¹] *He had a long-handled shovel over his shoulder, and we see the white patch on the old work-gown* 1896 TSD vii 360 (A duster or wrapper to protect the other clothes while at work. Comb. not in OED W S C. Cf. working-gown, below)

workhouse, sb. [AB²] *Eggs so unwholesome that the city physician seldom or never orders them for the workhouse* 1870 SNO (1875) 83 (OED 3. A prison or house of correction for petty offenders. *U.S.* 1888, only ex. So W H. Not A in S. This sense not in C)

working-folks, sb. [?AB¹] *They are poor working-folks, and ignorant* 1901 "Two Little Tales" (1928) 204 (Wr: The working-class. Comb. not in OED W S C. Cf. folks, above)

working-gown, sb. [?AB¹] *Uncle Silas's old faded green baize working-gown with the hood to it* 1896 TSD vi 358 (Cf. work-gown, above. Comb. not in OED W S C)

working-moment, sb. [B¹] *Opportunity had given me a chance working-moment or two* 1904 Autob (1924) I 245 (Comb. not in OED W S C. Cf. OEDS Working-day, 1813..)

working-people, sb. [?AB¹] *"In England the swell folks don't speak of the working-people as gentlemen and ladies"* 1892 AmCl xi 112 (Comb. not in OED W S C)

working-plans, sb. [?AB¹] *The ghastly desolation of the place was as tremendously complete as if Doré had furnished the working-plans for it* 1881 TA xxxiv 370 (C: same as *working-drawings.* Comb. not in OED W S. Cf. OED Working-drawings: The drawings made of the plan of a building, etc., from which the workmen carry out the construction)

worklike, a. [?AB¹] *There was something very real and worklike about the new phase of it* 1875 OTM 218 (Workmanlike, business-like. Not in OED W S C in this sense)

work-mule, sb. [?AB¹] *"De big house 'uz three mile back f'om de river en on'y work-mules to ride"* 1894 PW xviii 18 (Comb. not in OED W S C. Cf. work-animal, above)

work off, v. [?AB¹] *The astronomical apprentice worked off a section of the Milky Way on me for the Magellan Clouds* 1897 FE lxii 617. *He has not written as many plays as I have, but he has had that God-given talent, which I lack, of working them off on the manager* 1900 Speeches (1910) 164. *I was working off these humorous brilliancies on him and getting no return* 1906 Speeches (1910) 400 (W: To palm off, pass off. *slang.* So S. This sense not in OED C; cf. OED 37c. To perpetrate, 'play off;' as, "He worked off a swindle on me." 1891, only ex.)

work-parlor, sb. [B¹] *She tripped down-stairs every little while from her work-parlor* 1892 AmCl xx 206 (Comb. not in OED W S C. Cf. OED Work-room, 1828..)

works, sb. [?AB²] *"But here we're a-running on this way, and you hain't told me a word about Sis, nor any of them. Now I'll rest my works a little and you start up yourn"* 1884 HF xxxii 333. *Then it would bray, spreading its jaws till you could see down to its works. It was a disagreeable animal* 1885 "Private Hist. of Campaign" 196 (OED 20. Humorously applied to the internal organs of an animal, as *to take out the works* = to draw a fowl, etc. *colloq.* No ex. So U. This sense not in W S C)

work-stock, sb. [?AB²] *The people cared first for their work-stock... horses and mules were housed in a place of safety* 1883 LM App. A 603 (OED 1911, only ex. Comb. not in W S C. Cf. Work-animal and work-mule, above)

world, sb. **the world's people.** [?A] *"Is thy father willing thee should go away to a school of the world's people?"* 1873 GA xiv 134 (OED 4b. In the Society of Friends applied to those outside their own body. 1648.. 1867. So S. A in Th DN.IV. This sense not in W C)

world, adv. [?AC] *Trousers... a world too short* 1883 LM lvii 558 (OED 19b. Used advb. Infinitely, vastly. *arch.* 1600..1887. So S C U. This use not in W)

world, sb. **to think the world of.** [?AB²] *"They think the world of Mulberry"* 1892 AmCl iii 40 (OED 20e. To have the highest possible regard for. 1894.. Phr. not in W S C)

world-celebrated, a. [B¹] *Hadleyburg village woke up world-celebrated* 1899 "MCH" (1900) 18 (Given in W. Comb. not in OED S C; but cf. OED World-famed, modeled on German *weltberühmt,* 1866)

worlded, ppl.a. [B¹C] *"I think there is such a planet in one of the little new systems away out in one of the thinly worlded corners of the universe"* 1907 "Capt.Stormfield" 44 (S: Containing worlds. rare. So C. Not in OED W)

world-girdling, a. [B¹] *An embodied prodigy, a word, a phrase, a world-girdling Name* 1896 JA III iv 594 (Comb. not in OED W S C. Cf. German *Weltgürtel,* zone; *Weltumgürter,* Neptune)

World's Fair, sb. [B¹] *Save it for processions, and Chautauquas, and World's Fairs* 1905 Speeches (1910) 432 (Comb. not in OED W S C. Cf. Fair, above)

world-trade, sb. [B¹] *To go to the Amazon and open up a world-trade in coca* 1910 "Turning-Point of My Life" (1917) 133 (Comb. not in OED W S C. Cf. OED World, sb. 24b. Combinations with the meaning 'of or pertaining to the whole world, world-wide.' Orig. translating or modelled on German compounds, as *Welthandel,* world-commerce, 1905. Cf. also OEDS World-market, 1909)

world-wonder, sb. [B¹] *"Was this world-wonder in our familiar midst all these years?"* 1895 JA II ii 84 (Comb. not in OED W S C. Cf. German *Weltwunder,* wonder of the world)

worm-fashion, adv. [B[1]] *A heaped-up confusion of red roofs...with here and there a bit of ancient embattled wall bending itself over the ridges, worm-fashion* 1880 TA xxv 245 (Comb. not in OED W S C)

worrisome, a. [?AB[2]] "*I get a bit troubled and worrisome*" 1873 GA xxvii 245 (OED Given to worrying. 1893, only ex. this sense. So W S. A in B F Cl. This sense not in C)

worry along, v. [AB[2]] "*My friend, you seem to know pretty much all the tunes there are, and you worry along first rate*" 1871 SNO (1875) 296 (OED 8b. To contrive to 'keep going.' *U.S.* 1873.. Not A in W C U. This sense not in S)

worry down, v. [?AB[3]] "*I can swaller a thirteenth of the yarn, if you can worry down the rest*" 1883 LM iii 58 (OED With adv., e.g. *out, down:* To get into a specified condition by...dogged effort. U.S. quot. 1870, only ex. with *down.* Not A in W. This sense not in S C)

worsen, v. [?AC] "*Peace! and forbear to worsen our chances with dangerous speech*" 1881 PP xxiii 285. *Trying to better it, I've worsened it a hundred times* 1884 HF xxvii 275 (OED 1. Common in *dial*; reintroduced to literature c1800-1830 by writers like Southey and De Quincey as a racy vernacular substitute for *deteriorate* and the like. a1225..1670, 1806..1906. So W S U. *Rare* in C. A in Wr)

wot, v. [C] "*It would improve the sanity of some I wot of*" 1881 PP xv 123 (OED *arch.* To know. a1300..1874. So W S C U)

would God, v.phr. [C] "*Would God I had died or I saw this day*" 1889 CY iii 46 (OED Will, v. 37. *obs* or *rare arch.* c1375..c1600. Not *obs* or *arch* in W S C)

woundily, adv. [C] "*It were woundily hard to tell*" 1889 CY xi 129. "*The name of this valley doth woundily differ from the name of that one*" 1889 CY xxiv 303 (OED *obs* exc. *arch.* Excessively, extremely. 1706.. 1880. So W U. Not *obs* in S C)

wrapper, sb. [A] See *seed-leaf* 1910 (OED 4. Tobacco-leaf...used for the outer cover of cigars. Chiefly *U.S.* 1688.. Not A in W S C U)

write up, v. [?AB[3]] *The 'Sacramento Union' sent me to the Sandwich Islands for five or six months, to write up sugar* 1910 "Turning Point of My Life" (1917) 136 (OED 18e. To commend to notice or favor by appreciative writing; to laud by way of advertisement. 1824.. So W S C U. Cf. H: *write-up,* sb. Am. for Eng. *descriptive report*)

writing-gait, sb. [B[1]] *My writing-gait is twenty-four words per minute* 1899 "Simplified Alphabet" (1917) 260 (Comb. not in OED W S C)

writing-parlor, sb. [B[1]] *The busy gentlemen in the reporters' gallery jotted a line in their notebooks, ran to the telegraphic desk in a room which communicated with their own writing-parlor, and hurried back* 1873 GA xliii 390 (Room in the Senate building assigned for the use of correspondents; now usually called press-room. Comb. not in OED W S C)

X

xhvloj, sb. [B¹] See *kahkahponeeka* 1880 (Hum. invention)

xylaloes, sb. [C] See *afarabocca* 1894 (OED *obs* = Lign-aloes. 1545..1683. Not in W S C)

xylobalsamum, sb. Spelled **zylobalsamum.** [B¹E] *I will invent a name for him calculated to disenchant her* ..."*Well, then, I'll tell you about this man Snodgrass* ...*His—er—his initials are S.M....They—well, they stand for Spinal Meningitis*"..."*Why, it would be my name!*" "*Yes—Mrs. Spinal Meningitis Snodgrass... His brother, Zylobalsamum—*""*I never heard of such a name. Is it a disease?*" "*No...it's either Scriptural or ...it's anatomical*" 1892 AmCl xxiv 258. See also *afarabocca* 1894 (Nonsense use. Cf. OED The fragrant wood of the tree which yields the resin called Opobalsamum or Balm of Gilead. 1616..1868; so W S C U. S and C give *zylo-* as variant form)

Y

yacht, v.trans. [B¹] *Her husband would yacht me and my party around* 1895 *Letters* (1917) II xxxv 626 (The trans. use not in OED W S C. Cf. OED intr. To make a trip in a yacht. 1836..)

yachting-contest, sb. [B¹] *German papers...contain no information about...horse-races, walking-matches, yachting-contests* 1880 TA App. F 626 (Comb. not in OED W S C)

yam, sb. [AB³] *His mission had nothing more overpowering about it than the collecting of seeds, and uncommom yams, and extraordinary cabbages* 1869 IA ii 27 (OED 2(c). A variety of the sweet potato largely eaten by the negroes in America. 1862.. So W S C Wr B Cl M H DN.II, s.e.Mo.; DN.IV, New Orleans, Kansas; AS.IV.11. But only the OED confines the eating of yams to negroes!)

Yank, sb. [A] *Intruding upon a scene like this came the green-spectacled Yanks, with their flapping elbows and bobbing umbrellas* 1869 IA xlv 469. *Asked me where I was from. I answered, "New England." "Oh, a Yank!" said he* 1883 LM xxx 329. See also *South, down* 1894 (OED *colloq* abbrev. of Yankee. 1778.. So W S C U B F Cl M DN.II,III,IV)

yank, v. [AB³] *He'd yank a sinner outen* (Hades), *And land him with the blest* 1867 SNO (1875) 74. *He grabs his property viciously, yanks it this way, then that* 1880 TA xxii 216. *The rope sprang taut and yanked Sir Sagramor out of the saddle* 1889 CY xxxix 501 (OED 1. *dial* and *U.S.* To pull, to jerk. 1848.. So Wr B F Cl Th M. Not A in W S C U T)

Yankee, sb. [A] *A Connecticut Yankee in King Arthur's Court* (title) 1889 CY. *He found a keen-eyed Yankee engaged in repairing cheap chairs* 1892 AmCl iv 50. *The "Yankee" (citizen of the New England States) was hated with a splendid energy* 1899 "Concerning the Jews" (1900) 263. See also *trade,* sb. 1899; *bunco* 1905 (OED 1a. *U.S.* A nickname for a native or inhabitant of New England. 1765.. So W S C U B F Cl Th T M H DN.II,III,VI AS.IV.11)

Yankee, sb. [AB³] *"We say 'cow,' the Briton says 'kaow'; we—" "Oh, come! that is pure Yankee; everybody knows that." "Yes, it is pure Yankee; that is true. One cannot hear it in America outside the little corner called New England*" 1882 "Concerning the American Language" 266 (OED 2. The dialect of New England; loosely, American English generally. 1824.. So W. This sense not in S C)

Yankee-land, sb. [AB³] *I have no doubt small fortunes were made by certain delegates from Yankee land* 1856 Letter in *Iowa Journ. of Hist.* (1929) 423. *The little corner called New England, which is Yankee land* 1882 "Concerning the American Language" 266 (OED The land of Yankees, New England; loosely, the United States. 1803.. So W S C Th,1760. Comb. not in C)

yap, sb. [?AB¹] *He ordered me to "hold my yap"* 1870 CRG (1919) 85 (W: Talk, gab. *slang.* So S. A in Cl DN.II; but DN defines it as = 'Mouth.' This sense not in OED C; but cf. OEDS 2b. *slang.* A chat. 1930, only ex. The word is prob. a var. form of 'yawp,' q.v. below)

yare, v. [B¹] *It is my conviction that Shakespeare's sailor-talk would be Choctaw to...the captain of any sailing-vessel of our time. For instance—from "The Tempest"*: ..."*Boatswain. Heigh, my hearts! cheerly, cheerly, my hearts! yare, yare! Take in the topsail. Tend to the master's whistle...Down with the topmast! yare! lower, lower!*" *That will do for the present; let us yare a little now for a change* 1909 ISD vii 73 (Hum. nonsense use. Cf. OED Yare, adv. 1c. As exclamation: = Quick! esp. in nautical use. *arch.* 1606, Shakespeare..1867, Wm. Morris. Cf. M.T.'s own use of *snatch it* and *whale it,* above, for a modern parallel to the Elizabethan sailor-talk which he found so unconvincing)

yarning, vbl.sb. [B²] *The yarning and laughing and singing went on at a noble rate* 1895 JA I iv 692 (OEDS The action of 'spinning yarns.' 1916, only ex. So W S C)

yarn socks, sb. [AB¹] *Captain Hardy wore yarn socks* 1875 OTM 572 (A in DN.III, n.w.Ark. Comb. not in OED W S C; but cf. OED Yarn-stockings, 1704)

yawl, a. [B²] *He...climbed into the skiff that did "yawl" duty at the boat's stern* 1876 TS xv 129 (OED Yawl, sb. 4. attrib. 1894, only ex. For sb. use cf. OED 1. 1670.. not attrib. in W S C)

yawl, v. [B²C] *When we got to the village, they yawled us ashore* 1884 HF xxiv 242 (OED *nonce-wd.* To convey in a yawl. 1884, this quot, only ex. W: *rare.* Not in S C as verb)

yawp, sb. [?AB³] *Be so kind as to hold your yawp for about five minutes* 1877 *Speeches* (1910) 4 (OED b. *fig.* Applied in contempt to speech or utterance. 1884.. OEDS 1835.. All exs. U.S. A in B DN.I. So Mencken, ascribed to Whitman, tho it is much earlier, as the OEDS quots. show. This sense not in W S C)

yawp, v. [?AB³] *"Some people like to...moon around yawping at the lake or these mountains and things, but that ain't my way"* 1880 TA xxvii 278 (OED Chiefly *dial.* 3. To gape. Earliest ex. U.S. 1836.. A in M. Not A in W. This sense not in S C)

ye, art. [C] *Her Majestie, ye Queen* 1880 *Fireside Conversation of 1601* (OED Y (3): ye = the. In manuscript (e.g. in letter-writing) ye lasted well into the 19th c. It is still often used pseudo-archaically, jocularly, or vulgarly (pronounced as ye). So W S C U M)

ye, pron. [?ACE] *"My very words, Brer Penrod! I was a-sayin'—pass that-air sasser o' molasses, won't ye?"* 1884 HF xli 417 (OED Now in all uses only *dial, arch,* or *poet.* 2. Used instead of *thou* in addressing a single person. 1297..1878. So W S C U Wr. A in M)

ye, pron. [?ACE] *"Bless ye, my children!"* 1869 SNO (1875) 211 (OED 3. Used as objective instead of *you,* in plural or singular sense. Cf. above. So W S C U. A in M AS.V.255)

year-worn, a. [B¹] *Her year-worn advertisement had been answered* 1894 PW v 333 (Comb. not in OED W S C. Cf. OED Year-marked, 1873)

yellow, a. Spelled **yaller.** [AE] *Smiley had a yaller one-eyed cow* 1865 "Jumping Frog" (1875) 35. See *wench* 1874. *"If you let a pint of this yaller Mississippi water settle, you would have about half to three quarters of an inch of mud in the bottom"* 1883 LM iii 50. *He took up a little blue and yaller picture* 1884 HF v 32 (OED calls this sp. 19th c., esp. *U.S.* No ex. So DN.IV,V. Not A in W C. Not in S)

yellow-boy, sb. [AB¹] *A round ten thousand dollars in yellow boys* 1883 LM xxxvi 389. *When they found the bag they spilt it out on the floor, and it was a lovely sight, all them yaller-boys...They pawed the yaller-boys, and sifted them through their fingers; then...they counts it, and it comes out four hundred and fifteen dollars short* 1884 HF xxv 249 (Gold coins in U.S. money. So B Th DN.V. *Slang* in S C. Given in OED W only of British guineas or sovereigns; OED *slang. ?obs.* 1662..1840)

yellow-covered, ppl.a. [?AB¹] *"I have been in the editorial business going on fourteen years, and it is the first time I ever heard of a man's having to know anything in order to edit a newspaper...Who edit the agricultural papers?...Men, as a general thing, who fail in the poetry line, yellow-covered novel line, sensation-drama line, city-editor line, and finally fall back on agriculture as a temporary reprieve from the poor-house"* From "How I Edited an Agricultural Paper" 1870 *Screamers* (1871) 57 (Cf. W Yellow-covered literature: cheap, sensational, or trashy novels, magazines, etc.,—from the usual color of the covers. *colloq.* So S C. A in B. This sense not in OED; but cf. OED Yellow-back, sb.: A cheap yellow-backed (esp. French) novel. 1890, only ex.)

yellow-jacket, sb. [AB³] See *half-breed,* sb. 1872 (OED *U.S.colloq.* Name for a wasp or hornet. OEDS 1811.. So W S C B)

yellow-jacket, sb. [?AB¹] *It come out four hundred and fifteen dollars short..."Hold on," says the duke. "Let's make up the deffisit," and he begun to haul out yaller-boys out of his pocket. "It's a most amaz'n' good idea, duke"...says the king. "...and he begun to haul out yaller-jackets and stack them up* 1884 HF xxv 250 (Another name for 'yellow-boy,' q.v. above. Not in OED W S C in this sense)

yellow journalism, sb. [AB³] *He was the father of the William R. Hearst of to-day, and therefore grandfather of Yellow Journalism—that calamity of calamities* 1906 *Autob* (1924) II 14 (OED Yellow, a. 3. Orig. *U.S.* Applied to newspapers of a recklessly or unscrupulously sensational character. A use derived from the appearance in 1895 of a number of the *New York World* in which a child in a yellow dress ("The Yellow Kid") was the central figure of the cartoon. 1898.. So Cl H. Not A in W S. This use not in C.

The OED is doubtless right, as against M.T., in vindicating for Joseph Pulitzer, editor of the *New York World,* rather than for William R. Hearst, who was never anything but an imitator and a bad copyist, the dubious title of "Father of Yellow Journalism." Mark Twain himself, however, came within an ace of earning the honor of coining the phrase. By implication, at least, he associated the color "yellow" with sensational journalism nearly thirty years earlier than the earliest OED quot., when he described a forerunner of the species as a "mustard-plaster of a newspaper" (cf. OED Mustard-coloured, 1886; Mustard-yellow, 1904). The passage in which the phrase occurs demonstrates his familiarity also with the thing, by giving an excellent description of it, which has lost none of its applicability with the passage of time: *"The heaven-born mission of journalism is to disseminate truth; to eradicate error; to educate, refine, and elevate the tone of public morals and manners, and make all men more gentle, more virtuous, more charitable, and in all ways better, holier, and happier; and yet this black-hearted scoundrel degrades his great office persistently to the dissemination of falsehood, calumny, vituperation, and vulgarity . . . That mustard-plaster of a newspaper!"* From "Journalism in Tennessee" 1869 SNO (1875) 46.

It would also seem obvious that the journalistic application of the color-term was merely a transferred use from its earlier application to vulgar and sensational fiction. As M.T. intimates, in the quot. given above under *yellow-covered,* the practitioners of the one often graduated into the perpetrators of the other. The choice of the color "yellow" of course commended itself to Pulitzer and his colleagues on account of its exceptional conspicuousness; but this quality had already been discovered and utilized by the "Yellow-Backs." To them it is therefore likely that "The Yellow Kid" owed his complexion, at least in part; and if so, a portion of the paternity of Yellow Journalism must be traced back to certain disreputable French publishers!)

yellow-splotched, ppl.a. [B¹] *We were fairly within the straits of Gibraltar, the tall yellow-splotched hills of Africa on the right* 1869 IA vii 63 (Comb. not in OED S C. Given in W)

Yellow Terror, sb. [B¹] *In China...the Yellow Terror is threatening the world to-day* 1900 *Speeches* (1910) 355 (Cf. OED Yellow, a. 1d. In recent use also *transf.* in *yellow peril* and similar phrases, denoting a supposed danger of a destructive invasion of Europe by Asiatic peoples. 1900, only ex. (*yellow peril*); the comb. *yellow terror* not in OED W S C)

yes, adv. Spelled **yas.** [?AE] See *butternut* 1873. *"Going to renounce his lordship and be a man! Yas!"* 1892 AmCl i 25 (Given as *dial. var.* in W. So Wr. This form not in OED S C)

yesternight, adv. [C] *Yesternight toke Her Majestie, ye Queen, a fantasie* 1880 *Fireside Conversation of 1601.* *"Yesternight wert thou the Prince of Wales"* 1881 PP xiv 161 (OED Chiefly *arch* or *dial.* a1300..1888. So W U Wr. Not *arch* in S C)

yez, pron. [B¹] *"Phwat do yez want?" I told him I wanted to see Mr. Daly* 1890 *Speeches* (1910) 81 (Here incorrectly used to a single individual. Cf. OED Anglo-Irish. You; said to more than one. 1804.. So W. Not in S C)

yield, v. [C] *They would yield them to Queen Guinever's hands as captives* 1889 CY iii 44 (OED 15. *refl.* To give oneself up, surrender. Now *rare.* 1297..1847. This *refl.* use not in W S C)

yodel, sb. Spelled **jodel.** [?AB³E] *We were hearing for the first time the famous Alpine jodel in its own native wilds* 1880 TA xxviii 289 (OED Also jodel. A melody or musical phrase inarticulately sung with interchange of the ordinary and falsetto voice, as by Swiss and Tyrolese mountaineers. 1849.. So W S C U. A in M. Cf. Tyrolese warbling, above)

yodel, v. Spelled **jodel.** [?AB³E] *Now the jodeler appeared—a shepherd boy of sixteen—and in our gladness and gratitude we gave him a franc to jodel some more* 1880 TA xxviii 289 (OED Also jodel. 1838.. So W S C U. A in M. Cf. above)

yodeler, sb. Spelled **jodeler.** [?AB²E] See above (OED Also jodler. One who yodels. 1910, only ex. So W S C, but this sp. not given)

yodeling, vbl.sb. Spelled **jodeling.** [?AB³E] *The jodeling continued, and was very pleasant and inspiriting to hear* 1880 TA xxviii 289 (OED 1830.. No ex. this sp. So W S C. Cf. above)

yokky, sb. [B¹] See *kahkahponeeka* 1880 (Hum. invention)

yon, dem.adj. [?AC] *"Help me carry thy stricken brother to yon house"* 1881 PP xviii 227 (OED Now *arch* and *dial.* 1. Referring to a visible object at a distance but within view. *c*897..1890. So W S C U Wr. A in DN.II,III,V, s.e.Mo., n.w.Ark., N.C.)

yonder, adv. [?AB¹] *"Dey don't sell po' niggers down the river over yonder"* 1893 PW iii 238 (The other world; the habitation of the soul after death. This sense not in OED W S C)

yonder-way, adv. [?AC] *"You break for that light over yonder-way, and turn out west when you git there"* 1884 HF xiii 115 (OED †By that way. 1570, only ex. Comb. not in W S C)

you-all, pron. [AB²] *We-all send love to you-all* 1875 Letters (1917) I xv 268. *"Betwixt you, and the Colonel's wife, and Mrs. Captain Marsh,...you-all sitting around in the house, it's a wonder to me she comes along as well as she does"* 1906 "Horse's Tale" 541 (OEDS *U.S.* You (as sing. or pl.). 1919.. W: Said in addressing two or more persons or, sometimes, one person representing also another or others. *Colloq., Southern U.S.* So S M H DN.II,V AS.II.133,343,496; III.5, Ozarks; IV.54,347; VI.230; VII.94; XI.350. Comb. not in C. Of course M.T. knew Southern dialect too well to perpetrate the mistake of using *you-all* as a real singular; but cf. his error with the Irish *yez*, above)

Young America, sb. [AB¹] *He and the innocent chatterbox whom I met on the Swiss lake are the most unique and interesting specimens of Young America I came* across during my foreign tramping 1880 TA xxxviii **444** (W: American youth collectively. *Colloq. U.S.* So S C. Comb. not in OED. Cf. OED Young England: the typical young Englishman. 1843..)

Young-Man-Afraid-of-his-Shadow, sb. [?AB¹] *People of strange, hyphenated names—Six-Fingered Jake, Young-Man-Afraid-of-his-Shadow, and the like* [entries in dead cowboy's memorandum book] 1892 AmCl vii 75 (Not in OED W S C. Cf. M: Young-Man-Afraid-of-His-Wife, among hum. names used as a result of Indian example)

young-girl, a. [B²] *She was absorbed in her own thoughts, her own young-girl dreams* 1880 TA ix 78 (OED Young, a. 1b(b). Pertaining to a young girl. 1880, this quot., only ex. Comb. not in W S C)

yourn, poss.pron. [?AE] *"Shake hands—yourn'll come through the bars, but mine's too big"* 1876 TS xxiii 184. See also *share*, sb. 1876 (OED *dial*, as in *hern*, *ourn*, q.v. 1382..1858. W: *obs* exc. *dial.* A in C Wr M DN.II,III,V AS.III.5; V.267, Ozarks; XI.351. Not in S)

yours truly, pron.phr. [?AB³] *"Isaac and Jacob are good enough* [names] *for yours truly"* 1870 *Screamers* (1871) 42. *"I'm blamed if I can see through it. It's too many for yours truly"* 1894 PW xiii 777 (OED Yours, poss.pron. 1c. Humorously for 'I' or 'me.' 1860, only ex. So W C. This use not in S. Cf. subscriber, above)

Z

zedoary, sb. [D] See *afarabocca* 1894 (OED The aromatic tuberous root of one or more species of *Curcuma*, of the East Indies...used as a drug. *c*1475..1866—. So W S C U)

zenith-scouring, ppl.a. [B¹] *I had promised myself an easy and zenith-scouring triumph, and this was the outcome!* 1889 CY xxv 327 (Hum. variation on 'skytowering,' 'cloud-piercing.' Comb. not in OED W S C; but cf. OED Zenith-borne, 1886)

Zeus-worshipping, ppl.a. [B¹] *Try to Christianize the Zeus-worshipping pagans of Palmyra* 1898 "About Play-Acting" (1900) 214 (Comb. not in OED W S C but cf. OED Zeus-worship, 1839)

zinc-plated, ppl.a. [B¹] See *spiral twist* 1870 (Comb. not in OED W S C; but cf. OED Zinc-plate, 1823)

zip, int. [?AB³] *"When you're ready, zzip!—let her go!"* 1892 AmCl xvii 176 (OED 1. *colloq*, often reduplicated. A syllable expressing a light, sharp sound. 1875.. So W S C U. A in DN.V)

zoological, a. [?AB³] *Tracy's training had not fitted him to enjoy this hideous zoological clamor...this extraordinary outpouring of animal spirits* 1892 AmCl xii 118 (OED c. *transf.* Sometimes *humorous.* Animal. 1855.. U.S. quot, 1893, only ex. referring to animallike cries. So W. This sense not in S C)

Zug, sb. [B¹] See *bag*, v. 1880 (Nonce borrowing, with allusion to the multifarious senses of German *Zug*: pull, tug, draw, etc.)

APPENDIX

FINDING LIST FOR MARK TWAIN'S WORK

This is merely a finding list for the quotations actually used in the *Lexicon*. For a complete bibliography of Mark Twain's works and what has been written about him, see Dr. Emberson's *Mark Twain's Vocabulary: a General Survey*, Univ. of Missouri Studies, Vol. X, No. 3, 1935, pp. 35-53. Merle Johnson's *A Bibliography of the Work of Mark Twain*, revised and enlarged, 1935, should also be consulted, although its usefulness is diminished considerably by the palpable confusion in which it was left at its compiler's death.

The quotations given in the *Lexicon* are followed in each case by the date of first publication, delivery, or writing, and the title of the work from which the quotation is taken, abbreviated as indicated below. The title may be either that of the volume or that of a story, sketch, or article contained in a larger volume. Volume titles alone, in italics, are usually given for the heterogeneous collections entitled *The Jumping Frog and Other Sketches, Screamers, Sketches New and Old, The Curious Republic of Gondour, Speeches* (both the 1910 and the 1923 volumes) *Europe and Elsewhere*, and *Sketches of the Sixties*. In all other cases the individual title of the story, sketch, or article is given, in quotation marks. If the date of the volume used for reference is later than the date of first publication, delivery, or writing, the later date is added after the title in parentheses. After this is given the reference, including volume numbers or numbers of "Books" or "Parts," in Roman capitals; chapter numbers in small letters; and page numbers in Arabic numerals. The page number naturally applies only to the particular edition and volume used in each case; in the list given below, that edition and volume are always given first. Quotations may also be located, with some trouble, in other editions, with the aid of the volume and chapter numbers; and hence other editions of many items have been added, in parentheses, but there has been no attempt at completeness for later editions.

1893 "About All Kinds of Ships." In *Banknote*.

1878 "About Magnanimous-Incident Literature." In the *Atlantic*, May 1878, XLI 615-619. (Also in SWE)

1898 "About Play-Acting" (1900). In MCH (1900). (Also in the *Forum*, Oct. 1898, XXVI 143-151)

1856 or 1857 *Adv. of T. J. Snodgrass* (1928). = *The Adventures of Thomas Jefferson Snodgrass*, reprinted by P. Covici, Inc., Chicago, 1928. (First in the Keokuk *Saturday Post*, Nov. 1, 1856, and the Keokuk *Daily Post*, Nov. 29, 1856, and Apr. 10, 1857. Also reprinted in the *Iowa Journal of History*, 1929, XXVII 438-452)

1892 AmCl. = *The American Claimant*. (Chaps. i-xxv)

1906 "Amended Obituaries." In *Bequest*.

1917 "As Concerns Interpreting the Deity." In WIM.

1898 "At the Appetite Cure" (1900). In MCH (1900). (First in the *Cosmopolitan*, Aug. 1898, XXV 425-433)

1891 "At the Shrine of St. Wagner" (1917). In WIM. (First in the N. Y. *Sun*, Dec. 6, 1891)

1898 "Austrian Edison" (1900). = "The Austrian Edison Teaching School Again," in MCH (1900). (First in the *Century*, Aug. 1898, LVI 630-631)

—— *Autob* (1924). = *Mark Twain's Autobiography*, 2 vols., ed. by Albert Bigelow Paine, 1924. (The first date given for each quotation is the one assigned by the editor to its original dictation.)

1893 "Banknote" (1928). = "The £1,000,000 Banknote," in MCH (1928). (First in the *Century*, Jan. 1893, XLV 338-346. Also as title story in *Banknote*, 1893)

—— *Banknote* (1893). = *The £1,000,000 Banknote and Other New Stories*, 1893.

c1902 "The Bee" (1917). In WIM. (First published posthumously in 1917, but written, according to Mr. Paine, about 1902)

1902 "Belated Russ. Passport" (1928). = "The Belated Russian Passport," in MCH (1928). (First in *Harper's Weekly*, Dec. 1902, XLVI 4-9. Also in *Bequest*)

1904 "Bequest" (1906). = "The $30,000 Bequest," in *Bequest*. (First in *Harper's Weekly*, Dec. 1904, XLVIII 1870-1877)

—— *Bequest* (1906). = *The $30,000 Bequest and Other Stories*, 1906.

—— *Buyers' Manual* (1872). = *The Buyers' Manual and Business Guide*, 1872.

1893 "Californian's Tale" (1906). In *Bequest*. (First in *Liber Scriptorum: the First Book of the Authors' Club*, 1893. Also in *Harper's*, Mar. 1902, CIV 601-604)

1876 "Canvasser's Tale." In the *Atlantic*, Dec. 1876, XXXVIII 673-676.

1909 "Capable Humorist." In *Harper's Weekly*, Feb. 1909, LIII 130.

1877 "Captain's Story."   See "Some Rambling Notes."

1907 or 1908 "Capt. Stormfield."   = "Extract from Captain Stormfield's Visit to Heaven," in *Harper's*, Dec. 1907, CXVI 41-49, and Jan. 1908, CXVI 266-276. (Republished in book form, 1909. Also in MS (1922), q.v.)

1906 "Carl Schurz, Pilot."   In *Harper's Weekly*, May 1906, L 727.

1906 "Carnegie Spelling Reform."   In *Harper's Weekly*, Apr. 1906, L 488.

—— "Chaps. from Autob" (1906 or 1907).   = "Chapters from My Autobiography," in the *North American Review*, Sept. 1906 to Dec. 1907, vols. CLXXXIII-CLXXXVI. (References in the *Lexicon*, which are made only to the year and the page, may be located as follows: 1906, CLXXXIII 321-330, 449-460, 577-589, 705-716, 833-844, 961-970, 1089-1095, 1217-1224; 1907, CLXXXIV 1-14, 113-119, 225-232, 337-346, 449-463, 561-571, 673-682, 785-793; 1907, CLXXXV 1-12, 113-122, 241-251, 465-474, 689-698; 1907, CLXXXVI 8-21, 161-173, 327-336, 481-494. The first date given for each quotation is the one assigned as that of its original dictation. Since this magazine material was largely reprinted, although with many changes and omissions, in *Autob* (1924), the "Chaps. from Autob" have been used in the *Lexicon* only for passages not reprinted. For a useful analysis of the complicated bibliographical relations, and a table of passages not reprinted in *Autob* (1924), see the article by Prof. Delancey Ferguson, "The Uncollected Portions of Mark Twain's Autobiography," *American Literature*, Mar. 1936, VIII 37-46.)

1902 or 1903 "Chr. Sc."   = "Christian Science," in the *North American Review*, Dec. 1902, CLXXV 756-768; Jan. 1903, CLXXVI 1-9; Feb. 1903, CLXXVI 173-184. (Reprinted, in part, in CS)

1899 "Chr.Sc. and the Book."   = "Christian Science and the Book of Mrs. Eddy," in the *Cosmopolitan*, Oct. 1899, XXVII 585-594. (Reprinted, in part, in CS)

—— Clara Clemens, *My Father* (1931).   (The first date is that of the letters or other material here given.)

1882 "Concerning the American Language." In SWE.

1905 "Concerning Copyright."   In the *North American Review*, Jan. 1905, CLXXX 1-8.

1899 "Concerning the Jews" (1900).   In MCH (1900). (First in *Harper's*, Sept. 1899, XCIX 527-535)

c1893 "Concerning Tobacco" (1917).   In WIM. (Published posthumously in 1917, but first written, according to Mr. Paine, about 1893)

1895 "Cooper's Literary Offences."   = "Fenimore Cooper's Literary Offences," in the *North American Review*, July 1895, CLXI 1-12.

—— CRG (1919).   = *The Curious Republic of Gondour, and Other Whimsical Sketches*, 1919. (The first date in each case is that of original publication, mostly in the *Galaxy* and the Buffalo *Express*. Titles of the individual sketches have been omitted.)

1907 CS.   = *Christian Science*, 1907. (Book I, chaps. i-ix; Book II, chaps. i-xiv)

1893 "Cure for the Blues."   In *Banknote*.

1870 "Curious Dream" (1872).   In *A Curious Dream and Other Sketches*, 1872. (First in the Buffalo *Express*, Apr. 30 and May 7, 1870)

1881 "Curious Experience."   In the *Century*, Nov. 1881, XXIII, 35-46.

1875 "Curious Republic."   = "The Curious Republic of Gondour," in the *Atlantic*, Oct. 1875, XXXVI 461-463. (Also in CRG)

1889 CY.   = *A Connecticut Yankee in King Arthur's Court*, 1889. (Chaps. i-xliv)

1905 "Czar's Soliloquy."   In the *North American Review*, Mar. 1905, CLXXX 321-326.

1852 "Dandy Frightening the Squatter" (1930).   In *Tall Tales of the Southwest*, ed. by F. J. Meine, 1930. (First in *The Carpet Bag*, May 1, 1852)

1902 "DBDS" (1928).   = "A Double-Barrelled Detective Story," in MCH (1928). (First in *Harper's*, Jan. and Feb., 1902, CIV 254-270, 429-441. Also in *Bequest*)

1901 "Death Disk" (1928).   In MCH (1928). (First in *Harper's*, Dec. 1901, CIV 19-26. Also in *Bequest*)

1909 "Death of Jean" (1917).   In WIM. (First published in *Harper's*, Jan. 1911, CXXII 210-215. Written Dec. 26, 1909)

1882 "Decay of the Art of Lying."   In SWE.

1902 "Defence of Gen. Funston."   In the *North American Review*, May 1902, CLXXIV 613-624.

1894 "Defence of Harriet Shelley."   In the *North American Review*, July to Sept. 1894, CLIX 108-119, 240-251, 353-368.

1899 "Diplomatic Pay" (1928).   = "Diplomatic Pay and Clothes," in MCH (1928). (First in the *Forum*, Mar. 1899, XXVII 24-32. Also in *Bequest*)

1902 "Does the Race Love a Lord?"   = "Does the Race of Man Love a Lord?" in the *North American Review*, Apr. 1902, CLXXIV 433-444. (Also in *Bequest*)

1903 "Dog's Tale."   In *Harper's*, Dec. 1903, CVIII 11-19. (Also in *Bequest*)

—— E&E (1923).   = *Europe and Elsewhere*, 1923. (The first date in each case is that of original publication. Titles of the individual sketches have been omitted.)

1880 "Edward Mills."   = "Edward Mills and George Benton: a Tale," in the *Atlantic*, Aug. 1880, XLVI 226-229. (Also in *Bequest*)

1875 "Encounter with an Interviewer."   In *Lotos Leaves: Original Stories, Essays, and Poems*, 1875.

1887 "English as She Is Taught" (1917).   In WIM. (First in the *Century*, Apr. 1887, XXXIII 932-936)

1906 "Entertaining Article."   In *Bequest*.

1893 "Esquimau Maiden's Romance" (1900).   In MCH (1900). (First in the *Cosmopolitan*, Nov. 1893, XVI 53-63)

1905 "Eve's Diary."   In *Harper's*, Dec. 1905, CXII 25-32. (Also in *Bequest*)

1893 "Extracts from Adam's Diary" (1901).   In *Harper's*, Apr. 1901, CII 762-767. (First in the *Niagara Book*, 1893. Also in *Bequest*, 1906, but incomplete. Published separately in book form, 1907)

1909 "A Fable."   In *Harper's*, Dec. 1909, CXX 70-71. (Also in MS (1922), q.v.)

1876 "Facts Concerning the Recent Carnival of Crime in Connecticut."   In the *Atlantic*, June 1876, XXXVII 641-650.

1897 FE.   =*Following the Equator*, 1897. (Chaps. i-lxix. Chaps. lxii-lxiv, pp. 609-643, also appeared as "From India to South Africa" in *McClure's*, Nov. 1897, X 3-18)

1880 *Fireside Conversations of 1601*.   (Privately published)

1905 "First Writing-Machines" (1906).   In *Bequest*. (First in *Harper's Weekly*, Mar. 1905, XLIX 391, under title "From My Unpublished Autobiography")

1902 "Five Boons of Life" (1906).   In *Bequest*. (First in *Harper's Weekly*, July 1902, XLVI 866)

1866 "Forty-Three Days."   ="Forty-Three Days in an Open Boat," in *Harper's*, Dec. 1866, XXXIV 104-113. (Also, in part, in 1899 "My Debut," q. v.)

1897 "From India to South Africa."   See FE.

1898 "From the London *Times* of 1904" (1900).   In MCH (1900). (First in the *Century*, Nov. 1898, LVII 100-104)

1873 GA.   = *The Gilded Age: a Tale of Today*, 1873 (chaps. i-lxiii)

1868 "Gen. Washington's Negro Body-Servant" (1906).   In *Bequest*. (First in the *Galaxy*, Feb. 1868)

1893 "German Chicago."   In *Banknote*.

1896 "A Gift from India."   In the *Critic*, Apr. 1896, XXVIII 285.

1879 "Great Revolution in Pitcairn."   In the *Atlantic*, Mar. 1879, XLIII 295-302.

1852 or 1853 *Hannibal Journal*.   From *Mark Twain's Early Writings in Hannibal, Missouri, Papers, 1852-1853*. Photostats from the original papers . . . made by Willard S. Morse, Santa Monica, California, Jan. 1931.

1905 "Helpless Situation" (1906).   In *Bequest*. (First in *Harper's Bazaar*, Nov. 1905, XXXIX 979-981)

1884 HF.   = *The Adventures of Huckleberry Finn*, 1884. (Chaps. i-xlii, with chap. xliii appearing under the title "Chapter the Last." Parts of chaps. xix-xxix, pp. 179-295, also appeared under the title "Royalty on the Mississippi" in the *Century*, Feb. 1885, XXIX 544-567.)

1899 "Hist. Dates" (1917).   See "How to Make Hist. Dates Stick."

1906 "Horse's Tale."   In *Harper's*, Aug. and Sept. 1906, CXIII 327-342, 539-549. (Also in MS (1922), q.v.)

1906 "Howells" (1917).   = "William Dean Howells," in WIM. (First in *Harper's*, July 1906, CXIII 221-225)

1899 "How to Make Hist. Dates Stick" (1917).   In WIM. (Written in 1899, according to footnote on p. 146. Also in *Harper's*, Dec. 1914, CXXX 3-15)

1895 "How to Tell a Story" (1900).   In MCH (1900). (First in the *Youth's Companion*, Oct. 3, 1895)

1905 "Humane Word from Satan" (1906).   In *Bequest*. (First in *Harper's Weekly*, Apr. 1905, XLIX 496)

1906 "Hunting the Deceitful Turkey."   In *Harper's*, Dec. 1906, CXIV 57-58. (Also in MS (1922), q.v.)

1869 IA.   = *The Innocents Abroad: or, The New Pilgrim's Progress*, 1869. (Chaps. i-lx)

1867 "Inquiry about Insurances."   In *Jumping Frog*.

1882 *Innocents at Home*.   See RI.

1917. "Interpreting the Deity."   See "As Concerns Interpreting the Deity."

1882 "Invalid's Story."   In SWE, pp. 94-105, new matter added as an appendix to "Some Rambling Notes."

1909 ISD.   = *Is Shakespeare Dead?* 1909 (Chaps. i-xiii. Also in WIM)

1893 "Is He Living?" (1900).   = "Is He Living or Is He Dead?", in MCH (1900). (Also in the *Cosmopolitan*, Sept. 1893, XV 629-634)

1904 "Italian with Grammar" (1906).   In *Bequest*. (First in *Harper's*, Aug. 1904, CIX 397-400)

1904 "Italian without a Master" (1906).   In *Bequest*. (First in *Harper's Weekly*, Jan. 1904, XLVIII 18-19)

1895 or 1896 JA.   = *Personal Recollections of Joan of Arc*, in *Harper's*, Apr. to Dec. 1895, and Jan. to Apr. 1896, vols. XC-XCII. (References in the *Lexicon*, by year, part, chapter, and page, are to the original arrangement in *Harper's*, which was as follows. In 1895: Part I, chaps. i-ix, Apr. and May, XC 680-699, 845-858; Part II, chaps. i-xxiii, June to Nov., XCI 82-94, 227-239, 456-467, 543-555, 743-753, 879-894; Book II (*sic*), chaps. i-vi, Dec., XCII 135-150. In 1896: Book II, chaps. vii-xviii, Jan. and Feb., XCII 288-306, 432-445; Book III, chaps. i-xiii, Mar. and Apr., XCII 585-597, 655-673. When published in book form in 1896, and in subsequent editions, this confused plan was altered as follows: Book I, chaps. i-viii (the original first chap. being made an intro.); Book II, chaps. i-xli (thus combining the original "Part II" and "Book II"); Book III, chaps. i-xxiv (with the addition of eleven chapters, inserted between the original chaps. v and vi).)

1867 "Jim Wolfe" (1872).   = "Jim Wolfe and the Cats," in *Buyers' Manual*. (First in the *Californian*, Sept. 21, 1867)

1905 "John Hay and the Ballads."   In *Harper's Weekly*, Oct. 1905, XLIX 1530.

1865 "Jumping Frog" (1875).   = "The Celebrated Jumping Frog of Calaveras County," in SNO. (First in the *Saturday Press*, Nov. 18, 1865. Also as title story in *Jumping Frog*, 1867; in *Buyer's Manual*, 1872; separately published, 1903; and in countless other collections)

1867 *Jumping Frog.*   = *The Celebrated Jumping Frog of Calaveras County, and Other Sketches*, 1867. (Used only for a few sketches not included in SNO or other collections)

1905 *King Leopold's Soliloquy.*   (Published separately)

——— *Letters* (1917).   = *Mark Twain's Letters*, 2 vols., 1917. (Chaps. i-xlviii. The first date in each case is that of the individual letter.)

——— Letters, etc., in Clara Clemens, *My Father* (1931), q.v.

1872 "Letter to the Editor of the *Spectator*" (1911). In the *Bookman*, Apr. 1911, XXXIII 114-115. (Dated 1872)

——— Letters in *Iowa J. of Hist.* (1929).   In the *Iowa Journal of History*, July 1929, XXVII 410-431. (Three early letters, dated Oct. 26, 1853, May 25, 1856, and June 1, 1857)

1859 Letter in *New Orleans Daily Crescent.*   In the issue for May 17, 1859; headed "River Intelligence," and dated May 8, 1859.

——— Letters, etc., in Paine's *Biog.* (1912), q.v.

1906 "Letter to the Sec. of the Treas."   = "A Letter to the Secretary of the Treasury," in *Bequest*.

1889 Letter to Whitman (1926).   In *The Golden Day*, by Lewis Mumford, 1926, pp. 173-175. (Dated in 1889)

1876 "Literary Nightmare."   In the *Atlantic*, Feb. 1876, XXXVII 167-169.

1883 LM.   = *Life on the Mississippi*, 1883. (Chaps. i-lx. But all quotations from chaps. iv-xvii are cited in the *Lexicon* from their earlier publication in 1875 OTM, q.v.)

1878 "Loves of Alonzo and Rosannah."   = "The Loves of Alonzo Fitz Clarence and Rosannah Ethelton," in the *Atlantic*, Mar. 1878, XLI 320-330.

1891 "Luck."   In *Harper's*, Aug. 1891, LXXXIII 407-409.

1890 "Majestic Literary Fossil."   In *Harper's*, Feb. 1890, LXXX 439-444.

1868-1910 *Margins on "Swift"* (1935).   = *Mark Twain's Margins on Thackeray's "Swift,"* by Coley B. Taylor, 1935. (These marginal notes in M.T.'s copy of Thackeray's *English Humorists*, ed. of 1868, may have been written at any time between that year and his death in 1910.)

1899 "MCH" (1900).   = "The Man that Corrupted Hadleyburg," in MCH (1900). (First in *Harper's*, Dec. 1899, C 29-54)

——— MCH (1900).   = *The Man that Corrupted Hadleyburg and Other Stories and Essays*, 1900. (The first edition)

——— MCH (1928).   = *The Man that Corrupted Hadleyburg and Other Stories and Essays*, 1928. (This edition has been cited as the most convenient source for seven items not included in the first edition: "The Belated

Russian Passport," "The Death Disk," "Diplomatic Pay and Clothes," "A Double-Barrelled Detective Story," "The £1,000,000 Banknote," "A Petition to the Queen of England," and "Two Little Tales.")

1888 "Meisterchaft." In the *Century*, Jan. 1888, XXXV 457-467. (Also in *Merry Tales*, 1892)

1898 "Memorable Assassination" (1917). In WIM. (First published posthumously in 1917, but written, according to Mr. Paine's headnote, immediately after the assassination of the Empress of Austria on Sept. 10, 1898)

1891 "Mental Telegraphy." In *Harper's*, Dec. 1891, LXXXIV 95-104. (Also in *Banknote*)

1895 "Mental Telegraphy Again." In *Harper's*, Sept. 1895, XCI 521-524.

1906 "Monument to Adam." In *Bequest*. (Cf. Paine's *Biog.* III 1648-1650)

1903 "Mrs. Eddy in Error." In the *North American Review*, Apr. 1903, CLXXVI 505-517. (Reprinted, with changes, in CS)

1880 "Mrs. McWilliams and the Lightning" (1882). In SWE. (First in the *Atlantic*, Sept. 1880, XLVI 380-384)

*c*1898 MS (1916). = *The Mysterious Stranger*, 1916. (Chaps. i-xi. Written probably about 1898, according to Mr. Paine, although first published posthumously in 1916. Also in *Harper's*, May to Nov. 1916, CXXXII 813-818, CXXXIII 38-43, 236-241, 441-446, 574-581, 749-758, 883-892. Also in MS (1922), q. v. below)

—— MS (1922). = *The Mysterious Stranger and Other Stories*, 1922.

1872 "M.T. in New York." In *Buyers' Manual*.

1903 *M.T. Interviews Himself* (1920). = *Mark Twain, Able Yachtsman, Interviews Himself*. Privately printed, 1920. (First in the New York *Herald*, Aug. 30, 1903)

—— *M.T. the Letter Writer* (1932). = *Mark Twain the Letter Writer*, collected and edited by Cyril Clemens, 1932. (Chaps. i-xiv. The first date in each case is that of the individual letter.)

1900 "My Boyhood Dreams." In MCH (1900). (First in *McClure's*, Jan. 1900, XIV 286-290)

1899 "My Debut" (1900). = "My Debut as a Literary Person," in MCH (1900). (First in the *Century*, Dec. 1899, LIX 76-88)

1871 "My First Interview with Artemus Ward" (1872). In *Buyers' Manual*. (First in *Public and Private Readings*, Boston, 1871)

1899 "My First Lie" (1900). = "My First Lie and How I Got Out of It," in MCH (1900). (First in the New York *World*, Dec. 10, 1899)

1912 "My Platonic Sweetheart" (1922). In MS (1922). (First published posthumously in *Harper's*, Dec. 1912, CXXVI 14-20. Date of original composition unknown)

1861 "Nevada" (1929). In the *Iowa Journal of History*, July 1929, XXVII 453-456, where it is dated Oct. 26, 1861.

1909 "New Planet." In *Harper's Weekly,* Jan. 1909, LIII 13.

—— *Niagara Book* (1893). *The Niagara Book,* by W. D. Howells, Mark Twain, and others, Buffalo, 1893.

—— *Notebook* (1935). = *Mark Twain's Notebook,* ed. by Albert Bigelow Paine, 1935. (Chaps. i-xxxv. The first date for each quotation is the one assigned by the editor for the original note.)

1875 OTM. = *Old Times on the Mississippi,* in the *Atlantic,* Jan. to Aug., 1875, in Parts I-VII, vols. XXXV and XXXVI. (Also in book form, pirated, Toronto, 1876. Later included as chaps. iv-xvii in *Life on the Mississippi,* 1883. Quotations from OTM in the *Lexicon* are given merely with the page numbers in the *Atlantic;* but they may be located in LM by the following table:

1875 OTM   69- 71 (*Atlantic* XXXV, Part I, Jan.) = LM iv
1875 OTM   71- 73 (*Atlantic* XXXV, Part I, Jan.) = LM v
1875 OTM 217-221 (*Atlantic* XXXV, Part II, Feb.) = LM vi
1875 OTM 221-224 (*Atlantic* XXXV, Part II, Feb.) = LM vii
1875 OTM 283-286 (*Atlantic* XXXV, Part III, Mar.) = LM viii
1875 OTM 286-289 (*Atlantic* XXXV, Part III, Mar.) = LM ix
1875 OTM 446-449 (*Atlantic* XXXV, Part IV, Apr.) = LM x
1875 OTM 449-452 (*Atlantic* XXXV, Part IV, Apr.) = LM xi
1875 OTM 567-570 (*Atlantic* XXXV, Part V, May) = LM xii
1875 OTM 570-574 (*Atlantic* XXXV, Part V, May) = LM xiii
1875 OTM 721-724 (*Atlantic* XXXV, Part VI, June) = LM xiv
1875 OTM 724-730 (*Atlantic* XXXV, Part VI, June) = LM xv
1875 OTM 190-192 (*Atlantic* XXXVI, Part VII, Aug.) = LM xvi
1875 OTM 192-196 (*Atlantic* XXXVI, Part VII, Aug.) = LM xvii)

—— Paine's *Biog.* (1912). = Albert Bigelow Paine, *Mark Twain, a Biography,* 3 vols., 1912. (Contains numerous letters and reported conversations, and other material not elsewhere available, all of which are scrupulously dated by Mr. Paine.)

1879 "Pen-Picture" (1917). = "A Pen-Picture of Mark Twain's Brother," in *Current Opinion,* May 1917, LXII 351-352. (Extracts from a letter to W. D. Howells, dated Feb. 9, 1879, which is given in full in *Letters* (1917) I 352-357)

1887 "Petition to the Queen" (1928). = "A Petition to the Queen of England," in MCH (1928). (First in *Harper's,* Dec. 1887, LXXVI 157-158. Also in *Banknote*)

1893 "Playing Courier." In *Banknote.*

1881 PP. = *The Prince and the Pauper,* 1881. (Chaps. i-xxxiii)

1885 "Private Hist. of Campaign." = "Private History of a Campaign that Failed," in the *Century,* Dec. 1885, XXXI 193-204. (Also in *Merry Tales,* 1892)

1894 "Private History of the 'Jumping Frog' Story" (1900).   In MCH (1900).
    (First in the *North American Review*, Apr. 1894, CLVIII 446-453)

1878 "Punch, Brothers, Punch" (1882).   In SWE. (First in *Punch, Brothers,
    Punch! and Other Sketches*, 1878)

1893 or 1894 PW.   = *Pudd'nhead Wilson: a Tale*, in the *Century*, Dec. 1893
    to June 1894, vols. XLVII and XLVIII. (Chaps. i-iii appeared in
    1893, Dec., XLVII 233-240; chaps. iv-xxi in 1894, Jan. to June,
    XLVII 328-340, 548-557, 772-781, 816-822, and XLVIII 16-24, 232-
    240. First published in book form in *The Tragedy of Pudd'nhead
    Wilson and the Comedy of Those Extraordinary Twins*, 1894)

1872 RI.   = *Roughing It*, 1872. (Chaps. i-lxxix. Chaps. xlvi-lxxix of RI were
    published in Great Britain in 1882 under the title of *Innocents at
    Home*.)

1859 "River Intelligence."   See letter in *New Orleans Daily Crescent*.

1885 "Royalty on the Mississippi."   See HF.

1869 "Salutatory" (1923).   In E&E, under the title "Two Mark Twain Edi-
    torials." (First in the Buffalo *Express*, Aug. 21, 1869)

1894 "Scrap of Curious Hist." (1917).   = "A Scrap of Curious History," in
    WIM. (Written, according to M.T.'s statement in the first para-
    graph, in 1894. Also in *Harper's*, Oct. 1914, CXXIX 672-675)

—— *Screamers* (1871).   = *Screamers: a Gathering of Scraps of Humour*, 1871.
    (A pirated edition of fugitive pieces, published by Hotten, London)

1889 "Simplified Alphabet" (1917).   In WIM. (First published posthumously
    in 1917, but written, according to Mr. Paine, in the autumn of 1899)

1906 "Simplified Spelling."   In *Putnam's*, Nov. 1906, I 219-220.

1891 *Slovenly Peter* (1935).   = *Slovenly Peter (Struwwelpeter); or, Happy
    Tales and Funny Pictures. Freely translated, with Dr. Hoffman's
    Illustrations, from the Rare First Edition, by Fritz Kredel*. Harper
    & Bros., 1935. (M.T.'s translation was first published posthumously
    in 1935, but written, according to Mr. Paine, in 1891.)

—— SNO (1875).   = *Sketches New and Old*, 1875. (The first date in each
    case is that of first publication of the individual sketch. Titles of
    separate sketches have been omitted, with the exception of the "Jump-
    ing Frog.")

1877 or 1878 "Some Rambling Notes."   = "Some Rambling Notes of an Idle
    Excursion," in the *Atlantic*, Oct. 1877 to Jan. 1878, vols. XL and XLI.
    (Parts i-iv. Part i was published in Oct. 1877, XL 443-447; Part ii
    in Nov. 1877, XL 586-592; Part iii in Dec. 1877, XL 718-724; Part
    iv in Jan. 1878, XLI 12-19. The whole is published also in *Punch,
    Brothers, Punch! and Other Sketches*, 1878; also in SWE, 1882, with
    the addition at the end of "The Invalid's Story." A portion of Part
    iii is published separately in *Bequest*, 1906, under the title of "The
    Captain's Story.")

—— *Speeches* (1910).   = *Mark Twain's Speeches*, 1910. (The first date in each case is that of original delivery as stated in the head-notes.)

—— *Speeches* (1923).   = *Mark Twain's Speeches*, 1923. (Used, as above, for speeches not contained in the 1910 collection)

—— *Speeches at the Lotos Club* (1911).   = *After Dinner Speeches at the Lotos Club*, arranged by John Elderkin, Chester S. Lord, and Charles W. Price, New York, 1911. (Five speeches, delivered from 1901 to 1909, not contained except in part in the two collections above)

—— SS (1926).   = *Sketches of the Sixties*, by Bret Harte and Mark Twain, from the *Californian*, 1864-1867, San Francisco, 1926. (The first date in each case is that of first publication. Titles of the individual sketches have been omitted.)

1898 "Stirring Times" (1900).   = "Stirring Times in Austria," in MCH (1900). (First in *Harper's*, Mar. 1898, XCVI 530-540)

1882 "SWE."   = "The Stolen White Elephant," title story in SWE.

—— SWE (1882).   = *The Stolen White Elephant and Other Stories and Sketches*, Boston, 1882.

1891 "Switzerland" (1917).   = "Switzerland, the Cradle of Liberty," in WIM. (First published in the New York *Sun*, Mar. 15, 1892, but written, according to M.T.'s statement at the beginning, at Interlaken in 1891)

1880 TA.   = *A Tramp Abroad*, 1880. (Chaps. i-l)

*c*1880 "Taming the Bicycle" (1917).   In WIM. (First published posthumously in 1917, but written, according to Mr. Paine, "in the early eighties")

1880 "Telephonic Conversation."   In the *Atlantic*, June 1880, XLV 841-843. (Also in *Bequest*)

1894 TET.   = *Those Extraordinary Twins*. (Chaps. i-x. First in *The Tragedy of Pudd'nhead Wilson and the Comedy of Those Extraordinary Twins*, 1894)

1901 "To My Missionary Critics."   In the *North American Review*, Apr. 1901, CLXXII 520-534.

1901 "To the Person Sitting in Darkness."   In the *North American Review*, Feb. 1901, CLXXII 161-176.

1893 "Travelling with a Reformer" (1900).   In MCH (1900). (First in the *Cosmopolitan*, Dec. 1893, XVI 207-217)

1876 TS.   = *The Adventures of Tom Sawyer*, 1876. (Chaps. i-xxxv)

1893 or 1894 TSA.   = *Tom Sawyer Abroad*, in *St. Nicholas*, Nov. 1893 to Apr. 1894, vol. XXI. (Chaps. i-xiii. Chaps. i-v appeared in 1893, Nov. and Dec., pp. 20-29, 116-127; chaps. vi-xiii in 1894, Jan. to Apr., pp. 250-258, 348-356, 392-401, 539-548. First published in book form in *Tom Sawyer Abroad, Tom Sawyer, Detective, and Other Stories*, 1896)

1896 TSD.   = *Tom Sawyer, Detective*, in *Harper's*, Aug. and Sept. 1896, XCIII 344-361, 519-537. (Chaps. i-xi. First in book form in *Tom Sawyer Abroad, Tom Sawyer, Detective, and Other Stories*, 1896)

1910 "Turning-Point of My Life" (1917).   In WIM. (First in *Harper's Bazaar,* Feb. 1910, XLIV 118-119)

1901 "Two Little Tales" (1928).   In MCH (1928). (First in the *Century,* Nov. 1901, LXIII 24-32. Also in *Bequest*)

—— "Unpublished Chaps. from Autob" (1922).   = "Unpublished Chapters from the Autobiography of Mark Twain," in *Harper's,* Feb., Mar., and Aug. 1922, vols. CXLIV 273-280, 455-460, and CXLV 310-315. (Used in the *Lexicon* only for the parts omitted from the *Autob* (1924); cf. note above under "Chaps. from Autob," and see Professor Ferguson's article there cited.)

1904-05 "War Prayer" (1923).   In E&E, with the heading: "Dictated 1904-05." (Also, in part, in Paine's *Biog.* III 1232-3)

1902 "Was It Heaven?" (1906).   = "Was It Heaven? or Hell?" in *Bequest.* (First in *Harper's,* Dec. 1902, CVI 11-20)

1886 "What American Authors Think About Copyright."   In the *Century,* Feb. 1886, XXXI 634.

1895 "What Bourget Thinks."   = "What Paul Bourget Thinks of Us," in the *North American Review,* Jan. 1895, CLX 48-62.

1906 "WIM" (1917).   = "What Is Man?" title piece in WIM. (Chaps. i-vi. First published anonymously in a limited edition, as *What Is Man?* New York, 1906)

—— WIM (1917).   = *What Is Man? and Other Essays,* 1917.

1870 "Wit Inspirations" (1906).   = "Wit Inspirations of the 'Two-Year-Olds'," in *Bequest.* (First in the *Galaxy,* June 1870)

1890 "Wonderful Pair of Slippers."   In *St. Nicholas,* Feb. 1890, XVII 309-313. (Also in E&E)